QUICK REFERENCE TO PHYSICAL THERAPY

Julie A. Pauls
MS, PT, ICCE
President
PhysiCare for Women, PC
Predoctoral Fellow
Texas Woman's University

Kathlyn L. Reed
PhD, OTR, FAOTA, MLIS, AHIP
Education/Information
Services Librarian
Houston Academy of Medicine-
Texas Medical Center
Adjunct Professor
School of Occupational Therapy
Texas Woman's University
Houston, Texas

pro·ed
An International Publisher
8700 Shoal Creek Boulevard
Austin, Texas 78757-6897
800/897-3202 Fax 800/397-7633
www.proedinc.com

An International Publisher

© 1996 by PRO-ED, Inc.
8700 Shoal Creek Boulevard
Austin, Texas 78757-6897
www.proedinc.com

ISBN: 0-89079-901-6 (previously ISBN 0-8342-6654-4)

Printed in the United States of America

1   2   3   4   5   6   7   07   06   05   04   03   02

*This book is dedicated
to our fathers,
Dennis L. Hofts
and
Herbert C. Reed*

Table of Contents

Acknowledgments

We would like to thank the Acquisition and Developmental editors, Steve Zollo and Mary Anne Langdon, at Aspen Publishers, Inc. for their expertise and assistance in producing this text.

Introduction

PURPOSE

This book provides a synopsis of the diseases, disorders, and dysfunctions referenced in the physical therapy literature. The format used gives all therapists, whether they are students, clinicians, educators, or researchers, quick access to the information needed to assess, educate, and treat clients.

SOURCES

Most of the references cited were published from 1985 through 1995. Selected older sources supplement the current literature.To qualify for inclusion into the text, one of the authors of the article, chapter, or book had to be identified as a physical therapist. **Publications with no input by a physical therapist were excluded**. Authors who are not physical therapists appear only if the article was published in a physical therapy journal.

Classifications of the disorders were generally derived from the Medical Subject Headings (MeSH) list from the National Library of Medicine (NLM). Using these MeSH classifications, we compiled references from seven computer databases: Allied Alternative Medicine (AMED) from Data-Star, Cumulative Index to Nursing and Allied Health Literature (CINAHL), Current Contents, EMBASE, MEDLINE, NLM Locator, and RNdex. Bibliographies from these references led to a trail of additional references.

The journals researched were
- *Australian Journal of Physiotherapy*
- *British Journal of Physiotherapy*
- *Clinical Management in Physical Therapy*
- *Clinics in Physical Therapy*
- *Journal of Obstetric and Gynecologic Physical Therapy*
- *Journal of Orthopaedic and Sports Physical Therapy*
- *Journal of Physical Therapy Science*
- *National Association of Physical Therapy*
- *New Zealand Journal of Physiotherapy*
- *Orthopaedic Physical Therapy Clinics of North America*
- *Pediatric Physical Therapy*
- *Physical and Occupational Therapy in Geriatrics*
- *Physical and Occupational Therapy in Pediatrics*

- *Physical Therapy*
- *Physical Therapy Practice*
- *Physiotherapy (South Africa)*
- *Physiotherapy (England)*
- *Physiotherapy Canada*
- *Physiotherapy Theory and Practice*
- *PT Magazine of Physical Therapy*

Titles of the journals are listed in full in the text to facilitate reference location. Physical therapy journals cited should be available through standard library sources.

FORMAT

Each disorder is described according to the same format:

1. *Disorder:* The name of the disorder, followed by any additional names by which the condition is known. Some conditions, such as Raynaud's disease, were omitted because enough information was not found to complete the format. Other conditions, such as balance disorders and vestibular dysfunction, were included as problems of other disorders instead of being listed separately. When it was appropriate, similar conditions were grouped together because their assessment and treatment were the same.

2. *Description:* A brief summary of the disorder, based on the *Merck Manual* or selected references cited at the end of the section.

3. *Cause:* A review of the cause of the disorder, if known, based on the *Merck Manual* or selected references cited at the end of the section.

4. *Assessment*
    - *Areas:* A list outlining the scope of assessment categories. This list should be adapted to the client's condition. It may *not* be indicated or appropriate to include every area in the initial or subsequent assessments.
    - *Instruments/Procedures:* Published tools for evaluation or research, provided under corresponding categories. The tools listed offer a menu of tests, forms, and instrumentation that therapists can use as directed by the client's condition. These instruments were not necessarily invented by a physical therapist but are now cited in the therapeutic literature.

5. *Problems:* Clinical problems or complaints that a client can experience with each disorder.

6. *Treatment/management:* A synopsis of treatment and management options derived from selected references. This section is not intended to be a detailed treatment manual; rather, it is a rapid review of published procedures, protocols, and suggestions for therapeutic care. Therapists are encouraged to refer clients to the support groups listed in the appendices when needed.

7. *Precautions/contraindications:* Notes of caution mentioned by clinicians and researchers. This section is supplemented by a list of contraindications to physical agents and modalities in the appendices.

8. *Desired outcome/prognosis:* The goals of treatment, highlighted by bullets and followed by a mention of expectations found in the physical therapy literature.

9. *References:* A comprehensive list of articles and books, divided into references for treatment and references for instruments.

CONCLUSION

This reference guide is based on a survey of physical therapy publications that included contents from seven databases, 23 journal titles, and over 175 texts. It reflects the breadth of current practice and identifies areas in the literature that lack depth. Therapists are encouraged to continue contributions to the literature so as to refine the areas well established and to establish the emerging fields.

Julie Pauls

Chapter 1

Conditions in Athletic Injuries

- Anterior cruciate ligament tear
- Biceps tendon strain
- Hamstring muscle strain
- Hip contusion
- Iliotibial band friction syndrome
- Medial collateral ligament (of elbow) sprain
- Meniscal tear
- Osteitis pubis
- Rotator cuff tendinitis
- Ankle sprains

See also chapter "Musculoskeletal Conditions and Injuries"

Anterior Cruciate Ligament (ACL) Tear

DESCRIPTION

At the onset of injury to the anterior cruciate ligament (ACL), the athlete usually hears a popping noise. This is often followed by rapid swelling and decreased function, including the inability to walk. Other ligaments commonly torn include the posterior cruciate ligament, medial collateral ligament, and lateral collateral ligament. There is also a high incidence of accompanying patellofemoral pain.

CAUSE

In sports that involve jumping, twisting, and pivoting, the ACL is commonly injured through the following forces at the knee joint: valgus stress with external rotation of tibia, varus stress with internal rotation of the tibia, hyperextension, deceleration, or a crossover cut maneuver.

ASSESSMENT

Areas
- History
- Pain
- Gait
- Posture
- Balance
- Joint integrity and structural deviations
- Mobility: active and passive range of motion (ROM) and accessory motion
- Strength
- Neurological: sensation, proprioception, deep tendon reflexes, neural tension
- Skin and soft tissue: temperature, tenderness, tone, edema
- Functional level, including activities of daily living (ADLs)
- Special tests to which the PT may or may not have access

Instruments/Procedures (See References for Sources)

Balance
- Single-leg standing balance test

Functional Level
- Cincinnati Rating System
- Duocondylar Rating Scale
- Knee Society Rating Scale
- Lysholm Knee Rating Scale
- Modified Lysholm Knee Score

Joint Integrity and Structural Deviations. The following are orthopedic tests for the knee. Those recommended, especially for this condition, are marked with an asterisk.
- A-angle
- Anterolateral Rational Instability (ALRI)
- anterior drawer sign*
- Anteromedial Rotational Instability (AMRI)

- Apley grinding test
- apprehension test
- bounce home test
- brush or stroke (wipe) test
- Clark's sign
- crossover test
- Ely's test
- external rotation test
- flexion rotation drawer test
- fluctuation test
- gravity drawer test (posterior sag sign)
- hamstring length
- Helfet test
- Hughston plica test
- Hughston posterolateral drawer test
- Hughston test (jerk sign)
- hyperflexion-hyperextension test
- Jakob test (reverse pivot)
- Lachman test*
- lateral pull test
- limb-length discrepancy
- MacIntosh test (lateral pivot shift)*
- McConnell's test
- McMurray–Anderson test
- Noble's compression test
- Ober's test
- O'Donoghue's test
- patellar tap test
- patellar tilt test
- Perkin's test
- plica test
- posterior drawer sign
- posterior sag sign
- quadriceps active test
- reverse pivot shift
- Slocum test
- Steinman's test
- squat test
- tibial displacement test
- valgus stress test
- varus stress test
- Waldron test
- Wilson test

Mobility
- goniometry
- knee ligament arthrometer

- KT-1000 arthrometer

Pain
- palpation
- visual analogue scale

Skin and Soft Tissue
1. temperature, tenderness, tone
   - palpation
2. edema
   - tape measure
   - water displacement

Special Tests to Which the PT May or May Not Have Access
- arthroscopy

Strength
1. instrumentation
   - cable tensiometers
   - isokinetic dynamometers
   - strain gauge devices
2. manual muscle testing

PROBLEMS
- The athlete with knee instability is usually unable to bear weight normally.
- The athlete may report knee has a history of "giving way."
- There is usually weakness at the quadriceps muscle.
- The athlete will usually have pain with active movement of knee.
- There is limited ROM at the knee.
- There can be decreased proprioception.
- There may be an antalgic gait pattern.
- The athlete can have repeated episodes of pain and swelling at knee.

TREATMENT/MANAGEMENT

Acute Injury
The acronym **PRICEMM** outlines a general approach for pain and inflammation.

PRICEMM stands for the following:
- **P**rotection
- **R**est: eliminate aggravating activities
- **I**ce
- **C**ompression
- **E**levation
- **M**edication as prescribed by primary caregiver
- **M**odalities: high-voltage electrical stimulation, ultrasound, ice, heat

---

Knee Rehabilitation

Knee rehabilitation following ACL tears may follow a conservative, nonsurgical course of rehabilitation or, if the client elects surgery, a postsurgical course of rehabilitation. Conservative and postsurgical protocols vary. A therapist should work closely with the athlete's physician during the rehabilitation process.

In general, the phases of knee rehabilitation can be described as follows:

- *Phase 1:* Treat pain, inflammation, and intra-articular swelling.
- *Phase 2:* Regain limited motion and re-educate disused tissues. Control swelling and pain.
- *Phase 3:* Retrain function. Tissue realignment should be monitored for proper forces. Reduce risk of reinjury during ADLs.
- *Phase 4:* Begin light activity, progressing toward full functional retraining.
- *Phase 5:* Promote full return to activities and maintenance of progress.

The following general suggestions apply to any ACL rehabilitation program:

- Exercise should emphasize hamstring control of anterior tibial translation. Consider the use of closed-chain exercises, including proprioceptive neuromuscular facilitation (PNF), reclined squat, stair climber, and stationary bike. The quadriceps muscle should be exercised in a protected range of greater than 45 degrees flexion or with cocontraction. Surgical tubing can be used as an adjunct to exercise.
- Cryotherapy is often used for 15 to 20 minutes after an exercise session.
- Consider the use of transcutaneous electrical nerve stimulation (TENS) for pain.
- Consider the use of compression pump for swelling.
- The athlete may need an assistive device for ambulation using controlled weight bearing.
- Knee immobilizers can be used for a brief period. Assess the need for derotational bracing.
- Electrical stimulation can help with joint effusion and muscular control.

Conservative Management of ACL-Deficient Knee. See below for a sample eight-point rehabilitation protocol for the ACL-deficient knee. See references for additional protocols.

An eight-point rehabilitation protocol for the ACL-deficient knee is as follows:
1. Correct strength defects.
2. Increase muscular work and promote endurance.
3. Implement a high-speed dynamic-functional program to promote joint control.
4. Maintain reciprocal reflex speed.
5. Consider using a brace for sports activities.
6. Modify activities, especially any pivot shifting.
7. Promote weight loss to minimize effect of arthritis, if indicated.
8. Educate the patient regarding future progress.

Source: Reprinted with permission from B Sanders, *Sports Physical Therapy,* p. 440, © 1990, Appleton & Lange.

Postsurgical Management of the ACL-Reconstructed Knee. Below is a sample postoperative protocol for ACL reconstruction. See references for additional protocols.

Accelerated Rehabilitation for Anterior Cruciate Ligament Reconstruction

Postoperative Time	Exercise/Activity
0–1 d	Begin gait training and pain control
1-7 d	Monitor wound daily
	Cryo-cuff and PRICE as often as indicated
	Use immobilizer in full extension for sleeping and weight-bearing activities
	Start weight bearing as tolerated with crutches
	Use patellofemoral mobilization as tolerated
	Use wall slide exercise for flexion (< or = to 120 degrees as tolerated)
	Promote full terminal knee extension ASAP
7–14 d	Begin using closed kinematic chain for strengthening
	Use stationary bike for ROM and strengthening
	Consider pool exercises if wound is healed
	Start incisional mobilization ASAP
	Initiate progressive weight bearing to tolerance
	Continue PRICE as needed
	Offer electrical muscle stimulation as needed
	Provide proprioceptive balance board activities
2–6 w	Progress flexion to full as tolerated
	Continue weight bearing to full as tolerated
	Use progressive closed kinematic chain for strengthening
	Continue PRICE post exercise
6–12 w	Progress to jumping rope, sliding board, lateral shuffles
	Advance to pool running as tolerated
	Initiate light jogging
	Continue using closed kinematic chain for strengthening
12–24 w	Increase closed kinematic chain exercise, agility, and functional activities, such as running, jumping, and cutting, as tolerated
	Consider functional brace for sports or work

Source: Reprinted with permission from JP Tomberlin, and HD Saunders, *Evaluation, Treatment and Prevention of Musculoskeletal Disorders,* Vol. 2, p. 256, © 1994, The Saunders Group.

Prevention

Develop strength and endurance in musculature surrounding the knee to promote stability and prevention of injury.

PRECAUTIONS/CONTRAINDICATIONS

- Conservative and postsurgical protocols vary. A therapist should work closely with the athlete's physician/surgeon during the rehabilitation process.
- All protocols should be tailored to an athlete's individual problems.
- Unnecessary immobilization should be avoided. Consider use of continuous passive motion following surgery.
- The quadriceps should be strengthened with cocontraction or in a protective range (less than 45 degrees flexion).
- Do not progress athletes to the next level of rehabilitation unless they reach success at their current level. Progress depends on the rate of healing.
- See appendix for precautions for physical agents and modalities.

DESIRED OUTCOME/PROGNOSIS

- The athlete will have diminished or no pain, inflammation, or intra-articular swelling.
- The athlete will be educated in the avoidance of reinjury during ADLs.
- The athlete will not suffer loss of conditioning in uninjured areas of the body.
- The athlete will have full motion and function.
- Postsurgically, the athlete will avoid ligament failure, regain strength, and protect the articular surfaces.

If an athlete's goal is to continue with a sport or stressful work, he or she is usually a candidate for reconstructive surgery instead of conservative treatment.

REFERENCES

ASSESSMENT

Balance

Harrison EL, Duenkel N, Dunlop R, Russell G. Evaluation of single-leg standing following anterior cruciate ligament surgery and rehabilitation. *Physical Therapy*. 1994;74:245–252.

Functional Level

Barber SD, Noyes, FR, Mangine RE, et al. Quantitative assessment of functional limitations in normal and anterior cruciate ligament-deficient knee. *Clinical Orthopedics*. 1990;255:204–214.

Delitto A. Lower extremity: knee. In: Myers RS, ed. *Saunders Manual of Physical Therapy Practice*. Philadelphia, Pa: WB Saunders Co; 1995:1011. **[Modified Lysholm Knee Score]**

Lephart SC, Perrin DH, Fu FH, Gieck JH, McCue FC III, Irrgang JJ. Relationship between selected physical characteristics and functional capacity in the anterior cruciate ligament-insufficient athlete. *Journal of Orthopaedic and Sports Physical Therapy*. 1992;16:174–181.

Ranawat I, et al. Duocondylar Rating Scale. *Hospital for Special Surg Des*. 1976;77.

Tegner Y, Lysholm J. Rating systems in the evaluation of knee ligament injuries. *Clinical Orthopaedics and Related Research*. 1985;257:43–49. **[Lysholm Knee Rating Scale]**

Tomberlin JP, Saunders HD. *Evaluation, Treatment and Prevention of Musculoskeletal Disorders. Vol 2: Extremities*. Chaska, Minn: The Saunders Group; 1994:245. **[Cincinnati Rating System, Knee Society Rating Scale]**

Joint Integrity and Structural Deviations

Cooperman JM, Riddle DL, Rothstein J. Reliability and validity of judgments of the integrity of the anterior cruciate ligament of the knee using the Lachman's test. *Physical Therapy*. 1990;70:225–233.

Daniel DM, Stone ML, Malcom L, et al. Instrumented measurement of ACL disruption. *Orthopedic Resident Society.* 1983;8:12.

Daniel DM, Stone ML, Sachs R, Malcom L. Instrumented measurement of anterior knee laxity in patients with acute anterior cruciate ligament disruption. *American Journal of Sports Medicine.* 1985;13:401–407.

Jensen K. Manual laxity tests for anterior cruciate ligament injuries. *Journal of Orthopaedic and Sports Physical Therapy.* 1990;11:474–481.

McQuade KJ, Crutcher JP, Sidles JA, Larson RV. Tibial rotation in anterior cruciate deficient knees: an in vitro study. *Journal of Orthopaedic and Sports Physical Therapy.* 1989;11:146-149. [**Tibial displacement test**]

Rebman LW. Lachman's test: an alternative method clinical test to determine anterior cruciate deficiency. *Journal of Orthopaedic and Sports Physical Therapy.* 1988;9:381–382.

Rothstein JM, Roy SH, Wolf SL.*The Rehabilitation Specialist's Handbook.* Philadelphia, Pa: FA Davis Co; 1991:132–137. [**Apley grinding test, bounce home test, brush or stroke (wipe) test, Clark's sign, cross-over test, gravity drawer test (posterior sag sign), Helfet test, Hughston plica test, Hughston postero-lateral drawer test, Hughston test (jerk sign), Jakob test (reverse pivot), MacIntosh test (lateral pivot shift), O'Donoghue's test, Perkin's test, Slocum test, Waldron test, Wilson test**]

Shields CL, Silva I, Yee L, Brewster C. Evaluation of residual instability after arthroscopic meniscectomy in anterior cruciate-deficient knees. *American Journal of Sports Medicine.* 1987;15:129-131.

Tomberlin JP, Saunders HD. *Evaluation, Treatment and Prevention of Musculoskeletal Disorders. Vol 2: Extremities.* Chaska, Minn: The Saunders Group; 1994:233. [**ALRI, AMRI, apprehension test, brush or stroke (wipe) test, Ely's test, external rotation test, flexion rotation drawer, fluctuation test, ham-string length, hyperflexion-hyperextension test, Lachman's test, lateral pull test, McConnell's test, McIntosh test, McMurray-Anderson test, Noble's compression test, Ober's test, patellar tap, patellar tilt, plica test, posterior drawer sign, posterior sag sign, quadriceps active test, reverse pivot shift, Slocum's ALRI, squat test, Steinman's test, valgus stress, varus stress**]

Yack HJ, Collins CE, Whieldon TJ. Comparison of closed and open kinetic chain exercise in the anterior cruciate ligament-deficient knee. *American Journal of Sports Medicine.* 1993;21:49–54. [**Tibial displacement test**]

Mobility

Buss DD, Warren RF, Wickiewicz TL, Galinat BJ, Panariello R. Arthroscopically assisted reconstruction of the anterior cruciate ligament with use of autogenous patellar-ligament grafts: results after twenty-four to forty-two months. *Journal of Bone and Joint Surgery.* 1993;75A:1346–1355. [**KT-1000 Arthrometer**]

Hantsen WP, Pace MB. Reliability of measuring anterior laxity of the knee joint using a knee ligament arthrometer. *Physical Therapy.* 1987;67:357–359. [**Arthrometer**]

Rothstein JM, Miller PJ, Roetgger RF. Goniometric reliability in a clinical setting: elbow and knee measurements. *Physical Therapy.* 1983;63:1611–1615. [**Goniometry**]

Pain

Langely GB, Sheppeard H. The visual analogue scale: its use in pain measurement. *Rheumatology International.* 1985;5:145–148.

Skin and Soft Tissue

Edema

Delitto A. Lower extremity: knee. In: Myers RS, ed. *Saunders Manual of Physical Therapy Practice.* Phila-delphia, Pa: WB Saunders Co; 1995:1012. [**Tape measure, water displacement**]

Special Tests to Which the PT May or May Not Have Access

Arthroscopy

McClelland CJ. Arthroscopy and arthroscopic surgery of the knee. *Physiotherapy.* 1984;70:154–156.

Strength

Instrumentation

Delitto A. Lower extremity: knee. In: Myers RS, ed. *Saunders Manual of Physical Therapy Practice.* Philadelphia, Pa: WB Saunders Co; 1995:1019. [**Cable tensiometers, gravity-corrected isokinetic work, strain gauge devices**]

Gross MT, Tyson AD, Burns CB. Effect of knee angle and ligament insufficiency on anterior tibial translation during quadriceps muscle contraction: a preliminary report. *Journal of Orthopaedic and Sports Physical Therapy.* 1993;17:133–143. [**Dynamometry**]

Mayhew TP, Rothstein JM. Measurement of muscle performance with instruments. In: Rothstein JM, ed. *Clinics in Physical Therapy: Measurements in Physical Therapy.* New York, NY: Churchill Livingstone; 1985:57–102.

McComb FH, Kerr KM. Isokinetic strength of the thigh muscles following the dacron method of reconstruction of the anterior cruciate ligament. *Physiotherapy.* 1992;78:478–483.

Stratford P. Reliability of a peak knee extensor and flexor torque protocol: a study of post ACL reconstructed knees. *Physiotherapy Canada.* 1991;43:4:27–30.

Stratford P, Agostine V, Armstrong B, Stewart T, Weininger S. Diagnostic value of knee extension torque tracings in suspected anterior cruciate ligament tears. *Physical Therapy.* 1987;67:1533–1536.

Wilk KE, Andrews JR. The effects of pad placement and angular velocity on tibial displacement during isokinetic exercise. *Journal of Orthopaedic and Sports Physical Therapy.* 1993;17:24–30.

Wilk KE, Keirns MA, Andrews JR, et al. Anterior cruciate ligament reconstruction rehabilitation: a six month follow-up of isokinetic testing recreational athletes. *Isokinetic Exercise Science.* 1991;1:1:36–43.

Manual Muscle Testing

American Physical Therapy Association. A guide to physical therapist practice. Vol 1: A description of patient management. *Physical Therapy.* 1995;75:720–738. [**Muscle performance examination**]

Amundsen LR. *Muscle Strength Testing: Instrumented and Non-Instrumented Systems.* New York, NY: Churchill Livingstone; 1990.

Daniels L, Worthingham C. *Daniels and Worthingham's Muscle Testing Techniques of Manual Examination.* 6th ed. Philadelphia, Pa: WB Saunders Co; 1995.

Itoh H, Ichihashi N, Maruyama T, Kurosaka M, Hirohata K. Weakness of thigh muscles in individuals sustaining anterior cruciate ligament injury. *Kobe Journal of Medical Sciences.* 1992;38:2:93–107.

Kannus P. Ratio of hamstring to quadriceps femoris muscles' strength in the anterior cruciate ligament insufficient knee. *Physical Therapy.* 1988;68:961–965.

Kendall FP, McCreary EK, Provance PG. *Muscles, Testing and Function.* 4th ed. Baltimore, Md: Williams & Wilkins; 1993.

Kramer J, Nusca D, Fowler P, Webster-Bogaert S. Knee flexor and extensor strength during concentric and eccentric muscle actions after anterior cruciate ligament reconstruction using the semitendinosus tendon and ligament augmentation device. *American Journal of Sports Medicine.* 1993;21:285–291.

Snyder-Mackler L, Binder-Macleod SA, Williams PR. Fatiguability of human quadriceps femoris muscle following anterior cruciate ligament reconstruction. *Medicine and Science in Sports and Exercise.* 1993;25:783–789.

Snyder-Mackler L, Ladin Z, Schepsis AA, Young JC. Electrical stimulation of the thigh muscles after reconstruction of the anterior cruciate ligament: effects of electrically elicited contraction of the quadriceps femoris and hamstring muscles on gait and on strength of the thigh muscles. *Journal of Bone and Joint Surgery.* 1991;73A:1025–1036.

Wilk KE, Andrews JR, Clancy WG. Quadriceps muscular strength after removal of the central third patellar tendon for contralateral anterior cruciate ligament reconstruction surgery: a case study. *Journal of Orthopaedic and Sports Physical Therapy.* 1993;18:692–697.

Worrell TW, Borchert B, Erner K, Fritz J, Leerar P. Effect of a lateral step-up exercise protocol on quadriceps and lower extremity performance. *Journal of Orthopaedic and Sports Physical Therapy.* 1993;18:646–653.

TREATMENT

Anterior Cruciate Ligament

Antich TJ, Brewster CE. Rehabilitation of the nonreconstructed anterior cruciate ligament-deficient knee. *Clinics in Sports Medicine.* 1988;7:813–826.

Beard DJ, Fergusson CM. The conservative management of anterior cruciate ligament deficiency: a nationwide survey of current practice. *Physiotherapy.* 1992;78:181–186.

Currier DP, Ray JM, Nyland J, Rooney JG, Noteboom JT, Kellogg R. Effects of electrical and electromagnetic stimulation after anterior cruciate ligament reconstruction. *Journal of Orthopaedic and Sports Physical Therapy.* 1993;17:177–184.

Davies G, ed. *Rehabilitation of the Surgical Knee.* Ronkonkoma, NY: Cypress; 1984.

DeCarlo MS, Shelbourne KD, McCarroll JR, Rettig AC. Traditional versus accelerated rehabilitation following ACL reconstruction: a one-year follow-up. *Journal of Orthopaedic and Sports Physical Therapy.* 1992;15:309–316.

Delitto A, Rose SJ, McKowen JM, Lehman RC, Thomas JS, Shively RA. Electrical stimulation versus voluntary exercise in strengthening thigh musculature after anterior cruciate ligament surgery. *Physical Therapy.* 1988;68:660–663.

Draper V. Electromyographic biofeedback and recovery of quadriceps femoris muscle function following anterior cruciate ligament reconstruction. *Physical Therapy.* 1990;70:11–17.

Draper V, Ballard L. Electrical stimulation versus electromyographic biofeedback in the recovery of quadriceps femoris muscle function following anterior cruciate ligament surgery. *Physical Therapy.* 1991;71:455–461.

Einhorn AE, Sawyer M. The problem knee. Soft tissue considerations. In: Engle RP, ed. *Knee Ligament Rehabilitation.* New York, NY: Churchill Livingstone; 1991:197–219.

Einhorn AR, Sawyer M, Tovin B. Rehabilitation of intra-articular reconstructions. In: Greenfield BH, ed. *Rehabilitation of the Knee: A Problem-Solving Approach.* Philadelphia, Pa: FA Davis Co; 1993:288–303.

Engle RP, Canner GG. Proprioceptive neuromuscular facilitation (PNF) and modified procedures for anterior cruciate ligament (ACL) instability. *Journal of Orthopaedic and Sports Physical Therapy.* 1989;11:230–236.

Feagin JA, Curl WW. Isolated tear of the anterior cruciate ligament: five-year follow-up study. *Journal of Orthopaedic and Sports Physical Therapy.* 1990;12:232–235.

Friden T, Zatterstrom R, Lindstrand A, Moritz U. Anterior cruciate insufficient knees treated with physiotherapy: a three-year follow-up study of patients with late diagnosis. *Clinical Orthopaedics and Related Research.* 1991;263:190–199.

Fu FH, Woo SL, Irrgang JJ. Current concepts for rehabilitation following anterior cruciate ligament reconstruction. *Journal of Orthopaedic and Sports Physical Therapy.* 1992;15:270–278.

Jobe C, Jobe FW, Pink M. The sports medicine rehabilitation center. In: Nickel VL, Botte MJ, eds. *Orthopaedic Rehabilitation.* 2nd ed. New York, NY: Churchill Livingstone; 1992:207–221.

Lake DA. Neuromuscular electrical stimulation: an overview and its application in the treatment of sports injuries. *Sports Medicine.* 1992;13:320–336.

LoPresti C, et al. Quadriceps insufficiency following repair of the anterior cruciate ligament. *Journal of Orthopaedic and Sports Physical Therapy.* 1988;9:245–249.

Lysens RJ, de-Weerdt W, Nieuwboer A. Factors associated with injury proneness. *Sports Medicine.* 1991;12:281–289.

Mangine R, Heckman T. The knee. In: Sanders B, ed. *Sports Physical Therapy.* Norwalk, Conn: Appleton & Lange; 1990:434.

Mangine RE, Noyes FR. Rehabilitation of the allograft reconstruction. *Journal of Orthopaedic and Sports Physical Therapy.* 1992;15:294–302.

Mangine RE, Noyes FR, DeMaio M. Minimal protection program: advanced weight bearing and range of motion after ACL reconstruction—weeks 1 to 5. *Orthopedics.* 1992;15:504–515.

McCarthy MR, Yates CK, Anderson MA, Yates-McCarthy JL. The effects of immediate continuous passive motion on pain during the inflammatory phase of soft tissue healing following anterior cruciate ligament reconstruction. *Journal of Orthopaedic and Sports Physical Therapy.* 1993;17:96–101.

Norris CM. *Sports Injuries: Diagnosis and Management for Physiotherapists.* Boston, Mass: Butterworth-Heinemann; 1993.

Paulos L, Noyes FR, Grood E, Butler DL. Knee rehabilitation after anterior cruciate ligament reconstruction and repair. *Journal of Orthopaedic and Sports Physical Therapy.* 1991;13:60–68.

Schmidt G. Latest technique in ACL surgery and rehabilitation. *Journal of Orthopaedic and Sports Physical Therapy.* 1992;15:256–322.

Seto JL, Brewster CE, Lombardo SJ, Tibone JE. Rehabilitation of the knee after anterior cruciate ligament reconstruction. *Journal of Orthopaedic and Sports Physical Therapy.* 1989;11:8–18.

Shelbourne KD, Klootwyk TE, DeCarlo MS. Update on accelerated rehabilitation after anterior cruciate ligament reconstruction. *Journal of Orthopaedic and Sports Physical Therapy.* 1992;15:303–308.

Shelbourne KD, Nitz P. Accelerated rehabilitation after anterior cruciate ligament reconstruction. *Journal of Orthopaedic and Sports Physical Therapy.* 1992;15:256–264.

Stratford P. Reliability of a peak knee extensor and flexor torque protocol: a study of post anterior cruciate ligament reconstructed knees. *Physiotherapy Canada.* 1991;43:4:27–30.

Timm KE. Knee rehabilitation after anterior cruciate ligament reconstruction and repair. *Journal of Orthopaedic and Sports Physical Therapy.* 1991;13:69–70.

Tovin BJ, Tovin TS, Tovin M. Surgical and biomechanical considerations in rehabilitation of patients with intra-articular ACL reconstructions. *Journal of Orthopaedic and Sports Physical Therapy.* 1992;15:317–322.

Whieldon T, Yack, J, Colins C. Anterior tibial displacement during weight bearing and non-weight bearing rehabilitation exercises in the anterior cruciate deficient knee. *Physical Therapy.* 1989;69:Abstract 151:382.

Wilk KE, Andrews JR. Current concepts in the treatment of anterior cruciate ligament disruption. *Journal of Orthopaedic and Sports Physical Therapy.* 1992;15:279–293.

Zakaria D, Hartsell H. Efficacy of electrical muscle stimulation during protected immobilization following anterior cruciate ligament surgery. *Physiotherapy Canada.* 1993;45:2:89–93.

Posterior Cruciate Ligament and Medial Knee Ligament

Bandy WD, Timm KE. Relationship between peak torque, work, and power for knee flexion and extension in clients with grade I medial compartment sprains of the knee. *Journal of Orthopaedic and Sports Physical Therapy.* 1992;16:288–292.

Engle RP. Nonoperative posterior cruciate ligament rehabilitation. In: Engle RP, ed. *Knee Ligament Rehabilitation.* New York, NY: Churchill Livingstone; 1991:145.

Kannus P. Relationship between peak torque and angle-specific torques in an isokinetic contraction of normal and laterally unstable knees. *Journal of Orthopaedic and Sports Physical Therapy.* 1991;13:89–94.

Malone T. Surgical overview and rehabilitation process for ligamentous repair. In: Mangine RE, ed. *Physical Therapy of the Knee.* New York, NY: Churchill Livingstone; 1988:163.

McClure PW, Rothstein JM, Riddle DL. Intertester reliability of clinical judgements of medial knee ligament integrity. *Physical Therapy.* 1989;69:268–275.

Biceps Tendon Strain

DESCRIPTION

The biceps tendon can be strained or even ruptured during athletic activity. Strain and rupture of the biceps tendon is linked with an extremely strong elbow flexion force or a hyperextension force leading to elongation and stretch. Strains are graded as first, second, or third degree (mild, moderate, or severe).

- *First-degree strain* involves injury and irritation without any structural damage.
- *Second-degree strain* involves a certain degree of damage and functional loss, but the muscle-tendon unit is still intact.
- *Third-degree strain* involves a loss of function due to a complete tear. The onset can be sudden. If the biceps tendon is ruptured, resisted elbow flexion and forearm supination will be weak and painless. It is more common in athletes 50 years or older.

CAUSE

Typically, a hyperextension force causes the biceps tendon to elongate. Anterior and posterior joint capsule impingement may also occur with a hyperextension injury of the elbow. With a biceps tendon rupture, there may be a history of repeated corticosteroid injections.

ASSESSMENT

Areas

- History
- Pain
- Posture
- Joint integrity and structural deviations
- Mobility: active and passive range of motion (ROM) and accessory motion
- Strength: any muscle weakness and/or biomechanical abnormality in the rest of upper extremity that may be contributing to condition
- Neurological
- Skin and soft tissue: temperature, tenderness, tone, edema
- Functional level

Instruments/Procedures (See References for Sources)

Joint Integrity and Structural Deviations. The following areas are orthopedic tests for the elbow:

- golfer's elbow test
- ligamentous instability tests
- varus stress and valgus stress

Neurological

- elbow flexion test
- pinch test
- pronator teres syndrome
- Tinel's test

Mobility
- gonimetry

Pain
- Nirschl Pain Phase Scale

Skin and Soft Tissue
- palpation for temperature, tone, tenderness

Strength
1. instrumentation
   - grip test dynamometer
   - isokinetic testing
2. manual muscle testing

PROBLEMS
- The athlete may or may not complain of pain. With a strain, there is usually pain and tenderness.
- Usually if the biceps tendon ruptures, the athlete will have weakness in elbow flexion and forearm supination, but no pain.

TREATMENT/MANAGEMENT
- Use ice and compression immediately.
- A compression sleeve and taping can help limit elbow extension and promote healing in a shortened position.
- After healing, use passive stretching to work toward full extension.
- Protective splinting can be discontinued if symptoms are gone.
- Provide strengthening exercises initially with multiangle isometric work for biceps and supinators, and progress to isotonic and isokinetic muscular work. Eccentric biceps work should use an isotonic and isokinetic mode. Progress to coordination exercises and sport-specific training activities.
- Consider use of electrotherapy and hydrotherapy to increase circulation.
- To prevent further problems, instruct client in a stretching routine and use of taping before athletic activity.

PRECAUTIONS/CONTRAINDICATIONS
- Premature stress on tendon is contraindicated. Avoid massage or heat modalities to area during the early stages of treatment.
- Avoid hyperextension of the elbow.

DESIRED OUTCOME/PROGNOSIS
- The athlete will show no evidence of soft tissue inflammation, swelling, or ecchymosis.
- The athlete will have pain-free, normal joint mobility, and return of strength.

Muscles are highly vascularized and resilient. Unlike tendons, muscles rarely undergo fatigue degeneration. The decision of when the athlete can return to competition should be made in conjunction with the attending physician.

REFERENCES

ASSESSMENT

Joint Integrity and Structural Deviations
Rothstein JM, Roy SH, Wolf SL. *The Rehabilitation Specialist's Handbook*. Philadelphia, Pa: FA Davis Co; 1991:125–126. **[Ligamentous instability]**

Mobility
Rothstein JM, Roy SH, Wolf SL. *The Rehabilitation Specialist's Handbook*. Philadelphia, Pa: FA Davis Co; 1991:67–68. **[Goniometry]**
Tomberlin JP, Saunders HD. *Evaluation, Treatment and Prevention of Musculoskeletal Disorders. Vol 2: Extremities*. Chaska, Minn: The Saunders Group; 1994:113–138. **[Golfer's elbow, tennis elbow, varus stress and valgus stress]**

Neurological
Tomberlin JP, Saunders HD. *Evaluation, Treatment and Prevention of Musculoskeletal Disorders. Vol 2: Extremities*. Chaska, Minn: The Saunders Group; 1994:113–138. **[Pinch test, pronator teres syndrome, elbow flexion test, Tinel's test]**

Strength

Instrumentation
Buschbacher RM, ed. *Musculoskeletal Disorders: A Practical Guide for Diagnosis and Rehabilitation*. Boston, Mass: Andover Medical Publishers; 1994:160. **[Grip test dynamometer, isokinetic testing]**

Manual Muscle Testing
Daniels L, Worthingham C. *Muscle Testing Techniques of Manual Examination*. 6th ed. Philadelphia, Pa: WB Saunders Co; 1995.
Kendall FP, McCreary EK, Provance PG. *Muscles: Testing and Function*. 4th ed. Baltimore, Md: Williams & Wilkins; 1993.

Pain
Buschbacher RM. *Musculoskeletal Disorders: A Practical Guide for Diagnosis and Rehabilitation*. Boston, Mass: Andover Medical Publishers; 1994:158. **[Nirschl Pain Phase Scale]**

TREATMENT
Andrews JR, Whiteside JA. Common elbow problems in the athlete. *Journal of Orthopaedic and Sports Physical Therapy*. 1993;17:289–295.
Andrews JR, Wilk KE, Satterwhite YE, Tedder JL. Physical examination of the thrower's elbow. *Journal of Orthopaedic and Sports Physical Therapy*. 1993;17:296–304.
Dilorenzo CE, Parkes JC II, Chmelar RD. The importance of shoulder and cervical dysfunction in the etiology and treatment of athletic elbow injuries. *Journal of Orthopaedic and Sports Physical Therapy*. 1990;11:398–401.
Hertling D, Kessler RM. *Management of Common Musculoskeletal Disorders*. Philadelphia, Pa: JB Lippincott Co; 1990:78, 534.
Quarrier NF. Performing arts medicine: the musical athlete. *Journal of Orthopaedic and Sports Physical Therapy*. 1993;17:90–95.
Tomberlin JP, Saunders HD. *Evaluation, Treatment and Prevention of Musculoskeletal Disorders. Vol. 2: Extremities*. Chaska, Minn: The Saunders Group; 1994.
Werner SL, Fleisig GS, Dillman CJ, Andrews JR. Biomechanics of the elbow during baseball pitching. *Journal of Orthopaedic and Sports Physical Therapy*. 1993;17:274–278.

Wilk KE, Arrigo C, Andrews JR. Rehabilitation of the elbow in the throwing athlete. *Journal of Orthopaedic and Sports Physical Therapy.* 1993;17:305–317.

Wilk KE, Voight ML, Keirns MA, Gambetta V, Andrews JR, Dillman CJ. Stretch-shortening drills for the upper extremities: theory and clinical application. *Journal of Orthopaedic and Sports Physical Therapy.* 1993; 17:225–239.

Hamstring Muscle Strain

DESCRIPTION

The hamstring muscle (posterior femoral muscle) can be strained, pulled, or ruptured during athletic activity. The hamstring muscle extends the hip and flexes the knee during running and jumping and opposes the quadriceps muscle, which flexes the hip and extends the knee. The quadriceps muscle is stronger, but hamstring muscle strength should be at least 60% of or equal to the strength of the quadriceps muscle.

The strain usually occurs when the muscle is contracted quickly and vigorously. In addition to the hamstring muscle, other muscles prone to strain include the quadriceps muscle, the hip adductor muscles (gracilis, pectineus, and adductors longus, brevis, and magnus), the iliopsoas muscle, the rectus abdominis muscle, and the gluteus medius muscle.

Strains are classified into first, second, or third degree (mild, moderate, or severe).

- *First-degree strain* involves injury and irritation without any structural damage.
- *Second-degree strain* involves a certain degree of damage and functional loss, but the muscle–tendon unit is still intact.
- *Third-degree strain* involves a loss of function due to a complete tear.

CAUSE

Simultaneous contraction of the hamstrings and the quadriceps can lead to a hamstring tear if the hamstrings are too weak. Risk factors for a hamstring strain include poor posture, inflexibility, inadequate warm-up, neurological and muscular fatigue, improper techniques, strength imbalance, and poor neuromuscular control.

ASSESSMENT

Areas

- History
- Pain
- Posture
- Gait, including weight-bearing pattern
- Joint integrity and structural deviations
- Mobility: active and passive range of motion (ROM) and accessory motion
- Strength
- Neurological sensation, proprioception, deep tendon reflexes, neural tension
- Skin and soft tissue: temperature, tone, tenderness, edema
- Functional level, including activities of daily living (ADLs)

Instruments/Procedures (See References for Sources)

Joint Integrity and Structural Deviations. The following are orthopedic tests for the knee and hip:
- Craig's test
- Ely's test
- Fabere test
- hamstring tightness and muscle length
- iliotibial band length
- leg-length test
- Noble's compression test
- Ober's test
- piriformis test
- Thomas test
- Trendelenburg's sign

Mobility
- goniometry

Pain
- visual analogue scale

Skin and Soft Tissue
- palpation for temperature, tone, tenderness

Strength
- manual muscle testing

PROBLEMS
- The athlete usually reports hearing a "popping" sound with the muscle tear.
- There is intense pain and spasm proportional to the severity of injury.
- There may be tenderness, especially during a stretch of the hamstring muscle.
- There is usually pain with walking and using the stairs.
- The athlete may have ecchymosis, hemorrhage, and a muscle deficit if strain is severe.
- There is usually tightness and weakness in the hamstring muscle.

TREATMENT/MANAGEMENT

Acute Injury
- The acronym **RICE** (**R**est, **I**ce, **C**ompression, and **E**levation) is indicated for pain and inflammation.
- Physical agents can include cold whirlpool, high-voltage pulsed monophasic current, acupuncture point stimulation, phonophoresis, and ultrasound to local area. In the acute phase, a suggested treatment with pulsed 1 MHz ultrasound at an intensity of 0.5 W/cm^2 or less has been reported useful.
- Active ROM can be performed after the area has stabilized.
- Consider the use of progressive mobilization, friction massage, and stretching.
- Suggest alternative exercise for general fitness that will not stress the injured area.

Stable Injury
- Use scar massage with gentle stretching and phonophoresis.

- Consider cross-fiber friction massage.
- Consider mobilization of sacroiliac joint.
- Review athlete's technique to minimize avoidable stress.
- Pad over injury site with wrap before activity.
- Emphasize importance of flexibility, and instruct client in proper stretching techniques.
- Strengthen areas of weakness in a gradual and conservative progression.
- Warm-up exercises should include movements that mimic the actual sporting event.
- Cool-down exercises should reverse this technique.

PRECAUTIONS/CONTRAINDICATIONS
- Any attempt to "run off" a hamstring strain can increase the risk of causing a greater strain.
- A minimum wait of 5 to 7 days is recommended before resuming pain-free stretching after a mild second-degree tear. A second-degree tear can take at least 6 weeks to heal before return to full activity is permitted.
- Before returning to full activity, the client needs normal flexibility, strength, endurance, agility, and power. Adjacent muscles should also be checked.

DESIRED OUTCOME/PROGNOSIS
- The athlete will have an early stabilization of injury.
- The athlete will experience a reduction in pain.
- There will be a reduction of edema and promotion of healing.
- There will be minimal internal scar formation and muscle defect.
- Treatment will lead to improved remodeling of injury, with reduced cross-linking and random fiber alignment as the collagen repairs.
- Rehabilitation will prevent atrophy and maintain fitness.
- The athlete will maintain ROM in the lower extremities.
- The athlete will have minimal time lost from sport.

Collagen remodeling can take up to 3 weeks, and a gain of full strength may take even longer. Rehabilitation time of 2 to 3 weeks can be expected if injury is mild or 2 to 6 months if the injury is severe.

REFERENCES

ASSESSMENT

Joint Integrity and Structural Deviations
Gaidosik RL, Rieck MA, Sullivan DK, Wightman SE. Comparison of four clinical tests for assessing hamstring muscle length. *Journal of Orthopaedic and Sports Physical Therapy.* 1993;18:614–618.

Gogia PP, Braatz JH. Validity and reliability of leg length measurements. *Journal of Orthopaedic and Sports Physical Therapy.* 1986;8:185–188.

Melchione WE, Sullivan MS. Reliability of measurements obtained by use of an instrument designed to indirectly measure iliotibial band length. *Journal of Orthopaedic and Sports Physical Therapy.* 1993;18:511–515.

Tomberlin JP, Saunders HD. *Evaluation, Treatment and Prevention of Musculoskeletal Disorders. Vol 2: Extremities.* Chaska, Minn: The Saunders Group; 1994:200. [**Craig's test, Ely's test, Fabere, hamstring tightness, leg-length test, Noble's compression test, Ober's test, piriformis test, quadrant, Thomas test, Trendelenburg sign, torque test**]

Woerman AL, Binder-Macleod SA. Leg length discrepancy assessment: accuracy and precision in five clinical methods of evaluation. *Journal of Orthopaedic and Sports Physical Therapy.* 1984;230–239.

Mobility

Rothstein JM, Roy SH, Wolf SL. *The Rehabilitation Specialist's Handbook*. Philadelphia, Pa: FA Davis Co; 1991:67–68. **[Goniometry]**

Pain

Langely GB, Sheppeard H. The visual analogue scale: its use in pain measurement. *Rheumatology International*. 1985;5:145–148.

Strength

Manual Muscle Testing

Daniels L, Worthingham C. *Muscle Testing Techniques of Manual Examination*. 6th ed. Philadelphia, Pa: WB Saunders Co; 1995.

Kendall FP, McCreary EK, Provance PG. *Muscles: Testing and Function*. 4th ed. Baltimore, Md: Williams & Wilkins, 1993.

TREATMENT

Barker AT, Barlow PS, Porter J, et al. A double-blind clinical trial of low power pulsed shortwave therapy in the treatment of a soft tissue injury. *Physiotherapy*. 1985;71:500–504.

Brady WD, Sinning WE. Kinematic effects of heel lift use to correct lower limb length differences. *Journal of Orthopaedic and Sports Physical Therapy*. 1986;7:173–179.

Chadwick P. The significance of spinal joint signs in the management of groin strain and patellofemoral pain by manual techniques. *Physiotherapy*. 1987;73:507–513.

Cibulka MT. Rehabilitation of the pelvis, hip, and thigh. *Clinical Sports Medicine*. 1989;8:777-803.

Cibulka MT, Rose SJ, Delitto A, Sinacore DR. Hamstring muscle strain treated by mobilizing the sacroiliac joint. *Physical Therapy*. 1986;66:1220–1223.

Coole WG Jr, Gieck JH. An analysis of hamstring strains and their rehabilitation. *Journal of Orthopaedic and Sports Physical Therapy*. 1987;9:77–85.

Echternach JL, ed. *Physical Therapy of the Hip*. New York, NY: Churchill-Livingstone; 1990.

Kornberg C, Lew P. The effect of stretching neural structures on grade one hamstring injuries. *Journal of Orthopaedic and Sports Physical Therapy*. 1989;10:481–487.

Romero JA. The hip and pelvis. In: Sanders B, ed. *Sports Physical Therapy*. Norwalk, Conn: Appleton & Lange; 1990:397–421.

Satterfield MJ, Yasumura K, Abreu SH. Retro runner with ischial tuberosity enthesopathy. *Journal of Orthopaedic and Sports Physical Therapy*. 1993;17:191–194.

Stanton P, Purdam C. Hamstring injuries in sprinting: the role of eccentric exercise. *Journal of Orthopaedic and Sports Physical Therapy*. 1989;10:343–349.

Tonsolone PA. Chronic adductor tendinitis in a female swimmer. *Journal of Orthopaedic and Sports Physical Therapy*. 1993;18:629–633.

Hip Contusion

Also known as a *hip pointer*.

DESCRIPTION

Contusions are defined as direct blows leading to soft tissue trauma. When a blow occurs in the iliac crest region, usually at or near the anterior superior iliac spine, it is sometimes called a hip contusion. Avulsion of the external obliques is a common secondary problem. Other contusions in the hip region include sacroiliac joint contusion, coccygeal contusion, and contusion injuries to the groin.

CAUSE

A direct blow during a sport can cause muscle fibers to be crushed and separated, leading to bleeding and swelling.

ASSESSMENT

Areas
- History
- Pain
- Posture
- Gait, including weight-bearing pattern
- Joint integrity and structural deviations
- Mobility: active and passive range of motion (ROM) and accessory motion
- Strength
- Neurological: sensation, proprioception, deep tendon reflexes, neural tension
- Skin and soft tissue: temperature, tone, tenderness, edema
- Functional level

Instruments/Procedures (See References for Sources)

Joint Integrity and Structural Deviations. The following are orthopedic tests for the lower extremities:
- Craig's test
- Ely's test
- Fabere test
- hamstring tightness
- leg-length test
- Noble's compression test
- Ober's test
- piriformis test
- Thomas test
- torque test
- Trendelenburg's sign

Mobility
- goniometry

Pain
- visual analogue scale

Skin and Soft Tissue
- palpation for temperature, tone, tenderness

Strength
- manual muscle testing

PROBLEMS
- There is usually bleeding and edema.

- The athlete usually complains of pain with active trunk movement, coughing, sneezing, or laughing.

TREATMENT/MANAGEMENT
- Rest and ice are indicated, especially in early stages (48 to 72 hours post injury).
- Begin active ROM and a gradual return to function after there is a reduction of swelling and inflammation.
- Protective padding is usually indicated.
- Start gentle, graded stretching as symptoms subside.
- Consider transcutaneous electrical nerve stimulation (TENS) for pain.

PRECAUTIONS/CONTRAINDICATIONS
- Avoid aggravating the soft tissue injury by overly vigorous stretching.
- Contusions of the ischial tuberosity must be differentiated from avulsion fractures.
- Severe or chronic contusions can progress to myositis ossificans (a mineralization that forms in the hematoma and usually appears within 1 to 2 weeks following a severe contusion). Massage and stretching are generally contraindicated.

DESIRED OUTCOME/PROGNOSIS
- The athlete will experience a reduction in symptoms.
- The athlete will return to pain-free activities.

REFERENCES

ASSESSMENT

Echternach JL, ed. *Physical Therapy of the Hip*. New York, NY: Churchill-Livingstone; 1990:36. [**Hip pain algorithm**]

Hicklin SP, DePretis MC. Lower extremity: hip. In: Myers RS, ed. *Saunders Manual of Physical Therapy Practice*. Philadelphia, Pa: WB Saunders Co; 1995:962–968. [**Hip evaluation including orthopedic and neurological hip tests**]

Joint Integrity and Structural Deviations
Tomberlin JP, Saunders HD. *Evaluation, Treatment and Prevention of Musculoskeletal Disorders. Vol 2: Extremities*. Chaska, Minn: The Saunders Group; 1994:200. [**Trendelenburg's sign, piriformis test, Thomas test, Ely's test, Ober's test, Noble's compression test, hamstring tightness, quadrant test, Fabere test, torque test, Craig's test, leg-length test**]

Mobility

Goniometry
Rothstein JM, Roy SH, Wolf SL. *The Rehabilitation Specialist's Handbook*. Philadelphia, Pa: FA Davis Co; 1991:67–68.

Pain
Langely GB, Sheppeard H. The visual analogue scale: its use in pain measurement. *Rheumatology International*. 1985;5:145–148.

Strength

Manual Muscle Testing

Daniels L, Worthingham C. *Muscle Testing Techniques of Manual Examination.* 6th ed. Philadelphia, Pa: WB Saunders Co; 1995.

Kendall FP, McCreary EK, Provance PG. *Muscles: Testing and Function.* 4th ed. Baltimore, Md: Williams & Wilkins, 1993.

TREATMENT

Cibulka MT. Rehabilitation of the pelvis, hip, and thigh. *Clinical Sports Medicine.* 1989;8:777–803.

Cibulka MT, Delitto A. A comparison of two different methods to treat hip pain in runners. *Journal of Orthopedic and Sports Physical Therapy.* 1993;17:172–176.

Echternach JL, ed. *Physical Therapy of the Hip.* New York, NY: Churchill-Livingstone; 1990.

Hicklin SP, DePretis MC. Lower extremity: hip. In: Myers RS, ed. *Saunders Manual of Physical Therapy Practice.* Philadelphia, Pa: WB Saunders Co; 1995:982.

Pryor SR. *Getting Back on Your Feet: How to Recover Mobility and Fitness After Injury or Surgery to Your Foot, Leg, Hip, or Knee.* Post Mills, Vt: Chelsea Green Publishing Co; 1990.

Romero JA. The hip and pelvis. In: Sanders B, ed. *Sports Physical Therapy.* Norwalk, Conn: Appleton & Lange; 1990; 397–421.

Roy S, Irvin R. *Sports Medicine: Prevention, Evaluation, Management and Rehabilitation.* Englewood Cliffs, NJ: Prentice Hall; 1983:299–305.

Iliotibial Band Friction Syndrome

DESCRIPTION

Iliotibial band (ITB) friction syndrome is an overuse injury affecting two components at the lateral knee: the iliopatellar band and the iliotibial tract. This condition is a frequent source of knee pain in runners.

CAUSE

Excess friction, due to overuse of the knee, between the iliotibial band and the lateral femoral condyle lying underneath can be the cause of this problem. Iliotibial band friction syndrome can also be caused by a sudden unaccustomed stress to the knee. People prone to this condition include those with the following conditions: ITB tightness, pes cavus, genu varus, increased femoral rotation under the ITB, and a crossover gait pattern. Cycling or walking with the foot pronated can also affect the tightness of the ITB.

ASSESSMENT

Areas

- History
- Pain
- Posture

- Gait
- Joint integrity and structural deviations
- Mobility: active and passive range of motion (ROM) and accessory motion
- Strength
- Neurological: sensation, proprioception, deep tendon reflexes, neural tension tests
- Skin and soft tissue: temperature, tone, tenderness, edema
- Functional level and any training/performance errors
- Equipment, including footwear

Instruments/Procedures (See References for Sources)

Joint Integrity and Structural Deviations. The following are orthopedic tests for the knee. Those recommended especially for this condition are marked with an asterisk.

- A-angle
- Anteromedial Rotational Instability (AMRI)
- Anterolateral Rotational Instability (ALRI)
- Apley grinding test
- apprehension test
- bounce home test
- brush or stroke (wipe) test
- Clark's sign
- crossover test
- Ely's test
- external rotation test
- flexion rotation drawer text
- fluctuation test
- gravity drawer test (posterior sag sign)
- hamstring length
- Helfet test
- Hughston plica test
- Hughston posterolateral drawer test
- Hughston test (jerk sign)
- hyperflexion-hyperextension test
- Jakob test (reverse pivot)
- Lachman test
- lateral pull test
- leg-length discrepancy*
- MacIntosh test (lateral pivot shift)
- McConnell's test
- McMurray-Anderson test
- Noble's compression test*
- Ober's test*
- O'Donoghue's test
- patellar tap test
- patellar tilt test
- Perkin's test
- plica test

- posterior drawer sign
- posterior sag sign
- quadriceps active test
- reverse pivot shift
- Slocum test
- Steinman's test
- step-down test*
- squat test
- valgus stress test
- varus stress test
- Waldron test
- Wilson test

Mobility
- goniometry

Pain
- visual analogue scale

Skin and Soft Tissue
- palpation for temperature, tone, tenderness

Strength
- manual muscle testing

PROBLEMS
- The athlete usually complains of diffuse aching or tenderness at the lateral knee with activity. Pain may also be felt at the greater trochanter.
- Pain may have insidious onset but can also be triggered by athletic activity.
- The athlete may be unable to run secondary to pain.
- There is usually excessive tightness of the ITB.
- There can be point tenderness at the lateral femoral condyle.
- The athlete may complain of irritation during stair climbing.
- The athlete may be unable to run.
- There is usually weakness at quadriceps and gluteus medius muscles.

TREATMENT/MANAGEMENT
- Encourage rest.
- Physical agents and modalities can include ice, ultrasound, high-voltage pulsed monophasic current, and iontophoresis for symptoms.
- Stretch ITB and tensor fasciae latae tightness as indicated.
- Correct any structural limb-length inequality.
- Balance subtalar motion leading to any femoral internal rotation or genu varus.
- Consider an orthosis for any abnormalities in joint mechanics, especially the effect the foot position adds to any lateral stress at knee.
- Strengthen hip external rotators.
- Consider friction massage and soft tissue mobilization.
- Counsel athlete about avoiding activities or training errors that irritate the ITB.
- Resume normal athletic routine gradually.

PRECAUTIONS/CONTRAINDICATIONS
- Rule out femoral stress fracture, gluteal strain, lateral meniscal tear, piriformis syndrome, and popliteus tendinitis.
- The pain at the lateral knee will most likely increase if there is no modification of the repeated stress.
- Runners need to avoid too much sidehill running and unnecessary stair work.

DESIRED OUTCOME/PROGNOSIS
- The athlete will have a decrease in symptoms such as inflammation.
- The athlete will resume pain-free athletic activities and activities of daily living (ADLs). If the ITB is related to pes cavus, the recovery may take twice as long to resolve.

REFERENCES

ASSESSMENT
Joint Integrity and Structural Deviations
Blustein M, D'Amico JC. Limb length discrepancy: identification, clinical significance and management. *Physical Therapy.* 1985;75:200–206.

Melchione WE, Sullivan MS. Reliability of measurements obtained by use of an instrument designed to indirectly measure iliotibial band length. *Journal of Orthopaedic and Sports Physical Therapy.* 1993;18:511–515.

Myers RS, ed. *Saunders Manual of Physical Therapy Practice.* Philadelphia, Pa: WB Saunders Co; 1995:1349. **[Step-down test]**

Rothstein JM, Roy SH, Wolf SL. *The Rehabilitation Specialist's Handbook.* Philadelphia, Pa: FA Davis Co; 1991:132–137. **[Apley grinding test, bounce home test, brush or stroke (wipe) test, Clark's sign, cross-over test, gravity drawer test (posterior sag sign), Helfet test, Hughston plica test, Hughston postero-lateral drawer test, Hughston test (jerk sign), Jakob test (reverse pivot), MacIntosh test (lateral pivot shift), O'Donoghue's test, Perkin's test, Slocum test, Waldron test, Wilson test]**

Tomberlin JP, Saunders HD. *Evaluation, Treatment and Prevention of Musculoskeletal Disorders. Vol 2: Extremities.* Chaska, Minn: The Saunders Group; 1994:233. **[ALRI, AMRI, apprehension test, Ely's test, external rotation test, flexion rotation drawer, fluctuation test, functional knee status, hamstring length, hyperflexion-hyperextension test, Lachman's test, lateral pull test, McConnell's test, McIntosh test, McMurray-Anderson test, Noble's compression test, Ober's test, patellar tap, patellar tilt, plica test, posterior drawer sign, posterior sag sign, quadriceps active test, reverse pivot shift, Slocum's ALRI, squat test, Steinman's test, stroke test, valgus stress, varus stress]**

Mobility
Rothstein JM, Roy SH, Wolf SL. *The Rehabilitation Specialist's Handbook.* Philadelphia, Pa: FA Davis Co; 1991:67–68. **[Goniometry]**

Pain
Langely GB, Sheppeard H. The visual analogue scale: its use in pain measurement. *Rheumatology International.* 1985;5:145–148.

Strength
Manual Muscle Testing
Daniels L, Worthingham C. *Muscle Testing Techniques of Manual Examination.* 6th ed. Philadelphia, Pa: WB Saunders Co; 1995.

Kendall FP, McCreary EK, Provance PG. *Muscles: Testing and Function.* 4th ed. Baltimore, Md: Williams & Wilkins; 1993.

TREATMENT

Brown L, Yavorsky P. Locomotor biomechanics and pathomechanics: a review. *Journal of Orthopaedics and Sports Physical Therapy.* 1987;9:3–10.

Hertling D, Kessler RM. *Management of Common Musculoskeletal Disorders.* Philadelphia, Pa: JB Lippincott Co; 1990:351.

Mangine R, Heckman T. The knee. In: Sanders B, ed. *Sports Physical Therapy.* Norwalk, Conn: Appleton & Lange; 1990:438–439.

Pease B. Biomechanical assessment of the lower extremity. *Orthopaedic Physical Therapy Clinics of North America.* 1994;3:291–325.

Roy S, Irvin R. *Sports Medicine: Prevention, Evaluation, Management and Rehabilitation.* Englewood Cliffs, NJ: Prentice Hall; 1983.

Schwellnus MP, Mackintosh L, Mee J. Deep transverse frictions in the treatment of iliotibial band friction syndrome in athletes: a clinical trial. *Physiotherapy.* 1992;78:564–568.

Warren BL, Davis V. Determining predictor variables for running-related pain. *Physical Therapy.* 1988;68:647–651.

Medial Collateral Ligament (of elbow) Sprain

DESCRIPTION

The medial collateral ligament of the elbow may be sprained during throwing activities. Injury to the medial collateral ligament accompanied by medial elbow muscle hypertrophy is sometimes called "Little League elbow." In an adolescent whose growth plate has not fused, a repetitive valgus stress can lead to an avulsion injury of the medial epicondyle. Ligamentous injury has four stages: edema, scarring and disassociation of fibers, calcification, and finally ossification.

CAUSE

Throwing can place severe stress on the soft tissues of the elbow, resulting in an overuse injury. The acceleration phase of throwing is the most stressful to the elbow joint due to the valgus stress on the medial joint structures. This repeated valgus extension overload leads to microtraumatic injury. Factors influencing overuse injury risk may be both intrinsic and extrinsic:

- *Intrinsic factors* include malalignment, muscular imbalance, inflexibility, muscular weakness, and instability.
- *Extrinsic factors* include training errors, equipment, environment, technique, and sports-imposed deficiencies.

Injury can also be caused by a direct blow or elbow dislocation. A complete ligamentous rupture is usually associated with acute trauma.

ASSESSMENT

Areas

- History
- Pain
- Posture

- Joint integrity and structural deviations
- Mobility: active and passive range of motion (ROM) and accessory motion
- Strength: any muscle weakness and/or biomechanical abnormality in the rest of upper extremity that may be contributing to condition
- Neurological, including sensation, proprioception, and deep tendon reflexes
- Skin and soft tissue: temperature, tone, tenderness, edema
- Gait
- Functional level

Instruments/Procedures (See References for Sources)

Joint Integrity and Structural Deviations. The following are orthopedic tests for the elbow. Those recommended especially for this condition are marked with an asterisk.
- golfer's elbow test
- ligamentous instability tests
- tennis elbow test
- varus stress and valgus stress tests*

Neurological. The following are neurological tests of the elbow. See also "Strength," *grip test dynamometer* and *isokinetic testing.*
- elbow flexion test
- pinch test
- pronator teres syndrome
- Tinel's test

Pain
- Nirschl Pain Phase Scale

Skin and Soft Tissue
- palpation for temperature, tone, tenderness

Strength
1. instrumentation
   - grip test dynamometer
   - isokinetic testing
2. manual muscle testing

PROBLEMS
- The athlete usually has medial instability of the elbow joint with a valgus stress.
- The athlete usually has swelling of the elbow at the medial region.
- The athlete can have pain with throwing or pushing motions.
- The involved elbow may be painful to touch over the ulnar collateral ligament.

TREATMENT/MANAGEMENT
- Prescribe rest from stressful activities.
- Immobilization may be indicated if there is evidence of osteochondritis dissecans of the capitulum, if the athlete is post surgery, or if the symptoms are severe.
- Use physical agents and modalities as indicated.

- An exercise program can include a progression from passive exercise, including joint mobilization and stretching, to isometric, isotonic, and isokinetic work. One schedule recommends isokinetic work at three times per week for 10 to 30 seconds at 30 degree/second increments with 10 to 12 repetitions.
- Use proprioceptive exercise to prevent reinjury.
- Consider use of preventive taping or bracing.
- Teach proper mechanics of throwing.

PRECAUTIONS/CONTRAINDICATIONS
- During stages of healing, ligamentous rupture can still occur.
- Chronic valgus stress of the ligament, along with hyperextension at the humeroulnar joint, can lead to the formation of bone spurs and ossific bodies. Surgical removal of these spurs may be necessary for restoration of the function of the elbow.
- Surgical repair or reconstruction may be used with acute instability.
- Communication with surgeon about progression of rehabilitation is important.

DESIRED OUTCOME/PROGNOSIS
- The athlete will show no evidence of soft tissue inflammation or swelling.
- The athlete will have pain-free, normal joint mobility and return of strength.
- The athlete will be able to demonstrate a correct throwing technique.

The decision of when the athlete can return to competition should be made in conjunction with the primary caregiver.

REFERENCES

ASSESSMENT

Joint Integrity and Structural Deviations
Rothstein JM, Roy SH, Wolf SL. *The Rehabilitation Specialist's Handbook*. Philadelphia, Pa: FA Davis Co; 1991:125–126. [**Ligamentous instability tests**]
Tomberlin JP, Saunders HD. *Evaluation, Treatment and Prevention of Musculoskeletal Disorders. Vol 2: Extremities*. Chaska, Minn: The Saunders Group; 1994:113–138. [**Golfer's elbow test, tennis elbow test, varus stress and valgus stress tests**]

Neurological Features
Buschbacher RM, ed. *Musculoskeletal Disorders: A Practical Guide for Diagnosis and Rehabilitation*. Boston, Mass: Andover Medical Publishers; 1994:160. [**Grip test dynamometer, isokinetic testing**]
Tomberlin JP, Saunders HD. *Evaluation, Treatment and Prevention of Musculoskeletal Disorders. Vol 2: Extremities*. Chaska, Minn: The Saunders Group; 1994:113–138. [**Elbow flexion test, pinch test, pronator teres syndrome, Tinel's test**]

Pain
Buschbacher RM, ed. *Musculoskeletal Disorders: A Practical Guide for Diagnosis and Rehabilitation*. Boston, Mass: Andover Medical Publishers; 1994:158. [**Nirschl Pain Phase Scale**]

TREATMENT
Andrews JR, Whiteside JA. Common elbow problems in the athlete. *Journal of Orthopaedic and Sports Physical Therapy*. 1993;17:289–295.

Andrews JR, Wilk KE, Satterwhite YE, Tedder JL. Physical examination of the thrower's elbow. *Journal of Orthopaedic and Sports Physical Therapy.* 1993;17:296–304.

Bernhardt-Bainbridge D. Sports injuries in children. In: Campbell SK, ed. *Physical Therapy for Children.* Philadelphia, Pa: WB Saunders Co; 1994:383–422.

Dilorenzo CE, Parkes JC II, Chemlar RD. The importance of shoulder and cervical dysfunction in the etiology and treatment of athletic elbow injuries. *Journal of Orthopaedic and Sports Physical Therapy.* 1990;11:398–401.

Quarrier NF. Performing arts medicine: the musical athlete. *Journal of Orthopaedic and Sports Physical Therapy.* 1993;17:90–95.

Seto, Brewster CE, Randall CC, Jobe FW. Rehabilitation following ulnar collateral ligament reconstruction of athletes. *Journal of Orthopaedic and Sports Physical Therapy.* 1991;14:100–105.

Werner SL, Fleisig GS, Dillman CJ, Andrews JR. Biomechanics of the elbow during baseball pitching. *Journal of Orthopaedic and Sports Physical Therapy.* 1993;17:274–278.

Wilder RP, Nirschl PR, Sobel J. Elbow and forearm. In: Buschbacher RM, ed. *Musculoskeletal Disorders: A Practical Guide for Diagnosis and Rehabilitation.* Boston, Mass: Andover Medical Publishers; 1994:153–169.

Wilk KE, Arrigo C, Andrews JR. Rehabilitation of the elbow in the throwing athlete. *Journal of Orthopaedic and Sports Physical Therapy.* 1993;17:305–317.

Wilk KE, Voight ML, Keirns MA, Gambetta V, Andrews JR, Dillman CJ. Stretch-shortening drills for the upper extremities: theory and clinical application. *Journal of Orthopaedic and Sports Physical Therapy.* 1993;17:225–239.

Meniscal Tear

DESCRIPTION

A tear of the meniscus is common among athletes. The tear may be confined to the periphery or may involve the meniscal body. It is not uncommon to have an anterior cruciate ligament (ACL) injury concurrent with medial meniscal injury. The injury may be preceded by degenerative damage that leads to chronic pain.

CAUSE

Injury to the meniscus of the knee can be caused by varus or valgus contact with rotation but is usually triggered by noncontact knee stress. Often a quick change of direction can trigger injury. If the knee is twisted, in hyperflexion, or in hyperextension (as in jumping), it is more vulnerable to injury. Degenerative damage is usually due to repeated stress in a squatting or kneeling position.

ASSESSMENT

Areas
- History
- Pain
- Posture
- Gait

- Joint integrity and structural deviation
- Mobility: active and passive range of motion (ROM) and accessory motion
- Strength
- Neurological: sensation, proprioception, deep tendon reflexes, neural tension
- Skin and soft tissue: temperature, edema
- Functional level
- Equipment, including footwear

Instruments/Procedures (See References for Sources)

Functional Level
- Modified Lysholm Knee Score

Joint Integrity and Structural Deviations. The following are orthopaedic tests for the knee. Those commonly used with this condition are marked with an asterisk.
- A-angle
- Anteromedial Rotational Instability (AMRI)
- anterior drawer sign
- Anterolateral Rotational Instability (ALRI)
- Apley grinding test*
- apprehension test
- bounce home test
- brush or stroke (wipe) test
- Clark's sign
- crossover test
- Ely's test
- external rotation test
- flexion rotation drawer test
- fluctuation test
- gravity drawer test (posterior sag sign)
- hamstring length
- Helfet test*
- Hughston plica test
- Hughston posterolateral drawer test
- Hughston test (jerk sign)
- hyperflexion-hyperextension test
- Jakob test (reverse pivot)
- Lachman test
- lateral pull test
- limb-length discrepancy
- MacIntosh test (lateral pivot shift)
- McConnell test
- McMurray–Anderson test*
- Noble's compression test
- Ober's test
- O'Donoghue's test
- patellar tap
- patellar tilt

- Perkin's test
- plica test
- posterior drawer sign
- posterior sag sign
- quadriceps active test
- reverse pivot shift
- Slocum test
- Steinman's test
- squat test
- valgus stress test
- varus stress test
- Waldron test
- Wilson test

Mobility
- goniometry

Skin and Soft Tissue
1. temperature, tone, tenderness
   - palpation
2. edema
   - tape measure
   - water displacement

Strength
- manual muscle testing

PROBLEMS
- The athlete may complain of deep pain associated with a feeling of the joint "giving way."
- The athlete may report a feeling of the knee catching or locking.
- There may be pain at the knee joint line and with movement, especially with weight bearing.
- The athlete usually has an antalgic gait.
- There may be limited knee flexion.

TREATMENT/MANAGEMENT
- Treatment, in general, is based on the nature of the lesion, extent of degeneration, and residual joint stability.
- Use physical agents and modalities for symptom control.
- Gait activities may indicate the use of an assistive device. Usually, full weight bearing is allowed around 4 to 7 days postoperatively with a partial meniscectomy. Non-weight-bearing status is common for 3 to 6 weeks after meniscal repairs. Gradually return to full weight-bearing status.
- Exercise can include open-chain activities initially, progressing to closed-chain activities. Aquatic therapy and proprioceptive training can be useful.

PRECAUTIONS/CONTRAINDICATIONS
- Exercise should avoid excessive joint swelling or pain to prevent reinjury. The process of rehabilitation after surgery should be gradual, avoiding too strenuous activity.

- The therapist may be unable to perform McMurray's test if effusion restricts knee flexion or the Helfet test because of incomplete extension.

DESIRED OUTCOME/PROGNOSIS
- The athlete will have decreased or no symptoms.
- The athlete will have pain-free full ROM and resumption of activities of daily living (ADLs) including athletic activities.
  Nonoperative postmeniscal injury and partial meniscectomy rehabilitation lasts approximately 6 to 12 weeks. Recovery after surgical repair may last 6 months. In general, the more conditioned the athlete, the quicker the recovery.

REFERENCES

ASSESSMENT

Functional Level
Delitto A. Lower extremity: knee. In Myers RS, ed. *Saunders Manual of Physical Therapy Practice*. Philadelphia, Pa: WB Saunders Co; 1995:1011. **[Modified Lysholm Knee Score]**

Mobility
Delitto A. Lower extremity: knee. In: Myers RS, ed. *Saunders Manual of Physical Therapy Practice*. Philadelphia, Pa: WB Saunders Co; 1995:1012. **[Goniometry]**
Rothstein JM, Miller PJ, Roetgger RF. Goniometric reliability in a clinical setting: elbow and knee measurements. *Physical Therapy*. 1983:1611–1615. **[Goniometry]**

Joint Integrity and Structural Deviations
Rothstein JM, Roy SH, Wolf SL. *The Rehabilitation Specialist's Handbook*. Philadelphia, Pa: FA Davis Co; 1991:132–137. **[Apley's grinding test, bounce home test, brush or stroke (wipe) test, Clark's sign, crossover test, gravity drawer test (posterior sag sign), Helfet test, Hughston plica test, Hughston posterolateral drawer test, Hughston test (jerk sign), Jakob test (reverse pivot), MacIntosh test (lateral pivot shift), O'Donoghue's test, Perkin's test, Slocum test, Waldron test, Wilson test]**
Tomberlin JP, Saunders HD. *Evaluation, Treatment and Prevention of Musculoskeletal Disorders. Vol 2: Extremities*. Chaska, Minn: The Saunders Group; 1994:233. **[ALRI, AMRI, apprehension, Ely's test, external rotation test, flexion rotation drawer, fluctuation test, functional knee status, hamstring length, hyperflexion-hyperextension test, Lachman's test, lateral pull test, McConnell test, McIntosh test, McMurray-Anderson test, Noble's compression test, Ober's test, patellar tap, patellar tilt, plica test, posterior drawer sign, posterior sag sign, quadriceps active test, reverse pivot shift, Slocum's ALRI, squat, Steinman's test, stroke test, valgus stress, varus stress]**

Skin and Soft Tissue

Edema
Delitto A. Lower extremity: knee. In: Myers RS, ed. *Saunders Manual of Physical Therapy Practice*. Philadelphia, Pa: WB Saunders Co; 1995:1013. **[Tape measure, water displacement]**

Strength

Manual Muscle Testing
Daniels L, Worthingham C. *Muscle Testing Techniques of Manual Examination*. 6th ed. Philadelphia, Pa: WB Saunders Co; 1995.

Kendall FP, McCreary EK, Provance PG. *Muscles: Testing and Function*. 4th ed. Baltimore, Md: Williams & Wilkins; 1993.

TREATMENT

Campbell D, Glenn W. Rehabilitation of knee flexors and extensor muscle strength in patients with meniscectomies, ligamentous repairs, and chondromalacia. *Physical Therapy*. 1982;62:10–15.

David JM. Jumper's knee. *Journal of Orthopaedic and Sports Physical Therapy*. 1989;11:137–141.

Davies GJ, Wallace LA, Malone T. Mechanisms of selected knee injuries. *Physical Therapy*. 1980;60:1590.

Delitto A. Lower extremity: knee. In: Myers RS, ed. *Saunders Manual of Physical Therapy Practice*. Philadelphia, Pa: WB Saunders Co; 1995:1001–1029.

Farina NT. Isokinetics in knee rehabilitation. *Clinical Management in Physical Therapy*. 1991;11:6:58–63.

Forster DP, Frost CE. Cost-effectiveness of outpatient physiotherapy after medical meniscectomy. *British Medical Journal*. 1982;284:485–487.

Hertling D, Kessler RM. *Management of Common Musculoskeletal Disorders*. Philadelphia, Pa: JB Lippincott; 1990:342–344.

Mangine R, Heckman T. The knee. In: Sanders B, ed. *Sports Physical Therapy*. Norwalk, Conn: Appleton & Lange; 1990:434.

Meade TD. Meniscus tears: diagnosis and treatment. In: Engle RP. *Knee Ligament Rehabilitation*. New York, NY: Churchill Livingstone; 1991.

Moffet H, Richards CL, Malouin F, et al. Early and intensive physiotherapy accelerates recovery postarthroscopic meniscectomy: results of a randomized controlled study. *Archives of Physical Medicine and Rehabilitation*. 1994;75:415–426.

Poole, RM, Blackburn TA. Dysfunction, evaluation, and treatment of the knee. In: Donatelli RA, Wooden MJ, eds. *Orthopaedic Physical Therapy*. New York, NY: Churchill Livingstone; 1989:493.

Riddell AJ. Physiotherapy for sports injuries of the knee. *Physiotherapy*. 1984;70:157–160.

Osteitis Pubis

DESCRIPTION

Osteitis pubis is a chronic inflammatory condition of the pubic bone that leads to degeneration of the bony articulation. Small avulsion fractures can accompany the inflammation of the ligaments.

CAUSE

Forceful abduction of the legs, as in gymnastics, equestrian events, and water skiing, can stress the anterior aspect of the pelvis at the pubic symphysis joint. Single-leg weight-bearing stance can lead to downward shear forces. Pubic symphysitis may be a precursor or variation of osteitis pubis.

ASSESSMENT

Areas

• History

- Gait
- Joint integrity and structural deviations
- Mobility: including active and passive range of motion (ROM) and accessory motion
- Strength: abdominal, adductor, and lower back musculature
- Neurological
- Pain
- Skin and soft tissue: temperature, tone, tenderness, edema
- Functional level

Instruments/Procedures (See References for Sources)

Joint Integrity and Structural Deviation. The following are orthopedic tests for the lower quadrant:
- Craig's test
- Ely's test
- Fabere test
- hamstring tightness
- leg-length discrepancy
- Noble's compression test
- Ober's test
- piriformis test
- Thomas test
- Trendelenburg's sign

Strength
- manual muscle testing

PROBLEMS
- The athlete usually reports that pain comes on gradually after an accumulation of trauma.
- There may be joint tenderness and pain with adductor contraction or stretch.
- The athlete tends to ignore the symptoms.

TREATMENT/MANAGEMENT
- Encourage rest.
- Consider using ice followed by heat modalities.
- Begin gentle stretching of adductor muscles to tolerance.
- Swimming can be used as an alternative exercise if the athlete avoids kicks such as whip kicks, which can aggravate the condition.
- Gradually begin a progressive strengthening program after the acute phase.

PRECAUTIONS/CONTRAINDICATIONS
- The pain from osteitis pubis may be confused with referred pain from the viscera or the adductor muscles.
- Avoid cycling, which can aggravate symptoms.

DESIRED OUTCOME/PROGNOSIS
The athlete will return to a pain-free resumption of activities.

REFERENCES

ASSESSMENT

Evaluation
Echternach JL, ed. *Physical Therapy of the Hip*. New York, NY: Churchill Livingstone; 1990:36. **[Hip pain algorithm]**

Joint Integrity and Structural Deviations
Tomberlin JP, Saunders HD. *Evaluation, Treatment and Prevention of Musculoskeletal Disorders. Vol 2: Extremities*. Chaska, Minn: The Saunders Group; 1994:200. **[Craig's test, Ely's test, Fabere test, hamstring tightness, leg-length discrepancy, Noble's compression test, Ober's test, piriformis test, quadrant, Thomas test, torque test, Trendelenburg's sign]**

Strength

Manual Muscle Testing
Daniels L, Worthingham C. *Muscle Testing Techniques of Manual Examination*. 6th ed. Philadelphia, Pa: WB Saunders Co; 1995.

Kendall FP, McCreary EK, Provance PG. *Muscles: Testing and Function*. 4th ed. Baltimore, Md: Williams & Wilkins; 1993.

TREATMENT
Chadwick P. The significance of spinal joint signs in the management of groin strain and patellofemoral pain by manual techniques. *Physiotherapy*. 1987;73:507–513.

Cibulka MT. Rehabilitation of the pelvis, hip, and thigh. *Clinical Sports Medicine*. 1989;8:777–803.

Echternach JL, ed. *Physical Therapy of the Hip*. New York, NY: Churchill-Livingstone; 1990.

Romero JA. The hip and pelvis. In: Sanders B, ed. *Sports Physical Therapy*. Norwalk, Conn: Appleton & Lange; 1990:397–421.

Roy S, Irvin R. *Sports Medicine: Prevention, Evaluation, Management and Rehabilitation*. Englewood Cliffs, NJ: Prentice Hall; 1983.

Tonsolone PA. Chronic adductor tendinitis in a female swimmer. *Journal of Orthopaedic and Sports Physical Therapy*. 1993;18:629–633.

Rotator Cuff Tendinitis

Also known as *shoulder impingement syndrome, swimmer's shoulder, tennis shoulder,* and *pitcher's shoulder*.

DESCRIPTION
Rotator cuff tendinitis is a tearing and inflammation of the tendons of the rotator cuff muscles (supraspinatus, infraspinatus, subscapularis, and teres minor). It is common in sports in which the arm is repeatedly moved forward and overhead. Examples include the forward motion of the arm during the swimming strokes of freestyle, backstroke, and butterfly; overhead lifting in weightlifting; the serve in tennis; and the pitching motion in baseball. Rotator cuff tendinitis is the most common shoulder problem in sports medicine.

The disorder can be classified into the following stages:
* *Stage 1 lesion* is simple tendinitis of acute onset. Age of onset is usually under 25 years.
* *Stage 2 lesion* shows fibrosis and tendinitis. Age of onset is usually between 25 and 40 years, but can be any age.
* *Stage 3 lesion* demonstrates bone spurs and tendon rupture.
* *Stage 4 lesion* results in a complete-thickness rotator cuff tear.

CAUSE

Rotator cuff tendinitis is a progressive process, with overuse as the primary etiologic factor. Forward and overhead motion causes the humeral head of the anteriorly flexed shoulder to rub against the acromium and coracoacromial ligament, leading to friction and impingement at the supraspinatus tendon. This mechanical cause of impingement can also affect the adjacent biceps tendon, which may also become impinged. Structural causes of impingement include congenital abnormalities and/or degenerative alterations in the subacromial arch. Functional causes of impingement include glenohumeral capsular laxity or tightness, cervical spine dysfunction with radiculopathy, postural deviations, and inadequate rotator cuff function with diminished humeral head depression.

If the irritation is chronic, it can lead to subacromial bursitis, inflammation of the tendons, and tearing of the rotator cuff. If the patient ignores the pain and continues to exercise, the problem can progress to periostitis with avulsion of the tendons at their attachments.

ASSESSMENT

Areas
* History
* Pain
* Posture
* Joint integrity and structural deviations
* Mobility: active and passive range of motion (ROM) and accessory motion
* Strength
* Neurological: sensation, proprioception, deep tendon reflexes, neural tension tests
* Skin and soft tissue: temperature, tone, tenderness, edema
* Gait
* Functional level
* Special tests to which the PT may or may not have access

Instruments/Procedures (See References for Sources)

Functional Level
* shoulder pain and disability index

Joint Integrity and Structural Deviations/Neurological Involvement. The following are neurological and orthopedic tests for the upper extremity. Those commonly used with this condition are marked with an asterisk.
* differentiation tests
* impingement sign
* instability tests*
* lock test*
* neural tension tests

- rotator cuff resistive tests*
- shoulder quadrant test*

Mobility
- goniometry

Skin and Soft Tissue
- palpation for temperature, tone, tenderness

Special Tests to Which the PT May or May Not Have Access
- arthroscopic examination of the throwing shoulder
- electromyograph (EMG) analysis of posterior rotator cuff exercises
- EMG analysis of the upper extremity in pitching
- EMG maximal voluntary isometric contraction (MVIC)
- magnetic resonance imaging (MRI) anatomy of the shoulder

Strength
1. instrumentation
   - cable tensiometry
   - hand-held dynamometry
   - isokinetic assessment
2. manual muscle testing

PROBLEMS
See "Description" section for definition of stages

Stage 1
- The athlete may be unable to sleep on affected side.
- The involved joint can be warm to touch.
- The athlete usually has aching pain after a sporting activity.
- There is usually point tenderness over the greater tuberosity of the humerus.
- There may be tenderness over the anterior acromion.
- The athlete usually demonstrates the classic painful arch between 60 to 120 degrees of flexion.
- There can be involvement of the biceps tendon.

Stage 2
- The athlete usually has biceps tendon involvement.
- Usually symptoms progress to restricted movement and a refraining from activity that leads to pain.
- There is no relief with avoidance.
- The athlete can have increased tenderness over the acromioclavicular joint.
- The athlete may have pain and weakness with muscle testing, especially with supraspinatus.
- The athlete may complain of a painful catching sensation.

Stage 3
- There is usually increased involvement and frequency of earlier symptoms.
- Pain usually limits any athletic activity.

Stage 4
- The athlete usually reports prolonged history of shoulder problems.

- The athlete usually demostrates weakness and atrophy.
- The athlete usually has limited ROM, especially abduction and external rotation.
- There is usually difficulty initiating abduction.
- Usually the biceps tendon is involved.

TREATMENT/MANAGEMENT

Stage 1
- Encourage rest, and consider physical agents and modalities such as microcurrent, pulsed electromagnetic field therapy, iontophoresis, phonophoresis, cryotherapy, and transcutaneous electical nerve stimulator (TENS; low frequency) to decrease inflammation and pain.
- Initiate active assistive exercises of pendulum activity, pulley motion, and cane exercises with flexion to maintain mobility of glenohumeral, scapulothoracic, acromioclavicular, and sternoclavicular joints.
- Initiate modified isometric exercises. One schedule suggests three sets of 12 to 20 repetitions at a submaximal effort and in a slow, rhythmic action to prevent atrophy. Activities include external and internal rotation, abduction, flexion, extension, and scapular motions. Modified aerobic and non-weight-bearing arm activities can be prescribed as needed.
- Educate the patient about activities to avoid, and provide arm protection with support.
- Progress to next stage when client reports no pain at rest and no warmth of joint and tolerates stage 1 activities well.

Stage 2
- Physical agents and modalities to enhance circulation to the subacromial space can include
  1. ultrasound to supraspinatus fossa
  2. effleurage massage to supraspinatus and infraspinus muscles
  3. ice massage where indicated
  4. transverse friction massage if lesion is superficial
- Initiate abduction movement with rope and pulley and use of cane into external rotation at 90 degrees of abduction to increase ROM and flexibility.
- Consider progressive joint mobilization and self-stretching for shoulder capsule.
- Add total-arm-strengthening exercises to promote scapular stabilization, submaximal biceps, tricep, and forearm musculature. One suggested schedule uses light isotonic exercise of three sets of 10 repetitions progressing to 20 repetitions.
- Progress to stage 3 if client demonstrates normal ROM and is symptom-free with activites of daily living (ADLs), and shows improvement in muscle performance.

Stage 3
- Use joint mobilization (increasingly aggressive) to normalize arthokinematics. Client can use active assisted ROM with cane or T bar in all directions. Teach self-stretches for capsular stretch. Use arm ergometer before and after ROM exercises.
- Use arm ergometry and isotonic dumbbell program to regain shoulder muscle strength. A cable system is preferable if available. Can use surgical tubing as an equipment adjunct. Address proximal stability of scapula. Progress to sport specific training. Consider use of plyometrics to duplicate athletic activity and improve neuromuscular control.
- Progress to stage 4 if athlete regains full, nonpainful ROM, with no tenderness and with satisfactory strength on clinical examination.

Stage 4
- Athlete can perform functional activities, gradually progressing to full activity. Institute maintenance exercise program for flexibility and strengthening of arm.

PRECAUTIONS/CONTRAINDICATIONS
- Do not perform full ROM initially to avoid undue stress on the musculotendinous junctures.
- Rope and pulley exercises should start with flexion, with palm supinated and humerus externally rotated to avoid impingement. Avoid any discomfort with the movement.
- Grades 1 and 2 (mobilization) can be used in the glenohumeral joint to avoid the discomfort from the inflammatory process of the joint.
- Progressing too rapidly into stage 2 is a common fault in unsuccessful rehabilitation.

DESIRED OUTCOME/PROGNOSIS
- The athlete will be free of pain.
- The athlete will have a decrease in the inflammatory response and no swelling.
- The athlete will demonstrate a full range of active and passive motion.
- The athlete will demonstrate maximized shoulder function with coordinated neuromuscular timing.
- The athlete will be able to perform sport with proper technique.
- The athlete will wear properly fitted sports equipment.
- The athlete will have been instructed in correction or modification of joint abuse and prevention of recurrence.

    Tears of the supraspinatus occur before biceps ruptures in a 7:1 ratio.

    Steroid injections have been reported to weaken a normal tendon for up to 14 days. Athletes should be limited to light work activities for a minimum of 2 weeks post injection.

    An athlete who demonstrates structural changes and is not responding to rehabilitation may need surgery.

    Generally, 70% of athletes fit well into the rehabilitation program, 15% need to be accelerated, and 15% need to go slower.

REFERENCES

ASSESSMENT

Evaluation

Beach ML, Whitney SL, Dickoff-Hoffmen SA. Relationship of shoulder flexibility, strength, and endurance to shoulder pain in competitive swimmers. *Journal of Orthopaedic and Sports Physical Therapy.* 1992;16:262–268.

Boublik M, Hawkins RJ. Clinical examination of the shoulder complex. *Journal of Orthopaedic and Sports Physical Therapy.* 1993;18:379–385.

Chinn CJ, Priest JD, Kent BE. Upper extremity range of motion, grip strength, and girth in highly skilled tennis players. *Physical Therapy.* 1974;54:474–483.

Davies GJ, Gould JA, Larson RL. Functional examination of the shoulder girdle. *Physician and Sports Medicine.* 1981;9:82–104.

Diamond W. Upper extremity: shoulder. In: Myers RS, ed. *Saunders Manual of Physical Therapy Practice.* Philadelphia, Pa: WB Saunders Co; 1995:802–822.

Donatelli RA, ed. *Physical Therapy of the Shoulder.* 2nd ed. New York, NY: Churchill Livingstone; 1991:19–61. **[Algorithm for sequential shoulder girdle evaluation]**

Itoi E, Tabata S. Conservative treatment of rotator cuff tears. *Clinical Orthopedics and Related Research.* 1992:275:165–173. **[Wolfgang's criteria]**

Jobe FW, Pink M. Classification and treatment of shoulder dysfunction in the overhead athlete. *Journal of Orthopaedic and Sports Physical Therapy.* 1993;18:427–432. **[Classifications]**

Meister K, Andrews JR. Classification and treatment of rotator cuff injuries in the overhand athlete. *Journal of Orthopaedic and Sports Physical Therapy.* 1993;18:413–421. **[Classifications]**

Roach KE, Budiman-Mak E, Songsiridej, Lertratanakul Y. Development of a shoulder pain and disability index. *Arthritic Care and Research.* 1991;4:143–149. **[Classifications]**

Joint Integrity and Structural Deviations/Neurological Involvement

Diamond W. Upper extremity: shoulder. In: Myers RS, ed. *Saunders Manual of Physical Therapy Practice.* Philadelphia, Pa: WB Saunders Co; 1995:809–810. **[Rotator cuff resistive tests, instability tests, lock test, shoulder quadrant test, differentiation tests, neural tension tests]**

Slaughter D. Shoulder injuries. In: Sanders B, ed. *Sports Physical Therapy.* Norwalk, Conn: Appleton & Lange; 1990:343–367. **[Impingement sign]**

Mobility

Middleton K. Goniometry. In: Andrews JR, Harrelson GL, eds. *Physical Rehabilitation of the Injured Athlete.* Philadelphia, Pa: WB Saunders Co; 1991:59–84.

Middleton K. Range of motion and flexibility. In: Andrews JR, Harrelson GL, eds. *Physical Rehabilitation of the Injured Athlete.* Philadelphia, Pa: WB Saunders Co; 1991:59–84.

Special Tests to Which the PT May or May Not Have Access

Arthroscopy

Savoie FH. Arthroscopic examination of the throwing shoulder. *Journal of Orthopaedic and Sports Physical Therapy.* 1993;18:409–412.

EMG

Blackburn TA, McLeod WD, White BW, Wofford L. EMG analysis of posterior rotator cuff exercises. *Athletic Training.* 1990;25:40–45.

DiGiovine NM, Jobe FW, Pink M, Perry J. An electromyographic analysis of the upper extremity in pitching. *Journal of Shoulder Elbow Surgery.* 1992;1:15–25.

Jobe FW, Moynes DR, Tibone JE. An EMG analysis of the shoulder in pitching: a second report. *American Journal of Sports Medicine.* 1984;12:218–220.

Jobe FW, Tibone JE, Perry J, et al. An EMG analysis of the shoulder in throwing and pitching: a preliminary report. *American Journal of Sports Medicine.* 1983;11:3–5.

Mosely JB, Jobe FW, Pink M, et al. EMG analysis of the scapular muscles during a shoulder rehabilitation program. *American Journal of Sports Medicine.* 1992;20:128–134.

Moynes DR, Perry J, Antonelli DJ, Jobe FW. Electromyography and motion analysis of the upper extremity in sports. *Physical Therapy.* 1986;66:1905–1911.

Nuber GW, Jobe FW, Perry J, et al. Fine wire electromyography analysis of muscles in the shoulder in swimming. *American Journal of Sports Medicine.* 1986;14:7.

Pink M, Jobe FW, Perry J. Electromyographic analysis of the shoulder during the golf swing. *American Journal of Sports Medicine.* 1990;18:137–140.

Townsend H, Jobe FW, Pink M, Perry J. Electromyographic analysis of the glenohumeral muscles during a baseball rehabilitation program. *American Journal of Sports Medicine.* 1991;19:264–272.

Worrell TW, Corey BJ, York SL, Santiestaban J. An analysis of supraspinatus EMG activity and shoulder isometric force development. *Medicine and Science in Sports and Exercise.* 1992;24:744–748. **[EMG, maximal voluntary isometric contraction (MVIC)]**

MRI

Ho CP. Applied MRI anatomy of the shoulder. *Journal of Orthopaedic and Sports Physical Therapy.* 1993;18:351–359.

Strength

Instrumentation

Albert MS, Wooden MJ. Isokinetic evaluation and treatment of the shoulder. In: Donatelli R, ed. *Physical Therapy of the Shoulder*. New York, NY: Churchill Livingstone; 1987:63.

Alderink GJ, Kuck DJ. Isokinetic shoulder strength of high school and college aged pitchers. *Journal of Orthopaedic and Sports Physical Therapy*. 1986;7:163–172.

Connelly-Maddux RE, Kibler WB, Uhl T. Isokinetic peak torque and work values for the shoulder. *Journal of Orthopaedic and Sports Physical Therapy*. 1989;1:264–269.

Cook EE, Gray VL, Savinor-Nogue E, et al. Shoulder antagonistic agonist strength ratios: a comparison between college level baseball pitchers. *Journal of Orthopaedic and Sports Physical Therapy*. 1987;8:451–461.

Davies G. *A Compendium of Isokinetics in Clinical Usage*. 2nd ed. LaCrosse, Wis: S&S Publishers; 1985.

Ellenbecker TS. A total arm strength profile of highly skilled tennis players. *Isokinetics Exercise Science*. 1991;1:9–21.

Ellenbecker TS. Shoulder internal and external rotation strength and range of motion of highly skilled junior tennis players. *Isokinetics Exercise Science*. 1992;2:1–8.

Ellenbecker TS, Feiring DC, DeHart RL, Rich M. Isokinetic shoulder strength: coronal versus scapular plane testing in upper extremity unilaterally dominant athletes. *Physical Therapy*. 1992;72(suppl):580.

Elsner RC, Pedegana LR, Lang J. Protocol for strength testing and rehabilitation of the upper extremity. *Journal of Orthopaedic and Sports Physical Therapy*. 1983;4:229–235.

Falkel JE, Murphy TC, Murray TF. Prone positioning for testing shoulder internal and external rotation on the Cybex II isokinetic dynamometer. *Journal of Orthopaedic and Sports Physical Therapy*. 1987;8:368–370.

Greenfield BH, Donatelli R, Wooden MJ, Wilkens J. Isokinetic evaluation of shoulder rotational strength between plane of scapula and the functional plane. *American Journal of Sports Medicine*. 1990;18:124–128.

Greenfield B, Donatelli R, Wooden M, et al. Isokinetic evaluation of shoulder rotational strength between plane of scapula and the frontal plane. *American Journal of Sports Medicine*. 1990;18:2.

Hagemann PA, Mason DK, Rydlund KW, et al. Effects of positions and speed on eccentric and concentric isokinetic testing of the shoulder rotators. *Journal of Orthopaedic and Sports Physical Therapy*. 1989;11:64–69.

Hartsell SD. Postsurgical shoulder strength in the older patient. *Journal of Orthopaedic and Sports Physical Therapy*. 1993;18:667–672.

Malerba JL, Adam ML, Harris BA, Krebs DE. Reliability of dynamic and isometric testing of shoulder external and internal rotators. *Journal of Orthopaedic and Sports Physical Therapy*. 1993;18:543–552.

Malone TR. *Evaluation of Isokinetic Equipment. Sports Injury Management*. Vol 1, No 1. Baltimore, Md: Williams & Wilkins; 1988:1–92.

Malone TR. Elements of a standardized shoulder examination. In: Andrews JR, Wilk KE, eds. *The Athlete's Shoulder*. New York, NY: Churchill Livingstone; 1994:39–44. [**Isometric techniques of manual muscle testing, hand-held dynamometry, cable tensiometry; isotonic testing; isokinetic assessment; functional assessment**]

Ng LR, Kramer JS. Shoulder rotator torques in female tennis and nontennis players. *Journal of Orthopaedic and Sports Physical Therapy*. 1991;13:40–46.

Perrin DH, Robertson RJ, Ray RL. Bilateral isokinetic peak torque, torque acceleration energy, power, and work relationships in athletes and nonathletes. *Journal of Orthopaedic and Sports Physical Therapy*. 1987;9:184–189.

Soderberg GJ, Blaschek MJ. Shoulder internal and external rotation peak torque production through a velocity spectrum in differing positions. *Journal of Orthopaedic and Sports Physical Therapy*. 1987;8:518–524.

Tata GE, Ng L, Kramer JF. Shoulder antagonistic strength ratios during concentric and eccentric muscle actions in the scapular plane. *Journal of Orthopaedic and Sports Physical Therapy*. 1993;18:654–660.

Walmsley RP, Hartsell H. Shoulder strength following surgical rotator cuff repair: a comparative analysis using isokinetic testing. *Journal of Orthopaedic and Sports Physical Therapy.* 1992;15:215–222.

Walmsley RP, Szabo C. A comparative study of the torque generated by the shoulder internal and external rotators in different positions and at varying speeds. *Journal of Orthopaedic and Sports Physical Therapy.* 1987;9:217–222.

Weir JP, Wagner LL, Housh TJ, Johnson GO. Horizontal abduction and adduction strength at the shoulder of high school wrestlers across age. *Journal of Orthopaedic and Sports Physical Therapy.* 1992;15:183–186.

Wilk KE, Andrews JR, Arrigo CA, et al. The strength characteristics of internal and external rotators in professional baseball pitchers. *American Journal of Sports Medicine.* 1993;21:61–66.

Wilk KE, Arrigo CA. Isokinetic exercise and testing for the shoulder. In: Andrews JR, Wilk KE, eds. *The Athlete's Shoulder.* New York, NY: Churchill Livingstone; 1994:523–542.

Wilk KE, Arrigo CA. Isokinetic testing and exercises of microtraumatic shoulder injuries. In: Davies GJ, ed. *The Compendium of Isokinetics.* 4th ed. Onalaska, Wis: S&S Publishing; 1992.

Wilk KE, Arrigo CA. Isokinetic testing and exercise. In: Souza TA, ed. *Sports Injuries of the Shoulder.* New York, NY: Churchill Livingstone; 1994:237–256.

Wilk KE, Arrigo CA, Andrews JR. Standardized isokinetic testing protocol for the throwing shoulder: the throwers' series. *Isokinetic Exercise Science.* 1991;1:63–71.

Wilk KE, Arrigo CA, Keirns MA. Shoulder abduction/adduction isokinetic test results: window vs unwindow data collection. *Journal of Orthopaedic and Sports Physical Therapy.* 1992;15:107–112.

Manual Muscle Testing

Daniels L, Worthingham C. *Muscle Testing Techniques of Manual Examination.* Philadelphia, Pa: WB Saunders Co; 1995.

Kendall FP, McCreary EK, Provance PG. *Muscles: Testing and Function.* 4th ed. Baltimore, Md: Williams & Wilkins; 1993.

Wilk KE. Dynamic muscle strength testing. In: Amundsen LR, ed. *Muscle Strength Testing: Instrumental and Noninstrument Systems.* New York, NY: Churchill Livingstone; 1990:123.

TREATMENT

Andrews JR, Wilk KE, eds. *The Athlete's Shoulder.* New York, NY: Churchill Livingstone; 1994:523–542.

Blackburn TA. Off-season program for the throwing arm. In: Zarins B, Andrews JR, Carson WG, eds. *Injuries to the Throwing Arm.* Philadelphia, Pa: WB Saunders Co; 1985:277.

Blackburn TA. Throwing injuries to the shoulder. In: Donatelli R, ed. *Physical Therapy of the Shoulder.* New York, NY: Churchill Livingstone; 1991:239–270.

Bratatz JH, Gogia PP. The mechanics of pitching. *Journal of Orthopaedic and Sports Physical Therapy.* 1987;9:56–69.

Brewster C, Schwab ER. Rehabilitation of the shoulder following rotator cuff injury or surgery. *Journal of Orthopaedic and Sports Physical Therapy.* 1993;18:422–426.

Brewster CE, Shields CL, Seto JL, Morrissey MC. Rehabilitation of the upper extremity. In: Shields CL, ed. *Manual of Sports Surgery.* New York, NY: Springer-Verlag; 1987:62–90.

Burkhart SS. Arthroscopic treatment of massive rotator cuff tears. *Clinical Orthopaedics.* 1991;267:45–56.

Culham E, Peat M. Functional anatomy of the shoulder complex. *Journal of Orthopaedic and Sports Physical Therapy.* 1993;18:342–350.

Davies GJ, Dickoff-Hoffman S. Neuromuscular testing and rehabilitation of the shoulder complex. *Journal of Orthopaedic and Sports Physical Therapy.* 1993;18:427–432.

Davies GJ, Gould JA. *Orthopaedic and Sports Physical Therapy.* St Louis, Mo: CV Mosby Co; 1985.

Dillman CJ, Fleisig GS, Andrews JR. Biomechanics of pitching with emphasis upon shoulder kinematics. *Journal of Orthopaedic and Sports Physical Therapy.* 1993;18:402–408.

Ellenbecker TS, Derscheid GL. Rehabilitation of overuse injuries of the shoulder. *Clinical Sports Medicine.* 1989;8:583–604.

Elliott J. Shoulder pain and flexibility in elite water polo players. *Physiotherapy.* 1993;79:693–697.

Engle RP. Shoulder and glenoid labrum tears. *Clinical Management in Physical Therapy.* 1988;8:5:14–17.

Engle RP, Canner GC. Posterior shoulder instability: approach to rehabilitation. *Journal of Orthopaedic and Sports Physical Therapy.* 1989;10:488–494.

Falkel JE. Swimming injuries. In: Falkel, JE, Malone T, eds. *Sports Injury Management: Shoulder Injuries.* Baltimore, Md. Williams & Wilkins; 1988.

Falkel JE. Swimming injuries. In: Sanders B, ed. *Sports Physical Therapy.* Norwalk, Conn: Appleton & Lange; 1990:477.

Falkel JE, Murphy TC. Clinical evaluation of the shoulder complex. In: Falkel JE, Malone TR, eds. *Sports Injury Management: Shoulder Injuries.* Baltimore, Md: Williams & Wilkins; 1988:1:2:13–35.

Falkel JE, Murphy TC. Common injuries of the shoulder in athletes. In: Falkel JE, Malone TR, eds. *Sports Injury Management: Shoulder Injuries.* Baltimore, Md: Williams & Wilkins; 1988:1:2:66–108.

Falkel JE, Murphy TC. Principles of rehabilitation and prehabilitation. In: Falkel JE, Malone TR, eds. *Sports Injury Management: Shoulder Injuries.* Baltimore, Md: Williams & Wilkins; 1988:1:2:42–54.

Halbach J, Tank R. The shoulder. In: Gould JA, Davies GJ, eds. *Orthopedic and Sports Physical Therapy.* Vol 2. St Louis, Mo: CV Mosby Co; 1985:497–517.

Herrera-Lasso I, Mobarak L, Fernandez-Dominguez L, et al. Comparative effectiveness of packages of treatment including ultrasound or transcutaneous electrical nerve stimulation in painful shoulder syndrome. *Physiotherapy.* 1993;79:251–253.

Hertling D, Kessler RM. *Management of Common Musculoskeletal Disorders.* Philadelphia, Pa: JB Lippincott Co; 1990:169–204.

Jobe C, Jobe FW, Pink M. The sports medicine rehabilitation center. In: Nickel VL, Botte MJ, eds. *Orthopaedic Rehabilitation.* 2nd ed. New York, NY: Churchill Livingstone; 1992:207–221.

Jobe FW, Moynes DR. Delineation of diagnostic criteria and a rehabilitation program for rotator cuff injuries. *American Journal of Sports Medicine.* 1982;10:336-339.

Jobe FW, Moynes DR, Brewster CE. Rehabilitation of shoulder joint instabilities. *Orthopedic Clinics of North America.* 1987;18:473.

Lake DA. Neuromuscular electrical stimulation: an overview and its application in the treatment of sports injuries. *Sports Medicine.* 1992;13:320–336.

Leivseth G, Reikeras O. Changes in muscle fiber cross-sectional area and concentrations of Na, K-ATPase in deltoid muscle in patients with impingement syndrome of the shoulder. *Journal of Orthopaedic and Sports Physical Therapy.* 1994;19:146–149.

Litchfield R, Hawkins R, Dillman CJ, Atkins J, Hagerman G. Rehabilitation for the overhead athlete. *Journal of Orthopaedic and Sports Physical Therapy.* 1993;18:433–441.

Malone TR. *Evaluation of Isokinetic Equipment. Sports Injury Management,* Vol 1. No 1. Baltimore, Md: Williams & Wilkins; 1988:1–92.

McLean JM. Orthotron™ II and shoulder rehabilitation. *Clinical Management in Physical Therapy.* 1989;9:2:43.

McLeod WD, Andrews JR. Mechanisms of shoulder injuries. *Physical Therapy.* 1986;66:1901–1904.

Meador R. The treatment of shoulder pain and dysfunction in a professional viola player: implications of the latissimus dorsi and teres major muscles. *Journal of Orthopaedic and Sports Physical Therapy.* 1989;11:52–55.

Moynes DR. Prevention of injury to the shoulder through exercise and therapy. *Clinical Sports Medicine.* 1983;2:413–422.

Paine RM, Voight M. The role of the scapula. *Journal of Orthopaedic and Sports Physical Therapy.* 1993;18:386–391.

Perry J, Glousman R. Biomechanics of throwing. In: Nicholas JA, Hershman EB, eds. *The Upper Extremity in Sports Medicine.* St Louis, Mo: CV Mosby Co; 1990:735.

Pink M, Jobe FW. Shoulder injuries in athletes. *Clinical Management in Physical Therapy.* 1991;11:6:39–47.

Reid DC, Saboe L, Burnham R. Common shoulder problems in the athlete. In: Donatelli R, ed. *Physical Therapy of the Shoulder.* 2nd ed. New York, NY: Churchill Livingstone; 1991:225–237.

Simon ER, Hill JA. Rotator cuff injuries: an update. *Journal of Orthopaedic and Sports Physical Therapy.* 1989; 10:394–398.

Slaughter D. Shoulder injuries. In: Sanders B, ed. *Sports Physical Therapy.* Norwalk, Conn: Appleton & Lange; 1990;343–367.

Tomberlin JP, Saunders HD. *Evaluation, Treatment and Prevention of Musculoskeletal Disorders. Vol 2: Extremities.* Chaska, Minn: The Saunders Group; 1994:73–112.

Wilk KE, Andrews JR. Rehabilitation following arthroscopic shoulder subacromial decompression. *Orthopedics.* 1993;16:349–358.

Wilk KE, Arrigo C. Current concepts in the rehabilitation of the athletic shoulder. *Journal of Orthopaedic and Sports Physical Therapy.* 1993;18:365–378.

Wilk KE, Arrigo C, Courson R, et al. *Preventive and Rehabilitative Exercises for the Shoulder and Elbow.* 3rd ed. Birmingham, Ala: American Sports Medicine Institute; 1991.

Wilk KE, Voight ML, Keirns MA, et al. Plyometrics for the upper extremities: theory and clinical application. *Journal of Orthopaedic and Sports Physical Therapy.* 1993. May.

Wilk KE, Voight ML, Keirns MA, Gambetta V, Andrews JR, Dillman CJ. Stretch-shortening drills for the upper extremities: theory and clinical application. *Journal of Orthopaedic and Sports Physical Therapy.* 1993;17:225–239.

Wooden MJ, Greenfield, B, Johanson M, Litzelman L, Mundrane M, Donatelli RA. Effects of strength training on throwing velocity and shoulder muscle performance in teenage baseball players. *Journal of Orthopaedic and Sports Physical Therapy.* 1992;15:223–228.

Ankle Sprains

DESCRIPTION

Injury to the ligaments of the ankle is very common. Most ankle sprains (80–90%) involve injury to the lateral ligaments, including the anterior talofibular ligament, the posterior talofibular ligament, and the calcaneal fibular ligament. The anterior talofibular ligament is usually injured first. Less commonly, medial ankle ligaments may also be sprained.

Sprains can be classified by grade (grade 1, 2, or 3), degree (first, second, or third degree), or description (mild, moderate, or severe).

- In a *grade 1 or first-degree sprain,* there is some tearing of collagen fibers, and minimal hemorrhaging may occur. The ligament is still intact.
- In a *grade 2 or second-degree sprain,* part of the ligament or joint capsule is damaged; there is accompanying hemorrhaging and partial loss of function.
- In a *grade 3 or third-degree sprain,* the ligament is completely torn, with severe hemorrhaging, edema, and loss of function. There may be capsular disruption as well.

CAUSE

When the lateral ligament is injured, it is usually sprained in a plantar-flexed, inverted position with a twisting motion. Some clients with ligamentous laxity are more vulnerable to inversion injury.

ASSESSMENT

Areas
- History
- Pain

- Posture
- Gait
- Joint integrity and structural deviations
- Mobility: active and passive range of motion (ROM)
- Strength, including strength in weight bearing
- Balance: single-limb and double-limb balance, using stable and mobile surfaces
- Foot mechanics
- Neurological: sensation, proprioception, deep tendon reflexes, neural tension
- Skin and soft tissue: temperature, tone, tenderness, edema
- Functional level
- Equipment, including footwear
- Special tests to which the PT may or may not have access

Instruments/Procedures (See References for Sources)

Balance
- Chattecx balance systems

Gait
- dynamic assessment of foot mechanics
  1. dynamic plantar pressure distribution
  2. foot pressure EMED system
  3. pedabarograph three-dimensional kinematic analysis
- footprint analysis

Joint Integrity and Structural Deviations. The following are orthopedic tests of the ankle. Those commonly used for this condition are marked with an asterisk.
- Achilles tendon test
- anterior drawer sign*
- Homan's sign
- inversion stress test
- kinesthetic awareness
- Kleiger test
- talar tilt*
- Thomas test
- Thompson test

Mobility
- goniometric subtalar and ankle joint measurements
- open and closed kinetic chain subtalar joint neutral positions and navicular drop test
- visual estimates of ankle joint active range of motion

Posture
- postural responses to lateral perturbation
- postural sway following inversion sprain of the ankle

Skin and Soft Tissue
- palpation of temperature, tone, tenderness

Special Tests
- electromyography (EMG)

Strength
- Biodex dynamometer
- manual muscle testing

PROBLEMS
- The athlete usually has ankle edema.
- The athlete usually has pain, especially with weight bearing.
- The athlete may complain of tenderness over area of injured ligaments.
- The athlete may report a feeling of the joint "giving way."

TREATMENT/MANAGEMENT
In general:
- Control weight bearing as tolerated with assistive devices such as crutches. Progressively increase weight bearing.
- Consider ankle support or bracing. Keep damaged ligament in shortened position when supported.
- Use modalities, such as cryotherapy, for symptoms.
- Compression pumps or padding in key areas can decrease edema.
- Exercises can include proprioceptive exercises and open-chain exercises. Progress with closed-chain exercise as allowed by healing. Consider use of aquatic therapy.
- Stretch gastrocsoleus region.
  Treatment by degree of sprain is as follows:
- Grade 1
  1. Begin with non-weight-bearing activities, especially for a client with a muscle strength grade of fair or lower.
  2. Use compression such as orthotics or wrap with tape for support.
  3. Consider use of contrast baths for swelling.
- Grade 2
  1. Wrap with tape for support and felt pads over area for extra support.
  2. Consider use of balance board system, such as Biomechanical Ankle Platform System (BAPS) board, for proprioceptive training.
- Grade 3
  1. Avoid stretching ligaments in early stages.
  2. Gradually facilitate increase in ROM and strength.
  3. Consider use of balance board system, such as Biomechanical Ankle Platform System (BAPS) board, for proprioceptive training.

PRECAUTIONS/CONTRAINDICATIONS
- Subtalar and midtarsal joints should remain in a neutral position during measurement of ankle dorsiflexion.
- Be alert for signs of fracture with acute sprains. Signs of fracture include pain at the distal end of percussion and extreme sensitivity at one particular spot.
- Severe sprains may need surgery.

DESIRED OUTCOME/PROGNOSIS
- The athlete will have decreased pain.
- The athlete will have decreased edema.
- The athlete will restore normal ROM.

- The athlete will restore normal strength.
- The athlete will return to full function.
  Prolonged instability of ankle persists in 10% to 20% of patients with lateral ankle ruptures.

REFERENCES

ASSESSMENT

Balance
Feuerbach JW, Grabiner MD. Effect of the aircast on unilateral postural control: amplitude and frequency variables. *Journal of Orthopaedic and Sports Physical Therapy.* 1993;17:149–154. [**Chattecx balance systems**]

Functional Level
Giallonardo LM. Clinical evaluation of foot and ankle dysfunction. *Physical Therapy.* 1988;68:50–56.
Giallonardo LM. Lower extremity: ankle. In: Myers RS, ed. *Saunders Manual of Physical Therapy Practice.* Philadelphia, Pa: WB Saunders Co; 1995:1031–1053.
McPoil TG, Hunt GC. Evaluation and management of foot and ankle disorders: present problems and future directions. *Journal of Orthopaedic and Sports Physical Therapy.* 1995;21:381–388.

Gait
Donatelli R, ed. *The Biomechanics of the Foot and Ankle.* Philadelphia, Pa: FA Davis Co; 1990:148–152. [**Dynamic assessment of foot mechanics: dynamic plantar pressure distribution, foot pressure EMED system, pedabarograph, three-dimensional kinematic analysis**]
Shore M. Footprint analysis in gait documentation; an instructional sheet format. *Physical Therapy.* 1980; 60:1163–1167.

Special Tests to Which the PT May or May Not Have Access

Electromyography
Johnson MB, Johnson CL. Electromyographic response of peroneal muscles in surgical and nonsurgical injured ankles during sudden inversion. *Journal of Orthopaedic and Sports Physical Therapy.* 1993;18:497–501.
Soderberg GL, Cook TM, Rider SC, Stephenitch BL. Electromyographic activity of selected leg musculature in subjects with normal and chronically sprained ankles performing on a BAPS board. *Physical Therapy.* 1991;71:514–522.

Strength

Instrumentation
Chesworth BM, Vandervoort AA. Reliability of a torque motor system for measurement of passive ankle joint stiffness in control subjects. *Physiotherapy Canada.* 1988;40:300–303.

Manual Muscle Testing
Daniels L, Worthingham C. *Muscle Testing Techniques of Manual Examination.* 6th ed. Philadelphia, Pa: WB Saunders Co; 1995.
Kendall FP, McCreary EK, Provance PG. *Muscles: Testing and Function.* 4th ed. Baltimore, Md: Williams & Wilkins; 1993.

Joint Integrity and Structural Deviations
Rothstein JM, Roy SH, Wolf SL. *The Rehabilitation Specialist's Handbook.* Philadelphia: FA Davis Co; 1991:136–137. [**Achilles tendon test, Thompson test, Kleiger test**]

Tomberlin JP, Saunders HD. *Evaluation, Treatment and Prevention of Musculoskeletal Disorders. Vol 2: Extremities.* Chaska, Minn: The Saunders Group; 1994:265–306. **[Thomas test, anterior drawer sign, inversion stress test, talar tilt, Homan's sign, biomechanical assessment, swelling, effusion]**

Mobility

Bohannon RW, Tiberio D, Zitto M. Selected measures of ankle dorsiflexion range of motion: differences and intercorrelations. *Foot and Ankle.* 1989;10:2:99–103.

Elveru RA, Rothstein JM, Lamb RL. Goniometric reliability in a clinical setting: subtalar and ankle joint measurements. *Physical Therapy.* 1988;68:672.

Kleven D, Bornhoeft D, Thorp B. Assessing ankle dorsiflexion. *Clinical Management in Physical Therapy.* 1989;9:25–26.

Picciano AM, Rowlands MS, Worrell T. Reliability of open and closed kinetic chain subtalar joint neutral positions and navicular drop test. *Journal of Orthopaedic and Sports Physical Therapy.* 1993;18:553–558.

Simoneau GG. Isokinetic characteristics of ankle evertors and invertors in female control subjects using the Biodex dynamometer. *Physiotherapy Canada.* 1990;42:4:182–187.

Vandervoort AA, Chesworth BM, Cunningham DA, Rechnitzer PA, Paterson DH, Koval JJ. An outcome measure to quantify passive stiffness of the ankle. *Canadian Journal of Public Health.* 1992;83: Suppl 2: S19–23.

Youdas JW, Bogard CL, Suman VJ. Reliability of goniometric measurements and visual estimates of ankle joint active range of motion obtained in a clinical setting. *Archives of Physical Medicine and Rehabilitation.* 1993;74:1113–1118.

Neurological

Kinesthetic Awareness

Garn SN, Newton RA. Kinesthetic awareness in subjects with multiple ankle sprains. *Physical Therapy.* 1988;68:1667–1671.

Gross MT. Effects of recurrent lateral ankle sprains on active and passive judgements of joint position. *Physical Therapy.* 1987;67:1505–1509.

Sensation

Bullock-Saxton JE. Local sensation changes and altered hip muscle function following severe ankle sprain. *Physical Therapy.* 1994;74:17–28.

Posture

Brunt D, Andersen JC, Huntsman B, et al. Postural responses to lateral perturbation in healthy subjects and ankle sprain patients. *Medicine and Science in Sports and Exercise.* 1992;24:2:171–176.

Cornwall MW, Murrell P. Postural sway following inversion sprain of the ankle. *Journal of the American Podiatric Medical Association.* 1991;81:5:243–247.

TREATMENT

Ator R, Gunn K, McPoil TG, Knecht HG. The effect of adhesive strapping on medial longitudinal arch support before and after exercise. *Journal of Orthopaedic and Sports Physical Therapy.* 1991;14:18–23.

Case W. Ankle injuries. In: Sanders B, ed. *Sports Physical Therapy.* Norwalk, Conn: Appleton & Lange; 1990:451–476.

Cote DJ, Prentice WE, Hooker DN, Shields EW. Comparison of three treatment procedures for minimizing ankle swelling. *Physical Therapy.* 1988;68:1072–1076.

Evans P. Clinical biomechanics of the subtalar joint. *Physiotherapy.* 1990;76:47–51.

Falkel JE. Guidelines for running shoe selection to prevent running injuries. *Cardiopulmonary Recreation.* 1986;1:1:3–7.

Garn SN, Newton RA. Kinesthetic awareness in subjects with multiple ankle sprains. *Physical Therapy*. 1988;68:1667–1671.

Green TA, Wight CR. A comparative support evaluation of three ankle orthoses before, during, and after exercise. *Journal of Orthopaedic and Sports Physical Therapy*. 1990;11:453–473.

Gross MT, Ballard CL, Mears HG, Watkins EJ. Comparison of DonJoy Ankle Ligament Protector and Aircast Sport-Stirrup orthoses in restricting foot and ankle motion before and after exercise. *Journal of Orthopaedic and Sports Physical Therapy*. 1992;16:60–67.

Gross MT, Everts JR, Roberson SE, et al. Effect of DonJoy Ankle Ligament Protector and Aircast Sport-Stirrup orthosis on functional performance. *Journal of Orthopaedic and Sports Physical Therapy*. 1994;19:150–156.

Hamil J, Bates BT. A kinetic evaluation of the effects of in vivo loading on running shoes. *Journal of Orthopaedic and Sports Physical Therapy*. 1988;10:47–53.

Heil B. Lower limb biomechanics related to running injuries. *Physiotherapy*. 1992;78:400–406.

Hunt G, ed. *Physical Therapy of the Foot and Ankle*. New York, NY: Churchill Livingstone; 1988.

Lattanza L, Gray G, Kantner RM. Closed versus open kinematic chain measurements of subtalar joint eversion: implications for clinical practice. *Journal of Orthopaedic and Sports Physical Therapy*. 1988;9:310–314.

Leaman AM, Simpson DE. Treatment of sprained ankles by physiotherapists at professional soccer clubs. *Archives of Emergency Medicine*. 1988;5:177–179.

Lee JM. *Aids to Physiotherapy*. New York, NY: Churchill Livingstone; 1988:138.

Mascaro TB, Swanson LE. Rehabilitation of the foot and ankle. *Orthopedic Clinics of North America*. 1994;25:147–160.

McCulloch MU, Brunt D, Vander-Linden D. The effect of foot orthotics and gait velocity on lower limb kinematics and temporal events of stance. *Journal of Orthopaedic and Sports Physical Therapy*. 1993;17:2–10.

McPoil TG. Footwear. *Physical Therapy*. 1988;68:1857–1964.

McPoil T, Brocato R. The foot and ankle: Biomechanical evaluation and treatment. In: Gould J, Davis G, eds. *Orthopedic and Sports Physical Therapy*. St Louis, Mo: CV Mosby Co; 1985.

Rucinski TJ, Hooker DA, Prentice WE, Shields EW, Cote-Murray DJ. The effects of intermittent compression on edema in postacute ankle sprains. *Journal of Orthopaedic and Sports Physical Therapy*. 1991;14:65–69.

Scotece GG, Guthrie MR. Comparison of three treatment approaches for Grade I and II ankle sprains in active duty soldiers. *Journal of Orthopaedic and Sports Physical Therapy*. 1992;15:19–23.

Simpson DE. Management of sprained ankles referred for physiotherapy. *Physiotherapy*. 1991;77:314–316.

Tomberlin JP, Saunders HD. *Evaluation, Treatment and Prevention of Musculoskeletal Disorders. Vol 2: Extremities*. Chaska, Minn: The Saunders Group; 1994:265–302.

Weinstein ML. An ankle protocol for second-degree ankle sprains. *Military Medicine*. 1993;158:771–774.

Wilkerson GB, Horn-Kingery HM. Treatment of the inversion ankle sprain: comparison of different modes of compression and cryotherapy. *Journal of Orthopaedic and Sports Physical Therapy*. 1993;17:240–246.

Chapter 2
Cardiovascular Conditions

- Coronary artery disease
- Cardiac surgery
- Heart failure

Coronary Artery Disease

DESCRIPTION

Coronary artery disease (CAD) results from atherosclerotic lesions that affect the medium and large cardiac arteries. The narrowing and obstruction caused by the atheroma lead to an insufficient blood flow to the heart. CAD's primary complications are angina pectoris, myocardial infarction (MI), and sudden cardiac death.

Angina Pectoris

Angina pectoris is characterized by pressure or crushing pain in the midchest region triggered by exertion and relieved by rest. The pain may also radiate to the teeth, jaw, throat (tickling sensation), posterior neck, or shoulder blade areas. Unstable angina may not be associated with activity and can occur at rest.

Myocardial Infarction

Myocardial infarction results in ischemic myocardial necrosis. This leads to reduced cardiac output. It is usually triggered by a sudden decrease in coronary blood flow to a portion of the myocardium. The initial symptoms of an acute attack are usually deep, substernal, visceral pain that is described as pressure or aching. The pain can radiate into the jaw, left arm, or back.

Sudden Cardiac Death

Sudden cardiac death is defined as sudden death within 1 hour of initial symptoms.

CAUSE

Risk factors associated with CAD are age, gender, family history, high blood pressure, cigarette use, and high cholesterol. Other factors may include diabetes mellitus, sedentary lifestyle, obesity, and an aggressive personality.

Angina Pectoris

Angina pectoris is caused by transient myocardial ischemia without any death of myocardial cells.

Myocardial Infarction

For more than 90% of clients, an acute MI is usually triggered by a thrombus, caused by plaque rupture, that occludes an artery supplying the damaged area. The clot is thought to be formed by altered platelet function due to endothelial change in the atherosclerotic plaque.

Very rarely, MI can be caused by arterial embolization. Coronary spasm, which can be triggered by cocaine, can also lead to MI.

Sudden Cardiac Death

Sudden cardiac death is usually caused by ventricular fibrillation if known factors have been ruled out.

ASSESSMENT

Areas

General Cardiopulmonary Evaluation
• History, including medical and psychosocial history

- Vital signs, including temperature; heart rate; blood pressure; respiratory rate, rhythm, depth, and pattern
- Musculoskeletal, including skeletal system in general and specifically thoracic cage symmetry
- Cardiovascular: abnormal heart sounds, murmurs; abnormal pulsation, subcostal angle, ratio of anterior–posterior (AP) to lateral diameter, and areas of pain; endurance/exercise tolerance
- Respiratory, including AP to lateral diameter; excursion; positioning; breath sounds; dyspnea; fluid in lungs; vital capacity
- Skin, including facial appearance, skin coloration changes, edema
- Special tests to which the PT may or may not have access
- Functional level

Assessment Activities by Phase of Treatment (See "Treatment/Management")

- Phase 1
  1. Review history.
  2. Have client complete self-care evaluation.
  3. Assess activities of daily living (ADLs).
  4. Monitor vital signs: heart rate and blood pressure in rest in supine, sitting, standing, and effect of Valsalva.
  5. Ambulation: monitored ambulation; ambulating blood pressure reading; electrocardiogram via telemetry.
  6. Perform low- to moderate-level exercise test (heart rate of 120 to 140 beats per minute).
- Phase 2
  1. Monitor vital signs: heart rate, blood pressure, electrocardiogram (ECG), heart sounds, signs and symptoms.
  2. Monitor exercise sessions with continuous or intermittent portable radiotelemetry electrocardiographic equipment.
     a. Use continuous ECG monitoring for aerobic exercise sessions (for about 8 to 12 weeks if no complications).
     b. Use continuous ECG monitoring for beginning phase of anaerobic exercise sessions.
  3. Perform musculoskeletal assessment, especially in spine and lower extremities.
- Phase 3
  1. Review medical history.
  2. Review lab data: lipoprotein profile.
  3. Perform maximal symptom-limited exercise test. Determine target heart rate. Assess any variable present in relation to response to exercise, such as drop in blood pressure (especially systolic), angina, ST segment depression/elevation greater than 1 mm, extreme dyspnea, fatigue, and effect from medications.

Instrument/Procedures (See References for Sources)

Cardiovascular/Respiratory
1. breath sounds
   - auscultation
2. dyspnea
   - visual analogue scale
3. endurance/exercise tolerance
   a. endurance tests
   b. perceived exertion ratings
   c. response to exercise testing protocols

- Balke test
- bicycle test
- Bruce test
- Kottke–Kubicek Activity Test
- low-level functional test
- modified Naughton test
- self-paced walking test to predict $\dot{V}O_2$ max
- six-minute walking test
- submaximal exercise test protocols for elderly persons
- symptom-limited progressive exercise tolerance testing
- twelve-minute walking test

4. fluid in lungs
   - percussion
5. heart sounds
   - auscultation
6. pulsation, subcostal angle, ratio of AP to lateral diameter, areas of pain
   - palpation
7. vital capacity
   - pulmonary function testing

Functional Level
- Barthel ADL Index
- Functional Independence Measures
- Katz Index of Activities of Daily Living
- New York Functional and Therapeutic Classification of Heart Disease
- outcomes assessment measures
- PULSES profile

Special Tests to Which the PT May or May Not Have Access
- blood lipids
- chest x-ray
- cladication time
- electrocardiograms (ECGs)
- MB bands
- pulse oximetry
- serum enzymes
- telemetry

Vital Signs
- blood pressure
- heart rate
- respiratory rate, depth, rhythm, pattern

PROBLEMS

Angina
- Client reports pressure or crushing pain in the midchest region triggered by exertion and relieved by rest.

• The pain can also radiate to the teeth, jaw, throat (tickling sensation), posterior neck, or shoulder blade areas.
• Unstable angina may not be associated with activity and can occur at rest.

Myocardial Infarction
The client may describe symptoms in the following terms:
• burning
• chest tightness
• discomfort
• dizziness
• shortness of breath
• shoulder ache
• pain

TREATMENT/MANAGEMENT

Angina Pectoris
• Instruct client in exercise program as indicated.
• Educate client about risk factors.

Myocardial Infarction
• Rehabilitation is usually classified by phases of cardiac rehabilitation. During the acute MI, the client may also be treated medically with streptokinase, or t-PA (tissue plasminogen activator).
• The phases of cardiac rehabilitation also apply to clients with coronary insufficiency, which may also be treated with percutaneous transluminal coronary angioplasty (PTCA) or bypass surgery (coronary artery bypass graft [CABG]), and clients with pacemakers, heart valve repair, cardiac transplantation, heart failure, and arrhythmias.

Phase I. This phase usually begins as an inpatient program and ranges from 6 to 14 days in length.
• Phase 1 begins on day 4 post MI with a self-care evaluation. A client who executes activity levels 1 through 3 (see box below) with no complications can progress to monitored ambulation.
• Day 5 post MI: monitored ambulation. Place client on individualized, monitored walking program. Initial total walking distance can range from 10 feet to 100 yards and is usually 2 to 5 minutes in duration, progressing to 15 to 30 minutes in duration on treadmill or bicycle ergometer.
• Day 7 post MI: low-level exercise test.
• In general, supervise low-level exercises. Exercises may include active assistive ROM, progressing from supine to standing.
• In general, monitor cardiac response to ADLs. Low-level activities usually occur within the 1 to 3 metabolic equivalent range (METs). See Certo C, "Cardiovascular System," in references.
• Initiate stair climbing as indicated.

Activity Levels by Phase of Cardiac Rehabilitation

Level 1
- complete bed rest
- performs own morning care
- feeds self
- complete bed bath
- bedside commode

Level 2
- complete bed bath
- teaching material provided
- bedside commode
- up in chair for 20 to 30 minutes twice daily; blood pressure and pulse checked (flat, sitting, and standing) before moving to chair

Level 3
- bath responsibilities shared with nurse
- walks to bathroom with help; blood pressure and pulse (flat, sitting, and standing)
- walks to chair and sits for 30 to 60 minutes three times daily

Level 4. Same as level 3, plus:
- uses bathroom as needed
- monitored ambulation

Level 5
- self-administered sponge bath
- up in room as desired
- monitored ambulation

Level 6
- sit-down shower
- walks three times a day

Level 7
- up and down one flight of stairs

Level 8
- low-level treadmill test before discharge

Source: Reprinted with permission from LP Cahalin, RG Ice, and S Irwin, Program Planning and Implementation, in *Cardiopulmonary Physical Therapy*, S Irwin and JS Tecklin, p. 150, © 1990, Mosby-Yearbook, Inc.

Phase 2. Phase 2 usually begins after discharge from the hospital and lasts for up to 12 weeks after the initial cardiac event. Phase 2 candidates include clients who are post MI or post procedures such as coronary bypass surgery or PTCA, hypertrophic cardiomyopathy, mitral valve prolapse with ventricular dysrhythmias, latent coronary artery disease, or stable angina pectoris.
- Decrease myocardial oxygen demand with activity of the extremities for submaximal work. For lower extremities, use aerobic exercise via treadmill and bicycle ergometer. For upper extremities, train via arm ergometer unit and rowing machines.
- Phase 2 training intensity level of exercise is determined at a percentage of the maximum heart rate reached on the low-to-moderate exercise test performed at the end of phase 1. Sources report training at 80% to 90% rate reached on low-level test.

- During the first 2 to 4 weeks of phase 2, clients can try to increase duration of continuous exercise to 30 to 45 minutes.
- Clients with no complications can increase work levels and increase target heart rate by 10 beats per minute and continue to raise that amount every 1 to 2 weeks if no complications develop.
- Closer monitoring is needed in clients with complications such as angina, extreme hypertension or hypotension, ventricular or rapid supraventricular dysrhythmias, or extreme depression of left ventricular function.
- Progress client to independent, self-monitored exercise program 3 to 5 times per week in addition to supervised, monitored exercise 1 to 3 times per week.
- Progress to exercise duration of 45 to 60 minutes: 5 minutes of warm-up exercise, 30 to 45 minutes of continuous lower extremity exercise, 15 minutes continuous upper extremity exercise, and 5 minutes of cool-down exercise.
- Consider use of anaerobic training with weight-training program with high repetition and low weights. Wait 3 weeks post MI or surgery. PTCA patients may begin earlier.
- Continue to offer patient education in a formal manner, including individualized sessions and group activities such as a lecture series to cover risk factors, exercise, diet, medication, and stress management.
- Phase 2 can last at least 6 to 8 weeks and should include a maximal symptom-limited exercise test to assess a client's capacity to resume increased-intensity exercise, including sports. Clients who do well on the maximal exercise test will be assessed by the physician regarding return to work and participation in a phase 3 program.
- Before progressing to a phase 3 program, a client should be clinically stable with symptoms diminishing, be functioning at a 6 METs level or higher, have any arrhythmias controlled by medication, be able to self-regulate exercise, and be aware of any symptoms of cardiac distress.

Phase 3. This phase is generally a supervised outpatient program lasting around 4 to 6 months. Phase 3 may be named differently at different facilities. Clients include those who are post MI or bypass surgery *minimum* of 4 to 6 weeks, are post PTCA, have stable angina pectoris, have abnormal exercise tests, or are at high risk for coronary disease but are at present asymptomatic. Generally, clients are 3 to 6 months post the initial cardiac event. Phase 3 is a program of supervised conditioning exercise to facilitate clients' ability to reach an increased level of physical function.

- Promote lifelong exercise and inform client of lifestyle modification needed to diminish further risk of coronary problems.
- After assessment, determine target heart rate training intensity.
- Implement exercise program for client to produce peripheral and central cardiac improvement with aerobic exercise of at least 60% chronotropic reserve derived by using Karvonen's formula (target heart rate should be resting heart rate in addition to 60% of the difference between resting and maximum heart rate) in conjunction with variables listed under assessment.
- Provide advice on equipment needed. Aerobic exercise programs for clients with coronary artery disease can include bicycling, walking or jogging, aerobic dancing, roller skating or rollerblading, swimming, arm ergometer or rowing, jumping rope (on ground or on trampoline), or weight training in a circuit mode.
- The client needs reassessment after completing 6 months of rehabilitation.

- Emphasize increase in distance. Individually assess mode, intensity, frequency, and duration of client's exercise program.
- Gradually increase duration from 30 minutes to 45 to 60 minutes. Use telemetry monitoring in initial weeks with a new client.
- Work with interdisciplinary team to provide group educational sessions. The health care team often includes a nutritionist, a social worker, a psychologist, and medical speakers.
- Benefits of and compliance with program can be enhanced with evaluation of progress, blending program with client's schedule, setting goals, signing a participation agreement, and providing group support.
- Emphasize primary prevention programs. Include work-hardening evaluation.

For sample protocol, see Sixteen-Step Walk and Walk-Jog Program for Cardiac Patients in Phase 3 Exercise Program in Certo, "Cardiovascular system" (see references under "Treatment").

PRECAUTIONS/CONTRAINDICATIONS

In general, the following exercise testing precautions should be observed:

- Elderly persons with stable uncomplicated medical histories who report fatigue with exertion should be monitored, via respiratory rate, heart rate, blood pressure, and ECG, to assess closely their ability to participate in an exercise program.
- Additional monitoring can include resting and exercise pulmonary function, oxygen saturation, and analysis of expired gas at maximum exercise effort.
- Full 12-lead ECG monitoring is indicated if client has severe cardiac symptoms or specific medical complications such as respiratory infection.

Angina Pectoris

Clients with unstable angina are at increased risk during exercise due to lack of correlation between the cardiac system's response to exercise and perception of symptoms. It is important to follow strict use of target heart rate based on graded exercise test. **Never exercise during an angina attack.**

Myocardial Infarction

Phase 1

The following are contraindications to beginning a phase 1 treatment program (based on Cahalin, Ice, and Irwin, "Program Planning and Implementation"; see references):

- overt congestive heart failure
- MI or extension of infarction within the previous 2 days
- second- or third-degree heart block, coupled with PVCs or ventricular tachycardia at rest
- hypertensive resting blood pressure (systolic > 160 mm Hg, diastolic > 105 mm Hg)
- hypotensive resting blood pressure (systolic < 80 mm Hg)
- more than 10 to 15 PVCs per minute at rest, particularly if there is a variable coupling interval
- severe aortic stenosis (gradient of $\geq$ 80 mm Hg)
- unstable angina pectoris with recent changes in symptoms (< 24 hours)
- dissecting aortic aneurysm
- uncontrolled metabolic disease
- psychosis or other unstable psychological condition
  Modify or terminate phase 1 activities if any of the following occur:
- hypertensive blood pressure response (systolic > 180 mm Hg, diastolic > 110 mm Hg)
- hypotensive systolic blood pressure to <20 mm Hg between systolic and diastolic pressures

- development of coupled premature ventricular contractions (PVCs) or a salvo of three or more PVCs in a row (ventricular tachycardia)
- PVCs with R-on-T phenomenon during exercise
- level 1/4 angina pectoris
- onset of severe fatigue or dizziness
- 2+/4+ dyspnea with ambulation

Phase 2

The following are precautions for clients in this phase:
- Recent post-MI and postbypass clients may only tolerate 10 to 15 minutes of continuous low-intensity work. Post-PTCA clients may tolerate 20 to 30 minutes.
- Avoid the Valsalva maneuver during any weight training.

Phase 3

It is advisable to monitor electrocardiographically all phase 3 patients at intervals of 4 to 8 weeks.

DESIRED OUTCOME/PROGNOSIS

Angina Pectoris
- The client will experience a decrease or delay in episodes of angina.
- The client will improve in functional capacity.

Myocardial Infarction

Phase 1
- The client's electrocardiographic response to medication during activity will be monitored.
- The client's hemodynamic response during self-care activities will be determined.
- The client and family will be educated on behavior modification and risk factor reduction.
- The client's ability to progress to increasing levels of activity will be assessed.

Research has found that clients with no complications in the first 4 days post infarction usually do well in phase 1 and progress to phases 2 and 3 quickly.

Phase 2
- The client's cardiovascular response and medication effect to mild or moderate workloads will be determined.
- The client will increase physical work capacity and endurance.
- The client will maintain the continuity of his or her exercise program during the transition from inpatient to outpatient status.
- The client's understanding of cardiovascular fitness and ability to self-monitor activities will increase.
- The client will experience a decrease in the psychological stress of CAD.

Studies report no association between increased risk of morbidity or mortality with early exercise conditioning during phase 2. Clients post MI in a cardiac rehabilitation progam have returned to work an average of 40 days before those not undergoing rehabilitation, usually around 8 to 10 weeks post MI.

Phase 3
- The client will increase physical fitness and endurance levels.
- The client will increase understanding of CAD and health maintenance.

Studies report that cardiac rehabilitation post MI leads to around a 25% reduction in cardio-vascular mortality and death. But some feel that scientific data on the relationship between cardiac rehabilitation program and CAD are sparse.

REFERENCES

ASSESSMENT

Certo C. Cardiovascular system. In: Myers RS, ed. *Saunders Manual of Physical Therapy Practice*. Phila-delphia, Pa: WB Saunders Co; 1995:193–251. **[Differential diagnosis of chest pain, breathlessness, fatigue, irregular heartbeat, edema, angina]**

Goodman C, Snyder TE. *Differential Diagnosis in Physical Therapy*, Philadelphia, Pa: WB Saunders Co; 1990:332, 337, 357, 362–363.

Holloway V, Fick AW. Rehabilitation of the postsurgical cardiac patient. In: Payton OD, ed. *Manual of Physical Therapy*. New York, NY: Churchill Livingstone; 1989:593–609.

Irwin S, Blessey RL. Patient evaluation. In: Irwin S, Tecklin JS, eds. *Cardiopulmonary Physical Therapy*. 2nd ed. St Louis, Mo: CV Mosby Co; 1990:122. (3rd ed, 1995, available)

Cardiovascular/Respiratory

Breath Sounds

Auscultation

Aweida D, Kelsy CJ. Accuracy and reliability of physical therapists in auscultating tape-recorded lung sound. *Physiotherapy Canada*. 1990;42:279–282.

Brooks D, Wilson L, Kelsey C, et al. Accuracy and reliability of "specialized" physical therapists in ausculta-ting tape recorded lung sounds. *Physiotherapy Canada*. 1993;45:21–24.

Pasterkamp H, Montgomery M, Wiebicke W, et al. Nomenclature used by health care professionals to de-scribe breath sounds in asthma. *Chest*. 1987;92:346–352.

Dyspnea

Aitken RCB. Measurement of feelings using visual analogue scales. *Proceedings of the Royal Society of Medicine*. 1969;62:989–993.

Endurance/Exercise Tolerance

Endurance Tests

American Physical Therapy Association. A guide to physical therapist practice, Volume I: A description of patient management. *Physical Therapy*. 1995;75:720–738.

Perceived Exertion Ratings

Kowal M. Rating perceived exertion. *Clinical Management in Physical Therapy*. 1990;10:6:44–45.

Response to Exercise

Bassey EJ, Fenton PH, MacDonald IC. Self-paced walking as a method for exercise testing in elderly and young men. *Clinical Science and Molecular Medicine*. 1976;51:609–612. **[Self-paced walking test to predict $\dot{V}o_2$ max]**

Cahalin LP, Blessey RL, Kummer D, Simard M. The safety of exercise testing performed independently by physical therapists. *Journal of Cardiopulmonary Rehabilitation*. 1987;7:269–276. **[Treadmill exercise testing using Bruce protocol]**

Certo C. Cardiovascular system. In: Myers RS, ed. *Saunders Manual of Physical Therapy Practice*. Phila-delphia, Pa: WB Saunders Co; 1995:193–251. **[Twelve-minute walking test, modified Naughton test, Balke test, Bruce test, bicycle test]**

Cooper KH. A means of assessing maximal oxygen intake. *Journal of the American Medical Association*. 1968;203:135–138. **[Six-minute walking test]**

Ellingham CT, Amundsen LR. Cardiac considerations and physical training. In: Jackson O, ed. *Physical Therapy of the Geriatric Patient*. 2nd ed. New York, NY: Churchill Livingstone; 1989:213–238. **[Kottke–Kubicek Activity Test, submaximal exercise test protocols, symptoms-limited progressive exercise tolerance testing]**

Hamm LF, Stull GA, Ainsworth B, Serfass RC, Wolfe DR. Short- and long-term prognostic value of graded exercise testing soon after myocardial infarction. *Physical Therapy*. 1986;66:334–339.

Ice R, et al. Descriptive data on marathon runners with severe coronary artery disease: results from cardiac catheterization, exercise tests, and serum lipids. *Medicine and Science in Sports and Exercise*. 1978;10:35.

Irwin SC, Zadai CC. Cardiopulmonary rehabilitation of the geriatric patient. In: Lewis CB, ed. *Aging: The Health Care Challenge*. 2nd ed. Philadelphia, Pa: FA Davis Co; 1990:181–211. **[Twelve-minute walking test, low-level functional test, Balke test, Bruce test, bicycle test]**

Swerts PM, Mostert R, Wouters EF. Comparison of corridor and treadmill walking in patients with severe chronic obstructive pulmonary disease. *Physical Therapy*. 1990;70:439–442.

Fluid in Lungs

Percussion
Bourke S, Nunes D, Stafford F, Huvley G, Graham I. Percussion of the chest re-visited: a comparison of the diagnostic value of auscultatory and conventional chest percussion. *Irish Journal of Medical Science*. 1989;158:82–84.

Vital Capacity

Pulmonary Function Testing
American Thoracic Society. Lung function testing: selection of reference values and interpretive strategies. *American Review of Respiratory Disease*. 1991;144:1202–1218.

Functional Level

The Barthel Index
Mahoney BI, Barthel DW. Functional evaluation: the Barthel Index. *Maryland State Medical Journal*. 1965;14:61–65.

Wade DT, Collin C. The Barthel ADL Index: a standard measure of physical disability? *International Disability Studies*. 1988;10:2:64–67.

New York Heart Association Functional and Therapeutic Classification of Heart Disease
Certo C. Cardiovascular system. In: Myers RS, ed. *Saunders Manual of Physical Therapy Practice*. Philadelphia, Pa: WB Saunders Co; 1995:193–251.

Functional Independence Measures
Granger CV, Hamilton BB, Keith RA, et al. Advance in functional assessment for medical rehabilitation. *Topics in Geriatric Rehabilitation*. 1986;1:3:59–74.

Keith RA, Granger CV, Hamilton BB, Sherwins FS. The Functional Independence Measure. *Advances in Clinical Rehabilitation*. 1987;1:6–18.

Katz Index of Activities of Daily Living
Benjamin Rose Hospital Staff. Multidisciplinary studies of illness in aged persons: II. A new classification of functional status in activities of daily living. *Journal of Chronic Disease*. 1959;9:1:55–62.

Brorsson B, Ashberg KH. Katz Index of Independence in ADL: reliability and validity in short-term care. *Scandinavian Journal of Rehabilitation Medicine*. 1984;16:125–132.

Outcome Assessment Measures
Michel TH. Outcome assessment in cardiac rehabilitation. *International Journal of Technology Assessment in Health Care*. 1992;8:1:76–84.

NLN-PUBL. Outcome criteria for physical therapy, speech pathology, and occupational therapy: home health agencies. In: Rinke LT, et al. *Outcome Measures in Home Care Service*. 1987;21-2195:2:165–171.

Pashkow P, Ades, PA, Emery CF, et al. Outcome measurement in cardiac and pulmonary rehabilitation. *Journal of Cardiopulmonary Rehabilitation*. 1995;15:394–405.

PULSES Profile
Granger CV, Albrecht GL, Hamilton BB. Outcome of comprehensive medical rehabilitation: measurements by PULSES profile and the Barthel index. *Archives of Physical Medicine and Rehabilitation*. 1979;60:145–154.

Moskowitz RW, McCann CB. Classification of disability in the chronically ill and aging. *Journal of Chronic Disease*. 1957;5:342–346.

Special Tests to Which the PT May or May Not Have Access
Certo C. Cardiovascular system. In: Myers RS, ed. *Saunders Manual of Physical Therapy Practice*. Philadelphia, Pa: WB Saunders Co; 1995:193-251. **[Invasive tests: radionuclide studies, cardiac catheterization, coronary arteriography, percutaneous transluminal coronary angioplasty. Noninvasive tests: echocardiography, graded exercise test]**

DeTurk WE. Exercise and the intolerant heart. *Clinical Management in Physical Therapy*. 1992;12:1:67–73. **[Heart function tests]**

Vital Signs

Blood Pressure
Frohlich ED. Recommendations for human blood pressure determination by sphygmomanometers: report of a special task force appointed by the steering committee, American Heart Association. *Hypertension*. 1988;11:210A–222A.

Stolt M. Reliability of auscultory method of arterial blood pressure. *Hypertension*. 1990;3:697–703.

Heart Rate
Rothstein JM. *Measurement in Physical Therapy*. New York, NY: Churchill Livingstone; 1985.

Respiratory Rate
Simeos EAF, Roark R, Berman S, Esler L, Murphy J. Respiratory rate: measurement of variability over time and accuracy at different counting periods. *Archives of Disease in Childhood*. 1991;66:1199–1203.

TREATMENT
Atwood JA, Nielsen DH. Scope of cardiac rehabilitation: physical therapy involvement. *Physical Therapy*. 1985;65:1812–1819.

Booker H, Harries D, Rehahn M, et al. Progressive exercise training: subjective and objective changes. *Physiotherapy Practice*. 1985;1:31–36.

Certo C. Cardiovascular system. In: Myers RS, ed. *Saunders Manual of Physical Therapy Practice*. Philadelphia, Pa: WB Saunders Co; 1995:193–251.

Cohen M, Hoskin T. *Cardiopulmonary Symptoms in Physical Therapy Practice*. New York, NY: Churchill Livingstone; 1988.

Davidson DM, Maloney CA. Recovery after cardiac events. *Physical Therapy*. 1985;65:1820–1827.

DeTurk WE. The intolerant heart: part 2. *Clinical Management in Physical Therapy*. 1992;12:2:32–39.

Hillegass EA, Sadowsky HS. *Essentials of Cardiopulmonary Physical Therapy*. Philadelphia, Pa: WB Saunders Co; 1994.

Ice R, et al. The effects of long-distance bicycling on heart disease patients. In: Burke ER, Newsom MM, eds. *Medical and Scientific Aspects of Cycling*. Champaign, Ill: Human Kinetics Books; 1988.

Irwin S. Clinical manifestations and assessment of ischemic heart disease. *Physical Therapy*. 1985;65:1806–1811.

Irwin S, Tecklin JS, eds. *Cardiopulmonary Physical Therapy.* 2nd ed. St Louis, Mo: CV Mosby Co; 1990.

Irwin SC, Zadai CC. Cardiopulmonary rehabilitation of the geriatric patient. In: Lewis CB, ed. *Aging: The Health Care Challenge.* 2nd ed. Philadelphia, Pa: FA Davis Co; 1990:181–211.

Kehl P. A retrospective look at the effects of cardiac rehabilitation: post myocardial infarction. *Physiotherapy.* 1991;77:77–80.

Kispert CP, Nielsen DH. Normal cardiopulmonary responses to acute and chronic strengthening and endurance exercises. *Physical Therapy.* 1985;65:1828.

Lewis CB. Effects of aging on the cardiovascular system. *Clinical Management in Physical Therapy.* 1984;44:24–29.

Lindsay GM, Gaw A. Secondary prevention of coronary heart disease. *Physiotherapy.* 1995;81:398.

Newton M, Mutrie N, McArthur JD. The effects of exercise in a coronary rehabilitation programme. *Scottish Medical Journal.* 1991;36:2:38–41.

Nitz J, Cheras F. Transcutaneous electrical stimulation and chronic intractable angina pectoris. *Australian Journal of Physiotherapy.* 1993;39:2:109–113.

NLN-PUBL. Outcome criteria for physical therapy, speech pathology, and occupational therapy: home health agencies. In: Rinke LT, et al. *Outcome Measures in Home Care Service.* 1987;21-2195:2:165–171.

Ohshige T, Morimoto N, Tanaka H, Itjyo N. Risk management in physical therapy for cardiovascular diseases: applicability of Czermak-Hering reflex and Aschner reflex. *Journal of Physical Therapy Science.* 1995;7:1:9–13.

Oldridge NB. Compliance and dropout in cardiac rehabilitation. *Journal of Cardiac Rehabilitation.* 1984;4:166.

Ross J, Dean E. Integrating physiological principles into the comprehensive management of cardiopulmonary dysfunction. *Physical Therapy.* 1989;69:255.

Wallace C. Evaluation of a cardiac exercise programme: a pilot study. *New Zealand Journal of Physiotherapy.* 1987;15:8–10.

Watchie J. *Cardiopulmonary Physical Therapy: A Clinical Manual.* Philadelphia, Pa: WB Saunders Co; 1995.

Wenger NK, Froelicher ES, Smith LK, et al. *Cardiac Rehabilitation: Clinical Practice Guideline No. 17.* Rockville, Md: US Dept of Health and Human Services, Public Health Service, Agency for Health Care Policy and Research and the National Heart, Lung, and Blood Institute; 1995:22. AHCPR publication 96-0672. [Decision tree for cardiac rehabilitation services]

Williams T, Mueller K, Cornwall MW. Effect of acupuncture-point stimulation on diastolic blood pressure in hypertensive subjects: a preliminary study. *Physical Therapy.* 1991;71:523–529.

Cardiac Surgery

DESCRIPTION

Just as there are a variety of approaches to cardiac surgery, there are a variety of approaches to physical therapy after cardiac surgery. The therapist should work closely with the surgical team and client on treatment decisions. Clients undergoing cardiac surgery are at an increased risk for postoperative complications such as thrombosis or pneumonia. This section applies to the following surgeries:

- atrial septal defect
- complete transposition of the great vessels
- coronary artery bypass grafting (CABG)
- corrective surgery in adults

- pacemakers
- percutaneous transluminal coronary angioplasty (PTCA)
- pulmonary stenosis or aortic stenosis
- repair of ascending aortic aneurysm
- tetralogy of Fallot
- transplantation
- valve repair
- valve replacement
- ventricular aneurysmectomy
- ventricular septal defect
- ventricular tachycardia

CAUSE

Valvular lesions can be caused by complications from rheumatic fever, degenerative changes, congenital defects, or subacute bacterial endocarditis. Pulmonary valve problems are usually caused by congenital defects. Congenital defects are often a result of maternal disease, arrested development in utero, or genetic factors. See also "Pediatric Cardiac Conditions."

Congenital disorders are divided into acyanotic conditions and cyanotic conditions. Acyanotic conditions lead to excessive pulmonary blood flow, and cyanotic conditions lead to inadequate pulmonary blood flow. Acyanotic conditions include valvular stenosis, atrial septal defect, ventricular septal defect, persistent ductus arteriosus, and aortic coarctation. Cyanotic conditions include tetralogy of Fallot and transposition of great vessels.

The need for a pacemaker may be triggered by the following conditions: arrhythmias, heart block, hypersensitive carotid sinus syndrome, Stokes–Adams syndrome, and sick sinus syndrome. Arrhythmias are caused by abnormal conduction patterns.

ASSESSMENT

Areas

The following areas may be assessed postoperatively:
- History including operative notes, type of incision, use of any grafts
- Vital signs, including temperature; heart rate; blood pressure; arterial trace pulse rate; and respiratory rate, rhythm, depth, and pattern; also fluid intake and output, presence of any drainage tubes
- Cardiovascular: abnormal heart sounds and murmurs; abnormal pulsation, subcostal angle, ratio of anterior–posterior (AP) to lateral diameter, and areas of pain; endurance/exercise tolerance
- Respiratory, including AP to lateral diameter; excursion; positioning; fluid in lungs; vital capacity
- Skin, including skin coloration changes and edema
- Strength: little or no resistance to upper extremities after sternotomy
- Mobility, including bed mobility and transfers
- Functional level: activities of daily living (ADLs)
- Gait
- Special tests to which the PT may or may not have access

Instruments/Procedures (See References for Sources)

Cardiovascular/Respiratory
1. breath sounds

- auscultation
2. endurance/exercise tolerance
   - endurance testing
   - perceived exertion ratings
3. fluid in lungs
   - percussion
4. vital capacity
   - pulmonary function tests

Special Tests to Which the PT May or May Not Have Access
- blood gasses
- electrocardiograms (ECGs)
- electrolytes
- lab values

Vital Signs
- blood pressure
- heart rate
- respiratory rate, rhythm, depth, pattern

PROBLEMS

Postoperatively:
- The client is usually in pain.
- There can be diminished air entry.
- The client can have an increase in retained secretions.
- The client can have decreased extremity movement and general mobility, especially on the side from which the saphenous vein was donated for CABG.
- There can be brachial plexus injury.
- There can be weakness on one side, or foot drop.
- There can be edema.
Some of the possible complications from cardiac surgery include the following:
- anemia
- arrythmias
- cardiac arrest
- cerebral infarction
- embolus (peripheral or pulmonary)
- infection
- neurological deficits
- renal failure
- respiratory failure
- unstable sternum

TREATMENT/MANAGEMENT

Preoperatively:
- Explain equipment to client.
- Instruct client in range-of-motion (ROM) exercises, posture awareness, breathing exercises, effective cough and huffing techniques, and general mobility.
- Teach support of incision.

Postoperatively, in general:
- Be sure client is adequately medicated before starting treatment.
- Instruct in unilateral and bilateral deep breathing exercises; client may need IPPB.
- Consider unilateral, posterior shaking at base of lungs, huffing, and coughing with accompanying sternal support.
- May need percussion after the first 2 days if sputum is viscous.
- Instruct in active exercise to extremities one at a time, such as active ankle-pumping exercise.
- Instruct in ADLs for bed mobility and transfers.
- Begin gait activities a few days after surgery if physician approves.
- Stimulate progressive increase in mobility, and progress to exercise and stairs.
- Prescribe exercise as indicated. Monitor as per precautions.

Phases of cardiac rehabilitation, outlined in the previous section "Coronary Artery Disease," apply to clients with coronary insufficiency that may be treated with PTCA or CABG, as well as to clients with pacemakers, heart valve repair, cardiac transplantation, heart failure, and arrhythmias. See Certo, "Cardiovascular system," in references, for sample protocol for inpatient cardiac rehabilitation program following CABG surgery.

After transplantation surgery:
- Client may be isolated in room to avoid infection.
- Provide chest physical therapy postoperatively.
- During the first few days postoperatively, initiate transfers, gait training, and dangling feet at side of bed as indicated.
- Postural exercises are usually indicated, especially for weakened back musculature.
- Initiate ROM and strengthening exercises as tolerated by client.
- After sternum has healed, instruct client in activities to stretch anterior chest via scapular exercises.
- Begin aerobic conditioning program, such as walking or cycling, under close supervision. See "Precautions/Contraindications."

PRECAUTIONS/CONTRAINDICATIONS

Exercise
The American Heart Association recommends monitoring during exercise for the following signs that client is responding abnormally to exercise:
- flat or progressive decrease in systolic blood pressure
- bradycardia or excessive tachycardia
- significant arrhythmias
- angina
- undue shortness of breath
- dizziness
- confusion
- lower extremity claudication
- cyanosis
- pallor
- mottling of skin
- cold sweat
- ataxia
- glassy stare

- abnormal heart sounds
  The American Heart Association also lists the following contraindications to exercise:
- acute febrile illness
- uncontrolled, active chronic systemic disease
- anatomical abnormalities
- functional abnormalities, such as third-degree heart block

Intra-Aortic Balloon Pump
- Any interference of electrodes can interrupt the synchronization of the balloon pump.
- Avoid hyperextending the hip or flexing more than 50 degrees.

Pacemakers
- Pacemakers are subject to possible generator failure.
- Diathermy can interfere with pacemaker function.
- Temporary pacemaker wires should be kept dry.
- The physician may have client on limited ROM after pacemaker placement.
- Monitor blood pressure and any electrocardiogram (ECG) abnormalities during exercise for exercise intolerance.
- Use of rate of perceived exertion is helpful for clients with pacemakers.
- Avoid any excessive shortness of breath during exercise.
- Avoid forced coughing.

After Transplantation Surgery
- Client should avoid anyone with infection such as a cold.
- Avoid any stress on sternum.
- Consult with physician before initiating use of weights.
- Monitor exercise response using Borg's perceived levels of exertion and Stanford's dyspnea index.
- Be aware that a denervated heart may respond with little or no increase in heart rate to low levels of exercise.

DESIRED OUTCOME/PROGNOSIS
- The client will achieve maximum expansion of lungs and prevention of pulmonary complications.
- The client will prevent circulatory complications.
- The client will maintain maximum mobility.
- The client will increase endurance.
- The client will return to full activities of daily living.
  Improved normality of heart rate has been reported at 1 year post transplant.

REFERENCES

ASSESSMENT
Certo C. Cardiovascular system. In: Myers RS, ed. *Saunders Manual of Physical Therapy Practice*. Philadelphia, Pa: WB Saunders Co; 1995:193–251.

Holloway V, Fick AW. Rehabilitation of the postsurgical cardiac patient. In: Payton, OD, ed. *Manual of Physical Therapy*. New York, NY: Churchill Livingstone; 1989:593–609.

Irwin S, Blessey RL. Patient evaluation. In: Irwin S, Tecklin JS, eds. *Cardiopulmonary Physical Therapy*. 2nd ed. St Louis, Mo: CV Mosby Co; 1990:122. (3rd ed, 1995, available)

Pashkow P, Ades, PA, Emery CF, et al. Outcome measurement in cardiac and pulmonary rehabilitation. *Journal of Cardiopulmonary Rehabilitation*. 1995;15:394–405.

Cardiovascular/Respiratory

Breath Sounds

Auscultation

Aweida D, Kelsy CJ. Accuracy and reliability of physical therapists in auscultating tape-recorded lung sound. *Physiotherapy Canada*. 1990;42:279–282.

Brooks D, et al. Accuracy and reliability of specialized physical therapists in auscultating tape recorded lung sounds. *Physiotherapy Canada*. 1993;45:21-24.

Pasterkamp H, et al. Nomenclature used by health care professionals to describe breath sounds in asthma. *Chest*. 1993;92:346–352.

Endurance/Exercise Tolerance

Endurance Tests

American Physical Therapy Association. A guide to physical therapist practice, Volume I: A description of patient management. *Physical Therapy*. 1995;75:720–738.

Perceived Exertion Ratings

Kowal M. Rating perceived exertion. *Clinical Management in Physical Therapy*. 1990;10:6:44–45.

Fluid in Lungs

Percussion

Bourke S, et al. Percussion of the chest re-visited: a comparison of the diagnostic value of auscultatory and conventional chest percussion. *Irish Journal of Medical Science*. 1989;158:82–84.

Vital Capacity

Pulmonary Function Testing

American Thoracic Society. Lung function testing: selection of reference values and interpretive strategies. *American Review of Respiratory Disease*. 1991;144:1202–1218.

Vital Signs

Blood Pressure

Frohlich ED. Recommendations for human blood pressure determination by sphygmomanometers: report of a special task force appointed by the steering committee, American Heart Association. *Hypertension*. 1988;11:210A–222A.

Stolt M. Reliability of auscultory method of arterial blood pressure. *Hypertension*. 1990;3:697–703.

Heart Rate

Rothstein JM. *Measurement in Physical Therapy*. New York, NY: Churchill Livingstone; 1985.

Respiratory Rate

Simeos EAF, et al. Respiratory rate: measurement of variability over time and accuracy at different counting periods. *Archives of Disease in Childhood*. 1991;66:1199–1203.

TREATMENT

Barrell SE, Abbas HM. Monitoring during physiotherapy after open heart surgery. *Physiotherapy*. 1978;64:272–273.

Certo C. Cardiovascular system. In: Myers RS, ed. *Saunders Manual of Physical Therapy Practice.* Philadelphia, Pa: WB Saunders Co; 1995:193–251.

Clough P. The denervated heart. *Clinical Management in Physical Therapy.* 1990;10:4:14–17.

Downie PA. *Cash's Textbook of Chest, Heart and Vascular Disorders for Physiotherapists.* 4th ed. London, England: Faber & Faber; 1987.

Dull JL, Dull WL. Are maximal inspiratory breathing exercises or incentive spirometry better than early mobilization after cardiopulmonary bypass? *Physical Therapy.* 1983;63:655–659.

Howell S, Hill JD. Acute respiratory care in open heart surgery. *Physical Therapy.* 1972:52:253–260.

Jenkins SC, Soutar SA. A survey into the use of incentive spirometry following coronary artery bypass graft surgery. *Physiotherapy.* 1986;72:492–493.

Jenkins S, Soutar S, Gray B, Evans J. The acute effects of respiratory manoeuvres in postoperative patients. *Physiotherapy Practice.* 1988;4:63–68.

Jenkins SC, Soutar SA, Loukota JM, et al. A comparison of breathing exercise, incentive spirometry and mobilisation after coronary artery surgery. *Physiotherapy Theory and Practice.* 1990;6:117–126.

Jenkins SC, Soutar SA, Moxham J. The effects of posture on lung volumes in normal subjects and in patients pre- and post-coronary artery surgery. *Physiotherapy.* 1988;74:492–496.

King D. Physiotherapy and the ventricular assist device. *Physiotherapy.* 1991;77:255–258.

Lee JM. *Aids to Physiotherapy.* New York, NY: Churchill Livingstone; 1988;88–93.

Sadowsky H, Rohrkemper K, Quon S. Rehabilitation of cardiac and cardiopulmonary recipients: appendix I. *An Introduction for Physical and Occupational Therapists.* Stanford, Calif: Stanford University; 1986.

Semanoff T, Kleinfeld M, Castle P. Chest physical therapy as a preventive modality in cardiac surgery patients. *Archives of Physical Medicine.* 1981;62:506.

Sternweiler MR. Physiotherapy and the South African heart transplant patient. *Physical Therapy.* 1968;48:1399–1408.

Steven MH. Nasal intermittent positive pressure ventilation: a potential bridge to heart-lung transplantation. *Physiotherapy.* 1990;76:751–752.

Thornlow, DK. Is chest physiotherapy necessary after cardiac surgery? *Critical Care Nurse.* 1995;15:3:39–48.

Heart Failure

Also known as *congestive heart failure.*

DESCRIPTION

Heart failure (HF) is a progressive disease characterized by ineffective pumping of the heart, leading to a diminished and inadequate cardiac output. Initially this syndrome may be symptomatic only during exertion, but in later stages the symptoms of congestion and fatigue appear even when the client is at rest.

CAUSE

This disorder has multiple etiologies. Two causes are left ventricular failure and right ventricular failure.

Assessment

• History, including medical and psychosocial history

- Vital signs: temperature; blood pressure; heart rate; respiratory rate, rhythm, depth, and pattern
- Musculoskeletal, including skeletal system in general and thoracic cage symmetry specifically
- Cardiovascular, including abnormal heart sounds, murmurs; abnormal pulsation, subcostal angle, ratio of anterior–posterior (AP) to lateral diameter, and areas of pain; endurance/exercise tolerance
- Respiratory; including AP to lateral diameter; excursion; positioning; breath sounds; fluid in lungs
- Skin, including skin coloration, facial appearance, edema

Instruments/Procedures (See References for Sources)

Cardiovascular/Respiratory
1. breath sounds
   - auscultation
2. dyspnea
   - visual analogue scale
3. endurance/exercise tolerance
   a. endurance tests
   b. perceived exertion ratings
   c. exercise tolerance testing
      - Balke Test
      - bicycle test
      - Bruce test
      - Galke test
      - Kottke–Kubicek Activity Test
      - low-level functional test
      - modified Naughton test
      - six-minute walking test
      - self-paced walking test to predict $\dot{V}o^2$ max
      - submaximal exercise test protocols for elderly persons
      - symptom-limited progressive exercise tolerance testing
      - twelve-minute walking test
4. fluid in lungs
   - percussion
5. heart sounds
   - auscultation
6. pulsation, subcostal angle, ratio of AP to lateral diameter, areas of pain
   - palpation
7. vital capacity
   - pulmonary function testing

Functional Level
- Barthel ADL Index
- Functional Independence Measures
- Katz Index of Activities of Daily Living
- outcomes assessment measures

- PULSES profile

Special Tests to Which the PT May or May Not Have Access
- blood lipids
- chest x-ray
- cladication time
- electrocardiograms (ECGs)
- MB bands
- pulse oximetry
- serum enzymes
- telemetry

Vital Signs
- blood pressure
- heart rate
- respiratory rate, depth, rhythm, pattern

PROBLEMS
The client can display the following signs and symptoms:
- abdominal pain
- ankle swelling
- bloating
- cough (accompanied by rales) producing sputum with blood
- dyspnea and/or paroxysmal noctural dyspnea
- fatigue with orthopnea
- increased respiratory rate
- nausea

TREATMENT/MANAGEMENT
- Prescribe low-level exercise.
- Instruct in energy conservation techniques during acute phase.
- Progress through phases of cardiac rehabilitation as tolerated (see phases in previous section "Coronary Artery Disease")
- Consider use of oxygen.
- Consider use of chest physical therapy.

PRECAUTIONS/CONTRAINDICATIONS
The following precautions should be observed in exercise testing:
- Elderly persons with stable uncomplicated medical histories who report fatigue with exertion should be monitored, via respiratory rate, heart rate, blood pressure, and electrocardiogram, to assess closely their ability to participate in an exercise program.
- Additional monitoring can include resting and exercise pulmonary function, oxygen saturation, and analysis of expired gas at maximum exercise effort.
- Full 12-lead ECG monitoring is indicated if client has severe cardiac symptoms or specific medical complications such as respiratory infection.
- See additional precautions in previous section "CoronaryArtery Disease."

EXPECTED OUTCOME/PROGNOSIS
- Client will improve in cardiac output and performance.

REFERENCES

ASSESSMENT

Certo C. Cardiovascular system. In: Myers RS, ed. *Saunders Manual of Physical Therapy Practice*. Philadelphia, Pa: WB Saunders Co; 1995:193–251. [**Differential diagnosis of chest pain, breathlessness, fatigue, irregular heartbeat, edema, angina**]

Goodman C, Snyder TE. *Differential Diagnosis in Physical Therapy*. Philadelphia, Pa; 1990:332, 337, 357, 362–363.

Holloway V, Fick AW. Rehabilitation of the postsurgical cardiac patient. In: Payton OD, ed. *Manual of Physical Therapy*. New York, NY: Churchill Livingstone; 1989:593–609.

Irwin S, Blessey RL. Patient evaluation. In: Irwin S, Tecklin JS, eds. *Cardiopulmonary Physical Therapy*. 2nd ed. St Louis, Mo: CV Mosby Co; 1990:122. (3rd ed, 1995, available)

Cardiovascular/Respiratory

Breath Sounds

Auscultation

Aweida D, Kelsy CJ. Accuracy and reliability of physical therapists in auscultating tape-recorded lung sounds. *Physiotherapy Canada*. 1990;42:279–282.

Brooks D, et al. Accuracy and reliability of specialized physical therapists in auscultating tape recorded lung sounds. *Physiotherapy Canada*. 1993;45:21–24.

Pasterkamp H, et al. Nomenclature used by health care professionals to describe breath sounds in asthma. *Chest*. 1993;92:346–352.

Dyspnea

Aitken RCB. Measurement of feelings using visual analogue scales. *Proceedings of the Royal Society of Medicine*. 1969;62:989–993.

Endurance/Exercise Tolerance

Endurance Tests

American Physical Therapy Association. A guide to physical therapist practice, Volume I: A description of patient management. *Physical Therapy*. 1995;75:720–738.

Perceived Exertion Ratings

Kowal M. Rating perceived exertion. *Clinical Management in Physical Therapy*. 1990;10:6:44–45.

Response to Exercise Testing

Bassey EJ, Fenton PH, MacDonald IC. Self-paced walking as a method for exercise testing in elderly and young men. *Clinical Science and Molecular Medicine*. 1976;51:609–612. [**Self-paced walking test to predict $\dot{V}o_2$ max**]

Cahalin LP, Blessey RL, Kummer D, Simard M. The safety of exercise testing performed independently by physical therapists. *Journal of Cardiopulmonary Rehabilitation*. 1987;7:269–276. [**Treadmill exercise testing using Bruce protocol**]

Certo C. Cardiovascular system. In: Myers RS, ed. *Saunders Manual of Physical Therapy Practice*. Philadelphia, Pa: WB Saunders Co; 1995:193–251. [**Twelve-minute walking test, modified/Naughton test, Galke test, Bruce test, bicycle test**]

Cooper KH. A means of assessing maximal oxygen intake. *Journal of the American Medical Association*. 1968;203:135–138. [**Six-minute walking test**]

Ellingham CT, Amundsen LR. Cardiac considerations and physical training. In: Jackson O, ed. *Physical Therapy of the Geriatric Patient*. 2nd ed. New York, NY: Churchill Livingstone; 1989:213–238. [**Kottke–**

Kubicek Activity Test, submaximal exercise test protocols for elderly persons, symptom-limited progressive exercise tolerance testing]

Hamm LF, Stull GA, Ainsworth B, Serfass RC, Wolfe DR. Short- and long-term prognostic value of graded exercise testing soon after myocardial infarction. *Physical Therapy*. 1986;66:334–339.

Ice R, et al. Descriptive data on marathon runners with severe coronary artery disease: results from cardiac catheterization, exercise tests, and serum lipids. *Medicine and Science in Sports and Exercise*. 1978;10:35.

Irwin SC, Zadai CC. Cardiopulmonary rehabilitation of the geriatric patient. In: Lewis CB, ed. *Aging: The Health Care Challenge*. 2nd ed. Philadelphia, Pa: FA Davis Co; 1990:181–211. **[Twelve-minute walking test, low-level functional test, Balke test, Bruce test, bicycle test]**

Swerts PM, Mostert R, Wouters EF. Comparison of corridor and treadmill walking in patients with severe chronic obstructive pulmonary disease. *Physical Therapy*. 1990;70:439–442.

Fluid in Lungs

Percussion
Bourke S, et al. Percussion of the chest re-visited: a comparison of the diagnostic value of auscultatory and conventional chest percussion. *Irish Journal of Medical Science*. 1989;158:82–84.

Vital Capacity

Pulmonary Function Tests
American Thoracic Society. Lung function testing: selection of reference values and interpretive strategies. *American Review of Respiratory Disease*. 1991;144:1202–1218.

Functional Level

The Barthel Index
Mahoney BI, Barthel DW. Functional evaluation: The Barthel Index. *Maryland State Medical Journal*. 1965;14:61–65.

Wade DT, Collin C. The Barthel ADL index: a standard measure of physical disability? *International Disability Studies*. 1988;10:2:64–67.

New York Heart Association Functional and Therapeutic Classification of Heart Disease
Certo C. Cardiovascular system. In: Myers RS, ed. *Saunders Manual of Physical Therapy Practice*. Philadelphia, Pa: WB Saunders Co; 1995:193–251.

Functional Independence Measures
Granger CV, Hamilton BB, Keith RA, et al. Advance in functional assessment for medical rehabilitation. *Topics in Geriatric Rehabilitation*. 1986;1:3:59–74.

Keith RA, Granger CV, Hamilton BB, Sherwins FS. The Functional Independence Measure. *Advances in Clinical Rehabilitation*. 1987;1:6–18.

Katz Index of Activities of Daily Living
Benjamin Rose Hospital Staff. Multidisciplinary studies of illness in aged persons: II. A new classification of functional status in activities of daily living. *Journal of Chronic Disease*. 1959;9:1:55–62.

Brorsson B, Ashberg KH. Katz Index of Independence in ADL: reliability and validity in short-term care. *Scandinavian Journal of Rehabilitation Medicine*. 1984;16:125–132.

Outcomes Assessment Measures
Michel TH. Outcome assessment in cardiac rehabilitation. *International Journal of Technology Assessment in Health Care*. 1992;8:1:76–84.

NLN-PUBL. Outcome criteria for physical therapy, speech pathology, and occupational therapy: home health agencies. In: Rinke LT, et al., eds. *Outcome Measures in Home Care Service*. 1987;21-2195:2:165–171.

PULSES Profile

Granger CV, Albrecht GL, Hamilton BB. Outcome of comprehensive medical rehabilitation: measurements by PULSES profile and the Barthel index. *Archive of Physical Medicine and Rehabilitation.* 1979:60:145–154.

Moskowitz RW, McCann CB. Classification of disability in the chronically ill and aging. *Journal of Chronic Disease.* 1957;5:342–346.

Special Tests to Which the PT May or May Not Have Access

Certo C. Cardiovascular system. In: Myers RS, ed. *Saunders Manual of Physical Therapy Practice.* Philadelphia, Pa: WB Saunders Co; 1995:193–251. **[Invasive and noninvasive tests. Invasive: radionuclide studies, cardiac catheterization, coronary arteriography, percutaneous transluminal coronary angioplasty. Noninvasive: echocardiography, graded exercise tests]**

DeTurk WE. Exercise and the intolerant heart. *Clinical Management in Physical Therapy.* 1992;12:1:67–73.

Vital Signs

Blood Pressure

Frohlich ED. Recommendations for human blood pressure determination by sphygmomanometers: report of a special task force appointed by the steering committee, American Heart Association. *Hypertension.* 1988;11:210A–222A.

Stolt M. Reliability of auscultory method of arterial blood pressure. *Hypertension.* 1990;3:697–703.

Heart Rate

Rothstein JM. *Measurement in Physical Therapy.* New York, NY: Churchill Livingstone; 1985.

Respiratory Rate

Simeos EAF, et al. Respiratory rate: measurement of variability over time and accuracy at different counting periods. *Archives of Disease in Childhood.* 1991;66:1199–1203.

TREATMENT

Certo C. Cardiovascular system. In: Myers RS, ed. *Saunders Manual of Physical Therapy Practice.* Philadelphia, Pa: WB Saunders Co; 1995:193–251.

Collins JV. Clinical aspects of medical chest disease. I. Asthma: chronic airways obstruction: occupational lung diseases. In: Downie PA, ed. *Cash's Textbook of Chest, Heart and Vascular Disorders for Physiotherapists.* 4th ed. London, England: Faber & Faber;1987:471.

Chapter 3

Connective Tissue Conditions

- Ankylosing spondylitis
- Fibromyalgia
- Myofascial pain syndrome
- Osteoarthritis
- Rheumatoid arthritis

Ankylosing Spondylitis

DESCRIPTION

Ankylosing spondylitis (AS) is a type of systemic rheumatic arthritis producing symptoms of inflammation primarily in the axial skeleton, leading to complaints of recurrent back pain. Less typically, the disease begins with pain in the peripheral joints. It is seen three times more often in men than women. Onset is usually between the ages of 20 to 40.

CAUSE

Any neurological symptoms are usually the result of compression radiculitis or sciatica, cauda equina syndrome, or vertebral subluxation and fractures. Ankylosing spondylitis may also be associated with acute iritis, cardiovascular and pulmonary manifestations, Reiter's syndrome, ulcerative colitis, and Crohn's disease.

ASSESSMENT

Areas

- History, including height
- Pain
- Posture
- Cardiovascular, including endurance level
- Pulmonary capacity
- Mobility, including spinal mobility and active range of motion (ROM) in peripheral joints
- Functional level, including activities of daily living (ADLs), ergonomic factors, and sleep posture
- Health status

Instruments/Procedures (See References for Sources)

Functional Level
- Arthritis Self-Efficacy Scale
- Maximum work capacity by ergometry
- Functional Index (FI)

Health Status
- Health Assessment Questionnaire for the Spondylarthropathies
- Sickness Impact Profile (SIP)

Mobility
- cervical rotation
- chin-to-chest distance
- finger-to-floor distance
- occiput-to-wall distance
- Schöber test
- thoracolumbar flexibility

Pain
- visual analogue scale

Pulmonary Capacity
* chest expansion (CE)
* vital capacity (VC)

PROBLEMS
* The client usually has back pain, especially in the lumbar region.
* There may also be tenderness in the sacroiliac region.
* The client usually reports stiffness in the morning and after inactivity.
* The spine becomes progressively rigid.
* The client usually has postural changes such as forward head, increase in thoracic kyphosis, and loss of lumbar curve.
* There can be a decrease in chest expansion and a sunken chest appearance.
* The client can have flexion contractures at shoulders and hips.
* The client may complain of pain due to achilles tendonitis and plantar fasciitis.

TREATMENT/MANAGEMENT
* Consider use of modalities for pain relief such as heat and hydrotherapy.
* Stretch areas of tightness, especially at hips and shoulders.
* Prescribe land-based or aquatic exercises. Daily exercise should be encouraged. Include the following:
  1. breathing exercises and exercises for chest expansion
  2. spinal rotation, extension, and lateral movements
  3. hip and shoulder exercises
  4. postural exercises, especially extensor muscles
* Instruct in home program to be performed twice a day.
* Consider ergonomic applications to ADLs such as driving, working, and sleeping.
* Provide education about the disorder, refer to support groups, and provide long-term support.
* Reassess at least 1 month post treatment and again yearly.

PRECAUTIONS/CONTRAINDICATIONS
Diagnosis should be confirmed by x-ray.

EXPECTED OUTCOME/PROGNOSIS
* The client will improve posture and prevent deformity.
* The client will increase chest expansion and vital capacity.
* The client will maintain or improve mobility, fitness, functioning, and overall health.

In general, given proper treatment, a client with ankylosing spondylitis can expect to live a productive life.

REFERENCES

ASSESSMENT
Goodman C, Snyder TE. *Differential Diagnosis in Physical Therapy*. Philadelphia, Pa; 1990:332, 337, 357, 362–363.

Functional Level

Arthritis Self-Efficacy Scale
Lomi C, Nordholm LA. Validation of a Swedish version of the Arthritis Self-Efficacy Scale. *Scandinavian Journal of Rheumatology.* 1992;21:231–237.

Functional Index (FI)
Hidding A, van der Linden S, Boers M, et al. Is group physical therapy superior to individualized therapy in ankylosing spondylitis? *Arthritis Care and Research.* 1993;6:3:117–125.

Health Status

Sickness Impact Profile (SIP); Health Assessment Questionnaire for the Spondylarthropathies
Hidding A, van der Linden S, Boers M, et al. Is group physical therapy superior to individualized therapy in ankylosing spondylitis? *Arthritis Care and Research.* 1993;6:3:117–125.

Mobility
Kraag G, Stokes B, Groh J, Helewa A, Goldsmith C. The effects of comprehensive home physiotherapy and supervision of patients with ankylosing spondylitis: a randomized controlled trial. *Journal of Rheumatology.* 1990;17:228–233. **[Fingertip-to-floor distance]**
Vandervoort AA, Chesworth BM, Cunningham DA, et al. An outcome measure to quantify passive stiffness of the ankle. *Canadian Journal of Public Health.* 1992;83(suppl 2):S19–S23.
Viitanen JV, Suni J, Kautiainen H, et al. Effect of physiotherapy on spinal mobility in ankylosing spondylitis. *Scandinavian Jounal of Rheumatology.* 1992;21:38–41. **[Thoracolumbar flexibility (TFL), Schober test, occiput-to-wall distance, cervical rotation, chin-to-chest distance, finger-to-floor distance, chest expansion, vital capacity]**

Pain
Langely GB, Sheppeard H. The visual analogue scale: its use in pain measurement. *Rheumatology International.* 1985:5:145–148.

TREATMENT
Haralson K. Physical therapy and arthritis: origins and evolution. *Arthritis Care and Research.* 1990;3:4:173–177.
Hidding A, van der Linden S. Factors related to change in global health after group physical therapy in ankylosing spondylitis. *Clinical Rheumatology.* 1995;14:347–351.
Hidding A, van der Linden S, deWitts L. Therapeutic effects of individual physical therapy in ankylosing spondylitis related to duration of disease. *Clinical Rheumatology.* 1993;12:334–340.
Stucki G, von-Felten A, Speich R, Michel BA. Ankylosing spondylitis and sarcoidosis—coincidence or association? Case report and review of the literature. *Clinical Rheumatology.* 1992;11:436–439.
Tomlinson MJ, Barefoot J, Dixon AS. Intensive in-patient physiotherapy courses improve movement and posture in ankylosing spondylitis. *Physiotherapy.* 1986;72:238–240.
Viitanen JV, Suni J, Kautiainen H, Liimatainen M, Takala H. Effect of physiotherapy on spinal mobility in ankylosing spondylitis. *Scandinavian Journal of Rheumatology.* 1992;21:38–41.

Fibromyalgia

Also known as *fibrositis, fibromyositis.*

DESCRIPTION

Fibromyalgia is a nonarticular rheumatic condition. With fibromyalgia, there is pain in fibrous tissues such as muscles, ligaments, and tendons. It is characterized by extreme tenderness at a minimum of 11 of 18 specific tender points (see box for classification). The disorder occurs more frequently in females, reportedly 5 to 10 times more frequently. Although there are similarities, myofascial pain syndrome (MPS) is considered a separate disorder from fibromyalgia (see section "Myofascial Pain Syndrome"). Some clients may have symptoms of both disorders.

**American College of Rheumatology 1990 Criteria for the
Classification of Fibromyalgia**

1. History of widespread pain present for at least 3 months.
2. Pain in at least 11 of 18 tender point sites (9 bilateral points) on digital palpation:
- occiput
- low cervical
- trapezius
- supraspinatus
- second rib
- lateral epicondyle
- gluteal area
- greater trochanter
- knee

Source: Reprinted with permission from F Wolfe, et al, The American College of Rhematology 1990 Criteria for the Classification of Fibromyalgia, *Arthritis and Rheumatology*, pp. 160–172, © 1990, JB Lippincott.

CAUSE

The cause of fibromyalgia is still under investigation. The etiology has been associated with sleep disturbance, specifically a decrease of stage IV non-REM sleep. Some clients have a psychological component that aggravates the disorder. The disorder has also been linked with irritable bowel syndrome. In general, clients with fibromyalgia have an increased sensitivity to pain. Other pain triggers include stress, trauma, cold, and systemic disorders.

ASSESSMENT

Areas
- History, including detailed list of symptoms and results of other specialists' diagnostic tests
- Pain, including nature of pain and influence of motion and position
- Posture
- Joint integrity and structural deviations
- Mobility, including passive and active range of motion (ROM)

- Skin and soft tissue, including trigger points
- Special tests to which the PT may or may not have access

Instruments/Procedures (See References for Sources)

Pain
- body chart
- visual analogue scale

Skin and Soft Tissue
- palpation of trigger points

Special Tests to Which the PT May or May Not Have Access
- blood tests
- bone scan
- CT scan
- electrodiagnostic tests
- electromyography (EMG); integrated EMG
- phosphorus magnetic resonance imaging (MRI)
- radiographs

PROBLEMS
- The client is tender upon palpation of muscles, with tender points in at least 11 of 18 tender points (see criteria for classification in description).
- The client has chronic pain in muscles.
- The pain is usually diffuse and often described as stiffness or achiness.
- The client is usually fatigued.
- The client may report disturbed sleep.
- The client may report frequent headaches.
- Women may report painful menstrual periods.

TREATMENT/MANAGEMENT
- Symptoms usually respond to modalities, moderate activity, and stretching exercise.
- Modalities used to decrease symptoms can include
  1. heat packs before massage
  2. massage: concentrate on relaxing strokes such as stroking and kneading as client tolerates
  3. ice massage
  4. quick, cold stimulant such as vapocoolant spray or ice combined with stretching for trigger points
  5. electrical stimulation
  6. ultrasound
- Provide a carefully controlled, gradual program of conditioning, cardiovascular activity, flexibility, and posture re-education. Consider use of PNF techniques, muscle energy techniques, and manual therapies that employ use of gentle movement.
- Instruct in relaxation techniques that may include biofeedback.
- Teach pacing of activities to alternate work with frequent rest periods.
- Client education is a key component of treatment.
- Restful sleep is also a critical component of successful treatment.

PRECAUTIONS/CONTRAINDICATIONS
• Too vigorous an exercise program can worsen symptoms.
• Massage should not increase pain. Client will probably not be able to tolerate deep pressure.
• Contraindications to ice massage include a client who has an aversion or adverse reaction to cold or poor circulation. See also appendix for contraindications for physical agents and modalities.
• Contraindication to massage can include inflammation due to bacterial infection, signs of myositis ossificans, hematoma, traumatic arthritis, severe rheumatoid arthritis, massage of bursa, nerve entrapment, phlebitis, cellulitis, metastatic cancer, or infectious skin disease.

DESIRED OUTCOME/PROGNOSIS
• The client will experience a decrease in symptoms.
• The client will experience an increase in functional activity.
  Fibromyalgia has a tendency to become chronic.
  Efffective management depends on a client who engages in active self-care with home exercise activities.

REFERENCES

ASSESSMENTS

Pain
Miller B. Manual therapy treatment of myofascial pain and dysfunction. In: Rachlin ES, ed. *Myofascial Pain and Fibromyalgia*. St Louis, Mo: CV Mosby Co; 1993:455–472. **[Body chart and visual analogue scale]**

Special Tests to Which the PT May or May Not Have Access
Roy SH. Combined use of surface electromyography and 31P-NMR spectroscopy for the study of muscle disorders. *Physical Therapy*. 1993;73:892–901. **[Electromyography and phosphorus magnetic resonance]**
Stokes MJ, Colter C, Klestov A, Cooper RG. Normal paraspinal muscle electromyographic fatigue characteristics in patients with primary fibromyalgia. *British Journal of Rheumatology*. 1993;32:711–716. **[Integrated EMG]**

TREATMENT
Caldron PH. Screening for rheumatic disease. In: Boissonnault WG, ed. *Examination in Physical Therapy Practice*. Philadelphia, Pa: Churchill Livingstone; 1991:237–253. (2nd ed released in 1995)
Rachlin I. Therapeutic massage in the treatment of myofascial pain syndromes and fibromyalgia. In: Rachlin ES, ed. *Myofascial Pain and Fibromyalgia*. St Louis, Mo: CV Mosby Co; 1993:455–472.
Schutz L. Fibromyalgia and myofascial pain syndrome. In: Buschbacher RM, ed. *Musculoskeletal Disorders: A Practical Guide for Diagnosis and Rehabilitation*. Boston, Mass: Andover Medical Publishers; 1994:239–244.
Simons LS, Simons DG. Chronic myofascial pain syndrome. In: Tollison CD, ed. *Handbook of Chronic Pain Management*. Baltimore, Md: Williams & Wilkins; 1994:509–529.
Snyder-Mackler L, Barry AJ, Perkins AI, Soucek MD. Effects of helium-neon laser irradiation in skin resistance and pain in patients with trigger points in the neck or back. *Physical Therapy*. 1989;69:336–341.

Myofascial Pain Syndrome

DESCRIPTION

Myofascial pain syndrome (MPS) is muscular pain usually combined with trigger points and occasionally accompanied by autonomic symptoms. MPS is equally common in men and women.

CAUSE

MPS is thought to be caused by acute or chronic physical stress of muscle due to trauma, overstretching, or overwork fatigue. Mechanical factors such as poor posture or leg-length difference can contribute to or perpetuate the stress. Symptoms may be exacerbated by anxiety, infection, allergy, arthritis, or other underlying disorders.

ASSESSMENT

Areas

- History, including a detailed list of symptoms
- Pain, including nature of pain and influence of motion and position
- Posture
- Joint integrity and structural deviations
- Mobility, including passive and active range of motion (ROM)
- Skin and soft tissue, including trigger points
- Special tests to which the PT may or may not have access

Instruments/Procedures (See References for Sources)

Joint Integrity and Structural Deviations
- leg-length discrepancy

Pain
- body chart
- visual analogue scale

Skin
- trigger point palpation

Special Tests to Which the PT May or May Not Have Access
- blood tests
- bone scan
- electrodiagnostic tests
- magnetic resonance imaging (MRI)
- radiographs

PROBLEMS

- The client usually has complaints of regional muscle pain, but pain may also be localized.
- The muscles are tender during palpation.
- There are usually one or more trigger points characterized by a twitch response (involuntary contraction) and radiation of pain to referred zone.

- Trigger points may lead to headache.
- The trigger points may refer pain to arm or leg. (Radiculopathy should be ruled out.)

TREATMENT/MANAGEMENT

- Educate client about nature of disorder, posture, and body mechanics for activities of daily living (ADLs). Avoid muscle overwork.
- Instruct client in relaxation and stress management techniques.
- Therapeutic exercise may include traditional stretching and strengthening and conditioning exercise as well as movement therapy. Alternate voluntary contraction with passive stretch as well as contract-relax techniques. Emphasis is on optimal muscle control and active involvement of client.
- Consider use of manual therapy, including soft tissue mobilization, neurosensorimotor re-education, and joint mobilization. Soft tissue techniques vary depending on desired effect; they can be sustained or varied in rate and described as compressing or stripping.
- Assistive devices, such as tape, can be used for proper alignment of tissues. Rubber balls, foam, or cardboard rollers or tools can apply therapeutic pressure on tissues.
- Consult with physician on use of injections for trigger points.
- Address mechanical factors that can perpetuate stress, such as structural anatomical variations, postural abnormalities, and vocational factors.
- Massage may be helpful, including techniques of compression (especially useful for trigger points), friction, kneading, stroking, stripping, and digital pressure; also ice massage.
- Possible adjuncts to massage are
    1. vapocoolant sprays or ice combined with stretching
    2. accupressure
    3. ultrasound
    4. transcutaneous electrical nerve stimulation (TENS)
    5. electrical stimulation—generally recommended for electrodes to parallel the shape of tissue being treated
    6. cold laser

PRECAUTIONS/CONTRAINDICATIONS

- Contraindications to soft tissue manual therapy listed include acute infection, inflammation, neoplasm, fever, change in neurological status, instability, and recent injury to tissue. Contraindications are relative to the extent of condition and manner in which therapy is conducted.
- Soreness after treatment can be normal, but if soreness persists longer than 24 hours, it may indicate that treatment was too vigorous.
- It is important to address any underlying medical condition contributing to pain.

DESIRED OUTCOME/PROGNOSIS

- The client will have a decreased level of pain.
- The client will regain normal function of myofascial tissue with diminished hardened areas of the muscle.
- The client will have an inhibition of undesired muscle activity.
- The client will have an increased level of function.
- There will be improved efficiency of desired movement.

REFERENCES

ASSESSMENT

Pain
Miller B. Manual therapy treatment of myofascial pain and dysfunction. In: Rachlin ES, ed. *Myofascial Pain and Fibromyalgia*. St Louis, Mo: CV Mosby Co; 1993:455–472. **[Body chart and visual analogue scale]**

TREATMENT
Cantu RI, Grodin AJ. *Myofascial Manipulation: Theory and Clinical Application*. Gaithersburg, Md: Aspen Publishers, Inc; 1992.

Cottingham JT, Parges SW, Richmond K. Shifts in pelvic inclination angle and parasympathetic tone produced by rolfing soft tissue manipulation. *Physical Therapy*. 1988;68:1364–1369.

Headley BJ. EMG and myofascial pain. *Clinical Management in Physical Therapy*. 1990;10:443–446.

Kahn J. Electrical modalities in the treatment of myofascial conditions. In: Rachlin ES, ed. *Myofascial Pain and Fibromyalgia*. St Louis, Mo: CV Mosby Co; 1993:473–485.

Manheim CJ, Lavett DK. *The Myofascial Release Manual*. 2nd ed. Thorofare, NJ: Slack; 1994.

Miller B. Manual therapy treatment of myofascial pain and dysfunction. In: Rachlin ES, ed. *Myofascial Pain and Fibromyalgia*. St Louis, Mo: CV Mosby Co; 1993:415–454.

Schutz L. Fibromyalgia and myofascial pain syndrome. In: Buschbacher RM, ed. *Musculoskeletal Disorders: A Practical Guide for Diagnosis and Rehabilitation*. Boston, Mass: Andover Medical Publishers; 1994:239–244.

Simons LS, Simons DG. Chronic myofascial pain syndrome. In: Tollison CD, ed. *Handbook of Chronic Pain Management*. Baltimore, Md; Williams & Wilkins; 1994:509–529.

Snyder L, Meckler C, Borc L. The effect of cold laser on musculoskeletal trigger points. *Physical Therapy*. 1984; 64:745.

Snyder-Mackler L, Barry AJ, Perkins AI, Soucek MD. Effects of helium-neon laser irradiation in skin resistance and pain in patients with trigger points in the neck or back. *Physical Therapy*. 1989;69:336–341.

Osteoarthritis

Also known as *degenerative joint disease*.

DESCRIPTION
Osteoarthritis (OA) is the most frequent type of articular disorder. OA leads to the breakdown of hyaline cartilage followed by involvement of the subchondral bone and hypertrophy of surrounding tissues. Joints commonly affected include the cervical and lumbar spine, peripheral joints, and knee and hip joints.

CAUSE
The etiology of osteoarthritis is unknown, but factors influencing the course of the disease include aging, congenital joint abnormalities, genetic defects, and acute or chronic trauma to the joint. OA may also appear secondary to other joint diseases such as Legg–Calve–Perthes disease or slipped femoral capital epiphysis; diseases of the hyaline cartilage; or neuropathic, endocrine, metabolic, and infectious diseases.

ASSESSMENT

Areas

- History, including psychosocial evaluation if indicated
- Posture
- Pain
- Gait
- Joint integrity and structural deviations
- Mobility, including range of motion (ROM), hypermobility, and hypomobility
- Strength
- Neurological: position sense (if damage suggested by weakness or paresthesia)
- Skin and soft tissue: inflammation, temperature, edema
- Functional level, including activities of daily living (ADLs) and activity level
- Equipment, including shoes and any assistive devices
- Special tests to which the PT may or may not have access

Instruments/Procedures (See References for Sources)

Functional Level
- Arthritis Self-Efficacy Scale
- Functional Status Index
- Functional Independence Measure (FIM)
- Katz Index of Activities of Daily Living
- outcomes assessment measures
- Western Ontario and McMaster Universities Osteoarthritis Index (WOMAC)

Gait
- walking speed
- oxygen cost of walking

Health Status
- Sickness Impact Profile

Joint Integrity and Structural Deviations
- joint circumference as indicated
- leg-length discrepancy as indicated
- palpation for crepitus and laxity
- Patrick's test
- test for hip dislocation

Mobility
- relaxed oscillation test
- timed "up and go" test

Skin
- palpation for temperature, tenderness

Special Tests to Which the PT May or May Not Have Access
- electromyography (EMG)
- joint surface separation
- knee kinematics

- x-rays

Strength
- angular velocity testing
- dynamometer testing
- muscle endurance testing
- hand-held dynamometry
- isometric and isokinetic torque
- manual muscle testing

PROBLEMS
1. Early stages
   - The client usually reports pain with weight bearing, especially later in the day or with overexertion.
   - The client usually has mild limitation of ROM, especially into internal rotation, abduction, and extension at the hip.
2. Later stages
   - The client usually reports aching, even during sleep.
   - There is usually morning stiffness.
   - There are usually muscle spasms.
   - There can be joint swelling, which is usually moderate.
   - There is usually joint crepitus, sometimes audible.
   - Hip joint deformity usually follows a pattern of adduction, flexion, and lateral rotation.
   - Pain at hip joint varies depending upon stage of disease.
   - Knee joint deformity usually follows a pattern of varus or valgus deformity with flexion.
   - The client may have a leg-length discrepancy.
   - The client usually has a progressive loss of ROM.
   - The client may have an antalgic gait pattern.
   - The client may need assistive devices.
   - The client may report a decrease in balance.
   - The client may have decreased independence with ADLs such as dressing or stairs.

TREATMENT/MANAGEMENT
For treatment in general:
- Select modalities for pain such as heat or ice, ultrasound, interferential, and/or shortwave diathermy.
- Unload or modify excessive force patterns on joint.
- Provide careful prescription of exercise based on degree of joint damage.
- Encourage loss of any excessive weight.
  For treatment of the hip:
1. Early stages
   - Instruct in active ROM exercises.
   - Instruct in postural exercises as indicated.
   - Provide joint mobilization for ROM and decrease in pain.
   - Consider modalities for pain such as ultrasound and moist heat.
   - Instruct in strengthening exercises, especially for hip abductors. Consider use of isometric and isotonic exercise, graduated resistive exercise, proprioceptive neuromuscular facilitation (PNF) patterns, pendular exercise, and aquatic exercise.
   - Consider need for weight reduction to decrease stress on joints.

2. Later stages
    - Consider more vigorous mobilization such as grade 2 level.
    - Provide gait training as indicated.
    - Prescribe assistive device for weight-bearing activities and adaptive equipment such as raised toilet seat. Prescribe orthotics as indicated. Assess footwear.
    - People with hip disease should carry loads bilaterally to reduce force on hip joint.
    - The treatment modalities considered most effective for OA of hip include hydrotherapy, home exercises, and individual exercises.

    After a total hip replacement:
- Begin rehabilitation with isometric exercises like quadriceps setting and gluteal isometrics. Add ankle-pumping activity and diaphragmatic breathing as early as in recovery room.
- Initiate bed transfers at day 1 postoperatively.
- Perform gait training as indicated by weight-bearing status and client's response to surgery (usually partial weight bearing with uncemented hips and weight bearing as tolerated with cemented hips). Generally clients begin gait activities by using a walker or crutches to protect joint and then progress to cane.
- Instruct in transfers.
- Perform active ROM exercises for lower extremities within acceptable range.

    After a total shoulder replacement (TSR):
- Protect the surgical repair. Abduction brace may be indicated after rotator cuff repair.
- Prescribe individualized treatment program based on soft tissue constraints of client.
- Begin continuous passive motion if earlier mobilization is desired.
- After adequate healing, pendulum exercise may begin.
- Progress to pulley exercises and passive stretching.
- Mobilization and isometrics may also be included with caution.

PRECAUTIONS/CONTRAINDICATIONS

See also appendix for contraindications with physical agents.
- Heat from shortwave diathermy may aggravate condition.
- Use traction with caution.
- Consult with surgical team on recommended precautions after joint replacement surgery.
- After total hip replacement surgery, the client should avoid hip flexion (less than 90 degrees), adduction past midline, and internal rotation.
- After constrained total shoulder replacement, motion, particularly external rotation, should not be forced beyond the limits discovered at surgery. Vigorous or heavy use of shoulder could cause the prosthesis to loosen.

DESIRED OUTCOME/PROGNOSIS
- The client will experience pain relief.
- The client will gain increased mobility.
- The client will experience increased strength.
- The client will increase in functional independence.
- The client will be educated about OA.

    Within 3 months after total hip arthroplasty, the client should be independent in activities of daily living.

    Post total shoulder replacement, muscle-strengthening exercise must be continued for the rest of the patient's life. Total Shoulder Replacement (TSR) may relieve pain and increase function, but it may not return the client to normal strength or ROM.

    Repaired rotator cuff may need 6 to 12 weeks to heal before resuming active motion.

REFERENCES

ASSESSMENT

Functional Level

Lankhorst GJ, Van de Stadt R, Van der Korst JK. The relationship of functional capacity, pain, and isometric and isokinetic torque in osteoarthrosis of the knee. *Scandinavian Journal of Rehabilitation Medicine.* 1985;17:167–172.

Lankhorst GJ, Van de Stadt R, Van der Korst JK, et al. Relationship of isometric knee extension torque and functional variables in osteoarthrosis of the knee. *Scandinavian Journal of Rehabilitation Medicine.* 1982;14:7–10.

Arthritis Self-Efficacy Scale

Lomi C, Nordholm LA. Validation of a Swedish version of the Arthritis Self-Efficacy Scale. *Scandinavian Journal of Rheumatology.* 1992;21:231–237.

Functional Status Index

Fisher NM, Gresham, Pendergast DR. Effects of a quantitative progressive rehabilitation program applied unilaterally to the osteoarthritic knee. *Archives of Physical Medicine and Rehabilitation.* 1993;74:1319–1326.

Jette AM. Functional status index: reliability of a chronic disease evaluation instrument. *Archives of Physical Medicine and Rehabilitation.* 1980;61:395–401.

Functional Independence Measure

Granger CV, Hamilton BB, Keith RA, et al. Advance in functional assessment for medical rehabilitation. *Topics in Geriatric Rehabilitation.* 1986;1:3:59–74.

Keith RA, Granger CV, Hamilton BB, Sherwins FS. The Functional Independence Measure. *Advances in Clinical Rehabilitation.* 1987;1:6–18.

Katz Index of Activities of Daily Living

Benjamin Rose Hospital Staff. Multidisciplinary studies of illness in aged persons: II. A new classification of functional status in activities of daily living. *Journal of Chronic Disease.* 1959;9:1:55–62.

Brorsson B, Ashberg KH. Katz Index of Independence in ADL: reliability and validity in short-term care. *Scandinavian Journal of Rehabilitation Medicine.* 1984;16:125–132.

Outcomes Assessment Measures

Burckardt CS, Moncur C, Minor MA. Exercise tests as outcome measures. *Arthritis Care and Research.* 1994;7:4:169–175.

Western Ontario and McMaster Universities Osteoarthritis Index (WOMAC)

Bellamy N, Buchanon W, Goldsmith CH, et al. Validation study of WOMAC: a health status instrument for measuring clinically important patient relevant outcomes of antirheumatic drug therapy in patients with osteoarthritis of the hip or knee. *Journal of Rheumatology.* 1988;15:1833–1840.

Gait

Mattsson E, Olsson E, Brostrom LA. Assessment of walking before and after unicompartmental knee arthroplasty: a comparison of different methods. *Scandinavian Journal of Rehabilitation Medicine.* 1990;22:45–50.

Weidenhielm L, Mattsson E, Brostrom L, Wersall-Robertsson E. Effect of preoperative physiotherapy in unicompartmental prosthetic knee replacement. *Scandinavian Journal of Rehabilitation Medicine.* 1993;25:33–39. **[Walking speed and oxygen cost of walking]**

Health Status

Sickness Impact Profile

Mattsson E, Brostrom LA. The physical and psychosocial effect of moderate osteoarthrosis of the knee. *Scandinavian Journal of Rehabilitation Medicine*. 1991;23:215–218.

Joint Integrity and Structural Deviations

Rothstein JM, Roy SH, Wolf SL. *The Rehabilitation Specialist's Handbook*. Philadelphia, Pa: FA Davis Co; 1991:119. **[Patrick's test and test for hip dislocation]**

Mobility

Vandervoort AA, Chesworth BM, Cunningham DA, et al. An outcome measure to quantify passive stiffness of the ankle. *Canadian Journal of Public Health*. 1992;83(suppl 2):S19–S23.

Timed "Up and Go" Test

Podsiadlo D, Richardson S. The timed "up and go": A test of basic functional mobility for frail elderly persons. *Journal of the American Geriatric Society*. 1991;39:142–148.

Relaxed Oscillation Test

Oatis CA. The use of a mechanical model to describe the stiffness and damping characteristics of the knee joint in healthy adults. *Physical Therapy*. 1993;73:740–749.

Neurological

Marks R, Quinney AH, Wessel J. Reliability and validity of the measurement of position sense in women with osteoarthritis of the knee. *Journal of Rheumatology*. 1993;20:1919–1924. **[Position sense]**

Special Tests to Which the PT May or May Not Have Access

EMG

Neumann DA, Cook TM, Sholty RL, Sobush DC. An electromyographic analysis of hip abductor muscle activity when subjects are carrying loads in one or both hands. *Physical Therapy*. 1992;72:207–217.

Joint Surface Separation

Arvidsson I. The hip joint: forces needed for distraction and appearance of the vacuum phenomenon. *Scandinavian Journal of Rehabilitation Medicine*. 1990;22:157–161.

Knee Kinematics

Jevsevar DS, Riley PL, Hodge WA, Krebs DE. Knee kinematics and kinetics during locomotor activities of daily living in subjects with knee arthroplasty and in healthy control subjects. *Physical Therapy*. 1993;73:229–242.

Strength

Bohannon RW. Manual muscle test scores and dynamometer test scores of knee extension strength. *Archives of Physical Medicine and Rehabilitation*. 1986;67:380–392. **[MMT and dynamometry]**

Fisher NM, Gresham GE, Abrams M, Hicks J, Horrigan D, Pendergast DR. Quantitative effects of physical therapy on muscular and functional performance in subjects with osteoarthritis of the knees. *Archives of Physical Medicine and Rehabilitation*. 1993;74:840–847. **[Muscle function and functional assessment parameters]**

Fisher NM, Gresham GE, Pendergast DR. Effects of a quantitative progressive rehabilitation program applied unilaterally to the osteoarthritic knee. *Archives of Physical Medicine and Rehabilitation*. 1993;74:1319–1326. **[Strength, endurance, and angular velocity]**

Hayes KW, Falconer J. Reliability of hand-held dynamometry and its relationship with manual muscle testing in patients with osteoarthritis in the knee. *Journal of Orthopaedic and Sports Physical Therapy.* 1992;16:145–149.

Marks R. The effect of isometric quadriceps strength training in mid-range for osteo-arthritis of the knee. *New Zealand Journal of Physiotherapy.* 1993;21:2:16–19.

Vaz MD, Kramer JF, Rorabeck CH, Bourne RB. Isometric hip abductor strength following total hip replacement and its relationship to functional assessments. *Journal of Orthopaedic and Sports Physical Therapy.* 1993;18:526–531.

TREATMENT

Adler S. Self care in the management of the degenerative knee joint. *Physiotherapy.* 1985;71:58–60.

Allen SH, Minor MA, Hillman LS, et al. Effect of exercise on the bone mineral density and bone remodelling indices in women with rheumatoid arthritis. *Journal of Rheumatology.* 1993;20:1247–1249.

Arvidsson I. The hip joint: forces needed for distraction and appearance of the vacuum phenomenon. *Scandinavian Journal of Rehabiliation Medicine.* 1990;22:157–161.

Aubin M, Marks R. The efficacy of short-term treatment with transcutaneous electrical nerve stimulation for osteo-arthritic knee pain. *Physiotherapy.* 1995;81:669–676.

Banwell BF, Gall V, eds. *Physical Therapy Management of Arthritis.* New York, NY: Churchill Livingstone; 1988.

Clarke AK. *Rehabilitation Techniques in Rheumatology.* Baltimore, Md: William & Wilkins; 1987.

Donatelli RA, ed. *Physical Therapy of the Shoulder.* 2nd ed. New York, NY: Churchill Livingstone; 1991:341–354.

Falus A, Lakatos T, Smolen J. Dissimilar biosynthesis of interleukin-6 by different areas of synovial membrane of patients with rheumatoid arthritis and osteoarthritis. *Scandinavian Journal of Rheumatology.* 1992;21:116–119.

Fisher NM, Gresham GE, Abrams M, et al. Quantitative effects of physical therapy on muscular and functional performance in subjects with osteoarthritis. *Archives of Physical Medicine and Rehabilitation.* 1993;74:840–847.

Foldes K, Balint P, Gaal M, Buchanan WW, Balint GP. Nocturnal pain correlates with effusions in diseased hips. *Journal of Rheumatology.* 1992;19:1756–1758.

Green JR. Out-patient physiotherapy practice in osteo-arthritis of the hip joint. *Physiotherapy.* 1991;77:737–740.

Haralson K. Physical therapy and arthritis: origins and evolution. *Arthritis Care and Research.* 1990;3:4:173–177.

Harris C. Osteoarthritis and the weather. *Physiotherapy Practice.* 1987;3:179–184.

Hurley MV, Newham DJ. The influence of arthrogenous muscle inhibition on quadriceps rehabilitation of patients with early, unilateral osteoarthritic knees. *British Journal of Rheumatology.* 1993;32:127–131.

Jan MH, Lai JS. The effects of physiotherapy on osteoarthritic knees of females. *Journal of the Formosan Medical Association.* 1991;90:1008–1013.

Lechner DE. Rehabilitation of the knee with arthritis. In: Greenfield BH, ed. *Rehabilitation of the Knee: A Problem-Solving Approach.* Philadelphia, Pa: FA Davis Co; 1993:206–241.

Leivseth G, Torstensson J, Reikeras O. Effect of passive muscle stretching in osteoarthritis of the hip. *Clinical Science.* 1989;76:1:113–117.

Marks R. Peripheral articular mechanisms in pain production in osteoarthritis. *Australian Journal of Physiotherapy.* 1992;38:289–298.

Marks R. Muscles as a pathogenic factor in osteoarthritis. *Physiotherapy Canada.* 1993;45:251–259.

Marks R. Quadriceps strength training for osteo-arthritis of the knee: a literature review and analysis. *New Zealand Journal of Physiotherapy.* 1993;21:1:15–20.

Mattsson E, Brostrom LA. The physical and psychosocial effect of moderate osteoarthrosis of the knee. *Scandinavian Journal of Rehabilitation Medicine.* 1991;23:215–218.

Minor MA. Exercise in the management of osteoarthritis of the knee and hip. *Arthritis Care and Research.* 1994;7:4:198–204.

Minor MA, Brown JD. Exercise maintenance of persons with arthritis after participation in a class experience. *Health Education Quarterly.* 1993; 20:1:83–95.

Minor MA, Hewett JE, Webel RR, Anderson SK. Efficacy of physical conditioning exercise in patients with rheumatoid arthritis and osteoarthritis. *Journal of Rheumatology.* 1989;32:1396–1405.

Minor MA, Hewett JE, Webel RR, Dresinger TE, Kay DR. Exercise tolerance and disease related measures in patients with rheumatoid arthritis and osteoarthritis. *Journal of Rheumatology.* 1988;15:905–911.

Minor MA, Sanford MK. Physical interventions in the management of pain in arthritis: an overview for research and practice. *Arthritis Care and Research.* 1993;6:4:197–206.

Moncur C. Perceptions of physical therapy competencies in rheumatology: physical therapists versus rheumatologists. *Physical Therapy.* 1987; 67:331–339.

Moll JMH. *Manual of Rheumatology.* New York, NY: Churchill Livingstone; 1987.

Mortiz U. Physical therapy and rehabilitation. *Scandinavian Journal of Rheumatology.* 1982;43(suppl):49.

Reid JC, Minor MA, Mitchell JA, et al. OA rehab: designing a personalized exercise program for people with osteoarthritis. *Journal of the American Medical Informatics Association.* Vol. 272. 1994; (suppl): S987.

Smith CR, Lewith GT, Machin D. TNS and osteo-arthritic pain. *Physiotherapy.* 1983;69:266–268.

Sweeney GM, Clarke AK. Selecting easy chairs for people with arthritis and low back pain. *Physiotherapy.* 1991;77:509–511.

Threlkeld AJ, Currier DP. Osteoarthritis: effects on synovial joint tissues. *Physical Therapy.* 1988;68:364–370.

Triggs M. Orthopedic aquatic therapy. *Clinical Management in Physical Therapy.* 1991;11:1:30–31.

Arthroplasty

Basso DM, Knapp L. Comparison of two continuous passive motion protocols for patients with total knee implants. *Physical Therapy.* 1987;67:360–363.

Bohannon RW, Cooper J. Total knee arthroplasty: evaluation of an acute care rehabilitation program. *Archives of Physical Medicine and Rehabilitation.* 1993;74:1091–1094.

Bohannon RW, Chavis D, Larkin P, Lieber C, Riddick L. Effectiveness of repeated prolonged loading for increasing flexion in knees demonstrating postoperative stiffness. *Physical Therapy.* 1985;65:494.

Bolton-Maggs BG, Williams B. Total ankle arthroplasty. *Physiotherapy.* 1986;72:449–451.

Brimer MA. New clinical considerations in total knee replacement rehabilitation. *Clinical Management in Physical Therapy.* 1987:7:1:6,9.

Dalseth T, Lippincott C. Postoperative rehabilitation. In: Amsututz HC, ed. *Hip Arthroplasty.* New York, NY: Churchill Livingstone; 1991:379–389.

Fisher NM, Gresham GE, Abrams M, et al. Quantitative effects of physical therapy on muscular and functional performance in subjects with osteoarthritis of the knees. *Archives of Physical Medicine and Rehabilitation.* 1993;74:840–846.

Foldes K, Gaal M, Balint P, et al. Ultrasonography after hip arthroplasty. *Skeletal Radiology.* 1992;21:297–299.

Gateley-Jameson K, Barrow D, Bass D, et al. Cementless total-knee replacement. *Clinical Management in Physical Therapy.* 1988;8:6:21–23.

Givens-Heiss DL, Krebs DE, Riley PO, Strickland EM. In vivo acetabular contact pressures during rehabilitation: postacute phase. *Physical Therapy.* 1992;72:700–710.

Gose JC. Continuous passive motion in the postoperative treatment of patients with total knee replacement: a retrospective study. *Physical Therapy.* 1987;67:39–42.

Harms M, Engstrom B. Continuous passive motion as an adjunct to treatment in the physiotherapy management of the total knee arthroplasty patient. *Physiotherapy.* 1991;77:301–307.

Hughes K, Kuffner L, Dean B. Effect of weekend physical therapy treatment on postoperative length of stay following total hip and total knee arthroplasty. *Physiotherapy Canada.* 1993;45:245–249.

Hurley MV, Newham DJ. The influence of arthrogenous muscle inhibition on quadriceps rehabilitation of patients with early, unilateral osteoarthritic knees. *British Society for Rheumatology.* 1993;32:127–131.

Lakatos J, Csakanyi L. Comparison of complications of total hip arthroplasty in rheumatoid arthritis, ankylosing spondylitis, and osteoarthritis. *Orthopedics*. 1991;14:1:55–57.

Liang MH, Cullen KE, Larson MG, et al. Effects of reducing physical therapy services on outcomes in total joint arthroplasty. *Medical Care*. 1987;25:276–285.

Jevsevar DS, Riley PO, Hodge WA, Krebs DE. Knee kinematics during locomotor activities of daily living in subjects with knee arthroplasty and in healthy control subjects. *Physical Therapy*. 1993;73:229–239.

Johnsson R, Melander A, Onnerfalt R. Physiotherapy after total hip replacement for primary arthrosis. *Scandinavian Journal of Rehabilitation Medicine*. 1988;20:43–45.

Krebs DE, Elbaum L, Riley PO, et al. Exercise and gait effects on in vivo hip contact pressures. *Physical Therapy*. 1991;71:301–309.

Mattsson E, Brostrom LA, Linnarsson D. Changes in walking ability after knee replacement. *International Orthopaedics*. 1990;14:277–280.

Ogino T, Obata H, Ishii S. Tendon ball interposition arthroplasty for traumatic ankylosis of the MP joint. *Journal of Hand Surgery*. 1993;18B:704–707.

Ritter MA, Gandolf VS, Holston KS. Continuous passive motion versus physical therapy in total knee arthroplasty. *Clinical Orthopaedics and Related Research*. 1989;244:239–243.

Roush SE. Patient-perceived functional outcomes associated with elective hip and knee arthroplasties. *Physical Therapy*. 1985;65:1496–1500.

Strickland EM, Fares M, Krebs DE, et al. In vivo acetabular contact pressures during rehabilitation: acute phase. *Physical Therapy*. 1992;72:691–699, 706–710.

Udvarhelyi I. Arthroplasty using acetabular implants in secondary protrusioned hips. *Orthopedics*. 1991;14:1:25–27.

Viadero A, Harrison B, Farbent J. Postoperative care of the TSR patient: total shoulder replacement. *Clinical Management in Physical Therapy*. 1987;7:4:14–15.

Weidenheilm L, Mattsson E, Brostrom LA, Wersall-Robertsson E. Effect of preoperative physiotherapy in unicompartmental prosthetic knee replacement. *Scandinavian Journal of Rehabilitation Medicine*. 1993;25:33–39.

Rheumatoid Arthritis

DESCRIPTION

Rheumatoid arthritis (RA) is a chronic disorder that leads to inflammation of the peripheral joints, often progressing to destruction of the articular and periarticular structures of these joints. At the joint there is synovial inflammation, proliferation, thickening, and engorgement. The disease's severity can range from a few joints minimally involved to many joints affected by complete ankylosis. A joint is considered damaged if there is a loss of range of motion (ROM; 15 degrees or more), ligamentous laxity, gross crepitus, and/or joint deformity. Hands and feet are usually the first areas involved, typically at the second and third metacarpophalangeal (MP) joints and proximal interphalangeal joints (PIP). Women are affected 2 to 3 times more often than men.

CAUSE

The specific cause is unknown, but the immunologic changes that trigger the manifestations of RA are multifactorial.

ASSESSMENT

Areas

- History, including psychosocial evaluation if indicated
- Inflammation
- Pain
- Posture
- Mobility, including ROM, hypermobility, and hypomobility
- Strength
- Neurological, if indicated by weakness or paresthesia
- Joint integrity, including crepitus and laxity
- Skin and soft tissue: temperature, edema
- Balance
- Gait
- Functional level, including activities of daily living (ADLs)
- Equipment, including shoes and any assistive devices
- Special tests to which the PT may or may not have access

Instruments/Procedures (See References for Sources)

Functional Level
- Arthritis Self-Efficacy Scale
- Function Independence Measures
- functional inquiry joint examination by ARA classification system
- geriatric population tests
  1. Functional Life Scale
  2. Lawton's Activities of Daily Living Scale
  3. OARS Multidimensional Functional Assessment Questionnaire
  4. Philadelphia Geriatric Center Multilevel Assessment
- Katz Index of Activities of Daily Living
- MACTAR: Patient Preference Disability Questionnaire
- timed 50-feet walking test

Gait
- videotaped observational gait analysis assessments
- observational gait analysis

Inflammation
- duration of morning stiffness
- erythrocyte sedimentation rate
- number of active joints
- numerical scale for joint inflammation

Mobility
- fingertip-to-floor distances
- goniometry
- relaxed oscillation test
- timed "up and go" test
- Romberg test

- heel to shin test
- proprioception
- reflexes
- visual acuity
- mental status exam

Pain
- Numeric Pain Rating Scale (NPRS)
- Visual Analogue Scale (VAS)

Special Tests to Which the PT May or May Not Have Access
- modified Larsen's radiological index
- Ritchie's articular index

Strength
- hand-held dynamometer
- maximal isometric contraction
- modified sphygmomanometer
- manual muscle testing

PROBLEMS
1. General
   - The client usually complains of pain with movement.
   - The client usually complains of stiffness in the morning.
   - The joints are inflamed and tender.
   - The client usually reports loss of movement.
   - There is a tendency to flexion contractures.
   - The client may also have pulmonary problems of pleural effusions, pleuritis, or diffuse interstitial pneumonitis, leading to shallow breathing and chest pain during inspiration.
2. Hands
   - There can be dorsal subluxation of the ulnar head and palmar displacement of the extensor carpi ulnaris tendon.
   - There can be deformity in radiocarpal joint.
   - The client may have fusion of the wrist.
   - There may be deviation and subluxation of the finger metacarpophalangeal joints.
   - At finger interphalangeal joints or thumb joints (MP and PIP), there may be boutonniere deformity (PIP joint flexion and distal interphalangeal [DIP] joint extension) or swan-neck deformity (PIP joint extension, MP joint and DIP joint flexion).
3. Lower extremities
   - There is usually valgus deformity at the knees and ankles.
   - There may be a clawed-toes deformity.
   - The metatarsal heads may be callused.
   - Rheumatoid nodules may be visible on extensor surface with thinning of skin.

TREATMENT/MANAGEMENT

General

Acute Phase
1. Encourage rest as indicated.

2. Provide splints as indicated for rest and pain relief, especially at hands, wrists, knees, or ankles.
3. Consider use of ice or other modalities for pain, such as moist heat or paraffin wax for hands and hydrotherapy for relaxation.
4. Maintain ROM with active and active assistive movement within pain-free range, especially in the neck and shoulder region.
5. Do not move joint beyond limit of pain. Passive ROM is not advised during the acute phase.
6. Consider use of suspension devices for exercise or pendular exercises.
7. Educate the client about RA, including the following topics:
   - pathology
   - importance of rest
   - exercise program
   - protection of joints and energy pacing

Subacute Phase
1. Physical agents and modalities
   - cryotherapy, if tolerated
   - moist heat packs
   - paraffin wax
   - transcutaneous electrical nerve stimulation (TENS)
   - diathermy
   - galvanic muscle stimulation
   - ultrasound: may be used on localized soft tissue lesions, trigger points, bursae, and tendon sheaths but is not indicated over acute inflammatory lesions
   - massage, including friction, deep transverse friction, ice massage, and accupressure
   - traction (with caution)
2. Exercise
   - Begin with isometric exercise, progressing to active movement and concentrating especially on the postural muscles.
   - Use ROM exercises, and increase repetitions depending on degree of morning stiffness and degree of acute synovitis.
   - Consider use of hydrotherapy for relaxation and strengthening.
   - Exercises may include PNF patterns on land or in water.
   - Provide gait activities with weight bearing as tolerated.
3. Education
   - Offer group or individual educational sessions.
   - Encourage adequate rest periods.
   - Offer guidelines for lifestyle choices of recreation.

Chronic Phase
1. Continue to stress ROM activities; do not force areas with subluxation passively. ROM exercises are generally active or active assistive, with low repetition as tolerated by client.
2. Reduce contracture with splinting, mobilization, and gentle stretching. Include spray-and-stretch techniques.
3. Continue strengthening program, with hydrotherapy or isometric contractions. If pain persists for more than 2 hours after exercise, decrease intensity. No resistive exercise through full range if joint is swollen. Aerobic activities can include swimming, bicycling, walking, low-impact aerobics, and aquatics. Start slowly, and gradually increase to 45 minutes. Precede and conclude activity with warm-up exercise. Special adaptations for clients with ar-

thritis include the following: progress number of repetitions slowly, modify equipment as needed, use braces or other devices to protect joints, and avoid excess to avoid joint swelling.

4. Provide client with gait-assistive devices as indicated. Crutches should be used only if client can demonstrate sufficient hand grip strength, wrist dorsiflexion, elbow extensor strength, and latissimus dorsi strength. The client may find a platform crutch or a cane with a pistol grip or modified handle more suitable. Assess for the need for a wheelchair. Consider insoles for footwear or wedge to raise as needed for correction of leg-length discrepancy.
5. Assess home environment for needed changes such as handrails or alterations in furniture.
6. Encourage adequate rest periods. Provide improvements in functional capacity with assistive devices or energy conservation techniques.
7. Encourage weight management.
8. Consider physical agents and modalities for pain such as TENS.

Hands

Acute Phase
- Fit with splints, which may include cock-up or tripoint splints, for protection and rest.
- Use isometric hand exercises.
- Perform ROM exercises as tolerated.
- Provide modalities for edema and pain.
- Elastic gloves can be used at night to assist with swelling.

Subacute Phase
- Provide modalities for pain.
- Instruct in rest and protection of joints.
- Initiate active assistive exercises, progressing to isotonic exercises at MP joint, especially into extension.
- Fit with adaptive devices for ADLs as indicated.
- Provide education on RA.

Chronic Phase
- Consider splinting for ROM and prevention of contracture using a spring coil splint.
- Use isotonic exercise with mild resistance.
- Postsurgical protocols for procedures performed on MP joints vary among physicians. One protocol recommends the use of dynamic splints placed on day 3 after surgery and worn for 6 to 8 weeks. Switch to night use only until week 14 post surgery.

Physical Therapy Techniques Applied to RA	
Modality	Comments
Cold	Best for use on active joints, but exercise should not be performed using joints just anesthetized by cold
Heat	Best for use on chronic joint pain or muscle spasm

Transcutaneous electrical nerve stimulation (TENS)	Usually limited to one or two sites
Electrical muscle stimulation	Best for facilitation preceding strengthening exercise
Ice massage	Best for facilitation preceding strengthening exercise
Mobilizing exercise	Exercise to pain tolerance with active joint
Strengthening exercise	Use submaximal isometric for active joint
Conditioning exercise	Use low-impact or aquatics

Source: Adapted with permission from LG Pawlson and CB Lewis, Dysmobility, in *Aging and Clinical Practice: Musculoskeletal Disorders: A Regional Approach*, RR Karpman and J Baum, pp. 127–142, © 1988, Igakushoin.

See previous subchapter "Osteoarthritis" for a discussion of and references on joint arthroplasty.

PRECAUTIONS/CONTRAINDICATIONS

- Avoid overexertion.
- Do not have client engage in resistive exercise through full range when there is gross crepitus or when joint is swollen.
- Do not apply heat when joints are inflamed. Prolonged heat can lead to increase in edema and discomfort.
- Assess sensation before using ice. Ice should not be applied to the skin directly except when using ice massage. The body part involved should not be placed directly on the pack.
- TENS complications can include skin irritation, cutaneous burns, and electric shock. TENS is not to be used on clients with a demand cardiac pacemaker.
- Ultrasound is contraindicated over the spinal cord and anesthetic areas, areas of malignancy, and areas with compromised circulation and on clients with a demand cardiac pacemaker. Ultrasound may be contraindicated over metallic joint implants.
- Shortwave diathermy and microwave diathermy are contraindicated if client has a pacemaker.
- Splints should be removed at least daily, and client tolerance should be monitored closely.
- Manual therapy can be used with arthritis only after careful assessment of joint and recent x-rays. When a joint is in the acute phase, even gentle mobilization can lead to increased pain. Techniques should be used cautiously and modified as indicated.
- Isometric exercise is contraindicated in the rheumatoid hand because it may lead to ulnar subluxation.
- Temperature of water for hydrotherapy is recommended at 98 degrees F. Use hydrotherapy cautiously with clients with high blood pressure or recent myocardial disease. Hydrotherapy is of course contraindicated if the client is hydrophobic.

See also appendix for contraindications to physical agents.

EXPECTED OUTCOME/PROGNOSIS

- The client will experience a reduction in pain and swelling.
- Therapy will prevent further deterioration and deformity.
- There will be restoration and maintainance of normal motion and function.
- Cardiovascular conditioning will increase maximal aerobic power and aerobic capacity.

- The client will have enhanced endurance and fitness.
- The client will increase strength.
- The client may have an enhanced sense of well-being.
  The effectiveness of therapy for RA is closely related to the effectiveness of medications.

REFERENCES

ASSESSMENT

Balance

Ekdahl C. Postural control, muscle function and psychological factors in rheumatoid arthritis: are there any relations? *Scandinavian Journal of Rheumatology.* 1992;21:297–301.

Functional Level

Ellis JI, Orti M. Rheumatoid arthritis in the general hospital setting. In: Peat M, ed. *Current Physical Therapy.* 103–106. **[Timed 50-feet walk test, grip strength measurement, functional inquiry joint examination by ARA classification system, duration of morning stiffness]**

Arthritis Self-Efficacy Scale

Lomi C, Nordholm LA. Validation of a Swedish version of the Arthritis Self-Efficacy Scale. *Scandinavian Journal of Rheumatology.* 1992;21:231–237.

Pawlson LG, Lewis CB. Dysmobility. In: Karpman RR, Baum J, eds. *Aging and Clinical Practice. Musculoskeletal Disorders: A Regional Approach.* New York, NY: IGAKU-SHOIN; 1988:127–142. **[Functional Assessment Tests: timed walk, two steps up and down, time to climb stairs, overhead reach, picking up objects]**

Functional Independence Measures

Granger CV, Hamilton BB, Keith RA, et al. Advance in functional assessment for medical rehabilitation. *Topics in Geriatric Rehabilitation.* 1986;1:3:59–74.

Keith RA, Granger CV, Hamilton BB, Sherwins FS. The Functional Independence Measure. *Advances in Clinical Rehabilitation.* 1987;1:6–18.

Geriatric Population Tests

Jackson OL. Functional assessment of the aged. *Allied Health Behavioural Science.* 1979;2:47. **[Lawton's Activities of Daily Living Scale, OARS Multidimensional Functional Assessment Questionnaire, Functional Life Scale, Philadelphia Geriatric Center Multilevel Assessment]**

Katz Index of Activities of Daily Living

Benjamin Rose Hospital Staff. Multidisciplinary studies of illness in aged persons: II. A new classification of functional status in activities of daily living. *Journal of Chronic Disease.* 1959;9:55–62.

Brorsson B, Ashberg KH. Katz Index of Independence in ADL reliability and validity in short-term care. *Scandinavian Journal of Rehabilitation Medicine.* 1984;16:125–132.

MACTAR: Patient Preference Disability Questionnaire

Tugwell P, Bombardier C, Buchanen WW, Goldsmith CH, Grace E, Hanng B, et al. The MACTAR Patient Preference Disability Questionnaire: an individualized functional priority approach for assessing improvement in physical disability in clinical trials in rheumatoid arthritis. *Journal of Rheumatology.* 1987; 14:446–451.

Gait

Downey, CA. *Observational Gait Analysis Handbook.* Ranch Los Amigos Hospital, *Pathokinesiology Service and Physical Therapy Department,* 1989.

Eastlack ME, Arvidson J, Snyder-Mackler L, Danoff JV, McGarvey CL. Interrater reliability of videotaped observational gait-analysis assessments. *Physical Therapy.* 1991;71:465–472.

Pawlson LG, Lewis CB. Dysmobility. In: Karpman RR, Baum J, eds. *Aging and Clinical Practice. Musculoskeletal Disorders: A Regional Approach.* New York, NY: IGAKU-SHOIN; 1988:127–142. **[Gait and transfers]**

Inflammation

Helewa A, Smythe HA. Physical therapy in rheumatoid arthritis. In: Wolfe F, Pincus T, eds. *Rheumatoid Arthritis.* New York, NY: Marcel Dekker, Inc; 1994:419. **[Number of active joints, grip strength, duration of morning stiffness, erythrocyte sedimentation rate, pain with visual analogue scale, function]**

Pendelton TB, Coleman MR, Grossman BJ. Numerical scale for evaluation of the patient with inflammatory joint disease. *Physical Therapy.* 1973;53:373–380.

Mobility

Helewa A, Smythe HA. Physical therapy in rheumatoid arthritis. In: Wolfe F, Pincus T, ed. *Rheumatoid Arthritis.* New York, NY: Marcel Dekker, Inc; 1994:419. **[Goniometry, fingertip-to-floor distances]**

Pawlson LG, Lewis CB. Dysmobility. In: Karpman RR, Baum J, eds. *Aging and Clinical Practice: Musculoskeletal Disorders: A Regional Approach.* New York, NY: IGAKU-SHOIN; 1988:127–142. **[ROM and strength, Romberg test, heel-to-shin test; also tests for role of neurological, sensory, and psychological impairment]**

Podsiadlo D, Richardson S. The timed "up and go": a test of basic functional mobility for frail elderly persons. *Journal of the American Geriatric Society.* 1991;39:142-148. **[Timed "up and go" test]**

Oatis CA. The use of a mechanical model to describe the stiffness and damping characteristics of the knee joint in healthy adults. *Physical Therapy.* 1993;73:740–749. **[Relaxed oscillation test]**

Vandervoort AA, Chesworth BM, Cunningham DA, et al. An outcome measure to quantify passive stiffness of the ankle. *Canadian Journal of Public Health.* 1992;83(suppl 2): S19–S23.

Pain

Numeric Pain Rating Scale (NPRS)

Downie W, Leatham PA, Rhind VM. Studies with pain rating scales. *Annals of the Rheumatic Diseases.* 1978;37:378–381.

Jensen MP, Faroly P, Braver S. The measurement of clinical pain intensity: a comparison of six methods. *Pain.* 1986;27:117–126.

McGuire DB. The measurement of clinical pain. *Nursing Research.* 1984;33:152–156.

Visual Analogue Scale (VAS)

Dixon JS, Bird HA. Reproducibility along a 10 cm vertical visual analogue scale. *Annals of the Rheumatic Diseases.* 1981. 40:87–89.

Downie WW, Leatham PA, Rhind VM. Studies with pain rating scales. *Annals of the Rheumatic Diseases.* 1978;37:378–381.

Langely GB, Sheppeard H. The visual analogue scale: its use in pain measurement. *Rheumatology International.* 1985;5:145–148.

Scott J, Huskisson EC. Vertical or horizontal visual analogue scales. *Annals of the Rheumatic Diseases.* 1979;38:560.

Special Tests to Which the PT May or May Not Have Access

Radiographs

Stenstrom CH. Radiologically observed progression of joint destruction and its relationship with demographic factors, disease severity, and exercise frequency in patients with rheumatoid arthritis. *Physical Therapy.* 1994;74:32–39. **[Modified Larsen's radiological index, Ritchie's articular index]**

Strength

Ekdahl C. Muscle function in rheumatoid arthritis: assessment and training. *Scandinavian Journal of Rheumatology.* 1990;86(suppl):9–61. **[Muscle strength, endurance, balance, coordination]**

Giles C. The modified sphygmomanometer: an instrument to objectively assess muscle strength. *Physiotherapy Canada*. 1984;36:36–41.

Helewa A, Goldsmith CH, Smythe HA. The modified sphygmomanometer— an instrument to measure muscle strength: a validation study. *Journal of Chronic Disease*. 1981;34:353–361. **[Hand-held dynamometer, maximal isometric contraction, modified sphygmomanometer for measuring muscle strength]**

Helewa A, Goldsmith CH, Smythe HA. Patient, observer and instrument variation in the measurement of strength of shoulder abductor muscles in patients with rheumatoid arthritis using a modified sphygmomanometer. *Journal of Rheumatology*. 1986;13:1044–1049.

Helewa A, Goldsmith C, Smythe H, Gibson E. An evaluation of four different measures of abdominal strength: patient, order and instrument variation. *Journal of Rheumatology*. 1990;17:965–969.

Helewa A, Smythe HA. Physical therapy in rheumatoid arthritis. In: Wolfe F, Pincus T, eds. *Rheumatoid Arthritis*. New York, NY: Marcel Dekker, Inc; 1994:419.

TREATMENT

Axtell LA, Schoneberger MB. Physical therapy. In: Kemp B, Burmmel-Smith K, Ramsdell JW, eds. *Geriatric Rehabilitation*. Boston, Mass: Little, Brown & Company; 1990:157–175.

Banwell B, Gall V. *Physical Therapy Management of Arthritis*. New York, NY: Churchill Livingstone; 1988.

Bohannon RW, Chavis D, Larkin P, Lieber C, Riddick L. Effectiveness of repeated prolonged loading for increasing flexion in knees demonstrating postoperative stiffness. *Physical Therapy*. 1985;65:494.

Brozik M, Rosztoczy I, Meretey K, et al. Interleukin 6 levels in synovial fluids of patients with different arthritises: correlation with local IgM rheumatoid factor and systemic acute phase protein production. *Journal of Rheumatology*. 1992;19:63–68.

Bulstrade S, Clarke A, Harrison R. A controlled trial to study the effect of ice therapy on joint inflammation in chronic arthritis. *Physiotherapy Practice*. 1986;2:104–108.

Campion GV, Dixon A. *Rheumatology*. Boston, Mass: Blackwell Scientific Publications; 1989:256–259.

Clarke AK. *Rehabilitation Techniques in Rheumatology*. Baltimore, Md: William & Wilkins; 1987:177–195.

Crosbie WJ, Nicol AC. Aided gait in rheumatoid arthritis following knee arthroplasty. *Archives of Physical Medicine and Rehabilitation*. 1990;71:299–303.

Dacre JE, Beeney N, Scott DL. Injections and physiotherapy for the painful stiff shoulder. *Annals of the Rheumatic Diseases*. 1989;48:322–325.

Dalseth T, Lippincott C. Postoperative rehabilitation. In: Amstutz HC, ed. *Hip Arthroplasty*. New York, NY: Churchill Livingstone; 1991:379–389.

Edelstein JE. Foot care for the aging. *Physical Therapy*. 1988;68:1882–1886.

Falus A, Kramer J, Walcz E, et al. Unequal expression of complement C4A and C4B genes in rheumatoid synovial cells, human monocytoid and hepatoma-derived cell lines. *Immunology*. 1989;68:1:133–136.

Falus A, Lakatos T, Smolen J. Dissimilar biosynthesis of interleukin-6 by different areas of synovial membrane of patients with rheumatoid arthritis and osteoarthritis. *Scandinavian Journal of Rheumatology*. 1992;21:116–119.

Gibson KR. Rheumatoid arthritis of the shoulder. *Physical Therapy*. 1986;66:1920–1929.

Goto M, Yoshinoya S, Miyamoto T, et al. Stimulation of interleukin-1 alpha and interleukin-1 beta release from human monocytes by cyanogen bromide peptides of type II collagen. *Arthritis and Rheumatism*. 1988;31:1508–1514.

Haralson K. Physical therapy and arthritis: origins and evolution. *Arthritis Care and Research*. 1990;3:4:173–177.

Hayes KW. Heat and cold in the management of rheumatoid arthritis. *Arthritis Care and Research*. 1993;6:3:156–166.

Hawkes J, Care G, Dixon JS, Bird HA, Wright V. A comparison of three different physiotherapy treatments for rheumatoid arthritis of the hands. *Physiotherapy Practice*. 1986;2:155–160.

Helewa A, Bombardier C, Goldsmith CH, et al. Cost-effectiveness of inpatient and intensive outpatient treatment of rheumatoid arthritis. *Arthritis and Rheumatism*. 1989;32:1505–1514.

Helewa A, Smythe HA. Physical therapy in rheumatoid arthritis. In: Wolfe F, Pincus T, eds. *Rheumatoid Arthritis*. New York, NY: Marcel Dekker, Inc; 1994:415–433.

Helewa A, Smythe HA, Goldsmith CH, et al. The total assessment of rheumatoid polyarthritis: evaluation of a training program for physiotherapists and occupational therapists. *Journal of Rheumatology.* 1987;14:87–92.

Helliwell P, Wallace F, Evard F. Smoking and ice therapy in rheumatoid arthritis. *Physiotherapy.* 1989;75:551–552.

Hirohata S, Inoue T, Ito K. Development of rheumatoid arthritis after chronic hepatitis caused by hepatitis C virus infection. *Internal Medicine.* 1992;31:493–495.

Hirohata S, Lipsky PE. Regulation of B cell function by bucillamine, a novel disease-modifying antirheumatic drug. *Clinical Immunology and Immunopathology.* 1993;66:1:43–51.

Ishikawa H, Hirohata K. Posterior interosseous nerve syndrome associated with rheumatoid synovial cysts of the elbow joint. *Clinical Orthopedics & Related Research.* 1990;254:134–139.

Lakatos J, Csakanyi L. Comparison of complications of total hip arthroplasty in rheumatoid arthritis, ankylosing spondylitis, and osteoarthritis. *Orthopedics.* 1991;14:1:55–57.

Lechner DE. Rehabilitation of the knee with arthritis. In: Greenfield BH, ed. *Rehabilitation of the Knee: A Problem-Solving Approach.* Philadelphia, Pa: FA Davis Co; 1993:206–241.

Lewis CB, Knortz KA, eds. *Orthopedic Assessment and Treatment of the Geriatric Patient.* St. Louis, Mo: CV Mosby Co; 1993.

Mattsson E, Brostrom LA, Linnarsson D. Changes in walking ability after knee replacement. *International Orthopaedics.* 1990;14:277–280.

Mattsson E, Olsson E, Brostrom LA. Assessment of walking before and after unicompartmental knee arthroplasty: a comparison of different methods. *Scandinavian Journal of Rehabilitation Medicine.* 1990;22:45–50.

Mimori A, Takeuchi F, Tokunaga K, et al. Restriction fragment length polymorphism of complement C4 in Japanese patients with rheumatoid arthritis and normal Japanese. *Tissue Antigens.* 1990;35:5:197–202.

Minor MA, Hewitt JE, Webel RR, Anderson SK. Efficacy of physical conditioning exercise in patients with rheumatoid arthritis and osteoarthritis. *Arthritis and Rheumatism.* 1989;32:1396–1405.

Mody GM, Meyers OL. Therapeutic requirements in rheumatoid arthritis. *South African Medical Journal.* 1990;77:497–499.

Moll JMH. *Manual of Rheumatology.* New York, NY: Churchill Livingstone; 1987:245–249.

Moll JMH. *Rheumatology in Clinical Practice.* Boston, Mass: Blackwell Scientific Publications; 1987:708–712.

Moncur C. Perceptions of physical therapy competencies in rheumatology: physical therapists versus rheumatologists. *Physical Therapy.* 1987; 67:331–339.

Moncur C. Physical therapy competencies in rheumatology. *Physical Therapy.* 1985;65:1365–1372.

Moncur C, Williams HJ. Cervical spine management in patients with rheumatoid arthritis: review of the literature. *Physical Therapy.* 1988:68:509–515.

Oosterveld FG, Rasker JJ. The effect of pressure gradient and thermolactyl control gloves in arthritic patients with swollen hands. *British Journal of Rheumatology.* 1990;29:3:197–200.

Philips CA. Rehabilitation of the patient with rheumatoid hand involvement. *Physical Therapy.* 1989;69:1091–1098.

Sawada T, Hirohata S, Inoue T, Ito K. Correlation between rheumatoid factor and IL-6 activity in synovial fluids from patients with rheumatoid arthritis. *Clinical and Experimental Rheumatology.* 1991;9:363–368.

Shinohara S, Hirohata S, Inoue T, et al. Phenotypic analysis of peripheral blood monocytes isolated from patients with rheumatoid arthritis. *Journal of Rheumatology.* 1992;19:211–215.

Stenstrom CH. Radiologically observed progression of joint destruction and its relationship with demographic factors, disease severity, and exercise frequency in patients with rheumatoid arthritis. *Physical Therapy.* 1994;74:32–39.

Stenstrom CH, Lindell B, Swanberg E, et al. Intensive dynamic training in water for rheumatoid arthritis functional class II: a long term study of effects. *Scandinavian Journal of Rheumatology.* 1991;20:358–365.

Sweeney GM, Clarke AK. Office seating for people with rheumatoid arthritis, ankylosing spondylitis, and low back pain. *Physiotherapy.* 1990;76:203–206.

Swezey RL, Clements PJ, Policoff LD. Rehabilitation: physical therapy. In: Katz WA, ed. *Diagnosis and Management of Rheumatic Disease*. 2nd ed. Philadelphia, Pa: JB Lippincott Co; 1988:859–871.

Takeuchi F, Matsuta K, Watanabe Y, et al. Susceptibility epitope on HLA-DR beta chain for rheumatoid arthritis and the effect of the positivity on the clinical features. *Journal of Immunogenetics*. 1989;16:475–483.

Triggs M. Orthopedic aquatic therapy. *Clinical Management in Physical Therapy*. 1991;11:1:30–31.

Tsuchiya N, Endo T, Matsuta K, et al. Effects of glactose depletion from oligosaccharide chains on immunological activities of human IgG. *Journal of Rheumatology*. 1989;16:285–290.

Tsuchiya N, Endo T, Matsuta K, et al. Detection of glycosylation abnormality in rheumatoid IgG using N-acetylglucosamine-specific *Psathyrella velutina* lectin. *Journal of Immunology*. 1993;151:1137–1146.

Tsuchiya N, Endo T, Shiota M, et al. Distribution of glycosylation abnormality among serum IgG subclasses from patients with rheumatoid arthritis. *Clinical Immunology and Immunopathology*. 1994;70:1:47–50.

Tsuchiya N, Murayama T, Yoshinoya S, et al. Antibodies to human cytomegalovirus 65-kilodalton Fc-binding protein in rheumatoid arthritis: idiotypic mimicry hypothesis of rheumatoid factor production. *Autoimmunity*. 1993;15:1:39–48.

Wadsworth CT. Elbow, forearm, wrist and hand. In: Myers RS, ed. *Saunders Manual of Physical Therapy Practice*. Philadelphia, Pa: WB Saunders Co; 1995:888–891.

Wadsworth TG, Patel H. Joint reconstruction in the upper limb. *Physiotherapy*. 1987;73:679–684.

Williams J, Harvery J, Tannenebaum H. Use of superficial heat versus ice for the rheumatoid arthritic shoulder: a pilot study. *Physiotherapy Canada*. 1986;38:8–13.

Wright FV, Helewa A, Goldsmith CH, Doshi N. Observation variation in an audit of charts of patients with Rheumatoid Arthritis. *Physiotherapy Canada*. 1992;44:26–33.

Yamamoto K, Sakoda H, Nakajima T, et al. Accumulation of multiple T cell clonotypes in the synovial lesions of patients with rheumatoid arthritis revealed by a novel clonality analysis. *International Immunology*. 1992;4:1219–1223.

Chapter 4

Endocrine Disorders

- Diabetes mellitus

Diabetes Mellitus

DESCRIPTION

Diabetes mellitus (DM) is a disorder resulting in hyperglycemia due to a diminished effectiveness or secretion of insulin. Severe complications from DM include atherosclerotic coronary disease, nephropathy, peripheral arterial disease, peripheral neuropathy, and retinopathy. Clients with DM are at risk for diabetic ketoacidosis and nonketotic hyperglycemic-hyperosmolar coma. Over half of lower extremity amputations are a result of complications from diabetes.

DM is classified as insulin-dependent DM (IDDM, Type I DM) or non-insulin-dependent DM (NIDDM, Type II DM) on the basis of the tendency toward diabetic ketoacidosis, as well as other diagnostic criteria.

CAUSE

DM has varied etiology relating to genetic factors or environmental influences. DM can also occur secondary to the following disorders: endocrine disease, pancreatic disease, presence of beta-cell toxin, acanthosis nigricans, lipotrophic diabetes, and genetic disorders specific to insulin function.

ASSESSMENT

Areas

- History
- Cardiovascular, including pulse and blood pressure
- Pulmonary
- Neurological, including sensation, especially peripheral, and any retinopathy
- Vascular: any claudication
- Strength, including active motion
- Mobility, including active range of motion
- Skin: color changes, especially in lower legs and feet
- Functional level
- Special tests to which the PT may or may not have access

Instruments/Procedures

- efficacy measure for diabetic program

Special Tests to Which the PT May or May Not Have Access
- glucose fasting levels
- ketone levels

Mobility
- subtalar joint motion testing
- ankle dorsiflexion testing

Neurological
- sensation with Semmes–Weinstein monofilaments

PROBLEMS
- *Classic signs of DM*: polyuria, polydipsia, quick weight loss, ketouria, and extreme elevation of fasting and plasma glucose levels.
- Client can develop severe complications from DM, including atherosclerotic coronary disease, nephropathy, peripheral arterial disease, peripheral neuropathy, and retinopathy.

TREATMENT/MANAGEMENT
- Establish general program of exercise for fitness.
- Educate client about skin care, especially of the feet, and prevention of open wounds. Emphasize the need to keep skin clean and dry, and inspect frequently for signs of breakdown.
- Assess need for orthotics, especially for feet, and recommend proper footwear.
- Consider prescribing an accommodative shoe that has a rocker sole and a shock-absorbing insert.
- Early wound care may include warm soaks or whirlpool and relief of pressure. Consider use of modalities such as ultrasound; transcutaneous electrical nerve stimulation (TENS; high-voltage); pulsating diathermy; and low-voltage microcurrent stimulation, with negative treatment electrode followed by positive treatment electrode.

PRECAUTIONS/CONTRAINDICATIONS
- If a client has coronary disease in addition to diabetes, the clinician should be aware that beta blockers can mask the typical signs of impending insulin shock. If blood glucose level is lower than 70 mg/dl or higher than 240 mg/dl, the client should not exercise.
- When a client with diabetes is exercising, the increased glucose induced by exercise needs to be offset by the amount of insulin being administered. Administration directly into a muscle that will be exercised can increase absorption and effect of insulin. An insulin reaction can be caused by exercising at the peak action time of insulin (3 hours after regular insulin injection or 6 hours after Neutral Protamine Hagedorn (NPH) insulin injection).
- Excessive exercise may lead to dehydration and increase the risk of ketosis in a client with diabetes. If ketones are present in the urine, the client should not exercise.
- If the client has an eye condition, such as retinopathy, exercise can worsen the condition.

DESIRED OUTCOME/PROGNOSIS
- The client will alter glucose intolerance with exercise.
- The client will prevent ulcerations from diabetic peripheral vascular disease.
- The client will prevent end-stage kidney disease.
  Success depends on medical strategy for modification with diet control and medication.

REFERENCES

ASSESSMENT
Byl N, Pfalzer LA. Integumentary system screening, examination, and assessment. In: Myers RS, ed. *Saunders Manual of Physical Therapy Practice*. Philadelphia, Pa: WB Saunders Co; 1955:582. **[Glucose fasting levels]**

Certo C. Cardiovascular. In: Myers RS, ed. *Saunders Manual of Physical Therapy Practice*. Philadelphia, Pa: WB Saunders Co; 1995:243. **[Efficacy measure for diabetic program]**

Mueller MJ, Diamond, JE, Delitto A, Sinacore DR. Insensitivity, limited joint mobility, and plantar ulcers in patients with diabetes mellitus. *Physical Therapy*. 1989;69:453–459. **[Subtalar joint motion, ankle dorsiflexion, sensation with Semmes–Weinstein monofilaments]**

TREATMENT
Birke JA, Novick A, Graham SL, et al. Methods of treating plantar ulcers. *Physical Therapy*. 1991;71:116–122.
Frantz S, Lawton R, Schmagel C, Zimmerman C. The physical therapist's role in the treatment of diabetes. *Clinical Management in Physical Therapy*. 1987;1:30–31.
Jette DU. Physiological effects of exercise in the diabetic. *Physical Therapy*. 1984; 64:339–342.
Mueller MJ, Diamond JE, Sinacore DR, et al. Total contact casting in treatment of diabetic plantar ulcers: controlled clinical trial. *Diabetes Care*. 1989;12:384–388.
Mueller MJ, Minor SD, Diamond JE, Blair VP. Relationship of foot deformity to ulcer location in patients with diabetes mellitus. *Physical Therapy*. 1990;70:356–362.
Myers, RS, ed. *Saunders Manual of Physical Therapy Practice*. Philadelphia, Pa: WB Saunders Co; 1995:220, 243, 236, 414, 581–582, 629, 1190.
Shinabarger NI. Limited joint mobility in adults with diabetes mellitus. *Physical Therapy*. 1987;67:215–218.
Sinacore DR, Mueller MJ, Diamond JE, et al. Diabetic plantar ulcers treated by total contact casting. *Physical Therapy*. 1987;67:1543–1549.
Summers S. Exercise: a vital component for patients on the biostator treatment of diabetic patients. *Diabetes Educator*. 1984;10:2:22–24.
Wolfe PI, DiCarlo S. Fatigure rate during anaerobic and aerobic exercise in insulin-dependent diabetics and nondiabetics. *Physical Therapy*. 1983;63:500–504.

DIABETIC NEUROPATHY
Birke JA, Sims DS. The insensitive foot. In: Hunt GC, ed. *Physical Therapy of the Foot and Ankle*. New York, NY: Churchill Livingstone; 1988;133–168.
Diamond JE, Mueller MJ, Delitton A. Effect of total contact cast immobilization on subtalar and talocrural joint motion in patients with diabetes mellitus. *Physical Therapy*. 1993;73:310–315.
Diamond JE, Mueller MJ, Delitto A, Sinacore DR. Reliability of a diabetic foot evaluation. *Physical Therapy*. 1989;69:797–802.
Diamond JE, Sinacore DR, Mueller MJ. Molded double-rocker plaster shoe for healing a diabetic plantar ulcer: a case report. *Physical Therapy*. 1987;67:1150–1552.
Mueller MJ, Diamond JE. Biomechanical treatment approach to diabetic plantar ulcers: a case report. *Physical Therapy*. 1988;68:1917–1920.
Mueller MJ, Diamond JE, Delitto A, Sincacore DR. Insensitivity, limited joint mobility, and plantar ulcers in patients with diabetes mellitus. *Physical Therapy*. 1980;69:453–459.
Nawoczenski DA, Birke JA, Graham SL, Koziatek E. The neuropathic foot—a management scheme: a case report. *Physical Therapy*. 1980;69:287–291.
Sims DS Jr, Cavanagh PR, Ulbrecht JS. Risk factors in the diabetic foot: recognition and management. *Physical Therapy*. 1988;68:1887–1902.

Chapter 5
Hand Injuries

- Colles fracture
- deQuervain's disease
- Dupuytren's contracture
- Gamekeeper's thumb
- Tendon injury

Colles Fracture

DESCRIPTION

Colles fracture is the the most common fracture of the forearm/wrist/hand area. Colles fracture occurs at the distal 2 inches of the radius, leaving a dorsally angulated fracture, and may include ulnar fracture as well. It occurs most frequently in the elderly. A Smith fracture, or "reverse Colles," leaves a volarly angulated fracture of the radius. Other fractures in this area include scaphoid, metacarpal, and phalangeal fractures.

CAUSE

A Colles fracture results from a fall onto an outstretched hand when the wrist is extended. A Smith fracture results from a fall onto an outstretched hand when the wrist is flexed.

ASSESSMENT

Areas

- History, including occupation, hand dominance, details of injury, and psychosocial factors
- Pain
- Mobility, including active and passive range of motion (ROM), accessory motion, composite range of motion, and any fixed deformities
- Strength: compare with uninvolved hand, if applicable; power and precision
- Sensitivity
- Skin and soft tissue: trophic changes, edema, temperature, condition of nails
- Joint integrity and structural deviations
- Neurological, including deep tendon reflexes and sensation
- Functional level
- Vascular

Instruments/Procedures (See References for Sources)

Functional Level
- Demerit Point System: Colles' fractures
- Jebsen Test of Hand Function
- Physical Capacity Evaluation

Joint Integrity and Structural Deviations
1. orthopedic tests of the hand
    - Bunnell–Littler test
    - circle formation with tip opposition between thumb and index finger test
    - digit collateral ligamentous stress test
    - elbow collateral ligament test
    - Finklestein test
    - Froment's sign
    - lateral and medial epicondylitis test
    - lunate displacement test
    - oblique retinacular ligament test
    - trigger finger test

- triquestrolunate test
- ulnar snuff box test
- Watson's test
2. photography of joint deformity

MOBILITY
- goniometry
- Guidelines for Measurement from the American Society for Surgery of the Hand (all motions measured from neutral starting position)

Neurological/Sensitivity
- carpal and cubital tunnels
- Dellon modification of Moberg test
- distal ulnar tunnel
- Minnesota manual dexterity test
- Minnesota rate of manipulation test
- Moberg pick-up test
- nerve conduction velocity test
- O'Connor finger dexterity test
- Phalen's test
- pinch test
- point localization
- Purdue pegboard test
- ridge sensiometer
- Seddon coin test
- sensitivity to deep pressure
- sensitivity to light touch (Semmes–Weinstein monofilaments)
- sensitivity to pain
- sensitivity to temperature
- sudomotor test
- Tinel's sign
- two-pound discrimination test
- vibratory test
- wrinkle test

Skin and Soft Tissue
1. edema
   - tape measure
   - volumetric measurements
2. temperature
   - palpation

Strength
- grasp
- grip: sphygmomanometer and Jamar grip dynamometer
- pinch

Vascular
- Allen's test

- modified Allen's test
- capillary refill
- volumetric measures

PROBLEMS
- The client usually has pain.
- The client can have edema.
- The fracture can be unstable.
- The client can have complications with wound healing.

TREATMENT/MANAGEMENT
- Active ROM follows the period of immobilization, which is usually 4 to 6 weeks. Emphasize forearm, wrist, and thumb movements. Begin with gentle wrist flexion/extension and supination/pronation activities.
- Consider passive stretch to intrinsic musculature (metacarpophalangeal extension with interphalangeal flexion).
- Stretch extrinsic flexor tendons (combination extension of fingers and wrist).
- Use joint mobilization as indicated.
- Instruct in elevation and use of wrapping materials for edema of fingers and hand. Also consider retrograde massage for edema.
- Consider use of transcutaneous electrical nerve stimulation (TENS) or functional electrical stimulation for pain.
- Consider use of mild heat if stiffness is a problem.

PRECAUTIONS/CONTRAINDICATIONS
- Fingers must be observed for swelling after cast is applied.
- Uninjured parts should remain free and activity encouraged to prevent contracture. Metacarpal joints, in particular, should remain unrestricted for finger flexion and thumb opposition to little finger.

DESIRED OUTCOME/PROGNOSIS
- The client will have an increase in motion.
- The client will have increase in strength.
- The client will have a reduction of pain.
- The client will return to full function.

REFERENCES

ASSESSMENT
Flesch P, Macchiaverna J. Hand evaluation form for effective treatment of hand injuries. *Clinical Management in Physical Therapy.* 1982;2:28–29 (Summer).

Mitchell SS. An adjunctive method for wrist and hand assessment. *Clinical Management in Physical Therapy.* 1984;4:1:44.

Tubiana R, Thomine JM, Mackin E. *Examination of the Hand and Wrist.* New York, NY: CV Mosby Co;1996.

Functional Level

Demerit Point System: Colles' Fractures

Sarimento A, Pratt GW, Berry NC, Sinclair WF. Colles' fractures. *Journal of Bone and Joint Surgery*. 1975;57A:311–317.

Jebsen Test of Hand Function

Hackel ME, Wolfe GA, Bang SM, et al. Changes in hand function in the aging adult as determined by the Jebsen Test of Hand Function. *Physical Therapy*. 1992;72:373–377.

Jebsen RH, Taylor N, Trieschman RB, et al. An objective and standardized test of hand function. *Archives of Physical Medicine and Rehabilitation*. 1969;50:311–319.

Lynch KB, Bridle MJ. Validity of the Jebsen-Taylor Hand Function Test in predicting activities of daily living. *Occupational Therapy Journal of Research*. 1989;9:316–318.

Physical Capacity Evaluation

Bear-Lehman J, Abreu BC. Evaluating the hand: issues in reliability and validity. *Physical Therapy*. 1989;69:1025–1033.

Bell-Krotoski JA, Breger DE, Beach RB. Application of biomechanics for evaluation of the hand. In: Hunter JM, Schneider LH, Macklin EJ, Callahan AD, eds., *Rehabilitation of the Hand: Surgery and Therapy*. St. Louis, Mo: CV Mosby Co; 1990:139–166. **[Biomechanics]**

Wadsworth CT. Elbow, forearm, wrist, and hand. In: Myers RS, ed. *Saunders Manual of Physical Therapy Practice*. Philadelphia, Pa: WB Saunders Co; 1995:841–917.

Joint Integrity and Structural Deviations

Rothstein JM, Roy SH, Wolf SL. *The Rehabilitation Specialist's Handbook*. Philadelphia, Pa: FA Davis Co; 1991:126–127. **[Froment's sign intrinsic-plus test]**

Tomberlin JP, Saunders HD. *Evaluation, Treatment and Prevention of Musculoskeletal Disorders. Vol 2: Extremities*. Chaska, Minn: The Saunders Group; 1994:164. **[Finkelstein's test, trigger finger test, Bunnell–Littler test, retinacular test, Watson's test, triquestrolunate test, ulnar snuff box test, lunate displacement test]**

Wadsworth CT. Elbow, forearm, wrist, and hand. In: Myers RS, ed. *Saunders Manual of Physical Therapy Practice*. Philadelphia, Pa: WB Saunders Co; 1995:841–917. **[Bunnell–Littler test, circle formation with tip opposition between thumb and index finger test, digit collateral ligamentous stress test, elbow collateral ligaments, Finklestein test, Froment's sign, lateral and medial epicondylitis test, oblique retinacular ligament test, Phalen's test]**

Mobility

Cambridge CA. Range-of-motion measurements of the hand. In: Hunter JM, Schneider LH, Macklin EJ, Callahan AD, eds. *Rehabilitation of the Hand: Surgery and Therapy*. St. Louis, Mo: CV Mosby Co; 1990:82–92.

LaStayo PC, Wheeler DL. Reliability of passive wrist flexion and extension goniometric measurements: a multicenter study. *Physical Therapy*. 1994;74:162–174.

Mackin EJ. The role of the hand therapist. In: Lamb DW, Hooper G, Kuczynski K, eds. *The Practice of Hand Surgery*. Boston, Mass: Blackwell Scientific Publications; 1989:659–679. **[Guidelines for measurement from the American Society for Surgery of the Hand (all motions measured from neutral starting position)]**

Mints N, Dvir Z. Wrist complex mobility: a study of passive flexion and extension and accessory movements. *Physiotherapy Canada*. 1988;40:282–285. **[Goniometry]**

Wadsworth CT. Elbow, forearm, wrist, and hand. In: Myers RS, ed. *Saunders Manual of Physical Therapy Practice*. Philadelphia, Pa: WB Saunders Co; 1995:841–917. **[Composite ROM]**

Neurological/Sensitivity

Anthony MS. Sensory evaluation. In: Clark GL, Wilgis EF, Aiello B, et al, eds. *Hand Rehabilitation: A Practical Guide.* New York, NY: Churchill Livingstone; 1993:55–72.

Mackin EJ. The role of the hand therapist. In: Lamb DW, Hooper G, Kuczynski K, eds. *The Practice of Hand Surgery.* Boston, Mass: Blackwell Scientific Publications; 1989:659–679. **[Functional tests: Moberg pick-up test, point localization, and two-point discrimination. Modality tests: test pain, temperature, light touch (Semmes-Weinstein monofilaments), and deep pressure. Objective tests: nerve conduction velocity and wrinkle test]**

Tomberlin JP, Saunders HD. *Evaluation, Treatment and Prevention of Musculoskeletal Disorders. Vol 2: Extremities.* Chaska, Minn: The Saunders Group; 1994:170–171. **[Pinch test, Phalen's test, Tinel's sign, Jebsen–Taylor Hand Function Test, Minnesota rate of manipulation test, Purdue pegboard test, simulated ADL test]**

Wadsworth CT. Elbow, forearm, wrist, and hand. In: Myers RS, ed. *Saunders Manual of Physical Therapy Practice.* Philadelphia, Pa: WB Saunders Co; 1995:841–917. **[Carpal and cubital tunnels, distal ulnar tunnel. Modality test: Tinel's sign. Objective tests: sudomotor test, wrinkle test, nerve conduction velocity test. Subjective sensation: vibratory test, two-point discrimination test (static two-point discrimination, moving two-point discrimination), Semmes-Weinstein monofilament test. Functional tests: ridge sensiometer, Seddon coin test, Moberg pick-up test, Dellon modification of Moberg test. Standardized tests: Purdue pegboard test, Minnesota manual dexterity, O'Connor finger dexterity test]**

Skin

Edema

Mackin EJ. The role of the hand therapist. In: Lamb DW, Hooper G, Kuczynski K, eds. *The Practice of Hand Surgery.* Boston, Mass: Blackwell Scientific Publications; 1989:659–679. **[tape and volumetric measures]**

Mackin EJ, Byron PM. Postoperative management. In: McFarlane RM, McGrouther DA, Flint MH, eds. *Dupuytren's Disease.* New York, NY: Churchill Livingstone; 1990:370. **[tape and volumetric measures]**

Strength

Hamilton GF, McDonald C, Chenier TC. Measurement of grip strength: validity and reliability of the sphygmomanometer and Jamar grip dynamometer. *Journal of Orthopaedic and Sports Physical Therapy.* 1992;16:215–219.

Mackin EF, Byron PM. Postoperative management. In: McFarlane RM, McGrouther DA, Flint MH, eds. *Dupuytren's Disease.* New York, NY: Churchill Livingstone; 1990:370. **[Grasp measurements. Finger-to-palm distance and fingernail to distal palmar crease]**

Wadsworth CT. Elbow, forearm, wrist, and hand. In: Myers RS, ed. *Saunders Manual of Physical Therapy Practice.* Philadelphia, Pa: WB Saunders Co; 1995:841–917. **[Power grip, precision grip, hook grip, lateral pinch, cylinder grasp, pinch strength]**

Vascular

Greathouse DG, Underwood FB, Tuttle P. Roth technique—a new approach for measuring sensory neural conduction in the median and ulnar nerves: suggestion from the field. *Physical Therapy.* 1989;69:777–779.

Tomberlin JP, Saunders HD. *Evaluation, Treatment and Prevention of Musculoskeletal Disorders. Vol 2: Extremities.* Chaska, Minn: The Saunders Group; 1994:164. **[Allen's test, modified Allen's test, volumetric measures, capillary refill]**

Wadsworth CT. Elbow, forearm, wrist, and hand. In: Myers RS, ed. *Saunders Manual of Physical Therapy Practice.* Philadelphia, Pa: WB Saunders Co; 1995:841–917. **[Allen's test]**

TREATMENT

Barclay V, Collier RJ, Jones J. Treatment of various hand injuries by pulsed electromagnetic energy (diapulse). *Physiotherapy*. 1983;69:186–188.

Duncan RM. Basic principles of splinting the hand. *Physical Therapy*. 1989;69:1104–1116.

Durand LG, Ionescu GD, Banchard M, et al. Design and preliminary evaluation of a portable instrument for assisting physiotherapists and occupational therapists in the rehabilitation of the hand. *Journal of Rehabilitation Research and Development*. 1989;26:2:47–54.

Flowers KR. String wrapping versus massage for reducing digital volume. *Physical Therapy*. 1988;68:57–59.

Griffin JW, Newsome LS, Stralka SW, Wright PE. Reduction of chronic posttraumatic hand edema: a comparison of high voltage pulsed current, intermittent pneumatic compression, and placebo treatments. *Physical Therapy*. 1990;70:279–286.

Hunter JM, Mackin EJ. Oedema and bandaging. In: Hunter JM, Schneider LH, Mackin EJ, Callahan AD, eds. *Rehabilitation of the Hand*. 2nd ed. St. Louis, Mo: CV Mosby Co; 1984:146.

Mackin EJ. The therapist's point of view: prevention of complications in hand therapy. *Hand Clinics*. 1986;2:229–247.

Moran CA. Anatomy of the hand. *Physical Therapy*. 1989;69:1007–1013.

Morey KR, Watson AH. Team approach to treatment of the posttraumatic stiff hand: a case report. *Physical Therapy*. 1986;66:225–228.

Mullins PAT. Management of common chronic pain problems in the hand. *Physical Therapy*. 1989;69:1050–1058.

Parry CBW. Helping hands: rehabilitation in hand surgery. *Physiotherapy*. 1983;69:345–369.

Randall T, Portney L, Harris BA. Effects of joint mobilization on joint stiffness and active motion of the metacarpal-phalangeal joint. *Journal of Orthopaedic and Sports Physical Therapy*. 1992;16:30–36.

Saunders SR. Physical therapy management of hand fractures. *Physical Therapy*. 1989;69:1065–1076.

Sorenson MK. The edematous hand. *Physical Therapy*. 1989;69:1059–1064.

Tottenham VM. Hand therapy: a combined physical and occupational therapy approach. *Physiotherapy Canada*. 1989;41:156–157.

Wadsworth CT. Elbow, forearm, wrist, and hand. In: Myers RS, ed. *Saunders Manual of Physical Therapy Practice*. Philadelphia, Pa: WB Saunders Co; 1995:841–917.

de Quervain's Disease

Also known as *repetitive trauma of the hand*.

DESCRIPTION

de Quervain's disease is a type of tenosynovitis or inflammation of the abductor pollicis longus and extensor pollicus brevis tendons' sheath. Other hand conditions that can be caused by repetitive trauma include trigger finger and ganglia.

CAUSE

Etiology is unknown. de Quervain's disease may be caused by repetitive microtrauma or extreme trauma, strain, unaccustomed exercise, or the effects of aging. Specifically, overuse of activities of combined thumb and wrist movements may be implicated.

ASSESSMENT

Areas
- History, including occupation, hand dominance, details of injury, and psychosocial factors
- Pain
- Mobility, including active and passive range of motion (ROM), accessory motion, composite range of motion, and any fixed deformities
- Strength: compare with uninvolved hand, if applicable; power and precision
- Sensibility
- Skin and soft tissue: trophic changes, edema, temperature, condition of nails
- Joint integrity and structural deviations
- Neurological, including deep tendon reflexes, sensation
- Functional level
- Vascular

Instruments/Procedures (See References for Sources)

Functional Level
- impairment ratings
- Jebsen Test of Hand Function
- physical capacity evaluation

Joint Integrity and Structural Deviations
1. orthopedic tests of the hand
    - Bunnell–Littler test
    - circle formation with tip opposition between thumb and index finger test
    - digit collateral ligamentous stress test
    - elbow collateral ligament test
    - Finklestein test
    - Froment's sign
    - lateral and medial epicondylitis test
    - lunate displacement test
    - oblique retinacular ligament test
    - retinacular test
    - trigger finger test
    - triquestrolunate test
    - ulnar snuff box test
    - Watson's test
2. photography of joint deformity

Mobility
- goniometry
- Guidelines for Measurement from the American Society of Surgery of the Hand (all motions measured from neutral starting position)

Neurological/Sensibility
- carpal and cubital tunnels
- Dellon modification of Moberg test
- distal ulnar tunnel
- Minnesota manual dexterity test

- Minnesota rate of manipulation test
- Moberg pick-up test
- nerve conduction velocity test
- O'Connor finger dexterity test
- Phalen's test
- pinch test
- point localization
- Purdue pegboard test
- ridge sensiometer
- Seddon coin test
- sensitivity to deep pressure
- sensitivity to light touch (Semmes–Weinstein monofilaments)
- sensitivity to pain
- sensitivity to temperature
- sudomotor test
- Tinel's sign
- two-point discrimination test
- vibratory test
- wrinkle test

Skin and Soft Tissue
1. edema
   - tape measure
   - volumetric measures
2. temperature
   - palpation

Strength
- grasp
- grip: sphygmomanometer and Jamar grip dynamometer
- pinch

Vascular
- Allen's test
- modified Allen's test
- capillary refill
- volumetric measures

PROBLEMS
- The client usually has pain in wrist with activity.
- The client may have decreased use of hand due to pain.
- The client usually has swelling and tenderness around the wrist, first extensor compartment, or radial styloid process.
- The client usually has decreased ROM in direction of ulnar deviation.
- The client can have accompanying nerve irritation.

TREATMENT/MANAGEMENT

Acute Phase
- Instruct client in use of ice.

- Fit client with resting forearm splint.
- After 1 to 2 weeks, consider use of physical agents and modalities such as heat, phonophoresis, ultrasound, and friction massage.
- Begin mild stretching for wrist motion and active exercise.
- Consider soft tissue mobilization for neural problems.
- Educate client on benefits of activity modification of aggravating activities to prevent reinjury.

Postsurgical Rehabilitation
Active exercise usually begins 2 to 3 days post surgery after dressings are removed.

PRECAUTIONS/CONTRAINDICATIONS
de Quervain's disease must be differentiated from osteoarthrosis of the trapezium.

EXPECTED OUTCOME/PROGNOSIS
- The client will experience a decrease in symptoms.
- The client will progress to an increased functional level.
- The client will be instructed in avoiding aggravation of the condition and reinjury.

REFERENCES

ASSESSMENT
Flesch P, Macchiaverna J. Hand evaluation form for effective treatment of hand injuries. *Clinical Management in Physical Therapy*. 1982;2:28.

Mitchell SS. An adjunctive method for wrist and hand assessment. *Clinical Management in Physical Therapy*. 1984;1:44.

Tubiana R, Thomine JM, Mackin E. *Examination of the Hand and Wrist*. New York, NY: Mosby Co; 1996.

Functional Level

Impairment Rating
Ward RS. Impairment rating. *Clinical Management*. 1992;12:5:38–45.

Jebsen Test of Hand Function
Hackel ME, Wolfe GA, Bang SM, et al. Changes in hand function in the aging adult as determined by the Jebsen Test of Hand Function. *Physical Therapy*. 1992;72:373–377.

Jebsen RH, Taylor N, Trieschman RB, et al. An objective and standardized test of hand function. *Archives of Physical Medicine and Rehabilitation*. 1969;50:311–319.

Lynch KB, Bridle MJ. Validity of the Jebsen–Taylor Hand Function Test in predicting activities of daily living. *Occupational Therapy Journal of Research*. 1989;9:316–318.

Physical Capacity Evaluation
Bear-Lehman J, Abreu BC. Evaluating the hand: issues in reliability and validity. *Physical Therapy*. 1989;69:1025–1033.

Bell-Krotoski JA, Breger DE, Beach RB. Application of biomechanics for evaluation of the hand. In: Hunter JM, Schneider LH, Macklin EJ, Callahan AD, eds. *Rehabilitation of the Hand: Surgery and Therapy*. St. Louis, Mo: CV Mosby Co; 1990:139–166. **[Biomechanics]**

Wadsworth CT. Elbow, forearm, wrist, and hand. In: Myers RS, ed. *Saunders Manual of Physical Therapy Practice*. Philadelphia, Pa: WB Saunders Co; 1995:841-917.

Joint Integrity and Structural Deviations
Rothstein JM, Roy SH, Wolf SL. *The Rehabilitation Specialist's Handbook*. Philadelphia, Pa: FA Davis Co; 1991:126–127. **[Froment's sign intrinsic-plus test]**

Tomberlin JP, Saunders HD. *Evaluation, Treatment and Prevention of Musculoskeletal Disorders. Vol 2: Extremities.* Chaska, Minn: The Saunders Group; 1994:164. **[Finkelstein's test, trigger finger test, Bunnell–Littler test, retinacular test, Watson's test, triquestrolunate test, ulnar snuff box test, lunate displacement test]**

Wadsworth CT. Elbow, forearm, wrist, and hand. In: Myers RS, ed. *Saunders Manual of Physical Therapy Practice.* Philadelphia, Pa: WB Saunders Co; 1995:841–917. **[Bunnell–Littler test, circle formation with tip opposition between thumb and index finger test, digit collateral ligamentous stress test, elbow collateral ligaments, Finklestein test, Froment's sign, lateral and medial epicondylitis test, oblique retinacular ligament test, Phalen's test]**

Mobility

Cambridge CA. Range-of-motion measurements of the hand. In: Hunter JM, Schneider LH, Macklin EJ, Callahan AD, eds. *Rehabilitation of the Hand: Surgery and Therapy.* St. Louis, Mo: CV Mosby Co; 1990:82–92.

LaStayo PC, Wheeler DL. Reliability of passive wrist flexion and extension goniometric measurements: a multicenter study. *Physical Therapy.* 1994;74:162–174.

Mackin EJ. The role of the hand therapist. In: Lamb DW, Hooper G, Kuczynski K, eds. *The Practice of Hand Surgery.* Boston, Mass: Blackwell Scientific Publications; 1989:659–679. **[Guidelines for Measurement from the American Society for Surgery of the Hand (all motions measured from neutral starting position)]**

Mints N, Dvir Z. Wrist complex mobility: a study of passive flexion and extension and accessory movements. *Physiotherapy Canada.* 1988;40:282–285. **[Goniometry]**

Wadsworth CT. Elbow, forearm, wrist, and hand. In: Myers RS, ed. *Saunders Manual of Physical Therapy Practice.* Philadelphia, Pa: WB Saunders Co.; 1995:841–917. **[Composite ROM]**

Neurological/Sensitivity

Anthony MS. Sensory evaluation. In: Clark GL, Wilgis EF, Aiello B, et al, eds. *Hand Rehabilitation: A Practical Guide.* New York, NY: Churchill Livingstone; 1993:55–72.

Mackin EJ. The role of the hand therapist. In: Lamb DW, Hooper G, Kuczynski K, eds. *The Practice of Hand Surgery.* Boston, Mass: Blackwell Scientific Publications; 1989:659–679. **[Functional tests: Moberg pick-up test, point localization, and two-point discrimination. Modality tests: test pain, temperature, light touch (Semmes–Weinstein monofilaments), and deep pressure. Objective tests: nerve conduction velocity and wrinkle test]**

Tomberlin JP, Saunders HD. *Evaluation, Treatment and Prevention of Musculoskeletal Disorders. Vol 2: Extremities.* Chaska, Minn: The Saunders Group; 1994:170–171. **[Pinch test, Phalen's test, Tinel's sign, Jebsen-Taylor Hand Function Test, Minnesota rate of manipulation test, Purdue pegboard test, simulated ADL test]**

Wadsworth CT. Elbow, forearm, wrist, and hand. In: Myers RS, ed. *Saunders Manual of Physical Therapy Practice.* Philadelphia, Pa: WB Saunders Co; 1995:841–917. **[Carpal and cubital tunnels; distal ulnar tunnel. Modality tests: Tinel's sign. Objective tests: sudomotor test, wrinkle test, nerve conduction velocity test; subjective sensation: vibratory test, two-point discrimination test (static two-point discrimination, moving two-point discrimination), Semmes–Weinstein monofilament test. Functional tests: ridge sensiometer, Seddon coin test, Moberg pick-up test, Dellon modification of Moberg test. Standardized tests: Purdue pegboard test, Minnesota manual dexterity, O'Connor finger dexterity test]**

Skin

Edema

Mackin EJ. The role of the hand therapist. In: Lamb DW, Hooper G, Kuczynski K, eds. *The Practice of Hand Surgery.* Boston, Mass: Blackwell Scientific Publications; 1989:659–679. **[tape and volumetric measures]**

Mackin EF, Byron PM. Postoperative management. In: McFarlane RM, McGrouther DA, Flint MH, eds. *Dupuytren's Disease*. New York, NY: Churchill Livingstone; 1990:370. **[tape and volumetric measures]**

Strength
Hamilton GF, McDonald C, Chenier TC. Measurement of grip strength: validity and reliability of the sphygmomanometer and Jamar grip dynamometer. *Journal of Orthopaedic and Sports Physical Therapy*. 1992;16:215–219.

Mackin EF, Byron PM. Postoperative management. In: McFarlane RM, McGrouther DA, Flint MH, eds. *Dupuytren's Disease*. New York, NY: Churchill Livingstone; 1990:370. **[Grasp measurements. Finger-to-palm distance and fingernail to distal palmar crease]**

Wadsworth CT. Elbow, forearm, wrist, and hand. In: Myers RS, ed. *Saunders Manual of Physical Therapy Practice*. Philadelphia, Pa: WB Saunders Co; 1995:841–917. **[Power grip, precision grip, hook grip, lateral pinch, cylinder grasp, pinch strength]**

Vascular
Greathouse DG, Underwood FB, Tuttle P. Roth technique—a new approach for measuring sensory neural conduction in the median and ulnar nerves: suggestion from the field. *Physical Therapy*. 1989;69:777–779.

Tomberlin JP, Saunders HD. *Evaluation, Treatment and Prevention of Musculoskeletal Disorders. Vol 2: Extremities*. Chaska, Minn: The Saunders Group; 1994:164. **[Allen's test, modified Allen's test, volumetric measures, capillary refill]**

Wadsworth CT. Elbow, forearm, wrist, and hand. In: Myers RS, ed. *Saunders Manual of Physical Therapy Practice*. Philadelphia, Pa: WB Saunders Co; 1995:841–917. **[Allen's test]**

TREATMENT
Anderson M, Tichenor CJ. A patient with de Quervain's tenosynovitis: a case report using an Australian approach to manual therapy. *Physical Therapy*. 1994;74:314–326.

Barclay V, Collier RJ, Jones J. Treatment of various hand injuries by pulsed electromagnetic energy (diapulse). *Physiotherapy*. 1983;69:186–188.

Duncan RM. Basic principles of splinting the hand. *Physical Therapy*. 1989;69:1104–1116.

Durand LG, Ionescu GD, Banchard M, et al. Design and preliminary evaluation of a portable instrument for assisting physiotherapists and occupational therapists in the rehabilitation of the hand. *Journal of Rehabilitation Research and Development*. 1989;26:2:47–54.

Griffin JW, Newsome LS, Stralka SW, Wright PE. Reduction of chronic posttraumatic hand edema: a comparison of high voltage pulsed current, intermittent pneumatic compression, and placebo treatments. *Physical Therapy*. 1990;70:279–286.

Hertling D, Kessler RM. *Management of Common Musculoskeletal Disorders*. Philadelphia, Pa: JB Lippincott Co; 1990:226–271.

Hunter JM, Mackin EJ. Oedema and bandaging. In: Hunter JM, Schneider LH, Mackin EJ, Callahan AD, eds. *Rehabilitation of the Hand*. 2nd ed. St. Louis, Mo: CV Mosby Co; 1984;146.

Kisner C, Colby LA. *Therapeutic Exercise: Foundations and Techniques*. 2nd ed. Philadelphia, Pa: FA Davis Co; 1990:289–315.

Mackin EJ. The therapist's point of view: prevention of complications in hand therapy. *Hand Clinics*. 1986;2:229–247.

Moran CA. Anatomy of the hand. *Physical Therapy*. 1989;69:1007–1013.

Morey KR, Watson AH. Team approach to treatment of the posttraumatic stiff hand: a case report. *Physical Therapy*. 1986;66:225–228.

Mullins PAT. Management of common chronic pain problems in the hand. *Physical Therapy*. 1989;69:1050–1058.

Parry CBW. Helping hands: rehabilitation in hand surgery. *Physiotherapy*. 1983;69:345–369.

Pritchard-Roberts P. Tenosynovitis. *Physiotherapy*. 1986;72:293–294.

Randall T, Portney L, Harris BA. Effects of joint mobilization on joint stiffness and active motion of the metacarpal-phalangeal joint. *Journal of Orthopaedic and Sports Physical Therapy*. 1992;16:30–36.

Sorenson MK. The edematous hand. *Physical Therapy.* 1989;69:1059–1064.

Wilson DH. Tenosynovitis, tendovaginitis and trigger finger. *Physiotherapy.* 1983;69:350–352.

Tomberlin JP, Saunders HD. *Evaluation, Treatment and Prevention of Musculoskeletal Disorders. Vol 2: Extremities.* Chaska, Minn: The Saunders Group; 1994:141–182.

Tottenham VM. Hand therapy: a combined physical and occupational therapy approach. *Physiotherapy Canada.* 1989;41:156–157.

Dupuytren's Contracture

DESCRIPTION

Dupuytren's contracture is a spontaneous thickening of the palmar fascia that leads to flexion contracture, which is painless but prevents full use of fingers. It may also appear as a nodular lesion in the adipose tissue. There is an increased incidence in men over women and over the age of 40.

CAUSE

The fibrous thickening has an unknown etiology. Dupuytren's contracture may be affected by repeated microtrauma. This disorder can also accompany shoulder-hand syndrome. There appears to be an inherited tendency toward the disorder among those of European ancestry.

ASSESSMENT

Areas

- History, including occupation, hand dominance, details of injury, and psychosocial factors
- Pain
- Mobility, including active and passive range of motion (ROM), accessory motion, composite range of motion, and any fixed deformities
- Strength: compare with uninvolved hand, if applicable; power and precision
- Sensibility
- Skin and soft tissue: trophic changes, edema, temperature, condition of nails
- Joint integrity and structural deviations
- Neurological, including deep tendon reflexes and sensation
- Functional level
- Vascular

Instruments/Procedures (See References for Sources)

Functional Level
- Jebsen Test of Hand Function
- Physical Capacity Evaluation

Joint Integrity and Structural Deviations
1. orthopedic tests of the hand
    - Bunnell–Littler test
    - circle formation with tip opposition between thumb and index finger test

- digit collateral ligamentous stress test
- elbow collateral ligament test
- Finklestein test
- Froment's sign
- lateral and medial epicondylitis test
- lunate displacement test
- oblique retinacular ligament test
- retinacular test
- trigger finger test
- triquestrolunate test
- ulnar snuff box test
- Watson's test
2. photography of joint deformity

Mobility
- goniometry
- Guidelines for Measurement from the American Society for Surgery of the Hand (all motions measured from neutral starting position)

Neurological/Sensibility
- carpal and cubital tunnels
- Dellon modification of Moberg test
- distal ulnar tunnel
- Minnesota manual dexterity test
- Minnesota rate of manipulation test
- Moberg pick-up test
- nerve conduction velocity test
- O'Connor finger dexterity test
- Phalen's test
- pinch test
- point localization
- Purdue pegboard test
- ridge sensiometer
- Seddon coin test
- sensitivity to deep pressure
- sensitivity to light touch (Semmes–Weinstein monofilaments)
- sensitivity to pain
- sensitivity to temperature
- sudomotor test
- Tinel's sign
- two-point discimination test
- vibratory test
- wrinkle test

Skin and Soft Tissue
1. edema
    - tape measure
    - volumetric measures

2. temperature
   * palpation

Strength
* grasp
* grip: sphygmomanometer and Jamar grip dynamometer
* pinch

Vascular
* Allen's test
* modified Allen's test
* capillary refill
* volumetric measures

PROBLEMS
* There is flexion contracture of the palmar aponeurosis.
* Usually, the contractures affect the metacarpal phalangeal and proximal interphalangeal joints of the ring finger or little finger.
* The client usually is affected on both hands.
* The client can have loss of hand function because of stiffness.
* The client may have a lump in palmar aponeurosis.
* After surgery, the client can have complications such as edema, decreased ROM of the whole hand, and recurrence of flexion contracture.

TREATMENT/MANAGEMENT

Rehabilitation for Contracture or Stiffness
1. Consider use of massage with soft tissue mobilization techniques and joint mobilization.
2. Encourage use of splints, dynamic or static splints, between therapy sessions.
3. Use passive ROM and stretching techniques combined with heat followed by active exercise.
4. Encourage active mobilization.
5. Progress to resistive exercise. Begin with isometric exercises and progress to resistive isotonic exercises.
6. Graded resistive activity can progress using manual resistance PNF techniques or external resistance or weight and isoflex exercises.
7. Instruct in home program of self-stretching with automobilization techniques or reverse-stretching techniques.

Rehabilitation Following Surgical Release; Fasciectomy
1. Provide whirlpool for wound care combined with active flexion and extension exercises.
2. Post whirlpool, one suggested routine has client elevate hand while performing fist-making exercise for 1 minute, followed by interval rest of 3 to 5 minutes to prevent edema.
3. Client can consult with physician for home program of soaking hand in water and which type of dressings to use.
4. Fit client with dorsal splint after dressings are removed, as indicated. Splints must be carefully fitted and readjusted as indicated. Instruct client in proper use and fit of splints. See precautions.

5. Instruct client on proper positioning to prevent swelling, such as keeping hand elevated above level of heart after surgery. Avoid extreme elbow flexion for proper venous flow. Keep hand elevated during sleep if possible.
6. Severe pitting edema may indicate need for intermittent compression treatment. Mechanical compression can be followed by manual retrograde massage.
7. Elastic wraps or elastic glove can also be used to assist with edema.
8. Antiedema exercises can be instituted such as elevation of arms and making a fist, on a suggested schedule of 10 times every hour while awake.
9. Consider intermittent compression if edema is severe. Amount of pressure is adjusted as condition warrants. Mechanical massage may be followed by retrograde massage with lanolin.
10. Instruct client in passive and active exercise.
11. Active hand exercises may include
    • thumb opposition, abduction, and extension
    • finger abduction, adduction, extension, and flexion to thenar eminence
    • fist making
    • wrist flexion and extension
    • intrinsic extension
    • finger blocking: isolation of distal flexion with proximal joints held firm

Frequency of exercise: 10 repetitions, 3 to 4 times per day, is one recommended schedule, with increased precision as client increases in motion. Can add tendon gliding exercises at this time.

12. Client may begin putty-squeezing exercises at 4 to 6 weeks postoperatively if indicated.
13. Provide modification of scar tissue with direct pressure, serial or dynamic splints, ROM or stretching techniques. Scar management can be enhanced with massage with lotion and pressure forms for scars.
14. Instruct client in desensitization techniques if hypersensitive over healed area.

PRECAUTIONS/CONTRAINDICATIONS

In general:
• Suspect reflex sympathetic dystrophy if client reports edema and stiffness combined with extreme pain.
• Do not allow overexercise, which can lead to increased pain and edema.
• Avoid squeezing exercises.
• Avoid overstretching the capsules in the finger joints.
• Fingers should always be stretched individually. If stretching multijoint muscles, do not elongate all joints simultaneously.
• When using a splint, clients should be taught to look for signs of too much pressure, such as color changes in fingertips, feelings of tingling or numbness, or increased edema.
• When splinting, the traction must be perpendicular to the involved segment.
Postoperatively:
• Avoid having hand in a dependent position when in whirlpool.
• Exercise should not begin after surgery until from day 3 to day 21, as indicated.
• Avoid contaminating the wound area with lanolin or lotion during massage.
• Intermittent external compression can be used with open wounds if sterile dressings are in place.

DESIRED OUTCOME/PROGNOSIS

- The client will restore joint play and full range of motion of the involved hand.
- The client will have an increase in strength and endurance of the involved hand.
- The client will return to former activities/work.
  Postoperatively:
- Through therapy, the client will reduce or prevent edema.
- There will be a modification of scar tissue.

To maintain gains from surgery and achieve optimal results, therapy is critical and is usually needed for 1 month or more. The use of nighttime splints may be indicated for approximately 6 months.

Any diminished sensation usually resolves spontaneously.

REFERENCES

ASSESSMENT

Flesch P, Macchiaverna J. Hand evaluation form for effective treatment of hand injuries. *Clinical Management in Physical Therapy*. 1982;2:28.

Mitchell SS. An adjunctive method for wrist and hand assessment. *Clinical Management in Physical Therapy*. 1984;1:44.

Tubiana R, Thomine JM, Mackin E. *Examination of the Hand and Wrist*. New York, NY: CV Mosby Co;1996.

Functional Level

Jebsen Test of Hand Function

Hackel ME, Wolfe GA, Bang SM, et al. Changes in hand function in the aging adult as determined by the Jebsen Test of Hand Function. *Physical Therapy*. 1992;72:373–377.

Jebsen RH, Taylor N, Trieschman RB, et al. An objective and standardized test of hand function. *Archives of Physical Medicine and Rehabilitation*. 1969;50:311–319.

Lynch KB, Bridle MJ. Validity of the Jebsen–Taylor Hand Function Test in predicting activities of daily living. *Occupational Therapy Journal of Research*. 1989;9:316–318.

Physical Capacity Evaluation

Bear-Lehman J, Abreu BC. Evaluating the hand: issues in reliability and validity. *Physical Therapy*. 1989;69:1025–1033.

Bell-Krotoski JA, Breger DE, Beach RB. Application of biomechanics for evaluation of the hand. In: Hunter JM, Schneider LH, Macklin EJ, Callahan AD, eds. *Rehabilitation of the Hand: Surgery and Therapy*. St. Louis, Mo: CV Mosby Co; 1990:139–166. **[Biomechanics]**

Wadsworth CT. Elbow, forearm, wrist, and hand. In: Myers RS, ed. *Saunders Manual of Physical Therapy Practice*. Philadelphia, Pa: WB Saunders Co; 1995:841–917.

Joint Integrity and Structural Deviations

Rothstein JM, Roy SH, Wolf SL. *The Rehabilitation Specialist's Handbook*. Philadelphia, Pa: FA Davis Co; 1991:126–127. **[Froment's sign intrinsic-plus test]**

Tomberlin JP, Saunders HD. *Evaluation, Treatment and Prevention of Musculoskeletal Disorders. Vol 2: Extremities*. Chaska, Minn: The Saunders Group; 1994:164. **[Finkelstein's test, trigger finger test, Bunnell–Littler test, retinacular test, Watson's test, triquestrolunate test, ulnar snuff box test, lunate displacement test]**

Wadsworth CT. Elbow, forearm, wrist, and hand. In: Myers RS, ed. *Saunders Manual of Physical Therapy Practice*. Philadelphia, Pa: WB Saunders Co; 1995:841–917. **[Bunnell–Littler test, circle formation with tip opposition between thumb and index finger test, digit collateral ligamentous stress test,**

elbow collateral ligaments, Finklestein test, Froment's sign, lateral and medial epicondylitis test, oblique retinacular ligament test, Phalen's test]

Mobility

Cambridge CA. Range-of-motion measurements of the hand. In: Hunter JM, Schneider LH, Macklin EJ, Callahan AD, eds. *Rehabilitation of the Hand: Surgery and Therapy.* St. Louis, Mo: CV Mosby Co; 1990:82–92.

LaStayo PC, Wheeler DL. Reliability of passive wrist flexion and extension goniometric measurements: a multicenter study. *Physical Therapy.* 1994;74:162–174.

Mackin EJ. The role of the hand therapist. In: Lamb DW, Hooper G, Kuczynski K, eds. *The Practice of Hand Surgery.* Boston, Mass: Blackwell Scientific Publications; 1989:659–679. **[Guidelines for Measurement from the American Society for Surgery of the Hand (all motions measured from neutral starting position)]**

Mints N, Dvir Z. Wrist complex mobility: a study of passive flexion and extension and accessory movements. *Physiotherapy Canada.* 1988;40:282–285. **[Goniometry]**

Wadsworth CT. Elbow, forearm, wrist, and hand. In: Myers RS, ed. *Saunders Manual of Physical Therapy Practice.* Philadelphia, Pa: WB Saunders Co; 1995:841–917. **[Composite ROM]**

Neurological/Sensitivity

Anthony MS. Sensory evaluation. In: Clark GL, Wilgis EF, Aiello B, et al, eds. *Hand Rehabilitation: A Practical Guide.* New York, NY: Churchill Livingstone; 1993:55–72.

Mackin EJ. The role of the hand therapist. In: Lamb DW, Hooper G, Kuczynski K, eds. *The Practice of Hand Surgery.* Boston, Mass: Blackwell Scientific Publications; 1989:659–679. **[Functional tests: Moberg pick-up test, point localization, and two-point discrimination. Modality tests: test pain, temperature, light touch (Semmes–Weinstein monofilaments), and deep pressure. Objective tests: nerve conduction velocity and wrinkle test]**

Tomberlin JP, Saunders HD. *Evaluation, Treatment and Prevention of Musculoskeletal Disorders. Vol 2: Extremities.* Chaska, Minn: The Saunders Group; 1994:170–171. **[Pinch test, Phalen's test, Tinel's sign, Jebsen–Taylor hand function test, the Minnesota rate of manipulation test, Purdue pegboard test, simulated ADL test]**

Wadsworth CT. Elbow, forearm, wrist, and hand. In: Myers RS, ed. *Saunders Manual of Physical Therapy Practice.* Philadelphia, Pa: WB Saunders Co; 1995:841–917. **[Carpal and cubital tunnels; distal ulnar tunnel. Modality tests: Tinel's sign. Objective tests: sudomotor test, wrinkle test, nerve conduction velocity test; subjective sensation: vibratory test, two-point discrimination test (static two-point discrimination, moving two-point discrimination), Semmes–Weinstein monofilament test. Functional tests: ridge sensiometer, Seddon coin test, Moberg pick-up test, Dellon modification of Moberg test. Standardized tests: Purdue pegboard test, Minnesota manual dexterity, O'Connor finger dexterity test]**

Skin

Edema

Mackin EJ. The role of the hand therapist. In: Lamb DW, Hooper G, Kuczynski K, eds. *The Practice of Hand Surgery.* Boston, Mass: Blackwell Scientific Publications; 1989:659–679. **[tape and volumetric measures]**

Mackin EF, Byron PM. Postoperative management. In: McFarlane RM, McGrouther DA, Flint MH, eds. *Dupuytren's Disease.* New York, NY: Churchill Livingstone; 1990:370. **[tape and volumetric measures]**

Strength

Hamilton GF, McDonald C, Chenier TC. Measurement of grip strength: validity and reliability of the sphygmomanometer and Jamar grip dynamometer. *Journal of Orthopaedic and Sports Physical Therapy.* 1992;16:215–219.

Mackin EF, Byron PM. Postoperative management. In: McFarlane RM, McGrouther DA, Flint MH, eds. *Dupuytren's Disease*. New York, NY: Churchill Livingstone; 1990:370. **[Grasp measurements. Finger-to-palm distance and fingernail to distal palmar crease]**

Wadsworth CT. Elbow, forearm, wrist, and hand. In: Myers RS, ed. *Saunders Manual of Physical Therapy Practice*. Philadelphia, Pa: WB Saunders Co; 1995:841–917. **[Power grip, precision grip, hook grip, lateral pinch, cylinder grasp, pinch strength]**

Vascular

Greathouse DG, Underwood FB, Tuttle P. Roth technique—a new approach for measuring sensory neural conduction in the median and ulnar nerves: suggestion from the field. *Physical Therapy*. 1989;69:777–779.

Tomberlin JP, Saunders HD. *Evaluation, Treatment and Prevention of Musculoskeletal Disorders. Vol 2: Extremities*. Chaska, Minn: The Saunders Group; 1994:164. **[Allen's test, modified Allen's test, volumetric measures, capillary refill]**

Wadsworth CT. Elbow, forearm, wrist, and hand. In: Myers RS, ed. *Saunders Manual of Physical Therapy Practice*. Philadelphia, Pa: WB Saunders Co; 1995:841–917. **[Allen's test]**

TREATMENT

Barclay V, Collier RJ, Jones J. Treatment of various hand injuries by pulsed electromagnetic energy (diapulse). *Physiotherapy*. 1983;69:186–188.

Clark GL, Wilgis EF, Aiello B, et al, eds. *Hand Rehabilitation: A Practical Guide*. New York, NY: Churchill Livingstone; 1993.

Duncan RM. Basic principles of splinting the hand. *Physical Therapy*. 1989;69:1104–1116.

Durand LG, Ionescu GD, Banchard M, et al. Design and preliminary evaluation of a portable instrument for assisting physiotherapists and occupational therapists in the rehabilitation of the hand. *Journal of Rehabilitation Research and Development*. 1989;26:2:47–54.

Fietti VG, Mackin EJ. Open-palm technique on Dupuytren's disease. In: Hunter JM, Schneider LH, Mackin EJ, Callahan AD, eds. *Rehabilitation of the Hand*. 2nd ed. St. Louis, Mo: CV Mosby Co; 1984:624.

Flowers KR. String wrapping versus massage for reducing digital volume. *Physical Therapy*. 1988;68:57–59.

Griffin JW, Newsome LS, Stralka SW, Wright PE. Reduction of chronic posttraumatic hand edema: a comparison of high voltage pulsed current, intermittent pneumatic compression, and placebo treatments. *Physical Therapy*. 1990;70:279–286.

Hertling D, Kessler RM. *Management of Common Musculoskeletal Disorders*. Philadelphia, Pa: JB Lippincott Co; 1990:226–271.

Hunter JM, Mackin EJ. Oedema and bandaging. In: Hunter JM, Schneider LH, Mackin EJ, Callahan AD, eds. *Rehabilitation of the Hand*. 2nd ed. St. Louis, Mo: CV Mosby Co; 1984:146.

Hunter JM, Schneider LH, Macklin EJ, Callahan AD, eds. *Rehabilitation of the Hand: Surgery and Therapy*. St. Louis, Mo: CV Mosby Co; 1990.

Kisner C, Colby LA. *Therapeutic Exercise: Foundations and Techniques*. 2nd ed. Philadelphia, Pa: FA Davis Co; 1990:289–315.

Mackin EJ. The therapist's point of view: prevention of complications in hand therapy. *Hand Clinics*. 1986;2:429.

Mackin EF, Byron PM. Postoperative management. In: McFarlane RM, McGrouther DA, Flint MH, eds. *Dupuytren's Disease*. New York, NY: Churchill Livingstone; 1990:368–376.

Moran CA. Anatomy of the hand. *Physical Therapy*. 1989;69:1007–1013.

Morey KR, Watson AH. Team approach to treatment of the posttraumatic stiff hand: a case report. *Physical Therapy*. 1986;66:225–228.

Mullins PAT. Management of common chronic pain problems in the hand. *Physical Therapy*. 1989;69:1050–1058.

Parry CBW. Helping hands: rehabilitation in hand surgery. *Physiotherapy*. 1983;69:345–369.

Randall T, Portney L, Harris BA. Effects of joint mobilization on joint stiffness and active motion of the metacarpal-phalangeal joint. *Journal of Orthopaedic and Sports Physical Therapy.* 1992;16:30–36.

Salter M, ed. *Hand Injuries: A Therapeutic Approach.* New York, NY: Churchill Livingstone; 1987.

Sorenson MK. The edematous hand. *Physical Therapy.* 1989;69:1059–1064.

Stanley BG, Tribuzi SM. *Concepts in Hand Rehabilitation.* Philadelphia, Pa: FA Davis Co; 1992.

Tottenham VM. Hand therapy: a combined physical and occupational therapy approach. *Physiotherapy Canada.* 1989;41:156–157.

Wadsworth CT. Elbow, forearm, wrist, and hand. In: Myers RS, ed. *Saunders Manual of Physical Therapy Practice.* Philadelphia, Pa: WB Saunders Co; 1995:841–917.

Watson N. Dupuytren's contracture. *Physiotherapy.* 1983;69:353–354.

Gamekeeper's Thumb (Sprains and Dislocations of the Hand)

DESCRIPTION

Gamekeeper's thumb is the forceful rupture of the ulnar collateral ligament or volar plate insertion at the first metacarpal (MP) joint. Other areas prone to sprains and dislocations are the lunate bone, the second to fifth MP joints, the proximal interphalangeal (PIP) joints, and distal interphalangeal (DIP) joints.

CAUSE

First-MP-joint dislocation or sprain usually happens during a fall such as skiing. When the skiier lands on an abducted thumb, the joint is forced into hyperextension.

ASSESSMENT

Areas
- History, including occupation, hand dominance, details of injury, and psychosocial factors
- Pain
- Mobility, including active and passive range of motion (ROM), accessory motion, composite range of motion, and any fixed deformities
- Strength, compare with uninvolved hand, if applicable; power and precision
- Sensibility
- Skin and soft tissue: trophic changes, edema, temperature, condition of nails
- Joint integrity and structural deviations
- Neurological, including deep tendon reflexes and sensation
- Functional level
- Vascular

Instruments/Procedures (See References for Sources)

Functional Level
- Jebsen Test of Hand Function

• Physical Capacity Evaluation

Joint Integrity and Structural Deviations
1. orthopedic tests of the hand
   • Bunnell–Littler test
   • circle formation with tip opposition between thumb and index finger test
   • digit collateral ligamentous stress test
   • elbow collateral ligament test
   • Finklestein test
   • Froment's sign
   • lateral and medial epicondylitis test
   • lunate displacement test
   • oblique retinacular ligament test
   • retinacular test
   • trigger finger test
   • triquestrolunate test
   • ulnar snuff box test
   • Watson's test
2. photography of joint deformity

Mobility
• goniometry
• Guidelines for Measurement from the American Society for Surgery of the Hand (all motions measured from neutral starting position)

Neurological/Sensibility
• carpal and cubital tunnels
• Dellon modification of Moberg test
• distal ulnar tunnel
• Minnesota manual dexterity test
• Minnesota rate of manipulation test
• Moberg pick-up test
• nerve conduction velocity test
• O'Connor finger dexterity test
• Phalen's test
• pinch test
• point localization
• Purdue pegboard test
• ridge sensiometer
• Seddon coin test
• sensitivity to deep pressure
• sensitivity to light touch (Semmes–Weinstein monofilaments)
• sensitivity to pain
• sensitivity to temperature
• sudomotor test
• Tinel's sign
• two-point discrimination test
• vibratory test

- wrinkle test

Skin and Soft Tissue
1. edema
   - tape measure
   - volumetric measures
2. temperature
   - palpation

Strength
- grasp
- grip: sphygmomanometer and Jamar grip dynamometer
- pinch

Vascular
- Allen's test
- modified Allen's test
- capillary refill
- volumetric measures

PROBLEMS
- The client usually has pain and inflammation.
- The client usually has joint instability if there is complete rupture.
- The client may have loss of function.

TREATMENT/MANAGEMENT

Partial Rupture
- Initiate gentle ROM.
- Gradually progress to strengthening thumb exercises.

Complete Rupture
- A period of immobilization is usually 2 to 6 weeks, following manual or open reduction.
- After immobilization, begin treatment as in partial rupture.

PRECAUTIONS/CONTRAINDICATIONS
- If the adductor aponeurosis is caught between the ligament and the proximal phalanx, an open reduction is generally indicated.

DESIRED OUTCOME/PROGNOSIS
- The client will have a reduction in symptoms.
- The client will resume normal hand function.

REFERENCES

ASSESSMENT
Flesch P, Macchiaverna J. Hand evaluation form for effective treatment of hand injuries. *Clinical Management in Physical Therapy*. 1982;2:28.

Mitchell SS. An adjunctive method for wrist and hand assessment. *Clinical Management in Physical Therapy.* 1984;1:44.

Tubiana R, Thomine JM, Mackin E. *Examination of the Hand and Wrist.* New York, NY: CV Mosby Co;1996.

Functional Level

Jebsen Test of Hand Function

Hackel ME, Wolfe GA, Bang SM, et al. Changes in hand function in the aging adult as determined by the Jebsen Test of Hand Function. *Physical Therapy.* 1992;72:373–377.

Jebsen RH, Taylor N, Trieschman RB, et al. An objective and standardized test of hand function. *Archives of Physical Medicine and Rehabilitation.* 1969;50:311–319.

Lynch KB, Bridle MJ. Validity of the Jebsen–Taylor Hand Function Test in predicting activities of daily living. *Occupational Therapy Journal of Research.* 1989;9:316–318.

Physical Capacity Evaluation

Bear-Lehman J, Abreu BC. Evaluating the hand: issues in reliability and validity. *Physical Therapy.* 1989;69:1025–1033.

Bell-Krotoski JA, Breger DE, Beach RB. Application of biomechanics for evaluation of the hand. In: Hunter JM, Schneider LH, Macklin EJ, Callahan AD, eds. *Rehabilitation of the Hand: Surgery and Therapy.* St. Louis, Mo: CV Mosby Co; 1990:139–166. **[Biomechanics]**

Wadsworth CT. Elbow, forearm, wrist, and hand. In: Myers RS, ed. *Saunders Manual of Physical Therapy Practice.* Philadelphia, Pa: WB Saunders Co; 1995:841–917

Joint Integrity and Structural Deviations

Rothstein JM, Roy SH, and Wolf SL. *The Rehabilitation Specialist's Handbook.* Philadelphia, Pa: FA Davis Co; 1991:126–127. **[Froment's sign intrinsic-plus test]**

Tomberlin JP, Saunders HD. *Evaluation, Treatment and Prevention of Musculoskeletal Disorders. Vol 2: Extremities.* Chaska, Minn: The Saunders Group; 1994:164. **[Finkelstein's test, trigger finger test, Bunnell–Littler test, retinacular test, Watson's test, triquestrolunate test, ulnar snuff box test, lunate displacement test]**

Wadsworth CT. Elbow, forearm, wrist, and hand. In: Myers RS, ed. *Saunders Manual of Physical Therapy Practice.* Philadelphia, Pa: WB Saunders Co; 1995:841–917. **[Bunnell–Littler test, circle formation with tip opposition between thumb and index finger test, digit collateral ligamentous stress test, elbow collateral ligaments, Finklestein test, Froment's sign, lateral and medial epicondylitis test, oblique retinacular ligament test, Phalen's test]**

Mobility

Cambridge CA. Range-of-motion measurements of the hand. In: Hunter JM, Schneider LH, Macklin EJ, Callahan AD, eds. *Rehabilitation of the Hand: Surgery and Therapy.* St. Louis, Mo: CV Mosby Co; 1990:82–92.

LaStayo PC, Wheeler DL. Reliability of passive wrist flexion and extension goniometric measurements: a multicenter study. *Physical Therapy.* 1994;74:162–174.

Mackin EJ. The role of the hand therapist. In: Lamb DW, Hooper G, Kuczynski K, eds. *The Practice of Hand Surgery.* Boston, Mass: Blackwell Scientific Publications; 1989:659–679. **[Guidelines for Measurement from the American Society for Surgery of the Hand (all motions measured from neutral starting position)]**

Mints N, Dvir Z. Wrist complex mobility: a study of passive flexion and extension and accessory movements. *Physiotherapy Canada.* 1988;40:282–285. **[Goniometry]**

Wadsworth CT. Elbow, forearm, wrist, and hand. In: Myers RS, ed. *Saunders Manual of Physical Therapy Practice.* Philadelphia, Pa: WB Saunders Co; 1995:841–917. **[Composite ROM]**

Neurological/Sensibility

Anthony MS. Sensory evaluation. In: Clark GL, Wilgis EF, Aiello B, et al, eds. *Hand Rehabilitation: A Practical Guide*. New York, NY: Churchill Livingstone; 1993:55–72.

Mackin EJ. The role of the hand therapist. In: Lamb DW, Hooper G, Kuczynski K, eds. *The Practice of Hand Surgery*. Boston, Mass: Blackwell Scientific Publications; 1989:659–679. **[Functional tests: Moberg pickup test, point localization, and two-point discrimination. Modality tests: test pain, temperature, light touch (Semmes–Weinstein monofilaments), and deep pressure. Objective tests: nerve conduction velocity and wrinkle test]**

Tomberlin JP, Saunders HD. *Evaluation, Treatment and Prevention of Musculoskeletal Disorders. Vol 2: Extremities*. Chaska, Minn: The Saunders Group; 1994:170–171. **[Pinch test, Phalen's test, Tinel's sign, Jebsen–Taylor hand function test, Minnesota rate of manipulation test, Purdue pegboard test, simulated ADL test]**

Wadsworth CT. Elbow, forearm, wrist, and hand. In: Myers RS, ed. *Saunders Manual of Physical Therapy Practice*. Philadelphia, Pa: WB Saunders Co; 1995:841–917. **[Carpal and cubital tunnels; distal ulnar tunnel. Modality tests: Tinel's sign. Objective tests: sudomotor test, wrinkle test, nerve conduction velocity test; subjective sensation: vibratory test, two-point discrimination test (static two-point discrimination, moving two-point discrimination), Semmes–Weinstein monofilament test. Functional tests: ridge sensiometer, Seddon coin test, Moberg pick-up test, Dellon modification of Moberg test. Standardized tests: Purdue pegboard test, Minnesota manual dexterity, O'Connor finger dexterity test]**

Skin

Edema

Mackin EJ. The role of the hand therapist. In: Lamb DW, Hooper G, Kuczynski K, eds. *The Practice of Hand Surgery*. Boston, Mass: Blackwell Scientific Publications; 1989:659–679. **[tape and volumetric measures]**

Mackin EF, Byron PM. Postoperative management. In: McFarlane RM, McGrouther DA, Flint MH, eds. *Dupuytren's Disease*. New York, NY: Churchill Livingstone; 1990:370. **[tape and volumetric measures]**

Strength

Hamilton GF, McDonald C, Chenier TC. Measurement of grip strength: validity and reliability of the sphygmomanometer and Jamar grip dynamometer. *Journal of Orthopaedic and Sports Physical Therapy*. 1992;16:215–219.

Mackin EF, Byron PM. Postoperative management. In: McFarlane RM, McGrouther DA, Flint MH, eds. *Dupuytren's Disease*. New York, NY: Churchill Livingstone; 1990:370. **[Grasp measurements. Finger to palm distance and fingernail to distal palmar crease]**

Wadsworth CT. Elbow, forearm, wrist, and hand. In: Myers RS, ed. *Saunders Manual of Physical Therapy Practice*. Philadelphia, Pa: WB Saunders Co; 1995:841–917. **[Power grip, precision grip, hook grip, lateral pinch, cylinder grasp, pinch strength]**

Vascular

Greathouse DG, Underwood FB, Tuttle P. Roth technique—a new approach for measuring sensory neural conduction in the median and ulnar nerves: suggestion from the field. *Physical Therapy*. 1989;69:777–779.

Tomberlin JP, Saunders HD. *Evaluation, Treatment and Prevention of Musculoskeletal Disorders. Vol 2: Extremities*. Chaska, Minn: The Saunders Group; 1994:164. **[Allen's test, modified Allen's test, volumetric measures, capillary refill]**

Wadsworth CT. Elbow, forearm, wrist, and hand. In: Myers RS, ed. *Saunders Manual of Physical Therapy Practice*. Philadelphia, Pa: WB Saunders Co; 1995:841–917. **[Allen's Test]**

TREATMENT

Burnett WR. Rehabilitation techniques for ligament injuries of the hand. *Hand Clinics*. 1992;8:803–815.

Duncan RM. Basic principles of splinting the hand. *Physical Therapy*. 1989;69:1104–1116.

Griffin JW, Newsome LS, Stralka SW, Wright PE. Reduction of chronic posttraumatic hand edema: a comparison of high voltage pulsed current, intermittent pneumatic compression, and placebo treatments. *Physical Therapy*. 1990;70:279–286.

Hunter JM, Mackin EJ. Oedema and bandaging. In: Hunter JM, Schneider LH, Mackin EJ, Callahan, AD, eds. *Rehabilitation of the Hand*. 2nd ed. St. Louis, Mo: CV Mosby Co; 1984:146.

Mackin EJ. The therapist's point of view: prevention of complications in hand therapy. *Hand Clinics*. 1986;2:429.

Mullins PAT. Management of common chronic pain problems in the hand. *Physical Therapy*. 1989;69:1050–1058.

Randall T, Portney L, Harris BA. Effects of joint mobilization on joint stiffness and active motion of the metacarpal-phalangeal joint. *Journal of Orthopaedic and Sports Physical Therapy*. 1992;16:30-36.

Sorenson MK. The edematous hand. *Physical Therapy*. 1989;69:1059–1064.

Tottenham VM. Hand therapy: a combined physical and occupational therapy approach. *Physiotherapy Canada*. 1989;41:156–157.

Wadsworth CT. Elbow, forearm, wrist, and hand. In: Myers RS, ed. *Saunders Manual of Physical Therapy Practice*. Philadelphia, Pa: WB Saunders Co; 1995:841–917.

Tendon Injuries

DESCRIPTION

Tendon injuries such as avulsion injuries, tendon lacerations, and crush injuries disrupt tendons as well as nearby soft tissues, nerve, or bone.

CAUSE

Hand injuries usually have a thermal, traction, crush, or chemical mode of injury. Burns, sudden muscular contraction against resistance, trauma, and sharp cuts can lead to tendon injury.

ASSESSMENT

Areas

- History, including occupation, hand dominance, details of injury, and psychosocial factors
- Pain
- Mobility, including active and passive range of motion (ROM), accessory motion, composite range of motion, and any fixed deformities
- Strength: compare with uninvolved hand, if applicable; power and precision
- Sensibility
- Skin and soft tissue: trophic changes, edema, temperature, condition of nails
- Joint integrity and structural deviations
- Neurological, including deep tendon reflexes and sensation
- Functional level

- Vascular

Instruments/Procedures (See References for Sources)

Functional Level
- Jebsen Test of Hand Function
- Physical Capacity Evaluation

Joint Integrity and Structural Deviations
1. orthopedic tests of the hand
   - Bunnell–Littler test
   - circle formation with tip opposition between thumb and index finger test
   - digit collateral ligamentous stress test
   - elbow collateral ligament test
   - Finklestein test
   - Froment's sign
   - lateral and medial epicondylitis test
   - lunate displacement test
   - oblique retinacular ligament test
   - retinacular test
   - trigger finger test
   - triquestrolunate test
   - ulnar snuff box test
   - Watson's test
2. photography of joint deformities

Mobility
- goniometry
- Guidelines for Measurement from the American Society for Surgery of the Hand (all motions measured from neutral starting position)

Neurological/Sensibility
- carpal and cubital tunnels
- Dellon modification of Moberg test
- distal ulnar tunnel
- Minnesota manual dexterity test
- Minnesota rate of manipulation test
- Moberg pick-up test
- nerve conduction velocity test
- O'Connor finger dexterity test
- Phalen's test
- pinch test
- point localization
- Purdue pegboard test
- ridge sensiometer
- Seddon coin test
- sensitivity to deep pressure
- sensitivity to light touch (Semmes–Weinstein monofilaments)
- sensitivity to pain

- sensitivity to temperature
- sudomotor test
- Tinel's sign
- two-point discrimination test
- vibratory test
- wrinkle test

Skin and Soft Tissue
1. edema
   - tape measure
   - volumetric measures
2. temperature
   - palpation

Strength
- grasp
- grip: sphygmomanometer and Jamar grip dynamometer
- pinch

Vascular
- Allen's test
- modified Allen's test
- capillary refill
- volumetric measures

PROBLEMS
- The pain is usually localized.
- There is usually immediate functional loss of hand usage.

TREATMENT/MANAGEMENT
Treatment depends on zone of injury. Zones of injury are divided into flexor zones, extensor zones, and the zones of the thumb.

Flexor Zones of the Hand

Zone 1: Includes the fingertips, distal interphalangeal (DIP) joint, and distal half between the DIP and proximal interphalangeal (PIP) joint

Zone 2: Includes the proximal half between the DIP and PIP joint, the PIP joint, and the metacarpal phalangeal (MCP) point to the palmar crease

Zone 3: Includes the space between the palmar crease to a line drawn across the palm at the distal point where the thumb joins the hand

Zone 4: Includes the space between the line drawn across the palm at the distal point where the thumb joins the hand to the crease at the wrist

Zone 5: Begins at the crease at the wrist up the forearm

Source. Reed K. *Quick Reference to Occupational Therapy.* Gaithersburg, Md: Aspen Publishers; 1991:266.

Extensor Zones of the Hand

Zone 1: Distal interphalangeal joints (DIP) of digits 2 to 5
Zone 2: Space between the DIP and proximal interphalangeal (PIP) joints of digits 2 to 5
Zone 3: PIP joints of digits 2 to 5
Zone 4: Space between the PIP joints and the metacarpal phalangeal (MCP) joints of digits 2 to 5
Zone 5: MCP joints
Zone 6: Space between the MCP joints and the carpal bones of the wrist
Zone 7: Carpal bones of the wrist

Source: Reed K. *Quick Reference to Occupational Therapy.* Gaithersburg, Md: Aspen Publishers; 1991:267.

Zones of the Thumb

Zone T1: Interphalangeal (IP) joint
Zone T2: Space between the IP joint and the metacarpal phalangeal (MCP) joint
Zone T3: MCP joint
Zone T4: Space between the MCP joint and the carpal bones of the wrist
Zone T5: Area of the carpal bones on the thumb

Source: Reed K. *Quick Reference to Occupational Therapy.* Gaithersburg, Md: Aspen Publishers; 1991:267.

Rehabilitation of the flexor tendons after surgery is described below.

Rehabilitation of Flexor Tendons after Surgical Repair

Time Post Surgery	Treatment
Day 0 to day 3	Elevation
Day 4 to week 3.5	Wear dorsal protective splint; passive flexion, active extension, composite and isolated joint movement 8 times every 2 hours; edema control
Week 3.5 through week 5	Switch to wrist cuff with dynamic traction or adapt splint; gentle active finger flexion, active wrist extension with finger flexion, active finger extension with wrist flexion, composite wrist and finger extension to neutral 10 times every hour
Week 6 through week 8	Discontinue splint or cuff; active wrist flexion and extension; digital blocking exercise; differential tendon gliding 12 times per hour; begin scar management; use contracture control measures as needed; consider passive wrist and digit extension or extension splinting (week 7)

Week 9 through week 12		Progress to resistive exercise and work therapy

Source: Reprinted with permission from CT Wadsworth, Elbow, Forearm, Wrist, and Hand, in *Saunders Manual of Physical Therapy Practice*, pp. 841–917, © 1995, WB Saunders Co.

Rehabilitation of the extensor tendons after surgery is described below.

Rehabilitation of Extensor Tendons after Surgical Repair

Zone	Time	Treatment
1, 2	Day 0 to day 3	Elevation
	Day 4 through week 7	Splint DIP joint in hyperextension (0 to 10 degrees)
	Week 8 through week 9	Decrease use of splint, gentle active DIP flexion (20 to 40 degrees)
	Week 10 through week 11	Full ROM and function
3, 4	Day 0 through day 3	Elevate hand
	Day 4 through week 6	Splint PIP joint (0 degrees); start DIP joint extension for central slip injury
	Week 7 through week 8	Decrease use of splint, begin gentle active PIP joint flexion and extension (MP joint in extension)
	Week 9 through week 10	Isolated PIP active extension with increasing resistance
5,6	Day 0 through day 3	Elevate hand
	Day 4 through week 4	Volar forearm-hand splint (40 degrees wrist extension, 40 degrees wrist flexion, IP joint extension)
	Week 4	Active MP joint exercise, "clawing" exercise
	Week 5	Put splint in neutral position for 2 weeks; wrist ROM with finger extension, intrinsic muscle and "clawing" exercise
	Week 7 through week 9	Begin light resistive exercise
	Week 10 through week 11	Begin progressive resistive exercise
7	Day 0 through day 3	Elevate hand
	Day 4 through week 4	Volar forearm-hand splint (40 degrees wrist extension, 40 degrees MP flexion, IP joint extension if tendons injured)
	Week 4	Wrist flexion exercise (fingers extended) and finger flexion (wrist extended)
	Week 5 through week 6	Use splint with heavy activity; begin composite flexion and extension of wrist and fingers
	Week 7 through week 9	Begin light resistive exercise
	Week 10 through week 11	Begin progressive resistive exercise
Thumb	Day 0 through day 3	Elevate hand

1,2	Day 4 through week 6	Splint at IP joint (0 degrees)
	Week 7 through 8	Begin gentle active exercise
	Week 7 through week 9	Decrease use of splint
	Week 9 through week 11	Progress to full ROM and function
Thumb	Day 0 through day 3	Elevate hand
3,4	Day 4 through week 7	Splint MP joint (0 degrees) and wrist (30 degrees)
	Week 5 through week 6	Begin ROM
	Week 7 through week 8	Progress to full ROM and function
Thumb 5	Day 0 through day 3	Elevate hand
	Day 4 through week 4	Splint wrist in extension (40 degrees) and thumb extended
	Week 5 through week 6	Start active ROM
	Week 7 through week 8	Progress to full ROM and function

Source: Based on Wadsworth CT, Elbow, forearm, wrist, and hand. In: Myers RS, ed. *Saunders Manual of Physical Therapy Practice.* Philadelphia, Pa: WB Saunders Co; 1995:841–917.

PRECAUTIONS/CONTRAINDICATIONS
• Do not overstress healing tendon.

DESIRED OUTCOME/PROGNOSIS
• The client will return to normal function.

REFERENCES

ASSESSMENTS
Flesch P, Macchiaverna J. Hand evaluation form for effective treatment of hand injuries. *Clinical Management in Physical Therapy.* 1982;2:28.
Mitchell SS. An adjunctive method for wrist and hand assessment. *Clinical Management in Physical Therapy.* 1984;1:44.
Tubiana R, Thomine JM, Mackin E. *Examination of the Hand and Wrist.* New York, NY: CV Mosby Co; 1996.

Functional Level

Jebsen Test of Hand Function
Hackel ME, Wolfe GA, Bang SM, et al. Changes in hand function in the aging adult as determined by the Jebsen Test of Hand Function. *Physical Therapy.* 1992;72:373–377.
Jebsen RH, Taylor N, Trieschman RB, et al. An objective and standardized test of hand function. *Archives of Physical Medicine and Rehabilitation.* 1969;50:311–319.
Lynch KB, Bridle MJ. Validity of the Jebsen–Taylor Hand Function Test in predicting activities of daily living. *Occupational Therapy Journal of Research.* 1989;9:316–318.

Physical Capacity Evaluation
Bear-Lehman J, Abreu BC. Evaluating the hand: issues in reliability and validity. *Physical Therapy.* 1989;69:1025–1033.

Bell-Krotoski JA, Breger DE, Beach RB. Application of biomechanics for evaluation of the hand. In: Hunter JM, Schneider LH, Macklin EJ, Callahan AD, eds. *Rehabilitation of the Hand: Surgery and Therapy.* St. Louis, Mo: CV Mosby Co; 1990:139–166. **[Biomechanics]**

Wadsworth CT. Elbow, forearm, wrist, and hand. In: Myers RS, ed. *Saunders Manual of Physical Therapy Practice.* Philadelphia, Pa: WB Saunders Co; 1995:841–917.

Joint Integrity and Structural Deviations

Rothstein JM, Roy SH, Wolf SL. *The Rehabilitation Specialist's Handbook.* Philadelphia, Pa: FA Davis Co; 1991:126–127. **[Froment's sign intrinsic-plus test]**

Tomberlin JP, Saunders HD. *Evaluation, Treatment and Prevention of Musculoskeletal Disorders. Vol 2: Extremities.* Chaska, Minn: The Saunders Group; 1994:164. **[Finkelstein's test, trigger finger test, Bunnell–Littler test, retinacular test, Watson's test, triquestrolunate test, ulnar snuff box test, lunate displacement test]**

Wadsworth CT. Elbow, forearm, wrist, and hand. In: Myers RS, ed. *Saunders Manual of Physical Therapy Practice.* Philadelphia, Pa: WB Saunders Co; 1995:841–917. **[Bunnell–Littler test, circle formation with tip opposition between thumb and index finger test, digit collateral ligamentous stress test, elbow collateral ligaments, Finklestein test, Froment's sign, lateral and medial epicondylitis test, oblique retinacular ligament test, Phalen's test]**

Mobility

Cambridge CA. Range-of-motion measurements of the hand. In: Hunter JM, Schneider LH, Macklin EJ, Callahan AD. *Rehabilitation of the Hand: Surgery and Therapy.* St. Louis, Mo: CV Mosby Co; 1990:82–92.

LaStayo PC, Wheeler DL. Reliability of passive wrist flexion and extension goniometric measurements: a multicenter study. *Physical Therapy.* 1994;74:162–174.

Mackin EJ. The role of the hand therapist. In: Lamb DW, Hooper G, Kuczynski K, eds. *The Practice of Hand Surgery.* Boston, Mass: Blackwell Scientific Publications; 1989:659–679. **[Guidelines for Measurement from the American Society for Surgery of the Hand (all motions measured from neutral starting position)]**

Mints N, Dvir Z. Wrist complex mobility: a study of passive flexion and extension and accessory movements. *Physiotherapy Canada.* 1988;40:282–285. **[Goniometry]**

Wadsworth CT. Elbow, forearm, wrist, and hand. In: Myers RS, ed. *Saunders Manual of Physical Therapy Practice.* Philadelphia, Pa: WB Saunders Co; 1995:841–917. **[Composite ROM]**

Neurological/Sensibility

Anthony MS. Sensory evaluation. In: Clark GL, Wilgis EF, Aiello B, et al, eds. *Hand Rehabilitation: A Practical Guide.* New York, NY: Churchill Livingstone; 1993:55–72.

Mackin EJ. The role of the hand therapist. In: Lamb DW, Hooper G, Kuczynski K, eds. *The Practice of Hand Surgery.* Boston, Mass: Blackwell Scientific Publications; 1989:659–679. **[Functional tests: Moberg pick-up test, point localization, and two-point discrimination. Modality tests: test pain, temperature, light touch (Semmes–Weinstein monofilaments), and deep pressure. Objective tests: nerve conduction velocity and wrinkle test]**

Tomberlin JP, Saunders HD. *Evaluation, Treatment and Prevention of Musculoskeletal Disorders. Vol 2: Extremities.* Chaska, Minn: The Saunders Group; 1994:170–171. **[Pinch test, Phalen's test, Tinel's sign, Jebsen–Taylor Hand Function Test, Minnesota rate of manipulation test, Purdue pegboard test, simulated ADL test]**

Wadsworth CT. Elbow, forearm, wrist, and hand. In: Myers RS, ed. *Saunders Manual of Physical Therapy Practice.* Philadelphia, Pa: WB Saunders Co; 1995:841–917. **[Carpal and cubital tunnels; distal ulnar tunnel. Modality tests: Tinel's sign. Objective tests: sudomotor test, wrinkle test, nerve conduction velocity test; subjective sensation: vibratory test, two-point discrimination test (static two-point dis-**

crimination, moving two-point discrimination), Semmes–Weinstein monofilament test. Functional tests: ridge sensiometer, Seddon coin test, Moberg pick-up test, Dellon modification of Moberg test. Standardized tests: Purdue pegboard test, Minnesota manual dexterity, O'Connor finger dexterity test]

Skin

Edema
Mackin EJ. The role of the hand therapist. In: Lamb DW, Hooper G, Kuczynski K, eds. *The Practice of Hand Surgery*. Boston, Mass: Blackwell Scientific Publications; 1989:659–679. [tape and volumetric measures]

Mackin EF, Byron PM. Postoperative management. In: McFarlane RM, McGrouther DA, Flint MH, eds. *Dupuytren's Disease*. New York, NY: Churchill Livingstone; 1990:370. [tape and volumetric measures]

Strength
Hamilton GF, McDonald C, Chenier TC. Measurement of grip strength: validity and reliability of the sphygmomanometer and Jamar grip dynamometer. *Journal of Orthopaedic and Sports Physical Therapy*. 1992;16:215–219.

Mackin EF, Byron PM. Postoperative management. In: McFarlane RM, McGrouther DA, Flint MH, eds. *Dupuytren's Disease*. New York, NY: Churchill Livingstone; 1990:370. [Grasp measurements. Finger-to-palm distance and fingernail to distal palmar crease]

Wadsworth CT. Elbow, forearm, wrist, and hand. In: Myers RS, ed. *Saunders Manual of Physical Therapy Practice*. Philadelphia, Pa: WB Saunders Co; 1995:841–917. [Power grip, precision grip, hook grip, lateral pinch, cylinder grasp, pinch strength]

Vascular
Greathouse DG, Underwood FB, Tuttle P. Roth technique—a new approach for measuring sensory neural conduction in the median and ulnar nerves: suggestion from the field. *Physical Therapy*. 1989;69:777–779.

Tomberlin JP, Saunders HD. *Evaluation, Treatment and Prevention of Musculoskeletal Disorders. Vol 2: Extremities*. Chaska, Minn: The Saunders Group; 1994:164. [Allen's test, modified Allen's test, volumetric measures, capillary refill]

Wadsworth CT. Elbow, forearm, wrist, and hand. In: Myers RS, ed. *Saunders Manual of Physical Therapy Practice*. Philadelphia, Pa: WB Saunders Co; 1995:841–917. [Allen's test]

TREATMENT
Brandsma JW, Brand PW. Claw finger correction: considerations in choice of technique. *Journal of Hand Surgery*. 1992;17B:615–621.

Dovelle S, Heeter PK. The Washington regimen: rehabilitation of the hand following flexor tendon injuries. *Physical Therapy*. 1989;69:1034–1040.

Duncan RM. Basic principles of splinting the hand. *Physical Therapy*. 1989;69:1104–1116.

Durand LG, Ionescu GD, Banchard M, et al. Design and preliminary evaluation of a portable instrument for assisting physiotherapists and occupational therapists in the rehabilitation of the hand. *Journal of Rehabilitation Research and Development*. 1989;26:2:47–54.

Evans RB. Clinical application of controlled stress to the healing extensor tendon: a review of 112 cases. *Physical Therapy*. 1989;69:1041–1049.

Griffin JW, Newsome LS, Stralka SW, Wright PE. Reduction of chronic posttraumatic hand edema: a comparison of high voltage pulsed current, intermittent pneumatic compression, and placebo treatments. *Physical Therapy*. 1990;70:279–286.

Hayne CR, Orme JM. Physiotherapy for the severely traumatised hand. *Physiotherapy*. 1984;70:384–387.

Hunter JM, Mackin EJ. Oedema and bandaging. In: Hunter JM, Schneider LH, Mackin EJ, et al. eds. *Rehabilitation of the Hand*. 2nd ed. St. Louis, Mo: CV Mosby Co; 1984:146.

Hunter JM, Schneider LH, Mackin EJ, et al, eds. *Tendon Surgery in the Hand.* St. Louis, Mo: CV Mosby Co; 1987.

Jaeger SH, Mackin EJ. Primary care of the flexor tendons. In: Hunter JM, Schneider LH, Mackin EJ, et al., eds. *Rehabilitation of the Hand,* 2nd ed. St. Louis, Mo: CV Mosby Co; 1984:261.

Mackin EJ. The therapist's point of view: prevention of complications in hand therapy. *Hand Clinics.* 1986;2:429.

Mackin EJ, Byron PM. The role of the physical therapist. In: Lamb DW, Hooper G, Kuczynski K, eds. *The Practice of Hand Surgery.* Boston, Mass: Blackwell Scientific Publications; 1989:659–680.

Moran CA. Anatomy of the hand. *Physical Therapy.* 1989;69:1007–1013.

Morey KR, Watson AH. Team approach to treatment of the posttraumatic stiff hand: a case report. *Physical Therapy.* 1986;66:225–228.

Mullins PAT. Management of common chronic pain problems in the hand. *Physical Therapy.* 1989;69:1050–1058.

Parry CBW. Helping hands: rehabilitation in hand surgery. *Physiotherapy.* 1983;69:345–369.

Randall T, Portney L, Harris BA. Effects of joint mobilization on joint stiffness and active motion of the metacarpal-phalangeal joint. *Journal of Orthopaedic and Sports Physical Therapy.* 1992;16:30–36.

Robbins F, Reece T. Hand rehabilitation after great toe transfer from thumb reconstruction. *Archives of Physical Medicine and Rehabilitation.* 1985;66:109–112.

Sorenson MK. The edematous hand. *Physical Therapy.* 1989;69:1059–1064.

Tottenham VM. Hand therapy: a combined physical and occupational therapy approach. *Physiotherapy Canada.* 1989;41:156–157.

Wadsworth CT. Elbow, forearm, wrist, and hand. In: Myers RS, ed. *Saunders Manual of Physical Therapy Practice.* Philadelphia, Pa: WB Saunders Co; 1995:841–917.

Wilson RL, Reynolds CC. Joint stiffness. In: McFarlane RM, ed. *Unsatisfactory Results in Hand Surgery.* New York, NY: Churchill Livingstone; 1987:24–39.

Chapter 6
Infectious Disease Conditions

- HIV

Human Immunodeficiency Virus (HIV) Infection

DESCRIPTION

HIV is an infection resulting from a retrovirus that can lead to a spectrum of clinical manifestions. The spectrum ranges from being an asymptomatic carrier to having a debilitating, ultimately fatal, disorder. Acquired immunodeficiency syndrome (AIDS) is a secondary immunodeficiency syndrome at the extreme end of the HIV infection clinical presentations. AIDS can lead to a variety of symptoms, including infections, malignancies, and neurological dysfunction. There have been clients who have recovered from AIDS.

CAUSE

A retrovirus named human immunodeficiency virus (HIV); previously named human T-cell lymphotropic virus type III [HTLV-III], lymphadenopathy-associated virus [LAV], and AIDS-associated retrovirus [ARV]. HIV-1 and HIV-2, two related viruses, have also been discovered to cause AIDS. Transmission of the virus requires contact with bodily fluids that contain the infected cells or plasma. These bodily fluids, or exudates, include blood, breast milk, saliva, semen, and vaginal secretions. Documented transmission via saliva or droplets of nuclei that would be produced from coughing has not been established. In pregnant women, HIV can be transmitted through the placenta or perinatally.

ASSESSMENT

Areas
- History, including history of opportunistic infections and nature of social support system
- Pain
- Mobility, including joint active range of motion (ROM)
- Posture
- Gait, including any deviations
- Neurological: reflexes, sensation (light touch, pain, and temperature), proprioception, position, balance, cognition, vision, bowel and bladder function
- Cardiovascular/pulmonary: resting heart rates, target heart rate, blood pressure, MET level, and overall level of fitness
- Functional level: activities of daily living (ADLs) and possibly ability to roll, transfer, use assistive devices
- Special tests to which the PT may or may not have access

Instruments/Procedures (See References for Sources)

Special Test to Which the PT May or May Not Have Access
- body composition: percent body fat measurement
- electrophysiologic testing

Pain
- visual analogue scale

PROBLEMS
- The client with neuromuscular manifestations of HIV may have peripheral neuropathy or myopathy.

- The client with AIDS dementia complex may show motor symptoms of loss of balance and lower extremity weakness and may report "clumsiness." This can lead to a decrease in joint mobility, difficulty ambulating, and deconditioning.
- The client may have incontinence, headaches, diminished cognition, aphasia, seizures, hemiparesis, hemisensory loss, difficulty breathing, visual disturbances, incoordination, cranial neuropathies, and pain.
- The client may have various skin problems. Some include Karposi's sarcoma lesions, herpes simplex, herpes zoster, and psoriasis.
- The client may be depressed or have other mood disorder.
- Client may feel "untouchable."

TREATMENT/MANAGEMENT
Treatment involves
- working with a team of specialists that can include physicians, pharmacists, psychologists, recreational therapists, social workers, speech-language pathologists, AIDS project volunteers, dieticians, family members/significant others, nurses, occupational therapists, and community pastoral care services
- educating both professionals and client about the disease and community resources, as needed

Fitness
- Promote optimal fitness level with strength and conditioning activities.
- Maintain a flexible approach to treatment depending on client's stamina.
- Teach clients energy conservation measures, work simplification techniques, and stress management.

Emotions
- Give client "permission" to express feelings with statements like "It is common to be depressed about receiving a diagnosis of HIV."
- Express empathy through positive appropriate touch.

Function
- Assist client in gaining as much independence in function as possible. Provide ADL intervention and adaptive equipment as indicated. Assess and fit with splints, braces, or adaptive equipment. Provide mobility training.

Gait
- Provide gait training with assistive devices as needed.

Pain
- Assess for use of modalities to diminish pain. Consider use of transcutaneous electrical nerve stimulation (TENS), microcurrent electrical nerve stimulation (MENS), aquatics, relaxation exercises, and biofeedback for pain management. See precautions.

Joint Mobility
- Increase joint motion with stretching techniques, therapeutic exercise, postural training, functional movement patterns, and joint mobilization.

Central Nervous System
- Provide perceptual-motor training.

- Consider use of facilitation and inhibition techniques for abnormal muscle tone.

Respiratory
- Instruct in breathing exercises.
- Provide postural drainage and coughing techniques (except with *Pneumocystis carinii* pneumonia [PCP]).

Skin
- Promote mobility.
- Prevention is a key component of treatment. Use pressure-relieving devices, proper skin care, and good nutrition and hydration.
- Instruct client and caregivers in proper positioning.
- Use whirlpool for wound care as indicated. Try to minimize use due to force. See precautions.
- Consider use of occlusive dressings.

PRECAUTIONS/CONTRAINDICATIONS
In general:
- A client with hypersensitivity may not be able to tolerate electrotherapy, such as TENS. There is one report of reactivation of herpes simplex following TENS. Use modalities judiciously, and monitor results.
- Therapists should practice universal precautions if in contact with mucous membranes or other surfaces in contact with bodily fluids. Precautions are indicated for any contact with blood and body fluids from any client. See Centers for Disease Control, *Precautions* (in references) for latest guidelines.
- Generally sharp or chemical debridement is contraindicated when T-cell count is under 50 mm^3 or platelet count is under 50,000 mm^3. Sharp debridement is contraindicated when neutrophil count is at 900 mm^3 or higher. See Tucker, "Wound care" (in references) for specific guidelines.

Use of Whirlpools
- Follow guidelines from Center for Disease Control (in references) for current standards.
- Wash hands and use gloves both before putting wound area in whirlpool and immediately after.
- Use other protective devices, such as mask, gown, and goggles, as directed by guidelines.
- When client is out of whirlpool wear sterile gloves for wound care.
- Discard disposable items in plastic bag and seal properly.

To Disinfect
- An agent such as sodium hypochlorite at 500 to 5000 ppm has been suggested to inactivate HIV rapidly. Consult manufacturer for recommendations. Sterilize as for any other infections. See references for additional guidelines.

DESIRED OUTCOME/PROGNOSIS
- The client will have a decrease in pain.
- The client will increase or maintain ROM.
- The client will increase or maintain normal muscle strength and movement patterns.
- The client will be functionally independent in ADLs.
- The client will ambulate independently with normalized gait pattern.

- The client will breath efficiently.
- The client will have intact skin with no breakdown.
  HIV is an ultimately fatal disorder. Some clients have recovered from AIDS.

REFERENCES

ASSESSMENT

Galantino ML, Dellagatta R. HIV evaluation form. *Clinical Management in Physical Therapy*. 1990;10:6:30–36.

Goodman C, Snyder TE. *Differential Diagnosis in Physical Therapy*. Philadelphia, Pa; WB Saunders Co; 1990:332, 337, 357, 362–363.

Pain

Visual Analogue Scale (VAS)

Dixon JS, Bird HA. Reproducibility along a 10 cm. vertical visual analogue scale. *Annals of the Rheumatic Diseases*. 1981;40:87–89.

Downie WW, Leatham PA, Rhind VM. Studies with pain rating scales. *Annals of the Rheumatic Diseases*. 1978;37:378–381.

Langely GB, Sheppeard H. The visual analogue scale: its use in pain measurement. *Rheumatology International*. 1985:5:145–148.

Scott J, Huskisson EC. Vertical or horizontal visual analogue scales. *Annals of the Rheumatic Diseases*. 1979;38:560.

Special Tests to Which the PT May or May Not Have Access

Electrophysiologic Testing

Galantino ML, McReynolds M. Managing pain in HIV. *Clinical Management in Physical Therapy*. 1992;12:6:66–72.

TREATMENT

Anonymous. Public health service guidelines for counseling and antibody testing to prevent HIV infection and AIDS. *MMWR* 1987;31:509–515 Aug. 14.

Anonymous. Technical guidance on HIV counseling. Center for Disease Control and Prevention. *MMWR* 1993;42:RR-2:11-17 Jan. 15.

Brissette M, Iafolla B, Lu M. PTs and AIDS knowledge. *Clinical Management in Physical Therapy*. 1990; 10:1:27–29.

Butz L. Outpatient intervention in HIV. *Clinical Management in Physical Therapy*. 1992;12:6:51–53.

Coyne C. "It need not be this way": AIDS and HIV. *Clinical Management in Physical Therapy*. 1992;12:6:51–53.

Dike L. Physiotherapists' perceptions of risk of HIV transmission in clinical practice. *Physical Therapy*. 1993;79:3:178–185.

Galantino ML. An overview of the AIDS patient. *Clinical Management in Physical Therapy*. 1987;7:2:12–13.

Galantino ML. Pain management and neuromuscular reeducation for the HIV patient. *AIDS Patient Care*. 1991;5:2:81–84.

Galantino ML. *Clinical Assessment and Treatment of HIV: Rehabilitation of a Chronic Illness*. Thorofare, NJ: Slack; 1992.

Galantino ML, Dellagatta R. HIV evaluation form. *Clinical Management in Physical Therapy*. 1990;10:6:30–36.

Galantino ML, Levy JK. HIV infection: neurological implications for rehabilitation. *Clinical Management in Physical Therapy.* 1988;8:1:6, 8–10, 12–13.

Galantino ML, McReynolds M. The ever-changing challenge of HIV. *Clinical Management in Physical Therapy.* 1992;12:6:28–33.

Galantino ML, McReynolds M. Managing pain in HIV. *Clinical Management in Physical Therapy.* 1992;12:6:66–72.

Galantino ML, Pizzi M. Occupational and physical therapy for persons with HIV disease and their caregivers. *Journal of Home Health Care Practice.* 1991;3:3:46–57.

Harris-Copp M. The HIV-infected child: a critical need for physical therapy. Part 2. *Clinical Management in Physical Therapy.* 1988;8:1:16–19.

Hart M. More than just an infection: HIV. *Clinical Management in Physical Therapy.* 1992;12:6:42–50.

Hart M, Rogers EA. Acquired immunodeficiency syndrome. In: Fletcher GF, ed. *Rehabilitation Medicine: Contemporary Clinical Perspectives.* Philadelphia, Pa: Lea & Febiger; 1992:335–365.

Held SL. The effects of an AIDs education program on the knowledge and attitudes of a physical therapy class. *Physical Therapy.* 1993;73:156–164.

Lang C. Community physiotherapy for people with HIV/AIDS. *Physiotherapy.* 1993;79:163–167.

Lang C. Experience of community physiotherapy for people with HIV infection. *British Journal of Occupational Therapy.* 1993;56:213–216.

Lang C. Using relaxation and exercise as part of the care of people living with HIV/AIDS. *Physiotherapy.* 1993;79:379–384.

Law V, Baldwin C. Nutritional support in HIV disease. *Physiotherapy.* 1993;79:394–399.

McClure J. The role of physiotherapy in HIV and AIDS. *Physiotherapy.* 1993;79:388–393.

Okoli U, King JD. Attitude towards people with HIV and AIDs. *Physiotherapy.* 1993;79:168–173.

Pizzi M, Hinds-Harris M. Infants and children with HIV infection: perspectives in occupational and physical therapy. *Occupational Therapy in Health Care.* 1990;7:103–123.

Reynolds JP. The polio of the 21st century: HIV and AIDS. *Clinical Management in Physical Therapy.* 1992;12:6:10.

Rogers EA. The interdisciplinary HIV team. *Clinical Management in Physical Therapy.* 1992;12:6:38–41.

Romani-Ruby C. HIV: ethical considerations. *Clinical Management in Physical Therapy.* 1992;12:6:62–65.

Rosensweet E, Fink CJ. Physical therapy for the patient with acquired immunodeficiency syndrome. *Clinics in Podiatric Medicine and Surgery.* 1992;9:883–893.

Sim J, Purtilo RB. An ethical analysis of physical therapists' duty to treat persons who have AIDS: homosexual patients as a test case. *Physical Therapy.* 1991;71:650–655.

Smith K. Clinical features of HIV disease. *Physiotherapy.* 1993;79:375–378.

Smith K. HIV and the AIDS epidemic. *Physiotherapy.* 1993;79:3:159–162.

Smith K. HIV and the individual. *Physiotherapy.* 1993;79:371–375.

Spence DW, Galantino ML, Mossberg KA, Zimmerman, SO. Effect on muscle function and anthropometry of a select AIDS population. *Archives of Physical Medicine and Rehabilitation.* 1990;71:646–648.

Tucker RS. Wound care in patients with HIV. *Clinical Management in Physical Therapy.* 1992;12:6:73–77.

Chapter 7

Injuries

- Dislocation
- Fractures
- Head injury
- Lower extremity amputation
- Paraplegia
- Quadriplegia

Dislocation

DESCRIPTION

When a joint is dislocated, the articular surfaces are totally displaced. The joint structures that can be affected include the capsule, ligaments, tendons, bursae, nonarticular cartilage, and synovial fluid. The inflammation resulting from injury is usually acute, subacute, or chronic. The inflammatory process may also lead to fibrous adhesions. A client can also have a chronically dislocating joint in which there is no acute ligamentous injury. The shoulder is the most commonly dislocated joint in adults, followed by the elbow. In children, the elbow is the most commonly dislocated joint.

Joint displacement can also occur to a lesser degree. Subluxation is a partial joint separation possibly related to damage of the capsule and ligaments.

CAUSE

Dislocations are usually a result of disruptive forces from a long-lever-arm mechanism of injury. With smaller joints, dislocation is usually due to the approximation of surrounding tissues.

ASSESSMENT

Areas
- History
- Pain
- Posture, including symmetry and effect of injury on posture
- Skin and soft tissue: edema, temperature, color changes
- Gait, if applicable
- Joint integrity and structural deviations: crepitus, deformity, laxity
- Strength, including voluntary movements
- Mobility: active range of motion (ROM) within tolerance
- Functional level, including independence in activities of daily living (ADLs)
- Special tests to which the PT may or may not have access

Instruments/Procedures (See References for Sources)

Special Tests to Which the PT May or May Not Have Access
- subluxation measuring device
- x-rays

PROBLEMS
- The joint can appear misshapen.
- There is usually a limitation of movement.
- There can be muscle spasm.
- The client usually reports a tearing sensation.
- The client usually reports intense pain initially that later eases.
- There is usually a loss of function, and there may be muscle atrophy.

TREATMENT/MANAGEMENT
- Instruct client on proper positioning to avoid edema due to a dependent position.
- Initial treatment usually involves reduction of the dislocation, which may have already been performed before the client sees a therapist. This is usually followed by a period of immobilization. Provide sling, traction, or bed rest as needed.
- Consider use of early mobilization with passive ROM and active assistive ROM as indicated within pain tolerance and following any precautions due to direction of dislocation. Instruct client in movements allowed to prevent adhesions and atrophy.
- Progress to neuromuscular facilitation techniques, active movement, and resistive exercise.
- Modalities can include cold therapy, ultrasound, shortwave diathermy, and infrared.

PRECAUTIONS/CONTRAINDICATIONS
- Be aware of complications that can accompany dislocation, including fractures and injury to nerves, blood vessels, and surrounding tissues.
- See Appendix C for precautions when using physical agents and modalities.

DESIRED OUTCOME/PROGNOSIS
- There will be a reduction of the joint dislocation.
- The client will experience a decrease in symptoms.
- There will be a maintenance of allowable movement and prevention of atrophy.
- The client will return to normal function.
  Surgical repair may be indicated when there is a complete ligamentous tear.

REFERENCES

ASSESSMENT

Special Tests to Which the PT May or May Not Have Access
Hayes KW, Sullivan JE. Reliability of a new device used to measure shoulder subluxation. *Physical Therapy.* 1989;69:762–767.

TREATMENT
Bohannon RW. Effect of electrical stimulation to the vastus medialis muscle in a patient with chronically dislocating patellae. *Physical Therapy.* 1983;63:1445–1447.

Magarey M, Jones M. Clinical diagnosis and management of minor shoulder instability. *Australian Journal of Physiotherapy.* 1992;38:269–280.

McLeod WD, Andrews JR. Mechanism of shoulder injuries. *Physical Therapy.* 1986;66:1901–1904.

Myers RS, ed. *Saunders Manual of Physical Therapy Practice.* Philadelphia, Pa: WB Saunders Co; 1995:823, 824, 886, 897–900.

Ruys EC. Trochanteric girdle to prevent hip dislocation in standing: suggestion from the field. *Physical Therapy.* 1988;68:226–227.

Smith JJ. Compression bandage for shoulder subluxation. *Clinical Management in Physical Therapy.* 1987;7:6:36.

Smith RL, Brunolli J. Shoulder kinesthesia after anterior glenohumeral joint dislocation. *Physical Therapy.* 1989;69:106–112.

Wilk KE, Andrews JR. *Current Concepts in the Treatment of Shoulder Instability.* LaCrosse, Wis: Orthopaedic Physical Therapy Home Study Course; 1991.

Fractures

DESCRIPTION

A fracture is defined as discontinuity of bone structure. A fracture that occurs in an otherwise normal bone can be classified, in terms of the relationship of the fracture fragments to the external environment, as *closed* when the skin is intact or open (also called *compound*) when the skin has been injured.

CAUSE

A fracture can be caused by pathology or by trauma.
- *Pathological causes* include congenital defects, dysplasias, infective disease, metabolic disease, and neoplasms.
- *Traumatic causes* include direct or indirect force. Muscular force can also lead to fracture due to avulsion of the muscular attachment to the bone.

Stress fractures are also common and are associated with inadequate training and musculoskeletal malalignment.

ASSESSMENT

Areas
- History
- Pain
- Posture, including symmetry, effect of injury on posture
- Skin and soft tissue: edema, temperature, color changes
- Gait, if applicable—e.g., ambulation outcome after hip fracture
- Joint integrity and structural deviations: crepitus, deformity, laxity
- Strength, including voluntary movements
- Mobility, including active range of motion (ROM) within tolerance and precautions
- Functional level, including independence in activities of daily living (ADLs)
- Special tests to which the PT may or may not have access

Instruments/Procedures (See References for Sources)

Classifications
- Salter's fracture classification

Functional Level
- functional outcomes after hip fracture
- Harris Hip Score

Gait
- ambulation outcomes after hip fracture

Mobility
- passive stiffness of the ankle

Special Tests to Which the PT May or May Not Have Access
- acetabular contact pressure testing
- ultrasound

PROBLEMS
In general:
- The client usually has pain and tenderness.
- There is usually a loss of function or abnormal movement.
- There may be swelling or hemorrhage.
- There may be crepitus.
- There is usually deformity.

In the case of stress fracture:
- The client usually has extreme pain at site of injury.
- The client usually has skin irritation at site of injury.
- The client usually reports relief of pain with rest.

TREATMENT/MANAGEMENT
- After the fracture has been properly immobilized, which usually occurs before the client reaches therapy, treatment focuses on restoration and preservation of function.
- Provide modalities for pain reduction such as transcutaneous electrical nerve stimulation (TENS), ice, ultrasound, or moist heat.
- Instruct in gait training with assistive devices such as crutches, as indicated.
- Instruct in respiratory care for clients at risk for respiratory problems, such as clients with a thoracic area injury or spinal cord injury.
- During the immobilization period, consider the following:
  1. Encourage movement of noninvolved joints.
  2. Use isometric exercises for joint where movement is contraindicated.
  3. Encourage independence in ADLs.
  4. Instruct client in signs of proper use of cast/splint.
- When full mobilization is allowed, consider the following:
  1. Provide strengthening exercises for muscles, using resistive exercises and proprioceptive neuromuscular facilitation (PNF) patterns with resistance.
  2. Provide training in restoration of function.
  3. Provide mobilization as indicated with exercise, passive mobilization, and aquatic therapy.
  4. Instruct client in care of skin after cast/splint is removed.

PRECAUTIONS/CONTRAINDICATIONS
- Stress fracture injury may not appear on x-ray until 2 to 3 weeks after onset of symptoms.
- Remain alert for local and generalized complications affecting skin, viscera, bone, joints, muscles, tendons, nerves, and arteries.
- Local complications can include, but are not limited to, the following: lacerations, spinal cord injury, delayed union, avascular necrosis, infection, Sudek's atrophy, myositis ossificans, neuropraxia, thrombosis, and impaired arterial perfusion.
- General complications can include, but are not limited to, the following: fat or pulmonary embolism and venous thrombosis.

Signs of Impaired Arterial Perfusion

- Pain
- Pallor
- Paralysis
- Paresthesia
- Pulselessness

Source: Reprinted with permission from JM Lee, *Aids to Physiotherapy*, p. 103, © 1988, Churchill Livingstone, Inc.

PROGNOSIS/OUTCOME
- The client will preserve function in noninjured areas.
- The client will restore function to injured areas.
- The client will have normal movement.

A good index of rehabilitation outcome is the recovery of independent ambulation.

In general, stress fractures may take a period of healing equal to the period of symptoms.

REFERENCES

Classifications
Rothstein JM, Roy SH, Wolf SL. *The Rehabilitation Specialist's Handbook.* Philadelphia, Pa: FA Davis Co; 1991:45–46. **[Salter's fracture classification]**

EVALUATION
McGarvey CL. Effect of a thermoplastic orthosis in the rehabilitation of a patient with a scapular fracture. *Physical Therapy.* 1983;63:1289–1291.

Functional Level
Barnes B, Dunovan K. Functional outcomes after hip fracture. *Physical Therapy.* 1987;67:1675–1679.

Harris WH. Traumatic arthritis of the hip after dislocation and acetabular fractures: treatment by mold arthroplasty. *Journal of Bone and Joint Surgery.* 1969;51A:737–755.

Kauffman TL. Rehabilitation outcomes after hip fracture in persons 90 years old and older. *Archives of Physical Medicine and Rehabilitation.* 1987;68:369–371.

Partridge C, Johnston M. Perceived control of recovery from physical disability: measurement and prediction. *British Journal of Clinical Psychology.* 1989;1:53–59.

Gait
Barnes B. Ambulation outcomes after hip fracture. *Physical Therapy.* 1984;64:320–321.

Mobility
Vandervoort AA, Chesworth BM, Cunningham DA, Rechnitzer PA, Paterson DH, Koval JJ. An outcome measure to quantify passive stiffness of the ankle. *Canadian Journal of Public Health.* 1992;83:(suppl 2):S19–S23.

Special Tests to Which the PT May or May Not Have Access

Acetabular Contact Pressure Testing
Givens-Heiss DL, Krebs DE, Riley PO, et al. In vivo acetabular contact pressures during rehabilitation: postacute phase. *Physical Therapy.* 1992;72:700–710.

Krebs DE, Elbaum L, Riley PO, Hodge WA, Mann RW. Exercise and gait effects on in vivo hip contact pressures. *Physical Therapy.* 1991;71:301–309.

Strickland EM, Fares M, Krebs DE, et al. In vivo acetabular contact pressures during rehabilitation: acute phase. *Physical Therapy.* 1992;72:691–699.

Ultrasound

Lowdon A. Application of ultrasound to assess stress fractures. *Physiotherapy.* 1986;72:160–161.

TREATMENT

Bartosh RA, Dugdale TW, Neilsen R. Isolated musculocutaneous nerve injury complicating closed fracture of the clavicle: a case report. *American Journal of Sports Medicine.* 1992;20:356–359.

Burns A, Park K. Proximal femoral fractures in the female patient, a controlled trial: the role of the occupational therapist and the physiotherapist. *British Journal of Occupational Therapy.* 1992;55:397–400.

Camden P, Nade S. Fracture bracing the humerus. *Injury.* 1992;23:245–248.

Davies S. Effect of continuous passive movement and plaster of paris after internal fixation of ankle fractures. *Physiotherapy.* 1991;77:516–520.

Eppinghaus CE, Bloecher J. Incidence of sciatic nerve injury with acetabular fractures: a retrospective analysis and implications for the physical therapist. *Topics in Acute Care and Trauma Rehabilitation.* 1988;3:1:53–62.

Exler Y. Patella fracture: review of the literature and five case presentations. *Journal of Orthopaedic and Sports Physical Therapy.* 1991;13:177–183.

Grashion LA. Physiotherapy management of internal fixations of the spine with the Hartshill system. *Physiotherapy.* 1989;75:364–366.

Hielema F. Ambulation outcomes after hip fracture. *Physical Therapy.* 1984;64:320–321.

Jarnlo GB, Thorngren KG. Standing balance in hip fracture patients: 20 middle-aged patients compared with 20 healthy subjects. *Acta Orthopaedica Scandinavica.* 1991;62:427–434.

Jarnlo GB, Thorngren KG. Background factors to hip fractures. *Clinical Orthopaedics and Related Research.* 1993;287:41–49.

Kauffman TL, Albright L, Wagener C. Rehabilitation outcomes after hip fracture in persons 90 years old and older. *Archives of Physical Medicine and Rehabilitation.* 1987;68:369–371.

La Torre TR, Dahners LE, Wise MW. Adaptive device for increasing transfer mobility in a patient with multiple fractures. *Physical Therapy.* 1988;68:1121–1122.

Lowdon A. Application of ultrasound to assess stress fractures. *Physiotherapy.* 1986;72:160–161.

McClure PW, Flowers KR. Treatment of limited shoulder motion: a case study based on biomechanical considerations. *Physical Therapy.* 1992;72:929–936.

McPoil TG, Cornwall MW. Rigid versus soft foot orthoses: a single subject design. *Journal of the American Podiatric Medical Association.* 1991;81:638–642.

Meeds B, Pryor GA. Early home rehabilitation for the elderly patient with hip fracture: the Peterborough Hip Fracture Scheme. *Physiotherapy.* 1990;76:75–77.

Myers RS, ed. *Saunders Manual of Physical Therapy Practice.* Philadelphia, Pa: WB Saunders Co; 1995:80, 115, 175, 632–633, 885, 906–907, 1259, 1274, 1290.

Olson K. Rehabilitation: nonacute physical therapy. In: Hansen ST, Swiontkowski MF, eds. *Orthopaedic Trauma Protocols.* New York, NY: Raven Press; 1993:65–72.

Pachter S, Flics SS. Integrated care of patients with fractured hip by nursing and physical therapy. In: Scherubel JC, ed. *Patients and Purse Strings.* New York, NY: National League for Nursing Publications; 1988:Monograph Series 20-2191:441–443.

Ringsberg K, Johnell O, Obrant K. Balance and speed of walking of women with Colles' fractures. *Physiotherapy.* 1993;79:689-692.

Saunders SR. Physical therapy management of hand fractures. *Physical Therapy.* 1989;69:1065–1076.

Short J, Upadhyay SS. Does simple traction and functional bracing affect the outcome of a fractured femur as compared with the Thomas' splint method? *Physiotherapy.* 1984;70:350–354.

Smith RL, Brunolli J. Shoulder kinesthesia after anterior glenohumeral joint dislocation. *Physical Therapy.* 1989;69:106–112.

Twomey LT, Taylor JR, Taylor MM. Unsuspected damage to lumbar zygapophyseal (facet) joints after motor vehicle accidents. *Medical Journal of Australia.* 1989;151:210–212, 215–217.

Varga TL. Acute physical therapy. In: Hansen ST, Swiontkowski MF, eds. *Orthopaedic Trauma Protocols.* New York, NY: Raven Press; 1993:61–64.

Wells PA, Lessard E. Fractures and central nervous system disorders: a survey of students' clinical experiences. *Physiotherapy.* 1986;72:234–237.

Head Injury

DESCRIPTION

Problems caused from head injury can be due to primary damage and/or secondary effects. *Primary damage* refers to the brain trauma. *Secondary effects* refers to the damage caused by metabolic and physiologic events that occur after the initial trauma.

Men are more frequently injured than women. More than 500,000 hospitalizations each year are due to a head injury. Out of that number, 70,000 clients develop disabilities that hinder a normal independent life. Traumatic head injury is the number one cause of mortality in American children and young adults, with the typical victim being 15 to 24 years old.

CAUSE

Half of all traumatic head injuries are caused by motor vehicle accidents. The remainder are attributed to falls (21%), assaults and violence (12%), and sport or recreation (10%).

ASSESSMENT

Areas

- History
- Psychosocial
- Posture, including alignment in supine, side-lying, and sitting positions
- Cognition, including behavioral status
- Communication, including any aphasia, dysarthria, or hearing problems
- Cardiovascular, including heart rate and blood pressure changes with activity
- Pulmonary, including ventilator dependency, infection, need for suctioning
- Neurological, including sensation, proprioception, and reflexes (facial avoidance, rooting, asymmetric tonic neck reflex (ATNR), Babinski, tonic labyrinthine reflex, and associated movements)
- Mobility, including passive range of motion (ROM) and trunk mobility, especially lumbar/pelvic rotation; see precautions when testing cervical ROM
- Motor function, including tone, resistance to passive movement, spontaneous movement, and volitional movement
- Balance: static and dynamic

- Skin and soft tissue: discoloration, edema, pressure sores
- Gait, if indicated; include symmetry, coordination, and any extension in standing
- Functional level, including activities of daily living (ADLs), bed mobility, and transfers
- Equipment, including use of intracranial pressure (ICP) bolt and monitor, adaptive equipment, assistive devices, splints, orthotics, or wheelchair
- Special tests to which the PT may or may not have access

Instruments/Procedures (See References for Sources)

Balance
- clinical balance testing and clinical vestibular testing (functional testing and provocation of specific deficits)

Cardiovascular
- exercise testing

Cognition
- Rancho Los Amigos Levels of Cognitive Functioning (LOCF)

Communication
- speech and language assessment

Disability
- Rappaport's Disability Rating Scale

Functional Level
- Action Research Arm Test
- Glascow Coma Scale
- Institute of Medicine index
- Level of Rehabilitation Scale (LORS-II)
- Rivermeade ADL Assessment
- World Health Organization International Classification of Impairments, Disabilities, and Handicaps

Mobility
- mobility scale
- precasting assessment

Motor Function
- dynamometer

Neurological
- brain potentials
- finger-to-nose test

Special Tests to Which the PT May or May Not Have Access
- auditory testing
- cerebral blood flow (CBF) mapping
- computed tomography (CT) scan
- computed sinusoidal harmonic acceleration
- dynamic platform posturography
- electroencephalograms (EEGs)

- electronystagmogram
- magnetic resonance imaging (MRI)
- platform fistula testing
- sensory organization testing

PROBLEMS
- The client usually has a decreased level of consciousness.
- The client usually has learning, memory, and information-processing deficits.
- The client can have receptive and expressive communication disorders.
- The client usually has behavioral disorders.
- The client is usually deconditioned, with general weakness and loss of flexibility.
- The client can have hemiparesis or bilateral hemiparesis.
- The client usually has a balance deficit.
- The client can have unilateral or bilateral ataxia.
- The client usually has a coordination deficit.
- The client can have an intention tremor.
- The client can have associated injuries.
- If unconscious, the client can have impaired mucociliary clearance.

TREATMENT/MANAGEMENT

Acute Care
- Schedule frequent position changes.
- Assist to sitting, standing, or supported standing position.
- For chest PT, consider postural drainage, percussion, vibration and shaking, rib springing, or suction, as indicated.
- Use manual techniques to facilitate respiration, assisted sitting, and standing.
- Begin passive ROM.
- Consider use of splints or prophylactic short leg casts and passive standing using a tilt table.
- Consider continuous passive motion (CPM) for minimum time per day to achieve a beneficial effect.
- Begin functional mobility training after the client reaches a stable medical status.
- Consider sensory stimulation for clients in an unresponsive state.

Rehabilitation
Rehabilitation is based on level of cognitive function (LOCF) (see box).

Rancho Los Amigos Levels of Cognitive Functioning (LOCF)

LOCF1. No response. Appears to be in a deep sleep/completely unresponsive to any stimuli.
LOCF2. Generalized response. Reacts inconsistently and nonpurposefully to stimuli. Responses are limited.
LOCF3. Localized response. Reacts specifically but inconsistently to stimuli.
LOCF4. Confused-agitated. Heightened state of activity. Behavior is bizarre, and verbalizations are frequently incoherent.
LOCF5. Confused-inappropriate. Responds to simple commands somewhat consistently.
LOCF6. Confused-appropriate. Goal-directed behavior possible under direction.

LOCF7. Automatic-appropriate. Behavior appropriate but somewhat robotic.

LOCF8. Puposeful-appropriate. Can recall and integrate past and recent events and respond to environment.

Source: Reprinted with permission from P Leahy, Traumatic Head Injury, in *Physical Rehabilitation: Assessment and Treatment*, TJ Schmitz and SB O'Sullivan, p. 49, © 1994 FA Davis and Company.

LOCFs 1 to 3
- Evaluate the effectiveness of positioning devices. Consider casting if client is unresponsive for more than 2 weeks.
- Continue passive ROM to prevent contractures. Place in side-lying position for shoulder ROM slow controlled stretches.
- Consider use of sensory stimulation or sensory regulation, usually in short sessions of 15 to 30 minutes via one or two modalities at a time. Stimulation may be auditory, visual, olfactory, gustatory, tactile, or vestibular.

LOCF 4
- Continue with LOCF 1 to 3, and add transfers, ambulation, and other functional activities.
- Encourage active mobility as soon as the client is able.

LOCFs 5 and 6
- Increase ROM.
- Increase physical conditioning.
- Treat hemiparesis, nerve injury, or ataxia as for a patient without brain injury (see Chapter "Neurological disorders").

LOCFs 7 and 8
- Integrate cognitive, physical, and emotional skills.
- Continue problem-solving and planning activities for ADLs.
- Consider electrical stimulation.
- Address any need for strengthening with weights, proprioceptive neuromuscular facilitation (PNF), biofeedback, isokinetic exercisers, or sling suspension.
- To affect tone, consider inhibitory or facilitory techniques as indicated.
- Use coordination, balance, and sensation activities as indicated.
- For pain, consider use of ultrasound, ice, or transcutaneous electrical nerve stimulation (TENS).
- Encourage activities to build endurance.
- For edema, consider mild electrical stimulation for swelling.
- Facilitate increased mobility with wheelchair, transfers, and bed mobility activities.
- For ambulation training, use external support and assistance as needed.
- For respiratory problems, consider deep breathing and coughing exercises.
- If possible, consider the use of a therapeutic pool or hippotherapy.

PRECAUTIONS/CONTRAINDICATIONS
- Do not test cervical ROM if ventriculostomy or Richmond bolt is present. Consult with medical staff on other restrictions when these devices are in place.
- Avoid prolonged pressure over shunt if present.
- Generally the client is kept in a position with head elevated in the acute phase.

- Passive ROM should be used with caution due to client's low level of consciousness in LOCFs 1 to 3.
- Footboard may have counterproductive effect of increasing tone into a position of plantar flexion instead of the desired response of decreasing it.
- Secondary brain damage caused by late-occurring intracranial hematomas can turn a relatively mild injury into a life-threatening condition.
- A client's status can change quickly and dramatically. Maintain frequent communication with nurse.
- Sitting is contraindicated if the autoregulation of intracranial pressure or blood pressure is lost.
- Standing is contraindicated if unfixated, displaced fractures of long bones are present.
- Avoid ROM in area with arterial lines, and exercise caution so as not to dislodge other tubing when moving client.

DESIRED OUTCOME/PROGNOSIS
In general:
- The client's level of consciousness will increase.
- The client's musculoskeletal system will improve in flexibility.
- Contractures, respiratory distress, and skin breakdown will be prevented (loss of ROM may be so severe that it interferes with functional tasks if not prevented).
- Functional mobility training will increase the client's tolerance of upright posture and increase active movement.
- Client will achieve optimal function and minimize disability.

LOCF as an Outcome Predictor of Functioning
- LOCFs 1 to 3 may be considered a low level.
- LOCFs 4 to 6 may be considered midlevel.
- LOCFs 7 and 8 may be considered high level.

Physical Levels Defined by Impairment
- Minimal impairment: independent but with balance and coordination deficits
- Moderate impairment: ambulatory with assistance
- Severe impairment: dependent for ADLs

Predicted Outcome Based on a Combination of LOCF and Physical Levels
- Low-level cognitive skill and minimal impairment: acutely ill but fair prognosis
- High-level cognitive skill, but severe physical disability: high need for adaptive equipment
- Midlevel cognitive skill and minimal impairment: good prognosis, but need to educate family about residual deficits
    Outcome is influenced by preinjury level of function, degree of immediate damage to the brain (primary damage), and effect of secondary brain damage.
    One study found that unilateral compensatory treatments are not justified physiologically. They should be superseded by the treatments that guide axonal and dendritic development and facilitate the opening of new pathways. Long-term physical therapy can continue to enhance recovery.
    One study reported on head injury survivors at 3 months after the injury and found the following:
- 4% in a vegetative state

- 8% severely disabled
- 22% moderately disabled
- 66% showing good recovery

However, there are very few absolute predictors of success. Prevention is the only real "cure" for head injury.

REFERENCES

ASSESSMENT

Heiden JS, Small R, Caton W, Weiss M, Kurze T. Severe head injury: clinical assessment and outcome. *Physical Therapy*. 1983;63:1946–1951.

Balance

Newton R. Review of tests of standing balance abilities. *Brain Injury*. 1989;3:335–343.

Roland PS, Otto E. Vestibular dysfunction after traumatic brain injury: evaluation and management. In: Ashley MJ, Krych DK, eds. *Traumatic Brain Injury Rehabilitation*. New York, NY: CRC Press; 1995:131–186. **[Clinical balance testing and clinical vestibular testing (functional testing and provocation of specific deficits)]**

Cardiovascular

Exercise Testing

Hunter M, Tomberlin J, Kirkikis C, Kuna ST. Progressive exercise testing in closed head-injured subjects: comparison of exercise apparatus in assessment of a physical conditioning program. *Physical Therapy*. 1990;70:363–371.

Cognition

Rancho Los Amigos Levels of Cognitive Functioning (LOCF)

O'Sullivan SB, Schmitz TJ, eds. *Physical Rehabilitation: Assessment and Treatment*. 3rd ed. Philadelphia, Pa: FA Davis Co; 1994:494.

Communication

Leahy P. Head trauma in adults: problems, assessment and treatment. In: Lister, MJ, ed. *Contemporary Management of Motor Control Problems: Proceeding of the II Step Conference*. Fredricksburg, Va: Foundation for Physical Therapy; 1991:248–249. **[Speech and language assessment, visual-perceptual testing, behavioral analysis]**

Disability

Institute of Medicine Index

Institute of Medicine. *Disability in America*. Washington, DC: National Academy Press; 1991.

Equipment

Cammack S, Eisenberg MG, eds. *Key Words in Physical Rehabilitation: A Guide to Contemporary Usage*. New York, NY: Springer Publishing Co; 1995:45.

Functional Level

Bryan VL. Management of residual physical deficits. In: Ashley MJ, Krych DK, eds. *Traumatic Brain Injury Rehabilitation*. New York, NY: CRC Press; 1995:131–186.

Action Research Arm Test
Carrol D. A quantitative test of upper extremity function. *Journal of Chronic Disability.* 1965;18:479–491.
Lyle A. A performance test for assessment of upper limb function in physical rehabilitation treatment and research. *International Journal of Rehabilitation Research.* 1981;4:483–492.
de Weerdt WJG, Harrison MA. Measuring recovery of arm-hand function in stroke patients: a comparison of the Brunnstrom–Fugl–Meyer test and the action research arm test. *Physiotherapy Canada.* 1985;37:65–70.

Glascow Coma Scale
Jennett B, Teasdale G. *Management of Head Injuries.* Philadelphia, Pa: FA Davis Co; 1981:80.
Rothstein JM, Roy SH, Wolf SL. *The Rehabilitation Specialist's Handbook.* Philadelphia, Pa: FA Davis Co; 1991: 379–383. **[Glascow Coma Scale and diagnostic features of comalike states]**

Level of Rehabilitation Scale (LORS-II)
Carey RG, Posavac EJ. Program evaluation of a physical medicine and rehabilitation unit: a new approach. *Archives of Physical Medicine and Rehabilitation.* 1978;59:330–337.
Carey RG, Posavac EJ. *Manual for the Level of Rehabilitation Scale II.* Park Ridge, Ill: Lutheran General Hospital; 1980.

Rappaport's Disability Rating Scale
Rappaport M, Hall KM, Hopkins K, Bellezy T, Cope DN. Disability Rating Scale for Severe Head Trauma: coma to community. *Archives of Physical Medicine and Rehabilitation.* 1982;63:118.
Eliason MR, Topp BW. Predictive validity of Rappaport's Disability Rating Scale in subjects with acute brain dysfunction. *Physical Therapy.* 1984;64:1357–1360.

Rivermeade ADL Assessment
Lincoln N, Edmans JA. A revalidation of the Rivermeade ADL scale for elderly patients with stroke. *Age and Aging.* 1990;19:19–24.

World Health Organization International Classification of Impairments, Disabilities, and Handicaps
World Health Organization. *International Classification of Impairments, Disabilities, and Handicaps.* Geneva, Switzerland: World Health Organization; 1980.

Mobility

Mobility Scale
Myerly LM, Dillon WJ, Hilbers SM. A mobility scale for rehabilitation of patients with head injuries. *Clinical Management in Physical Therapy.* 1988:8:5:27–31.

Precasting Assessment
Leahy P. Precasting work sheet—an assessment tool: a clinical report. *Physical Therapy.* 1988;68:72–74.

Motor Function

Dynamometer
Bohannon RW. Documentation of tremor in patients with central nervous system lesions: a clinical report. *Physical Therapy.* 1986;66:229–230.
Riddle DL, Finucane SD, Rothstein JM, Walker ML. Intrasession and intersession reliability of hand-held dynamometer measurements taken on brain-damaged patients. *Physical Therapy.* 1989;69:192–194.

Neurological
Mayo NE, Sullivan SJ, Swaine B. Observer variation in assessing neurophysical signs among patients with head injuries. *American Journal of Physical Medicine and Rehabilitation.* 1991;70:118–123.

Nativ A. Brain potentials associated with movement in traumatic brain injury. *Physical Therapy.* 1991;71:48–59.

Swain BR, Sullivan SJ. Reliability of the scores for the finger-to-nose test in adults with traumatic brain injury. *Physical Therapy.* 1993;73:71–78.

Special Tests to Which the PT May or May Not Have Access

Roland PS, Otto E. Vestibular dysfunction after traumatic brain injury: evaluation and management. In: Ashley MJ, Krych DK, eds. *Traumatic Brain Injury Rehabilitation.* New York, NY: CRC Press; 1995:131–186. **[Auditory testing, electronystagmogram, computed sinusoidal harmonic acceleration, dynamic platform posturography, sensory organization testing, platform fistula testing]**

Leahy P. Traumatic head injury. In: O'Sullivan SB, Schmitz TJ, eds. *Physical Rehabilitation: Assessment and Treatment.* 3rd ed. Philadelphia, Pa: FA Davis Co; 1994:494–496. **[Electroencephalograms (EEG), computed tomography (CT) scan, magnetic resonance imaging (MRI), cerebral blood flow (CBF) mapping]**

TREATMENT

Ada L, Canning C, Paratz J. Care of the unconscious head-injured patient. In: Ada L, Canning C, eds. *Key Issues in Neurological Physiotherapy.* London, England: Butterworth Heinemann; 1990:237–248.

Alderman N, Shepherd J, Youngson H. Increasing standing tolerance and posture quality following severe brain injury using a behaviour modification approach. *Physiotherapy.* 1992;78:335–343.

Bach y Rita P, Bjelke B. Lasting recovery of motor function, following brain damage, with a single dose of amphetamine combined with physical therapy: changes in gene expression? *Scandinavian Journal of Rehabilitation Medicine.* 1991;23:219–220.

Booth BJ, Doyle M, Montgomery J. Serial casting for the management of spasticity in the head-injured adult. *Physical Therapy.* 1983;63:1960–1965.

Boughton A, Ciesla N. Physical therapy management of the head-injured patient in the intensive care unit. *Topics in Acute Care and Trauma Rehabilitation.* 1986;1:1:1–18.

Bryan VL. Management of residual physical deficits. In: Ashley MJ, Krych DK, eds. *Traumatic Brain Injury Rehabilitation.* New York, NY: CRC Press; 1995:131–186.

Carey CD, Homm CL. Cognitive remediation expanding into physical therapy. *Clinical Management in Physical Therapy.* 1986;6:6:20–25.

Davis CW, Kerrick RC. Treatment of head-injured patients in the acute stages. *Clinical Management in Physical Therapy.* 1985;5:5:16–18, 20–21, 23.

Durham DP. Occupational and physical therapists' perspective of the perceived benefits of a therapeutic home visit program. *Physical and Occupational Therapy in Geriatrics.* 1992;10:3:15–33.

Ellis E. Respiratory function following head injury. In: Ada L, Canning C, eds. *Key Issues in Neurological Physiotherapy.* London, England: Butterworth Heinemann; 1990:237–248.

Edwards S. Rehabilitation after severe head injury. *Physiotherapy Practice.* 1986;2:1:45–46.

Edwards SM, Williams CL. Comprehensive treatment programs for severely disabled brain-injured patients classified as level III on the Rancho Los Amigos scale. *Clinical Management in Physical Therapy.* 1987;7:5:6, 8–10.

Ersson U, Carlson H, Mellstrom A, Ponten U, Hedstrand U. Observations on intracranial dynamics during respiratory physiotherapy in unconscious neurosurgical patients. *Acta Anaesthesiologica Scandinavica.* 1990;34:2:99–103.

Fisher B. Effect of trunk control and alignment on limb function. *Journal of Head Trauma Rehabilitation.* 1987;2:2:72–79.

Giles GM, Gent A. Conductive education and motor learning. In: Fussey I, Giles GM, eds. *Rehabilitation of the Severely Brain-Injured Adult: A Practical Approach.* London, England: Croom Helm Ltd; 1988:130–149.

Garland DE, Keenan MAE. Orthopedic strategies in the management of the adult head-injured patient. *Physical Therapy.* 1983;63:2004–2009.

Giles GM, Gent A. Conductive education and motor learning. In: Fussey I, Giles GM, eds. *Rehabilitation of the Severely Brain-Injured Adult.* London, England: Croom Helm Ltd; 1988:131–148.

Hall M, Brandys C, Yetman L. Multidisciplinary approaches to management of acute head injury. *Journal of Neuroscience Nursing.* 1992;24:4:199–204.

Herdman SJ. Treatment of vestibular disorders in traumatically brain-injured patients. *Journal of Head Trauma Rehabilitation.* 1990;5:4:63–76.

Jackson H. Psychological aspects of physical rehabilitation after severe head injury: a case study. *Physiotherapy Practice.* 1986;2:1:47–51.

Krus LH. Cognitive and behavioural skills retraining of the brain-injured patient. *Clinical Management in Physical Therapy.* 1988;8:2:24–26, 31.

Lamperski CA, Domholdt E. Learning to cope: a workshop for PTs on brain-injury units. *Clinical Management in Physical Therapy.* 1989;9:2:16–20.

Leahy P. Traumatic head injury. In: O'Sullivan SB, Schmitz TJ, eds. *Physical Rehabilitation: Assessment and Treatment.* 3rd ed. Philadelphia, Pa: FA Davis Co; 1994:491–508.

Leahy P. Head trauma in adults: problems, assessment, and treatment. In: Lister MJ, ed. *Contemporary Management of Motor Control Problems: Proceedings of the II STEP Conference.* Fredricksburg, Va; Foundation for Physical Therapy; 1991:247–251.

Lehmkuhl LD, Krawczyk L. Physical therapy management of the minimally responsive patient following traumatic brain injury: coma stimulation. *Neurology Report.* 1993;17:10–17.

Lehmkuhl D. *Brain Injury Glossary.* Houston, Tex: HDI Publishers; 1992.

Lovejoy D, Minkler D. Taking cognition into consideration: effective physical therapy with the head-injured patient. *Clinical Management in Physical Therapy.* 1986;6:1:26–27.

MacKay-Lyons M. Low-load, prolonged stretch in treatment of elbow flexion contractures secondary to head trauma: a case report. *Physical Therapy.* 1989;69:292–296.

Montgomery J. *Physical Therapy for Traumatic Brain Injury.* New York, NY: Churchill Livingstone; 1995.

Murdock KR, Klein P. Physical therapy intervention for acute head injury. *Physical Therapy Practice.* 1994;3:19–36.

Newton RA. Evaluation and treatment of balance problems associated with traumatic brain injury. *Physical Therapy Practice.* 1994;3:218–226.

Orest M. Patients with a low level of responsiveness. In: Myers RS, ed. *Saunders Manual of Physical Therapy Practice.* Philadelphia, Pa: WB Saunders Co; 1995:405–410.

Orest M. Casting protocol for patients with neurological dysfunction. *PT—Magazine of Physical Therapy.* 1993;1:51–55.

Pope PM. A model for evaluation of input in relation to outcome in severely brain damaged patients. *Physiotherapy.* 1988;74:647–650.

Roland PS, Otto E. Vestibular dysfunction after traumatic brain injury: evaluation and management. In: Ashley MJ, Krych DK, eds. *Traumatic Brain Injury Rehabilitation.* New York, NY: CRC Press; 1995:131–186.

Slater B, Kendricken M, Zoltan B. *Coping with Head Injury.* Thorofare, NJ: Slack Inc; 1988.

Smutok MA, Grafman J, Salazar AM, et al. Effects of unilateral brain damage on contralateral and ipsilateral upper extremity function in hemiplegia. *Physical Therapy.* 1989;69:195–203.

Stephenson R. A review of neuroplasticity: some implications for physiotherapy in the treatment of lesions of the brain. *Physiotherapy.* 1993;79:699–704.

Tangeman PT, Wheeler J. Inner ear concussion syndrome: vestibular implications and physical therapy treatment. *Topics in Acute Care and Trauma Rehabilitation.* 1986;1:1:72–83.

Trettin H. Craniocerebral trauma caused by sports: pathogenic mechanism, clinical aspects and physical therapy with special reference to manual lymph drainage. *Journal of Lymphology.* 1993;17:2:36–40.

Wolf SL, LeCraw DE, Barton LA. Comparison of motor copy and targeted biofeedback training techniques for restitution of upper extremity function among patients with neurologic disorders. *Physical Therapy.* 1989;69:719–735.

Woltersdorf MA. Beyond the sensorimotor strip. *Clinical Management in Physical Therapy.* 1992;12:3:63–69.

Wright KL, Veroff AE. Integration of cognitive and physical hierarchies in head injury rehabilitation. *Clinical Management in Physical Therapy.* 1988;8:4:6, 8–9.

Lower Extremity Amputation

DESCRIPTION

Amputation is the removal of a limb or appendage from the body. Levels of amputation are usually listed by anatomical consideration. Levels of amputation are from the Task Force on Standardization of Prosthetic and Orthotic Terminology:

- A below-knee (transtibial) amputation leaves a limb of between 20% and 50% of the original tibial length.
- A short below-knee amputation leaves a limb of less than 20% of tibial length.
- An above-knee (transfemoral) amputation leaves a limb of between 35% and 60% of femoral length.
- A long above-knee amputation leaves a limb of more than 60% of femoral length.

Other levels include the following:

Level	Description
Toe disarticulation	Disarticulation at the metatarsal phalangeal joint
Syme's	Ankle disarticulation with attachment of heel pad to distal end of tibia; may include removal of malleoli and distal tibial/fibular flares
Knee disarticulation	Amputation through the knee joint; femur intact
Hip disarticulation	Amputation through hip joint; pelvis intact

Source: Reprinted with permission from SB O'Sullivan and TJ Schmitz, *Physical Rehabilitation*, p. 376, © 1994, FA Davis & Company.

CAUSE

The main cause of amputation in the lower extremity is peripheral vascular disease, especially associated with smoking and diabetes. The next leading cause is trauma, such as gunshot wound or motor vehicle accident, followed by malignant tumor, infections, and limb discrepancies.

ASSESSMENT

Areas
- History

- Psychosocial, including depression and discharge plans
- Residual limb girth, length, shape, level of amputation
- Skin and soft tissue, including edema and scars
- Vascular
- Neurological, including sensation
- Pain, including phantom pain and phantom sensation
- Pulmonary
- Mobility, including range of motion (ROM)
- Strength
- Balance
- Gait
- Functional level, including ADLs, bed mobility, transfers, wheelchair mobility and management, and elevations
- Equipment: assess prosthesis if available

Instruments/Procedures (See References for Sources)

Equipment
- prosthetic requirements examination

Functional Level
- Barthel ADL Index
- Functional Independence Measure
- Katz Index of Activities of Daily Living
- Level of Rehabilitation Scale (LORS-II)
- PULSES profile

Gait
- gait recovery pattern assessment
- measurement of energy cost of walking

Mobility
- goniometry

Strength
- manual muscle testing

PROBLEMS
- The client usually has pain of intrinsic origin, such as bone or vascular pain, or extrinsic origin, such as pressure from a cast or phantom limb pain.
- There will be grief, and the client may experience depression.
- There can be adherent scar tissue.
- There can be edema in the residual limb.
- The client may have loss of strength, balance, and coordination.
- There can be functional loss.
- There can be medical complications.
- With forefoot amputation, the client can have balance loss, weight-bearing loss, proprioceptive loss, and loss of leverage.

TREATMENT/MANAGEMENT

Treatment Post Surgery

Immediate postoperative care can include the following: deep breathing exercises, coughing, stump dressing care, positioning, exercise program, transfer procedures, and early ambulation. Treatments for specific levels of amputation are as follows:

- *Toe disarticulation:* Cautiously mobilize (manually) any adherent scar tissue.
- *Forefoot amputation:* Stretch medial border of residual foot. Consider scar mobilization.
- *Ankle disarticulation (Syme's):* Stump end must be protected postsurgically. Client should not be allowed to bear weight without a heel pad.
- *Below-knee amputation:* Enhance weight bearing with slight flexion on stance to place weight bearing on patellar tendon.
- *Knee disarticulation:* Emphasize hip extension.
- *Above-knee (transfemoral) amputation:* Prevent contractures. Before gait training, check for stump socket wall contact on all four sides. Prepare for gait training with stump exercises, balance exercise, and step practice.
- *Hip disarticulation:* Reduce edema in tissues surrounding the disarticulation. Exercise program before initiation of gait training should include uninvolved leg exercise, trunk range of motion (ROM), pelvic tilt, bilateral arm exercise, and scar mobilization.

In general:

- Instruct client to use firm support when lying and sitting. Have a client use a firm mattress, and provide client with a wheelchair board.
- To prepare for ambulation, emphasize the following muscles: trunk extensors, abdominals, hip and knee extensors, hip and knee flexors. Use isometric exercises progressing to isotonic action.
- Teach the following transfers: bed to chair, with prosthesis, and with an overhead device.
- Promote early ambulation activities, including weight-bearing tolerance activities. Prior to receiving a prosthesis, a client with a unilateral amputation can use a three-point gait pattern.
- Assess socket position, suspension system, and alignment of temporary prosthetic device.
- Preparation for prosthetic fitting involves
  1. educating the client about the prosthetic process
  2. facilitating stump maturation or healing of any stump skin problems; consider use of whirlpool, ultraviolet, suture line taping, bandaging, splinting, reapplication of the rigid dressing
- Provide gait training by beginning in parallel bars. Progress with weight-shifting activities, heel-strike to foot-flat position, foot-flat to midstance position, and step-through. Monitor skin tolerance carefully.
- For edema, consider the use of elastic bandaging, shrinker sock application, rigid dressings, air splint, intermittent pressure pumping, pneumatic walking aid, and weight bearing without ambulation device.
- For any decrease in strength, consider a graded exercise regimen.
- For any decrease in ROM, consider the use of heat or cold, as indicated, with caution; manual stretching techniques such as passive, active, and contract-relax; splinting with serial casting; active exercises; and ambulation with prosthesis.

- For any sensory impairment, consider desensitization with vibration, stroking, percussion, and touching. Increase proprioceptive awareness with biofeedback and education to prevent skin trauma.
- For stump pain, consider the use of positioning, desensitization techniques, thermal modalities, transcutaneous electrical nerve stimulation (TENS), and weight-bearing activities.

Prosthetic Management

Management of the prosthesis includes the following:
- educating the client on maintenance and usage
- performing the prescription assessment
- adding to the prosthetic prescription as indicated
- assessing the prosthesis
- promoting acceptance
- training the client in donning, doffing, balance and coordination, gait and activities of daily living (ADLs), transfers, climbing, maintenance, and monitoring of skin response to use of prosthesis

PRECAUTIONS/CONTRAINDICATIONS

- Clients with bilateral amputations who are often in a sitting position are more likely to develop flexion contractures. Pillows under a stump should probably be discarded.
- A postoperative plaster cast can allow early weight bearing, but if it loosens, it should not be pushed back onto the stump. The upward pushing effort can cause the suture line to split. Adjustments to a prosthetic device must be performed by an experienced professional.
- The residual stump should be elevated only if there is excessive bleeding postoperatively. Circulatory impairment restricts the use of thermal modalities. See precautions for modality usage in Appendix C.
- A client with claudication pain should be counseled to walk within comfort level. After pain begins, the client should rest the leg completely before resuming. Closely monitor skin response to prosthesis.
- Bandages should never be applied in a circular motion because that can lead to restricted circulation.
- Caution should be used when prescribing exercise for clients with cardiac disease or hypertension.

DESIRED OUTCOME/PROGNOSIS

Before Prosthetic Fitting
- The client will achieve as high a level of function as possible.
- The client will be physically and psychologically ready for prosthetic rehabilitation.
- The client will prevent or reduce edema of residual limb.
- The client will prevent contracture.
- The client will maintain or increase strength in affected and remaining extremities.
- The client will be independent in mobility and ADLS.

After Prosthetic Training
- The client will maintain full ROM.
- The client will reach achievable muscular strength.

- The client will be able to care for the residual limb properly.
- The client will reach residual limb shrinkage.
- The client will reach potential for independence with bed mobility, transfers, and ambulation without the prosthesis.
- The client will reach independence with wheelchair.
- The client will be independent in use of prosthesis for ADLs, dressing, transfers, wearing, and ambulation.
- The client will be informed about support available.

Achievement may be limited by age, strength, endurance level of amputation, length of time after amputation, general medical status, pain, motivation, contractures, and any joint pathology.

REFERENCES

ASSESSMENT
Patrick DG. Prosthetics. In: Myers RS, ed. *Saunders Manual of Physical Therapy Practice*. Philadelphia, Pa: WB Saunders Co; 1995:1124–1130. **[Leg-length measurements, girth measurements, classifications of residual skin, classifications of residual limb subcutaneous tissue, sensation, phantom pain and phantom sensation]**

Equipment

Prosthetic Requirements Examination
American Physical Therapy Association. A guide to physical therapist practice, Volume I: a description of patient management. *Physical Therapy.* 1995;75:720–738.

Functional Level

Barthel ADL Index
Mahoney BI, Barthel DW. Functional evaluation: the Barthel index. *Maryland State Medical Journal.* 1965;14:61-65.
Wade DT, Collin C. The Barthel ADL Index: a standard measure of physical disability? *International Disability Studies.* 1988;10:2:64–67.

Functional Independence Measure
Granger CV, Hamilton BB, Keith RA, et al. Advance in functional assessment for medical rehabilitation. *Topics in Geriatric Rehabilitation.* 1986;1:3:59–74.
Keith RA, Granger CV, Hamilton BB, Sherwins FS. The Functional Independence Measure. *Advances in Clinical Rehabilitation.* 1987;1:6–18.

Katz Index of Activities of Daily Living
Benjamin Rose Hospital Staff. Multidisciplinary studies of illness in aged persons: II. A new classification of functional status in activities of daily living. *Journal of Chronic Disease.* 1959;9:55–62.
Brorsson B, Ashberg KH. Katz Index of Independence in ADL: reliability and validity in short-term care. *Scandinavian Journal of Rehabilitation Medicine.* 1984;16:125–132.

Level of Rehabilitation Scale (LORS-II)
Carey RG, Posavac EJ. Program evaluation of a physical medicine and rehabilitation unit: a new approach. *Archives of Physical Medicine and Rehabilitation.* 1978;59:330–337.
Carey RG, Posavac EJ. *Manual for the Level of Rehabilitation Scale II.* Park Ridge, Ill: Lutheran General Hospital; 1980.

PULSES Profile

Granger CV, Albrecht GL, Hamilton BB. Outcome of comprehensive medical rehabilitation: measurements by PULSES profile and the Barthel index. *Archives of Physical Medicine and Rehabilitation.* 1979:60:145–154.

Moskowitz RW, McCann CB. Classification of disability in the chronically ill and aging. *Journal of Chronic Disease.* 1957;5:342–346.

Gait

Baker PA, Hewison SR. Gait recovery pattern of unilateral lower limb amputees during rehabilitation. *Prosthetics and Orthotics International.* 1990;14:2:80–84.

Waters RL, Perry J, Antonelli DE, Hislop H. Energy cost of walking of amputees: the influence of level of amputation. *Journal of Bone and Joint Surgery.* 1976;58A:42–46.

Weaver CJ. Terminology: assisted gaits. *Clinical Management in Physical Therapy.* 1992;12:1:32–37.

Mobility

Gajdosik RL, Bohannon RW. Clinical measurement of range of motion: review of goniometry emphasizing reliability and validity. *Physical Therapy.* 1987;67:1867–1872. **[Goniometry]**

Pain

Phantom Pain

Cammack S, Eisenberg MG, eds. *Key Words in Physical Rehabilitation: A Guide to Contemporary Usage.* New York, NY: Springer Publishing Co; 1995:92.

Patrick DG. Prosthetics. In: Myers RS, ed. *Saunders Manual of Physical Therapy Practice.* Philadelphia, Pa: WB Saunders Co; 1995;1112–1130.

Strength

Bohannon RW. Manual muscle testing of the limbs: consideration, limitations, and alternative. *Physical Therapy Practice.* 1992;2:11–21.

Bohannon RW. Nature, implications, and measurement of limb muscle strength in patients with orthopaedic or neurologic disorders. *Physical Therapy Practice.* 1992;2:22–31.

Daniels L, Worthingham C. *Muscle Testing Techniques of Manual Examination.* 6th ed. Philadelphia, Pa: WB Saunders Co; 1995.

Kendall FP, McCreary EK, Provance PG. *Muscles, Testing and Function.* 4th ed. Baltimore, Md: Williams & Wilkins; 1993.

TREATMENT

Baker PA, Hewison SR. Gait recovery pattern of unilateral lower limb amputees during rehabilitation. *Prosthetics and Orthotics International.* 1990;14:2:80–84.

Barr AE, Siegel KL, Danoff JV, et al. Biomechanical comparison of the energy-storing capabilities of SACH and Carbon Copy II prosthetic feet during the stance phase of gait in a person with below-knee amputation. *Physical Therapy.* 1992;72:344–354.

Beekman DE, Axtell LA. Prosthetic use in elderly patients with dysvascular above-knee and through-knee amputations. *Physical Therapy.* 1987;67:1510–1516.

Booker H, Smith S. The AK/BK revisited. *Physiotherapy.* 1988;74:366–368.

Buttershaw P. Amputees benefit from teamwork. *Therapy Weekly.* 1991;17:41:2.

Cirullo JA. Prosthetic training for the elderly amputee. *Clinical Management in Physical Therapy.* 1985;5:30–31.

Clark GS, Blue B, Bearer JB. Rehabilitation of the elderly amputee. *Journal of the American Geriatrics Society.* 1983;31:439–448.

Cooney DFM. Gait training of the lower extremity amputee. In: Peat M, ed. *Current Physical Therapy.* Philadelphia, Pa: BC Decker Inc; 1988:107–110.

Cooney DFM, Vinnecour K. An advanced approach toward improved prosthetic fitting. *Clinics in Prosthetics and Orthotics.* 1985;9:3.

Culham EG, Peat M, Newell E. Analysis of gait following below-knee amputation: a comparison of the SACH and single-axis foot. *Physiotherapy Canada.* 1984;36:237–242.

Donn J. Use of the TES belt as an alternative means of suspension with the PPAM aid. *Physiotherapy.* 1991;77:591–592.

Edelstein JE. Prosthetic feet: state of the art. *Physical Therapy.* 1988;68:1874–1881.

Edelstein JE. Prosthetic and orthotic gait. In: Smidt GL, ed. *Gait in Rehabilitation.* New York, NY: Churchill Livingstone; 1990.

Edelstein JE. Prosthetic assessment and management. In: O'Sullivan SB, Schmitz TJ, eds. *Physical Rehabilitation.* 3rd ed. Philadelphia, Pa: FA Davis Co; 1994:397–419.

Ellis M. Amputation rehabilitation: physiotherapy. *CONA Journal.* 1984;6:4:10–15.

Engstrom B, Van de Ven C. *Physiotherapy for Amputees.* 2nd ed. New York, NY: Churchill Livingstone; 1993.

Falkel JE. Amputation as a consequence of diabetes mellitus: an epidemiological review. *Physical Therapy.* 1983;63:960–964.

Hadley AW, McDowell AD, Whitlock BD. Calibration of physiotherapy PPAM aids. *Physiotherapy.* 1991;77:179–180.

Ham R. Improvements possible in the management of the amputee in line with the McColl Report. *Physiotherapy.* 1986;72:520–522.

Ham R, Richardson P. The King's amputee stump board: Mark II. *Physiotherapy.* 1986;72:124.

Ham R, Thornberry DJ, Regan JC, et al. Rehabilitation of the vascular amputee: one method evaluated. *Physiotherapy Practice.* 1985;1:6–13.

Ham R, Van de Ven C. The management of the lower limb amputee in England and Wales today. *Physiotherapy Practice.* 1986;2:94–100.

Hubbard WA. Rehabilitation outcomes for elderly lower limb amputees. *Australian Journal of Physiotherapy.* 1989;35:219–224.

Karacoloff LA. *Lower Extremity Amputation.* Rockville, Md: Aspen Publishers, Inc; 1986.

Kay J. Domiciliary rehabilitation of elderly amputees. *Physiotherapy.* 1991;77:60–61.

Krebs DE, Edelstein JE, Thornby MA. Prosthetic management of children with limb deficiencies. *Physical Therapy.* 1991;71:920–934.

Levin A. How are physiotherapists using the Vessa Pneumatic Post-Amputation Mobility Aid? *Physiotherapy.* 1992;78:318–322.

May BJ. Assessment and treatment of individuals following lower extremity amputation. In: O'Sullivan SB, Schmitz TJ, eds. *Physical Rehabilitation.* 3rd ed. Philadelphia, Pa: FA Davis Co; 1994:533–576.

Mensch G. Aids and equipment: prosthetic update. *Physiotherapy Canada.* 1986;38:369–371.

Mensch G, Ellis P. The Terry Fox Running Prosthesis. *Physiotherapy Canada.* 1984;36:245–246.

Mensch L, Ellis PM. *Physical Therapy Management of Lower Extremity Amputation.* Rockville, Md: Aspen Publishers, Inc; 1986.

Mitchell CA, Versluis TL. Management of an above-knee amputee with complex medical problems using the CAT-CAM prosthesis. *Physical Therapy.* 1990;70:389–393.

Mouratoglou VM. Amputees and phantom limb pain: a literature review. *Physiotherapy Practice.* 1986;2:177–185.

Mueller MJ, Delitto A. Selective criteria for successful long-term prosthetic use. *Physical Therapy.* 1985;65:1037–1040.

Palma T, Hoyle D. Lower-extremity amputation. *Clinical Management in Physical Therapy.* 1992;12:3:96–99.

Patrick DG. Prosthetics. In: Myers RS, ed. *Saunders Manual of Physical Therapy Practice.* Philadelphia, Pa: WB Saunders Co; 1995:1121–1182.

Penington G, Warminton S, Hull S, Freijah N. Rehabilitation of lower limb amputees and some implications for surgical management. *Australian and New Zealand Journal of Surgery.* 1992;62:774–779.

Ramsey EM. A clinical evaluation of the LIC Femurett as an early training device for the primary above-knee amputee. *Physiotherapy.* 1988;74:598–560.

Rausch RW, Khalili AA. Air splint in preprosthetic rehabilitation of lower extremity amputated limbs: a clinical report. *Physical Therapy.* 1985;65:912–914.

Rehabilitation Institute of Chicago. *Lower Extremity Amputation: A Guide to Functional Outcomes in Physical Therapy Management.* Rockville, Md: Aspen Publishers, Inc; 1986.

Rizzo N. Physical therapy management of diabetics undergoing lower extremity amputation. *Diabetes Educator.* 1983;8:4:24–29.

Roth EJ, Wiesner SL, Green D, Wu YC. Dysvascular amputee rehabilitation: the role of continuous noninvasive cardiovascular monitoring during physical therapy. *American Journal of Physical Medicine and Rehabilitation.* 1990;69:1:16–22.

Tilbury B, Slack HN, Mancey C. The Exeter amputee stump support board. *Physiotherapy.* 1985;71:477.

Spinal Cord Injuries: Paraplegia

DESCRIPTION

Paraplegia is the partial or complete loss of neurologic function due to a spinal injury. Injury may result in a lesion at the level of the thoracic or lumbar spinal cord or at the sacral roots. With a complete lesion, no sensory or motor function remains below the level of the lesion. Typically the level of the lesion is defined as the most distal uninvolved nerve root segment with normal function at the corresponding skeletal level.

Incomplete lesions include the Brown–Sequard syndrome, anterior cord syndrome, central cord syndrome, and posterior cord syndrome. Approximately 54% of the spinal cord injuries occurring in the United States are classified as incomplete. This classification is given if there is any motor or sensory function intact more than three levels below the level of neurologic injury.

CAUSE

Traumatic spinal cord injuries usually result from a fall, sporting activity, diving accident, motor vehicle accident, or gunshot wound. Complete lesions are caused by transection with a severing action or by severe compression. Incomplete lesions usually result from contusions. Nontraumatic damage can also occur, such as vascular impairment to the cord, but it is not as common as damage due to trauma. Eighty percent of all spinal cord injuries occur in people under the age of 40.

ASSESSMENT

Areas

- History
- Psychosocial
- Pain
- Pulmonary, including muscle strength and tone of respiratory muscles, chest expansion and mobility, breathing pattern and respiratory rate, cough effectiveness, vital capacity, and tidal volume and posture
- Cardiovascular, including endurance and heart rate
- Skin and soft tissue

- Neurological, including sensation and reflexes
- Motor control, including muscle tone
- Strength
- Mobility, including passive range of motion (ROM)
- Gait, as indicated, including ambulation potential
- Functional assessment, including activities of daily living (ADLs)
- Equipment, including home environment
- Special tests to which the PT may or may not have access

Instruments/Procedures (See References for Sources)

Functional Level
- Barthel ADL Index
- Functional Independence Measure
- Katz Index of Activities of Daily Living
- Level of Rehabilitation Scale (LORS-II)

Gait
- based on motor scores of muscular strength

Motor Control
- modified Ashworth scale of muscle spasticity

Special Tests to Which the PT May or May Not Have Access
- sacral sparing
- spinal canal assessment
- hydrostatic weight measurement

Strength
- manual muscle testing
- shoulder torque

Six-Point Scale for Grading Muscles

0	=	total paralysis
1	=	palpable or visible contraction
2	=	active movement, full ROM with gravity eliminated
3	=	active movement, full ROM against gravity
4	=	active movement, full ROM against moderate resistance
5	=	(normal) active movement, full ROM against full resistance
NT	=	not testable

Courtesy of the American Spinal Injury Association, Chicago, Illinois.

PROBLEMS

Primary Problems
- The client will usually have motor deficits and sensory loss.

- The client will usually have impaired temperature control.
- The client can have respiratory impairment.
- The client can have spasticity.
- The client will usually have bladder and bowel dysfunction.
- The client will usually have sexual dysfunction.

Secondary Problems
- The client can develop autonomic dysreflexia.
- The client can develop contractures.
- The client can develop deep-vein thrombosis.
- The client can develop heterotopic bone formation.
- The client usually experiences postural hypotension.
- The client can develop pressure sores.
- The client usually has some complaints of pain; sources can be nerve root, physical trauma, spinal cord, or musculoskeletal.

TREATMENT/MANAGEMENT

Acute Phase

Strengthening of Selected Musculature
- Strengthen upper extremity muscles, with emphasis on triceps, latissimus dorsi, and shoulder depressors and on functional activities.
- Exercise techniques in the early phase can include manual resistance in straight-plane motions or upper extremity proprioceptive neuromuscular facilitation (PNF) patterns, progressing to resistive exercise with cuffed weights.
- Pulley weight systems and sports can be used in the later phases of rehabilitation. Bilateral activities should be emphasized.
- Biofeedback can be used to augment the exercise program.

ROM
- Except for areas contraindicated (see precautions), full ROM exercises should be performed daily. It is preferable for ROM to be done in both prone and supine positions if possible.
- Use selective stretching to allow development of selected tightness to enhance function. A tenodesis grasp, for example, in a patient with a C-6 and C-7 quadriplegia, is formed by allowing mild tightness of long finger flexors to develop. This improves grasp by allowing fingers to close upon wrist extension and the fingers to open upon wrist flexion (with assistance from gravity).

Positioning
- After the fracture site is stabilized, gradual acclimation to an upright posture is indicated. To facilitate acclimation, the patient may need an abdominal binder, elastic stockings, and/or elastic wraps.
- Consider splints for wrists, hands, and fingers, as well as ankle splints or boots. Gradually increase tolerance to prone position.

Respiratory Care
- Respiratory care can include the following activities: deep breathing exercises, glossopharyngeal breathing (for high-level cervical lesions), airshift chest expansion and chest mobility,

diaphragm-strengthening exercises, assisted coughing, and stretching of pectoral and chest wall muscles.
- Consider the use of an abdominal support.
- Intervention strategies can include postural drainage and chest PT techniques such as vibration and percussion.

Subacute Phase
- Continue respiratory management, ROM, and positioning.
- Expand resistive exercises for innervated muscles.
- Include interval training, with upper extremity aerobic activity, for cardiovascular training.
- Teach independence in mobilization.
- Mat programs can be initiated after patient is cleared for activity. Mat programs are varied and can include facilitating mastery of the components of functional skills. Component skills may involve activities such as rolling; transition to side-lying, prone-on-elbows, prone-on-hands, or supine-on-elbows position, pull-ups (with quadriplegia), transition to sitting (long and short), transition to quadriped position (in paraplegia), and kneeling (in paraplegia). Consider using group mat activities.
- Independent transfer training can be initiated after adequate sitting balance is achieved. Transfer training can include two-person lift, stand-pivot transfer, airlift, sliding board transfer, and lateral and forward transfers. Basic functional transfer activities include the following:
  1. wheelchair to bed, car, toilet or chair
  2. chair to bath or floor (an advanced-level skill)
- Prescribe wheelchair and teach management skills. Basic wheelchair skills include weight shifting; propelling the wheelchair; managing brakes, armrests, and legrest/footrests; and picking up objects off the floor. Advanced wheelchair skills include wheelies, ramps and curbs, stairs, getting wheelchair into the car, and controlled falling.

Ambulation
- Determine if patient is a candidate for ambulation.
- Prescribe orthotics; usually ankle and/or knee bracing is adequate, but low thoracic lesions, level T-9 to T-12, will need knee-ankle-foot orthoses (KAFOs).
- Consider use of functional electrical stimulation (FES). This modality can assist with ambulation and endurance activities but is still in the experimental stage and not widely available.
- Ambulation training includes donning and doffing orthoses, sit-to-stand activities, trunk balancing, push-ups, turning around, jackknifing, and parallel bars activities. Teach gait patterns such as four-point, two-point, swing-to and swing-through patterns, elevation activities, and controlled falling.

Treatment of Pressure Sores
- Use topical therapy debridement and dressing technique for pressure sores, grade 3 or grade 4, a minimum of twice daily.
- Consider use of whirlpool, hyperbaric oxygen, electrical stimulation, and laser therapy.

Grades of Pressure Sores

Grade 1: limited to superficial epidermis and dermal layers
Grade 2: involves the epidermal and dermal layers and extends into the adipose tissue

Grade 3:   extends through the superficial structures and adipose tissue down to and including muscle

Grade 4:   destroys all soft tissue structures down to bone, with communication with bone or joint structures or both

Courtesy of the National Spinal Cord Injury Association, Thorofare, New Jersey.

Skin Care Management Dos and Don'ts

- Do lift in the chair every 10 minutes.
- Do lift the paralyzed limbs when transferring.
- Do use a mirror for detection of marks, abrasions, blisters, and redness on buttocks, back of legs, and malleoli.
- Do watch for marks on the penis from the condom.
- Do protect the arms and legs from excessive cold.
- Do watch the temperature of bathwater; avoid too hot water.
- Don't expose the body to strong sunlight.
- Don't knock arms or legs against a hard object.
- Don't rest arms or legs against a warm object or sit too close to a fire.

Source: Reprinted with permission from I Bromley, *Tetraplegia and Paraplegia: A Guide for Physiotherapy,* © 1985, Churchill Livingstone, Inc.

Psychosocial Issues
- Although physical therapy deals primarily with the physical and functional losses that a patient experiences, therapists need to be aware of the psychosocial issues facing a spinal-cord-injured patient.
- Physical therapists should work closely with other team members to address psychosocial issues such home modifications, community re-entry, driving, communication skills, feeding, hygiene, bladder training, dressing, and other ADLs.
- Address psychosocial issues, including normalization, promoting independence, positive atmosphere and interactions with the rehabilitation team, education, and social support.
- Formal strategies for discharge include counseling, education, social skills training, bladder and bowel retraining for postacute management, recreation training, pharmaceutical planning, and postdischarge planning.
- Psychosexual treatment involves physical evaluation, education, behavioral treatment, counseling, and prescription of physical aids for penile erectile dysfunction.

PRECAUTIONS/CONTRAINDICATIONS
- Avoid allowing the patient to maintain a posture in bed of constant shoulder flexion, adduction, internal rotation, elbow flexion, and forearm pronation.
- Redness over bony prominences should be gone within 30 minutes of the position change.
- Surgical intervention may be needed for pressure sores if conservative measures are not successful.
- Unresolved pressure sores may lead to chronic localized infection, osteomyelitis, sepsis, or even death.

- During the acute period, caution should be used during muscle strengthening to avoid stress at the fracture site, especially at the hips and trunk in paraplegia.
- Avoid asymmetric rotational stresses on the spine.
- Extreme ROM should be avoided, especially at the hip or knee (only 45 degrees of abduction should be allowed at hip).
- Support medial side of knee to avoid excessive stress.
- Do not combine flexion of the wrist and fingers.
- With paraplegia, trunk motion and some hip motions are contraindicated. In general, straight leg raise (SLR) greater than 60 degrees and hip flexion beyond 90 degrees should be avoided during the acute phase. Avoid overstretching of the low back because mild tightness facilitates transfer activity.
- It is critical to prevent secondary shoulder pain because of the importance of the shoulder in functional activities.
- Testing or monitoring of patients who may have impaired cardiovascular adaptation during exercise is indicated because of the demands of wheelchair propulsion.
- Symptoms of autonomic dysreflexia should be considered a medical emergency. Immediate assessment of the bladder drainage system should be performed.
- Some experts state that ambulation is contraindicated for 6 months post fracture stabilization.
- Contraindications for FES application in spinal-cord-injured patients include the following:
    1. peripheral lesions
    2. osteoporosis
    3. heterotopic ossifications
    4. contractures
    5. severe atrophy of muscles and no response to restrengthening
    6. pressure sores
    7. obesity
    8. severe spasticity
    9. inadequate sitting balance
    10. lack of patient interest

DESIRED OUTCOME

Acute

- The client will improve ventilation, increase effectiveness of cough, prevent chest tightness and substitute breathing patterns, maintain adequate bronchial hygiene, and develop coordination of breathing with activity.
- The client will maintain ROM, especially alignment of fingers, thumb, and wrist for functional activities or dynamic splints, and will maintain alignment and prevent heel cord tightness.
- The client will maintain skin integrity and prevent pressure sores.
- The client will have improved bladder drainage.
- The client will maintain strength of remaining musculature.

Subacute

- The client will have increased responsibility for skin inspection.
- The client will have relief of pressure and maintenance of proper hygiene.
- There will be an increase in wheelchair mobility.

- The client will develop motor control and muscle re-education techniques.
- The client will regain postural control and balance.
- The client will improve cardiovascular response to exercise.
- The client will have functional skills, achieve stability, and progress to controlled mobility that leads to mobility skill.
  Outcomes for ambulation are as follows:
- The client will achieve functional ambulation and increase tolerance to standing.
- For KAFO users, the desired outcome is to master a swing-through gait pattern.

PROGNOSIS

General

Prognosis for recovery, in general, relates directly to the extent of the spinal cord damage and the prevention of additional compromise during the acute phase. With a complete lesion, there is no expectation of motor improvement except what may accompany motor root return. Most incomplete lesions begin to show improvement after spinal shock has subsided.

Gait

Gait training can take 3 to 6 weeks or longer.

FES long-term follow-up data are not available at this time. It remains undetermined whether FES-facilitated ambulation is more practical than wheelchair mobility.

Psychosocial

After a period of adjustment to the profound loss, most people adapt to spinal cord injury and can have a positive self-concept and be generally satisfied with life. Research offers conflicting reports on whether depression is more common among cord-injured people than the general population.

Fertility

Fertility generally remains unchanged in a woman. Complications from a pregnancy for spinal-cord-injured women can include
- autonomic dysreflexia during labor (with lesions above T-7)
- lack of awareness of labor contractions due to sensory loss (with lesions above T-6)
- increased risk of anemia
- urinary tract infection
- decubiti
- deep-vein thrombosis
- rapid labor
- high incidence of premature labor

There is, however, no major threat and no increased need for cesarean delivery. Most women can deliver healthy babies vaginally.

Male fertility is lower following spinal cord injury, with incidence of paternity at 5% or lower.

REFERENCES

ASSESSMENT

Cardiovascular

Hooker SP, Greenwood JD, Hatae DT, Husson RP, Matthiesen TL, Waters AR. Oxygen uptake and heart rate relationship in persons with spinal cord injury. *Medicine and Science in Sports and Exercise.* 1993;25:1115–1119.

Functional Level

Rothstein JM, Roy SH, Wolf SL. *The Rehabilitation Specialist's Handbook*. Philadelphia, Pa: FA Davis Co; 1991:430–439. [**Functional expectations for spinal-cord-injured patients**]

Barthel Index

Mahoney BI, Barthel DW. *Maryland State Medical Journal*. 1965;14:61–65.

Wade DT, Collin C. The Barthel ADL Index: a standard measure of physical disability? *International Disability Studies*. 1988;10:2:64–67.

Functional Independence Measure

Granger CV, Hamilton BB, Keith RA, et al. Advance in functional assessment for medical rehabilitation. *Topics in Geriatric Rehabilitation*. 1986;1:3:59–74.

Keith RA, Granger CV, Hamilton BB, Sherwins FS. The Functional Independence Measure. *Advances in Clinical Rehabilitation*. 1987;1:6–18.

Roth E, Davidoff G, Haughton J, Ardner M. Functional assessment in spinal cord injury: a comparison of the modified Barthel Index and the adapted Functional Independence Measure. *Clinical Rehabilitation*. 1990;4:277–285.

Katz Index of Activities of Daily Living

Benjamin Rose Hospital Staff. Multidisciplinary studies of illness in aged persons: II. A new classification of functional status in activities of daily living. *Journal of Chronic Disease*. 1959;9:55–62.

Brorsson B, Ashberg KH. Katz Index of Independence in ADL: reliability and validity in short-term care. *Scandinavian Journal of Rehabilitation Medicine*. 1984;16:125–132.

Level of Rehabilitation Scale (LORS-II)

Carey RG, Posavac EJ. Program evaluation of a physical medicine and rehabilitation unit: a new approach. *Archives of Physical Medicine and Rehabilitation*. 1978;59:330–337.

Carey RG, Posavac EJ. *Manual for the Level of Rehabilitation Scale II*. Park Ridge, Ill: Lutheran General Hospital; 1980.

Gait

Ambulation Potential

Waters RL, Adkins R, Yakura J, et al. Prediction of ambulatory performance based on motor scores derived from standards of the American Spinal Injury Association. *Archives of Physical Medicine and Rehabilitation*. 1994;75:756–760.

Motor Control

Muscle Tone

Bohannon R, Smith M. Interrator reliability of a modified Ashworth scale of muscle spasticity. *Physical Therapy*. 1987;67:206–207.

Special Tests to Which the PT May or May Not Have Access

Sacral Sparing

Schmitz TJ. Traumatic spinal cord injury. In: O'Sullivan SB, Schmitz TJ, eds. *Physical Rehabilitation*. 3rd ed. Philadelphia, Pa: FA Davis Co; 1994:537.

Spinal Canal Assessment

Rothstein JM, Roy SH, Wolf SL.*The Rehabilitation Specialist's Handbook*. Philadelphia, Pa: FA Davis Co; 1991:205–206. [**Cross sectional views of the spinal tracts and lamina of Rexed, relationship between spinal and vertebral segments of spinal cord**]

Twomey L, Taylor J. Age changes in the lumbar spinal and intervertebral canals. *Paraplegia*. 1988;26:238–249.

Hydrostatic Weight Measurement
George CM, Wells CL, Dugan NL, Hardison R. Hydrostatic weights of patients with spinal injury: reliability of measurements in standard sit-in and Hubbard tanks. *Physical Therapy.* 1987;67:921–925.

Strength

Manual Muscle Testing
Daniels L, Worthingham C. *Muscle Testing Techniques of Manual Examination.* 5th ed. Philadelphia, Pa: WB Saunders Co;1986.
Kendall F, McCreary E. *Muscles: Testing and Function.* 3rd ed. Baltimore, Md: Williams & Wilkins; 1983.

Shoulder Torque
Powers CM, Newsam CJ, Gronley JK, et al. Isometric shoulder torque in subjects with spinal cord injury. *Archives of Physical Medicine and Rehabilitation.* 1994;75:761–765.

TREATMENT
Adkins HV. *Spinal Cord Injury.* New York, NY: Churchill Livingstone; 1985.
Bohannon RW. Tilt table standing for reducing spasticity after spinal cord injury. *Archives of Physical Medicine and Rehabilitation.* 1993;74:1121–1122.
Bromley I. *Tetraplegia and Paraplegia: A Guide for Physiotherapy.* 3rd ed. New York, NY: Churchill Livingstone; 1985.
Butler PB, Major R. The ParaWalker: a rational approach to the provision of reciprocal ambulation for paraplegic patients. *Physiotherapy.* 1987;73:393–397.
Clough P. Respiratory care for the spinal cord injured patient. In: Peat M, ed. *Current Physical Therapy.* Philadelphia, Pa: BC Decker Inc; 1988:33–42.
Clough P, Lindenauer D, Hayes M, Zekany B. Guidelines for routine respiratory care of patients with spinal cord injury: a clinical report. *Physical Therapy.* 1986;66:1395–1402.
Coogler C. Clinical decision making among neurologic patients: spinal cord injury. In: Wolf S, ed. *Clinical Decision Making in Physical Therapy.* Philadelphia, Pa: FA Davis Co; 1985:149–170.
Crum NA. Signs of temporomandibular joint dysfunction in spinal cord injured patients wearing halo braces: a clinical report. *Physical Therapy.* 1990;70:132–137.
Curtis KA, Hall KM. Spinal cord injury community follow-up role of the physical therapist. *Physical Therapy.* 1986;1370–1375.
Davis G, Plyley MJ, Shephard RJ. Gains of cardiorespiratory fitness with arm-crank training in spinally disabled men. *Canadian Journal of Sport Sciences.* 1991;16:1:64–72.
DonTigny RL. Seat angles and support. *Physical Therapy.* 1988;68:1682–1686.
Duffus A, Wood J. Standing and walking for the T6 paraplegic. *Physiotherapy.* 1983;69:45–46.
Edelstein JE. Orthoses. In: Myers RS, ed. *Saunders Manual of Physical Therapy Practice.* Philadelphia, Pa: WB Saunders Co; 1995:1198–1203.
Engen T. Lightweight modular orthosis. *Prosthetics and Orthotics International.* 1989;13:3:125–129.
Ferguson ACB, Granat MH. Evaluation of functional electrical stimulation for an incomplete spinal cord injured patient. *Physiotherapy.* 1992;78:253–256.
Garvey LA. Spinal cord injury and aquatics. *Clinical Management in Physical Therapy.* 1991;11:1:21–24.
Gerhart KA. Personal perspectives. In: Whiteneck GG, Charlifue SW, Gerhart KA, et al, eds. *Aging With Spinal Cord Injury.* New York, NY: Demos Publications; 1993:343–352.
Greenfield JM, Davidson V. Group treatment sessions for paraplegic patients. *Clinical Management in Physical Therapy.* 1988;8:2:32, 34–35, 38.
Griffen JW, Tooms RE, Mendius RA, Clifft JK, Vander-Zwaag R, el Zeky F. Efficacy of high voltage pulsed current for healing of pressure ulcers in patients wih spinal cord injury. *Physical Therapy.* 1991;71:433–442.
Gordon T, Mao J. Muscle atrophy and procedures for training after spinal cord injury. *Physical Therapy.* 1994;74:50–60.

Gunduz S, Kalyon TA, Dursun H, Mohur H, Bilgic F. Peripheral nerve block with phenol to treat spasticity in spinal cord injured patients. *Paraplegia.* 1992;30:808–811.

Harnish LA. Functional gains in SCI. *Clinical Management in Physical Therapy.* 1990;10:2:35–38.

Harries R. Personal experience of pressure sores. *Physiotherapy.* 1987;73:448–450.

Hilbers P, White T. Effects of wheelchair design on metabolic and heart rate responses during propulsion by persons with paraplegia. *Physical Therapy.* 1987;67:1355–1358.

Hughes CJ, Weimar WH, Sheth PN, Brubaker CE. Biomechanics of wheelchair propulsion as a function of seat position and user-to-chair interface. *Archives of Physical Medicine and Rehabilitation.* 1992;73:263–269.

Imle PC. Physical therapy for acute spinal cord injury. *Physical Therapy Practice.* 1994;3:11–18.

Imle PC, Boughton AC. The physical therapist's role in the early management of acute spinal cord injury. *Topics in Acute Care and Trauma Rehabilitation.* 1987;1:3:32–47.

McAteer MF. Some aspects of grief in physiotherapy. *Physiotherapy.* 1989;75:55–58.

McDermott AL. Functional electrical stimulation in spinal cord injury. In: Peat M, ed. *Current Physical Therapy.* Philadelphia, Pa: BC Decker Inc; 1988:180–183.

McEwen-Hill J. Rehabilitation in spinal cord injury. In: Peat M, ed. *Current Physical Therapy.* Philadelphia, Pa: BC Decker Inc; 1988:165–173.

McGarry J, Woolsey RM, Thompson CW. Autonomic hyperreflexia following passive stretching to the hip joint. *Physical Therapy.* 1982;62:30.

Minor M, Minor S. *Patient Care Skills: Positioning, Range of Motion, Transfers, Wheelchairs and Ambulation.* Reston, Va: Reston Publishing; 1984.

Nawoczenski DA. Pressure sores: prevention and management. In: Buchanan LE, Nawoczenski DA, eds. *Spinal Cord Injury: Concepts and Management.* Baltimore, Md: Williams & Wilkins; 1987:99–121.

Nawoczenski DA, Rinehart M, Duncanson P, Brown B. Physical management. In: Buchanan LE, Nawoczenski DA, eds. *Spinal Cord Injury: Concepts and Management.* Baltimore, Md: Williams & Wilkins; 1987:123–184.

Nixon V. *Spinal Cord Injury: A Guide to Functional Outcomes in Physical Therapy Management. Rehabilitation Institute of Chicago Procedure Manual.* Rockville, Md: Aspen Publishers, Inc; 1985.

Phillips CA. Medical criteria for active physical therapy: physician guidelines for patient participation in a program of functional electrical rehabilitation. *American Journal of Physical Medicine.* 1987;66:269–286.

Phillips CA. Functional electrical stimulation and lower extremity bracing for ambulation exercise of the spinal cord injured individual: a medically prescribed system. *Physical Therapy.* 1989;60:842–849.

Rinehart M, Nawoczenski D. Respiratory care. In: Buchanan L, Nawoczenski E, eds. *Spinal Cord Injury: Concepts and Management.* Baltimore, Md: Williams & Wilkins; 1987:61–79.

Schmitz TJ. Traumatic spinal cord injury. In: O'Sullivan SB, Schmitz TJ, eds. *Physical Rehabilitation.* 3rd ed. Philadelphia, Pa: FA Davis Co; 1994:533–576.

Shields RK, Cook TM. Lumbar support thickness: effect on seated buttock pressure of individuals with and without spinal cord injury. *Physical Therapy.* 1992;72:218–226.

Shindo N, Jones R. Reciprocal patterned electrical stimulation of the lower limbs in severe spasticity. *Physiotherapy.* 1987;73:579, 581.

Somers MF. *Spinal Cord Injury: Functional Rehabilitation.* Norwalk, Conn: Appleton & Lange; 1992.

Sorg RJ. HDL-cholesterol:exercise formula: results of long-term (6 year) strenuous swimming exercise in a middle-aged male with paraplegia. *Journal of Orthopaedic and Sports Physical Therapy.* 1993;17:195–199.

Sullivan P, Markos P, Minor M. *An Integrated Approach to Therapeutic Exercises: Therapy and Clinical Application.* Reston, Va: Reston Publishing; 1982.

Tuel SM, Cross LL, Meythaler JM, et al. Interdisciplinary management of hemicorporectomy after spinal cord injury. *Archives of Physical Medicine and Rehabilitation.* 1992;73:669–673.

Twist DJ. Acrocyanosis in a spinal cord injured patient—effects of computer-controlled neuromuscular electrical stimulation: a case report. *Physical Therapy.* 1990;70:45–49.

Voss D, Ionta M, Meyers B. *Proprioceptive Neuromuscular Facilitation.* 3rd ed. Philadelphia, Pa: Harper & Row; 1985.

Walker JB, Harris M. GM-1 ganglioside administration combined with physical therapy restores ambulation in humans with chronic spinal cord injury. *Neuroscience Letter.* 1993;161:174–178.

Waters RL, Sie ID, Adkins RH. The musculoskeletal system. In: Whiteneck GG, et al, eds. *Aging With Spinal Cord Injury.* New York, NY: Demos Publications; 1993;53–71.

Watkins EM, Edwards DE, Patrick JH. ParaWalker paraplegic walking. *Physiotherapy.* 1987;73:99–100.

Yang JF, Fung J, Edamura M, Blunt R, Stein RB, Barbeau H. H-reflex modulation during walking in spastic paretic subjects. *Canadian Journal of Neurological Sciences.* 1991;18:443–452.

Young JH. Implications of elbow arthrodesis for individuals with paraplegia. *Physical Therapy.* 1993;73:194–201.

Spinal Cord Injuries: Quadriplegia

Also known as *tetraplegia.*

DESCRIPTION

Quadriplegia is damage of the cervical spinal cord resulting in partial or complete motor and/or sensory function of all extremities and the trunk, including respiratory muscles.

CAUSE

Traumatic spinal cord injuries result from a fall, sporting activity, diving accident, motor vehicle accident, or gunshot wound. Complete lesions are caused by a transection with a severing action or by severe compression. Incomplete lesions usually result from contusions. Nontraumatic damage can also occur, such as vascular impairment to the cord, but it is not as common as damage due to trauma. Eighty percent of all spinal cord injuries occur to people under the age of 40.

ASSESSMENT

Areas
- History, including medications, gastrointestinal complaints, and visual disturbances
- Psychosocial, including behavior
- Communication
- Balance
- Pain
- Posture (sitting)
- Respiratory status and function, including muscle strength and tone of respiratory muscles, chest expansion and mobility, breathing pattern and respiratory rate, cough effectiveness, vital capacity, and tidal volume
- Cardiovascular, including endurance and heart rate
- Skin and soft tissue, including any edema
- Neurological, including sensation and DTRs
- Motor control, including muscle tone

- Strength, especially of shoulder flexors, abductors, elbow flexors and extensors, and wrist extensors
- Genitourinary, including bowel and bladder continence schedule
- Mobility, including passive range of motion (ROM)
- Gait: ambulation potential
- Functional assessment, including mobility and activities of daily living (ADLs)
- Equipment, including assistive devices and assessment of home environment
- Special tests to which the PT may or may not have access

Instruments/Procedures (See References for Sources)

Cardiovascular
- arm ergometry

Functional Level
- Barthel ADL Index
- Functional Independence Measure
- Katz Index of Activities of Daily Living
- Level of Rehabilitation Scale (LORS-II)

Gait
- based on motor scores of muscular strength

Motor Control
- modified Ashworth scale of muscle spasticity

Respiratory Status and Function
- maximal inspiratory pressure
- spirometric measurements

Special Test to Which the PT May or May Not Have Access
- sacral sparing
- spinal canal assessment
- hydrostatic weight assessment

Strength
- manual muscle testing
- shoulder torque

Six-Point Scale for Grading Muscles

0	=	total paralysis
1	=	palpable or visible contraction
2	=	active movement, full ROM with gravity eliminated
3	=	active movement, full ROM against gravity
4	=	active movement, full ROM against moderate resistance
5	=	(normal) active movement, full ROM against full resistance
NT	=	not testable

Courtesy of the American Spinal Injury Association, Chicago, Illinois.

PROBLEMS

Primary Problems
- The client will usually have motor deficits and sensory loss.
- The client will usually have impaired temperature control.
- The client can have respiratory impairment.
- The client can have spasticity.
- The client will usually have bladder and bowel dysfunction.
- The client will usually have sexual dysfunction.

Secondary Problems
- The client can develop autonomic dysreflexia.
- The client can develop contractures.
- The client can develop deep-vein thrombosis.
- The client can develop heterotopic bone formation.
- The client usually experiences postural hypotension.
- The client can develop pressure sores.
- The client usually has some complaints of pain; sources can be nerve root, physical trauma, spinal cord, or musculoskeletal.

TREATMENT/MANAGEMENT

Acute Phase

Strengthening of Selected Musculature
- Strengthen upper extremity muscles, with emphasis on anterior deltoids, shoulder extensors, biceps, and lower trapezius muscles and on functional activities.
- Exercise techniques in the early phase can include manual resistance in straight-plane motions or upper extremity proprioceptive neuromuscular facilitation (PNF) patterns, progressing to resistive exercise with cuffed weights.
- Pulley weight systems and sports can be used in the later phases of rehabilitation. Bilateral activities should be emphasized.

ROM
- Except for areas contraindicated (see precautions), full ROM exercises should be performed daily. It is preferable for ROM to be done in both prone and supine positions if possible.
- Use selective stretching to allow development of selected tightness to enhance function. A tenodesis grasp, for example, in a patient with a C-6 and C-7 quadriplegia, is formed by allowing mild tightness of long finger flexors to develop. This improves grasp by allowing fingers to close upon wrist extension and the fingers to open upon wrist flexion (with assistance from gravity).

Positioning
- After the fracture site is stabilized, gradual acclimation to an upright posture is indicated. To facilitate acclimation, the patient may need an abdominal binder, elastic stockings, and/or elastic wraps.
- Consider splints for wrists, hands, and fingers, as well as ankle splints or boots. Gradually increase tolerance to prone position.

Respiratory Care
- Respiratory care can include the following activities: deep breathing exercises, glossopharyngeal breathing (for high-level cervical lesions), airshift chest expansion and chest mobility, diaphragm-strengthening exercises, assisted coughing, and stretching of pectoral and chest wall muscles.
- Consider the use of an abdominal support.
- Intervention strategies can include postural drainage and chest PT techniques such as vibration and percussion.

Subacute Phase
- Continue respiratory management, ROM, and positioning.
- Expand resistive exercises for innervated muscles.
- Include interval training, with upper extremity aerobic activity, for cardiovascular training.
- Teach independence in mobilization.
- Mat programs can be initiated after patient is cleared for activity. Mat programs are varied and can include facilitating mastery of the components of functional skills. Component skills may involve activities such as rolling; transition to side-lying, prone-on-elbows, prone-on-hands, or supine-on-elbows position, pull-ups, and transition to sitting (long and short). Consider using group mat activities.
- Independent transfer training can be initiated after adequate sitting balance is achieved. Transfer training can include two-person lift, stand-pivot transfer, airlift, sliding board transfer, and lateral and forward transfers. Basic functional transfer activities include the following:
  1. wheelchair to mat
  2. removal of footplates
  3. chair to bed or car; chair to toilet or bath if patient has use of triceps
- Prescribe wheelchair and teach management skills. Basic wheelchair skills include weight shifting; propelling the wheelchair; managing of brakes, armrests, and legrest/footrests; and picking up objects off the floor. Advanced wheelchair skills include wheelies, ramps and curbs, stairs, getting wheelchair into the car, and controlled falling.

Treatment of Pressure Sores
- Use topical therapy debridement and dressing technique for pressure sores, grade 3 or grade 4, a minimum of twice daily.
- Consider use of whirlpool, hyperbaric oxygen, electrical stimulation, and laser therapy.

Grades of Pressure Sores

Grade 1: limited to superficial epidermis and dermal layers
Grade 2: involves the epidermal and dermal layers and extends into the adipose tissue
Grade 3: extends through the superficial structures and adipose tissue down to and including muscle
Grade 4: destroys all soft tissue structures down to bone, with communication with bone or joint structures or both

Courtesy of the National Spinal Cord Injury Association, Thorofare, New Jersey.

Skin Care Management Dos and Don'ts

- Do lift in the chair every 10 minutes.
- Do lift the paralyzed limbs when transferring.
- Do use a mirror for detection of marks, abrasions, blisters, and redness on buttocks, back of legs, and malleoli.
- Do watch for marks on the penis from the condom.
- Do protect the arms and legs from excessive cold.
- Do watch the temperature of bathwater; avoid too hot water.
- Don't expose the body to strong sunlight; quadriplegic patients should wear a hat.
- Don't knock arms or legs against a hard object.
- Don't rest arms or legs against a warm object or sit too close to a fire.

Source: Adapted with permission from I Bromley, *Tetraplegia and Paraplegia: A Guide for Physiotherapy*, © 1985, Churchill Livingstone, Inc.

Psychosocial Issues
- Although physical therapy deals primarily with the physical and functional losses that a patient experiences, therapists need to be aware of the psychosocial issues facing a spinal-cord-injured patient.
- Physical therapists should work closely with other team members to address psychosocial issues such as home modifications, community re-entry, driving, communication skills, feeding, hygiene, bladder training, dressing, and other ADLs.
- Address psychosocial issues, including normalization, promoting independence, positive atmosphere and interactions with the rehabilitation team, education, and social support.
- Formal discharge strategies include counseling, education, social skills training, bladder and bowel retraining for postacute management, recreation training, pharmaceutical planning, and postdischarge planning.
- Psychosexual treatment involves physical evaluation, education, behavioral treatment, counseling, and prescription of physical aids for penile erectile dysfunction.

PRECAUTIONS/CONTRAINDICATIONS
- Avoid allowing the patient to maintain a posture in bed of constant shoulder flexion, adduction, internal rotation, elbow flexion, and forearm pronation.
- Redness over bony prominences should be gone within 30 minutes of the position change. Surgical intervention for pressure sores may be needed if conservative measures are not successful.
- Unresolved pressure sores may lead to chronic localized infection, osteomyelitis, sepsis, or even death.
- During the acute period, caution should be used during muscle strengthening to avoid stress at the fracture site, especially at the scapula and shoulder with quadriplegia.
- Avoid asymmetric rotational stresses on the spine.
- Extreme ROM should be avoided, especially at the hip or knee (only 45 degrees of abduction should be allowed at hip).
- Support medial side of knee to avoid excessive stress.
- Do not combine flexion of the wrist and fingers.
- Testing or monitoring of patient who may have impaired cardiovascular adaptation during exercise is indicated during wheelchair propulsion.

- Symptoms of autonomic dysreflexia should be considered a medical emergency. Immediate assessment of the bladder drainage system should be performed.
- Dependence on upper extremities for mobility may lead to acceleration of degenerative changes in joints and upper extremity pain.

DESIRED OUTCOME/PROGNOSIS

Acute
- The client will improve ventilation, increase effectiveness of cough, prevent chest tightness and substitute breathing patterns, maintain adequate bronchial hygiene, and develop coordination of breathing with activity.
- The client will maintain ROM, especially alignment of fingers, thumb, and wrist for functional activities or dynamic splints, and will maintain alignment and prevent heel cord tightness.
- The client will maintain skin integrity and prevent pressure sores.
- The client will have improved bladder drainage.
- The client will maintain strength of remaining musculature.

Subacute
- The client will have increased responsibility for skin inspection.
- The client will have relief of pressure and maintenance of proper hygiene.
- There will be an increase in wheelchair mobility.
- The client will develop motor control and muscle re-education techniques.
- The client will regain postural control and balance.
- The client will improve cardiovascular response to exercise.
- The client will have functional skills, achieve stability, and progress to controlled mobility leading to skill.

PROGNOSIS

General Prognosis
Prognosis for recovery, in general, relates directly to the extent of the spinal cord damage and the prevention of additional compromise during the acute phase. With a complete lesion, there is no expectation of motor improvement except what may accompany motor root return. Most incomplete lesions begin to show improvement after spinal shock has subsided. The highest level to achieve independence in transfers are quadriplegics at the C-6 level. Muscle strength score higher than 3 out of 5 in upper extremities may indicate good prognosis for functional independence.

Psychosocial Prognosis
After a period of adjustment to the profound loss, most people adapt to spinal cord injury and can have a positive self-concept and be generally satisfied with life. Research offers conflicting reports on whether depression is more common among cord-injured people than the general population.

Aging
Changes in musculoskeletal system due to age may lead to changes in functional status.

REFERENCES

ASSESSMENT

Cromwell S. Patients with quadriplegia. In: Myers RS, ed. *Saunders Manual of Physical Therapy Practice.* Philadelphia, Pa: WB Saunders Co; 1995:396. **[American Spinal Injury Association standard neurological classification of spinal cord injury form]**

Cardiovascular

DiCarlo SE. Effect of arm ergometry training on wheelchair propulsion endurance of individuals with quadriplegia. *Physical Therapy.* 1988;68:40–44.

Hooker SP, Greenwood JD, Hatae DT, Husson RP, Matthiesen TL, Waters AR. Oxygen uptake and heart rate relationship in persons with spinal cord injury. *Medicine and Science in Sports and Exercise.* 1993;25:1115–1119.

Functional level

Rothstein JM, Roy SH, Wolf SL. *The Rehabilitation Specialist's Handbook.* Philadelphia, Pa: FA Davis Co; 1991:430–439. **[Functional expectations for spinal cord-injured patients]**

Barthel Index

Mahoney BI, Barthel DW. Functional evaluation: the Barthel index. *Maryland State Medical Journal.* 1965;14:61–65.

Wade DT, Collin C. The Barthel ADL Index: a standard measure of physical disability? *International Disability Studies.* 1988;10:2:64–67.

Functional Independence Measure

Whiteneck GG. A functional independence measure trial in SCI model systems. *American Spinal Injury Association Proceedings.* 1982:48.

Granger CV, Hamilton BB, Keith RA, et al. Advance in functional assessment for medical rehabilitation. *Topics in Geriatric Rehabilitation.* 1986;1:3:59–74.

Keith RA, Granger CV, Hamilton BB, Sherwins FS. The Functional Independence Measure. *Advances in Clinical Rehabilitation.* 1987;1:6–18.

Roth E, Davidoff G, Haughton J, Ardner M. Functional assessment in spinal cord injury: a comparison of the Modified Barthel Index and the adapted Functional Independence Measure. *Clinical Rehabilitation.* 1990;4:277–285.

Katz Index of Activities of Daily Living

Benjamin Rose Hospital Staff. Multidisciplinary studies of illness in aged persons: II. A new classification of functional status in activities of daily living. *Journal of Chronic Disease.* 1959;9:55–62.

Brorsson B, Ashberg KH. Katz Index of Independence in ADL: reliability and validity in short-term care. *Scandinavian Journal of Rehabilitation Medicine.* 1984;16:125–132.

Level of Rehabilitation Scale (LORS-II)

Carey RG, Posavac EJ. *Manual for the Level of Rehabilitation Scale II.* Park Ridge, Ill: Lutheran General Hospital; 1980.

Carey RG, Posavac EJ. Program evaluation of a physical medicine and rehabilitation unit: a new approach. *Archives of Physical Medicine and Rehabilitation.* 1978;59:330–337.

Gait

Ambulation Potential

Waters RL, Adkins R, Yakura J, et al. Prediction of ambulatory performance based on motor scores derived from standards of the the American Spinal Injury Association. *Archives of Physical Medicine and Rehabilitation.* 1994;75:756–760.

Motor Control

Muscle Tone

Bohannon R, Smith M. Interrater reliability of a modified Ashworth scale of muscle spasticity. *Physical Therapy.* 1987;67:206–207.

Respiratory Status and Function

Hornstein S, Ledsome JR. Ventilatory muscle training in acute quadriplegia. *Physiotherapy Canada.* 1986;38:145–149. [**Maximal inspiratory pressure and vital capacity**]

Stiller K, Simionato R, Rice K, Hall B. The effect of intermittent positive pressure breathing on lung volumes in acute quadriparesis. *Paraplegia.* 1992;30:2:121–126.

Spirometric Measurements

Derrickson J, Ciesla N, Simpson N, Imle PC. A comparison of two breathing exercise programs for patients with quadriplegia. *Physical Therapy.* 1992;72:763–769.

Special Tests to Which the PT May or May Not Have Access

Sacral Sparing

Schmitz TJ. Traumatic spinal cord injury. In: O'Sullivan SB, Schmitz TJ, eds. *Physical Rehabilitation.* 3rd ed. Philadelphia, Pa: FA Davis Co; 1994:537.

Spinal Canal Assessment

Rothstein JM, Roy SH, Wolf SL. *The Rehabilitation Specialist's Handbook.* Philadelphia, Pa: FA Davis Co; 1991:205–206. [**Cross-sectional view of the spinal tracts and lamina of Rexed, relationship between spinal and vertebral segments of spinal cord**].

Twomey L, Taylor J. Age changes in the lumbar spinal and intervertebral canals. *Paraplegia.* 1988;26:238–249.

Hydrostatic Weight Measurement

George CM, Wells CL, Dugan NL, Hardison R. Hydrostatic weights of patients with spinal injury: reliability of measurements in standard sit-in and Hubbard tanks. *Physical Therapy.* 1987;67:921–925.

Strength

Manual Muscle Testing

Daniels L, Worthingham C. *Muscle Testing Techniques of Manual Examination.* 5th ed. Philadelphia, Pa: WB Saunders Co; 1986.

Kendall F, McCreary E. *Muscles: Testing and Function.* 3rd ed. Baltimore, Md: Williams & Wilkins; 1983.

Shoulder torque

Powers CM, Newsam CJ, Gronley JK, et al. Isometric shoulder torque in subjects with spinal cord injury. *Archives of Physical Medicine and Rehabilitation.* 1994;75:761–765.

TREATMENT

Adkins HV. *Spinal Cord Injury.* New York, NY: Churchill Livingstone; 1985.

Biss S, Fox B. Functional electrical stimulation in incomplete tetraplegia. *Physiotherapy Practice.* 1988;4:163–167.

Bohannon RW. Tilt table standing for reducing spasticity after spinal cord injury. *Archives of Physical Medicine and Rehabilitation.* 1993;74:1121–1122.

Bromley I. *Tetraplegia and Paraplegia: A Guide for Physiotherapy.* 3rd ed. New York, NY: Churchill Livingstone; 1985.

Brownlee S, Williams SJ. Physiotherapy in the respiratory care of patients with high spinal injury. *Physiotherapy.* 1987;73:148–152.

Carroll SG, Bird SF, Brown DJ. Electrical stimulation of the lumbrical muscles in an incomplete quadriplegic patient: case report. *Paraplegia*. 1992;30:223–226.

Carroll SG, Meeny CF. Electrical stimulation for restoring independent feeding in a man with quadriplegia. *American Journal of Occupational Therapy*. 1993;47:739–742.

Clough P, Lindenauer D, Hayes M, Zekany B. Guidelines for routine respiratory care of patients with spinal cord injury: a clinical report. *Physical Therapy*. 1986;66:1395–1402.

Clough P. Respiratory care for the spinal cord injured patient. In: Peat M, ed. *Current Physical Therapy*. Philadelphia, Pa: BC Decker Inc; 1988:33–42.

Coogler C. Clinical decision making among neurologic patients: spinal cord injury. In: Wolf S, ed. *Clinical Decision Making in Physical Therapy*. Philadelphia, Pa: FA Davis Co; 1985:149–170.

Cromwell S. Patients with quadriplegia. In: Myers RS, ed. *Saunders Manual of Physical Therapy Practice*. Philadelphia, Pa: WB Saunders Co; 1995:393–403

Crum NA. Signs of temporomandibular joint dysfunction in spinal cord injured patients wearing halo braces: a clinical report. *Physical Therapy*. 1990;70:132–137.

Curtis KA, Hall KM. Spinal cord injury community follow-up role of the physical therapist. *Physical Therapy*. 1986;66:1370–1375.

Derrickson J, Ciesla N, Simpson N, Imle PC. A comparison of two breathing exercise programs for patients with quadriplegia. *Physical Therapy*. 1992;72:763–769.

DonTigny RL. Seat angles and support. *Physical Therapy*. 1988;68:1682–1686.

Engen T. Lightweight modular orthosis. *Prosthetics and Orthotics International*. 1989;13:3:125–129.

Ferguson ACB, Granat MH. Evaluation of functional electrical stimulation for an incomplete spinal cord injured patient. *Physiotherapy*. 1992;78:253–256.

Findlater KA. A behavioural approach to the rehabilitation of long-standing hysterical quadriplegia: a case report. *Physiotherapy Canada*. 1986;38:216–222.

Garvey LA. Spinal cord injury and aquatics. *Clinical Management in Physical Therapy*. 1991;11:1:21–24.

Gerhart KA. Changing the adaptive environment. Whiteneck GG, Charlifue SW, Gerhart KA, et al, eds. *Aging With Spinal Cord Injury*. New York, NY: Demos Publications; 1993:343–351.

Griffen JW, Tooms RE, Mendius RA, Clifft JK, Vander-Zwaag R, el Zeky F. Efficacy of high voltage pulsed current for healing of pressure ulcers in patients with spinal cord injury. *Physical Therapy*. 1991;71:433–442.

Gordon T, Mao J. Muscle atrophy and procedures for training after spinal cord injury. *Physical Therapy*. 1994;74:50–60.

Harnish LA. Functional gains in SCI. *Clinical Management in Physical Therapy*. 1990;10:2:35–38.

Hornstein S, Ledsome J. Ventilatory muscle training in acute quadriplegia. *Physiotherapy Canada*. 1986;38:145–149.

Hughes CJ, Weimar WH, Sheth PN, Brubaker CE. Biomechanics of wheelchair propulsion as a function of seat position and user-to-chair interface. *Archives of Physical Medicine and Rehabilitation*. 1992;73:263–269.

Imle PC, Boughton AC. The physical therapist's role in the early management of acute spinal cord injury. *Topics in Acute Care and Trauma Rehabilitation*. 1987;1:3:32–47.

Ince LP, Leon MS, Christidis D. EMG biofeedback for improvement of upper extremity function: a critical review of the literature. *Physiotherapy Canada*. 1985;37:12–17.

Lehr RP, Silver JR. A three-hour electromyographic investigation of generalised spasms in a tetraplegic patient: a preliminary report. *Physiotherapy*. 1991;77:411–414.

McAteer MF. Some aspects of grief in physiotherapy. *Physiotherapy*. 1989;75:55–58.

McDermott AL. Functional electrical stimulation in spinal cord injury. In: Peat M, ed. *Current Physical Therapy*. Philadelphia, Pa: BC Decker Inc; 1988:180–183.

McEwen-Hill J. Rehabilitation in spinal cord injury. In: Peat M, ed. *Current Physical Therapy*. Philadelphia, Pa: BC Decker Inc; 1988:165–173.

Millington P, Ellingsen J, Hauswirth B, Fabian P. Thermoplastic Minerva body jacket: a practical alternative to current methods of cervical spine stabilization. *Physical Therapy*. 1987;67:223–225.

Minor M, Minor S. *Patient Care Skills: Positioning, Range of Motion, Transfers, Wheelchairs and Ambulation.* Reston, Va: Reston Publishing; 1984.

Nawoczenski DA. Pressure sores: prevention and management. In: Buchanan LE, Nawoczenski, DA, eds. *Spinal Cord Injury: Concepts and Management.* Baltimore, Md: Williams & Wilkins; 1987:99–121.

Nawoczenski DA, Rinehart M, Duncanson P, Brown B. Physical management. In: Buchanan LE, Nawoczenski, DA, eds. *Spinal Cord Injury: Concepts and Management.* Baltimore, Md: Williams & Wilkins; 1987:123–184.

Nixon V. *Spinal Cord Injury: A Guide to Functional Outcomes in Physical Therapy Management. Rehabilitation Institute of Chicago Procedure Manual.* Rockville, Md: Aspen Publishers, Inc; 1985.

O'Daniel B, Krapfl B. Spinal cord injury. In: Payton O, ed. *Manual of Physical Therapy.* New York, NY: Churchill Livingstone; 1989:69–172.

Phillips CA. Medical criteria for active physical therapy: physician guidelines for patient participation in a program of functional electrical rehabilitation. *American Journal of Physical Medicine.* 1987;66:269–286.

Phillips CA. Functional electrical stimulation and lower extremity bracing for ambulation exercise of the spinal cord injured individual: a medically prescribed system. *Physical Therapy.* 1989;60:842–849.

Rinehart M, Nawoczenski D. Respiratory care. In: Buchanan L, Nawoczenski E, eds. *Spinal Cord Injury: Concepts and Management.* Baltimore, Md: Williams & Wilkins; 1987:61–79.

Schmitz TJ. Traumatic spinal cord injury. In: O'Sullivan SB, Schmitz TJ, eds. *Physical Rehabilitation.* 3rd ed. Philadelphia, Pa: FA Davis Co; 1994:533–576.

Somers MF. *Spinal Cord Injury.* Norwalk, Conn: Appleton & Lange; 1992.

Shields RK, Cook TM. Lumbar support thickness: effect on seated buttock pressure of individuals with and without spinal cord injury. *Physical Therapy.* 1992;72:218–226.

Shindo N, Jones R. Reciprocal patterned electrical stimulation of the lower limbs in severe spasticity. *Physiotherapy.* 1987;73:579, 581.

Sullivan P, Markos P, Minor M. *An Integrated Approach to Therapeutic Exercises: Therapy and Clinical Application.* Reston, Va: Reston Publishing; 1982.

Twist DJ. Acrocyanosis in a spinal cord injured patient—effects of computer-controlled neuromuscular electrical stimulation: a case report. *Physical Therapy.* 1990;70:45–49.

Voss D, Ionta M, Meyers B. *Proprioceptive Neuromuscular Facilitation.* 3rd ed. Philadelphia, Pa: Harper & Row; 1985.

Walker JB, Harris M. GM-1 ganglioside administration combined with physical therapy restores ambulation in humans with chronic spinal cord injury. *Neuroscience Letter.* 1993;161:2:174–178.

Waters RL, Sie IH, Adkins RH. The musculoskeletal system. In: Whiteneck GG, Chalifue SW, Gerhart KA, et al., eds. *Aging With Spinal Cord Injury.* New York, NY: Demos Publications; 1993:53–70.

Chapter 8

Musculoskeletal Disorders

- Achilles tendinitis
- Adhesive capsulitis
- Epicondylitis
- Hammer toes
- Hip capsular sprain
- Iliopectinal bursitis
- Interdigital neuroma
- Medial tibial stress syndrome
- Patellar tendinitis
- Patellofemoral stress syndrome
- Pes cavus
- Pes planus
- Piriformis syndrome
- Plantar fasciitis
- Plica syndrome
- Prepatellar bursitis
- Retrocalcaneal bursitis
- Shoulder bursitis
- Shoulder tendinitis
- Temporomandibular joint (TMJ) dysfunction
- Trochanteric bursitis

See also chapters on Back Pain and Athletic Injuries.

Achilles Tendinitis

DESCRIPTION
Inflammation of the Achilles tendon.

CAUSE
Unknown etiology. Achilles tendinitis may be caused by the effects of aging, repetitive microtrauma, extreme trauma, strain, an inflexible gastrocsoleus complex, unaccustomed exercise, or malalignment of the foot structure. The tendon or the paratendon (a sleeve like structure surrounding the Achilles tendon) becomes inflamed and painful. Tissue thickening also occurs in the area of the tendon. Abnormal alignment may predispose the tendon to injury.

ASSESSMENT

Areas
• History
• Pain
• Posture
• Gait
• Strength
• Neurological, including sensation
• Joint integrity and structural deviations
• Mobility, including active and passive range of motion (ROM) and accessory motion
• Skin and soft tissue: temperature, edema
• Equipment, including footwear

Instruments/Procedures (See References for Sources)

Gait
• dynamic assessment of foot mechanics
  1. dynamic plantar pressure distribution
  2. foot pressure EMED system
  3. pedabarograph
  4. three-dimensional kinematic analysis
• footprint analysis
• gait velocity measurement
• stance phase analysis

Joint Integrity and Structural Deviations
• tibial varum assessment

Mobility
• goniometry
• open and closed kinetic chain subtalar joint neutral positions
• subtalar and ankle joint measurements
• visual estimates of ankle joint active ROM

Strength
• instrumentation
• manual muscle testing

PROBLEMS
- The client usually has pain proximal to the heel.
- The pain may be experienced at rest but is usually associated with activity, especially weight bearing.
- The client can have tenderness.
- The ankle can be edematous; there is usually localized swelling.
- The client can feel crepitus with active motion.

TREATMENT/MANAGEMENT
For treatment of foot and ankle problems in general:
- Exercises progress from passive ROM to active assisted and active ROM to resisted ROM.
- Begin non-weight-bearing strengthening activities after pain-free ROM is achieved.
- Isometric, isotonic, and isokinetic exercise can be used.
- Consider eccentric loading.
- Progress to jogging, running, and athletic maneuvers as indicated.
- Address preventive measures, such as stretching, choice of shoes, and use of adhesive strapping during athletic activities.

For Achilles tendinitis specifically, the foundation of treatment is indicated by the acronym **PRICEMM** (see box).

The acronym **PRICEMM** outlines a general approach useful for treating pain and inflammation:
- **P**rotection
- **R**est: eliminate aggravating activities
- **I**ce
- **C**ompression
- **E**levation
- **M**edication: as prescribed
- **M**odalities: high-voltage electrical stimulation, ultrasound, ice, heat

---

In addition:
- Use physical agents as indicated.
- Whirlpools should be cold.
- Soft tissue mobilization may be indicated.
- Consider heel lift or orthotics. Consider an ankle-foot arthosis (AFO) with limited-motion ankle joints placed in a shoe that also has a heel lift.
- Modify daily activities as needed.
- Progress to active stretching.
- Use gastrocsoleus strengthening exercises, including eccentric exercises.
- Consider the use of a balance board.
- If available, use aquatic exercise progressing to weight-bearing activities.
- Ice may be indicated after activity.
- Assess footwear; consider counterforce straps.
- Implement a home program of strength maintenance and flexibility.
- Consider protective taping for athletic activities.

PRECAUTIONS/CONTRAINDICATIONS
See appendix for precautions applicable to the use of modalities.

DESIRED OUTCOME/PROGNOSIS
- Symptoms, such as edema and inflammation, will be controlled and healing.
- The client will gain adequate flexibility and strength and reduce tension on the sural nerve and Achilles tendon.
- The client will return to normal function and activity, and recurrence will be prevented.

Most acute Achilles tendinitis responds well to conservative therapy. Symptoms lasting longer than 6 to 8 weeks may mean that adhesions have formed in the tendoachilles region. Chronic Achilles tendinitis may need immobilization.

REFERENCES

ASSESSMENT
McPoil TG, Hunt GC. Evaluation and management of foot and ankle disorders: present problems and future directions. *Journal of Orthopaedic and Sports Physical Therapy.* 1995;21:381–388.

Gait
Cerny K, Perry J, Walker JM. Effect of an unrestricted knee-ankle foot orthosis on the stance phase of gait in healthy persons. *Orthopedics.* 1990;13:1121–1127.
Donatelli R, ed. *The Biomechanics of the Foot and Ankle.* Philadelphia, Pa: FA Davis Co; 1990:148–152.
[Dynamic assessment of foot mechanics: dynamic plantar pressure distribution, foot pressure EMED system, pedabarograph; three-dimensional kinematic analysis]
McCulloch MU, Brunt D, Vander-Linden D. The effect of foot orthotics and gait velocity on lower limb kinematics and temporal events of stance. *Journal of Orthopaedic and Sports Physical Therapy.* 1993;17:1:2–10.
Shore M. Footprint analysis in gait documentation: an instructional sheet format. *Physical Therapy.* 1980;60:1163–1167.

Joint Integrity and Structural Deviations
McPoil TG, Schuit D, Knecht HG. A comparison of three positions used to evaluate tibial varum. *Journal of American Podiatric Medical Association.* 1988;78:22–28.
Rothstein JM, Roy SH, Wolf SL. *The Rehabilitation Specialist's Handbook.* Philadelphia, Pa: FA Davis Co; 1991:136–137.
Tomberlin JP, Saunders HD. *Evaluation, Treatment and Prevention of Musculoskeletal Disorders. Vol 2: Extremities.* Chaska, Minn: The Saunders Group; 1994:265–306.

Mobility
Bohannon RW, Tiberio D, Zitto M. Selected measures of ankle dorsiflexion range of motion: differences and intercorrelations. *Foot and Ankle.* 1989;10:2:99–103.
Chesworth BM, Vandervoort AA. Reliability of a torque motor system for measurement of passive ankle joint stiffness in control subjects. *Physiotherapy Canada.* 1988;40:300–303.
Creighton D, Olson V. Evaluation of range of motion of first metatarsophalangeal joint in runners with plantar fasciitis. *Journal of Orthopaedic and Sports Physical Therapy.* 1987;8:357–361.
Elveru RA, Rothstein JM, Lamb RL. Goniometric reliability in a clinical setting: subtalar and ankle joint measurements. *Physical Therapy.* 1988;68:672–677.
Kleven D, Bornhoeft D, Thorp B. Assessing ankle dorsiflexion. *Clinical Management in Physical Therapy.* 1989;9:25–26.

Picciano AM, Rowlands MS, Worrell T. Reliability of open and closed kinetic chain subtalar joint neutral positions and navicular drop test. *Journal of Orthopaedic and Sports Physical Therapy*. 1993;18:553–558.

Vandervoort AA, Chesworth BM, Cunningham DA, et al. An outcome measure to quantify passive stiffness of the ankle. *Canadian Journal of Public Health*. 1992;83(suppl 2):S19–S23.

Youdas JW, Bogard CL, Suman VJ. Reliability of goniometric measurements and visual estimates of ankle joint active range of motion obtained in a clinical setting. *Archives of Physical Medicine and Rehabilitation*. 1993;74:1113–1118.

Strength

Instrumentation

Lee WA, Michaels CF, Pai YC. The organization of torque and EMG activity during bilateral handle pulls by standing humans. *Experimental Brain Research*. 1990;82:304–314.

Simoneau GG. Isokinetic characteristics of ankle evertors and invertors in female control subjects using the Biodex dynamometer. *Physiotherapy Canada*. 1990;42:182–187.

Manual Muscle Testing

Daniels L, Worthingham C. *Muscle Testing Techniques of Manual Examination*. 6th ed. Philadelphia, Pa: WB Saunders Co; 1995.

Kendall FP, McCreary EK, Provance PG. *Muscles: Testing and Function*. 4th ed. Baltimore, Md: Williams & Wilkins, 1993.

TREATMENT

Ballantyne BT, Kukulka CG, Soderberg GL. Motor unit recruitment in human medial gastrocnemius muscle during combined knee flexion and plantar flexion isometric contractions. *Experimental Brain Research*. 1993;93:492–498.

Brown LP, Yavorsky P. Locomotor biomechanics and pathomechanics: a review. *Journal of Orthopaedic and Sports Physical Therapy*. 1987;9:3–10.

Donatelli R. Abnormal biomechanics of the foot and ankle. *Journal of Orthopaedic and Sports Physical Therapy*. 1987;9:11–16.

Donatelli R, ed. *The Biomechanics of the Foot and Ankle*. Philadelphia, Pa: FA Davis Co; 1990:258–259.

Donatelli R, Hurlbert C, Conway P, et al. Biomechanical foot orthotics: a retrospective study. *Journal of Orthopaedic and Sports Physical Therapy*. 1988;10:205–212.

Donatelli R, Wooden MJ, eds. *Orthopaedic Physical Therapy*. New York, NY: Churchill Livingstone; 1989. (2nd ed, 1994)

Doxey GE. Clinical use and fabrication of molded thermoplastic foot orthotic devices. *Physical Therapy*. 1985;65:1679–1680.

Giallonardo LM. Clinical evaluation of foot and ankle dysfunction. *Physical Therapy*. 1988;68:1850–1856.

Grisogono V. Physiotherapy treatment for Achilles tendon injuries. *Physiotherapy*. 1989;75:562–572.

Gould JA, Davies GJ, eds. *Orthopaedic and Sports Physical Therapy*. St Louis, Mo: CV Mosby Co; 1985:317.

Hertling D, Kessler RM. *Management of Common Musculoskeletal Disorders*. Philadelphia, Pa: JB Lippincott Co; 1990:359–410.

Hunt GC, ed. *Physical Therapy of the Foot and Ankle*. New York, NY: Churchill Livingstone; 1988.

Kisner C, Colby LA. *Therapeutic Exercise: Foundations and Techniques*. 2nd ed. Philadelphia, Pa: FA Davis Co; 1990:385–407.

Lattanza L, Gray GW, Kantner R. Closed vs open kinematic chain measurements of subtalar joint eversion: implications for clinical practice. *Journal of Orthopaedic and Sports Physical Therapy*. 1988;9:310–314.

Leard J, Massie DL, Brautigam J, Buschbacher R. Lower leg, ankle, and foot. In: Buschbacher RM, ed. *Musculoskeletal Disorders: A Practical Guide for Diagnosis and Rehabilitation*. Boston, Mass: Andover Medical Publishers; 1994:216–235.

Lockard MA. Foot orthoses. *Physical Therapy.* 1988;68:1866–1873.

Maitland GD. *Peripheral Manipulation.* 3rd ed. Boston, Mass: Butterworths; 1990.

McPoil TG. Footwear. *Physical Therapy.* 1988;68:1857–1865.

McPoil TG, Knecht HG. Biomechanics of the foot in walking: a functional approach. *Journal of Orthopaedic and Sports Physical Therapy.* 1985;7:2:69–72.

Oatis CA. Biomechanics of the foot and ankle under static conditions. *Physical Therapy.* 1988;68:1815–1821.

Palmer M, Epler M. *Clinical Assessment Procedures in Physical Therapy.* Philadelphia, Pa: JB Lippincott Co; 1990.

Riddle DL, Freeman DB. Management of a patient with a diagnosis of bilateral plantar fasciitis and Achilles tendinitis: a case report. *Physical Therapy.* 1988;68:1913–1916.

Riegger CL. Anatomy of the ankle and foot. *Physical Therapy.* 1988;68:1802–1814.

Sabbahi MA, Fox AM, Druffle C. Do joint receptors modulate the motorneuron excitability? *Electromyography and Clinical Neurophysiology.* 1990;30:387–396.

Sammarco GJ, ed. *Foot and Ankle Manual.* Philadelphia, Pa: Lea & Febiger; 1991:350–358.

Tiberio D. The effect of excessive subtalar joint pronation on patellofemoral mechanics: a theoretical model. *Journal of Orthopaedic and Sports Physical Therapy.* 1987;9:160–165.

Tiberio D. Pathomechanics of structural foot deformities. *Physical Therapy.* 1988;68:1840–1849.

Tomberlin JP, Saunders HD. *Evaluation, Treatment and Prevention of Musculoskeletal Disorders. Vol 2: Extremities.* Chaska, Minn: The Saunders Group; 1994:265–305.

Wessling KC, DeVane DA, Hylton CR. Effects of static stretch versus static stretch and ultrasound combined on triceps surae muscle extensibility in healthy women. *Physical Therapy.* 1987;67:674–679.

Woodman R, Pare L. Evaluation and treatment of soft tissue lesions of the ankle and forefoot using the Cyriax approach. *Physical Therapy.* 1982;62:1144.

Adhesive Capsulitis

Also known as *frozen shoulder* or *periarthritis.*

DESCRIPTION

Adhesive capsulitis is the inflammation of the shoulder capsule. Adhesive capsulitis leads to inflammation between the joint capsule and the shoulder's articular cartilage. Shoulder pain from adhesive capsulitis may be due to one pathologic process or a combination of disorders of adhesive capsulitis, tendinitis, and bursitis.

CAUSE

No specific cause of adhesive capsulitis may be determined. Possible causes are immobilization, reflex sympathetic dystrophy, trauma, alteration in scapulohumeral alignment, rheumatoid arthritis, or, rarely, degenerative joint disease. It occurs in middle-aged and older persons more frequently than in the young. Women are more often affected than men.

ASSESSMENT

Areas

• History

- Pain
- Posture
- Joint integrity and structural deviations
- Skin and soft tissue
- Movements, including active and passive range of motion (ROM) and accessory motion
- Strength
- Neurological
- Circulation
- Functional level: use of arm
- Special tests to which the PT may or may not have access

Instruments/Procedures (See References for Sources)

Joint Integrity/Structural Deviations and Neurological Involvement
- acromioclavicular instability test
- anterior apprehension test
- anterior drawer sign
- anterior stability test
- active impingement test
- Adson's test
- Allen's test
- clunk test
- costoclavicular syndrome test
- drop arm test
- Feagin test
- fulcrum test
- Gilchrist's sign
- Halstead maneuver
- Hawkin's test
- hyperabduction syndrome test
- jerk test
- lateral scapular glide
- Lippman's test
- locking test
- Ludington's test
- Neer's test
- Norwood stress test
- posterior apprehension test
- posterior drawer sign
- push-pull test
- quadrant test
- relocation test
- Roo's test (EAST test)
- Rockwood test
- Rowe test
- Speed's test (bicep's test)
- sulcus sign

- suprascapular nerve entrapment test
- transverse humeral ligament rupture test
- upper limb tension test
- upper quarter screen
- Yergason's test

Pain
- body chart
- visual analogue scale

Special Tests to Which the PT May or May Not Have Access
- electromyography (EMG)

Strength
- isokinetic evaluation
- manual muscle testing

Temperature
- thermography

PROBLEMS
- The client usually reports gradual increase in pain and stiffness.
- The client usually has decreased active and passive motion in shoulder in a capsular pattern, especially in external rotation and abduction. The restriction leads to an inability to reach behind the back with hand.
- The client can have some decreased ROM in flexion and internal rotation.
- There is usually painless resisted motion.
- The client can have difficulty with activities of daily living due to decreased functional usage.
- The client usually has disturbed sleep secondary to pressure on involved side in acute phase.
- The client usually has pain at extremes of shoulder ROM or with lifting, especially overhead.
- There can be decreased shoulder strength.

TREATMENT/MANAGEMENT

Acute
- Use ice or superficial heat if indicated.
- Consider gentle joint mobilization.
- Maintain and try to increase ROM.
- Begin strength training with isometric exercises, progressing to isotonic and then resistive exercises.
- Instruct client in posture training. Emphasize avoidance of kyphotic and protracted shoulder postures.

Chronic
- Consider use of ultrasound if indicated.
- Consider joint mobilization and automobilization techniques.

PRECAUTIONS/CONTRAINDICATIONS
- Brachial plexus peripheral entrapment at the thoracic outlet or the shoulder can be mistakenly identified as musculoskeletal pain of the shoulder.

- Avoid self-stretching into abduction until sufficient gains in external rotation are reached to prevent traumatization of subacromial tissues.
- Ill-timed or overly aggressive therapy can extend the symptoms.

DESIRED OUTCOME/PROGNOSIS

- The client will experience a decrease in symptoms.
- Painless functional ROM will be restored (regaining full movement may not be possible).
- The client will increase shoulder movement and be independent in self-mobilization techniques.
- The client will be independent in a home ROM plan to maintain progress.

Therapy for 3 to 4 months should bring satisfactory results. However, improvement usually follows a nonlinear pattern of recovery. Some report spontaneous recovery on an average of 12 months to 2 years after onset. When frozen shoulder is caused by sympathetic dystrophy, it can be very resistant to conservative management.

REFERENCES

ASSESSMENT

Donatelli RA, ed. *Physical Therapy of the Shoulder*. 2nd ed. New York, NY: Churchill Livingstone; 1991:19–61. [Algorithm for sequential shoulder girdle evaluation]

Elsner RC, Pedegrana LR, Lang J. Protocol for strength testing and rehabilitation of the upper extremity. *Journal of Orthopaedic Sports and Physical Therapy*. 1983;4:229.

Joint Integrity and Structural Deviations/Neurological Involvement

Donatelli RA, ed. *Physical Therapy of the Shoulder*. 2nd ed. New York, NY: Churchill Livingstone; 1991:19-61. [Transverse homeral ligament rapture test, upper quarter screen]

Grant R, ed. *Physical Therapy of the Cervical and Thoracic Spine*. New York, NY: Churchill Livingstone; 1988:167–194. [Upper limb tension test]

Hertling D, Kessler RM. *Management of Common Musculoskeletal Disorders*. Philadelphia, Pa: JB Lippincott Co; 1990:192–194. [Locking test, quadrant test, anterior stability test, isokinetic tests, nerve conduction studies]

Rothstein JM, Roy SH, Wolf SL. *The Rehabilitation Specialist's Handbook*. Philadelphia, Pa: FA Davis Co; 1991:124–125. [Thoracic outlet syndrome: Adson's test, Allen's test, costoclavicular syndrome test, Halstead maneuver, hyperabduction syndrome test, Speed's test (bicep's test), suprascapular nerve entrapment test, Yergason's test]

Tomberlin JP, Saunders HD. *Evaluation, Treatment and Prevention of Musculoskeletal Disorders. Vol 2: Extremities*. Chaska, Minn: The Saunders Group; 1994:91. [Joint/ligamentous: anterior apprehension test, Rockwood test, relocation test, anterior drawer sign, fulcrum test, clunk test, posterior apprehension test, posterior drawer sign, jerk test, Norwood stress test, push-pull test, sulcus sign, Feagin test, Rowe test for multidimensional instability, lateral scapular glide, acromioclavicular instability test, Neer's test, Hawkin's test, active impingement test, drop arm test, Speed's test, Gilchrist's sign, Lippman's test, Ludington's test; neurological: Adson's test, costoclavicular syndrome test, hyperabduction syndrome test, Roo's test (EAST test)]

Pain

Donatelli RA, ed. *Physical Therapy of the Shoulder*. 2nd ed. New York, NY: Churchill Livingstone; 1991:19–61. [Pain visual analogue scale and body chart]

Special Tests to Which the PT May or May Not Have Access

EMG

Ballantyne BT, O'Hare SJ, Paschall JL, et al. Electromyographic activity of selected shoulder muscles in commonly used therapeutic exercises. *Physical Therapy*. 1993;73:668–682.

Strength

Isokinetic Evaluation

Donatelli RA, ed. *Physical Therapy of the Shoulder*. 2nd ed. New York, NY: Churchill Livingstone; 1991:19–61.

Hageman PA, Mason DK, Rylund KW, et al. Effects of position and speed on eccentric and concentric isokinetic testing of the shoulder rotators. *Journal of Orthopaedic Sports and Physical Therapy*. 1989;11:64–69.

Maddux REC, Kibler WB, Uhl T. Isokinetic peak torque and work values for the shoulder. *Journal of Orthopaedic Sports and Physical Therapy*. 1989;1:264–269.

Soderberg GJ, Blaschak MJ. Shoulder internal and external rotation peak torque production through a velocity spectrum in differing positions. *Journal of Orthopaedic and Sports Physical Therapy*. 1987;8:518–524.

Wilk KE, Arrigo CA, Andrews JR. Isokinetic testing of the shoulder abductors and adductors: windowed vs non-windowed data collection. *Journal of Orthopaedic and Sports Physical Therapy*. 1992;15:107–112.

Manual Muscle Testing

Daniels L, Worthingham C. *Muscle Testing Techniques of Manual Examination*. 6th ed. Philadelphia, Pa: WB Saunders Co; 1995.

Kendall FP, McCreary EK, Provance PG. *Muscles: Testing and Function*. 4th ed. Baltimore, Md: Williams & Wilkins; 1993.

Temperature

Middleditch A, Jarman P. An investigation of frozen shoulders using thermography. *Physiotherapy*. 1984;70:433–439.

TREATMENT

Boissonnault WG, Janos, SC. Dysfunction, evaluation, and treatment of the shoulder. In: Donatelli R, Wooden MJ, eds. *Orthopaedic Physical Therapy*. New York, NY: Churchill Livingstone; 1989.

Boublik M, Hawkins RJ. Clinical examination of the shoulder complex. *Journal of Orthopaedic and Sports Physical Therapy*. 1993;18:379–385.

Burstein D. Joint compression for treatment of shoulder pain. *Clinical Management in Physical Therapy*. 1985;5:2:6–9.

Culham E, Peat M. Functional anatomy of the shoulder complex. *Journal of Orthopaedic and Sports Physical Therapy*. 1993;18:342–350.

Corrigan B, Maitland GD. *Practical Orthopaedic Medicine*. Boston, Mass: Butterworth; 1985.

Dacre JE, Beeney N, Scott DL. Injections and physiotherapy for the painful stiff shoulder. *Annals of the Rheumatic Diseases*. 1989;48:322–325.

Davies G, Dickoff-Hoffman S. Neuromuscular testing and rehabilitation of the shoulder complex. *Journal of Orthopaedic and Sports Physical Therapy*. 1993;18:449–458.

Donatelli RA, ed. *Physical Therapy of the Shoulder*. 2nd ed. New York, NY: Churchill Livingstone; 1991:19–62, 63–79, 91–116.

Donatelli RA, Greenfield B. Rehabilitation of a stiff and painful shoulder: a biomechanical approach. *Journal of Orthopaedic and Sports Physical Therapy*. 1987;9:118–126.

Engle RP, Canner GC. Shoulders and glenoid labrum tears. *Clinical Management in Physical Therapy*. 1988;8:5:14–17.

Gould J, Davies G, eds. *Orthopedic and Sports Physical Therapy*. St Louis, Mo: CV Mosby Co; 1985.

Grant LW, Ritch JM. Rx: rubber tubing. *Clinical Management in Physical Therapy*. 1988;8:6:10–15.

Grant R. *Physical Therapy of the Cervical and Thoracic Spine*. New York, NY: Churchill Livingstone; 1988.

Grieve GP, ed. *Modern Manual Therapy of the Vertebral Column*. New York, NY: Churchill Livingstone; 1986.

Grubbs N. Frozen shoulder syndrome: a review of literature. *Journal of Orthopaedic and Sports Physical Therapy*. 1993;18:479–487.

Hart DL, Carmichael SW. Biomechanics of the shoulder. *Journal of Orthopaedic and Sports Physical Therapy.* 1985;6:229–234.

Hertling D, Kessler RM. *Management of Common Musculoskeletal Disorders.* Philadelphia, Pa: JB Lippincott Co; 1990:169–204, 532–541.

Kisner C, Colby LA. *Therapeutic Exercise: Foundations and Techniques.* 2nd ed. Philadelphia, Pa: FA Davis Co; 1990:241–270.

McLean JM, Credit L. Orthotron II and shoulder rehabilitation. *Clinical Management in Physical Therapy.* 1989;9:2:43.

Nicholson G. The effects of passive joint mobilization on pain and hypermobility associated with adhesive capsulitis of the shoulder. *Journal of Orthopaedic Sports and Physical Therapy.* 1985;6:238–246.

Nitz AJ. Physical therapy management of the shoulder. *Physical Therapy.* 1986;66:1912–1919.

Palmer M, Epler M. *Clinical Assessment Procedures in Physical Therapy.* Philadelphia, Pa: JB Lippincott Co; 1990.

Peat M. Functional anatomy of the shoulder complex. *Physical Therapy.* 1986;66:1855–1865.

Tomberlin JP, Saunders HD. *Evaluation, Treatment and Prevention of Musculoskeletal Disorders. Vol 2: Extremities.* Chaska, Minn: The Saunders Group; 1994:73–111.

Schneider G. Restricted shoulder movement: capsular contracture or cervical referral—a clinical study. *Australian Journal of Physiotherapy.* 1989;35:2:97–100.

Schenkman M, Rugo de Cartaya V. Kinesiology of the shoulder complex. *Journal of Orthopaedic and Sports Physical Therapy.* 1993;18:442–448.

Simmons TC, Skyhair MJ. Rehabilitation of the shoulder. In: Nickel VL, Botte MJ, eds. *Orthopaedic Rehabilitation.* New York, NY: Churchill Livingstone; 1992:747.

Strang MH. Physiotherapy of the shoulder complex. *Baillieres Clinical Rheumatology.* 1989;3:669–680.

Wadsworth CT. Frozen shoulder. *Physical Therapy.* 1986;66:1878–1883.

Wilk KE, Arrigo CA. An integrated approach to upper extremity exercises. In Timm K, ed. Exercise Principles. *Orthopaedic Physical Therapy Clinics of North America.* 1992;2:337–360.

Voss DE, Knott M, Kabat M. Application of neuromuscular facilitation in the treatment of shoulder disabilities. *Physical Therapy Review.* 1953;33:536.

Lateral Epicondylitis and Medial Epicondylitis

DESCRIPTION

Lateral epicondylitis is also known as *tennis elbow* or *backhand tennis elbow*. In lateral humeral epicondylitis, the lateral forearm muscles (or their tendinous attachments) are strained close to their origin on the lateral epicondyle of the humerus. Tennis elbow occurs more frequently in men than women.

Medial epicondylitis is also known as *golfer's elbow, forehand tennis elbow, baseball elbow*, and *suitcase elbow*. In medial epicondylitis, the ventral forearm muscles and their attachments are strained.

CAUSE

Etiology is uncertain. The tissues may undergo degenerative changes called angiofibroblastic tendonosis.

Lateral epicondylitis may be caused by repetitive wrist action against resistance during extension and supination. *Medial epicondylitis* may be caused by repetitive stress during forceful wrist flexion and pronation.

Overuse injury risk factors

Intrinsic factors: malalignment, muscular imbalance, inflexibility, muscular weakness, instability

Extrinsic factors: training errors, equipment, environment, technique, sports-imposed deficiencies

Source: Adapted with permission from RM Buschbacher, *Musculoskeletal Disorders: A Practical Guide for Diagnosis and Rehabilitation*, p. 163, © 1994, Andover Medical Publishers.

ASSESSMENT

Areas
- History
- Pain
- Joint integrity and structural deviations
- Mobility: active and passive range of motion (ROM) and accessory motion
- Strength: any muscle weakness and biomechanical abnormality in rest of upper extremity that may be contributing to condition
- Neurological, including sensation
- Skin and soft tissue, including edema
- Functional level, including activities of daily living (ADLs)
- Special tests to which the PT may or may not have access

Instruments/Procedures (See References for Sources)

Joint Integrity and Structural Deviations/Neurological Involvement. The following neurological and orthopedic tests for the elbow may be performed:
- elbow flexion test
- golfer's elbow test
- ligamentous instability tests
- modification of passive extension-adduction tests
- neural tissue tension test
- pinch test
- pronator teres syndrome
- Tinel's sign
- tennis elbow tests
- varus stress test
- valgus stress test

Pain
- Nirschl Pain Phase Scale

Special Tests to Which the PT May or May Not Have Access
- integrated electromyography (IEMG)

Strength
- grip test dynamometer
- isokinetic testing
- manual muscle testing

PROBLEMS

Lateral Epicondylitis
- The client usually has localized tenderness medial and distal to the lateral epicondyle or at the lateral epicondyle.
- The client can have pain that extends along the extensor muscle distally.
- Usually pain is associated with gripping or repetitive motion.
- The client can also have neck pain or symptoms involving the radial nerve.
- The client can have decreased wrist extension with wrist flexed and ulnarly deviated and with fingers flexed.

Medial Epicondylitis
- The client usually has tenderness at the medial epicondyle.
- The client usually has pain and loss of strength with gripping or repetitive motion.
- The client can complain of neck pain or symptoms involving the median or ulnar nerve.

TREATMENT/MANAGEMENT

General Treatment Approach

The acronym **PRICEMM** summarizes treatments useful for pain and inflammation:
Protection
Rest: eliminate aggravating activities
Ice
Compression
Elevation
Medication: as prescribed
Modalities: high-voltage electrical stimulation, ultrasound, ice, heat

---

- Implement rehabilitative exercises, aerobic exercise, and general conditioning.
- Initially use isometric strengthening of elbow flexors and wrist extensors.
- Emphasize the pronators and supinators for lateral injury and the wrist flexors for medial injury.
- Progress to isotonic exercise and then to resistive exercise.
- Isoflex resistance tubing may begin after patient can perform exercise tolerating a 3# weight. Flexibility exercises can be started after 80% of normal strength is achieved.

Lateral Epicondylitis
- Consider use of modalities, such as cryotherapy or high-voltage galvanic stimulation for inflammation and electrical stimulation for mobilization. Ultrasound or phonophoresis can also promote healing.
- Provide friction massage to site of lesion.

- Use soft tissue mobilization to lateral forearm.
- Eliminate aggravating condition and avoid strong gripping activities in acute stage.
- Consider bracing to modify these conditions and combine with gentle ROM exercise when brace is off.
- Include flexibility stretching exercises and strengthening as tolerated, including both eccentric and concentric exercises.
- Emphasize high-repetition, low-resistance exercises. Can use freeweight elastic tubing if desired.
- Perform grip-strengthening exercises in functional power grip position.
- Consider appropriate neck, shoulder, and posture exercises.
- Consider ergonomic changes necessary to prevent injury recurrence.
- Ultrasound and friction massage can be useful in chronic conditions.
- Treatment following surgery usually includes gentle active ROM for approximately 3 weeks. Gradually progress to increase in ROM and resistance for strengthening exercises.

Medial Epicondylitis
- Generally, use same treatments as with lateral tennis elbow, but directed at the appropriate location.
- Avoid extreme repetitive flexion (if nerve is subluxating).
- Emphasize forearm flexor strength and endurance.
- Consider protection with elbow pad.

PRECAUTIONS/CONTRAINDICATIONS
- Progress cautiously with exercises to avoid aggravation of condition.
- Some other conditions that can cause similar pain and can be labeled as tennis elbow include pulled or pushed elbow, pinched synovial fringe, meniscal lock, periosteal bruise, and rotated elbow.
- Pain over the posterior aspect of the elbow may signal posterior tennis elbow, a rare condition.

DESIRED OUTCOME/PROGNOSIS
- The client will experience control of pain, edema, or spasm.
- The client will maintain soft tissue and joint mobility.
- The client will restore strength and extensibility to muscle tendon complex.
- Therapy will promote maturation of the healed area of the tendon.
- The client will progress to functional recovery.
- The client will have restoration of normal, painless use of the involved arm.
- The client will prevent recurrence.

In lateral epicondylitis, rehabilitation usually lasts a minimum of 3 months. A patient who ranks phase 5 or less on the Nirschl Pain Phase Scale may respond better to the rehabilitation program. Exercise appears to be the critical factor in recovery.

In medial epicondylitis, if the client does not respond to the conservative management after 3 to 4 months, the client may need to consider surgery.

REFERENCES

ASSESSMENT

Stratford PW, Levy DR, Gowland C. Evaluative properties of measures used to assess patients with lateral epicondylitis at the elbow. *Physiotherapy Canada*. 1993;45:160–164.

Joint Integrity and Structural Deviation/Neurological Involvement

Hyland S, Nitschke J, Matyas TA. The extension-adduction test in chronic tennis elbow: soft tissue components and joint biomechanics. *Australian Journal of Physiotherapy.* 1990;36:147–153. **[Modification of passive extension-adduction tests]**

Rothstein JM, Roy SH, Wolf SL. The *Rehabilitation Specialist's Handbook.* Philadelphia, Pa: FA Davis Co; 1991:125–126. **[Elbow flexion test, golfer's elbow test, tennis elbow tests, ligamentous instability tests]**

Stratford PW, Levy DR, Gowland C. Evaluative properties of measures used to assess patients with lateral epicondylitis at the elbow. *Physiotherapy Canada.* 1993;45:160–164.

Tomberlin JP, Saunders HD. *Evaluation, Treatment and Prevention of Musculoskeletal Disorders. Vol 2: Extremities.* Chaska, Minn: The Saunders Group; 1994:113–138. **[Golfer's elbow, tennis elbow, pinch test, pronator teres syndrome, elbow flexion test, Tinel's sign, varus stress test, valgus stress test]**

Yaxley GA, Jull GA. Adverse tension in the neural system: a preliminary study of tennis elbow. *Australian Journal of Physiotherapy.* 1993;39:1:15–22. **[Neural tissue tension test]**

Pain

Nirschl Pain Phase Scale

Buschbacher RM, ed. *Musculoskeletal Disorders: A Practical Guide for Diagnosis and Rehabilitation.* Boston, Mass: Andover Medical Publishers; 1994:158.

Special Tests to Which the PT May or May Not Have Access

Integrated EMG

Snyder-Mackler L, Epler M. Effect of standard and Aircast tennis elbow bands on integrated electromyography of forearm extensor musculature proximal to the bands. *American Journal of Sports Medicine.* 1989;17:278–281.

Strength

Grip Testing and Isokinetic Testing

Buschbacher RM, ed. *Musculoskeletal Disorders: A Practical Guide for Diagnosis and Rehabilitation.* Boston, Mass: Andover Medical Publishers; 1994:160.

Stratford PW, Norman GR, McIntosh JM. Generalizability of grip strength measurements in patients with tennis elbow. *Physical Therapy.* 1989;69:276–281.

Manual Muscle Testing

Daniels L, Worthingham C. *Muscle Testing Techniques of Manual Examination.* 6th ed. Philadelphia, Pa: WB Saunders Co; 1995.

Kendall FP, McCreary EK, Provance PG. *Muscles: Testing and Function.* 4th ed. Baltimore, Md: Williams & Wilkins; 1993.

TREATMENT

Almekinders LC, Almekinders SV. Outcome in the treatment of chronic overuse sports injuries: a retrospective study. *Journal of Orthopaedic and Sports Physical Therapy.* 1994;19:157–161.

Corrigan B, Maitland GD. *Practical Orthopaedic Medicine.* Boston, Mass: Butterworth; 1985.

Gould J, Davies G, eds. *Orthopedic and Sports Physical Therapy.* St Louis, Mo: CV Mosby Co; 1985.

Halle JS, Franklin RJ, Karalfa BL. Comparison of four treatment approaches for lateral epicondylitis of the elbow. *Journal of Orthopaedic and Sports Physical Therapy.* 1986;8:62–68.

Hertling D, Kessler RM. *Management of Common Musculoskeletal Disorders.* Philadelphia, Pa: JB Lippincott Co; 1990:216.

Kisner C, Colby LA. *Therapeutic Exercise: Foundations and Techniques.* 2nd ed. Philadelphia, Pa: FA Davis Co; 1990:280–283.

Palmer M, Epler M. *Clinical Assessment Procedures in Physical Therapy.* Philadelphia, Pa: JB Lippincott Co; 1990.

Stratford P, Levy DR, Gauldie S, Levy K, Miseferi D. Extensor carpi radialis tendinitis: a validation of selected outcome measures. *Physiotherapy Canada*. 1987;39:250–255.

Stratford PW, Levy DR, Gauldie S, Miseferi D, Levy K. The evaluation of phonophoresis and friction massage as treatments for extensor carpi radialis tendinitis: a randomized controlled trial. *Physiotherapy Canada*. 1989;41:93–99.

Stroyan M, Wilk K. The functional anatomy of the elbow complex. *Journal of Orthopaedic and Sports Physical Therapy*. 1993;17:279–288.

Tomberlin JP, Saunders HD. *Evaluation, Treatment and Prevention of Musculoskeletal Disorders. Vol 2: Extremities*. Chaska, Minn: The Saunders Group; 1994:113–138.

Vasseljen O. Low-level laser versus traditional physiotherapy in the treatment of tennis elbow. *Physiotherapy*. 1992;78:329–334.

Wadsworth CT. Elbow, forearm, wrist, and hand. In: Myers RS, ed. *Saunders Manual of Physical Therapy Practice*. Philadelphia, Pa: WB Saunders Co; 1995:841–917.

Wadsworth CT, Nelson DH, Burns LT, et al. Effect of the counterforce armband on wrist extension and grip strength and pain in subjects with tennis elbow. *Journal of Orthopaedic and Sports Physical Therapy*. 1989;11:192–197.

Wilder RP, Nirschl PR, Sobel J. Elbow and forearm. In: Buschbacher RM, ed. *Musculoskeletal Disorders: A Practical Guide for Diagnosis and Rehabilitation*. Boston, Mass: Andover Medical Publishers; 1994:153–169.

Yaxley GA, Jull GA. Adverse tension in the neural system: a preliminary study of tennis elbow. *Australian Journal of Physiotherapy*. 1993;39:1:15–22.

Hammer Toes

DESCRIPTION

Hammer toes are a deformity of the metatarsophalangeal joint resulting in flexion of the proximal interphalangeal joint.

CAUSE

Hammer toes are usually caused by wearing ill-fitting shoes. Malalignment of the joint surfaces leads to subluxations, capsular and synovial impingement, and destruction of joint cartilage.

ASSESSMENT

Areas

- History
- Posture
- Pain
- Gait
- Equipment, including footwear
- Strength
- Neurological
- Joint integrity and structural deviations

- Mobility, including active and passive range of motion (ROM) and accessory motion
- Skin and soft tissue, including edema

Instruments/Procedures (See References for Sources)

Mobility
- goniometry

Skin: Edema
- palpation

PROBLEMS

The client usually finds the condition painful.

TREATMENT/MANAGEMENT

In treatment of foot and ankle problems in general:
- Exercises progress from passive ROM to active assisted and active ROM to resisted ROM.
- Begin non-weight-bearing strengthening activities after pain-free ROM is achieved.
- Isometric, isotonic, and isokinetic exercise can be used.
- Consider eccentric loading.
- Progress to jogging, running, and athletic maneuvers as indicated.
- Address preventive measures, such as stretching, choice of shoes, and use of adhesive strapping during athletic activities.
  For hammer toes specifically:
- Fit with shoes with a deep toe box.
- Use muscle-strengthening exercises for foot intrinsic muscles.

PRECAUTIONS

- No precautions were identified.

DESIRED OUTCOME/PROGNOSIS

The client will experience relief of pressure on the dorsum of the flexed joints.
Surgery may be indicated in severe cases.

REFERENCES

ASSESSMENT
Giallonardo LM. Clinical evaluation of foot and ankle dysfunction. *Physical Therapy.* 1988;68:1850–1856.
McPoil TG, Hunt GC. Evaluation and management of foot and ankle disorders: present problems and future directions. *Journal of Orthopaedic and Sports Physical Therapy.* 1995;21:381–388.

TREATMENT
Boissonnault W, Donatelli R. The influence of hallux extension on the foot during ambulation. *Journal of Orthopaedic and Sports Physical Therapy.* 1984;5:240–242.
Brown LP, Yavorsky P. Locomotor biomechanics and pathomechanics: a review. *Journal of Orthopaedic and Sports Physical Therapy.* 1987;9:3.
Buschbacher RM, ed. *Musculoskeletal Disorders: A Practical Guide for Diagnosis and Rehabilitation.* Boston, Mass: Andover Medical Publishers; 1994:216–235.

Cibulka MT. Management of a patient with forefoot pain: a case report. *Physical Therapy*. 1990;70:41–44.

Donatelli R. Normal biomechanics of the foot and ankle. *Journal of Orthopaedic and Sports Physical Therapy*. 1985;7:91–95.

Donatelli R. Abnormal biomechanics of the foot and ankle. *Journal of Orthopaedic and Sports Physical Therapy*. 1987;9:11–16.

Donatelli R, ed. *The Biomechanics of the Foot and Ankle*. Philadelphia, Pa: FA Davis Co; 1990:258–259.

Donatelli R, Hurlbert C, Conway P, et al. Biomechanical foot orthotics: a retrospective study. *Journal of Orthopaedic and Sports Physical Therapy*. 1988;10:205–212.

Donatelli R, Wooden MJ, eds. *Orthopaedic Physical Therapy*. New York, NY: Churchill Livingstone; 1989.

Doxey GE. Clinical use and fabrication of molded thermoplastic foot orthotic devices. *Physical Therapy*. 1985;65:1679–1682.

Giallonardo LM. Clinical evaluation of foot and ankle dysfunction. *Physical Therapy*. 1988;68:1850–1856.

Gould JA, Davies GJ, eds. *Orthopaedic and Sports Physical Therapy*. St Louis: CV Mosby Co; 1985:317.

Hertling D, Kessler RM. *Management of Common Musculoskeletal Disorders*. Philadelphia, Pa: JB Lippincott Co; 1990:359–410.

Hunt GC, ed. *Physical Therapy of the Foot and Ankle*. New York, NY: Churchill Livingstone; 1988.

Kahn J. Electrotherapy with podiatric conditions. *Clinical Management in Physical Therapy*. 1988;8:3:6–9.

Kisner C, Colby LA. *Therapeutic Exercise: Foundations and Techniques*. 2nd ed. Philadelphia, Pa: FA Davis Co; 1990:385–407.

Lockard MA. Foot orthoses. *Physical Therapy*. 1988;68:1866–1873.

Maitland GD. *Peripheral Manipulation*, 3rd ed. Boston, Mass: Butterworths; 1990.

McPoil TG. The cobra pad: an orthotic alternative for the PT. *Journal of Orthopaedic and Sports Physical Therapy*. 1983;5:30.

McPoil TG. Footwear. *Physical Therapy*. 1988;68:1857–1865.

McPoil TG, Knecht HG. Biomechanics of the foot in walking: a functional approach. *Journal of Orthopaedic and Sports Physical Therapy*. 1985;7:69–72.

Oatis CA. Biomechanics of the foot and ankle under static conditions. *Physical Therapy*. 1988;68:1815–1821.

Palmer M, Epler M. *Clinical Assessment Procedures in Physical Therapy*. Philadelphia, Pa: JB Lippincott Co; 1990.

Riegger CL. Anatomy of the ankle and foot. *Physical Therapy*. 1988;68:1802–1814.

Sammarco GJ, ed. *Foot and Ankle Manual*. Philadelphia, Pa: Lea & Febiger; 1991:350–358.

Tiberio D. Pathomechanics of structural foot deformities. *Physical Therapy*. 1988;68:1840–1849.

Tomberlin JP, Saunders HD. *Evaluation, Treatment and Prevention of Musculoskeletal Disorders. Vol 2: Extremities*. Chaska, Minn: The Saunders Group; 1994:265–305.

Viel ER, Desmarets JJ. Mechanical pull of the peroneal tendons on the fifth ray of the foot. *Journal of Orthopaedic and Sports Physical Therapy*. 1985;7:102–106.

Hip Capsular Sprain

DESCRIPTION

Wrenching of the hip joint with disruption of the joint capsule.

CAUSE

Hip capsular sprain may have an insidious onset or be caused by minor trauma, such as a twisting motion.

ASSESSMENT

Areas
- History
- Pain
- Posture
- Joint integrity and structural deviations
- Gait
- Mobility: active and passive range of motion (ROM) and accessory motion
- Strength
- Neurological
- Skin and soft tissue, including edema
- Functional level

Instruments/Procedures (See References for Sources)

Joint Integrity and Structural Deviations. The following orthopedic tests may be performed:
- Craig's test
- Ely's test
- Fabere test
- hamstring tightness
- leg-length measurements
- Noble's compression test
- Ober's test
- piriformis test
- quadrant tests
- Thomas test
- Trendelenburg's sign

Mobility
- goniometry

Posture
- clinical measurement of postural control
- pelvic tilt measurement

Skin: Edema
- palpation

Strength
- maximal isometric hip abductor muscles torques
- manual muscle testing

PROBLEMS
- The client will usually have pain with weight bearing.
- The client may have decreased range of motion at hip.
- The client may be unable to tolerate weight bearing or may have shorter stride length.
- The client may have decreased capacity for activities of daily living.

TREATMENT/MANAGEMENT
- Use modalities for pain relief and tissue management.

- Consider gentle mobilization; progress as tolerated.
- The therapist can use external support, such as hip spica wrap and cane, crutches, or walker for support with weight-bearing activities.
- Begin strengthening exercises as tolerated. These can include active and resistive exercise. Consider proprioceptive neuromuscular facilitation (PNF) or aquatic therapy.
- Initiate ROM exercises early.

PRECAUTIONS/CONTRAINDICATIONS
- See Appendix C for precautions for modality usage.

DESIRED OUTCOME/PROGNOSIS
- The client will return to pain-free activities of daily living.
- The client will prevent any further capsular stiffness and degenerative changes.

Acute symptoms may resolve spontaneously, but any lingering capsular tightness may lead to further hip problems.

REFERENCES

ASSESSMENT
Echternach JL, ed. *Physical Therapy of the Hip*. New York, NY: Churchill Livingstone; 1990:36. [**Hip pain algorithm**]

Joint Integrity and Structural Deviations/Neurological Involvement
Gogia PP, Braatz JH. Validity and reliability of leg length measurements. *Journal of Orthopaedic and Sports Physical Therapy*. 1986;8:185–188.
Tomberlin JP, Saunders HD. *Evaluation, Treatment and Prevention of Musculoskeletal Disorders. Vol 2: Extremities*. Chaska, Minn: The Saunders Group; 1994:200. [**Trendelenburg's sign, piriformis test, Thomas test, Ely's test, Ober's test, Noble's compression test, hamstring tightness, quadrant test, Fabere test, torque test, Craig's test, leg-length test**]
Woerman AL, Binder-MacLeod SA. Leg length discrepancy assessment accuracy and precision in five clinical methods of evaluation. *Journal of Orthopaedic and Sports Physical Therapy*. 1984;5:230–239.

Mobility
Rothstein JM, ed. *Measurement in Physical Therapy*. New York, NY: Churchill Livingstone; 1985:103.
VanRoy P, Borms J, Haentjens A. Goniometric study of the maintenance of hip flexibility resulting from hamstring stretches. *Physiotherapy Practice*. 1987;3:2:52–59.

Posture
Horak FB. Clinical measurement of postural control in adults. *Physical Therapy*. 1987;67:1881–1885.
Gajdosik R, Simpson R, Smith R, DonTigny R. Pelvic tilt, intertester reliability of measuring the standing position and range of motion. *Physical Therapy*. 1985;65:169–174.

Strength
Neumann DA, Soderberg GL, Cook TM. Comparison of maximal isometric hip abductor muscles torques between hip sides. *Physical Therapy*. 1988;68:496–502.
Neumann DA, Soderberg GL, Cook TM. Electromyographic analysis of hip abductor musculature in healthy right-handed persons. *Physical Therapy*. 1989;69:431–440.

Manual Muscle Testing

Daniels L, Worthingham C. *Muscle Testing Techniques of Manual Examination.* 6th ed. Philadelphia, Pa: WB Saunders Co; 1995.

Kendall FP, McCreary EK, Provance PG. *Muscles: Testing and Function.* 4th ed. Baltimore, Md: Williams & Wilkins, 1993.

TREATMENT

Bandy WD, Sinning WE. Kinematic effect of heel lift use to correct lower limb length. *Journal of Orthopaedic and Sports Physical Therapy.* 1986;7:173–179.

Cibulka MT. Rehabilitation of the pelvis, hip and thigh. *Clinics in Sports Medicine.* 1989;8:777–803.

Donatelli R, Wooden MJ, eds. *Orthopaedic Physical Therapy.* New York, NY: Churchill Livingstone; 1989:403.

Echternach JL, ed. *Physical Therapy of the Hip.* New York, NY: Churchill Livingstone; 1990.

Hertling D, Kessler RM. *Management of Common Musculoskeletal Disorders.* Philadelphia, Pa: JB Lippincott Co; 1990:272–297.

Kisner C, Colby LA. *Therapeutic Exercise: Foundations and Techniques.* 2nd ed. Philadelphia, Pa: FA Davis Co; 1990:317–344.

Kornberg C, McCarthy T. The effect of neural stretching technique on sympathetic outflow to the lower limbs. *Journal of Orthopaedic and Sports Physical Therapy.* 1992;16:269–274.

Maitland GF. *Peripheral Manipulation.* 3rd ed. London, England: Butterworths, 1990:203.

Markos PD. Ipsilateral and contralateral effects of proprioceptive neuromuscular facilitation techniques on hip motion and electromyographic activity. *Physical Therapy.* 1979;59:1366.

Newton RA. Effects of vapocoolants on passive hip flexion in healthy subjects. *Physical Therapy.* 1985;65:1034–1036.

Palmer M, Epler M. *Clinical Assessment Procedures in Physical Therapy.* Philadelphia, Pa: JB Lippincott Co; 1990.

Tomberlin JP, Saunders HD. *Evaluation, Treatment and Prevention of Musculoskeletal Disorders. Vol 2: Extremities.* Chaska, Minn: The Saunders Group; 1994:187–212.

Iliopectineal Bursitis

DESCRIPTION

Acute or chronic inflammation of the iliopectineal bursa. Iliopectineal bursitis is less common than trochanteric bursitis.

CAUSE

Onset is insidious but can be associated with osteoarthritis. Iliopectineal bursitis may be caused by tightness in the iliopsoas muscle.

ASSESSMENT

Areas
- History
- Pain

- Posture
- Joint integrity and structural deviations
- Gait
- Mobility: active and passive range of motion (ROM) and accessory motion
- Strength
- Neurological
- Skin and soft tissue: edema
- Functional level

Instruments/Procedures (See References for Sources)

Joint Integrity and Structural Deviations
- Craig's test
- Ely's test
- Fabere test
- hamstring tightness
- leg-length measurements
- Noble's compression test
- Ober's test
- piriformis test
- Thomas test
- Trendelenburg's sign
- quadrant test

Mobility
- goniometry

Posture
- clinical measurement of postural control
- pelvic tilt

Skin: Edema
- palpation

Strength
- maximal isometric hip abductor muscles torques
- manual muscle testing

PROBLEMS
- This condition closely resembles trochanteric bursitis, but pain is with hip flexion against resistance or passive hip extension.
- The client usually has pain in the groin area.
- There can be pain that radiates to the L-2 or L-3 segment level.

TREATMENT/MANAGEMENT
- Use modalities, such as ice, ultrasound, and iontophoresis, if indicated.
- Avoid aggravating activities.
- Discuss sleep posture adaptations with pillows.
- Assess for muscular imbalance and stretch (iliotibial band tightness), and strengthen accordingly.

- Refer to section on osteoarthritis if this condition is an aggravating factor.

PRECAUTIONS/CONTRAINDICATIONS
Refer to Appendix C for precautions concerning the use of modalities.

PROGNOSIS/OUTCOME
- The client will return to pain-free activities of daily living.
- The inflammation and pain will decrease, and recurrence will be prevented.
  Ultrasound may offer quite effective relief in three to six sessions.

REFERENCES

ASSESSMENT
Echternach JL, ed. *Physical Therapy of the Hip*. New York, NY: Churchill Livingstone; 1990:36. **[Hip pain algorithm]**

Hicklin SP, DePretis MC. Lower extremity: hip. In: Myers RS, ed. *Saunders Manual of Physical Therapy Practice*. Philadelphia, Pa: WB Saunders Co; 1995:955–999. **[Algorithm]**

Joint Integrity and Structural Deviations
Gogia PP, Braatz JH. Validity and reliability of leg length measurements. *Journal of Orthopaedic and Sports Physical Therapy*. 1986;8:185.

Tomberlin JP, Saunders HD. *Evaluation, Treatment and Prevention of Musculoskeletal Disorders. Vol 2: Extremities*. Chaska, Minn: The Saunders Group; 1994:200. **[Trendelenburg's sign, piriformis test, Thomas test, Ely's test, Ober's test, Noble's compression test, hamstring tightness, quadrant test, Fabere test, torque test, Craig's test, leg-length test]**

Woerman AL, Binder-MacLeod SA. Leg length discrepancy assessment accuracy and precision in five clinical methods of evaluation. *Journal of Orthopaedic and Sports Physical Therapy*. 1984;5:230.

Mobility
Johnston R. Hip motion measurements for selected activities of daily living. *Clinical Orthopedics*. 1970;72:205–216.

Rothstein JM, ed. *Measurement in Physical Therapy*. New York, NY: Churchill Livingstone; 1985:103.

VanRoy P, Borms J, Haentjens A. Goniometric study of the maintenance of hip flexibility resulting from hamstring stretches. *Physiotherapy Practice*. 1987;3:52–59.

Posture
Gajdosik R, Simpson R, Smith R, DonTigny R. Pelvic tilt, intertester reliability of measuring the standing position and range of motion. *Physical Therapy*. 1985;65:169.

Horak FB. Clinical measurement of postural control in adults. *Physical Therapy*. 1987;67:1881.

Strength
Neumann DA, Soderberg GL, Cook TM. Comparison of maximal isometric hip abductor muscles torques between hip sides. *Physical Therapy*. 1988;68:596.

Neumann DA, Soderberg GL, Cook TM. Electromyographic analysis of hip abductor musculature in healthy right-handed persons. *Physical Therapy*. 1989;69:431.

Manual Muscle Testing
Daniels L, Worthingham C. *Muscle Testing Techniques of Manual Examination*. 6th ed. Philadelphia, Pa: WB Saunders Co; 1995.

Kendall FP, McCreary EK, Provance PG. *Muscles, Testing and Function*. 4th ed. Baltimore, Md: Williams & Wilkins; 1993.

TREATMENT

Bandy WD, Sinning WE. Kinematic effect of heel lift use to correct lower limb length. *Journal of Orthopaedic and Sports Physical Therapy*. 1986;7:173.

Boyle AM. The Bad Ragaz ring method. *Physiotherapy*. 1981;67:265.

Cibulka MT. Rehabilitation of the pelvis, hip and thigh. *Clinics in Sports Medicine*. 1989;8:777–803.

Donatelli R, Wooden MJ, eds. *Orthopaedic Physical Therapy*. New York, NY: Churchill Livingstone; 1989:403.

Echternach JL, ed. *Physical Therapy of the Hip*. New York, NY: Churchill Livingstone; 1990.

Hertling D, Kessler RM. *Management of Common Musculoskeletal Disorders*. Philadelphia, Pa: JB Lippincott Co; 1990:272–297.

Kisner C, Colby LA. *Therapeutic Exercise: Foundations and Techniques*. 2nd ed. Philadelphia, Pa: FA Davis Co; 1990:317–344.

Kornberg C, McCarthy T. The effect of neural stretching technique on sympathetic outflow to the lower limbs. *Journal of Orthopaedic and Sports Physical Therapy*. 1992;16:269–274.

Maitland GF. *Peripheral Manipulation*, 3rd ed. London, England: Butterworths; 1990:203.

Newton RA. Effects of vapocoolants on passive hip flexion in healthy subjects. *Physical Therapy*. 1985;65:1034.

Palmer M, Epler M. *Clinical Assessment Procedures in Physical Therapy*. Philadelphia, Pa: JB Lippincott Co; 1990.

Tomberlin JP, Saunders HD. *Evaluation, Treatment and Prevention of Musculoskeletal Disorders. Vol 2: Extremities*. Chaska, Minn: The Saunders Group; 1994:187–212.

Interdigital Neuroma

Also known as *Morton's neuroma* or *metatarsalgia*.

DESCRIPTION

Neuroma is a benign fibrous tissue formation. Interdigital neuroma usually occurs at the third plantar interdigital nerve, although other locations are possible. Interdigital neuroma is more likely to be unilateral than bilateral and is more common in women than men.

CAUSE

This condition may begin with a lack of neural mobility and progress to the formation of a neuroma. It may be caused by excessive compression and the shearing force accompanying weight bearing. Undue pronation during the stance phase of weight bearing has also been implicated.

ASSESSMENT

Areas
- History
- Posture
- Pain
- Gait
- Strength
- Neurological
- Joint integrity and structural deviations

- Mobility, including active and passive range of motion (ROM) and accessory motion
- Skin and soft tissue
- Equipment, including footwear

Instruments/Procedures (See References for Sources)

Gait
- dynamic assessment of foot mechanics
  1. dynamic plantar pressure distribution
  2. foot pressure EMED system
  3. pedabarograph
  4. three-dimensional kinematic analysis
- footprint analysis in gait documentation

PROBLEMS
- The client usually has pain at the metatarsal head, especially the third or fourth, with weight bearing.
- The client can demonstrate extreme pronation of the subtalar joint.
- The client can have tenderness to touch at the third or fourth metatarsal head or at any metatarsal head.
- The metatarsal bone can demonstrate either hypo- or hypermobility.
- Usually the pain worsens with activity.

TREATMENT/MANAGEMENT
- Use physical agents, such as local ice application, if indicated.
- Consider joint mobilization for intermetatarsal joint.
- Use neural mobilization if indicated.
- Assess footwear. Consider custom-made shoes with support for proximal to metatarsal heads.
- Assess need for orthotics such as metatarsal arch pads.
- Assess and possibly change any fitness training techniques.
- Use strengthening and flexibility exercises.
- If the client is postoperative, consider mobility exercises.

PRECAUTIONS/CONTRAINDICATIONS
See Appendix C for precautions for modality usage.

DESIRED OUTCOME/PROGNOSIS
- The client will experience control of symptoms.
- There will be an improved joint glide.
- Therapy will control forefoot hypermobility and excessive pronation.

Sometimes surgical removal of the neuroma is indicated. Postoperative care may prevent scar tissue formation.

REFERENCES

ASSESSMENT
McPoil TG, Hunt GC. Evaluation and management of foot and ankle disorders: present problems and future directions. *Journal of Orthopaedic and Sports Physical Therapy.* 1995;21:381–388.

Gait

Donatelli R, ed. *The Biomechanics of the Foot and Ankle.* Philadelphia, Pa: FA Davis Co; 1990:148–152.
   [Dynamic assessment of foot mechanics: dynamic plantar pressure distribution, foot pressure EMED system, pedabarograph, three-dimensional kinematic analysis]

Shore M. Footprint analysis in gait documentation: an instructional sheet format. *Physical Therapy.* 1980;60:1163–1167.

Joint Integrity and Structural Deviations

Rothstein JM, Roy SH, Wolf SL. *The Rehabilitation Specialist's Handbook.* Philadelphia, Pa: FA Davis Co; 1991:136–137.

Tomberlin JP, Saunders HD. *Evaluation, Treatment and Prevention of Musculoskeletal Disorders. Vol 2: Extremities.* Chaska, Minn: The Saunders Group; 1994:265–306.

TREATMENT

Billing HE, Brennan RL. Foot pains. *NAPT Journal.* 1984;16:18 (Jan-Feb).

Brown LP, Yavorsky P. Locomotor biomechanics and pathomechanics: a review. *Journal of Orthopaedic and Sports Physical Therapy.* 1987;9:3.

Buschbacher RM, ed. *Musculoskeletal Disorders: A Practical Guide for Diagnosis and Rehabilitation.* Boston, Mass: Andover Medical Publishers; 1994:216–235.

Cibulka MT. Management of a patient with forefoot pain: a case report. *Physical Therapy.* 1990;70:41–44.

Donatelli R. Normal biomechanics of the foot and ankle. *Journal of Orthopaedic and Sports Physical Therapy.* 1985;7:91.

Donatelli R. Abnormal biomechanics of the foot and ankle. *Journal of Orthopaedic and Sports Physical Therapy.* 1987;9:11–16.

Donatelli R, ed. *The Biomechanics of the Foot and Ankle.* Philadelphia, Pa: FA Davis Co; 1990:258–259.

Donatelli R, Hurlbert C, Conway P, et al. Biomechanical foot orthotics: A retrospective study. *Journal of Orthopaedic and Sports Physical Therapy.* 1988;10:205–212.

Donatelli R, Wooden MJ, eds. *Orthopaedic Physical Therapy.* New York, NY: Churchill Livingstone; 1989.

Doxey GE. Clinical use and fabrication of molded thermoplastic foot orthotic devices. *Physical Therapy.* 1985;65:1679.

Giallonardo LM. Clinical evaluation of foot and ankle dysfunction. *Physical Therapy.* 1988;68:1850–1856.

Gould JA, Davies GJ, eds. *Orthopaedic and Sports Physical Therapy.* St Louis: CV Mosby Co; 1985:317.

Hertling D, Kessler RM. *Management of Common Musculoskeletal Disorders.* Philadelphia, Pa: JB Lippincott Co; 1990:359–410.

Hunt GC, ed. *Physical Therapy of the Foot and Ankle.* New York, NY: Churchill Livingstone; 1988.

Kahn J. Electrotherapy with podiatric conditions. *Clinical Management in Physical Therapy.* 1988;8:3:6–9.

Kisner C, Colby LA. *Therapeutic Exercise: Foundations and Techniques.* 2nd ed. Philadelphia, Pa: FA Davis Co; 1990:385–407.

Lockard MA. Foot orthoses. *Physical Therapy.* 1988;68:1866–1873.

Maitland GD. *Peripheral Manipulation.* 3rd ed. Boston, Mass: Butterworths; 1990.

McPoil TG. Footwear. *Physical Therapy.* 1988;68:1857.

McPoil TG, Knecht HG. Biomechanics of the foot in walking: a functional approach. *Journal of Orthopaedic and Sports Physical Therapy.* 1985;7:69.

Oatis CA. Biomechanics of the foot and ankle under static conditions. *Physical Therapy.* 1988;68:1815.

Palmer M, Epler M. *Clinical Assessment Procedures in Physical Therapy.* Philadelphia, Pa: JB Lippincott Co; 1990.

Riegger CL. Anatomy of the ankle and foot. *Physical Therapy.* 1988;68:1802–1814.

Sammarco GJ, ed. *Foot and Ankle Manual.* Philadelphia, Pa: Lea & Febiger; 1991:350–358.

Tiberio D. Pathomechanics of structural foot deformities. *Physical Therapy.* 1988;68:1840–1849.

Tomberlin JP, Saunders HD. *Evaluation, Treatment and Prevention of Musculoskeletal Disorders. Vol 2: Extremities.* Chaska, Minn: The Saunders Group; 1994:265–305.

Viel ER, Desmarets JJ. Mechanical pull of the peroneal tendons on the fifth ray of the foot. *Journal of Orthopaedic and Sports Physical Therapy.* 1985;7:102.

Woodman R, Pare L. Evaluation and treatment of soft tissue lesions of the ankle and forefoot using the Cyriax approach. *Physical Therapy.* 1982;62:1144.

Medial Tibial Stress Syndrome

Also known as *anterolateral* or *posteromedial shin splints.*

DESCRIPTION

An overuse syndrome leading to damage to the anterior compartment muscles or posteromedial compartment muscles. The tibialis posterior tendon is the most commonly affected structure.

CAUSE

This overuse syndrome can be caused by irritation of the tibial periosteum. Tendinitis can also cause this complaint. Extreme pronation of the subtalar joint can cause this condition in the posteromedial compartment. Factors also influencing medial tibial stress syndrome include repetitive microtrauma, footwear, flexibility, muscle imbalance, and structural malalignment.

ASSESSMENT

Areas

- History
- Pain
- Posture
- Gait
- Strength
- Neurological
- Joint integrity and structural deviations
- Mobility, including active and passive range of motion (ROM) and accessory motion
- Skin and soft tissues
- Equipment, including footwear

Instruments/Procedures (See References for Sources)

Gait
- dynamic assessment of foot mechanics
  1. dynamic plantar pressure distribution
  2. foot pressure EMED system
  3. pedabarograph
  4. three-dimensional kinematic analysis
- stance phase analysis
- gait velocity
- footprint analysis in gait documentation

Joint Integrity and Structural Deviations
• tibial varum assessment

Mobility
• assessment of ankle dorsiflexion
• goniometry
• visual estimates of ankle joint active ROM

Pain
• palpation

Strength
• isokinetic testing
• manual muscle testing

PROBLEMS

Anterolateral
• The client usually has pain and tenderness at the lateral border and distal half of the medial tibial crest of the tibia.
• Usually the pain increases with active dorsiflexion and passive stretch of ankle dorsiflexors.

Posteromedial
• The client usually has shin pain posteromedially, 4 to 6 inches proximal to the medial malleolus with activity, especially weight bearing.
• There can be tenderness along the posteromedial border of the tibia, especially distally.
• The client may have a tendency toward excessive subtalor pronation.
• The client usually has a tight soleus muscle.

TREATMENT/MANAGEMENT
For treatment of foot and ankle problems in general:
• Exercises progress from passive ROM to active assisted and active ROM to resisted ROM.
• Begin non-weight-bearing strengthening activities after pain-free ROM is achieved.
• Isometric, isotonic, and isokinetic exercise can be used.
• Eccentric loading should not be overlooked.
• Progress to jogging, running, and athletic maneuvers as indicated.
• Address preventive measures, such as stretching, choice of shoes, and use of adhesive strapping during athletic activities.
For medial tibial stress syndrome specifically:
• Use physical agents, such as ice, as indicated.
• Consider use of compression.
• Avoid weight bearing; the client may need gait-assistive devices.
• Instruct in flexibility and strengthening exercises.
• Assess for orthotics.
• Teach activity modification with return to activity as pain allows.

PRECAUTIONS/CONTRAINDICATIONS
This condition can mimic tibial or fibular stress fracture, tibial stress reaction, or anterior compartment syndrome.

DESIRED OUTCOME/PROGNOSIS
- The client will experience control of symptoms such as edema, pain, and inflammation.
- The client will decrease stress with activity modification.
- There will be a decrease in excessive pronation, and shock will be absorbed with orthotics.
- Therapy will improve flexibility of the heel cord and the first metatarsal phalangeal joint to reduce excessive pronatatory forces.
- Therapy will strengthen the plantarflexors and inverters of the foot.
- The client will prevent recurrence.

REFERENCES

ASSESSMENT

Gait
Cerny K, Perry J, Walker JM. Effect of an unrestricted knee-ankle-foot orthosis on the stance phase of gait in healthy persons. *Orthopedics*. 1990;13:1121–1127.

Donatelli R, ed. *The Biomechanics of the Foot and Ankle*. Philadelphia, Pa: FA Davis Co; 1990:148–152.
[Dynamic assessment of foot mechanics: dynamic plantar pressure distribution, foot pressure EMED system, pedabarograph, three-dimensional kinematic analysis]

McCulloch MU, Brunt D, Vander-Linden D. The effect of foot orthotics and gait velocity on lower limb kinematics and temporal events of stance. *Journal of Orthopaedic and Sports Physical Therapy*. 1993;17:2–10.

Shore M. Footprint analysis in gait documentation: an instructional sheet format. *Physical Therapy*. 1980;60:1163–1167.

Joint Integrity and Structural Deviations
McPoil TG, Schuit D, Knecht HG. A comparison of three positions used to evaluate tibial varum. *Journal of the American Podiatric Medical Association*. 1988;78:22–28.

Rothstein JM, Roy SH, Wolf SL. *The Rehabilitation Specialist's Handbook*. Philadelphia, Pa: FA Davis Co; 1991:136–137.

Tomberlin JP, Saunders HD. *Evaluation, Treatment and Prevention of Musculoskeletal Disorders. Vol 2: Extremities*. Chaska, Minn: The Saunders Group; 1994:265–306.

Mobility
Bohannon RW, Tiberio D, Zitto M. Selected measures of ankle dorsiflexion range of motion: differences and intercorrelations. *Foot and Ankle*. 1989;10:2:99–103.

Elveru RA, Rothstein JM, Lamb RL. Goniometric reliability in a clinical setting: subtalar and ankle joint measurements. *Physical Therapy*. 1988;68:672.

Kleven D, Bornhoeft D, Thorp B. Assessing ankle dorsiflexion. *Clinical Management in Physical Therapy*. 1989;9:6:25–26.

Youdas JW, Bogard CL, Suman VJ. Reliability of goniometric measurements and visual estimates of ankle joint active range of motion obtained in a clinical setting. *Archives of Physical Medicine and Rehabilitation*. 1993;74:1113–1118.

Strength

Isokinetic Testing
Lee WA, Michaels CF, Pai YC. The organization of torque and EMG activity during bilateral handle pulls by standing humans. *Experimental Brain Research*. 1990;82:304–314.

Simoneau GG. Isokinetic characteristics of ankle evertors and invertors in female control subjects using the Biodex dynamometer. *Physiotherapy Canada*. 1990;42:182–187.

Manual Muscle Testing
Daniels L, Worthingham C. *Muscle Testing Techniques of Manual Examination*. 6th ed. Philadelphia, Pa: WB Saunders Co; 1995.
Kendall FP, McCreary EK, Provance PG. *Muscles: Testing and Function*. 4th ed. Baltimore, Md: Williams & Wilkins, 1993.

TREATMENT
Ballantyne BT, Kukulka CG, Soderberg GL. Motor unit recruitment in human medial gastrocnemius muscle during combined knee flexion and plantar flexion isometric contractions. *Experimental Brain Research*. 1993;93:492–498.
Brown LP, Yavorsky P. Locomotor biomechanics and pathomechanics: a review. *Journal of Orthopaedic and Sports Physical Therapy*. 1987;9:3–10.
Buschbacher RM, ed. *Musculoskeletal Disorders: A Practical Guide for Diagnosis and Rehabilitation*. Boston, Mass: Andover Medical Publishers; 1994:216–235.
Donatelli R. Normal biomechanics of the foot and ankle. *Journal of Orthopaedic and Sports Physical Therapy*. 1985;7:91.
Donatelli R. Abnormal biomechanics of the foot and ankle. *Journal of Orthopaedic and Sports Physical Therapy*. 1987;9:11–16.
Donatelli R, ed. *The Biomechanics of the Foot and Ankle*. Philadelphia, Pa: FA Davis Co; 1990:258–259.
Donatelli R, Hurlbert C, Conway P, et al. Biomechanical foot orthotics: a retrospective study. *Journal of Orthopaedic and Sports Physical Therapy*. 1988;10:205–212.
Donatelli R, Wooden MJ, eds. *Orthopaedic Physical Therapy*. New York, NY: Churchill Livingstone; 1989.
Doxey GE. Clinical use and fabrication of molded thermoplastic foot orthotic devices. *Physical Therapy*. 1985;65:1679–1682.
Gans A. The relationship of heel contact in ascent and descent from jumps to the incidence of shin splints in ballet dancers. *Physical Therapy*. 1985;65:1192–1196.
Giallonardo LM. Clinical evaluation of foot and ankle dysfunction. *Physical Therapy*. 1988;68:1850–1856.
Gould JA, Davies GJ, eds. *Orthopaedic and Sports Physical Therapy*. St Louis: CV Mosby Co; 1985:317.
Hertling D, Kessler RM. *Management of Common Musculoskeletal Disorders*. Philadelphia, Pa: JB Lippincott Co; 1990:359–410.
Hunt GC, ed. *Physical Therapy of the Foot and Ankle*. New York, NY: Churchill Livingstone; 1988.
Kisner C, Colby LA. *Therapeutic Exercise: Foundations and Techniques*. 2nd ed. Philadelphia, Pa: FA Davis Co; 1990:385–407.
Kues J. The pathology of shin splints. *Journal of Orthopaedic and Sports Physical Therapy*. 1990;12:115–121.
Lockard MA. Foot orthoses. *Physical Therapy*. 1988;68:1866–1873.
Maitland GD. *Peripheral Manipulation*. 3rd ed. Boston, Mass: Butterworths; 1990.
McPoil TG. Footwear. *Physical Therapy*. 1988;68:1857–1865.
McPoil TG, Knecht HG. Biomechanics of the foot in walking: a functional approach. *Journal of Orthopaedic and Sports Physical Therapy*. 1985;7:69–72.
Oatis CA. Biomechanics of the foot and ankle under static conditions. *Physical Therapy*. 1988;68:1815–1821.
Palmer M, Epler M. *Clinical Assessment Procedures in Physical Therapy*. Philadelphia, Pa: JB Lippincott Co; 1990.
Riegger CL. Anatomy of the ankle and foot. *Physical Therapy*. 1988;68:1802–1814.
Sammarco GJ, ed. *Foot and Ankle Manual*. Philadelphia, Pa: Lea & Febiger; 1991:350–358.
Tiberio D. The effect of excessive subtalar joint pronation on patellofemoral mechanics: a theoretical model. *Journal of Orthopaedic and Sports Physical Therapy*. 1987;9:160–165.

Tiberio D. Pathomechanics of structural foot deformities. *Physical Therapy*. 1988;68:1840–1849.

Tomberlin JP, Saunders HD. *Evaluation, Treatment and Prevention of Musculoskeletal Disorders. Vol 2: Extremities*. Chaska, Minn: The Saunders Group; 1994:265–305.

Vander-Linden DW, Kukulka CG, Soderberg GL. The effect of muscle length on motor unit discharge characteristics in human tibialis anterior muscle. *Experimental Brain Research*. 1991;84:210–218.

Varelas FL, Wessel J, Clement DB, Doyle DL, Wilery JP. Muscle function in chronic compartment syndrome of the leg. *Journal of Orthopaedic and Sports Physical Therapy*. 1993;18:586–589.

Viel ER, Desmarets JJ. Mechanical pull of the peroneal tendons on the fifth ray of the foot. *Journal of Orthopaedic and Sports Physical Therapy*. 1985;7:102–106.

Woodman R, Pare L. Evaluation and treatment of soft tissue lesions of the ankle and forefoot using the Cyriax approach. *Physical Therapy*. 1982;62:1144.

Patellar Tendinitis

Also known as *jumper's knee, popliteal tendinitis*, and *semimembranosus tendinitis*.

DESCRIPTION

Inflammation of patellar, popliteal, or semimembranosus tendons. There is usually a higher incidence in clients involved in athletic activities.

CAUSE

Popliteal tendinitis, semimembranosus tendinitis, and patellar tendinitis are of unknown etiology, but overuse is considered an irritating factor. These conditions may be caused by the effects of aging, repetitive microtrauma, extreme trauma, strain, or unaccustomed exercise.

Patellar Tendinitis

Patellar tendinitis (jumper's knee) is an overuse syndrome often caused by repetitive jumping. It is often associated with tracking problems.

Popliteal and Semimembranosus Tendinitis

Popliteal tendinitis and semimembranosus tendinitis are often associated with running. Downhill running and hyperpronation of the foot may lead to popliteal or bicipital tendinitis at the knee.

ASSESSMENT

Areas

- History
- Pain
- Posture, including any pronation of feet and internal rotation at hip
- Joint integrity and structural deviations
- Mobility, including active and passive range of motion (ROM), and accessory motion
- Strength, including quadriceps and gluteus medius muscles
- Neurological

- Skin and soft tissue, including edema
- Gait
- Functional level

Instruments/Procedures (See References for Sources)

Functional Level
- modified Lysholm knee score

Joint Integrity and Structural Deviations. The following orthopaedic tests of the knee may be used. Those most recommended are marked with an asterisk.
- A-angle
- ALRI test
- AMRI test
- Apley grinding test
- apprehension test
- bounce home test
- brush or stroke (wipe) test
- Clark's sign
- crepitus*
- crossover test
- dynamic Q-angle*
- Ely's test
- external rotation test
- flexion rotation drawer sign
- fluctuation test
- gravity drawer test (posterior sag sign)
- hamstring length
- Helfet test
- Hughston plica test
- Hughston posterolateral drawer test
- Hughston test (jerk sign)
- hyperflexion-hyperextension test
- Jakob test (reverse pivot)
- Lachman test
- lateral pull test
- limb-length discrepancy
- MacIntosh test (lateral pivot shift)
- McConnell test
- McMurray–Anderson test
- Noble's compression test
- Ober's test
- O'Donoghue's test
- patellar tap
- patellar tilt
- patellofemoral grind test*
- Perkin's test
- plica test
- posterior drawer sign

- posterior sag test
- quadriceps active test
- reverse pivot shift test
- Slocum test
- Steinman's test
- squat test
- valgus stress test
- varus stress test
- Waldron test
- Wilson test

Skin and Soft Tissue: Edema
- thigh measurement

Special Tests to Which the PT May or May Not Have Access
- arthrography and arthroscopy
- computed tomography (CT)
- joint aspiration
- magnetic resonance imaging (MRI)
- x-ray studies
- ultrasonography

Strength
- cable tensiometers
- isokinetic dynamometers
- strain gauge devices
- manual muscle testing

PROBLEMS

Patellar Tendinitis
- The client usually reports pain and tenderness at the inferior end of the patella.
- The client can have swelling.
- There is usually pain when using the stairs and with any forceful knee extension.
- The client may complain of the knee's getting stiff and sore with prolonged sitting.

Popliteal and Semimembranosus Tendinitis
- The client usually reports pain on the lateral aspect of the knee.

TREATMENT/MANAGEMENT

Patellar Tendinitis
- Encourage rest.
- Use ice massage if indicated.
- Begin progressive resistive exercise strengthening program with emphasis on vastus medialis obliquus (VMO) and on eccentric exercises. Assess also for weakness of dorsiflexors.
- Implement flexibility exercises, including hamstring and gastrocnemius stretching.
- Consider phonophoresis with 10% hydrocortisone ointment. Other modalities include ultrasound or high-voltage pulsed monophasic current to patellar tendon.
- Consider an orthosis, patellar taping, or infrapatellar straps.

- Consider patellofemoral knee sleeve for edema control and reduction of mobility of patella tendon during activity.
- Advise client on modification of recreational and occupational activities.

Popliteal and Semimembranosus Tendinitis
- Encourage rest.
- Try intermittent use of ice for at least the first 72-hour period, if indicated.
- Consider use of ultrasound.
- Begin flexibility and strengthening exercises.
- Assess training techniques and footwear.

PRECAUTIONS/CONTRAINDICATIONS
- X-rays should be consulted to rule out any potential fractures.
- Carefully consider the nature of the problem before examination so you do not aggravate the condition with the test procedures.
- Avoid aggressive kinetic open-chain quadriceps exercise, which may aggravate tendinitis.
- Popliteal and semimembranosus tendinitis can mimic a meniscal injury.

DESIRED OUTCOME/PROGNOSIS
- The client will have a reduction in symptoms.
- The client will have pain-free full function of the knee.
  If tendinitis continues without treatment, the tendon may rupture.

REFERENCES

ASSESSMENT
Davies G, Malone T, Basett F. Knee examination. *Physical Therapy.* 1980;60:1565–1574.
Delitto A. Lower extremity: knee. In: Myers RS, ed. *Saunders Manual of Physical Therapy Practice.* Philadelphia, Pa: WB Saunders Co; 1995:1001–1029.
Myers RS, ed. *Saunders Manual of Physical Therapy Practice.* Philadelphia, Pa: WB Saunders Co; 1995:1352. **[Physical therapy diagnosis, patellar tendinitis]**

Functional Level
Delitto A. Lower extremity: knee. In: Myers RS, ed. *Saunders Manual of Physical Therapy Practice.* Philadelphia, Pa: WB Saunders Co; 1995:1011. **[Modified Lysholm knee score]**

Joint Integrity and Structural Deviations
Arno S. The A angle: a quantitative measurement of patella alignment and realignment. *Journal of Orthopaedic and Sports Physical Therapy.* 1990;12:237–242.
Baumgaertner J. Quadriceps active test for posterior cruciate ligament injuries. *Clinical Management in Physical Therapy.* 1991;11:2:84-85.
Blustein M, D'Amico JC. Limb length discrepancy: identification, clinical significance and management. *Physical Therapy.* 1985;75:200–206.
Buschbacher RM, ed. *Musculoskeletal Disorders: A Practical Guide for Diagnosis and Rehabilitation.* Boston, Mass: Andover Medical Publishers; 1994:206–208. **[Q-angle measurements, thigh measurement, x-ray studies, joint aspiration, MRI, CT, arthrography and arthroscopy]**
Caylor D, Fites R, Worrell TW. The relationship between quadriceps angle and anterior knee pain syndrome. *Journal of Orthopaedic and Sports Physical Therapy.* 1993;17:11–16.

DiVeta JA, Vogelbach WD. The clinical efficacy of the A-angle in measuring patellar alignment. *Journal of Orthopaedic and Sports Physical Therapy.* 1992;16:136–139.

Noyes FR, Grood ES, Butler DL, et al. Knee ligament tests. *Physical Therapy.* 1980;60:1578–1581.

Rothstein JM, Roy SH, Wolf SL. *The Rehabilitation Specialist's Handbook.* Philadelphia, Pa: FA Davis Co; 1991:132–137. **[Apley grinding test, bounce home test, brush or stroke (wipe) test, Clark's sign, crossover test, gravity drawer test (posterior sag sign), Helfet test, Hughston plica test, Hughston posterolateral drawer test, Hughston test (jerk sign), Jakob test (reverse pivot), MacIntosh test (lateral pivot shift), O'Donoghue's test, Perkin's test, Slocum test, Waldron test, Wilson test]**

Tomberlin JP, Saunders HD. *Evaluation, Treatment and Prevention of Musculoskeletal Disorders. Vol 2: Extremities.* Chaska, Minn: The Saunders Group; 1994:233. **[Functional knee status exam, stroke test, fluctuation test, patellar tap, hamstring length, Ely's test, Ober's test, Noble's compression test, patellar tilt, lateral pull test, McConnell test, apprehension test, varus stress test, valgus stress test, Lachman test, posterior sag test, posterior drawer sign, quadriceps active test, AMRI, ALRI, flexion rotation drawer sign, Slocum's ALRI, McIntosh test, external rotation test, reverse pivot shift test, squat test, Steinman's test, hyperflexion-hyperextension test, McMurray–Anderson test, plica test]**

Special Tests to Which the PT May or May Not Have Access

Ultrasonography

Stokes M, Young A. Measurement of quadriceps cross-sectional area by ultrasonography: a description of the technique and its applications in physiotherapy. *Physiotherapy Practice.* 1986;2:1:31–36.

Strength

Instrumentation

Afzali L, Kuwabara F, Zachazewski J, Browne P, Robinson B. A new method for the determination of the characteristic shape of an isokinetic quadriceps femoris muscle torque curve. *Physical Therapy.* 1992;72:585–595.

Charteris J. An isometric normative database to facilitate restoration of function in knee-injured active young adults. *South African Journal of Physiotherapy.* 1993;49:2:28–34. **[Simple strain-gauge measure of isometric torque using knee flexor-extensor capacities, dominance ratios, contralateral asymmetries, and sexual dimorphism ratios]**

Chung F. Effect of two input adapters used with the Orthotron II on knee torque. *Physiotherapy Canada.* 1988;40:356–360.

Durand A, Malouin F, Richards CL, Bravo G. Intertrial reliability of work measurements recorded during concentric isokinetic knee extension and flexion in subjects with and without meniscal tears. *Physical Therapy.* 1991;71:804–812.

Gross MT, McGrain P, Demilio N, et al. Relationship between multiple predictor variables and normal knee torque production. *Physical Therapy.* 1989;69:54.

Kramer J, Clarkson H. Comparison of muscle capability and the resistance patterns provided by Nautilus leg extension and leg curl machines. *Physiotherapy Canada.* 1989;41:256–261.

Kramer JF, Hill K, Jones IC, Sandrin M, Vyse M. Effect of dynamometer application arm length on concentric and eccentric torques during isokinetic knee extension. *Physiotherapy Canada.* 1989;41:100–106.

Steiner LA, Harris BA, Krebs DE. Reliability of eccentric isokinetic knee flexion and extension measurements. *Archives of Physical Medicine and Rehabilitation.* 1993;74:1327–1335.

Wessel J, Gray G, Luongo F, Isherwood L. Reliability of work measurements recorded during concentric and eccentric contractions of the knee extensors in healthy subjects. *Physiotherapy Canada.* 1989;41:250–253.

Wilk KE, Andrew JR. The effects of pad placement and angular velocity on tibial displacement during isokinetic exercise. *Journal of Orthopaedic and Sports Physical Therapy.* 1993;17:24–30.

Manual Muscle Testing

Daniels L, Worthingham C. *Muscle Testing Techniques of Manual Examination.* 6th ed. Philadelphia, Pa: WB Saunders Co; 1995.

Kendall FP, McCreary EK, Provance PG. *Muscles: Testing and Function.* 4th ed. Baltimore, Md: Williams & Wilkins, 1993.

TREATMENT

Buschbacher RM, ed. *Musculoskeletal Disorders: A Practical Guide for Diagnosis and Rehabilitation.* Boston, Mass: Andover Medical Publishers; 1994:197–215.

DuBois M. Functional knee extension. *Clinical Management in Physical Therapy.* 1990;10:4:57–58.

Farina NT. Isokinetics in knee rehabilitation. *Clinical Management in Physical Therapy.* 1991;11:6:58–63.

Gerrard B. The patellofemoral pain syndrome: a clinical trial of the McConnell programme. *Australian Journal of Physiotherapy.* 1989;35:70–80.

Hertling D, Kessler RM. *Management of Common Musculoskeletal Disorders.* Philadelphia, Pa: JB Lippincott Co; 1990:298–358.

Jensen K, DiFabio RP. Evaluation of eccentric exercise in the treatment of patellar tendinitis. *Physical Therapy.* 1989;69:211–216.

Karst GM, Jewett PD. EMG analysis of exercise proposed for differential activation of medial and lateral quadricep femoris muscle components. *Physical Therapy.* 1993;73:286–299.

Kisner C, Colby LA. *Therapeutic Exercise: Foundations and Techniques.* 2nd ed. Philadelphia, Pa: FA Davis Co; 1990:345–384.

Mangine RE, ed. *Physical Therapy of the Knee.* New York, NY: Churchill Livingstone; 1988.

McLeod WD, Hunter S. Biomechanical analysis of the knee: primary functions as elucidated by anatomy. *Physical Therapy.* 1980;60:1561.

Nelson EM. Knee rehabilitation with office stools. *Clinical Management in Physical Therapy.* 1991;11:3:53–54.

Palmer M, Epler M. *Clinical Assessment Procedures in Physical Therapy.* Philadelphia, Pa: JB Lippincott Co; 1990.

Paulos L, Rusche K, Johnson C, et al. Patellar malalignment: a treatment rationale. *Physical Therapy.* 1980;60:1627–1632.

Puniello MS. Iliotibial band tightness and medial patellar glide in patients with patellofemoral dysfunction. *Journal of Orthopaedic and Sports Physical Therapy.* 1993;17:144–148.

Selkowitz DM. Improvement in isometric strength of the quadriceps femoris muscle after training with electric stimulation. *Physical Therapy.* 1985;65:186–196.

Shelton GL, Thigpen LK. Rehabilitation of patellofemoral dysfunction: a review of literature. *Journal of Orthopaedic and Sports Physical Therapy.* 1991;14:243–249.

Soderberg GL, Minor SD, Nelson RM, et al. Electro-myographic analysis of knee exercises in healthy subjects and in patients with knee pathologies. *Physical Therapy.* 1987;67:1691–1696.

Stratford P. Electromyography of the quadriceps femoris muscles in subjects with normal knees and acutely effused knees. *Physical Therapy.* 1981;62:279–283.

Tomberlin JP, Saunders HD. *Evaluation, Treatment and Prevention of Musculoskeletal Disorders. Vol 2: Extremities.* Chaska, Minn: The Saunders Group; 1994:217–264.

Woodall W, Welsh J. A biomechanical basis for rehabilitation programs involving the patello-femoral joint. *Journal of Orthopaedic and Sports Physical Therapy.* 1990;11:535–542.

Patellofemoral Stress Syndrome

Also known as *patellofemoral instability, patellar tracking dysfunction*, or *patellofemoral pain syndrome*.

DESCRIPTION

Patellofemoral stress syndrome is a condition in which the patella does not follow the normal path of tracking between the femoral condyles but articulates against the femur instead. This syndrome occurs more frequently in adolescent girls and in clients with anterior cruciate ligament problems.

CAUSE

The most common cause of patellofemoral problems is repetitive trauma. Patellofemoral stress syndrome can also be caused by patella alta (high-riding patella), plicas, or tightness in any of the following structures: hamstrings, heel cords, vastus lateralis, iliotibial tract, or lateral retinaculum. Weakness of the vastus medialis and a Q angle (angle between the long axis of the thigh and patella tendon) greater than 15 degrees can also be the cause. A common cause is a lateral pull of the patella combined with excessive pronation. While the lower leg turns medially during pronation, the three quadriceps muscles pull laterally on the patella. This pulling causes the patella to articulate against the femur.

ASSESSMENT

Areas

- History
- Pain
- Posture, including any pronation of feet or internal rotation at femurs
- Joint integrity and structural deviations
- Mobility, including active and passive ROM, and accessory motion
- Strength: especially note any vastus medialis obliquus (VMO) weakness
- Neurological
- Skin and soft tissue
- Gait
- Special tests to which the PT may or may not have access

Instruments/Procedures (See References for Sources)

Functional Level
- Lysholm knee rating scale

Joint Integrity and Structural Deviations. The following orthopedic tests of the knee may be performed:
- A-angle
- ALRI
- AMRI
- Apley grinding test
- apprehension test
- bounce home test

- brush or stroke (wipe) test
- Clark's sign
- crepitus
- crossover test
- Ely's test
- external rotation test
- flexion rotation drawer sign
- fluctuation test
- gravity drawer test (posterior sag sign)
- hamstring length
- Helfet test
- Hughston plica test
- Hughston posterolateral drawer test
- Hughston test (jerk sign)
- hyperflexion-hyperextension test
- Jakob test (reverse pivot)
- Lachman test
- lateral pull test
- limb-length discrepancy
- MacIntosh test (lateral pivot shift)
- McConnell test
- McMurray–Anderson test
- Noble's compression test
- Ober's test
- O'Donoghue's test
- patellar tap
- patellar tilt
- patellofemoral grind test
- Perkin's test
- plica test
- posterior drawer sign
- posterior sag test
- quadriceps active test
- reverse pivot shift test
- Slocum test
- Steinman's test
- step-down test
- squat test
- valgus stress test
- varus stress test
- Waldron test
- Wilson test

Pain
- palpation

Skin and Soft Tissue: Edema
- thigh measurement

Special Tests to Which the PT May or May Not Have Access
- arthrography and arthroscopy
- computed tomography (CT) scan
- magnetic resonance imaging (MRI)
- x-ray studies
- joint aspiration
- ultrasonography

Strength
- dynamometer
- eccentric isokinetic knee flexion and extension measurements
- manual muscle testing
- Nautilus
- Orthotron II
- simple strain-gauge measure of isometric torque
- work measurements

PROBLEMS
- The client usually complains of anterior knee pain.
- The client usually finds pain worse with weight bearing or standing right after prolonged sitting.
- The client can report episodes of kneecap "going out" and a feeling of weakness.
- The client can report hearing crepitus (or noise) in the joint.
- The client can complain of swelling around patella on medial side.

TREATMENT/MANAGEMENT
- Most knee conditions can be treated conservatively with ice, stretch, and exercise.
- Consider patellar taping or infrapatellar straps in acute stage.
- Consider immobilization for 3 to 7 days to several weeks if dislocated. Immobilization is followed by strengthening program.
- While immobilized, the client may be on crutches with partial weight bearing.
- The client may want to wear a brace in the early stage of rehabilitation.
- Begin with closed kinematic chain exercises done in pain-free ROM. Closed kinematic chain exercise can include biking, stairs, or balance exercises on a board.
- Treat any edema.
- Stretching exercise should be included if tightness is found in piriformis, hamstring, or gastrocsoleus muscles or iliotibial band (ITB).
- Implement VMO re-education through electrical stimulation, biofeedback, and patellofemoral taping. Role of VMO is critical to proper tracking of patella.
- Assess foot and ankle mechanics for proper footwear and orthosis.
- Include proprioceptive training in the treatment program.

PRECAUTIONS/CONTRAINDICATIONS
- X-rays should be consulted to rule out any potential fractures.
- Consult orthopedic surgeon if major ligament damage or meniscal tear is suspected or if hemarthosis or sudden effusion of joint develops.
- Carefully consider the nature of the problem before examination so you do not aggravate the condition with the test procedures.

- Open-chain exercises may predispose patella to lateral subluxation.
- Popliteal and semimembranosis tendinitis and patella tendon tendinitis can mimic a meniscal injury.
- Inflamed plica can sometimes be mistaken for meniscal tear or patellofemoral dysfunction.

DESIRED OUTCOME/PROGNOSIS
- Any acute dislocation of the patella will be reduced, and further dislocation will be prevented.
- The client will experience a reduction in symptoms and increased patellar stability.

Patients usually respond well to a conservative program. For continued success, the therapist must treat the source of the pain and not just the symptoms.

REFERENCES

ASSESSMENT
Davies G, Malone T, Basett F. Knee examination. *Physical Therapy*. 1980;60:1565–1574.
MacIntyre DL, Hopkins PM, Harris SR. Evaluation of pain and functional activity in patellofemoral pain syndrome: reliability and validity of two assessment tools. *Physiotherapy Canada*. 1995;47:164–172.

Functional Level
Harrison E, Quinney H, Magee D, et al. Analysis of outcome measures used in the study of patellofemoral pain syndrome. *Physiotherapy Canada*. 1995;47:264–272. **[Outcomes assessment]**
Ranawat I, et al. Duocondylar Rating Scale. *Journal of Bone and Joint Surgery*. 1976;58A:754–765. **[Functional knee evaluation]**
Tegner Y, Lysolm J. Rating systems in the evaluation of knee ligament injuries. *Clinical Orthopaedics and Related Research*. 1985;43–49. **[Lysolm Knee Rating Scale]**

Joint Integrity and Structural Deviations
Arno S. The A angle: a quantitative measurement of patella alignment and realignment. *Journal of Orthopaedic and Sports Physical Therapy*. 1990;12:237–242.
Baumgaertner J. Quadriceps active test for posterior cruciate ligament injuries. *Clinical Management in Physical Therapy*. 1991;11:2:84–85.
Blustein M, D'Amico JC. Limb length discrepancy: identification, clinical significance and management. *Physical Therapy*. 1985;75:200–206.
Buschbacher RM, ed. *Musculoskeletal Disorders: A Practical Guide for Diagnosis and Rehabilitation*. Boston, Mass: Andover Medical Publishers; 1994:206–208. **[Q-angle measurements, thigh measurement, x-ray studies, joint aspiration, MRI, CT, arthrography and arthroscopy]**
Caylor D, Fites R, Worrell TW. The relationship between quadriceps angle and anterior knee pain syndrome. *Journal of Orthopaedic and Sports Physical Therapy*. 1993;17:11–16.
DiVeta JA, Vogelbach WD. The clinical efficacy of the A-angle in measuring patellar alignment. *Journal of Orthopaedic and Sports Physical Therapy*. 1992;16:136–139.
Myers RS, ed. *Saunders Manual of Physical Therapy Practice*. Philadelphia, Pa: WB Saunders Co; 1995:1351. **[Step-down test, patellofemoral grind test, crepitus]**
Noyes FR, Grood ES, Butler DL, et al. Knee ligament tests. *Physical Therapy*. 1980;60:1578–1581.
Rothstein JM, Roy SH, Wolf SL. *The Rehabilitation Specialist's Handbook*. Philadelphia, Pa: FA Davis Co; 1991:132–137. **[Apley grinding test, bounce home test, brush or stroke (wipe) test, Clark's sign, crossover test, gravity drawer test (posterior sag sign), Helfet test, Hughston plica test, Hughston posterolateral drawer test, Hughston test (jerk sign), Jakob test (reverse pivot), MacIntosh test (lateral pivot shift), O'Donoghue's test, Perkin's test, Slocum test, Waldron test, Wilson test]**

Tomberlin JP, Saunders HD. *Evaluation, Treatment and Prevention of Musculoskeletal Disorders. Vol 2: Extremities.* Chaska, Minn: The Saunders Group; 1994:233. **[Functional knee status exam, stroke test, fluctuation test, patellar tap, hamstring length, Ely's test, Ober's test, Noble's compression test, patellar tilt, lateral pull test, McConnell test, apprehension test, varus stress test, valgus stress test, Lachman test, posterior sag test, posterior drawer sign, quadriceps active test, AMRI, ALRI, flexion rotation drawer sign, Slocum's ALRI, McIntosh test, external rotation test, reverse pivot shift test, squat test, Steinman's test, hyperflexion-hyperextension test, McMurray–Anderson test, plica test]**

Special Tests to Which the PT May or May Not Have Access

Ultrasonography
Stokes M, Young A. Measurement of quadriceps cross-sectional area by ultrasonography: a description of the technique and its applications in physiotherapy. *Physiotherapy Practice.* 1986;2:1:31–36.

Strength

Instrumentation
Afzali L, Kuwabara F, Zachazewski J, Browne P, Robinson B. A new method for the determination of the characteristic shape of an isokinetic quadriceps femoris muscle torque curve. *Physical Therapy.* 1992;72:585–595.

Charteris J. An isometric normative database to facilitate restoration of function in knee-injured active young adults. *South African Journal of Physiotherapy.* 1993;49:2:28–34. **[Simple strain-gauge measure of isometric torque using knee flexor-extensor capacities, dominance ratios, contralateral asymmetries, and sexual dimorphism ratios]**

Chung F. Effect of two input adapters used with the Orthotron II on knee torque. *Physiotherapy Canada.* 1988;40:356–360.

Durand A, Malouin F, Richards CL, Bravo G. Intertrial reliability of work measurements recorded during concentric isokinetic knee extension and flexion in subjects with and without meniscal tears. *Physical Therapy.* 1991;71:804–812.

Gross MT, McGrain P, Demilio N, et al. Relationship between multiple predictor variables and normal knee torque production. *Physical Therapy.* 1989;69:54.

Kramer J, Clarkson H. Comparison of muscle capability and the resistance patterns provided by Nautilus leg extension and leg curl machines. *Physiotherapy Canada.* 1989;41:256–261.

Kramer JF, Hill K, Jones IC, Sandrin M, Vyse M. Effect of dynamometer application arm length on concentric and eccentric torques during isokinetic knee extension. *Physiotherapy Canada.* 1989;41:100–106.

Steiner LA, Harris BA, Krebs DE. Reliability of eccentric isokinetic knee flexion and extension measurements. *Archives of Physical Medicine and Rehabilitation.* 1993;74:1327–1335.

Wessel J, Gray G, Luongo F, Isherwood L. Reliability of work measurements recorded during concentric and eccentric contractions of the knee extensors in healthy subjects. *Physiotherapy Canada.* 1989;41:250–253.

Wilk KE, Andrew JR. The effects of pad placement and angular velocity on tibial displacement during isokinetic exercise. *Journal of Orthopaedic and Sports Physical Therapy.* 1993;17:24–30.

Wyatt MP, Edwards AM. Comparison of quadriceps and hamstring torque values during isokinetic exercises. *Journal of Orthopaedic and Sports Physical Therapy.* 1981;3:2:48–56.

Manual Muscle Testing
Daniels L, Worthingham C. *Muscle Testing Techniques of Manual Examination.* 6th ed. Philadelphia, Pa: WB Saunders Co; 1995.

Kendall FP, McCreary EK, Provance PG. *Muscles: Testing and Function.* 4th ed. Baltimore, Md: Williams & Wilkins; 1993.

TREATMENT

Blackburn TA, Eiland WG, Bandy WG. An introduction to the plica. *Journal of Orthopaedic and Sports Physical Therapy*. 1982;3:171–177.

Bohannon RW. Effect of electrical stimulation to the vastus medialis muscle in a patient with chronically dislocating patellae. *Physical Therapy*. 1983;63:1445–1447.

Buschbacher RM, ed. *Musculoskeletal Disorders: A Practical Guide for Diagnosis and Rehabilitation*. Boston, Mass: Andover Medical Publishers; 1994:197–215.

DuBois M. Functional knee extension. *Clinical Management in Physical Therapy*. 1990;10:4:57–58.

Farina NT. Isokinetics in knee rehabilitation. *Clinical Management in Physical Therapy*. 1991;11:6:58–63.

Gerrard B. The patellofemoral pain syndrome: a clinical trial of the McConnell programme. *Australian Journal of Physiotherapy*. 1989;35:70–80.

Hertling D, Kessler RM. *Management of Common Musculoskeletal Disorders*. Philadelphia, Pa: JB Lippincott Co; 1990:298–358.

Jensen K, DiFabio RP. Evaluation of eccentric exercise in the treatment of patellar tendinitis. *Physical Therapy*. 1989; 69:211–216.

Johanson MA, Donatelli R, Greenfield BH. Rehabilitation of microtrauma injuries. In: Greenfield BH, ed. *Rehabilitation of the Knee: A Problem-Solving Approach*. Philadelphia, Pa: FA Davis Co; 1993:139–176.

Karst GM, Jewett PD. EMG analysis of exercise proposed for differential activation of medial and lateral quadricep femoris muscle components. *Physical Therapy*. 1993;73:286–299.

Kisner C, Colby LA. *Therapeutic Exercise: Foundations and Techniques*. 2nd ed. Philadelphia, Pa: FA Davis Co; 1990:345–384.

Mangine RE, ed. 2nd ed. *Physical Therapy of the Knee*. New York, NY: Churchill Livingstone; 1995.

McConnell J. The management of chondromalacia patellae: a long-term solution. *Australian Journal of Physiotherapy*. 1986;32:215–223.

McLeod WD, Hunter S. Biomechanical analysis of the knee: primary functions as elucidated by anatomy. *Physical Therapy*. 1980;60:1561.

McMullen W, Roncarati A, Koval P. Static and isokinetic treatments of chondromalacia patellae: a comparative investigation. *Journal of Orthopaedic and Sports Physical Therapy*. 1990;12:256–266.

Nelson EM. Knee rehabilitation with office stools. *Clinical Management in Physical Therapy*. 1991;11:3:53–54.

Palmer M, Epler M. *Clinical Assessment Procedures in Physical Therapy*. Philadelphia, Pa: JB Lippincott Co; 1990.

Puniello MS. Iliotibial band tightness and medial patellar glide in patients with patellofemoral dysfunction. *Journal of Orthopaedic and Sports Physical Therapy*. 1993;17:144–148.

Selkowitz DM. Improvement in isometric strength of the quadriceps femoris muscle after training with electric stimulation. *Physical Therapy*. 1985;65:186–196.

Shelton GL, Thigpen LK. Rehabilitation of patellofemoral dysfunction: a review of literature. *Journal of Orthopaedic and Sports Physical Therapy*. 1991;14:243–249.

Soderberg GL, Minor SD, Nelson RM, et al. Electro-myographic analysis of knee exercises in healthy subjects and in patients with knee pathologies. *Physical Therapy*. 1987;67:1691–1696.

Tomberlin JP, Saunders HD. *Evaluation, Treatment and Prevention of Musculoskeletal Disorders. Vol 2: Extremities*. Chaska, Minn: The Saunders Group; 1994:217–264.

Woodall W, Welsh J. A biomechanical basis for rehabilitation programs involving the patello-femoral joint. *Journal of Orthopaedic and Sports Physical Therapy*. 1990;11:535–542.

Pes Cavus

DESCRIPTION

Pes cavus is a condition in which the foot is highly arched or abnormally supinated. A highly arched foot structure (either flexible or rigid) predisposes the patient to problems caused by lack of shock absorption.

CAUSE

Abnormal supination is caused by the inability of the foot to pronate. This leads to prolonged supination during the stance phase of gait.

ASSESSMENT

Areas

- History
- Posture
- Pain
- Gait
- Strength
- Neurological
- Joint integrity and structural deviations
- Mobility, including active and passive range of motion (ROM) and accessory motion
- Skin and soft tissue
- Equipment, including footwear

Instruments/Procedures (See References for Sources)

Gait
- dynamic assessment of foot mechanics
- dynamic plantar pressure distribution
- foot pressure EMED system
- pedabarograph
- three-dimensional kinematic analysis
- footprint analysis in gait documentation

Joint Integrity and Structural Deviations. The following orthopedic tests may be performed:
- Achilles tendon test
- anterior drawer sign
- Homan's sign
- Kleiger test
- talar tilt test
- Thompson test

PROBLEMS

- The client usually complains of foot pain.
- The client may have related stress fracture, metatarsalgia, plantar fasciitis, and Achilles tendinitis.

TREATMENT/MANAGEMENT

For treatment of foot and ankle problems in general:
- Exercises progress from passive ROM to active assisted and active ROM to resisted ROM.
- Begin non-weight-bearing strengthening activities after pain-free ROM is achieved.
- Isometric, isotonic, and isokinetic exercise can be used.
- Eccentric loading should not be overlooked.
- Progress to jogging, running, and athletic maneuvers as indicated.
- Address preventive measures, such as stretching, choice of shoes, and use of adhesive strapping during athletic activities.

For pes cavus specifically:
- Consider rigid orthotic device with forefoot valgus post.
- Begin a lower extremity flexibility program of stretching, mobilization, and exercises.

PRECAUTIONS/CONTRAINDICATIONS

No precautions were identified.

DESIRED OUTCOME/PROGNOSIS

- The client will have pain-free function of the foot.
- The client will experience a relief of foot pressure and lessen strain on lower extremities.

Flexible cavus foot responds well to orthotic foot control. Rigid cavus foot may need a special shock-absorbing material.

REFERENCES

ASSESSMENT

Giallonardo LM. Clinical evaluation of foot and ankle dysfunction. *Physical Therapy*. 1988;68:1850–1856.
McPoil TG, Hunt GC. Evaluation and management of foot and ankle disorders: present problems and future directions. *Journal of Orthopaedic and Sports Physical Therapy*. 1995;21:381–388.

Gait

Donatelli R, ed. *The Biomechanics of the Foot and Ankle*. Philadelphia, Pa: FA Davis Co; 1990:148–152. **[Dynamic assessment of foot mechanics: dynamic plantar pressure distribution, foot pressure EMED system, pedabarograph, three-dimensional kinematic analysis]**
Shore M. Footprint analysis in gait documentation: an instructional sheet format. *Physical Therapy*. 1980;60:1163–1167.

Joint Integrity and Structural Deviations

Rothstein JM, Roy SH, Wolf SL. *The Rehabilitation Specialist's Handbook*. Philadelphia, Pa: FA Davis Co; 1991:136–137. **[Achilles tendon test, anterior drawer sign, Homan's sign, Kleiger test, talar tilt, Thompson test]**
Tomberlin JP, Saunders HD. *Evaluation, Treatment and Prevention of Musculoskeletal Disorders. Vol 2: Extremities*. Chaska, Minn: The Saunders Group; 1994:265-306.

TREATMENT

Brown LP, Yavorsky P. Locomotor biomechanics and pathomechanics: a review. *Journal of Orthopaedic and Sports Physical Therapy*. 1987;9:3–10.
Buschbacher RM, ed. *Musculoskeletal Disorders: A Practical Guide for Diagnosis and Rehabilitation*. Boston, Mass: Andover Medical Publishers; 1994:216–235.
Cibulka MT. Management of a patient with forefoot pain: a case report. *Physical Therapy*. 1990;70:41–44.

Donatelli R. Normal biomechanics of the foot and ankle. *Journal of Orthopaedic and Sports Physical Therapy.* 1985;7:91–95.

Donatelli R. Abnormal biomechanics of the foot and ankle. *Journal of Orthopaedic and Sports Physical Therapy.* 1987;9:11–16.

Donatelli R, Hurlbert C, Conway P, et al. Biomechanical foot orthotics: a retrospective study. *Journal of Orthopaedic and Sports Physical Therapy.* 1988;10:205–212.

Donatelli R, Wolf SL, eds. *The Biomechanics of the Foot and Ankle.* Philadelphia, Pa: FA Davis Co; 1990:258–259.

Donatelli R, Wooden MJ, eds. *Orthopaedic Physical Therapy.* New York, NY: Churchill Livingstone; 1989.

Doxey GE. The semi-flexible foot orthotic: fabrication and guidelines for use. *Journal of Orthopaedic and Sports Physical Therapy.* 1983;5:526.

Doxey GE. Clinical use and fabrication of molded thermoplastic foot orthotic devices. *Physical Therapy.* 1985;65:1679–1682.

Giallonardo LM. Clinical evaluation of foot and ankle dysfunction. *Physical Therapy.* 1988;68:1850–1856.

Gould JA, Davies GJ, eds. *Orthopaedic and Sports Physical Therapy.* St Louis: CV Mosby Co; 1985:317.

Hertling D, Kessler RM. *Management of Common Musculoskeletal Disorders.* Philadelphia, Pa: JB Lippincott Co; 1990:359–410.

Hunt GC, ed. *Physical Therapy of the Foot and Ankle.* 2nd ed. New York, NY: Churchill Livingstone; 1995.

Kahn J. Electrotherapy with podiatric conditions. *Clinical Management in Physical Therapy.* 1988;8:3:6–9.

Kisner C, Colby LA. *Therapeutic Exercise: Foundations and Techniques.* 2nd ed. Philadelphia, Pa: FA Davis Co; 1990:385–407.

Lockard MA. Foot orthoses. *Physical Therapy.* 1988;68:1866–1873.

Maitland GD. *Peripheral Manipulation.* 3rd ed. Boston, Mass: Butterworths; 1990.

McPoil TG. Footwear. *Physical Therapy.* 1988;68:1857–1865.

McPoil TG, Knecht HG. Biomechanics of the foot in walking: a functional approach. *Journal of Orthopaedic and Sports Physical Therapy.* 1985;7:69–72.

Oatis CA. Biomechanics of the foot and ankle under static conditions. *Physical Therapy.* 1988;68:1815–1821.

O'Conner PL. Physical therapy. In: Sammarco GJ, ed. *Foot and Ankle Manual.* Philadelphia, Pa: Lea & Febiger; 1991:351–358

Palmer M, Epler M. *Clinical Assessment Procedures in Physical Therapy.* Philadelphia, Pa: JB Lippincott Co; 1990.

Riegger CL. Anatomy of the ankle and foot. *Physical Therapy.* 1988;68:1802–1814.

Sammarco GJ, ed. *Foot and Ankle Manual.* Philadelphia, Pa: Lea & Febiger; 1991:350–358.

Tiberio D. Pathomechanics of structural foot deformities. *Physical Therapy.* 1988;68:1840–1849.

Tomberlin JP, Saunders HD. *Evaluation, Treatment and Prevention of Musculoskeletal Disorders. Vol 2: Extremities.* Chaska, Minn: The Saunders Group; 1994:265–305.

Viel ER, Desmarets JJ. Mechanical pull of the peroneal tendons on the fifth ray of the foot. *Journal of Orthopaedic and Sports Physical Therapy.* 1985;7:102–106.

Pes Planus

Also known as *flat foot, pronated foot,* and *pes planovalgus.*

DESCRIPTION

Pes planus results in a flattened medial longitudinal arch.

CAUSE

This condition may be caused by muscle weakness, ligamentous laxity, trauma, paralysis, or postural deformity, or it may be congenital. Local structural disorder or structural deviations elsewhere contribute to the problem.

ASSESSMENT

Areas
- History
- Pain
- Posture
- Gait
- Strength
- Neurological, including sensation
- Joint integrity and structural deviations
- Mobility, including active and passive range of motion (ROM) and accessory motion
- Skin and soft tissue
- Equipment, including footwear

Instruments/Procedures (See References for Sources)

Gait
- dynamic assessment of foot mechanics
  1. dynamic plantar pressure distribution
  2. foot pressure EMED system
  3. pedabarograph
  4. three-dimensional kinematic analysis

Joint Integrity and Structural Deviations. The following orthopedic tests for the lower extremities may be used:
- Achilles tendon test
- anterior drawer sign
- Homan's sign
- Kleiger test
- talar tilt
- Thompson test

PROBLEMS
- The client usually has pain over the plantar aspect of the foot.
- Usually fatigue stress is felt over the sole of the foot, especially on the medial side.
- Related knee pain is common.
- Forefoot pain is also common.

TREATMENT/MANAGEMENT
- Begin strengthening exercises of the intrinsic foot muscles.
- Add flexibility exercises for the gastrocsoleus complex.
- Consider an orthotic device. Options may include an insert, such as the University of California Biomechanical Laboratory insert, a semirigid scaphoid pad insert, or a medial heel wedge (possibly in combination with a medial forefoot wedge) insert.

- Provide advice on appropriate activity level.
- Include proprioceptive balance training.
- Consider the use of strapping, usually a valgus correction strap attached to an ankle-foot orthosis.
- Use ultrasound and friction massage, if indicated.

PRECAUTIONS/CONTRAINDICATIONS
- See Appendix C for precautions for modality usage.

DESIRED OUTCOME/PROGNOSIS
- The client will have foot restored to normal alignment.
- The client will have pain-free function of foot.
- Provide arch support and calcaneal control.

A rigid pes planus usually cannot be changed with an orthosis, although use of a heel wedge has been suggested. Selective reduction of abnormal stress reduces the frequency and/or magnitude of stress on the foot.

REFERENCES

ASSESSMENT
Giallonardo LM. Clinical evaluation of foot and ankle dysfunction. *Physical Therapy*. 1988;68:1850–1856.
McPoil TG, Hunt GC. Evaluation and management of foot and ankle disorders: present problems and future directions. *Journal of Orthopaedic and Sports Physical Therapy*. 1995;21:381–388.

Gait
Donatelli R, ed. *The Biomechanics of the Foot and Ankle*. Philadelphia, Pa: FA Davis Co; 1990:148–152. **[Dynamic assessment of foot mechanics: dynamic plantar pressure distribution, foot pressure EMED system, pedabarograph, three-dimensional kinematic analysis]**
Shore M. Footprint analysis in gait documentation: an instructional sheet format. *Physical Therapy*. 1980;60:1163–1167.

Joint Integrity and Structural Deviations
Rothstein JM, Roy SH, Wolf SL. *The Rehabilitation Specialist's Handbook*. Philadelphia, Pa: FA Davis Co; 1991:136–137. **[Achilles tendon test, anterior drawer sign, Homan's sign, Kleiger test, talar tilt, Thompson test]**
Tomberlin JP, Saunders HD. *Evaluation, Treatment and Prevention of Musculoskeletal Disorders. Vol 2: Extremities*. Chaska, Minn: The Saunders Group; 1994:265–306.

TREATMENT
Brown LP, Yavorsky P. Locomotor biomechanics and pathomechanics: a review. *Journal of Orthopaedic and Sports Physical Therapy*. 1987;9:3–10.
Buschbacher RM, ed. *Musculoskeletal Disorders: A Practical Guide for Diagnosis and Rehabilitation*. Boston, Mass: Andover Medical Publishers; 1994:216–235.
Cibulka MT. Management of a patient with forefoot pain: a case report. *Physical Therapy*. 1990;70:41–44.
Donatelli R. Normal biomechanics of the foot and ankle. *Journal of Orthopaedic and Sports Physical Therapy*. 1985;7:91–95.
Donatelli R. Abnormal biomechanics of the foot and ankle. *Journal of Orthopaedic and Sports Physical Therapy*. 1987;9:11–16.
Donatelli R, ed. *The Biomechanics of the Foot and Ankle*. Philadelphia, Pa: FA Davis Co; 1990:258–259.

Donatelli R, Hurlbert C, Conway P, et al. Biomechanical foot orthotics: a retrospective study. *Journal of Orthopaedic and Sports Physical Therapy*. 1988;10:205–212.

Donatelli R, Wooden MJ, eds. *Orthopaedic Physical Therapy*. New York, NY: Churchill Livingstone; 1989.

Doxey GE. Clinical use and fabrication of molded thermoplastic foot orthotic devices. *Physical Therapy*. 1985;65:1679–1682.

Edelstein JE. Orthoses. In: Myers RS, ed. *Saunders Manual of Physical Therapy Practice*. Philadelphia, Pa: WB Saunders Co; 1995:1189.

Giallonardo LM. Clinical evaluation of foot and ankle dysfunction. *Physical Therapy*. 1988;68:1850–1856.

Gould JA, Davies GJ, eds. *Orthopaedic and Sports Physical Therapy*. St Louis: CV Mosby Co; 1985:317.

Hertling D, Kessler RM. *Management of Common Musculoskeletal Disorders*. Philadelphia, Pa: JB Lippincott Co; 1990:359–410.

Hunt GC, ed. *Physical Therapy of the Foot and Ankle*. 2nd ed. New York, NY: Churchill Livingstone; 1995.

Kahn J. Electrotherapy with podiatric conditions. *Clinical Management in Physical Therapy*. 1988;8:3:6–9.

Kisner C, Colby LA. *Therapeutic Exercise: Foundations and Techniques*. 2nd ed. Philadelphia, Pa: FA Davis Co; 1990:385–407.

Lockard MA. Foot orthoses. *Physical Therapy*. 1988;8:1866–1873.

Maitland GD. *Peripheral Manipulation*. 3rd ed. Boston, Mass: Butterworths; 1990.

McPoil TG. Footwear. *Physical Therapy*. 1988;68:1857–1865.

McPoil TG, Knecht HG. Biomechanics of the foot in walking: a functional approach. *Journal of Orthopaedic and Sports Physical Therapy*. 1985;7:69–72.

Oatis CA. Biomechanics of the foot and ankle under static conditions. *Physical Therapy*. 1988;68:1815–1821.

Palmer M, Epler M. *Clinical Assessment Procedures in Physical Therapy*. Philadelphia, Pa: JB Lippincott Co; 1990.

Riegger CL. Anatomy of the ankle and foot. *Physical Therapy*. 1988;68:1802–1814.

Sammarco GJ, ed. *Foot and Ankle Manual*. Philadelphia, Pa: Lea & Febiger; 1991:350–358.

Tiberio D. Pathomechanics of structural foot deformities. *Physical Therapy*. 1988;68:1840–1849.

Tomberlin JP, Saunders HD. *Evaluation, Treatment and Prevention of Musculoskeletal Disorders. Vol 2: Extremities*. Chaska, Minn: The Saunders Group; 1994:265–305.

Viel ER, Desmarets JJ. Mechanical pull of the peroneal tendons on the fifth ray of the foot. *Journal of Orthopaedic and Sports Physical Therapy*. 1985;7:102–106.

Piriformis Syndrome

DESCRIPTION

With the piriformis syndrome, the sciatic nerve is irritated by the overlying piriformis muscle. In 15% to 20% of the population, the nerve pierces the muscle. Piriformis syndrome is more common in women than men.

CAUSE

The sciatic nerve can be mechanically irritated when it is trapped between the muscle and the ischium or when it lies within the belly of the muscle.

ASSESSMENT

Areas

• History

- Pain
- Posture
- Joint integrity and structural deviations
- Gait
- Mobility, including active and passive range of motion (ROM), and accessory motion
- Strength
- Neurological
- Skin and soft tissue
- Functional level
- Special tests to which the PT may or may not have access

Instruments/Procedures (See References for Sources)

Joint Integrity and Structural Deviations. The following orthopedic tests for the lower quadrant may be performed:
- Craig's test
- Ely's test
- Fabere test
- hamstring tightness
- leg-length measurements
- Ober's test
- Noble's compression test
- piriformis test
- Thomas test
- torque test
- Trendelenburg's sign
- quadrant test

Mobility
- goniometry
- hip flexibility

Posture
- clinical measurement of postural control
- pelvic tilt and the standing position

Special Tests to Which the PT May or May Not Have Access
- electromyographic analysis of hip abductor musculature

Strength
- maximal isometric hip abductor muscles torques
- manual muscle test

PROBLEMS
- The client may complain of pain in posterior hip area.
- Usually, resisted hip rotation (external) produces pain.
- The client may also complain of pain in leg, lumbar spine, or pelvis.
- The client usually has diminished tolerance to sitting and weight bearing.
- The client can have a decreased ROM in internal rotation with adduction.

- Usually, passive internal rotation produces pain.

TREATMENT/MANAGEMENT
- Use modalities, such as ice or ultrasound, if indicated.
- Encourage rest in acute stage.
- Consider soft tissue mobilization or neural mobilization techniques.
- Assess activities of daily living (ADLs) and posture, especially of hip.
- Introduce gradual, gentle stretching of piriformis muscle in side-lying or sitting position.
- Maintain piriformis mobility with stretching to prevent recurrence.

PRECAUTIONS/CONTRAINDICATIONS
- See Appendix C for cautions to use with physical agents and modalities.

DESIRED OUTCOME/PROGNOSIS
- The client will experience relief of symptoms.
- The client will experience a decreased stress on muscle.

Addressing contributing factors and maintaining piriformis muscle mobility are critical to the prevention of recurrence.

In a report on 12 selected cases of chronic piriformis syndrome, 10 reported improvement post surgery.

REFERENCES

ASSESSMENT
Echternach JL, ed. *Physical Therapy of the Hip.* New York, NY: Churchill Livingstone; 1990:36. **[Hip pain algorithm]**
Hicklin SP, DePretis MC. Lower extremity: hip. In: Myers RS, ed. *Saunders Manual of Physical Therapy Practice.* Philadelphia, Pa: WB Saunders Co; 1995:955–990. **[Trigger points in piriformis muscle]**

Joint Integrity and Structural Deviations
Gogia PP, Braatz JH. Validity and reliability of leg length measurements. *Journal of Orthopaedic and Sports Physical Therapy.* 1986;8:185–188.
Tomberlin JP, Saunders HD. *Evaluation, Treatment and Prevention of Musculoskeletal Disorders. Vol 2: Extremities.* Chaska, Minn: The Saunders Group; 1994:200. **[Trendelenburg's sign, piriformis test, Thomas test, Ely's test, Ober's test, Noble's compression test, hamstring tightness, quadrant test, Fabere test, torque test, Craig's test, leg-length test]**
Woerman AL, Binder-MacLeod SA. Leg length discrepancy assessment accuracy and precision in five clinical methods of evaluation. *Journal of Orthopaedic and Sports Physical Therapy.* 1984;5:230–239.

Mobility
Rothstein JM, ed. *Measurement in Physical Therapy.* New York, NY: Churchill Livingstone; 1985:103.
VanRoy P, Borms J, Haentjens A. Goniometric study of the maintenance of hip flexibility resulting from hamstring stretches. *Physiotherapy Practice.* 1987;3:2:52–59.

Posture
Gajdosik R, Simpson R, Smith R, DonTigny R. Pelvic tilt, intertester reliability of measuring the standing position and range of motion. *Physical Therapy.* 1985;65:169–174.
Horak FB. Clinical measurement of postural control in adults. *Physical Therapy.* 1987;67:1881–1885.

Strength

Neumann DA, Soderberg GL, Cook TM. Comparison of maximal isometric hip abductor muscles torques between hip sides. *Physical Therapy.* 1988;68:596.

Neumann DA, Soderberg GL, Cook TM. Electromyographic analysis of hip abductor musculature in healthy right-handed persons. *Physical Therapy.* 1989;69:431.

Manual Muscle Testing

Daniels L, Worthingham C. *Muscle Testing Techniques of Manual Examination.* 6th ed. Philadelphia, Pa: WB Saunders Co; 1995.

Kendall FP, McCreary EK, Provance PG. *Muscles: Testing and Function.* 4th ed. Baltimore, Md: Williams & Wilkins; 1993.

TREATMENT

Bandy WD, Sinning WE. Kinematic effect of heel lift use to correct lower limb length. *Journal of Orthopaedic and Sports Physical Therapy.* 1986;7:173–179.

Cibulka MT. Rehabilitation of the pelvis, hip and thigh. *Clinics in Sports Medicine.* 1989;8:777–803.

Cookson JC, Kent BE. Orthopedic manual therapy: an overview. Part 1. The extremities. *Physical Therapy.* 1979;59:135.

Echternach JL, ed. *Physical Therapy of the Hip.* New York, NY: Churchill Livingstone; 1990.

Grieve GP. The hip. *Physiotherapy.* 1983;69:196–204.

Henricson AS, Fredriksson K, Persson I, et al. The effect of heat and stretching on the range of hip motion. *Journal of Orthopaedic and Sports Physical Therapy.* 1984;6:110.

Hertling D, Kessler RM. *Management of Common Musculoskeletal Disorders.* Philadelphia, Pa: JB Lippincott Co; 1990:272–297.

Hicklin SP, DePretis MC. Lower extremity: hip. In: Myers RS, ed. *Saunders Manual of Physical Therapy Practice.* Philadelphia, Pa: WB Saunders Co; 1995:976.

Kisner C, Colby LA. *Therapeutic Exercise: Foundations and Techniques.* 2nd ed. Philadelphia, Pa: FA Davis Co; 1990:317–344.

Kornberg C, McCarthy T. The effect of neural stretching technique on sympathetic outflow to the lower limbs. *Journal of Orthopaedic and Sports Physical Therapy.* 1992;16:269–274.

Maitland GF. *Peripheral Manipulation.* 3rd ed. Boston, Mass: Butterworths; 1990:203.

Newton RA. Effects of vapocoolants on passive hip flexion in healthy subjects. *Physical Therapy.* 1985;65:1034–1036.

Palmer M, Epler M. *Clinical Assessment Procedures in Physical Therapy.* Philadelphia, Pa: JB Lippincott Co; 1990.

Tomberlin JP, Saunders HD. *Evaluation, Treatment and Prevention of Musculoskeletal Disorders. Vol 2: Extremities.* Chaska, Minn: The Saunders Group; 1994:187–212.

Plantar Fasciitis

DESCRIPTION

Inflammation at the inner border of the plantar fascia that leads to pain.

CAUSE

The most irritating causative factor is overuse. Plantar fasciitis can also be triggered by excessive stretching. Flat feet and contracted heel cords are associated with this disorder. In runners, this condition can also be associated with limited range of motion (ROM) of the first metatarsal phalangeal (MTP) joint. Training errors, repetitive trauma, and hyperpronation (of the subtalar joint) have been implicated as well.

ASSESSMENT

Areas
- History
- Pain
- Posture
- Gait
- Strength
- Neurological, including sensation
- Joint integrity and structural deviations
- Mobility, including active and passive ROM and accessory motion
- Skin and soft tissue
- Equipment, including footwear

Instruments/Procedures (See References for Sources)

Gait
- dynamic assessment of foot mechanics
  1. dynamic plantar pressure distribution
  2. foot pressure EMED system
  3. pedabarograph
  4. three-dimensional kinematic analysis
- footprint analysis in gait documentation

Joint Integrity and Structural Deviations
- tibial varum evaluation

Mobility
- goniometric subtalar and ankle joint measurements
- open and closed kinetic chain subtalar joint neutral positions and navicular drop test

Strength
- instrumentation
- manual muscle testing

PROBLEMS
- The client usually has pain in heel with weight-bearing activities.
- Usually, the pain increases with the first steps taken upon rising but is better after a few hours and then worse again.
- The client usually has pain with passive dorsiflexion and great toe extension.
- There is usually tenderness on the medial side of the heel and pain along the anteromedial aspect of the plantar surface of the calcaneus.
- The client may report that the foot is extremely stiff or hypermobile.

TREATMENT/MANAGEMENT
For treatment of foot and ankle problems in general:

- Exercises progress from passive ROM to active assisted and active ROM to resisted ROM.
- Begin non-weight-bearing strengthening activities after pain-free ROM is achieved.
- Isometric, isotonic, and isokinetic exercise can be used.
- Consider eccentric loading.
- Progress to jogging, running, and athletic maneuvers as indicated.
- Address preventive measures, such as stretching, choice of shoes, and use of adhesive strapping during athletic activities.
  For plantar fasciitis specifically:
- Use physical agents, such as ice massage or immersion (3–4 times per day), as indicated.
- Consider taping.
- Use foot orthotics during the healing phase.
- Consider long-term use of orthotics and inserts. One option is an insert that has a heel elevation, scaphoid pad, and a flexible top cover.
- Mobilize immobile first MTP, if needed.
- Stretch gastrocsoleus complex in pain-free range flexibility program for lower extremities.
- Use strengthening exercise for gastrocnemius and arch musculature.
- Treat any neural tension.
- Try cross-friction massage with slow passive stretching.

PRECAUTIONS/CONTRAINDICATIONS
- This condition can mimic tibial nerve entrapment and/or medial plantar nerve entrapment, and these conditions should be ruled out. Pain under the plantar surface probably signals heel contusion, not plantar fasciitis.

DESIRED OUTCOME/PROGNOSIS
- The client will experience a reduction in symptoms and decreased stress on the plantar fascia.
- The client will prevent reinjury.
  It is not unusual for plantar fasciitis to resist conservative therapy. All related elements must be addressed to promote successful treatment.

REFERENCES

ASSESSMENT
Fromherz WA. Examination. In: Hunt GC, ed. *Physical Therapy of the Foot and Ankle*. New York, NY: Churchill Livingstone; 1988:133–138.
Giallonardo LM. Clinical evaluation of foot and ankle dysfunction. *Physical Therapy*. 1988;68:1850–1856.
McPoil TG, Brocato RS. The foot and ankle: biomechanical evaluation and treatment. In: Gould JA, ed. *Orthopaedic and Sports Physical Therapy*. St Louis: CV Mosby Co; 1990:395–421.
McPoil TG, Hunt GC. Evaluation and management of foot and ankle disorders: present problems and future directions. *Journal of Orthopaedic and Sports Physical Therapy*. 1995;21:381–388.

Gait
Cerny K, Perry J, Walker JM. Effect of an unrestricted knee-ankle foot orthosis on the stance phase of gait in healthy persons. *Orthopedics*. 1990;13:1121–1127.
Donatelli R, ed. *The Biomechanics of the Foot and Ankle*. Philadelphia, Pa: FA Davis Co; 1990:148–152.
  [Dynamic assessment of foot mechanics: dynamic plantar pressure distribution, foot pressure EMED system, pedabarograph, three-dimensional kinematic analysis]

McCulloch MU, Brunt D, Vander-Linden D. The effect of foot orthotics and gait velocity on lower limb kinematics and temporal events of stance. *Journal of Orthopaedic and Sports Physical Therapy.* 1993;17:2–10.

Shore M. Footprint analysis in gait documentation: an instructional sheet format. *Physical Therapy.* 1980;60:1163–1167.

Joint Integrity and Structural Deviations

McPoil TG, Schuit D, Knecht HG. A comparison of three positions used to evaluate tibial varum. *Journal of the American Podiatric Medical Association.* 1988;78:22–28.

Rothstein JM, Roy SH, Wolf SL. *The Rehabilitation Specialist's Handbook.* Philadelphia, Pa: FA Davis Co; 1991:136–137.

Tomberlin JP, Saunders HD. *Evaluation, Treatment and Prevention of Musculoskeletal Disorders. Vol 2: Extremities.* Chaska, Minn: The Saunders Group; 1994:265–306.

Mobility

Bohannon RW, Tiberio D, Zitto M. Selected measures of ankle dorsiflexion range of motion: differences and intercorrelations. *Foot and Ankle.* 1989;10:99–103.

Creighton D, Olson V. Evaluation of range of motion of first metatarsophalangeal joint in runners with plantar fasciitis. *Journal of Orthopaedic and Sports Physical Therapy.* 1987;8:357–361.

Elveru RA, Rothstein JM, Lamb RL. Goniometric reliability in a clinical setting: subtalar and ankle joint measurements. *Physical Therapy.* 1988;68:672–677.

Kleven D, Bornhoeft D, Thorp B. Assessing ankle dorsiflexion. *Clinical Management in Physical Therapy.* 1989;9:6:25–26.

Picciano AM, Rowlands MS, Worrell T. Reliability of open and closed kinetic chain subtalar joint neutral positions and navicular drop test. *Journal of Orthopaedic and Sports Physical Therapy.* 1993;18:553–558.

Vandervoort AA, Chesworth BM, Cunningham DA, Rechnitzer PA, Paterson DH, Koval JJ. An outcome measure to quantify passive stiffness of the ankle. *Canadian Journal of Public Health.* 1992;83(suppl 2):S19–S23.

Youdas JW, Bogard CL, Suman VJ. Reliability of goniometric measurements and visual estimates of ankle joint active range of motion obtained in a clinical setting. *Archives of Physical Medicine and Rehabilitation.* 1993;74:1113–1118.

Strength

Instrumentation

Lee WA, Michaels CF, Pai YC. The organization of torque and EMG activity during bilateral handle pulls by standing humans. *Experimental Brain Research.* 1990;82:304–314.

Simoneau GG. Isokinetic characteristics of ankle evertors and invertors in female control subjects using the Biodex dynamometer. *Physiotherapy Canada.* 1990;42:182–187.

Manual Muscle Testing

Daniels L, Worthingham C. *Muscle Testing Techniques of Manual Examination.* Philadelphia, Pa: WB Saunders Co; 1995.

Kendall FP, McCreary EK, Provance PG. *Muscles: Testing and Function.* 4th ed. Baltimore, Md: Williams & Wilkins; 1993.

TREATMENT

Ballantyne BT, Kukulka CG, Soderberg GL. Motor unit recruitment in human medial gastrocnemius muscle during combined knee flexion and plantar flexion isometric contractions. *Experimental Brain Research.* 1993;93:492–498.

Billing HE, Brennan RL. Foot pains. *NAPT Journal*. (Jan–Feb), 1984;16:18.

Brown LP, Yavorsky P. Locomotor biomechanics and pathomechanics: a review. *Journal of Orthopaedic and Sports Physical Therapy*. 1987;9:3–10.

Buschbacher RM, ed. *Musculoskeletal Disorders: A Practical Guide for Diagnosis and Rehabilitation*. Boston, Mass: Andover Medical Publishers; 1994:216–235.

Cibulka MT. Management of a patient with forefoot pain: a case report. *Physical Therapy*. 1990;70:41–44.

Donatelli R. Normal biomechanics of the foot and ankle. *Journal of Orthopaedic and Sports Physical Therapy*. 1985;7:91–95.

Donatelli R. Abnormal biomechanics of the foot and ankle. *Journal of Orthopaedic and Sports Physical Therapy*. 1987;9:11–16.

Donatelli R, ed. *The Biomechanics of the Foot and Ankle*. Philadelphia, Pa: FA Davis Co; 1990:258–259.

Donatelli R, Hurlbert C, Conway P, et al. Biomechanical foot orthotics: a retrospective study. *Journal of Orthopaedic and Sports Physical Therapy*. 1988;10:205–212.

Donatelli R, Wooden MJ, eds. *Orthopaedic Physical Therapy*. New York, NY: Churchill Livingstone; 1989.

Doxey GE. The semi-flexible foot orthotic: fabrication and guidelines for use. *Journal of Orthopaedic and Sports Physical Therapy*. 1983;5:526.

Doxey GE. Clinical use and fabrication of molded thermoplastic foot orthotic devices. *Physical Therapy*. 1985;65:1679–1682.

Giallonardo LM. Clinical evaluation of foot and ankle dysfunction. *Physical Therapy*. 1988;68:1850–1856.

Gould JA, Davies GJ, eds. *Orthopaedic and Sports Physical Therapy*. St Louis: CV Mosby Co; 1985:317.

Goulet MJ. Role of soft orthosis in treating plantar fasciitis: suggestion from the field. *Physical Therapy*. 1984;64:1544.

Hertling D, Kessler RM. *Management of Common Musculoskeletal Disorders*. Philadelphia, Pa: JB Lippincott Co; 1990:359–410.

Hunt GC, ed. *Physical Therapy of the Foot and Ankle*. New York, NY: Churchill Livingstone; 1988.

Kahn J. Electrotherapy with podiatric conditions. *Clinical Management in Physical Therapy*. 1988;8:3:6–9.

Kaltenborn FM. *Manual Mobilization of the Extremity Joints*. 4th ed. Oslo, Norway: Olaf Norlis Bokhandel; 1989:152–159.

Kisner C, Colby LA. *Therapeutic Exercise: Foundations and Techniques*. 2nd ed. Philadelphia, Pa: FA Davis Co; 1990:385–407.

Kosmahl EM, Kosmahl HE. Painful plantar heel, plantar fasciitis, and calcaneal spur: etiology and treatment. *Journal of Orthopaedic and Sports Physical Therapy*. 1987;9:17–24.

Lattanza L, Gray GW, Kantner R. Closed vs open kinematic chain measurements of subtalar joint eversion: implications for clinical practice. *Journal of Orthopaedic and Sports Physical Therapy*. 1988;9:310–314.

Lockard MA. Foot orthoses. *Physical Therapy*. 1988;68:1866–1873.

Maitland GD. *Peripheral Manipulation*. 3rd ed. Boston, Mass: Butterworths; 1990.

McPoil TG. Footwear. *Physical Therapy*. 1988;68:1857–1865.

McPoil TG, Knecht HG. Biomechanics of the foot in walking: a functional approach. *Journal of Orthopaedic and Sports Physical Therapy*. 1985;7:69–72.

Monney M, Maffey-Ward L. All heel pain is not plantar fasciitis. *Physiotherapy Canada*. 1995;47;185–189.

Oatis CA. Biomechanics of the foot and ankle under static conditions. *Physical Therapy*. 1988;68:1815–1821.

Palmer M, Epler M. *Clinical Assessment Procedures in Physical Therapy*. Philadelphia, Pa: JB Lippincott Co; 1990.

Riddle DL, Freeman DB. Management of a patient with a diagnosis of bilateral plantar fasciitis and Achilles tendinitis: a case report. *Physical Therapy*. 1988;68:1913–1916.

Riegger CL. Anatomy of the ankle and foot. *Physical Therapy*. 1988;68:1802–1814.

Sammarco GJ, ed. *Foot and Ankle Manual*. Philadelphia, Pa: Lea & Febiger; 1991:350–358.

Tiberio D. Pathomechanics of structural foot deformities. *Physical Therapy*. 1988;68:1840–1849.

Tomberlin JP, Saunders HD. *Evaluation, Treatment and Prevention of Musculoskeletal Disorders. Vol 2: Extremities*. Chaska, Minn: The Saunders Group; 1994:265–305.

Viel ER, Desmarets JJ. Mechanical pull of the peroneal tendons on the fifth ray of the foot. *Journal of Orthopaedic and Sports Physical Therapy.* 1985;7:102–106.
Wessling KC, DeVane DA, Hylton CR. Effects of static stretch versus static stretch and ultrasound combined on triceps surae muscle extensibility in healthy women. *Physical Therapy.* 1987;67:674–679.

Plica Syndrome

DESCRIPTION

The plica syndrome is a thickening of the medial synovial plica (this plica is found in 60% of normal knees).

CAUSE

This thickening of the medial synovial plica combined with fibrotic changes causes anteromedial knee pain and noise.

ASSESSMENT

Areas
- History
- Posture
- Pain
- Joint integrity and structural deviations
- Mobility, including active and passive range of motion (ROM) and accessory motion
- Strength
- Neurological
- Skin and soft tissue
- Gait
- Functional level
- Special tests to which the PT may or may not have access

Instruments/Procedures (See References for Sources)

Functional Level
- modified Lysholm knee score

Joint Integrity and Structural Deviations. The following orthopedic tests for the knee may be performed:
- A-angle
- ALRI test
- AMRI test
- Apley grinding test
- apprehension test
- bounce home test
- brush or stroke (wipe) test

- Clark's sign
- crossover test
- Ely's test
- external rotation test
- flexion rotation drawer sign
- fluctuation test
- gravity drawer test (posterior sag sign)
- hamstring length
- Helfet test
- Hughston plica test
- Hughston posterolateral drawer test
- Hughston test (jerk sign)
- hyperflexion-hyperextension test
- Jakob test (reverse pivot)
- Lachman test
- lateral pull test
- limb-length discrepancy
- MacIntosh test (lateral pivot shift)
- McConnell test
- McMurray–Anderson test
- Noble's compression test
- Ober's test
- O'Donoghue's test
- patellar tap
- patellar tilt
- Perkin's test
- plica test
- posterior drawer sign
- posterior sag
- quadriceps active test
- reverse pivot shift
- Slocum test
- Steinman's test
- squat test
- valgus stress test
- varus stress test
- Waldron test
- Wilson test

Mobility
- goniometric knee measurements

Special Tests to Which the PT May or May Not Have Access
- arthrography and arthroscopy
- computed tomography (CT) scan
- magnetic resonance imaging (MRI)
- x-ray studies
- joint aspiration

- ultrasonography

Strength
- instrumentation
- manual muscle testing

PROBLEMS
- The client usually complains of anteromedial knee pain.
- The client may report that pain worsens with running. Pain may also worsen with prolonged sitting but then resolve after a few steps.
- In acute cases, the client may report clicking, swelling, catching, and feeling of weakness.

TREATMENT/MANAGEMENT

Acute
- Encourage rest.
- Strengthen the quadriceps muscle (especially the articularis genu to assist with pulling synovial membrane away from the joint during knee extension).

PRECAUTIONS/CONTRAINDICATIONS
- X-rays should be consulted to rule out any potential fractures.
- Consult orthopedic surgeon if major ligament damage or meniscal tear is suspected or if there is hemarthosis or sudden effusion of the joint.
- Carefully consider the nature of the problem before examination so you do not aggravate the condition with the test procedures.
- Inflamed plica can sometimes be mistaken for meniscal tear or patellofemoral dysfunction.

DESIRED OUTCOME/PROGNOSIS
- The client will have a reduction in symptoms.
- The client will have full knee function.

Conservative care reportedly offers good results. However, arthroscopic resection may be needed for unresponsive cases.

REFERENCES

ASSESSMENT
Delitto A. Lower extremity: knee. In: Myers RS, ed. *Saunders Manual of Physical Therapy Practice*. Philadelphia, Pa: WB Saunders Co; 1995:1001–1029.

Functional Level
Delitto A. Lower extremity: knee. In: Myers RS, ed. *Saunders Manual of Physical Therapy Practice*. Philadelphia, Pa: WB Saunders Co; 1995:1011. **[Modified Lysholm knee score]**

Joint Integrity and Structural Deviations
Arno S. The A angle: a quantitative measurement of patella alignment and realignment. *Journal of Orthopaedic and Sports Physical Therapy*. 1990;12:237–242.
Baumgaertner J. Quadriceps active test for posterior cruciate ligament injuries. *Clinical Management in Physical Therapy*. 1991;11:2:84–85.

Blustein M, D'Amico JC. Limb length discrepancy: identification, clinical significance and management. *Physical Therapy.* 1985;75:200–206.

Caylor D, Fites R, Worrell TW. The relationship between quadriceps angle and anterior knee pain syndrome. *Journal of Orthopaedic and Sports Physical Therapy.* 1993;17:11–16.

DiVeta JA, Vogelbach WD. The clinical efficacy of the A-angle in measuring patellar alignment. *Journal of Orthopaedic and Sports Physical Therapy.* 1992;16:136–139.

Noyes FR, Grood ES, Butler DL, et al. Knee ligament tests. *Physical Therapy.* 1980;60:1578–1581.

Rothstein JM, Roy SH, Wolf SL. *The Rehabilitation Specialist's Handbook.* Philadelphia, Pa: FA Davis Co; 1991:132–137. **[Apley grinding test, bounce home test, brush or stroke (wipe) test, Clark's sign, crossover test, gravity drawer test (posterior sag sign), Helfet test, Hughston plica test, Hughston posterolateral drawer test, Hughston test (jerk sign), Jakob test (reverse pivot), MacIntosh test (lateral pivot shift), O'Donoghue's test, Perkin's test, Slocum test, Waldron test, Wilson test]**

Tomberlin JP, Saunders HD. *Evaluation, Treatment and Prevention of Musculoskeletal Disorders. Vol 2: Extremities.* Chaska, Minn: The Saunders Group; 1994:233. **[Functional knee status exam, stroke test, fluctuation test, patellar tap, hamstring length, Ely's test, Ober's test, Noble's compression test, patellar tilt, lateral pull test, McConnell test, apprehension test, varus stress test, valgus stress test, Lachman test, posterior sag test, posterior drawer sign, quadriceps active test, AMRI, ALRI, flexion rotation drawer sign, Slocum's ALRI, MacIntosh test, external rotation test, reverse pivot shift, squat test, Steinman's test, hyperflexion-hyperextension test, McMurray–Anderson test, plica test]**

Mobility

Goniometry

Rothstein JM, Miller PJ, Roetgger RF. Goniometric reliability in a clinical setting: elbow and knee measurements. *Physical Therapy.* 1983;63:1611–1615.

Special Tests to Which the PT May or May Not Have Access

Buschbacher RM, ed. *Musculoskeletal Disorders: A Practical Guide for Diagnosis and Rehabilitation.* Boston, Mass: Andover Medical Publishers; 1994:206–208. **[Q-angle measurements, thigh measurement, x-ray studies, joint aspiration, MRI, CT, arthrography and arthroscopy]**

Stokes M, Young A. Measurement of quadriceps cross-sectional area by ultrasonography: a description of the technique and its applications in physiotherapy. *Physiotherapy Practice.* 1986;2:1:31–36. **[Ultrasonography]**

Strength

Instrumentation

Afzali L, Kuwabara F, Zachazewski J, Browne P, Robinson B. A new method for the determination of the characteristic shape of an isokinetic quadriceps femoris muscle torque curve. *Physical Therapy.* 1992;72:585–595.

Charteris J. An isometric normative database to facilitate restoration of function in knee-injured active young adults. *South African Journal of Physiotherapy.* 1993;49:2:28–34. **[Simple strain-gauge measure of isometric torque using knee flexor-extensor capacities, dominance ratios, contralateral asymmetries and sexual dimorphism ratios]**

Chung F. Effect of two input adapters used with the Orthotron II on knee torque. *Physiotherapy Canada.* 1988;40:356–360.

Durand A, Malouin F, Richards CL, Bravo G. Intertrial reliability of work measurements recorded during concentric isokinetic knee extension and flexion in subjects with and without meniscal tears. *Physical Therapy.* 1991;71:804–812.

Gross MT, McGrain P, Demilio N, et al. Relationship between multiple predictor variables and normal knee torque production. *Physical Therapy.* 1989;69:54.

Kramer J, Clarkson H. Comparison of muscle capability and the resistance patterns provided by Nautilus leg extension and leg curl machines. *Physiotherapy Canada.* 1989;41:256–261.

Kramer JF, Hill K, Jones IC, Sandrin M, Vyse M. Effect of dynamometer application arm length on concentric and eccentric torques during isokinetic knee extension. *Physiotherapy Canada.* 1989;41:100–106.

Steiner LA, Harris BA, Krebs DE. Reliability of eccentric isokinetic knee flexion and extension measurements. *Archives of Physical Medicine and Rehabilitation.* 1993;74:1327–1335.

Wessel J, Gray G, Luongo F, Isherwood L. Reliability of work measurements recorded during concentric and eccentric contractions of the knee extensors in healthy subjects. *Physiotherapy Canada.* 1989;41:250–253.

Wilk KE, Andrew JR. The effects of pad placement and angular velocity on tibial displacement during isokinetic exercise. *Journal of Orthopaedic and Sports Physical Therapy.* 1993;17:24-30.

Wyatt MP, Edwards AM. Comparison of quadriceps and hamstring torque values during isokinetic exercises. *Journal of Orthopaedic and Sports Physical Therapy.* 1981;3:2:48–56.

Manual Muscle Testing

Daniels L, Worthingham C. *Muscle Testing Techniques of Manual Examination.* 6th ed. Philadelphia, Pa: WB Saunders Co; 1995.

Kendall FP, McCreary EK, Provance PG. *Muscles; Testing and Function.* 4th ed. Baltimore, Md: Williams & Wilkins; 1993.

TREATMENT

Blackburn TA, Eiland WG, Bandy WG. An introduction to the plica. *Journal of Orthopaedic and Sports Physical Therapy.* 1982;3:171–177.

Buschbacher RM, ed. *Musculoskeletal Disorders: A Practical Guide for Diagnosis and Rehabilitation.* Boston, Mass: Andover Medical Publishers; 1994:197–215.

DuBois M. Functional knee extension. *Clinical Management in Physical Therapy.* 1990;10:4:57–58.

Gerrard B. The patellofemoral pain syndrome: a clinical trial of the McConnell programme. *Australian Journal of Physiotherapy.* 1989;35:70–80.

Hertling D, Kessler RM. *Management of Common Musculoskeletal Disorders.* Philadelphia, Pa: JB Lippincott Co; 1990:298–358.

Jensen K, DiFabio RP. Evaluation of eccentric exercise in the treatment of patellar tendinitis. *Physical Therapy.* 1989;69:211–216.

Karst GM, Jewett PD. EMG analysis of exercise proposed for differential activation of medial and lateral quadricep femoris muscle components. *Physical Therapy.* 1993;73:286–299.

Kisner C, Colby LA. *Therapeutic Exercise: Foundations and Techniques.* 2nd ed. Philadelphia, Pa: FA Davis Co; 1990:345–384.

Mangine RE, ed. *Physical Therapy of the Knee.* New York, NY: Churchill Livingstone; 1988.

McConnell J. The management of chondromalacia patellae: a long-term solution. *Australian Journal of Physiotherapy.* 1986;32:215–223.

McMullen W, Roncarati A, Koval P. Static and isokinetic treatments of chondromalacia patellae: a comparative investigation. *Journal of Orthopaedic and Sports Physical Therapy.* 1990;12:256–266.

Palmer M, Epler M. *Clinical Assessment Procedures in Physical Therapy.* Philadelphia, Pa: JB Lippincott Co; 1990.

Puniello MS. Iliotibial band tightness and medial patellar glide in patients with patellofemoral dysfunction. *Journal of Orthopaedic and Sports Physical Therapy.* 1993;17:144–148.

Selkowitz DM. Improvement in isometric strength of the quadriceps femoris muscle after training with electric stimulation. *Physical Therapy.* 1985;65:186–196.

Shelton GL, Thigpen LK. Rehabilitation of patellofemoral dysfunction: a review of literature. *Journal of Orthopaedic and Sports Physical Therapy.* 1991;14:243–249.

Soderberg GL, Minor SD, Nelson RM, et al. Electro-myographic analysis of knee exercises in healthy subjects and in patients with knee pathologies. *Physical Therapy.* 1987;67:1691–1696.

Tomberlin JP, Saunders HD. *Evaluation, Treatment and Prevention of Musculoskeletal Disorders. Vol 2: Extremities.* Chaska, Minn: The Saunders Group; 1994:217–264.
Woodall W, Welsh J. A biomechanical basis for rehabilitation programs involving the patellofemoral joint. *Journal of Orthopaedic and Sports Physical Therapy.* 1990;11:535–542.

Prepatellar Bursitis

Also known as *housemaid's knee.*

DESCRIPTION
Acute or chronic inflammation of the prepatellar bursa.

CAUSE
Unknown etiology. May be caused by trauma, such as a direct fall on the knee, or chronic overuse from persistent kneeling. Acute or chronic infection or arthritis can also be involved. This condition is the most common bursitis of the knee joint.

ASSESSMENT

Areas
- History
- Posture
- Pain
- Joint integrity and structural deviations
- Mobility, including active and passive range of motion (ROM) and accessory motion
- Strength
- Neurological
- Skin and soft tissue
- Gait
- Functional level
- Special tests to which the PT may or may not have access

Instruments/Procedures (See References for Sources)

Functional Level
- Lysholm knee score
- modified Lysholm knee score

Joint Integrity and Structural Deviations. The following orthopedic tests of the knee may be performed:
- A-angle
- ALRI test
- AMRI test
- Apley grinding test

- apprehension test
- bounce home test
- brush or stroke (wipe) test
- Clark's sign
- crossover test
- Ely's test
- external rotation test
- flexion rotation drawer sign
- fluctuation test
- gravity drawer test (posterior sag sign)
- hamstring length
- Helfet test
- Hughston plica test
- Hughston posterolateral drawer test
- Hughston test (jerk sign)
- hyperflexion-hyperextension test
- Jakob test (reverse pivot)
- Lachman test
- lateral pull test
- limb-length discrepancy
- MacIntosh test (lateral pivot shift)
- McConnell test
- McMurray–Anderson test
- Noble's compression
- Ober's test
- O'Donoghue's test
- patellar tap
- patellar tilt
- Perkin's test
- plica test
- posterior drawer sign
- posterior sag test
- quadriceps active test
- Q-angle measurements
- reverse pivot shift
- Slocum test
- Steinman's test
- squat test
- valgus stress test
- varus stress test
- Waldron test
- Wilson test

Mobility
- goniometry

Special Tests to Which the PT May or May Not Have Access
- x-ray studies

- joint aspiration
- magnetic resonance imagery (MRI)
- CT scan
- arthrography and arthroscopy

Strength
- instrumentation
- manual muscle testing

PROBLEMS
- The client usually complains of anterior knee pain.
- The client may have an antalgic gait.
- The client may complain of weakness in quadriceps and tightness in hamstring and gastrocnemius/soleus muscles.

TREATMENT/MANAGEMENT
- Use physical modalities, such as ice, as indicated.
- Consider the use of compression.
- Avoid persistent kneeling or direct fall on knee.

PRECAUTIONS/CONTRAINDICATIONS
- X-rays should be consulted to rule out any potential fractures.
- Carefully consider the nature of the problem before examination so you do not aggravate the condition with the test procedures.

DESIRED OUTCOME/PROGNOSIS
- Relieve symptoms such as inflammatory response.
- The client will have pain-free knee function.

REFERENCES

ASSESSMENT
Davies G, Malone T, Basett F. Knee examination. *Physical Therapy*. 1980;60:1565–1574.
Delitto A. Lower extremity: knee. In: Myers RS, ed. *Saunders Manual of Physical Therapy Practice*. Philadelphia, Pa: WB Saunders Co; 1995:1001–1029.

Functional level
Delitto A. Lower extremity: knee. In: Myers RS, ed. *Saunders Manual of Physical Therapy Practice*. Philadelphia, Pa: WB Saunders Co; 1995:1011. **[Modified Lysholm knee score]**
Tegner Y, Lysholm J. Rating systems in the evaluation of knee ligament injuries. Vol 198. *Clinical Orthopaedics and Related Research*. 1985;43–49. **[Lysholm Knee Rating Scale]**

Joint Integrity and Structural Deviations
Arno S. The A angle: a quantitative measurement of patella alignment and realignment. *Journal of Orthopaedic and Sports Physical Therapy*. 1990;12:237–242.
Blustein M, D'Amico JC. Limb length discrepancy: identification, clinical significance and management. *Physical Therapy*. 1985;75:200–206.
Caylor D, Fites R, Worrell TW. The relationship between quadriceps angle and anterior knee pain syndrome. *Journal of Orthopaedic and Sports Physical Therapy*. 1993;17:11–16.

DiVeta JA, Vogelbach WD. The clinical efficacy of the A-angle in measuring patellar alignment. *Journal of Orthopaedic and Sports Physical Therapy.* 1992;16:136–139.

Noyes FR, Grood ES, Butler DL, et al. Knee ligament tests. *Physical Therapy.* 1980;60:1578–1581.

Rothstein JM, Roy SH, Wolf SL.*The Rehabilitation Specialist's Handbook.* Philadelphia, Pa: FA Davis Co; 1991:132–137. [**Apley grinding test, bounce home test, brush or stroke (wipe) test, Clark's sign, cross-over test, gravity drawer test (posterior sag sign), Helfet test, Hughston plica test, Hughston postero-lateral drawer test, Hughston test (jerk sign), Jakob test (reverse pivot), MacIntosh test (lateral pivot shift), O'Donoghue's test, Perkin's test, Slocum test, Waldron test, Wilson test**]

Tomberlin JP, Saunders HD. *Evaluation, Treatment and Prevention of Musculoskeletal Disorders. Vol 2: Extremities.* Chaska, Minn: The Saunders Group; 1994:233. [**Functional knee status exam, stroke test, fluctuation test, patellar tap, hamstring length, Ely's test, Ober's test, Noble's compression test, pa-tellar tilt, lateral pull test, McConnell test, apprehension test, varus stress test, valgus stress test, Lachman sign, posterior sag test, posterior drawer sign, quadriceps active test, AMRI, ALRI, flexion rotation drawer sign, Slocum's ALRI, McIntosh test, external rotation test, reverse pivot shift test, squat test, Steinman's test, hyperflexion-hyperextension test, McMurray–Anderson test, plica test**]

Mobility

DuBois M. Functional knee extension. *Clinical Management in Physical Therapy.* 1990;10:4:57–58. [**Range of motion**]

Rothstein JM, Roy SH, Wolf SL. *The Rehabilitation Specialist's Handbook.* Philadelphia, Pa: FA Davis Co; 1991:67–68. [**Goniometry**]

Special Tests to Which the PT May or May Not Have Access

Buschbacher RM, ed. *Musculoskeletal Disorders: A Practical Guide for Diagnosis and Rehabilitation.* Bos-ton, Mass: Andover Medical Publishers; 1994:206–208. [**Q-angle measurements, thigh measurement, x-ray studies, joint aspiration, MRI, CT, arthrography and arthroscopy**]

Strength

Instrumentation

Charteris J. An isometric normative database to facilitate restoration of function in knee-injured active young adults. *South African Journal of Physiotherapy.* 1993;49:2:28–34. [**Simple strain-gauge measure of iso-metric torque using knee flexor-extensor capacities, dominance ratios, contralateral asymmetries and sexual dimorphism ratios**]

Steiner LA, Harris BA, Krebs DE. Reliability of eccentric isokinetic knee flexion and extension measure-ments. *Archives of Physical Medicine and Rehabilitation.* 1993;74:1327–1335.

Manual Muscle Testing

Daniels L, Worthingham C. *Muscle Testing Techniques of Manual Examination.* 6th ed. Philadelphia, Pa: WB Saunders Co; 1995.

Kendall FP, McCreary EK, Provance PG. *Muscles: Testing and Function.* 4th ed. Baltimore, Md: Williams & Wilkins; 1993.

TREATMENT

Buschbacher RM, ed. *Musculoskeletal Disorders: A Practical Guide for Diagnosis and Rehabilitation.* Bos-ton, Mass: Andover Medical Publishers; 1994:197–215.

Hertling D, Kessler RM. *Management of Common Musculoskeletal Disorders.* Philadelphia, Pa: JB Lippincott Co; 1990:298–358.

Johanson MA, Donatelli R, Greenfield BH. Rehabilitation of microtrauma injuries. In: Greenfield BH, ed. *Rehabilitation of the Knee: A Problem-Solving Approach.* Philadelphia, Pa: FA Davis Co; 1993:139–176.

Kisner C, Colby LA. *Therapeutic Exercise: Foundations and Techniques.* 2nd ed. Philadelphia, Pa: FA Davis Co; 1990:345–384.

Mangine RE, ed. *Physical Therapy of the Knee.* New York, NY: Churchill Livingstone; 1988.

Nelson EM. Knee rehabilitation with office stools. *Clinical Management in Physical Therapy.* 1991;11:3:53–54.

Palmer M, Epler M. *Clinical Assessment Procedures in Physical Therapy.* Philadelphia, Pa: JB Lippincott Co; 1990.

Tomberlin JP, Saunders HD. *Evaluation, Treatment and Prevention of Musculoskeletal Disorders. Vol 2: Extremities.* Chaska, Minn: The Saunders Group; 1994:217–264.

Woodall W, Welsh J. A biomechanical basis for rehabilitation programs involving the patellofemoral joint. *Journal of Orthopaedic and Sports Physical Therapy.* 1990;11:535–542.

Retrocalcaneal Bursitis

DESCRIPTION

Acute or chronic inflammation of the retrocalcaneal bursa. This acute or chronic inflammation can appear in the superficial retrocalcaneal bursa between the skin and the Achilles tendons or in the deep bursae between the Achilles tendon and the calcaneus. It occurs more frequently in young women but can also be present in men.

CAUSE

Deep bursa irritation is caused by excessive compensatory subtalar joint pronation or direct trauma. Footwear can also cause irritation through compressive forces.

ASSESSMENT

Areas
- History
- Pain
- Posture
- Gait
- Strength
- Neurological
- Joint integrity and structural deviations
- Mobility: active and passive range of motion (ROM) and accessory motion
- Skin and soft tissue
- Equipment, including footwear

Instruments/Procedures (See References for Sources)

Gait
- dynamic assessment of foot mechanics
  1. dynamic plantar pressure distribution
  2. foot pressure EMED system

3. pedabarograph
4. three-dimensional kinematic analysis
- gait velocity

Joint Integrity and Structural Deviations. The following orthopedic tests for the leg and foot may be performed:
- Achilles tendon test
- anterior drawer sign
- Homan's sign
- Kleiger test
- talar tilt
- Thompson test
- tibial varum evaluation

Mobility
- selected measures of ankle dorsiflexion
- goniometric measurements
- open and closed kinetic chain subtalar joint neutral positions and navicular drop test
- visual estimates of ankle joint active range of motion

Strength
- dynamometer
- manual muscle testing

PROBLEMS
- The client usually complains of pain.
- The client usually has swelling.
- The client can have inflammation over posterior calcaneus.

TREATMENT/MANAGEMENT
- Use physical agents, such as ice, as indicated.
- Consider orthotics or supportive counters in the shoes.
- Implement heel cord stretching.
- Assess footwear.
- Encourage enforced rest if there is a partial tear.

PRECAUTIONS/CONTRAINDICATIONS
- Do not overstress the tendon for up to 6 weeks if it has been injected with a steroid anesthetic because it may be prone to rupture during this period.

DESIRED OUTCOME/PROGNOSIS
- The client will reduce superficial bursa irritation and decreased inflammation.
- The client will have normal function.
  Surgery may be indicated in severe cases.

REFERENCES

ASSESSMENT
Giallonardo LM. Clinical evaluation of foot and ankle dysfunction. *Physical Therapy.* 1988;68:1850–1856.

McPoil TG, Hunt GC. Evaluation and management of foot and ankle disorders: present problems and future directions. *Journal of Orthopaedic and Sports Physical Therapy.* 1995;21:381–388.

Whitlock R, Eggart JE. A simple test for differentiating retrocalcaneal bursitis from calcaneal tendonitis. *Clinical Management in Physical Therapy.* 1985; 5:2:50. **[Differential diagnosis]**

Gait

Donatelli R, ed. *The Biomechanics of the Foot and Ankle.* Philadelphia, Pa: FA Davis Co; 1990:148–152. **[Dynamic assessment of foot mechanics: dynamic plantar pressure distribution, foot pressure EMED system, pedabarograph, three-dimensional kinematic analysis]**

McCulloch MU, Brunt D, Vander-Linden D. The effect of foot orthotics and gait velocity on lower limb kinematics and temporal events of stance. *Journal of Orthopaedic and Sports Physical Therapy.* 1993;17:2–10.

Joint Integrity and Structural Deviations

McPoil TG, Schuit D, Knecht HG. A comparison of three positions used to evaluate tibial varum. *Journal of the American Podiatric Medical Association.* 1988;78:22–28.

Rothstein JM, Roy SH, Wolf SL. *The Rehabilitation Specialist's Handbook.* Philadelphia, Pa: FA Davis Co; 1991:136–137. **[Achilles tendon test, anterior drawer sign, Homan's sign, Kleiger test, talar tilt, Thompson test]**

Tomberlin JP, Saunders HD. *Evaluation, Treatment and Prevention of Musculoskeletal Disorders. Vol 2: Extremities.* Chaska, Minn: The Saunders Group; 1994:265–306.

Mobility

Bohannon RW, Tiberio D, Zitto M. Selected measures of ankle dorsiflexion range of motion: differences and intercorrelations. *Foot and Ankle.* 1989;10:2:99–103.

Elveru RA, Rothstein JM, Lamb RL. Goniometric reliability in a clinical setting: subtalar and ankle joint measurements. *Physical Therapy.* 1988;68:672–677.

Kleven D, Bornhoeft D, Thorp B. Assessing ankle dorsiflexion. *Clinical Management in Physical Therapy.* 1989;9:6:25–26.

Lattanza L, Gray GW, Kantner R. Closed vs open kinematic chain measurements of subtalar joint eversion: implications for clinical practice. *Journal of Orthopaedic and Sports Physical Therapy.* 1988;9:310–314.

Picciano AM, Rowlands MS, Worrell T. Reliability of open and closed kinetic chain subtalar joint neutral positions and navicular drop test. *Journal of Orthopaedic and Sports Physical Therapy.* 1993;18:553–558.

Youdas JW, Bogard CL, Suman VJ. Reliability of goniometric measurements and visual estimates of ankle joint active range of motion obtained in a clinical setting. *Archives of Physical Medicine and Rehabilitation.* 1993;74:1113–1118.

Strength

Instrumentation

Lee WA, Michaels CF, Pai YC. The organization of torque and EMG activity during bilateral handle pulls by standing humans. *Experimental Brain Research.* 1990;82:304–314.

Simoneau GG. Isokinetic characteristics of ankle evertors and invertors in female control subjects using the Biodex dynamometer. *Physiotherapy Canada.* 1990;42:182–187.

Manual Muscle Testing

Daniels L, Worthingham C. *Muscle Testing Techniques of Manual Examination.* 6th ed. Philadelphia, Pa: WB Saunders Co; 1995.

Kendall FP, McCreary EK, Provance PG. *Muscles: Testing and Function.* 4th ed. Baltimore, Md: Williams & Wilkins, 1993.

TREATMENT

Buschbacher RM, ed. *Musculoskeletal Disorders: A Practical Guide for Diagnosis and Rehabilitation.* Boston, Mass: Andover Medical Publishers; 1994.

Donatelli R. Abnormal biomechanics of the foot and ankle. *Journal of Orthopaedic and Sports Physical Therapy.* 1987;9:11–16.

Donatelli R, ed. *The Biomechanics of the Foot and Ankle.* Philadelphia, Pa: FA Davis Co; 1990:258–259.

Donatelli R, Hurlbert C, Conway P, et al. Biomechanical foot orthotics: a retrospective study. *Journal of Orthopaedic and Sports Physical Therapy.* 1988;10:205.

Donatelli R, Wooden MJ, eds. *Orthopaedic Physical Therapy.* New York, NY: Churchill Livingstone; 1989.

Doxey GE. Clinical use and fabrication of molded thermoplastic foot orthotic devices. *Physical Therapy.* 1985;65:1679–1682.

Grisogono V. Physiotherapy treatment for Achilles tendon injuries. *Physiotherapy.* 1989;75:562–572.

Gould JA, Davies GJ, eds. *Orthopaedic and Sports Physical Therapy.* St Louis, Mo: CV Mosby Co; 1985:317.

Hertling D, Kessler RM. *Management of Common Musculoskeletal Disorders.* Philadelphia, Pa: JB Lippincott Co; 1990:359–410.

Hunt GC, ed. *Physical Therapy of the Foot and Ankle.* 2nd ed. New York, NY: Churchill Livingstone; 1995.

Kisner C, Colby LA. *Therapeutic Exercise: Foundations and Techniques.* 2nd ed. Philadelphia, Pa: FA Davis Co; 1990:385–407.

Lockard MA. Foot orthoses. *Physical Therapy.* 1988;68:1866–1873.

Maitland GD. *Peripheral Manipulation.* 3rd ed. Boston, Mass: Butterworths; 1990.

McPoil TG. Footwear. *Physical Therapy.* 1988;68:1857–1865.

McPoil TG, Knecht HG. Biomechanics of the foot in walking: a functional approach. *Journal of Orthopaedic and Sports Physical Therapy.* 1985;7:69–72.

Oatis CA. Biomechanics of the foot and ankle under static conditions. *Physical Therapy.* 1988;68:1815–1821.

Palmer M, Epler M. *Clinical Assessment Procedures in Physical Therapy.* Philadelphia, Pa: JB Lippincott Co; 1990.

Riddle DL, Freeman DB. Management of a patient with a diagnosis of bilateral plantar fasciitis and Achilles tendinitis: a case report. *Physical Therapy.* 1988;68:1913–1916.

Riegger CL. Anatomy of the ankle and foot. *Physical Therapy.* 1988;68:1802–1814.

Sammarco GJ, ed. *Foot and Ankle Manual.* Philadelphia, Pa: Lea & Febiger; 1991:350–358.

Tiberio D. The effect of excessive subtalar joint pronation on patellofemoral mechanics: a theoretical model. *Journal of Orthopaedic and Sports Physical Therapy.* 1987;9:160–165.

Tiberio D. Pathomechanics of structural foot deformities. *Physical Therapy.* 1988;68:1840–1849.

Tomberlin JP, Saunders HD. *Evaluation, Treatment and Prevention of Musculoskeletal Disorders. Vol 2: Extremities.* Chaska, Minn: The Saunders Group; 1994:265–305.

Wessling KC, DeVane DA, Hylton CR. Effects of static stretch versus static stretch and ultrasound combined on triceps surae muscle extensibility in healthy women. *Physical Therapy.* 1987;67:674–679.

Shoulder Bursitis

DESCRIPTION

Acute or chronic inflammation of the shoulder bursa. Bursitis of the shoulder may include the subacromial or subdeltoid bursas. Shoulder pain from bursitis may be due to one pathologic process or a combination of the following disorders: adhesive capsulitis, tendinitis, and bursitis.

CAUSE

Unknown etiology. Shoulder bursitis may be caused by trauma, chronic overuse, inflammatory arthritis, or acute or chronic infection.

ASSESSMENT

Areas

- History
- Pain
- Posture
- Joint integrity and structural deviations
- Skin and soft tissue
- Mobility: active and passive range of motion (ROM) and accessory motion
- Strength
- Neurological
- Vascular
- Functional level, including functional use of arm
- Special tests to which the PT may or may not have access

Instruments/Procedures (See References for Sources)

Joint Integrity and Structural Deviations/Neurological Involvement. The following neurological and orthopedic tests of the upper extremity may be performed:

- acromioclavicular instability test
- anterior apprehension sign
- anterior drawer sign
- anterior stability test
- active impingement test
- Adson's test
- Allen's test
- clunk test
- costoclavicular syndrome test
- drop arm test
- Feagin test
- fulcrum test
- Gilchrist's sign
- Halstead maneuver
- Hawkin's test
- hyperabduction syndrome test
- jerk test
- lateral scapular glide
- Lippman's test
- locking test
- Ludington's test
- Neer's test
- Norwood stress test
- posterior apprehension test
- posterior drawer sign

- push-pull test
- quadrant test
- relocation test
- Roo's test (EAST test)
- Rockwood test
- Rowe test
- Speed's test (bicep's test)
- sulcus sign
- suprascapular nerve entrapment test
- transverse humeral ligament rupture test
- upper limb tension test
- upper quarter screen
- Yergason's test

Pain
- body chart
- palpation
- visual analogue scale

Special Tests to Which the PT May or May Not Have Access
- electromyography (EMG)
- thermography

Strength
- isokinetic peak torque and work values
- isokinetic testing of the shoulder rotators
- manual muscle testing

PROBLEMS
- The client usually has constant, intense pain, which may radiate down the arm.
- The client can have disturbed sleep because of pain.
- The client may be unable to use the arm secondary to pain.
- There is usually a decreased ROM in active flexion and abduction.
- The client can have a decrease in internal and external rotation.

TREATMENT/MANAGEMENT

Exercise in General
- Isokinetic rehabilitation can begin when the client's shoulder can tolerate resisted exercise through specific ROM.
- Progress exercise from submaximal isometrics to maximum-effort isometrics. Proceed from submaximal concentric isokinetics to isotonics. Proceed from maximal isokinetics through partial-range to full-ROM isokinetics at submaximal level. Progress from isotonics at full ROM to maximal effort isokinetics at full ROM.

Acute
- Use ice or superficial heat if indicated.
- Consider external support for arm via sling.
- Begin gentle active assisted exercises and pendulum exercises.
- Use gentle joint mobilization techniques if indicated.

Chronic
- Use ultrasound if indicated.
- Consider joint mobilization.
- Begin a home program of strength training exercises and ROM exercises.
- Educate on proper usage to prevent recurrence.

PRECAUTIONS/CONTRAINDICATIONS
- Brachial plexus peripheral entrapment at the thoracic outlet or the shoulder can be mistakenly identified as shoulder tendinitis or musculoskeletal pain of the shoulder.
- Rule out pre-existing calcific rotator cuff tendinitis.
- Do not begin isokinetic exercise progression until after lesion is well healed and painless ROM is achieved.

DESIRED OUTCOME/PROGNOSIS
- The client will have an absence of pain at rest.
- The client will have active flexion to 90 degrees or more.
- Any chronic inflammatory process will be resolved, and full ROM, joint play, and strength will be restored.

This condition is usually self-limiting after several weeks.

REFERENCES

ASSESSMENT
Boublik M, Hawkins RJ. Clinical examination of the shoulder complex. *Journal of Orthopaedic and Sports Physical Therapy.* 1993;18:379–385.

Diamond W. Upper extremity: shoulder. In: Myers RS, ed. *Saunders Manual of Physical Therapy Practice.* Philadelphia, Pa: WB Saunders Co; 1995:802–822.

Donatelli RA, ed. *Physical Therapy of the Shoulder.* 2nd ed. New York, NY: Churchill Livingstone; 1991:19–61. [Algorithm for sequential shoulder girdle evaluation]

Jobe FW, Pink M. Classification and treatment of shoulder dysfunction in the overhead athlete. *Journal of Orthopedic and Sports Physical Therapy.* 1993;8:427–432.

Joint Integrity and Structural Deviations/Neurological Involvement
Donatelli RA, ed. *Physical Therapy of the Shoulder.* 2nd ed. New York, NY: Churchill Livingstone; 1991:19–61. [Transverse humeral ligament rupture test, upper quarter screen]

Elvey RL. Brachial plexus tension tests and the pathoanatomical origin of arm pain. In: Glascow E, Twomey LT, eds. *Aspects of Manipulative Therapy.* 2nd ed. New York, NY: Churchill Livingstone; 1985:105–110.

Grant R, ed. *Physical Therapy of the Cervical and Thoracic Spine.* New York, NY: Churchill Livingstone; 1988:167–194. [Upper limb tension test]

Hertling D, Kessler RM. *Management of Common Musculoskeletal Disorders.* Philadelphia, Pa: JB Lippincott Co; 1990:192–194. [Locking test, quadrant test, anterior stability test, isokinetic testing, nerve conduction studies]

Rothstein JM, Roy SH, Wolf SL. *The Rehabilitation Specialist's Handbook.* Philadelphia, Pa: FA Davis Co; 1991:124–125. [Thoracic outlet syndrome: Adson's test, Allen's tests, costoclavicular syndrome test, Halstead maneuver, hyperabduction syndrome test, Speed's test (bicep's test), suprascapular nerve entrapment test, Yergason's test]

Tomberlin JP, Saunders HD. *Evaluation, Treatment and Prevention of Musculoskeletal Disorders. Vol 2: Extremities.* Chaska, Minn: The Saunders Group; 1994:91. [Joint/ligamentous: anterior apprehension test, Rockwood test, relocation test, anterior drawer sign, Rowe test, fulcrum test, clunk test, posterior apprehension test, posterior drawer sign, jerk test, Norwood stress test, push-pull test, sulcus sign, Feagin test, Rowe test for multidimensional instability, lateral scapular glide, acromioclavicular instability test. **Musculotendinous:** Neer's test, Hawkin's test, active impingement test, drop arm test, Speed's test, Gilchrist's sign, Lippman's test, Ludington's test. **Neurological:** Adson's test, costoclavicular syndrome test, hyperabduction syndrome test, Roo's test (EAST test).]

Pain

Donatelli RA, ed. *Physical Therapy of the Shoulder.* 2nd ed. New York, NY: Churchill Livingstone; 1991:19-61. [Pain visual analogue scale and body chart]

Special Tests to Which the PT May or May Not Have Access

EMG

Ballantyne BT, O'Hare SJ, Paschall JL, et al. Electromyographic activity of selected shoulder muscles in commonly used therapeutic exercises. *Physical Therapy.* 1993;73:668–682.

Moseley JB, Jobe FW, Pink M, et al. EMG analysis of the scapular muscles during a shoulder rehabilitation program. *American Journal of Sports Medicine.* 1992;20:128–135.

Thermography

Middleditch A, Jarman P. An investigation of frozen shoulders using thermography. *Physiotherapy.* 1984;70:433–439.

Strength

Instrumentation

Maddux REC, Kibler WB, Uhl T. Isokinetic peak torque and work values for the shoulder. *Journal of Orthopaedic Sports and Physical Therapy.* 1989;1:264.

Donatelli RA, ed. *Physical Therapy of the Shoulder.* 2nd ed. New York, NY: Churchill Livingstone; 1991:19–61.

Hageman PA, Mason DK, Rylund KW, et al. Effects of position and speed on eccentric and concentric isokinetic testing of the shoulder rotators. *Journal of Orthopaedic Sports and Physical Therapy.* 1989;11:64–69.

Soderberg GJ, Blaschak MJ. Shoulder internal and external rotation peak torque production through a velocity spectrum in differing positions. *Journal of Orthopaedic and Sports Physical Therapy.* 1987;8:518–524.

Wilk KE, Arrigo CA, Andrews JR. Isokinetic testing of the shoulder abductors and adductors: windowed vs non-windowed data collection. *Journal of Orthopaedic and Sports Physical Therapy.* 1992;15:107–112.

Manual Muscle Testing

Daniels L, Worthingham C. *Muscle Testing Techniques of Manual Examination.* 6th ed. Philadelphia, Pa: WB Saunders Co; 1995.

Elsner RC, Pedegrana LR, Lang J. Protocol for strength testing and rehabilitation of the upper extremity. *Journal of Orthopaedic Sports and Physical Therapy.* 1983;4:229.

Kendall FP, McCreary EK, Provance PG. *Muscles: Testing and Function.* 4th ed. Baltimore, Md: Williams & Wilkins; 1993.

TREATMENT

Boissonnault WG, Janos SC. Dysfunction, evaluation, and treatment of the shoulder. In: Donatelli R, Wooden MJ, eds. *Orthopaedic Physical Therapy.* New York, NY: Churchill Livingstone; 1989.

Burstein D. Joint compression for treatment of shoulder pain. *Clinical Management in Physical Therapy.* 1985;5:2:6–9.

Corrigan B, Maitland GD. *Practical Orthopaedic Medicine*. Boston, Mass: Butterworth; 1985.

Culham E, Peat M. Functional anatomy of the shoulder complex. *Journal of Orthopaedic and Sports Physical Therapy*. 1993;18:342–350.

Dacre JE, Beeney N, Scott DL. Injections and physiotherapy for the painful stiff shoulder. *Annals of the Rheumatic Diseases*. 1989;48:322–325.

Davies G, Dickoff-Hoffman S. Neuromuscular testing and rehabilitation of the shoulder complex. *Journal of Orthopaedic and Sports Physical Therapy*. 1993;18:449–458.

Donatelli RA, ed. *Physical Therapy of the Shoulder*. 2nd ed. New York, NY: Churchill Livingstone; 1991:19–62, 63-79, 91–116.

Donatelli RA, Greenfield B. Rehabilitation of a stiff and painful shoulder: a biomechanical approach. *Journal of Orthopaedic and Sports Physical Therapy*. 1987;9:118–126.

Downing DS, Weinstein A. Ultrasound therapy of subacromial bursitis: a double blind trial. *Physical Therapy*. 1986;66:194–199.

Gould J, Davies G, eds. *Orthopedic and Sports Physical Therapy*. St Louis, Mo: CV Mosby Co; 1985.

Grant R. *Physical Therapy of the Cervical and Thoracic Spine*. New York, NY: Churchill Livingstone; 1988.

Grant LW, Ritch JM. Rx: rubber tubing. *Clinical Management in Physical Therapy*. 1988;8:6:10–15.

Grieve GP, ed. *Modern Manual Therapy of the Vertebral Column*. New York, NY: Churchill Livingstone; 1986.

Grubbs N. Frozen shoulder syndrome: a review of literature. *Journal of Orthopaedic and Sports Physical Therapy*. 1993;18:479–487.

Haig SV. *Shoulder Pathophysiology: Rehabilitation and Treatment*. Gaithersburg, Md: Aspen Publishers, Inc; 1996.

Hart DL, Carmichael SW. Biomechanics of the shoulder. *Journal of Orthopaedic and Sports Physical Therapy*. 1985;6:229–234.

Hertling D, Kessler RM. *Management of Common Musculoskeletal Disorders*. Philadelphia, Pa: JB Lippincott Co; 1990:169–204, 532–541.

Kisner C, Colby LA. *Therapeutic Exercise: Foundations and Techniques*. 2nd ed. Philadelphia, Pa: FA Davis Co; 1990:241–270.

McLean JM, Credit L. Orthotron II and shoulder rehabilitation. *Clinical Management in Physical Therapy*. 1989;9:2:43.

Nitz AJ. Physical therapy management of the shoulder. *Physical Therapy*. 1986;66:1912–1919.

Oldham G. The occupational health physiotherapist's role in assessing fitness for work. *Physiotherapy*. 1988;74:422–425.

Palmer M, Epler M. *Clinical Assessment Procedures in Physical Therapy*. Philadelphia, Pa: JB Lippincott Co; 1990.

Peat M. Functional anatomy of the shoulder complex. *Physical Therapy*. 1986;66:1855–1865.

Schenkman M, Rugo de Cartaya V. Kinesiology of the shoulder complex. *Journal of Orthopaedic and Sports Physical Therapy*. 1993;18:442–448.

Schneider G. Restricted shoulder movement: capsular contracture or cervical referral—a clinical study. *Australian Journal of Physiotherapy*. 1989;35:97–100.

Simmons TC, Skyhair MJ. Rehabilitation of the shoulder. In: Nickel VL, Botte MJ, eds. *Orthopaedic Rehabilitation*. New York, NY: Churchill Livingstone; 1992:747.

Strang MH. Physiotherapy of the shoulder complex. *Baillieres Clinical Rheumatology*. 1989;3:669–680.

Tomberlin JP, Saunders HD. *Evaluation, Treatment and Prevention of Musculoskeletal Disorders. Vol 2: Extremities*. Chaska, Minn: The Saunders Group; 1994:73–111.

Wilk KE, Arrigo CA. An integrated approach to upper extremity exercises. In Timm K, ed. Exercise Principles. *Orthopaedic Physical Therapy Clinics of North America*. 1992;2:337–360.

Voss DE, Knott M, Kabat M. Application of neuromuscular facilitation in the treatment of shoulder disabilities. *Physical Therapy Review*. 1953;33:536.

Shoulder Tendinitis

DESCRIPTION

Shoulder tendinitis is the inflammation of a tendon. Shoulder pain from shoulder tendinitis may be due to one pathologic process or a combination of disorders: adhesive capsulitis, bursitis, and tendinitis.

CAUSE

Unknown etiology. Shoulder tendinitis may be caused by the effects of aging, repetitive microtrauma, extreme trauma, strain, or unaccustomed exercise. It occurs in young and old and about equally in females and males.

ASSESSMENT

Areas

- History
- Pain
- Posture
- Joint integrity and structural deviations
- Skin and soft tissue
- Mobility, including active and passive range of motion (ROM) and accessory motion
- Strength
- Neurological
- Vascular
- Functional level, including functional use of arm
- Special tests to which the PT may or may not have access

Instruments/Procedures (See References for Sources)

Joint Integrity and Structural Deviations/Neurological Involvement. The following neurological and orthopedic tests of the upper extremity may be performed:
- acromioclavicular instability test
- anterior apprehension test
- anterior drawer sign
- anterior stability test
- active impingement test
- Adson's test
- Allen's test
- clunk test
- costoclavicular syndrome test
- drop arm test
- Feagin test
- fulcrum test
- Gilchrist's sign
- Halstead maneuver
- Hawkin's test
- hyperabduction syndrome test

- jerk test
- lateral scapular glide
- Lippman's test
- locking test
- Ludington's test
- Neer's test
- Norwood stress test
- posterior apprehension test
- posterior drawer sign
- push-pull test
- quadrant test
- relocation test
- Roo's test (EAST test)
- Rockwood test
- Rowe test
- Speed's test (bicep's test)
- sulcus sign
- suprascapular nerve entrapment test
- transverse humeral ligament rupture test
- upper limb tension test
- upper quarter screen
- Yergason's test

Pain
- body chart
- visual analogue scale

Special Tests to Which the PT May or May Not Have Access
- EMG
- thermography

Strength
- isokinetic peak torque and work values
- isokinetic testing of the shoulder rotators
- manual muscle testing

PROBLEMS
- The client usually has intense lateral brachial pain, which may radiate into arm.
- Usually the pain is associated with increased arm usage and specific movements, especially reaching behind the back.
- The client usually has pain with resisted motions, specifically shoulder abduction, internal and external rotation, elbow flexion, and forearm supination.

TREATMENT/MANAGEMENT
- Use physical modalities, such as ultrasound or friction massage, if indicated.
- Provide education in proper activity level.
- Begin strength training of rotator cuff muscles, progressing from isometric to isotonic to resistive exercise.
- Consider aquatic therapy.

- Teach automobilization techniques.
- Address total body fitness considerations.
- Prevent impingement via shoulder shrugs and push-ups with arm abducted to 90 degrees.

PRECAUTIONS/CONTRAINDICATIONS
- Brachial plexus peripheral entrapment at the thoracic outlet or the shoulder can be mistakenly identified as shoulder tendinitis or musculoskeletal pain of the shoulder.
- Avoid activities that require repeated arm elevation to 90 degrees or more.
- Rotator cuff muscles should be strong before initiating shoulder elevation above 90 degrees.
- It is preferable to perform exercises with arm close to side to avoid impingement in early phase of recovery.

DESIRED OUTCOME/PROGNOSIS
- The client will obtain pain relief.
- The client will be able to return to normal use of shoulder.
- There will be restoration of normal joint mechanics at shoulder.
- There will be restoration of normal strength and endurance.

If shoulder tendinitis is caused by a degenerative process, the pain will tend to be chronic. The condition may respond quite well to a treatment program but is unlikely to recover spontaneously. If the client has a surgical repair of the rotator cuff, the rehabilitation process is often slow. An athlete may average 12 to 14 months before obtaining prior activity status.

REFERENCES

ASSESSMENT
Boublik M, Hawkins RJ. Clinical examination of the shoulder complex. *Journal of Orthopaedic and Sports Physical Therapy*. 1993;18:379-385.

Diamond W. Upper extremity: shoulder. In: Myers RS, ed. *Saunders Manual of Physical Therapy Practice*. Philadelphia, Pa: WB Saunders Co; 1995:802–822.

Donatelli RA, ed. *Physical Therapy of the Shoulder*. 2nd ed. New York, NY: Churchill Livingstone; 1991:19–61. [**Algorithm for sequential shoulder girdle evaluation**]

Jobe FW, Pink M. Classification and treatment of shoulder dysfunction in the overhead athlete. *Journal of Orthopedic and Sports Physical Therapy*. 1993;8:427–432.

Joint Integrity and Structural Deviations/Neurological Involvement
Donatelli RA, ed. *Physical Therapy of the Shoulder*. 2nd ed. New York, NY: Churchill Livingstone; 1991:19–61. [**Transverse humeral ligament rupture test, upper quarter screen**]

Elvey RL. Brachial plexus tension tests and the pathoanatomical origin of arm pain. In: Glascow E, Twomey LT, eds. *Aspects of Manipulative Therapy*. 2nd ed. New York, NY: Churchill Livingstone; 1985:105–110.

Grant R, ed. *Physical Therapy of the Cervical and Thoracic Spine*. New York, NY: Churchill Livingstone; 1988:167–194. [**Upper limb tension test**]

Hertling D, Kessler RM. *Management of Common Musculoskeletal Disorders*. Philadelphia, Pa: JB Lippincott Co; 1990:192–194. [**Locking test, quadrant test, anterior stability tests, isokinetic testing, nerve conduction studies**]

Rothstein JM, Roy SH, Wolf SL. *The Rehabilitation Specialist's Handbook*. Philadelphia, Pa: FA Davis Co; 1991:124–125. [**Speed's test (bicep's test), suprascapular nerve entrapment test, Yergason's test. Thoracic outlet syndrome: Adson's test, Allen's test, costoclavicular syndrome test, Halstead maneuver, hyperabduction syndrome test**]

Tomberlin JP, Saunders HD. *Evaluation, Treatment and Prevention of Musculoskeletal Disorders. Vol 2: Extremities.* Chaska, Minn: The Saunders Group; 1994:91. **[Joint/ligamentous: anterior apprehension test, Rockwood test, relocation test, anterior drawer test, Rowe test, fulcrum test, clunk test, posterior apprehension test, posterior drawer test, jerk test, Norwood stress test, push-pull test, sulcus sign, Feagin test, Rowe test for multidimensional instability, lateral scapular glide, acromioclavicular instability test. Musculotendinous: Neer's test, Hawkin's test, active impingement test, drop arm test, Speed's test, Gilchrist's sign, Lippman's test, Ludington's test. Neurological: Adson's test, costoclavicular syndrome test, hyperabduction syndrome test, Roo's test (EAST test).]**

Pain
Donatelli RA, ed. *Physical Therapy of the Shoulder.* 2nd ed. New York, NY: Churchill Livingstone; 1991:19–61. **[Pain visual analogue scale and body chart]**

Special Tests to Which the PT May or May Not Have Access

EMG
Ballantyne BT, O'Hare SJ, Paschall JL, et al. Electromyographic activity of selected shoulder muscles in commonly used therapeutic exercises. *Physical Therapy.* 1993;73:668–682.

Moseley JB, Jobe FW, Pink M, et al. EMG analysis of the scapular muscles during a shoulder rehabilitation program. *American Journal of Sports Medicine.* 1992;20:128–135.

Thermography
Middleditch A, Jarman P. An investigation of frozen shoulders using thermography. *Physiotherapy.* 1984;70:433–439.

Strength

Instrumentation
Donatelli RA, ed. *Physical Therapy of the Shoulder.* 2nd ed. New York, NY: Churchill Livingstone; 1991:19–61.

Hageman PA, Mason DK, Rylund KW, et al. Effects of position and speed on eccentric and concentric isokinetic testing of the shoulder rotators. *Journal of Orthopaedic Sports and Physical Therapy.* 1989;11:64–69.

Maddux REC, Kibler WB, Uhl T. Isokinetic peak torque and work values for the shoulder. *Journal of Orthopaedic Sports and Physical Therapy.* 1989;1:264–269.

Soderberg GJ, Blaschak MJ. Shoulder internal and external rotation peak torque production through a velocity spectrum in differing positions. *Journal of Orthopaedic and Sports Physical Therapy.* 1987;8:518–524.

Wilk KE, Arrigo CA, Andrews JR. Isokinetic testing of the shoulder abductors and adductors: windowed vs non-windowed data collection. *Journal of Orthopaedic and Sports Physical Therapy.* 1992;15:107–112.

Manual Muscle Testing
Elsner RC, Pedegrana LR, Lang J. Protocol for strength testing and rehabilitation of the upper extremity. *Journal of Orthopaedic Sports and Physical Therapy.* 1983;4:229.

Daniels L, Worthingham C. *Muscle Testing Techniques of Manual Examination.* 6th ed. Philadelphia, Pa: WB Saunders Co; 1995.

Kendall FP, McCreary EK, Provance PG. *Muscles: Testing and Function.* 4th ed. Baltimore, Md: Williams & Wilkins; 1993.

TREATMENT
Almekinders LC, Almekinders SV. Outcome in the treatment of chronic overuse sports injuries: a retrospective study. *Journal of Orthopaedic and Sports Physical Therapy.* 1994;19:157–161.

Boissonnault WG, Janos, SC. Dysfunction, evaluation, and treatment of the shoulder. In: Donatelli R, Wooden MJ, eds. *Orthopaedic Physical Therapy*. New York, NY: Churchill Livingstone; 1989.

Burstein D. Joint compression for treatment of shoulder pain. *Clinical Management in Physical Therapy*. 1985;5:2:6–9.

Corrigan B, Maitland GD. *Practical Orthopaedic Medicine*. Boston, Mass: Butterworth; 1985.

Culham E, Peat M. Functional anatomy of the shoulder complex. *Journal of Orthopaedic and Sports Physical Therapy*. 1993;18:342–350.

Dacre JE, Beeney N, Scott DL. Injections and physiotherapy for the painful stiff shoulder. *Annals of the Rheumatic Diseases*. 1989;48:322–325.

Davies G, Dickoff-Hoffman S. Neuromuscular testing and rehabilitation of the shoulder complex. *Journal of Orthopaedic and Sports Physical Therapy*. 1993;18:449–458.

Donatelli RA, ed. *Physical Therapy of the Shoulder*. 2nd ed. New York, NY: Churchill Livingstone; 1991:19–62, 63–79, 91–116.

Donatelli, RA, Greenfield B. Rehabilitation of a stiff and painful shoulder: a biomechanical approach. *Journal of Orthopaedic and Sports Physical Therapy*. 1987;9:118–126.

Fowler C, Potter GE. An uncommon shoulder injury. *British Journal of Sports Medicine*. 1990;24:125–126.

Gould J, Davies G, eds. *Orthopedic and Sports Physical Therapy*. St Louis, Mo: CV Mosby Co; 1985.

Grant R. *Physical Therapy of the Cervical and Thoracic Spine*. New York, NY: Churchill Livingstone; 1988.

Grant LW, Ritch JM. Rx: rubber tubing. *Clinical Management in Physical Therapy*. 1988;8:6:10–15.

Grieves GP, ed. *Modern Manual Therapy of the Vertebral Column*. New York, NY: Churchill Livingstone; 1986.

Grubbs N. Frozen shoulder syndrome: a review of literature. *Journal of Orthopaedic and Sports Physical Therapy*. 1993;18:479–487.

Hart DL, Carmichael SW. Biomechanics of the shoulder. *Journal of Orthopaedic and Sports Physical Therapy*. 1985;6:229–234.

Hertling D, Kessler RM. *Management of Common Musculoskeletal Disorders*. Philadelphia, Pa: JB Lippincott Co; 1990:169–204, 532–541.

Kisner C, Colby LA. *Therapeutic Exercise: Foundations and Techniques*. 2nd ed. Philadelphia, Pa: FA Davis Co; 1990:241–270.

McLean JM, Credit L. Orthotron II and shoulder rehabilitation. *Clinical Management in Physical Therapy*. 1989;9:2:43.

Nitz AJ. Physical therapy management of the shoulder. *Physical Therapy*. 1986;66:1912–1919.

Palmer M, Epler M. *Clinical Assessment Procedures in Physical Therapy*. Philadelphia, Pa: JB Lippincott Co; 1990.

Peat M. Functional anatomy of the shoulder complex. *Physical Therapy*. 1986;66:1855–1865.

Schenkman M, Rugo de Cartaya V. Kinesiology of the shoulder complex. *Journal of Orthopaedic and Sports Physical Therapy*. 1993;18:442–448.

Schneider G. Restricted shoulder movement: capsular contracture or cervical referral—a clinical study. *Australian Journal of Physiotherapy*. 1989;35:97–100.

Simmons TC, Skyhair MJ. Rehabilitation of the shoulder. In: Nickel VL, Botte MJ, eds. *Orthopaedic Rehabilitation*. New York, NY: Churchill Livingstone; 1992:747.

Strang MH. Physiotherapy of the shoulder complex. *Baillieres Clinical Rheumatology*. 1989;3:669–680.

Tomberlin JP, Saunders HD. *Evaluation, Treatment and Prevention of Musculoskeletal Disorders. Vol 2: Extremities*. Chaska, Minn: The Saunders Group; 1994:73–111.

Voss DE, Knott M, Kabat M. Application of neuromuscular facilitation in the treatment of shoulder disabilities. *Physical Therapy Review*. 1953;33:536.

Wilk KE, Arrigo CA. An integrated approach to upper extremity exercises. In Timm K, ed. Exercise Principles. *Orthopaedic Physical Therapy Clinics of North America*. 1992;9:337.

Wilk KE, Arrigo C. Current concepts in the rehabilitation of the athletic shoulder. *Journal of Orthopaedic and Sports Physical Therapy*. 1993;18:365–378.

Temporomandibular Joint (TMJ) Dysfunction

DESCRIPTION
The temporomandibular joint (TMJ) is subject to a variety of disorders, such as internal derangement and ankylosis as well as arthritis, dislocation, congenital anomalies, fractures, and neoplastic diseases. The more common lesions seen by physical therapists include TMJ internal derangement, dislocation, and arthritis.

CAUSE
Internal disc derangement can be caused by chronic muscle spasm, trauma, or changes in the articulating surfaces due to arthritis. Anklyosis is usually caused by trauma or infection but may be congenital or may occur with rheumatoid arthritis.

The TMJ can also be affected by other craniomandibular disorders involving dentition. The masticatory system can be disrupted by malocclusion and stress.

ASSESSMENT

Areas
- History, including screening history
- Pain
- Posture
- Cranial nerve exam
- Strength, including lips/cheek, tongue, and masticatory musculature
- Periarticular tissue and muscles, including
    1. digastric
    2. masseter
    3. medial pterygoid
    4. mylohyoid
    5. lateral pterygoid
    6. levator scapula
    7. posterior cervical
    8. scaleni
    9. sternocleidomastoid
    10. temporalis
- Joint integrity and structural deviations of TMJ
- Mobility, including joint play and functional movement (opening, protrusion, lateral deviation)
- Respiration, including normal diaphragmatic versus upper chest breathing
- Swallowing, including hyoid movement and tongue position
- Pain, including headaches
- Special tests to which the PT may or may not have access

Instruments/Procedures (See References for Sources)

Joint Integrity and Structural Deviations
- resting vertical dimension (anterior and posterior)

- condyle-meniscus relationship (opening click, closing click, force closing click, crepitus)
- TMJ loading
- upper quarter screen

Periarticular Tissue and Muscles
- palpation

Special Tests to Which the PT May or May Not Have Access
- arthrography
- CT scan
- dental examination
- magnetic resonance imaging (MRI)
- occlusal examination
- x-rays

PROBLEMS
Problems that can be indicative of TMJ dysfunction in general include the following:
- cervical pain
- dizziness
- headache
- hyperalgesia
- symptoms in sinuses or eyes
- ringing in ears (tinnitus)
  In TMJ derangement:
- The client may report a single click.
- The client may report an audible, reciprocal click when mandible opens.
  In TMJ functional dislocation with reduction:
- The client has limited mouth opening.
- There is no report of audible noise with opening.
- The client may report joint catching or locking.
- The client usually reports pain in jaw.
  In TMJ functional dislocation with no reduction:
- The client reports limited jaw opening and restriction of movement to the unaffected side.
- The mandible is usually pulled to the affected side.
  In anklyosis:
- The client usually reports painless restriction of movement.
- The condition is usually chronic.

TREATMENT/MANAGEMENT
In general:
- Consider use of physical agents and modalities. Modalities may include moist heat, ultrasound, ice, vapocoolant sprays, electrical stimulation, electrogalvanic stimulation, transcutaneous electrical nerve stimulation (TENS), acupuncture point stimulation, soft tissue manipulation, massage, stretching, and joint mobilization through unloading in the closed pack position.
- Provide advice on TMJ joint protection:

1. Open jaw within painless range.
2. Avoid taking big bites of food and choose soft foods, when possible.
3. Avoid clenching and grinding teeth.
- Prescribe exercise regimens, which can include
  1. Passive range of motion (ROM) within client's pain-free range
  2. Active assistive stretching exercises with gentle intermittent pressure
  3. Self-stretch home program
  4. Combined stretch and vapocoolant spray treatment
  5. Resistive exercises, usually for 10 repetitions, five times a day
  6. Isometric resisted jaw opening against fist

  For displacements and dislocation with reduction:
- Consider fitting client with anterior repositioning appliance, which is worn continuously for several months as dictated by the extent of the damage.

  For dislocation without reduction:
- Consider manipulation to reduce dislocation.
- Successful reduction is facilitated by relaxation of superior lateral pterygoid muscle, extreme forward condylar position, and increased disk space.
- Self-manipulation may be performed by moving the mandible in a side-to-side motion.
- Use modalities for pain as indicated such as ultrasound, phonophoresis, high-voltage pulsed current, and moist heat.

  For arthritis:
- Consider use of appliance.
- Modalities for pain include moist heat and ultrasound.
- Use gentle active exercise for mandibular ROM.

PRECAUTIONS/CONTRAINDICATIONS
- Anterior displacement of disk that does not self-reduce is usually an indication for surgery.

DESIRED OUTCOME/PROGNOSIS
- The client will obtain optimal joint position to promote healing.
- The client will experience a reduction in symptoms.
- The client will have unrestricted mandibular function.

  The client may be a candidate for surgery if conservative treatment fails.

  Post surgery:
- The client will experience a normalization of ROM.
- The client will experience the elimination of pain.
- The client will experience a reduction in inflammation.
- The client will have unrestricted mandibular function.

  The majority of evidence is clinical without well-controlled studies. One study reports greater ROM with patients who receive physical therapy postoperatively.

REFERENCES

ASSESSMENT
Bourbon B. Craniomandibular examination and treatment. In: Myers RS, ed. *Saunders Manual of Physical Therapy Practice*. Philadelphia, Pa: WB Saunders Co; 1995:669–718. **[Screening history, cranial nerve exam]**

Goodman C, Snyder TE. *Differential Diagnosis in Physical Therapy*. Philadelphia, Pa: WB Saunders Co; 1990:332, 337, 357, 362–363.
Myers S. Appendix E. In: Myers RS, ed. *Saunders Manual of Physical Therapy Practice*. Philadelphia, Pa: WB Saunders Co; 1995:1331–1345.

Mobility
Austin BD, Shupe SM. The role of physical therapy in recovery after temporomandibular joint surgery. *Journal of Oral and Maxillofacial Surgery*. 1993;51:495–498. **[ROM]**

TREATMENT
Austin BD, Shupe SM. The role of physical therapy in recovery after temporomandibular joint surgery. *Journal of Oral and Maxillofacial Surgery*. 1993;51:495–498.
Bertolucci LE. Physical therapy post-arthroscopic TMJ management (update). *Cranio*. 1992;10:130–137.
Bertolucci LE. Postoperative physical therapy in temporomandibular joint arthroplasty. *Cranio*. 1992;10:211–220.
Bertolucci LE, Uriell P, Swaffer C. Postoperative physical therapy in temporomandibular joint arthroplasty. *Journal of Cranio-Mandibular Practice*. 1989;7:214–222.
Bourbon B. Craniomandibular examination and treatment. In: Myers RS, ed. *Saunders Manual of Physical Therapy Practice*. Philadelphia, Pa: WB Saunders Co; 1995:669–718.
Braun BL. Treatment of an acute anterior disk displacement in the temporomandibular joint: a case report. *Physical Therapy*. 1987;67:1234–1236.
Darling DW, Kraus S, Glasheen-Wray MB. Relationship of head posture and the rest position of the mandible. *Journal of Prosthetic Dentistry*. 1984;52:111–114.
Ellis JJ, Makofsky HW. Balancing the upper quarter through awareness of RTTPB: Relax, Teeth apart, Tongue on palate, Posture, Breath system. *Clinical Management in Physical Therapy*. 1987;7:6:20–23.
Fast J. Physical therapy evaluation and treatment and auricular pain. In: Ferrer-Brechnier T, ed. *Common Problems in Pain Management*. Chicago, Ill: *Year Book Medical Publishers*; 1990:99–104.
Grieves GP, ed. *Modern Manual Therapy of the Vertebral Column*. New York, NY: Churchill Livingstone; 1986.
Hansson T, Minor CAC, Taylor DLW. *Physical Therapy in Craniomandibular Disorders*. Chicago, Ill: Quintessence Publishing Co; 1992.
Hargreaves A. Dysfunction of the temporomandibular joints. *Physiotherapy*. 1986;72:209–212.
Heinrich S. The role of physical therapy in craniofacial pain disorders: an adjunct to dental pain management. *Cranio*. 1991;9:71–75.
Hertling D. The temporomandibular joint. In: Herling D, Kessler RM, eds. *Management of Common Musculoskeletal Disorders*. 2nd ed. Philadelphia, Pa: JB Lippincott Co; 1990:411–447.
Kirk WS, Calabrese DK. Clinical evaluation of physical therapy in the management of internal derangement of the temporomandibular joint. *Journal of Oral and Maxillofacial Surgery*. 1989;47:113–119.
Kraus S. Temporomandibular joint. In: Saunders HD. *Evaluation, Treatment and Prevention of Musculoskeletal Disorders*. Bloomington, Minn: Educational Opportunities; 1985:171–194.
Kraus SL, ed. *TMJ Disorders: Management of Craniomandibular Complex*. 2nd ed. New York, NY: Churchill Livingstone; 1994.
Kronn E. The incidence of TMJ dysfunction in patients who have suffered a cervical whiplash injury following a traffic accident. *Journal of Orofacial Pain*. 1993;7:209–213.
Morrone L, Makofsky H. TMJ home exercise program. *Clinical Management in Physical Therapy*. 1991;11:2:20–26.
Osborne JJ. A physical therapy protocol for orthognathic surgery. *Journal of Cranio-Mandibular Practice*. 1989;7:132–136.
Paquet JB. Treatment for TMJ dysfunction. *Clinical Management in Physical Therapy*. 1991;11:2:27–29.
Passero PL, Wyman BS, Bell JW, Hirschey SA, Schlosser WS. Temporomandibular joint dysfunction syndrome: a clinical report. *Physical Therapy*. 1985;65:1203–1207.

Rocabado M. Diagnosis and treatment of abnormal craniomandibular mechanics. In: Solberg W, Clark G, eds. *Abnormal Jaw Mechanics: Diagnosis and Treatment.* Chicago, Ill: Quintessence Publishing Co; 1984.

Rocabado M. Physical therapy for the postsurgical TMJ patient. *Journal of Cranio-Mandibular Disorders.* 1989;3:75–82.

Root GR, Kraus SL, Razook SJ, et al. Effect of an intraoral appliance on head and neck posture. *Journal of Prosthetic Dentistry.* 1987;58:90–95.

Santiesteban AJ. Isometric exercises and a simple appliance for temporomandibular joint dysfunction: a case report. *Physical Therapy.* 1989;69:463–466.

Sporton JJM. The treatment of temporomandibular joint dysfunction by physiotherapy. *Physiotherapy.* 1986;72:212–214.

Sturdivant J, Fricton JR. Physical therapy for temporomandibular disorders and orofacial pain. *Current Opinion in Dentistry.* 1991;1:485–496.

Trott PH, Goss AN. Physiotherapy in diagnosis and treatment of the myofascial dysfunction syndrome. *International Journal of Oral Surgery.* 1978;7:360–365.

Uriell P, Bertolucci L, Swaffer C. Physical therapy in the postoperative management of temporomandibular joint arthroscopic surgery. *Journal of Cranio-Mandibular Practice.* 1989;7:27–32.

Van Dyke AR, Goldman SM. Manual reduction of displaced disk. *Cranio.* 1990;8:350–352.

Waide FL, Bade DM, Lovasko J, Montana J. Clinical management of a patient following temporomandibular joint arthroscopy. *Physical Therapy.* 1992;72:355–364.

Wang K. A report of 22 cases of temporomandibular joint dysfunction syndrome treated with acupuncture and laser radiation. *Journal of Traditional Chinese Medicine.* 1992;12:116–118.

Wilk BR, Stenback JT, McCain JP. Postarthroscopy physical therapy management of a patient with temporomandibular joint dysfunction. *Journal of Orthopaedic and Sports Physical Therapy.* 1993;18:473–478.

Trochanteric Bursitis

DESCRIPTION

Acute or chronic inflammation of the trochanteric bursa. Trochanteric bursitis is the most common bursitis in the hip area. This type of bursitis is seen often in dancers, gymnasts, and runners—those who use repetitive motion of hip flexion with external rotation. The condition is more common in women than men.

CAUSE

Unknown etiology. Trochanteric bursitis may be caused by trauma, chronic overuse, inflammatory arthritis, or acute or chronic infection. Onset is usually insidious but may be linked to a fall on the lateral hip or feeling a "snap" in the lateral hip. Factors influencing tendency toward condition include the following: iliotibial band tightness, muscular imbalance, postural imbalance, leg-length difference, and improper athletic footwear or running surface.

ASSESSMENT

Areas
- History
- Pain

- Posture
- Joint integrity and structural deviations
- Gait
- Mobility: active and passive range of motion (ROM), and accessory motion
- Strength
- Neurological
- Skin and soft tissue
- Functional level
- Special tests to which the PT may or may not have access

Instruments/Procedures (See References for Sources)

Joint Integrity and Structural Deviations. The following orthopedic tests for the lower extremity may be performed:
- Craig's test
- Ely's test
- Fabere test
- hamstring tightness
- leg-length measurements
- Ober's test
- Noble's compression test
- piriformis test
- Thomas test
- torque test
- Trendelenburg's sign
- quadrant test

Mobility
- goniometry
- hip flexibility

Posture
- clinical measurement of postural control

Special Tests to Which the PT May or May Not Have Access
- electromyographic (EMG) analysis of hip abductor musculature

Strength
- maximal isometric hip abductor muscles torques
- manual muscle testing

PROBLEMS
- The client usually reports tenderness over area of lateral thigh and posterolateral trochanter. The area usually has an increase in temperature.
- The client can have pain radiating to lumbosacral region on the same side.
- The client usually has pain with sitting and weight-bearing activities, especially climbing the stairs.
- The client may be unable to tolerate side-lying position, so sleep is diminished.
- Usually pain is described as "deep" as opposed to "sharp."

- The client can have pain with adduction.
- Hip abduction with resistance is usually painful.

TREATMENT/MANAGEMENT
- Use modalities, such as ice, ultrasound, phonophoresis, and iontophoresis, if indicated.
- Avoid aggravating activities.
- Discuss sleep posture adaptations with pillows.
- Assess for muscular imbalance and stretch and strengthen accordingly (iliotibial band tightness).

PRECAUTIONS/CONTRAINDICATIONS
- The pain pattern for trochanteric bursitis is very similar to that for an L-5 lesion.

DESIRED OUTCOME/PROGNOSIS
The inflammation and pain will decrease, and recurrence will be prevented.

Ultrasound may offer quite effective relief in three to six sessions. The key component of treatment is identifying the predisposing cause of injury.

Chronic conditions may need surgical treatment.

REFERENCES

ASSESSMENT
Hicklin SP, DePretis MC. Lower extremity: hip. In: Myers RS, ed. *Saunders Manual of Physical Therapy Practice*. Philadelphia, Pa: WB Saunders Co; 1995:955–999.
Echternach JL, ed. *Physical Therapy of the Hip*. New York, NY: Churchill Livingstone; 1990:36. **[Hip pain algorithm]**

Joint Integrity and Structural Deviations
Gogia PP, Braatz JH. Validity and reliability of leg length measurements. *Journal of Orthopaedic and Sports Physical Therapy*. 1986;8:185–188.
Tomberlin JP, Saunders HD. *Evaluation, Treatment and Prevention of Musculoskeletal Disorders. Vol 2: Extremities*. Chaska, Minn: The Saunders Group; 1994:200. **[Trendelenburg's sign, piriformis test, Thomas test, Ely's test, Ober's test, Noble's compression test, hamstring tightness, quadrant test, Fabere test, torque test, Craig's test, leg-length test]**
Woerman AL, Binder-MacLeod SA. Leg length discrepancy assessment accuracy and precision in five clinical methods of evaluation. *Journal of Orthopaedic and Sports Physical Therapy*. 1984;5:230–239.

Mobility
Rothstein JM, ed. *Measurement in Physical Therapy*. New York, NY: Churchill Livingstone; 1985:103.
VanRoy P, Borms J, Haentjens A. Goniometric study of the maintenance of hip flexibility resulting from hamstring stretches. *Physiotherapy Practice*. 1987;3:2:52–59.

Posture
Horak FB. Clinical measurement of postural control in adults. *Physical Therapy*. 1987;67:1881–1885.

Strength
Neumann DA, Soderberg GL, Cook TM. Comparison of maximal isometric hip abductor muscles torques between hip sides. *Physical Therapy*. 1988;68:496–502.

Neumann DA, Soderberg GL, Cook TM. Electromyographic analysis of hip abductor musculature in healthy right-handed persons. *Physical Therapy.* 1989;69:431–440.

Manual Muscle Testing

Daniels L, Worthingham C. *Muscle Testing Techniques of Manual Examination.* 6th ed. Philadelphia, Pa: WB Saunders Co; 1995.

Kendall FP, McCreary EK, Provance PG. *Muscles: Testing and Function.* 4th ed. Baltimore, Md: Williams & Wilkins; 1993.

TREATMENT

Bandy WD, Sinning WE. Kinematic effect of heel lift use to correct lower limb length. *Journal of Orthopaedic and Sports Physical Therapy.* 1986;7:173–179.

Cibulka MT. Rehabilitation of the pelvis, hip and thigh. *Clinics in Sports Medicine.* 1989;8:777–803.

Corrigan B, Maitland GD. *Practical Orthopaedic Medicine.* Boston, Mass: Butterworths; 1983.

Donatelli R, Wooden MJ, eds. *Orthopaedic Physical Therapy.* New York, NY: Churchill Livingstone; 1989:403.

Echternach JL, ed. *Physical Therapy of the Hip.* New York, NY: Churchill Livingstone; 1990.

Grieve GP. The hip. *Physiotherapy.* 1983;69:196–204.

Halkovich LR, Personius WJ, Clamann HP, Newton RA. Effect of fluorimethane spray on passive hip flexion. *Physical Therapy.* 1981;61:185–189.

Henricson AS, Fredriksson K, Persson I, et al. The effect of heat and stretching on the range of hip motion. *Journal of Orthopaedic and Sports Physical Therapy.* 1984;6:110–115.

Hertling D, Kessler RM. *Management of Common Musculoskeletal Disorders.* Philadelphia, Pa: JB Lippincott Co; 1990:272–297.

Hicklin SP, DePretis MC. Lower extremity: hip. In: Myers RS, ed. *Saunders Manual of Physical Therapy Practice.* Philadelphia, Pa: WB Saunders Co; 1995:975–976.

Kisner C, Colby LA. *Therapeutic Exercise: Foundations and Techniques.* 2nd ed. Philadelphia, Pa: FA Davis Co; 1990:317–344.

Kornberg C, McCarthy T. The effect of neural stretching technique on sympathetic outflow to the lower limbs. *Journal of Orthopaedic and Sports Physical Therapy.* 1992;16:269–274.

Maitland GF. *Peripheral Manipulation.* 3rd ed. Boston, Mass: Butterworths; 1990:203.

Newton RA. Effects of vapocoolants on passive hip flexion in healthy subjects. *Physical Therapy.* 1985;65:1034–1036.

Palmer M, Epler M. *Clinical Assessment Procedures in Physical Therapy.* Philadelphia, Pa: JB Lippincott Co; 1990.

Singleton MC, LeVeau BF. The hip joint: Structure, stability and stress. *Physical Therapy.* 1975;55:957.

Tomberlin JP, Saunders HD. *Evaluation, Treatment and Prevention of Musculoskeletal Disorders. Vol 2: Extremities.* Chaska, Minn: The Saunders Group; 1994:187–212.

Chapter 9

Conditions in Back Pain

- Cervical dysfunction/thoracic dysfunction
- Low back pain

See also the sections "Connective Tissue Disorders" and "Women's Health Disorders."

Cervical Dysfunction/Thoracic Dysfunction

DESCRIPTION

Cervical dysfunction can lead to local, distant, or referred pain. It may include paresthesias, muscle weakness, and reflex or sensory loss.

Thoracic dysfunction is also known as thoracic postural stabilizing syndrome. Complaints vary by region but may include aching across the supraspinous fossa or along the spine of the scapula to the superior posterior border of the shoulder and posterolateral upper arm region. The client may feel anterior chest discomfort that may be confused with cardiac involvement and may have unilateral or bilateral low back pain with radiating pain. The T-7 level may refer pain into the mid- and upper abdominal area.

CAUSE

Cervical dysfunction may be caused by a pathologic process or a combination of abnormalities. Trauma, such as a motor vehicle accident, can also lead to cervical dysfunction.

Thoracic dysfunction may be caused by hypomobility at the thoracic level or levels.

ASSESSMENT

Areas
- History, including nature of symptoms
- Posture, including resting posture
- Pain, including reproduction of symptoms
- Cervical spine: vertebral position
- Skin and soft tissues and associated structures such as peripheral joints, viscera, and paravertebral muscles
- Joint integrity and structural deviations
- Mobility: active cervical range of motion (ROM), combined movements, and repeated movements
- Strength
- Neurological: especially indicated if client has referred pain, weakness, paresthesia, signs of upper motor neuron lesion; include reflexes, sensation, and Babinski's sign, and check for clonus
- Functional level

Instruments (See References for Sources)

Cervical Spine
- palpation examination of vertebral position
- mechanical diagnosis

Functional Level
- Neck Disability Index

Joint Integrity/Structural Deviations and Neurological Involvement. The following neurological and orthopedic tests of the cervical and thoracic region may be performed:
- adverse mechanical tension of the nervous system assessment
- brachial plexus tension test

- carpal tunnel test
- distraction test
- dizziness tests
- foraminal compression test
- ischemic vertigo
- L'hermitte's sign
- passive accessory intervertebral movement tests (PAIVMs)
- passive physiologic intervertebral movement tests (PPIVMs)
- scalenus anticus and thoracic outlet syndrome tests
- shoulder abduction test
- shoulder depression test
- slump test
- Spurling test
- upper limb tension test
- Valsalva test
- vertebral artery test

Mobility
1. craniovertebral hypermobility syndrome testing
2. ROM testing
   - tape measure
   - Myrin gravity reference goniometer

Pain
- visual analogue scales

Posture
- cervical ROM device
- pendulum goniometer
- triaxial electrogoniometer

Skin and Soft Tissues
- palpation for temperature, tone, tenderness

PROBLEMS

Cervical Dysfunction

Acute Disk Bulge
- The client usually has a sudden onset of severe pain in the neck. The problem may progress to muscle spasm.
- The client may be unable to rotate the neck unilaterally.
- The client usually has limitation of rotation and flexion to one side but more movement to opposite side.

Cervical Degenerative Changes
- The client may have decreased motion in the neck.
- The client may have pain into the shoulders and arms.
- The client may have pain bilaterally; usually one side is more involved.
- The client may describe the pain as worse in the morning and again in the evening.

- There is usually extreme restriction of motion into extension. The restriction is less with side bending, rotation, and flexion.
- The client may have pain at extremes of joint ROM.

Cervical Nerve Root Impingement
- The client usually has unilateral pain in the neck, scapula, or arm.
- The client usually has paresthesia into the fingers.
- The client may have sharp or aching arm pain.
- Usually, the pain is intense and worse with weight bearing.

Localized Cervical Joint Restriction in Facet Joint (Zygapophyseal Joint)
- The client may have aching in the scapula, usually unilateral.
- The pain is usually worse at the end of the day.
- The pain is usually worse with sustained muscular tension.
- The client usually has pain with extremes of joint ROM in rotation and side bending.
- The client may have pain on extension.

Thoracic Dysfunction
- The client usually has a gradual onset of symptoms.
- The client may report symptoms after being in a prolonged stooped position with repetitive upper extremity work.
- The client may complain of central discomfort and tightness or dull ache into the anterior lower thoracic rib cage.

T-4 Syndrome
- The client may have a feeling of tightness in the posterior mid thoracic area.
- The client usually has a dull pain with aching and discomfort and may have paresthesia in the arm.
- The client may also have posterior neck discomfort accompanied with a dull headache.

TREATMENT/MANAGEMENT

Cervical Dysfunction

Disk Bulge
   In acute cases:
- Usually the position of comfort is a combined movement of extension and lateral flexion to the opposite side.
- Traction may make the condition more comfortable.
- To increase ROM and decrease pain, try a position of tolerable extension and manual traction. Begin ROM while using traction to the symptom-free side.
- After achieving full ROM on the symptom-free side, begin on the painful side.
- Soft cervical support may be useful for a few days.
- After acute symptoms recede, more advanced therapy can be undertaken.
   In subacute cases:
- Use gentle manual traction, use a soft collar temporarily, and avoid flexion if painful.
- Use gentle mobilization techniques as tolerated.
- Moist warmth may be helpful.
- Correct muscle imbalance and any forward head posture.

- Teach self-treatment techniques.

Cervical Degenerative Changes
- Try positional traction.
- Provide activities of daily living (ADLs) instruction on how to avoid unwanted mechanical stress.
- Consider mobilization of adjacent segments.
- Relaxation exercises can reduce tension.
- Use external support collar if symptoms are acute.
- Strengthen muscle, beginning with isometric exercise in the pain-free range.

Cervical Nerve Root Impingement
- Traction can be used as tolerated.
- Consider passive mobilization.
- Consider McKenzie mechanical treatment and self-treatment if pain falls into one of the following categories: posture syndrome, dysfunction, or derangement.

Localized Cervical Joint Restriction in Facet Joint (Zygapophyseal Joint)
- Use manual traction with slow oscillation as a reciprocal relaxation technique.
- Mechanical traction may also be indicated.
- Spinal mobilization and manipulation are treatment options. Use gentle unilateral oscillatory pressure over appropriate zygapophyseal joints. Bilateral treatment may be necessary. Progress to firm pressure as tolerated.
- Use transverse thrust manipulation to open locked joint, if no contraindications exist.
- Use unilateral oscillatory pressures for appropriate joint, and consider use of ultrasound.
- Provide soft collar as needed.
- Instruct client in self-mobilization, strength, and coordination training if there is recurrent locking of zygapophyseal joints.

Thoracic Dysfunction
- Mobilize or manipulate appropriate hypomobile segments. Treat adjacent structures.

T-4 syndrome
- Perform direct palpation of spinous processes at T-3 to T-6 level, using gentle oscillatory pressures and progressing to more forceful techniques if indicated.

PRECAUTIONS/CONTRAINDICATIONS

Cervical Dysfunction
- Structural integrity must be known before one treats the cervicothoracic spine.
- Any anatomical variation on normal can contraindicate therapy, especially passive movement.
- Prior to initiating mechanical treatment, upper cervical ligament integrity should be tested.
- Nerve root pain or musculoskeletal pain in neck can actually be peripheral entrapment of the brachial plexus at the thoracic outlet.
- Vertebral arteries should be tested individually prior to using traction or mobilization techniques on the upper cervical spine. See the orthopedic tests listed in "Instruments."
- With existing degenerative joint disease, extension and extension with rotation can lead to further narrowing of the foramina and spinal canal and should be avoided.

• If neurological symptoms are present, the client should be reassessed frequently, perhaps at each treatment session.

Thoracic Dysfunction
• Because these symptoms are often vague and nonspecific and because their onset cannot be reproduced by movement, one must rule out a potential visceral source of symptoms.

DESIRED OUTCOME/PROGNOSIS

Cervical Dysfunction
• The client will have pain-free full cervical ROM.
• The client will have normal strength.
• The client will have normal cervical function.
An acute disc bulge can sometimes resolve spontaneously in a few days.

Thoracic Dysfunction
• The client will experience a reduction in symptoms.
• The client will have normal strength.
• The client will have normal thoracic function.

REFERENCES

ASSESSMENT

Cervical Dysfunction

Cervical Spine
Anderson M, Stevens B, Richards J, Jensen G. Cervical spine. In: Myers RS, ed. *Saunders Manual of Physical Therapy Practice*. Philadelphia, Pa: WB Saunders Co; 1995:727–787. **[Subjective and objective examination, neurological examination, dizziness testing, adverse mechanical tension tests for upper limb, and differentiation of cervical and shoulder problems]**
Goodman C, Snyder TE. *Differential Diagnosis in Physical Therapy*. Philadelphia, Pa; WB Saunders Co; 1990:332, 337, 357, 362–363.
Maitland GD. Palpation examination of the posterior cervical spine: the ideal, average and abnormal. *Australian Journal of Physiotherapy*. 1982;28:3–12.
Stevens BJ, McKenzie RA. Mechanical diagnosis and treatment of the cervical spine. *Clinics in Physical Therapy*. 1988;17:271–289.

Functional Level
Vernon H, Mior S. The Neck Disability Index: a study of reliability and validity. *Journal of Manipulative and Physiological Therapeutics*. 1991;14:409–415.

Joint Integrity/Structural Deviations and Neurological Involvement
Aspinall W. Clinical testing for cervical mechanical disorders which produce ischemic vertigo. *Journal of Orthopaedic and Sports Physical Therapy*. 1989;11:176–182. **[Ischemic vertigo]**
Butler DS. Adverse mechanical tension of the nervous system: a model for assessment and treatment. *Australian Journal of Physiotherapy*. 1989;35:227–238.
Butler DS, Gifford L. The concept of adverse mechanical tension in the nervous system. Part 1: testing of dural tension. *Physiotherapy*. 1989;75:622–636.
Elvey RL. Brachial plexus tension signs and the pathoanatomical origin of arm pain. In: Glascow EF, Twomey LT, Scull ER, eds. *Aspects of Manipulative Therapy*. New York, NY: Churchill Livingstone; 1985.

Grant R, ed. *Physical Therapy of the Cervical and Thoracic Spine.* New York, NY: Churchill Livingstone; 1988:62, 75, 97–98, 111–124, 167–194. **[Dizziness tests, neuromeningeal mobility tests (slump test, upper limb tension test), passive accessory intervertebral movement tests (PAIVMs), passive physiologic intervertebral movement tests (PPIVMs)]**

Hertling D, Kessler RM. *Management of Common Musculoskeletal Disorders: Physical Therapy Principles and Methods.* 2nd ed. Philadelphia, Pa: JB Lippincott Co; 1990:510–511. **[Spurling test, carpal tunnel test, scalenus anticus and thoracic outlet, and vertebral artery test]**

Kenneally M, Rubenach H, Elvey RL. The upper limb tension test: the SLR of the arm. *Clinics in Physical Therapy.* 1988;17:167–194.

Maitland GD. The slump test: examination and treatment. *Australian Journal of Physiotherapy.* 1985;31:215. **[Slump test]**

Rothstein JM, Roy SH, Wolf SL. *The Rehabilitation Specialist's Handbook.* Philadelphia, Pa: FA Davis Co; 1991:123. **[Brachial plexus tension test, distraction test, foraminal compression test, L'hermite's sign, shoulder abduction test, shoulder depression test, Valsalva test, vertebral artery test]**

Stevens BJ, McKenzie RA. Mechanical diagnosis and treatment of the cervical spine. *Clinics in Physical Therapy.* 1988;17:271–289.

Mobility

Aspinall W. Clinical testing for the craniovertebral hypermobility syndrome. *Journal of Orthopaedic and Sports Physical Therapy.* 1990;12:47–54.

Balogun JA, Abereoje OK, Olaogun MO, Obajuluwa VA. Inter and intratester reliability of measuring neck motions with tape measure and Myrin gravity reference goniometer. *Journal of Orthopaedic and Sports Physical Therapy.* 1989;10:248–253. **[ROM]**

Pain

Dalton PA, Jull GA. The distribution and characteristics of neck-arm pain in patients with and without a neurological deficit. *Australian Journal of Physiotherapy.* 1989;35:3–8.

Visual Analogue Scale (VAS)

Langely GB, Sheppeard H. The visual analogue scale: its use in pain measurement. *Rheumatology International.* 1985;5:145–148.

Scott J, Huskisson EC. Vertical or horizontal visual analogue scales. *Annals of the Rheumatic Diseases.* 1979;38:560.

Posture

American Physical Therapy Association. A guide to physical therapist practice, Volume I: a description of patient management. *Physical Therapy.* 1995;75:720–738. **[Posture examination]**

Garrett TR, Youdas JW, Madson TJ. Reliability of measuring forward head posture in a clinical setting. *Journal of Orthopaedic and Sports Physical Therapy.* 1993;17:155–160.

Griegel-Morris P, Larson K, Mueller-Klaus K, Oatis CA. The incidence of common postural abnormalities in the cervical, shoulder, and thoracic regions and their association with pain in two age groups of healthy subjects. *Physical Therapy.* 1992;72:425–431.

Herrmann DB. Validity study of head and neck flexion-extension motion comparing measurements of a pendulum goniometer and roentgenograms. *Journal of Orthopaedic and Sports Physical Therapy.* 1990;11:414–418.

Hertling D, Kessler RM. *Management of Common Musculoskeletal Disorders: Physical Therapy Principles and Methods.* 2nd ed. Philadelphia, Pa: JB Lippincott Co; 1990:507.

Malouin F, Prefontaine J, Richards CL. Quantitative evaluation of head posture and movements with a triaxial electrogoniometer: a reproducibility study. *Physiotherapy Canada.* 1989;41:294–301.

Rheault W, Albright B, Byers C, et al. Intertester reliability of the cervical range of motion device. *Journal of Orthopaedic and Sports Physical Therapy.* 1992;15:147–150.

Schneider G, Pardoe M. Translation of the facets during coupled motion in the cervical spine: a pilot study. *Australian Journal of Physiotherapy.* 1985;31:39.

TREATMENT

Cervical Dysfunction

Anderson M, Stevens B, Richards J, Jensen G. Cervical spine. In: Myers RS, ed. *Saunders Manual of Physical Therapy Practice*. Philadelphia, Pa: WB Saunders Co; 1995:727–787.

Axen K, Haas R, Schicchi J, Merrick J. Progressive resistance neck exercises using a compressible ball coupled with an air pressure gauge. *Journal of Orthopaedic and Sports Physical Therapy*. 1992;16:275–280.

Bognuk N. The innervation of the vertebral column. *Australian Journal of Physiotherapy*. 1985;31:89.

Corrigan B, Maitland GD. *Practical Orthopaedic Medicine*. London: Butterworth; 1983.

Curillo JA. Aquatic physical therapy approaches for the spine. *Orthopedic Physical Therapy Clinics of North America*. 1994;3:179–208.

Edwards BC. *Manual of Combined Movements: Their Use in the Examination and Treatment of Mechanical Vertebral Column Disorders*. New York, NY: Churchill Livingstone; 1992:42–97.

Grant R, ed. *Physical Therapy of the Cervical and Thoracic Spine*. New York, NY: Churchill Livingstone; 1988:219–241, 243–270, 271–289. (2nd ed, 1994, available)

Griegel-Morris P, Larson K, Mueller-Klaus K, Oatis CA. Incidence of common postural abnormalities in the cervical, shoulder, and thoracic regions and their association with pain in two age groups of healthy subjects. *Physical Therapy*. 1992;72:425–431.

Grieve G, ed. *Modern Manual Therapy of the Vertebral Column*. New York, NY: Churchill Livingstone; 1986:53, 182, 289, 350, 359, 370, 377, 481, 503, 512, 530, 561, 656, 873.

Hertling D, Kessler RM. *Management of Common Musculoskeletal Disorders: Physical Therapy Principles and Methods*. 2nd ed. Philadelphia, Pa: JB Lippincott Co; 1990:496–531, 532–540.

Jette DU, Falkel JE, Trombly C. Effect of intermittent, supine cervical traction on the myoelectric activity of the upper trapezius muscle in subjects with neck pain. *Physical Therapy*. 1985;65:1173–1176.

Kisner C, Colby LA. *Therapeutic Exercise: Foundations and Techniques*. 2nd ed. Philadelphia, Pa: FA Davis Co; 1990:473–499.

Levoska S, Keinanen-Kiukaaniemi S. Active or passive physiotherapy for occupational cervicobrachial disorders? A comparison of two treatment methods with a 1-year follow-up. *Archives of Physical Medicine and Rehabilitation*. 1993;74:425–430.

Maitland GD. *Vertebral Manipulation*. 5th ed. London, England: Butterworth; 1986.

McKenzie RA. *Treat Your Own Neck*. Waikanae, New Zealand: Spinal Publications; 1983.

McKinney LA, Cornan JO, Ryan M. The role of physiotherapy in the management of acute neck sprains following road-traffic accidents. *Archives of Emergency Medicine*. 1989;6:1:27–33.

Murphy MJ. Effects of cervical traction on muscle activity. *Journal of Orthopaedic and Sports Physical Therapy*. 1991;13:220–225.

Pennie BH, Agambar LJ. Whiplash injuries: a trial of early management. *Journal of Bone and Joint Surgery*. 1990;72B:277–279.

Pennie B, Agambar L. Patterns of injury and recovery in whiplash. *Injury*. 1991;22:1:57–59.

Rundcrantz BL, Johnsson B, Moritz U. Occupational cervico-brachial disorders among dentists: analysis of ergonomics and locomotor function. *Swedish Dental Journal*. 1991;15:3:105–115.

Schneider G, Pardoe M. Translation of the facets during coupled motion in the cervical spine: a pilot study. *Australian Journal of Physiotherapy*. 1985;31:39.

Snyder-Mackler L, Barry AJ, Perkins AI, Soucek MD. Effects of helium-neon laser irradiation in skin resistance and pain in patients with trigger points in the neck or back. *Physical Therapy*. 1989;69:336–341.

Tan JC, Nordin M. Role of physical therapy in the treatment of cervical disk disease. *Orthopedic Clinics of North America*. 1992;23:435–449.

Twomey LT, Taylor JR. The whiplash syndrome: pathology and physical treatment. *Journal of Manual and Manipulative Therapy*. 1993;1:1:26–29.

Thoracic Dysfunction

Grant R, ed. *Physical Therapy of the Cervical and Thoracic Spine*. New York, NY: Churchill Livingstone; 1988.

Low Back Pain

DESCRIPTION

Pain experienced in the lower lumbar, lumbosacral, or sacroiliac region of the back. Pain can also be accompanied by sciatica.

CAUSE

There are multiple causes of back pain. These can include (1) acute ligamentous sprain; (2) acute muscular strain or tear of paraspinous muscle; (3) chronic muscular strain secondary to faulty posture, poor conditioning, or mechanical factors such as pregnancy, obesity, or excessive use; (4) chronic fibromyalgia; (5) chronic osteoarthritis; (6) chronic ankylosing spondylosis; (7) congenital defects of the low lumbar and upper sacral spine; (8) ruptured or protruding intervertebral disk; (9) traumatic ligament rupture; (10) stress fracture of the pars interarticularis; (11) fracture, infection, or tumor involving the back, pelvis, or retroperitoneum; (12) spondylolisthesis with loss of substance in the pars interarticularis bilaterally and resultant forward slippage of one vertebra on another; (13) spinal stenosis with narrowing of spinal canal; (14) osteitis condensans ilii; and (15) visceral disease causing referred pain.

ASSESSMENT

Areas

- History, including social/psychological issues
- Pain
- Posture
- Gait
- Mobility, including active and passive range of motion (ROM)
- Joint integrity and structural deviations
- Neurological, including sensation and reflexes
- Strength
- Skin and soft tissue: palpation of trigger points
- Cardiovascular: endurance
- Functional level, including use of assistive devices and activities of daily living (ADLs), and health status
- Health status
- Special tests to which the PT may or may not have access

Instruments/Procedures (See References for Sources)

Cardiovascular

- aerobic capacity testing

Evaluations
- algorithms and classification systems
- differential diagnosis
- McKenzie assessment algorithm
- National Institute for Occupational Safety and Health (NIOSH) Low Back Atlas of Standardized Tests and Measurements
- Toronto-Hamilton Lumbar Database (THLD)

Functional Level
- functional status exam

Gait
- visual gait assessment

Health Status
- Sickness Impact Profile
- Roland and Morris Disability Index
- Oswestry Low Back Pain Questionnaire
- Waddell and Main Disability Index
- Dallas Pain Questionnaire

Joint Integrity and Structural Deviations
1. low back orthopedic tests
- bowstring test
- Brudzinski's test
- cram test
- femoral nerve traction test
- Hoover's sign
- Kernig's sign
- Naffziger test
- popliteal pressure sign
- prone knee flexion test (or reverse Lasegue test)
- sitting root test
- straight-leg-raising test
2. sacroiliac joint tests
- Gillet test
- palpation of anterior superior iliac spines (sitting, standing)
- palpation of iliac crests (sitting, standing)
- palpation of posterior superior iliac spines (sitting, standing)
- prone knee flexion test
- side-lying iliac compression test
- sitting flexion test
- standing flexion test
- standing Gillet test
- supine iliac gapping test
- supine long sitting test

Mobility
- fingertip-to-floor measurements
- flexicurves
- goniometric measurement
- inclinometer
- double inclinometer
- Leighton flexometer
- modified fingertip-to-floor method
- optical methods
- PRIDE ROM

- radiologic ROM measures
- stiffness measures
- tape measure methods (Schöber, modified Schöber)
- three-dimensional digitizer

Neurological
- deep-tendon reflexes
- electromyography (EMG)
- motor tests
- sensory (dermatomal) tests

Outcome/Measures
- outcomes on ambulation, activity level, and pain
- outcome predictors

Pain
- Beck Depression Inventory
- Coping Strategy Questionnaire
- McGill Pain Questionnaire
- Modified Pain Rating Chart
- pain drawings
- Pain Rating Chart
- Oswestry Low Back Pain Questionnaire
- visual analogue pain scale
- West Haven–Yale Multidimensional Pain Inventory

Posture
- photography

Special Tests to Which the PT May or May Not Have Access
1. computed-tomography (CAT) scan
2. electromyography (EMG)
3. ergonomics
   a. ergonomics or body mechanics examination
   b. mattress evaluation
   c. functional task performance
- commercial lift testing units
- commercial work evaluation systems
- functional measurement laboratory
- multiple-tasks obstacle course
- progressive isoinertial lifeline evaluation (PILE)
- physiological work performance testing

Strength
1. manual muscle testing
2. modified sphygmomanometer
3. partial sit-up/curl-up protocol
4. pressure biofeedback
5. Sorensen test
6. trunk strength testing

- lifting dynanometers
- isokinetic dynanometers
- commercial trunk strength units

PROBLEMS

Ankylosing Spondylitis
- The client usually has decreased ROM of lumbar flexion and extension.
- The client usually has decreased lumbar lordosis.
- The client can have restricted sacroiliac joint motion.
- The condition can involve stiffening of entire spine and hips.

Chronic Back Pain
- The client can have altered muscle recruitment patterns.
- The client can have shortened muscle groups.
- The client can have reduced levels of endorphins.
- The client can have demineralization of spine.

Degenerative Joint Disease (Osteoarthritis/Spondylosis)
- The client usually has pain with movement.
- The client usually has loss of active and passive mobility.
- The client can be hypermobile instead of hypomobile.

Disk Herniation
- The client can have neurological involvement (reflexes, myotome and/or dermatome).
- The client can have pain and/or paresthesia distal to the knee.
- The client may find that mechanism of onset involves lumbar flexion.
- The client can have pain aggravated by sitting.

Facet-Joint Derangement—Acute
- The client usually has sudden onset of pain.
- The client usually has pain aggravated by movement.
- The client usually has loss of active and passive motion in specific directions.

Fracture
- The client can have pain with active lumbar motion.
- The client may need radiographic confirmation.

Hypomobility Dysfunction
- The client usually has accessory motion at one or more levels less than normal.
- The client usually has flexion and/or extension ROM less than normal.
- The client usually has pain and/or stiffness with no paresthesia.
- The client can have passive intervertebral ROM restricted.
- The client can have pain at end of ROM.
- The client usually has limitation of movement in one or two directions only.
- The client usually has a reduction in lumbar spine lateral flexion associated with either extension or flexion.

- The client usually has pain that is localized in the back but may be referred into the leg or abdominal areas.
- There may be no neurological signs.

Infection
- The client may have a fever.
- Confirmation with a bone scan is needed.

Ligamentous Sprain—Acute
- The client usually has a loss of active and passive mobility.
- The client usually has localized pain with movement.
- The client can experience pain radiating distally.

Lower Lumbar Disc Herniation (Extrusion) With Nerve Root Impingement
- The client can have unilateral leg pain, but bilateral pain is possible.
- The client usually feels leg pain in the posterolateral thigh and the anterior lateral or posterior aspect of the lower leg.
- The client can have back pain alone; a combination of back and leg pain is less common.
- Usually lumbar extension will peripheralize pain. Extremity pain is usually worse than back pain.
- The client usually has mild segmental neurologic deficit, indicated by the presence of specific dermatome sensory loss or specific motor weakness.
- Rarely, rupture of the nerve root leads to decreased pain but increased neurological signs.

Muscle Spasm
- The client usually has decreased ROM and pain and tenderness over the muscle.
- The client can have increased tone in muscles.
- The client may find that continued spasm becomes a source of additional pain due to a self-perpetuating cycle.

Muscle Strain—Acute
- The client may have localized swelling.
- The client usually has pain with movement.
- The client usually has decreased and painful ROM.
- Usually passive movement is within normal limits.
- The client may show painful recovery from movement.
- The client can have unilateral pain.
- The client can have pain radiate distally.

Nerve Root Adhesion
- The client usually has a minimum of one previous episode of back pain and /or current pain of at least 2 months' duration.
- The client usually finds that flexion and/or flexion with side flexion away from pain aggravates pain and/or paresthesia.
- The client can have reflex and/or motor deficit.

Nerve Root Irritation
- The client usually has lower extremity pain aggravated by one or more lumbar movements.
- The client usually has a subjective complaint of paresthesia.
- The client may have lower extremity pain distal to the knee.

Posterolateral Disk Prolapse—Acute
- The client can have sudden onset of unilateral lumbosacral pain.
- The client usually reports that pain is severe, but pain may be dull and aching or knifelike.
- The client may have aching into the leg, usually unilateral.
- The pain is usually worse with sitting or sudden straining, and it may be hard to stand up.
- The client usually has lumbar deformity with loss of lordosis.
- The client usually has lumbar scoliosis (convexity on the involved side).
- There is usually marked, painful restriction of spinal movement with decrease of extension mobility.
- Usually the pain increases with repeated flexion and/or sustained flexion.
- Usually the mechanism of onset involves flexion.

Postural Syndrome
- The client usually finds that pain eases with activity.
- Usually standing or sitting posture is habitually beyond normal limits.
- The client may feel pain only during sustained positions of spine.

Pregnancy/Postpartum
- The client usually has low back pain that worsens with fatigue, with static postures, and as the day progresses.
- The client may be more prone to injury.
- The client usually has increased pelvic mobility.
- The client can have a combination of low back pain and dysfunction of the sacroiliac joint.
- The client can have gait dysfunction, pain, and tenderness of the sacroiliac joint.
- The client usually has sacroiliac joint pain that is worse with prolonged posture or activity, unilateral weight bearing, or twisting activities.
- The pain may accompany pubic symphysial pain.

Referred Visceral
- Usually lumbar examination is negative and visceral findings are positive.

Sacroiliac Joint Dysfunction
- The client usually complains of pain with sitting.
- The client usually has pain when leaning forward.
- The client can have pain with increase in intra-abdominal pressure.
- The client usually experiences a sudden onset of unilateral sacroiliac pain.
- The client may feel pain in the posterior thigh.
- The client may have anterior hip pain.
- The client may report paresthesia in the absence of neurological signs.
- There can be ipsilateral sacroiliac dysfunction present with L3–4 or L4–5 lesions.

Sacroiliac Hypomobility
- The client usually has pelvic asymmetry.

- The client may have unilateral buttock and/or posterior thigh pain.
- The client may have restricted sacroiliac accessory motion.

Scheurmann's Disease
- There may be thoracic kyphosis.
- Accessory motion can be restricted.

Scoliosis
- There is usually an observed spinal curve in coronal plane.
- Scoliosis may be present in standing but alter its configuration on movement.
- There is usually postural deviation that includes asymmetry in the shoulders, and the convex side of the curve shows a prominent scapula.
- There is unilateral hip protrusion and pelvic obliquity.
- Lumbar lordosis can be seen to increase with prominent erector spinae musculature on the side of the convexity.
- Diminished flexibility can be seen in spinal, abdominal, intercostal, and hip musculature and spinal ligaments.
- Weakness in musculature can be seen on the convex side of the curve. Abdominals, trunk extensors, and hip muscles may also weaken.

Segmental Hypermobility
- The client may report that sustained positions aggravate pain.
- Usually accessory motion has a late onset of resistance and/or increased ROM.
- The client may have abnormal segmental spinal muscle activity patterns.
- The client may find that activity eases pain.
- The client may find that extension from a flexed position reproduces pain.
- Passive intervertebral ROM may indicate hypermobility.

Spinal Congenital Anomaly
(Sacralization of L-5 Transverse Processes, Abnormal Intervertebral Facets)
- Radiographic confirmation is needed.

Spinal Stenosis
- The client usually reports that extension reproduces and aggravates pain and/or paresthesia.
- Usually flexion relieves pain.
- The client may have bilateral lower extremity pain.
- Usually pain in one or both legs is brought on by walking.
- The client may find that pain is associated with weakness and/or paresthesias.
- Symptoms may be vague or diffuse.

Spondylolisthesis
- The client may have pain coincidental with the level of radiographic results.
- The client may find that extension positions aggravate pain.
- The client may have a palpable step.

Tumor
- The client may have constant pain.
- The client may find that low back pain is not relieved by rest.

- The pain may mimic musculoskeletal pain.
- The client may find that the pain increases at night.
- The pain may not be associated with activity.
- The pain may migrate or have insidious onset.

TREATMENT/MANAGEMENT

General Treatment Considerations

Therapists generally treat low back pain using exercise, education, and physical agents or modalities such as massage, heat, transcutaneous electrical nerve stimulation (TENS), interferential therapy, and shortwave diathermy. Additional approaches include manipulative and mechanical therapies: spinal manipulative therapy (SMT), mobilization, and traction (intermittent and autotraction). Active measures also include biofeedback, assessment of ADLs, and work hardening.

Exercise

Movement and exercise are critical to develop and maintain musculoskeletal strength. Types of exercise therapy include the following:
- Extension exercise can be useful to increase or maintain lordosis and to diminish and centralize pain.
- Flexion exercise can be useful in treating paravertebral musculature and the posterior facet syndrome.
- Proprioceptive neuromuscular facilitation (PNF) is used to produce increased muscular excitation or inhibition. In the lumbar spine, the psoas-iliacus muscle, hamstrings, quadratus lumborum, piriformis, lumbar spine extensors, and trunk extensors and flexors may be targeted.
- Muscle energy techniques are used to restore optimal static and dynamic posture.
- Stabilization exercise routines and posture education are used for instability.
- An aerobic fitness program may include brisk walking, cycling, aquatics, swimming, cross-country skiing, or low-impact aerobics.

Education

Education is important to facilitate recovery and prevent recurrence through information on back care strategies or through a back school. Goals of back schools, in general, include the following:
- *Provision of information:* anatomy, biomechanics, pain, drugs, sex, stress, physical fitness, holistic health, resources
- *Rehabilitation/prevention:* posture, awareness, movement, body/mind inter-relatedness, self-help techniques, physical interventions
- *Teaching ergonomic principles:* human considerations, environmental conditions, work dynamics, relevance of person to equipment

---

The Basic Rules of Lifting

Stance: Lifter should be well balanced over a stable base. Face in direction of lift with feet apart and one foot in front of the other.
Posture: Keep shoulders and pelvis aligned.

Grip: Use handles when possible. If not, use intrinsic grip with as many fingers as possible.

Picking up: Bend knees to squat. Straddle load between knees and grip firmly. Pulling is easier than pushing.

Lifting: Get as close to the load as possible. The lift must be powered by the legs.

Moving the load: Lean back to balance the load.

There is no exact agreement on the best position of the spine during heavy lifting. Positions recommended include fully extended, fully straight, and fully flexed. A balance between the two extremes—midway between flexion and extension—has also been recommended.

Source: Data from LT Twomey and JR Taylor, *Physical Therapy of the Low Back*, © 1987, Churchill Livingstone.

Manual Therapy

Manual therapy has several major physical therapist contributors, including Kaltenborn, Maitland, and McKenzie. All three advocate treatment strategies utilizing mobilization and manipulation, exercise, and patient education. Differences include the following:

- Kaltenborn emphasizes testing intervertebral joint motion and treating through motion. He advocates traction, distraction, and soft tissue mobilization.
- Maitland emphasizes the pain-range-spasm relationship. Treatment also emphasizes continual assessment, adverse neural tissue mobilization, and traction.
- McKenzie's system classifies low back pain problems as postural, dysfunction, and derangement. Low back pain etiology may be caused by three predisposing factors: poor sitting posture, loss of extension, and frequency of flexion. Patient can self-treat using repeated movements.

Other therapists contributing to manual therapy approaches include

- Edwards: combined-movements techniques
- Grieve: major contributions as a clinician, teacher, and author
- Saunders: outlines a classification system based on anatomic structures
- Paris: developed structured training system

Treatment of Specific Conditions

Ankylosing Spondylitis

- Provide client education.
- Instruct client to avoid heavy lifting (and occupations involving heavy lifting).
- Teach proper positioning.
- Educate client on exercises to avoid, such as flexion of spine and possibly hip flexion.
- Encourage client to sleep on firm mattress (avoid sleeping in flexed, "fetal" position)
- Encourage client to use lumbar roll support when seated.
- Consider manual mobilization to promote extension.
- Provide physical agents and modalities, along with external support during acute flare-ups.

Chronic Back Pain

- Consider use of TENS.
- Promote overall fitness. A fitness program is critical for chronic low back pain.

- Encourage increased levels of activity as appropriate.

Degenerative Joint Disease
- Consider use of ultrasound, mobilization, traction, and exercise if client is hypomobile.
- Provide external support for hypermobility.
- Initiate muscle-strengthening exercises and postural training for either hypomobility or hypermobility.
- Provide physical agents and modalities for pain.
- Generally exercise should proceed in a direction opposite the area of aggravation.
- Instruct in preventive measures and postures to relieve mechanical stress.

Disk Herniation. In the case of protrusion with neurological signs:
- Provide physical agents and modalities as indicated.
- Encourage rest.
- Avoid aggravation with postures causing increased intradiscal pressure (especially sitting and flexion).
- Consider use of heavy traction.
- Encourage client to maintain correct posture.
- Provide client education.
- Assess for external support.
- Consider trial of extension exercises.
  In the case of extrusion:
- Consider use of TENS for pain.
- Consider trial of heavy traction if condition cannot be differentiated from nerve root syndrome.

Facet-Joint Derangement—Acute
- Use mobilization techniques as indicated.
- Consider manual or mechanical traction.

Fracture
- After healing, restore functional mobility and strength.

Hypomobility Dysfunction
- Use ultrasound as indicated.
- Use mobilization as indicated.
- Consider use of traction.

Muscle Strain. In acute cases:
- Encourage rest.
- Use ice and other physical agents and modalities, as well as muscle-setting techniques to elongate as tolerated.
  In subacute cases:
- Begin gentle movement.
- Heat and massage can be added.
- Progress to full movement.
- Use gentle stretching techniques, graded isometric exercise, and resistive dynamic exercise.
- Correct posture abnormalities with kinesthetic training.
- Correct flexibility and strength imbalances.

Muscle Spasm. In acute cases:
- Provide passive support, but avoid overdependence.
- Encourage elongation of muscle to tolerance via positioning. Use reverse muscle action techniques.
- Provide passive to active ROM in pain-free range.
- Consider use of ice or cold packs.
  In subacute and chronic cases:
- Consider use of moist heat, diathermy, electrical stimulation, ice, cold packs, and/or massage.
- Progress exercise program as tolerated.
- Provide postural retraining with kinesthetic awareness.
- Teach client relaxation exercises.
- Provide education on condition.
- Search for underlying cause.

Posterolateral Disk Derangement
- Reduce derangement with appropriate movement; client may find pain reduced with repeated extension.
- Maintain reduction with posture correction and restore function.
- Correct posture with education in prevention.
- Self-treatment with repeated movements can be tried first. Progress to mobilization and, if necessary, manipulation.
- Consider use of traction.
- Consider use of modalities for pain such as TENS, interferential, and diathermy.
- Client may find that a crook-lying position eases pain.

Postural Syndrome
- Teach postural exercises.
- Initiate general conditioning exercises.
- Offer physical agents and modalities as indicated.
- Use external support for severe cases.

Pregnancy/Postpartum. In cases of acute low back pain:
- Encourage decreased activity.
- Offer gentle heat and massage of muscle spasm while client is positioned side-lying.
- Provide obstetric back school.
- Initiate land- or water-based exercise program.
- Use stabilization exercises as indicated.
- For diastasis recti, splint during stressful activity or abdominal exercise.
  In cases of sacroiliac joint dysfunction:
- Provide education on vulnerability of the back.
- Offer posture and body mechanics education.
- Instruct client to avoid high heels and prolonged standing.
- Strengthen pelvic floor muscles and abdominal musculature.
- Teach proper relaxation positions. (Avoid supine position for prolonged periods after 20 weeks gestation.)
- Use gentle mobilization or muscle energy techniques.
- Provide external support to stabilize or relieve stress.
- Avoid unilateral weight bearing.

- Consider use of heel lift if needed for leg-length discrepancy.
  In cases of pubic symphysis pain:
- Use moist heat or cold pack for pain.
- Avoid having legs spread in extremely wide position.
- Client may need crutches or walker for weight bearing.
- Provide binder around hips for support as tolerated.
- Consider gentle mobilization.
- Use muscle energy techniques as indicated.

Nerve Root Adhesion
- Use straight-leg stretch as tolerated.
- Use ultrasound as indicated.
- Consider unilateral traction.

Nerve Root Irritation
- Use physical agents and modalities as indicated.

Sacroiliac Hypermobility
- Provide external support.
- Encourage rest if condition inflamed.

Sacroiliac Hypomobility
- Use ultrasound as indicated.
- Consider mobilization.
- Encourage rest and provide external support if condition is acute.

Scoliosis
- Exercise is used in conjunction with bracing, casting, or traction.
- Exercise alone for very mild idiopathic scoliosis may be useful.
- Consider lateral electrical surface stimulation or nighttime intermittent neuromuscular stimulation.
  (See also the chapter "Pediatric Disorders.")

Segmental Hypermobility
- Initiate muscle-strengthening exercises and posture instruction.
- Provide external support.
- Use physical agents and modalities for pain relief as indicated.

Spinal Stenosis
- Provide patient education on avoiding irritation (client can rest or be in spinal flexion).
- Use lumbar bracing for support.
- Use modalities for pain.
- Flexibility exercises may be useful.

Spondylolisthesis
- Provide postural instruction.
- Begin abdominal exercises.
- Use physical agents and modalities for pain, as indicated.
- Provide external support if condition is severe.
- Assess for additional musculoskeletal conditions.

Tumor
- Consult with physician.

PRECAUTIONS/CONTRAINDICATIONS

Cancer
- Cancer can mimic musculoskeletal complaints. Unexplained response to treatment or symptoms that cannot be categorized should lead you to suspect a more serious pathology. Modalities, manual therapy, and spinal traction may be contraindicated with tumor or neoplasm.

Manipulation
- The joint should not be forcibly thrust in a direction guarded by muscle spasm.
- Avoid manipulation with herniated nucleus pulposus protrusion with nerve root impingement.
- Use caution with degenerative joint disease. Due to the narrowed spinal canal, extension and extension with rotation could further narrow the canal and should be avoided.

Mobilization
- Excessive force in young children may disrupt the epiphyseal plate, possibly leading to a secondary deformity. Pediatric therapists have been advised to be cautious in the use of joint mobilization.
- Avoid aggressive treatment of nerve root irritation if there is a history of severe trauma.

Modalities
- Modalities can be overused, particularly with musculoskeletal strain or sprain and inflammation. Pain relief through modalities should not cause you to ignore loss of motion and strength.
- See Appendix C for general precautions for use of modalities.

Movement
- Correction of lateral shift may cause increased back pain (a centralization effect) but should not cause increased leg pain. Discontinue extension exercise if this happens. Extension of spine is contraindicated if it does not decrease or centralize the pain, if bladder weakness is present or if there is paresthesia in the saddle region, or if the client is unable to assume position due to pain.
- Avoid flexion if it increases pain or peripheralizes the symptoms. Flexion positions and exercises may harm clients who have herniated nucleus pulposus with protrusion.
- If any increase in mobility increases pain or an inflammatory response, try another approach.
- Clients with pain and stiffness usually progress in improvement. If the client is not following patterns of improvement, this may be an alert to consider an organic disease or psychogenic disorder.

Pregnancy-Related Precautions
- Ultrasound or electrical stimulation over the sacral sulci is contraindicated during pregnancy.
- TENS for pain relief in pregnancy has not been approved by FDA and should be used only as a last resort. But TENS has been used successfully, and the benefit may outweigh any potential risk. *(See also the chapter "Women's Health Disorders.")*

- Special precautions should be taken when using mobilization during pregnancy. Adequate posturing of the client needs to be considered. Although some consider pregnancy a contraindication to mobilization, Maitland reports that clients can usually be treated with an appropriate mobilizing technique without any complication. See Maitland and Corrigan, *Practical Orthopaedic Medicine*, in Treatment references.

DESIRED OUTCOME/PROGNOSIS
- The client's pain and symptoms will decrease.
- The client will increase ROM, and function will be restored.
- Contracture and adhesion formation will be prevented or minimized.
- The client will avoid progression of disorder and recurrence.

Reportedly 70% to 80% of patients improve within 1 month of therapy. Recurrent back pain occurs in 30% of clients. Reports of recurrent pain vary from 11% to 30% after 1 month to 50% to 62% 1 year after an episode of acute back pain. The chance of successful rehabilitation decreases to 40% if the patient has had low back pain for more than 3 months. This is thought to be due to alteration of the client's affect. Often a specific cause for low back pain cannot be identified. Activity-related pain is often nonspecific and is usually mechanical in origin. Ninety-two percent of clients are better in 2 months.

In general, there is an absence of research to substantiate the use of one treatment over another. Physical agents and modalities do not alter the natural history of mechanical pain in the back.

Preliminary Profile of Patient Most Likely To Benefit From Treatment With Manual Therapy

- acute symptom onset and less than 1 month's duration of symptoms
- central or paravertebral pain distribution
- no previous exposure to spinal manipulation
- no pending litigation or workers' compensation

Source: Data from RP DiFabio, Efficacy of Manual Therapy, *Physical Therapy*, Vol. 72, No. 12, pp. 853–864, © 1992, American Physical Therapy Association.

REFERENCES

ASSESSMENT

Evaluation

Algorithms, Classification Systems

Bigos S, Bowyer O, Braen G, et al. *Acute Low Back Problems in Adults: Clinical Practice Guideline*. Rockville, Md: US Dept of Health and Human Services, Public Health Service, Agency for Health Care Policy and Research; 1994. AHCPR Pub. No. 95-0643, Quick Reference Guide No. 14. [**Algorithm for initial evaluation of acute low back pain**]

Binkley J, Finch E, Hall J, Black T, Gowland C. Diagnostic classification of patients with low back pain: report on a survey of physical therapy experts. *Physical Therapy*. 1993;73:138–150. [**Diagnostic classification system for low back pain**]

Delitto A, Shulman AD, Rose SJ. On developing expert-based decision-support systems in physical therapy: The NIOSH Low Back Atlas. *Physical Therapy*. 1989;69:554–558. [**National Institute for Occupational Safety and Health (NIOSH) Low Back Atlas of Standardized Tests and Measurements**]

Echternach JL, Rothstein JM. Hypothesis-oriented algorithms. *Physical Therapy*. 1989;69:559–564. **[Low back pain algorithm]**

Gill C, Sandford J, Binkley J, Stratford P, Finch E. Low back pain: program description and outcome in a case series. *Journal of Orthopaedic and Sports Physical Therapy*. 1994;20:11–16. **[Toronto–Hamilton Lumbar Database (THLD)]**

Differential Diagnosis

Goodman C, Snyder TE. *Differential Diagnosis in Physical Therapy*. Philadelphia, Pa; WB Saunders; 1990:332, 337, 357, 362–363.

Mayer TG, Mooney V, Gatchel RJ. *Contemporary Conservative Care for Painful Spinal Disorders*. Philadelphia, Pa: Lea & Febiger; 1993:216. **[McKenzie assessment algorithm]**

Outcomes Measures

Beekman CK, Axtell L. Ambulation, activity level, and pain: outcomes of a program for spinal pain. *Physical Therapy*. 1985;65:1649–1655.

Fredrickson BE, Trief PM, VanBeveren P, et al. Rehabilitation of the patient with chronic back pain: a search for outcome predictors. *Spine*. 1988;13:351–353. **[Strength, flexibility, endurance, body mechanics, EMG levels, work and activity levels, subjective pain assessment]**

Gottlieb HJ, Koller R, Alperson BL. Low back pain comprehensive rehabilitation program: a followup study. *Archives of Physical Medicine and Rehabilitation*. 1982;63:458–461. **[Reduction in pain, work time, relaxation skills, and doctor visits]**

Screens

Diastasis Recti of Pregnancy (See Also Chapter "Women's Health Disorders")
Kisner C, Colby LA. *Therapeutic Exercise: Foundations and Techniques*. 2nd ed. Philadelphia, Pa: FA Davis Co; 1990:555.

Scoliosis (See Also Chapter "Pediatric Disorders")
Kisner C, Colby LA. *Therapeutic Exercise: Foundations and Techniques*. 2nd ed. Philadelphia, Pa: FA Davis Co; 1990:525.

Cardiovascular

Aerobic Capacity Testing

Lindström I, Ohlund C, Eek C, Wallin L, Peterson L, Nachemson A. Mobility, strength, and fitness after a graded activity program for patients with subacute low back pain. *Spine*. 1992;17:641–652. **[Lumbar range of motion, muscular endurance, and cardiovascular fitness]**

Functional Level

Cammack S, Eisenberg MG, eds. *Key Words in Physical Rehabilitation: A Guide to Contemporary Usage*. New York, NY: Springer Publishing Co; 1995:57–58.

Deyo RA. Measuring the functional status of patients with low back pain. *Archives of Physical Medicine and Rehabilitation*. 1988;69:1044–1053.

Gait

Patla AE, Proctor J, Morson B. Observations on aspects of visual gait assessment: a questionnaire study. *Physiotherapy Canada*. 1987;39:311–316.

Health Status

Bergner M, Bobbitt RA, Carter WB, Gilson BS. The Sickness Impact Profile: development and final revision of a health status measure. *Medical Care*. 1981;19:787–805.

Delitto A. Are measures of function and disability important in low back care? *Physical Therapy*. 1994;74:452–462. **[Sickness Impact Profile, Roland and Morris Disability Index, Oswestry Low Back Pain Questionnaire, Waddell and Main Disability Index, Dallas Pain Questionnaire]**

Lawlis GF, Cuencas R, Selby D, et al. The development of the Dallas Pain Questionnaire, an assessment of the impact of spinal pain on behavior. *Spine*. 1981;14:512–515. **[Dallas Pain Questionnaire]**

Roland MO, Jenner JR, eds. *Back Pain: New Approaches to Rehabilitation and Education*. New York, NY: Manchester University Press; 1989:187–204. **[Oswestry Low Back Pain Questionnaire]**

Roland M, Morris R. A study of the natural history of back pain, Part 1: development of a reliable and sensitive measure of disability in low-back pain. *Spine*. 1983;8:141–144. **[Disability Questionnaire]**

Roland M, Morris R. A study of the natural history of back pain, Part 2: development of guidelines for trials of treatment in primary care. *Spine*. 1983;8:141–144.

Waddell G, Main CJ, Morris EW, DiPoala M, Gray IC, et al. Chronic low back pain, psychological distress and illness behavior. *Spine*. 1984;9:209–213. **[Waddell and Main Disability Index]**

Mobility

Beattie P, Rothstein JM, Lamb RL. Reliability of the attraction method for measuring lumbar spine backward bending. *Physical Therapy*. 1987;67:364–369. **[Schöber method]**

Gauvin MG, Riddle DL, Rothstein JM. Reliability of clinical measurements of forward bending using the modified fingertip to floor method. *Physical Therapy*. 1990;70:443–447.

Lee M, Svensson NL. Measurement of stiffness during simulated spinal physiotherapy. *Clinical Physics and Physiological Measurement*. 1990;11:201–207.

Leighton JR. The Leighton flexometer and flexibility test. *Journal of the Association for Physical and Mental Rehabilitation*. 1958;20:127–130.

Loebl WY. Measurement of spinal posture and range of spinal movement. *Annals of Physical Medicine*. 1967;9:104–110. **[Inclinometer method]**

MacRae I, Wright V. Measurements of back movement. *Annals of the Rheumatic Diseases*. 1969;28:584. **[Modified Schöber method]**

Mayer TG, Mooney V, Gatchel RJ. *Contemporary Conservative Care for Painful Spinal Disorders*. Philadelphia, Pa: Lea & Febiger; 1993:290–307. **[Goniometric, fingertip-to-floor, flexicurves, three-dimensional digitizer, inclinometers, radiologic ROM measures, optical methods, PRIDE ROM, tape measure method]**

Miller SA, Mayer T, Cox R, Gatchel RJ. Reliability problems associated with the modified Schober technique for true lumbar flexion measurement. *Spine*. 1992;17:345–348. **[Schöber method]**

Newton M, Waddell G. Reliability and validity of clinical measurement of the lumbar spine in patients with chronic low-back pain. *Physiotherapy*. 1991;77:796–800. **[Inclinometer method]**

Schöber P. Lendenwerelsaule and Kreuzschmergen. *Munch Med Wschr*. 1937;84:336. **[Schöber method]**

Stokes BA, Helewa A, Goldsmith CH, Groh JD, Kraag GR. Reliability of spinal mobility measurements in ankylosing spondylitis patients. *Physiotherapy Canada*. 1988;40:338–344.

Williams R, Binkley J, Bloch R, Goldsmith CH, Minuk T. Reliability of the Modified-Modified Schöber and double inclinometer methods for measuring lumbar flexion and extension. *Physical Therapy*. 1993;73:33–44. **[Modified-Modified Schöber and double inclinometer methods]**

Joint Integrity and Structural Deviations

Cummings GS, Crowell RC. Source of error in clinical assessment of innominate rotation. *Physical Therapy*. 1988;68:77–78.

DonTigny R. Measuring PSIS movement. *Clinical Management in Physical Therapy*. 1990;10:3:34–40.

Rothstein JM, Roy SH, Wolf SL. *The Rehabilitation Specialist's Handbook*. Philadelphia, Pa: FA Davis Co; 1991:127–131; 170–182. **[Low back orthopedic tests: bowstring test, Brudzinski's test, cram test, femoral nerve traction test, Hoover's sign, Kernig's sign, Naffziger test, popliteal pressure sign, prone knee flexion test (or reverse Lasegue test), sitting root test, and straight leg–raising test. Sacroiliac joint tests: Gillet test; palpation of anterior superior iliac spines (patient sitting), palpation of ante-**

rior superior iliac spines (patient standing), palpation of iliac crests (patient sitting, patient standing), palpation of posterior superior iliac spines (patient sitting, patient standing), prone knee flexion test, side-lying iliac compression test, sitting flexion test, standing flexion test; standing Gillet test; supine iliac gapping test; supine long sitting test. Palpation of trigger points]

Walker JM. The sacroiliac joint: a critical review. *Physical Therapy.* 1992;72:903–916. [**Sacroiliac joint mobility tests: gross examination and manual pressure, roentgenography, tomography, kinematics, stereophotogrammetry, stress radiology, Kirschner wires, holography, loading computer generated biomechanical model simulations**]

Neurological

Rothstein JM, Roy SH, Wolf SL. *The Rehabilitation Specialist's Handbook.* Philadelphia, Pa: FA Davis Co; 1991:208–209. [**Sensory (dermatomal) tests, motor tests, deep-tendon reflexes**]

Pain

Beck AT, Ward CH, Mendelson M, Mock J, Erbaugh J. An inventory for measuring depression. *Archives of General Psychiatry.* 1961;4:561–571. [**Beck Depression Inventory**]

Brill MM, Whiffen JR. Application of 24-hour burst TENS in a back school. *Physical Therapy.* 1985;65:1355–1357. [**Morphine use length of stay, and pain reduction**]

Budzynski TH, Stoyra JM, Adler CS, Mullaney OJ, et al. EMG biofeedback and tension headache: a controlled outcome study. *Psychosomatic Medicine.* 1973;35:484–496. [**Pain Rating Chart**]

Delitto A, Cibulka MT, Erhard RE, Bowling RW, Tenhula JA. Evidence for use of an extension-mobilization category in acute low back syndrome: a prescriptive validation pilot study. *Physical Therapy.* 1993;73:216-222. [**Oswestry Low Back Pain Questionnaire**]

Denning ML. Retrospective review of long-term transcutaneous nerve stimulation in the management of chronic back pain. *Physiotherapy.* 1988;74:149–151. [**Visual analogue pain scale**]

Elton D. *Psychological Control of Pain.* New York: Grune & Stratton; 1983. [**Modified Pain Rating Chart**]

Fairbanks JCT, Davies JB, Couper J, O'Brien JP. The Oswestry Low Back Pain Disability Questionnaire. *Physiotherapy.* 1980;66:271–273.

Greenough CG, Fraser RD. Comparison of eight psychometric instruments in unselected patients with back pain. *Spine.* 1991;16:1068–1074.

Kerns RD, Turk DC, Rudy TE, et al. The West Haven–Yale Multidimensional Pain Inventory (WHYMPI). *Pain.* 1985;23:345–356.

Koes BW, Bouter LM, van Mameren H, et al. The effectiveness of manual therapy, physiotherapy, and treatment by the general practitioner for nonspecific back and neck complaints: a randomized clinical trial. *Spine.* 1992;17:1:28-35. [West Haven–Yale Multidimensional Pain Inventory]

Koes BW, Bouter LM, van Mameren H, et al. Randomized clinical trial of manipulative therapy and physiotherapy for persistent back and neck complaints: results of one year follow up. *British Medical Journal.* 1992;304:601–605. [**Global perceived effect**]

Margolis RB, Tait RC, Krause SJ. A rating system for the use with patient pain drawings. *Pain.* 1986;24:57–65.

Melzak R, Veter P, Finch L. Transcutaneous electrical nerve stimulation for low-back pain: a comparison of TENS and massage for pain and range of motion. *Physical Therapy.* 1983;63:489–493. [**McGill Pain Questionnaire**]

Mitchell J, Ness D, Whitelock S. Low back pain in pregnancy: a comparative study of two pain-rating scales. *South African Journal of Physiotherapy.* 1992;48:3:33–35.

Nicholas MK, Wilson PH, Goyen J. Comparison of cognitive-behavioral group treatment and an alternative non-psychological treatment for chronic low back pain. *Pain.* 1992;48:339–347. [**Pain Rating Chart, Beck Depression Inventory, Pain Beliefs Questionnaire, Coping Strategy Questionnaire, Sickness Impact Profile—Self, Pain Self-Efficacy Questionnaire**]

Ransford AO, Cairns D, Mooney V. The pain drawing as an aid to the psychologic evaluation of patients with low-back pain. *Spine.* 1976;1:127–134.

Rosenstiel AK, Keefe FJ. The use of coping strategies in chronic low back pain patients: relationship to patient characteristics and current adjustment. *Pain.* 1983;17:33–44. **[Coping Strategy Questionnaire]**

Posture
Mitchell J. A new method of measuring the degree of lumbar spine curvature in pregnant women. *South African Journal of Physiotherapy.* 1992;48:4:51–55. **[photography]**

Skin and Soft Tissue
Kisner C, Colby LA. *Therapeutic Exercise: Foundations and Techniques.* 2nd ed. Philadelphia, Pa: FA Davis Co; 1990:214. **[Grades of tissue injury: first, second and third degree definitions]**

Special Tests to Which the PT May or May Not Have Access

CT Scan
Halkovich R. Using the CAT scan for lumbar neuromuscular diagnosis. *Clinical Management in Physical Therapy.* 1985;52:22.

Electromyography
Headley B. Self-assessment quizzes: EMG and postural dysfunction. *Clinical Management in Physical Therapy.* 1990;10:3:14–17.

Ergonomics
American Physical Therapy Association. A guide to physical therapist practice, Volume I: A description of patient management. *Physical Therapy.* 1995;75:720–738. **[Ergonomics or body mechanics examination]**

Dubb IBM, Driver HS. Ratings of sleep and pain in patients with low back pain after sleeping on mattresses of different firmness. *Physiotherapy Canada.* 1993;45:26–28.

Functional Task Performance
Mayer TG, Gatchel RJ, Kishino N, et al. Objective assessment of lumbar function following industrial injury. *Spine.* 1985;10:482–493.

Mayer TG, Mooney V, Gatchel RJ. *Contemporary Conservative Care for Painful Spinal Disorders.* Philadelphia, Pa: Lea & Febiger; 1993:290–307. **[Commercial lift testing units, progressive isoinertial lifting evaluation (PILE), functional measurement laboratory, multiple tasks obstacle course, commercial work evaluation systems]**

Thomas LK, Hislop HJ, Waters RL. Physiological work performance in chronic low back disability. *Physical Therapy.* 1980;60:407–411.

Strength

Manual Muscle Testing
Daniels L, Worthingham C. *Muscle Testing Techniques of Manual Examination.* 6th ed. Philadelphia, Pa: WB Saunders Co; 1995.

Kendall FP, McCreary EK, Provance PG. *Muscles: Testing and Function.* 4th ed. Baltimore, Md. Williams & Wilkins; 1993.

Modified Sphygmomanometer
Giles C. The modified sphygmomanometer: an instrument to objectively assess muscle strength. *Physiotherapy Canada.* 1984;36:36–41.

Helewa A, Goldsmith CH, Smythe HA. The modified sphygmomanometer—an instrument to measure muscle strength: a validation study. *Journal of Chronic Disease.* 1981;34:353–361.

Helewa A, Goldsmith C, Smythe H, Gibson E. An evaluation of four different measures of abdominal strength: patient, order and instrument variation. *Journal of Rheumatology.* 1990;17:965–969.

Partial Sit-Up/Curl-Up Protocol

Faulkner RA, Sprigings EJ, McQuarrie A, Bell RD. A partial curl-up protocol for adults based on an analysis of two procedures. *Canadian Journal of Sport Science.* 1989;14:3:135–141.

Richardson C, Toppenberg R, Jull G. An initial evaluation of eight abdominal exercises for their ability to provide stabilization for the lumbar spine. *Australian Physiotherapy.* 1990;36:1:6-11.

Sorensen Test

Biering-Sorensen F. Physical measurement as risk indicators for low-back trouble over a one-year period. *Spine.* 1984;9:106–119.

Nordin M, Kahanovitz N, Verderame R. Normal trunk muscle strength and endurance in women and the effects of exercise and electrical stimulation. Part 1: normal endurance and trunk muscle strength in 101 women. *Spine.* 1987;12:105–111.

Pressure Biofeedback

Richardson C, Jull G, Poppenberg R, Comerford M. Techniques for active lumbar stabilization for spinal protection: a pilot study. *Australian Physiotherapy.* 1992:38:105–112.

Richardson C, Toppenberg R, Jull G. An initial evaluation of eight abdominal exercises for their ability to provide stabilization for the lumbar spine. *Australian Physiotherapy.* 1990;36:1:6–11.

Trunk Strength Testing

Beimborn DS, Morrissey MC. A review of the literature related to trunk muscle performance. *Spine.* 1988;13:655–660.

Graves JE, Fix CK, Pollock ML, Leggett SH, Foster DN, Carpenter DM. Comparison of two restraint systems for pelvic stabilization during isometric lumbar extension strength testing. *Journal of Orthopaedic and Sports Physical Therapy.* 1992;15:37–42.

Hurri H. The Swedish back school in chronic low back pain. *Scandinavian Journal of Rehabilitative Medicine.* 1989;21:33–40. **[Dynamometrical measurements]**

Lifting Dynamometers

Mayer T, Gatchel RJ. *Functional Restoration for Spinal Disorders: A Sports Medicine Approach.* Philadelphia, Pa: Lea & Febiger; 1988.

Isokinetic Dynamometers

Fenety A, Kumar S. Isokinetic trunk strength and lumbosacral range of motion in elite female field hockey players reporting low back pain. *Journal of Orthopaedic and Sports Physical Therapy.* 1992;16:129–135.

Kort HD, Hendriks ERH. A comparison of selected isokinetic trunk strength parameters of elite male judo competitors and cyclists. *Journal of Orthopaedic and Sports Physical Therapy.* 1992;16:92–96.

Mayer TG, Smith SS, Kondraske G, et al. Quantification of lumbar function, part 3: preliminary data on isokinetic torso rotation testing with myoelectric spectral analysis in normal and low-back pain subjects. *Spine.* 1985;10:912–920.

Commercial Trunk Strength Units

Mayer TG, Mooney V, Gatchel RJ. *Contemporary Conservative Care for Painful Spinal Disorders.* Philadelphia, Pa: Lea & Febiger; 1993:290–307.

TREATMENT

Abram SE, Hebar RL. Radiculopathy. In: Abram SE, ed. *The Pain Clinic Manual.* Philadelphia, Pa: JB Lippincott Co; 1990:105–117.

Apts DW. *Back Injury Prevention Handbook.* Chelsea, Mich: Lewis Publications; 1992.

Binkley J, Finch E, Hall J, Black T, Gowland C. Diagnostic classification of patients with low back pain: report on a survey of physical therapy experts. *Physical Therapy.* 1993;73:138–150.

Boissonnault WG, ed. *Examination in Physical Therapy Practice: Screening for Medical Disease.* New York, NY: Churchill Livingstone; 1991:219.

Curillo JA. Aquatic physical therapy approaches for the spine. *Orthopedic Physical Therapy Clinics of North America.* 1994;3:179–208.

D'Orazio BP. *Back Pain Rehabilitation.* Boston, Mass: Andover Medical Publishers; 1993.

Delitto A, Cibulka MT, Erhard RE, Bowling RW, Tenhula J. Evidence for use of an extension-mobilization category in acute low back pain syndrome: a prescriptive validation pilot study. *Physical Therapy.* 1993;73:216–228.

DonTigney RL. Function and pathomechanics of the sacroiliac joint: a review. *Physical Therapy.* 1985;65:35–44.

Edwards BC. *Manual of Combined Movements.* New York, NY: Churchill Livingstone; 1992.

Farrell JP, Jensen GM. Manual therapy: a critical assessment of role in the profession of physical therapy. *Physical Therapy.* 1992; 72:843–852.

Gee R. Back fitness pyramid. *Clinical Management in Physical Therapy.* 1990;10:5:26–29.

Grieve GP, ed. *Modern Manual Therapy of the Vertebral Column.* New York, NY: Churchill Livingstone; 1986:605–655.

Grieve GP. *Common Vertebral Joint Problems.* New York, NY: Churchill Livingstone; 1988:495, 508.

Hammill JM. Relief cushion for coccygeal pain. *Clinical Management in Physical Therapy.* 1988;8:5:27.

Hansen FR, Bendix T, Skov P, et al. Intensive, dynamic back-muscle exercises, conventional physiotherapy, or placebo-control treatment of low-back pain. *Spine.* 1993;18:98–108.

Homer S, Mackintosh S. Injuries in young female elite athletes. *Physiotherapy.* 1992;78:804–808.

Hopper D, Elliott B. Lower limb and back injury patterns of elite netball players. *Sports Medicine.* 1993;16:148–162.

Jackson CP. Physical therapy for lumbar disc disease. *Seminars in Spine Surgery.* 1:1:1989;28–94.

Jackson CP. Historic perspective on patient education and its place in acute spinal disorders. In: Mayer TG, Mooner V, Gatchel RJ, eds. *Contemporary Conservative Care for Painful Spinal Disorders.* Philadelphia, Pa: Lea & Febiger; 1991:221–234.

Jette AM, Smith K, Haley SM, Davis KD. Physical therapy episodes of care for patients with low back pain. *Physical Therapy.* 1994;74:101–115.

Kessler RM, Hertling D. *Management of Common Musculoskeletal Disorders: Physical Therapy Principles and Methods.* 2nd ed. Philadelphia, Pa: Harper & Row; 1990:592–597.

Kirkaldy-Willis W, ed. *Managing Low Back Pain.* 2nd ed. New York, NY: Churchill Livingstone; 1988:345–354.

Kisner C, Colby LA. *Therapeutic Exercise: Foundations and Techniques.* 2nd ed. Philadelphia, Pa: FA Davis Co; 1990:214–215, 480, 489–493, 507, 527–543, 556.

Klaber Moffett JA. Back schools. In: Roland MO, Jenner JR, eds. *Back Pain: New Approaches to Rehabilitation and Education.* New York, NY: Manchester University Press; 1989:33–49, 50–62.

Koes BW, Bouter LM, van Mameren H, et al. Randomized clinical trial of manipulative therapy and physiotherapy for persistent back and neck complaints: results of one year follow up. *British Medical Journal.* 1992;304:601–605.

Lindsay DM, Meeuwisse WH, Vyse A, et al. Lumbosacral dysfunctions in elite cross-country skiers. *Journal of Orthopaedic and Sports Physical Therapy.* 1993;18:580–585.

Lindström I, Ohlund C, Eek C, Wallin L, Peterson L, Nachemson A. Mobility, strength, and fitness after a graded activity program for patients with subacute low back pain. *Spine.* 1992;17:641–652.

Lindström I, Ohlund C, Eek C, et al. The effect of graded activity on patients with subacute low back pain: a randomized prospective clinical study with an operant-conditioning behavioural approach. *Physical Therapy.* 1992;72:279–293.

Maitland GD, Corrigan B. *Practical Orthopaedic Medicine.* Cambridge, England: Butterworth; 1983:267–268, 281, 283–286, 288–297, 315.

Mayer TG, Mooney V, Gatchel RJ. *Contemporary Conservative Care for Painful Spinal Disorders.* Philadelphia, Pa: Lea & Febiger; 1993:211, 222, 226.

McKenzie RA. *The Lumbar Spine: Mechanical Diagnosis and Therapy.* Waikanae, New Zealand: Spinal Publications; 1981.

McQuarrie A. Physical therapy. In: Kirkaldy-Willis W, ed. *Managing Low Back Pain*. 2nd ed. New York, NY: Churchill Livingstone; 1988:345–354.

Nwuga G, Nwuga V. Relative therapeutic efficacy of the Williams and McKenzie protocols in back pain management. *Physiotherapy Practice*. 1985;1:99–105.

Oliver J. *Back Care: An Illustrated Guide*. Oxford, England; Butterworth-Heinemann; 1994.

Overman SS, Larson JW, Dickstein DA, Rockey PH. Physical therapy care for low back pain. *Physical Therapy*. 1988;68:199–207.

Pollock RA, Sounder HD, Melnik MS. *Your Healthy Back: Supervising to Prevent and Manage Back Injuries*. Minneapolis, Minn: Educational Opportunities; 1991.

Porterfield JA, DeRosa C. *Mechanical Low Back Pain: Perspectives in Functional Anatomy*. Philadelphia, Pa: WB Saunders Co; 1991.

Pullen S. Myofascial pain: a review. *South African Journal of Physiotherapy*. 1992;48:3:37–39.

Roland MO, Jenner JR. *Back Pain: New Approaches to Rehabilitation and Education*. New York, NY: Manchester University Press; 1988:33–62.

Saunders HD. *Evaluation, Treatment and Prevention of Musculoskeletal Disorders*. Bloomington, Minn: Educational Opportunities; 1985:13–75, 138–141. (2nd ed, 1993)

Sikorski JM. A rationalized approach to physiotherapy for low-back pain. *Spine*. 1985;10:571–579.

Stankovic R, Johnell O. Conservative treatment of acute low-back pain: a prospective randomized trial. McKenzie method of treatment versus patient education in "Mini Back School." *Spine*. 1990;15:120–123.

Stuberg W. Manual therapy in pediatrics: some considerations. *PT Magazine of Physical Therapy*. 1993;1:54–56.

Timm KE, Malone TR, eds. *Back Injuries and Rehabilitation*. Baltimore, Md: Williams & Wilkins; 1990.

Twomey LT. A rationale for the treatment of back pain and joint pain by manual therapy. *Physical Therapy*. 1992;72:885–892.

Twomey LT, Taylor JR. *Physical Therapy of the Low Back*. New York, NY: Churchill Livingstone; 1987:131, 157–173, 279–316. (2nd ed, 1994)

Videman T, Batti'e M. Current research on spinal disorders. In: Mayer TG, Mooner V, Gatchel RJ, eds. *Contemporary Conservative Care for Painful Spinal Disorders*. Philadelphia, Pa: Lea & Febiger; 1991:113–121.

Walker JM. The sacroiliac joint: a critical review. *Physical Therapy*. 1992;72:903–916.

Weber MD, Woodall WR. Spondylogenic disorders in gymnasts. *Journal of Orthopaedic and Sports Physical Therapy*. 1991;14:6–13.

White TL, Malone TR. Effects of running on intervertebral disc height. *Journal of Orthopaedic and Sports Physical Therapy*. 1990;12:139–146.

Williams MM, Hawley JA, McKenzie RA, van Wijmen PM. A comparison of the effects of two sitting postures on back and referrred pain. *Spine*. 1991;16:1185–1191.

Wilson DJ. Diagnosis and treatment of sacro-iliac joint dysfunction. *Physiotherapy*. 1989;75:500–501.

Chronic Back Pain

Denning ML. Retrospective review of long-term transcutaneous nerve stimulation in the management of chronic back pain. *Physiotherapy*. 1988;74:149–151.

Fredrickson BE, Trief PM, VanBeveren P, Yuan HA. Rehabilitation of the patient with chronic back pain: a search for outcome predictors. *Spine*. 1988;13:351.

Kirkaldy-Willis W, ed. *Managing Low Back Pain*. 2nd ed. New York, NY. Churchill Livingstone; 1988:345–354.

Miller DJ. Comparison of electromyographic activity in the lumbar paraspinal muscles of subjects with and without chronic low back pain. *Physical Therapy*. 1985;65:1347–1354.

Roland MO, Jenner JR. *Back Pain: New Approaches to Rehabilitation and Education*. New York, NY: Manchester University Press; 1988:58–59.

Manual Therapy

Erhard RE, Delitto A, Cibulka MT. Relative effectiveness of an extension program and a combined program of manipulation and flexion and extension exercises in patients with acute low back syndrome. *Physical Therapy.* 1994;74:1093–1100.

Valid Efficacy Studies

Cibulka MT, Delitto A, Koldehoff RM. Changes in innominate tilt after manipulation of the sacroiliac joint in patients with low back pain: an experimental study. *Physical Therapy.* 1988;68:1359–1363.

Evans DP, Burke MS, Lloyd KN, et al. Lumbar spinal manipulation on trial, part I: clinical assessment. *Rheumatology and Rehabilitation.* 1978;17:46–53.

Farrell J, Twomey LT. Acute low back pain: comparison of two conservative treatment approaches. *Medical Journal of Australia.* 1982;1:160–164.

Fisk JW. A controlled trial of manipulation in a selected group of patients with low back pain favoring one side. *New Zealand Medical Journal.* 1979;90:288–291.

Glover JR, Morris JG, Khosla T. Back pain: a randomized clinical trial of rotational manipulation of the trunk. *British Journal of Industrial Medicine.* 1974;31:59–64.

Hadler NM, Curtis P, Gillings DB, Stinnett S. A benefit of spinal manipulation as adjunctive therapy for acute low-back pain: a stratified controlled trial. *Spine.* 1987;12:703–706.

Hoehler FK, Tobis JS, Buerger AA. Spinal manipulation for low back pain. *Journal American Medical Association.* 1981;245:1835–1838.

Howe DH, Newcombe RG, Wade MT. Manipulation of the cervical spine: a pilot study. *Journal of the Royal College of General Practice.* 1983;33:574–579.

Mathews JA, Mills SB, Jenkins VM, et al. Back pain and sciatica: controlled trial of manipulation, traction, sclerosant and epidural injections. *British Journal of Rheumatology.* 1987;26:416–423.

Mead TW, Dyer S, Browne W, et al. Low back pain of mechanical origin: randomized comparison of chiropractic and hospital outpatient treatment. *British Medical Journal.* 1990;300:1431–1437.

Nwuga VCB. Relative therapeutic efficacy of vertebral manipulation and conventional treatment in back pain management. *American Journal of Physical Medicine.* 1982;61:273–278.

Ongley MJ, Klein RG, Dorman TA, et al. A new approach to the treatment of chronic low back pain. *Lancet.* 1987;18:143–146.

Parker G, Pryor D, Tupling H. New Zealand inquiry into chiropractic. *Australian and New Zealand Journal of Medicine.* 1978;8:589–593.

Sanders GE, Reinert O, Tepe R, Maloney P. Chiropractic adjustive manipulation on subjects with acute low back pain: visual analog pain scores and plasma beta-endorphin levels. *Journal of Manipulative and Physiological Therapeutics.* 1990;13:391–395.

Source:Based on DiFabio RP. Efficacy of Manual Therapy. *Physical Therapy.* 1992;72:12:853-864.

Pregnancy-Related

Gleeson P, Pauls J. Obstetrical physical therapy: review of the literature. *Physical Therapy.* 1988;68:1699–1702.

Mantle MJ, Greenwood RM, Currey HLF. Backache in pregnancy. *Rheumatology and Rehabilitation.* 1977;16:95–101.

Mantle MJ, Holmes J, Currey HLF. Backache in pregnancy. II. Prophylactic influence of back care classes. *Rheumatology and Rehabilitation.* 1981;20:227–232.

O'Connor L, Gourley R. *Obstetric and Gynecologic Care in Physical Therapy.* Thorofare, NJ: Slack Inc; 1990.

Pauls J. *Therapeutic Approaches to Women's Health: A Program of Exercise and Education.* Gaithersburg, Md; Aspen Publishers, Inc; 1995.

Paulsen TE. The conservative treatment of pain in the sacroiliac region during pregnancy: a case study. *South African Journal of Physiotherapy.* 1993;49:1:14–17.

Polden M, Mantle J. *Physiotherapy in Obstetrics and Gynaecology.* London, England: Butterworth-Heinemann; 1990.

Work Hardening/Work Conditioning/Industry

Aberg J. Evaluation of an advanced back pain rehabilitation program. *Spine.* 1984;9:317–318.

Bennet DL, Gillis DK, Portney LG, et al. Comparison of integrated electromyographic activity and lumbar curvature during standing and during sitting in three chairs. *Physical Therapy.* 1989;69:902–913.

Bigos SJ, Batti'e MC. Surveillance of back problems in industry. In: Hadler NM, ed. *Clinical Concepts in Regional Musculoskeletal Illness.* New York, NY: Grune & Stratton, Inc; 1987:299–315.

Bullock MI. *Ergonomics: The Physiotherapist in the Workplace.* New York, NY: Churchill Livingstone; 1990.

Caruso LA, Chan DE, Chan A. The management of work-related back pain. *American Journal of Occupational Therapy.* 1987;41:112–117.

Frey JK, Tecklin JS. Comparison of lumbar curves when sitting on the Westnofa Balans Multi-chair, sitting on a conventional chair, and standing. *Physical Therapy.* 1986;66:1365–1369.

Hazard RG, Fenwick JW, Kalisch SM, et al. Functional restoration with behavioral support: a one-year prospective study of patients with chronic low-back pain. *Spine.* 1989;14:157–161.

Industrial Physical Therapy: APTA Resource Guide. Alexandria, Va: American Physical Therapy Association; 1991.

Isernhagen S. Functional capacity evaluation. In: Isernhagen S, ed. *Work Injury: Management and Prevention.* Rockville, Md: Aspen Publishers, Inc; 1988.

Isernhagen S. The role of functional capacity assessment after rehabilitation. In: Bullock M, ed. *Ergonomics: The Physiotherapist in the Workplace.* New York, NY: Churchill Livingstone; 1989.

Isernhagen S. Industrial physical therapy. *Orthopaedic Physical Therapy Clinics of North America.* 1992;1:1.

Isernhagen S. Advancements in functional capacity evaluation. In: D'Orazio BP, ed. *Back Pain Rehabilitation.* Boston, Mass: Andover Medical Publishers; 1993:180–204.

Key G. Work capacity analysis. In: Scully R, Barnes M, eds. *Physical Therapy.* Philadelphia, Pa: JB Lippincott Co; 1989;652–669.

Lechner DE. Work hardening and work conditioning interventions: do they affect disability? *Physical Therapy.* 1994;74:472–493.

Lindstrom I, Ohlund C, Eek C, et al. The effect of graded activity on patients with subacute low back pain: a randomized prospective clinical study with an operant-conditioning behavioral approach. *Physical Therapy.* 1992;72:279–293.

Linton SJ, Kamwendo K. Low back schools: a critical review. *Physical Therapy.* 1987;67:1375–1383.

Mayer TG, Gatchel RJ, Kishino N, et al. Objective assessment of spine function following industrial injury: a prospective study with comparison group and one-year follow-up. *Spine.* 1985;10:483–493.

McReynolds M. Early return to work. *Clinical Management in Physical Therapy.* 1990;10:5:10–11.

Mitchell RI, Carmen GM. Results of a multi-center trial using an intensive active exercise program for the treatment of acute soft tissue and back injuries. *Spine.* 1990;15:514–521.

Nosse LJ, Sobush DC, McCrimmon C. Spinal effects of head-down tilting. Part I—low-back contour changes. *Physical Therapy.* 1988;68:60–66.

Oland G, Tvetien G. A trial of modern rehabilitation for chronic low-back pain and disability: vocational outcome and effect of pain modulation. *Spine.* 1991;16:457–459.

Richardson B, Eastlake A. *Physiotherapy in Occupational Health: Management, Prevention, and Health Promotion in the Work Place.* Boston, Mass: Butterworth-Heinemann; 1994.

Rothman J, Levine RE. *Prevention Practice: Strategies for Physical Therapy and Occupational Therapy.* Philadelphia, Pa: JB Saunders Co; 1992.

Twelves JW. Physical therapy in industry. *Clinical Management in Physical Therapy.* 1990;5:14.

Chapter 10

Neurological Disorders

- Alzheimer's disease
- Amyotrophic lateral sclerosis
- Carpal tunnel syndrome
- Chronic pain
- Facial palsy
- Guillain–Barre syndrome
- Huntington's disease
- Late effects of polio
- Multiple sclerosis
- Parkinson's disease
- Peripheral nerve injury
- Reflex sympathetic dystrophy
- Stroke
- Thoracic outlet syndrome

Alzheimer's disease

Also known as *Alzheimer-type dementia.*

DESCRIPTION

Alzheimer's disease is a gradual deterioration of the cerebral cortex, basal forebrain, and other areas of the brain. The most typical early symptom is memory loss. This disease is progressive, reaching an advanced state in 2 to 3 years.

CAUSE

Alzheimer's disease is caused by the degeneration of the brain cells, characterized by a smoothing and flattening of the sulci and gyri and by plaque formations.

ASSESSMENT

Areas
- History
- Cognition, including orientation, level of recall, and cognitive and dementia screening, if indicated
- Posture
- Gait
- Mobility
- Neurological, including sensation
- Skin and soft tissues
- Functional level, including activities of daily living (ADLs)
- Environmental assessment

Instruments/Procedures (See References for Sources)

Cognition
- Mini-Mental State exam
- Short Portable Mental Status Questionnaire (SPMSQ)

Functional Level
- Barthel ADL Index
- Physical ADL (PADL)
- Structural Assessment of Independent Living Skills (SAILS)

PROBLEMS
- The client usually has diminished motor planning skills. There may be cognitive inability to follow gait-training instructions.
- The client can have a decreased incentive to walk.
- There can be ataxia of gait.
- The client can have diminished coordination.
- The client can have diminished balance.
- The client can have a decreased ability to use assistive devices.
- The client usually has a decreased awareness of safety issues.

TREATMENT/MANAGEMENT
- Treatment focuses on addressing symptoms and planning a realistic program.

- Work with a multidisciplinary team.
- Provide activities to stimulate coordination.
- Provide gait training as indicated.
- Assess safety factors related to client's living environment.

PRECAUTIONS/CONTRAINDICATIONS
- Stress safety issues with client and caregiver.

EXPECTED OUTCOME/PROGNOSIS
- The client will have an increased incentive to walk and improved motor planning skills.
- The client will maintain ability to use assistive devices as needed.
- The client will maintain coordination and balance.
- The client and any caregivers will have an increased awareness of safety issues.

REFERENCES

ASSESSMENT

Cognition

American Physical Therapy Associaition. A guide to physical therapist practice, Volume I: a description of patient management. *Physical Therapy.* 1995;75:720–738.

Folstein MF, Folstein SE, McHugh PR. Mini-Mental State: a practical method for grading the cognitive state of patients for the clinicians. *Journal of Psychiatric Research.* 1975;12:189–198. **[Mini-Mental State exam]**

Pfeiffer E. A Short Portable Mental Status Questionnaire for the assessment of organic brain deficit in elderly patients. *Journal of the American Geriatrics Society.* 1975;23:433–441.

Environmental Assessment

Pawlson LG, Lewis CB. Dysmobility. In: Karpman RR, Baum J, eds. *Aging and Clinical Practice: Musculoskeletal Disorders: A Regional Approach.* New York, NY: IGAKU-SHOIN; 1988:127–142.

Functional Level

Granger CV, Greer DS. Functional status measurement and medical rehabilitation outcomes. *Archives of Physical Medicine and Rehabilitation.* 1976;57:103–109. **[Adaptation of Barthel Index and physical condition, upper extremities, lower extremities, excretory, mental and emotional status (PULSES) scales]**

Kane RA, Kane RL. *Assessing the Elderly: A Practical Guide to Measurement.* Lexington, Mass: Lexington Books; 1984. **[ADLs]**

Katz S, Akpom CA. A measure of primary sociobiological functions. *International Journal of Health Services.* 1976;6:493–507. **[Physical ADL (PADL)]**

Mahurin RK, DeBettignies BH, Pirozzolo FJ. Structural assessment of independent living skills: preliminary report of a performance measure of functional abilities in dementia. *Journal of Gerontology.* 1991;46:2:P58–66. **[SAILS: Structural assessment of independent living skills]**

National Institute on Disability and Rehabilitation Research. *Digest of Data on Persons With Disabilities.* Washington, DC: US Dept of Education; 1992.

TREATMENT

Davis CM. The role of the physical and occupational therapist in caring for the victim of Alzheimer's disease. *Physical and Occupational Therapy in Geriatrics.* 1986;4:3:15–28.

Everett T, Dennis M, Ricketts E. *Physiotherapy in Mental Health: A Practical Approach.* Boston, Mass: Butterworth-Heinemann; 1995.

Jamieson N. Hand contractures in mental illness. *Physiotherapy.* 1989;75:496–500.

Mace NL, Hardy SR, Rabins PV. Alzheimer's disease and the confused patient. In: Jackson O, ed. *Physical Therapy of the Geriatric Patient.* New York, NY: Churchill Livingstone; 1989:129–144.

Oddy R. Promoting mobility in patients with dementia: some suggested strategies for physiotherapy. *Physiotherapy Practice.* 1987;3:1:18–27.

Pomeroy VM. The effect of physiotherapy input on mobility skills of elderly people with severe dementing illness. *Clinical Rehabilitation.* 1993;7:163–170.

Price CC. Confusion, depression, dementia. *Physiotherapy.* 1986;72:165–168.

Taira ED. *The Mentally Impaired Elderly: Strategies and Interventions to Maintain Function.* New York, NY: Haworth Press; 1991.

Amyotrophic Lateral Sclerosis

DESCRIPTION

Amyotrophic lateral sclerosis (ALS) is a progressive motor neuron disorder leading to eventual degeneration of corticospinal tracts and/or bulbar motor nuclei and/or anterior horn cells. ALS affects both upper and lower motor neurons, resulting in a combination of spasticity along with lowered tone, weakness, and atrophy. The initial signs are often muscle cramps and/or muscular fasciculations. The progression of muscular weakness and atrophy is asymmetric, but sensory systems, voluntary eye movements, and urinary sphincters remain unaffected. The disease is more common in men than women, generally beginning at age 55. The disease is fatal for 50% of clients within 3 to 4 years after onset.

CAUSE

The cause is unknown.

ASSESSMENT

Areas

- History, including medications and metabolic status
- Cardiovascular, including endurance to activities
- Cognition, including behavioral factors
- Posture
- Pain
- Mobility, including active and passive range of motion (ROM)
- Motor control, including strength
- Pulmonary status
- Skin and soft tissue, including edema and open wounds
- Neurological, including sensation
- Gait
- Functional level, including, but not limited to, activities of daily living (ADLs), bed mobility, sitting, transfers, and standing

- Equipment, including appliances and assistive devices, and environmental assessment of needs upon discharge
- Special tests to which the PT may or may not have access

Instruments/Procedures (See References for Sources)

Functional Level
- Barthel Index
- PULSES Profile

Motor Control
- maximum voluntary isometric contraction
- manual muscle testing
- motor unit estimating methodology

Pulmonary Status
- manual muscle testing
- palpation
- pulmonary tests

Special Tests to Which the PT May or May Not Have Access
- electromyography (EMG)

PROBLEMS
- The client usually complains first of painful muscle cramps after exercise or certain movements. These cramps can also occur at night.
- Fasciculations are also a common initial complaint of ALS.
- The client usually complains of weakness and muscle atrophy, initally in the small muscles of the hand and forearm. At onset, the weakness can be unilateral, but the other side will be affected soon after. Other muscles that can be involved in the early stages include the shoulder, serratus anterior, and pectoralis major muscles.
- Usually the pelvic and lower extremity muscles weaken and atrophy at a later stage.
- If bulbar paralysis is present, there may be unilateral wasting of the tongue.
- In later stages, the client can have difficulty with dysphagia, dysarthria, and mastication.
- Pseudobulbar reflexes can be triggered, leading to complusive crying, compulsive laughing, and a brisk masseter reflex.
- Speech impairment may be present and may lead to total anarthria.
- In the final phase, the client may have paralysis and impaired breathing but is usually conscious.

TREATMENT/MANAGEMENT
When planning an exercise program, the therapist should regard the following:
- nature and rate of disease progression
- level of activity and physical condition of client
- level of fatigue of client
- psychological factors

The therapist should prescribe an exercise plan according to client's individual needs and modify accordingly. Exercise/treatment activities may include

- General conditioning: mild to moderate exercise of multiple muscle groups via swimming, stationary bike, rowing, or walking
- Isometric exercise: for use when spasticity from upper motor neuron involvement is present and causes discomfort. Recommend that the client hold contraction for maximum of 5- to 10-second intervals unless the client fatigues earlier.
- Isotonic exercise
- Postural training
- Dynamic balance activities
- Active assistive exercise
- Passive range of motion

Instruct in breathing exercises for conditioning of primary muscles of inspiration such as diaphragm and external intercostals. Primary muscles of expiration include the abdominal and internal intercostal muscles. These may be strengthened through partial sit-ups, rolling from supine to side-lying, pelvic tilt, posterior neck flexion, huffing, slow controlled exhale, coughing, and general conditioning. Use manual assistive compression over lateral costal or epigastric regions if cough is weak. Consider postural drainage, especially for clients with bulbar dysfunction, if indicated. Vibration is usually tolerated better than percussion. Other respiratory techniques to consider include incentive spirometry to decrease atelectasis and manual techniques for chest wall mobility, such as stretching, squeezing, and posterior lifts.

Provide gait training and assess need for ambulation aids and orthotics. Aids should ideally be lightweight yet stable.

Provide functional training.

PRECAUTIONS/CONTRAINDICATIONS
- Endurance training is recommended when muscular weakness is minimal and should be performed at a submaximal level.
- Swimming is not recommended for clients with bulbar involvement due to risk of choking episodes.
- Isometric exercise may induce cramping in clients who do not have upper motor neuron symptoms.
- Isotonic and isokinetic exercise should be monitored closely to avoid overfatigue. Areas with extreme weakness are prone to cramping; resistive exercise should be avoided in these areas.

DESIRED OUTCOME/PROGNOSIS
- The client will function physically at the peak of his or her neuromuscular capacity.
- The client will ambulate independently with inhibition of unwanted tone.
- Contractures will be prevented.
- Breathing exercises will assist in conditioning of the primary muscles of inspiration and expiration to obtain maximal ventilatory muscle strength.
- Functional training will enable client to perform optimal ADLs.

Clinical studies addressing the effect of exercise on ALS are limited. Clients who demonstrate gains in strength through exercise are generally in the early or moderate stage of ALS, with the disease progressing slowly, and were inactive before the exercise program began.

REFERENCES

ASSESSMENT

Functional Level
Zawodniak J. Functional profiles based on clinical variations in amyotrophic lateral sclerosis. In: Caroscio JT, ed. *Amyotrophic Lateral Sclerosis: A Guide to Patient Care*. New York, NY: Thieme Medical Publishers, Inc; 1986:173–187.

Barthel Index
Mahoney BI, Barthel DW. Functional evaluations: the Barthel Index. *Maryland State Medical Journal*. 1965;14:61–65.

Wade DT, Collin C. The Barthel ADL Index: a standard measure of physical disability? *International Disability Studies*. 1988;10:2:64–67.

PULSES Profile
Granger CV, Albrecht GL, Hamilton BB. Outcome of comprehensive medical rehabilitation: measurements by PULSES Profile and the Barthel Index. *Archives of Physical Medicine and Rehabilitation*. 1979;60:145–154.

Moskowitz RW, McCann CB. Classification of disability in the chronically ill and aging. *Journal of Chronic Disease*. 1957;5:342–346.

Motor Control

Maximum Voluntary Isometric Contraction and Manual Muscle Testing
Munsat TL, Andres P, Skerry L. Therapeutic trials in amyotrophic lateral sclerosis. In: Rose FC, ed. *Amyotrophic Lateral Sclerosis*. New York, NY: Demos Publications; 1990:65–76.

Munsat TL, Hollander D, Andres P, Finison L. Clinical trials in ALS: measurement and natural history. *Advances in Neurology*. 1991;56:515–519.

Motor Unit Estimating Methodology
McComas AJ, Galea V, de Bruin H. Motor unit populations in healthy and diseased muscles. *Physical Therapy*. 1993;73:868–877.

Special Tests to Which the PT May or May Not Have Access

EMG
Bethlem J, Knobbout CE. *Neuromuscular Disease*. Oxford, England: Oxford University Press; 1987:38.

TREATMENT
Bethlem J, Knobbout CE. *Neuromuscular Disease*. Oxford, England: Oxford University Press; 1987:33–38.

Bohannon RW. Results of resistance exercise on a patient with amyotrophic lateral sclerosis: a case report. *Physical Therapy*. 1983;63:965–968.

McComas AJ, Galea V, de-Bruin H. Motor unit populations in healthy and diseased muscles. *Physical Therapy*. 1993;73:868–877.

Munsat TL, Andres P, Skerry L. Therapeutic trials in amyotrophic lateral sclerosis. In: Rose FC, ed. *Amyotrophic Lateral Sclerosis*. New York, NY: Demos Publications; 1990:65–76.

Munsat TL, Hollander D, Andres P, Finison L. Clinical trials in ALS: measurement and natural history. *Advances in Neurology*. 1991;56:515–519.

Thibodeau LM, Andres LP. Physical therapy management of patients with ALS. *Clinical Management in Physical Therapy*. 1987;7:4:6, 8–9.

Zawodniak J. Exercise, ambulation, and pulmonary physical therapy for the amyotrophic lateral sclerosis patient. In: Caroscio JT, ed. *Amyotrophic Lateral Sclerosis: A Guide to Patient Care.* New York, NY: Thieme Medical Publishers, Inc; 1986:219–244.

Carpal Tunnel Syndrome

DESCRIPTION

Carpal tunnel syndrome is a type of peripheral neuropathy leading to compression of the median nerve on the volar side of the wrist. This compression occurs between the forearm flexor muscle tendons and the transverse superficial carpal ligament and produces hand pain. Carpal tunnel syndrome is more common in women than men and more common after age 40.

CAUSE

The cause often remains undetermined, but the condition can stem from vascular insufficiency of the median nerve at the carpal tunnel or direct pressure on the nerve. Possible causes include structural changes, cumulative effect of overuse, trauma, and physiological disorders. Disorders such as arthritis, hypothyroidism, acromegaly, and myxedema have been associated with CTS. CTS is also associated with work that demands repeated forceful flexion of the wrist. The fluid changes that accompany pregnancy can also trigger CTS.

ASSESSMENT

Areas
(See also "General Hand Evaluation" in Chapter "Hand Injuries.")
- History
- Posture
- Pain
- Joint integrity
- Soft tissue, including tenderness, mobility, circulation, and edema, especially volar swelling
- Skin, including condition of nails
- Mobility, including active and passive range of motion (ROM) and accessory motion
- Strength, including grip strength, and thenar atrophy
- Neurological, including sensation, dexterity, coordination, and median nerve pressure reactions
- Functional level
- Special tests to which the PT may or may not have access

Instruments/Procedures (See References for Sources)

Neurological
- Tinel's sign
- Phalen's sign

Special Tests to Which the PT May or May Not Have Access
- nerve conduction studies
- cervical nerve root involvement testing

Strength
- manual muscle testing
- dynanometry

PROBLEMS
- The client usually has pain and paresthesias, or pins-and-needles sensation, into the first 3 or 4 fingers and on the radial aspect of the hand, along with the wrist and possibly the forearm and shoulder. This pain usually starts out gradually and can progress to a constant sensation.
- The client usually has decreased sensation in the affected hand.
- The pain is usually worse at night, waking the client up during sleep.
- There may be weakness in hand muscles, especially the thenar muscles.
- The client may report "clumsiness" when using fingers.
- The client may complain of limitation in daily activities due to symptoms.
- The client may also have cervical symptoms.

TREATMENT/MANAGEMENT
The acronym **PRICEMM** outlines a general approach for pain and inflammation.

PRICEMM: Treatment for Pain and Inflammation

- **P**rotection
- **R**est: eliminate aggravating activities
- **I**ce
- **C**ompression
- **E**levation
- **M**edication: as prescribed
- **M**odalities: as indicated

Specifically:
- Recommend rest if disorder is linked to unaccustomed excessive use.
- Prescribe resting splint (neutral or up to 20 degrees of extension) for work and at night. A splint may only be needed at night, especially after the first few weeks of symptom relief (avoid pressure over median nerve at wrist).
- Consider use of physical agents and modalities, such as iontophoresis.
- Soft tissue mobilization, joint mobilization, and neural mobilization may be indicated.
- Education and activity modifications are very important. Adapt work positions and body mechanics to avoid aggravating symptoms. Consider work height, altered posture, frequent rest periods, early treatment, and ergonomic assessment as indicated.
  For treatment post surgery, consider the following:
- elevation for 3 to 4 days
- early passive mobilization of hand and wrist (begin active finger exercises for the first few weeks; exercises may include making a full fist, making a flat fist, making a hook fist, and extending thumb)

- mobilization of carpal bones
- neural tissue mobilization
- soft tissue mobilization of transverse carpal ligament and at incision site

PRECAUTIONS/CONTRAINDICATIONS
- Teach client how to don and doff splint without fastening straps too tightly, which can interfere with circulation.
- Consider referral to surgeon if there is rapid progression of symptoms that would necessitate the surgical release of the transverse carpal ligament.

DESIRED OUTCOME/PROGNOSIS
- The client will have pain-free full use of upper extremity.
- Postsurgically, therapy will prevent adhesions that would interfere with space needed for median nerve within the carpal tunnel.
  Early intervention assists in more effective management.

REFERENCES

ASSESSMENT

Functional Level
Hertling D, Kessler RM. *Management of Common Musculoskeletal Disorders*. Philadelphia, Pa: JB Lippincott Co; 1990:254–256. **[Median nerve pressure tests]**
Levine DW. A self-administered questionnaire for the assessment of severity of symptoms and functional status in carpal tunnel syndrome. *Journal of Bone and Joint Surgery*. 1993;75A:1585–1592.

Neurological
Rothstein JM, Roy SH, Wolf SL. *The Rehabilitation Specialist's Handbook*. Philadelphia, Pa: FA Davis Co; 1991:245, 274, 277. **[Tinel's sign, Phalen's sign]**
Tomberlin JP, Saunders HD. *Evaluation, Treatment and Prevention of Musculoskeletal Disorders. Vol 2: Extremities*. Chaska, Minn: The Saunders Group; 1994:233.

Special Tests to Which the PT May or May Not Have Access
Hertling D, Kessler RM. *Management of Common Musculoskeletal Disorders*. Philadelphia, Pa: JB Lippincott Co; 1990:254–256. **[Nerve conduction studies]**

TREATMENT
Gleeson P, Pauls J. Carpal tunnel syndrome during pregnancy and lactation. *PT Magazine of Physical Therapy*. 1993;9: 52–54.
Headley BJ. Carpal tunnel syndrome. *Advance for Directors in Rehabilitation*. 1994;3:2:19–23.
Hertling D, Kessler RM. *Management of Common Musculoskeletal Disorders*. Philadelphia, Pa: JB Lippincott Co; 1990:256.
Nagai L, Eng J. Overuse injuries incurred by musicians. *Physiotherapy Canada*. 1992;44:23–30.
Nathan PA, Meadows KD, Keniston RC. Rehabilitation of carpal tunnel surgery patients using a short surgical incision and an early program of physical therapy. *Journal of Hand Surgery*. 1993;18:1044–1050.
Nitz AJ, Dobner JJ. Upper extremity tourniquet effects in carpal tunnel release. *Journal of Hand Surgery*. 1989;14:499–504.
Quarrier NF. Performing arts medicine: the musical athlete. *Journal of Orthopaedic and Sports Physical Therapy*. 1993;17:90–95.

Vanderpool HE, Friis EA, Smith BS, Harms KL. Prevalence of carpal tunnel syndrome and other work-related musculoskeletal problems in cardiac sonographers. *Journal of Occupational Medicine*. 1993;35:604–610.

Wadsworth CT. Elbow, forearm, wrist, and hand. In: Myers RS, ed. *Saunders Manual of Physical Therapy Practice*. Philadelphia, Pa: WB Saunders Co; 1995:891–892.

Chronic Pain

DESCRIPTION

Pain is usually classified as chronic when it continues for more than 3 to 6 months. The pain is no longer serving its role as a signal of biological injury or damage. Chronic pain is the pain that remains even after the initial damage has been physically healed. Even if little or no organic cause is identified, the pain is still quite "real." Clients with chronic pain may also display somatic symptoms such as weight change, sleep disturbance, and diminished libido. Depression is common. For many clients, the psychological state affects impairment more than any organic disease.

CAUSE

The cause of chronic pain is often unclear, but one system classifies the pathogenesis of pain as either nociceptive, neuropathic, or psychogenic.

- *Nociceptive:* somatic or visceral pain caused by activation of pain-reactive nerve fibers
- *Neuropathic:* central, peripheral, or sympathetically mediated pain caused by damage to afferent nerve pathways
- *Psychogenic:* usually involves pain without an organic lesion and includes somatization disorder, psychogenic pain, and hypochondriasis; this category also includes syndromes in which there is an organic component

Musculoskeletal disorders in the spine leading to chronic pain include the following: postural pain, derangement, degenerative joint disease, facet joint pathology, compression fracture, spinal fusion, arachnoiditis, postoperative scarring, spondylolisthesis, piriformis syndrome, and cervical spine pain. Other pain syndromes include reflex sympathetic dystrophy, postherpetic neuralgia, amputation, and chronic abdominal pain.

ASSESSMENT

Areas

- History, including mental status, daily schedule, work history, medical status, and surgical history
- Vital statistics: blood pressure, heart rate, pulse
- Pain, including aggravating factors, remitting factors, nature of pain over a 24-hour period, sleep, quality of pain
- Headache (if applicable)
- Posture

- Gait
- Mobility, including active and passive range of motion (ROM) and accessory movements
- Strength
- Coordination
- Neurological, including sensation, reflexes, dural tension signs, and Babinski
- Skin and soft tissue
- Cardiovascular, including endurance and fitness level
- Functional level
- Health status
- Special tests to which the PT may or may not have access, including diagnostic tests

Instruments/Procedures (See References for Sources)

Functional Level
- Functional Interference Estimate
- Functional Assessment Screening Questionnaire

Headache
- Mood Adjective Check List
- passive accessory intervertebral mobility (PAIVM) exam
- plumbline postural assessment

Health Status
- Sickness Impact Profile

Pain
- body diagrams
- forceps algometer
- McGill Pain Questionnaire (MPQ)
- McGill Melzack Short Form
- Multidimensional Pain Inventory (MPI)
- Numeric Pain Rating Scale
- Pain Disability Index
- pain threshold measures
- Pain and Impairment Relationship Scale (PAIRS)
- palpation
- Pressure dolorimeter
- Symptom Checklist 90 (SCL-90)
- visual analogue scale

Special Tests to Which the PT May or May Not Have Access
- electromyography (EMG)

PROBLEMS
- The client has pain that may be accompanied by musculoskeletal and neuromuscular dysfunction.
- The client can have selected joint and soft tissue restriction.
- There can be areas of muscular weakness, instability, or imbalance.
- The client can have muscle spasm.

- The client can have related gait abnormalities.
- The client usually has accompanying postural deviations.
- The client usually has decreased independence in functional activities.
- The client usually has decreased cardiovascular fitness.
- The client reports tension, and there is usually difficulty with relaxation response.

Psychophysiologic Dimensions of Chronic Pain

Autonomic dysfunction
- increased sympathetic activity
- increased muscle tone
- hypersensitivity

CNS dysfunction
- decreased pain tolerance and threshold
- decreased endorphin levels

Metabolic change in affected tissue
- decreased blood flow
- increased edema

Motor control dysfunction
- decreased movement skill and strategies
- decreased proprioception

Self
- decreased sense of self-worth
- identity crisis
- feeling overwhelmed and out of control

Psychological
- depression
- somaticization
- sleep deprivation
- interrelational stress
- moving toward a vegetative state

Source: Reprinted with permission from SB O'Sullivan and TJ Schmitz, *Physical Rehabilitation*, p. 590, © 1994, FA Davis & Company.

TREATMENT/MANAGEMENT

Treatment should be designed with a client's individual needs in mind. Physical therapy is one component of a team approach that may also include behavior modification and family education.

Consider referral to vocational counseling, a support group, and counseling.

Recognize that pain-relieving techniques are often the secondary issue; the primary concern is the management of a client with chronic pain that also has a psychological or psychiatric component. Teach the client the concept that pain relief is not the primary goal, but part of working to criterion.

Consider the following strategy:
- Provide information on origin of pain and exacerbating factors.

- Encourage the client to be an active participant in treatment.
- Consider behavioral factors when applying traditional physical therapy techniques, with emphasis on areas in which the client is motivated to attempt to improve function.
- Involve family and friends, as indicated.
- Provide a clear plan for cessation of treatment.

Individualize the client's treatment by choosing from the appropriate physical agents and modalities to modify pain, such as the following (see precautions and appendix for contraindications):

1. cold
   - ethyl chloride spray
   - ice massage
   - ice pack
   - chemical cold pack
2. combination cold/heat
   - contrast baths
3. electrical stimulation
   - alternating or direct current
   - high-voltage galvanic stimulation
   - iontophoresis
   - transcutaneous electrical nerve stimulation (TENS)
4. exercise
   - active
   - active assistive
   - coordination
   - passive
   - proprioceptive neuromuscular facilitation
   - resistive
   - lifestyle modifications that include a general fitness exercise program
5. heat
   - hydrocollator packs, hydrotherapy, or paraffin bath for superficial heating
   - diathermy, microwave or shortwave, or ultrasound for deep heating
6. manual therapy
   - mobilization
   - muscle energy techniques
7. massage
   - effleurage
   - friction
   - petrissage
   - percussion
   - soft tissue mobilization
   - trigger point deactivation
   - vibration
   - accupressure
   - deep tissue massage
8. pacing
   - endurance activities
   - functional training

- work hardening (see also section "Low Back Pain")
- proper body mechanics
9. relaxation
  - breathing techniques
  - EMG biofeedback
  - progressive relaxation
  - autogenic training
  - stress management
10. sensory training
  - desensitization
11. traction
  - intermittent
  - manual
  - positional
  - static

Factors That Can Raise a Pain Threshold

- antidepressants
- analgesics
- anxiety reduction
- anxiolytics
- companionship
- diversional activities
- mood elevation
- relaxation
- rest/sleep
- sympathy
- symptom relief

Source: Reprinted with permission from LA Pflazer, Oncology: Examination, Diagnosis, and Treatment; Medical and Surgical Considerations, in *Saunders Manual of Physical Therapy and Practice*, RS Myers, p. 78, © 1995, WB Saunders Company.

PRECAUTIONS/CONTRAINDICATIONS

The following precautions are taken from Fairchild et al., "Physical Therapy" (see Treatment references). See also contraindications to physical agents in Appendix C.

- Contrast baths: contraindicated in clients with Berger's disease, Raynaud's disease, or sensory loss.
- Cryotherapy: contraindicated with Raynaud's disease.
- Diathermy: same as with other heat modalities. Additionally, diathermy should not be used over areas of poor circulation, malignancies, pregnant uterus, thrombophlebitis, or hemorrhagic diathesis. Use with special caution if sensation is diminished or if client is debilitated. Microwave diathermy is contraindicated in areas of eyes. Shortwave diathermy can be used, with caution, if contact lenses are taken off.

- *Electrical stimulation:* primarily contraindicated in a client with a cardiac disease that requires use of demand-type pacemakers or a client prone to arrhythmias due to electrical stimulation; contraindicated with phlebothrombosis and skin disorders.
- *Hydrocollator packs:* use cautiously; may be contraindicated over areas of inflammation, with areas with decreased sensation, or over open lesions.
- *Hydrotherapy:* use cautiously. May be contraindicated in clients with infections with swelling, peripheral vascular disease, or rash, or in clients who cannot withstand any increase in core temperature.
- *Massage:* use with caution. May be contraindicated with acute circulatory disorder, infection, malignancies, and select skin diseases.
- *Mobilization:* contraindicated with active disk prolapse with herniation with no neurologic signs, acute arthritis, hypermobility, malignancy, osteoporosis, fractures, osteomyelitis, ruptured ligaments, scoliosis, spondylosis, spondylolisthesis, and tuberculosis. Use with caution if client is debilitated, has ligamentous laxity, is pregnant, or has upper respiratory tract infection.
- *Paraffin baths:* use cautiously. May be contraindicated over areas of decreased circulation or sensation, infection, malignancies, or open lesions.
- *Traction:* contraindicated with acute trauma, acute inflammation, hemorrhage, malignancy, acute lumbago (as per source). Use cautiously with clients with neurological disorders.
- *Ultrasound:* contraindicated over areas of diminished circulation; over area of growth center of bone until growth is complete; over area of pacemaker implantation, healing fracture, pregnant uterus, or malignancy; over the eye; or over the spinal cord.

DESIRED OUTCOME/PROGNOSIS
- The client will be educated about pain reduction techniques.
- The client will eliminate or reduce pain. Caution client not to expect complete alleviation of the pain.
- Therapy will reduce stress on structures involved and promote healing.
- The client will control any edema formation and prevent secondary loss and disability.
- The client will restore function and increase stamina, endurance, and tolerance to functioning even when there is pain.
- The client will modify neuronal activity and stimulate release of endorphins.
- The client will promote autonomic homeostasis.
- The client will increase in movement awareness, muscle skill, strength, flexibility, and normalization strategies.
- The client will identify pain behaviors and work to eliminate them.
- Therapy will facilitate adaptation to any permanent disability.

  Some clients do not seem to gain a favorable outcome from therapy. These clients may be affected by the following factors:
- incongruity between history and objective exam
- uncooperativeness with treatment
- unrealistic expectations
- litigation (this does not necessarily affect outcome, but may be a factor)
- no interest in returning to work or ADLs

  Functional improvement should be compared to client's baseline and not to the average person's schedule.

The most common types of pain treated at pain treatment centers are cervical pain, lower back pain, headache, nerve root injury, and myofascial syndromes.

REFERENCES

ASSESSMENT

General Assessment
American Physical Therapy Association. A guide to physical therapist practice, Volume I: a description of patient management. *Physical Therapy.* 1995;75:720–738. **[Pain examination]**

Bowsher D. Acute and chronic pain and assessment. In: Wells PE, Frampton V, Bowsher D, eds. *Pain Management in Physical Therapy.* 2nd ed. Norwalk, Conn: Appleton & Lange; 1988.

Echternack JL. Clinical evaluation of the patient in pain. *Physical Therapy Practice.* 1993;2:3:14–16.

Differential Diagnosis
Goodman C, Snyder TE. *Differential Diagnosis in Physical Therapy.* Philadelphia, Pa; WB Saunders; 1990:332, 337, 357, 362–363.

Rothstein JM, Roy SH, Wolf SL.*The Rehabilitation Specialist's Handbook.* Philadelphia, Pa: FA Davis Co; 1991:442–443. **[Pain referred from viscera]**

Measures
Beekman CE, Deusinger RH. Ambulation, activity level, and pain: outcomes of a program for spinal pain. *Physical Therapy.* 1985;65:1656–1657.

Functional Level

Functional Interference Estimate
Toomey TC, Mann JD, Hernandez JT, Abashian SW. Psychometric characteristics of a brief measure of pain-related functional impairment. *Archives of Physical Medicine and Rehabilitation.* 1993;74:1305–1308.

Functional Assessment Screening Questionnaire
Millard RW. The Functional Assessment Screening Questionnaire: application for evaluating pain-related disability (FASQ). *Archives of Physical Medicine and Rehabilitation.* 1989;70:303–307.

Headache

Mood Adjective Check List
Carlsson J, Augustinsson LE, Blomstrand C, Sullivan M. Health status in patients with tension headache treated with acupuncture or physiotherapy. *Headache.* 1990;30:593–599.

Passive Accessory Intervertebral Mobility (PAIVM) Exam
Watson DH, Trott PH. Cervical headache: an investigation of natural head posture and upper cervical flexor muscle performance. *Cephalalgia.* 1993;13:272–284.

Plumbline Postural Assessment
Griegel-Morris P, Larson K, Mueller-Klaus K, Oatis CA. Incidence of common postural abnormalities in the cervical, shoulder, and thoracic regions and their association with pain in two age groups of healthy subjects. *Physical Therapy.* 1992;72:425–431.

Health Status

Sickness Impact Profile
Carlsson J, Augustinsson LE, Blomstrand C, Sullivan M. Health status in patients with tension headache treated with acupuncture or physiotherapy. 1990;30:593–599.

Pain
Simmonds M, Wessel J, Scudds R. The effect of pain quality on the efficacy of conventional TENS. *Physiotherapy Canada*. 1992;44:35–40. **[Pressure dolorimeter, forceps algometer, McGill Pain Questionnaire (MPQ)]**

Body Diagrams
Headley BJ. Chronic pain management. In: O'Sullivan SB, Schmitz TJ, eds. *Physical Rehabilitation*. 3rd ed. Philadelphia, Pa: FA Davis Co; 1994:577–602.

McGill Pain Questionnaire (MPQ)
Melzack R. The McGill Pain Questionnaire: major properties and scoring methods. *Pain*. 1975;1:277–299.
Melzack R. The Short-Form McGill Pain Questionnarie. *Pain*. 1987;30:191–197. **[Short-Form McGill Pain Questionnaire]**

Multidimensional Pain Inventory (MPI)
Headley BJ. Chronic pain management. In: O'Sullivan SB, Schmitz TJ, eds. *Physical Rehabilitation*. 3rd ed. Philadelphia, Pa: FA Davis Co; 1994:577–602.

Neuromuscular Electrical Stimulation
Delitto A, Strube MJ, Shulman AD, Minor SD. A study of discomfort with electrical stimulation. *Physical Therapy*. 1992;72:410–424.

Numeric Pain Rating Scale
Jensen MP, Faroly P, Braver S. The measurement of clinical pain intensity: a comparison of six methods. *Pain*. 1986;27:117–126.
McGuire DB. The measurement of clinical pain. *Nursing Research*. 1984;33:152–156.

Pain Disability Index
Tait RC, Pollard A, Margolis RB, Krause SJ. Pain Disability Index: psychometric and validity data. *Archives of Physical Medicine and Rehabilitation*. 1987;68:438–441.

Pain Threshold Measures
Hogeweg JA, Langereis MJ, Bernards AT, et al. Algometry: measuring pain threshold, method and characteristics in healthy subjects. *Scandinavian Journal of Rehabilitation Medicine*. 1992;24:99–103.

Pain and Impairment Relationship Scale (PAIRS)
Riley JF, Ahern DK, Follick MJ. Chronic pain and functional impairment: assessing beliefs about their relationship. *Archives of Physical Medicine and Rehabilitation*. 1988;69:579–582.
Slater MA, Hall HF, Atkinson H, Garfin SR. Pain and impairment beliefs in chronic low back pain: validation of the Pain and Impairment Relationship Scale (PAIRS). *Pain*. 1991;44:51–56.

Palpation
Levoska S, Keinanen-Kiukaanniemi S, Bloigu R. Repeatability of measurement of tenderness in the neck-shoulder region by a dolorimeter and manual palpation. *Clinical Journal of Pain*. 1993;9:229–235.

Symptom Checklist 90 (SCL-90)
Headley BJ. Chronic pain management. In: O'Sullivan SB, Schmitz TJ, eds. *Physical Rehabilitation*. 3rd ed. Philadelphia, Pa: FA Davis Co; 1994:577–602.

Visual Analogue Scale
Carlsson AM. Assessment of chronic pain, Part I: aspects of the reliability and validity of the visual analogue scale. *Pain*. 1983;16:87–101.
Longobardi AG, Clelland JA, Knowles CJ, Jackson JR. Effects of auricular transcutaneous electrical nerve stimulation on distal extremity pain. *Physical Therapy*. 1989;69:10–17.

Special Tests to Which the PT May or May Not Have Access

EMG

Headley BJ. Chronic pain management. In: O'Sullivan SB, Schmitz TJ, eds. *Physical Rehabilitation*. 3rd ed. Philadelphia, Pa: FA Davis Co; 1994:590.

TREATMENT

Bending J. TENS in a pain clinic. *Physiotherapy*. 1989;75:292–294.

Bengston R. Physical therapy. In: Warfield CA, ed. *Manual of Pain Management*. Philadelphia, Pa: JB Lippincott Co; 1991:286–290.

Biggers J. Physical therapy in the treatment of chronic pain syndrome. *Clinical Management in Physical Therapy*. 1986;6:6:6,9–10.

Blossom BM. The role of the physical therapist. In: Brena SF, Chapman SL, eds. *Management of Patients With Chronic Pain*. New York, NY: SP Medical and Scientific Books; 1983:211-216.

Butler D, Gifford L. The concept of adverse mechanical tension in the nervous system: testing for "dural treatment," part 1. *Physiotherapy*. 1989;75:622–629.

Butler D, Gifford L. The concept of adverse mechanical tension in the nervous system: examination and treatment, part 2. *Physiotherapy*. 1989;75:629–636.

Clelland J, Savinar E, Shepard KF. The role of the physical therapist in chronic pain management. In: Burrows GB, Elton D, Stanley GV, eds. *Handbook of Chronic Pain Management*. New York, NY: Elsevier Science Publishers; 1987:243–258.

Denning ML. Retrospective review of long-term transcutaneous nerve stimulation in the management of chronic back pain. *Physiotherapy*. 1988;74:149–151.

Doleys D, Crocker M, Patton D. Response of patients with chronic pain to exercise quota. *Physical Therapy*. 1982;62:1111–1114.

Doliber CM. Role of the physical therapist at pain treatment centers: a survey. *Physical Therapy*. 1983;69:266–268.

Ehrenkranz CE. A coordinated physical therapy/movement therapy approach to treatment of the chronic pain patient. *Clinical Management in Physical Therapy*. 1986;6:2:24–29.

Eick WC. Habitual tension: challenge for the physical therapist. *Clinical Management in Physical Therapy*. 1981;1:4:7–8.

Fairchild VM, Salerno LM, Wedding SL, Weinberg E. Physical therapy. In: Raj PP, ed. *Practical Management of Pain*. Chicago, Ill: Year Book Medical Publishers, Inc; 1986:839–852.

Finneran J. A biofeedback program for the patient with pain. *Clinical Management in Physical Therapy*. 1985;5:1:6,9.

French S, ed. *Physiotherapy: A Psychosocial Approach*. London, England: Butterworth-Heinemann; 1992.

Gersch MR, Wolf SL. Applications of transcutaneous electrical nerve stimulation in the management of patients with pain: state of the art update. *Physical Therapy*. 1985;65:314–336.

Harding V, Williams ACD. Extending physiotherapy skills using a psychological approach: cognitive-behavioural management of chronic pain. *Physiotherapy*. 1995;81:681–688.

Headley BJ. Self-efficacy and chronic pain. *Clinical Management in Physical Therapy*. 1990;10:4:47–50.

Headley BJ. The use of biofeedback in pain management. *Physical Therapy Practice*. 1993;2:2:49–56.

Hertling D, Jones D. The revival of relaxation techniques and the development of related techniques. In: Hertling D, Kessler RM, eds. *Management of Common Musculoskeletal Disorders*. 2nd ed. Philadelphia, Pa: JB Lippincott Co; 1990:202–230.

Injury Specialists Physical Therapy Manual. Bridgeton, Mo: Physicians' Pain Management Center; 1994.

Langridge JC, Phillips D. Group hydrotherapy exercises for chronic back pain sufferers. *Physiotherapy*. 1988;74:269–273.

Lawrence LM. Musculoskeletal changes in chronic pain patients. In: France RD, Krishnan KRR, eds. *Chronic Pain*. Washington, DC: American Psychiatric Press, Inc; 1988:245–255.

Lein DH Jr, Clelland JA, Knowles CJ, Jackson JR. Comparison of effect of transcutaneous electrical nerve stimulation of auricular, somatic, and the combination of auricular and somatic acupuncture points on experimental pain threshold. *Physical Therapy*. 1989;69:671–678.

Leseberg KA, Schunk C. TENS and geriatrics. *Clinical Management in Physical Therapy*. 1990;10:6:23–25.

Longobardi AG, Clelland JA, Knowles CJ, Jackson JR. Effects of auricular transcutaneous electrical nerve stimulation on distal extremity pain. *Physical Therapy*. 1989;69:10–17.

McCombe WS, Mushi R. Physical therapy in the multidisciplinary pain treatment center. *Physical Therapy Practice*. 1993;2:3:57–60.

McDonald AJR, Coates TW. The discovery of transcutaneous spinal electroanalgesia and its relief of chronic pain. *Physiotherapy*. 1995;81:653–661.

Meilman PW. Chronic pain: basic assumptions regarding treatment. *Journal of Orthopaedic and Sports Physical Therapy*. 1984;5:312–315.

Meilman PW. Legitimizing chronic pain. *Journal of Orthopaedic and Sports Physical Therapy*. 1984;5:308–310.

Melzack R, Vetere P, Finch L. TENS for low back pain. *Physical Therapy*. 1983;63:489–493.

Miller DJ. Comparison of electromyographic activity in the lumbar paraspinal muscles of subjects with and without chronic low back pain. *Physical Therapy*. 1985;65:1347–1354.

Moon MH. The muscle pain of conflict, submissiveness, and grief. *Physiotherapy Practice*. 1986;2:3:128–131.

Nolan MF. Pain: the experience and its expression. *Clinical Management in Physical Therapy*. 1990;10:1:22–25.

Nolan MF. Contemporary perspectives on pain and discomfort. *Physical Therapy Practice*. 1993;2:3:1–6.

O'Brien WJ, Rutan FM, Sanborn C, Omer GE. Effect of transcutaneous electrical nerve stimulation on human blood beta-endorphin levels. *Physical Therapy*. 1984;64:1367–1374.

Oliveri AC, Clelland J, Jackson J, Knowles C. The effects of auricular transcutaneous electrical nerve stimulation on experimental pain threshold. *Physical Therapy*. 1985;66:12–16.

Prip K. *Physiotherapy to Torture Survivors*. Copenhagen, Denmark: International Rehabilitation Council for Torture Victims; 1994.

Ryskalczyk RJ. An operant conditioning program for the treatment of chronic pain. *Clinical Management in Physical Therapy*. 1983;3:1:11–14.

Sanders PL. Breaking the chronic pain cycle. *Clinical Management in Physical Therapy*. 1991;11:4:72–79.

Showers MC. Relaxation of muscles in patients with chronic pain. *Clinical Management in Physical Therapy*. 1981;1:1:18.

Simmonds M, Wessel J, Scudds R. The effect of pain quality of the efficacy of conventional TENS. *Physiotherapy Canada*. 1992;44:35–40.

Siracusano G. The physical therapist's use of exercise in the treatment of chronic pain. *Journal of Orthopaedic and Sports Physical Therapy*. 1984;6:72–88.

Siracusano G. Problems faced by the physical therapist in the treatment of chronic pain. *Journal of Orthopaedic and Sports Physical Therapy*. 1984;6:2–5.

Smith LM. Physiotherapy. In: Tyrer SP, ed. *Psychology, Psychiatry, and Chronic Pain*. London, England: Butterworth-Heinemann; 1992:179–187.

Smith P. An educational tool for the patient with chronic pain. *Clinical Management in Physical Therapy*. 1988;8:4:10.

Solomon P, Tunks E. The role of litigation in predicting disability outcomes in chronic pain patients. *Clinical Journal of Pain*. 1991;7:300–304.

Trumble EA, Krengel MP. Physical therapy. In: Raj PP, ed. *Pain Medicine: A Comprehensive Review*. New York, NY: CV Mosby Co; 1996:335–338.

von Nieda K, Michlovitz S. The application of physical agents in the treatment of patients with pain. *Physical Therapy Practice*. 1993;2:3:45–50.

Wasserman JB. Physical therapy in the treatment of chronic pain syndrome. *Clinical Management in Physical Therapy*. 1986;6:6:6–10.

Wells PE, Frampton V, Bowsher D. *Pain Management by Physiotherapy.* 2nd ed. Boston, Mass: Butterworth-Heinemann; 1994.

Williams JI. Illness behaviour to wellness behaviour: the "School for Bravery" approach. *Physiotherapy.* 1989;75:2–7.

Wolff MS, Michel TH, Krebs DE, Watts NT. Chronic pain assessment of orthopedic physical therapists' knowledge and attitudes. *Physical Therapy.* 1991;71:207–214.

Headache

Bremiller W. Headache: a multimodal approach to diagnosis and treatment. *Clinical Management in Physical Therapy.* 1985:5:2:30.

Carlsson J, Augustinsson LE, Blomstrand C, Sullivan M. Health status in patients with tension headache treated with acupuncture or physiotherapy. *Headache.* 1990;30:593–599.

Carlsson J, Fahlcrantz A, Augustinsson LE. Muscle tenderness in tension headache treated with acupuncture or physiotherapy. *Cephalalgia.* 1990;10:131–141.

Carlsson J, Rosenhall U. Oculomotor disturbances in patients with tension headache treated with acupuncture or physiotherapy. *Cephalalgia.* 1990;10:123–129.

Griegel-Morris P, Larson K, Mueller-Klaus K, Oatis CA. Incidence of common postural abnormalitites in the cervical, shoulder, and thoracic regions and their association with pain in two age groups of healthy subjects. *Physical Therapy.* 1992;72:425–431.

Hellsing A, Linton S. Chronic headache treatment in an occupational setting: a pilot study. *Physiotherapy Practice.* 1989;5:1:3–8.

Rundcrantz BL, Johnsson B, Moritz U. Cervical pain and discomfort among dentists: epidemiological, clinical, and therapeutic aspects. Part 1: a survey of pain and discomfort. *Swedish Dental Journal.* 1990;14:2:71–80.

Watson DH, Trott PH. Cervical headache: an investigation of natural head posture and upper cervical flexor muscle performance. *Cephalalgia.* 1993;13:272–284.

Substance Abuse

Bruckner J. Physical therapists as double agents: ethical dilemmas of divided loyalties. *Physical Therapy.* 1987;67:383–387.

Conaty J. Physiotherapy with alcohol and drug dependent patients: implications for general settings. *Physiotherapy Canada.* 1992;44:31–34.

Cornell CJ. Basic counseling techniques for physical therapists. *Clinical Management in Physical Therapy.* 1982:2:3:16.

Warren E. Addiction. In: French S, ed. *Physiotherapy: A Psychosocial Approach.* London, England: Butterworth-Heinemann; 1992.

Facial Palsy

Also known as *Bell's palsy.*

DESCRIPTION

Facial palsy is a peripheral lesion of the seventh cranial nerve leading to unilateral facial weakness or paralysis. Sensory changes usually appear before motor changes. This type of peripheral nerve lesion is categorized as a neuropraxia, or localized blockage of the nerve conduction.

CAUSE

Facial palsy may be caused by pressure from inflammation of the seventh cranial nerve inside its canal. This inflammation can be caused by conditions affecting the middle ear, by herpes zoster of the geniculate ganglion, or by an immune disease. Facial palsy can also be idiopathic.

ASSESSMENT

Areas

- History
- Communication, including speech
- Pain
- Strength, including active motion of facial muscles and facial expression, especially muscles used in raising eyebrows, smiling, and showing lower teeth
- Neurological, including facial nerve and sensation, especially ability to distinguish between sugar and salt
- Functional level
- Special tests to which the PT may or may not have access

Instruments/Procedures (See References for Sources)

Neurological
- cranial nerve testing
- electromyography (EMG)

Special Tests to Which the PT May or May Not Have Access
- nerve conduction velocity tests

Strength
- manual muscle testing

PROBLEMS

- The client may complain of pain behind the ear before rapidly developing unilateral facial weakness.
- The client will usually have a unilateral loss of facial expression.
- The client will usually be unable to purse lips or smile.
- The client may complain of loss of taste.
- The client will usually be unable to close eye.

TREATMENT/MANAGEMENT

- Instruct client in active and active assistive facial exercises.
- Consider use of neuromuscular facilitation techniques.
- Use surface EMG to facilitate relearning of facial motor control.
- Encourage use of mirror as feedback during facial motion exercises.
- Work with psychological or psychiatric services and support groups to address the disfigurement that accompanies facial palsy, if indicated.

PRECAUTIONS/CONTRAINDICATIONS

- Refer to occupational therapy and/or speech therapy if client has persistent difficulty with eating, drinking, or speech.

DESIRED OUTCOME/PROGNOSIS
* The client will restore form, movement, and function of face.
  The majority of clients with facial palsy recover in 4 weeks.

REFERENCES

ASSESSMENT
Bourbon B. Craniomandibular examination and treatment. In: Myers RS, ed. *Saunders Manual of Physical Therapy Practice*. Philadelphia, Pa: WB Saunders Co; 1995:698–699.
Shores M. Bell's palsy assessment chart. *Clinical Management in Physical Therapy.* 1982;2:3:21.

Neurological

Cranial Nerve Testing
American Physical Therapy Association. A guide to physical therapist practice, Volume I: a description of patient management. *Physical Therapy.* 1995;75:720–738.
Isaacs ER, Bookout MR. Screening for pathologic origins of head and facial pain. In Boissonnault WG, ed. *Examination in Physical Therapy Practice: Screening for Medical Disease*. New York, NY: Churchill Livingstone; 1991:185. **[Facial nerve (cranial nerve VII) testing]**

Special Tests to Which the PT May or May Not Have Access

Nerve Conduction Velocity Tests and EMG
Portney LG. Electromyography and nerve conduction velocity tests. In: O'Sullivan SB, Schmitz TJ, eds. *Physical Rehabilitation: Assessment and Treatment*. 3rd ed. Philadelphia, Pa: FA Davis Co; 1994:150.

Strength
Daniels L, Worthingham C. *Muscle Testing Techniques of Manual Examination*. Philadelphia, Pa: WB Saunders Co; 1972. (new edition available)
Kendall FP, McCreary EK, Provance PG. *Muscles: Testing and Function*. 4th ed. Baltimore, Md: Williams & Wilkins; 1993.

TREATMENT
Lee JM. *Aids to Physiotherapy*. 2nd ed. New York, NY: Churchill Livingstone; 1988:57.
Novak CB, Ross B, Mackinnon SE, Nedzelski JM. Facial sensibility in patients with unilateral facial nerve paresis. *Otolaryngology and Head and Neck Surgery.* 1993;109:506–513.
Vanswearingen J. Tracing a clinical path for saving face. *Advance/Rehabilitation.* 1994;4:10:45–47.

Guillain Barre Syndrome

DESCRIPTION
Guillain Barre syndrome (GBS) is an acute polyneuropathy leading to muscular weakness and mild sensory loss.

CAUSE

Cause is unknown, but the syndrome is thought to have an autoimmune basis. When GBS appears, it usually occurs within a few days or weeks following a respiratory tract infection, influenza, immunization, or surgery.

ASSESSMENT

Areas
- History, including medications and metabolic status
- Communication, including speech, reading, and writing
- Vision
- Cognition, including behavioral factors
- Pain
- Posture, including any asymmetry
- Pulmonary, including dyspnea and ventilator dependency
- Cardiovascular status, including endurance to activities
- Genitourinary status, including incontinence
- Mobility, including active and passive range of motion (ROM)
- Motor control, including tone (resting and dynamic), reflexes (tonic reflexes, righting reflexes, equilibrium responses), balance and postural reactions, and active movement control, including coordination, patterned movement, and isolated movement
- Strength, especially cranial nerve function; testing may be delayed until client is stable
- Neurological, including sensation and sensory component of cranial nerves I, V, and VII through X
- Skin and soft tissue, including atrophy, edema, pressure sores, or open wounds
- Functional level, including but not limited to activities of daily living (ADLs), bed mobility, sitting, transfers, standing, and gait, if indicated
- Equipment, including appliances and assistive devices, and environmental needs upon discharge

Instruments/Procedures (See References for Sources)

Functional Level
- Barthel Index
- PULSES Profile

Strength
- manual muscle testing

PROBLEMS
- The client can have respiratory insufficiency if intercostal muscles are affected. In severe cases, the client can also have acute respiratory failure.
- The client usually has bilateral muscular weakness, especially in the lower extremities, ranging from slight decline to total paralysis.
- About 50% of clients have facial palsy, which can be bilateral.
- About 50% of clients have paresthesia of feet that moves proximally; possibly felt in hands.

• The client usually has symptoms related to autonomic nervous system dysfunction, such as arrhythmia, tachycardia, orthostatic hypotension, hyperhydrosis, urine retention, and possibly diminished reflexes.

TREATMENT/MANAGEMENT
• Perform passive ROM and proper positioning.
• Instruct in exercises for strength and endurance.
• Provide gait training as indicated.
• Prescribe orthotics if needed.
• Perform respiratory therapy as indicated for enhanced elimination of secretions. Train muscles of respiration for strength and endurance by breathing against mouthpiece that applies inspiratory resistance.
• Initiate exercises that progressively increase in difficulty from passive to active assistive to active exercise as tolerated. Avoid fatigue. In the early stages, only one or two repetitions are indicated. Begin strengthening and aerobic exercises, but not to overexertion.
• Instruct client in modification of ADLs as needed. Include weight shifting, rolling, bed mobility skills, and transfer training. Teach client pressure relief techniques to avoid skin breakdown.
• Consider gait training with assistive devices as indicated.
• Assess needs for adaptive equipment for home environment.
• Instruct client in wheelchair independence if indicated.
• Reassess status frequently.

PRECAUTIONS/CONTRAINDICATIONS
• Limit physical activity in the acute phase to avoid exacerbating symptoms.
• Avoid overexertion during assessment.
• Be alert for signs of autonomic dysreflexia (sudden increase in blood pressure), orthostatic hypotension, or deep-vein thrombosis.

EXPECTED OUTCOME/PROGNOSIS
• The client will avoid secondary problems of contractures and decubitis ulcers.
• The client will return to normal activities of daily living.
  Maximal paralysis usually peaks at 1 to 3 weeks after onset. Approximately 30% of clients experience residual weakness at 3 years post onset.

REFERENCES

ASSESSMENT

Functional Level

Barthel Index
Mahoney BI, Barthel DW. Functional evaluation: the Barthel Index. *Maryland State Medical Journal.* 1965;14:61–65.
Wade DT, Collin C. The Barthel ADL Index: a standard measure of physical disability? *International Disability Studies.* 1988;10:2:64–67.

PULSES Profile
Granger CV, Albrecht GL, Hamilton BB. Outcome of comprehensive medical rehabilitation: measurements by PULSES profile and the Barthel Index. *Archive of Physical Medicine and Rehabilitation.* 1979;60:145–154.
Moskowitz RW, McCann CB. Classification of disability in the chronically ill and aging. *Journal of Chronic Disease.* 1957;5:342–346.

Strength
Daniels L, Worthingham C. *Muscle Testing Techniques of Manual Examination.* Philadelphia, Pa: WB Saunders Co; 1972.
Kendall FP, McCreary EK, Provance PG. *Muscles: Testing and Function.* 4th ed. Baltimore, Md: Williams & Wilkins; 1993.

TREATMENT
Bethlem J, Knobbout CE. *Neuromuscular Disease.* Oxford, England: Oxford University Press; 1987:44.
Karni Y, Archdeacon L, Mills KR, Wiles CM. Clinical assessment and physiotherapy in Guillain–Barre syndrome. *Physiotherapy.* 1984;70:288–292.
Umphred DA. *Neurological Rehabilitation.* 2nd ed. St. Louis, Mo: CV Mosby Co; 1990.

Huntington's Disease

Also known as *Huntington's chorea.*

DESCRIPTION

Huntington's disease (HD) is a neurodegenerative disease characterized by choreiform movements and progressive dementia. Usually beginning in a client's 40s, it affects men and women at similar rates of 6.5 per 100,000 people.

CAUSE

HD is an inherited autosomal-dominant neurodegenerative disease. The abnormal Huntington gene has been located on the short arm of chromosome 4.

ASSESSMENT

Areas
- History
- Communication
- Cognition, including orientation
- Posture
- Mobility
- Neurological, including sensation
- Skin and soft tissue
- Gait
- Functional level including activities of daily living (ADLs)
- Environmental needs

Instruments/Procedures (See References for Sources)

Functional Level
- Barthel Index
- PULSES Profile

PROBLEMS
- The client may have memory loss, cognitive impairment, and personality changes.
- There may be dysarthria and dysphagia.
- The gait is usually ataxic, with choreiform or choreoathetoid movements.
- In later stages, the client usually has rigidity and akinesia.

TREATMENT/MANAGEMENT
- Use range of motion (ROM) and strengthening exercises to promote joint stability.
- Offer facilitation and inhibition techniques.
- Biofeedback and relaxation techniques can be useful in the early stages of disease.
- At later stages of the disease, the choreiform movements of the mouth can be decreased with slow rocking and neutral warmth.
- Select adaptive equipment as needed for ADLs, or consult with an occupational therapist.
- Education and support are crucial, especially for family members and caregivers.

PRECAUTIONS/CONTRAINDICATIONS
- See Appendix C for contraindications for physical agents and modalities.

DESIRED OUTCOME/PROGNOSIS
- The client will have stabilized proximal joint musculature.
- The client will function at the highest level possible.

REFERENCES

ASSESSMENT

Environmental Assessment
Pawlson LG, Lewis CB. Dysmobility. In: Karpman RR, Baum J, ed. *Aging and Clinical Practice: Musculoskeletal Disorders: A Regional Approach.* New York, NY: IGAKU-SHOIN; 1988:127–142.

Functional Level

Barthel Index
Mahoney BI, Barthel DW. Functional evaluation: the Barthel Index. *Maryland State Medical Journal.* 1965;14:61–65.
Wade DT, Collin C. The Barthel ADL Index: a standard measure of physical disability? *International Disability Studies.* 1988;10:2:64–67.

PULSES Profile
Granger CV, Albrecht GL, Hamilton BB. Outcome of comprehensive medical rehabilitation: measurements by PULSES Profile and the Barthel Index. *Archives of Physical Medicine and Rehabilitation.* 1979;60:145–154.
Moskowitz RW, McCann CB. Classification of disability in the chronically ill and aging. *Journal of Chronic Disease.* 1957;5:342–346.

TREATMENT

Corcos DM. Strategies underlying the control of disordered movement. *Physical Therapy.* 1991;71:25–38.

Imbriglio S, Peacock IW. Huntington's disease at mid-stage. *Clinical Management in Physical Therapy.* 1992;12:5:62–72.

Peacock IW. A physical therapy program for Huntington's disease patients. *Clinical Management in Physical Therapy.* 1987;7:1:22–23,34.

Stelmach GE, Phillips JG. Movement disorders: limb movement and the basal ganglia. *Physical Therapy.* 1991;71:60–67.

van Vliet P, Wing AM. A new challenge: robotics in the rehabilitation of the neurologically motor impaired. *Physical Therapy.* 1991;71:39–47.

Late Effects of Poliomyelitis

Also known as *late motor neuron degeneration, postpolio progressive muscular atrophy, postpolio muscular atrophy, postpolio sequelae, chronic anterior poliomyelitis,* and *forme fruste amyotrophic lateral sclerosis.*

DESCRIPTION

Late effects of poliomyelitis are symptoms that occur years after the onset of poliomyelitis, usually 30 to 40 years after. Twenty-five percent or more of clients who contracted polio during the poliomyelitic epidemics of the 1940s and 1950s are reporting new symptoms. Symptoms may include choking and dysphagia (problems swallowing), cold sensitivity, difficulty breathing, diminished endurance, fatigue, pain, psychological problems, and weakness.

CAUSE

The cause of late effects of polio is not fully established, but effects are triggered when remaining motor units become gradually more dysfunctional.

ASSESSMENT

Areas
- History, including medications and metabolic status
- Pain
- Posture
- Cardiovascular, including endurance to activities
- Pulmonary
- Mobility: active and passive range of motion (ROM)
- Motor function
- Strength
- Neurological, including sensation
- Skin and soft tissue
- Gait
- Functional level, including, but not limited to, activities of daily living (ADLs), bed mobility, sitting, transfers, and standing

- Equipment, including use of orthotics, appliances, and assistive devices, and environmental needs upon discharge
- Special tests to which the PT may or may not have access

Instruments/Procedures (See References for Sources)

Functional Level
- Barthel ADL Index
- PULSES profile

Motor Function
- motor unit estimating methodology

Mobility
- goniometry

Special Tests to Which the PT May or May Not Have Access
- electromyography (EMG)
- muscle biopsy
- nerve conduction studies
- serologic tests

Strength
- Cybex testing
- manual muscle testing

PROBLEMS
- The client usually reports a gradual pattern of fatigue that can be either generalized or localized but is most pronounced in the afternoon.
- The client may report diminished mental alertness.
- The client usually reports muscle weakness, especially in those muscles previously weakened.
- The client may notice muscular atrophy.
- The client may describe the appearance of fasciculations, especially in recently weakened muscles.
- The client usually has muscle pain often described as aching or cramping.
- The client usually has joint pain that is exacerbated by activity.
- The client may report intolerance to cold.
- The client's symptoms can interfere with ADLs such as walking, climbing stairs, and dressing.
- The client can have difficulty with breathing.
- The client can have difficulty with swallowing.

TREATMENT/MANAGEMENT
- Instruct client in lifestyle modifications such as energy conservation techniques and pacing activities with rest to reduce chronic overuse.
- Instruct in proper body mechanics.
- Assess and treat for any secondary musculoskeletal dysfunction.
- Prescribe orthotics for joints that are overstressed.

- Assess gait pattern, and perform gait training as indicated.
- Assess for partial or full-time use of wheelchair.
- Exercise: Promote activity as indicated. Prescribe supervised nonfatiguing exercise program if client is deconditioned due to disuse. Reduce overactivity if chronic overuse is exacerbating symptoms.
- Provide sources of psychosocial support and counseling to cope with new changes in symptoms.

PRECAUTIONS/CONTRAINDICATIONS
- Carefully monitor any exercise program.
- Encourage client to balance low-intensity exercise with rest.

DESIRED OUTCOME/PROGNOSIS
- The client will function at optimal level.
- Therapy will provide optimal joint function.

One report says clients may see increase in muscle strength through resistance exercise that is nonfatiguing. The report cautions, however, that muscles should be tested every 3 months to ensure that the muscles are not undergoing overwork weakness. The influence of chronic overuse on weakness and pain is not fully understood. No research was found to support conventional muscle strengthening programs.

REFERENCES

ASSESSMENT
Peach PE. Late effects of poliomyelitis. In: Fletcher GF, Banja JD, Jann BB, Wolf SL. *Rehabilitation Medicine: Contemporary Clinical Perspectives*. Philadelphia, Pa: Lea & Febiger; 1992:128–135. **[Spinal cord examination]**

Functional Level

Barthel Index
Mahoney BI, Barthel DW. Functional evaluation: the Barthel Index. *Maryland State Medical Journal*. 1965;14:61–65.
Wade DT, Collin C. The Barthel ADL Index: a standard measure of physical disability? *International Disability Studies*. 1988;10:2:64–67.

PULSES Profile
Granger CV, Albrecht GL, Hamilton BB. Outcome of comprehensive medical rehabilitation: measurements by PULSES profile and the Barthel index. *Archives of Physical Medicine and Rehabilitation*. 1979;60:145–154.
Moskowitz RW, McCann CB. Classification of disability in the chronically ill and aging. *Journal of Chronic Disease*. 1957;5:342–346.

Motor Function

Motor Unit Estimating Methodology
McComas AJ, Galea V, de Bruin H. Motor unit populations in healthy and diseased muscles. *Physical Therapy*. 1993;73:868–877.

Special Tests to Which the PT May or May Not Have Access
Peach PE. Late effects of poliomyelitis. In: Fletcher GF, Banja JD, Jann BB, Wolf SL. *Rehabilitation Medicine: Contemporary Clinical Perspectives*. Philadelphia, Pa: Lea & Febiger; 1992:128–135. **[EMG, muscle biopsy, nerve conduction study/electromyelogram, serologic tests]**

Strength

Cybex Testing
Peach PE. Late effects of poliomyelitis. In: Fletcher GF, Banja JD, Jann BB, Wolf SL, eds. *Rehabilitation Medicine: Contemporary Clinical Perspectives*. Philadelphia, Pa: Lea & Febiger; 1992:128–135.

Manual Muscle Testing
Daniels L, Worthingham C. *Muscle Testing Techniques of Manual Examination*. Philadelphia, Pa: WB Saunders Co; 1972.

Kendall FP, McCreary EK, Provance PG. *Muscles: Testing and Function*. 4th ed. Baltimore, Md: Williams & Wilkins; 1993.

TREATMENT
Babaniyi OA, Yeya-Agba B, Parakoyi DB. Monitoring impact of oral poliovirus vaccine on poliomyelitis trends from physiotherapy records, Ilorin, Nigeria, 1981–1988. *East African Medical Journal*. 1991;68:642–648.

Dean E. Clinical decision making in the management of the late sequelae of poliomyelitis. *Physical Therapy*. 1991;71:752–761.

Fillyaw MJ, Badger GJ, Goodwin GD, et al. The effects of long-term non-fatiguing resistance exercise in subjects with post-polio syndrome. *Orthopedics*. 1991;14:1253–1256.

Greetham CJ. Poliomyelitis among Afghan refugees. *Physiotherapy*. 1991;77:421–422.

Gross MT, Schuch CP. Exercise programs for patients with post-polio syndrome: a case report. *Physical Therapy*. 1989;69:72-76. (For published erratum, see *Physical Therapy*. 1989;69:301. For comments, see Dean E, Ross J, MacIntyre D. A rejoinder to "Exercise Programs for Patients With Post-Polio Syndrome: a case report." *Physical Therapy*. 1989;69:695–698; discussion, 698–699.)

Perry J, Barns G, Gronely JK. Post-polio muscle function. *Birth Defects*. 1987;23:315.

Twist DJ, Ma DM. Physical therapy management of the patient with post-polio syndrome: a case report. *Physical Therapy*. 1986;66:1403–1406.

Multiple Sclerosis

DESCRIPTION
Multiple sclerosis (MS) is a gradually progressive disease of the central nervous system. MS is also known as *disseminated sclerosis* due to disseminated spots of demyelination in the brain and spinal cord. The neurological problems reported by clients with MS demonstrate considerable variability. Women are affected slightly more frequently than men, with the age of onset occurring between 20 to 40.

CAUSE

Etiology is unknown, but MS is thought to be caused by an immunologic defect. There is also evidence suggesting genetic susceptibility. Environment may influence incidence, as MS occurs more frequently in temperate climates.

ASSESSMENT

Areas
- History, including medications and metabolic status
- Pain
- Posture
- Pulmonary
- Cardiovascular, including endurance to activities
- Mobility, including active and passive range of motion (ROM)
- Strength
- Spasticity
- Neurological, including sensation
- Skin and soft tissue, including open wounds
- Gait
- Functional level, including, but not limited to, activities of daily living (ADLs), bed mobility, sitting, transfers, and standing
- Equipment, including use of orthotics, appliances, and assistive devices, and environmental needs upon discharge

Instruments/Procedures (See References for Sources)

Functional Level/Disability
- Barthel Index
- Expanded Disability Scale (expansion of the Disability Status Scale [DSS])
- Functional Independence Measure (FIM)
- Katz Index of Activities of Daily Living
- Level of Rehabilitation Scale (LORS-II)
- Minimum Record of Disability (MRD)
- PULSES Profile

Mobility
- timed "up and go" test

Spasticity
- Wartenberg pendulum test
- Ashworth grading scale

PROBLEMS

The problems reported by clients with MS demonstrate considerable variability.
- The client usually reports persistent fatigue.
- The client usually reports visual disturbances. Specific disorders of diplopia, optic neuritis, scotoma, and nystagmus are common.
- The client usually has impaired bowel, bladder, and sexual function. Specifically, reports of urinary incontinence, retention, or urgency are common, along with sexual dysfunction.

- The client usually has muscle weakness that varies from mild to total paralysis (due to upper motor neuron [UMN] syndrome or disuse atrophy).
- The client usually reports altered sensations, such as a pins-and-needles sensation (paresthesia) or numbness. The client may report an electric-shock-like sensation triggered when the neck is flexed (L'hermitte's sign).
- Position sense and vibratory sense may be reduced.
- The client may report hypersensitivity to a minor stimulus or an abnormal burning or painful sensation.
- There can be severe facial pain.
- The client usually has spasticity that varies from mild to severe.
- The client can have intention tremors, varying in severity from mild to large involuntary movements, that usually interfere with functional activities.
- The client may demonstrate movement disorders like dysmetria, dysdiadochokinesia, and ataxia if the cerebellum is involved.
- The client may experience vestibular dysfunction such as balance impairment, dizziness, or vertigo.
- The client may demonstrate mental or behavioral impairment, usually ranging from mild to moderate disturbance of function.
- The client usually has difficulty with coordination of speech and swallowing musculature. Secondary problems may include
- cardiovascular deconditioning
- decreased respiratory endurance
- impaired mobility secondary to contractures
- osteoporosis with resultant fractures
- heterotopic ossification
- decubitus ulcers

TREATMENT/MANAGEMENT
- Provide sensory retraining for a client with diminished sensation. Techniques may include vigorous rubbing or tapping or use of alternate sensory systems to provide feedback. Biofeedback, for example, can provide alternate visual or auditory feedback.
- Provide education, care, and protection of desensitized areas through proper skin care.

Suggestions for Skin Care

Keep skin clean and dry.
Follow a proper diet with plenty of fluids.
Inspect skin a minimum of once each day.
Provide systematic pressure relief.
Prevention is key.

Source: Reprinted with permission from SB O'Sullivan and TJ Schmitz, *Physical Rehabilitation: Assessment and Treatment*, p. 459, © 1994, FA Davis & Company.

- Also, encourage client to change positions every 2 hours while in bed or every 15 minutes when in a wheelchair. Provide pressure-reducing assistive devices as needed.
- If a decubitus ulcer is present, provide cleansing and debridement of wound. Hydrotherapy and wound dressings are usually used to augment medical management of antibiotic therapy.

- Instruct in postural retraining and correction, using orthotic devices as needed.
- Secondary musculoskeletal pain may necessitate the use of modalities along with exercise and education.
- Treat spasticity with use of therapeutic exercise, modalities, and positioning. Modalities can include cold therapy. Provide stretching and ROM on land or in water. Relaxation techniques, selected proprioceptive neuromuscular facilitation (PNF) techniques like rhythmic initiation, neurodevelopment key points of control, or other techniques can be used to reduce tone. Positioning should include the use of postures that reduce tone. Facilitate the antagonist of the spastic muscle.
- Functional electrical stimulation and biofeedback procedures can be used to inhibit spasticity.
- The client should receive passive ROM several times a day; some references suggest at least daily for immobilized joints. Teach client active and active assistive ROM exercises.
- Consider use of splinting or casting to achieve optimal positioning.
- Consider use of manual passive stretching or prolonged static stretching if the contracture is severe.
- Exercise prescriptions will vary with each client's individual needs and can include resistive training with progressive resistance exercise or isokinetics. Tone reduction activities are more appropriate if spasticity overrides.
- Instruct client in energy conservation techniques. Offer a low-stimulation environment.
- Consider use of facilitation techniques such as PNF patterns, weights (with caution), Frenkl's exercises, stationary bike, and aquatic therapy to promote stability.
- Gait training: strengthen weakened areas, such as quadriceps; prescribe assistive devices and orthosis as needed, such as ankle-foot orthosis, or rocker shoes or modified Danish clogs, canes, crutches, or walkers.
- For functional impairments, prescribe adaptive equipment such as a wheelchair, with attention to proper pressure relief and devices, especially for toileting, eating, dressing, and communication activities.
- Instruct client in respiratory exercises.
- Direct client to group and individual support for psychological and social issues.

PRECAUTIONS/CONTRAINDICATIONS
- Avoid trauma to the skin.
- Transcutaneous electrical nerve stimulation (TENS) for pain relief with MS has produced varied results, with some clients experiencing an increase in symptoms.
- Avoid prolonged time in a static posture if the client has spasticity.
- For functional electrical stimulation to be considered, the client must have an intact reflex arc and intersegmental reciprocal relationship.
- Caution should be used when stretching muscles. Avoid overstretching.
- Clients with MS fatigue easily, so choose activities that can optimally achieve goals. It is contraindicated to exercise to fatigue.
- Avoid warm environments for exercise.

DESIRED OUTCOME/PROGNOSIS
- The client and family will be educated about the psychosocial aspects of MS and be provided support.
- The client will maintain or increase in ROM.
- The client will have increased sensory awareness.

- The client will be educated on skin care.
- The client will increase muscular strength and motor control.
- The client will experience decreased spasticity.
- The client will increase functional independence.
- The client will ambulate independently with assistive devices as needed.
  The course that MS follows is unpredictable and variable.

REFERENCES

ASSESSMENT

Functional Level

Barthel Index
Mahoney F, Barthel D. Functional evaluation: the Barthel Index. *Maryland State Medical Journal*. 1965;14:61–65.
Wade DT, Collin C. The Barthel ADL Index: a standard measure of physical disability? *International Disability Studies*. 1988;10:2:64–67.

Expanded Disability Scale (Expansion of the Disability Status Scale [DSS])
Kurtzke J. Rating neurological impairment in multiple sclerosis: an expanded disability status scale (EDSS). *Neurology*. 1983;33:1444.

Functional Independence Measure (FIM)
Granger CV, Cotter A, Hamilton BB, et al. Functional assessment scales: a study of persons with multiple sclerosis. *Archives of Physical Medicine and Rehabilitation*. 1990;71:870–875.
Granger CV, Hamilton BB, Keith RA, et al. Advance in functional assessment for medical rehabilitation. *Topics in Geriatric Rehabilitation*. 1986;1:3:59–74.
Keith RA, Granger CV, Hamilton BB, Sherwins FS. The Functional Independence Measure. *Advances in Clinical Rehabilitation*. 1987;1:6–18.

Katz Index of Activities of Daily Living
Benjamin Rose Hospital Staff. Multidisciplinary studies of illness in aged persons: II. A new classification of functional status in activities of daily living. *Journal of Chronic Disease*. 1959;9:55–62.
Brorsson B, Ashberg KH. Katz Index of Independence in ADL: reliability and validity in short-term care. *Scandinavian Journal of Rehabilitation Medicine*. 1984;16:125–132.

Level of Rehabilitation Scale (LORS-II)
Carey RG, Posavac EJ. Program evaluation of a physical medicine and rehabilitation unit: a new approach. *Archives of Physical Medicine and Rehabilitation*. 1978;59:330–337.
Carey RG, Posavac EJ. *Manual for the Level of Rehabilitation Scale II*. Park Ridge, Ill: Lutheran General Hospital; 1980.

Minimum Record of Disability (MRD)
Haber A, LaRocca N, eds. *Minimal Record of Disability for Multiple Sclerosis*. New York, NY: National Multiple Sclerosis Society; 1985. **[Includes subscales of Incapacity Status Scale (ISS) and Environmental Status Scale (ESS)]**

PULSES Profile
Granger CV, Albrecht GL, Hamilton BB. Outcome of comprehensive medical rehabilitation: measurements by PULSES Profile and the Barthel Index. *Archives of Physical Medicine and Rehabilitation*. 1979;60:145–154.

Moskowitz RW, McCann CB. Classification of disability in the chronically ill and aging. *Journal of Chronic Disease*. 1957;5:342–346.

Mobility

Timed "Up and Go" Test

Podsiadlo D, Richardson S. The timed "up and go": a test of basic functional mobility for frail elderly persons. *Journal of the American Geriatric Society*. 1991;39:142–148.

Spasticity

De Souza LH, Musa I. The measurement and assessment of spasticity. *Clinical Rehabilitation*. 1987;1:89–96.

Leslie GC, Muir C, Part N, Roberts RC. A comparison of the assessment of spasticity by the Wartenberg pendulum test and the Ashworth grading scale in patients with multiple sclerosis. *Clinical Rehabilitation*. 1992;6:41–48.

Strength

Footh WK. Clinical observations: patterns of muscle weakness in patients with multiple sclerosis. *Clinical Management in Physical Therapy*. 1983;3:3:32–34.

TREATMENT

Ashburn A, De Souza LH. An approach to the management of multiple sclerosis. *Physiotherapy Practice*. 1988;4:139–145.

Bohannon RW. Physical rehabilitation in neurologic diseases. *Current Opinion in Neurology*. 1993;6:765–772.

Brosseau L, Philippe P, Methot G, Duquette P, Haraoui B. Drug abuse as a risk factor of multiple sclerosis: case-control analysis and a study of heterogeneity. *Neuroepidemiology*. 1993;12:1:6–14.

Costello E, Alexander J. Physical and surgical therapy. In: Scheinberg LC, Holland NJ, eds. *Multiple Sclerosis: A Guide for Patients and Their Families*. 2nd ed. New York, NY: Raven Press; 1987:79–107.

De Souza LH. A different approach to physiotherapy for multiple sclerosis patients. *Physiotherapy*. 1984;70:429–432.

De Souza LH. *Multiple Sclerosis: Approaches to Management*. New York, NY: Chapman & Hall; 1990:34–53.

De Souza LH, Simpson KE. Therapy oriented self-help groups for people with multiple sclerosis. *Physiotherapy Practice*. 1985;1:1:23–26.

Fawcett J, Sidney JS, Hanson MJ, Riley-Lawless K. Use of alternative health therapies by people with multiple sclerosis: an exploratory study. *Holistic Nursing Practice*. 1994;8:2:36–42.

Gehlsen GM, Grigsby SA, Winanat DM. Effects of an aquatic fitness program on the muscular strength and endurance of patients with multiple sclerosis. *Physical Therapy*. 1984;64:653–657.

Livesley E. Effects of electrical neuromuscular stimulation on functional performance in patients with multiple sclerosis. *Physiotherapy*. 1992;78:914–917.

Madonna MG, Holland NJ, Wiesel-Levison P. The value of physical therapy in improving gait in multiple sclerosis: a research design. *Rehabilitation Nursing*. 1985;10:5:32–34.

Menendez P. Evaluation and prescription for wheelchairs and seating. In: Myers RS, ed. *Saunders Manual of Physical Therapy Practice*. Philadelphia, Pa: WB Saunders Co; 1995:419–425.

O'Sullivan SB, Schmitz TJ, eds. *Physical Rehabilitation: Assessment and Treatment*. Philadelphia, Pa: FA Davis Co; 1994:451–471.

Shaw CA. Spasticity: its functional implication in multiple sclerosis. *Axon*. 1988;9:4:63–65.

Szorbor A. Treatment of multiple sclerosis. *Therapia Hungarica*. 1989;37:2:67–82.

Parkinson's Disease

Also known as *paralysis agitans* and *shaking palsy*.

DESCRIPTION

Parkinson's disease is a gradually progressive degenerative disease of the central nervous system (CNS). It is characterized by tremor at rest, postural instability, ridigity, and bradykinesia. The mean age of onset is 57, but an earlier onset, even in childhood, is possible.

CAUSE

Parkinson's disease can be caused by a depletion of the pigmented neurons in the brain stem dopaminergic cell groups, such as the substantia nigra, which leads to a loss of dopamine. Dopamine loss or interference can also occur in the basal ganglia secondary to degenerative disease, metabolic conditions, medications, or toxins. Structural lesions, hematoma, or hydrocephalus can also lead to parkinsonism. Parkinson's disease can also be idiopathic.

ASSESSMENT

Areas
- History, including medications and metabolic status
- Communication, including dysarthria
- Pain
- Posture
- Pulmonary
- Cardiovascular, including endurance to activities
- Mobility: active and passive range of motion (ROM)
- Motor control, including tone (resting and dynamic), rigidity, reflexes (tonic reflexes, righting reflexes, equilibrium responses), balance and postural reactions, and active movement control, including strength, coordination, patterned movement, and isolated movement
- Neurological, including sensation
- Skin and soft tissue, including edema or open wounds
- Gait
- Functional level, including, but not limited to, activities of daily living (ADLs), bed mobility, sitting, transfers, and standing
- Equipment, including use of orthotics, appliances, and assistive devices, and environmental needs upon discharge
- Special tests to which the PT may or may not have access

Instruments/Procedures (See References for Sources)

Functional Level
- Barthel Index
- Functional Independence Measure (FIM)
- Kate Index of ADLs
- PULSES Profile

Gait
- gait and balance examination
- stopwatch test

Mobility
- timed "up and go" test

Motor Control
1. balance
   - Berg Balance Assessment
   - gait and balance examination
2. rigidity
   - isokinetic dynamometry
   - joint angular stiffness (torque to joint-angle ratio) as an index of rigidity
   - relaxed oscillation test

Special Tests to Which the PT May or May Not Have Access
- electromyography (EMG)

PROBLEMS

- The client usually has trouble balancing when standing, walking, or turning. Falls are common. There may be an absence of equilibrium and righting responses and diminished associated reaction.
- The client usually has a delay in initiating movement, or akinesia, and demonstrates a decreased speed of execution of movement, or bradykinesia. This bradykinesia can lead to a severe freezing of movement.
- The client usually complains of rigidity, either a jerky, "cogwheel" type or a constant, "lead pipe" type.
- The client may demonstrate tremor, especially with a "pill-rolling" motion of the hand. Tremors can also appear in the tongue, lips, jaw, and feet.
- The client usually complains of fatigue.
- The client may be unable to perform two or more simultaneous movements.
- The hypokinesia, or poverty of movement, common to clients usually leads to a deviated gait pattern that is slow and shuffling. Festination, or an abnormal increase in walking speed in order to avoid falling forward, is typical.
- A masklike facial expression is common.
- The client can have impaired swallowing.
- The client usually has dysarthria, or impaired speech.
- The client can have orthostatic hypotension and low blood pressure.
- The client may demonstrate dementia.
- Perceptual motor deficits may appear.
- The client may experience a sensory loss or abnormal sensation. Autonomic dysfunction may also occur.
- The deconditioning common to clients can lead to musculoskeletal problems such as kyphosis, osteoporosis, muscular atrophy, and decreased ROM, leading to contracture. Other musculoskeletal abnormalities, such as scoliosis, can limit postural control.
- Circulatory changes such as edema and decubitus ulcers can also occur.

TREATMENT/MANAGEMENT
- Provide education related to the disorder to the client and family.
- Prescribe appropriate exercise, such as walking or bicycling, for cardiovascular conditioning.
- Provide activities that are progressively more complex, such as weight shifting on a mat and then on a gymnastic ball, to promote balance.
- Instruct client in exercises for mobility that promote functional movement patterns. Activities should stress postural control and can engage multiple body segments simultaneously, such as patterns found in proprioceptive neuromuscular facilitation (PNF).
- Gait training techniques used may include
  1. high stepping with alternating dorsiflexion of ankle with support
  2. weight shifting
  3. cues on floor for step length or width
  4. blocks on floor to promote floor clearance
  5. wooden support in hand of both client and therapist to promote reciprocal arm swing
  6. music to promote rhythm
  7. weights or orthotic support for balance
  8. PNF patterns for coordination
  9. use of treadmill to provide multisensory and mechanical input
- Encourage group support activities.
- Teach client ROM exercises that can be performed several times a day and continue with home ROM exercise program, with or without adaptive equipment.
- Utilize gentle rocking and rhythmic techniques to promote relaxation, and teach self-care relaxation techniques such as Jacobsen's progressive relaxation.
- Instruct client in deep-breathing respiratory exercises.
- Provide training in ADLs, and prescribe assistive devices as indicated.
- Explore the use of complex response speeds, directions, and amplitudes in varied environmental situations to elicit the ability to adapt.
- Vary timing and intensity of stimuli, especially auditory or visual, given before movement to stimulate change in client's motor response.

PRECAUTIONS/CONTRAINDICATIONS
- No excessive stretching or painful stretching activities.
- Remember when planning ROM activities, that the client with Parkinson's disease may also have undiagnosed osteoporosis.
- High levels of resistance are contraindicated for clients with increased tone.

DESIRED OUTCOME/PROGNOSIS
- The client will have functional ROM.
- The client will not develop contractures.
- The client will demonstrate correct posture.
- The client will be aware of safety factors related to impaired balance reactions.
- The client will ambulate with a functional gait pattern.
- The client will maintain or improve respiratory capacity.
- The client will maintain or improve speech function.
- The client will improve energy level and cardiovascular endurance.
- The client will maintain or improve independence in activities of daily living.

- The client and family will be assisted in psychological adjustment to a chronic illness. Neuromuscular control of the ankle is critical to functional gait.

REFERENCES

ASSESSMENT

Bain PG, Findley LJ, Atchinson P, et al. Assessing tremor severity. *Journal of Neurology, Neurosurgery, and Psychiatry.* 1993;56:868–873. **[Severity of Tremor: Clinical Rating Scale]**

O'Sullivan SB, Schmitz TJ, eds. *Physical Rehabilitation: Assessment and Treatment.* Philadelphia, Pa: FA Davis Co; 1994:477, 488–490. **[Hoehn-Yahr Classification of Disability Scale, Unified Parkinson's Disease Rating Scale]**

Communication

Dysarthria

Cammack S, Eisenberg MG, eds. *Key Words in Physical Rehabilitation: A Guide to Contemporary Usage.* New York, NY: Springer Publishing Co; 1995:45–47.

Functional Level

Barthel Index

Mahoney BI, Barthel DW. Functional evaluation: the Barthel Index. *Maryland State Medical Journal.* 1965;14:61–65.

Wade DT, Collin C. The Barthel ADL Index: a standard measure of physical disability? *International Disability Studies.* 1988;10:2:64–67.

Functional Independence Measure (FIM)

Granger CV, Hamilton BB, Keith RA, et al. Advance in functional assessment for medical rehabilitation. *Topics in Geriatric Rehabilitation.* 1986;1:3:59–74.

Keith RA, Granger CV, Hamilton BB, Sherwins FS. The Functional Independence Measure. *Advances in Clinical Rehabilitation.* 1987;1:6–18.

Katz Index of Activities of Daily Living

Benjamin Rose Hospital Staff. Multidisciplinary studies of illness in aged persons: II. A new classification of functional status in activities of daily living. *Journal of Chronic Disease.* 1959;9:55–62.

Brorsson B, Ashberg KH. Katz Index of Independence in ADL: reliability and validity in short-term care. *Scandinavian Journal of Rehabilitation Medicine.* 1984;16:125–132.

PULSES Profile

Granger CV, Albrecht GL, Hamilton BB. Outcome of comprehensive medical rehabilitation: measurements by PULSES Profile and the Barthel Index. *Archives of Physical Medicine and Rehabilitation.* 1979;60:145–154.

Moskowitz RW, McCann CB. Classification of disability in the chronically ill and aging. *Journal of Chronic Disease.* 1957;5:342–346.

Gait

American Physical Therapy Association. A guide to physical therapist practice, Volume I: a description of patient management. *Physical Therapy.* 1995;75:720–738.

Bowes SG, Charlett A, Dobbs RJ, et al. Gait in relation to aging and idiopathic parkinsonism. *Scandinavian Journal of Rehabilitation Medicine.* 1992;24:181–186.

Franklyn S. User's guide to the physiotherapy assessment form for Parkinson's disease. *Physiotherapy.* 1986;72:359–361.

Schenkman M, Butler RB. A model for multisystem evaluation treatment of individuals with Parkinson's disease. *Physical Therapy.* 1989;69:932–943.

O'Sullivan SB, Schmitz TJ, eds. *Physical Rehabilitation: Assessment and Treatment.* Philadelphia, Pa: FA Davis Co; 1994:479. **[Stopwatch test]**

Mobility

Timed "Up and Go" Test

Podsiadlo D, Richardson S. The timed "up and go": a test of basic functional mobility for frail elderly persons. *Journal of the American Geriatric Society.* 1991;39:142–148.

Motor Control

Balance

Berg Balance Assessment

Berg K, Maki B, Williams JI, et al. Clinical and laboratory measures of postural balance in an elderly population. *Archives of Physical Medicine and Rehabilitation.* 1992;73:1073–1083.

Berg K, Wood-Dauphinee S, Williams JI, Gayton D. Measuring balance in the elderly: preliminary development of an instrument. *Physiotherapy Canada.* 1989;41:304–311.

Gait and Balance Examination

American Physical Therapy Association. A guide to physical therapist practice, Volume I: a description of patient management. *Physical Therapy.* 1995;75:720–738.

Rigidity

Mortimer JA, Webster DD. Evidence for a quantitative association between EMG stretch responses and Parkinsonian rigidity. *Brain Research.* 1979;162;169-173. **[Joint angular stiffness (torque to joint-angle ratio)]**

Oatis CA. The use of a mechanical model to describe the stiffness and damping characteristics of the knee joint in healthy adults. *Physical Therapy.* 1993;73:740–749. **[Relaxed oscillation test]**

O'Sullivan SB, Schmitz TJ, eds. *Physical Rehabilitation: Assessment and Treatment.* Philadelphia, Pa: FA Davis Co; 1994:479. **[Isokinetic dynamometry]**

VanDillen LR, Roach KE. Interrater reliability of a clinical scale of rigidity. *Physical Therapy.* 1988;68:1679–1681.

Special Tests to Which the PT May or May Not Have Access

EMG

Traub MM, Rothwell JC, Marsden CD. Anticipatory postural reflexes in Parkinson's disease and other akinetic-rigid syndromes and in cerebellar ataxia. In: Lister MJ, ed. *Contemporary Management of Motor Control Problems: Proceedings of the II STEP Conference.* Fredricksburg, Va: Foundation for Physical Therapy; 1991:195–208.

TREATMENT

Ada L, Canning C. *Key Issues in Neurological Physiotherapy.* Boston, Mass: Butterworth-Heinemann; 1990.

Bagley S, Kelly B, Tunnicliffe N, Turnbull GI, Walker JM. The effect of visual cues on the gait of independently mobile Parkinson's disease patients. *Physiotherapy.* 1991;77:415–420.

Bohannon RW. Physical rehabilitation in neurologic disease. *Current Opinion Neurology.* 1993;6:765–772.

Brown R, Frith C. Some psychological factors relevant to physiotherapy in patients with Parkinson's disease. *Physiotherapy.* 1986;72:335–337.

Burford K. The physiotherapist's role in Parkinson's disease. *Geriatric Nursing and Home Care.* 1988;8:1:14–16.

Carpenter JR. Physical Therapy. In: Hutton JT, Dippel RL, eds. *Caring for the Parkinson Patient: A Practical Guide.* Buffalo, NY: Prometheus Books; 1989:81–96.

Chan J, Lee J, Neubert C. Physiotherapy intervention in Parkinsonian gait. *New Zealand Journal of Physiotherapy.* 1993;21:1:23–28.

Coles JA. The drug treatment of Parkinson's disease. *Physiotherapy.* 1986;72:338–339.

Corcos DM. Strategies underlying the control of disordered movement. *Physical Therapy.* 1991;71:25–38.

Crossley SM. Intensive physiotherapy for Parkinson's disease in a holiday environment. *Physiotherapy.* 1986;72:383–384.

Formisano R, Pratesi L, Modarelli FT, Bonifati V, Meco G. Rehabilitation and Parkinson's disease. *Scandinavian Journal of Rehabilitation Medicine.* 1992;24:3:157–160.

Franklyn S. An introduction to physiotherapy for Parkinson's disease. *Physiotherapy.* 1986;72:379–380.

Gibberd FB. The clinical findings and pathology in Parkinson's disease. *Physiotherapy.* 1986;72:333–335.

Gibberd FB, Page NGR, Spencer KM, et al. Controlled trial of physiotherapy and occupational therapy for Parkinson's disease. *British Medical Journal.* 1981;282:1196.

Glendinning DS, Enoka RM. Motor unit behaviour in Parkinson's disease. *Physical Therapy.* 1994;74:61–70.

Handford F. The Flewitt–Handford exercises for Parkinsonian gait. *Physiotherapy.* 1986;72:382.

Handford F. Parkinsonian gait. *Physiotherapy.* 1986;72:341–342.

Homberg V. Motor training in the therapy of Parkinson's disease. *Neurology.* 1993;43:12(suppl 6):45–46.

Horak FB, Diener HC, Nashner LM. Influence of central set on human postural response. *Journal of Neurophysiology.* 1989;62:841–853.

Horak FB, Nashner LM, Nutt JG. Postural instability in Parkinson's disease: motor coordination and sensory organization. *Society for Neuroscience Abstracts.* 1984;10:634.

Kinnear E. Long-term management of Parkinson's disease. *Physiotherapy.* 1986;72:340–341.

Kinsman R. Video assessment of the Parkinson patient. *Physiotherapy.* 1986;72:386–389.

Kinsman R, Verity R, Waller J. A conductive education approach for adults with neurological dysfunction. *Physiotherapy.* 1988; 74:227–230.

Krasilovsky G, Gianutsos J. Effect of video feedback on the performance of a weight shifting controlled tracking task in subjects with parkinsonism and neurologically intact individuals. *Experimental Neurology.* 1991;113:192–201.

Mackaylyons M, Turnbull G. Physical therapy in Parkinson's disease. *Neurology.* 1995;45:1:205.

McNiven DR. Rotational impairment of movement in the Parkinsonian patient. *Physiotherapy.* 1986;72:381–382.

Pai YC, Rogers MW. Control of body mass transfer as a function of speed of ascent in sit-to-stand. *Medicine and Science in Sports and Exercise.* 1990;22:378–384.

Palmer SS, Martimer JA, Webster DO, Bisterin R, Dickson, DL. Exercise therapy in Parkinson's disease. *Archives of Physical Medicine and Rehabilitation.* 1986;67:741.

Rogers MW. Control of posture and balance during voluntary movements in Parkinson's disease. In: Duncan PW, ed. *Balance.* Alexandria, Va: American Physical Therapy Association; 1990:79–86.

Rogers MW. Motor control problems in Parkinson's disease. In: Lister MJ, ed. *Contemporary Management of Motor Control Problems: Proceedings of the II STEP Conference.* Fredricksburg, Va: Foundation for Physical Therapy; 1991:195–208.

Rogers MW, Chan CWY. Motor planning is impaired in Parkinson's disease. *Brain Research.* 1986;386;183–196.

Rogers MW, Kukulka CG, Soderberg GL. Postural adjustments preceding rapid arm movements in Parkinsonian subjects. *Neuroscience Letters.* 1987;75:246–251.

Schenkman M, Butler RB. A model for multisystem evaluation treatment of individuals with Parkinson's disease. *Physical Therapy.* 1989;69:932–943.

Schenkman M, Donovan J, Tsubota J, et al. Management of individuals with Parkinson's disease: rationale and case studies. *Physical Therapy.* 1989;69:944–955.

Stelmach GE, Phillips JG. Movement disorders: limb movement and the basal ganglia. *Physical Therapy.* 1991;71:60–67.

Szekely BC, Kosanovich NN, Sheppard W. Adjunctive treatment in Parkinson's disease: physical therapy and comprehensive group therapy. *Rehabilitation Literature.* 1982;43:72–76.

Turnbull GI. *Physical Therapy Management of Parkinson's Disease.* New York, NY: Churchill Livingstone; 1992.

van Vliet P, Wing AM. A new challenge: robotics in the rehabilitation of the neurologically motor impaired. *Physical Therapy.* 1991;71:39–47.

Weissenborn S. The effect of using a two-step verbal cue to a visual target above eye level on the Parkinsonian gait: a case study. *Physiotherapy.* 1993;79:26–31.

Whitney SL, Blatchly CA. Dizziness and balance disorders. *Clinical Management in Physical Therapy.* 1991;11:1:42–44.

Winter DA. Concerning the scientific basis for the diagnosis of pathological gait and for rehabilitation protocols. *Physiotherapy Canada.* 1985;37:245–252.

Yekutiel MP. Patients' fall records as an aid in designing and assessing therapy in Parkinsonism. *Disability and Rehabilitation.* 1993;15:4:189–193.

Peripheral Nerve Injury

DESCRIPTION

Peripheral nerve injury leads to sensory and motor loss at the involved site. Peripheral nerve injuries can be divided into three categories:

- *Neuropraxia* is a transient paralysis and sensory loss at a point of localized blockage. There may be nerve conduction above and below the lesion. Motor function may be more affected than sensory function.
- *Axonotmesis* results from Wallerian degeneration below the level of injury. However, the Schwann nerve sheath is left intact. After Wallerian degeneration, axons regrow to corresponding end organs. Deficit depends on the number of axons affected.
- *Neurotmesis* is a total disruption of axon and nerve sheath, with no conduction below the level of the lesion.

CAUSE

- Neuropraxia is caused by a crushing injury or by compression disorders.
- Axonotmesis is caused by stretch or compression of the axon. It may be a progressive result of chronic neuropraxia.
- Neurotmesis is caused by a cut separating the axon and epineurium that eliminates conduction.

ASSESSMENT

Areas

- History, including medications and metabolic status

- Pain
- Motor function, including nerve conduction testing until day 21, strength duration curve after the 21st day
- Strength
- Neurological, including sensation, proprioception, temperature, touch, and two-point discrimination
- Skin and soft tissue
- Mobility: range of motion (ROM)
- Functional level
- Equipment, including appliances and assistive devices, and environmental needs upon discharge
- Special tests to which the PT may or may not have access

Instruments/Procedures (See References for Sources)

Functional Level
- Functional Independence Measure
- Katz Index of Activities of Daily Living

Special Tests to Which the PT May or May Not Have Access
- modality tests and quantitative assessment
- motor unit estimating methodology

Strength
- manual muscle testing

PROBLEMS

General Problems
- The client may have paralysis with no tone.
- The client usually has muscular atrophy.
- There can be contracture of uninvolved muscle groups.
- There is usually loss of sensation and proprioception.
- There can be localized inability to sweat.
- The client can have localized hair loss.
- The client can have poor wound healing.
- The client's skin will usually demonstrate change in temperature.
- The client's nails are often brittle.

Specific Nerve Lesions

Axillary Nerve Lesion
- There is usually atrophy or flattening of the shoulder area.
- The client complains of inability to abduct or elevate the arm.

Median Nerve
- There is usually an "ape-hand" or "monkey" deformity, with thumb lying on the same plane as the hand.
- There is thenar eminence atrophy.

- There is loss of the ability to use indicating gesture; flexion of index finger along with partial inability to flex middle finger.
- There is loss of precision grip.
- There is usually loss of proprioception on the radial aspect of the hand.

Ulnar Nerve
- The hand assumes a clawing position, with hyperextension of fourth and fifth metacarpophalangeal joints and interphalangeal joint flexion.
- There is fifth-finger abduction.
- There is atrophy of the hypothenar eminence and interossei.
- The client complains of a weakened power grip.
- There is loss of finger precision movements.

Radial Nerve Injury
- There is atrophy of forearm extensor muscles.
- There is wrist drop.
- The client reports inability to put objects on a flat surface.
- The client complains of loss of flexor grip.

Common Peroneal Nerve
- The client has foot drop.
- There is a high-stepping gait.
- There is equinovarus foot positioning.

TREATMENT/MANAGEMENT
- Stimulate circulation with massage, elevation, and general exercise.
- Perform ROM activities as indicated with passive, active assistive, and active movements.
- Stimulate strength in both affected and unaffected musculature with balance activities, active exercise, resistive exercise, aquatic therapy, and neuromuscular facilitation techniques. Motor training can be used post tendon transfer.
- Provide sensory re-education or desensitization.
- Promote functional training.
- Prescribe splints as indicated. Usually the affected area is immobilized for 3 to 4 weeks. In general, a static splint is used to provide stability, whereas a dynamic splint is used to enhance mobility. A cock-up splint, with or without an outrigger, is used for a radial nerve injury. A thumb opponens splint is used for a median nerve injury. A dorsal-based splint is used for an ulnar nerve injury.
- With neurotomesis, surgical repair is necessary for healing. During weeks 1 to 3 postsurgically, maintain circulation and promote activity in unaffected areas. During weeks 3 to 8 postsurgically, perform ROM within prescribed limits and increase strength in unaffected musculature.

PRECAUTIONS/CONTRAINDICATIONS
- When using a splint, be especially alert for possible skin breakdown if sensation is impaired.

DESIRED OUTCOME/PROGNOSIS

Nerve Regeneration
- Identify extent of loss of return and functional ability.

- The client will maintain or improve ROM.
- The client will maintain or increase circulation.
- The client will increase strength.
- Provide sensory re-education.
- The client will improve in function.
  In cases of neuropraxia, the client will usually recover in 6 weeks.
  In cases of axonotmesis, recovery is usually good, but time depends on lesion location and length between injury site and receptors or muscle.
  In cases of neurotmesis, recovery is variable. Recovery of function depends on axon recovery.

REFERENCES

ASSESSMENT

Functional Level

Functional Independence Measure
Granger CV, Hamilton BB, Keith RA, et al. Advance in functional assessment for medical rehabilitation. *Topics in Geriatric Rehabilitation.* 1986;1:3:59–74.
Keith RA, Granger CV, Hamilton BB, Sherwins FS. The Functional Independence Measure. *Advances in Clinical Rehabilitation.* 1987;1:6–18.

Katz Index of Activities of Daily Living
Benjamin Rose Hospital Staff. Multidisciplinary studies of illness in aged persons: II. A new classification of functional status in activities of daily living. *Journal of Chronic Disease.* 1959;9:1:55–62.
Brorsson B, Ashberg KH. Katz Index of Independence in ADL: reliability and validity in short-term care. *Scandinavian Journal of Rehabilitation Medicine.* 1984;16:125–132.

Special Tests to Which the PT May or May Not Have Access
Wadsworth CT. Elbow, forearm, wrist, and hand. In: Myers R, ed. *Saunders Manual for Physical Therapy Practice.* Philadelphia, Pa: WB Saunders Co; 1995:911. **[Modality tests and quantitative assessment]**
McComas AJ, Galea V, de Bruin H. Motor unit populations in healthy and diseased muscles. *Physical Therapy.* 1993;73:868–877. **[Motor unit estimating methodology]**

Strength
Daniels L, Worthingham C. *Muscle Testing Techniques of Manual Examination.* Philadelphia, Pa: WB Saunders Co; 1972.
Kendall FP, McCreary EK, Provance PG. *Muscles: Testing and Function.* 4th ed. Baltimore, Md: Williams & Wilkins, 1993.

TREATMENT
Doucette SA, Goble EM. The effect of exercise on patellar tracking in lateral patellar compression syndrome. *American Journal of Sports Medicine.* 1992;20:434–440.
Lee JM. *Aids to Physiotherapy.* 2nd ed. New York, NY: Churchill Livingstone; 1988:58–65.
Silliman JF, Dean MT. Neurovascular injuries to the shoulder complex. *Journal of Orthopaedic and Sports Physical Therapy.* 1993;18:442–448.
Wadsworth CT. Elbow, forearm, wrist, and hand. In: Myers RS, ed. *Saunders Manual for Physical Therapy Practice.* Philadelphia, Pa: WB Saunders Co; 1995:911.

Reflex Sympathetic Dystrophy

Also known as *sympathetically maintained pain, shoulder hand syndrome, post-traumatic dystrophy, post-traumatic neuralgia, Sudeck's atrophy,* and *minor causalgia.*

DESCRIPTION
Reflex sympathetic dystrophy (RSD) is a neurovascular syndrome in which pain accompanies autonomic changes and/or dystrophic changes in skin and bone and can lead to contracture in an extremity. The pain with RSD exceeds the level expected by initial injury or disease. Pain may start immediately or in hours or weeks after the initial event.

RSD is three times more common in women than in men and usually afflicts clients age 35 to 60. Three stages appear with RSD: acute, dystrophic, and atrophic.

CAUSE
Etiology is unknown. Predisposing factors may include surgery, trauma (especially shoulder injury or injury to the lower extremity), lesions, neurological disorders, or neuropathy. Possible causes also include a defect between sympathetic efferent fibers and sensory afferent fibers, which leads to a cycle of additional sympathetic outflow and increased pain sensation.

ASSESSMENT

Areas
- History
- Pain
- Posture
- Skin and soft tissue, including edema, and any dystrophic changes such as skin atrophy or hair loss
- Mobility, including active range of motion (ROM)
- Strength
- Functional level, including activities of daily living (ADLs)

Instruments/Procedures (See References for Sources)

Pain
- Sickness Impact Profile
- McGill Pain Questionnaire
- Multidisciplinary Pain Inventory
- visual analogue scale

PROBLEMS
- The client usually complains initially of a burning pain; later it may be described as aching or crushing pain.
- In the upper extremity, the client usually has changes in the hand that include edema and a mottled, slightly cyanotic, appearance of the hand in the early stages. This is later replaced by warmth, reddening, and dryness of skin.
- In later stages, the client usually experiences atrophy, contracture, and trophic skin changes. The client usually has pain with motion and capsular restriction of all or most upper extremity joints in differing degrees.

- The client may have edema of the lower extremity if injured in this area.
- The client usually has dyesthesias, with pain and hypersensitivity to slight touch.
- After about 9 months, the client can experience a decrease in pain, but joint ankylosis, severe osteoporosis, and functional loss can occur.

TREATMENT/MANAGEMENT
- Educate client about skin protection.
- Work within pain-free range to increase ROM of shoulder and hand or, where indicated, use joint mobilization, muscle inhibition techniques, and soft tissue stretching.
- Begin movement with passive ROM, progressing to active assistive and then active movement.
- Encourage independence in movement. Encourage active muscle contraction via isotonic and isometric exercise.
- Use light weight-bearing activities. Begin progressive schedule of compression and traction with weight bearing on affected extremity. One suggested schedule starts with 3 to 5 minutes three times daily. Add traction, such as carrying a weight in hand, for 10 minutes three times daily. Increase compression and traction forces as indicated.
- Set up a home program for ROM, ADLs, and general conditioning.
- Consider use of ice for pain.
- Consider use of intermittent pneumatic compression or elevation and elastic compression for edema.
- Alter feedback loop by encouraging hypostimulation with relaxation techniques and biofeedback, or try hyperstimulation with environmental changes such as contrast baths or spray-and-stretch techniques.
- Consider transcutaneous electrical nerve stimulation (TENS), using conventional mode first. You may need to try a variety of treatment parameters with electrode placement and setting parameters.
- Modalities may also include contrast baths, massage, and electrical stimulation.
- Work with attending physician on rehabilitation plan following nerve block.

PRECAUTIONS/CONTRAINDICATIONS
- Exercise caution when using physical agents and modalities due to trophic changes. See Appendix C for contraindications.

DESIRED OUTCOME/PROGNOSIS
- The client will have an increase in circulation.
- The client will have a decrease in pain.
- The areas involved will be desensitized in order to promote autonomic homeostasis.

Preventative measures include frequent active exercise of uninvolved joints with elevation of extremity as well.

Condition may resolve spontaneously but can linger for months or even years.

Early assessment and treatment are critical to break the pain cycle of RSD. Prognosis is improved if treatment begins at least 6 months from onset.

Pain associated with RSD is a definitive, physically driven pain, as opposed to cases of chronic pain, in which the pain is often poorly localized.

REFERENCES

ASSESSMENT

Pain

Cammack S, Eisenberg MG, eds. *Key Words in Physical Rehabilitation: A Guide to Contemporary Usage.* New York, NY: Springer Publishing Co; 1995:91.

Headley BJ. Chronic pain management. In: O'Sullivan SB, Schmitz TJ, eds. *Physical Rehabilitation.* 3rd ed. Philadelphia, Pa: FA Davis Co; 1994:577–602. **[Sickness Impact Profile, McGill Pain Questionnaire, Multidisciplinary Pain Inventory, Visual Analogue Scale]**

TREATMENT

Bilkey AJ. Screening for psychological disorders. In: Boissonnault WG, ed. *Examination in Physical Therapy Practice.* New York, NY: Churchill Livingstone; 1991:250.

Burkman K, Tanner ED. Shoulder pain. In: Kaplan PE, Tanner ED, eds. *Musculoskeletal Pain and Disability.* East Norwalk, Conn: Appleton & Lange; 1988:111–112, 125.

Gersch MR. Reflex sympathetic dystrophy syndrome: a model for the multidisciplinary management of patients with pain. *Physical Therapy Practice.* 1993;2:3:34–44.

Gobelet C, Waldburger M, Meier JL. The effect of adding calcitonin to physical treatment on reflex sympathetic dystrophy. *Pain.* 1992;48:171–175.

Headley BJ. Historical perspective of causalgia: management of sympathetically maintained pain. *Physical Therapy.* 1987;67:1370.

Headley BJ. Chronic pain management. In: O'Sullivan SB, Schmitz TJ, eds. *Physical Rehabilitation.* 3rd ed. Philadelphia, Pa: FA Davis Co; 1994:577–602.

Hertling D, Kessler RM. *Management of Common Musculoskeletal Disorders.* Philadelphia, Pa: JB Lippincott Co; 1990:259–261.

Kisner C, Colby LA. *Therapeutic Exercise: Foundations and Techniques.* 2nd ed. Philadelphia, Pa: FA Davis Co; 1990:259–260.

Lawrence LM. Musculoskeletal changes in chronic pain patients. In: France RD, Krishnan KRR, eds. *Chronic Pain.* Washington, DC: American Psychiatric Press, Inc; 1988:245–255.

Mullins PA. Management of common chronic pain problems in the hand. *Physical Therapy.* 1989;69:1050–1058.

Reddy MP. Bilateral shoulder-hand syndrome associated with phenobarbital administration: a case report. *Physical Therapy.* 1985;65:201–202.

Wadsworth CT. Elbow, forearm, wrist, and hand. In: Myers RS, ed. *Saunders Manual of Physical Therapy Practice.* Philadelphia, Pa: WB Saunders Co; 1995:887–888.

Wattay E. Reflex sympathetic dystrophy syndrome. *Clinical Management in Physical Therapy.* 1989;9:1:28.

Stroke

Also known as *cerebrovascular accident* or *cerebrovascular disease.*

DESCRIPTION

Cerebrovascular disease leads to vascular injury of the brain due to interruption of cerebral circulation followed by neurologic disability. Cerebrovascular disease can be divided into four main types: arteriovenous malformation, cerebral insufficiency (ischemia), hemorrhage, and infarction.

Stroke usually refers to an ischemic lesion. A *stroke in evolution* refers to an enlarging infarction with neurological deficits that increase over a period of 24 to 48 hours. A *completed stroke* refers to an infarction of brain tissue of abrupt onset followed by neurological defects of variable outcome but stable symptoms.

CAUSE

A stroke can occur in conjunction with other diseases, but cerebrovascular disease is usually due to hypertension, atherosclerosis, or both. The mechanisms involved in causing the stroke include embolism, hemorrhage secondary to trauma or aneurysm, and thrombus. Major risk factors for cerebrovascular disease include diabetes, heart disease, high blood pressure, cigarette smoking, and transient ischemic attacks (TIAs). A TIA is a sudden, brief dysfunction of the arterial system. Secondary risk factors include elevated cholesterol and lipid levels, excessive alcohol consumption, obesity, and physical inactivity.

ASSESSMENT

Areas

- History, including medications and metabolic status
- Psychosocial, including depression and family support
- Vision
- Communication, including aphasia
- Cognition
- Pain
- Posture, including sitting, standing, and supine positions and any asymmetry
- Cardiovascular, including blood pressure, heart rate, endurance, and any vascular compromise
- Pulmonary, if indicated
- Urogenital, including incontinence
- Skin and soft tissue, including edema or pressure sores
- Mobility, including active and passive range of motion (ROM)
- Joint integrity, including any shoulder subluxation
- Motor control, including tone (resting and dynamic); reflexes (tonic reflexes, righting reflexes, equilibrium responses); balance and postural reactions; hemiplegia and active movement control components, such as strength, coordination, patterned movement, and isolated movement
- Neurological, including proprioception, sensation, DTRs, Babinski, and clonus; kinesthesia, level of consciousness (if indicated)
- Functional level, including activities of daily living (ADLs), bed mobility, sitting, transfers, standing, and use of wheelchair
- Gait
- Equipment, including use of orthotics, appliances, and assistive devices, and environmental assessment of needs upon discharge
- Health status

Instruments/Procedures (See References for Sources)

References with an asterisk are the preferred standard instruments for patient assessment in stroke.

Balance
- Berg Balance Assessment*
- adaptability measures
- balance response to external displacement
- balance response to volitional movement
- sway excursion
- verticality measures
- Clinical Test for Sensory Interaction on Balance (CTSIB)
- functional reach
- postural control evaluation
- "Get up and go" test
- Tinetti test

Cognition
- Activity Index
- Folstein Mini-Mental State Examination*
- Neurobehavioural Cognition Status Exam (NCSE)*

Communication
- Boston Diagnostic Aphasia Examination*
- Boston Naming Test
- Communicative Abilities in Daily Living Test
- Functional Communication Profile
- Promoting Aphasic's Communicative Effectiveness (PACE)
- Minnesota Test for Differential Diagnosis of Aphasia
- Porch Index of Communicative Ability (PICA)*
- Token Test
- Western Aphasia Battery*

Disability
- Chedoke–McMaster Stroke Assessment (Chedoke), to be used in conjunction with Uniform Data System for Medical Rehabilitation (UDS)
- Functional Autonomy Measurement System (SMAF)
- Rankin Scale* and modified Rankin Scale
- NIH Stroke Scale*
- World Health Organization International Classification of Impairment, Disability and Handicap

Functional Level
1. Action Research Arm Test
2. Acute Care Index for Function
3. ADLs: Activity Index
   - Barthel Index
   - Frenchay Activities Index*
   - Katz Index of ADLs
   - Kenny Self-Care Evaluation
   - Klein–Bell ADL scale
   - PGC Instrumental Activities of Daily Living*
   - Rivermeade ADL Assessment
4. Functional Index Measure (FIM; a component of Uniformed Data System for Medical Rehabilitation)*

5. Level of Rehabilitation Scale (LORS-II)—revision of LORS-I
6. Patient Evaluation Conference System (PECS); a modification of PECS is the Clinical Outcome Variable Scale [COVS])
7. PULSES Profile
8. Geriatric assessments
   - Lawton's Activities of Daily Living Scale
   - Older Americans Resources & Services (OARS) Multidimensional Functional Assessment Questionnaire
   - Functional Life Scale
   - Philadelphia Geriatric Center Multilevel Assessment Instrument

Gait
- Functional Ambulation Profile (FAP)
- gait analysis
- Gait Assessment Rating Sheet (GARS)
- Tinetti test

Health Status
- Medical Outcomes Study (MOS) 36-Item Short-Form Health Survey*
- Sickness Impact Profile (SIP)*

Mobility
- goniometry
- Rivermeade Mobility Index*
- timed "up and go" test

Motor Control and Muscular Performance
1. General
   - Activity Index
   - manual muscle testing
   - Motoricity Index Score*
   - Motor Assessment Scale*
   - Modified Motor Assessment Scale (MMAS)
2. Hemiplegia
   - Bobath and modified Bobath methods of assessment of postural and movement patterns
   - Brunnstrom method of assessment
   - Fugl-Meyer Assessment (FMA; expansion of Brunnstrom)*
3. Tone
   - Ashworth Scale of Muscle Spasticity
   - isokinetic dynamometer
   - myometer

Neurological
- Canadian Neurological Scale*
- Glasgow Coma Scale*

Psychosocial
1. depression
   - Beck Depression Inventory (BDI)*
   - Center for Epidemiologic Studies—Depression (CES-D)*

- Geriatric Depression Scale (GDS)*
- Hamilton Depression Scale*
2. family support
  - Family Assessment Device (FAD)*

Vision
- visual scanning test

PROBLEMS

Psychosocial
- The client may have poststroke mood disorder, especially depression (more with left-hemisphere injury), emotional lability, irritability, confusion, and, if multiple infarcts have occurred, dementia.

Vision
- Visual defects, such as loss of depth perception and homonymous hemiannopsia, or visual field defect, commonly accompany hemiplegia. There may also be forced gaze deviation.

Communication
- The client can have communication impairment. Aphasia, or acquired communication disorder, is usually associated with left hemispheric lesion (right hemiplegia).
- The client can also have dysarthria, or impairment of speech production.

Cognition
- The client can have cognitive deficits. Deficits can affect orientation, attention span, ability to process information, conceptualizing ability, memory, and activity tolerance.
- The client may demonstrate perceptual deficits. These include distorted body image, unilateral neglect, and visuospatial distortions like topographical disorientation.

Pain
- Knee pain can accompany any hyperextension with gait.
- The client often has shoulder subluxation and pain. Reflex sympathetic dystrophy may accompany the pain (see precautions).

Cardiovascular
- The client with cardiac disease may also demonstrate cardiac decompensation, along with deconditioning and limited exercise tolerance.
- Deep-venous thrombosis and pulmonary embolism may occur if the client is immobilized.

Urogenital
- The client may have bladder and bowel dysfunction.

Skin
- There may be edema and pain.

Mobility
- The client may have decreased ROM and joint contractures.

- The client usually has impaired mobility influenced by motor programming deficits. Functional ability impairment leads to difficulty with rolling, sitting, standing, gait (see "Common gait problems following stroke"), and ADLs.

Motor Control
- The client will usually have paresis or weakness.
- The client may have impairment of motor power. Hypotonicity is initially common and then replaced by hypertonicity, hyperreflexia, and mass patterns of movement.
- The client may have weak or absent muscle strength.
- The client may have ataxia, or incoordination.
- The client may have apraxia, or inability to perform purposive movements, usually associated with left hemispheric lesion (right hemiplegia).

Neurological
- The client usually has sensory impairment, without total loss, on hemiplegic side.
- The client may have symptoms of crossed anesthesia, defined as ipsilateral facial impairments with contralateral trunk and limb deficits, usually associated with brain stem lesions.
- The client may have proprioceptive loss. There can also be loss of superficial touch, along with pain and altered temperature sensation.
- The client may lose combined sensations such as two-point discrimination.
- Initial contralateral sensory loss may be followed by burning pain on the hemiplegic side, called thalamic syndrome.

Common Gait Problems Post Stroke

Trunk/pelvis
- weak hip extension
- flexion contracture
- lack of pelvic rotation with swing phase
- weak abdominals
- weak ankle flexor muscles

Hip
- adduction or flexon of hip during stance phase
- weak abductor muscles
- spasticity in adductors and quadriceps
- inadequate flexion during swing phase
- weak hip flexor, abdominal, and hip adductor muscles
- excess hip flexion
- possible circumduction, external rotation, adduction, toe drag, during swing phase

Knee
- flexion during forward progression of stance phase
- hyperextension during forward progression of stance phase
- inadequate or delayed flexion at knee during swing phase
- weak knee extensors

Ankle
- equinus gait, in which heel does not touch the ground in stance phase
- varus foot
- unequal step lengths
- lack of dorsiflexion in stance phase
- exaggerated dorsiflexion in the swing phase

Source: Reprinted with permission from SB O'Sullivan and TJ Schmitz, *Physical Rehabilitation: Assessment and Treatment*, p. 342, © 1994, FA Davis & Company.

Comparison of Left and Right Hemiplegia

Right Hemiplegia
- Verbal communication difficulties, such as receptive or expressive or global aphasia
- Right visual field deficit
- Decreased computation (mathematics) skills
- Left/right confusion
- Deficits in memory
- Depression
- Motorapraxia

Left Hemiplegia
- Visual, perceptual deficits
- Left visual field deficit
- Distractable
- Denial of problem with left side of body
- Impulsive behavior
- Dressing apraxia
- Difficulty crossing midline of body

Source: Reed KL. *Quick Reference to Occupational Therapy.* Gaithersburg, Md: Aspen Publishers;1991:134.

TREATMENT/MANAGEMENT

Treatment Approaches

Recent theories and principles have led to revised treatment approaches for clients with neurological deficits. The main approaches used include the compensatory approach, the muscle re-education approach, the neurotherapeutic facilitation approach, and the contemporary task-oriented approach (also called motor control/motor learning). Many therapists use an integrated approach utilizing any or all of these various approaches depending on the individual needs of the client. General treatment considerations are listed here; see references for detailed treatment plans.

Compensatory Approach
- Focus on improving function instead of individual impairment by structuring task to be performed in a predictable environment.

Muscle Re-Education Approach
- Focus on individual muscle isolation of muscle action.
- Avoid secondary impairments.
- Teach client to avoid compensatory movement patterns.
- Teach functional activities.
- Use orthopedic supports as indicated.
- Increase strength of intact motor units.

Neurotherapeutic Facilitation Approach
- Provide proprioceptive input to facilitate normal movement patterns.
- Normalize tone.
- Break up abnormal synergies.
- Inhibit primitive reflexes and any abnormal tone.
- Prevent learning of abnormal movement patterns.
- Therapist provides hands-on sensory feedback to correct movement patterns.

Contemporary Task-Oriented Approach
- Teach client motor problem-solving skills appropriate to context needed.
- Explore effective compensation.
- Practice functional activities in varied environmental conditions, and vary the tasks performed.
- Encourage client to achieve task goals through problem solving and error detection. Allow client to make mistakes and analyze outcome.
- Use developmental sequence activities only in a manner appropriate to the clients' age and activity.
- Feedback should be task specific and designed to discourage overdependency of the client on the therapist.
- Posturing of extremities focuses on maintaining the necessary muscle length needed for ADLs using passive ROM or serial casting.

General Considerations in the Acute Stage

Positioning
- Prevent hip and knee contractures when client is on bed rest.
- Use egg-crate mattress for pressure relief.
- Client should be turned every 2 to 3 hours in early stage if on prolonged bed rest.
- Assume upright posture as soon as possible and when client is stable.
- Avoid pulling on weakened extremity.
- Protect hemiplegic shoulder from downward displacement through a scapular position of slight protraction and upward rotation.
- Arrange room to maximize the client's awareness of the hemiplegic side.

ROM
- Perform full ROM in all areas of deficit. Upper extremity motions should include external rotation of the arm and scapular mobilization and upward rotation during shoulder elevation activities.
- Assess for temporary use of sling.
- Consider use of neurotherapeutic facilitation to promote joint stability.
- Consider use of inflated pressure splint to promote optimal positioning and sensory re-education.

Mobility
- Encourage early mobilization, after the client is medically stable, to prevent secondary impairments like psychological problems, decreasing ROM, contracture and deformity, deep-venous thrombosis, pain, shoulder dysfunction, and deconditioning.
- Encourage use of both sides of the body.
- Encourage client to participate actively in movement as soon as possible.
- Concentrate on functional activities like rolling, sitting up, bridging, standing, and transfers.
- Consider use of extremity movement patterns to improve rolling.
- Encourage weight-bearing activity on the hemiplegic side.
- Upright activities should promote stability, followed by controlled mobility and then dynamic balance challenges.
- Promote normalization of chewing, expressive, respiratory, and swallowing functions.

General Considerations During the Postacute Stage
Provide education about the disease and the rehabilitation program for client and family. Offer counseling in the areas of need, including recreational, psychological, sexual, and vocational counseling. Provide discharge planning.

Motor Control
- Stress function that is meaningful to client.
- Incorporate bilateral activities when possible.
- Mental rehearsal of activities may be indicated.
- Encourage movement patterns that are out of synergy, and permit completion of functional tasks.
- Inhibit unwanted muscle activity.
- Select postures that promote desired motion, and reduce any unwanted excess in tone or interference from reflexes. Progress to more challenging postures.
- Activate muscles in a variety of patterns and situations.
- Emphasize a balanced interaction between agonists and antagonists.
- Use stimuli to facilitate hypotonia; exteroceptive, proprioceptive, and reflex stimulation techniques can be considered.
- Continue static control and balance activities started in acute stage.
- Promote control of upper extremity and lower extremity.
- Initiate gait training early. Consider use of assistive device.
- Identifiy and correct specific movement deficits.
- Advanced gait training emphasizes selective movement control combined with normal timing. Practice gait activities in varied directions and on surfaces.
- Practice elevation activities.
- Consider use of an orthosis, most often an ankle-foot orthosis.
- Control knee problems by adjustment of ankle position.
- Continue functional training in ADLs.
- Establish cardiovascular conditioning program for those who are candidates.
- Consider use of isokinetic training to stimulate improved lower extremity reciprocal movement during gait activities.
- Consider use of neuromuscular electrical stimulation (NMES) to facilitate voluntary motor control or functional electrical stimulation (FES) to re-establish normal joint alignment.
- Consider use of biofeedback to improve motor function.

Sensory Loss
- Encourage use of affected side.
- Present repeated sensory stimuli, such as stretch, stroking, deep and superficial pressure, along with weight bearing.
- Utilize localization of touch.
- Consider electrical stimulation to activate sensorimotor response.
- Avoid adverse effects with excessive intensity.
- Consider use of pressure splints or in severe cases, intermittent pressure therapy.
- Educate client on issue of anesthetic limbs.

PRECAUTIONS/CONTRAINDICATIONS

Positions To Avoid

1. Lateral side flexion of the head and trunk toward the affected side with head rotation toward the unaffected side
2. Depression and retraction of the scapula, internal rotation and adduction of the arm, elbow flexion and forearm pronation, wrist and finger flexion
3. Retraction and elevation of the hip, with hip and knee extension and hip adduction; or hip and knee flexion with hip abduction. Ankle plantarflexion is common to both.

Source: Reprinted with permission from SB O'Sullivan and TJ Schmitz, *Physical Rehabilitation: Assessment and Treatment*, p. 343, © 1994, FA Davis & Company.

- Overhead pulleys are usually contraindicated for self ROM to avoid shoulder impingement or rotator cuff injury.
- Monitor circulation when using sling, especially figure-eight harness-type sling. Sling is often contraindicated with spasticity.
- Watch for depression, and refer for psychological/psychiatric support as indicated. Client may need medical treatment for depression.
- Generally, it is advisable to arrange the room to maximize the client's awareness of the hemiplegic side, but this strategy is contraindicated with clients who have unilateral neglect or anosognosia because this may actually stimulate withdrawal.

DESIRED OUTCOME/PROGNOSIS
- The client will be aware of and use the hemiplegic side.
- The client will be functionally mobile.
- The client will be independent with ADLs.
- The client will have adequate cardiopulmonary endurance.
- The client will maintain ROM and prevent deformity.
- The client will regain oromotor function.
- The client will have postural control, balance, and control of elective movements.
- The client will engage in socialization activities.
- Secondary complications will be prevented.

Studies report improved functional outcome and increased independence after physical therapy, but no single optimal approach has been identified. Approximately 75% to 85% of clients are discharged back home. Clients who generally do not respond well to rehabilitation efforts include those with the following problems:

- diminished alertness and ability to learn
- severe anosognosis
- severe medical complications
- severe language impairment

Approximately 30% of stroke victims die in the acute phase. Of those who survive, approximately 30% to 40% are left with severe disability.

Early diagnosis of reflex sympathetic dystrophy (RSD) is critical to optimal outcome. Watch for swelling and tenderness of hand and fingers and accompanying shoulder pain. The skin may appear red and glossy and be warm to touch, with fingernails appearing white or opaque. In later stages of the problem, the skin turns cool, cyanotic, and contracted.

The first 6 weeks to 2 months is generally the period of optimal spontaneous recovery for speech abilities.

Clients with thalamic syndrome generally have a poor functional outcome.

REFERENCES

ASSESSMENT

Campbell SK. Measurement in developmental therapy: past, present, and future. In: Miller LJ, ed. *Developing Norm-Referenced Standardized Tests.* New York, NY: Haworth Press Inc; 1989:1–13. [**Standardized testing**]

Lennon S. Using standardised scales to document outcome in stroke rehabilitation. *Physiotherapy.* 1995;81:200–202.

Cognition

Folstein Mini-Mental State Examination

Folstein MF, Folstein SE, McHugh PR. "Mini-Mental State": a practical method for grading the cognitive state of patients for the clinician. *Journal of Psychiatric Research.* 1975;12:189–198.

Neurobehavioural Cognition Status Exam (NCSE)

Kiernan RJ, Mueller J, Langston JW, Van Dyke C. The Neurobehavioral Cognitive Status Examination: a brief but differentiated approach to cognitive assessment. *Annals of Internal Medicine.* 1987;107:481–485.

Communication

Cammack S, Eisenberg MG, eds. *Key Words in Physical Rehabilitation: A Guide to Contemporary Usage.* New York, NY: Springer Publishing Co; 1995:26. [**Boston Diagnostic Aphasia Examination, Boston Naming Test, Communicative Abilities in Daily Living Test, Functional Communication Profile, PACE, Minnesota Test for Differential Diagnosis of Aphasia, Porch Index of Communicative Ability (PICA), Token Test, Western Aphasia Battery**]

Disability

Ashburn A. A physical assessment for stroke patients. *Physiotherapy.* 1982;68:109–113.

Ashburn A. Methods of assessing the physical disabilities of stroke patients. *Physiotherapy Practice.* 1986;2:2:47–51.

Chedoke–McMaster Stroke Assessment

Gowland C, Stratford P, Ward M, Moreland J, Torresin W. Measuring physical impairment and disability with the Chedoke–McMaster Stroke Assessment. *Stroke.* 1993;24:1:58–61.

NIH Stroke Scale
Brott T, Adams HP, Olinger CP, et al. Measurements of acute cerebral infarction: a clinical examination scale. *Stroke*. 1989;20:864–870.

Rankin and Modified Rankin Scales
Bonita R, Beaglehoe R. Recovery of motor function after stroke. *Stroke*. 1988;19:1497–1500. **[Modified Rankin Scale]**
Rankin J. Cerebral vascular accidents in patients over the age of 60. *Scottish Medical Journal*. 1957;2:200–215. **[Rankin Scale]**

World Health Organization International Classification of Impairments, Disabilities, and Handicaps (WHO-ICIDH)
International Classification of Impairments, Disabilities and Handicaps. World Health Organization; Geneva, Switzerland: 1980.

Functional Level

Action Research Arm Test
Carrol D. A quantitative test of upper extremity function. *Journal of Chronic Disability*. 1965;18:479–491.
DeWeerdt WJG, Harrison MA. Measuring recovery of arm-hand function in stroke patients: a comparison of the Brunnstrom–Fugl-Meyer test and the action research arm test. *Physiotherapy Canada*. 1985;37:65–70.
Lyle RC. A performance test for assessment of upper limb function in physical rehabilitation treatment and research. *International Journal of Rehabilitation Research*. 1981;4:483–492.

Acute Care Index for Function
Roach KE, Van Dillen LR. Development of an acute care index of functional status for patients with neurologic impairment. *Physical Therapy*. 1988;68:1102–1108.
Van Dillen LR, Roach KE. Reliability and validity of the Acute Care Index for Function for patients with neurologic impairment. *Physical Therapy*. 1988;68:1098–1101.

ADLs
Bohannon RW, Learey KM, Cooper J. Independence in floor-to-stand transfers soon after stroke. *Topics in Geriatric Rehabilitation*. 1995;11:1:6–9.
Chiou IF, Burnett CN. Values of activities of daily living: a survey of stroke patients and their home therapists. *Physical Therapy*. 1985;65:901–806.

Activity Index
Stott DH, Moyes FA, Henderson SE. *Test of Motor Impairment*. Guelph, Ontario: Brook Educational Publishing Ltd; 1972.

Barthel Index
DeWeerdt WJG, Harrison MA. Measuring recovery of arm-hand function in stroke patients. *Physiotherapy Canada*. 1985;37:65–70.
DeWeerdt W, Harrison M, Smith P, et al. The Nottingham Balance Platform: a practical application of microcomputers in physiotherapy. *Physiotherapy Practice*. 1988;4:1:9–17.
Mahoney BI, Barthel DW. Functional evaluation: the Barthel Index. *Maryland State Medical Journal*. 1965;14:61–65.
Partridge C, Edwards S. Recovery curves as a basis for evaluation. *Physiotherapy*. 1988;74:141–143.
Wade DT, Collen FM, Rob GF, Warlow CP. Physiotherapy intervention late after stroke and mobility. *British Medical Journal*. 1992;304:609–613.
Wade DT, Collin C. The Barthel ADL Index: a standard measure of physical disability? *International Disability Studies*. 1988;10:2:64–67.

Frenchay Activities Index
Holbrook M, Skilbeck CE. An activities index for use with stroke patients. *Age and Aging.* 1983;12:166–170.

Katz Index of Activities of Daily Living
Ashberg KH, Nydevik I. Early prognosis of stroke outcome by means of Katz Index of Activities of Daily Living. *Scandinavian Journal of Rehabilitation Medicine.* 1991;23:187–191.
Benjamin Rose Hospital Staff. Multidisciplinary studies of illness in aged persons: II. A new classification of functional status in activities of daily living. *Journal of Chronic Disease.* 1959;9:55–62.
Brorsson B, Ashberg KH. Katz Index of Independence in ADLL reliability and validity in short-term care. *Scandinavian Journal of Rehabilitation Medicine.* 1984;16:125–132.

Kenny Self-Care Evaluation
Donaldson SW, Wagner CC, Gresham GE. A unified ADL evaluation form. *Archives of Physical Medicine and Rehabilitation.* 1973;54:175–179.
Grodeon EE, Drenth V, Jarvis L, et al. Neurophysiologic syndromes in stroke as predictors of outcomes. *Archives of Physical Medicine and Rehabilitation.* 1978;59:399–409.
Kerner JF, Alexander J. Activities of daily living: reliability and validity of gross versus specific ranges. *Archives of Physical Medicine and Rehabilitation.* 1981;62:161–166.

Klein–Bell Activities of Daily Living
Klein RM, Bell B. Self-care skills: behavioural measurement with Klein–Bell ADL Scale. *Archives of Physical Medicine and Rehabilitation.* 1982;63:335–338.
Klein RM, Bell B. *Klein-Bell Activities of Daily Living Scales.* 1979. Seattle, Wa: University of Washington Medical School Health Sciences Resource Center, 56.

PGC Instrumental Activities of Daily Living
Lawton MP. Assessing the competence of older people. In: Kent D, Kastenbaum R, Sherwood S, eds. *Research Planning and Action for the Elderly.* New York, NY: Behavioral Publications; 1972.

Rivermeade ADL Assessment
Lincoln N, Edmans JA. A re-validation of the Rivermeade ADL scale for elderly patients with stroke. *Age and Aging.* 1990;19:19–24.

Functional Index Measure (FIM)
Cammack S, Eisenberg MG, eds. *Key Words in Physical Rehabilitation: A Guide to Contemporary Usage.* New York, NY: Springer Publishing Co; 1995:53–54, 57–58. **[FIM, functional assessment, and functional limitation]**
Granger CV, Hamilton BB, Keith RA, et al. Advance in functional assessment for medical rehabilitation. *Topics in Geriatric Rehabilitation.* 1986;1:3:59–74.
Hamilton BB, Granger CV. Disability outcomes following inpatient rehabilitation for stroke. *Physical Therapy.* 1994;74:494-503.
Keith RA, Granger CV, Hamilton BB, Sherwin FA. The Functional Independence Measure: a new tool for rehabilitation. *Advances in Clinical Rehabilitation.* 1987;1:6–18.
Seitz RH, Allred KE, Backus ME, Hoffman JA. Functional changes during acute rehabilitation in patients with stroke. *Physical Therapy.* 1987;67:1685–1690.
Smith ME, Garraway WM, Smith DL, Akhtar AJ. Therapy impact on functional outcome in a controlled trial of stroke rehabilitation. *Archives of Physical Medicine and Rehabilitation.* 1982;63:21–24.

Level of Rehabilitation Scale (LORS-II)
Carey RG, Posavac EJ. Program evaluation of a physical medicine and rehabilitation unit: a new approach. *Archives of Physical Medicine and Rehabilitation.* 1978;59:330–337.
Carey RG, Posavac EJ. *Manual for the Level of Rehabilitation Scale II.* Park Ridge, Ill: Lutheran General Hospital; 1980.

Patient Evaluation Conference System (PECS)

Harvey RF, Jellinek HM. Functional performance assessment: a program approach. *Archives of Physical Medicine and Rehabilitation.* 1981;62:456–461.

Korner-Bitensky N, Mayo N, Cabot R, et al. Motor and functional recovery after stroke: accuracy of physical therapists' predictions. *Archives of Physical Medicine and Rehabilitation.* 1989;70:95–99.

PULSES Profile

Granger CV, Albrecht GL, Hamilton BB. Outcome of comprehensive medical rehabilitation: measurements by PULSES Profile and the Barthel Index. *Archives of Physical Medicine and Rehabilitation.* 1979;60:145–154.

Moskowitz RW, McCann CB. Classification of disability in the chronically ill and aging. *Journal of Chronic Disease.* 1957;5:342–346.

Rivermeade Motor Assessment/Rivermeade Mobility Index

Collen FM, Wade DT, Robb GF, Bradshaw CM. The Rivermeade Mobility Index: a further development of the Rivermeade Motor Assessment. *International Disability Studies.* 1991;13:50–54.

Lincoln N, Leadbitter D. Assessment of motor function in stroke patients. *Physiotherapy.* 1979;15:48–51.

Wade DT, Collen FM, Robb GP, Warlow CP. Physiotherapy intervention late after stroke and mobility. *British Medical Journal.* 1992;304:609–613.

Geriatric Assessments

Jackson OL. Functional assessment of the aged. *Allied Health and Behavioral Sciences.* 1979;2:47. [**Lawton's Activities of Daily Living Scale, OARS Multidimensional Functional Assessment Questionnaire, Functional Life Scale, Philadelphia Geriatric Center Multilevel Assessment Instrument**]

Gait

Bogataj U, Gros N, Malezic M, et al. Restoration of gait during two to three weeks of therapy with multichannel electrical stimulation. *Physical Therapy.* 1989;69:319–327.

Craik RL, Oatis CA. Gait assessment in the clinic: issues and approaches. In: Rothstein JM, ed. *Clinics in Physical Therapy: Measurement in Physical Therapy.* New York, NY: Churchill Livingstone; 1985;47:169–206.

Holden MK, Gill KM, Magliozzi MR. Gait assessment for neurologically impaired patients: standards for outcome assessment. *Physical Therapy.* 1986;66:1530–1539.

Lemkuhl D, Smith L. *Brunnstrom's Clinical Kinesiology*, 4th ed. Philadelphia, Pa: FA Davis Co; 1984.

Musa I. Evaluation and re-education of gait following stroke. *Physiotherapy Practice.* 1986;2:2:63–73.

Olney SJ, Colborne GR, Martin CS. Joint angle feedback and biomechanical gait analysis in stroke patients: a case report. *Physical Therapy.* 1989;69:863–870.

Pathokinesiology Service Observational Gait Analysis. Downey, Calif: Rancho Los Amigos Medical Center; 1993.

Perry J. *Gait Analysis: Normal and Pathological Function.* Thorofare, NJ: Slack; 1992.

Functional Ambulation Profile (FAP)

Glaser L. Effects of isokinetic training on the rate of movement during ambulation in hemiparetic patients. *Physical Therapy.* 1986;66:673–676.

Nelson AJ. Functional Ambulation Profile. *Physical Therapy.* 1974;54:1059–1064.

Gait Assessment Rating Sheet (GARS)

Wolfson L, Whipple R, Amerman P, Tobin JN. Gait assessment in the elderly: a gait abnormality rating scale and its relation to falls. *Journal of Gerontology.* 1990;45:1:M12–M19.

Tinetti Test

Tinetti ME. Performance-oriented assessment of mobility problems in elderly patients. *Journal of the American Geriatric Society.* 1986;34:119–126.

Health Status

Medical Outcomes Study (MOS) 36-Item Short-Form Health Survey

Ware JE, Sherbourne CD. The MOS 36-Item Short-Form Health Survey (SF-36): I. Conceptual framework and item selection. *Medical Care.* 1992;30:473–483.

Sickness Impact Profile (SIP)

Bergner M, Bobbitt RA, Carter WB, et al. The Sickness Impact Profile: development and final revision of a health status measure. *Medical Care.* 1981;19:787–805.

Mobility

Goniometry

Andrews AW, Bohannon RW. Decreased shoulder range of motion on paretic side after stroke. *Physical Therapy.* 1989;69:768–772.

Norkin CC, White DJ. *Measurement of Joint Motion: A Guide to Goniometry.* Philadelphia, Pa: FA Davis Co; 1985.

Rivermeade Mobility Index

Collen FM, Wade DT, Robb GF, Bradshaw CM. The Rivermeade Mobility Index: a further development of the Rivermeade Motor Assessment. *International Mobility Studies.* 1991;13:50–54.

Timed "Up and Go" Test

Podsiadlo D, Richardson S. The timed "up and go": a test of basic functional mobility for frail elderly persons. *Journal of the American Geriatric Society.* 1991;39:142–148.

Motor Control

General

Manual Muscle Testing

Daniels L, Worthingham C. *Muscle Testing Techniques of Manual Examination.* Philadelphia, Pa: WB Saunders Co; 1986.

Kendall FP, McCreary EK, Provance PG. *Muscles: Testing and Function.* 4th ed. Baltimore, Md: Williams & Wilkins; 1993.

Motoricity Index Score

Collin C, Wade D, Bradshaw C. Mobility after stroke: reliability of measurements of impairment and disability. *International Disability Studies.* 1990;12:6.

Motor Assessment Scale

Carr JH, Shepherd RB, Nordholm L, Lynne D. Investigation of a new motor assessment scale for stroke patients. *Physical Therapy.* 1985;65:175–180.

Modified Motor Assessment Scale (MMAS)

Loewen SC, Anderson BA. Reliability of the Modified Motor Assessment Scale and the Barthel Index. *Physical Therapy.* 1988; 68:1077–1081.

Balance

Berg K, Maki B, Williams JI, et al. Clinical and laboratory measures of postural balance in an elderly population. *Archives of Physical Medicine and Rehabilitation.* 1992;73:1073–1083. **[Berg Balance Assessment]**

Berg K, Wood-Dauphinee S, Williams JI, Gayton D. Measuring balance in the elderly: preliminary development of an instrument. *Physiotherapy Canada.* 1989;41:304–311.

Cromwell S. Balance instability. In: Myers RS, ed. *Saunders Manual of Physical Therapy Practice*. Philadelphia, Pa: WB Saunders; 1995:376. **[Adaptability, balance response to external displacement, balance response to volitional movement, sway excursion, verticality]**

Duncan PW, Weiner DK, Chandler J, Studenski S. Assessing the influence of sensory interaction of balance. *Journal of Gerontology*. 1990;45:M192–M197. **[Functional reach]**

Flores AM. Objective measurement of standing balance. *Neurology Report*. 1992;16:1:17–21. **[Equipment]**

Goldie PA, Matyas TA, Spencer KL, McGinley RB. Postural control in standing following stroke: test-retest reliability of some quantitative clinical tests. *Physical Therapy*. 1990;70:234–243.

Mathias N, Nayak USL, Isaacs B. Balance in elderly patients: the "get-up and go" test. *Archives of Physical Medicine and Rehabilitation*. 1986;67:387. **["Up and go" test]**

Shumway-Cook A, Horak F. Assessing the influence of sensory interaction of balance. *Physical Therapy*. 1986;66:1548–1550. **[Clinical Test for Sensory Interaction on Balance (CTSIB)]**

Tinetti ME. Performance-oriented assessment of mobility problems in elderly patients. *Journal of the American Geriatric Society*. 1986;34:119–126. **[Tinetti test]**

Hemiplegia

Bohannon RW. Relative decreases in knee extension torque with increased knee extension velocities in stroke patients with hemiparesis. *Physical Therapy*. 1987;67:1218–1220.

Bohannon RW, Larkin PA, Smith MB, Horton MG. Relationship between static muscle strength deficits and spasticity in stroke patients with hemiparesis. *Physical Therapy*. 1987;67:1068–1071.

Bohannon RW, Smith MB. Assessment of strength deficits in eight paretic upper extremity muscle groups of stroke patients with hemiplegia. *Physical Therapy*. 1987;67:522–525.

Dickstein R, Hocherman S, Amdor G, Pillar T. Reaction and movement times in patients with hemiparesis for unilateral and bilateral elbow flexion. *Physical Therapy*. 1993; 73:374–380.

Dickstein R, Nissan M, Pillar T, Scheer D. Foot-ground pressure pattern of standing hemiplegic patients: major characteristics and patterns of improvement. *Physical Therapy*. 1984;64:19–23.

DiFabio RP, Badke MB. Relationship of sensory organization to balance function in patients with hemiplegia. *Physical Therapy*. 1990;70:542–548.

DiFabio RP, Badke MB. Stance duration under sensory conflict conditions in patients with hemiplegia. *Archives of Physical Medicine and Rehabilitation*. 1991;72:292–295.

LaVigne J. Hemiplegia sensorimotor assessment. *Physical Therapy*. 1974;54:128–134.

Rogers MW, Hedman LD, Pai Y. Kinetic analysis of dynamic transitions in stance support accompanying voluntary leg flexion movements in hemiparetic adults. *Archives of Physical Medicine and Rehabilitation*. 1993;74:19–25.

Rosecrance JC, Giuliani CA. Kinematic analysis of lower-limb movement during ergometer pedaling in hemiplegic and nonhemiplegic subjects. *Physical Therapy*. 1991;71:334–343.

Tripp EJ, Harris SR. Test-retest reliability of isokinetic knee extension and flexion torque measurements in persons with spastic hemiparesis. *Physical Therapy*. 1991;71:390–396.

Wagenaar RC, Beek WJ. Hemiplegic gait: a kinematic analysis using walking speed as a basis. *Journal of Biomechanics*. 1992;25:1007–1015.

Watkins MP, Harris BA, Kozlowski BA. Isokinetic testing in patients with hemiparesis: a pilot study. *Physical Therapy*. 1984;64:184–189.

Bobath and Modified Bobath Methods of Assessment

Arsenault AB, Dutil E, Lambert J, Corriveau H, Guarna F, Drowin G. An evaluation of the hemiplegic subject based on the Bobath approach, III: a validation study. *Scandinavian Journal of Rehabilitation Medicine*. 1988;20:13–16.

Bobath B. *Adult Hemiplegia: Evaluation and Treatment*. 2nd ed. London, England: William Heinemann Medical Books Ltd; 1978. **[Bobath method]**

Corriveau H, Guarna F, Dutil E, Riley E, Arsenault AB, Drowin G. An evaluation of the hemiplegic subject based on the Bobath approach, II: the evaluation protocol. *Scandinavian Journal of Rehabilitation Medicine*. 1988;20:5–11.

Guarna F, Corriveau H, Chamberland J, Arsenault AB, Dutil E, Drowin G. An evaluation of the hemiplegic subject based on the Bobath approach, I: the model. *Scandinavian Journal of Rehabilitation Medicine.* 1988;20:1–4.

Brunnstrom Method of Assessment

Brunnstrom S. Motor testing procedures in hemiplegia based on recovery stages. *Journal of American Physical Therapy Association.* 1966;46:357.

Duncan PW, Goldstein LB, Matchar D, et al. Measurement of motor recovery after stroke: outcome assessment and sample size requirements. *Stroke.* 1992;23:1084–1089.

Fugl-Meyer Assessment (FMA)

Fugl-Meyer AR, Jaasko L, Leyman I, et al. The post-stroke hemiplegia patient. I. A method for evaluation of physical performance. *Scandinavian Journal of Rehabilitation Medicine.* 1975;7:13–31.

Sanford J, Moreland J, Swanson LR, Stratford PW, Gowland C. Reliability of the Fugl-Meyer Assessment for testing motor performance in patients following stroke. *Physical Therapy.* 1993;73:447–454.

Spasticity

Bohannon RW. Variability and reliability of the pendulum test for spasticity using a Cybex II isokinetic dynamometer. *Physical Therapy.* 1987;67:659–661.

Bohannon RW, Larkin PA. Cybex II isokinetic dynamometer for the documentation of spasticity: suggestion from the field. *Physical Therapy.* 1985;65:46–47.

Bohannon RW, Smith MB. Interrater reliability of a modified Ashworth scale of muscle spasticity. *Physical Therapy.* 1987;67:206–207.

Dvir Z, Panturin E. Measurement of spasticity and associated reactions in stroke patients before and after physiotherapeutic intervention. *Clinical Rehabilitation.* 1993;7:1:15–21. **[isokinetic dynamometer]**

Livesley E. The intra-observer reliablity of the hand-held myometer in the measurement of isotonic muscle strength in chronic spasticity. *Physiotherapy.* 1992;78:918–921.

Neurological

Canadian Neurological Scale

Cote R, Hachinski VC, Shurvell BL, et al. The Canadian Neurological Scale: a preliminary study in acute stroke. *Stroke.* 1986;17:731–737.

Kinesthesia

Sartor-Glittenberg C, Powers R. Quantitative measurement of kinesthesia following cerebral vascular accident. *Physiotherapy Canada.* 1993;45:179–186.

Level of Consciousness

Glascow Coma Scale

Teasdale G, Jennett B. Assessment of coma and impaired consciousness: a practical scale. *Lancet.* 1974;2:81–83.

Teasdale G, Murray G, Parker L, Jennett B. Adding up the Glascow Coma Scale. *Acta Neurochirurgica.* 1979;28(suppl):13–16.

Psychosocial

Depression

Beck Depression Inventory (BDI)

Beck AT, Steer RA. *Beck depression inventory: manual.* rev ed. New York, NY: Psychological Corporation; 1987.

Beck AT, Ward CH, Mendelson M, Mock J, Erbaugh J. An inventory for measuring depression. *Archives of General Psychiatry.* 1961;4:561–571.

Center for Epidemiologic Studies—Depression (CES-D)
Radloff LS. The CES-D Scale: a self-report depression scale for research in the general population. *Journal of Applied Psychological Measures.* 1977;1:385–401.

Geriatric Depression Scale (GDS)
Yesavage JA, Brink TL, Rose TL, et al. Development and validation of a geriatric depression screening scale: a preliminary report. *Journal of Psychiatric Research.* 1982–1983;17:1:37–49.

Hamilton Depression Scale
Hamilton M. A rating scale for depression. *Journal of Neurology, Neurosurgery and Psychiatry.* 1960;23:56–62.
Hamilton M. Development of a rating scale for primary depressive illness. *British Journal of Social and Clinical Psychology.* 1967;6:278–296.

Family Support
Epstein NB, Baldwin LM, Bishop DS. The McMaster Family Assessment Device. *Journal of Marital and Family Therapy.* 1983;9:171–180.

Vision

Visual Scanning Test
Wagenaar RC, vanWieringen PC, Netelenbos JB, et al. The transfer of scanning training effects in visual inattention after stroke: five single-case studies. *Disability and Rehabilitation.* 1992;14:51–60.

TREATMENT

Ada L, Canning C, eds. *Key Issues in Neurological Physiotherapy.* London: Butterworth-Heinemann; 1990.
Axtell LA, Schoneberger MB. Physical therapy. In: Kemp B, Brummel-Smith K, Ramsdell JW, eds. *Geriatric Rehabilitation.* Boston, Mass: Little, Brown & Co; 1990:157–175.
Baker LL, Parker K. Neuromuscular electrical stimulation of the muscles surrounding the shoulder. *Physical Therapy.* 1986;66:1930–1937.
Basmajian JV, Gowland CA, Finlayson MAJ, et al. Stroke treatment of integrated behavioural physical therapy vs traditional physical therapy programs. *Archives of Physical Medicine and Rehabilitation.* 1987;68:267–272.
Bate PJ, Matyas TA. Negative transfer of training following brief practice of elbow tracking movements with electromyographic feedback from spastic antagonists. *Archives of Physical Medicine and Rehabilitation.* 1992;73:1050–1058.
Bethlem J, Knobbout CE. *Neuromuscular Diseases.* New York, NY: Oxford University Press; 1987.
Bobath B. *Abnormal Postural Reflex Activity Caused by Brain Lesions.* Rockville, Md: Aspen Publishers, Inc; 1985.
Bogataj U, Gros N, Malizic M, et al. Restoration of gait during two to three weeks of therapy with multichannel electrical stimulation. *Physical Therapy.* 1989;69:319–327.
Bohannon RW. Physical rehabilitation in neurologic disease. *Current Opinion in Neurology.* 1993;6:765–772.
Bruckner J. Design for a soft orthosis: suggestion from the field. *Physical Therapy.* 1985;65:1522–1523.
Caldwell C, MacDonald D, MacNeil K, et al. Symmetry of weight distribution in normals and stroke patients using digital weigh scales. *Physiotherapy Practice.* 1986;2:3:109–116.
Carr JH, Shepherd RB. *Physiotherapy in Disorders of the Brain.* Rockville, Md; Aspen Publishers, Inc; 1980.
Carr JH, Shepherd RB, eds. *A Motor Relearning Programme for Stroke.* Rockville, MD: Aspen Publishers, Inc; 1983.

Carr JH, Shepherd RB. A motor learning model for stroke rehabilitation. *Physiotherapy.* 1989;75:372–380.

Chan CWY. Motor and sensory deficits following a stroke: relevance to a comprehensive evaluation. *Physiotherapy Canada.* 1986;38:29–34.

Corcos DM. Strategies underlying the control of disordered movement. *Physical Therapy.* 1991;71:25–38.

Crisostoma EA, Duncan PW, Propst M, Dawson DV, Davis JN. Evidence that amphetamine with physical therapy promotes recovery of motor function in stroke patients. *Annals of Neurology.* 1988;23:94–97.

Delitto A, Snyder-Mackler L. Two theories of muscle strength augmentation using percutaneous electrical stimulation. *Physical Therapy.* 1990;70:158–164.

DeWeerdt W, Harrison MC. The efficacy of electromyographic feedback for stroke patients: a critical review of the main literature. *Physiotherapy.* 1986;72:108–118.

Dickstein R, Hocherman S, Pillar T, Shaham R. Stroke rehabilitation: three exercise therapy approaches. *Physical Therapy.* 1986;66:1233–1238.

Duncan PW. Stroke: physical therapy assessment and treatment. In: Lister MJ, ed. *Contemporary Management of Motor Control Problems: Proceedings of the II STEP Conference.* Alexandria, Va: Foundation for Physical Therapy; 1991:209–218.

Duncan PW, Badke MB, eds. Therapeutic strategies for rehabilitation of motor deficits. In: *Stroke Rehabilitation: The Recovery of Motor Control.* Chicago, Ill: Year Book Medical Publishers Inc; 1987:161.

Engardt M, Olsson E. Body weight-bearing while rising and sitting down in patients with stroke. *Scandinavian Journal of Rehabilitation Medicine.* 1992;24:67–74.

Engardt M, Ribbe T, Olsson E. Vertical ground reaction force feedback to enhance stroke patients' symmetrical body-weight distribution while rising/sitting down. *Scandinavian Journal of Rehabilitation Medicine.* 1993;25:41–48.

Ernst E. A review of stroke rehabilitation and physiotherapy. *Stroke.* 1990;21:1081–1085.

Ferguson J, Davis C. Group programs in physical therapy. *Clinical Management in Physical Therapy.* 1988;8:3:20–24.

Fletcher GF, Banja JD, Jann BB, Wolf SL, eds. *Rehabilitation Medicine: Contemporary Clinical Perspectives.* Philadelphia, Pa; Lea & Febiger; 1992.

Forster A, Young J. The role of community physiotherapy for stroke patients. *Physiotherapy.* 1990;76:495–497.

Gaimer JE. Development of a stroke support group. *Clinical Management in Physical Therapy.* 1986;66:26–29.

Gentile AM. Skill acquisition: action, movement, and neuromotor processes. In: Carr JH, Shepherd RB, Gordon J, et al, eds. *Movement Science: Foundations for Physical Therapy in Rehabilitation.* Rockville, Md: Aspen Publishers, Inc; 1987:93–154.

Giuliani CA. Understanding AHCPR Clinical Practice Guideline No. 16: post-stroke rehabilitation. *PT— Magazine of Physical Therapy.* 1995;3:10:51–83.

Gladman JR, Lomas S, Lincoln NB. Provision of physiotherapy and occupational therapy in outpatient departments and day hospitals for stroke patients in Nottingham. *International Disability Studies.* 1991;13:2:38–41.

Gordon JH. Assumptions underlying physical therapy intervention: theoretical and historical perspectives. In: Carr JH, Shepherd RB, Gordon J, et al, eds. *Movement Science: Foundations for Physical Therapy in Rehabilitation.* Rockville, Md: Aspen Publishers Inc; 1987:1–30.

Gowland C, deBruin H, Basmajian JV, et al. Agonist and antagonist activity during voluntary upper-limb movement in patients with stroke. *Physical Therapy.* 1992;72:624–633.

Gresham GE, Duncan PW, Stason WB, et al. *Post-Stroke Rehabilitation: Assessment, Referral, and Patient Management. Clinical Practice Guideline.* Rockville, Md: US Dept of Health and Human Services, Agency for Health Care Policy and Research; 1995. AHCPR Pub. No 95-0663, Quick Reference Guide for Clinicians, No. 16.

Hogue R, McCandless S. Endurance exercise for adult stroke patients. *Clinical Management in Physical Therapy.* 1987;7:4:28–30.

Horak FB. Clinical assessment of postural control in adults. *Physical Therapy.* 1987;67:1881–1885.

Horak FB. Comparison of cerebellar and vestibular loss on scaling of postural responses. In: Brandt T, Paulus W, Les W, et al, eds. *Disorders of Posture and Gait*. New York, NY: Georg Thieme Verlag; 1990:370–373.

Horak FB, Diener HC, Nashner LM. Influence of central set on human postural responses. *Journal of Neurophysiology*. 1989;62:841–853.

Hurley R, Turner C. Neurology and aquatic therapy. *Clinical Management in Physical Therapy*. 1991;11:1:26–29.

John J. Failure of electrical myofeedback to augment the effects of physiotherapy in stroke. *International Journal of Rehabilitation*. 1986;9:1:35–45.

Johnstone M. *Home Care for the Stroke Patient*. 2nd ed. New York, NY: Churchill Livingstone; 1987.

Johnstone M. *Restoration of Motor Function in the Stroke Patient: A Physical Therapist's Approach*. 3rd ed. New York, NY: Churchill Livingstone; 1987.

Johnstone M. *Stroke Patient: A Team Approach*. 3rd ed. New York, NY: Churchill Livingstone; 1987.

Johnstone M. *Therapy for Stroke: Building on Experience*. New York, NY: Churchill Livingstone; 1991.

Keshner EA. Reevaluating the theoretical model underlying the neurodevelopmental treatment approach. *Physical Therapy*. 1981;61:1035–1040.

Kinsman R. A conductive education approach to stroke patients at Barnet General Hospital. *Physiotherapy*. 1989;75:418–421.

Knott M, Voss D. *Proprioceptive Neuromuscular Facilitation*. New York, NY: Harper & Row; 1968.

Lewis Y. Use of the gymnastic ball in adult hemiplegia. *Physiotherapy*. 1989;75:421–424.

Lindmark B, Hamrin D. Evaluation of functional capacity after stroke as a basis for active intervention. *Scandinavian Journal of Rehabilitation Medicine*. 1988;20:103–109.

Malouin F, Potvin M, Prevost J, et al. Use of an intensive task-oriented gait training program in a series of patients with acute cerebrovascular accidents. *Physical Therapy*. 1992;72:781–793.

Moreland J, Thomson MA. Efficacy of electromyographic biofeedback compared with conventional physical therapy for upper-extremity function in patients following stroke: a research overview and meta-analysis. *Physical Therapy*. 1994;74:534–547.

Morris ME, Matyas TA, Bach TM, Goldie PA. Electrogoniometric feedback; its effect on genu recurvatum in stroke. *Archives of Physical Medicine and Rehabilitation*. 1992;73:1147–1154.

Musa I. Evaluation and re-education of gait following stroke. *Physiotherapy Practice*. 1986;2:2:63–73.

Ostrosky K. Facilitation vs. motor control. *Clinical Management in Physical Therapy*. 1990;3:10:34–40.

O'Sullivan SB. Stroke. In: O'Sullivan SB, Schmitz TJ, eds. *Physical Rehabilitation: Assessment and Treatment*. 3rd ed. Philadelphia, Pa: FA Davis Co; 1994:327–373.

Ottenbacher KJ. *Evaluating Clinical Change: Strategies for Occupational and Physical Therapists*. Baltimore, Md: Williams & Wilkins; 1986.

Packman-Braun R. Relationship between functional electrical stimulation duty cycle and fatigue in wrist extensor muscles of patients with hemiparesis. *Physical Therapy*. 1988;68:51–56.

Price SJ, Reding MJ. Physical therapy philosophies and strategies. In: Good DC, Couch JR, eds. *Handbook of Neurorehabilitation*. New York, NY: Marcel Dekker Inc; 1994:181–197.

Richards CL, Malouin F, Wood-Dauphinee S, et al. Task-specific physical therapy for optimization of gait recovery in acute stroke patients. *Archives of Physical Medicine and Rehabilitation*. 1993;74:612–620.

Riddoch MJ, Humphreys GW. Unilateral neglect. *Physiotherapy*. 1986;72:425–428.

Riddoch MJ, Humphreys GW, Bateman A. Stroke: issues in recovery and rehabilitation. *Physiotherapy*. 1995;81:689–695.

Robichaud JA, Agostinucci J, Vander-Linden DW. Effect of air-splint application on soleus muscle motorneuron reflex excitability in nondisabled subjects and subjects with cerebrovascular accidents. *Physical Therapy*. 1992;72:176–185.

Rogers MW, Hedman LD, Pai YC. Kinetic analysis of dynamic transitions in stance support. *Archives of Physical Medicine and Rehabilitation*. 1993;74:19–25.

Sackley CM, Baguley BI, Gent S, Hodgson P. The use of a balance performance monitor in the treatment of weight-bearing and weight-transference problems after stroke. *Physiotherapy*. 1992;78:907–913.

Seitz RH, Allred KE, Backus ME, Hoffman JA. Functional changes during acute rehabilitation in patients with stroke. *Physical Therapy.* 1987;67:1685–1690.

Shumway-Cook A, Horak FB. Assessing the influence of sensory interaction on balance. *Physical Therapy.* 1986;66:1548–1550.

Shumway-Cook A, Horak FB. Rehabilitation strategies for patients with vestibular deficits. *Neurology Clinics.* 1990;8:441–457.

Sullivan PE, Markos PD, Minor MAD. *An Integrated Approach to Therapeutic Exercise: Theory and Clinical Application.* Reston, Va: Reston Publishing Co; 1982.

Sunderland A, Tinson DJ, Bradley EL, Fletcher D. Enhanced physical therapy improves recovery of arm function after stroke. *Journal of Neurology, Neurosurgery and Psychiatry.* 1992;5:530–537.

Tangemen PT, Banaitis DA, Williams AK. Rehabilitation of chronic stroke patients: changes in functional performance. *Archives of Physical Medicine and Rehabilitation.* 1990;71:876–880.

Twist DJ. Effects of a wrapping technique on passive range of motion in a spastic upper extremity. *Physical Therapy.* 1985;65:299–304.

VanSant A. Rising from a supine position to erect stance: description of adult movement and a developmental hypothesis. *Physical Therapy.* 1988;68:185–192.

Visintin M, Barbeau H. The effects of body weight support on the locomotor pattern of spastic paretic patients. *Canadian Journal of Neurological Sciences.* 1989;16:315–325.

Wade DT, Collen FM, Robb GF, Warlow CP. Physiotherapy intervention late after stroke and mobility. *British Medical Journal.* 1992;304:609–613.

Wagenaar RC, Meijer OF, vanWieringen PCW, et al. The functional recovery of stroke: a comparison between neuro-developmental treatment and the Brunnstrom method. *Scandinavian Journal of Rehabilitation Medicine.* 1990;22:1–8.

Wolf SL, LeCraw DE, Barton LA. Comparison of motor copy and targeted biofeedback training techniques for restitution of upper extremity function among patients with neurologic disorders. *Physical Therapy.* 1989;69:719–735.

Woo E, Proulx SM, Greenblatt DJ. Differential side effect profile of trizolam versus flurazepam in elderly patients undergoing rehabilitation therapy. *Journal of Clinical Pharmacology.* 1991;31:168–173.

Wood-Dauphinee S. The epidemiology of stroke: relevance for physical therapists. *Physiotherapy Canada.* 1985;37:377–386.

Young J, Forster A. Day hospital and home physiotherapy for stroke patients: a comparative cost-effectiveness study. *Journal of the Royal College of Physicians of London.* 1993;27:252–258.

Hemiplegia

Andrews AW, Bohannon RW. Decreased shoulder range of motion on paretic side after stroke. *Physical Therapy.* 1989;69:768–772.

Bobath B. *Adult Hemiplegia: Evaluation and Treatment.* 2nd ed. London, England: William Heinemann Medical Books Ltd; 1978.

Bohannon RW, Larkin PA. Passive ankle dorsiflexion increases in patients after a regimen of tilt table-wedge board standing: a clinical report. *Physical Therapy.* 1985;65:1676–1678.

Borello-France DF, Burdett RG, Gee ZL. Modification of sitting posture of patients with hemiplegia using seat boards and backboards. *Physical Therapy.* 1991;68:71–87.

Brown DA, DeBacher GA. Bicycle ergometer and electromyographic feedback for treatment of muscle imbalance in patients with spastic hemiparesis: suggestions from the field. *Physical Therapy.* 1987;67:1715–1719.

Brunnstrom S. *Movement Therapy in Hemiplegia: A Neurophysiological Approach.* New York, NY: Harper & Row Publishers; 1970.

Bruton JD. Shoulder pain in stroke patients with hemiplegia or hemiparesis following a cerebrovascular accident. *Physiotherapy.* 1985;71:2–4.

Burdett RG, Borello-France D, Blatchly C, Potter C. Gait comparison of subjects with hemiplegic walking unbraced, with ankle-foot orthosis, and with air-stirrup brace. *Physical Therapy.* 1988;68:1197–1203.

Diamond MF, Ottenbacher KJ. Effect of a tone-inhibiting dynamic ankle-foot orthosis on stride characteristics of an adult with hemiparesis. *Physical Therapy*. 1990;70:423–430.

Garland SJ, Hayes KC. Effects of brushing on electromyographic activity and ankle dorsiflexion in hemiplegic subjects with foot drop. *Physiotherapy Canada*. 1987;39:239–247.

Horak FB, Anderson M, Esselman P, Lynch K. The effects of movement velocity, mass displaced and task certainty on associated postural adjustments made by normal and hemiplegic individuals. *Journal of Neurology, Neurosurgery and Psychiatry*. 1989;62:841–853.

Hui Chan CW, Levin MF. Stretch reflex latencies in spastic hemiparetic subjects are prolonged after transcutaneous electrical nerve stimulation. *Canadian Journal of Neurological Sciences*. 1993;20:2:97–106.

Moodie NB, Brisbain J, Morgan AMG. Subluxation of the glenohumeral joint in hemiplegia: evaluation of supportive devices. *Physiotherapy Canada*. 1986;38:151–157.

Mueller K, Cornwall M, McPoil JT, et al. Effect of a tone-inhibiting dynamic ankle-foot orthosis on the foot-loading pattern of a hemiplegic adult: a preliminary study. *Journal of Prosthetics and Orthotics*. 1992;4:2:86–92.

Olney SJ, Jackson VG, George SR. Gait re-education guidelines for stroke patents with hemiplegia using mechanical energy and power analyses. *Physiotherapy Canada*. 1988;40:242–248.

Packman-Braun R. Relationship between functional electrical stimulation duty cycle and fatigue in wrist extensor muscles of patients with hemiparesis. *Physical Therapy*. 1988;68:51–56.

Prevost R. Bobath axillary support for adults with hemiplegia: a biomechanical analysis. *Physical Therapy*. 1988;68:228–232.

Riddoch MJ, Humphreys GW, Bateman A. Cognitive deficits following stroke. *Physiotherapy*. 1995;81:465–473.

Smutok MA, Grafman J, Salazar AM, et al. Effects of unilateral brain damage on contralateral and ipsilateral upper extremity function in hemiplegia. *Physical Therapy*. 1989;69:195–203.

Trueblood PR, Walker JM, Perry J, Gronely JK. Pelvic exercise and gait in hemiplegia. *Physical Therapy*. 1989;69:18–26.

Van-Langenberghe HVK, Partridge CJ, Edwards MS, Mee R. Shoulder pain in hemiplegia: a literature review. *Physiotherapy Practice*. 1988;4:3:155–162.

Waagford J, Levangie PK, Certo CM. Effects of treadmill training on gait in a hemiparetic patient. *Physical Therapy*. 1990;70:549–558.

Wang RY. Effect of proprioceptive neuromuscular facilitation on the gait of patients with hemiplegia of long and short duration. *Physical Therapy*. 1994;74:1108–1115.

Williams R, Taffs L, Minuk T. Evaluation of two support methods for the subluxated shoulder of hemiplegic patients. *Physical Therapy*. 1988;68:1209–1214.

Thoracic Outlet Syndrome

Also known as *neurovascular compression syndromes of the shoulder girdle, scalenus anticus syndrome*, and *cervical rib syndrome*.

DESCRIPTION

Thoracic outlet syndrome (TOS) is a combination of symptoms noted by pain and paresthesias that usually appear gradually in the neck, shoulder, arm, or hand and possibly in the anterior chest wall. Some clients experience severe vascular-autonomic changes in the hand. Age of onset is usually between 35 and 55, with the condition occurring more frequently in women.

CAUSE

Etiology is uncertain. Thoracic outlet syndrome can be due to compression of the neurovascular bundle that includes the brachial plexus, axillary artery, and the subclavian vessels. The presence of a cervical rib, an abnormal first thoracic rib, or abnormal insertion of the scalene muscle can lead to narrowing of the thoracic outlet where the compression occurs.

ASSESSMENT

Areas
- History
- Pain
- Posture
- Joint integrity
- Skin and soft tissue
- Mobility, including active and passive range of motion (ROM) and accessory motion
- Arterial compression
- Strength, including grip strength
- Functional level, including activities of daily living (ADLs)
- Special tests to which the PT may or may not have access

Instruments/Procedures (See References for Sources)

Arterial Compression
- Adson's test
- Allen maneuver
- costoclavicular test
- Halstead maneuver
- hyperabduction test
- Roo's test (EAST)

Special Tests to Which the PT May or May Not Have Access
- nerve conduction studies for carpal tunnel syndrome
- dexterity and coordination tests
- x-rays
- magnetic resonance imaging (MRI)
- arteriograms and venograms
- plethysmography
- tests for cervical nerve root involvement

Strength
- manual muscle testing

PROBLEMS
- The client usually reports that using arms overhead leads to fatigue.
- The client usually reports a feeling of arm falling asleep or "pins-and-needles" sensation.
- The symptoms are usually aggravated by sleeping with arms overhead.
- Pain usually begins distally and progresses proximally.
- The pain and parethesia lead to functional limitations.
- There can be cold sensitivity at a later stage.

TREATMENT/MANAGEMENT
- Instruct client in postural correction.
- Suggest modification of work and sleep postures.
- Teach scapular stabilization exercises.
- Consider modalities as indicated.
- Consider mobilization of first cervical rib and clavicle.
- Stretch scalenes, pectoralis minor, or other involved musculature.
- Instruct in self-stretches.
- Avoid repetitive movements.

PRECAUTIONS
- Presence of cyanosis in one or more fingers can indicate presence of emboli, and the therapist should refer the client to a doctor.
- Refer to Appendix C for precautions when using physical agents and modalities.

DESIRED OUTCOME/PROGNOSIS
- The client will experience a decrease in pressure on involved structures.
- Therapy will promote proper upright posture.
  Condition often takes weeks or even months to resolve. Compliance with a home program is critical.

REFERENCES

ASSESSMENT
Jackson P. Thoracic outlet syndrome evaluation and treatment. *Clinical Management in Physical Therapy.* 1987;67:6,8,10.

Arterial Compression
Rothstein JM, Roy SH, Wolf SL.*The Rehabilitation Specialist's Handbook*. Philadelphia, Pa: FA Davis Co; 1991:124. [**Adson maneuver, Allen maneuver, costoclavicular syndrome test, hyperabduction syndrome test, Halstead maneuver**]
Tomberlin JP, Saunders HD. *Evaluation, Treatment and Prevention of Musculoskeletal Disorders. Vol 2: Extremities.* Chaska, Minn: The Saunders Group; 1994:108. [**Adson's test, costoclavicular test, hyperabduction test, Roo's test (EAST)**]

Special Tests to Which the PT May or May Not Have Access
Tomberlin JP, Saunders HD. *Evaluation, Treatment and Prevention of Musculoskeletal Disorders. Vol 2: Extremities.* Chaska, Minn: The Saunders Group; 1994:108. [**X-rays, MRI, arteriograms, venograms, plethysmography**]

Strength

Manual Muscle Testing
Daniels L, Worthingham C. *Muscle Testing Techniques of Manual Examination*. 6th ed. Philadelphia, Pa: WB Saunders Co; 1995.
Kendall FP, McCreary EK, Provance PG. *Muscles: Testing and Function*. 4th ed. Baltimore, Md: Williams & Wilkins; 1993.

TREATMENT

Aligne C, Barral X. Rehabilitation of patients with thoracic outlet syndrome. *Annals of Vascular Surgery.* 1992;6:381–389.

Baker CL Jr, Liu SH. Neurovascular injuries to the shoulder. *Journal of Orthopaedic and Sports Physical Therapy.* 1993;18:360–364.

Frampton VM. Management of brachial plexus lesions. *Physiotherapy.* 1984;70:388–392.

Hama H, Matsusue Y, Ito H, Yamamuro T. Thoracic outlet syndrome associated with an anomalous coracoclavicular joint: a case report. *Journal of Bone and Joint Surgery.* 1993;75A:1368–1369.

Jackson P. Thoracic outlet syndrome: evaluation and treatment. *Clinical Management in Physical Therapy.* 1987;7:6:6–10.

Kamkar A, Irrgang JJ, Whitney SL. Nonoperative management of secondary shoulder impingment syndrome. *Journal of Orthopaedic and Sports Physical Therapy.* 1993;17:212–224.

Kenny RA, Traynor GB, Withington D, Keegan DJ. Thoracic outlet syndrome: a useful exercise treatment option. *American Journal of Surgery.* 1993;165:282–284.

Levoska S, Keinanen-Kiukaanniemi S. Active or passive physiotherapy for occupational cervicobrachial disorders: a comparison of two treatment methods with a 1-year follow-up. *Archives of Physical Medicine and Rehabilitation.* 1993;74:425–430.

Novak CB, Collins ED, Mackinnon SE. Outcome following conservative management of thoracic outlet syndrome. *Journal of Hand Surgery.* 1995;20A:542–548.

Rundcrantz BL, Johnsson B, Moritz U. Occupational cervico-brachial disorders among dentists: analysis of ergonomics and locomotor functions. *Swedish Dental Journal.* 1991;15:3:105–115.

Silliman JF, Dean MT. Neurovascular injuries to the shoulder complex. *Journal of Orthopaedic and Sports Physical Therapy.* 1993;18:442–448.

Totten PA, Hunter JM. Therapeutic techniques to enhance nerve gliding in thoracic outlet syndrome and carpal tunnel syndrome. *Hand Clinics.* 1991;7:505–520.

Chapter 11
Oncology

- Breast cancer
- Head and neck cancer
- Leukemia
- Lung cancer
- Soft tissue sarcoma

Breast Cancer

DESCRIPTION

Cancer is a cellular malignancy characterized by the loss of the usual controls. This allows unrestricted cellular proliferation that can invade normal tissues as well as metastasize to other sites. If left untreated, this uncontrolled spread of abnormal cells can lead to death.

Around 180,000 women in the United States are diagnosed with breast cancer each year. Medical treatment for breast cancer varies depending on the diagnosis. Systemic treatments, such as chemotherapy and hormone therapy, may control cancer cells throughout the body. Localized treatments include radiation and surgery. Surgery, however, is the most common choice for treating breast cancer.

CAUSE

Breast cancer is influenced by the following risk factors:
- for women, age, breast disease, family history, and reproductive history
- for men, age, cancer therapy, genetic predisposition, gynecomastia, and Klinefelter's syndrome

ASSESSMENT

Areas
- History, including hand dominance and type of surgery, particularly breast reconstruction
- Psychosocial
- Chest wall: swelling, appearance in general
- Pain
- Posture
- Cardiopulmonary screen, including peripheral pulses, vital signs during activity, respiration
- Mobility: active range of motion (ROM), including neck, shoulder, and upper extremities
- Skin and soft tissue: color changes, edema, and scar, including any adhesions
- Neurological, including sensation
- Strength, especially upper quarter region, with emphasis on thorax and shoulder
- Balance
- Functional level, including activities of daily living (ADLs)
- Special tests, including available diagnostic tests, to which the PT may or may not have access

Instruments/Procedures (See References for Sources)

Functional Level
- Katz Index of Activities of Daily Living
- Barthel Mobility Index for ADL disturbance
- Functional Independence Measure

Pain
- finger dynameter
- pain intensity number scale
- visual analogue scale

Skin and Soft Tissue
1. edema
   - circumferential measurements
   - volumetrics

Special Tests to Which the PT May or May Not Have Access
- breast exam
- needle aspiration
- mammography
- imaging techniques
- diaphanoscopy
- biopsy
- hormone receptor tests
- chest x-ray films
- blood tests

PROBLEMS
- The client can develop lymphedema.
- The client usually has pain.
- The client can have spasm in the posterior cervical region and shoulder girdle.
- The client can have neurological symptoms, such as hyperesthesia, parethesia, throbbing pain, weakness, and skin trophic changes, that are secondary to nerve damage during surgery, radiotherapy, or chemotherapy.
- The client can have weakness, especially in the involved upper extremity.
- The client can develop contracture secondary to immobilization of upper extremity.
- The client can have sensory loss with radiating pain or aching.
- The client can develop postural asymmetry.
- The client can have difficulty with psychological adjustment to body image and sexual functioning.
- The client can have menopausal symptoms such as hot flashes, interrupted periods, or vaginal dryness due to hormone therapy.

TREATMENT/MANAGEMENT

Lymphedema Treatment
- Design treatment to meet individual needs.
- Lymphedema prevention involves arm mobilization, shoulder strengthening, prevention and treatment of upper extremity edema, and education on arm function.
- Consider use of manual lymph drainage, elevation, compression, and retrograde massage with a good skin conditioner.
- Consider use of complex physical therapy: a combination of skin hygiene, lymphatic massage, compression bandaging and garment, and specific exercises to supplement massage.
- Modalities for edema include intermittent compression, massage, tapping, exercise, continual elevation, and elastic gradient support garments or bandages.
- One suggested pumping program consists of mechanical pumping, 1 to 3 days for 8 to 10 hours per day, and then fitting client with a custom compression garment. Switch to progressively smaller garments every 4 to 6 weeks.

Postsurgical Treatment
- The client should receive pain medication shortly before treatment.
- Instruct the client in positioning. If the client is on bed rest, the arm may be in slight shoulder abduction and flexion, with distal elevation and support.
- Encourage active movement of the hand, wrist, forearm, and elbow.
- Begin with passive and active assistive ROM activities for the shoulder without harming healing of suture area.
- Educate the client to avoid holding affected arm in flexed protective posture against body.
- On day 4 or 5 post surgery, begin active exercises. Include neck ROM, shoulder shrugs, shoulder rotation, flexion and abduction to tolerance, and protraction and retraction of scapula. Use unaffected arm to assist as needed.
- Modalities for pain, relaxation, or edema include cold packs, mechanical compression, and massage (not with bone tumor).
- Initiate stretching activities. Neuropathic symptoms may be relieved by stretching adhesions and increasing ROM.
- Instruct the client to watch for signs of edema: increased fullness in arm; change in color, usually more reddened; increase in skin temperature. See box for specific instructions.

Skin Care Tips To Avoid Lymphedema

For the breast cancer patient who is at risk of lymphedema or who has developed lymphedema:
- Don't ignore any slight increase of swelling in the arm, hand, fingers, or chest wall (consult with your doctor immediately).
- Don't allow an injection or a blood drawing in the affected arm(s).
- Don't have blood pressure checked in the affected arm.
- Do keep the edemic or "at-risk" arm very clean. Use lotion after bathing. When drying, be gentle, but thorough.
- Avoid vigorous, repetitive movements against resistance with the affected arm.
- Avoid heavy lifting with the affected arm.
- Don't wear tight jewelry or elastic bands around affected fingers or arm(s).
- Avoid extreme temperature changes. Do keep the arm protected from the sun.
- Avoid any type of trauma, such as insect bites or cat scratches.
- Do wear gloves while doing work that could result in even a minor injury.
- Avoid cutting your cuticles when manicuring your nails.
- Although exercise is important, don't overtire an at-risk arm; if it starts to ache, lie down and elevate it. Recommended exercises: walking, swimming, light aerobics, bike riding, and specially designed ballet or yoga. (Do not lift more than 12 lb.)
- If you have lymphedema, wear a well-fitted compression sleeve, especially when traveling.
- Patients with large breasts should wear light breast prostheses and a well-fitted bra that is not too tight and has no wire support.
- Warning: If you notice a rash, blistering, redness, increase of temperature, or fever, see your physician immediately. An inflammation or infection in the affected arm could be the beginning of lymphedema or a worsening of lymphedema.

- Maintain your ideal weight. Lymphedema is a high-protein edema, but eating too little protein will not reduce the protein element in the lymph fluid; rather, this will weaken the connective tissue and worsen the condition. The diet should contain protein that is easily digested, such as chicken and fish.
- Avoid smoking and alcoholic beverages.

Source: Reprinted from S Thiadens, National Lymphcdema Network; Skin Care Tips to Avoid Lymphedema, in *Therapeutic Approaches to Women's Health: A Program of Exercise and Education*, J Pauls, p. 7-1:26, © 1995, Aspen Publishers, Inc.

- Use orthotic and assistive devices as indicated for ADLs.
- Prescribe exercise program with emphasis on strength, flexibility, and endurance. Types of exercise may include shoulder shrugging, ROM for cervical spine and shoulder with shoulder circle exercises, and exercises for spinal extensor musculature and upper extremity strength. Manual isotonic resistance exercise may be initiated with physician consultation, usually on the 4th day post surgery.
- Consider use of joint mobilization for glenohumeral joint and scapulothoracic joint.
- Emphasize postural instruction.
- Provide gait training if indicated.
- Clients who are at increased risk of pathological fractures—those with bone metastases—should be instructed in prevention of falls and consider use of prophylactic orthotics.

PRECAUTIONS/CONTRAINDICATIONS
- See Pfalzer, "Physical Agents and the Patient with Cancer," in Treatment references.
- Heat and cold modalities are contraindicated in the area of the axilla if it was irradiated.
- Tissue should not blanch when stretched.
- Modify exercise as indicated if client also has bone metastases or osteoporosis.
- See Appendix C for contraindications with physical agents and modalities.

DESIRED OUTCOME/PROGNOSIS
- The client will prevent lymphedema formation.
- The client will prevent postural deficits.
- The client will prevent contractures.
- The client will improve symmetry in posture.
- The client will protect skin and monitor own status.
- The client will be independent in ADLs.
- The client will have a decrease in pain and symptoms.
- The client will have an increased ability to cope with the diagnosis.
- The client will have a well-healed wound site.
- The client will have adaptive equipment, such as a prosthesis, if needed.

In general, if cancer is detected at an early stage, it is usually curable. One study reports that early intervention offers a significant increase in return to normal function post mastectomy with no increased incidence of postoperative complications or increase in hospital stay.

One study reports a highly significant decrease in edema post use of complex PT. Sensory loss with radiating pain or aching usually diminishes within 6 months to a year.

REFERENCES

ASSESSMENT

Adcock JL. Rehabilitation of the breast cancer patient. In: McGarvery CL, ed. *Physical Therapy for the Cancer Patient: Clinics in Physical Therapy*. New York, NY: Churchill Livingstone; 1990:67–84. **[Upper extremity measuring sheet]**

Goodman C, Snyder TE. *Differential Diagnosis in Physical Therapy*. Philadelphia, Pa: WB Saunders Co; 1990:332, 337, 357, 362–363.

Konecne SM. Postsurgery breast cancer inpatient program. *Clinical Management in Physical Therapy*. 1992;12:4:42–49.

Pfalzer LA. Oncology: examination, diagnosis, and treatment. Medical and surgical considerations. In: Myers RS, ed. *Saunders Manual of Physical Therapy Practice*. Philadelphia, Pa: WB Saunders Co; 1995:65–147.

Pfalzer LA. Oncology: examination, diagnosis, and treatment. Physical therapy considerations. In: Myers RS, ed. *Saunders Manual of Physical Therapy Practice*. Philadelphia, Pa: WB Saunders Co; 1995:149–190.

Functional Level

Katz Index of Activities of Daily Living

Benjamin Rose Hospital Staff. Multidisciplinary studies of illness in aged persons: II. A new classification of functional status in activities of daily living. *Journal of Chronic Disease*. 1959;9:55–62.

Brorsson B, Ashberg KH. Katz Index of Independence in ADL: reliability and validity in short-term care. *Scandinavian Journal of Rehabilitation Medicine*. 1984;16:125–132.

Barthel Mobility Index

Yoshioka H. Rehabilitation for the terminal cancer patient. *American Journal of Physical Medicine and Rehabilitation*. 1994;73:199–206.

Functional Independence Measure

Granger CV, Hamilton BB, Keith RA, et al. Advance in functional assessment for medical rehabilitation. *Topics in Geriatric Rehabilitation*. 1986;1:3:59–74.

Keith RA, Granger CV, Hamilton BB, Sherwins FS. The Functional Independence Measure. *Advances in Clinical Rehabilitation*. 1987;1:6–18.

Pain

Wilkie D, Lovejoy N, Dodd M, Tesler M. Cancer pain intensity measurement: concurrent validity of three tools—finger dynameter, pain intensity number scale, visual analog scale. *Hospice Journal*. 1990;6:1:1–13.

Skin and Soft Tissue

Edema

Circumferential Measurements

Gerber L, Lampert M, Wood C, et al. Comparison of pain, motion, and edema after modified radical mastectomy vs local excision with axillary dissection and radiation. *Breast Cancer Research and Treatment*. 1992;21:139–145.

TREATMENT

Adcock JL. Rehabilitation of the breast cancer patient. In: McGarvery CL, ed. *Clinics in Physical Therapy: Physical Therapy for the Cancer Patient*. New York, NY: Churchill Livingstone; 1990:67–84.

Balzarini A, Pirovano C, Diazzi G, et al. Ultrasound therapy of chronic arm lymphedema after surgical treatment of breast cancer. *Lymphology.* 1993;26:128–134.

Boyd-Walton J. The role of rehabilitation services in oncology. *Clinical Management in Physical Therapy.* 1985;5:2:24–25.

Cammack JM. Interdisciplinary care of the patient with cancer in a community hospital. *Clinical Management in Physical Therapy.* 1984;2:4:7–12.

Dean JT, Davidson G. Trismus after radiation therapy. *Clinical Management in Physical Therapy.* 1992;12:4:70–76.

Delisa JA, Miller RM, Melnick RR, et al. Rehabilitation of the cancer patient. In: DeVita VT Jr., Hellman S, Rosebert SA, et al, eds. *Cancer: Principles and Practice of Oncology.* 3rd ed. Philadelphia, Pa: JB Lippincott Co; 1989:2333–2368.

Etherington ME. Physical therapy management of the cancer patient. *Clinical Management in Physical Therapy.* 1987;7:3:12, 14–15.

Flomenhoft D. Understanding and helping people who have cancer: a special communication. *Physical Therapy.* 1984;64:1232–1234.

Frankiel M. The physical therapist and post-mastectomy rehabilitation. *Journal of Obstetric and Gynecologic Physical Therapy.* 1992;16:1:9–11.

Gudas SA. Directives in cancer rehabilitation. *Clinical Management in Physical Therapy.* 1992;12:4:32–36.

Gutman H, Kersz T, Barzilai T, Haddad M, Reiss R. Achievements of physical therapy in patients after modified radical mastectomy compared with quadrantectomy, axillary dissection, and radiation for carcinoma of the breast. *Archives of Surgery.* 1990;125:389–391.

Hamburgh RR. Principles of cancer treatment. *Clinical Management in Physical Therapy.* 1992;12:4:37–41.

Har-El G, Krespi YP, Har-El R. Physical rehabilitation after myocutaneous flaps. *Head and Neck.* 1990;12:218–224.

Hicks JE. Exercise for cancer patients. In: Basmajian JV, Wolf SL, eds. *Therapeutic Exercise.* 5th ed. Baltimore, Md: Williams & Wilkins; 1990:28–31.

Hladiuk M, Huchcroft S, Temple W, Schnurr BE. Arm function after axillary dissection for breast cancer: a pilot study to provide parameter estimates. *Journal of Surgical Oncology.* 1992;50:1:47–52.

Hock K. Ambulatory oncology program. *Clinical Management in Physical Therapy.* 1992;12:4:87–91.

Konecne SM. Postsurgery breast cancer inpatient program. *Clinical Management in Physical Therapy.* 1992;12:4:42–49.

Kuchler T, Wood-Dauphines S. Working with people who have cancer: guidelines for physical therapists. *Physiotherapy Canada.* 1991;43:4:19–23.

Luk KH, Drennan T, Anderson K. Potential role of physical therapists in hyperthermia in cancer therapy: the need for further training. *Physical Therapy.* 1986;66:340–343.

Mason M. The treatment of lymphoedema by complex physical therapy. *Australian Journal of Physical Therapy.* 1993;39:1:41–45.

Marcant D, Rapin CH. Role of the physiotherapist in palliative care. *Journal of Pain and Symptom Management.* 1993;8:2:68–71.

McLoughlin WJ, Holz S. Cancer rehabilitation is an integrated support system. *Clinical Management in Physical Therapy.* 1985;5:6:10–12.

Miller LT. Postsurgery breast cancer outpatient program. *Clinical Management in Physical Therapy.* 1992;12:4:50–56.

Molinaro J, Kleinfeld M, Lebed S. Physical therapy and dance in the surgical management of breast cancer: a clinical report. *Physical Therapy.* 1986;66:967–969.

Myers RS, ed. *Saunders Manual of Physical Therapy Practice.* Philadelphia, Pa: WB Saunders Co; 1995:94–95, 124–126, 179–182, 184–186.

Pauls J. Mastectomy. In: Pauls J. *Therapeutic Approaches to Women's Health: A Program of Exercise and Education.* Gaithersburg, Md: Aspen Publishers, Inc; 1995:7-1:1.

Pfalzer LA. Aerobic exercise for patients with disseminated cancer. *Clinical Management in Physical Therapy.* 1988;8:2:351–370.

Pfalzer L. Physical agents and the patient with cancer. *Clinical Management in Physical Therapy.* 1992;12:4:83–86.

Pfalzer L, Walter J. Facts and fiction: cancer in the 1990's. *Clinical Management in Physical Therapy.* 1992;12:4:26–31.

Pomerantz E. Speaking with and listening to the breast cancer patient. *Journal of Obstetric and Gynecologic Physical Therapy.* 1992;16:1:12–13.

Sicard-Rosenbaum L, Danoff J. Cancer and ultrasound: a warning letter. *Physical Therapy.* 1993;73:404–406.

Snyder R. Physical therapy in terminal illness. *Clinical Management in Physical Therapy.* 1992;12:4:96–100.

Tool JL. Physical therapy in the care of patients with a diagnosis of cancer. *Clinical Management in Physical Therapy.* 1992;12:4:96–100.

Watchie J. Cardiopulmonary complications of cancer. *Clinical Management in Physical Therapy.* 1992;12:4:92–95.

Wingate L. Efficacy of physical therapy for patients who have undergone mastectomies. *Physical Therapy.* 1985;65:896–900.

Wingate L, Croghan I, Natarajan N, Michalek AM, Jordan C. Rehabilitation of the mastectomy patient: a randomized, blind, prospective study. *Archives of Physical Medicine and Rehabilitation.* 1989;70:21–24.

Woods EN. Reaching out to patients with breast cancer. *Clinical Management in Physical Therapy.* 1992;12:4:58–63.

Yoshioka H. Rehabilitation for the terminal cancer patient. *American Journal of Physical Medicine and Rehabilitation.* 1994;73:199–206.

Lymphedema

Balzarini A, Pirovano C, Diazzi G, et al. Ultrasound therapy of chronic arm lymphedema after surgical treatment of breast cancer. *Lymphology.* 1993;26:128–134.

Carriere B. Edema: its development and treatment using lymph drainage massage. *Clinical Management in Physical Therapy.* 1988:8:5:19–21.

Casley-Smith JR, Casley-Smith JR. Modern treatment of lymphoedema. 1. Complex physical therapy: the first 200 Australian limbs. *Australian Journal of Dermatology.* 1992;33:2:61–68.

Casley-Smith JR, Casley-Smith JR, Morgan RG. Physical therapy for lymphoedema. *Medical Journal of Australia.* 1989;150:542–543.

Gerber L, Lampert M, Wood C, et al. Comparison of pain, motion, and edema after modified radical mastectomy vs local excision with axillary dissection and radiation. *Breast Cancer Research and Treatment.* 1992;21:139–145.

Gray RC. The management of limb oedema in patients with advanced cancer. *Physiotherapy.* 1987;73:504–506.

Mark B. Lymphedema: etiology and management techniques. *Journal of Obstetric and Gynecologic Physical Therapy.* 1994;18:2:5–8.

Mark B, Feltman B. Case studies in the management of post-mastectomy lymphedema. *Journal of Obstetric and Gynecologic Physical Therapy.* 1994;18:3:5–9.

Morgan RG, Casley-Smith JR, Mason MR, Casley-Smith JR. Complex physical therapy for the lymphoedematous arm. *Journal of Hand Surgery.* 1992;17B:437–441.

Swedborg I, Norrefalf JR, Piller NB, Asard C. Effectiveness of combined methods of physiotherapy for post-mastectomy lymphoedema. *Scandinavian Journal of Rehabilitation Medicine.* 1980;12:77–85.

Head and Neck Cancer

DESCRIPTION

Cancer is a cellular malignancy characterized by the loss of the usual controls. This allows unrestricted cellular proliferation that can invade normal tissues as well as metastasize to other sites. If left untreated, this uncontrolled spread of abnormal cells can lead to death.

Cancers of the head and neck are cancers that affect the upper aerodigestive tract. The most common sites for these cancers are the larynx, oral cavity, pharynx, and salivary glands. The lips, nose, sinuses, and ears may also be affected. Reportedly, 80% of head and neck cancers originate in the mucosa of the aerodigestive tract. The squamous cell carcinoma is the most common type of malignant neoplasm of the head and neck region.

CAUSE

Cancers of the head and neck are usually caused by tobacco and alcohol abuse. Nasopharyngeal cancer is also linked to Epstein–Barr virus.

ASSESSMENT

Areas
- History
- Psychosocial factors
- Pain
- Posture
- Skin and soft tissue, including wound assessment, color, and edema
- Pulmonary: as indicated
- Mobility, including active and passive range of motion (ROM), especially in head, neck, and shoulder area
- Strength
- Neurological, including sensation
- Functional level

Instruments/Procedures (See References for Sources)

Functional Level
- Karnofsky Performance Scale
- Performance Status Scale for Head and Neck Cancer Patients
- Katz Index of Activities of Daily Living
- Barthel Mobility Index for ADL disturbance
- Functional Independence Measure

Pain
- finger dynameter
- pain intensity number scale
- visual analogue scale

PROBLEMS
- The client usually has diminished or lost function in the area of the head, neck, and shoulder due to radical or modified dissection of muscle, nerve, vessels, and lymphatic groups.

- The client can have pain in the shoulder.
- The client usually has trapezius muscle dysfunction or paralysis.
- The scapula can be medially rotated and laterally deviated.
- The client can have clavicle subluxation.
- The client can have scapular fixation that limits active motion to 130 degrees flexion and 90 degrees abduction.
- The client can have diminished sensation in the upper extremities.

TREATMENT/MANAGEMENT
- The therapist should be part of a team approach to rehabilitation.
- Educate area musculature to substitute in shoulder motions of elevation, retraction, and stabilization during flexion and abduction.
- Instruct the client in an exercise program that can be followed on an outpatient or home care basis, to be adapted to individual needs. This may include chin retraction, cervical flexion, rotation, sidebending, circumduction, upper extremity flexion, and pendulum exercises.
- Educate the client about the potential dangers due to sensory deficits, especially extreme temperatures.
- Respiratory treatment may include cough instruction, pursed lip breathing, and energy conservation techniques.
- Address issues of social and psychological impact if facial disfigurement is involved. See Appendix D for addresses.

PRECAUTIONS/CONTRAINDICATIONS
- Until the wound is properly healed, the client should be well supported on the affected shoulder and neck area to avoid unnecessary trapezius muscle stretching.
- Exercise program should be delayed in the client with fistula formation, delayed wound healing, or carotid "blowout."
- Use physical agents and modalities with caution. See Appendix C for precautions. In general, heat modalities are contraindicated.

DESIRED OUTCOME/PROGNOSIS
- The client will increase ROM in neck and shoulder areas to within normal limits.
- The client will increase the strength of the neck and affected arm to the highest capacity possible and will maintain scapular alignment.
- The client will maintain shoulder alignment and prevent postural problems.

A grade of "good" is commonly reached in shoulder musculature. Usually the wound is healed enough in 10 to 14 days to permit initiation of an exercise program. No one muscle group can completely compensate for the loss of trapezius musculature.

REFERENCES

ASSESSMENT
Pfalzer LA. Oncology: examination, diagnosis, and treatment. Medical and surgical considerations. In: Myers RS, ed. *Saunders Manual of Physical Therapy Practice*. Philadelphia, Pa: WB Saunders Co; 1995:65–147. **[Performance Status Scale for Head and Neck Cancer Patients]**
Pfalzer LA. Oncology: examination, diagnosis, and treatment. Physical therapy considerations. In: Myers RS, ed. *Saunders Manual of Physical Therapy Practice*. Philadelphia, Pa: WB Saunders Co; 1995:149–190.

Roberts WL. Rehabilitation of the head and neck cancer patient. In: McGarvery CL, ed. *Physical Therapy for the Cancer Patient: Clinics in Physical Therapy.* New York, NY: Churchill Livingstone; 1990:47–65. Adapted from Snow JB. [**Karnofsky Performance Scale. Surgical management of head and neck cancer.** *Seminars in Oncology.* **1988;15:20**]

Functional Level

Katz Index of Activities of Daily Living
Benjamin Rose Hospital Staff. Multidisciplinary studies of illness in aged persons: II. A new classification of functional status in activities of daily living. *Journal of Chronic Disease.* 1959;9:1:55–62.
Brorsson B, Ashberg KH. Katz Index of Independence in ADL: reliability and validity in short-term care. *Scandinavian Journal of Rehabilitation Medicine.* 1984;16:125–132.

Barthel Mobility Index
Yoshioka H. Rehabilitation for the terminal cancer patient. *American Journal of Physical Medicine and Rehabilitation.* 1994;73:199–206.

Functional Independence Measure
Granger CV, Hamilton BB, Keith RA, et al. Advance in functional assessment for medical rehabilitation. *Topics in Geriatric Rehabilitation.* 1986;1:3:59–74.
Keith RA, Granger CV, Hamilton BB, Sherwins FS. The Functional Independence Measure. *Advances in Clinical Rehabilitation.* 1987;1:6–18.

Pain
Wilkie D, Lovejoy N, Dodd M, Tesler M. Cancer pain intensity measurement: concurrent validity of three tools—finger dynameter, pain intensity number scale, visual analog scale. *Hospice Journal.* 1990;6:1:1–13.

TREATMENT
Barrett NV, Martin JW, Jacob RF, et al. Physical therapy techniques in the treatment of the head and neck patient. *Journal of Prosthetic Dentistry.* 1988;59:343–346.
Boyd-Walton J. The role of rehabilitation services in oncology. *Clinical Management in Physical Therapy.* 1985;5:2:24–25.
Bussieres A, Cassidy JD, Dzus A. Spinal cord astrocytoma presenting as torticollis and scoliosis. *Journal of Manipulative and Physiological Therapeutics.* 1994;17:113–118.
Dean JT, Davidson G. Trismus after radiation therapy. *Clinical Management in Physical Therapy.* 1992;12:4:70–76.
Delisa JA, Miller RM, Melnick RR, et al. Rehabilitation of the cancer patient. In: DeVita VT Jr, Hellman S, Roseberg SA, et al, eds. *Cancer: Principles and Practice of Oncology.* 3rd ed. Philadelphia, Pa: JB Lippincott Co; 1989;2333–2368.
Etherington ME. Physical therapy management of the cancer patient. *Clinical Management in Physical Therapy.* 1987;7:3:12, 14–15.
Gallon A. Physiotherapy following oesophagectomy. *Physiotherapy.* 1992;78:353–356.
Gray RC. The management of limb oedema in patients with advanced cancer. *Physiotherapy.* 1987;73:504–506.
Gudas SA. Directives in cancer rehabilitation. *Clinical Management in Physical Therapy.* 1992;12:4:32–36.
Hamburgh RR. Principles of cancer treatment. *Clinical Management in Physical Therapy.* 1992;12:4:37–41.
Har-El G, Krespi YP, Har-El R. Physical rehabilitation after myocutaneous flaps. *Head and Neck.* 1990;12:218–224.
Herring D, King AL, Connelly M. New rehabilitation concepts in management of radical neck dissection syndrome: a clinical report. *Physical Therapy.* 1987;67:1095–1099.
Hicks JE. Exercise for cancer patients. In: Basmajian JV, Wolf SL, eds. *Therapeutic Exercise.* 5th ed. Baltimore, Md: Williams & Wilkins; 1990:28–31.

Hock K. Ambulatory oncology program. *Clinical Management in Physical Therapy.* 1992;12:4:87–91.

Kuchler T, Wood-Dauphines S. Working with people who have cancer: guidelines for physical therapists. *Physiotherapy Canada.* 1991;43:4:19–23.

Luk KH, Drennan T, Anderson K. Potential role of physical therapists in hyperthermia in cancer therapy: the need for further training. *Physical Therapy.* 1986;66:340–343.

Lynch PD, Schaefer S, Eckert D. Cancer rehabilitation issues for occupational and physical therapists: a conference report. *Progress in Clinical and Biological Research.* 1983;130:443–453.

Marcant D, Rapin CH. Role of the physiotherapist in palliative care. *Journal of Pain and Symptom Management.* 1993;8:2:68–71.

McLoughlin WJ, Holz S. Cancer rehabilitation is an integrated support system. *Clinical Management in Physical Therapy.* 1985;5:6:10–12.

Pfalzer L. Physical agents and the patient with cancer. *Clinical Management in Physical Therapy.* 1992;12:4:83–86.

Pfalzer L, Walter J. Facts and fiction: cancer in the 1990's. *Clinical Management in Physical Therapy.* 1992;12:4:26–31.

Quan KM, Shiran M, Watmough DJ. Applicators for generating ultrasound-induced hyperthermia in neoplastic tumours and for use in ultrasound physiotherapy. *Physics in Medicine and Biology.* 1989;34:1719–1731.

Ridder T. Orofacial physiotherapy after radiotherapy in the head and neck region. *Cranio.* 1993;11:242–244.

Roberts WL. Rehabilitation of the head and neck cancer patient. In: McGarvery CL, ed. *Physical Therapy for the Cancer Patient: Clinics in Physical Therapy.* New York, NY: Churchill Livingstone; 1990:47–65.

Sicard-Rosenbaum L, Danoff J. Cancer and ultrasound: a warning letter. *Physical Therapy.* 1993;73:404–406.

Snyder R. Coping: you and your patient with cancer. *Clinical Management in Physical Therapy.* 1992;12:4:64–69.

Snyder R. Physical therapy in terminal illness. *Clinical Management in Physical Therapy.* 1992;12:4:96–100.

Tool JL. Physical therapy in the care of patients with a diagnosis of cancer. *Clinical Management in Physical Therapy.* 1992;12:4:96–100.

Watchie J. Cardiopulmonary complications of cancer. *Clinical Management in Physical Therapy.* 1992;12:4:92–95.

Yoshioka H. Rehabilitation for the terminal cancer patient. *American Journal of Physical Medicine and Rehabilitation.* 1994;73:199–206.

Leukemia

DESCRIPTION

Leukemia is defined as a malignant neoplasm of the blood-forming tissues. This disorder leads to production of abnormal white blood cells in the blood and bone marrow. Leukemia is designated as acute or chronic depending on cellular maturity. Acute leukemia is mainly undifferentiated cell groups, and chronic leukemias are further developed cell populations. There are four major types of leukemia: acute lymphoblastic leukemia (ALL), acute myelogenous leukemia (AML), chronic myelogenous leukemia (CML), and chronic lymphocytic leukemia (CLL).

CAUSE

The cause of leukemia is not clearly defined. Two viruses have been identified, the Epstein–Barr virus and the human acute leukemia/lymphoma virus. Exposure to some chemical and ionizing radiation has also been associated with an increased risk of leukemia. Other factors include immunological and genetic disorders.

ASSESSMENT

Areas
- History
- Psychosocial
- Pain
- Posture
- Cardiopulmonary, including endurance
- Musculoskeletal, including joint integrity
- Strength
- Mobility, including range of motion (ROM)
- Neurological
- Genitourinary
- Skin, including color, edema, and any wounds
- Functional level, including activities of daily living (ADLs)

Instruments/Procedures (See References for Sources)

Functional Level
- Katz Index of Activities of Daily Living
- Barthel Mobility Index for ADL disturbance
- Functional Independence Measure

Pain
- finger dynameter
- pain intensity number scale
- visual analogue scale

PROBLEMS
Acute symptoms are as follows:
- The client usually has joint pain.
- There can be cyanosis.
- The client can have frequent infections.
- There is a tendency to bleed or bruise easily.
- There can be enlarged lymph nodes, spleen, testicles, and liver.
- There can be headache, diplopia, cranial nerve palsy, papilledema, or mental changes.
  Due to prolonged hospitalization:
- The client usually has loss of strength and endurance.
- Osteoporosis can develop secondary to bed rest.
- The client can have activity restriction secondary to nausea and vomiting.

TREATMENT/MANAGEMENT
- Adjust treatment to accommodate diagnosis, age, and course of treatment for cancer. The client may be undergoing chemotherapy or radiation treatment that can affect physical therapy treatment.
- Provide preventive care to counteract problems triggered by prolonged hospitalization.

- Educate the client about an exercise program of active exercise and walking.
- For clients with neuropathies, consider splinting, stretching exercise, and orthosis such as ankle or foot to prevent contractures and maintain function.

Physical Therapy Treatment in Conjunction With Bone Marrow Transplantation (BMT)
- Provide comprehensive exercise program. Include upper extremity, weight bearing, back extension, ambulation, and proximal musculature strengthening.
- Add ROM, balance, strengthening, endurance, and progressive ambulation activities as indicated.

PRECAUTIONS/CONTRAINDICATIONS

In Conjunction With Chemotherapy
- Side effects of chemotherapy can include lowered blood counts, nausea, vomiting, loss of hair, adult respiratory distress syndrome, cardiotoxic effects, peripheral neuropathies, proximal muscle weakness, aseptic necrosis of hips or shoulder joint, joint pain, neuropsychologic effects, and encephalopathy.
- Monitor vital signs closely during exercise and activity.
- Low white cell count can mean that the client is at an increased risk for infection.
- Low platelet count may place the client at increased risk for bleeding and may contraindicate resistive exercise.
- Clients with low blood volume may be able to tolerate only gentle bedside exercise.

In Conjunction With BMT
- BMT may lead to the side effects of impaired renal, cardiovascular, or neuromuscular function, increased risk for lung infection, hepatic veno-occlusive disease, mucositis, and graft-versus-host disease (GVHD).
- The treatment of GVHD with the use of steroids in high doses increases risk of aseptic necrosis, osteoporosis, and steroid myopathies.

General Hematologic Guidelines
- Avoid resistive exercise when platelet counts are below $50,000/mm^3$.
- Avoid all activity when platelet counts are below $20,000/mm^3$ or hematocrit is below 25%, hemoglobin is below 8 mg/dl, or white blood cells are below $500/mm^3$.
- Exercise should be mild when hemoglobin is as low as 8 to 10 mg/dl.
- Other factors that affect tolerance to activity include dialysis, intubation, prolonged bed rest, and presence of any intracranial bleeding.

DESIRED OUTCOME/PROGNOSIS
- Neuropathies secondary to chemotherapy usually resolve spontaneously after 1 to 2 years with support provided by treatment mentioned earlier.

REFERENCES

ASSESSMENT

Functional Level

Katz Index of Activities of Daily Living
Benjamin Rose Hospital Staff. Multidisciplinary studies of illness in aged persons: II. A new classification of functional status in activities of daily living. *Journal of Chronic Disease.* 1959;9:1:55–62.

Brorsson B, Ashberg KH. Katz Index of Independence in ADL: reliability and validity in short-term care. *Scandinavian Journal of Rehabilitation Medicine.* 1984;16:125–132.

Barthel Mobility Index
Yoshioka H. Rehabilitation for the terminal cancer patient. *American Journal of Physical Medicine and Rehabilitation.* 1994;73:199–206.

Functional Independence Measure
Granger CV, Hamilton BB, Keith RA, et al. Advance in functional assessment for medical rehabilitation. *Topics in Geriatric Rehabilitation.* 1986;1:3:59–74.

Keith RA, Granger CV, Hamilton BB, Sherwins FS. The Functional Independance Measure. *Advances in Clinical Rehabilitation.* 1987;1:6–18.

Pain
Wilkie D, Lovejoy N, Dodd M, Testler M. Cancer pain intensity measurement: concurrent validity of three tools—finger dynameter, pain intensity number scale, visual analog scale. *Hospice Journal.* 1990;6:1:1–13.

TREATMENT
Boyd-Walton J. The role of rehabilitation services in oncology. *Clinical Management in Physical Therapy.* 1985;5:2:24–25.

Dean JT, Davidson G. Trismus after radiation therapy. *Clinical Management in Physical Therapy.* 1992;12:4:70–76.

Delisa JA, Miller RM, Melnick RR, et al. Rehabilitation of the cancer patient. In: DeVita VT Jr, Hellman S, Roseberg SA, et al, eds. *Cancer: Principles and Practice of Oncology.* 3rd ed. Philadelphia, Pa: JB Lippincott Co; 1989:2333–2368.

Etherington ME. Physical therapy management of the cancer patient. *Clinical Management in Physical Therapy.* 1987;7:3:12, 14–15.

Gray RC. The management of limb oedema in patients with advanced cancer. *Physiotherapy.* 1987;73:504–506.

Gudas SA. Implications of oncology in the aged. In: Lewis CB, ed. *Aging: The Health Care Challenge.* 2nd ed. Philadelphia, Pa: FA Davis Co; 1990; 212–240.

Gudas SA. Directives in cancer rehabilitation. *Clinical Management in Physical Therapy.* 1992;12:4:32–36.

Hamburgh RR. Principles of cancer treatment. *Clinical Management in Physical Therapy.* 1992;12:4:37–41.

Hicks JE. Exercise for cancer patients. In: Basmajian JV, Wolf SL, eds. *Therapeutic Exercise.* 5th ed. Baltimore, Md: Williams & Wilkins; 1990;28–31.

Hock K. Ambulatory oncology program. *Clinical Management in Physical Therapy.* 1992;12:4:87–91.

Holtzman L, Chesney K. Rehabilitation of the breast cancer patient. In: McGarvery CL, ed. *Physical Therapy for the Cancer Patient: Clinics in Physical Therapy.* New York, NY: Churchill Livingstone; 1990:85–110.

Kuchler T, Wood-Dauphines S. Working with people who have cancer: guidelines for physical therapists. *Physiotherapy Canada.* 1991;43:4:19–23.

Luk KH, Drennan T, Anderson K. Potential role of physical therapists in hyperthermia in cancer therapy: the need for further training. *Physical Therapy.* 1986;66:340–343.

Marcant D, Rapin CH. Role of the physiotherapist in palliative care. *Journal of Pain and Symptom Management.* 1993;8:2:68–71.

McLoughlin WJ, Holz S. Cancer rehabilitation is an integrated support system. *Clinical Management in Physical Therapy.* 1985;5:6:10–12.

Pfalzer LA. Aerobic exercise for patients with disseminated cancer. *Clinical Management in Physical Therapy.* 1988;8:2:351–370.

Pfalzer L. Physical agents and the patient with cancer. *Clinical Management in Physical Therapy.* 1992;12:4:83–86.

Pfalzer L, Walter J. Facts and fiction: cancer in the 1990's. *Clinical Management in Physical Therapy.* 1992;12:4:26–31.

Sayre RS, Marcoux BC. Exercise and autologous bone marrow transplants. *Clinical Management in Physical Therapy.* 1992;12:4:78–82.

Sicard-Rosenbaum L, Danoff J. Cancer and ultrasound: a warning letter. *Physical Therapy.* 1993;73:404–406.

Snyder R. Coping: you and your patient with cancer. *Clinical Management in Physical Therapy.* 1992;12:4:64–69.

Snyder R. Physical therapy in terminal illness. *Clinical Management in Physical Therapy.* 1992;12:4:96–100.

Tool JL. Physical therapy in the care of patients with a diagnosis of cancer. *Clinical Management in Physical Therapy.* 1992;12:4:96–100.

Watchie J. Cardiopulmonary complications of cancer. *Clinical Management in Physical Therapy.* 1992;12:4:92–95.

Yoshioka H. Rehabilitation for the terminal cancer patient. *American Journal of Physical Medicine and Rehabilitation.* 1994;73:199–206.

Lung Cancer

DESCRIPTION

Cancer is a cellular malignancy characterized by the loss of the usual controls. This allows unrestricted cellular proliferation that can invade normal tissues as well as metastasize to other sites. If left untreated, this uncontrolled spread of abnormal cells can lead to death.

Lung cancer usually begins in the epithelium of the bronchial and bronchioalveolar surfaces as well as in the bronchial mucous glands. Lung cancer is the most common cause of death from cancer.

CAUSE

The main cause of lung cancer is cigarette smoking. Other factors include exposure to chemicals such as chromium, arsenic, and nickel, as well as to compounds such as asbestos dust, chloromethyl ethers, and vinyl chloride.

ASSESSMENT

Areas
Assessment should be performed preoperatively, concerning client's tolerance.
- History
- Psychosocial, including family and social support, employment history, and history of exposure to carcinogenic agents
- Pain
- Posture
- Strength, including trunk and abdominal musculature
- Mobility, including active range of motion (ROM)
- Functional level

- Pulmonary, including rate, rhythm, and pattern of respiration; chest mobility; structure of thorax; degree of dyspnea, cough productivity and effectiveness; type and amount of sputum; breath sounds
- Cardiovascular, including endurance
- Special tests to which the PT may or may not have access

Instruments/Procedures (See References for Sources)

Functional Level
- Katz Index of Activities of Daily Living
- Barthel Mobility Index for ADL disturbance
- Functional Independence Measure

Pain
- finger dynameter
- pain intensity number scale
- visual analogue scale

Special Tests to Which the PT May or May Not Have Access
- arterial blood gases
- blood chemistry
- bone scan
- computed tomography (CT) scan
- electrocardiogram
- magnetic resonance imaging (MRI)
- mediastinoscopy
- pulmonary function test
- x-rays

PROBLEMS
Problems associated with the postsurgical client are as follows:
- The client usually has an ineffective and unproductive cough.
- The client usually has a decreased chest expansion.
- The client usually has a poor breathing ratio.
- The client can have decreased trunk mobility.
- There can be decreased tolerance for ambulation.

TREATMENT/MANAGEMENT
Physical therapy intervention in the client with lung cancer usually relates to recovery from surgery, although the client may also undergo chemotherapy and/or radiation therapy.

Preoperative Instruction
- Instruct the client in manual assistive and independent coughing techniques to be performed every 30 minutes and with every position change (ideally 20 minutes post change). Teach independent coughing utilizing huffing techniques.
- Teach proper breathing techniques, including diaphragmatic, pursed-lip, and segmental breathing techniques. Instruct in active and isometric lower extremity exercises and postural considerations.

Postoperative Exercise Program
- Breathing exercise program begins post extubation with diaphragmatic, pursed-lip, and segmental patterns. Begin in supine position, and progress to sitting and then standing as tolerated by the client. Encourage maximal chest expansion. May need to use transcutaneous electrical nerve stimulation (TENS) for analgesia.
- Progressive ambulation may begin on day 2 with assistance as needed.
- Begin trunk mobility exercises after chest tubes are removed. Include flexion, extension, lateral flexion, and rotation exercises.
- Stress continued awareness of posture.
- Continue emphasis on chest expansion, trunk mobility, and endurance for ambulation. Address the need for pain management, as indicated.
- Follow progression of exercise program, including a home self-care program.

PRECAUTIONS/CONTRAINDICATIONS
- Coughing with knees and hips flexed can help avoid overstressing abdominal musculature.

DESIRED OUTCOME/PROGNOSIS
- The client will demonstrate an effective and productive cough.
- The client will resume preoperative chest expansion in the proportion appropriate to the amount of lung resection.
- The client will demonstrate appropriate breathing pattern and ratio.
- The client will resume preoperative level of trunk mobility.
- The client will tolerate ambulation of at least 1,000 feet with no dyspnea.
- The client will be able to manage pain.

REFERENCES

ASSESSMENT
Pfalzer LA. Oncology: examination, diagnosis, and treatment. Medical and surgical considerations. In: Myers RS, ed. *Saunders Manual of Physical Therapy Practice*. Philadelphia, Pa: WB Saunders Co; 1995:65–147.
Pfalzer LA. Oncology: examination, diagnosis, and treatment. Physical therapy considerations. In: Myers RS, ed. *Saunders Manual of Physical Therapy Practice*. Philadelphia, Pa: WB Saunders Co; 1995:149–190.

Functional level

Katz Index of Activities of Daily Living
Benjamin Rose Hospital Staff. Multidisciplinary studies of illness in aged persons: II. A new classification of functional status in activities of daily living. *Journal of Chronic Disease*. 1959;9:55–62.
Brorsson B, Ashberg KH. Katz Index of Independence in ADL: reliability and validity in short-term care. *Scandinavian Journal of Rehabilitation Medicine*. 1984;16:125–132.

Barthel Mobility Index
Yoshioka H. Rehabilitation for the terminal cancer patient. *American Journal of Physical Medicine and Rehabilitation*. 1994;73:199–206.

Functional Independence Measure
Granger CV, Hamilton BB, Keith RA, et al. Advance in functional assessment for medical rehabilitation. *Topics in Geriatric Rehabilitation*. 1986;1:3:59–74.

Keith RA, Granger CV, Hamilton BB, Sherwins FS. The Functional Independence Measure. *Advances in Clinical Rehabilitation.* 1987;1:6–18.

Pain

Wilkie D, Lovejoy N, Dodd M, Tesler M. Cancer pain intensity measurement: concurrent validity of three tools—finger dynameter, pain intensity number scale, visual analog scale. *Hospice Journal.* 1990;6:1:1–13.

TREATMENT

Boyd-Walton J. The role of rehabilitation services in oncology. *Clinical Management in Physical Therapy.* 1985;5:2:24–25.

Dean JT, Davidson G. Trismus after radiation therapy. *Clinical Management in Physical Therapy.* 1992;12:4:70–76.

Delisa JA, Miller RM, Melnick RR, et al. Rehabilitation of the cancer patient. In: DeVita VT Jr, Hellman S, Roseberg SA, et al, eds. *Cancer: Principles and Practice of Oncology.* 3rd ed. Philadelphia, Pa: JB Lippincott Co; 1989:2333–2368.

Etherington ME. Physical therapy management of the cancer patient. *Clinical Management in Physical Therapy.* 1987;7:3:12, 14–15.

Gray RC. The management of limb oedema in patients with advanced cancer. *Physiotherapy.* 1987;73:504–506.

Gudas SA. Directives in cancer rehabilitation. *Clinical Management in Physical Therapy.* 1992;12:4:32–36.

Hamburgh RR. Principles of cancer treatment. *Clinical Management in Physical Therapy.* 1992;12:4:37–41.

Hicks JE. Exercise for cancer patients. In: Basmajian JV, Wolf SL, eds. *Therapeutic Exercise.* 5th ed. Baltimore, Md: Williams & Wilkins, 1990:28–31.

Hock K. Ambulatory oncology program. *Clinical Management in Physical Therapy.* 1992;12:4:87–91.

Kuchler T, Wood-Dauphines S. Working with people who have cancer: guidelines for physical therapists. *Physiotherapy Canada.* 1991;43:4:19–23.

Luk KH, Drennan T, Anderson K. Potential role of physical therapists in hyperthermia in cancer therapy: the need for further training. *Physical Therapy.* 1986;66:340–343.

Marcant D, Rapin CH. Role of the physiotherapist in palliative care. *Journal of Pain and Symptom Management.* 1993;8:2:68–71.

McLoughlin WJ, Holz S. Cancer rehabilitation is an integrated support system. *Clinical Management in Physical Therapy.* 1985;5:6:10–12.

Pfalzer L. Physical agents and the patient with cancer. *Clinical Management in Physical Therapy.* 1992;12:4:83–86.

Pfalzer L, Walter J. Facts and fiction: cancer in the 1990's. *Clinical Management in Physical Therapy.* 1992;12:4:26–31.

Shea BD, VLad G. Rehabilitation of the breast cancer patient. In: McGarvery CL, ed. *Physical Therapy for the Cancer Patient: Clinics in Physical Therapy.* New York, NY: Churchill Livingstone; 1990:29–45.

Sicard-Rosenbaum L, Danoff J. Cancer and ultrasound: a warning letter. *Physical Therapy.* 1993;73:404–406.

Snyder R. Coping: you and your patient with cancer. *Clinical Management in Physical Therapy.* 1992;12:4:64–69.

Snyder R. Physical therapy in terminal illness. *Clinical Management in Physical Therapy.* 1992;12:4:96–100.

Tool JL. Physical therapy in the care of patients with a diagnosis of cancer. *Clinical Management in Physical Therapy.* 1992;12:4:96–100.

Watchie J. Cardiopulmonary complications of cancer. *Clinical Management in Physical Therapy.* 1992;12:4:92–95.

Yoshioka H. Rehabilitation for the terminal cancer patient. *American Journal of Physical Medicine and Rehabilitation.* 1994;73:199–206.

Soft Tissue Sarcoma

DESCRIPTION

Cancer is a cellular malignancy characterized by the loss of the usual controls. This allows unrestricted cellular proliferation that can invade normal tissues as well as metastasize to other sites.

Soft tissue sarcoma is a malignant tumor that begins in the soft connective tissue area. There are 30 types of sarcomas. These are usually named after the cell of origin, such as liposarcoma, arising from adipose tissue. The types of soft tissue sarcomas include fibrosarcomas, malignant fibrous histiocytomas, synovial sarcomas, rhabdomyosarcomas, liposarcomas, and leiomyosarcomas.

CAUSE

Risk factors for soft tissue sarcoma include exposure to phenoxyacetic acids, vinyl chloride, and high doses of radiation; rare genetic defects; certain inherited diseases, such as von Rechlinghausen's disease; and a retrovirus in the case of Kaposi's sarcoma.

ASSESSMENT

Areas
- History
- Psychosocial
- Pain
- Posture
- Cardiopulmonary, including endurance
- Musculoskeletal, including joint integrity
- Strength
- Mobility, including active range of motion (ROM)
- Neurological
- Genitourinary
- Skin, including color, edema, and open wounds
- Functional level: including activities of daily living (ADLs)

Instruments/Procedures (See References for Sources)

Functional Level
- Katz Index of Activities of Daily Living
- Barthel Mobility Index for ADL disturbance
- Functional Independence Measure

Pain
- finger dynameter
- pain intensity number scale
- visual analog scale

PROBLEMS

Problems Related to Side Effects of Cancer Medical Treatment Protocols
- The client may have nausea, vomiting, alopecia, cardiomyopathy, peripheral neuropathy (mixed sensorimotor), mucositis, myelosuppression, delayed healing, decreased endurance, amenorrhea, and sexual dysfunction.

Complications due to Preoperative Radiation
- There may be a predisposition of long bones to fracture due to devascularization and delayed healing.
- Usually there are radiation reactions of dermatitis or erythema. There may be fibrosis of connective tissue, leading to joint contracture.
- The client may have edema, pain, and decreased function due to bone necrosis, endarteritis, and decreased elasticity of lymphatic channels. The client may have edema in the lower extremities.
- If the glenoid complex is intact, the upper extremity is probably normal. Glenoid removal leads to decreased arm ROM, especially beyond 90 degrees.
- Usually there is pain and fatigue.

Problems Post Buttock Resection
- Client may complain of pain at the incision site.
- The client can have difficulty climbing stairs.
- The client can have altered sexual function.
- The client can have altered bowel habits.
- The client usually has an altered body image.

Problem in Soft Tissue Sarcoma of the Thigh
- The client can develop pain.
- The client can have joint dysfunction.
- The client can have drainage at the site of excision.
- The client can develop chronic lymphedema.
- The client can have altered sexual function.

Problems Post Medial Excision
- The client usually has pain.
- The client can have edema.
- There may be excision of the hamstring muscle.
- The client may have stiffness after prolonged sitting.

TREATMENT/MANAGEMENT
- Provide whirlpool/debridement for burns or open wound.
- Encourage an active exercise program.

For Limb-Sparing Treatment
- Rehabilitation should begin at diagnosis and continue for life.
- Make assistive devices available, such as over-the-bed trapezes for bed mobility, seating cushioning, and grab bars for safety.
- Consider transcutaneous electrical nerve stimulation (TENS) for pain.
- Instruct the client in use of support hose for lower extremity edema.

Post Buttock Resection
- Strengthen remaining hip musculature.
- Supply seat cushion or other assistive devices.
- Consider a prosthetic buttock device.

Internal Hemipelvectomy
- Provide shoe lifts immediately after bed rest restrictions are removed (often not for 3–6 weeks post surgery).
- Provide gait training using partial weight bearing with crutches. The client may be on crutches for 6 months or until sufficient bone union occurs.
- Exercise distal musculature and upper extremities with active exercise.

Soft Tissue Sarcoma of the Thigh
- The client stays in bed with a knee immobilizer until more activity is allowed. Ankle motion can be performed at this time.
- When ambulation has been approved, begin with partial weight bearing with splint. Consider use of ankle-foot orthosis at about 2 weeks post surgery.
- As drainage diminishes and drainage tubing is removed, therapy can become more aggressive, with ambulation and exercise.
- Apply splint to knee and foot as needed to protect the wound.

Sarcoma of the Medial Thigh, Resulting in Excision of the Adductor Muscles
- Activities are usually minimal.
- Support stockings are indicated for upright activities.
- Instruct the client in proper care of skin and positioning to diminish edema and precautions to prevent injury leading to infection.

PRECAUTIONS/CONTRAINDICATIONS
If the ambulation occurs without the brace (after removal of the quadriceps muscle), the joint may hyperextend the knee, and there may be a subsequent increase in lumbar lordosis, with an increased risk of falling, loss of balance, and back pain.

DESIRED OUTCOME/PROGNOSIS
- The client will experience a reduction in pain.
- The client will control edema formation.
- The client will prevent infection.
- The client will achieve a maximum level of function.

Change can occur up to 6 months after cancer treatment. Most of the side effects are reversible over time. Active stretching may reverse muscle fibrosis. Chronic changes may be irreversible.

REFERENCES

ASSESSMENT
Pfalzer LA. Oncology: examination, diagnosis, and treatment. Medical and surgical considerations. In: Myers RS, ed. *Saunders Manual of Physical Therapy Practice*. Philadelphia, Pa: WB Saunders Co; 1995:65–147.

Pfalzer LA. Oncology: examination, diagnosis, and treatment. Physical therapy considerations. In: Myers RS, ed. *Saunders Manual of Physical Therapy Practice*. Philadelphia, Pa: WB Saunders Co; 1995:149–190.

Functional Level

Katz Index of Activities of Daily Living
Benjamin Rose Hospital Staff. Multidisciplinary studies of illness in aged persons: II. A new classification of functional status in activities of daily living. *Journal of Chronic Disease.* 1959;9:55–62.
Brorsson B, Ashberg KH. Katz Index of Independence in ADL: reliability and validity in short-term care. *Scandinavian Journal of Rehabilitation Medicine.* 1984;16:125–132.

Barthel Mobility Index
Yoshioka H. Rehabilitation for the terminal cancer patient. *American Journal of Physical Medicine and Rehabilitation.* 1994;73:199–206.

Functional Independence Measure
Granger CV, Hamilton BB, Keith RA, et al. Advance in functional assessment for medical rehabilitation. *Topics in Geriatric Rehabilitation.* 1986;1:3:59–74.
Keith RA, Granger CV, Hamilton BB, Sherwins FS. The Functional Independence Measure. *Advances in Clinical Rehabilitation.* 1987;1:6–18.

Pain
Wilkie D, Lovejoy N, Dodd M, Tesler M. Cancer pain intensity measurement: concurrent validity of three tools—finger dynameter, pain intensity number scale, visual analog scale. *Hospice Journal.* 1990;6:1:1–13.

TREATMENT
Boyd-Walton J. The role of rehabilitation services in oncology. *Clinical Management in Physical Therapy.* 1985;5:2:24–25.
Dean JT, Davidson G. Trismus after radiation therapy. *Clinical Management in Physical Therapy.* 1992;12:4:70–76.
Delisa JA, Miller RM, Melnick RR, et al. Rehabilitation of the cancer patient. In: DeVita VT Jr, Hellman S, Roseberg SA, et al, eds. *Cancer: Principles and Practice of Oncology.* 3rd ed. Philadelphia, Pa: JB Lippincott Co; 1989:2333–2368.
Etherington ME. Physical therapy management of the cancer patient. *Clinical Management in Physical Therapy.* 1987;7:3:12, 14–15.
Gerber LH, McGarvey CL III. Musculoskeletal deficits and rehabilitation intervention in the cancer patient. In: Wittes RE, ed. *Manual of Oncologic Therapeutics.* Philadelphia, Pa: JB Lippincott Co; 1989–1990.
Gray RC. The management of limb oedema in patients with advanced cancer. *Physiotherapy.* 1987;73:504–506.
Gudas SA. Directives in cancer rehabilitation. *Clinical Management in Physical Therapy.* 1992;12:4:32–36.
Hamburgh RR. Principles of cancer treatment. *Clinical Management in Physical Therapy.* 1992;12:4:37–41.
Hicks JE. Exercise for cancer patients. In: Basmajian JV, Wolf SL, eds. *Therapeutic Exercise.* 5th ed. Baltimore, Md: Williams & Wilkins; 1990:28–31.
Hock K. Ambulatory oncology program. *Clinical Management in Physical Therapy.* 1992;12:4:87–91.
Kemp HBS. Bone tumours of the appendicular skeleton. *Physiotherapy.* 1986;66:340–343.
Kuchler T, Wood-Dauphines S. Working with people who have cancer: guidelines for physical therapists. *Physiotherapy Canada.* 1991;43:4:19–23.
Lampert MK, Gahagen C. Rehabilitation of the sarcoma patient. In: McGarvery CL, ed. *Physical Therapy for the Cancer Patient: Clinics in Physical Therapy.* New York, NY: Churchill Livingstone; 1990:111–135.

Luk KH, Drennan T, Anderson K. Potential role of physical therapists in hyperthermia in cancer therapy: the need for further training. *Physical Therapy*. 1986;66:340–343.

Marcant D, Rapin CH. Role of the physiotherapist in palliative care. *Journal of Pain and Symptom Management*. 1993;8:2:68–71.

Mattsson E, Brostrom LA, Linnarsson D. Changes in walking ability after knee replacement. *International Orthopaedics*. 1990;14:277–280.

McLoughlin WJ, Holz S. Cancer rehabilitation is an integrated support system. *Clinical Management in Physical Therapy*. 1985;5:6:10–12.

Pfalzer LA. Aerobic exercise for patients with disseminated cancer. *Clinical Management in Physical Therapy*. 1988;8:2:351–370.

Pfalzer L. Physical agents and the patient with cancer. *Clinical Management in Physical Therapy*. 1992;12:4:83–86.

Pfalzer L, Walter J. Facts and fiction: cancer in the 1990's. *Clinical Management in Physical Therapy*. 1992;12:4:26–31.

Quan KM, Shiran M, Watmough DJ. Applicators for generating ultrasound-induced hyperthermia in neoplastic tumors and for use in ultrasound physiotherapy. *Physics in Medicine and Biology*. 1989;34:1719–1731.

Sicard-Rosenbaum L, Danoff J. Cancer and ultrasound: a warning letter. *Physical Therapy*. 1993;73:404–406.

Snyder R. Coping: you and your patient with cancer. *Clinical Management in Physical Therapy*. 1992;12:4:64–69.

Snyder R. Physical therapy in terminal illness. *Clinical Management in Physical Therapy*. 1992;12:4:96–100.

Tool JL. Physical therapy in the care of patients with a diagnosis of cancer. *Clinical Management in Physical Therapy*. 1992;12:4:96–100.

Watchie J. Cardiopulmonary complications of cancer. *Clinical Management in Physical Therapy*. 1992;12:4:92–95.

Yoshioka H. Rehabilitation for the terminal cancer patient. *American Journal of Physical Medicine and Rehabilitation*. 1994;73:199–206.

Chapter 12
Pediatric Disorders

- Arthrogryposis multiplex congenita
- Asthma
- Brachial plexus injury
- Burns—child
- Cerebral palsy
- Congenital heart disease
- Congenital dislocation of the hip
- Cystic fibrosis
- Deaf-blindness
- Down syndrome
- Dysphagia
- Failure to thrive
- Fetal alcohol syndrome
- Foot deformities
- Genetic disorders
- Hemophilia
- High-risk or at-risk infants
- Infectious disorders of the brain
- Juvenile rheumatoid arthritis
- Learning disorders
- Legg–Calve–Perthes
- Limb deficiencies and amputations
- Limb-length discrepancy
- Mental retardation
- Muscular dystrophy
- Near-drowning
- Neoplasms—child
- Osgood–Schlatter disease

- Osteogenesis imperfecta
- Pain in childhood
- Pediatric HIV/AIDS
- Poliomyelitis
- Premature and low-birth-weight infants
- Reflex sympathetic dystrophy in children
- Respiratory disorders in children
- Rett syndrome
- Scoliosis
- Slipped capital femoral epiphysis
- Spina bifida/meningomyelocele/myelodysplasia
- Spinal cord injury—child
- Spinal muscular atrophy
- Torticollis, congenital muscular
- Traumatic head injuries—child
- Ventilator dependency—child

Arthrogryposis Multiplex Congenita

Also known as multiple congenital contractures.

DESCRIPTION

Arthrogryposis multiplex congenita (AMC) is a nonprogressive, congenital disorder present at birth that is characterized by fibrous ankylosis of multiple joints, multiple joint contractures, and muscle weakness. Major forms include amyoplastic or myogenic (classic form), contracture syndrome, neuromuscular or neurogenic syndrome, distal arthrogryposis, congenital anomalies, and chromosomal abnormalities. (See Donohoe & Bleakney, "Arthrogryposis Multiplex Congenita," p. 261, in references.)

CAUSE

The cause is unknown except for the distal arthrogryposis form, which is inherited as an autosomal-dominant trait. Insult is thought to occur during the first trimester of pregnancy. There may be a relationship to impaired movement during fetal life. The neurogenic form may be caused by a disorder in the anterior horn cell. Other possibilities include hyperthermia of the fetus caused by maternal fever, prenatal viral infection, vascular compromise between mother and fetus, or a septum of the uterus. Other contributing factors may be fetal crowding or constraint in multiple births, breech position, and oligohydramnios (reduced volume of amniotic fluid).

ASSESSMENT

Areas
- Mobility, including joint range of motion (ROM)
- Muscle strength
- Ambulation skills
- Soft tissue fibrosis
- Functional skills
- Developmental milestones

Instruments/Procedures

Developmental Milestones
- photographs and videos of the initial position and periodic follow-ups to document changes

Mobility
- goniometric assessment of joint motion, active passive and functional (hand to mouth)

Muscle Strength
- manual muscle testing to determine whether limitation in function is due to muscle weakness or absence of muscles

PROBLEMS
- Joint rigidity and contractures are present. Multiple, symmetrical joints are involved. Contractures are nonprogressive. Some joint mobility improves with age.
- Hips may be dislocated or subluxed and usually are flexed, abducted, and externally rotated.

- Knees are either extended or flexed, with few degrees or no motion. The patellae may be dislocated or absent.
- Feet are often in the equinovarus position (clubfeet).
- Shoulders generally are adducted and internally rotated. This limits shoulder abduction and external rotation.
- Elbows are either flexed or extended, with few degrees of motion.
- Wrists usually are flexed and ulnarly deviated; this decreases hand manipulation skills.
- Fingers and digits are flexed.
- Muscles are hypoplastic or atrophied. Deltoids, biceps, and forearm muscles may be inactive.
- Some extremities may have few or no features.
- Some extremities may be cylindrical or tubular.
- Some muscle groups may be absent.
- Some skin creases may be absent.
- Soft tissue webbing is sometimes present over the ventral aspects of the flexed joints.
- Deep tendon reflexes are absent or reduced.
- The child may have feeding disorders due to structural disorders of the tongue and jaw.
- The child usually needs assistive devices and equipment for ambulation and manipulation.
- Intelligence and speech are usually normal, and sensation is usually intact.
- Associated abnormalities include scoliosis, cleft palate, cryptorchidism (undescended testes), cardiac lesions, congenital heart disease, dimpling of skin over joints, hemangiomas, absent or decreased finger creases, facial abnormalities, respiratory problems leading to frequent infections, abdominal hernias, urinary tract malformations, constipation, and failure to thrive.

TREATMENT/MANAGEMENT

AMC is a complex disorder that requires the combined efforts of an interdisciplinary team. The physical therapist works in cooperation with the team, which should include the child.

- Increase ROM and improve mobility.
  1. Provide stretching exercise to increase ROM, especially during the neonatal period and continuing through the first 3 years. Sessions should be short periods of time several times per day.
  2. Serial casting may be used to promote and maintain ROM.
  3. Progressive splints may be needed.
  4. Use passive ROM to maintain joint mobility in older children.
- Provide therapeutic exercise to increase muscle strength.
- Positioning is important to decrease deformity and increase function.
- Improve motor control, especially in ambulation.
- Promote functional skills and maximize independent activities of daily living (ADLs).
  1. Provide exercises to increase upper extremity range and mobility.
  2. Use splinting and serial casting where useful.
  3. In cooperation with an occupational therapist, recommend adapted equipment for feeding and other daily activities.
- Optimize lower extremity for ambulation.
  1. Provide activities to promote motor development.
  2. Decrease joint contractures with exercise, casting, or splinting in hip, knee, ankle, and foot.
  3. Increase weight-bearing activities using standing devices.
  4. Provide pregait training with alternating kick activities and weight transfer.

5. Participate in bracing of feet and legs to provide stability.
- Increase performance of gross motor skills.
- Assist in determining need for orthotic and assistive devices. Equipment needs to be as light-weight as possible to facilitate use and increase compliance.
- Follow up for surgery for clubfoot, dislocated hip, knee joint contractures, elbow extension to provide flexion, wrist fusion, and scoliosis.
- Maximize opportunity for cognitive and social development.
  1. Provide early ambulation aids such as modified child seats to assist family in taking child along.
  2. Provide adapted devices to permit child to explore environment and play alone or with others.

PRECAUTIONS/CONTRAINDICATIONS
- Progress is slow and requires patience and persistence.
- Rigid splinting of the lower extremity should be avoided where possible to facilitate mobility.

DESIRED OUTCOME/PROGNOSIS
- Lower extremities will have well-aligned joints for weight bearing.
- Upper extremity function will enable the child to gain independence in ADLs.
- Parents will be educated and instructed regarding exercises.
- Exercise will be performed following surgical procedures to improve function.

REFERENCES

Donohoe M, Bleakney DA. Arthrogryposis multiplex congenita. In: Campbell SK, ed. *Physical Therapy for Children*. Philadelphia, Pa: WB Saunders Co; 1994:261–277.

Hall JG. Arthrogryposis. *American Family Physician*. 1989;39:113–119.

Moore P, Major R, Stallard J, Butler PB. Contracture correction device for arthrogryposis. *Physiotherapy*. 1990;76:303–305.

Robinson RO, Cartwright R, Fixsen JA, Jones M. Arthrogryposis. In: McCarthy GT, ed. *Physical Disability in Childhood: An Interdisciplinary Approach to Management*. New York, NY: Churchill Livingstone; 1992:293–303.

Shepherd RB. Arthrogryposis multiplex congenita. In: Shepherd RB, ed. *Physiotherapy in Paediatrics*. 3rd ed. Oxford, England: Butterworth-Heinemann; 1995:235–237.

Tecklin JS. Arthrogryposis multiplex congenita. In: Tecklin JS, ed. *Pediatric Physical Therapy*. 2nd ed. Philadelphia, Pa: JB Lippincott Co; 1994:298–302.

Asthma

DESCRIPTION

Asthma is a lung disease characterized by (1) airways obstruction that is usually reversible either spontaneously or with treatment, (2) airways inflammation, and (3) increased airways responsiveness to a variety of stimuli. More boys than girls are affected. Incidence in blacks is higher than in whites, and incidence in urban areas is higher than in rural. Use of chest physical therapy with asthma conditions is controversial. There are mixed results in research studies. See Asher, et al, "Effects of Chest Physical Therapy," Edenbrandt et al, "Effect of Physiotherapy," and Eid et al, "Chest Physiotherapy," in Treatment references.

CAUSE

The airways obstruction in asthma is due to a combination of factors that include (1) spasm of airways smooth muscle, (2) edema of airways mucosa, (3) increased mucus secretion, (4) cellular infiltration of the airways walls, and (5) injury and loss of squamous cells in the airways epithelium. Genetic research has shown that the gene responsible for asthma is on the long arm of chromosome 11. Inheritance is through an autosomal-dominant pattern with variable patterns of expression.

ASSESSMENT

Areas
- Range of motion (ROM), especially the shoulder
- Respiratory: lung inflation during inspiration, use of accessory muscles, breath sounds, dyspnea; in infants, signs of increased respiratory muscle activity, such as flaring nostrils, sternal paradox, and rib recession; for children under age 3, differences between resting and stressful conditions such as during feeding, crying, hospital procedures, and handling
- Muscle strength
- Posture
- Exercise tolerance: heart rate, oxygen saturation, respiratory rate, breathing patterns, blood pressure, exhaled gas, end-tidal CO_2 minute ventilization, O_2 consumption, and respiratory exchange ratio

Instruments/Procedures (See References for Sources)

Exercise Tolerance (See also "Respiratory")
- Borg Scale of Rating of Perceived Exertion (RPE)
- ergometer or exercise bicycle
- stair climbing test
- treadmill test

Respiratory
- spirometer
- visual analogue scale for dyspnea
- Wright Peak Flow Meter
- pulmonary function tests (PFT)
  1. forced expiratory volume in one (FEV1)
  2. vital capacity (VC)
  3. volume of trapped gas (VTG)
  4. expiratory reserve volume (ERV)
  5. functional residual capacity (FRC)
  6. residual volume (RV)
  7. total lung capacity (TLC)
  8. peak expiratory flow rate (PEFR)

9. maximum midexpiratory flow (FEF 25–75)
10. maximum oxygen consumption (VO_2 max)
11. peak work capacity (PWC)
12. saturation (percentage) of oxygen (SaO_2)

PROBLEMS
- There may be dyspnea or shortness of breath.
- There may be wheezing, especially after exercise or following a minor respiratory tract infection.
- There may be coughing episodes, including nocturnal coughing.
- There may be chest tightness.
- Child may feel out of breath.
- Child may lack endurance.
- There may be muscle weakness.
- There may be excessive use of accessory muscles in breathing.
- There may be excessive use of abnormal muscles in breathing.
- Child may be hypersensitive to stimuli that are *extrinsic* (allergic), such as mold, pollen, dander, dust, animal dander (cats, dogs, feathers), cigarette smoke, foods, drugs, and strong odors, or *intrinsic* (nonallergic), such as changes in weather or climate, emotional stress, exercise, inhalation of irritating substances, or viral infections.
- Child may be absent from school due to wheezing.
- Child may have difficulty with speaking due to wheezing.
- Child may feel fear, frustration, and anger related to the asthma attacks and its symptoms and limitations.
- There may be limitations on physical activities such as running or jogging.
- Child may have difficulty falling asleep and staying asleep.
- Child may have difficulty concentrating on school work.
- Child may not be allowed to have pets.

TREATMENT/MANAGEMENT
- Improve breathing control and lung function.
  1. Recommend learning to swim to encourage breathing exercises such as swimming face down in the water and diving to the floor to pick up objects.
  2. Teach breathing exercises that emphasize full, deep, and efficient expansion on inspiration, concentrating on the diaphragm, followed by passive relaxed expiration.
- Teach inhaler usage.
  1. Show child how to use spacer inhaler device (nebuhaler or volumatic) with face mask.
  2. Teach suck, breath-hold, and breathing out in preparation for using patient-activated inhalers such as rotahalers, diskhalers, and spinhalers.
- Improve exercise tolerance and physical activity if child's working capacity is below predicted normal values.
  1. Use conditioning exercises in swimming pool.
  2. Use exercise or stationary bicycle.
  3. Show child how to warm up before exercise and cool down after exercise.
- Prevent thoracic and spinal deformity.
  1. Suggest exercises for thoracic mobility such as swimming or singing lessons.
  2. Encourage good posture.

- Maintain or increase ROM.
- Increase muscle strength.
- Encourage relaxation to reduce fear and anxiety while increasing feeling of control. Jacobson's relaxation techniques may be useful.
  1. Work with family to develop an emergency plan for acute attacks.
  2. Positioning techniques: While waiting for the bronchodilator to take effect, the child can learn to lean forward in a relaxed position, with the arms supported on a table, or against a wall, the edge of a bed, or a railing, while attempting to breathe quietly, with emphasis on deep inspiration and relaxed expiration.
  3. Increase lateral costal breathing and/or diaphragmatic breathing.
  4. Teach relaxation of the shoulder girdle.
- Use and teach techniques to clear secretions.
  1. postural drainage
  2. percussion
  3. vibrations
  4. forced expiration technique
  5. arm "wing" flapping
  6. coughing
- Educate the patient and family.
  1. Assist in teaching the child to coordinate effective inhalation with the spray mechanism on an aerosol dispenser.
  2. Assist in teaching the child how to blow his or her nose one nostril at a time.
  3. Teach the child and family to recognize early signs of an asthma attack.
  4. Teach the parents drainage positions and manual techniques.
- Group activities in small groups of four or five children enable the therapist to assess how effective the child is in coping with exercise and activities when other children are present.

PRECAUTIONS/CONTRAINDICATIONS
- Asthma attacks should be taken seriously. Get medical assistance if normal management techniques for the particular child are not working.
- Exercise testing with a child under 3 years is not recommended because the child usually has difficulty participating and cooperating.
- Care should be taken in selecting the proper protocol for exercise testing on the basis of the child's age, disease severity, level of physical activity, and purpose for performing the test so that the test does not aggravate or bring on an asthma attack.
- Discontinue exercise testing if the patient requests it, if pallor or extreme dyspnea is observed, if ECG dysrhythmias occur, if there is a decrease in systolic or pulse pressure with increasing effort, if systolic pressure is greater than 250 mm Hg, or if diastolic pressure is greater than 110 mm Hg.
- Discontinue treatment if the child is in status asthmaticus. Resume treatment as status asthmaticus wanes (decrease in severe bronchospasm).

DESIRED OUTCOME/PROGNOSIS
- The value of physical therapy in working with childhood asthma has not been established.
- The child will be able to perform independently normal physical activities such as daily self-care tasks and chores.
- The child's attendance at school will improve, and days absent due to asthma will decrease.

- The child will be able to participate in selected recreational activities.
- The sleep cycle will normalize due to decreased incidence of wheezing.
- The number of days in bed due to asthma will decrease.

REFERENCES

ASSESSMENT

Exercise Tolerance
Borg GV. Psychophysical bases of perceived exertion. *Medical Science and Sports Exercise*. 1982;14:377–387.

Respiratory
Stark RD, Gambles SA, Chatterjee SS. An exercise test to assess clinical dyspnoea: estimation of reproducibility and sensitivity. *British Journal of the Chest*. 1982;76:269–274.

TREATMENT
Asher MI, Douglas C, Airy M, Andrews D, Trenholme A. Effects of chest physical therapy on lung function in children recovering from acute severe asthma. *Pediatric Pulmonology*. 1990;9:146–151.

Darbee J, Cerny F. Exercise testing and exercise conditioning for children with lung dysfunction. In: Irwin S, Tecklin JS, eds. *Cardiopulmonary Physical Therapy*. St Louis, Mo: CV Mosby Co; 1995:563–578.

Edenbrandt L, Olseni L, Swevonious E, Jonson G. Effect of physiotherapy in asthmatic children: a one-year follow-up after physical training once a week. *Acta Paediatrica Scandinavica*. 1990;79:973–975.

Eid N, Buchheit J, Neuling M, Phelps H. Chest physiotherapy in review. *Respiratory Care*. 1991;36:270–282.

Magee CL. Asthma. In: Campbell SK, ed. *Physical Therapy for Children*. Philadelphia, Pa: WB Saunders Co; 1994:717–736.

Shepherd RB. Respiratory disorders in childhood. In: Shepherd RB, ed. *Physiotherapy in Paediatrics*. 3rd ed. Oxford, England: Butterworth-Heinemann; 1995:350–362.

Tecklin JS. Asthma. In: Tecklin JS, ed. *Pediatric Physical Therapy*. 2nd ed. Philadelphia, Pa: JB Lippincott Co; 1994:271–275.

Brachial Plexus Injury

DESCRIPTION

Brachial plexus injury is an injury to nerve roots and peripheral nerves that causes temporary or permanent paralysis of the upper extremity. Erb's palsy is an upper brachial plexus (C5–6) injury causing adduction and internal rotation of the shoulder with pronation of the forearm; ipsilateral paralysis of the diaphragm is common. Klumpke's palsy is a lower plexus injury (C7–8 and T1) resulting in paralysis of the hand and wrists, often with ipsilateral Horner's syndrome (miosis, ptosis, anhidrosis). The Erb–Klumpke type includes the whole arm (C5–T1).

CAUSE

Brachial plexus injury arises from a difficult birth that results in stretching of an upper extremity caused by shoulder dystocia, breech extraction, or hyperabduction of the neck in cephalic presentations. The injury can be due to simple stretching, hemorrhage within a nerve, tearing of the nerve or root, or avulsion of the roots, with associated cervical cord injury.

ASSESSMENT

Areas
- Mobility: passive range of motion (ROM)
- Motor function patterns of the upper extremity, especially reaching to grasp
- Motor control of spontaneous movement and posture of the infant in the supine and prone positions and while moved around, cuddled, and talked to
- Neurological, including sensory function and loss and reflex testing, especially the Moro reflex, the placing reaction of the hands, the Galant (trunk incurvation) reflex, the neck-righting reaction, and the parachute reaction

Instruments/Procedures

Mobility
- observation of passive movement to gauge the length of muscles

Motor Function/Motor Control
- recording on videotape, cine film, or still photograph
- observation of muscle contraction and of movement in comparison with normal function at the child's age
- electromyograph (EMG) or muscle chart documentation of muscle activity

Neurological
- O'Rain's wrinkle test: Fingers are immersed in water at 40 degrees centigrade for 30 minutes; normal skin wrinkles, but denervated skin does not
- Aesthesiometer: may be used for two-point discrimination in older children, but the functional significance is questionable

PROBLEMS
- There may be atrophy if recovery of function is delayed.
- There may be contractures of the shoulder or elbow.
- There may be muscle weakness in external rotation, extension, and abduction of the shoulder; elbow flexion and forearm supination; and wrist extension.
- Upper-arm-type dysfunction involves rhomboids, levator scapulae, serratus anterior, deltoid, supraspinatus, infraspinatus, biceps brachii, brachioradialis, brachialis, supinator, and long extensors of the wrist, fingers, and thumb.
- Lower-arm-type dysfunction involves the intrinsic muscles of the hand and the extensors and flexors of the wrist and fingers.
- There may be muscle imbalance.
- There may be paralysis or weakness of certain muscles or muscle groups.
- There may be unopposed activity of muscles.
- There may be persistent and abnormal movement substitutions.
- There may be abnormal posturing of the arm.
- There may be abnormal arm movements due to muscle imbalance and substitution of incorrect motor activity. Neonate usually has adducted, medially rotated shoulder, pronated fore-

arm, and flexed wrist; this changes to an elevated, slightly abducted, medially rotated, and pronated arm.
- In whole-arm paralysis, the problems are caused by the dependent position of the arm, with resultant stretch of soft tissues and lack of muscle activity with which to preserve the integrity of the glenohumeral joint.
- In "learned nonuse," paralysis occurs because the arm has not been used.
- Delays may be noted in achieving certain milestones, such as independent sitting and performance of two-handed actions.
- There may be soft tissue contracture due to paralysis or weakness of the shoulder abductors and flexors and the scapular retractors and protractors and the overactivity of the unopposed shoulder adductors and medial rotators; or due to paralysis of the rhomboideus muscle, together with the unopposed activity of the muscles that link the humerus to the scapula, which causes the scapula to adhere to the humerus.
- There may be glenohumeral subluxation or dislocation.
- There may be posterior displacement of the humeral epiphysis.
- There may be posterior radial dislocation.
- There may be skeletal deformity.
- There may be poor bone growth.
- Sensory loss may not correspond to the pattern of motor loss.
- Respiratory dysfunction may occur if the phrenic nerve is paralyzed.
- Hemiparalysis of the diaphragm may be present if atelectasis and unilateral diaphragmatic elevation occur.

TREATMENT/MANAGEMENT
- Expand ROM. Use gentle ROM exercises during the first 2 weeks, and continue ROM through activity and gentle passive exercise to the shoulder girdle, shoulder, and hand.
- Instruct the parents to position the involved upper extremity in a neutral position. Pin the sleeve of the baby's T-shirt to the diaper.
- Position the infant in adduction, internal rotation, and supination to prevent further damage.
- Splinting of the elbow, wrist, or hand may be useful.
- Elicit active muscle function using age-appropriate developmental activities and dynamic weight bearing. Neuromuscular electrical stimulation may be helpful. Temporary restriction of the uninvolved side may facilitate use of the involved.

PRECAUTIONS/CONTRAINDICATIONS
- Avoid overstretching of flaccid muscles, tendons, and ligaments.
- Do not mobilize the glenohumeral joint to more than 30 degrees if the scapula is manually held.
- Splinting of the shoulder is controversial.
- Shoulder subluxation and contractures may develop secondary to muscle imbalance.

DESIRED OUTCOME/PROGNOSIS
- The child will be able to reach out in front of self and overhead to grasp objectives.
- The child will be able to use one hand or both hands effectively to grasp, hold, and release objectives.
- The child will be able to perform age-appropriate activities.

REFERENCES

Shepherd RB. Brachial plexus injury. In: Campbell SK, ed. *Pediatric Neurologic Physical Therapy*. 2nd ed. New York, NY: Churchill Livingstone; 1992:101–130.

Shepherd RB. Brachial plexus lesions in infancy. In: Shepherd RB, ed. *Physiotherapy in Paediatrics*. 3rd ed. Oxford, England: Butterworth-Heinemann; 1995:196–203.

Burns—Child

DESCRIPTION

A burn is a partial- or full-thickness soft tissue injury. The result is protein denaturation, burn wound edema, and loss of intravascular fluid volume due to increased permeability. Systemic effects, such as hypovolemic shock, infection, or respiratory tract injury, are greater threats to life than the local area of burn.

CAUSE

Tissue injury may be caused by thermal (flame, scalding liquid, flash), chemical, radiation, or electrical contact. More boys than girls are burned. About 10% of child abuse cases are burn injuries.

ASSESSMENT

Areas

- Chart records: type, location, extent, and depth of burn, and surgeries performed, such as escharotomies
- Range of motion (ROM) with and without dressing bandages (note: during the emergent phase of treatment, ROM may need to be "eyeballed" due to extent of injury; more accurate measurement will be possible later)
- Endurance
- Edema
- Soft tissue injury, including scarring and contracture
- Posture and positioning
- Orthotic devices such as splints
- Activities of daily living (ADLs)
- Developmental level

Instruments/Procedures (See References for Sources)

Developmental Level
- Denver Developmental Screening Test
- Early Intervention Profile

ROM
- Goniometry

Soft Tissue Injury
- Vancouver Burn Scar Assessment

PROBLEMS
- There may be pain.
- There may be loss of ROM.
- There may be lack of mobility, from joint contractures, muscle atrophy, and/or decreased cardiopulmonary function.
- There may be a loss of skin elasticity secondary to pain, edema, skin grafting, and scarring; also, inelastic eschar and edema may compromise lymphatic and vascular flow, leading to distal ischemia.
- There may be changes in physical appearance due to skin grafting, scarring, and possible amputation.
- There may be loss of function skills due to lack of mobility.
- There may be loss of developmental skills.
- There may be hypovolemia.
- There may be respiratory distress.

TREATMENT/MANAGEMENT
   Burn management is usually conducted through use of the team concept. The physical therapist must work in coordination with other team members to determine goals and implement treatment objectives.

Phases of Rehabilitation

Emergent Phase: First 48 to 72 Hours
- Have protocol established with surgery department, requiring a consult upon admission.
- If indicated, start controlling edema.
- Begin and maintain motion and mobility.
- Consider splinting and positioning.
- Start training in ADLs.
- Begin promoting normal development.

Acute Phase
- Use splinting and positioning to increase ROM by counteracting the force of contracting tissue.
- Institute ROM exercises and activities to counter the contracting forces of healthy tissue.
- Check condition of exposed tendons and joints.
- Help child participate in ADLs.

Skin Graft Phase
- Splinting may be necessary to immobilize a joint during grafting, but splint should be in an anticontracture position.
- ROM needs to be adjusted to state of graft healing. ROM may be discontinued for 3 to 5 days to permit healing.
- Begin discharge planning.

Rehabilitation Phase
- Begin weight bearing and ambulation.

- Teach skin care.
- Evaluate scar and recommend pressure garments.

Splints
- Resting splints are used to prevent hand contractures.
- Splint should be reviewed at least daily to determine whether it should be continued, modified, or discarded.
- Splint should fit properly. Check to be sure it is not impinging on nerve or blood supply.

ROM
- Initially emphasize maintaining ROM, not regaining it.
- Begin daily joint mobility exercises as soon as possible.
- Encourage team cooperation for ROM, even during life-saving phase of treatment.

Mobility
- Identify and provide means for self-mobility as early as medically possible.
- Secure team member support for early self-mobility.

Positioning
- Provide splints to prevent or reduce contractures and to promote functional position.
- Promote placement of body and especially extremities in positions of function, not positions of comfort.
- Hands should be placed in plastic or permeable-membrane bags or gloves.

Plaster Casting and Serial Casting
- Casting can be used postoperatively to immobilize a body part and prevent graft movement.
- Casting can be used to minimize scar contracture formation during the remodeling phase.
- Serial casting can be used to correct plantar-flexion contractures during wound healing.
- Serial casting can be used to increase ROM when mobility is limited due to scar tissue.

Hydrotherapy
- Whirlpool may be useful in debridement.

Pressure Garments (Tubular or Lycra)
- Pressure garments prevent or reduce hypertrophic scarring, contractures, and edema.
- Pressure garments should be replaced every 2 to 3 months. They are usually worn 23 out of 24 hours for about 18 months.
- Size is very important because the pressure must be the right amount. The garment is too big or loose if it bags or does not cling to the child, and it is too tight if it leaves deep indentations in the skin or restricts circulation.

Skin Care
- Silicone gel to the affected area can improve cosmetic appearance.
- The client should be advised to avoid sun or hot temperatures (bathwater, sunbathing), which might damage new skin.
- Regular creaming (lanolin or paraffin-based cream) and massage three to four times daily can help relieve itching (pruritus) and keep the skin soft and supple.
- If itching continues, an oral antipruritic may be necessary.

Classification of Burns by Thickness

Partial-Thickness Burns (Formerly First- and Second-Degree Burns)

A. Superficial
1. Involve the epidermis and upper portion of the dermal papillae
2. Appear red, are painful, and usually blister
3. Heal in about 2 weeks without scarring
B. Deep
1. Injure the dermis
2. Appear waxy white, are pliable, may be insensitive to light touch but are painful to deep pressure
3. Heal in about 3 to 6 weeks but usually produce scar tissue

Full-Thickness Burns (Formerly Third-Degree Burns)

A. All layers of skin destroyed
B. May appear cherry-red, white, or brown and leathery, with visible veins; are anesthetic to touch because nerve ends in the skin have been destroyed

Source: Reprinted with permission from SK Campbell, *Physical Therapy for Children*, p. 764, © 1994, WB Saunders Co.

Classification by Comparison of Burns by Size (Total Body Surface Area, TBSA)

	Adult	**Child**
Head	9%	18%
Arms	18%	
Legs	36%	27%
Trunk	36%	

Source: Reprinted with permission from LG de Linde, Rehabilitation of the Child With Burns, in JS Tecklin, *Pediatric Physical Therapy*, p. 213, © JP Lippincott.

Burn Prevention

1. Lower water heater temperature to 120 degrees.
2. Keep electrical cords out of reach of young children (coffee pots, toaster, etc).
3. Keep children in a safe place during food preparation and serving (playpen, high chair, another room with flexible gate).
4. Turn pot handles on stove toward back of stove, and use rear burners as much as possible.
5. Always supervise children in the bathtub, and test bathwater with a thermometer before placing the child in the tub.
6. Place safety caps on all electrical outlets.
7. Teach young children that matches are not toys, and keep any matches out of children's reach.
8. Teach older children and adolescents about the dangers of high-voltage wires and flammable liquids such as gasoline.

Source: Reprinted with permission from LG de Linde, Rehabilitation of the Child With Burns, in JS Tecklin, *Pediatric Physical Therapy*, p. 210, © JB Lippincott.

Pain Control
- Have child help with or perform exercises by him- or herself as much as possible.
- Coordinate exercise time with administration of pain control medication.
- Tell the child exactly what exercise is going to be done, how it is going to be done, and how many repetitions will be performed. Then do exactly what was said.

Relationship With Child, Family, and Caregivers
- Be truthful in explaining the treatment, and do what you say.
- Give the child as many choices as possible to permit some control, such as the order of the exercises or the time of day.
- Learn what food or activities the child likes, and always end treatment with something that the child wants to do for fun.

Promoting Independence and a Sense of Competence
- Encourage the child to learn to do exercises.
- Facilitate the child's attempt at self-help activities as much as possible.

Instructing Parents or Caregivers
- Involve the parents in exercise and positioning activities.
- Help the parents find play activities and functional activities that they can do with the child.
- As skin heals, parents can help with creaming and massage of skin.

PRECAUTIONS/CONTRAINDICATIONS
- Assessment tools such as goniometers should not touch an open wound.
- Avoid allowing the child to assume positions of comfort that are not compatible with function.
- Avoid long periods of static positioning.

DESIRED OUTCOME/PROGNOSIS
- The child will be able to use functional ROM and mobility to participate in a regular daily routine.
- The child will have endurance to engage in a regular daily routine.
- The child will be able to attend school at the grade level consistent with his or her intellectual development.
- The child will be able to perform, independently or with assistive technology, ADLs including mobility, feeding, and dressing.
- The child will be able to perform age-appropriate activities and skills.
- The child will be able to participate in social and recreational activities.

REFERENCES

ASSESSMENT

Developmental Level
Frankenburg WK, Dodds JB. *Denver Developmental Screening Test*. rev ed. Denver, Colo: La Doca Foundation; 1990.

Rogers S, D'Eugenio DB. *Developmental Programming for Infants and Young Children: Early Intervention Profile*. 2nd ed. Vols 2, 5. Ann Arbor, Mich: University of Michigan Press; 1990.

Soft Tissue Injury

Sullivan T, Smith J, Kermode, J, et al. Rating the burn scar. *Journal of Burn Care and Rehabilitation.* 1990;11:256–260. **[Vancouver Burn Scar Assessment]**

TREATMENT

de Linde LG. Rehabilitation of the child with burns. In: Tecklin JS, ed. *Pediatric Physical Therapy.* 2nd ed. Philadelphia, Pa: JB Lippincott Co; 1994:208–248.

Eigsti H, Aretz M, Shannon L. Pediatric physical therapy in a rehabilitation setting. *Pediatrician.* 1990;17:267–277.

Johnson J, Silverberg R. Serial casting of the lower extremity to correct contractures during the acute phase of burn care. *Physical Therapy.* 1995;75:262–266.

Moore ML. The burn unit. In: Campbell SK, ed. *Physical Therapy for Children.* Philadelphia, Pa: WB Saunders Co; 1994:763–786.

Raeside F. Physiotherapy management of burned children: a pilot study. *Physiotherapy.* 1992;78:891–895.

Reeves SU, Wareden G, Staley MJ. Management of the pediatric burn patient. In: Richard RL, Staley MJ, eds. *Burn Care and Rehabilitation: Principles and Practice.* Philadelphia, Pa: FA Davis Co; 1994:499–530.

Ricks NR, Meagher DP Jr. The benefits of plaster casting for lower-extremity burns after grafting in children. *Journal of Burn Care and Rehabilitation.* 1992;13:465–468.

Shepherd RB. Burns in childhood. In: Shepherd RB, ed. *Physiotherapy in Paediatrics.* Oxford, England: Butterworth-Heinemann; 1995:322–331.

Cerebral Palsy

Also known as Little's disease.

DESCRIPTION

Cerebral palsy is a broad term used to describe a number of motor disorders resulting from prenatal developmental abnormalities or perinatal or postnatal central nervous system (CNS) damage occurring before age 5 years and characterized by impaired voluntary movement. The term is not a diagnosis but provides a useful therapeutic classification for children with nonprogressive spasticity, athetoid, ataxia, or mixed forms who will require complex training and therapy to attain their optimum potential.

Spastic syndromes represent about 70% of cases. The spasticity is due to upper motor neuron involvement and may affect motor function mildly or severely. *Hemiplegia* denotes involvement of both limbs on one side; the arm usually is more involved than the leg. *Paraplegia* denotes involvement of both legs, with relative or complete sparing of the arms. *Quadriplegia* or *tetraplegia* denotes involvement of all limbs to a similar degree. *Diplegia* refers to a form intermediate between para- and quadriplegia, with predominant involvement of the legs.

Athetoid or dyskinetic syndromes occur in about 20% of patients and result from basal ganglia involvement. The resultant slow, writhing, involuntary movements may affect the extremities (athetoid) or the proximal parts of the limbs and the trunk (dystonic); abrupt, jerky, distal movements (choreiform) also may occur. The movements increase with emotional tension and disappear during sleep. Dysarthria is present and often severe.

Ataxic syndromes are uncommon (10%) and result from involvement of the cerebellum or its pathways. Weakness, incoordination, and intention tremor produce unsteadiness, a wide-based gait, and difficulty with rapid or fine movements.

Mixed forms are common: most often, spasticity and athetosis; less often, ataxia and athetosis.

CAUSE

Between 1% and 2% of children have cerebral palsy syndromes; up to 1% of premature or small-for-gestational-age babies are affected. The cause often is hard to establish, but in utero disorders, neonatal jaundice, birth trauma, and neonatal asphyxia are contributing factors.

ASSESSMENT

Areas
- Muscle and postural tone: hypertonicity or hypotonicity, distribution, tone under stimulation, interactions of tone and movement patterns, effect of sensory input on tone
- Motor control: stereotyped and limited patterns of movement
- Mobility, including active and passive joint range of motion (ROM)
- Functional muscle strength
- Postural alignment and patterns of weight bearing
- Developmental skills and motor milestones
- Oral-motor function
- Speech delay and difficulties in articulation
- Ocular motor disorders such as strabismus
- Need for adapted equipment and assistive technology
- Positioning: neck hyperextension; Soutler retraction; ability to bear weight on the forearms while prone; ability to maintain a stable head position unsupported or independent sitting; ability to assume antigravity position of the head, trunk, and extremities, especially flexing of the hips
- Reflex development: primitive reflexes, especially the startle reflex, the Moro reflex, palmar grasp, rooting, sucking, and the asymmetric tonic neck reflex; postural reflexes, including righting reflexes and equilibrium reactions
- Contractures due to abnormal reflex activity, weakness, or static positioning
- Gait and ambulation

Instruments/Procedures (See References for Sources)

Developmental Skills/Motor Function
- Barthel Index
- Bayley Scales of Infant Development
- Bruininks–Oseretsky Test of Motor Proficiency
- Gross Motor Function Measures
- Vineland Adoptive Behavior Scale
- Vulpe Assessment Battery

PROBLEMS

Spastic Hemiplegia
- There is hypertonicity on one side of the body.
- There are abnormal movement patterns, including limited patterns of movement and stereotyped movements on one side of the body.
- The upper extremity is more involved than the lower.
- Sensory deficit usually is present also.
- There is decreased activity and passive ROM on the involved side.

- There is persistence of primitive and tonic reflexes on the involved side.
- Postural reflexes on the involved side are poorly developed.
- The child may ignore or fail to use the involved side and use the sound side for most or all activities and weight bearing.
- Strabismus may be present, especially esotropia due to ocular muscle imbalance.
- Oral-motor dysfunction may be present.
- Somatosensory dysfunction (akinesia, astereognosis) may be present.
- Perceptual and learning disorders may be present.
- Seizures often develop as the child grows older.

Spastic Diplegia
- Hypertonicity is present throughout the body but with greater involvement in the trunk and lower extremities.
- Stereotyped and limited patterns of movement are present, especially in the lower extremities.
- Active and passive ROM are decreased.
- There is persistence of primitive and tonic reflexes.
- Postural reflexes are poorly developed.
- Strabismus may be present, especially bilateral esotropia due to ocular muscle imbalance.
- Oral-motor dysfunction may be present.
- Speech problems may be present.
- Often one side is more involved than the other (double hemiplegia), particularly in the lower extremities.

Spastic Quadriplegia
- Muscle tone abnormalities are present throughout the body, with the arms as involved as or more involved than the legs.
- Muscle imbalance across joints may lead to limitations in ROM in
  1. scapular protraction and depression
  2. glenohumeral flexion, abduction, external rotation
  3. elbow, wrist, and finger extension
  4. hip extension, abduction, and external rotation
  5. knee extension
  6. ankle dorsiflexion and supination
- Hypotonia is often present in the infant.
- In severe cases, the abnormal tone dominates the child's posture and movement.
- Ability to move against gravity is very limited due to abnormalities in postural muscle tone.
- Contractures are present. The most common sites are
  1. shoulder—adduction and internal rotation contractures
  2. elbow—flexion contractures
  3. forearm—pronation contracture
- There are positioning problems:
  1. spine—lordosis, kyphosis, or scoliosis
  2. hip—subluxation or dislocation
- There are deformities, such as
  1. persistent shortening of a muscle or group of muscles from spasticity without adequate activation of antagonists
  2. abnormal or persistent reflexes, muscle weakness, and static positioning

- Stereotyped and limited patterns of movement are present such as "scissor" gait.
- Active and passive ROM are decreased.
- There is persistence of primitive and tonic reflexes.
- Postural reflexes are poorly developed.
- There are abnormal movements:
  1. *Choreiform movements*—rapid, irregular, jerky motions most commonly seen in the face and extremities
  2. *Ballismus*—coarse flailing or flinging motion of the extremities characterized by a wide amplitude of motion
  3. *Tremor*—fine shaking motion of the head and extremities
- Other possible associated problems are strabismus, oral-motor dysfunction, hearing defects, mental retardation, perceptual and learning disorders, and seizures.

Athetosis (Dyskinetic Syndromes)
- There are four types of dyskinetic syndromes:
  1. *Nontension athetoid*—involuntary movements without increased muscle tone
  2. *Dystonic athetoid*—abnormal positioning of limbs, head, and trunk, with unpredictable increased tone
  3. *Choreoathetoid*—involuntary, unpredictable, small movements of the distal parts of the extremities
  4. *Tension athetoid*—increased muscle tone, which usually blocks involuntary movements
- Muscle tone is variable (fluctuates).
- Purposeful movement is poorly executed and coordinated.
- Postural alignment is difficult to sustain (instability).
- Involvement is often asymmetrical.
- Hypotonia precedes onset of athetosis.
- Involuntary movements are exaggerated by voluntary movement, postural adjustments, changes in emotions, and anxiety or speech.
- Other possible associated problems are speech impairment, poor respiratory control, oral-motor dysfunction, and high-frequency hearing loss.

Ataxia
- Sustained control against gravity is difficult due to low postural tone (hypotonia), defective postural function, disturbed equilibrium, and cocontraction.
- Diplegic distribution affects trunk and legs more than arms and hands.
- There are postural balance problems: poor balance when standing and walking, wide-based stance and gait, and increased ataxia and dyscoordination as base of support is decreased.
- Intentional use of the hands produces tremor.
- Movement is uncoordinated for both gross and fine motor tasks.
- There may be joint hypermobility in infancy.
- Stress or attempts to speed up movement increase incoordination.
- Spastic diplegia or athetosis is often concomitant.
- Ataxia often follows the initial stage of hypotonia.
- Nystagmus may be present.
- Poor eye tracking may be present.
- Delayed and poorly articulated speech may be present.

Flaccid Musculature and Hypotonia
- Muscle tone is decreased.
- There is real or apparent muscle weakness.
- ROM is increased.
- There is difficulty moving against gravity.
- Excessive joint flexibility indicates severe hypotonia.
- In the supine position, the child lies in "frog-leg" position.
- In sitting position, the child stabilizes the body with the hands and sits between the legs to provide a wider base of support and accommodate for postural instability in the trunk.

Mixed Forms
Problems depend on type and degree of mix.

Associated Problems

Oculomotor Problems
- *Strabismus:* imbalance of muscle tone/strength in the eye muscles, either lateral or vertical. Present in 20% to 60% of cases, with the highest incidence in children with diplegia and quadriplegia. Esotropia, deviation of eyes toward midline, is more prevalent than exotropia.
- *Homonymous hemianopsia:* neglect of objects viewed in one field of vision, often the left. It is seen in 25% of children with hemiplegia.
- *Nystagmus:* involuntary rapid oscillation of the eyeballs in a horizontal, vertical, or rotary direction; occurs in children with ataxia.

Oral-Motor Control
- Abnormal tone and poor control of the muscles of the face, mouth, and respiratory system cause difficulties with feeding and communication.

Growth Disturbances
- Both longitudinal and cross-sectional growth disturbances are involved. Longitudinal growth reductions are greatest in the radius, followed by the humerus and tibia. Cross-sectional area of the limbs may be decreased by 16% to 19%.

Respiratory Complications/Inefficiency
- Lung expansion is often compromised as a result of abnormal muscle tone and lack of anti-gravity control and strength of the muscles of the trunk.
- Lack of full development of the ribs reduces the mechanical advantage of the intercostals and diaphragm.
- Weakness of the abdominals and lack of balance between the trunk flexors and extensors further limit thoracic strength and expansion.

Cognitive Disorders
- Mental retardation occurs in 40% to 60% of cases but is most common in children with quadriplegia, rigidity, and atonia.
- All categories of mental retardation may occur, including mild, moderate, and severe.

Seizure Disorders
- Seizures occur in about 50% of children.
- Both petit mal and grand mal may occur.

Communication Disorders
- Some are secondary to poor oral-motor control, central language dysfunction, hearing impairment, or cognitive deficits.

TREATMENT/MANAGEMENT
Many different approaches to the treatment of cerebral palsy have been advanced. Current approaches are based on the work of the Bobaths (neurodevelopmental treatment), Ayres (sensory integration), Peto (conductive education), and others. No one approach has produced sufficient efficacy to be considered the best approach.

In general:
- Maximize development of normal movement patterns.
- Identify and respond to tone abnormality to facilitate movement.
- Facilitate oral-motor function.
- Prevent contractures.
- Minimize or prevent sequelae to skeletal alignment.
- Recommend aids for ambulation.
- Provide developmental activities.
  For the child with spasticity:
- Increase postural tone in trunk musculature.
- Reduce tone throughout the extremities where hypertonicity is present.
- Promote full ROM in extremities.
- Increase spinal mobility.
- Promote varied and differentiated movement patterns, including varying positions, speed, direction, and use of equipment.
- Provide weight-bearing experience with movement.
- Inhibit associated reactions.
- Avoid static postures.
- Promote muscle elongation, joint mobility, proximal stability, and active function of muscles around the joint.
- Encourage child to initiate movement.
  For the child with athetosis:
- Balance postural tone to increase tone in hypotonic muscle groups and decrease tone in hypertonic groups.
- Promote midline and symmetric muscle action.
- Increase muscle control in ranges away from the midline position.
- Improve postural and motor control in various positions and during movement transitions.
- Facilitate smooth grading of movement.
- Promote development of smoothly coordinated automatic reactions.
  For the child with ataxia:
- Promote balanced postural tone.
- Facilitate midline and sustained holding through range of movement.
- Develop smoothly coordinated automatic reactions.
  For the child with hypotonia:
- Increase postural tone.
- Improve head and trunk control against gravity.
- Improve automatic reactions.

- Facilitate smooth coordinated movement of the extremities in gravity-eliminated positions and in positions against gravity with the trunk stabilized.
- Permit child to react to imposed movement.
- Promote stabilization of joints in neutral alignment.

PRECAUTIONS/CONTRAINDICATIONS

- Although cerebral palsy is not a progressive disorder, the dynamics of growth and development change the type and degree of deformities. Regular reassessment is important to prevent new deformities from occurring.
- The variety of treatment approaches is confusing to parents as well as therapists. Because there is no research that has shown one method to be superior to another, therapists should be careful in telling parents that one method is wrong or bad as opposed to another.
- Therapists need to know and use good lifting techniques and body mechanics to avoid injury to themselves.
- Therapists need to understand that working with families and chronically disabled children is emotionally stressful. Therapists need to learn and use stress management techniques.
- Therapists need to know and convey to parents that there are no magic cures for cerebral palsy available today. Therapy assists the development of better movement and coordination but does not make the cerebral palsy "go away." Also, therapists need to help parents identify the positive aspects of the child's abilities while minimizing the negative aspects because this combination is most likely to help the child achieve maximum potential.
- Ethical issues regarding new treatment techniques and new equipment must be addressed realistically in relation to research or available resources.

DESIRED OUTCOME/PROGNOSIS

- The child will have independent movement of the head on a stable trunk.
- The child will be able to perform a variety of normal or near-normal movements and simple skills appropriate to the child's stage of development.
- The child will be able to perform functional sensorimotor skills such as activities of daily living and independent living.
- The child will be able to perform a variety of sensorimotor skills necessary to participate successfully in play and work activities.

REFERENCES

ASSESSMENT

Ashton B, Piper MC, Warren S, Stewin L, Byrne P. Influence of medical history on assessment of at-risk infants. *Developmental Medicine and Child Neurology.* 1991;33:412–418.

Bower E, McLellan DL. Evaluating therapy in cerebral palsy. *Child: Care, Health and Development.* 1994;20:409–419.

Boyce WF, Gowland C, Hardy S, et al. Development of a quality-of-movement measure for children with cerebral palsy: commentary by Kreshner EA, Scholz JP with author response. *Physical Therapy.* 1991;71:820–828; discussion, 828–832.

Boyce WF, Gowland C, Rosebaum P, et al. Measuring quality of movement in cerebral palsy: a review of instruments. *Physical Therapy.* 1991;71:813–819.

Burns YR, O'Callaghan M, Tudehope DI. Early identification of cerebral palsy in high risk infants. *Australian Paediatric Journal.* 25:215–219.

Dvir Z, Bar Haim S, Arbel N. Intertester agreement in static resistance measurement using a simple uniaxial dynamometer. *Physical and Occupational Therapy in Pediatrics*. 1990;10:3:59–67.

Harris SR. Early diagnosis of spastic diplegia, spastic hemiplegia, and quadriplegia. *American Journal of Diseases of Children*. 1989;143:1356–1360; comments, 144:958–959.

Harris SR. Movement analysis: an aid to early diagnosis of cerebral palsy. *Physical Therapy*. 1991;71:215–221.

Harris SR. Early identification of cerebral palsy. In: Gottlieb MI, Williams JE, eds. *Developmental-Behavioral Disorders*. Vol 3. New York, NY: Plenum Press; 1911:67–77.

Myhr U, von Wendt L, Sandberg KW. Assessment of sitting in children with cerebral palsy from videofilm: a reliability study. *Physical and Occupational Therapy in Pediatrics*. 1993;12:4:21–35.

Myklebust BM. A review of myotatic reflexes and the development of motor control and gait in infants and children: a special communication. *Physical Therapy*. 1990;70:188–203.

Rosenbaum PL, Russell DJ, Cadman DT, Gowland C, Jarvis S, Hardy S. Issues in measuring change in motor function in children with cerebral palsy: a special communication. *Physical Therapy*. 1990;70:125–131.

Stuberg WA, Colerick VL, Blanke DJ, Bruce W. Comparison of a clinical gait analysis method using videography and temporal-distance measures with 16mm cinematography. *Physical Therapy*. 1988;68:1221–1225.

Tardieu C, Lespargot A, Tabary C, Bret MD. Toe-walking in children with cerebral palsy: contributions of contracture and excessive contraction of triceps surae muscle. *Physical Therapy*. 1989;69:656–662.

Woollacott MH, Burtner PA. Sensorimotor deficits associated with posture control in children with cerebral palsy. In: Sussman MD, ed. *The Diplegic Child: Evaluation and Management*. Rosewood, Ill: American Academy of Orthopaedic Surgeons; 1991:87–97.

Developmental Skills/Motor Function

Scales of Infant Development
Piper MC, Darrah J. *Motor Assessment of the Developing Infant*. Philadelphia, Pa: WB Saunders Co; 1994.

Barthel Index
Mahoney FI, Barthel DW. *Maryland Medical Journal*. 1965;14:61–65.

Bayley Scales of Infant Development
Bayley Scales of Infant Development. *Bayley*. Bayley, N. San Antonio, Tex: Psychological Corporation; 1993.

Bruininks–Oseretsky Test of Motor Proficiency
Bruininks, RH. *Bruininks-Oseretsky Test of Motor Proficiency*. Circle Pines, Minn: American Guidance Service; 1978.

Gross Motor Function Measure
Russell D, Rosenbaum P, Cadman D, Gowland D, Hardy S, Jarvis S. The Gross Motor Function Measure: A means to evaluate the effects of physical therapy. *Developmental Medial and Child Neurology*. 1989;31:341–352.

Movement Assessment of Infants (MAI)
Chandler LS, Andrew MS, Swanson MW. *Movement Assessment of Infants: A Manual*. Rolling Bay, Wash: Infant Movement Research; 1980.

Vineland Adaptive Behavior Scales
Sparrow SS, Balla DA, Ciccetti DV. *Vineland Adaptive Behavior Scales*. Circle Pines, Minn: American Guidance Service; 1984.

Vulpe Assessment Battery

Vulpe, S.G. *Vulpe Assessment Battery*. Toronto, Ontario, Canada: National Institute on Mental Retardation; 1982.

Muscle Tone

Wilson JM. Cerebral palsy. In: Campbell SK, ed. *Pediatric Neurological Physical Therapy*. New York, NY: Churchill Livingstone. 1991:313–314.

TREATMENT

Anderson J, Campbell SK, Gardner HG. Correlates of physician utilization of physical therapy. *International Journal of Technology Assessment in Health Care*. 1992;8:1:10–19.

Barbeau H, Fung J. New experimental approaches in the treatment of spastic gait disorders. In: Forssbert H, Hirschfeld H, eds. *Movement Disorders in Children*. Basel, Switzerland: Karger; 1992:234–246.

Bertoti DB. Effects of therapeutic horseback riding on posture in children with cerebral palsy. *Physical Therapy*. 1988;68:1505–1512.

Bower E. Hip abduction and spinal orthosis in cerebral palsy. *Physiotherapy*. 1990;76:658–659.

Bower E, McLellan DL. Effect of increased exposure to physiotherapy on skill acquisition of children with cerebral palsy. *Developmental Medicine and Child Neurology*. 1992;34:25–39.

Butler PB, Nene AV. The biomechanics of fixed ankle foot orthoses and their potential in the management of cerebral palsied children. *Physiotherapy*. 1991;77:81–88.

Butler PB, Thompson N, Major RE. Improvement in walking performance of children with cerebral palsy: preliminary results. *Developmental Medicine and Child Neurology*. 1992;34:567–576.

Campbell SK. Efficacy of neurodevelopmental therapy (NDT) in the treatment of children with cerebral palsy. *Physical and Occupational Therapy in Pediatrics*. 1989;9:2:1–4. Editorial.

Campbell SK. Consensus conference on efficacy of physical therapy in the management of cerebral palsy. *Pediatric Physical Therapy*. 1990;2:123–124.

Campbell SK. Efficacy of physical therapy in improving postural control in cerebral palsy. *Pediatric Physical Therapy*. 1990;2:135–140.

Campbell SK. Expected outcomes of physical therapy for children with cerebral palsy: the evidence and the challenge. In: Sussman MD, ed. *The Diplegic Child: Evaluation and Management*. Rosemont, Ill: American Academy of Orthopaedic Surgeons; 1991:221–227.

Campbell SK, Anderson JC, Gardner HG. Use of survey research methods to study clinical decision making: referral to physical therapy of children with cerebral palsy. *Physical Therapy*. 1989;69:610–615.

Campbell SK, Anderson J, Gardner G. Physicians' beliefs in the efficacy of physical therapy in the management of cerebral palsy. *Pediatric Physical Therapy*. 1990;2:169–173.

Carmick J. Clinical use of neuromuscular electrical stimulation for children with cerebral palsy, part 1: lower extremity. *Physical Therapy*. 1993;73:505–513.

Carmick J. Clinical use of neuromuscular electrical stimulation for children with cerebral palsy, part 2: upper extremity. Commentary by Chech DJ, and McEwen IR, with author response. *Physical Therapy*. 1993;73:514–522; discussion, 523–527.

Chakerian DL, Larson MA. Effects of upper-extremity weight-bearing on hand-opening and prehension patterns in children with cerebral palsy. *Developmental Medicine and Child Neurology*. 1993;5:216–229.

Colborne GR, Wright FV, Naumann S. Feedback of triceps surae EMG in gait of children with cerebral palsy: a controlled study. *Archives of Physical Medicine and Rehabilitation*. 1994;75:40–45.

Eigsti H, Aretz M, Shannon L. Pediatric physical therapy in a rehabilitation setting. *Pediatrician*. 1990;17:267–277.

Fetters L. Cerebral palsy: contemporary treatment concepts. In: Leiter N, ed. *Contemporary Management of Motor Control Problems: Proceedings of the II STEP Conference*. Arlington, Va: Foundation for Physical Therapy; 1991:219–224

Fetters L. Measurement and treatment in cerebral palsy: an argument for a new approach. *Physical Therapy*. 1991;71:244–247.

Fetters L, Holt K. Efficiency of movement: biomechanical and metabolic aspects. *Pediatric Physical Therapy.* 1990;2:155–159.

Goodgold-Edwards SA. Cognitive strategies during coincident timing tasks. *Physical Therapy.* 1991;71:236–243.

Graves P. Therapy methods for cerebral palsy. *Journal of Paediatric Child Health.* 1995;31:24–28.

Harris SR. Commentary on "The effects of physical therapy on cerebral palsy: a controlled trial in infants with spastic diplegia." *Physical and Occupational Therapy in Pediatrics.* 1989;9:3:1–4.

Harris SR. Efficacy of physical therapy in promoting family functioning and functional independence for children with cerebral palsy. *Pediatric Physical Therapy.* 1990;2:160–164.

Harris SR. Joint mobilization for children with central nervous system disorders; indications and precautions. *Physical Therapy.* 1991;71:890–896.

Harris SR, Atwater SW, Crowe TK. Accepted and controversial neuromotor therapies for infants at high risk for cerebral palsy. *Journal of Perinatology.* 1988;8:1:3–13.

Harryman SE. Rationale for physical therapy in the management of children with spastic diplegia. In: Sussman MD, ed. *The Diplegic Child: Evaluation and Management.* Rosewood, Ill: American Academy of Orthopaedic Surgeons; 1991:209–220.

Harryman SE. Lower-extremity surgery for children with cerebral palsy: physical therapy management. *Physical Therapy.* 1992;72:16–24.

Hedges K. The Bobath and conductive education approaches to cerebral palsy treatment: management and education models. *New Zealand Journal of Physiotherapy.* 1988;16:1:6–12.

Hinderer KA, Harris SR, Purdy AH et al. Effects of "tone-reducing" vs standard plaster casts on gait improvement of children with cerebral palsy. *Developmental Medicine and Child Neurology.* 1988;30:370–377.

Hinojosa J, Anderson J. Mothers' perceptions of home treatment programs for their preschool children with cerebral palsy. *American Journal of Occupational Therapy.* 1991;45:273–279.

Hoffer MM, Lehman M, Mitani M. Surgical indications in children with cerebral palsy. *Hand Clinics.* 1989;5:69–74.

Horton SV, Taylor DC. The use of behavior therapy and physical therapy to promote independent ambulation in a preschooler with mental retardation and cerebral palsy. *Research in Developmental Disabilities.* 1989;10:363–375.

Hsu LD, Li HS. Distal hamstring elongation in the management of spastic cerebral palsy. *Journal of Pediatric Orthopedics.* 1990;10:378–381.

Hulme JB, Sain B, Hardin M, McKinnon A, Waldron D. The influence of adaptive seating devices on vocalization. *Journal of Communication Disorders.* 1989;22:137–145.

Hurvitz EA. Stretching soleus muscle to prevent contractures. *Developmental Medicine and Child Neurology.* 1989;31:117–118.

Keshner EA. Can changing concepts enhance efficacy in physical therapy? *Pediatric Physical Therapy.* 1990;2:141–144.

Kluzik J, Fetters L, Coryell J. Quantification of control: a preliminary study of the effects of neurodevelopmental treatment on reaching in children with cerebral palsy. *Physical Therapy.* 1990;70:65–74; discussion, 76–78.

Koman LA, Gelberman RH, Hoby EB, Poehling GG. Cerebral palsy: management of the upper extremity. *Clinical Orthopaedics and Related Research.* 1990;253:62–74.

Koop SE, Stout JL, Drinken WH, Starr RC. Energy cost of walking in children with cerebral palsy. *Physical Therapy.* 1989;69:386.

Kramer JF, Ashton B, Brander R. Training of head control in the sitting and semi-prone positions. *Child: Care Health and Development.* 1992;18:365–376.

Kramer JF, MacPhail HEA. Relationships among measures of walking efficiency gross motor ability and isokinetic strength in adolescents with cerebral palsy. *Pediatric Physical Therapy.* 1994;6:3–8.

Kurtson LM, Clark DE. Orthotic devices for ambulation in children with cerebral palsy and myelomeningocele. *Physical Therapy.* 1991;71:947–960.

Kurtz LA, Schull SA. Rehabilitation for developmental disabilities. *Pediatric Clinics of North America.* 1993;40:629–643.

Law M, Cadman D, Rosenbaum P, Walter S, Russell D, DeMatteo C. Neurodevelopmental therapy and upper-extremity inhibitive casting for children with cerebral palsy. *Developmental Medicine and Child Neurology.* 1991;33:379–387; comments, 33:377–378.

Law M, King G. Parent compliance with therapeutic interventions for children with cerebral palsy. *Developmental Medicine and Child Neurology.* 1993;35:983–990.

Leonard CT, Moritani T. H-reflex testing to determine the neural basis of movement disorders of neurologically impaired individuals. *Electromyography and Clinical Neurophysiology.* 1992;32:341–349.

Levangie PK, Guihan MF, Meyer P, Stuhr K. Effect of altering handle position of a rolling walker on gait in children with cerebral palsy. *Physical Therapy.* 1989;69:130–134.

Mackey S. The use of computer-assisted feedback in a motor control task for cerebral palsied children. *Physiotherapy.* 1989;75:143–148.

Mayo NE. The effect of physical therapy for children with motor delay and cerebral palsy: a randomized clinical trial. *American Journal of Physical Medicine and Rehabilitation.* 1991;70:258–267.

Mazur JM, Shanks DE, Cummings RJ, McCluskey WP, Federico L, Goins M. Nonsurgical treatment of tight Achilles tendon. In: Sussman MD, ed. *The Diplegic Child: Evaluation and Management.* Rosewood Ill: American Academy of Orthopedic Surgeons; 1991:343–354.

McEwen IR. Assistive positioning as a control parameter of social-communicative interactions between students with profound multiple disabilities and classroom staff. *Physical Therapy.* 1992;72:634–644: discussion, 644–647.

McLoughlin KM. The Niagara therapy bench for children. *Physiotherapy.* 1990;76:295.

Meadows CB, Meyerink I, Farley R, Silmour A. The Arrow walker. *Physiotherapy.* 1992;78:679–680.

Mettler JL. Efficacy of neurodevelopmental therapy (NDT) in the treatment of children with cerebral palsy. *Physical and Occupational Therapy in Pediatrics.* 1989;9:2:5–8. Editorial.

Miedaner J, Finuf L. Effects of adaptive positioning on psychological test scores for preschool children with cerebral palsy. *Pediatric Physical Therapy.* 1993;5:177–182.

Molnar GE. Rehabilitation in cerebral palsy. *Western Journal of Medicine.* 1991;154:569–572.

Mossbert KA, Linton KA, Friske K. Ankle-foot orthoses: effect on energy expenditure of gait in spastic diplegic children. *Archives of Physical Medicine and Rehabilitation.* 1990;71:490–494.

Mulcahy C, Pountney T, Billington G. Adapted tricycle. *Physiotherapy.* 1991;77:660.

Myhr U, von Wendt L. Improvement of functional sitting position for children with cerebral palsy. *Developmental Medicine and Child Neurology.* 1991;33:246–256; comments, 33:648.

O'Connell DG, Barnhart R, Parks L. Muscular endurance and wheelchair propulsion in children with cerebral palsy or myelomeningocele. *Archives of Physical Medicine and Rehabilitation.* 1992;73:709–711.

Okawa A, Kajiura I, Hiroshia K. Physical therapeutic and surgical management in spastic diplegia: a Japanese experience. *Clinical Orthopaedics and Related Research.* 1990;253:38–44.

Olney SJ. Efficacy of physical therapy in improving mechanical and metabolic efficiency of movement in cerebral palsy. *Pediatric Physical Therapy.* 1990;2:145–149, 152–154.

Olney SJ. Cerebral palsy. In: Campbell SK, ed. *Physical Therapy in Children.* Philadelphia, Pa: WB Saunders Co; 1994:489–523.

Olney SJ, MacPhail HA, Hedden DM, Boyce WF. Work and power in hemiplegic cerebral palsy gait. *Physical Therapy.* 1990;70:431–438.

Oppenheim WL, Staudt LA, Peacock WJ. The rationale for rhizotomy. In: Sussman MD, ed. *The Diplegic Child: Evaluation and Management.* Rosemont, Ill: American Academy of Orthopaedic Surgeons; 1991:271–285.

Ottenbacher KJ. Efficacy of physical therapy: rate of motor development in children with cerebral palsy. *Pediatric Physical Therapy.* 1990;2:131–134.

Palmer FB, Shapiro BK, Allen MC, et al. Infant stimulation curriculum for infants with cerebral palsy: effects on infant temperament, parent-infant interaction, and home environment. *Pediatrics.* 1990;85:411–415.

Palmer FB, Shapiro BK, Capute AJ. Physical therapy for infants with spastic diplegia. *Developmental Medicine and Child Neurology.* 1989;31:128–129. Letter to the editor.

Palmer FB, Shapiro BK, Wachtel RC, et al. The effects of physical therapy on cerebral palsy: a controlled trial in infants with spastic diplegia. *New England Journal of Medicine.* 1988;318:803–808.

Patrick J. Cerebral palsy diplegia: improvements for walking. *British Medical Journal.* 1989;299:115–116.

Parette HP Jr. Frequency and duration of therapeutic intervention with young children with cerebral palsy. *Psychological Reports.* 1990;67:697–698.

Parette HP, Hendricks MD, Rock SL. Efficacy of therapeutic intervention intensity with infants and young children with cerebral palsy—including commentary by Hanft B, Royeen CB, and Harris SR. *Infants and Young Children.* 1991;4:2:1–19.

Perry J, Newsam C. Function of the hamstrings in cerebral palsy. In: Sussman MD, ed. *The Diplegic Child: Evaluation and Management.* Rosemont, Ill: American Academy of Orthopaedic Surgeons. 1991;299–307.

Phillips WE. Stress and coping in the family of the child with cerebral palsy: the role of the physical therapist. *Pediatric Physical Therapy.* 1990;2:166–168.

Phillips WE, Audent M. Use of serial casting in the management of knee joint contractures in an adolescent with cerebral palsy. *Physical Therapy.* 1990;70:521–523.

Piper MC. Efficacy of physical therapy: rate of motor development in children with cerebral palsy. *Pediatric Physical Therapy.* 1990;2:126–130.

Reddihough D, Bach T, Burgess G, Oke L, Hudson I. Comparison of subjective and objective measures of movement performance of children with cerebral palsy. *Developmental Medicine and Child Neurology.* 1991;33:578–584.

Richards CL. Spasticity control in the therapy of cerebral palsy. In: Forssbert H, Hirschfeld H, eds. *Movement Disorders in Children.* Basel, Switzerland; Karger; 1992:217–224.

Richards CL, Malouin F, Dumas F. Effects of a single session of prolonged plantarflexor stretch on muscle activations during gait in spastic cerebral palsy. *Scandinavian Journal of Rehabilitation Medicine.* 1991;23:103–111.

Robison RO, McCarthy G, Little TM. Conductive education at the Peto Institute, Budapest. *British Medical Journal.* 1989;299:1145–1149; comments, 299:1461–1462.

Rose SA, Ounpuu S, DeLuca PA. Strategies for the assessment of pediatric gait in the clinical setting. *Physical Therapy.* 1991;71:961–980.

Ross K, Thomson B. An evaluation of parents' involvement in the management of their cerebral palsy children. *Physiotherapy.* 1993;79:561–565.

Rothberg AD, Goodman M, Jacklin LA, Cooper PA. Six-year follow-up of early physiotherapy intervention in very low birth weight infants. *Pediatrics.* 1991;88:547–552.

Scholz JP. Quantification of control: a preliminary study of effects of neurodevelopmental treatment on reaching in children with spastic cerebral palsy. *Physical Therapy.* 1990;70:76–78.

Scrutton D. The Bobaths. *Developmental Medicine and Child Neurology.* 1991;33:565–566. Editorial.

Sharma S, Mishra KS, Dutta A, Kulkarni SK, Nair MN. Intrapelvic obturator neurectomy in cerebral palsy. *Indian Journal of Pediatrics.* 1989;56:259–265.

Sharman A, Ponton T. The social, functional and physiological benefits of intimately-contoured customized seating: the Matrix body support system. *Physiotherapy.* 1990;76:187–191.

Short DL, Schkade JK, Herring JA. Parent involvement in physical therapy: a controversial issue. *Journal of Pediatric Orthopedics.* 1989;9:444–446.

Singhi PD. Cerebral palsy: approach and principles of management. *Indian Pediatrics.* 1988;25:282–287.

Smithers JA. Facilitation of rolling in a child with athetoid cerebral palsy: a single-subject design. *Physiotherapy.* 1991;77:243–248.

Sparling J. Efficacy of neurodevelopmental therapy (NDT) in the treatment of children with cerebral palsy. *Physical and Occupational Therapy in Pediatrics.* 1989;9:2:8–9. Editorial.

Styer-Acevedo J. Physical therapy for the child with cerebral palsy. In: Tecklin JS, ed. *Pediatric Physical Therapy.* 2nd ed. Philadelphia, Pa: J.B. Lippincott Co; 1994:89–134.

Tirosh E, Rabino S. Physiotherapy for children with cerebral palsy: evidence for its efficacy. Comments by Stine SB. *American Journal of Diseases of Children*. 1989;143:552–555. Comments, 144:519–520.

Todd JE. Conductive education: the continuing challenge. Observations drawn from a recent period of study at the Peto Institute, Budapest. *Physiotherapy*. 1990;76:13–16.

Trevelyan J. Aquatots. *Nursing Times*. 1990;86:15:46–47.

Turnbull JD. Early intervention for children with or at risk of cerebral palsy. *American Journal of Diseases of Children*. 1993;147:54–59: comments, 147:12–15.

van der Weel FR, van der Meer AL, Lee DN. Effect of task on movement control in cerebral palsy: implications for assessment and therapy. *Developmental Medicine and Child Neurology*. 1991;33:419–426.

Wilson JM. Cerebral palsy. In: Campbell SK, ed. *Pediatric Neurologic Physical Therapy*. 2nd ed. New York, NY: Churchill Livingstone; 1991;301–360.

Rhizotomy

Arens LJ, Peacock WJ, Peter J. Selective posterior rhizotomy: a long-term follow-up study. *Childs Nervous System*. 1989;5:148–152.

Giuliani CA. Dorsal rhizotomy for children with cerebral palsy: support for concepts of motor control. *Physical Therapy*. 1991;71:248–259.

Giuliani CA. Dorsal rhizotomy as a treatment for improving function in children with cerebral palsy. In: Forssbert HJ, Hirschfeld H, eds. *Movement Disorders in Children*. Basel, Switzerland: Karger; 1992;247–254.

Sled EA. Selective posterior rhizotomy to treat spastic cerebral palsy: a literature review. *Physiotherapy Canada*. 1991;43:22–25.

Staudt LA, Peacock WJ, Oppenheim W. The role of selective posterior rhizotomy in the management of cerebral palsy. *Infants and Young Children*. 1990;2:3:48–58.

Congenital Heart Disease

DESCRIPTION

Congenital heart disease is any structural cardiovascular disorder that occurs in utero during the first 2 months of fetal life.

Acyanotic Defects (Excessive Pulmonary Blood Flow)

- *Aortic stenosis*—Narrowing of the left ventricular outflow tract near the aortic valve
- *Atrial septal defect*—single or multiple openings in the wall separating the two atria, decreasing blood flow going directly to ventricles and resulting in mild to moderate left-to-right shunt
- *Atrioventricular septal defect*—partial or complete (atrioventricular canal) defect of the atrioventricular septum at the junction of the atrial and ventricular septa, which creates a left-to-right shunt and is associated with Down syndrome
- *Coarctation of the aorta*—narrowing of the aorta in close approximation to the ductus arteriosus, which increases resistance to blood flow in the left ventricle and decreases blood flow to the extremities
- *Patent ductus arteriosus*—failure of the ductus arteriosus to close after birth, allowing blood flow from high-pressure aorta to low-pressure pulmonary artery and a left-to-right shunt

- *Ventricular septal defect*—single or multiple opening in the wall separating the two ventricles, which usually results in significant left-to-right shunt

Cyanotic Defects (Inadequate Pulmonary Blood Flow)
- *Heart transplantation*—surgical implantation of a donor heart to replace an underdeveloped or severely damaged heart in an infant
- *Heart—lung transplantation*—surgical implantation of a donor heart and lung (single or double lung) to replace an underdeveloped or severely damaged heart and lung (or lungs) in an infant
- *Hypoplastic left-sided heart syndrome*—left heart incapable of providing sufficient blood flow to maintain life
- *Pulmonary atresia*—failure of the pulmonary valve to develop, which results in obstruction of blood flow from the right heart to the lungs
- *Tetralogy of Fallot*—includes ventricular septal defect, pulmonary stenosis, and resulting right ventricular hypertrophy and aortic dextroposition
- *Total anomalous pulmonary venous return*—failure of the pulmonary veins to connect with the left atrium, and their connection instead to the coronary sinus of the right atrium or one of the systemic veins, which may lead to congestive heart failure
- *Transposition of the great arteries*—incomplete division of embryonic exit trunk, so that the aorta comes from the right ventricle and the pulmonary artery from the left ventricle
- *Tricuspid atresia*—failure of the tricuspid valve to develop, which results in obstruction of blood flow between the right atrium and right ventricle
- *Truncus arteriosus*—failure of the aorta and pulmonary artery to separate in utero, and their formation instead of a common trunk arising from both ventricles

Congenital Conditions Associated With Increased Pressure
- *Aortic stenosis*—left ventricular outflow tract obstruction
- *Coarctation of the aorta*—constriction of the aorta, most commonly just distally to the origin of the left subclavian artery
- *Pulmonary stenosis*—defect in fusion of the valve, causing a right ventricular outflow tract obstruction

CAUSE
Rubella infection is a known cause, but other maternal infections and maternal diabetes may be contributory. Genetic disorders such as Down syndrome may be related.

ASSESSMENT
Prior to surgery, the purpose of assessment is to establish a baseline performance. After surgery the purpose is to document progress toward goals.

Areas
- Postural alignment
- Range of motion (ROM), especially of the neck, shoulder, and thorax
- Gross motor development
- Fine motor development
- Ability to cough effectively
- After surgery, incision site and position of chest drains
- Blood pressure and cardiac status
- Breath sounds

Instruments/Procedures

No specific tests or procedures were named.

PROBLEMS

- There may be limited exercise and activity tolerance. The degree of limitation depends on the severity of cardiopulmonary distress. There are limitations in mobility, especially ambulation.
- There may be gross and fine motor development delay. Therapy is not usually effective until surgical correction has occurred.
- There may be pain, especially upon exertion.
- ROM and joint mobility are restricted; there are movement limitations in the neck, shoulder, and thorax.

TREATMENT/MANAGEMENT

Physical therapy is most effective after corrective surgery. Prior to surgery, the objective would be to maintain level of function, which may be very compromised, to clear the airways, to maintain cardiopulmonary status, and to establish a good relationship with the child. After surgery, the focus is on increasing and improving function.

- Work remedially with gross and fine motor developmental delay.
  1. Use age-appropriate activities geared to the activity tolerance level of the child.
  2. Select and provide assistive devices that will facilitate independence.
  3. Focus on mobility and ambulation skills.
- Increase ROM and joint mobility.
  1. Use exercises to maintain or increase neck, shoulder, and thorax mobility.
  2. Use games to promote neck and shoulder mobility.
  3. Begin ROM as soon as possible to reduce guarding of incision.
- Provide demonstration and instruction on how to facilitate aeration and mobilize secretion.
  1. Demonstrate coughing, postural drainage, vibration, compression, and percussion to caregivers and child if child is old enough to cooperate in treatment.
  2. Facilitate coughing and drainage in child who is fearful of pain by using reassurance and gentle persuasion. Coughing can be simulated by putting a soft tube down the nose and into the larynx, or by gentle lateral pressure on the trachea.
  3. Teach child deep breathing by blowing balloons, paper toys, and pinwheels (windmills).
  4. To remove secretions, turn child on side and give gentle percussion or vibration.
  5. Removal of secretions is sometimes difficult and may require manual hyperinflation or "bag squeezing."
  6. Yawn maneuver or prolonged inspiration with increased inflation can assist in preventing atelectasis.
  7. Segmental expansion—placing a hand over a particular segment and allowing it to move with the ventilator or respiratory cycle—can reduce postoperative complications and increase segmental aeration.
- Increase endurance and activity tolerance as cardiopulmonary system improves.
- Achieve optimal pulmonary hygiene and gas exchange.
  1. Work with caregivers and child to optimize hygiene care.
  2. When moving a child on continuous positive airways pressure (CPAP), the tubing must remain in a dependent position behind the child's head to prevent condensation from the humidified air from draining into the respiratory tract.

3. If child is kept warm by an overhead radiant heat warmer with pericardial drains carrying blood to underwater-seal drainage bottles, frequent checks of blood gases and electrolytes will be necessary to check progress.
- Improve postural alignment if needed.
- Work with team members to prepare the child and family for the hospital stay and routine.

PRECAUTIONS/CONTRAINDICATIONS
- Do not exercise the child beyond cardiopulmonary status prior to surgery during assessment or treatment periods.
- Watch for signs of pain and neck, thoracic, or shoulder movement limitations that may result in life-threatening respiratory infection.
- Confirm signs of cardiorespiratory distress for each child with the physician.
- The head-down position is generally contraindicated immediately after surgery.
- Monitor the child for changes in respiratory rate or color at all times during treatment to detect sudden changes.
- Postoperative pain discourages deep breathing. Alert physician if pain continues to interfere with breathing exercises and activities.

DESIRED OUTCOME/PROGNOSIS
- The child will attain age-appropriate gross and fine motor skills.
- The child will have functional ROM in the neck, shoulder, and thorax.
- The child and family will be able to manage any continuing need for monitoring respiratory functions.
- The child's endurance and activity tolerance will be within normal limits or at best level given residual limitations.

REFERENCES

Bastow V. Respiratory conditions and cardiothoracic disorders: respiratory problems associated with cardiac abnormalities. In: Eckersley PM, ed. *Elements of Paediatric Physiotherapy*. New York, NY: Churchill Livingstone; 1993:109–114.

Howell BA. Thoracic surgery. In: Campbell SK, ed. *Physical Therapy for Children*. Philadelphia, Pa: WB Saunders Co; 1994;735–760.

Hussey J. Effects of chest physiotherapy for children in intensive care after surgery. *Physiotherapy*. 1992;78:109–113.

Johnson, BA. Postoperative physical therapy in the pediatric cardiac surgery patient. *Pediatric Physical Therapy*. 1991;2:14–22.

Parker A. Paediatrics: congenital heart disease and cardiac surgery in infants and children. In: Webber BA, Pryor JA, eds. *Physiotherapy for Respiratory and Cardiac Problems*. New York, NY: Churchill Livingstone; 1993:309–315.

Shepherd RB. Physical evaluation and treatment. In: Shepherd RB, ed. *Physiotherapy in Paediatrics*. 3rd ed. Oxford, England: Butterworth-Heinemann; 1995;363–384.

Tecklin JS. Evaluation of the cardiopulmonary system in the neonate. In: Wilhelm IJ, ed. *Physical Therapy Assessment in Early Infancy*. New York, NY; Churchill Livingstone; 1993:133–143.

Congenital Dislocation of the Hip

DESCRIPTION

A dislocated hip exists when the femoral head is found completely outside the acetabulum. A subluxed hip is one is which the femoral head is partially but not completely outside the acetabulum. A teratologic hip is one in which structural changes in the hip joint (femoral head, joint capsule, or acetabulum) have occurred that will require surgery. The condition is more common in females than males by a ratio of approximately 5 to 1. White infants are diagnosed with congenital hip dislocation more often than blacks. The left hip is more commonly involved if the dislocation is unilateral. Congenital dislocation of the hip is usually identified in neonatal screening examinations. (See Tecklin, "Orthopedic Disorders," p. 291, in references.)

CAUSE

Exact cause is unknown. The disorder is associated with breech presentation, a positive family history, first-born status, or a hip click. It may be related to laxity of the ligaments about the hip joint or to in utero positioning that results in stress on the leg-folding mechanism.

ASSESSMENT

Areas
- Pain: dull pain in the groin, the anteriomedial aspects of the thigh, and/or the knee
- Mobility: limitation in hip range of motion (ROM)
- Joint integrity and structural deviations
  1. Unilateral dislocation
     a. decreased passive abduction in one hip
     b. asymmetrical gluteal skin folds
     c. asymmetrical skin folds in the adductor region
     d. leg-length discrepancy; dislocated or subluxed hip may be shorter
     e. on palpation, one greater trochanter felt to be higher than the other
     f. limp due to apparent shortness of the limb and lateral hip instability
     g. telescoping of the flexed and adducted thigh on the pelvis
  2. Bilateral dislocation
     a. wide perineum
     b. wide pelvis
     c. increased lumbar lordosis
     d. waddling gait due to lateral hip instability

Instruments/Procedures

Mobility
- goniometry, especially of the hip joints; restriction of hip abduction in flexion greater than 30 degrees is indicative of congenital hip dislocation

Joint Integrity and Structural Deviations. The following orthopedic tests may be performed:
- Ortolani's sign
  1. Placing the infant in a supine position, the examiner flexes the hips and knees and abducts the hips; a positive test indicated by a palpable jerk and click.

2. The infant is unable to abduct the thigh completely to the surface of the examining table when the hip and knee are flexed.
3. Use only in the first few weeks after birth.
- Barlow's test
  1. The infant is placed in a supine position with knees and hips flexed to 90 degrees.
  2. The examiner grasps the thigh with the thumb medially over the lesser trochanter while the other hand stabilizes the pelvis.
  3. With the hip in midrotation, pressure is applied longitudinally down toward the table.
  4. If a click or jerk is felt, the head of the femur has slipped posteriorly.
- Trendelenburg's sign
  1. When the child is in a standing position, the pelvis drops on the unaffected side of the body at the moment of heel strike on the affected side.
  2. Pelvic drop during the walking cycle lasts until heel strike on the unaffected side and is accompanied by an apparent lateral protrusion of the affected hip.
  3. Positive test is associated with weakness of the gluteus medius.
  4. The test is used with older children who are walking.
- Galeazzi's sign
  1. The infant is placed supine with hips and knees flexed and feet flat on the table; a positive test indicated by one knee higher than the other.
  2. Use with children aged 3 to 18 months with unilateral dislocation only.
- Telescoping sign
  1. The infant is placed supine with hips and knees flexed to 90 degrees. The examiner pushes down on femur toward the table and lifts up.
  2. A positive test is indicated by excessive movement.

PROBLEMS
- Pain is associated with the groin, thigh, and knee. The infant may respond by fretting or crying.
- There is limited motion in hip internal rotation and hip flexion.
- There is antalgic gait.
- Condition may cause developmental delay due to difficulty in weight bearing.

TREATMENT
According to Tecklin ("Orthopedic Disorders"; see references), there are three types of dislocated hips. Lateral displacement occurs at birth and reduces easily, responding well to simple treatment. Dislocation due to neuromuscular origin reduces easily, but tends to redislocate due to muscle imbalance. Teratologic dislocation is the most serious. Dislocation occurs laterally and proximally, and the head will not reduce into the acetabulum. Surgery is often necessary to remold a good acetabulum.

Prevention
- Goals are to prevent further slippage of the femoral head from the acetabulum, and to prevent secondary deformities caused by avascular necrosis.

Splints
- The Von Rosen splint holds the legs in flexion and abduction to 90 degrees.
- Teach parents to watch skin carefully to prevent pressure sores.

Harnesses
- *Pavlik*—webbing harness used during the first 9 months of life and worn for 8 weeks and holds the hips in flexion and abduction, thereby allowing the child to creep.
- *Denis Browne*—holds hips in flexion and abduction but permits a little movement at the hips.

Braces
- *A-frame*—non-weight-bearing, unilateral double upright long-leg brace with pelvic band; the medial uprights connect by a horizontal bar under the groin so that the hips are positioned in abduction and internal rotation, the knees in extension, and the feet in neutral. It is useful for children aged 9 months to 4 years.
- *Scottish Rite*—a pelvic band with plastic thigh sockets that places the hip in abduction but does not control rotation. It is used with children older than 4 years.

Frejka Pillow
- This consists of a molded piece of firm rubber or felt covered with waterproof material.

Plaster Hip Spica Cast
- Preceded by 2 to 3 weeks of traction to stretch soft tissue and enable the hip to be replaced in the acetabulum.
- Parents and caregivers must be taught proper lifting techniques because of the weight of the cast.

Traction
- *Buck or split Russell*—pulls the hips into extension and abduction, and may be used unilaterally or bilaterally.
- *Bryant*—applied bilaterally to place the hips in a position of flexion and abduction and is used with infants weighing less than 35 lbs.

Exercise Program to Increase ROM
- Concentrate on hip flexion, abduction, and internal rotation. External rotation is allowed only to a neutral position because greater magnitude will tend toward dislocation.
- A Salter osteotomy or Steele triple osteotomy often causes limitation in hip flexion.
- The Chiari procedure causes a lack of hip abduction.
- Aquatic therapy or hydrotherapy in therapeutic pool is often the best starting point. Activities can include walking, jumping, kicking on a body board, and swimming.
- Exercises should include weight-bearing activities through the feet as much as possible.

Gait Training
- Weight bearing through standing or ambulation is encouraged to deepen the acetabulum.
- Gait training should begin when the hip is stable: muscle strength is rated as fair or better and ROM has reached a plateau.
- The child in an A-frame brace can use a walker or crutches. Crutches are placed one in front and the other in back, and a modified four-point gait is used. First, one foot is lifted and advanced, then the contralateral crutch, then the opposite foot followed by the remaining crutch.
- The child in a Scottish Rite brace tends to ambulate with the hips slightly abducted and externally rotated, the knees slightly flexed, and the feet in normal position.

- A slow-moving treadmill can be useful with an older child to practice walking. An added advantage is increased endurance.

Muscle Strengthening to Decrease Muscle Atrophy
- Both hips should be strengthened, since the normal hip may have been immobilized during the healing process.
- Concentrate on gluteus maximus, iliopsoas, gluteus medius, quadriceps, and hamstrings.

Pain Management
- Ice packs or cold hydrocolator packs may be used.
- Heat is not commonly used, especially with younger children; nor are electrical agents.
- If infant is fearful of movement because of pain, aquatic therapy can be helpful.

PRECAUTIONS/CONTRAINDICATIONS
- Avoid weight bearing until subluxation and dislocation are resolved.
- Generally immobilization through traction, orthotics, and casting is ineffective.
- Abduction splints have been associated with damage to the capital femoral epiphysis and avascular necrosis.
- Vigorous exercise should be avoided because of possible strain on the reduced hip.
- Medical follow-up is important until skeletal maturity occurs to ensure that the hip and acetabulum continue to develop and function properly.

DESIRED OUTCOME/PROGNOSIS
- The child will be able to walk with a normal gait pattern.
- The child will be able to combine other activities with standing and walking such as lifting and carrying.

REFERENCES

Fiddian NJ, Gardiner JC. Screening for congenital dislocation of the hip by physiotherapists: results of a ten-year study. *Journal of Bone and Joint Surgery.* 1994;76B:458–459.

Shepherd RB. Congenital dislocation of the hip. In: Shepard RB, ed. *Physiotherapy in Paediatrics.* Oxford, England: Butterworth-Heinemann; 1995:228–233.

Tecklin JS. Orthopedic disorders in children and their physical therapy management. In: Tecklin JS, ed. *Pediatric Physical Therapy.* 2nd ed. Philadelphia, Pa: JB Lippincott Co; 1994:286–298.

Cystic Fibrosis

DESCRIPTIONS

Cystic fibrosis (CF) is an inherited disease of the exocrine glands, primarily affecting the gastrointestinal and respiratory systems, and usually characterized by the triad of chronic obstructive pulmonary disease, exocrine pancreatic insufficiency, and abnormally high sweat electrolytes. The disorder was first described by DH Anderson in 1938. Diagnosis is confirmed by a positive sweat test with sweat sodium concentration in excess of 60 mmol/l. Misdiagnoses include asthma, allergy, celiac disease, and chronic diarrhea. Incidence is about 1 in 2000 births among whites but is lower in other races.

CAUSE

CF is carried as an autosomal recessive trait by about 5% of the white population. The gene responsible for CF has been localized to the long arm of chromosome 7q. It encodes a membrane-associated protein called the *cystic fibrosis transmembrane conductance regulator* (CFTR), which appears to be closely involved with chloride transport across epithelial membranes. Most children are diagnosed by their third birthday.

ASSESSMENT

Areas
- History of disorder
- Postural assessment: watch for barrel-shaped chest with increase in the normal thoracic kyphosis and scapular protraction
- Exercise tolerance
- Respiration: abnormal breath sounds including wheezes, harsh breath sounds, and crackles; muscular pattern of breathing; ability to cough
- Chest mobility, including thoracic index, thoracic girth, and rib motion
- Oral-motor skills, especially swallowing

Instruments/Procedures (See Reference for Sources)

Respiratory Function Tests (RFT)
1. forced vital capacity (FVC)
2. peak expiratory flow rate (PEFR)
3. maximal sustainable ventilatory capacity (MSVC)
4. vital capacity (VC) measured by spirometry
5. total lung capacity (TLC) measured by spirometry
6 inspiratory reserve volume (IRV) measured by spirometry
7. expiratory reserve volume (ERV) measured by spirometry
8. forced expiration volume (FEV)
9. residual volume (RV)
10. functional reserve capacity (FRC)

Other Tests
1. auscultation for breath sounds
2. Shwachman score (see Schwachman in references)

Exercise Tolerance
- cycle egometers
- treadmill tests for younger children
- Borg Scale of Ratings of Perceived Exertion

PROBLEMS
- Pulmonary problems include the following:
  1. dilation and hypertrophy of mucus-secreting goblet cells

  2. impaired mucociliary clearance
  3. repeated respiratory tract infections due to *Staphylococcus aureus, Hemophilus influenza,* and *Pseudomonas aeruginosa*
  4. recurrent pneumonia, bronchitis, bronchiectasis, and bronchiolitis
  5. airway obstruction due to chronic bronchorrhea (abnormally large quantities of sticky mucus secretions)
  6. progressive inflammation secondary to chronic bacterial colonization
  7. coughing that may be paroxysmal
  8. breathing that is shallow and rapid
  9. bronchospasm
- There may be failure to thrive—an inability to gain weight despite an apparently adequate food intake due to pancreatic deficiency.
- Pancreatic and nutritional problems include the following:
  1. pancreatic insufficiency or defect due to obstruction of the ducts that results in failure of the pancreas to secrete the enzymes (trypsin, lipase, and amylase) necessary to break down fats, which in turn leads to nutritional insufficiency
  2. nutritional losses through steatorrhea
  3. incomplete digestion—meconium ileus, which is an obstruction of the intestine in the newborn due to the presence of sticky meconium in the bowel
- The sweat gland defect results in excessive secretion of sodium and chloride.

TREATMENT/MANAGEMENT
Treatment is symptomatic, since there is no cure. "Conventional" physical therapy includes postural drainage, percussion, and vibration.
- Use bronchial hygiene to remove airway secretions.
  1. Use postural drainage positions (two to four times per day) for lung areas, with emphasis on those identified as congested by auscultation.
     a. For infants up to 15 months, treatment can be done on the parent's knee. Include apical segments of the upper lobes.
     b. For children from over age 15 months to age 4, a small, high-density form wedge with a PVC cover is useful.
     c. For children from over age 4 to 9 years, a large foam wedge is needed. Include middle and lingular lobe.
     d. For persons over age 9, a postural drainage table such as the Chesham tipping table is needed. Include anterior segments of the upper lobes.
  2. Use manual or mechanical percussion of segmental lobes.
  3. Use vibratory facilitation of the ciliary function.
  4. Use directed breathing techniques such as forced expiration and assisted deep coughing.
  5. Nose blowing should be practiced as part of the postural drainage routine.
  6. Use positive expiratory pressures (PEP) mask therapies.
  7. Use suctioning, if necessary.
  8. Use intermittent aerosol therapy—a liquefier to liquefy secretions, usually three times per day. Bronchodilator and antibiotics can be given via the nebulizer also.
  9. An intermittent positive pressure ventilator may be used in cases of segmental collapse, but use is controversial and considered by some to be contraindicated in treatment of infants and children with cystic fibrosis.

- Increase chest wall mobility.
  1. Minimize hyperinflation by consistent bronchial hygiene.
  2. Teach breathing exercises to maintain balanced proportions of rib cage.
  3. Minimize use of accessory muscles of respiration by positioning, relaxation, and retraining.
- Optimize postural alignment.
  1. Provide exercises and postural awareness.
  2. Anticipate and prevent or minimize forward head and elevated and forward shoulders.
  3. Anticipate and prevent or minimize kyphosis and scoliosis.
- Teach breathing exercises.
  1. At 3 years, encourage "tummy" (relaxed or diaphragmatic) breathing, deep breathing, and coughing.
  2. Encourage expectoration as early as possible.
  3. Forced expiration technique can be introduced at age 4 or 5.
  4. At age 9 or 10 the child can take some responsibility for his or her own treatment, such as postural drainage.
- Increase cardiopulmonary conditioning.
  1. Encourage appropriate sports and recreational activities such as swimming, cycling, gymnastics, and walking.
  2. As physical ability decreases, introduce activities such as table tennis.
- In the case of lung transplants and heart-lung transplants, provde a conditioning program before surgery to maximize functional ability and exercise tolerance and to provide emotional well-being.
- During terminal care, recommend humidification to help with dry mouth and nose, and provide gentle chest drainage in position of maximum comfort.
- Provide family education.
  1. Demonstrate and explain techniques and exercises needed for the child.
  2. Encourage parents not to overprotect child but to promote normal exploratory play. Active games can loosen secretions.
  3. Teach parents the postural drainage routine.
  4. Instruct the family to avoid items that might be inhaled, such as small toys, beads, and coins, and food items such as peanuts, that might cause inflammation.
  5. Recommend that parents become involved with a support group.

PRECAUTIONS/CONTRAINDICATIONS
- Look for signs of atelectasis, and refer to physician immediately.
- Look for signs of increased airway resistance.
- Avoid suctioning in the terminal stage of care.
- Never permit the child to play with small items that might be inhaled.
- Physical therapy is contraindicated in the presence of an untreated, progressing, or tension pneumothorax.

DESIRED OUTCOME/PROGNOSIS
- The child will be able to participate in functional activities for as long as possible.
- The child will be performing age-appropriate activities.

REFERENCES

ASSESSMENT

Exercise Tolerance

Borg Scale of Ratings of Perceived Exertion
Borg GAV. Psychophysical bases of perceived exertion. *Medicine and Science in Sports and Exercise.* 1982;14:377–381.

Respiratory

Forced Vital Capacity
Pryor JA, Webber BA, Hodson ME, Batten JC. Evaluation of the forced expiratory technique as an adjunct to postural drainage in treatment of cystic fibrosis. *British Medical Journal.* 1979;2:417–418.

Peak Expiratory Flow Rate
Hofnyer JL, Webber BA, Hodson ME. Evaluation of positive expiratory pressure as an adjunct to chest physiotherapy in the treatment of cystic fibrosis. *Thorax.* 1986;41:951–954.

Maximal Sustainable Ventilatory Capacity
Keens TG, Krastins ERB, Wannamaker EM, et al. Ventilatory muscle endurance training in normal subjects and patients with cystic fibrosis. *American Review of Respiratory Diseases.* 1977;116:853–860.

Schwachman Score
Shwachman H, Kulczycki, LL. Long-term study of 105 patients with cystic fibrosis. *American Journal of Diseases of Children.* 1958;96:6–15.

TREATMENT
Ashwell JA, Agnew-Coughlin JL, Boyd S, Brooks D. Cystic fibrosis. In: Campbell SK, ed. *Physical Therapy for Children.* Philadelphia, Pa: WB Saunders Co; 1994:687–715.

Bastow V. Respiratory conditions and cardiothoracic disorders: cystic fibrosis. In: Eckersley PM, ed. *Elements of Paediatric Physiotherapy.* New York, NY: Churchill-Livingstone; 1993:100–104.

Boyd S, Brooks D, Agnew-Coughlin J, Ashwell J. Evaluation of the literature on the effectiveness of physical therapy modalities in the management of children with cystic fibrosis. *Pediatric Physical Therapy.* 1994;6:2:70–74.

Cerny FJ. Relative effects of bronchial drainage and exercise for in-hospital care of patients with cystic fibrosis. *Physical Therapy.* 1989;69:633–639.

Cerny F, Armitage L, Hirsch JA, Bishop, B. Respiratory and abdominal muscle responses to expiratory threshold loading in cystic fibrosis. *Journal of Applied Physiology.* 1992;72:842–850.

Eid N, Buchheit J, Neuling M, Phelps H. Chest physiotherapy in review. *Respiratory Care.* 1991;36:270–282.

Liska SA. Cystic fibrosis. In: Scully RM, Barnes MR, eds. *Physical Therapy.* Philadelphia, Pa: JB Lippincott Co; 1989;1209–1218.

Mortensen J, Falk M, Groth S, Jensen C. The effects of postural drainage and positive expiratory pressure physiotherapy on tracheobronchial clearance in cystic fibrosis. *Chest: The Cardiopulmonary Journal.* 1991;100:1350–1357.

Parker AE, Young CS. The physiotherapy management of cystic fibrosis in children. *Physiotherapy.* 1991;77:584–586.

Prasad SA. Current concepts in physiotherapy. *Journal of the Royal Society of Medicine.* 1993;86(suppl 20):23–29.

Pryor JA, Webber BA. Physiotherapy for cystic fibrosis: which technique? *Physiotherapy.* 1992;78:105–108.

Steven MH, Pryor JA, Weber BA, Hodson MR. Physiotherapy versus cough alone in the treatment of cystic fibrosis. *New Zealand Journal of Physiotherapy.* 1992;20:2:31, 37.

Tecklin JS. Cystic fibrosis. In: Tecklin JS, ed. *Pediatric Physical Therapy.* 2nd ed. Philadelphia, Pa: JB Lippincott Co; 1994:275–281.

Webber BA, Pryor JA. Bronchiectasis, primary ciliary dyskinesia and cystic fibrosis. In: Webber BA, Pryor JA, eds. *Physiotherapy for Respiratory and Cardiac Problems.* New York, NY: Churchill Livingstone; 1993:399–417.

Deaf-Blindness

Related terms are deafness, hearing loss, hearing impairment, visual impairment, blindness.

DESCRIPTION

The child has both an auditory impairment and a visual impairment that are present from birth or acquired in infancy. The degree of loss is quite variable. The combination can cause severe communication and other developmental and education problems that require programs solely for deaf-blind children. In the United States, the federal government defines *deaf-blindness* as concomitant hearing and visual impairments, the combination of which causes such severe communication and other developmental and education problems that children with this condition cannot be accommodated in special education programs solely for children with deafness or children with blindness (See the *Federal Register,* Sept 19, 1992, pp. 44801–44802).

CAUSE

Hearing loss is divided into conductive and sensorineural types. A conductive (structural) hearing loss is due to middle ear dysfunction. A sensorineural hearing loss is due to neurological (inner ear and/or auditory nerve) factors.

ASSESSMENT

No specific areas, instruments, or procedures are described in the literature.

PROBLEMS

- Development of visual skills may be delayed in the following areas:
  1. Scanning—looking rapidly around (up/down and side to side) the environment
  2. Focusing—selecting a target to examine
  3. Binocular vision—focusing the two eyes together on a target
  4. Discriminating—selecting one object to become the foreground while everything else becomes background
  5. Visual imagery—"seeing" an object without it being present or in view
  6. Part-whole discrimination—understanding the relation of a part to the whole of an object
  7. Object permanence—understanding that objects exist whether or not they are present or visible at a particular moment

- Development of auditory and hearing skills may be delayed in the following areas:
  1. direction of sound
  2. discriminating one sound from another
  3. recognizing familiar sounds
- Development of gross and fine motor skills may be delayed.
- Development of perceptual motor skills may be delayed in the following areas:
  1. learning to imitate
  2. spatial relationships
- Development of cognitive skills may be delayed in the following areas:
  1. understanding of cause and effect
  2. development of concepts and categories
     a. similarities and differences
     b. function of objects
     c. object constancy of form
  3. listening skills
     a. following directions
     b. understanding the relationship of objects, actions, and words
- Development of communication skills may be delayed in the following areas:
  1. preverbal
     a. babbling
     b. imitating sounds, including tone and pitch
  2. verbal
     a. *Symbolic*—Use of language to represent objects and events
     b. *Thought and action*—use of language to convey thinking and doing processes
     c. *Reflective*—use of language to "talk to oneself"
  3. nonverbal
     a. body movements
     b. vocalizations such as crying
     c. facial expressions
  4. sociocultural use of expressive and receptive language
     a. organizing the syntax of language
     b. understanding the meaning of language

TREATMENT/MANAGEMENT

Treatment and management require a partnership with parents and participation on an interdisciplinary team of professionals to develop an approach and provide continuity of handling.

- Use hands-on learning.
- Use familiar daily routines.
- Use backward chaining learning—for example, (1) removing spoon from mouth, (2) closing lips and removing food from spoon, (3) putting spoon in mouth, (4) raising spoon to mouth, (5) loading spoon, (6) putting spoon in bowl, (7) holding and stabilizing the bowl, (8) lifting the spoon, (9) grasping the spoon handle, and (10) finding the spoon.
- Increase movement awareness and skills.
  1. Develop awareness of movement.
  2. Develop static and dynamic balance.
  3. Develop direction of movement: over and under, across, up and down, along, around.
  4. Encourage the initiation of movement.

  5. Improve sitting balance.
  6. Facilitate walking.
  7. Increase skill in getting from sitting to standing.
- Develop tactile, kinesthetic, and proprioceptive skills as compensation for visual: perception of shape, texture, weight, density, height, length.
- Use purposeful play.
  1. *Preparation for play*—singing, rocking, tossing child in air, and turning upside down
  2. *Games involving movement*—nursery rhymes with actions, dancing using "round and round," and jumping
  3. *Sitting and exploring play*—use different textures, shapes, and sounds; play on different surfaces; and use common objects
  4. *Hiding, searching, and finding games*
  5. *Hand skills play*—poking, rolling, tearing, pushing, squeezing, patting, swiping, rubbing, punching, picking up smaller and smaller objects
  6. *Skill games*—picking up and placing, nesting toys, and taking off lids and putting them back on
- Assist in encouraging communication skills.
  1. *Signals*—personal symbols representing significant people, tapping shoulder before picking child up, dabbing hands in water before washing, and touching hips in downward direction before pulling down clothes
  2. *Signs*—touching self or other person for "me" and "you"
  3. *Finger spelling*—spelling words for symbols
  4. *Vocalizing*
- Assist in providing visual training:
  1. visual attention
  2. focus and fixation of gaze
  3. tracking
  4. ocular coordination
  5. visual memory
- Assist in providing auditory/listening skills in the areas of paying auditory attention, recognizing everyday sounds, detecting vibrations, distinguishing sounds, and recognizing complex sounds.
- Instruct parents.

PRECAUTIONS/CONTRAINDICATIONS
- Encourage the child to choose whenever possible; selecting for the child fosters dependency.
- Integrate communication as much as possible so that the child is able to think of communication as a means of influencing the environment.
- Observe safety precautions.

DESIRED OUTCOME/PROGNOSIS
- The child will be able to move about and explore the environment.
- The child will be able to walk when led by the hand.
- The child will be able to manipulate and identify familiar objects.
- The child will be able to use other sensory systems to substitute for deficits in vision and hearing.

REFERENCES

Crowe TK, Horak FB. Motor proficiency associated with vestibular deficits in children with hearing impairments. *Physical Therapy*. 1988;68:1493–1499.

Freeman P. Sensory disorders: the deaf and blind child. In: Eckersley PM, ed. *Elements of Paediatric Physiotherapy*. New York, NY: Churchill Livingstone; 1993;247–265.

Shepherd RB. The blind infant. In: Shepherd RB, ed. *Physiotherapy in Paediatrics*. Oxford, England: Butterworth-Heinemann. 1995;397–398.

Down Syndrome

DESCRIPTION

Down syndrome is a chromosomal disorder of having 47 instead of 46 chromosomes, resulting in neuropathology, hypotonia, and musculoskeletal differences. Sensory and/or cardiopulmonary anomalies may also be present. The most common type, found in 95% of cases, is called trisomy 21 because there is a third chromosome 21. Common signs and symptoms are hypotonia, poor Moro response, joint hyperflexibility, excess skin on the back of the neck, flat facial profile, upslanted palpebral fissures, external ear anomalies, pelvic hypoplasia with shallow acetabular angle, dysplasia of the midphalanx of the fifth finger, and simian crease (single midpalmar crease). Other types are translocation, in which there is breakage of two chromosomes and subsequent reattachment of the broken pieces to other chromosome pairs, and mosaicform, which is characterized by mixed 46- and 47-chromosome cells.

CAUSE

The cause is unknown but is related to developmental errors leading to alteration in chromosomal patterns and is associated with births to very young mothers and to older mothers over the age of 35.

ASSESSMENT

Areas
- Current medical history for cardiac status, risk of atlantoaxial dislocation, history of seizures, visual and auditory examinations
- Muscle tone, especially hypotonia
- Development assessment of gross and fine motor skills
- Movement patterns: quality of patterns, hypermobility
- Reflex development: integration of primitive reflexes, use of automatic reflexes, development of postural reflexes
- Grip strength
- Muscle contraction
- Functional assessment: self-care activities
- Range of motion (ROM)

- Oral-motor reflexes and skills: sucking, swallowing, tongue and lip control, chewing, and drinking
- Parental goals and expectations

Instruments/Procedures (See References for Sources)
- Bayley Scales of Infant Development
- Bruininks–Oseretsky Test of Motor Proficiency
- Movement Assessment of Infants (MAI)
- Peabody Developmental Motor Scales
- Revised Gesell and Amatruda Developmental and Neurological Examination
- Stott–Moyes–Henderson Test of Motor Impairment

PROBLEMS

Neurological
- There may be generalized hypotonia.
- Reflex development may be delayed.
- Motor development may be delayed.
- Other possible delays include speech and cognition.

Musculoskeletal
- There may be linear growth deficits.
  1. Velocity of growth in stature shows the greatest deficiency between 6 and 24 months of age.
  2. The major deficiency in stature is due to leg-length reduction.
  3. Metacarpal bones and phalanges are 10% to 30% reduced.
- There may be ligamentous laxity, which results in pes planus, patellar instability, and scoliosis.
- There may be atlantoaxial instability, subluxation, or dislocation related to increased laxity of transverse ligaments between the atlas and odontoid process. When joint interval is 6 to 10 mm, the following may also occur:
  1. pyramidal tract signs
  2. hyper-reflexia: positive Babinski sign and ankle clonus
  3. muscle weakness
  4. abnormal gait
  5. limitation of cervical ROM with torticollis
  6. pain
- Some muscle variations are
  1. absent palmaris longus
  2. extra supernumerary forearm flexors
  3. lack of differentiation of distinct muscle bellies for zygomaticus major and minor
- There may be muscle weakness and hypotonia of neck and trunk antigravity musculature.
- There may be acetabular dysplasia.
- Iliac crest may be widened or flared.
- The acetabulum roof may be flattened.
- Ischia may be long and tapered, resulting in decreased acetabular and iliac angles.
- Gross motor development may be delayed.

- Development of functional skills, including self-help skills such as feeding, may be delayed.
- There may be orthopedic problems such as pes planus, metatarsus varus, scoliosis, patellar subluxation or dislocation, and hip subluxation or dislocation.

Cardiopulmonary
- Cardiac anomalies are present in 40% of individuals with Down syndrome; these may be ventricular septal defects or atrioventricular canal defects.

Cognitive
- There may be microcephaly (reduced head circumference).
- There may be a smaller brain side with a less complex gyral pattern and abnormal synaptic morphology.
- There may be perceptual deficits.
- There may be decreased myelination of fibers in the precentral areas and frontal lobes.

Sensory—Visual and Auditory
- Visual defects are often present, including strabismus (usually esotropia), nystagmus, and myopia.
- Otitis media is a frequent source of hearing loss that presents in over 60% of children.

Speech
- Tongue protrusion and lax mouth closure may contribute to speech delay.
- Oral-motor development may be delayed.

Other
- Other possible problems are obesity, which may contribute to motor delay; seizures; duodenal stenosis; leukemia; and senile dementia.

TREATMENT/MANAGEMENT
Information is lacking on both the best type(s) of intervention techniques and the efficacy of physical therapy for Down syndrome. The following is a summary of techniques found in the literature, but there is no attempt to rank the items in any order of importance (based on research studies).
- Improve muscle strength, especially the antigravity muscles.
  1. Encourage positioning and weight-shifting activities in prone position to facilitate neck extension and rotation, weight bearing on arms, reaching, pivoting, and rolling.
  2. Place activities and toys overhead with child in supine or supported sitting position to promote reaching eye-hand coordination and midline manual activity.
  3. Use rolling from supine to side-lying positions and pull-to-sit activities, starting with neck support to develop neck and anterior trunk strength against gravity.
  4. Have child hold weighted objects or weights in pockets to emphasize trunk extension to increase axial tone.
  5. Use dynamic rather than static positions when working on sitting and standing activities, but watch alignment.
- Facilitate attainment of developmental skills.
  1. Integrate activities that require fine motor and cognitive skills while working on antigravity gross motor skills.

2. Provide toys that require hand and finger manipulation while child is in prone, sitting, or standing positions.
3. Games with cognitive requirements can be used during antigravity activities.

- Provide appropriate splinting or orthotic intervention.
  1. Orthoses may be needed to ensure foot alignment during early standing.
  2. In cooperation with a speech pathologist, a dietician, and an occupational therapist, determine what other orthotic devices may be useful, such as feeding equipment.
  3. Refer for other orthopedic assessment as needed.
- Facilitate effective oral-motor function.
  1. Promote lip sealing on nipple and sucking by swiping the upper and lower lips and sides.
  2. Utilize gentle tactile cues to promote sucking. Place forefinger horizontally and apply pressure just below the lower lip.
  3. Use activities such as imitation of kissing or puckering to encourage mouth closure.
  4. Use sucking with a straw to transition between bottle to cup.
- Provide sensory and gross motor stimulation.
  1. Provide vestibular stimulation of the horizontal and vertical canals to facilitate righting reflexes and neck and back extension by tilting the child on the therapist's knee or using a beach ball.
  2. Use vibrators to stimulate weak extensor muscles and oral facilitation.
- Provide education to parent and client.
  1. Promote parents' attachment and adjustment to the child.
  2. Recommend a support group to promote acceptance and guidance.
  3. Recommend publications sponsored by national associations concerned with Down syndrome and mental retardation.
  4. Provide consultation regarding the child's educational placement and participation in public schools.
  5. Provide or recommend sources of information about vocational training and living arrangements for young adults.
  6. Advise, if asked, that megavitamin therapy is not proven to be effective according to the National Down Syndrome Congress.
  7. Advise parents that "cell therapy" or injections of fetal tissue into the brain have not proven to be effective and may be life threatening.
  8. Advise parents that "patterning therapy" based on Doman and Delacato has not proven to be effective.
  9. Advise parents that facial reconstructive (plastic) surgery to normalize appearance has not been researched enough to be given a sound opinion. The therapist should get up-to-date information on this subject.

PRECAUTIONS/CONTRAINDICATIONS
- Contact sports, gymnastics, diving, and any activities that can lead to cervical spine injury are contraindicated.
- Avoid emphasis on body flexion activities, which tend to reduce tone.
- Avoid foods that particularly difficult to chew, swallow, and digest. Celery, carrots, popcorn, and peanuts are not recommended for a child under the age of 6 years.

DESIRED OUTCOME/PROGNOSIS
- The child will be able to participate in play and recreational activities appropriate for age and other health restrictions (no tackle games if neck instability is present).

- The child will be able to perform independently or with orthotic devices all self-care skills appropriate to age and other health considerations.
- The child will be able to attend school and benefit from education and training.
- The child will be able to perform chores and other activities required of a member of a family or living group.

REFERENCES

ASSESSMENT

Bayley N. *Bayley Scales of Infant Development*. 2nd ed. San Antonio, Tex: Psychological Corporation; 1993.

Bruininks, RH. *Bruininks–Oseretsky Test of Motor Proficiency*. Circle Pines, Minn: American Guidance Service; 1978.

Chandler LS, Andrews MS, Swanson MW. *Movement Assessment of Infants: A Manual*. Rolling Bay, Wash: Children Development and Mental Retardation Center; 1980.

Dichter CG, Darbee JC, Effgen SK, Palisano RJ. Assessment of pulmonary function and physical fitness in children with Down syndrome. *Pediatric Physical Therapy*. 1993;5:3–8.

Folio MR, Dubose RF. *Peabody Developmental Motor Scales*. Allen, Tex: DLM Teaching Resources; 1983.

Knoblock H, Stevens F, Malone A. *Manual of Developmental Diagnosis: The Administration and Interpretation of the Revised Gesell and Amatruda Developmental and Neurological Examination*. Houston, Tex: Gesell Developmental Materials; 1987.

Stott DH, Moyes FA, Henderson SE. *Stott–Moyes–Henderson Test of Motor Impairment*. Guelph, Ontario, Canada: Brook Educational Publishing; 1966.

Ulrich BD, Ulrich DA, Collier DH. Alternating stepping patterns: hidden abilities of 11-month-old infants with Down syndrome. *Developmental Medicine and Child Neurology*. 1992;34:233–239.

Ulrich BD, Ulrich DA, Collier DH, Cole EL. Developmental shifts in the ability of infants with Down syndrome to produce treadmill steps. *Physical Therapy*. 1995;75:14–23.

TREATMENT

Almeida GL, Corcos DM, Latash ML. Practice and transfer effects during fast single-joint elbow movements in individuals with Down syndrome. *Physical Therapy*. 1994;74;1000–1016.

Brenneman SK, Stanger M, Bertoti DB. Age-related considerations: pediatric. In: Myers RS, ed. *Saunders Manual of Physical Therapy Practice*. Philadelphia Pa: WB Saunders Co; 1995:1229–1282.

Connolly BM, Morgan SB, Russell FF, Fulliton WL. A longitudinal study of children with Down syndrome who experienced early intervention programming: commentary by Shea AM. *Physical Therapy*. 1993;73:170–179, discussion, 179–181.

Corcos DM. Strategies underlying the control of disordered movement. *Physical Therapy*. 1991;71:25–38.

Eigsti H, Aretz M, Shannon L. Pediatric physical therapy in a rehabilitation setting. *Pediatrician*. 1990;17: 267–277.

Glatz NE, Berg R. Oral dysfunction in children with Down's syndrome: an evaluation of treatment effects by means of video registration. *European Journal of Orthodontics*. 1991;13:446–451.

Harris SR, Shea AM. Down syndrome. In: Campbell SK, ed. *Pediatric Neurologic Physical Therapy*. New York, NY: Churchill Livingstone; 1991:131–68.

Limbrock GJ, Fischer-Brandies H, Avalle D. Castillo-Morales' orofacial therapy: treatment of 67 children with Down syndrome. *Developmental Medicine and Child Neurology*. 1991;33:296–303.

Linkous LW, Stutts RM. Passive tactile stimulation effects on the muscle tone of hypotonic, developmentally delayed young children. *Perceptual and Motor Skills*. 1990;71:951–954.

Millar AL, Fernhall B, Burkett LN. Effects of aerobic training in adolescents with Down syndrome. *Medicine and Science in Sports and Exercise*. 1993;25:270–274.

Shea AM. Motor attainments in Down syndrome. In: Leiter N, ed. *Contemporary Management of Motor Control Problems: Proceedings of the II Step Conference.* Alexandria, Va: Foundation for Physical Therapy; 1991:225–236.

Sellers JS, Capt B. Use of abduction restraint in facilitating selected motor patterns in a child with Down syndrome: a case report. *Physical and Occupational Therapy in Pediatrics.* 1989;9:63–68.

Dysphagia

Related terms are *deglutition disorders, swallowing disorders,* and *oral-motor disorders.*

DESCRIPTION

Dysphagia is a subjective awareness of difficulty in swallowing due to impaired progression of matter from the pharynx to the stomach. Dysphagia is the major symptom of esophageal transport disorders. There are several types. *Pre-esophageal dysphagia* is difficulty emptying material from the oral pharynx into the esophagus. *Esophageal dysphagia* is difficulty passing food down the esophagus. *Achalasia* (called also *cardiospasm, esophageal aperistalsis,* and *megaesophagus*) is symptomatic diffuse esophageal spasm causing impairment of esophageal peristalsis and lower esophageal sphincter relaxation. *Dysphagia lusoria* is compresssion of the esophagus. *Sideropenic dysphagia* (called also *esophageal webs, Plummer–Vison syndrome,* and *Patterson–Kelly syndrome*) is due to a thin, mucosal membrane that grows across the lumen of the esophagus.

CAUSE

Pre-esophageal dysphagia is associated with neurologic or muscular disorders that affect skeletal muscles, such as dermatomyositis, bulbar poliomyelitis, cerebral palsy, myasthenia gravis, muscular dystrophy, pseudobulbar palsy, and other central nervous system lesions. Esophageal dysphagia is associated with obstructive disorders, such as carcinoma, benign peptic stricture, and lower esophageal ring, or with motor disorders of smooth muscle, such as scleroderma. Achalasia is associated with malfunction of the myenteric plexus of the esophagus that results in denervation of the esophageal muscle. The exact cause is unknown. Dysphagia lusoria is associated with congenital vascular abnormalities, of which the most common is an aberrant right subclavian artery arising from the left side of the aortic arch. The disorder may appear in childhood or develop later due to arteriosclerotic changes in the aberrant vessel. Sideropenic dysphagia may develop in untreated severe iron-deficiency anemia, but the exact cause is unknown.

ASSESSMENT

Areas

- History of feeding patterns
- Oral muscle control, tongue control, lip closure control
- Suckling-swallowing reflex
- Control of swallowing
- Neck and trunk control

- Oral sensation inside and around the mouth, including responses to texture, taste, and temperature
- Muscle tone, especially strong extensor tone, which restricts movement and causes asymmetry, setting the stage for problems in oral-motor develpment and dysphagia
- Body symmetry
- Postural reactions
- Primitive reflexes, especially asymmetrical tonic neck reflex (ATNR), a pattern of head and neck hyperextension and shoulder elevation that causes the head and shoulders to move as one unit instead of separately and limits the ability of the child to lift the head against gravity
- Spinal mobility
- Abdominal activity
- Breathing patterns
- Range of motion (ROM), especially of the upper extremity
- Shoulder girdle stability
- Total patterns of movement
- Functional patterns available

Instruments/Procedures (See References for Sources)

History of Feeding Patterns
- Screening questions
  1. How long does it take to feed the baby?
  2. Does the baby push food out of the mouth with the tongue?
  3. Does the baby suckle well?
  4. Does the baby choke or gag, or vomit after meals?
  5. Does the baby push the head back when feeding?
  6. Is the baby able to keep food in the mouth?
- Physical Therapy Assessment for Feeding
- Seating Positioning Assessment

Motor Function/Motor Control
- Gross motor assessment

PROBLEMS
- There is nasal regurgitation.
- There is tracheal aspiration.
- There is coughing or choking.
- Food "gets stuck" on the way down the throat (esophagus).
- There is pain in the throat (esophagus) area.
- Child has difficulty swallowing solids primarily (obstructive esophageal dysphagia).
- Child has intermittent difficulty swallowing (lower esophageal ring).
- Child had poor motor control, especially ability to establish and maintain stability of the neck and shoulder girdle.
- There is hypotonia (low or floppy muscle tone).
- There is a history of abnormal oral development such as poor sucking.
- There is a predominance of primitive reflexes that affect alignment of the head and body, such as the asymmetrical and symmetrical tonic neck reflexes.
- There are exaggerated oral reflexes.

- There is open mouth and drooling.

TREATMENT/MANAGEMENT
Treatment techniques are based on neurodevelopmental therapy (Bobath).
- Teach positioning to reduce symptoms.
  1. To reduce gastroesophageal reflux:
     a. Feed child on the right side.
     b. Use a reflux wedge, which holds child prone at a 30- to 45-degree angle.
  2. In general:
     a. Promote chin tuck, abdominal control, and balance of flexion and extension for upright head control; bring the tongue and lips into more forward position and reduce inappropriate posturing of the mouth and pharynx.
     b. Promote mastery of fine postural adjustments around the vertebral midline to improve mouth symmetry and control.
     c. Use external support for seating and positioning to inhibit poor postures and facilitate more normal movement.
- Strengthen the abdominal muscles to promote stability and mobility of the rib cage for improved respiration.
- Promote upper body and abdominal stability to reduce excessive burping and gastroesophageal reflux.
- Maintain pharyngeal airway.
  1. Use prone-lying or forward side-lying position during feeding to prevent problem of tongue falling back into airway.
- Facilitate integration of primitive reflexes and movement patterns.
  1. Promote righting reactions to improve postural control against gravity and bring head into proper position in space.
  2. Facilitate neck extension and flexion to permit chin tuck, neck elongation and face into vertical and mouth into horizontal position.
  3. Encourage independent movement of the head and trunk through integration of the neck-righting reflex.
- Facilitate purposeful movement.
  1. Encourage movement of head separate from shoulder girdle.
  2. Modify tone and posture through handling techniques to facilitate normal movement patterns.

PRECAUTIONS/CONTRAINDICATIONS
- Feeding involves the total system. Positioning, sensory system, seating, reflex development, and postural tone are important to the total control of dysphagia. Parents and caregivers must understand the interrelations.
- Reassessment of feeding program should be scheduled frequently to ensure that the treatment provided is eliciting the desired response for swallowing and the child's other functional needs.

DESIRED OUTCOME/PROGNOSIS
- The child will be able to feed without gagging.
- The child will be able to keep food down without reflux occurring.
- The child will be able to assume a position that maximizes oral-motor skills in feeding.

REFERENCES

Woods EK. The influence of posture and positioning on oral motor development and dysphagia. In: Rosenthal RS, Sheppard JJ, Lotze M, eds. *Dysphagia and the Child with Developmental Disabilities: Medical Clinical and Family Interventions.* San Diego, Calif: Singular Publishing Group; 1995;153–187. **[Physical Therapy Assessment for Feeding, Seating Positioning Assessment]**

ASSESSMENT

Screening Questions
Shepherd RR. *Physiotherapy in paediatrics.* 3rd ed. Oxford: Butterworth–Heinemann; 1995.

Failure To Thrive

DESCRIPTION

   Failure to thrive (FTT) is a disorder characteristic of infants and young children who do not grow at a rate normal for their age, sex, or race. FTT is usually defined in terms of (1) weight consistently below the third percentile for age; (2) weight under 80% of ideal weight for height-age; (3) progressive fall-off in weight to below the third percentile; or (4) a decrease in expected rate of growth along the child's previously defined growth curve irrespective of its relationship to the third percentile. Weight is used as the growth parameter because it is the most sensitive indicator of nutritional status. Subtypes include organic failure to thrive (OFTT) and nonorganic failure to thrive (NOFTT).

CAUSE

   The causes may be organic, nonorganic, or a combination of the two *(mixed etiology).* Examples of organic causes include defects in the gastrointestinal system, such as short-bowel syndrome, renal failure, congenital cardiac disease, chronic lung disease, cystic fibrosis, biliary atresia, certain genetic disorders, chromosome abnormalities, and chronic infections. Nonorganic causes are external to the infant or child and include trauma, neglect, rejection, a poor mother-infant relationship, inadequate mothering skills, and family stress due to divorce, unemployment, poverty, and overcrowded living conditions.

ASSESSMENT

Areas
• Initial impression, including infant's affect or mood and parental presence
• Chart history, including past weight gains and social history
• Range of motion (ROM): asymmetries, hypermobility, or hypomobility
• Functional ability
   1. *Gross motor skills*—may tolerate supine position better than prone position or have poor prone and transitional skills from one position to another
   2. *Fine motor skills*—may be at a higher level than gross motor
   3. *Communication skills*—language may be delayed or absent

4. *Social skills* such as smiling, eye contact, eye tracking, motivation to move
- Gait: should be assessed if not appropriate for age and development
- Neurological: asymmetries and imbalance of muscle tone, comparison of reflex response to gross motor skills
- Posture: posture against gravity in supine and prone, extremity held in an unusual position, position of hands and face
- Skin and soft tissue: loose skin folds indicating loss of subcutaneous fat
- Behavior: differences in response when parent is present or absent from the room
- Socialization
  1. *Severe case:* when approached, infant avoids eye contact, may ruminate, lacks vocalizations, and shields face with upper arm
  2. *Moderate case:* when approached, infant avoids eye contact, ruminates, and decreases vocalization
  3. *Mild case:* infant avoids eye contact and decreases vocalization

Instruments/Procedures
No specific tests are listed or discussed. Developmental assessment and functional assessment may be performed.

PROBLEMS
- ROM is limited.
- Developmental and functional skills—gross motor, communication, and socialization skills, especially smiling—are delayed.
- Endurance is limited.
- Child withdraws from interaction by such actions as avoiding eye contact, ruminating, shielding face with upper arm, and decreasing vocalization.

TREATMENT/MANAGEMENT
Frequency of treatment depends on severity: twice a day, 7 days a week for severely affected infants, less frequent for moderately or mildly affected infants.
- Use ROM activities to decrease abnormal posturing, improve postural alignment, and facilitate acquisition of motor skills.
- Inhibition techniques may be used with ROM activities to decrease abnormal posturing and improve postural alignment.
- Work on gross motor activities.
  1. Work in the position the infant prefers, with minimum handling during early treatment to avoid overstressing the infant with difficult tasks that may cause withdrawal.
  2. If infant prefers the supine position, begin with kicking in supine and introduce rolling to side-lying.
  3. If infant is able to sit with support or independently, work on pivoting and transition from sitting to prone.
  4. If handling stresses infant, delay activities for crawling, creeping, and standing.
- Increase social stimulation.
  1. The quality of interaction with the infant is the most important aspect of treatment.
  2. The goal is to achieve eye contact, smiling, and vocalization.
  3. Begin by approaching the infant from a distance, and move slowly into the infant's field of vision. An infant seat may be useful if the infant is unable to sit independently.

4. If eye contact is achieved, reinforce with verbal praise.
5. If the infant withdraws, diverts gaze, or shields eyes, retreat slightly, but continue talking.
6. Continue to watch the infant's reactions, and gradually approach the infant as favorable response (eye contact, smiling, or vocalization) is noted.
7. Smiling begins with corners of the mouth turning up, then there is smiling with entire mouth, and finally there is a total face reaction.
- Educate parent/family.
  1. Instruct parents and family members in techniques for handling the infant.
  2. Stress person-to-person interaction.
  3. Facilitate the learning of parenting skills through demonstration.
- Start a home program.
  1. Emphasize positive interaction between parent and infant during feeding and other activities.
  2. Provide samples of developmental activities appropriate to the functional level of the infant.
- Use a team approach.
  1. Work with a team to determine the best intervention approach, especially for nonorganic and mixed etiologies.
  2. Include parents or caregivers in treatment planning and implementation.

PRECAUTIONS/CONTRAINDICATIONS
- Malnutrition may limit the infant's endurance. Initial assessment and treatment may need to be brief.
- Avoid overwhelming the infant with stimulation during initial sessions. If reflux or rumination occurs, stop the interaction.
- Avoid use of toys in treatment sessions until interaction with people is established.

DESIRED OUTCOME/PROGNOSIS
- The infant will be able to interact with parents or caregivers by maintaining eye contact, smiling, and vocalizing.
- The infant's movements will be smooth and coordinated.
- The infant's gross motor skills will be age-appropriate.
- The parents or caregivers will be able to interact successfully with the infant.

REFERENCES
Bezner J, Rogers H. Nonorganic failure to thrive protocol. In: *Physical Therapy Protocols: Guidelines for Rehabilitation*. Tucson, Ariz: Therapy Skills Builders; 1991:155–158.

Fetal Alcohol Syndrome

DESCRIPTION

The most serious consequence of fetal alcohol syndrome (FAS) is severe mental retardation due to impaired brain development. Affected neonates have growth retardation and are microcephalic. Multiple malformations may occur, including microphthalmia, short palpebral tissues, midfacial phyoplasia, abnormal palmar creases, cardiac defects, and joint contractures. FAS is also called *alcohol-related birth defects (ARBD)*. The diagnosis depends on three categories of symptoms: prenatal and/or postnatal growth retardation, central nervous system (CNS) impairment, and characteristic facial dysmorphology. There is no typical pattern. The disorder was first described in 1973. Incidence is highest among Native American and African American ethnic groups.

CAUSE

Maternal alcohol abuse during pregnancy is the most common cause of drug-induced teratogenesis. Smoking and alcohol abuse tend to increase the potential for infant disorders. The mental retardation is thought to be part of ethanol teratogenesis, since infants of alcoholic women are often retarded even if raised in foster homes.

ASSESSMENT

Areas
- Musculoskeletal function
- Developmental milestones
- Behavior
- Feeding and drinking

Instruments/Procedures (See References for Sources)
- Bayley Scales of Infant Development
- Movement Assessment of Infants (MAI)
- Peabody Developmental Motor Scales

PROBLEMS
- There may be growth retardation/short stature.
- Possible craniofacial deformities include brachycephaly; epicanthal folds; flat nasal bridge; low-set ears; small nose; flat, smooth philtrum; thin upper lip; microphthalmia (small eyes); flat midface (maxilla); and short palpebral fissures.
- Possible abnormal hand features include abnormal palmar creases and small fifth fingers.
- There may be hypotonia or hypertonia.
- Problems in reflex development may include persistent primitive reflexes (asymmetrical tonic neck reflex, palmar grasp, and tonic labyrinthine reflex-supine) and delayed head-righting reactions.
- Other possible motor problems include tremors, hyperactivity, and slowed reaction time.
- Possible skeletal deformities include pectus excavatum (funnel chest) with depressed sternum, talipes equinovarus, and tibial bowing.
- There may be astasia (refusal to bear weight on the feet when placed in supported standing).

- Possible sensory problems include tactile and oral hypersensitivity, auditory hyposensitivity, and inconsistent response to auditory and visual stimuli.
- There may be developmental delay in gross and fine motor milestones, or in language.
- Possible cognitive disorders include mental retardation, problems with judgment (eg, concerning safety of self), poor comprehension, and poor short-term memory.
- There may be episodes of profuse sweating (diaphoresis).
- Feeding and drinking difficulties include gagging on anything except pureed food, drinking from a bottle long after normal age, vomiting, and constipation.
- Possible behavioral problems include failure to show response to objects in the environment, attention deficit disorder, and flat affect.
- There may be mood fluctuations: fussiness to smiling and laughing, autisticlike behaviors such as stranger anxiety, unusual fears of inanimate objects, or outbursts of temper.
- Child may engage in perseverant and self-stimulatory behaviors: perseverant motor behaviors and vocalizations, rocking, hand waving, and obsessive interest in spinning, pulling out hair, or hitting self.
- There may be withdrawal symptoms such as irritability.
- Other possible problems and symptoms are bilateral hair whorls, periods of apnea, and seizures.

TREATMENT/MANAGEMENT

Since there is limited information available on treatment and management of FAS, the following should be considered suggestions rather than indications of good management.
- Promote hands-to-midline.
- Promote hands-to-knees.
- Encourage active trunk rotation.
- Encourage movement into and out of sitting.
- Facilitate quadrupedal and kneel-standing activities.
- Encourage independent walking.
- Enhance postural and balance activities using balance board and balance beam.
- Provide developmentally appropriate play activities.
- Encourage spontaneous play.
- Promote gross and fine motor activities.
- Desensitize oral area.

PRECAUTIONS/CONTRAINDICATIONS

None were specifically mentioned.

DESIRED OUTCOME/PROGNOSIS

- The child will be able to perform developmental gross and fine motor skills within normal limits as assessed on a test of normal development.
- Orthopedic problems will be corrected with orthopedic devices and/or surgery.
- The child will be able to feed and drink using techniques appropriate for age.
- The child will be able to perform tasks related to the family, school, recreation, and the community.

REFERENCES

Harris SR, Osborn JA, Weinberg J, Loock C, Junaid K. Effects of prenatal alcohol exposure on neuromotor and cognitive development during early childhood: a series of case reports. *Physical Therapy*. 1993;73:608–617.

Osborn JA, Harris SR, Weinberg J. Fetal alcohol syndrome: review of the literature with implications for physical therapists. *Physical Therapy.* 1993;73:599–607.

ASSESSMENT

Bayley N. *Bayley Scales of Infant Development.* New York, NY: Psychological Corporation; 1969.
Bayley N. *Bayley Scales of Infant Development.* 2nd ed. San Antonio, Tex: Psychological Corporation; 1993.
Chandler LS, Andrews MS, Swanson MW. *Movement Assessment of Infants: A Manual.* Rolling Bay, Wash: Infant Movement Research; 1980.
Folio MR, Fewell RR. *Peabody Developmental Motor Scales.* Allen, Tex: DLM Teaching Resources; 1983.

Foot Deformities

See also the sections "Cerebral Palsy," "Legg–Calves–Perthes Disease," "Slipped Capital Femoral Epiphysis," "Spina Bifida," and "Spinal Muscular Atrophy."

DESCRIPTION

Foot deformities include structural disorders such as the following:
- *Calcaneovalgus:* hyperdorsiflexed foot; the forefoot is curved out laterally (banana shaped), while the hindfoot is in valgus
- *Cavus foot or pes cavus:* muscle imbalance associated with peroneal muscular atrophy, spina bifida, and poliomyelitis
- *Equinovarus or clubfoot:* fixed plantar flexion, inversion of the heel with adduction and varus of the forefoot
- *Equinus deformity:* muscular imbalance between the plantar flexors and dorsiflexors
- *Equinus foot or pes equinus:* imbalance of muscle pull on one or both feet
- *Metatarsus adductas or metatarsus varus:* compression of forefoot when legs are flexed across the body during late gestation
- *Pes equinus:* a foot deformity in which the toes are extremely flexed
- *Pes planus:* abnormal but common condition characterized by flattening out of the arch of the foot, called *flatfoot*
- *Pes valgus:* eversion, plantar flexion, and inclination of the calcaneus with abduction of the forefoot
- *Talipes calcaneovalgus:* a congenital deformity in which the foot is held in dorsiflexion at the ankle joint and in eversion at the subtaloid joint and cannot be moved passively into full inversion or plantarflexion
- *Talipes calcaneovarus:* see *calcaneovarus*
- *Talipes cavus:* see *cavus foot, pes cavus*
- *Talipes equinovarus* (TEV): foot is plantarflexed at the ankle, inverted and abducted at the subtaloid (talocalcaneal) and midtarsal joints; TEV may be the only deformity or one of many in a congenital disorder
- *Talipes equinus:* see *pes equinus*
- *Varus deformity:* result of imbalance between weak peroneal muscles and spastic posterior or anterior tibialis muscles

CAUSE

Foot abnormalities occur in 1 of every 100 births. The majority are functional, such as metatarsus adducts, rather than structural, such as talipes varus or metatarsus varus. The exact cause is frequently unknown, although explanations include uterine position, genetic or hereditary factors, neurological disorders, and changes in muscle pull and position related to angulations, rotations, and longitudinal growth.

ASSESSMENT

Areas

Joint Integrity and Structural Deviations
- *Rotation:* a movement of one or both joint segments in a plane that is perpendicular to the axis of the motion, such as medial rotation toward the midline or lateral rotation away from the midline
- *Torsion:* a structural, osseous state of twist in a bone along its longitudinal axis such as *medial femoral torsion,* which describes a femur with a medial twist of the distal-on-proximal end, or *lateral femoral torsion,* which describes a lack of normal medial torsion to a true lateral twist of the distal-on-proximal ends of the femur
- *Version:* the act or process of turning something or changing direction; eg, the femoral head and neck are described as anteverted when the head lies anterior to the frontal plane and as retroverted when the head lies posterior to the frontal plane
- *Genicular position:* an abnormality in the relative ranges of medial or lateral axial tibiofibular rotation with the knee joint flexed 90 degrees

Instruments/Procedures (See References for Sources)

Joint Integrity and Structural Deviations
- foot progression angle test
- pelvic rotation test
- Ryder's test
- hip rotation mobility test
- thigh-foot angle test
- transmalleolar axis-thigh angle test
- tibiofibular torsion test
- axial tibiofibular rotation test
- foot configuration test

PROBLEMS
- There may be muscle imbalance.
- There may be structural deformity.
- Range of motion (ROM) may be limited.
- The following biomechanical factors may contribute to lower extremity malalignment:
  1. pelvic rotation in the transverse plane
  2. immature acetabular anteversion
  3. soft tissue restriction limiting mobility of the hip joint in medial or lateral rotation
  4. abnormal magnitude of femoral torsion

5. abnormal activity of the medial hamstring muscles
6. medial or lateral genicular position
7. abnormal magnitude of tibiofibular torsion
8. abnormal transverse-plane alignment of the talar body with the ankle mortise
9. persistent talar neck adduction relative to the talar body
10. abnormal foot pronation, resulting in midtarsal joint abduction
11. abnormal foot supination, resulting in midtarsal joint adduction
12. metatarsus adduction
13. overpull of the abductor hallucus muscle (searching toe)

TREATMENT/MANAGEMENT
- Use corrective positioning to prevent soft tissue deformities or contractures from occurring.
  1. Taping joint into correct position is useful with newborn infants whose joints are too small to provide enough leverage for a splint.
  2. Splints or casts can be used to correct positions with older infants or young children. They must be checked frequently to insure proper fit.
- Use corrective positioning to decrease effect of tonus abnormalities and facilitate correct joint alignment.
- Use corrective positioning to prevent bone structure deformities whenever possible to reduce need for surgery.
- Use supportive orthoses to facilitate balance.
  1. Orthoses should be used to control undesirable motion of supporting segments while faciliting motion wherever it occurs normally.
  2. Orthoses can be used as training aids.
- Provide opportunity for standing and walking using biomechanical support when needed.
  1. Protect weak stabilizing muscles with splints as needed.
  2. Splints provide support for ambulatory children weighing 50 lbs or less. Such splints should be made so that they are easily revised or replaced to accommodate changes in functional ability or growth.
- Use corrective orthoses to correct soft tissue deformities.
  1. Night splints that are lightweight and easily fabricated and revised are useful to correct soft tissue deformities.
  2. Serial casting is useful for correcting soft tissue deformities in young children.
- Use postoperative orthoses to maintain correct positioning during healing process especially for knees and ankles.

PRECAUTIONS/CONTRAINDICATIONS
Changing the position of the foot may cause related changes in muscle pull and alignment of other joints in the lower extremity. The therapist should continually reassess changes in the foot in relation to the rest of the body.

DESIRED OUTCOME/PROGNOSIS
- The child will be about to ambulate with or without orthoses.
- The child will be able to perform age-appropriate gross motor activities.
- The child will be able to perform functional activities.

REFERENCES

ASSESSMENT
Cusick BD, Stuberg WA. Assessment of lower-extremity alignment in the transverse plane: implications for management of children with neuromotor dysfunction. *Physical Therapy* 1992;72:3–15.

TREATMENT
Cusick BD. Splints and casts: managing foot deformity in children with neuromotor disorders. *Physical Therapy.* 1988;68:1903–1912.

Leach J. Orthopaedic conditions. In: Campbell SK, ed. *Physical Therapy for Children*. Philadelphia, Pa: WB Saunders Co; 1994:353–361.

McGreary G, Bjornson KR. Taping to facilitate fabrication of lower extremity. *Pediatric Physical Therapy.* 1989;1:138–139.

Samson PG, Harris SR. Congenital clubfoot: review of the literature on clinical assessment and physiotherapy intervention. *Physiotherapy Canada.* 1994;46:249–254.

Shepherd RB. Talipes equinovarus. In: Shepherd, RB, ed. *Physiotherapy in Paediatrics*. 3rd ed. Oxford, England: Butterworth-Heinemann.1995;207–223.

Shepherd RB. Talipes calcaneovalgus. In: Shepherd, RB, ed. *Physiotherapy in Paediatrics*. 3rd ed. Oxford, England: Butterworth-Heinemann; 1995:224–227.

Genetic Disorders

DESCRIPTION

Genetic disorders are divided into two major categories: chromosomal abnormalities and specific gene defects. Chromosomal abnormalities can be further subdivided into autosomal trisomies, sex chromosome abnormalities, and partial deletion syndromes. Genetic defects are transmitted through three different modes of inheritance: autosomal dominant, autosomal recessive, and sex linked. (See Naganuma et al, "Genetic Disorders," p. 288, in references.)

CAUSE

The exact cause of many genetic disorders is unknown, although the genetic and chromosomal abnormalities and defects are being identified. Most chromosomal abnormalities appear as an extra chromosome or as a missing chromosome. Most genetic abnormalities appear as a result of gene defects related to the three major types of genetic inheritance. Factors thought to be contributing to chromosomal and genetic abnormalities include advanced maternal age (past 35), toxins, poisons, family genetic inheritance, and spontaneous mutation.

ASSESSMENT

Areas
- Hypertonicity
- Hypotonicity
- Hyperextensible joints

- Contractures and deformities
- Respiratory problems
- Hip dislocation
- Spinal deformities
- Upper extremity deformities
- Motor delays
- Cognitive delays
- Cerebral dysfunction
- Other defects

Instruments/Procedures (See References for Sources)
- *Discriminative assessments:* used to distinguish between individuals with or without a particular feature of interest. Such assessments are useful in determining eligibility for services but generally do not provide information specific enough for planning or evaluating therapy programs.
  1. Bayley Scales of Infant Development
  2. Bruininks–Oseretsky Test of Motor Proficiency
  3. Gesell and Amatruda Developmental and Neurological Examination-Revised
  4. Peabody Development Motor Scales
  5. Stott–Moyes–Henderson Test of Motor Impairment
- *Predictive assessments:* used to classify individuals according to a set of established categories and to verify whether an individual has been classified correctly; may be used to predict future performance, as in detection of early signs of motor impairment.
  1. Movement Assessment of Infants (MAI)
- *Evaluative assessments:* used to document change within an individual over time or change as the result of intervention.
  1. Functional Independence Measure (FIM)
  2. Hawaii Early Learning Profile (HELP)
  3. Pediatric Assessment of Disability Inventory (PEDI)
  4. Tufts Assessment of Motor Performance (TAMP)
  5. WeeFIM (FIM for children)

PROBLEMS
- *Cri-du-chat syndrome (cat-cry syndrome):* high-pitched cry due to abnormal laryngeal development that disappears after a few years, hypotonicity, hypertonicity, microcephaly, intrauterine growth retardation, heart defects, hypertelorism (wide-set eyes), strabismus (crossed eyes), "moon face," hip dislocation, scoliosis, clubfeet, hyperextensibility of fingers and toes, syndactyly, motor delays, severe mental retardation, cognitive delays, severe respiratory problems, feeding problems, facial asymmetry, and malocclusion
- *Hurler syndrome:* hypertonicity, hip dislocation, spinal deformities, upper extremity deformities, motor delays, cognitive delays, large skull, corneal clouding, hirsutism, gargoylelike facial features, growth retardation, mental retardation, spastic paraparesis or paraplegia, thoracolumbar kyphosis, genu valgum, pes cavus, claw hands secondary to joint deformities, possible restriction of neck flexion and extension resulting from hypoplasia of the odontoid process, deafness, hydrocephaly, an enlarged tongue, hepatosplenomegaly, respiratory involvement; mental and physical deterioration is progressive

- *Klinefelter syndromes:* type XXY usually do not require physical therapy; types XXXY and XXXXY may have mental retardation, microcephaly, hypertelorism, strabismus, cleft palate, radioulnar synostosis, genu valgum, and pes planus
- *Kugelberg–Welander syndrome:* see "Spinal Muscular Atrophy"
- *Lesch–Nyham syndrome:* hypertonicity, hip dislocation, motor delays, cognitive delays, cerebellar dysfunction, choreoathetosis, self-mutilation, progressive spastic paresis and athetosis, ballismus, tremor, hyperactive deep-tendon reflexes, severe dysarthria and dysphagia, growth retardation, moderate to severe mental retardation, and kidney damage
- *Lowe syndrome:* hypotonicity, motor delays, cognitive delays, progressive mental deterioration, renal tubular dysfunction, cortical cataracts, joint hyperextensibility, growth retardation, failure to thrive, shrill cry, scaphocephaly (long, narrow skull), diminished or absent deep-tendon reflexes, and muscle hypoplasia with fatty infiltration
- *Neurofibromatosis:* hypertonicity, light brown skin patches called cafe au lait spots, neurofibromas or connective tissue tumors that can lead to optic and acoustic nerve damage and muscle weakness or paralysis, incoordination, learning disorders, possible scoliosis or kyphosis, other skeletal deformities including pseudoarthrosis of the tibia and fibula, tibial bowing, craniofacial and vertebral dysplasia, rib fusion, and dislocation of the radius and ulna
- *Osteogenesis imperfecta:* see separate section
- *Phenylketonuria* (PKU), untreated: hypertonicity, motor delays, cognitive delays, severe mental retardation, growth retardation, cerebellar dysfunction, seizures, pigment deficiency of hair and skin, hyperactive reflexes, hyperkinesis, and tremors
- *Prader–Willi syndrome:* hypotonicity, obesity that can contribute to impaired breathing, short stature, dysmorphic facial features, compulsive preoccupation with food, expressionless face, little spontaneous movement, scoliosis, motor delays, poor coordination, cognitive delays, mental retardation, feeding difficulties, slow weight gain, behavioral problems such as temper tantrums, aggressiveness, self-abuse, and emotional lability
- *Rett syndrome:* see separate section
- *Trisomy 13* (Patau's syndrome): hypotonicity, hypertonicity, flexion contractures of the fingers, polydactyly of hands and feet, motor delays, myelomeningocele, microcephaly, hydrocephaly, severe mental retardation, cognitive delays, deafness, ocular abnormalities including retinal dysplasia and microphthalmia, cleft lip or palate
- *Trisomy 18* (Edwards syndrome): hypotonicity, hypertonicity, scoliosis, rocker-bottom feet, talipes equinovarus, flexion deformities of the fingers, joint hyperextensibility, motor delays, microencephaly, myelomeningocele, profound mental retardation, cognitive delays, cardiovascular malformations, gastrointestinal malformations, urogenital malformations, cleft palate, and poor oral-motor skills, including sucking
- *Trisomy 21* (Down syndrome): see separate section
- *Tuberous sclerosis:* hypertonicity, motor delay, in some cases rigidity or hemiplegia, cognitive delays, mental retardation, speech delay, seizures of the myoclonic type initially that progress to grand mal type, tumors in the ventricles that are often the source of the seizures, sebaceous adenomas, retinal tumors and hemorrhages, glaucoma, corneal opacities, cyst formation in long bones and finger and toe bones that contributes to osteoporosis, reports of cardiac and kidney involvement
- *Turner syndrome* (gonadal dysgenesis, XO syndrome): hip dislocations, pes planus, pes equinovarus, dislocated patella, deformity of the medial tibial condyles, osteoporosis, decreased lumbar lordosis, idiopathic scoliosis, decreased gustatory and olfactory sensitivity, deficits in spatial perception and orientation, moderate hearing loss, chronic otitis media,

spinal deformities, webbed neck, cubitus valgus, dorsal edema of hands and feet, growth retardation, upper extremity deformities, and congenital heart disease; may or may not have normal intelligence
- *Werdnig–Hoffman syndrome:* see "Spinal Muscular Atrophy"
- *Wolf–Hirschhorn syndrome:* hypotonicity, hip dislocation, scoliosis, severe psychomotor retardation, growth retardation, seizures, clubfeet, microcephaly, craniofacial anomalies, ocular malformation, cleft lip or palate, heart malformations, proximal radioulnar synostosis, motor delays, and cognitive delays

TREATMENT/MANAGEMENT
- Increase or maintain functional skills.
- Recommend assistive technology devices.
- Improve motor skills.
  1. Develop normal patterns of movement.
  2. Prevent abnormal patterns from occurring.
- Decrease hypertonicity.
  1. Decrease reliance on use of reflexes to imitate movement patterns by teaching alternate method.
  2. If child is unable to learn alternate method, some reflex imitative patterns may be necessary.
  3. Increase range of motion.
- Increase hypotonicity.
  1. Decrease dependence on locking joints and broad base of support.
  2. Increase postural control.
  3. Increase muscle strength.
  4. Increase endurance.
- Compensate for hyperextensible joints.
  1. Modify activities or provide external support to avoid undue stress on these joints and surrounding ligaments, tendons, and fascia. For example, positions that allow knee or elbow joints to lock into extension should be modified so weight bearing occurs through neutral alignment.
  2. Techniques include specific placement of toys and support surfaces, providing physical assistance, and using adaptive equipment.
  3. Foot-ankle orthoses may provide sufficient support to permit functional activities in standing.
  4. Vertical stander may permit knee hyperextension and allow the child to stand and play.
- Compensate for contractures and deformities.
  1. With other team members, work to detect and prevent the progression of the disorder, using knowledge of the factors that contribute to the development of specific deformities. For example, a child with hypertonicity is at risk for developing joint contracture because movement is limited to the range around the joint. The solution is to increase the range of movement. Or, for example, a child with hypotonicity is at risk for developing soft tissue restrictions and contractures due to habitual positioning such as "frog" sitting (wide abduction, external rotation, and flexion at the hips). The solution is to teach long-leg sitting or cross-leg.
  2. The position of adduction, flexion, and internal rotation of hips places the child at risk for hip subluxation or dislocation.

3. Abnormal or asymmetrical tone causes spinal deformities such as lumbar lordosis, thoracic kyphosis, and scoliosis.
- Decrease respiratory problems.
  1. Provide mobilization techniques, deep breathing exercises, chest expansion exercises, and postural drainage.
  2. If child is unable to tolerate one position for an extended time, rotate or alter positions.
- Increase developmental milestones.
  1. Correct expectation for degree of prematurity.
  2. Order of skill acquisition does not have to follow normal acquisition exactly.
- Normalize muscle tone by using alternate positions or varied external support.
- Improve sensory integration—an occupational therapist can assist with or recommend sensory integrative activities.
- Instruct parents, teachers, and other caregivers in proper lifting, carrying, and handling techniques and proper positioning.
- Assist in controlling behavioral problems of noncompliance, self-stimulation, and self-abuse.
- Develop a home program if the family is able and wants to participate in the treatment/management program.
- Assist in providing family support.
  1. Work with the family to understand and incorporate family priorities into treatment/management plan as much as possible to encourage the family's participation in the treatment/management program.
  2. Acknowledge family culture and values regarding views of disability, child-rearing practices, decision making, family life, future planning, and need for privacy.
  3. Incorporate family members as part of treatment/management team in goal setting, planning of service delivery, and program evaluation.
  4. Build on family and community resources.
     a. Provide information and encouragement to facilitate the family's decision making concerning the child.
     b. Allow the family to provide as many services as the family wishes to provide to the child.
     c. Recommend community resources that can assist the family to expand service delivery.

PRECAUTIONS/CONTRAINDICATIONS
- Try to avoid restricting the child's repertoire of normal activities. Use alternate activities or provide support to achieve better postural alignment or movement pattern.
- A limited variety of postures and movement patterns is the primary cause of deformities and contractures. Any child with a limited number of postures and movement patterns should be considered at risk.
- A child who has hypotonicity or hypertonicity or is compromised due to chest and skeletal deformities is at risk for respiratory problems and should be treated before major respiratory problems occur.

DESIRED OUTCOME/PROGNOSIS
- The child will attain all major motor milestones consistent with chronological age, corrected for immaturity if born premature.
- The child will be able to perform basic functional skills independently or with minimal assistance (cueing).

- The child will be able to use assistive devices and technology, if needed.
  Exceptions in which limited progress is expected are
- *Trisomy 13*—Infant usually dies before first birthday.
- *Trisomy 18*—Infant usually dies before first birthday.
- *Wolf–Hirschhorn syndrome*—Infant usually dies before second birthday.

Types of Genetic Disorders

Chromosomal Abnormalities
    Autosomal trisomy
        Trisomy 21 (Down syndrome; see separate chapter)
        Trisomy 18 (Edwards' syndrome)
        Trisomy 13 (Patau's syndrome)
    Sex chromosome abnormalities
        Turner syndrome
        Klinefelter syndrome
    Partial deletion syndromes
        Wolf–Hirshhorn syndrome (4p-)
        Cri-du-chat syndrome (5p-)
        Prader–Willi syndrome (15q-)
Specific Gene Defects
    Autosomal dominant
        Osteogenesis imperfecta (see separate chapter)
        Tuberous sclerosis
        Neurofibromatosis
    Autosomal recessive
        Hurler syndrome (gargoylism, mucopolysaccharidosis I)
        Phenylketonuria (PKU)
        Werdneg–Hoffmann disease (acute infantile spinal muscular atrophy; see
            section "Spinal Muscular Atrophy")
        Kugelberg Welander disease (intermediate spinal muscular atrophy; see
            section "Spinal Muscular Atrophy")
    Sex-linked
        Lowe syndrome (oculocerebrorenal syndrome)
        Lesch–Nyham syndrome
    Other genetic disorders
        Rett syndrome (see separate chapter)

Source: Naganuma GM, Harris SK, Tada WL. Genetic disorders. In: Umphred DA, ed. *Neurological Rehabilitation*. 3rd ed. St Louis, Mo: CV Mosby Co; 1995:287–311.

REFERENCES

Donnai D, Kerzin-Storrar L, Wigmore P. Genetics and embryology. In: Eckersley PM, ed. *Elements of Paediatric Physiotherapy*. New York, NY: Churchill Livingstone; 1993:19–33.

Harris SR, Tada WL. Genetic disorders. In: Umphred DA, ed. *Neurological Rehabilitation*. 2nd ed. St Louis, Mo: CV Mosby Co; 1990:259–281.

Naganuma GM, Harris SR, Tada WL. Genetic disorders. In: Umphred DA, ed. *Neurological Rehabilitation.* 3rd ed. St Louis, Mo: CV Mosby Co; 1995:287–311.

ASSESSMENT

Discriminative Assessments
Bayley N. *Bayley Scales of Infant Development.* 2nd ed. San Antonio, Tex: Psychological Corporation; 1993.
Bruininks RH. *Bruininks–Oseretsky Test of Motor Proficiency.* Circle Pines, Minn: American Guidance Service; 1978.
Folio MR, Fewell RR. *Peabody Development Motor Scales.* Allen, Tex: DLM Teaching Resources; 1983.
Knobloch H, Stevens F, Malone A. *Manual of Developmental Diagnosis: The Administration and Interpretation of the Revised Gesell and Amatruda Developmental and Neurological Examination.* Houston, Tex: Gesell Developmental Materials, Inc; 1987.
Stott, DH, Moyes FA, Henderson SE. *Stott–Moyes–Henderson Test of Motor Impairment.* Guelph, Ontario, Canada: Brook Educational Publishing Ltd; 1984.

Predictive Assessments
Chandler LS, Andrews MS, Swanson MW. *Movement Assessment of Infants: A Manual.* Rolling Bay, Wash: Infant Movement Research; 1980.

Evaluative Assessments
Furno S, O'Reilly KA, Hosaka CM, Inatsuka TT, Aeisloft-Falbey B, Allman T. *Hawaii Early Learning Profile (HELP).* Palo Alto, Calif: VORT Corporation; 1979.
Gans BM, et al. Description and interobserver reliability of the Tufts Assessment of Motor Performance. *American Journal of Physical Medicine and Rehabilitation.* 1988; 67:202–207.
Granger CV. Guide for the Use of the Uniform Data Set for Medical Rehabilitation. Buffalo, NY: Research Foundation, State University of New York; 1986. **[Functional Independence Measure (FIM)]**
Granger CV. *Guide for the Use of the Functional Independence Measure (WeeFIM) of the Uniform Data Set for Medical Rehabilitation.* Buffalo, NY: Research Foundation, State University of New York; 1988.
Haley SM, Coster WJ, Ludlow LH, Haltiwanger J, Andrellos PJ. *Pediatric Evaluation of Disability Inventory (PEDI).* Boston, Mass: New England Medical Center Publications; 1992.

Hemophilia

DESCRIPTION
Hemophilia is the term used to collectively identify several X-linked disorders, recessive inheritance type, of bleeding due to clotting factor deficiencies. The most common of these are factor VIII deficiency or hemophilia A, composing 80% to 90% of the population with hemophilia, and factor IX deficiency or hemophilia B (see McGee, "Hemophilia," p. 227, in references.) Because a major treatment for hemophilia is blood transfusion, many persons with hemophilia have acquired HIV and AIDS from infected blood products prior to the development and widespread use of the blood screening test for the virus.

CAUSE

Hemophilia A (factor VIII deficiency), which affects about 80% of hemophiliacs, and hemophilia B (factor IX deficiency) have identical clinical manifestations, screening test abnormalities, and sex-linked genetic transmission. Specific factor assays are required to distinguish the two. Hemophilia results from many different mutations of genes for factors VIII (hemophilia A) and IX (hemophilia B). Because both factors are located on the X chromosome, most affected individuals are male. Note: Females may have von Willebrand's disease, which is an autosomal disorder characterized by superficial bleeding into mucocutaneous tissue.

ASSESSMENT

Areas

- General assessment
  1. Joint range of motion (ROM)
  2. Muscle strength: gross muscle test for all groups and specific manual muscle test for problem joints using isokinetics only
  3. Level of pain tolerance
  4. Any gross neurological abnormalities
  5. Problems in posture and gait
  6. Skin and soft tissue: hematomas, edema, ecchymosis, or muscle wasting
  7. Cardiac and respiratory abnormalities
  8. Developmental milestones
  9. Functional abilities and skills, especially in activities of daily living (ADLs)
- Specific assessment after hemorrhage
  1. History of hemorrhages
  2. Level of activity prior to hemorrhage
  3. Factors occurring before hemorrhage began
  4. Previous state of joint
  5. Level of pain tolerance
  6. Mobility: active ROM only
  7. Gait and posture (if lower extremity is involved)

Instruments/Procedures (See References for Sources)

- Bruininks–Oseretsky Test of Motor Proficiency
- Denver II Screening Manual
- Peabody Developmental Motor Scales and Activity Cards

PROBLEMS

- There may be hemarthrosis (bleeding into the joints).
- There may be hemorrhaging (bleeding into tissues, including muscle).
- There may be pseudotumors (encapsulated hematomas that usually must be surgically removed).
- There may be pain in and around joints, especially if hemarthrosis or hemorrhaging has occurred.
- Chronic pain can be present if arthritis has occurred because of multiple hemarthrosis incidents or hemorrhaging.

- ROM may be limited in hinge joints such as knee, elbow, and ankle, especially after hemarthrosis has occurred.
- Muscle weakness may occur, especially if hemorrhaging into muscle tissue has occurred.
- Developmental delay is usually the result of multiple hospitalizations for problems related to the control of hemophilia.

TREATMENT/MANAGEMENT

Equipment
- Equipment can include weights, surgical tubing, isokinetic exercise equipment, bike, swimming pool, gym equipment, elastic bandages, ice, and biofeedback and electrical stimulation equipment for muscle re-education.

Prophylactic Treatment
- Instruct child and family about minimizing joint and other hemorrhages.
- Learn about replacement therapy for factor VIII and/or factors II, VII, IX, X, and XIII. This is often referred to as *cryoprecipitate medium therapy* because the preparation in which the factors are stored must be kept frozen and then thawed just before transfusion into the person.
- Teach techniques and ideas of joint protection for avoiding injuries in the home, school, and community environments.
- Provide muscle strengthening exercises.
  1. Young children can benefit from proactive strengthening exercises and activities before hemarthrosis has occurred.
  2. Older children may need strengthening exercises after bleeding has occurred.
- Provide information about physical fitness and conditioning, including cardiopulmonary fitness, strengthening, and mobility. Explore and recommend recreational and sports activities that can assist in maintaining or regaining fitness, such as swimming.
- Develop a home program for involved joint or joints.
  1. Phase 1: Select exercises consisting of isometrics to strengthen muscles and maintain or increase active ROM around the involved joint.
  2. Phase 2: Continue exercising by adding progressive weights to exercises in phase 1.
  3. Phase 3: Provide functional retraining of the involved joint, including flexibility exercises when needed.
- Periodically reassess.

Treatment Post Hemarthrosis
In hemarthrosis, hinge joints are most commonly involved, beginning with the knee, elbow, and ankle.

Ice
- Use only during acute bleeds; not for chronic conditions.
- Use crushed ice in a towel for 5 to 20 minutes 6 to 8 times per day.
- Always examine skin for redness or pressure.

Splinting
- Immediately after hemarthrosis has occurred, immobilize joint in the position the client prefers to protect the joint, decrease pain, and prevent further loss of motion.
- After replacement therapy, modify splint as pain decreases and client regains ROM.
- Final resting or night splint should be full extension for knee or elbow and in dorsiflexion for the ankle.

Progressive Exercises
- Begin exercise when the factor level is sufficient (usually 35% to 40% for factor VIII or IX) and the pain has decreased.
- Perform only isometrics for 1 to 2 days.
- If there is no bleeding or increased pain, begin active assistive exercises.
- Begin exercises with weights when isometrics and active motion can be repeated 60 to 80 times.

Gait
- Provide or assist in serial casting, splinting, or bracing prior to ambulation.
- Begin progress gait training as physician approves.
- For partial weight bearing, use lateral support or begin training in a swimming pool.
- Provide exercises to increase lower extremity strength and endurance to improve mobility.

Hematoma Treatment

Ice
Protocol is the same as for hemarthrosis.

Compression
This may be performed with elastic bandage wrapping to decrease edema.

Splinting
- Use splint to immobilize joint or joints until hemorrhage in muscle has stopped.
- Serial splinting can be started when the muscle is no longer firm to the touch or painful and the factor level is adequate to maintain the ROM attained during therapy.
- The final splint should be used as a resting or night splint to maintain muscle length and ROM.

Progressive Exercise
- Begin progressive exercises when the factor level (usually 25% to 30% of factor VIII or IX) is adequate and the muscle contracts without pain.
- Start with isometrics, then active assistive ROM, then active ROM, and finally progressive resistive exercise.
- If stretching is needed, begin with active contraction of the antagonist, and then move to passive stretch.

Gait
- Initial training may be non-weight-bearing activities.
- When physician approves, begin weight bearing.

Peripheral Nerve Palsy Treatment

Splinting
Protocol is the same as with hematoma.

Exercise
Protocol is the same as with hematoma. Use muscle re-education techniques for muscles affected by palsy.

Ice
Protocol is the same as with hemarthrosis.

Gait

Protocol is the same as with hematoma. Consider recommending bracing or lateral support if palsy compromises gait pattern or mobility.

PRECAUTIONS/CONTRAINDICATIONS
- Educate the child and family about the danger of contact sports such as football or hockey, which could result in injury and serious bleeding problems.
- Do not force involved joints through ROM.
- With ice, check skin to avoid skin damage, and use protective layers between ice and skin.
- If the client is aware that a bleed is starting, stop therapy and report bleed to physician.
- If the client develops antibodies to factor VIII, exercise may not be possible. Use ice to relieve pain.
- Short, frequent sessions may be preferable to reduce pain and stress.

DESIRED OUTCOME/PROGNOSIS
- The child will regain or maintain active and passive ROM.
- The child will regain or maintain muscle strength.
- The child will have normal gait.
- The child will have a normal level of function.
- The child will have normal posture.
- The child will have normal skin and soft tissue.
- The child and family will be able to carry out a written home exercise program.

REFERENCES

ASSESSMENT
Bruininks RH. *Bruininks–Oseretsky Test of Motor Proficiency*. Circle Pines, Minn: American Guidance Service; 1987.

Folio MR, & Fewell RR. *Peabody Developmental Motor Scales and Activity Cards*. Allen, Tex: DLM Teaching Resources; 1983.

Frankenburg WK, Dodds JB, Archer P, et al. *Denver II Screening Manual*. Denver, Colo: Denver Developmental Materials; 1990.

TREATMENT
Bezner J, Rogers H, eds. Pediatric hemophilia protocol. In: *Physical Therapy Protocols: Guidelines for Rehabilitation*. Tucson, Ariz: Therapy Skill Builders; 1991:159–164.

Cintas HL. Pediatric disorders: hemophilia. In: Long TM, Cintas ML, eds. *Handbook of Pediatric Therapy*. Baltimore, Md: Williams & Wilkins; 1995:129–130.

Gregosiewicz A, Wo'sko I, Kandziershi G. Intraarticular bleeding in children with hemophilia: the prevention of arthropathy. *Journal of Pediatric Orthopedics*. 1989; 9:182–185.

Holdredge S, Cotta S. Physical therapy and rehabilitation in the care of the adult and child with hemophilia. In: Hilgartner MW, Pochedly C, eds. *Hemophilia in the Child and Adult*. New York, NY: Raven Press; 1989:235–262.

Kasper CK. Hemophilia care in the near future. *Progress in Clinical and Biological Research*. 1990; 324:291–293.

McGee SM. Hemophilia. In: Campbell, SK, ed. *Physical Therapy for Children*. Philadelphia, Pa: WB Saunders Co; 1994:227–237.

Nelson IW, Atkins RM, Allen AL. The management of knee flexion contractures in hemophilia: brief report. *Journal of Bone and Joint Surgery*. 1989;71B:327–328.

Petrini P, Lindvall N, Egberg N, Blomback M. Prophylaxis with factor concentrates in preventing hemophilic arthropathy. *American Journal of Pediatric Hematology/Oncology.* 1991;13:280–287.

Timmermans H. The role of the physiotherapist. In: Gilbert MS, Greene WB. *Musculoskeletal Problems in Hemophilia.* New York, NY: National Hemophilia Foundation; 1990:115–121.

High-Risk or At-Risk Infants

DESCRIPTION
A high-risk infant is any newborn or young infant who has a high probability of manifesting in childhood sensory or motor deficit and/or mental handicap (see Parmelee and Haber, in references).

CAUSE
Typical causes for being considered at risk or high-risk are very low birth weight, intraventricular hemorrhage, bronchopulmonary dysplasia, birth asphyxia, respiratory distress syndrome, meconium aspiration, specific congenital anomalies or syndromes, metabolic acidosis, hyperbilirubinemia, patent ductus arteriosus, substance abuse, infants with abnormal movement or abnormal postures, or possible delay in motor development.

ASSESSMENT

Areas
- Autonomic system: respiratory rhythms, color changes, visceral signals
- Overall development status: neonatal development, motor development
- Motor behavior and control: movement patterns, postural reactions, muscle tone, muscle strength, joint range of motion (ROM), reflex development, oral-motor development
- Sensory perception
- Physical strength and endurance
- Behavioral state (state organizational system): patterns of state changes, range of available states, differentiation and lability of states
- Attentional/interactive system

Instruments/Procedures (See References for Sources)
Apgar Score—should be available from infant's chart; compare 1-minute and 5-minute results
- Assessment of Preterm Infant's Behavior (APIB)
- Bayley Scales of Infant Development
- Gesell and Amatruda Developmental and Neurologic Examination
- Milani–Comparetti Motor Development Screening Test
- Morgan Neonatal Neurobehavioral Examination
- Neonatal Behavioral Assessment Scale
- Neonatal Individualized Developmental Care and Assessment Program (NIDCAP)
- Neonatal Oral-Motor Assessment Scale (NOMAS)
- Obstetric and Postnatal Complications Scales

- Peabody Developmental Motor Scales
- Problem-Oriented Perinatal Risk Assessment Systems

PROBLEMS
- Birth weight may be low.
- Possible brain disorders and injuries include periventricular leukomalacia, periventricular hemorrhagic infarction, intraventricular hemorrhage, and neonatal seizures.
- There may be sepsis neonatorum.
- There may be respiratory distress syndrome.
- There may be symptoms of withdrawal from maternal substance abuse.
- There may be suboptimal head growth (microcephaly secondary to inadequate brain growth).
- Motor control problems include the following:
  1. poorly coordinated movement
  2. difficulty inhibiting motor activity
  3. difficulty maintaining motor control while attending to other stimuli
  4. abnormal tone—may be hypotonic, hypertonic, or fluctuating
  5. oral-motor skills weak or absent
  6. difficulty changing positions especially against gravity
  7. difficulty maintaining a flexed posture
  6. nursery-acquired positional malformations
     a. elevated and retracted scapulae, abducted shoulders, and flexed elbows ("W" position of upper extremities)
     b. flexed, abducted, and externally rotated hips ("frog" position of the lower extremities)
     c. neck hyperextension

TREATMENT/MANAGEMENT
Treatment models vary depending on the view of high-risk infants. The "extrauterine fetus" view suggests that treatment should mimic the intrauterine environment. The "inadequately functioning neonate" view suggests that treatment should stimulate the infant. The "deprivation" view suggests that treatment should include sensory enrichment. The "sensory overload" view suggests that treatment should decrease input. The "discordant and strive" view suggests that treatment should be rhythmic and contingent.
- Promote state organization; especially enhance quiet state with non-nutritive sucking and vestibular input using waterbeds, hammocks, and rocking. Position infant in prone.
- Promote appropriate parent-infant or caregiver-infant interaction through instruction and demonstration.
- Enhance self-regulatory behavior through environmental modification. Show parent or caregiver skin-to-skin contact, called "kangaroo care." Infant is held directly against parent's body at about a 60 degree angle from upright. This may assist in promoting regular sleep and homeostasis and decreasing crying.
- Prevent iatrogenic musculoskeletal abnormalities, and promote postural alignment and more normal patterns of movement through therapeutic handling and positioning. Facilitate flexion of trunk and limbs. Use symmetric postures and midline orientations. Use side-lying position to avoid extension and abduction of the trunk and extremities.
- Provide selected stimulation using tactile-kinesthetic input. Tactile stimulation may be used to arouse infant. Neonatal massage and stroking may increase awake time, alertness, muscle

tone, and heart and respiratory rates. Tactile-kinesthetic stimulation may assist in orientation, motor functions, and improved state.

- Enhance oral-motor skills and assist with oral feedings.
- Improve visual and auditory reactions.
- Promote weight gain through selected stimulation: tactile-kinesthetic stimulation, non-nutritive sucking, and vestibular-proprioceptive stimulation.
- Neonatal hydrotherapy may reduce extension tone, increase spontaneous movement, and decrease hypersensitivity to touch.
- Provide appropriate remediation of orthopedic complications.
- Provide consultation to team members regarding developmental intervention.
- Participate in interagency collaboration to facilitate transition from hospital to home environment.

PRECAUTIONS/CONTRAINDICATIONS

Therapists should exercise caution in assessing and treating high-risk infants so as not to cause injury or problems.

- Motor aspects include fractures, dislocation, and joint effusion.
- Homeostatic disturbances include apnea, bradycardia, and hypothermia during movement therapy.
- Regurgitation or aspiration may occur during oral-motor therapy.
- There may be propagation of infection.
- Apnea and bradycardia may occur during feeding.
- Heart and respiratory rates may increase during tactile-kinesthetic stimulation.
- Respiratory distress may occur during chest physical therapy.

DESIRED OUTCOME/PROBLEMS

- The infant or child will develop normal motor skills.
- The infant or child will achieve developmental milestones.
- The infant or child will be able to function in normal age-appropriate daily activities.

REFERENCES

ASSESSMENT

Amiel-Tison C. Neurologic evaluation of the infant and newborn. *Archives of Diseases in Children.* 1968;43:89–93.

Amiel-Tison C, Grenier A. *Neurological Evaluation Within the First Years of Life.* New York, NY: Oxford University Press; 1986.

Ashton B, Piper MC, Warren S, Stein L, Borne P. Influence of medical history on assessment of at-risk infants. *Developmental Medicine and Child Neurology.* 1991;33:412–418.

Dubowitz L, Dubowitz V. Neurological assessment of the full-term and preterm newborn infant. *Clinics in Developmental Medicine* No. 79. Philadelphia, Pa: JB Lippincott Co; 1981.

Dubowitz LMS, Dubowitz V, and Goldbert D. Clinical assessment of gestational age in the newborn infant. Journal of Pediatrics. 1970;77:1–10.

Hislop HJ, Montgomery J. *Daniel's and Worthingham's Muscle Testing and Techniques of Manual Examination.* Philadelphia, Pa: WB Saunders; 1995.

Zausmer E. Evaluation of strength and motor development in infants. Part 1. *Physical Therapy Review.* 1953;33:575.

Assessment of Preterm Infant's Behavior
Als H, Lester BM, Tronick EZ, Brazelton TB. Toward a research instrument for the assessment of preterm infants' behavior (APIB). In: Fitzgerald H, Lester GM, Yogman MW, eds. *Theory and Research in Behavioral Pediatrics.* Vol 1. New York, NY; Plenum Press; 1982:65–132.

Bayley Scales of Infant Development
Bayley N. *Bayley Scales of Infant Development.* 2nd ed. San Antonio, Tex: Psychological Corporation; 1993.

Gesell Development Schedules
Knoblock H. *Gesell and Amatruda Developmental and Neurologic Examination.* New York, NY: Harper & Row; 1980.
Knobloch H, Stevens F, Malone A. *Manual of Developmental Diagnosis: The Administration and Interpretation of the Revised Gesell and Amatruda. Developmental and Neurological Examination.* Houston, Tex: Developmental Evaluation Materials, Inc; 1987.

Milani–Comparetti Motor Development Screening Test
Studberg WA, White RJ, Miedaner JA, Dehne PR. *Milani–Comparetti Motor Development Screening Test.* 3rd ed, rev. Omaha, Neb: University of Nebraska Medical Center; 1992.

Morgan Neonatal Neurobehavioral Examination
Morgan A. Neurodevelopmental approach to the high-risk neonate. In: Tecklin JS, ed. *Pediatric Physical Therapy.* Philadelphia, Pa: JP Lippincott Co; 1994:71–73.

Neonatal Behavioral Assessment Scale
Brazelton TB. Neonatal Behavioral Assessment Scale. *Clinics in Developmental Medicine No. 88.* Philadelphia, Pa: JP Lippincott Co; 1984.

Neonatal Individualized Developmental Care and Assessment Program (NIDCAP)
Als H. *Manual for the Naturalistic Observation of Newborn Behavior (Preterm and Fullterm Infants).* Boston, Mass: Children's Hospital; 1984.

Neonatal Oral-Motor Assessment Scale (NOMAS)
Braun MA, Palmer MM. A pilot study of oral-motor dysfunction in "at-risk" infants. *Physical and Occupational Therapy in Pediatrics.* 1986;5:4:13–25.

Obstetric and Postnatal Complications Scales
Parmelee A, Kopp C, Sigmon M. Selection of developmental assessment techniques. *Merrill-Palmer Quarterly.* 1976;22:177.

Peabody Developmental Motor Scales
Folio MR, Fewell RR. *Peabody Developmental Motor Scales.* Allen, Tex: DLM Teaching Resources; 1983.

Problem-Oriented Perinatal Risk Assessment System
Hoebel CJ. Identification of the patient at risk. In: Bolognese RJ, Schwarz RH, Schneider J, eds. *Perinatal Medicine: Management of the High Risk Fetus and Neonate.* Baltimore, Md: Williams & Wilkins; 1982:31.

TREATMENT
Cocrane CG, Farley BG, Wilhelm IJ. Preparation of physical therapists who work with handicapped infants and their families: current status and training needs. *Physical Therapy.* 1990;70:372–380.

DeSantis AM. Sensory, motor, and regulatory problems: behavior and early intervention strategies. In: Ensher GL, Clark DA, eds. *Newborn at Risk: Medical Care and Psychoeducation Intervention.* 2nd ed. Gaithersburg, Md: Aspen Publishers, Inc; 1994:295–322.

Hayes MJ, Ensher GL. Intervening in intensive care nurseries. In: Ensher GL, Clark DA, eds. *Newborns at Risk: Medical Care and Psychoeducation Intervention.* 2nd ed. Gaithersburg, Md: Aspen Publishers, Inc; 1994:227–248.

Heriza CB. Implications of a dynamical systems approach to understanding infant kicking behavior. *Physical Therapy.* 1991;71:222–235.

Osborne PS. Physical therapy. In *Follow-up Management of the High-Risk Infant,* ed. H.W. Taeusch and M.W. Yogman. Boston: Little Brown & Co; 1987;127–34.

Parmelee AH, Haber A. Who is the "risk infant"? *Clinical Obstetrics & Gynecology.* 1973;16(1):376–387.

Rothberg AD, Goodman M, Jacklin LA, Cooper PA. Six-year follow-up of early physiotherapy intervention in very low birth weight infants. *Pediatrics.* 88(3);547–552.

Sheahan MS, Brockway NF. The high-risk infant. *Pediatric Physical Therapy,* 2nd ed. Philadelphia, Pa: J.B. Lippincott Co; 56–88.

Sweeney JK. Assessment of the special care nursery environment: effects on the high-risk infant. In: Wilhelm IJ, ed. *Physical Therapy Assessment in Early Infancy.* New York, NY: Churchill-Livingstone 13–34.

Washington KA, Harris SR. Mental and motor performance of low-birthweight infants with normal developmental outcomes. *Pediatric Physical Therapy.* 1(4):159–165.

Wilhelm IJ. Neurobehavioral assessment of the high-risk neonate. In: Wilhelm IJ, ed. *Physical therapy assessment in early infancy.* New York, NY: Churchill-Livingstone; 1993; 71–104.

Infectious Disorders of the Brain

More specific terms include *brain abscess, meningitis, leptomeningitis, pachymeningitis, encephalitis,* and *encephalomyelitis.*

DESCRIPTION

In a brain abscess, the brain parenchyma shows a poorly localized, inflammatory response *(cerebritis)* that subsequently become necrotic and encapsulated by glia and fibroblasts. Days or weeks later, edema around the abscess gives rise to increased intracranial pressure, with signs and symptoms resembling those seen in brain tumor.

Meningitis or *leptomeningitis* denotes an infection spread through the cerebrospinal fluid, with the inflammatory process involving the pia and arachnoid maters, the subarachnoid space, and the adjacent superficial tissues of the brain and spinal cord. *Pachymeningitis* denotes an inflammatory process involving the dura mater. Types of meningitis are acute bacterial meningitis, acute viral encephalitis, aseptic meningitis, and neonatal meningitis (see Porter, "Therapeutic management," 1995 edition, p. 536, in references).

Encephalitis is an acute inflammatory disease of the brain due to direct viral invasion or to hypersensitivity initiated by a virus or other foreign protein.

Encephalomyelitis is the same disorder as encephalitis except that the spinal cord structures as well as the brain are involved.

CAUSE

A brain abscess is caused by microorganisms reaching brain tissue by a penetrating wound to the brain, by extension of local infection such as sinusitis or otitis, or by hematogenous spread from a distant site of infection.

Causes of meningitis include *Escherichia coli,* group B streptococci, *Hemophilus influenza, Neisseria meningitides,* and *Streptococcus pneumonia.*

Viral infection may cause encephalitis as a primary manifestation or as a secondary complication. Primary encephalitis may be epidemic or sporadic. Secondary encephalitis (parainfectious or postinfectious encephalitides, acute toxic encephalopathy, or acute disseminated encephalomyelitis), usually a complication of viral infection, is considered to have an immunologic mechanism and follows disorders such as measles, chicken pox, rubella, and some vaccinations. It occurs 5 to 10 days after onset of illness.

ASSESSMENT

Areas
- Medical history
- Vital signs: pulse, respiration, blood pressure
- Pain
- Movement abilities: ability to assume, maintain, and move within and out of postures, including supine, prone, prone on elbows, prone on extended arms, long sitting, all fours, side sitting, knee standing, half kneeling, and standing; gait
- Sensory abilities including cutaneous, olfactory, gustatory, vestibular, proprioceptive, auditory, visual, and multichannel processing
- Cognitive status: level of consciousness, communication abilities, cognitive abilities, perceptual abilities, motor learning within and between sessions
- Functional abilities: progression through function sequence, activities of daily living (ADLs), eating sequence, oral-motor function

Instruments/Procedures (See References for Sources)
- Glasgow Coma Scale
- Southern California Nystagmus Test
- Kernig's sign: Infant or child is supine with thigh flexed on the abdomen and knee extended. The pull on the sciatic nerve, which pulls the spinal cord, causes pain.
- Hoppenfeld test: Infant or child is supine with leg raised straight.
- Kernig's test: Infant or child is supine. Cervical area of spine is flexed. Test is positive if there is pain.
- Brudzinski's sign—refers to the flexion of the hips and knees elicited when cervical flexion is performed.

PROBLEMS
- Physiological signs are headache, nausea, vomiting, and papilledema.
- Neuromotor signs are seizures, local neurologic deficits, difficulty with movement patterns, and changes in postural tone from hypotonia to hypertonia.
- Sensorimotor problems include hyperresponsiveness to sensory stimuli and perceptual motor problems.
- Cognitive problems include difficulty following instructions.
- Personality changes include agitation, ranging mild to severe, and lethargy.

TREATMENT/MANAGEMENT
Treatment is generally provided by an interdisciplinary team. The approach to treatment is based on a systems model (Bernstein) of interrelated problems and solutions, as opposed to the

Bobath (neurodevelopmental treatment) approach, which is based on a strict hierarchical model of the nervous system using reflexes or reactions to imitate movement sequences. Integration of sensory input is based on Ayres (sensory integration).

- Promote and improve postural control, as demonstrated by ability to maintain a position against gravity, ability to adjust automatically before and continuously during movement, and decreasing hypertonicity and increasing hypotonicity as needed to facilitate movement.
  1. Sequences may be initiated with primitive reflexes if no nonreflex method works, but use of reflex-initiated movement should be phased out as soon as possible.
  2. Develop selective control of movement through repetition in several positions and different activities.
  3. Provide opportunity to make a response within a variety of environmental constraints and conditions. For example, to improve eccentric hamstring control in a variety of conditions, (1) roll from supine to side-lying position with "hamstring control leg" held in the air and knee slightly bent but not touching the surface; (2) roll from side-lying to prone position with controlled leg held in the air, and knee slightly bent but not touching the surface; (3) stand on one leg, using eccentric hamstring contraction (therapist should place hand on hip to facilitate balance); and (4) control hamstring activity during swing phase of gait.
- Promote and improve selective, voluntary movement patterns within functional activities. For example, for movement sequence from supine to sitting: (1) begin with supine position, (2) roll child to side-lying, (3) assist in head up and propping on forearms, (4) move to side sitting with propping patterns on hands, and (5) assist child to attain symmetrical sitting position.
  1. Decrease stereotypical linkages developed in postural control, and increase ability to activate certain muscle groups selectively.
  2. Improve both mobility and stability patterns of the extremities.
  3. Decrease stereotypical posturing of upper extremities by changing the position (repositioning) before initiating movement.
  4. Reduce spasticity by applying approximation through the long axis of the extremity such as weight bearing on the heel of the hand placed on a table. Fist may be used if hand cannot open yet. After spasticity is reduced, move the extremity to an alternate resting position.
  5. Encourage child to assist with a movement, but the therapist must be ready to control the response so that a massive effort or overactivation does not occur.
  6. Electrical simulation can be used as an adjunct, if needed, to facilitate specific components of a pattern.
  7. Neutral warmth and diagonal patterns of proprioceptive neuromuscular facilitation (PNF) may help mobility of the scapula.
  8. Movement patterns should progress toward the ability to reverse the direction of movement or sequence to avoid stereotyped movement sequences.
- Enhance progression through the sequence of functional activities.
  1. Increase the sequence of functional activities required of the child.
  2. The therapist should focus on observing the child's ability to assume a posture, maintain it, move within it, and move out of it.
  3. Continue to practice activities with different environments to enhance generalization of learning.
  4. The development sequence provides a guide for increasing the amount and complexity of functional activities.

- Foster integration of sensory input.
  1. Begin by having the child respond adaptively to a single sensory system input. Usually vestibular, proprioceptive, or kinesthetic is started first.
  2. Have the child respond to a single input in the presence of multiple-system input.
  3. Have the child respond adaptively to inputs from two or more sources.
  4. Verbal commands should be concise, sparse, and appropriately timed.
  5. The therapist should watch for correct responses, not just the number of responses.
  6. At the highest level, the child can respond to cross-modal input such as identifying an object with the hand (touch) from seeing a picture (visual) of the object but not seeing the actual object.
  7. The therapist must watch for substitute or compensatory responses, eg, is the child actually crossing the midline of the body or simply rotating the midline of the body to avoid crossing it? The hand or leg must cross over the midline of the body.
  8. Balance can be disturbed when sensory integration of the equilibrial triad (visual, vestibular, and somatosensory systems) is missing one of the systems. The therapist should provide opportunities to practice responding to the specific deletion of one of the triad, as in blindfolding child or having child walk on a soft compliant surface.
- Promote and improve cognitive and psychosocial responses.
  1. Agitation is not conducive to good attention to movement. Reduce agitated state before treatment. Techniques to calm and quiet the nervous system, such as providing neutral warmth or rhythmic rocking and reducing stimuli in the environment, may be useful.
  2. As the child improves, increase the number of problem-solving tasks the child does, but have the child participate more in selecting tasks and deciding how to do them.
- Work with the interdisciplinary team to provide a coordinated and integrated plan of treatment.
  1. The therapist should reinforce goals of other services whenever possible.
  2. Some activities can be done collaboratively with other therapies.

PRECAUTIONS/CONTRAINDICATIONS
- Do not proceed with treatment when the child is agitated. Calm the child down first, or reschedule treatment.
- Do not leave the child alone or unattended even for a few minutes. The child should always be in line of sight.

DESIRED OUTCOME/PROGNOSIS
- The child will be able to ambulate independently with or without assistive devices.
- The child will be able to perform functional activities within level of residual ability.
- The child will be able to perform age-appropriate activities within level of residual ability.

REFERENCES

ASSESSMENT

Glasgow Coma Scale
Teasdale G, Jennett B. Assessment of coma and impaired consciousness: a practical scale. *Lancet.* 1974;2:81–84.

Southern California Post-Rotatory Nystagmus Test
Ayres AJ. *Southern California Post-Rotatory Nystagmus Test.* Los Angeles, Calif: Western Psychological Services; 1975.

TREATMENT
Porter RE. Therapeutic management of the client with inflammatory and infectious disorders of the brain. In: Umpherd DA, ed. *Neurological Rehabilitation*. 2nd ed. St Louis, Mo: CV Mosby Co; 1990:485–507.
Porter RE. Therapeutic management of the client with inflammatory and infectious disorders of the brain. In: Umpherd DA, ed. *Neurological Rehabilitation*. 3rd ed. St Louis, Mo: CV Mosby Co; 1995:535–555.

Juvenile Rheumatoid Arthritis

DESCRIPTION

Juvenile rheumatoid arthritis (JRA) is arthritis beginning before 16 years of age. JRA is divided into three subtypes (systemic, pauciarticular, polyarticular), each presenting with different clinical features. The disease tends to affect both large and small joints, which may result in interference with growth and development. About 20% of children have a systemic onset (called also *Still's disease*). Pauciarticular onset affects about 40% of children. The other 40% have a polyarticular onset. The systemic form affects both males and females in about equal distribution; the pauciarticular form is more common in young girls 4 years and under and boys 10 years and older; and the polyarticular form is most common in girls.

CAUSE

The cause is unknown. Some possible factors include infection, autoimmunity, trauma, stress, and genetic predisposition. The systemic onset is marked by high fever, rash, splenomegaly, generalized adenopathy, serositis, and a neurophilic leukocytosis.

ASSESSMENT

Areas
- History and chart review
- Mobility range of motion (ROM)
- Strength of functional muscle groups
- Posture and postural control
- Gait: stride length, step length, width of base of support, deviations such as decreased velocity, cadence, and anterior pelvic tilt
- Signs of muscle atrophy
- Joint swelling, edema, proliferation of synovial tissue
- Joint integrity and structural deviations: joint malalignments
- Function, including activities of daily living (ADLs)

Instruments/Procedures (See References for Sources)

Function/Disability
- Children's Seashore House Physical Therapy Department Evaluation for Juvenile Rheumatoid Arthritis
- Functional Independence Measure for Children (WeeFIM)
- Health Assessment Questionnaire (HAQ)

- Juvenile Arthritis Functional Assessment Scale (JAFAS)
- Pediatric Evaluation of Disability Inventory (PEDI)

Joint Integrity and Structural Deviations
- Thomas test to identify hip flexion contractures
- Adams bend-over test to identify scoliosis
- valgus and varus stress at the knee
- anterior and posterior drawer signs
- Ober test on the hip for iliotibial band
- leg-length discrepancy

Mobility
- goniometer

Skin and Soft Tissue
- palpation for temperature, tone, tenderness, proliferation of synovial tissue

Strength
- manual muscle testing of functional muscle groups

PROBLEMS

Systemic Type
- There is pain and inflammation in many joints.
- Involved joints have mobility limitations.
- Gait is dysfunctional and antalgic (painful), with decreased velocity and decreased stride length.
- There is decreased performance of ADLs if upper extremities are involved.
- There is usually multisystem or organ involvement, such as pericarditis, myocarditis, or hepatosplenomegaly.

Pauciarticular Type
- There is joint pain and inflammation in four joints or fewer.
- Involved joints have mobility limitations.
- Gait is dysfunctional and antalgic (painful), with decreased velocity and decreased stride length.
- There is decreased performance of ADLs if upper extremities and/or vision is involved.
- In young girls, there is a high risk of blindness called *iridocyclitis.*
- Males typically have hip joint involvement that may spread to pelvis and spine.

Polyarticular Type
- There is pain and inflammation in five joints or more, usually symmetrically.
- Mobility is limited in involved joints.
- Gait is dysfunctional and antalgic (painful), with decreased velocity and decreased stride length.
- Knees and ankles are most frequently involved, elbows, wrists, and fingers less often, and temporomandibular and cervical spine rarely.
- There is decreased performance of ADLs if upper extremities are involved.
- Females primarily are affected.

TREATMENT/MANAGEMENT
- Attain and maintain joint mobility and ROM.
    1. Establish and monitor a joint exercise program that includes moving all joints through their available ROM at least once a day.
    2. Use multiple-joint rather than single-joint exercises when possible.
    3. Target specific joints for increased ROM when they limit or interfere with function.
    4. Stretching exercises may be used if the disease process is under control.
    5. The contract-relax technique may be used for muscle elongation.
- Attain and maintain muscle strength.
    1. Select strengthening activities that minimize joint destruction or pain.
    2. Isometric activities may be preferred.
- Maintain or improve ambulation skills.
- Assist in controlling pain.
    1. Stabilize and immobilize joints that cause pain.
    2. Distal joints may be allowed to fuse naturally if pain is a continuing problem.
- Maintain or improve ability to perform ADLs independently.
- Monitor joint alignment.
    1. Watch for signs of deformities, such as genu valgus of the knee and ulnar drift of the hand.
    2. Educate the child and family on methods to minimize activities that lead to deformities, such as twisting jar lids open with right hand.
    3. Avoid selecting or recommending ROM exercises that can lead to known deformities.
    4. Recommend activities that exercise joints in opposing directions to avoid deformities.
    5. Select trunk posture and extremity elongation activities to optimize alignment.
- Intervene to promote proper joint alignment.
    1. If alignment problems are occurring, try to find contributing factors, and revise activity program to reduce opportunity for dysfunctional activities to occur.
    2. Use naturally occurring activities whenever possible. Verbal cues may be ignored or viewed as nagging.
    3. Extension in lower extremities can usually be maintained by having the child lie in a prone position for 20 minutes with hips and knees fully extended and feet over the edge of a mattress.
- Increase cardiopulmonary fitness and endurance.
    1. Select and use activities that will maintain physical fitness, such as swimming drills and water relay games.
- Educate the child and family about management of problems.
    1. Encourage the child and family to cooperate in planning a program of activities. Active participation improves compliance.
    2. Encourage optimal sitting alignment, especially at school.
    3. Encourage use of a thin, flat pillow or no pillow to reduce change of flexion contractures of the neck with sleeping in supine.
- Start a home program.
    1. Select exercises and recreational activities within the child's and family's interest whenever possible, such as swimming and aquatic therapy activities.
    2. Emphasis and recommend normal activities rather than contrived whenever possible to promote normal rather than disabled living.
    3. Select activities that can be done in multiple environments with a minimal amount of special equipment. Use clinic time for special or complicated exercises that require spe-

cialized equipment.
* Cooperate with team to coordinate treatment.
  1. Report to physician if medications are working or may need adjustment and change.

PRECAUTIONS/CONTRAINDICATIONS
* Modify muscle testing to avoid undue stress on inflamed joints. Use resistance judiciously. Preferred method is break testing of groups of muscles using isometric contraction rather than individual muscles.
* The child should be cautioned to move and change positions regularly throughout the day to avoid contractures.

DESIRED OUTCOME/PROGNOSIS
* The child will be able to move with controlled or no pain.
* The child will be able to ambulate independently with or without assistive technology.
* The child will be able to perform self-care tasks independently with or without assistive technology.
* The child will be able to participate in the family, school, recreational activities, and the community.

Range of Motion for Children

1. Arms above the head
2. Hands behind the head (external rotation)
3. Hands behind the back (internal rotation)
4. Palms up
5. Palms down
6. Hands in a position of prayer
7. Opening and closing the hands
8. Bending down to pick up a toy

Source: Reprinted with permission from SA Schull, Juvenile Rheumatoid Arthritis, in *Pediatric Physical Therapy*, JS Tecklin, p. 345, © 1994, JB Lippincott.

REFERENCES

ASSESSMENT

Function/Disability

Children's Seashore House Physical Therapy Department Evaluation for Juvenile Rheumatoid Arthritis
Scull SA. Juvenile rheumatoid arthritis. In: Tecklin JS, ed. *Pediatric Physical Therapy*. Philadelphia, Pa: JB Lippincott Co; 1994:342–344.

Functional Independence Measure for Children (WeeFIM)
Granger CV. *Guide for the Use of the Uniform Data Set for Medical Rehabilitation Including the Functional Independence Measure for Children (WeeFIM)*. Buffalo, NY: Research Foundation, State University of New York; 1991.

Health Assessment Questionnaire (HAQ)

Scull SA. Juvenile rheumatoid arthritis. In: Tecklin JS, ed. *Pediatric Physical Therapy*. Philadelphia, Pa: JB Lippincott Co; 1994:348–351.

Juvenile Arthritis Functional Assessment Scale (JAFAS)

Lovell DJ, Howe S, Shear E, et al. Development of a disability measurement tool for juvenile rheumatoid arthritis: the Juvenile Arthritis Functional Assessment Scale. *Arthritis and Rheumatism*. 1989;32:1390–1395.

Pediatric Evaluation of Disability Inventory (PEDI)

Hayley SM, Coster WJ, Fass RM. A content validity study of the Pediatric Evaluation of Disability Inventory. *Pediatric Physical Therapy*. 1991;3:177–189.

TREATMENT

Ansell BM. The First International Workshop on Physiotherapy in Juvenile Chronic Arthritis. *Clinical and Experimental Rheumatology*. 1992;72:365–372.

Bacon MC, Nicholson C, Binder H, White PH. Juvenile rheumatoid arthritis: aquatic exercise and lower-extremity function. *Arthritis Care and Research*. 1991;4:102–105.

Giannini J, Protas EJ, Exercise response in children with and without juvenile rheumatoid arthritis: a case-comparison study. *Physical Therapy*. 1992;72:365–372.

Lloyd J, Aldrich S. Second workshop on physiotherapy in JCA Garmisch-Partenkirchen. *British Journal of Rheumatology*. 1993;32:425.

Page-Goertz SS. Even children have arthritis. *Pediatric Nursing*. 1989;15:1:11–16, 30.

Rhodes VJ. Physical therapy management of patients with juvenile rheumatoid arthritis. *Physical Therapy*. 1991;71:910–919.

Scull SA. Juvenile rheumatoid arthritis. In: Tecklin JS, ed. *Pediatric Physical Therapy*. Philadelphia, Pa: JB Lippincott Co; 1994:337–362.

Scull SA. Juvenile rheumatoid arthritis. In: Campbell SK, ed. *Physical Therapy for Children*. Philadelphia, Pa: WB Saunders Co; 1994:207–225.

Shepherd RB. Inflammatory disorders of soft tissues and joints. In: Shepherd RB, ed. *Physiotherapy in Pediatrics*. Oxford, England: Butterworth-Heinemann; 1995:311–321.

Learning Disorders

Related disorders are developmental coordination disorder and minimal brain dysfunction.

DESCRIPTION

Because of their interrelatedness, the three disorders are considered together. The treatment approaches used by physical therapy appear to overlap so that separation is not practical.

Learning disorder is the inability to acquire, retrain, or generalize specific skills or sets of information because of deficiencies or defects in attention, memory, or reasoning or deficiencies in producing responses associated with desired and skilled behavior.

Developmental coordination disorder is diagnosed when motor coordination is markedly below expected levels, significantly interferes with academic achievement or activities of daily living (ADLs), and is not due to known physical disorders (see David, "Developmental Coordination Disorders," p. 425, in references).

Minimal brain dysfunction (MBD) includes one or more of the following deficits: dyslexia (difficulty reading), attention deficit, learning disability, and motoric clumsiness (see Shepherd, "Minimal Brain Dysfunction," p. 154, in references). Other terms include *minimal cerebral dysfunction (MCD)* and *minor neurological dysfunction (MND)*.

CAUSE

Learning disorders are multidimensional, and affected children are heterogeneous. No single cause has been defined, but neurologic deficits are presumed. Genetic influences may be obvious or subtle. Males outnumber females 5 to 1 suggesting familial and biologic influences.

The cause of developmental coordination disorders is not known.

ASSESSMENT

Areas

- History from parents and teachers
- Motor and movement control: frequency and pattern: synergistic, normal (flexion, extension, rotation), abnormal (dyskinesia, spasticity, ataxia), atypical (immature, repetitive, apraxic)
- Reflex development: primitive, righting, protective, and equilibrium
- Motor development—developmental milestones: gross and fine motor skills
- Muscle function: strength and endurance, tone (hypertonicity or hypotonicity)
- Structure: posture and postural control, joint range of motion (ROM), limb length and configuration (dislocation, clubfoot)
- Sensory and perception: visual, auditory, tactile, proprioceptive and kinesthetic, vestibular, and spatial
- Cognition, language, and emotion
- Health and fitness: cardiopulmonary status, nutritional status, immune system status
- Family: coping skills, strengths and weakness

Instruments/Procedures (See References for Sources)

- Basic Motor Ability Test-Revised
- Bayley Scales of Infant Development
- Brigance Diagnostic Inventory of Early Development
- Bruininks-Oseretsky Test of Motor Proficiency
- Frostig Development Test of Visual Perception
- Gesell Developmental Schedules
- Gubbay Tests of Motor Proficiency (Gubbay Short Screening Test)
- Hughes Basic Gross Motor Assessment
- Kaufman Assessment Battery for Children
- Milani-Comparetti and Gidoni Developmental Examination
- Miller Assessment for Preschoolers
- Movement Assessment of Infants (MAI)
- Peabody Developmental Motor Scales
- Pediatric Evaluation of Disability Inventory (PEDI)
- Southern California Sensory Integration Tests
- Stott–Moyes–Henderson Test of Motor Impairment

PROBLEMS

- Academic problems include dyslexia (difficulty with language and reading), dyscalculia (difficulty with arithmetic), and dysgraphia (difficulty with spelling).

- Cognitive processing deficits include attention deficits (distractibility) and difficulty following verbal directions.
- Sensory perceptual problems (inadequate sensory discrimination) include visual perception deficits such as visuospatial orientation, oculomotor deficits (difficulty dissociating eye and head movements, poor control of saccadic eye movements, poor visual pursuit), poor tactile perception, inadequate body scheme, problems in stereognosis, poor joint position, and poor two-point discrimination.
- Sensory integrative dysfunction problems include vestibular and bilateral integration dysfunction, developmental apraxia, and generalized dysfunction.
- Psychosocial problems include loss of self-esteem and fear of failure.
- Motor control problems include poor body coordination and developmental dyspraxia and apraxia (impairment in performing new skilled or nonhabitual tasks).
- Motor skill development problems include poor gross motor skills, especially balance and postural control (standing balance), and poor fine motor skills, especially hand control (grip strength, especially to control grasp; difficulty maintaining thumb in abducted position; poor pincer grasp; inaccurate reaching; difficulty with rapid repetitive movements; and difficulty catching and throwing a ball).
- There may be delayed or immature postural reactions and control, such as absent or poorly elicited backward protective extension; poor trunk extension; balance adjustments, including an inability to stand on one leg without excessive movement of the body, difficulty walking on a balance beam when control of speed is required, loss of balance when visual inputs are eliminated, and only a small perimeter in which balance can be maintained.
- Joint problems include joint laxity, scapular winging, elbow hyperextension, and hypermobile fingers.
- Acquisition of daily living skills is delayed.

TREATMENT/MANAGEMENT

Controversy continues as to whether treatment should be directed toward the underlying impairments, the existing disability, or functional limitations.

Underlying Impairments

- Increase muscle strength and coordination in hand muscles for handwriting.
- Use verbal cues to remember the sequence for a task such as tying shoe laces.
- Improve visual perception in preparation for scissor cutting, printing or writing, or coloring/drawing.
- Practice attending behavior to various sensory stimuli.
- Provide feedback on motor skill performance.

Existing Disability

- Increase quality of gross and fine motor skills, such as hopping, jumping, ball skills, and threading beads.
- Improve quality of gait.
- Provide opportunity for play activities with peers.
- Increase self-esteem by praising success.
- Increase attention span and concentration by reducing distraction and focusing on task.

Functional Limitations
- Increase self-help skills.
- Improve ability to participate with peers in physical education activities. Work on specific skills required in physical education class.
- Improve written communication skills through facilitation of motor control and/or adapted equipment such as built-up handle for pencil.
- With team members, develop a program to increase language skills. Increased motor activity and skill may facilitate communication.
- With team members, develop a program to increase academic achievement. Increased motor control of the hand in printing, coloring, and cutting is useful.
- With team members, develop a program to increase socialization. Group play may promote social skills.

PRECAUTIONS/CONTRAINDICATIONS
- Use of vestibular stimulation with children who have seizures may be contraindicated. Check with physician before using vestibular stimulation with any child known or suspected of having a seizure disorder.

DESIRED OUTCOME/PROGNOSIS
- The child will be able to perform coordinated movements.
- The child will be able to perform age-appropriate motor skills.
- The child will be able to function in family, school, recreational, and community activities.

Developmental Coordination Disorders

1. Performance in daily activities that require motor coordination is substantially below that expected given the person's chronological age and measured intelligence. This may be manifested by marked delays in achieving motor milestones (eg, walking, crawling, sitting) dropping things, "clumsiness," poor performance in sports, or poor handwriting.
2. The disturbance in criterion 1 significantly interferes with academic achievement or activities of daily living.
3. The disturbance is not due to a general medical condition (eg, cerebral palsy, hemiplegia, or muscle dystrophy) and does not meet criteria for pervasive developmental disorder.
4. If mental retardation is present, the motor difficulties are in excess of those usually associated with it.

Source: Reprinted with permission from *Diagnostic and Statistical Manual of Mental Disorders,* © 1994, American Psychiatric Press, Inc.

REFERENCES

ASSESSMENT
Beery KE. *Development of Visual Motor Integration.* 3rd ed. Cleveland, Ohio: Modern Curriculum Press; 1989.

Blackman JA, Lough LK, Huntley JS. *Assessment of Neuromotor Dysfunction in Infants: A Computer Videodisc Program.* Baltimore, Md: Williams & Wilkins; 1985.

Laugh LK. Measures of motor development. In: Walraich ML, ed. *The Practical Assessment and Management of Children With Disorders of Development and Learning.* Chicago, Ill: Year Book Medical Publishers; 1987:64–84.

Basic Motor Ability Test—Revised
Arnheim DD, Sinclar WA. *The Clumsy Child: A Program of Motor Therapy.* 2nd ed. St Louis, Mo: CV Mosby Co; 1979.

Bayley Scales of Infant Development
Bayley N. *Bayley Scales of Infant Development.* 2nd ed. San Antonio, Tex: Psychological Corporation; 1993.

Brigance Diagnostic Inventory of Early Development
Brigance AH. *Brigance Diagnostic Inventory of Early Development.* North Billerica, Mass: Curriculum Associates; 1978.

Bruininks–Oseretsky Test of Motor Proficiency
Bruininks RH. *Bruininks–Oseretsky Test of Motor Proficiency.* Circle Pines, Minn: American Guidance Service; 1978.

Frostig Development Test of Visual Perception
Frostig M. *Frostig Development Test of Visual Perception.* Los Angeles, Calif: Consulting Psychology Press; 1963.

Gesell Developmental Schedules—Revised
Knobloch H, Stevens F, Malone AF. *Manual of Developmental Diagnosis: The Administration and Interpretation of the Revised Gesell and Amatruda Developmental and Neurologic Examination.* New York, NY: Gesell Developmental Materials; 1987.

Gubbay Tests of Motor Proficiency (Gubbay Short Screening Test)
Gubbay SS. In: Arnheim DD, Sinclair WW, eds. *The Clumsy Child: A Study of Developmental Apraxic and Agnosic Ataxia.* New York, NY: WB Saunders Co; 1975:155–156.

Hughes Basic Gross Motor Assessment
Hughes JE. *Hughes Basic Gross Motor Assessment.* Yonkers, NY: GE Miller; 1979.

Kaufman Assessment Battery for Children
Kaufman AS, Kaufman NL. *Kaufman Assessment Battery for Children.* Circle Pines, Minn: American Guidance Service; 1993.

Milani-Comparetti and Gidoni Developmental Examination
Milani-Comparetti A, Gidoni EA. Routine developmental examination in normal and retarded children. *Developmental Medicine and Child Neurology.* 1967;9:631–638.

Miller Assessment for Preschoolers
Miller LJ. *Miller Assessment for Preschoolers.* San Antonio, Tex: Psychological Corporation; 1982.

Movement Assessment of Infants (MAI)
Chandler LS, Andrews MS, Swanson MW. *Movement Assessment of Infants: A Manual.* Rolling Bay, Wash: Infant Movement Research; 1980.

Peabody Developmental Motor Scales
Folio MR, Fewell RR. *Peabody Developmental Motor Scales and Activity Cards Manual*. Allen, Tex: DLM Teaching Resources; 1983.

Pediatric Evaluation of Disability Inventory (PEDI)
Haley SM, Faas RM. Coster WJ, Gans BM, Webster HM. *Pediatric Evaluation of Disability Inventory (PEDI)*. Boston, Mass: New England Medical Center; 1989.

Southern California Sensory Integration Tests
Ayres AJ. *Southern California Sensory Integration Tests*. Los Angeles, Calif: Western Psychological Services; 1980.

Stott–Moyes–Henderson Test of Motor Impairment
Stott DH, Moyes F, Henderson S. *Stott–Moyes–Henderson Test of Motor Impairment*. Guelph, Ontario, Canada: Brook Education Publishing; 1984.

TREATMENT
David KS. Developmental coordination disorders. In: Campbell SK, ed. *Physical Therapy in Children*. Philadelphia, Pa: WB Saunders Co; 1994:425–458.

Eckersley P. The clumsy child. In: Eckersley PM, ed. *Elements of Paediatric Physiotherapy*. New York, NY: Churchill Livingstone; 1993:286–294..

Orner CE, Turner D, Worrell T. Effect of foot orthoses on the balance skills of a child with a learning disability. *Pediatric Physical Therapy*. 1994;6:1:10–14.

Palisano RJ. Comparison of two methods of service delivery for students with learning disabilities. *Physical and Occupational Therapy in Pediatrics*. 1989;9:79–100.

Rennie J, Flynn M. A prototype seating harness for people with a severe learning disability and physical handicap: an evaluation of effectiveness. *Physiotherapy*. 1992;78:740–744.

Seyhan S, Kayihan H. Differentiation of motor planning ability in normal and learning-disabled children. *Clinical Rehabilitation*. 1993;7:119–123.

Shepherd RB. Minimal brain dysfunction: learning disability, attention deficit disorder, clumsiness. In: Shepherd RB, ed. *Physiotherapy in Paediatrics*. Oxford, England: Butterworth-Heinemann; 1995:154–164.

Unwin J. Current perspectives on minimal cerebral dysfunction. *Australian Journal of Physiotherapy*. 1995;41:109–112.

Woltersdorf MA. Beyond the sensorimotor strip. *Clinical Management*. 1992;12:3:63–69.

Legg-Calve-Perthes Disease

Also called *Perthes disease.*

DESCRIPTION
Legg–Calve–Perthes disease (LCPD) is a self-limiting disease of the hip produced by ischemia and varying degrees of necrosis of the femoral head. Subchondral stress fracture of the necrotic bone initiates the clinical onset of the disease and the process of resorption of dead bone. The medial femoral circumflex artery is the principal vessel within the complex vascular distribution of the femur. Natural progression of the disease is through four stages: an initial phase of vascu-

lar compromise and fragmentation of the femoral head with possible deformation; a second phase of healing or reossification that can last up to 2 years; a third phase of remodeling of the femoral head and acetabulum; and a fourth phase, the definitive period in which the femoral head is revascularized but permanent deformity may exist. LCPD is the most common of the osteochondroses. It occurs primarily in males (4:1 male-to-female ratio) between ages 5 and 10 years and usually affects only one hip. Four grades are recognized. Grade 1 is characterized by no obvious necrosis, and only the anterior portion of the femoral head is involved. Grade 2 has a larger portion of the anterior epiphysis involved, with necrosis and subsequent collapse. Grade 3 is characterized by necrosis and collapse of a major portion of the femoral head but with a normal medial and lateral border. Grade 4 involves necrosis and destruction of all of the femoral head and neck. LCPD is named for Arthur T. Legg in the United States, Georg Perthes in Germany, and Jacques Calve in France.

CAUSE

The cause is unknown. Genetic and environmental factors probably are involved. The pathogenesis appears to be an interruption of the blood supply to the femoral head. A familial link occurs in 20% to 24% of cases. There is a correlation between low birth weight and LCPD.

ASSESSMENT

Areas
- Passive range of motion (ROM) of hip in all planes
- Gait

Instruments/Procedures
- goniometer
- clinical gait analysis
- Trendelenburg sign

PROBLEMS
- There may be limping.
- The child may complain of mild pain, often referred to the groin, anteromedial thigh, and knee, which is aggravated by activity and relieved by rest.
- ROM of the hip, especially hip abduction and internal rotation, may be decreased with hip flexion contracture.
- There may be muscle weakness related to lack of or restricted activity.
- There may be gait deviation due to pain.

TREATMENT/MANAGEMENT

Treatment is controversial because the condition is self-limiting. The question is whether treatment can improve the quality of the outcome: that is, a good fit or "containment" of the femoral head in the acetabulum, normal contouring of the femoral head, correct centering of the femoral head in the acetabulum, full ROM, and no pain.
- Work toward achieving a normal, congruent hip joint with full ROM restored through exercises.
  1. Maintain hip ROM through active motion of the hip while wearing a containment orthosis such as Petrie casts (two long-leg casts with a bar between, holding the hips abducted).

2. Restore full hip motion through traction.
- Prevent secondary degenerative arthritis.
- In milder forms, monitor the involvement of the femoral head and fit in acetabulum.
- Assist in resumption of weight bearing.
  1. Initial aim is to reduce forces acting on the femoral head. Provide a walker for younger children and crutches for older children.
  2. Provide gait training. If an orthosis is present, vary gait training accordingly.
- Instruct child and family in techniques for putting on and taking off the orthotic device if one is required.

PRECAUTIONS/CONTRAINDICATIONS
- The child with a brace may have difficulty maintaining peer and social relations and academic skills. The therapist should assist the family to find methods to minimize the potential loss.

DESIRED OUTCOME/PROGNOSIS
- The child will have no pain while performing normal activities appropriate for age.
- The child will be able to move hip in all planes of movement needed to perform normal activities.
- The child will be able to participate in the family, school, recreational activities, and community.

Grade Levels of LCPD

Grade I	No clear sign of necrosis
	Involvement of anterior portion of femoral head only
	No evidence of sequestrum, subchondral fracture line, metaphyseal abnormalities
Grade II	Greater portion of the anterior epiphysis involved
	Necrosis and subsequent collapse of the femoral head are beginning to occur
	Sequestrum formation, anterolateral metaphyseal lesions, subchondral fracture line
	Clear junction between the involved and uninvolved areas
Grade III	Necrosis and collapse of major portion of femoral head have occurred
	Medial and lateral border of femoral head is normal
	Large sequestrum involving three quarters of the femoral head
	Junction between the involved and uninvolved portions is sclerotic
	Metaphyseal lesions are diffuse
Grade IV	Necrosis and destruction of entire femoral head and neck
	Subluxation places additional stress and deformity on the femoral head

Source: Reprinted with permission from SR Tippet, Referred Knee Pain in a Young Athlete: A Case Study, *Journal of Orthopaedic Sports Physical Therapy*, Vol. 9, No. 2, pp. 117–120, © 1994, JB Lippincott.

REFERENCES

Brenneman SK, Stanger M, Bertoti DB. Aged-related considerations: pediatrics–osteochondroses. In: Meyers RS, ed. *Saunders Manual of Physical Therapy*. Philadelphia, Pa: WB Saunders Co; 1995:1269.

Leach J. Orthopaedic conditions: Perthes disease. In: Campbell SK, ed. *Physical Therapy for Children.* Philadelphia, Pa: WB Saunders Co; 1994:369–370.

Shepherd RB. Disorders of bones, joints, muscles and skin. In: Shepherd RB, ed. *Physiotherapy in Paediatrics.* 3rd ed. Oxford, England: Butterworth-Heinemann; 1995:276–277.

Tecklin JS. Orthopedic disorders in children and their physical therapy management: Legg–Calve–Perthes disease. In: Tecklin JS, ed. *Pediatric Physical Therapy.* Philadelphia, Pa: JB Lippincott Co; 1994:305–311.

Tippett SR. Referred knee pain in a young athlete: a case study. *Journal of Orthopaedic Sports Physical Therapy.* 1994;19:117–120.

Limb Deficiencies and Amputations

Also termed *congenital amputations* or *traumatic amputations.*

DESCRIPTION

Congenital limb deficiencies or amputations are transverse or longitudinal deficiencies due to primary intrauterine growth inhibition or secondary intrauterine destruction of normal embryonic tissues. In transverse deficiencies, all parts of limb beyond or below a certain level are absent: thus the limb resembles a residuum or stump. In longitudinal deficiencies, specific development problems occur such as complete or partial absence of a bone (radius, fibula, or other bone). Traumatic and/or surgical amputation is usually the result of injury, accident, or gangrene related to an injury or accident. More boys than girls (about 60:40) are affected, and more congenital limb reductions occur on the left side.

CAUSE

Causes of congenital limb deficiencies are often unclear, but teratogenic agents (eg, thalidomide) and amniotic bands are two known causes. Congenital limb deficiencies probably occur between the fourth and eighth gestational week when the limb buds are forming. Congenital limb deficiencies are more likely to be bilateral, trimembral, or quadrimembral than other causes and are more likely to involve upper extremities. The most common cause of traumatic injury is traffic accidents. Other causes are tumors and various diseases. Causes other than congenital are more likely to involve lower extremities.

ASSESSMENT

Areas
- Range of motion (ROM)
- Muscle strength
- Functional skills (with and without prosthetic devices)
- Temperament
- Developmental profile
- Prosthetic device(s)

Instruments/Procedures
- goniometry
- dynamometry

- functional assessment
- developmental assessment
- prosthetic checkout

PROBLEMS
- There may be function limitations:
  1. *Lower*—balance, mobility, gait, ambulation
  2. *Upper*—balance, coordination, hands together, grasp and release, manipulation, dexterity
- There may be developmental delays in milestones.
- The child may experience problems around being and looking different.
- Bony overgrowth can cause pain and skin penetration.
- There may be a lack of or reduced effectiveness of protective reactions in falling.
- Prosthetic device(s) may be of poor quality or ill-fitting.
- There may be phantom limb sensation and pain.

TREATMENT/MANAGEMENT
Technology to enhance the ability of the persons with limb deficiencies is rapidly expanding. Children should be referred to pediatric amputation centers for specialized treatment and management as early as possible but at least by 6 months of age. Quarterly revisits are suggested for young children and semiannual revisits for adolescents. The statements below should be considered as guidelines to treatment and management for therapists who see limb-deficient children when they are not at a pediatric amputation center. If limb lengthening is recommended, see section on "Limb-Length Discrepancy."

General
- Maintain or increase ROM in all remaining joints.
- Facilitate ability to change positions to explore the environment.
- Encourage play behavior and activities in the environment, using whatever sensorimotor abilities (hand, stump or residuum, mouth, body, and feet) are available.
- Promote development of normal skills and abilities, using whatever functions the child has, including compensatory and substitute skills.
- Work on developing balance in sitting and then in standing. A crash helmet is useful protection until balance skills are perfected.
- When balance is achieved, mobility should be encouraged, including stairs, curbs, and steps.
- Recommend and encourage participation in sports and recreational activities, making whatever adaptations are needed.
- Children with trimembral or quadrimembral amputation will need assistive devices whether or not prostheses are used.
- Watch for signs of distal end bone overgrowth in residuums that contain vestigial articulations and epiphyseal growth plates. Symptoms include localized pain and a palpable and irregular stiff spike below the skin at the residuum end. Firm prosthetic contact may reduce bone overgrowth, but this concept is still controversial.

Education and Instruction of Parents
- Parents should be encouraged to attend and participate in therapy sessions, with emphasis on how and when to assist the child in carrying out an activity or a task.

- Parents should be taught how to put on, take off, care for, and maintain the prosthesis. This knowledge should be transferred to the child as he or she is able to understand and follow through.
- Parents and child should be taught a home program of residuum care and exercises to maintain ROM and muscle strength.
- Help parents cope with grief, disappointment, guilt, shame, fear, anxiety, and rejection. Focus on ability, not disability.

Lower Extremity
- Provide protection to bony areas involved in ambulation (feet, buttocks, knees) with extra padding or "spats."
- If both lower extremities are involved, using the wall to lean against while negotiating steps may be helpful.

Upper Extremity
- For children with missing upper extremities, standing frames or baby walkers may be needed to provide enough practice in balance to overcome lack of arm protection in falling.
- Children with congenital amputation or amputations that occurred very early in life often learn to feed and care for themselves by developing skills in prehension and manipulation with their feet or "prehensile toes."

PRECAUTIONS/CONTRAINDICATIONS
- Teeth may be used to substitute for holding and compensate for lack of grip. These extra activities are hard on teeth, so good, frequent dental care is extra important.
- Limb deficiencies reduce the sweating surfaces of the body, so heat can be a serious problem. Lightweight, loose-fitting clothing is important in summer or heated areas. Prevent dehydration with plenty of fluids.

DESIRED OUTCOME/PROGNOSIS
- The child will be independent in mobility.
- The child will have achieved maximum degree of independence in daily living activities.
- The child will be able to perform functional skills in the home, school, and community.

Definitions

Acheiria—absence of a hand
Amelia—complete absence of a limb
Apodia—absence of a foot
Ectrodactyly—partial or complete absence of a digit
Ectromelia—complete absence of a limb
Hemimelia—absence of some portion of a limb
Intercalary limb deficit—only the middle part of the limb is affected
Meromelia—absence of some portion of a limb
Phocomelia—the top portion of the limb is absent, and the terminal part of the limb is attached higher than would be expected
Polydactyly—extra digits are present on the hand or foot

Proximal focal femoral deficiency (PFFD)—partial form of phocomelia in which the shaft of the femur is always shorter than normal
Syndactyly—digits are fused together
Terminal limb deficit—there are no parts below the affected portion of the limb

Source: Reprinted with permission from TM Long and HL Cintas, *Handbook of Pediatric Physical Therapy*, p. 104, © 1995, Williams & Wilkins.

Classification of Upper Extremity Transverse Deficiencies

Shoulder total
Upper arm total
Upper arm middle third
Forearm total
Forearm upper third
Carpal total
Carpal partial
Phalangeal total
Phalangeal partial

Source: From HJ Day: The ISO/ISPO classification of congenital limb deficiency. In American Academy of Orthopedic Surgeons: Atlas of Limb Prosthetics: Surgical, Prosthetic, and Rehabilitation Principles, 2nd ed, 1992, St. Louis, Mosby-year Book, Inc.

REFERENCES

Brenneman SK, Stanger M, Bertoti DB. Aged-related considerations: pediatric. In: Myers RS, ed. *Saunder's Manual for Physical Therapy Practice*. Philadelphia, Pa: WB Saunders Co; 1995:1261–1264.

Cintas HL. Pediatric disorders: amputations and limb deficiencies specific to children. In: Long TM, Cintas HL, eds. *Handbook of Pediatric Physical Therapy*. Baltimore, Md: Williams & Wilkins; 1995:104–106.

Fletcher I, Cartwright R, Jones M, Limb deficiency. In: McCarthy GT, ed. *Physical Disability in Childhood: An Interdisciplinary Approach to Management*. New York, NY: Churchill Livingstone; 1992:305–329.

Krebs DE, Edelstein JE, Thornby MA. Prosthetic management of children with limb deficiencies. *Physical Therapy*. 1991;71:920–934.

Shepherd RB. Congenital limb deficiencies. In: Shepherd RB, ed. *Physiotherapy in Paediatrics*. 3rd ed. Oxford, England: Butterworth-Heinemann. 1995:261–271.

Stanger, M. Limb deficiencies and amputations. In: Campbell SK, ed. *Physical Therapy in Children*. Philadelphia, Pa: WB Saunders Co. 1994:325–351.

Limb-Length Discrepancy

DESCRIPTION

A limb-length discrepancy is generally a leg-length inequality of 2.5 cm (about 1 inch) or greater (see "Orthopaedic Conditions," Leach, p. 375, in references). The Ilizarov method of limb lengthening originated in 1943 in Russia by Gavriil Abramovich Ilizarov. Discrepancies of 2 cm or less are not considered clinically significant and can be easily corrected without surgery.

CAUSE
Congenital or developmental leg-length discrepancy is often secondary to hip dislocation; hemimelia, in which one segment is shorter; or hemihypertrophy, in which one side of the body is larger. Acquired leg-length discrepancy is usually secondary to paralysis; due to vascular differences in each leg; caused by neoplasms, especially Wilm's tumor; or due to growth plate damage as a result of trauma, infection, or fracture.

ASSESSMENT

Areas
- True versus apparent leg-length discrepancy
- Muscle strength
- Range of motion (ROM)
- Sensation
- Girth measurements bilaterally
- Joint stability
- Deformities
- Posture and gait
- Functional mobility

Instruments/Procedures

Mobility
- goniometry

Muscle Strength
- manual muscle testing

True Versus Apparent Leg-Length Discrepancy
- True leg-length discrepancy is often evident upon visual comparison of femoral lengths when patient is in supine position with hips and knees in 90 degrees flexion and feet flat on the surface (Galeazzi sign). One knee will be higher than the other. Also, measurement from anterior superior iliac spine to medial malleolus is different. In standing, a block under one foot is necessary to make the pelvis level on both sides.
- Apparent leg-length discrepancy is associated with scoliosis and pelvic obliquity, hip abduction or flexion contracture, or knee or ankle contracture. The measure from the xiphoid process to the medial malleolus is different on each side.

PROBLEMS

Preoperative Period
- There may be gait dysfunction (awkward gait and limping).
- There may be postural alignment deformities.
- There may be back pain.
- Walking may require increased energy expenditure.
- There may be scoliosis.
- There may be potential for premature arthrosis.

During Lengthening Procedure
- Muscles may have contractures, especially if they cross two joints, as the hamstrings do.
- There may be decreased ROM.
- Joint subluxation may be present, especially in preexisting unstable joints such as the knee.
- There may be axial or angular deviation, which is usually corrected with adjustment to the hardware.
- Neurological or vascular insult may cause pain or signs of vascular compromise. It is usually corrected by decreasing the daily amount of distraction (length) of the apparatus.
- Premature consolidation may require additional surgical intervention.
- Delayed consolidation may increase the time the fixator must be worn.
- Refracture also may increase the time the fixator must be worn.
- Pin-site infection which must be treated to avoid osteomyelitis.
- There may be discomfort and pain.
- There may be a loss of independence and change in lifestyle.
- There may be psychological adjustment difficulties such as frustration, fear, and anger.

TREATMENT/MANAGEMENT
- In *conservative management*, work with the orthopedist regarding
  1. shoe lift
     a. Difference of 1 to 2 cm: lift can be placed inside the shoe.
     b. Difference of 2 to 4 cm: lift must be placed outside the shoe.
     c. Difference of 5 cm or more: lift not recommended because it is unstable and cosmetically unappealing.
  2. orthotic modification
  3. exercises to improve limited joint mobility or postural alignment
- In surgical management, work with the orthopedist to
  1. regain normal postural alignment
  2. regain muscle strength
- Before lengthening:
  1. Prevent joint and soft tissue contractures.
  2. Decrease pain and edema.
  3. Increase ROM of affected limb.
  4. Increase muscle strength.
  5. Prevent or minimize gait deviations.
  6. Restore functional mobility and independence.
  7. Use pain management.
- Instruct patient in a home exercise program including isometric, active, and passive exercises for muscles that cross the joint above and below the segment to be lengthened.
- Instruct patient in postoperative positioning and splinting.
- Instruct patient in stretching and strengthening exercises prior to surgery, including gluteal sets, straight-leg raising, hip abduction in side-lying position, hip extension and knee flexion in prone position, short-arc quadriceps femoris muscle sets, knee flexion and extension in a sitting position, ankle dorsiflexion and plantar flexion, and passive heel cord stretching using a towel or TheraBand in a long-sitting position.

PRECAUTIONS/CONTRAINDICATIONS
- Each pin site must be cleaned individually, and care must be followed for about 7 days to avoid infection.

- Generally patient must not bathe for 8 days and must not soak the fixator as it may cause oxidation.

DESIRED OUTCOME/PROGNOSIS
- Limb length will be equal or within 1 inch of longer limb.
- Angular deformity will have been corrected.
- The child will be able to walk without noticeable limp if lower extremity was lengthened.
- The child's posture will be symmetrical.
- The child's gait will be smooth and coordinated.

REFERENCES

TREATMENT

Brenneman SK, Stanger M, Bertoti DB. Age-related considerations: pediatric leg-length discrepancy. In: Myers RS, ed. *Saunders Manual of Physical Therapy Practice*. Philadelphia, Pa: WB Saunders Co; 1995:1270–1271.

Cintas HL. Pediatric disorders: leg length discrepancy. In: Long TM, Cintas HL, eds. *Handbook of Pediatric Physical Therapy*. Baltimore, Md: Williams & Wilkins; 1995:132–133.

Leach J. Orthopaedic conditions: leg length inequality. In: Campbell SK, ed. *Physical Therapy for Children*. Philadelphia, Pa: WB Saunders Co; 1994:375–380.

Simard S, Marchant M, Mencio G. The Ilizarov procedure: limb lengthening and its implications. *Physical Therapy*. 1992;72:35–44.

Tecklin JS. Orthopedic disorders in children and their physical therapy management: limb length discrepancy. In: Tecklin JS, ed. *Pediatric Physical Therapy*. 2nd ed. Philadelphia, Pa: J.B. Lippincott Co; 1994:314–320.

Mental Retardation

Related terms are *mentally retarded, mental deficiency,* and *intellectually disabled.*

DESCRIPTION

Mental retardation (MR), according to the *Merck Manual,* is subaverage intellectual ability present from birth or early infancy, manifested by abnormal development and associated with difficulties in learning and social adaptation. According to the American Association on Mental Retardation (AAMR), it is significantly subaverage intellectual functioning existing concurrently with deficits in adaptive behavior and manifested during the developmental period. Mental retardation is classified as mild (Wechsler Quotient Range 55–69), moderate (40–54), severe (25–39), and profound (0–24). Generally persons with severe and profound retardation are most likely to need therapy.

CAUSE

Intelligence is determined by multiple interactive processes. In 80% of cases, the cause of MR is unknown, but over 200 conditions are known to cause retardation. Factors causing MR may occur in the prenatal, perinatal, and postnatal periods. Prenatal factors include genetic metabolic disorders, genetic neurologic disorders, congenital infections, teratogens (drugs and other chemical agents), radiation, and chromosomal abnormalities. Perinatal complications are related to prematurity; bleeding in the central nervous system, especially the brain; periventricular leukomalacia; breech or high-forceps delivery; multiple births; placenta previa; preeclampsia; and asphyxia neonatorum. Postnatal factors include viral and bacterial encephalitides, meningitides, poisoning with lead or mercury, and accidents that result in severe head injuries or asphyxia. Prenatal nutrition in the mother may also contribute if the malnutrition affects brain development.

ASSESSMENT

Areas
- History: background information from family, teachers, and other professionals who have interacted with the child
- Sensory processing
  1. Visual tracking using flashlight or toy 7–15 inches from eyes in horizontal, vertical, and diagonal patterns; watch eyes as they cross the midline. Note nystagmus or cortical blindness.
  2. Auditory orientation to and moving toward stimuli such as a bell
  3. Tactile response to stimuli
  4. Vestibular response to postrotary nystagmus
  5. Self-stimulation
  6. Perception
- Motor control: reflex maturation, gross and fine motor skills, developmental milestones, muscle tone, muscle strength, range of motion (ROM), positioning
- Adaptive equipment
- Behavior
- Functional skills
- Processes underlying the observed skills and behaviors of motor development and movement skills
- Play

Instruments/Procedures (See References for Sources)
- Adaptive Behavior Curriculum
- AAMD Adaptive Behavior Scales
- Balthazar Scales of Adaptive Behavior
- Bayley Scales of Infant Development
- Behavior Rating Inventory for the Retarded
- Camelot Behavioral Checklist
- Early Intervention Development Profile
- Hawaii Early Learning Profile
- Peabody Developmental Motor Scales
- Prescriptive Behavioral Checklist for the Severely and Profoundly Retarded
- Southern California Postrotary Nystagmus Test
- TMR Performance Profile for the Severely and Moderately Retarded
- Vineland Adaptive Behavior Scale

- Vulpe Assessment Battery

Muscle Strength
- Dynamometry and manual muscle testing are difficult to do on the severely and profoundly retarded. Usually muscle strength must be estimated from observation.

Range of Motion
- goniometry

PROBLEMS

Motor Control
- Reflexes may be immature and unintegrated.
- Muscles may be weak, especially in the hip extensors and abdominals, and hip flexors or hamstrings may be tight.
- Joint limitation problems include contractures, especially flexor contractures of the knee; subluxation; dislocation of the patellae; ligamentous and joint laxity; and genu valgum of the knee.
- Developmental milestones may be delayed.
- There may be muscle hypotonia.
- Spinal problems may include scoliosis; kyphosis due to tight hamstrings or increased lumbar lordosis, and lordosis due to weak abdominals.

Sensory and Perceptual
- There may be difficulty in monitoring the intensity of sensory input.
- Perceptiveness to incoming stimuli may be reduced.
- There may be difficulty in visual tracking or inability to track, especially across the midline.
- There may be difficulty orienting and/or moving toward sound.
- There may be aversion to tactile stimulation—tactile defensiveness or hypersensitivity.
- There may be hyper- or hyporesponsiveness to postrotary nystagmus.

Cognition
- Child may have a short attention span.
- Child may have low motivation.
- Child may have little curiosity.
- Child may have a limited will to achieve.
- Child may be slow to learn new tasks.

Seizures
- All types of seizures may be seen.
- Side effects of medication for seizures may increase other problems, such as hypotonia.

Oral-Motor Functioning
   Problems include drooling, mouth closure, and separation of jaw motions from lips.

Communication Skills
- There may be problems with both receptive and expressive language.

Behavior and Personality
• May be difficult to motivate.
• May display self stimulatory or self injurious behavior.

TREATMENT/MANAGEMENT

Treatment should focus on the development and reinforcement of appropriate adaptive behaviors that are interesting, fun, and pleasurable. All goals must be coordinated and carried out by all members of the treatment team, including the child, parents, teachers, aides, and other therapists (transdisciplinary team approach). Because children with severe and profound mental retardation must repeat a task many times to learn it, tasks practiced only during physical therapy are unlikely to be successful. Likewise, the physical therapist must know what communication techniques and behavior modification approaches are being used by other team members in order to complement and build upon existing learned behavior.

Neurophysiologic and developmental models, including neurodevelopmental therapy (Bobath), sensorimotor therapy (Rood), sensory integrative therapy (Ayres), and neuromuscular reflex therapy (Doman–Delacato), have been used most often in treating children with mental retardation. The motor control model (Bernstein) presents a significant challenge to therapists to convey a cognitive-motor task to a child who does not function well at the cognitive level.
• Develop sensory integration skills.
  1. Visual skills
     a. Improve midline, symmetrical gaze.
     b. Increase visual exploratory behavior.
  2. Auditory skills
     a. Use vestibular stimulation to enhance auditory integration and vocalization.
  3. Tactile skills
     a. Use heavy touch and pressure or weight bearing to decrease tactile hypersensitivity and increase proximal joint stability.
  4. Vestibular and proprioceptive-kinesthetic input
     a. Improve postural mechanisms.
  5. Body image, body scheme, and sensory awareness
     a. Increase self-awareness.
     b. Increase knowledge of body parts.
• Develop oral-motor control and skills.
  1. Best feeding position is a 45-degree tilt while child is seated with hips and knees at 90 degrees, head balanced in a neutral position between flexion and extension. Deformities and dysphagia will necessitate modifications from the ideal.
  2. Recommend in cooperation with team a consistent feeding position, best utensils to use, and type, texture, and temperature of food.
• Develop postural balance and control.
  1. Have child practice walking between rows of chairs on bleachers or on a balance beam.
  2. Facilitate postural adjustment reactions.
• Develop cognitive and affective skills.
  1. Use repetition and consistency to reinforce learning.
  2. Use games to improve attention and focus on another goal.
  3. Instruct child in imitative learning.
• Promote ambulation and normal gait patterns.
  1. Decrease "crouched posture" in walking.
  2. Decrease toe walking.

3. Decrease "high guard" of the arms.
4. Facilitate reciprocal, coordinated movements of arms and legs.
- Organize presentation of activities to maximize learning.
  1. Keep in treatment area only those items needed for treatment activities.
  2. Present tasks clearly and simply. Break activities down into easy-to-understand steps.
  3. Start with simple tasks, then progress to more complex.
  4. Explain what is expected of the child.
  5. Give immediate feedback and positive reinforcement.
  6. Repeat instructions as often as needed until the child understands the expected behavior and performance.
  7. Check accuracy of performance often.
  8. Provide opportunities to demonstrate and practice new skills independently.
- Facilitate communication skills.
  1. Encourage imitation.
  2. Use nonspeech communication, including mime, manual sign language, Blissymbolics, or communication boards.
- Provide assistive technology.
  1. Use orthotic devices to correct postural deformities and foot orthoses specifically to permit weight bearing.
  2. Assist with determining mobility aids such as tricycles, Irish Mails, scooter boards, walkers, or wheelchairs.
  3. Provide adaptive seating systems as needed.
  4. Provide equipment for adaptive supported weight bearing, such as a standing frame or standing box.
  5. Provide adaptive systems for lying down, such as bolsters, wedges, or side-lyers.
- Use behavior modification techniques to reinforce motivation.
- Reduce self-injurious behavior and self-stimulation behavior.
  1. Use sensory stimulation, including visual, auditory, tactile, vestibular, proprioceptive, and vibratory, depending on which the child responds to best.
  2. Decrease the overall stimulation (increase the homeostasis) in the environment and increase a focused area of stimulation (toys in visual field and in easy reach that are attached to prevent throwing).
- Prevent deformity and respiratory problems.
  1. Stress best handling techniques.
  2. Identify best positioning techniques and equipment needed to achieve the positions.
  3. Establish an exercise program.
  4. Evaluate and recommend assistive technology.
- Educate parents and child in a home program.
- Suggest community and national resources.
  1. Assist in providing parents with information about public laws and the rights of persons with disabilities, including accessibility to public places and buildings.
  2. Provide information about group homes, respite care, home care with day school, and national groups such as the Association for the Severely Handicapped and Association for Retarded Citizens.

PRECAUTIONS AND CONTRAINDICATIONS
- Avoid light touch or stimuli that tickle or irritate.
- Do not work in distracting environments.

- Avoid hyperextension of neck (called "bird-feeding position") during feeding because the glottis is not able to close effectively over the trachea, and thus there is an open channel for aspiration of food into the lungs.

DESIRED OUTCOME/PROGNOSIS
- The child will be able to perform adaptive behaviors within level of functional ability.
- The child will have achieved motor skills within level of ability.
- The child will have achieved developmental milestones within level of ability.

REFERENCES

ASSESSMENT

Adaptive Behavior Curriculum
Popovich D, Laham SL, eds. *Adaptive Behavior Curriculum: Prescriptive Behavior Analysis for Moderately, Severely and Profoundly Handicapped Students*. Baltimore, Md: Paul H Brooks; 1982.

AAMD Adaptive Behavior Scales
Nihira K, Foster R, Shellhass M, Leland H. *AAMD Adaptive Behavior Scales*. rev. ed. Washington, DC: American Association on Mental Deficiency; 1974.

Balthazar Scales of Adaptive Behavior
Balthazar EE. *Balthazar Scales of Adaptive Behavior*. Champaign, Ill: Research Press; 1976.

Bayley Scales of Infant Development
Bayley N. *Bayley Scales of Infant Development*. New York, NY: Psychological Corporation; 1969.
Bayley N. *Bayley Scales of Infant Development*. 2nd ed. San Antonio, Tex: Psychological Corporation; 1993.

Behavior Rating Inventory for the Retarded
Sparrow SS, Cichetti CV. *Behavior Rating Inventory for the Retarded*. New Haven, Conn: Child Study Center; 1978.

Camelot Behavioral Checklist
Foster RW. *Camelot Behavioral Checklist*. Lawrence, Kan: Camelot Behavioral Systems; 1974.

Early Intervention Developmental Profile
Rogers SJ, Donovan CM, D'Eugenia DB, et al. *Developmental Programming for Infants and Young Children: Early Intervention Developmental Profile*. Vol 2. Ann Arbor, Mich: University of Michigan Press; 1981.

Hawaii Early Learning Profile (HELP)
Furuno S, O'Reilly KA, Hosaka CM, Inatsuka TT, Aeisloft-Falbey B, Allman T. *Hawaii Early Learning Profile*. Palo Alto, Calif: VORT Corporation; 1979.

Peabody Developmental Motor Scales
Folio MR, Fewell RR. *Peabody Developmental Motor Scales and Activity Cards*. Allen, Tex: DLM Teaching Resources; 1983.

Prescriptive Behavioral Checklist for the Severely and Profoundly Retarded
Popovich D. *Prescriptive Behavioral Checklist for the Severely and Profoundly Retarded.* Baltimore, Md: University Park Press; 1977.

Southern California Postrotary Nystagmus Test
Ayres AJ. *Southern California Postrotary Nystagmus Test.* Los Angeles, Calif: Western Psychological Services; 1975.

TMR Performance Profile for the Severely and Moderately Retarded
DiNola AJ, Kaminsky B, Sternfeld AE. *TMR Performance Profile for the Severely and Moderately Retarded.* Ridgefield, NJ: Educational Performance Associates.

Vineland Adaptive Behavior Scales
Sparrow SS, Balla DA, Chichetti CV. *Vineland Adaptive Behavior Scales.* Circle Pines, Minn: American Guidance Services; 1984.

Vulpe Assessment Battery
Vulpe S. *Vulpe Assessment Battery.* Toronto, Ontario, Canada: National Institute on Mental Retardation; 1982.

TREATMENT
Bell E, Lamond JE. Profound and multiple disability. In: Eckersley PM, ed. *Elements in Paediatric Physiotherapy.* New York, NY: Churchill Livingstone; 1993:167–186.

Bertoti DB. Physical therapy for the child with mental retardation. In: Tecklin JS, ed. *Pediatric Physical Therapy.* Philadelphia, Pa: JB Lippincott Co; 1994:363–389.

Cameron R. Helping parents to help children. *Physiotherapy.* 1987;93;172–175.

Hearn PM. The role of the physiotherapist in the Portage home teaching schema. *Physiotherapy.* 1987;73;169–171.

McEwen I. Mental retardation. In: Campbell SK, ed. *Physical Therapy in Children.* Philadelphia, Pa: WB Saunders Co; 1994:459–488.

Rennie J. Evolution of the motor pattern from birth to puberty in genetic microcephaly. *Physiotherapy.* 1989;75;358–353.

Woods M. Impressions of home-based Portage services. *Physiotherapy.* 1987;73;175–176.

Resources for Planning Therapy Programs
Falvey MA. *Community-Based Curriculum Strategies for Students with Severe Handicaps.* Baltimore, Md: Paul H Brooks; 1985.

Fraser BA, Hensinger RN. *Managing Physical Handicaps: A Practical Guide for Parents, Care Providers and Educators.* Baltimore, Md: Paul H Brooks; 1983.

Galka G, Fraser B. *Gross Motor Management of Severely Impaired Students. Vol 2. Curriculum Model.* Baltimore, Md: University Park Press; 1980.

Jaeger L. *Home Program Instruction Sheets for Infants and Young Children.* Tucson, Ariz: Therapy Skill Builders; 1987.

Jegard S, Anderson L, Glazer C, Zaleski WA. *A Comprehensive Program for Multihandicapped Children.* Saskatchewan, Canada: Alvin Buckwold Centre; 1980.

Kissinger EM. A Sequential Curriculum for the Severely and Profoundly Mentally Retarded/Multihandicapped. Springfield, Ill: Charles C Thomas; 1981.

Popovich D, Laham SL. eds. *The Adaptive Behavior Curriculum.* Vol. 2. Baltimore, Md: Paul H Brooks; 1982.

Shanely E, ed. *Mental Handicaps: A Handbook of Care.* New York, NY: Churchill Livingstone; 1986.

Muscular Dystrophy

Also known as *Duchenne muscular dystrophy, pseudohypertrophic muscular dystrophy,* and *Becker muscular dystrophy.*

DESCRIPTIONS

Duchenne muscular dystrophy (DMD) is an X-linked recessive disorder typically presenting in boys aged 3 to 7 years as proximal muscle weakness causing waddling gait, toe walking, lordosis, frequent falls, and difficulty in standing up and climbing stairs. The pelvic girdle is affected first, then the shoulder girdle. Progression is steady, and most patients are confined to a wheelchair by age 10 to 12. Cardiac involvement is common. A firm pseudohypertrophy of the calves is due to fatty and fibrous infiltration of the muscle. The average IQ is 1 standard deviation below the mean. Flexion contractures and scoliosis ultimately occur, and most patients die by age 20 years. Respiratory failure alone or secondary to infection is the most common cause of death.

Becker muscular dystrophy (BMD) is a clinical variant that is also an X-linked disorder with the same genomic mutation at Xp21, but the BMD patients have dystrophin of abnormal molecular weight. Clinically, BMD is less severe. Very few patients are in wheelchairs by age 16 years, and more than 90% are alive at age 20 years.

CAUSE

Duchenne muscular dystrophy is caused by a mutation at the Xp21 locus that results in the absence of the gene product dystrophin. The protein is normally localized to the sarcolemma of muscle cells.

ASSESSMENT

Areas
- Serial muscle strength assessment to monitor progression of disease, influence of strength on functional ability, and effectiveness of medical treatment and physical therapy
- Serial goniometric assessment to prevent contractures
- Cardiac functioning
- Respiratory functioning, especially weak muscles
- Cognitive skills
- Perceptual and perceptual-motor skills
- Developmental milestones
- Functional status

Instruments/Procedures (See References for Sources)
- manual muscle testing
- goniometry
- scoliometer
- functional testing
- Gower's maneuver: child gets up from the floor by using arms to crawl up own legs

PROBLEMS
- There may be muscle weakness.

1. Muscles may atrophy.
2. There may be asymmetrical muscle development and muscle tone imbalance.
3. There is primary involvement of proximal musculature to distal beginning with weakness of the pelvic and shoulder girdle and then trunk and extremity muscles. The lower extremity muscles become progressively more weak. Hypertrophy of the calf muscle usually occurs by age 5.
4. Cranial nerves (except the sternocleidomastoid) are not involved.
5. Progressive loss of the anterior neck musculature affects functional activities, including head control and upper extremity activities.
6. There is arching of the back (lordosis) and protrusion of abdomen as posterior hip muscles weaken.
7. As the quadriceps weaken, the child uses hyperextension of the knees.
8. Severe equinovarus deformities occur when ambulation and weight bearing stop.
- There may be feeding difficulties.
- There may be dysphagia.
- Contractures may be present, especially of the hip flexors, iliotibial band, knee flexors, and ankle plantar flexors.
- Spinal deformities of scoliosis and lordosis may develop.
- There may be cardiac dysfunction.
- There is low normal intelligence (75 to 85), nonprogressive.
- There is mild delay in achieving milestones, then loss of skills.
- There may be low frustration tolerance.

TREATMENT/MANAGEMENT
There is no specific medical management. Usually the child is managed by a team of specialists. Therapy needs to be based on the problems of the individual child.
- Prevent deformity and contractures.
  1. Anticipate progression pattern and rate of the disorder.
  2. Apply passive and active range of motion (ROM) to maintain flexibility of joints.
  3. Continue stretching exercises to prevent flexion contractures of the hips and knees and equinovarus deformities of the feet.
  4. Continue strengthening exercises to maintain muscle strength as long as possible.
  5. Teach value of positioning.
  6. Provide appropriate splints, orthotics, and adaptive equipment.
  7. Recommend ordering special cushions for wheelchair to prevent skin breakdown.
- Maintain ambulation.
  1. Maintain flexibility and strength of both lower and upper extremities.
  2. Assist in recommending knee-ankle-foot orthoses when needed.
  3. Assist in recommending a wheelchair when needed.
- Encourage use of good positioning.
  1. Good positioning can prevent or delay the onset of scoliosis. The child's wheelchair may need to be equipped with lateral trunk supports, head rests, and trays to obtain optimal alignment.
  2. Assist in developing a seating system in the wheelchair to continue best posture consistent with respiration and functional use of upper extremities.
  3. Assist in designing and maintaining a back brace, if needed, to slow scoliosis.
  4. The wheelchair should have ability to recline for rest periods.

- Teach energy conservation techniques to child and parents.
  1. A reclining wheelchair reduces the need to transfer the child from chair to bed during the day.
  2. A mechanical lift can be used to reduce the need to lift the child manually as he or she grows older and gains weight.
  3. Work with the family to explore ways of modifying the home to facilitate care.
- Maintain functional abilities.
  1. Use orthotics and assistive devices as needed to facilitate self-care activities.
  2. Assist in recommending assistive technology to facilitate school work.
- Make recommendations for an exercise and recreation program.
  1. Establish a home exercise program to maintain flexibility, strength, and function.
  2. Suggest recreational activities to decrease boredom, maintain positive attitude, and expend energy to work off calories and keep weight down.
- Assist the child and family in dealing with learning, perceptual, and psychosocial issues.
  1. Keep instruction simple for learning compensatory strategies.
  2. Reduce the problem of low frustration tolerance by concentrating on the positive skills and not focusing on the loss of skills.
  3. Consultation with an occupational therapist is useful in dealing with these issues.
- Provide instruction to the family on management techniques.
  1. Encourage the family to watch caloric intake, which is likely to be less than normal, to reduce obesity.
  2. Instruct parents in ROM and positioning techniques.
- Assist the family to adapt home and school.
  1. Identify and recommend methods to eliminate architectural barriers.
  2. Recommend installation of mechanical lifts.
  3. Suggest other environmental adjustments that can facilitate care.

PRECAUTIONS/CONTRAINDICATIONS
- Make sure that the family understands the value of stretching exercises in relation to facilitating continuing care. For example, equinovarus deformities of the feet make putting on shoes very difficult.

DESIRED OUTCOME/PROGNOSIS
- The child will be able to maintain independent ambulation with or without assistive devices for as long as possible.
- The child will be able to maintain functional abilities with or without assistive devices and energy conservation techniques for as long as possible.
- The child will not have deformities that limit functional ROM.
- The family will demonstrate knowledge of the techniques needed to maintain the child in the family, school, and community.

Stages in Muscular Dystrophy

1. *Ambulation*—Has mild waddling gait and lordosis but walks without assistance.
   Running—Can run with effort.
   Stairs or curbs—Can climb up and down without assistance.

Chair—Has no difficulty sitting down or getting up.

Floor—Can rise from floor.

Upper extremities—Starting with arms at sides, can abduct the arms in a full circle until they touch above the head.

2. *Ambulation*—Has moderate waddling gait and lordosis but walks without assistance.

Running—Cannot run.

Stairs or curbs—Has some difficulty climbing up and down; uses railing for assistance.

Chair—Has no difficulty sitting down or getting up.

Floor—Rises from floor using Gower's maneuver.

Upper extremities—Can raise arms above head only by flexing the elbow or using accessory muscles.

3. *Ambulation*—Has moderately severe waddling gait and lordosis, but walks without assistance.

Stairs or curbs—Has difficulty ascending or descending stairs or curbs independently and climbs slowly.

Chair—Can get up from chair independently.

Floor—Cannot rise from floor independently.

Upper extremities—Cannot raise hands above head but can raise a glass of water to mouth.

4. *Ambulation*—Walks independently but may need some assistance with balance, or walks with bilateral knee-ankles-foot orthoses but needs a wheelchair for community mobility.

Stairs or curbs—Cannot climb stairs or curb.

Chair—Can rise from a chair without assistance.

Self care—Is independent, but may need assistance if time is important.

Upper extremities—About the same as in stage 3.

5. *Ambulation*—Can walk independently only for very short distances. Can propel manual chair slowly, but motorized wheelchair is preferable.

Stairs or curbs—Cannot climb stairs or curb.

Chair—Cannot rise from chair.

Transfers—Is independent in transfers from bed to chair, in and out of bath or shower.

Self-care—Is independent.

Upper extremities—About the same as in stage 3.

6. *Ambulation*—Walks short distances only with assistance or with long leg braces. Independent in motorized chair but may need trunk support or orthosis.

Self-care—Needs assistance with dressing, toileting, and bathing but is independent in grooming.

Upper extremities—Can raise hands to mouth but cannot raise a glass of water to mouth.

Bed—May need assistance in turning and can use a pressure relief mattress.

7. *Ambulation*—Walks short distances in long leg braces but requires assistance for balance. Independent in motorized chair but may need to recline.

Self-care—Is dependent in all activities requiring upper extremity control.

Upper extremities—Cannot raise hand to mouth but can hold pen or pick up small objects from table.

8. *Ambulation*—Cannot walk even with assistance but can stand. Needs wheelchair for all functional ambulation.

Self-care—Uses two hands for single hand activities; one hand supports the working hand or arm. Needs arm support for self-feeding.

Upper extremities—Can perform simple table-level hand activities.

9. *Ambulation*—Is confined to a wheelchair or gurney.

Self-care—May have some hand control if arms are supported.

Bed mobility—Needs assistance with turning over at night.

Respiration—May need nighttime ventilatory support or intermittent positive pressure ventilation (IPPV) during the day.

10. *Ambulation*—None. Is confined to bed. Cannot tolerate upright position.

Respiration—Needs ventilator, and a tracheostomy is useful.

Self-care—None. Needs 24-hour care.

Upper extremities—Has no useful function of hands.

Source: Data from A Hallum, Neuromuscular Diseases, in *Neurological Rehabilitation*, DA Umphred, © 1995, CV Mosby and MH Brooke et al, and Duchenne Muscular Dystrophy: Patterns of Clinical Progression and Effects of Supportive Therapy, *Neurology*, Vol. 39, p. 475, © 1989, Advanstar Communications, Inc.

REFERENCES

ASSESSMENT

Amendt LE, Ause-Elias KL, Eybers JL, Wadsworth CT, Nielsen DH, Weinstein SL. Validity and reliability testing of the scoliometer. *Physical Therapy.* 1990;70:108–117.

Brooke MH, Griggs RC, Mendell JR, et al. Clinical trial in Duchenne dystrophy: I. The design of the protocol. *Muscle and Nerve.* 1981;4:186–197. Reprinted in: Campbell SK, ed. *Physical Therapy for Children.* Philadelphia, Pa: WB Saunders Co; 1994:324. **[Protocol for functional testing]**

Brussock CM, Haley SM, Munsat TL, Bernhardt DB. Measurement of isometric force in children with and without Duchenne's muscular dystrophy. Commentary by DJ Cech with author response. *Physical Therapy.* 1992;72:105–114, 122–124.

Florence JM, Pandya S, King WM, et al. Intrarater reliability of manual muscle test (Medical Research Council scale) grades in Duchenne's muscular dystrophy. Commentary by DJ Cech with author response. *Physical Therapy.* 1992;72:115–122, discussion, 122–126.

Hiller LB, Wade CK. Upper extremity functional assessment scales in children with Duchenne muscular dystrophy: a comparison. *Archives of Physical Medicine and Rehabilitation.* 1992;73:527–534.

TREATMENT

Brenneman SK, Stanger M, Bertoti DB. Aged-related considerations: pediatric. In: Myers RS, ed. *Saunders Manual of Physical Therapy Practice.* Philadelphia, Pa: WB Saunders Co; 1995:1229–1283.

Brooke MH, Fenichel GM, Griggs RC, et al. Duchenne muscular dystrophy: patterns of clinical progression and effects of supportive therapy. *Neurology.* 1989;39:475–481.

Florence JM. Neuromuscular disorders in childhood and physical therapy intervention. In: Tecklin JS, ed. *Pediatric Physical Therapy*, 2nd ed. Philadelphia, Pa: JB Lippincott Co; 1994:390–411.

Griffiths RD. Controlling weight in muscle disease to reduce the burden. *Physiotherapy.* 1989;75:190–192.

Hallum A. Neuromuscular diseases: muscular dystrophy. In: Umphred DA, ed. *Neurological Rehabilitation.* 3rd ed. St Louis, Mo: CV Mosby Co; 1995:403–420.

Heckmatt J, Rodillo E, Dubowitz V. Management of children: pharmacological and physical. *British Medical Bulletin*. 1989;45:788–801.

Kurtz LA, Schull SA. Rehabilitation for developmental disabilities. *Pediatric Clinics of North America*. 1993;40:629–643.

Scott OM, Hyde SA, Vrbova G, Dubowitz V. Therapeutic possibilities of chronic low frequency electrical stimulation in children with Duchenne muscular dystrophy. *Journal of the Neurological Science*. 1990;95:171–182.

Shepherd RB. Muscle disorders (myopathies). In: Shepherd RB, ed. *Physiotherapy in Paediatrics*. Oxford, England: Butterworth-Heinemann; 1995:280–292.

Siegel IM. Update on Duchenne muscular dystrophy. *Comprehensive Therapy*. 1989;15:3:45–52.

Stern LM, Marin AJ, Jones H, Garrett R, Yeates J. Training inspiratory resistance in Duchenne dystrophy using adapted computer games. *Developmental Medicine and Child Neurology*. 1989;31:494–500.

Stuberg WA. Muscular dystrophy and spinal muscular atrophy. In: Campbell SK, ed. *Physical Therapy in Children*. Philadelphia, Pa: WB Saunders Co; 1994:295–324.

Stuberg WA. Considerations related to weight-bearing programs in children with development disabilities. *Physical Therapy*. 1992;72:45–50.

Near-Drowning

DESCRIPTION

Near-drowning is an episode in which someone survives a period of submersion under water. If the near-drowning occurred in water less than 20 degrees C, the diving reflex occurs and may protect the brain from ischemia. The diving reflex causes peripheral vasoconstriction and bradycardia, which shunts the blood to the brain, reducing the effect of anoxic encephalopathy.

CAUSE

Near-drowning occurs because of such factors as lack of supervision, lack of experience, lack of swimming skills, lack of flotation devices, or lack of knowledge on the part of rescuers about cardiopulmonary resuscitation.

ASSESSMENT

No specific areas were identified. Items listed under the section "Traumatic Injuries" may be useful.

No specific tests or procedures were identified.

PROBLEMS

- Cardiac problems include ischemia and cardiac arrest.
- Central nervous system complications include asphyxia, hypoxic-ischemic brain injury, cerebral edema, and herniation of tissue from the brain through the foramen magnum.
- Respiratory problems include respiratory distress syndrome and atelectasis.

TREATMENT/MANAGEMENT

- Provide passive range of motion to extremities.

- Facilitate righting and equilibrium reactions. Begin with head righting, and progress to sitting, kneeling, and standing.
- Position to decrease spasticity: side-lying in bed and prone on ball.
- Inhibitive casting may be used to decrease spasticity.
- Improve mobility skills.
    1. A wheelchair may be necessary during initial stages of recovery. If balance does not improve, a wheelchair may be needed on a long-term basis.
    2. Begin with rolling.
- Encourage stability and midline functions.
- Instruct parents in stretching exercises.

PRECAUTIONS/CONTRAINDICATIONS
No specific precautions were stated.

DESIRED OUTCOME/PROGNOSIS
- Child will be able to ambulate independently.
- The child will have attained developmental milestones.
- The child will be able to perform activities of daily living independently.
- The child will be able to attend school and participate in community and recreational activities.
- The child will have been provided with assistive devices or technology, if needed.

REFERENCES
Phillips WE. Brain tumors, traumatic head injuries, and near-drowning. In: Campbell SK, ed. *Physical Therapy for Children*. Philadelphia, Pa: WB Saunders Co; 1994:549–569.

Neoplasms

DESCRIPTION

Childhood neoplasms include leukemia, brain tumors, lymphomas, neuroblastoma, Wilms' tumor, bone tumors (osteosarcoma and Ewing's sarcoma), soft tissue tumors (rhabdomyosarcoma), and retinoblastoma.

Leukemia is a malignant disease of the blood that originates in the bone marrow, the substance found in the inner cavities of long bone. There are three subtypes of leukemia: *acute lymphoblastic leukemia (ALL), acute myelogenous leukemia (AML),* and *chronic myelogenous leukemia (CML).*

Brain tumors are the most common form of solid tumors in children. *Medulloblastoma* occurs predominantly in the cerebellum. *Astrocytoma* occurs in astrocytes and has two forms: *cerebellar astrocytoma* and *supratentorial astrocytoma. Ependymoma* occurs in the posterior fossa and cerebral hemispheres. *Gliomas* often occur in the brain stem. *Craniopharyngiomas* occur primarily in the midline suprasellar region.

Lymphomas include Hodgkin's disease and non-Hodgkin's lymphoma. *Hodgkin's disease* occurs primarily in peripheral lymph nodes and in young adults. *Non-Hodgkin's lymphoma* is a group of disorders most frequently found in the abdomen and mediastinum and occurs in children 7 to 11 years of age.

Neuroblastoma is a tumor that develops from neural crest cells and may arise anywhere in the sympathetic nervous system. The common sites are the adrenal glands or paraspinal ganglion. Typical age range is 1 to 5 years.

Wilms' tumor or *nephroblastoma* is a tumor that originates in the kidney and occurs in both hereditary and nonhereditary forms. Most tumors occur in children ages 1 to 4 years, although cases have been reported up to age 15.

Bone tumors include osteosarcoma and Ewing's sarcoma. *Osteosarcoma* is a bone tumor derived from bone-forming mesenchyme in which the malignant cell produces osteoid tissue or immature bone. Peak incidence coincides with the pubertal growth spurt from age 10 to 20 years. The most common sites are the distal femur, proximal tibia, and proximal humerus. *Ewing's sarcoma* is an undifferentiated round cell tumor that infiltrates bone marrow and adjacent soft tissue. Primary sites are weight-bearing bones of the lower extremity or pelvis.

Soft tissue sarcomas are tumors derived from skeletal muscle *(rhabdomyosarcoma)* or connective tissue. *Nonrhabdomyosarcoma* soft tissue sarcomas of young children exhibit benign behavior and may be managed with surgery alone.

Retinoblastoma is a tumor of the eye that may or may not be hereditary. About one third are bilateral and usually occur before age 2.

Diagnosis of neoplasms is made through biopsy and histologic examination and radiologic evaluation.

CAUSE

The exact cause of tumors is unknown. Environmental factors such as ionizing radiation or certain chemical and genetic factors, both hereditary and nonhereditary, have been associated.

ASSESSMENT

Areas
- Medical history
- Range of motion (ROM), especially cervical mobility
- Joint mobility
- Muscle strength
- Posture
- Sensation and sensory function, including visual proprioceptive, kinesthetic, and tactile
- Pain
- Muscle tone
- Reflexes
- Deformities such as scoliosis, kyphosis, and leg-length discrepancies
- Balance and coordination
- Cranial nerve function
- Gait analysis
- Developmental status
- Functional status
- Respiratory status
- Cardiovascular endurance

Instruments/Procedures
- chart review
- goniometry
- manual muscle testing
- developmental testing
- *pain*—facial expressions for younger children and body mapping or visual analogue scales for older children

PROBLEMS
- There may be pain at the site of the tumor with or without a palpable mass.
- A mass or swelling may be present but not in all cases.
- Fever is present in 25% of children with Ewing's sarcoma at the time of diagnosis; it may be mistaken for chronic osteomyelitis.
- Neurologic changes may be present, including headaches.
- Sensory changes may be present, especially visual disturbances in the case of brain tumors.
- Skin changes may occur, such as easy bruising or pallor.
- ROM may be decreased due to immobilization or surgery.
- Muscle strength may be decreased due to immobilization or surgery.
- Sensation may decrease or be lost, especially if a brain tumor was removed.
- There may be contractures or tight muscles due to immobilization.
- There may be postural problems such as head tilt, kyphosis, scoliosis, and leg-length discrepancies, especially if radiation has damaged the epiphyseal plates or brain tumor.
- The child may fatigue easily and have low endurance.

TREATMENT/MANAGEMENT
The treatment and management techniques given here are general. Morgan ("Pediatric Oncology," in references) discusses some specific techniques for selected types of neoplasms. Brenneman et al. ("Age-Related Considerations," p. 1273, in references) have a chart of commonly used cancer drugs, their side effects, and therapy concerns.
- Maintain or increase ROM.
  1. Emphasize maintaining hip and knee extension.
  2. Emphasize maintaining hip adductor ROM of the residual limb.
  3. Provide resting knee extension splints for child with below-knee amputation.
- Prevent secondary deformities resulting from chemotherapy regimen.
  1. Know the chemotherapy regimen and possible side effects.
  2. Monitor the skin very closely if the child is wearing a prosthesis.
  3. Provide preventive splints for wrists or ankles if initial symptoms of peripheral neuropathy develop.
- Maintain or increase strength and activity.
  1. Begin with isometrics, and progress to resistive exercises as appropriate.
  2. Emphasize hip extensors and abductors for the child with above-knee amputation.
  3. Provide extremity strengthening after limb-sparing procedure.
  4. Increase overall strength and activity level secondary to effects of bed rest and general malaise.
- Increase independence with mobility.
  1. Minimize gait deviations, especially compensations of the trunk.
  2. Emphasize symmetrical posture.

3. Provide assistive devices if needed.
- Maintain or increase activities of daily living.
  1. Maintain independence when residual disease exists and progressive disability is anticipated.
  2. Increase independence if recovery is expected.
- Promote activity to counteract effects of lethargy secondary to effects of radiotherapy and chemotherapy.
- Maximize motor return in patients with deficits.
- Provide palliative care for patients with terminal disease.
- Assist in providing orthotic and assistive devices to prevent deformity and encourage more independent functioning.

PRECAUTIONS/CONTRAINDICATIONS
- If the child is thrombocytopenic, be careful to avoid bruises and bleeding into a muscle or joint.
- Differential diagnosis may require careful assessment and analysis of data, as in the case of Ewing's sarcoma.
- Therapists should be aware of responses to cancer drugs, including side effects and adverse reactions that can affect therapy.

DESIRED OUTCOME/PROGNOSIS
- The child will be able to ambulate independently with or without assistive devices.
- The child will be able to perform functional activities independently within the limits imposed by residual disease and possible progressive disability.
- The child's level of development will be age-appropriate given residual disability.
- The child will be as comfortable and independent as terminal illness permits.

REFERENCES
Brenneman SK, Stanger M, Bertoti DB. Age-related considerations: pediatric. In: Myers RS, ed. *Saunders Manual of Physical Therapy*. Philadelphia, Pa: WB Saunders Co; 1995:1271–1273.

Dincer F, Dincer C, Baskaya MK. Results of the combined treatment of paediatric intraspinal tumours. *Paraplegia*. 1992;30;718–728.

Fulton CL. Physiotherapists in cancer care: a framework for rehabilitation of patients. *Physiotherapy*. 1994;80;830–834.

Morgan CR. Pediatric oncology. In: Tecklin JS, ed. *Pediatric Physical Therapy*. 2nd ed. Philadelphia, Pa: JB Lippincott Co; 1994:187–207.

Phillips WE. Brain tumors, traumatic head injuries, and near-drowning. In: Campbell SK, ed. *Physical Therapy for Children*. Philadelphia, Pa: WB Saunders Co; 1994:549–557.

Stanger M. Limb deficiencies and amputations: disease-related amputations. In: Campbell SK, ed. *Physical Therapy in Children*. Philadelphia, Pa: WB Saunders Co; 1994:329–333.

Osgood-Schlatter Disease

DESCRIPTION

Osgood–Schlatter disease is characterized by activity-related pain and swelling at the insertion of the patellar tendon on the tibial tubercle. It usually occurs between ages 10 and 15 years and is more common in boys. The problem tends to occur during a rapid growth spurt when the tibial tubercle is susceptible to stress. The disorder is self-limiting and ceases when the tibial tubercle ossifies to the diaphysis of the tibia at about age 15 (see Leach, "Orthopaedic Conditions," p. 372, in references).

CAUSE

The etiology is thought to be trauma, from excessive traction caused by prolonged overuse and chronic avulsion of fragments, to the patella tendon at the immature epiphyseal insertion on the tibial tubercle. A lateral radiograph of the knee should show fragmentation of the tibial tubercle.

ASSESSMENT

Areas

- The complaint is localized to the knee region, but a general assessment of other joints and regions of the body should be included to determine that no systemic disturbance or other localized area is involved.
- There should be a history of pain aggravated by physical activity.
- Direct pressure over the tibial tubercle should elicit a response of pain and protection.
- Tightness of the gastrocsoleus complex, hamstring, and quadriceps musculature often is present, but there should be no contractures.
- Note limping during walking on the involved leg as a protection mechanism in response to the pain, swelling, and tenderness.
- Observe skin over the tibial tubercle for signs of redness.

Instruments/Procedures

- Apply pressure using thumb or fingers over the tibial tubercle. Response should be pain, tenderness to touch, and a protective reaction.

PROBLEMS

- There may be pain, swelling, and tenderness over the area of the tibial tubercle at the patellar tendon insertion, especially during activity.
- The child may limp in response to the pain, swelling, and tenderness.

TREATMENT/MANAGEMENT

- Rest and decreased activity level should resolve acute symptoms of pain, swelling, and tenderness within weeks or months.
- Provide stretching of tight musculature, especially the quadriceps mechanism, to decrease the pull over the tibial tubercle.
- Ice applied on the site may reduce pain.

- Immobilization in long-leg cast over the knee region and an injection of hydrocortisone may be necessary if symptoms persist.
- A Neoprene knee brace may be used to limit movement.
- Surgery is rarely necessary but may include excision of the tubercle, excision of loose ossicles, and grafting.

PRECAUTIONS/CONTRAINDICATIONS
- Sports and excessive exercise involving deep knee bends, squatting, and jumping should be avoided.

DESIRED OUTCOME/PROGNOSIS
- The tibial tubercle will have fused to the main body of the tibia; this usually occurs at age 15.
- The symptoms of pain, swelling, and tenderness at the site of the patellar tendon and tibial tubercle will have disappeared.

REFERENCES

Brenneman SK, Stanger M, Bertoti DB. Age-related considerations: pediatric. In: Myers RS, ed. *Saunders Manual of Physical Therapy*. Philadelphia, Pa: WB Saunders Co; 1995:169–170.

Leach J. Orthopaedic conditions. In: Campbell SK, ed. *Physical Therapy for Children*. Philadelphia, Pa: WB Saunders Co; 1994:372.

Osteogenesis Imperfecta

Also known as *brittle bone disease* and *fragilitas ossium*.

DESCRIPTION
Osteogenesis imperfecta (OI) is characterized by an abnormal weakness and fragility of bone due to failure to produce organized collagen. It is an inherited disorder of collagen synthesis affecting all connective tissue. Severity and type of the disease are usually based on the age at which the fractures first occurred. Current classification by Silence in 1981 includes four types: OI type 1 or fetal form, OI type 2 or infantile form, OI type 3, and OI type 4. The diagnostic triad includes blue sclera, dentinogenesis imperfecta, and generalized osteoporosis with fractures and bowing of the long bones. A triangular facial appearance is often present, as is wormian (multiple small bones) in the occipital region upon radiographic examination. Intelligence is usually normal, but social isolation by the family may result in difficulty with peer relations, adjustment to school, independent living, and vocational planning. No effective medications are available to strengthen skeletal structures and prevent fractures (see Bleakney and Donohoe, "Osteogenesis Imperfecta," pp. 279–280, in references).

CAUSE
Osteogenesis imperfecta is a genetic disorder with some forms caused by autosomal-dominant inheritance and others caused by autosomal-recessive inheritance.

ASSESSMENT

Areas
- Medical history of fractures and types of immobilization used
- Caregiving
- Range of motion (ROM)
- Muscle strength
- Developmental level

Instruments/Procedures (See References for Sources)
- medical chart review
- observation of caregiver's handling and positioning techniques during dressing, diapering, and bathing
- goniometry for active ROM and functional ROM; do not do passive ROM
- observation of muscle strength and palpation of contracting muscles; do not do standard manual muscle test
- tests of gross motor skills
  1. Bayley Scales of Infant Development
  2. Peabody Developmental Motor Scales
  3. Pediatric Evaluation of Disability Inventory (PEDI)
- orthopaedic tests generally contraindicated

PROBLEMS

General
- There is ligament laxity of the joints.
- There are weak muscles.
- There is diffuse osteoporosis.
- Scoliosis is present in 80–90% of cases.
- Bowing deformities of the lower extremities can impair standing and ambulation abilities.
- There may be fractures and nonunion of fractures.
- There may be defective dentinogenesis of primary and secondary teeth.
- There may be conductive hearing loss secondary to fractures of the ossicles.
- There may be excessive sweating.
- There may be hernias.
- The child may bruise easily.
- Family members may overprotect the child.
- The child may be socially isolated.

Type 1—Accounts for 80% of Cases and Is Autosomal Dominant
- There is hypermobility and laxity of joints.
- There is generalized osteoporosis with bone fragility.
- Dentinogenesis imperfecta may be present.
- The child has normal stature at birth but does not attain normal height as adult.
- Blue sclerae are present throughout life.
- The child may have presenile conductive hearing loss.
- Fractures may or may not appear at birth.

Type 2—Probably Autosomal Recessive
* The infant is born with multiple fractures.
* Gross limb deformities are present.
* The bones are extremely fragile, with minimal mineralization.
* Ossification of the skull and face is markedly delayed.
* The child is small for his or her age.
* Often the outcome is death in infancy.

Type 3—Probably Autosomal Recessive
* There is progressive development of deformities of long bones, skull, and spine.
* Children often develop a kyphoscoliosis and resulting respiratory compromise.
* The bones are very narrow and fragile, but sclerae are normal in adult life.
* Dentinogenesis imperfecta may occur.
* The child is usually unable to walk.
* Stature is very short, with severe growth retardation.
* Hearing loss is common.
* Death in childhood occurs due to respiratory compromise.

Type 4—Probably Autosomal Dominant but Rarest Type
* The child has short stature.
* The child has normal sclerae.
* The child may have abnormal teeth.
* The child may have mild to moderate deformity.
* Bone fragility is variable.
* Hearing loss is variable.
* Prognosis for ambulation is excellent.

TREATMENT/MANAGEMENT
* Provide parental instruction on handling and positioning.
  1. Demonstrate and provide instruction on proper and safe methods of handling the child for bathing, dressing, and carrying.
     a. The head and trunk should be fully supported, with arms and legs draped across the supporting arm, or use a pillow on which to carry the infant. Change the position periodically to avoid accommodation.
     b. Recommend loose-fitting clothes with Velcro closures. Encourage parents not to over-dress the child because of excess sweating.
     c. Roll the infant off the diaper rather than lifting by the ankles. Lift by the buttocks.
     d. Recommend a padded carrier with support for head, trunk, and extremities, such as a one-piece molded thoracolumbosacral orthosis (TLSO) fabricated from polyethylene.
  2. Help parents understand that fractures can occur with the best of care.
  3. Help parents deal with guilt or anger about the child's disease.
* Positioning should emphasize symmetry of head and spine and alignment of extremities.
  1. For infants, towel rolls may be used to maintain side-lying position.
  2. For older children, support in seating (strollers and wheelchairs) is important to promote head and trunk alignment.
  3. Baby walkers and jumping seats should not be used because they do not provide enough support. The child should be fitted snugly to prevent falling, and feet should be supported, not left dangling.

- Provide ROM exercises.
  1. Gentle passive ROM should be used after fracture or surgery.
  2. Use low weight with high repetitions.
  3. Aquatic exercise is useful, but the temperature of the water should be monitored to avoid raising the body temperature.
- Encourage development activities.
  1. Infants should be placed in a variety of positions, including prone and side-lying, as they play.
  2. Prone positioning promotes development of neck and upper trunk musculature, leading to head control. A towel roll can be placed under the hips to reduce stress on knees (called "prone-on-a-roll" position).
  3. Reaching should be encouraged from supine and side-lying positions to develop upper extremity strength.
  4. Rolling must be done with care to avoid trapping an arm under the child's trunk.
  5. Trunk extension and symmetry are important when sitting.
  6. Sitting can be encouraged by straddling a leg or roll.
  7. Use roll to transfer from prone to sit; do not pull by arms to sitting position.
  8. Handling should be through pelvis, trunk, and shoulder.
  9. Toys should be selected that are safe for the child and can be adapted for various positions of play.
- Strengthening is achieved through active movement.
  1. Resistive weights can be initiated with school-aged children. Increase weight in small increments; place weights near large joints to avoid a long-lever arm and potential fractures.
  2. Water is an excellent medium to incorporate active movement.
- Provide orthotic devices.
  1. Splinting of upper extremities with low-temperature plastics is used to decrease bowing deformities.
  2. Bracing of lower extremities is used to protect long bones against additional fractures and deformity while assisting in ambulation.
- Provide standing and gait training.
  1. Parapodiums, tilt tables, prone or supine standers, or long-leg braces may be used to promote weight bearing. Stress promotes formation of osteoblasts, which can promote healing of fractures.
  2. Knee-ankle-foot orthoses (KAFOs) can be used with children who have moderate to severe types of OI.
  3. Unsupported ambulation is discouraged for children with Type III OI.
  4. Fitting for braces to be used for standing and ambulation is usually done between 2 and 3 years of age.
  5. Braces should be lightweight, Chamsehill type, with quadrilateral cuffs to support the long bones fully.
  6. Pneumatic Rouser splints have been used but may not be tolerated as well by a child with OI because of the child's tendency to sweat profusely.
  7. Begin training in parallel bars, and move to various assistive devices such as walkers or crutches.
  8. Axillary and Lofstrand crutches are used commonly. The four-point gait pattern is preferred, but swing-to and swing-through patterns are also used.

- Provide assistive technology.
  1. Mobility often requires the use of a manual or power wheelchair for independence and function.
  2. Molded seating is useful to prevent scoliosis.
  3. If walkers are used, splints may be helpful to prevent bowing deformities of the radius and ulna.
- Thermal modalities including heat and cold may be used to reduce pain and edema.
- Fracture management should encourage mobilization as soon as possible to prevent cycle of osteoporosis and increased fractures in the future.
- Surgical management involves inserting Bailey–Dubow rods in the long bones. The rods can be lengthened as the child grows. Harrington rods may be used to control scoliosis.

PRECAUTIONS/CONTRAINDICATIONS
- Prevent cardiorespiratory compromise.
- Watch for signs of bowing as body weight is applied.
- Watch for signs of fractures such as warmth at the site, edema, pain, bruising, irritability, and deformity.
- If child with an intramedullary rod suddenly loses ROM, refer to a physician immediately because the rod may have moved.

DESIRED OUTCOME/PROGNOSIS
- The child will be able to attend school and participate in a normal educational environment.
- The child will be able to perform functional skills within limitations of musculoskeletal ability.
- The child will be learning skills that will facilitate independent living as an adult.
- The child will be learning skills that will facilitate vocational planning and choice as an adult.
- The child will be able to participate in social and recreational activities within limitations of musculoskeletal ability.

REFERENCES

ASSESSMENT
Bayley N. *Bayley Scales of Infant Development.* 2nd ed. San Antonio, Tex: Psychological Corporation; 1993.
Folio MR, Fewell RR. *Peabody Developmental Motor Scales.* Allen, Tex: DLM Teaching Resources; 1983.
Haley SM, Faas RM, Coster WJ, Webster H, Gans BM. *Pediatric Evaluation of Disability Inventory.* Boston, Mass: New England Medical Center; 1989.

TREATMENT
Bender LH. Part 2: osteogenesis imperfecta. *Orthopedic Nursing.* 1991;10:4:23–32.
Binder H, Conway A, Gerber LH. Rehabilitation approaches to children with osteogenesis imperfecta: a ten-year experience. *Archives of Physical Medicine and Rehabilitation.* 1993;74:386–390.
Binder H, Conway A, Hason S, et al. Comprehensive rehabilitation of the child with osteogenesis imperfecta. *American Journal of Medical Genetics.* 1993;45:265–269.
Bleakney DA, Donohoe M. Osteogenesis imperfecta. In: Campbell SK, ed. *Physical Therapy for Children.* Philadelphia, Pa: WB Saunders Co; 1994:279–294.
Brenneman SK, Stanger M, Bertoti DB. Age-related considerations: pediatric. In: Myers RS, ed. *Saunders Manual of Physical Therapy Practice.* Philadelphia, Pa: WB Saunders Co; 1995:1229–1283.

Stuberg WA. Considerations related to weight-bearing programs in children with developmental disabilities. *Physical Therapy*. 1992;72;45–50.

Tecklin JS. Osteogenesis imperfecta. In: Tecklin JS, ed. *Pediatric Physical Therapy*. 2nd ed. Philadelphia, Pa: JB Lippincott Co; 1994:302–305.

Pain in Childhood

DESCRIPTION

Pain is, according to the International Association for the Study of Pain (IASP), an unpleasant sensory and emotional experience associated with actual or potential tissue damage or described in terms of such damage (see Merskey, "Classification of Chronic Pain," in references). Pain must always be viewed within the total clinical picture as expected or unexpected. Expected pain can be dealt with using established protocols. Unexpected or excessive pain alerts the therapist to the possibility that additional assessment or intervention may be needed.

CAUSE

Causes include cancer, burns, juvenile rheumatoid arthritis (JRA), and reflex sympathetic dystrophy. See also individual sections on each disease or disorder.

ASSESSMENT

In assessing a child, it is important to establish a trusting relationship by informing the child of the purpose and rationale for each test procedure. Also, the therapist must be flexible in administering the assessment and alter the sequence or technique depending on the response of the child and the child's attention span. In addition, doing as many tests as possible in the sitting or standing position provides the child with a sense of control and is thus less threatening.

Areas
- Medical history
- Range of motion (ROM) and flexibility, especially for areas where pain is reported
- Strength: discrepancies between the two sides of the body, partial paralysis
- Sensory (touch/tactile, proprioceptive, vestibular, visual): hemiparesis, proximal versus distal discrepancies, hypersensitivity, diplopia (double vision), and visual field deficits
- Posture: scoliosis, kyphosis, leg-length discrepancies, and head tilt
- Muscle tone
- Postural reflexes
- Balance: muscle splinting and weight shifting as techniques to avoid pain
- Gait: asymmetry, ataxia, high steppage
- Gross motor skill development
- Function: ask child about getting to and from school, responsibility for chores at home, leisure activity, eating and sleeping habits
- Cardiovascular/respiratory status: heart rate, respiratory rate, blood pressure, oxygen saturation

- Skin and soft tissue: discoloration, dryness, excessive sweating, scarring, shininess, hair growth or loss, temperature; edema; soft tissue contractures
- Contractures: may be evidence of protective reaction to pain
- Pain: behavioral responses, self-reports

Instruments/Procedures (See References for Sources)

History
- medical chart review

Pain: Behavioral Responses
- Children's Hospital of Eastern Ontario Pain Scale (CHEOPS)

Pain: Self-Reports
- Beyer–Aradine Scale
- Eland Color Scale
- Visual analogue scale

ROM
- goniometer

Strength
- manual muscle testing
- dynamometer.

Skin and Soft Tissue
- observation
- palpation for hypersensitivity, pitting characteristics, temperature differences, types of touch tolerated
- girth measurements for edema

PROBLEMS
- There may be joint pain.
- There may be swelling/edema.
- There may be scar tissue.
- There may be adhesions and contractures.
- There may be muscle weakness.
- There may be hypersensitivity.
- There may be fractures.
- There may be sores.
- There may be referred pain.
- There may be emotional responses to pain.

TREATMENT/MANAGEMENT

Pain management requires a team approach including pharmacologic agents, relaxation techniques, hypnosis, behavior modification, and activity.
- Reduce pain, including swelling and soreness.
  1. Use ultrasound to provide thermal and nonthermal effects to subcutaneous tissues including muscle, tendon, and bursa.
     a. Continuous ultrasound provides heat to the tissues.

   b. Pulsed ultrasound provides acoustical streaming (steaming).

   c. Phonophoresis is a method of using ultrasound to apply substances such as hydrocortisone topically through the skin.

  2. Transcutaneous electrical nerve stimulation (TENS) is used for partially or completely blocking the pain.

  3. Biofeedback can help with the re-education of muscles for relaxation or for motor unit recruitment.

  4. Use hydrotherapy, warm or cool whirlpool, for local relief of pain or whole-body submersion. Contrast baths may be used to promote circulation.

  5. Sleeping in a sleeping bag or blanket-sleeper pajama may be useful in maintaining the body's natural heat.

  6. Paraffin bath is useful for small joints of the wrist and hand.

  7. Hydrocollator packs may be used for the cervical or lumbar spine.

- Restore physical function.

  1. Use electrical stimulation, direct and alternating currents, to change muscle function and tissue homeostasis.

  2. Pool therapy with toys that float encourages exercise.

  3. A warm tub bath or shower in the morning can reduce morning stiffness.

- Manage activities of daily living.
- Educate patient and family.
- Assist in teaching relaxation techniques.

PRECAUTIONS

- Ultrasound is contraindicated in younger children if there are epiphyseal (growth) plates.
- Ultrasound and diathermy are contraindicated in pediatric patients with JRA because of their potential for increasing inflammation and accelerating the bioenzymatic chain of events that leads to destruction of cartilage.

DESIRED OUTCOME/PROGNOSIS

- The child will be able to hold positions and move without pain, with reduced pain, or with pain within tolerable limits.
- The child will be able to perform activities of daily living appropriate to age and within limits of disease or disability.
- The child will be able to function as a family member, student, and peer in the home, school, and community.
- The child and family will have demonstrated learning designed to reduce pain or keep it within tolerable limits.

REFERENCES

Merskey H. Classification of chronic pain: descriptions of chronic pain syndromes and definitions of pain terms. *Pain* (suppl 3):S217.

ASSESSMENT

Pain

Behavioral Responses

Children's Hospital of Eastern Ontario Pain Scale (CHEOPS)
McGrath, PA. An assessment of children's pain: a review of behavior, physiological and direct scaling techniques. *Pain*. 1987;31:147–176.

Self-Reports

Beyer–Aradine Scale

Beyer JE, Aradine CR. Patterns of pediatric pain intensity: a methodological investigation of a self-report scale. *Clinical Journal of Pain.* 1987;3:130–341. **[Child selects a picture of a facial expression on a scale to represent intensity of pain; useful for children as young as 3 years.]**

Eland Color Scale

Eland JM. The child who is hurting. *Seminars in Oncology Nursing.* 1985;1:116–122. **[Child uses different colors of crayons to represent four levels of pain; useful for school-age children]**

Visual Analogue Scale

Abu-Saad H, Holzemer W. Measuring children's self-assessment of pain. *Issues in Comprehensive Pediatric Nursing.* 1988;14:21–24. **[Useful for children age 9 and above]**

ROM

Heck CV, Hendryson IE, Rowe CR. *Joint Motion: Method of Measuring and Recording.* Chicago, Ill: American Academy of Orthopaedic Surgeons; 1965.

Strength

Daniels L, Worthingham C. *Muscle Testing: Techniques of Manual Examination.* Philadelphia, Pa: WB Saunders Co; 1995.

Kendall PF, McCreary ER. *Muscles: Testing and Function.* 3rd ed. Baltimore, Md: Williams & Wilkins; 1983.

TREATMENT

Allen J, Jedlinsky BP, Wilson TL, McCarthy CF. Physical therapy management of pain in children. In: Schechter NL, Berde CB, Yaster M, eds. *Pain in Infants, Children and Adolescents.* Baltimore, Md: Williams & Wilkins; 1993:317–329.

Cooper J. Food intolerance and joint symptoms: historical review and present-day application. *Physiotherapy.* 1991;77:847–858.

Tippett SR. Referred knee pain in a young athlete: a case study. *Journal of Orthopaedic and Sports Physical Therapy.* 1994;19:117–120.

Pediatric HIV/AIDS

DESCRIPTION

Pediatric HIV/AIDS is the presence of the HIV virus or symptoms of acquired immunodeficiency syndrome (AIDS) in infants and children usually under the age of thirteen. The child usually was born with the virus but may have been infected by other means. There tends to be two categories of neurologic findings: static encephalopathy and progressive deterioration. The course of the disease may follow any of the following patterns: subacute progressive, plateau, plateau followed by further deterioration, plateau followed by improvement, and nonprogressive delayed acquisition of developmental milestones. There is no typical pattern of progression of the disorder. Evidence of encephalopathy is the most common reason for referral to rehabilitation and physical therapy (see Harris, "Physical Therapy," pp. 85–86, in references).

CAUSE

Contact with the HIV virus is through intrauterine infection, congenital factors, blood transfusion, or exchange of bodily fluids, as in breast feeding or child sexual abuse. Infection is caused by a cytopathic human retrovirus, resulting in a continuously changing and progressive spectrum of immunologic deterioration and associated clinical conditions, of which the end stage is AIDS-related complex (ARC), a prodromal stage.

ASSESSMENT

Areas
- Pertinent medical history
  1. number of opportunistic infections, including cytomegalovirus (CMV), pneumocystis pneumonia, and disseminated candida infection
  2. nutritional status: oral-motor skills, feeding difficulties
- Neurologic dysfunction: changes in postural tone and motor control
- Gross motor skills development and/or delays: level of milestones attained, degree of mobility in changing position, fear of movement, motivation to move
- Postural competence: balance recovery; coordination of the two sides of the body; righting reactions in vertical suspension, sitting, and prone; need for external support
- Fine motor skills: play skills, manipulation skills, grasp-and-release skills, use of hands to support body
- Movement patterns: variety of movement patterns
- Potential for deformities
- Potential for contractures
- Physical fitness and energy expenditure
  1. cardiac status
  2. respiratory dysfunction, especially presence of *Pneumocystis carinii* pneumonia
  3. vital signs and color
  4. oxygen saturation
  5. degree of pulmonary compromise
  6. breath sounds
  7. congestion
- Psychosocial: degree of irritability, degree of consolability, response to handling
- Problems associated with substance withdrawal: jitteriness, lethargy
- Need for assistive devices
- Functional communication and language skills
- Self-help skills attainment
- Perceptual disorders
- Intellectual dysfunction
  Note: If mother is HIV-positive, be aware of potential difficulties with caregiving skills.

Instruments/Procedures (See References for Sources)
- Bayley Scales of Infant Development: Motor Scale
- Movement Assessment of Infants (MAI)
- Neonatal Behavior Assessment Scale
- Observation of child at play
- Peabody Developmental Motor Scales

PROBLEMS
- Motor signs include pseudobulbar palsy, truncal hypertonia, aspastic diplegia or quadriplegia, hyperreflexia, pyramidal signs, myoclonus, and appearance of primitive reflexes that were previously integrated.
- Movement deficits related to axial tone dysfunction include difficulty with righting skills against gravity, impaired postural reactions, posturing of the lower extremities, difficulty with weight bearing, difficulty transitioning from one position to another, and lack of spontaneous movement.
- Motor deficits include disturbances in hand functions (reach against gravity, grasp and release) and disordered sequencing of movement (apraxia).
- Developmental problems include impaired functional skills development, delay and/or loss of motor developmental milestones, intellectual deficits, impaired brain growth.
- Pyramidal tract signs usually appear in later stages.
- There may be general weakness and a poor level of fitness.
- There may be chronic respiratory problems due to opportunistic infections.
- There may be ataxia.
- There may be seizures—focal or generalized.
- There may be progressive generalized apathy.
- There may be loss of functional skills such as feeding skills.

TREATMENT/MANAGEMENT
Harris ("Physical Therapy," in references) suggests there are seven categories of HIV disease (see box).
- Facilitate postural reactions.
- Facilitate normal motor patterns for attainment of developmental milestones, using developmental activities.
- Prevent deformities and contractures by
  1. instruction in positioning, handling, and carrying
  2. splinting or casting
  3. adaptive equipment
- Facilitate motor control and functional movement skills in the following areas:
  1. mobility
  2. reaching, grasping, and manipulation of objects
  3. balance reactions and adaptation to movement
  4. normalization of sensation and perception
  5. play skills: positions, motivation, and toy selection
- Facilitate feeding by monitoring
  1. oral-motor development and control
  2. sucking, swallowing, and breathing coordination
  3. food textures
  4. nutritional status
- Maintain respiratory status:
  1. breathing pattern
  2. congestion status
  3. energy expenditure and oxygen saturation during activities
- Maintain health status in coordination with physician, especially if drug therapy is being used.

- Select or fabricate assistive devices and equipment.
- Educate caregivers and staff.

PRECAUTIONS/CONTRAINDICATIONS
- The child may fatigue quickly if general fitness is compromised.
- Be sensitive to the child and to the family or caregivers' need to determine the level and amount of care by professionals.

DESIRED OUTCOME/PROGNOSIS
- Because the course is quite variable, the outcome depends on the category and degree of severity.
- Increase and maintain motor and movement skills as long as possible.
- Develop and maintain functional skills as long as possible.
- Continue to monitor status.

Categories of HIV Disease

Category 1: Rapidly Progressive
- Diagnosis is made within the first few months of life.
- The infant has frequent opportunistic infections.
- Neurologic deterioration is rapidly progressive.
- Prognosis is poor. Death occurs between 6 months and 2 years.

Category 2: Subacute Relentlessly Progressive
- Diagnosis is made at about age 1.
- Deterioration alternates with periods of plateau.
- The infant has frequent severe respiratory infections.
- Severe extensor tone changes to hypotonia in final stage.
- There is marked global developmental delay.
- Intelligence is considered to be severely mentally retarded.
- There are marked deficits in postural reactions.
- There are persistent primitive reflexes.
- There is oral-motor hypersensitivity.
- Respiratory status is poor, with shallow, rapid open-mouth breathing.
- Crying is high-pitched with no verbal sounds.
- The child is irritable and difficult to console.
- The child dies at around age 2 years.

Category 3: Subacute Progressive With Plateau
- Similar to category 2, but deterioration is slower, with longer periods of plateaus.

Category 4: Static Encephalopathy
- The child is relatively medically stable.
- Encephalopathy may have resulted from HIV infection of the central nervous system in utero.
- The course is marked by severe developmental, cognitive, and neurologic deficits, including motor development, autonomic reactions, muscle tone, sensory function, language, feeding skills, and respiratory function.
- The course is quite variable, and the child may shift between the previous categories.

Category 5: Moderately Impaired
- The child has moderate motor, perceptual, sensory, cognitive, and behavioral deficits.
- The child has frequent mild infections, high fevers of undetermined origin, chronic respiratory disorders and asymptomatic lymphadenopathy.
- Medical problems may require frequent trips to the emergency room and absences from school but do not leave residual impairment or loss of achieved skills.
- The child does not require physical therapy unless there is specific movement or respiratory dysfunction or decline in functional ability.
- The child should be referred for evaluation in occupational and recreational therapy and speech pathology.

Category 6: Mildly Impaired
- The child has mild-to-moderate deficits in one or more areas: fine and gross motor skills and behavioral, sensory, and social development.
- The child may benefit from early intervention.
- The child should be re-evaluated because of potential for insidious deterioration.
- Ninety percent of cases eventually develop neurologic and cognitive deficits and lose developmental milestones and functional skills.
- Watch for abrupt changes in muscle tone; increase of spasticity, especially in the lower extremities; increase in truncal flexor or extensor tone; decrease in postural tone in the trunk; loss of tone in the upper extremities; changes in behavior; loss of functional skills; loss of postural reactions; clumsiness, frequent falls; and changes in eating or feeding patterns.
- Rapid onset of spasticity or rigidity may progress quickly to contractures and loss of function.
- Adaptive equipment may facilitate continued function.

Category 7: Normal Mental and Motor Neurologic Course
- Baseline evaluation is useful, but ongoing therapy is not needed.
- Assessment should include motor pattern analysis, attainment of developmental milestones, functional skills, feeding, range of motion, muscle tone, automatic reactions/postural adjustment, primitive reflexes, coordination, balance, behavior, reaction to stimuli, and ability to integrate sensory data.
- The child may not be identified until preschool age or later.

Source: Adapted with permission from MH Harris, Physical Therapy in Pediatric HIV Infection, in *Rehabilitation for Patients with HIV Disease*, pp. 353–356, © 1991, McGraw-Hill.

REFERENCES

ASSESSMENT
Lord D, Danoff JV, Smith MR. Motor assessment of infants with human immunodeficiency virus infection: a retrospective review of multiple cases. *Pediatric Physical Therapy*. 1995;7:1:9–13.

Bayley Scales of Infant Development—Motor Scale
Bayley N. *Bayley Scales of Infant Development*. New York, NY: Psychological Corporation; 1969.

Movement Assessment of Infants (MAI)
Chandler LS, Andrews MS, Swanson MW. *Movement Assessment of Infants.* Rolling Bay, Wash: Infant Development Center; 1980.

Neonatal Behavior Assessment Scale
Brazelton TB. *Neonatal Behavior Assessment Scale.* 2nd ed. Clinics in Developmental Medicine, No. 88. Philadelphia, Pa: JB Lippincott Co; 1984.

Peabody Developmental Motor Scales
Folio RM, Fewell RR. *Peabody Developmental Motor Scales and Activity Cards.* Allen, TX: DLM Teaching Resources; 1983.

TREATMENT
Diamond GW, Cohen HJ. HIV infection in children; medical and neurological aspects. *Pediatric Physical Therapy.* 1990;2:1:34–38.
Harris MH. Physical therapy in pediatric HIV infection. In: Mukand J, ed. *Rehabilitation for Patients With HIV Disease.* New York, NY: McGraw-Hill Book Co; 1991:343–357.
Harris MH. Habilitative and rehabilitative needs of children with HIV infection. In: Crocker AC, Cohen HJ, Hastner TA, eds. *HIV Infection and Developmental Disabilities: A Resource for Service Providers.* Baltimore, Md: Paul H Brooks; 1992:85–94.

Poliomyelitis

Also known as *anterior poliomyelitis, acute anterior poliomyelitis, infantile paralysis, polio.*

DESCRIPTION
Poliomyelitis is an acute viral infection with a wide range of manifestations, including non-specific minor illness, aseptic meningitis (nonparalytic poliomyelitis), and flaccid weakness of various muscle groups (paralytic poliomyelitis). Poliomyelitis is rare in the United States since the vaccine became widely available in the 1960s but does occur in a few children without immunization. It still occurs regularly in underdeveloped countries in areas where children have not received vaccinations. Recovery from paralytic poliomyelitis occurs in three stages: healing of damaged motor units (short term), hypertrophy of remaining muscle fibers (intermediate term), and re-innervation of muscles (long term). Postpolio syndrome problems should alert health care professionals to the fact that poliomyelitis results in a chronic disorder that lasts a lifetime.

CAUSE
Poliovirus is an enterovirus belonging to the Picornaviridae. Of the three immunologically distinct poliovirus serotypes, type 1 is the most paralytogenic and the most common cause of epidemics. Infection occurs through direct contact, and the virus is highly contagious. The virus enters through the mouth. The spinal cord and brain are the only sites of significant virus-induced pathology. The motor neurons of the anterior horn of the spinal cord and the medulla are most involved sites, although other parts of the brain can be involved, including the cerebellum and motor cortex. Damage to neurons elicits an intense inflammatory response and eventually

neuronophagia. Factors predisposing to serious neurologic damage include increased age, recent tonsillectomy, inoculations such as DTP, pregnancy, and physical exertion concurrent with the onset of the central nervous system phase.

ASSESSMENT

Areas
Full assessment is not possible until the acute stage of the illness is past. Periodic reassessments are useful to determine need for orthotics, braces, and assistive devices.
• Muscle strength—The following muscles have been found to be more susceptible to paralysis: tibialis anterior, tibialis posterior, the long toe flexors and extensors, the peronei, the calf muscles, intrinsic muscles of the hand, and the deltoid and triceps brachii
• Range of motion (ROM) and muscle length
• Respiratory function, especially muscles of respiration
• Pain and tenderness, especially in muscles

Instruments/Procedures (See References for Sources)
• electromyography (if available)
• goniometry
• muscle strength testing
• muscle length assessment
• palpation

PROBLEMS
• ROM may be limited.
• There may be muscle spasms.
• There may be muscle pain.
• There may be muscle weakness and paralysis.
• There may be breathing problems.
• There may be positioning problems.
• Possible deformities include drop foot, genu valgum, genu recurvatum, limb-length discrepancy, external rotation of the hip, lumbar lordosis, kyphosis, and scoliosis.
• Child may lack endurance.
• Child may experience pain upon exertion.
• Child can fatigue quickly upon exertion.
• Child can quickly become malnourished.

TREATMENT/MANAGEMENT
All treatment and management techniques should be undertaken with the knowledge that poliomyelitis results in a lifelong disorder. Short-term achievements in function must be weighed against the potential for long-term impairment. Total independence for a few years may result in increased dependence in later years. The therapist should be realistic in setting short- and long-term goals.

Acute Stage: Complete Bed Rest
• Maintain ROM through gentle passive exercise during the acute febrile stage. If muscles are weak and flaccid, one session per day is probably enough.

- Reduce muscle spasms and muscle pain using heat packs, although the type of heat, optimal therapeutic temperature, and application parameters are still not known.
- Maintain anatomical position of function to prevent deformity.
- Facilitate rest during the acute stages of the disorder.
- Maintain airway by using facilitated coughing and body positioning.
  1. Respiratory and swallowing status must be evaluated several times a day to ensure breathing and avoid aspiration.
  2. If paralysis of respiratory muscles occurs, the preferred method of ventilation is intermittent positive pressure ventilation (IPPV) because it is relatively free from infection.
  3. If paralysis of swallowing muscles occurs, a tracheostomy must be performed to keep mucus and food from oral cavity from getting into the lungs.

Postacute Period
- Continue passive ROM and add active ROM.
- Provide muscle strengthening, starting with body weight only and progressing to dynamic moderate resistive exercise. Exercise machines that provide feedback about the level of effort provide motivation for the child. Games are also useful such as throwing, tossing, or hitting the ball with hands to use elbow extension.
- Denervated muscles may be helped by using electrical stimulation to maintain viability until nerve regeneration occurs. Use long-duration pulse width (greater than 10 milliseconds) or a low frequency (less than 10 Hz) sine-wave alternating current.
- Improve balance and equilibrium reactions by using a balance board or stepping up on and down off a stool.
- Increase endurance by using exercises and games such as riding a prone scooter, playing a toss game while lying down, or pool activities to facilitate movement if muscles are very weak at first and later adding pool walking for resistance.
- Improve respiration by using games that require holding the breath, as in a pool or as in blowing a sailboat across the water. Teach glossopharyngeal or "frog" breathing to reduce ventilator dependence.
- Prevent deformity through positioning and selective use of electrical stimulation.
  1. The bed should have a firm mattress, although a sheepskin mattress may be used.
  2. The child's position should be changed frequently.
  3. Splints may be used to maintain a position such as 2 or 3 degrees flexion of the knee.
- Educate caregivers regarding necessity of
  1. maintaining good positioning in bed
  2. alternating hip when carrying the child
  3. continuing exercise at home
  4. maintaining good skin care to avoid skin ulceration
  5. maintaining body temperature, especially in cold weather when muscle mass is poor
  6. caring for splints, braces, and assistive devices if still needed
- Teach trick and substitute movements to compensate for lost function, such as thrusting the pelvis forward to gain stability that was lost due to loss of hip muscles.
- Promote normal sensorimotor developmental activities as much as possible by using positioning and play activities.
- Provide temporary orthotic devices to facilitate function while return of muscle activity is expected and permanent orthotic devices if function is not expected to return.

- Assist child and parents to cope with loss of or decreased functional ability, and encourage adjustment to residual impairment.

PRECAUTIONS/CONTRAINDICATIONS
- Always provide support for joints when exercising to the outer limit of the range.
- Avoid overexertion and fatigue from too much or too long a period of exercise, especially during the first 6 months after acute onset.
- Avoid heavy resistive exercise, which may contribute to muscle irritation, pain, and muscle damage especially during first 6 months.
- Do not use electrical stimulation if muscle responds to a lower pulse width (under 10 milliseconds). Muscle is innervated and does not need electrical stimulation.
- Pay close attention to signs of deformity during growth spurts.
- Avoid a soft mattress and avoid putting a pillow under knees to reduce chances of contractures.
- If aquatic activities are used, the water temperature should be 32 to 34 degrees centigrade to avoid overheating muscles, which is enervating, or chilling muscles, which inhibits muscle action.
- The full degree of loss of function may not be apparent until several years after the acute phase due to progressive deformities that become more acute as the child grows and develops or as the mechanical advantage changes due to changes in the musculoskeletal system.
- Postpolio syndrome problems will occur unless the child is reassessed regularly and steps are taken to remediate small problems as they occur.

DESIRED OUTCOME/PROGNOSIS
- The child has a means of effective mobilization consistent with degree of recovery including, for example, independent walking, walking with crutches, or use of a wheelchair.
- The child is independent in activities of daily living with assistive devices, if necessary.
- The child has attained maximum functional independence consistent with degree of recovery.

Techniques for Eliciting Contraction of the Tibialis Anterior

1. Have the child sit up from a semireclined or supine position with feet held (start with semireclined position if abdominals are weak also).
2. Use manual or electrical stimulation on the belly of the muscle plus pressure on the dorsum of the foot while the child attempts to dorsiflex the foot.
3. Have the child sit on a stool with feet on the floor; manually stimulate the bottom of the toes to facilitate any potential of the dorsiflexor muscle and toe extensors to contract.
4. Have the child lie supine, and hold the plantar surface of the heel in hand while pushing the heel down into the hand as though to elongate the leg.
5. Have the child lie supine and resist hip and knee flexion with resistance given at the thigh while the other hand is holding the dorsum of the foot.
6. Have the child alternately stand up and sit down, modifying the height of the seat as needed.

Source: Adapted with permission from RB Shepherd, *Physiotherapy for Pediatrics*, p. 190, © 1995, Butterworth-Heinemann.

REFERENCES

ASSESSMENT

Ada L, Canning C. Anticipating and avoiding muscle shortening. In: Ada L, Canning C, eds. *Key Issues in Neurological Physiotherapy*. Oxford, England: Butterworth-Heinemann; 1990:219–236.

Kendall FP, McCreary EK. *Muscle testing and function*. 4th ed. Baltimore, Md: Williams & Wilkins; 1993.

Moseley A, Adams R. Measurement of passive ankle dorsiflexion: procedure and reliability. *Australian Journal of Physiotherapy*. 1991;37:175–181.

Babaniyi OA, Yeya-Agba B, Parakoyi DB. Monitoring impact of oral poliovirus vaccine on poliomyelitis trends from physiotherapy records, Ilorin, Nigeria, 1981–1988. *East African Medical Journal*. 1991;68:642–648. (statistical data only)

Dean E, Agboatwalla M, Dallimore M, Habib A, Akram D. Poliomyelitis, part 1: an old problem revisited. *Physiotherapy*. 1995;81:17–22.

Dean E, Agboatwalla M, Dallimore M, Habib A, Arkam D. Poliomyelitis, part 2: revised principles of management. *Physiotherapy*. 1995;81:22–28.

Miles M. Monitoring polio trends from physiotherapy records: independent sentinel surveillance in Pakistan. *Tropical Doctor*. 1989;19:1:3–5. (statistical data only)

Shepherd RB. Infections of the nervous system. In: Shepherd RB, ed. *Physiotherapy in Paediatrics*. 3rd ed. Oxford, England: Butterworth-Heinemann; 1995:185–195.

Premature and Lower Birth Weight Infants

DESCRIPTION

Any infant born before 37 weeks gestation. Current frames of reference for treatment are based on Als et al's synactive model of infant behavior, which is based on four subsystems in a hierarchical pattern progressing from autonomic to motor, to state, to attentional/interactive (see box).

Synactive Theory of Neurobehavioral Organization

Autonomic Level: Digestion, heart rate, respiration, and temperature control/regulation. Example: an infant struggling to maintain cardiopulmonary homeostasis cannot maintain an alert state or interact with the environment.

Motor Level: Activity and movement of the extremities, head, and trunk; posture; and tone. Example: active movements can contribute to instability of the autonomic system.

State Level: Behavioral/mood range of states available to the infant, the transition from one state to another, and the clear definition or differentiation of states. Example: ability to change quickly from stress reaction to calmness indicates a better adaptive response.

Attention/Interaction Level: Ability to assume and maintain an alert state and to take in and respond appropriately to environmental input, including social, cognitive, and emo-

---

tional input. Example: long intervals of attending/interacting behavior indicate a better adaptive response.

Source: Data from H Als, BM Better, EZ Tronick, and TB Brazelton, in *Theory and Research in Behavioral Pediatrics*, H Fitzgerald, et al, © 1982, 1985 Plenum Publishing Company.

CAUSE

In most cases, the cause of premature labor or premature rupture of the membranes followed by premature labor is unknown. Many maternal histories show low socioeconomic status, inadequate prenatal medical care, poor nutrition, poor education, unwed state, and intercurrent, untreated illness or infection.

ASSESSMENT

Areas
- Gestational/postconceptual age
- Range of motion (ROM): note existence of flexion contractures
- Functional ability
- State of arousal: irritability, consolability
- Sensorimotor skills: head and trunk control, oral-motor skills, visual orientation, auditory orientation
- Neurological
- Cardiorespiratory
- Postural alignment
- Skin and soft tissue

Instruments/Procedures (See References for Sources)
- Chart review, especially Apgar scores (see box)

The Apgar Score

Clinical Feature	Score 0	Score 1	Score 2
Heart rate	0 (absent)	<100 (slow)	>100
Respiration	Absent	Gasping, slow, or irregular	Regular or crying lustily
Color of trunk	White, pale	Blue	Pink
Muscle tone	Limp, flaccid	Diminished	Normal, active
Response to oral suction	Nil	Grimace	Cough

Total score: 0–3 = severe distress, 4–6 = moderate difficulty, 7–10 = absence of stress.

Source: Reprinted with permission from V Apgar, Proposal for New Method of Evaluation of Newborn Infant, *Anesthesia and Analgesia*, Vol. 32, p. 269, Williams & Wilkins.

- Clinical Assessment of Gestational Age of the Newborn Infant
- Milani-Comparetti Motor Development Screening Test
- Morgan Neonatal Neurobehavioral Examination
- Movement Assessment of Infants (MAI)
- Neonatal Behavioral Assessment Scale
- Neurological Assessments

PROBLEMS
- There is global hypotonia, with the level depending on the degree of prematurity due to lack of neuromuscular development.
- There is limited active ROM, related to degree of prematurity due to lack of neuromuscular development.
- Typical postural position is extension and abduction with decreased flexor patterns and midline orientation due to lack of time in the uterus in a compacted position, which normally produces physiologic flexion.
- Muscle weakness, especially in antigravity movements, tends to add to the appearance of extension and abduction postures.
- Muscle imbalance between extensor and flexor groups is related to lack of development of flexor tone to offset the already developed extensor tone.
- There is difficulty with midrange control postures—for example, maintaining the head in alignment with the body and bringing the hands together at midline—due to lack of muscle balance.
- Primitive reflexes may be absent, reduced, or inconsistent due to lack of development of the neuromuscular system.
- Spontaneous movement may be minimal due to lack of neuromuscular development.
- If there is ventilator dependence, infants may show increased hypertension of neck, scapular elevation, shoulder retraction, arching of the trunk, and immobility of the pelvis.

TREATMENT/MANAGEMENT
Treatment and management are based on the rationale that passive movement and stimulation by the therapist can strengthen movement and speed development of tone and automatic movement patterns in the infant; that positioning in midrange can facilitate movement while reducing undesirable tone and preventing malformation; that an altered state is necessary for the infant to benefit from treatment; and that pelvic tilt is the basis for trunk and head control.

ROM
- Move joints through full-ROM exercise and proprioceptive input. Note abnormal tone or contractures, and make specific effort to range such joints. If pain is noted, joint pathology is present and should be referred for medical assessment.

Positioning
- Swaddling the infant inside a blanket with legs and arms flexed provides external stability and reduces sensory input, thereby improving feeding and visual skills.
- Rolled linens can be used to support proximal joints in 30 degrees of flexion with the head in midline.
- When the infant is in supine position, place rolls under the back to support the arms in shoulder flexion and under the knees to keep the hips and knees flexed but not laterally rotated.

- When the infant is in side-lying position, place rolls in front of the infant to increase flexion and a second roll behind the infant to prevent extension.

Arousal
- Gently pat the infant on the back, or flex the lower extremities and rock the pelvis gently to arouse the infant from states I or II (see box for state definitions).
- Add auditory input (talking) as the infant begins to awaken.
- States III and IV are optimal for motor, visual, and auditory skills. Use stimulation to bring the infant into these states, and stop when the infant can no longer maintain states IV or V.

States of Arousal and Their Defining Signs

State I. Deep Sleep
- regular breathing
- eyes closed
- no spontaneous activity
- no eye movements

State II. Light Sleep
- eyes closed
- rapid eye movements
- irregular respiration

State III. Drowsy
- semidozing
- eyes open or closed
- activity variable
- movements usually smooth

State IV. Alert 1
- bright look in eyes
- minimal motor activity

State V. Alert 2
- bright look in eyes
- considerable motor activity

State VI. Crying

Source: Adapted with permission from J Bezner, and H Rogers, *Physical Therapy Protocols: Guidelines for Rehabilitation*, pp. 167–177, © 1995, Therapy Skills Builders.

Reflex Facilitation
- Use proprioceptive placing, palmar grasp, and traction to increase upper extremity flexion.
- Use proprioceptive placing, inversion, plantar grasp, and flexor withdrawal to increase lower extremity flexion.
- Use crossed extension anteversion reflexes to facilitate lower extremity extension.
- Use the umbilical reflex to facilitate abdominal and hip flexion.
- Use Galant, rooting, and neonatal positive supporting reflexes to facilitate trunk extension.
- Use the asymmetric tonic neck reflex to facilitate flexion and extension of all extremities: head position must be alternated in both directions to balance tone.

- Use the suck-swallow and rooting reflexes to strengthen oral-motor skills to improve feeding.
- Use the finger-sequencing and avoidance reflexes to develop finger extension, but only after flexor tone is established.
- Gently rock the pelvis anteriorly and posteriorly, and stimulate reflexes to encourage active flexion and extension.

Head Control
- Begin with the gravity-eliminated position, using stimulation to the anterior neck muscles to promote neck flexion.
- Continue with the gravity-eliminated position, using stroking of the posterior neck musculature and anterior pelvic tilt to facilitate neck and upper trunk extension.
- Watch for good upper trunk extension, not just extension of the neck.
- Flexor tone and anterior pelvic tilt are considered prerequisites to the development of voluntary neck extension.

Visual and Auditory Orientation
- Begin with the infant about 12 inches away from your face.
- While continuing to talk to the infant, move slowly away from the infant's midline.
- Eliminate as much extraneous input as possible to allow the infant to attend to your stimulation.

Sensory Accommodation
- Proprioceptive and vestibular awareness and response develop early in utero and usually are tolerated well from birth. Positioning and rocking are useful stimuli.
- Tactile and visual awareness and response are considered to develop later and should be introduced after the infant is able to tolerate proprioceptive and vestibular input. Holding, stroking, and looking at faces are useful stimuli.
- Auditory awareness and response are considered to be intermediate. Talking and singing are useful stimuli.

Parent Education
- Teach parents or caregivers handling techniques. Show them, then let them practice with consultation from you.
- Provide a written home program as soon as the parents are ready to assume responsibility for interacting with and caring for the infant.

PRECAUTIONS/CONTRAINDICATIONS

Handling
- Infants should not be handled within 1 hour after gavage or oral feeding; usually between the second or third hour is acceptable.
- Infants on continuous drip feeding generally can be handled at any time.
- Therapy should be avoided immediately after other treatment.

Minimal Stimulation
- The caution of minimal stimulation generally means the infant is unstable and responds poorly to handling. Check with nursing staff prior to assessment.

Oxygen Saturation
- Hypoxia can lead to an intraventricular hemorrhage; stop handling the infant if oxygen saturation cannot be maintained above 80%.

Sensory Overload
The following are signs of overload, which should be avoided:
- color fluctuation, such as pallor, mottling, cyanosis around the mouth, duskiness, or plethora (overfilling of blood vessels)
- cardiorespiratory alteration, such as irregular respiration, hiccups, tachypnea (abnormally rapid rate of breathing), apnea, or bradycardia (slow heart rate)
- motility symptoms such as stiffness of limbs, increased startling or jerky limb movements, regurgitation, or hypotonia
- attentional symptoms such as staring, gaze aversion, fussing, or crying

Knee-to-Chest Position
- Avoid holding the infant in the knee-to-chest position to decrease the chance of raising blood pressure and decreasing oxygen saturation.

Hyperextension or Hyperflexion of the Neck
- Avoid either position; either can occlude the infant's airway.

Heat Loss
- Avoid loss of heat, which can reduce growth and weight gain.

Central and Peripheral Lines
- Lines should be handled with care, since the infant may be dependent on them for long periods of time.

Chest Tubes
- Precautions with chest tubes should be obtained from the physician or nursing staff.

Arousal
- In general, premature infants are more difficult to arouse and calm due to their lack of ability to modulate behavior and use protective responses.
- Avoid suddenly rolling or picking up sleeping infants because the sudden movement may startle them, making it difficult to calm them down.

Moro Reflex
- Avoid using the Moro reflex to facilitate phasic and tonic muscle contractions because it tends to agitate infants.

Lights and Noise
- Avoid bright lights and loud noises, which may cause the infant to shut down and avoid all sensory input.

DESIRED OUTCOME/PROGNOSIS
- ROM will be within normal range for age, corrected for prematurity, and there will be no contractures.
- Reflex development will be within normal range for age, corrected for prematurity.
- Response to sensory stimulation will be within normal range for age, corrected for prematurity.

- The infant's ability to modulate behavior state to calm self and alert self will be within normal range for age, corrected for prematurity.
- Motor control of stability and movement patterns will be within normal range for age, corrected for prematurity.
- The parents will be able to follow the home program independently.

REFERENCES

ASSESSMENT

Ashton B, Piper MC, Warren S, Stewin L, Byrne P. Influence of medical history on assessment of at risk infants. *Developmental Medicine and Child Neurology.* 1991;33:412–418.

Mandich M, Simons CJ, Ritchie S, Schmidt D, Mullett M. Motor development, infantile reactions and postural responses of preterm, at risk infants. *Developmental Medicine and Child Neurology.* 1994;36:397–405.

Clinical Assessment of Gestational Age of the Newborn Infant

Dubowitz LMS, Dubowitz V, Goldberg C. Clinical assessment of gestational age in the newborn infant. *Journal of Pediatrics.* 1970; 77:1–10.

Milani–Comparetti Motor Development Screening Test

Stuberg WA, White PJ, Miedaner JA, Dehne PR. Item reliability of the Milani–Comparetti Motor Development Screening Test. *Physical Therapy.* 1989;69:328–335.

White PJ, Miedaner JA, Dehne PA, et al. *Milani—Comparetti Motor Development Screening Test.* 3rd ed. Omaha, Neb: University of Nebraska Medical Center; 1992.

Morgan Neonatal Neurobehavioral Examination

Morgan A. *Morgan Neonatal Neurobehavioral Examination.* In: Tecklin JS, ed. *Pediatric Physical Therapy.* Philadelphia, Pa: JB Lippincott Co; 1994:71–73.

Movement Assessment of Infants (MAI)

Chandler LS, Andrews MS, Swanson MW. *Movement Assessment of Infants.* Rolling Bay, Wash: Infant Development Center; 1980.

Neonatal Behavioral Assessment Scale

Brazelton TB. Clinics in Developmental Medicine. *Neonatal Behavioral Assessment Scale.* 2nd ed. Philadelphia, Pa: JB Lippincott Co; 1984:88.

Neurological Assessments

Andre-Thomas CY, Saint-Anne Dargassies S. Little Club Clinics in Developmental Medicine. *Neurological Examination of the Infant.* London, England: National Spastics Society; 1960:1.

Dubowitz L. Neurological assessment of the full-term and preterm newborn infant. In: Harel S, Anastastiow N, eds. *The At-Risk Infant.* Baltimore, Md: Paul H Brooks; 1985:185–196.

Prechtl H. Clinics in Developmental Medicine. *Neurological Assessment of the Full-Term Newborn Infant.* 2nd ed. Philadelphia, Pa: JB Lippincott Co; 1977:77.

TREATMENT

Bartlett D, Piper MC. Neuromotor development of preterm infants through the first year of life: implications for physical and occupational therapists. *Physical and Occupational Therapy in Pediatrics.* 1993;12:4:37–55.

Bezner J, Rogers H. Premature baby protocol. In: *Physical Therapy Protocols: Guidelines for Rehabilitation*. Tucson, Ariz: Therapy Skill Builders; 1995:165–177.

Crane LD. Physical therapy for the neonate with respiratory disease. In: Irwin S, Tecklin JS, eds. *Cardiopulmonary Physical Therapy*. St Louis, Mo: CV Mosby Co; 1995:486–515.

Downs JA, Edwards AD, McCormick DC, Roth SC, Stewart AL. Effect of intervention on development of hip posture in very preterm babies. *Archives of Disease in Childhood*. 1991;66:797–801.

Eigsti H, Aretz M, Shannon L. Pediatric physical therapy in a rehabilitation setting. *Pediatrician*. 1990;17:267–277.

Harris MB, Simons CJR, Ritchie SK, Mullett MD, Myerberg DZ. Joint range of motion development in premature infants. *Pediatric Physical Therapy*. 1991;2:185–191.

Heriza CB. Implications of a dynamical systems approach to understanding infant kicking behavior. *Physical Therapy*. 1991;71: 222–235.

Jonkey BW, Bolava DG. Model for physical therapy in the NICU. *Journal of Perinatology*. 1990;10:185–187.

Kelly MK, Palisano RJ, Wolfson MR. Effect of a development physical therapy program on oxygen saturation and heart rate in preterm infants. *Physical Therapy*. 1989;69:467–474; comment, 69:988–989.

Maier CL. Developmental program for neonates questioned. *Physical Therapy*. 1989;69:988–989. Comment, letter.

Paratz J, Burns Y. Intracranial dynamics in pre-term infants and neonates: implications for physiotherapists. *Australian Journal of Physiotherapy*. 1993;39, 171–178.

Parker A. Expert handling. *Nursing Times*. 1990;86:35–37.

Parker A. Neonatal problems and the neonatal unit. In: Eckersley PM, ed. *Elements of Paediatric Physiotherapy*. New York, NY: Churchill Livingstone; 1995:79–96.

Portela ALM. Massage as a stimulation technique for premature infants: an annotated bibliography. *Pediatric Physical Therapy*. 1990;2:2:80–86.

Rothberg AD, Goodman M, Jacklin LA, Cooper PA. Six-year follow-up of early physiotherapy intervention in very low birth weight infants. *Pediatrics*. 1991;88:547–552.

Sheahan MS, Brockway NF. The high-risk infant. In: Tecklin JS, ed. *Pediatric Physical Therapy*. 2nd ed. Philadelphia, Pa: JB Lippincott Co; 1994:56–88.

Turnbull JD. Early intervention for children with or at risk of cerebral palsy. *American Journal of Diseases of Children*. 1993;147:1:54–59. Comment.

Unwin JF. Long-term sequelae of bronchopulmonary dysplasia: a review of the literature. *Physiotherapy*. 1993;79:633–636.

Reflex Sympathetic Dystrophy in Children

Also known as Sudeck's atrophy, minor causalgia, post-traumatic neuralgia, shoulder-hand syndrome, reflex neurovascular dystrophy, and causalgia.

DESCRIPTION

Reflex sympathetic dystrophy (RSD) is a disorder characterized by pain in an extremity associated with autonomic dysfunction that occurs following injury to bone and soft tissue. It is most characterized by nonprotective, nonfunctional pain. The system that monitors and modulates pain is dysfunctional, interpreting signals for skin and joint receptors incorrectly and thereby inhibiting normal function. The disorder was first described in 1864 by Silas Mitchell, a neurologist. RSD is rare before age 8 and is more common in girls than boys.

CAUSE

The factors that trigger the autonomic dysfunction are unknown, although the syndrome usually occurs secondary to a preexisting condition related to trauma or surgery to the lower extremities. Disagreement continues as to whether RSD is caused by dysfunction of the sympathetic system or if increased sympathetic tone is due to altered pain responses.

ASSESSMENT

Areas General (See Boxes for Specific Criteria and Stages)

- Pain: degree, duration, inciting event
- Skin and soft tissue: skin color changes, especially dependent rubor and mottling; skin temperature changes; altered degree of perspiration or sweating; skin texture or appearance changes; edema; hyper- or hyposensitivity to touch
- Hair growth pattern changes
- Range of motion (ROM) limitations

Diagnostic Criteria for Pediatric RSD

1. Pain out of proportion to the inciting event
2. Evidence of neurovascular dysfunction, as manifested by three or more of the following:
   - dependent edema
   - dependent rubor
   - mottling of skin
   - hypersensitivity of skin to light touch
   - skin temperature change
   - altered degree of perspiration
   - changes in patterns of hair growth

Source: Reprinted with permission from RP Stanton et al, Orthopedics, Vol. 16, No. 7, p. 774, © 1993, Slack Inc.

Instruments/Procedures

No specific tests or procedures were named.

PROBLEMS

The following are symptoms and problems of RSD (not all symptoms or problems occur in every child):

- burning pain
- hyperalgesia (increased sensitivity to noxious stimuli)
- allodynia (pain provoked by stimuli not usually considered painful, such as light touch)
- dysesthesia (may be hyperesthesia or hypesthesia)
- paresthesia
- cyanosis, coldness, or dependent rubor of the skin
- mottling
- dependent edema
- altered, increased or decreased, perspiration or sweating

- abnormal or changes in patterns of growth of hair
- diffuse swelling not confined to the vicinity of joints
- atrophy of muscles
- demineralization of bone and osteopenia, seen on radiographs
- contractures (in stages II and III)
- psychological disturbances and emotional dysfunction
- delayed functional recovery

Stages of RSD

Stage I
1. There is localized pain, allodynia, edema, vasomotor spasms, and pain with initiation of movement.
2. Vasomotor spasms are responsible for causing transient, unilateral temperature and color changes in the affected limb.
3. This stage may resolve with intervention or degenerate to stage II.

Stage II
1. Pain becomes more diffuse, constant, and exaggerated.
2. Poor circulation is evident in decreased hair growth, increased edema, and drawn, shiny skin.
3. Muscle wasting becomes more evident, and osteoporosis may be evident on x-ray.
4. Treatment can limit this state, but if it is not provided, the patient may progress to stage III.

Stage III
1. Joints become ankylosed with severe osteoporosis and swelling.
2. Pain may or may not be present.
3. Epiphyseal plate bone growth may be affected.

Source: Adapted with permission from NL Schechter, CB Berde, and M Yaster, *Pain in Infants, Children, and Adolescents*, p. 326, © 1993, Williams & Wilkins.

TREATMENT/MANAGEMENT

No single treatment approach appears to be successful in a majority of cases. Each patient's situation must be determined separately. All of the techniques below have been used successfully in various combinations. Average length of treatment is 9 months according to Stanton et al, "Reflex Sympathetic Dystrophy" (see references). Initially, twice-daily treatments are recommended by Stanton et al. Inpatient and outpatient treatment may be needed.

- transcutaneous electrical nerve stimulation (TENS)
- biofeedback for muscle tension or spasms
- desensitization to tactile stimuli, such as pressure desensitization
- thermal modalities, both heat and cold
- whirlpool
- passive and active ROM exercises to maintain muscle and joint integrity (eg, riding a stationary bicycle)
- neuroaugmentation, including counterirritation (brisk rubbing of the affected part)
- active muscle strengthening

- physical conditioning (aquatic therapy may be useful)
- for lower extremities, progressive weight bearing to maintain proper mineralization of the bones while regaining ambulation skills
- progressive ambulation to retain function
- for tight Achilles tendon, stretching exercises
- possible casting or splinting to regain function
- constant passive motion (CPM) to facilitate motion
- behavior modification, such as rewards for "working hard" in PT
- work with other disciplines and the family to resolve major psychological stresses in child's life, and development of more effective coping mechanisms, such as deep breathing exercises and massage
- work with the family to clarify what they can expect from rehabilitation and physical therapy

PRECAUTIONS/CONTRAINDICATIONS
- Psychological stress is likely to increase the severity of symptoms of RSD.
- Rule out any possible organic cause.
- Avoid use of protective devices, including crutches, splints, and slings. Use these only if they are essential to promote return to functional performance of normal activity.
- The family may resist participation in rehabilitation because they believe that time is needed for the "injury" to heal (organic disease model). Work with family to understand the need for and participation in a rehabilitation model.

DESIRED OUTCOME/PROGNOSIS
   Average length of treatment is 9 months according to Stanton et al, "Reflex Sympathetic Dystrophy" (See references). Initially, twice-daily treatments are recommended by Stanton et al. Inpatient and outpatient treatment may be needed.
- The child will be able to participate in age-appropriate physical activities, including school, physical education, and extracurricular activities.
- The child with lower extremity involvement will progress from no weight bearing to unassisted walking.
- The child will be able to perform all functional skills within age range and remaining capacity if injury has altered performance.

REFERENCES

Allen J, Jedlinsky BR, Wilson TL, McCarthy CF. In: Schechter NL, Gerde CB, Yaster M, eds. *Pain in Infants, Children, and Adolescents*. Baltimore, Md: Williams & Wilkins; 1993:317–329.

Kesler RW, Saulsbury FT, Miller LT, Rowlingston JC. Reflex sympathetic dystrophy in children: treatment with transcutaneous electric nerve stimulation. *Pediatrics*. 1988;82:728–732.

Stanton RP, Malcolm JR, Wesdock KA, Singsen BH. Reflex sympathetic dystrophy in children: an orthopedic perspective. *Orthopedics*. 1993;16:773–779.

Wilder RT, Berde CB, Wolohan M, Vieyra MA, Masek BJ, Micheli LJ. Reflex sympathetic dystrophy in children. Clinical characteristics and follow-up of seventy patients. *Journal of Bone and Joint Surgery*. 1992;74A:910–919.

Respiratory Disorders in Children

DESCRIPTION

- *Asthma:* See separate chapter.
- *Bronchiectasis:* Irreversible, focal bronchial dilation, usually accompanied by infection. Congenital bronchiectasis is a rare condition in which the lung periphery fails to develop, resulting in cystic dilation of developed bronchi.
- *Bronchiolitis:* An acute viral infection of the lower respiratory tract affecting infants and young children and characterized by respiratory distress, expiratory obstruction, wheezing, and crackles due to the respiratory syncytial virus (RSV), parainfluenza virus, adenovirus, and *Mycoplasma pneumonia.*
- *Bronchopulmonary dysplasia (BPD)* or *respiratory distress syndrome (RDS):* Has four stages: the first corresponds with hyaline membrane disease, and the fourth is consistent with changes seen in chronic lung disease (Crane, "Neonate and Child," p. 671; see references). BPD is a chronic lung disorder in infants who have been treated for respiratory distress with intermittent mandatory ventilation.
- *Congenital central hypoventilation syndrome (CCHS):* Chronic respiratory failure in the absence of primary pulmonary or neuromuscular disease. Hypoventilation occurs when the volume of air that enters the alveoli and takes part in gas exchanges is not adequate for the metabolic needs of the body.
- *Cystic fibrosis:* See separate chapter.
- *Diaphragmatic hernia:* Protrusion of abdominal contents into the thorax through a defect in the diaphragm, usually occurring on the left side and in the posterolateral portion.
- *Esophageal atresia* and *tracheoesophageal fistula (TE):* Most commonly a fistula from near the carina of the trachea to the lower esophageal segment.
- *Gastroesophageal reflux (GER):* Reflux of gastric contents into the esophagus. The presence of GER indicates incompetence of the lower esophageal sphincter.
- *Idiopathic or infant respiratory distress syndrome (IRDS)* or *hyaline membrane disease (HMD):* Inadequate level of pulmonary surfactant is available to stabilize terminal air spaces by decreasing alveolar surface tension, causing alveolar collapse (Crane, "Neonate and Child," p. 669; see references).
- *Iatrogenic infection:* Can cause apnea, cyanosis, bradycardia, retractions, vomiting, difficulty feeding, and unstable temperature (Crane, "Physical Therapy," p. 492; see references).
- *Immotile cilia syndrome (ICS)* or *primary ciliary dyskinesia:* Infant is prone to upper and lower airway infection because of ciliary immotility due to absence of dyneine arms in the ciliary microstructure (Crane, "Physical Therapy," p. 673; see references). The disorder is a rare, inherited (autosomal recessive) condition (Parker, "Pediatrics," p. 307; see references).
- *Inhaled foreign body:* Inhaled object may cause widespread inflammation (Barstow, "Respiratory Conditions," p. 104; see references).
- *Meconium-aspiration syndrome (MAS):* Aspiration of meconium that has entered the amniotic sac, leading to a chemical pneumonitis and mechanical obstruction of bronchi.
- *Mikity–Wilson syndrome (MW)* or *pulmonary dysmaturity:* Occurs in very premature infants and is believed to be associated with unequal distribution of ventilation in the immature lung (Crane, "Physical Therapy," p. 492; see references).
- *Neonatal pneumonia:* Caused by group B streptococcus and *Hemophilus influenza* and mimics HMD in clinical presentation (Crane, "Neonate and Child," p. 670; see references).

- *Subglottic and bronchial stenosis:* Associated with prolonged intubation and frequent endotracheal suctioning; the narrowing can result in mild or pronounced upper airway obstruction (Crane, "Physical Therapy," p. 492; see references).
- *Transient tachypnea:* Associated with delayed clearance of amniotic fluid from the lungs (Crane, "Neonate and Child," p. 671; see references).
- *Tracheoesophageal fistula:* see *esophageal atresia,* above.
- *Tracheostomy:* Surgical opening in the trachea to facilitate breathing.
- *Whooping cough (pertussis):* Infection may cause necrosis of the surface epithelium of the respiratory tract, which becomes covered by thick mucopurulent exudate (Barstow, "Respiratory Conditions," p. 105; see references).

CAUSE

Respiratory failure can be due to central nervous system disorders, intrinsic muscle disease, intrinsic cardiac or pulmonary disease, or congenital airway abnormalities. Respiratory failure is associated with preterm delivery, low birth weight, perinatal problems such as asphyxia or meconium aspiration, and congenital abnormalities.

ASSESSMENT

Areas

- Chart history (Crane, "Physical Therapy," p. 495; see references).
  1. Complete history of labor and delivery
  2. Assessment of infant, including Apgar scores and Dubowitz gestational age scores
  3. Clinical course of infant from birth to present
  4. History of respiratory distress and use of oxygen and ventilation assistance provided since birth
  5. Arterial blood gas history
  6. Report on previous chest radiographs
  7. Mode and frequency of nutrition and feedings
  8. Physician orders
- Central nervous system: coma, headache, irritability, papilledema, restlessness, seizures
- Cardiac: bradycardia, cardiac arrest, hypertension, hypotension, tachycardia
- Respiratory
  1. Altered depth and pattern of respiration (deep, shallow, apnea, or irregular)
  2. Barrel-shaped thoracic cage—result of hyperinflation and air trapping within the lung
  3. Chest wall retractions or recession—the sternum and ribs are severely pulled into the thorax
  4. Cyanosis—unreliable sign because it depends on the relative amount and type of hemoglobin in the blood and adequacy of peripheral circulation; use only in combination with other signs
  5. Decreased or absent breath sounds
  6. Expiratory grunting—noise made by breathing out against a partially closed glottis
  7. Head bobbling—attempt to use sternocleidomastoid and scalene muscles as accessory muscles of respiration; occurs because infant is not strong enough to stabilize head to prevent the movement
  8. Nasal flaring—dilation of the nostrils by the dilatores naris muscle
  9. Neck extension—extension of neck lessens airway resistance, but overextension may collapse trachea

10. Pallor—sign may indicate hypoxemia or other problems such as anemia; use only in combination with other signs
11. Stridor—harsh sound made when there is partial obstruction of the upper trachea and/or larynx
12. Tachypnea—respiratory rates greater than or equal to 60 breaths/min (normal is 35–40 breaths/min)
13. Wheezing or prolonged expiration

- Excessive sweating
- State: fatigue; quiet alertness; sits but does not play
- Reluctance of feed—needing to take frequent pauses from sucking because of tachypnea
- Primitive reflexes
- Muscle tone
- Limb movements and postures
- Sucking and swallowing
- Deep tendon reflexes
- Behavior: irritability, agitation
- Joint range of motion (ROM)

Instruments/Procedures
- Auscultation—head should be in midline position
- Chest palpation—limited to palpating for the position of the mediastinum for subcutaneous emphysema, edema, or rib fracture
- Mediate percussion—limited to using one finger directly on the chest to check for presence of pneumothoraces, diaphragmatic hernia, enlarged liver and masses

PROBLEMS
Problems may be present in the following areas: handling (handling a severely ill infant causes the condition to deteriorate)
- parent-infant bonding
- periventricular hemorrhage
- periventricular leucomalacia
- temperature control
- infection
- jaundice
- feeding difficulties
- delayed development
- failure to thrive

TREATMENT/MANAGEMENT
The following treatments may be helpful:
- chest percussion
- vibration and shaking
- postural drainage (gravity-assisted positioning)
- manual hyperinflation
- breathing exercises
- coughing
- suction

- ventilation
- positional rotation—frequent changes of position to help avoid or treat pooling of secretions by preventing the prolonged dependency of one portion of the lung; side-lying and supine positions are used, but not prone

PRECAUTIONS/CONTRAINDICATIONS
- Generally, the child should not be treated prior to feeding or for at least 1 hour following feed to avoid aspiration.
- Use percussion cautiously with infants who have rickets, osteoporosis, softening of bones, or deformities to avoid breaking ribs.
- Do not use percussion or vibration on infants with extremely thin skin that can be easily bruised or damaged.
- Vibrations during expiration should not be continued beyond functional residual capacity.
- In positioning, watch for signs of rapid deterioration if the affected area of thorax is positioned up (on top) during side-lying.
- Infant with raised intracranial pressure or at risk for periventricular hemorrhage should never be tipped head down.
- Infants with abdominal distention do not tolerate the head-down position because their diaphragm cannot work effectively.
- Newborns are better oxygenated when tilted slightly head up.
- Medically unstable infants should not have their position changed.
- Manual hyperinflation should be used only with extreme care with children who have hyperinflation conditions (asthma, bronchiolitis) because infants lack the alveolar and bronchiolar connect channels; thus air will not diffuse from inflated to collapsed alveoli, and a pneumothorax could result.
- The therapist must work around equipment that limits access to the infant. Equipment may include endotracheal tubes, nasopharyngeal tube (nasal prong), incubators, radiant warmers, headboxes, humidifiers, phototherapy units, transcutaneous oxygen monitors, electrocardiogram, respiratory and blood pressure monitors, and transcutaneous carbon dioxide monitors.

DESIRED OUTCOME/PROGNOSIS
- The child will be able to breathe without assistance of suctioning, percussion, vibration, drainage, or special positioning performed by therapists.
- The parents will be able to manage the child's care at home.
- The child will be able to perform age-appropriate developmental skills, corrected for prematurity, if necessary.
- The child will be able to perform functional skills appropriate for his or her age.

REFERENCES
Andersen JB, Falk M. Chest physiotherapy in the pediatric age group. *Respiratory Care*. 1991;36:546–554.

Barstow V. Respiratory conditions and cardiothoracic disorders. In: Eckersley PM, ed. *Elements of Paediatric Physiotherapy*. New York, NY: Churchill Livingstone; 1993:97–114.

Cheng M, Williams PD. Oxygenation during chest physiotherapy of very-low-birth-weight infants: relations among fraction of inspired oxygen levels, number of hand ventilizations, and transcutaneous oxygen pressure. *Journal of Pediatric Nursing: Nursing Care of Children and Families*. 1989;4:411–418.

Crane LD. The neonate and child. In: Frownfelter DL, ed. *Chest Physical Therapy and Pulmonary Rehabilitation: An Interdisciplinary Approach*. 2nd ed. Chicago, Ill: Year Book Medical Publisher; 1987:666–697.

Crane LD. Physical therapy for the neonate with respiratory disease. In: Irwin S, Tecklin JS, eds. *Cardiopulmonary Physical Therapy*. 3rd ed. St Louis, Mo: CV Mosby Co; 1995:486–515.

Darbee J, Cerny F. Exercise testing and exercise conditioning for children with lung dysfunction. In: Irwin S, Tecklin JS, eds. *Cardiopulmonary Physical Therapy*. 3rd ed. St. Louis, Mo: CV Mosby Co: 1995:563–578.

DeCesare JA, Graybill-Tucker CA, Gould AL. Physical therapy for the child with respiratory dysfunction. In: Irwin S, Tecklin JS, eds. *Cardiopulmonary Physical Therapy*. St. Louis, Mo: CV Mosby Co: 1995:516–562.

Eid N, Buchheit J, Neurling M, Phelps H. Chest physiotherapy in review. *Respiratory Care*. 1991;36:270–282.

Eigsti H, Aretz M, Shannon L. Pediatric physical therapy in a rehabilitation setting. *Pediatrician*. 1990;17:267–277.

Fitzpatrick MP, Bullock MI, Tudehope DI. Chest physiotherapy for intubated infants with hyaline membrane disease. *New Zealand Journal of Physiotherapy*. 1988:16:2:15–18.

Kelly MK. Children with ventilator dependence. In: Campbell SK, ed. *Physical Therapy for Children*. Philadelphia, Pa: WB Saunders Co; 1994:669–671.

Parker A. Paediatrics. In: Webber BA, Pryor JA, eds. *Physiotherapy for Respiratory and Cardiac Problems*. New York, NY: Churchill Livingstone; 1993:281–318.

Shepherd RB. Respiratory disorders in childhood. In: Shepherd RB, *Physiotherapy in Paediatrics*. 3rd ed. Oxford, England: Butterworth-Heinemann; 1995:350–362.

Shepherd RB. Respiratory disorders in the neonatal period and infancy. In: Shepherd RB, *Physiotherapy in Paediatrics*. 3rd ed. Oxford, England: Butterworth-Heinemann; 1995:344–349.

Tecklin JS. Pulmonary disorders in infants and children and their physical therapy management. In: Tecklin JS, ed. *Pediatric Physical Therapy*. 2nd ed. Philadelphia, Pa: JB Lippincott Co; 1994:249–285.

Webber BA, Pryor JA. Bronchiectasis, primary ciliary dyskinesia and cystic fibrosis. In: Webber BA, Pryor JA, eds. *Physiotherapy for Respiratory and Cardiac Problems*. New York, NY: Churchill Livingstone; 1993:399–417.

Rett Syndrome

DESCRIPTION

Rett syndrome is a neurological disorder found exclusively in females. It was first described in 1966 by Andreas Rett, a pediatrician, in the German medical literature, but the article was not translated into English until 1977. The course of the syndrome has been divided into four stages. The Early Onset Stagnation State begins between 6 and 18 months, when developmental arrest and delay occurs. In the second stage, called the Rapid Destruction Stage, which occurs between 1 and 4 years, marked developmental deterioration occurs. During the third stage, called the Pseudostationary Stage, which can last for several years, some "progress" may occur, especially in the psychosocial areas. During the fourth stage, called the Late Motor Deterioration Stage, there is marked loss of neuromotor skills, and malnutrition often occurs.

CAUSE

Genetic factors are implicated because girls are exclusively affected, but the exact cause is not known, and no biological marker has been identified. Possible causes are a fragile site on the X chromosome or possibly an X-chromosome dominant mutation.

ASSESSMENT

Areas
- Neuromotor developmental level
- Muscle tone
- Motor control
- Reflex testing
- Gross motor development level
- Fine motor development level—hand skills and functions
- Mobility and ambulation skills
- Functional range of motion (ROM)
- Oral-motor/feeding skills
- Sensory and perceptual skills
- General cognitive skills
- General social skills

Instruments/Procedures
No specific instruments or procedures were identified.

PROBLEMS

Muscle Tone
- There is hypotonia in infancy that changes to hypertonia.
- There are muscle tone abnormalities.
- There is dystonia.
- There is spasticity, especially in the gastrocnemius-soleus muscles.
- There is clonus.

Gross Motor Skills
- There may be a loss of acquired skills as spasticity and apraxia increase.
- Motor apraxia, especially in initiating movement, may seem blocked.
- There may be a loss of transitional movements—rolling, coming to sitting position, coming to standing, and transferring weight.

Motor Control
- There is choreoathetosis.
- There is a progression from hyperkinesia to bradykinesia with age.
- Reaction time is slow.
- Decreased postural stability leads to compensatory increased tone, resulting in abnormal movement patterns.
- Righting reactions and equilibrium responses are retained but may be so slow, and the range so decreased, that the reactions and responses, such as protective extension, become ineffective.

ROM
- Loss of lateral rotation in the trunk may be related to voluntary rigidity of the spine.

Hand Skills
- Stereotypical hand movements (clapping, wringing, clenching) are involuntary and increase with intent.

- There is a loss of purposeful hand movements (reach, grasp, manipulation, and release).
- The child may substitute head, elbow, or foot for loss of hand movement and control.

Spinal Deformities
- Kyphosis may be present.
- Scoliosis may be present.
- Voluntary spinal rigidity may be compensatory for loss of truncal/axial stability.

Mobility and Gait
- There is a loss of functional mobility related to spasticity, ataxia, apraxia, and compensatory spinal rigidity.
- Loss of ambulation skills may be due to loss of ability to shift weight from one foot to the other.
- There may be toe walking.
- There may be ataxia.
- The child may rely on a compensatory wide base of support.
- Weight shift may be achieved by lateral rocking while trunk rotation disappears.
- Asymmetries may develop, such as one leg's being stiffer or weaker.
- Rocking on feet may occur, with one foot forward and other behind.
- Stepping may occur by bringing one foot up to the other but never past. Only one foot is moved forward.

Perceptual Skills
- Spatial disorientation in upright position may cause leaning backward, forward, or laterally.
- Spatial awareness, proprioception, and kinesthetic senses may be dysfunctional.

Oral-Motor Skills
- There may be regression in feeding skills.
- There may be drooling and involuntary rhythmic tongue movements and deviation.

Behavioral Changes
- The child may show withdrawal and autisticlike behavior.
- The child may show minimal variability in facial expression.
- Behavioral changes may be related to dementia and retardation.
- The child may hyperventilate or grind teeth under pressure to perform.
- Agitation and resistance may occur when the child is being moved.

Other
- The child may have seizures.
- The child may have sleep and breathing abnormalities.
- The child may have foot deformities.

TREATMENT/MANAGEMENT
- Develop, maintain, or regain ambulation skills. Walking (independent or with assistance) should be encouraged.
  1. Use neurodevelopmental framework for younger girls.
  2. For older girls, working on isolated skills may be more successful.

3. Provide slow, firm, graded assistance to perform movements to diminish anxiety and reduce resistance.
4. Maintain close physical contact to provide security and guidance.
5. Give verbal direction, encouragement, and reinforcement.
6. Wait for a response. A very long latency is to be expected—up to 60 seconds or more.
7. Reward partial response.
8. Be aware that cognitive disability/dementia may result in failure to understand directions and requests for action.
- Develop, maintain, or regain transition skills, including rolling to prone, getting to a sitting position, pulling to stand, and shifting weight.
  1. Use of a large therapy ball may facilitate getting to prone position, leaning forward, shifting weight, and experiencing the upright position. A small bench seat may also be used to promote hip flexion.
- Elicit righting and equilibrium responses, using a large therapy ball on which the child can sit while the therapist controls the speed, direction, duration, and excursion of the movements.
- Gait symmetry may be improved by changing the stride position and putting the nonpreferred leg first.
- Prevent or reduce deformities.
  1. For scoliosis, use tone reduction activities: gentle lengthening of the concave side and activation of the convex side through elicitation of equilibrium reactions. Have the child lie on the concave side.
- Alleviate discomfort and irritability when the child is moving or being moved. Provide passive and active motions, especially in spinal flexion, hip rotation, and knee flexion.
- Improve independence.
- Use of rhythmic, repetitive music may be helpful in controlling the stereotypic movements and facilitating voluntary movement.
- Use techniques or behaviors that are incompatible or that compete with the stereotypic movements, such as placement in prone position, use of elbow splints, use of a walker, or holding one hand.

PRECAUTIONS/CONTRAINDICATIONS
- Do not use aversive consequences in attempts to alter stereotypical hand movements. The movements are involuntary and not attempts at self-stimulation. Since the movements are not under voluntary control, behavior modification cannot be expected to be effective.

DESIRED OUTCOME/PROGNOSIS
Rett syndrome is a fatal disease. Desired outcomes relate to improving and maintaining psychomotor skills as long as possible.

REFERENCES

Hanks SB. Motor disabilities in the Rett syndrome and physical therapy strategies. *Brain and Development.* 1990;12:157–161.

Stewart KB, Brady DK, Crowe TK, Naganuma GM. Rett syndrome: a literature review and survey of parents and therapists. *Physical and Occupational Therapy.* 1989;9:3:35–55.

Tuten H, Miedaner J. Effect of hand splints on stereotypic hand behavior of girls with Rett syndrome: a replication study. *Physical Therapy.* 1989;69:1099–1103.

Scoliosis

DESCRIPTION

Scoliosis is a structural lateral curvature of the spine. It is more common in girls than boys. Idiopathic scoliosis is the most common. It is usually diagnosed during pre- or early adolescence. Congenital scoliosis is rare. Infantile idiopathic scoliosis is rare in the United States but is more common in England and northern Europe. The juvenile and adolescent idiopathic scoliosis are more common. Disorders associated with scoliosis are leg-length discrepancy, muscular dystrophy, osteogenesis imperfecta, spina bifida, and spinal cord injuries. Scoliosis is classified by magnitude, location, direction, and etiology. A right thoracic curve, idiopathic type, is the most common form in adolescents. The degree of curvature is usually measured using the Cobb system of measurement.

CAUSE

The cause of idiopathic scoliosis is unknown. It is generally considered to be familial, inherited as a multifactorial genetic disorder. Theories regarding the exact mechanism revolve around skeletal growth disturbances or central nervous system dysfunction. Paralytic scoliosis is due to spinal muscle imbalance from a disorder such as poliomyelitis, myelomeningocele, or cerebral palsy. Scoliosis may also be described as functional (due to postural factors) or structural (fixed).

ASSESSMENT

Early detection through school screening programs has been the most successful method of identifying scoliosis in children.

Areas

- Spine: spine position when person bends forward, especially the thoracic and lumbar areas; most common is convex curve to right in thorax and left curve in lumbar region
- Reflexes: presence of asymmetrical tonic neck reflex (ATNR)
- Posture: asymmetries in natural, relaxed standing posture in the anterior, posterior, and lateral views—unequal shoulder level, scapular prominence, uneven waist lines/hip prominence, pelvic asymmetry, unequal distance between arms and body, unequal knee level
- Balance: changes when balance is challenged
- Leg length: real measurement from the anterior superior iliac crest to the medial malleolus and apparent measurement from the umbilicus to the medial malleolus
- Range of motion (ROM), especially hip flexor, hamstring, tensor facia latae, and low back muscles and the trunk and shoulder girdle; any inequalities on the two sides of the body
- Muscle strength: emphasis on the abdominal musculature; any inequalities on the two sides of the body
- Breathing pattern: history of asthma or other respiratory disorders
- Functional activity level: baseline for returning child to former activity level

Instruments/Procedures (See References for Sources)

- scoliometer (SCOL): this inclinometer is especially sensitive to rotational deformities but does yield false positives
- back-contour device (BCD)

- Moire topographic imaging (MTI) technique consists of superimposing dark and light fringes on an object by lighting and observing the object through a screen of fine opaque lines to produce a three-dimensional contour image; requires training to use
- Polaroid HealthCam System: film has an embedded grid to permit the clinician to examine postural problems while providing a visual record for documentation
- integrated shape imaging system (ISIS)
- plumb line for observation of postural asymmetries
- manual muscle testing
- Orthopaedic tests
  1. Adams forward bending test
     a. Sit or kneel behind the child so that your eyes are level to the child's waist.
     b. Ask the child to bend forward from the waist until the spine is approximately parallel with the floor, knees are straight, and arms are straight with palms together.
     c. Observe for compensatory unilateral rib hump.
  2. Thomas test—excess flexibility of the hip.
  3. Risser sign—method of determining skeletal maturity that grades the amount of ossification of the iliac crest, using grades 0 to 5. Grades 1 to 4 are measured from 25% to 100%, starting at the anterior superior iliac spine. Grades 0, 1, and 2 represent skeletal immaturity; grade 3, progressing skeletal maturity; grade 4, the end of spinal growth; and grade 5, the end of growth in height.
  4. Cobb method—method of measuring spinal curvature. The measurement depends on identifying the end vertebrae of the top and bottom of the curve. The end vertebrae are described as the top vertebra of a curve whose upper surface maximally tilts toward the curve's concavity and the most bottom vertebra with maximal tilt toward the concavity. Lines are drawn as extension of the end vertebra from either end plate or pedicle. The degree of curvature is measured as the angle formed by the intersection of the lines perpendicular to orthoses and vertebral lines. Minimal degree of curvature for diagnosis is 10 degrees.

PROBLEMS
- Curvature, lateral and rotational, of the spine is especially noticeable when the person bends forward at greater than 25 degrees.
- There may be fatigue in the lumbar region after prolonged sitting or standing.
- There may be muscular backaches in areas of strain such as the lumbosacral angle.
- Pain may become persistent as irritation of the ligaments increases. It occurs most often in structural curves.
- Physical shortening of height may occur in structural curves.
- There may be reduced lung capacity, especially on the concave side. Severe reduction in vital capacity can be life threatening.
- Paraparesis or paraplegia can occur in gross curves.
- The child may feel different and left out of peer activities.
- The child may experience loss of self-image due to wearing a body cast or brace.
- The child may be concerned about loss of independence during hospitalization and following surgery.

TREATMENT/MANAGEMENT
Physical therapy alone does not appear to be effective in preventing progression of the curvature.

Interventions include the following:
- Lateral electrical surface stimulation—application of intermittent electrical stimulation by use of surface electrodes
- Orthotic management—usually necessary for curves greater than 25 degrees
  1. Milwaukee brace (MWB) or cervical-thoracic-lumbar-sacral orthosis (CTLSO)
     a. Used where the curve has its apex at T-8 or above
     b. Provides pressure over the point of maximum convexity, traction between the occiput and the pelvis
  2. Boston bracing system (BBS) or thoracolumbosacral orthosis (TLSO)
     a. Pads are applied laterally below the apex of the curve
     b. There is no superstructure with headpiece
     c. Works best with curves that have an apex lower than T-9
  3. Other thoracolumbar-sacral orthoses (TLSO)
     a. Wilmington—achieves maximal spinal correction by the tight contact and fit, not by pads and relief areas
     b. Lyon—used to treat idiopathic scoliosis presenting with thoracic hypohyphosis
     c. Charleston—worn only at night
  4. Plaster of Paris cast
     a. Risser localizer plaster—used to treat younger children or milder curves in older children
     b. Cotrel EDF (elongation, derotation, and flexion) localizer cast
  5. Adaptive seating using seat molds
     a. Provide static equilibrium to replace or supplement inadequate muscular force or postural control
     b. Usually include a seat port, trunk support, lateral and medial thigh support, foot support, and chest and pelvic belts
  6. Denis Browne splint—used for infants that lie with the spine curved in the direction opposite the deformity
- Exercise program
  1. Develop postural awareness
  2. Maintain respiration patterns and chest mobility
  3. Maintain strength of muscles, especially the abdominal muscles
  4. Maintain joint ROM, especially spinal flexibility
  5. Swimming is an excellent activity
- Instruction in functional activity while wearing the brace
- Surgery
  1. Used for curves greater than 35 to 40 degrees
  2. Spine is fused posteriorly, in most cases with Harrington or Luque rods
  3. Anterior fusion may be used for scoliosis due to neuromuscular disease, using the Dwyer or Zielke procedures

PRECAUTIONS/CONTRAINDICATIONS
- Parents should know how to give postural drainage if infection develops.

DESIRED OUTCOME/PROGNOSIS
- The child will be able to perform functional activities related to the family, school, recreation, and community.
- The child will be able to perform age-appropriate activities.
- The child will be able to perform motor and movement activities.

Types of Scoliosis

I. Idiopathic
   A. Infantile idiopathic—0–3 years
   B. Juvenile idiopathic—4–6 years
   C. Adolescent idiopathic—7–16 years
II. Congenital
III. Neuromuscular
   A. Neuromuscular
   B. Myopathic
IV. Adult-form

Source: Data from WC Warner, Surgical Treatment of Children With Idiopathic Scoliosis. Physical Therapy Practice, Vol. 3, No. 3, pp. 127–135, © 1994, Buterworth-Heinemann.

Seating Principles

I. Provision of proximal joint stability
   A. Pelvic positioning
      1. Ideal position is a stable, midline, symmetrical alignment of the pelvis, with neutral or slight anterior pelvic tilt and a minimum of rotation.
      2. Exceptions
         a. In the case of a strong, asymmetrical tonic neck reflex or tonic labyrinthine prone or supine reflex, head alignment must be considered first.
         b. A severe pelvic and lower extremity deformity may require compromise on midline pelvic alignment to permit the head and upper trunk to be positioned in midline.
   B. Hip joint positioning
      1. Ideal position is a wide base of support with hip flexion, 85 to 95 degrees hip rotation, and neutral or slight abduction.
      2. Exceptions
         a. If extensor tone predominates, increasing hip flexion beyond 90 degrees may reduce tone and improve alignment.
         b. If there is excessive pressure of the ischial tuberosities or sacrum, reduce hip flexion below 90 degrees.
         c. Trunk positioning
      1. Ideal position provides proximal stability with upright, midline, and symmetrical alignment of the trunk.
      2. Exceptions
         a. If severe fixed trunk deformity is present, midline and symmetrical positions may be impossible to achieve; maximal function and comfort should be the goal.
         b. If pressure from the support system required to maintain upright positioning is intolerable, positioning for maximal function and comfort should be considered.
II. Orientation in space

A. The posture should be as upright as possible, but optimal posture will vary with the individual and the tasks to be performed.

B. Variations in upright posture include reclined back and tilt to right or left.

C. Considerations in orientation-in-space posture include muscle tone, function, pressure distribution, vision, feeding, postural control, head position, physiological function (breathing, digestion), and primitive reflexes.

III. Alignment of the head and body

A. The head should be centered over the body in a midline, symmetrical, and upright posture, with the eyes in the same frontal and horizontal plane.

B. The neck should have a slight lordotic curve.

C. If the child is not comfortable in the optimal position, check for altered visual fields, impairments in balance and perception, self-stimulating behavior, discomfort due to deformity, primitive reflexes, or individual preference.

IV. Alignment of body on body

A. The body should be in midline, balanced over a stable base of support, upright, with shoulders symmetrical and centered over the pelvis.

B. If scoliosis is severe, this position may be resisted or impossible to achieve, but the closest approximation should be attempted.

V. Alignment of distal joints of the extremities

A. Optimal position is 90 degrees' flexion of the knees with neural alignment of the ankles.

B. If this position is impossible, trunk alignment should be considered before extremities.

C. Orthoses may assist in promoting better alignment.

Source: Reprinted with permission from RD Mulvany, Adaptive Seating for Individuals with Scoliosis, *Physical Therapy Practice*, Vol. 3, No. 3, pp. 175–195, © 1994, Butterworth-Heinemann.

REFERENCES

ASSESSMENT

Byl NN, Gray JM. Complex balance reactions in different sensory conditions: adolescents with and without idiopathic scoliosis. *Journal of Orthopaedic Research.* 1993;11:215–227.

Connolly BH, Stralka SW, Zeno MB. Interrater reliability of the Polaroid HealthCam System in assessing scoliosis. *Physical Therapy Practice.* 1994;3:3:196–202.

Pearsall DJ, Reid JG, Hedden DM. Comparison of three noninvasive methods for measuring scoliosis. *Physical Therapy.* 1992;72:648–657.

Stralka SW. Clinical implications of ISIS scanning. *Physical Therapy Practice.* 1994;3:3:156–162.

TREATMENT

Banks GM, Garvey TA. The non-operative treatment of idiopathic scoliosis. *Physical Therapy Practice.* 1994;3:3:136–147.

Cassella MC. Non-operative treatment of children with adolescent idiopathic scoliosis using the Boston brace: a case study. *Physical Therapy Practice.* 1994;3:3:163–174.

Cassella MC, Hall JE. Current treatment approaches in the nonoperative and operative management of adolescent idiopathic scoliosis. *Physical Therapy.* 1991;71:879–909.

Granata C, Merlini L, Magni E, Marini ML, Stagni SB. Spinal muscular atrophy: natural history and orthopaedic treatment of scoliosis. *Spine*. 1989;14:760–762.

Hansen PD, Woods L, Blaszczyk JW. A model for the neurological findings in idiopathic scoliosis. *Physical Therapy Practice*. 1994;3:3:148–155.

Lehnert-Schroth C. Introduction to the three-dimensional scoliosis treatment according to Schroth. *Physiotherapy*. 1992;78:810–815.

Mulvany RD. Adaptive seating for individuals with scoliosis. *Physical Therapy Practice*. 1994;3:3:175–195.

Patrick C. Spinal conditions. In: Campbell SK, ed. *Physical Therapy in Children*. Philadelphia, Pa: WB Saunders Co; 1994:239–251.

Shepherd RB. Structural scoliosis. In: Shepherd RB, *Physiotherapy in Paediatrics*. 3rd ed. New York, NY: Churchill Livingstone; 1995:303–310.

Tecklin JS. Orthopedic disorders in children and their physical therapy management: scoliosis. In: Tecklin JS, ed. *Pediatric Physical Therapy*. 2nd ed. Philadelphia, Pa: JB Lippincott Co; 1994;320–327.

Warner WC. Surgical treatment of children with idiopathic scoliosis. *Physical Therapy Practice*. 1994;3:3:127–135.

Weiss HR. The progression of idiopathic scoliosis under the influence of a physiotherapy rehabilitation programme. *Physiotherapy*. 1992;78:815–821.

Slipped Capital Femoral Epiphysis

DESCRIPTION

Slipped capital femoral epiphysis is characterized by a disturbance in the growth plate of the capital epiphysis, an associated weakening of the structure, and subsequent displacement of the femoral head from the femoral neck. Usually the shift is in an inferior and posterior direction, and even though the head remains in the acetabulum, it is externally rotated. The disorder is more common in black boys, obese children, and children with delayed skeletal and sexual maturity. Boys are usually between 12 and 16, while girls are between 10 and 13. The disorder is characterized by grades. In Grade 1, the femoral head is displaced less than one third of the width of the neck. In Grade II, the displacement is between one third and one half of the width of the femoral neck. In Grade III, the displacement is more than one half of the width of the femoral neck. Usually one hip is involved, but about 20% of cases have bilateral slips (Tecklin, "Orthopedic Disorders," p. 311; see references).

CAUSE

The cause is unknown but appears to be related to growth and mechanical factors such as shear stress. Other factors are hormonal, infection, trauma, and genetic predisposition.

ASSESSMENT

Areas
- Range of motion (ROM)
- Gait
- Pain

Instruments/Procedures
* goniometry

PROBLEMS
* The child may experience sudden or chronic pain in the hip, knee, buttock, or groin.
* The child may have an antalgic gait or limp.
* There may be muscle spasms.
* There may be ROM limitations in hip internal rotation, abduction, and sometimes flexion.
* A small leg-length discrepancy may be present.

TREATMENT/MANAGEMENT
* During treatment, weight bearing should be stopped.
* Immobilization through traction, orthotics, or casting is usually ineffective.
* Exercises and gait training are helpful.

PRECAUTIONS/CONTRAINDICATIONS
* No specific precautions were stated.

DESIRED OUTCOMES/PROGNOSIS
* The child will be able to bear weight and walk without a limp.
* The child will be able to participate in normal activities without pain.

REFERENCES

Brenneman SK, Stanger M, Bertoti DB. Age-related considerations: pediatric—slipped capital femoral epiphysis. In: Myers RM, ed. *Saunders Manual of Physical Therapy Practice*. Philadelphia, Pa: WB Saunders Co; 1995:1270.

Leach J. Orthopaedic conditions: slipped capital femoral epiphysis. In: Campbell SK, ed. *Physical Therapy for Children*. Philadelphia, Pa: WB Saunders Co; 1994:371–372.

Tecklin JS. Orthopedic disorders in children and their physical therapy management: slipped capital femoral epiphysis. In: Tecklin JS, ed. *Pediatric Physical Therapy*. 2nd ed. Philadelphia, Pa: JB Lippincott Co; 1994:311–314.

Spina Bifida/Meningomyelocele/ Myelodysplasia

DESCRIPTION
Spina bifida is one of the neural tube defect disorders in which there is a defective closure of the vertebral column. Severity varies from the occult type (spina bifida oculta) with no findings to a type featuring a completely open spine (spina bifida aperta, rachischisis), resulting in severe neurologic disability and death. In spina bifida cystica, the protruding sac can contain meninges (meningocele), spinal cord (myelocele), or both (myelomeningocele). Spina bifida is most com-

mon in the lumbar, low thoracic, or sacral region and usually extends for three to six vertebral segments. Spinal deformities are present in 90% of children with myelomeningocele (Hinderer et al, "Myelodysplasia," p. 571–573, see references).

CAUSE

Spina bifida appears to be a genetic disorder that is affected by environmental factors. The exact relationship is unknown.

ASSESSMENT

Areas
- Range of motion (ROM)
- Muscle strength (in infants, grade P = present or A = absent)
- Deep tendon reflexes
- Neonatal reflexes
- Level of sensory innervation
- Functional abilities
- Developmental abilities
- Skin and soft tissue
- Posture
- Possible asymmetries or spinal deformities (scoliosis)
- Possible Arnold–Chiari malformation
- Possible hip dislocation
- Possible hydrocephalus
- Possible hydromyelia
- Possible tethered cord
- Possible occult fractures

Instruments/Procedures
- goniometry
- muscle testing
- reflex testing
- sensory acuity testing
- development profile testing

PROBLEMS
- In *kyphosis,* curves may be greater than 65 degrees, which can severely limit sitting and ambulation abilities, lead to skin ulcerations, and impair respiratory function.
- In *scoliosis,* the curvature may be greater than 30 degrees at birth, which can interfere with sitting balance and ambulation potential, leading to skin ulcerations, and can affect respiratory function.
- Lordosis can develop as a secondary impairment to hip flexion contractures or weak hip extensors.
- Hip deformities occur as a result of muscle imbalances and/or dysplasia of the acetabulum, femoral head, or femoral neck.
  1. Adduction contracture occurs with spasticity of the hip adductor musculature. Unilateral adduction contracture produces pelvic obliquity with resultant hip subluxation or disloca-

tion and possible scoliosis. Unopposed hip adductor muscle action may result from higher level lumbar lesions as a result of flaccid or weak hip abductors and hip extensor musculature.

2. High lumbar/thoracic-level lesions result in unopposed action of the hip flexors and cause flexion contractures due to positioning, especially from sitting or lying supine with legs flexed for long periods of time. Flexion contractures can interfere with bracing and ambulation. They may cause increased pelvic tilt with excessive lumbar lordosis and may be associated with knee flexion contractures.

3. Subluxation and dislocation may be the result of a congenital or teratological defect that causes a dysplastic acetabulum and/or femoral head. It may result in paralysis that leads to muscle imbalance.

- Knee deformities are most common in children with high lumbar and thoracic lesions.
    1. Flexion contracture—watch for the following:
        a. Lying supine in frog-legged posture
        b. Sitting in wheelchair for extended periods of time
        c. Crouched-stance posture as result of weak ankle plantar flexors
        d. Hamstring spasticity accompanying "tethered cord syndrome"
    2. Extension contractures may occur with a history of breech presentation. They may result from fibrosis of quadriceps mechanisms or muscle imbalance, with quadriceps stronger than hamstring musculature.
    3. Genu valgus is associated with high lumbar lesions and contracture of the iliotibial band. It may interfere with fitting of orthotic devices.
- Foot and ankle deformities may be congenital, as a result of intrauterine positioning and paralysis, or acquired, resulting from muscle imbalances, spasticity, and the influence of positioning, gravity, and growth. Common deformities include clubfoot, equinus, equinovarus, calcaneovalgus, and a vertical talus.
- Pathological fractures are most common in children with thoracic or high lumbar lesions.
- Frog-legged position—hip flexion, abduction, and external rotation contractures secondary to paralysis.

TREATMENT/MANAGEMENT

Spinal Deformities
- Slow or limit progression of deformity.
- Prevent skin breakdown.
- Improve functional posture for sitting or standing activities.
- In cases of kyphosis, the use of orthotics is not recommended.
- In cases of scoliosis, viewpoints conflict.
    1. Orthotics may be beneficial in limiting or slowing the progression of a scoliosis and are indicated if the curve is greater than 20 degrees.
    2. Orthotics to limit scoliosis may be incorporated into the child's bracing system for ambulation or standing and for positioning when seated.
    3. Orthotics has little role in scoliosis secondary to the inability to halt progression of a curve and the difficulty of maintaining pressure over insensitive skin.
- For frog-legged position, institute ROM exercises; use side-lying or prone positioning. Instruct parents on gentle wrapping of the lower extremities at night and on adduction straps and splints.

Hip Subluxation/Dislocation
- Work toward a level pelvis and free motion of the hips.
- Abduction splints, such as a Frejka pillow or Pavlik harness, are generally not recommended.
- If surgery is performed, watch for infection, pathological fractures, skin ulceration, loss of ROM, decrease in function, and failure to maintain relocation of the hip.

Joint Contractures
- Use ROM exercises and positioning.
- Serial casting, splinting, and/or surgical correction may be necessary.

Standing and Ambulation
- Begin by positioning the child upright in a standing frame or parapodium at 1 year of age, increasing tolerance to the full day.
- At 2 years, a "swivel" gait may be used with a rolling walker.
- At 3 years, the child may learn a "swing-through" gait with a rolling walker.
- At 5 years the child should have mastered a swing-through gait and be ready for crutch walking. The child should be able to lock and unlock leg braces and be learning transfers.
- Low-level lesions may need ankle or foot orthoses or no device.
- The nonambulatory child should be fitted with a wheelchair.

Instruction to Caregivers
- Instruct parents and teachers in ambulation and standing activities, ROM exercises, positioning, handling, transfers, developmental activities, and signs of malfunction.

Prevention of Contractures and Fractures
- Administer a standing program for at least 60 minutes, 4 to 5 times per week.

Equipment
- Measure, order, and modify equipment to provide for maximum mobility.

PRECAUTIONS/CONTRAINDICATIONS
- In the case of osteoporosis, use caution with ROM exercises.
- In the case of hip dislocation, avoid simultaneous adduction and flexion of the hip.
- Lack of sensation may prevent recognition of occult fractures. Watch for signs of redness, local heat, swelling, deformity of limb, and fever.
- Watch for signs of hydrocephalus/shunt malformation.
  1. Infants: bulging fontanelle, change in appetite, edema or redness along shunt, high-pitched cry, irritability, lethargy, sunset eyes, or vomiting
  2. Toddlers: edema or redness along the shunt, headache, irritability, lethargy, new appearance of squinting or nystagmus, seizures, or vomiting
  3. Older children: all items above, decreased school performance, decreased sensory or motor function, handwriting changes, or memory changes
- Watch for signs of hydromyelia, including progressive upper extremity weakness and hypertonus, pressure necrosis of peripheral nerve and muscle tissue, and scoliosis.

- Watch for signs of tethered cord, including scoliosis in persons with a lesion below T-12 and a decrease in motor function.

DESIRED OUTCOME/PROGNOSIS
- The child will develop normal abilities and skills with the limitations of the neurological deficit.
- The parents or caregivers will learn appropriate handling, positioning techniques, and ROM activities to prevent or reduce muscle imbalance, hip dislocation, and scoliosis.

REFERENCES

Bedford S. Disorders of the central nervous system: spina bifida cystica. In: Eckersley PM, ed. *Elements in Paediatric Physiotherapy*. New York, NY: Churchill-Livingstone; 1993:131–143.

Bezner J, Rogers H. Newborn spina bifida protocol. In: *Physical Therapy Protocols: Guidelines for Rehabilitation*. Tucson, Ariz: Therapy Skill Builders; 1991:151–154.

Bezner J, Rogers H. Spina bifida outpatient clinic screening protocol. In: *Physical Therapy Protocols: Guidelines for Rehabilitation*. Tucson, Ariz: Therapy Skill Builders; 1991:179–183.

Brenneman SK, Stanger M, Bertoti DB. Age-related consideration: pediatric. In: Myers RS, ed. *Saunders Manual of Physical Therapy Practice*. Philadelphia, Pa: WB Saunders Co; 1995:1229–1283.

Canale G, Scarsi J, Mastragostino S. Hip deformity and dislocation in spina bifida. *Italian Journal of Orthopaedics and Traumatology*. 1992;18:155–165.

Charney EB, Melchionni JE, Smith DR. Community ambulation by children with myelomeningocele and high-level paralysis. *Journal of Pediatric Orthopedics*. 1992;11:579–582.

Effgen SK, Brown DA. Long-term stability of hand-held dynamometric measurements in children who have myelomeningocele. *Physical Therapy*. 1992;72:458–465.

Eigsti H, Aretz M, Shannon L. Pediatric physical therapy in a rehabilitation setting. *Pediatrician*. 1990;17:267–277

Feldman AB, Haley SM, Coryell J. Concurrent and construct validity of the Pediatric Evaluation of Disability Inventory. *Physical Therapy*. 1990;70:602–610.

Franks CA, Palisano RJ, Darbee JC. The effect of walking with an assistive device and using a wheelchair on school performance in students with myelomeningocele. *Physical Therapy*. 1991;71:570–577, discussion, 577–579.

Garber JB. Myelodysplasia. In: Campbell SK, ed. *Pediatric Neurologic Physical Therapy*. New York, NY: Churchill Livingstone; 1991:169–212.

Hinderer KA, Hinderer SR, Shurtleff DB. Myelodysplasia. In: Campbell SK, ed. *Physical Therapy for Children*. Philadelphia, Pa: WB Saunders Co; 1994:571–619.

Kahn-D'Angelo L. The reciprocation-gait orthosis for children with myelodysplasia. *Physical and Occupational Therapy in Pediatrics*. 1989;9:107–117.

Karmel-Ross K, Cooperman DR, Van Doren CL. The effect of electrical stimulation on quadriceps femoris muscle torque in children with spina bifida. *Physical Therapy*. 1992;72:723–730.

Knutson LM, Clark DE. Orthotic devices for ambulation in children with cerebral palsy and myelomeningocele. *Physical Therapy*. 1991;71:947–960.

Kurtz LA, Schull SA. Rehabilitation for developmental disabilities. *Pediatric Clinics of North America*. 1993;40:629–643.

Long TM, Cintas HL. Pediatric disorders: spina bifida. In: *Handbook of Pediatric Physical Therapy*. Baltimore, Md: Williams & Wilkins; 1995:138–141.

Muller EB, Nordwall A, von Wendt L. Influence of surgical treatment of scoliosis in children with spina bifida on ambulation and motoric skills. *Acta Paediatrica*. 1992;81:173–176.

O'Connell DG, Barnhart R, Parks L. Muscular endurance and wheelchair propulsion in children with cerebral palsy or myelomeningocele. *Archives of Physical Medicine and Rehabilitation*. 1992;73:709–711.

Parsch K. Origin and treatment of fractures in spina bifida. *European Journal of Pediatric Surgery*. 1991;1:298–305.

Robinson RO, McCarthy GT, Little TM. Conductive education at the Peto Institute, Budapest. *British Medical Journal*. 1989;299:1145–1149; comments, 299:1461–1462.

Ryan KD, Ploski C, Emans JB. Myelodysplasia: the musculoskeletal problem: habilitation from infancy to adulthood. *Physical Therapy*. 1991;71:935–946.

Schneider JW, Krosschell K, Gabriel KL. Congenital spinal cord injuries. In: Umphred DA, ed. *Neurological Rehabilitation*. 3rd ed. St. Louis, Mo: CV Mosby Co; 1995:454–483.

Shepherd RB. Spina bifida. In: Shepherd RB, *Physiotherapy in Paediatrics*. Oxford, England: Butterworth-Heinemann; 1995:238–260.

Sonnino RE, Reinberg O, Bensoussan AL, Laberge JM, Blanchard H. Gracilis muscle transposition for anal incontinence in children: long-term follow-up. *Journal of Pediatric Surgery*. 1991;26:1219–1223; comments, 27:795–796.

Tappit-Emas E. Spina bifida. In: Tecklin JS, ed. *Pediatric Physical Therapy*. 2nd ed. Philadelphia, Pa: JB Lippincott Co; 1994:135–186.

Spinal Cord Injury

DESCRIPTION

Loss of neurologic function after a spinal injury can result briefly from concussion or more lastingly from compression of the spinal cord to contusion or hemorrhage, as well as permanently from lacerations or transection. In contusion, rapid edematous swelling of the cord with a rise in intradural pressure can result in several days of severe dysfunction followed by spontaneous improvement, although some residual disability may remain. Hemorrhage usually is confined to the cervical central gray matter (hematomyelia). The result includes signs of lower motor neuron damage (muscle weakness and wasting, fasciculation, diminished tendon reflexes) that usually are permanent. The motor weakness often is proximal rather than distal and accompanied by selective impairment of pain and temperature sensations. Extradural, subdural, or subarachnoid hemorrhage also can occur. Lacerations or transection almost always leave permanent dysfunction. More boys than girls are affected.

CAUSE

Major causes of spinal cord injury in children are automobile accidents, sports injuries, diving, gunshot wounds, and falls from high places. Other causes include birth trauma, child abuse, tumors of the spine, and transverse myelitis.

ASSESSMENT

Areas

- Motor functions, including ability to reach, roll and position in bed, come to sitting, balance in sitting, scoot, crawl, transfer, come to kneel, stand, and ambulate
- Strength
- Cardiovascular endurance

Instruments/Procedures (See References for Sources)
- Function/Disability
  1. ASIA Impairment Scale
  2. Functional Independence Measure for Children (WeeFIM)
  3. Pediatric Evaluation of Disability Inventory (PEDI)
- Cardiovascular endurance
  1. assessment of length of play time
- Strength
  1. manual muscle testing (Note: considered unreliable in children under 5; estimates must be based on play activities)

Include parents in the assessment process so they can understand what is planned and participate.

PROBLEMS
- Muscle weakness and/or paralysis
- Loss of range of motion (ROM)
- Altered muscle tone
- Sensory loss and/or impairment
- Decreased endurance
- Poor postural control
- Altered cardiovascular responses: autonomic dysreflexia, orthostatic hypotension

TREATMENT/MANAGEMENT
- Direct therapy involves
  1. maintaining joint ROM and muscle length
  2. strengthening of spared innervated muscles
  3. monitoring and treating postural deformities and contractures
- Equipment includes
  1. orthoses for trunk and seating
  2. orthoses for standing and ambulation
  3. mobility aids such as wheelchair or scooter
  4. orthoses for upper extremity function, such as adapted eating utensils, writing and keyboarding adaptations, personal hygiene aids, and tenodesis splint
- The family can be instructed in
  1. lifting and handling techniques
  2. correct use of equipment
  3. skin care
- The child can be instructed in
  1. mobility skills appropriate to neurological level of function
  2. transfer skills appropriate to neurological level
  3. compensatory strategies for lost function
  4. skill acquisition through play, such as lying prone on scooter
- Cooperation with interdisciplinary team is necessary to manage and coordinate
  1. medical care
  2. rehabilitation services
  3. educational pursuits
  4. vocational training for older children

- Follow-up is required for
  1. adaptations for access and function in the home, school, community, and transportation
  2. family and individual adjustment to permanent disability
  3. instruction to adapted recreational activities and wheelchair sports

PRECAUTIONS/CONTRAINDICATIONS
- Check skin frequently for signs of breakdown, including redness.

DESIRED OUTCOME/PROGNOSIS
- The child will have an independent means of mobility.
- The child will have attained age-appropriate development given functional limitation.
- The child will be able to function as a family member, peer, and student.

ASIA System of Muscle Grades

0 = absence, total paralysis
1 = trace, palpable or visible contraction
2 = poor, active movement though full ROM with gravity eliminated
3 = fair, active movement through full ROM against gravity
4 = good, active movement through full ROM against resistance
5 = normal

Courtesy of the American Spinal Injury Association, Chicago, Illinois.

Key Muscles for Motor Level Classification

C-5	Elbow flexors (biceps, brachialis)
C-6	Wrist extensors (extensor carpi radialis longus and brevis)
C-7	Elbow extensors (triceps)
C-8	Finger flexors to the middle finger (flexor digitorum profundus)
T-1	Small finger abductors (adductor digiti minimi manus)
L-2	Hip flexors (iliopsoas)
L-3	Knee extensors (quadriceps)
L-4	Ankle dorsiflexors (tibialis anterior)
L-5	Long toe extensors (extensor hallucis longus)
S-1	Ankle plantar flexors (gastrocnemius, soleus)

Courtesy of the American Spinal Injury Association, Chicago, Illinois.

ASIA Impairment Scale

A   *Complete*—No sensory or motor function below the neurological level of injury
B   *Incomplete*—Sensory but not motor function preserved below the neurological level of injury

C   *Incomplete*—Motor function preserved below the neurological level, and the majority of key muscles below the neurological level have a muscle grade less than 3

D   *Incomplete*—Motor function preserved below the neurological level, and the majority of key muscles below the neurological level have a muscle grade greater than or equal to 3

E   *Normal*—Sensory and motor function normal

Courtesy of the American Spinal Injury Association, Chicago, Illinois.

Theories of Recovery From Injury to the CNS

Diaschisis theory assumes that a period of shock and edema follows the injury and that the area of edema is wider than the actual lesion. Thus, as the system recovers from the shock and the edema recedes, function is restored.

Supersensitivity theory assumes that target neurons enhance their ability to function in response to neurotransmitters and thus produce a degree of recovery.

Vicariation or *equipotentiality theory* proposes that undamaged parts of the nervous system may take over functions previously serviced by the damaged areas.

Axonal sprouting (synaptogenesis) theory proposes that damaged axons may regrow or new undamaged axons may sprout to take over vacated synaptic sites. Some new pathways may be maladaptive, as in hyperreflexia, if appropriate experience is not available. "Appropriate experience" has not been fully clarified.

Compensation theory suggests that functions previously serviced by the damaged area may recover but are mediated by different means. The nature of the means is not clarified.

Source: Reprinted with permission from RB Shepherd, *Physiotherapy in Pediatrics*, p. 103, © 1995, Butterworth-Heinemann.

REFERENCES

ASSESSMENT

ASIA Impairment Scale
ASIA Impairment Scale. Chicago, Ill: American Spinal Injury Association; 1992.

Functional Independence Measure for Children (Wee-FIM)
Granger CV, Hamilton BB, Kayton R. *Guide for the Use of the Functional Independence Measure for Children (Wee-FIM) of the Uniform Data Set for Medical Rehabilitation*. Buffalo, NY: State University of New York, Research Foundation; 1988.

Pediatric Evaluation of Disability Inventory (PEDI)
Haley SM, Faas RM, Coster WJ, Webster H, Gans BM. *Pediatric Evaluation of Disability Inventory*. Boston, Mass: New England Medical Center; 1989.

TREATMENT
Flett PJ. The rehabilitation of children with spinal cord injury. *Journal of Paediatrics and Child Health.* 1992;28:141–146.

Southard RL, Massagli TL. Spinal cord injury. In: Campbell SK, ed. *Physical Therapy in Children*. Philadelphia, Pa: WB Saunders Co; 1994:525–547.

Wetzel JL, Lunsford BR, Peterson MJ, Alvarez SE. In: Irwin S, Tecklin JS, eds. *Cardiopulmonary Physical Therapy*. 3rd ed. St. Louis, Mo: CV Mosby Co; 1995:579–603.

Spinal Muscular Atrophy

DESCRIPTION

Spinal muscular atrophy (SMA) comprises a group of disorders beginning in infancy or childhood, characterized by skeletal muscle wasting due to progressive degeneration of anterior horn cells in the spinal cord and motor nuclei in the brain stem, leading to lower motor neuron disorders. Most cases are inherited. Three main variants are recognized. *Acute childhood-onset SMA* (type I, infantile SMA, or Werdnig–Hoffman disease) is an autosomal recessive disorder. Symptoms appear between 2 and 4 months of age. Most infants are hypotonic at birth. All affected infants have delayed motor milestones by 3 months. Most children die before age 1 due to respiratory failure and apnea. The term *chronic childhood-onset SMA* (type II, intermediate SMA, or chronic Werdnig–Hoffman disease) is applied to infants and children who are symptomatic by age 4. One quarter of such children learn to sit, but few learn to crawl or walk. Regardless of age of onset, children are hypotonic with flaccid muscle weakness, absent deep tendon reflexes, and fasciculation. Dysphagia may be present. The disease often is fatal in early life, frequently from respiratory complication. Some cases show spontaneous arrest that leaves the child with a chronic, nonprogressive weakness. *Juvenile-onset SMA* (type III or Wohlfart–Kugelbert–Welander disease) begins between 5 and 10 years of age with similar pathologic findings and mode of inheritance but a slower evolution and longer life expectancy. Weakness and wasting are most evident in the legs, with onset in the quadriceps and hip flexors. Later the arms are affected. Weakness often progresses from proximal to distal parts. Some familial cases may be secondary to specific enzyme defects. Type IV is applied to adult onset. Type I was originally described in 1891 by Werdnig and in 1893 by Hoffman. Type III was described by Wohlfart in 1955 and by Kugelberg and Welander in 1956. SMA is often confused with muscular dystrophy. Intelligence is usually normal, and characteristics of upper motor neuron disorders are not present.

CAUSE

Most cases are due to autosomal recessive inheritance. The genetic defect is located on chromosome 5 and affects the anterior horn cell. The number of cells is reduced, and there is progressive degeneration of the remaining cells.

ASSESSMENT

Area

• Muscle development

- Muscle strength
- Developmental milestones

Instruments/Procedures
- Gower's sign: child stands up by placing hands on legs and "walking" up the legs until upright.
- Special tests to which the PT may or may not have access
  1. muscle biopsy
  2. electromyography (EMG)

PROBLEMS

Acute or Infantile Form
- Motor problems include the following:
  1. hypotonicity
  2. muscle atrophy
  3. progressive, symmetrical muscle weakness secondary to progressive loss of anterior horn cells
  4. lack of spontaneous movement
  5. possible involvement of cranial nerve functions
  6. contractures, especially related to limited fetal movement
- Facial appearance is usually alert and responsive.
- Reflex abnormalities may include absent or decreased deep tendon reflexes and flexor or absent plantar responses.
- There is developmental delay, especially in motor milestones. Children rarely learn to crawl or walk.
- There are no sensory or intelligence losses or abnormalities.
- Feeding problems include difficulty with chewing and swallowing, atrophy of the tongue, and fasciculation, or "jumpiness," of the tongue.
- There is respiratory distress and greater use of abdominal versus thoracic muscles in breathing ("belly breathing").
- There is failure to thrive.
- Survival beyond 3 years is rare.

Childhood Form
- Motor problems include
  1. "floppy" or hypotonic movements, especially antigravity movements of the shoulder girdle and pelvic musculature
  2. posturing in antigravity positions
  3. muscle atrophy and weakness, especially in the extremities and trunk musculature in proximal muscle groups (but functional ambulation with assistive devices possible)
  4. fine motor tremor called minipolymyoclonus
  5. contractures and scoliosis
- Motor milestones are delayed. Children have difficulty learning to crawl or walk.
- Feeding and swallowing are not usually a problem.
- There is respiratory insufficiency.
- The child is easily fatigued.

Juvenile Form
- Motor problems include progressive weakness, beginning in the proximal muscle groups, progressive wasting or atrophy, and fasciculation.
- Deep tendon reflexes may be weak or absent.
- Generally, contractures are not a problem.
- Generally, spinal deformities are not a problem.

TREATMENT/MANAGEMENT

Infantile Form
- Encourage sitting using supports to maintain alignment. An elastic binder may be useful for children who demonstrate decreased oxygen saturation in the seated position.
- Maintain or increase joint mobility and range of motion (ROM).
- Promote alignment and posture: prevent scoliosis as long as possible. Use rolled towels or bolsters to keep upper extremities positioned in midline and to prevent lower extremity abduction and external rotation.
- Implement an exercise program to promote light strengthening of muscles, using lightweight toys or rattles. Velcro straps around wrist or mobiles positioned close to the hands are useful. A hammock may be used to promote movement.
- Promoting development of milestones and developmental activities is controversial but may be justified because a few type II SMA children show signs of progress in early infancy. Generally Type I children do not attain lifting of the head from a prone position or prone on elbows.
- Promote feeding. Several small meals may be necessary because of fatigue. Breast-feeding may be difficult and need extra support.
- Promote respiratory function by using wedges in the supine but not the prone position unless head righting is established. Provide suctioning, assisted coughing, and postural drainage as needed.

Childhood Form
- Facilitate and maintain walking for as long as possible (generally up to about 5 years of age).
- Teach use of manual wheelchair when walking is no longer possible.
- Encourage development of gross motor skills.
- Prevent contractures and kyphoscoliosis as long as possible.
- Provide information to family on problems related to decreasing functional independence due to spinal instability that requires the use of the upper extremities for trunk support. When upper extremities are not available for "table top activities" spinal surgery may be indicated.
- After surgery, determine if orthotic devices can be used to counter the loss of upper extremity function.
- Provide information to the family about the benefits of cardiovascular fitness.
- Inform family that loss of function is typical in children after spinal fusion surgery due to the loss of proximal flexibility of the spine which reduces shoulder and arm flexibility.

Juvenile Form
- Provide training in wheelchair mobility.
- Develop skills in transfers, rolling, and sitting.
- Promote independence in feeding, bathing, dressing, hygiene, and toileting.

- Orthoses including mobile arm supports (MAS), reachers, and lap boards may be added to the wheelchair for additional function skills, especially after spinal fusion surgery.
- Participate in a program to help the child regain as much skill as possible after spinal fusion surgery (Harrington rod or Luque rod instrumentation procedures).

PRECAUTIONS/CONTRAINDICATIONS
- Watch for signs of aspiration and secondary respiratory problems.

DESIRED OUTCOME/PROGNOSIS
- The child will have developed the maximum degree of motor skills consistent with type of SMA and will be able to use motor skills effectively.
- The child will be able to function in the family, school, recreation, and the community.
- The child will have achieved developmental milestones to the maximum level consistent with type of SMA.

REFERENCES

Brown JC, Zeller JL, Swank SM, Furumasu J, Warath SL. Surgical and functional results of spine fusion in spinal muscular atrophy. *Spine*. 1989;14:763–770.

Furumasu J, Swank SM, Brown JC, Gilfogg I, Warath S, Zeller J. Functional activities in spinal muscular atrophy patients after spinal fusion. *Spine*. 1989;14:771–775.

Stuberg WA. Muscular dystrophy and spinal muscular atrophy. In: Campbell SK, ed. *Physical Therapy for Children*. Philadelphia, Pa: WB Saunders Co; 1995:295–323.

Tecklin JS. Neuromuscular disorders in childhood and physical therapy intervention: spinal muscular atrophy. In: Tecklin JS, ed. *Pediatric Physical Therapy*. 2nd ed. Philadelphia, Pa: JB Lippincott Co; 1994:407–408.

Torticollis/Congenital Muscular Torticollis

Also known as infantile torticollis, congenital torticollis, muscular torticollis, "wry neck."

DESCRIPTION

Congenital muscular torticollis (CMT) is a musculoskeletal disorder in which there is restricted neck range of motion (ROM) and shortening of the sternocleidomastoid (SCM) due to fibrosis in the SCM, which often appears as a nodule in the neck. The condition, although present at birth, usually does not appear until a few days after birth. The incidence is between 0.3% and 1.9%. There is an association of torticollis with Down syndrome, myelodysplasia, cerebral palsy, and spinal muscular atrophy. CMT should be differentiated from torticollis due to neurological (spasmodic torticollis) or structural (congenital hemivertebrae) defects or associated with parotiditis. CMT should also be differentiated from septic deep glands, subluxation of the atlantoaxial joint, visual defects, plagiocephaly without SCM involvement, and brain injury, all of which may cause the infant to hold the head to one side (Emery, "Determinants," pp. 921–922; see references).

CAUSE

The exact cause is unknown. Several theories have been advanced. One is neck trauma during delivery that results in hematoma, fibrosis, and constriction of the SCM muscle. Another is that of intrauterine malpositioning of the neck, with resultant local ischemia of the sternomastoid. Relationship to breech delivery and birth trauma has also been noted, although torticollis has been found in cesarean sections. Familial factors may also be involved. The fibrous mass may be caused by fibrotic changes in muscle tissue.

ASSESSMENT

Areas

- Head pulled to one side; usually flexed to one side and rotated to the other (appears a few days or weeks after birth).
- SCM: in some but not all cases, a nontender mass or nodule in the segment nearest the occiput; if present, the mass is most obvious during the second and third week and usually disappears by 6 months
- ROM: passive rotation of the neck through 180 degrees usually possible, but active range by the infant limited to the midline position of the neck
- Facial and in some cases cranial asymmetry that occasionally persists
- Signs of pain, such as crying, when head is rotated
- General development, in particular any other persistent asymmetries and asymmetrical or abnormal reflex activity such as a Moro, Galant, or grasp reflex

Instruments/Procedures

- goniometry: goniometer may be modified to include carpenter's levels attached to its stationary arm, one placed parallel to the arm and the other perpendicular
- use of toy or object to attract the infant's attention during observation of active ROM
- palpation of SCM

PROBLEMS

- There is limited ROM. Often the head cannot be rotated beyond the midline to the opposite side.
- The head tilts toward the side of the shortened muscle.
- The head rotates toward the contralateral side.
- There are facial asymmetries. The face on the side of the affected muscle tends to flatten if the child lies prone with the head turned to the opposite side.
- Plagiocephaly (askewed head) is present. This is a congenital malformation of the skull in which premature or irregular closure of the coronal or lambdoidal sutures results in asymmetric growth of the head, giving it a twisted, lopsided appearance so that the maximum length is not along the midline but on a diagonal.
- Pain occurs in some cases, as evidenced by crying when the head is rotated.
- Contracture of the SCM occurs if treatment is not begun early in the course of the disorder.

TREATMENT/MANAGEMENT

Treatment should begin before age 2 to avoid permanent asymmetry. Conservative treatment should begin as soon as the CMT is identified. The best methods of treatment are not fully investigated. Controversy still exists. Severe cases and those not treated early usually require surgery followed by physical therapy.

- Use passive and active SCM stretching of the neck while flexing the neck laterally and rotating to the opposite side. One method of treatment is to place the infant on a padded surface in supine with the affected side away from the therapist, who sits facing the table and holding the legs and body with one arm. The hand holds the shoulder, thereby fixing the sternoclavicular attachment of the SCM and allowing the flexion of the head to perform the stretch. The other hand is used to hold the head (avoiding holding the ear) and to pull it into as much side (lateral) flexion as possible. The stretch is repeated with the addition of rotation as needed. Note that rotation is most likely to be painful. Alternating flexion only and flexion with rotation is helpful. Also note that the maximum stretch need not be applied as one motion. Rather, move the head until resistance is felt. Let the infant relax. Then continue the stretch. Distracting the infant may help relax him or her. If the parent is present, encourage him or her to provide distraction. Talking to the infant is sometimes helpful. Stretching should be done several times daily for approximately 5 minutes at a time. Use toys and games to promote active flexion to the opposite side and rotation.
- Provide muscle-strengthening exercises for the contralateral SCM muscle.
- With older children, use equilibrium reactions such as head righting to encourage lateral bend to the uninvolved side.
- Educate parents in the importance of continuing exercises until the neck ROM is normal. A sample home stretching program for parents is presented in Emery ("Determinants," p. 924; see references). Emery recommends that two people assist in stretching the infant's neck. One person holds the infant's shoulders to stabilize the clavicle while the other does the stretching. Hand placement is stressed. If the torticollis is right-sided, the parent or therapist cups the left side of the infant's face. Support the skull under the occipital region with the right hand. Use the same hand placement for right rotation and left lateral flexion. Use slight traction to promote relaxation prior to starting full rotation of the head to the right through the ROM available. Hold the stretch at the end of the ROM. Lateral flexion stretch is started with the application of slight traction, followed by slight forward flexion and 10 degrees of right rotation. Then the head is moved laterally toward the left side in a position where the left ear approaches the left shoulder. Stretching position is held for 10 seconds and stretching exercises are repeated five times each twice a day.
- Recommend that the child sleep in a side-lying position on the side of the tight SCM muscle to provide a gentle stretch of the contracted muscle.
- Suggest that the child play in a prone position with the neck extended to encourage bilateral SCM muscle elongation.
- If the child is 4 months or older, promote strengthening of the opposite SCM using the lateral righting response in upright, rolling, and side-lying activities.
- If the child is 4.5 months or older and head tilt is 6 degrees or greater, a tubular orthosis for torticollis, made by soft tubing, can be provided (usually by occupational therapy). See Emery, "Determinants," p. 925 (in references) for an illustration.
- Prevent associated adaptive skull, face, eye, and trunk asymmetries through corrective positioning when the infant is carried as well as when he or she is resting or sleeping.
- Reduce parental anxiety about the possible deformity by assuring them the treatment generally is effective and by showing them how to handle the infant most effectively to assist in treatment and prevent additional problems and deformities. Shepherd ("Torticollis"; see references) provides several suggestions on p. 299.

- Splinting is used only with severe asymmetries, especially if surgery is required. The splint consists of a cap made from webbing and attached to a jacket using Velcro to provide lateral flexion and rotation in the opposite direction.
- Treatment is the same if surgery is required, beginning about 36 hours after surgery.

PRECAUTIONS/CONTRAINDICATIONS
- If left untreated, the soft tissues may not grow in relation to the child's skeletal growth.
- Deep cervical fascia, carotid sheath, and vessels can thicken.
- Compensatory thoracic scoliosis may occur as a result of the cervical displacement.
- Note that occasionally a visual problem may be the cause of the head tilt. Recommend an eye examination to rule this out.
- Care in observation and general assessment is especially important if no mass or nodule is present to be sure that the torticollis is not part of a more extensive neurological or musculoskeletal abnormality such as cerebral palsy.
- If pain is present, the stretching technique should be modified and applied gently to reduce resistance and crying. Holding the stretch if the infant struggles is not recommended.
- If stretching results in the nodule's pressing against a blood vessel, care must be taken to avoid cyanosis. Rotation may need to be limited until the nodule has decreased in size.
- Always observe for signs of SCM rupture, bruising, or clavicle fracture. Discontinue treatment until the physician recommends restarting.

DESIRED OUTCOME/PROGNOSIS
- If a nodule is present but there is no limitation in ROM, the desired outcome is to prevent head tilt and restricted neck movement.
- If restricted neck movement has occurred, then the desired outcome is the achievement of full passive ROM.
- Note that there is a correlation between severity of restriction (greater than 30 degrees of rotation) and treatment duration and between presence of a mass and treatment duration.
- There is spontaneous resolution of the facial asymmetry once the head position has been corrected.

REFERENCES

Binder H, Eng GD, Gaiser JF, Koch D. Congenital muscular torticollis: results of conservative management with long-term follow-up of 85 cases. *Archives of Physical Medicine and Rehabilitation.* 1987;68:222–225.

Davids MM. Congenital muscular torticollis: a preliminary survey. *Physiotherapy.* 1989;43:2:45–46.

Emery C. The determinants of treatment duration for congenital muscular torticollis. *Physical Therapy.* 1994;74:921–929.

Shepherd RB. Torticollis. In: Shepherd RB, *Physiotherapy in Paediatrics.* 3rd ed. Oxford, England: Butterworth-Heinemann; 1995:293–302.

Traumatic Head Injuries

DESCRIPTION

Craniocerebral trauma and its complications are a leading cause of injury and death in children. Injury to the central nervous system often results in residual impairment of physical, cognitive, and emotional functions. Loss of consciousness includes concussion, which is a transient and rapidly reversible state of neuronal dysfunction, and contusion, which is a focal bruising or tearing of cerebral tissue accompanied by parenchymatous hemorrhage and local edema. Skull fracture may cause a subdural hematoma, which is a collection of blood beneath the dura mater, usually associated with a significant contusion of the brain, or an epidural hematoma, which is a collection of blood between the dura mater and the skull resulting from arterial or venous injury.

CAUSE

Head injury is the second most common form of trauma in children, especially boys, aged 1 to 15 years, that requires hospitalization. Frequently occurring causes of head injury are motor vehicle and bicycle accidents, falls, diving accidents, birth injuries, and contact sports. The injury is due to mechanical forces of acceleration (a moving object such as a ball hits the stationary head), deceleration (the head hits a stationary object such as the pavement), or rotation (when a blow to the head, such as the impact of a fist, is asymmetrical). The effect on the brain may be concussion, cerebral contusion or laceration, intracranial hemorrhage, subdural hematoma, or subarachnoid hemorrhage. There are several theories about the mechanism of recovery from head injury, including theories of diaschis, equipotentiality, compensation, vicariation, and/or collateral regeneration and hypersensitivity (see box in section "Spinal Cord Injury" for a description of these theories).

ASSESSMENT

Areas

- History: preinjury behavior; cognitive abilities; favorite activities; family status; cause, location, and severity of injury; length of coma
- Motor control of movement in response to controlled stimulation: timing, force, duration, direction, location
- Sensory awareness and sensation in response to controlled stimulation: auditory, visual, olfactory, gustatory, pain, proprioception, tactile (two-point discrimination, sharp/dull, hypersensitivity)
- Sensorimotor integration
- Range of motion (ROM)
- Muscle tone
- Cardiopulmonary status
- Postural control and positioning
- Oral-motor control
- Cognitive skills: ability to follow instructions, level of arousal, judgment, problem solving
- Other: behavioral status, post-traumatic seizures, intellectual functioning, learning ability

Instruments/Procedures (See References for Sources)

- Bruininks–Oseretsky Test of Motor Proficiency

- Children's Coma Scale
- Children's Orientation and Amnesia Test
- Functional Independence Measure for Children (WeeFIM)
- Glasgow Coma Scale (Scale is considered difficult to apply to infants and young children; see Ewing-Cobb)
- Ommaya Scale
- Peabody Developmental Motor Scales
- Pediatric Evaluation of Disability Inventory (PEDI)
- Rancho Levels of Cognitive Functioning

PROBLEMS
- The child may be in a coma (see Ommaya classification of levels of consciousness, in box).

Ommaya Scale of Levels of Consciousness

Level V	No response to stimuli
	Unable to respond to verbal commands
Level IV	Generalized response to sensory stimuli
	Unable to respond to verbal commands
Level III	Consistent localized response to a stimulus
	Unable to respond to verbal commands
Level II	Responsive to the environment
	Able to respond to simple, one-step commands, but distractable
Level I	Oriented to self, time, and place and recording ongoing events
	Able to respond to and follow directions in a controlled environment

Source: Adapted with permission from J Blaskey, Head Trauma, in *Pediatric Neurologic Physical Therapy*, 2nd ed., SK Campbell, pp. 229–230, © 1991, Churchill-Livingstone.

Rancho Levels of Cognitive Functioning

Level I	No response to stimuli
	No response to verbal commands
Level II	Generalized response to stimuli
	No response to verbal commands
Level III	Consistent localized response to stimuli
	No response to verbal commands
Level IV	Confused agitated
	Heightened state of activity
	Demonstrates bizarre and nonpurposeful behavior relative to the environment
Level V	Confused inappropriate
	Can follow simple commands but is inconsistent
	Shows general attention to the environment but is easily distracted
	Lacks ability to focus attention on a specific task
	Memory impaired so that new information is not maintained
Level VI	Confused appropriate

Shows goal-directed behavior
Responds appropriately to the environment
Memory still impaired, but may remember some tasks performed from one session to the next if reminded
Can follow simple commands
Still dependent on external clues for direction
Shows little or no transfer of training or generalization

Level VII   Automatic appropriate
Behavior appropriate
Child is oriented to self and environment
Is able to perform daily routine tasks automatically, but needs supervision to initiate activity
Recent memory still impaired, resulting in limited recall of activities and decreased rate of learning for new information
Judgment is impaired

Level VIII   Appropriate
Can recall and integrate past and recent activities
Can adapt responses to the changing environment
Can remember activities from one session to the next
Can perform without supervision
Still has deficits in abstract reasoning
Still has limited tolerance to stress
Still has some impairment in judgment

Source: Adapted with permission from J Blaskey, Head Trauma, in *Pediatric Neurologic Physical Therapy*, 2nd ed., SK Campbell, pp. 219, © 1991, Churchill-Livingstone.

- Motor control problems may include the following:
  1. ataxia (dyssynergia, dysmetria); child may be viewed as clumsy
  2. diadochokinesis (difficulty performing rapid movement)
  3. time force production
  4. spasticity (hyperreflexia)
  5. muscle tone imbalance
  6. weakness
  7. visual-motor dysfunction
- Musculoskeletal problems may include ROM limitations; heterotopic ossification, especially around the shoulders, elbows, hips, and knees, due to prolonged coma; and soft tissue contractions, due to immobility and persistent posturing.
- There may be visual and auditory sensory deficits.
- Cognitive deficits may include fluctuating levels of alertness and consciousness, impaired attention span, distractibility, impaired orientation and memory, amnesia, impaired judgment, poor problem-solving skills, and impaired intelligence.
- Behavior and personality changes may include aggression, poor impulsive control and impulsivity, destructive behavior, hyperactivity, poor social judgment, emotional lability, low frustration tolerance, and temper tantrums.
- The child may require supervision.

- Functional skill limitations may include problems in transfer and limitations in ambulation.
- Other problems may include cerebral edema, headaches, vertigo, post-traumatic epilepsy, spinal cord injury, brachial plexus injury, and fractures.

TREATMENT/MANAGEMENT

The timing, frequency, and type of treatment for effective outcome from head injuries has not been determined. Treatment based on neurodevelopmental therapy (Bobath techniques) is reported but has not been shown to be effective. Treatment based on biomechanical models, motor learning, and movement science (Carr and Shepherd) has shown some success. Recovery from head injury continues for at least 2 to 3 years and probably longer, although the rate slows. However, a young child who makes an apparent good recovery may not show the problems in cognition until adolescence.

Respiratory Management
- Ensure clear airways with modified bronchial drainage and assisted breathing exercises.
- Use modified postural drainage, since head-dependent position is contraindicated (increased intracranial pressure).
- Manual techniques of percussion and vibration assist in mobilizing secretions.

ROM
- Use positioning, myofascial stretch, joint mobilization, static stretch, cast, splints, orthoses, and/or electric stimulation to facilitate or manage problems in ROM.
- Compensatory techniques may be useful until heterotopic ossification or soft tissue contractures are resolved.

Soft Tissue Management
- Prevent soft tissue contractures, especially in hip and knee flexors, ankle plantarflexors, and adductors and flexors of the upper extremities.
- Discourage supine position, as it stimulates dystonic posturing.
- Passive ROM exercises appear not to prevent contractures, but talking with the child about the movements may help establish contact with the environment.
- Serial casting of calf muscle contractures and possibly other joints is effective.

Active Exercise
- Active exercise or active assistive exercise should be started as soon as possible.
- Active exercise is important with serial casting so the child regains muscle control and does not lose the gains made by the serial cast.
- Passive stretching appears not to be effective in improving muscle activation or functional activity.

Motor Learning (Adapted From Tecklin)
- The goal must be identified and relevant to the child.
- The child must be an active participant in learning the movement through experiencing the feel of the movement.
- The therapist assists with the inhibition of unnecessary activity.
- Normal postural reactions necessary to maintain balance and position against gravity permit progression from stability to controlled mobility.

- Guided and controlled practice, variability in practice, motivation and knowledge of results, and feedback on performance are used to enhance learning.
- Feedback must be specific, quantitative, and appropriate to the cognitive level of the child.
- Practice sessions must challenge the child to solve problems and adapt to different situations and environments.
- After the child practices a single movement, it must be incorporated into functional movement tasks immediately to maximize learning.
- Activities should be task and context specific.
- Activities used should be everyday actions such as sit-to-stand, walking, reaching, and manipulation.
- Supervised and nonsupervised activities should be observed as treatment progresses.

Oral-Motor Function
- Desensitize hypersensitivity to reduce effect of bionic bite and gag. Use firm pressure on the lips, firm stroking of the gums, and firm stroking and pressure with a tongue blade intraorally.
- Increase stimulation for hyposensitivity using quick strokes periorally and intraorally prior to feeding and lemon ice or chilled utensils to facilitate awareness and completion of swallow.
- Maintain trunk and head in good alignment.

Attention Control Training
- Have the child make eye contact while the task is explained and when verbal feedback is provided.
- Modify the task as needed to permit some degree of success.
- Decrease distractions initially, and then gradually add them back as attention improves.
- Try to arrange carryover of improved performance outside therapy session.

Behavior Management Techniques
- Motivation may be enhanced by selecting activities that are relevant and challenging to the child.
- The activities should be achievable, and feedback that the child likes should always be provided for success.

Level III and IV (Ommaya Scale)
- Determine the need for assistive devices and equipment.
- Prevent contractures, especially if the child is in a wheelchair.
- Position to maintain body alignment and prevent deformities. A program using the tilt table may be necessary if the child has been prone for a long period of time.
- Maintain ROM and joint flexibility using ROM and stretching exercises. Serial casting may be necessary.
- Teach family members to do respiratory-postural drainage-vibration program.
- Instruct the family on good body mechanics when assisting in transfers.

Level II (Ommaya Scale)
- Help the child to relearn automatic activities such as rolling, sitting, crawling, standing, walking, and self-feeding.
- Instruct the family on the need for safety and supervision.

Level I (Ommaya Scale)
- Help the child relearn mobility by promoting normal postural reactions needed for balance and position against gravity and progressing from standing to controlled ambulation.
- Help the child relearn self-care activities by using guided and controlled practice and a variety of practice situations and by providing knowledge of results and feedback on performance.
- Provide exercise therapy to increase muscle strength by using games and activities of interest to the child.

Parent and Client Education
- Instruct parents and caregivers in all aspects of the child's care.
- Help the parents to be realistic in their expectations.
- Identify structure barriers and safety hazards in the home environment.
- Assist the family in identifying adaptive equipment needs.
- Help the family identify community and national resources.

Team Management
  Work with other team members to provide a total rehabilitation program.
- The speech pathologist assesses and treats the cognitive and language problems.
- Social workers, psychologists, and psychiatrists may provide family counseling to deal with behavioral and personality changes.
- Social workers assess and intervene with family support systems to facilitate family adjustment.
- A nurse or therapist familiar with the educational system can facilitate necessary testing and referrals for reentry into school.
- The occupational therapist emphasizes fine motor, self-care, and perceptual skills, age-appropriate socialization, and play skills.

PRECAUTIONS/CONTRAINDICATIONS
- Do not use the head-dependent position for postural drainage because it may increase intracranial pressure.
- If serial casting is used with a child who is nonverbal or nonresponsive, special attention must be made to ensure skin integrity because the child will not be able to report pain or discomfort.
- If serial casting is used with a child, be sure that alignment of the foot is preserved to avoid rocker shape by force applied to the forefoot instead of the ankle joint.
- Safety is especially important with a child who is mobile but not cognitively able to judge hazards in the environment.
- Physical skills are not a good indicator of recovery. Cognitive deficits can remain even when physical recovery is complete. Do not overstate expected outcome.

DESIRED OUTCOME/PROGNOSIS
- The child will be able to perform mobility activities appropriate for age or preinjury status in levels I and II (Ommaya Scale; see box) and for physical and cognitive considerations in levels III and IV.
- The child will be able to perform functional activities appropriate for age or preinjury status in levels I and II and for physical and cognitive considerations in levels III and IV.

- The child will be able to perform developmental activities appropriate for age or preinjury status in levels I and II and for physical and cognitive considerations in levels III and IV.
- The child will be able to continue education appropriate for age or preinjury status in levels I and II and for physical and cognitive considerations in levels III and IV.
- The child at level II will be able to follow commands, initiate purposeful activity, and perform automatic activities appropriate for age or preinjury status.
- The child at level I will be able to function independently in all activities appropriate for age or preinjury status. Some supervision may be needed for cognitive tasks requiring problem solving, judgment, and impulse control.
- Family or caregivers will be able to manage the child's needs if level of function is III or IV.

REFERENCES

ASSESSMENT

Bruininks–Oseretsky Test of Motor Proficiency
Bruininks RH. *Bruininks–Oseretsky Test of Motor Proficiency.* Circle Pines, Minn: American Guidance Service; 1978.

Children's Coma Scale
Raimondi AJ, Hirschauer J. Head injury in infant and toddler: coma scoring and outcome scale. *Child's Brain.* 1984;11:12–35.

Children's Orientation and Amnesia Test (COAT)
Ewing-Cobb L, Lewin HS, Fletcher JM, Miner ME, Eisenbert HM. Post-traumatic amnesia in children: assessment and outcome. Presented at the meeting of the International Neuropsychological Society; 1989: Vancouver, BC, Canada.

Functional Independence Measure for Children (WeeFIM)
Braun SL, Granger CV. A practical approach to functional assessment in pediatrics. *Occupational Therapy Practice.* 1991; 2:46–51.

Glascow Coma Score
Teasdale G, Jennett B. Assessment of coma and impaired consciousness. *Lancet.* 1974;2:81–84.

Ommaya Scale
Ommaya AK. Trauma to the nervous system. *Annals of the Royal College of Surgery in England.* 1966;39:317–347.
Carlidge NEF, Shaw DA. Head injury. *Major Problems in Neurology.* 10;42–51.

Peabody Developmental Motor Scales
Folio MR, Fewell RR. *Peabody Developmental Motor Scales and Activity Cards.* Allen, Tex: DLM Teaching Resources; 1983.

Pediatric Evaluation of Disability Inventory (PEDI)
Haley SM, Coster WJ, Ludlow LH, Haltiwangtee JT, Andrellos PH. *Pediatric Evaluation of Disability Inventory.* Boston, Mass: New England Medical Center Publications; 1992.

Rancho Levels of Cognitive Functioning
Hagen C, et al. Levels of cognitive function. In: Hagen C, et al. *Rehabilitation of the Head-Injured Adult: Comprehensive Physical Management.* Downey, Calif: Professional Staff Association of Rancho Los Amigos Hospital; 1979:87–90.

TREATMENT
Blaskey J. Head trauma. In: Campbell SK, ed. *Pediatric Neurologic Physical Therapy.* 2nd ed. New York, NY: Churchill Livingstone; 1994:213–249.
Middleton J, Jones M, Moffat V, Wintle L, Russell P. Rehabilitation after acute neurological trauma. In: McCarthy GT, ed. *Physical Disability in Childhood: An Interdisciplinary Approach to Management.* New York, NY: Churchill Livingstone; 1992:249–268.
Phillips WE. Brain tumors, traumatic head injuries, and near-drowning. In: Campbell SK, ed. *Physical Therapy for Children.* Philadelphia, Pa: WB Saunders Co; 1994:557–564.
Shepherd RB. Acute brain injury. In: Shepherd RB, *Physiotherapy in Paediatrics.* Oxford, England: Butterworth-Heinemann; 1995:145–153.

Ventilator Dependency

DESCRIPTION
A ventilator-dependent child needs a ventilator to provide most or all of the support in breathing at night only or throughout the 24-hour day. Ventilator dependency is defined as having been on the ventilator for at least 6 months and without obvious prospect of dispensing with this support (Robinson et al, "Ventilator-Dependent Child," p. 269; see references). The US Government Office of Technology Assessment (OTA) defines the technology-dependent child as "one who needs both a medical device to compensate for the loss of a vital body function and substantial and ongoing nursing care to avert death or further disability" (OTA, Ventilator-Dependent Children; see references). Mechanical ventilization is broadly classified into two types. Positive-pressure ventilation, the most common type, operates by inflating the lungs with increased airway pressures above atmospheric pressure. The peak inflation pressure generated depends on lung and thorax compliance, airway resistance, tidal volume delivered and inspiratory flow rate, and baseline level of continuous positive airway pressure from the ventilator. Negative-pressure ventilization, rarely used today, functions by using a subatmospheretic pressure gradient that is created around the body while the nose and mouth are exposed to atmospheric (ambient) pressure. As a result of the difference in pressure, air enters the lung.

Types of Ventilation

Assisted control ventilation (ACV): Ventilator is triggered by the child's spontaneous efforts to breathe or by a timing device that acts as a backup in the event of apnea to initiate breathing.

Assisted mechanical ventilation (AMV): Ventilator will not deliver a breath unless the patient intimates a spontaneous breathing effort. Also called "patient-triggered" positive-pressure ventilation.

Continuous positive airway pressure ventilation (CPAP): Used in conjunction with spontaneous breaths but can be used with mechanical ventilation if needed.

Continuous positive-pressure ventilation (CPPV): Delivers a preselected ventilatory rate, tidal volume, and inspiratory flow rate independent of spontaneous attempts to breathe, but airway pressure never returns to zero.

Controlled mechanical ventilation (CMV): Same as CPPV, except that airway pressure drops to zero.

Expiratory positive-pressure ventilation (EPPV): Similar to CPAP, except that airway pressure is zero or negative during inhalation but increases at the end of exhalation to a preset positive pressure.

Extracorporeal membrane oxygenation (ECMO): Used for infants with severe reversible respiratory failure who do not respond well to other forms of ventilatory support.

High-frequency positive-pressure ventilation (HFPPV): Delivers compressed gas through a small-bore cannula at rates of between 180 and 300 pulses per minute.

High-frequency jet ventilation (HFJV): Used with patients who have respiratory distress syndrome, pulmonary interstitial emphysema, or pulmonary dysplasia due to diaphragmatic hernia.

High-frequency oscillation (HFO): Uses a pump oscillator or airflow interrupter to deliver pulses of gas at a fixed rate between 180 and 300 pulses per minute.

Intermittent mandatory ventilation (IMV): Child breathes spontaneously with a mechanical inflation provided at preset intervals that the child cannot influence. Used to maintain normal alveolar ventilization and $PaCO_2$.

Intermittent positive-pressure ventilation (IPPV): Respiratory support is provided on a set time on and off, usually through a tracheotomy.

Mandatory minute ventilation (MMV): Child is guaranteed a preselected minute volume either through spontaneous ventilation or by the positive-pressure ventilator.

Negative extrathoracic pressure ventilation (NEPV): Used for respiratory failure due to myopathy or neuromuscular disorder, congenital central hypoventilation (Ondine's curse), bilateral phrenic nerve damage, weaning from positive pressure ventilation, and prevention of further lung damage.

Synchronized intermittent mandatory ventilation (SIMV): Similar to IMV, but mandatory breath is synchronized to begin with the next spontaneous inhalation to avoid the phenomenon of "breath staking."

Sources: Data from MK Kelly, Children with Ventilator Dependence, in *Physical Therapy For Children*, SK Campbell, ed., pp. 669–671, © 1991, WB Saunders and Co. and A Parker, Pediatrics, Ventilation of the Newborn, in *Physiotherapy for Respiratory and Cardiac Problems*, BA Webber, and JA Pryor, eds., pp. 298–301, © 1993, Churchill-Livingstone.

CAUSE

Primary causes of ventilator dependence are severe lung disease, usually secondary to cardiac problems, or severe neuromuscular conditions such as high spinal cord injuries or generalized neuromuscular weakness. Common pathophysiologic mechanisms leading to chronic respiratory failure are central nervous system disorders such as apnea of prematurity or intracranial hemorrhage, intrinsic muscle disease such as Duchenne's muscular dystrophy or myasthenia gravis, intrinsic pulmonary disease such as congenital heart disease or bronchopulmonary dysplasia, and congenital airway abnormalities such as tracheoesophageal fistula or laryngomalacia. Respiratory failure itself is classified into two types. Type I failure is hypoxemia with a normal or low arterial PCO_2, usually caused by a mismatch between the rate of ventilation and perfusion. Type II failure is alveolar hypoventilation, in which the levels of arterial carbon dioxide are elevated in addition to hypoxemia. Type II failure is most often associated with ventilator dependence.

ASSESSMENT

Areas
- History: complications associated with mechanical ventilation, including respiratory, circulatory, metabolic, renal, and equipment malfunction
- Respiratory: response to activity and general status; signs of respiratory distress, such as skin color changes indicative of hypoxia, changes in respiratory rate, changes in breathing pattern, symmetry of chest expansion, posture, general level of comfort, shoulder retraction, nasal flaring, expiratory grunting, and stridor or high-pitched sound
- Neuromuscular and neurodevelopmental: musculoskeletal status; muscle strength; posture; movement competencies, such as rolling, getting to prone on elbows, coming to sit
- Function: age-appropriate basic and instrumental activities of daily living; general mobility skills; communication skills; role within the family and community

Instruments/Procedures

Respiratory
- cardiorespiratory monitors
- pulse oximeters
- ventilator alarms
- transcutaneous PO_2 and PCO_2
- oxygen analyzers on the ventilator
- sphygmomanometer

PROBLEMS
- Continuing need for respiratory support
  1. In the most severe cases, mechanical ventilation may be needed throughout life.
  2. Positive airway pressure methods may be needed, such as continuous positive airway pressure (CPAP), or positive and expiratory pressure (PEEP) may be needed for moderate involvement.
  3. Supplemental nasal oxygen may suffice for milder problems.
- Sensory defensiveness
- Generalized weakness
- Poor cardiopulmonary endurance
- Soft tissue tightness or contracture
- Muscle tightness or contracture
- Developmental delay
  1. Motor development delay related to being tethered
     a. Limited mobility due to being tethered to the equipment, which limits opportunity for exploration and practice

b. Delay in gross and fine motor skills

c. Delay in reflex and reactions: primitive reflex integration, use of righting and equilibrium

d. Delay in postural stability and midline functions

e. Delay in shifting from static to dynamic postures

2. Sensory development delay related to limited mobility

3. Cognitive development delay related to limited mobility

4. Communication and speech development delay, in part due to tracheotomy

5. Delay in development of oral-motor skills: hypersensitivity, poor reflex development in suck, poor oral-motor control

- Separation from "normal" environment due to long hospitalizations and physical constraints due to the equipment
- Poor endurance for physical activity
- Poor nutrition intake relative to energy expenditure to breathe
- Failure to thrive syndrome

TREATMENT/MANAGEMENT

There is no single approach to treating and managing children who are dependent on ventilators. The major concept is based on preventing a vicious cycle in which inactivity leads to reluctance to move and explore which decreases endurance and physical fitness, which leads to inactivity, and so forth. A related concept is the idea that if the child associates movement with negative experiences such as fatigue, hypoxia, and pain, his or her motivation to move and explore will be reduced. However, very little is known about the limits ventilators put on the system. Normally, cardiac function limits exercise, but the ventilator may be the primary factor that limits exercise in the child who is dependent on a ventilator.

- Increase the variety of opportunities the child has to explore and experience the environment through movement and practice.
  1. Develop gross and fine motor skills.
  2. Develop reflexes and reactions.
  3. Emphasize midline functions, including scapular protraction and trunk rotation.
  4. Emphasize weight shift across the midline to change posture.
- Increase endurance and physical fitness through developmental activities.
  1. Gradually increase treatment length and intensity while staying within the cardiopulmonary limits.
  2. Gradually increase demands for environmental exploration.
- If motor impairments such as lower extremity weakness and spasticity are present, assist in providing assistive devices to facilitate ambulation.
- Recommend approaches to staff and parents to "normalize" the environment (reduce the impact of machines and equipment) and facilitate the normal acquisition of functional skills.
  1. Assist family or caregivers with ideas on how to alter the environment to reduce the physical limitations to infant/child movement.
  2. Fabricate or provide design for furniture that will accommodate ventilator and tubing while allowing the infant maximum opportunity for practicing skill development.
- Teach parents how to increase environmental (people and toy) interaction.
- Prevent deprivation of sensory and motor experience, which may lead to secondary disability not specifically related to the primary respiratory problems.
- Work with the interdisciplinary team to reduce the developmental risk of the child and improve the potential for a sense of well-being, social productivity, and self-actualization.

- Instruct parents in all aspects of care in which physical therapy has been involved.
- Assist the parents and interdisciplinary team in decisions regarding home care versus residential care. Weaning the child from a ventilator may take 2 or 3 years from supplemental oxygen.

PRECAUTIONS/CONTRAINDICATIONS
- Watch for pneumothorax due to high peak inspiratory pressure, positive end expiratory pressure, long inflation times, and active expiration.
- Pulmonary interstitial emphysema (PIE) occurs when gas leaks from an alveolus, travels along the cardiovascular bundle, and becomes trapped, forming an interstitial gas pocket.
- Subglottic stenosis can occur following prolonged intubation and lead to upper airway obstruction.
- Retinopathy of prematurity or hemorrhage of the capillaries in the retina can lead to fibrosis and scarring of the retina, which may lead to permanent visual impairment.
- Watch for signs of bronchopulmonary dysplasia (BD) or chronic lung disease (CLD), as well as for signs of pulmonary congestion, edema, and decreased lung compliance.
- Watch for signs of fatigue and cardiopulmonary stress.

DESIRED OUTCOME/PROGNOSIS
- The child will be able to breathe without the assistance of a ventilator or, if the respiratory system is paralyzed or severely compromised, the assistance given will be the minimum needed consistent with the disorder.
- The child will have age-appropriate skills or will have attained the skills possible given restrictions imposed by the physiologic and ventilation systems.
- The child will able to perform functional activities in the family, school, and community or to perform all activities possible given the restrictions imposed by the physiologic and ventilation systems.

REFERENCES

Kelly MK. Children with ventilator dependence. In: Campbell SK, ed. *Physical Therapy for Children*. Philadelphia, Pa: WB Saunders Co; 1994:663–685.

Office of Technology Assessment. *Technology-Dependent Children: Home Versus Hospital Care. A Technical Memorandum*. Washington, DC: Government Printing Office; 1987.

Parker A. Paediatrics: ventilation of the newborn. In: Webber BA, Pryor JA, eds. *Physiotherapy for Respiratory and Cardiac Problems*. New York, NY: Churchill Livingstone; 1993:298–301.

Robinson RO, Cartwright R, Fuller W, Jones M, Samuels M. The ventilator dependent child. In: McCarthy GT, ed. *Physical Disability in Childhood: An Interdisciplinary Approach to Management*. New York, NY: Churchill Livingstone; 1992:269–277.

Chapter 13
Pulmonary Disorders

- Asthma
- Bronchiectasis
- Chronic bronchitis
- Emphysema
- Pneumonia

Asthma

DESCRIPTION

Asthma is a disease of excessive airway responsiveness to stimuli that are otherwise harmless. This hyperreactivity leads to recurrent inflammation and narrowing of the airways that can be reversed with medication or spontaneously. Asthma is one of a number of disorders considered obstructive, including bronchiectasis, chronic bronchitis, cystic fibrosis, and emphysema.

CAUSE

Obstructive diseases are caused by either reversible factors, such as inflammation, or irreversible factors, such as damaged alveoli. A localized lesion, such as a foreign body, can also cause airway obstruction. Causes can be considered extrinsic or intrinsic. Extrinsic asthma is caused by hypersensitivity to a triggering substance and usually develops early in life. Intrinsic asthma begins in adulthood and is considered more intense and harder to control with treatment. Factors that can trigger or exacerbate asthma include anxiety, history of stress at birth or early hospitalization, respiratory irritants like smoke, exercise-induced temperature change in airways, premenstrual changes, hyperventilation, changes in weather temperature, and certain foods such as dairy foods, caffeine drinks, or products with the additives of salt or aspirin.

ASSESSMENT

Areas

- History, including any drug or oxygen therapy and fluid balance
- Vital signs, including temperature, blood pressure, and heart rate
- General appearance
- Cardiovascular, including results of exercise testing
- Equipment, including use of oxygen, humidification, drips, and any chest tubes
- Musculoskeletal, including posture, head and neck musculature, and chest shape
- Skin and soft tissue, including edema and condition of hands, especially nails
- Pulmonary, including breathing rate, pattern, and speech; position of trachea, chest motion, fremitus (vibration from the voice or secretion transmitted to chest wall), chest pain, diaphragmatic movement; breath sounds, extrapulmonary adventitious sounds, voice sounds; lung density and diaphragmatic excursion
- Functional level, including activities of daily living (ADLs)
- Special tests to which the PT may or may not have access

Instruments/Procedures (See References for Sources)

Functional Level
- Chronic Respiratory Disease Questionnaire
- classes of respiratory impairment
- visual analogue scale for dyspnea

Pulmonary
- palpation of abdomen, position of trachea, fremitus, scalene muscles, chest pain, diaphragmatic movement
- auscultation of breath sounds, extra-pulmonary adventitious sounds, voice sounds
- percussion of lung density and diaphragmatic excursion

Special Tests to Which the PT May or May Not Have Access
- arterial blood gases
- bacterial and cytological tests of sputum
- chest x-ray
- exercise tests
- Respiratory Function Tests (RFTs)
    1. airways resistance
    2. body plethysmography
    3. diffusing capacity
    4. exercise testing
    5. expiratory reserve volume (ERV)
    6. flow-volume loops
    7. forced expiratory volume in 1 second
    8. forced vital capacity (FVC)
    9. functional residual capacity (FRC)
    10. helium dilution method
    11. inspiratory reserve volume (IRV)
    12. nitrogen washout test
    13. peak expiratory flow rate (PEFR)
    14. residual volume (RV)
    15. spirogram
    16. spirometry
    17. tidal volume
    18. total lung capacity (TLC)
    19. vital capacity (VC)
    20. ventilation/perfusion scan

PROBLEMS

Acute Asthma
- The client usually feels breathless, and breathing is labored.
- The client may have overexpansion of the chest.
- The client can have prolonged expiration.
- The client may feel anxious.
- The client usually has decreased breath sounds and wheezing.

Severe Acute Asthma
- The wheeze usually lessens.
- The client usually has difficulty in talking.
- The skin can feel clammy.
- The client can look blue and have a rapid heart rate.
- The client can feel confused.
- The client usually has tachypnea.
- The client usually has increased use of accessory muscle tone.
- The client may have increased secretions.
- There may be pulsus paradoxus.

Chronic Asthma
- The client usually has a dry cough at night or morning wheezing.

- The client can have an exaggerated bronchial response to a cold room at night, leading to a morning dip in peak flow.

TREATMENT/MANAGEMENT

Acute Asthma
Aim to control the disease. Attacks may be avoided by the following suggested instructions to the client:
- Assess peak expiratory flow rate (PEFR) upon waking (within 1/2 hour) daily if chronic; may need to seek medical help if PEFR is below 80 and does not rise to above 200 following medication.
- Keep a log of symptoms to gain better understanding of when to seek medical help.
- If in a high-risk group, be prepared for an attack with equipment needed for self-treatment. Provide the following instructions to the client on how to deal with an attack:
- Lean forward with arms supported in an upright position. An alternative position is to straddle a chair facing backwards.
- Fresh air, but not too cold, may help.
- Try to breathe slowly through the nose, controlling the rate and rhythm of breath.
- Place emphasis on exhalation, perhaps using pursed-lip breathing.
- Use relaxation techniques.
- Use secretion removal techniques as indicated.

Chronic Asthma
- Provide the client with education about the disease.
- Help the client identify avoidable precipitating factors.
- Encourage regular exercise.
- Teach relaxation and stress reduction techniques.
- Encourage the client to try different sleeping postures and temperatures if he or she has nocturnal asthma.
- Inform the client about support groups.

PRECAUTIONS
- Deep breathing can exacerbate bronchospasm in those with acute asthma.
- Improperly used nebulizers can trigger bronchospasm.

DESIRED OUTCOME/PROGNOSIS
- The client will experience a reduction in the number and intensity of asthma attacks.
- The client will have an increased capacity for ADLs.
- The client will have an increased sense of control over symptoms.

REFERENCES

ASSESSMENT
American Physical Therapy Association. A guide to physical therapist practice, volume I: a description of patient management. *Physical Therapy*. 1995;75:720–738. **[Ventilation, respiration, and circulation examination]**

Goodman C, Snyder TE. *Differential Diagnosis in Physical Therapy*. Philadelphia, Pa: WB Saunders;1990:332, 337, 357, 362–363.

Functional Level

Chronic Respiratory Disease Questionnaire

Guyatt G, Berman LB, Townsend M, Pugsley SO. A measure of quality of life for clinical trials in chronic lung disease. *Thorax.* 1987;42:773–778.

Classes of Respiratory Impairment

Rothstein JM, Roy SH, Wolf SL. *The Rehabilitation Specialist's Handbook.* Philadelphia, Pa: FA Davis Co; 1991:585–626.

Visual Analogue Scale for Dyspnea

Aitken RCB. Measurement of feelings using visual analogue scales. *Proceedings of the Royal Society of Medicine.* 1969;62:989–993.

Pulmonary

Auscultation

Aweida D, Kelsey CJ. Accuracy and reliability of physical therapists in auscultating tape-recorded lung sound. *Physiotherapy Canada.* 1990;42:279–282.

Brooks D, Wilson L, Kelsey C, et al. Accuracy and reliability of specialized physical therapists in auscultating tape recorded lung sounds. *Physiotherapy Canada.* 1993;45:21–24.

Pasterkamp H, Montgomery M, Wiebicke W, et al. Nomenclature used by health care professionals to describe breath sounds in asthma. *Chest.* 1993;92:346–352.

Percussion

Bourke S, Nunes D, Stafford F, Hurley G, Graham I, et al. Percussion of the chest re-visited: a comparison of the diagnostic value of auscultatory and conventional chest percussion. *Irish Journal of Medical Science.* 1989;158:82–84.

Special Tests to Which the PT May or May Not Have Access

Mackenzie CF, Shin B, McAslan TC. Chest physiotherapy: the effect on arterial oxygenation. *Anesthesia and Analgesia.* 1978;57:28–30. **[Arterial blood gases; chest x-ray]**

Respiratory Function Tests (RFTs)

American Thoracic Society. Lung function testing: selection of reference values and interpretive strategies. *American Review of Respiratory Disease.* 1991;144:1202–1218. **[Vital capacity]**

Downie PA. *Cash's Textbook of Chest, Heart and Vascular Disorders for Physiotherapists.* 4th ed. Philadelphia, Pa: JB Lippincott Co; 1987:83–101. **[Ventilatory function: helium dilution method, whole-body plethysmography, and radiological. Tests of forced expiration: peak expiratory flow rate (PEFR), forced expiratory volume in 1 second (FEV1), and flow-volume loops]**

Hough A. *Physiotherapy in Respiratory Care: A Problem-Solving Approach.* London, England: Chapman & Hall; 1991:37–41. **[Peak expiratory flow rate (PEFR), total lung capacity (TLC), vital capacity (VC), forced vital capacity (FVC), forced expiratory volume in 1 second (FEV 1 *Little*), FEV1/FVC, tidal volume, functional residual capacity (FRC), inspiratory reserve volume (IRV), expiratory reserve volume (ERV), residual volume (RV), spirometry, inspiratory muscle function, airways resistance, lung volumes, and exercise testing]**

O'Rourke PP, Schena JA, Thompson JE. The effects of pulmonary physiotherapy on delivered tidal volume. *Critical Care Medicine.* 1984;88:286. Abstract.

Rothstein JM, Roy SH, Wolf SL. *The Rehabilitation Specialist's Handbook.* Philadelphia, Pa: FA Davis Co; 1991:585–626. **[Pulmonary function terminology, common pulmonary function tests such as spirometry, diffusing capacity, body plethysmography, nitrogen washout test, ventilation/perfusion scan, spirogram and lung volumes, low-volume loops, and normal arterial blood gas values]**

Singh S. The use of field walking tests for assessment of functional capacity in patients with chronic airways obstruction. *Physiotherapy.* 1992;78:102–104.

Vital Signs

Blood Pressure

Frohlich ED. Recommendations for human blood pressure determination by sphygmomanometers: report of a special task force appointed by the steering committee, American Heart Association. *Hypertension.* 1988;11:210A–222A.

Stolt M. Reliability of auscultory method of arterial blood pressure. *Hypertension.* 1990;3:697–703.

Heart Rate

Rothstein JM. *Measurement in Physical Therapy.* New York, NY: Churchill Livingstone; 1985.

Respiratory Rate

Simeows EAF, Roark R, Berman S, Ester L, Murphy J. Respiratory rate: measurement of variability over time and accuracy at different counting periods. *Archives of Disease in Childhood.* 1991;66:1199–1203.

TREATMENT

Booker HA. Exercise training and breathing control in patients with chronic airflow limitation. *Physiotherapy.* 1984;70:258–260.

Cohen M, Hoskin TM. *Cardiopulmonary Symptoms in Physical Therapy.* New York, NY: Churchill Livingstone; 1988.

Dean E. Effect of body position on pulmonary function. *Physical Therapy.* 1985;65:613–618.

DeGarmo C, Cerny F, Conboy K, Ellis EF. In vivo effects of theophylline on diaphragm, bicep, and quadricep strength and fatigability. *Journal of Allergy and Clinical Immunology.* 1988;82:1041–1046.

Downie PA. *Cash's Textbook of Chest, Heart and Vascular Disorders for Physiotherapists.* 4th ed. Philadelphia, Pa: JB Lippincott Co; 1987.

Ellis E, Alison J. *Key Issues in Cardiorespiratory Physiotherapy.* Boston, Mass: Butterworth-Heinemann; 1992.

Frownfelter D. *Chest Physical Therapy and Pulmonary Rehabilitation: An Interdisciplinary Approach.* Chicago, Ill: Year Book; 1987:239–259.

Hough A. *Physiotherapy in Respiratory Care.* London, England: Chapman & Hall; 1991.

Irwin S, Tecklin JS, eds. *Cardiopulmonary Physical Therapy.* 2nd ed. St Louis, Mo: CV Mosby Co; 1990.

Kigin C. *Advances in Chest Physical Therapy.* Park Ridge, Ill: American College of Chest Physicians; 1984.

Kigin C. Evolution of pulmonary physical therapy in the United States. *Physiotherapy Practice.* 1986;2:22–30.

Pryor JA. *Respiratory Care.* New York, NY: Churchill Livingstone; 1991.

Tyler ML. Complications of positioning and chest physiotherapy. *Respiratory Care.* 1982;27:458–466.

Webber BA. *The Brompton Hospital Guide to Chest Physiotherapy.* 5th ed. London, England: Blackwell Scientific Publications; 1988.

Webber BA, Pryor JA. *Physiotherapy for Respiratory and Cardiac Problems.* New York, NY: Churchill Livingstone; 1993.

Witt PL, MacKinnon J. Trager psychophysical integration: a method to improve chest mobility of patients with chronic lung disease. *Physical Therapy.* 1986;66:214–217.

Zadai CC. Exercise testing and training for the pulmonary impaired patient. In: Basmajian JV, Wolf S, eds. *Therapeutic Exercise.* 5th ed. Baltimore, Md: Williams & Wilkins; 1990.

Zadai CC. *Pulmonary Management in Physical Therapy.* New York, NY: Churchill Livingstone; 1992.

Bronchiectasis

DESCRIPTION

Bronchiectasis is an obstruction of airways that have become damaged and chronically dilated. Airway obstruction is characterized by an increased resistance to airflow occurring during forced expiration. Other disorders considered obstructive include asthma, chronic bronchitis, cystic fibrosis, and emphysema.

CAUSE

Obstructive diseases are caused by either reversible factors, such as inflammation, or irreversible factors, such as damaged alveoli. A localized lesion, such as a foreign body, may cause airway obstruction. Bronchiectasis can be caused by accidental inhalation of a foreign object or by a viral infection such as severe pneumonia.

ASSESSMENT

Areas
- History, including any drug or oxygen therapy and fluid balance
- Vital signs, including temperature, blood pressure, and heart rate
- General appearance
- Cardiovascular, including results of exercise testing
- Equipment, including use of oxygen, humidification, drips, and any chest tubes
- Musculoskeletal, including posture, head and neck musculature, and chest shape
- Skin and soft tissue, including edema and condition of hands, especially nails
- Pulmonary, including breathing rate, pattern, and speech; position of trachea, chest motion, fremitus (vibration from the voice or secretion transmitted to chest wall), chest pain, diaphragmatic movement; breath sounds, extrapulmonary adventitious sounds, voice sounds; lung density and diaphragmatic excursion
- Functional level, including activities of daily living (ADLs)
- Special tests to which the PT may or may not have access

Instruments (See References for Sources)

Functional level
- Chronic Respiratory Disease Questionnaire
- classes of respiratory impairment
- visual analogue scale for dyspnea

Pulmonary
- palpation of abdomen, position of trachea, fremitus, scalene muscles, chest pain, diaphragmatic movement
- auscultation of breath sounds, extrapulmonary adventitious sounds, voice sounds
- percussion of lung density and diaphragmatic excursion

Special Tests to Which the PT May or May Not Have Access
- arterial blood gases
- chest x-ray
- exercise tests

- bacterial and cytological tests of sputum
- Respiratory Function Tests (RFTs)
  1. airways resistance
  2. body plethysmography
  3. diffusing capacity
  4. exercise testing
  5. expiratory reserve volume (ERV)
  6. flow-volume loops
  7. forced expiratory volume in 1 second
  8. forced vital capacity (FVC)
  9. functional residual capacity (FRC)
  10. helium dilution method
  11. inspiratory reserve volume (IRV)
  12. nitrogen washout test
  13. peak expiratory flow rate (PEFR)
  14. residual volume (RV)
  15. spirogram
  16. spirometry
  17. tidal volume
  18. total lung capacity (TLC)
  19. vital capacity (VC)
  20. ventilation/perfusion scan

PROBLEMS
- The client usually has hoarse wheezes and altered breath sounds.
- There may be clubbing at the fingers.
- The client may be short of breath and fatigued.
- There can be a large quantity of pus-filled sputum that may also contain blood.

TREATMENT/MANAGEMENT
- Educate the client in sputum clearance.
- Encourage daily exercise if the disease is in the moderate stage.
- The client will probably need daily postural drainage to improve impaired sputum clearance.

Chest PT in General
- Provide education on disease control and pain management.
- Provide clearance of secretions via hydration, humidification, nebulization, mobilization, breathing exercises, postural drainage, manual techniques, mechanical aids, cough and forced expiratory techniques, and nasopharyngeal suction.
- Consider mechanical devices to aid ventilation, such as continuous positive airways pressure (CPAP) and intermittent positive-pressure breathing (IPPB). In general, additional oxygen therapy is needed only for hypoxemia. It can be delivered through low-flow or high-flow masks, large-capacity masks, reservoir bags, nasal cannulas, transtracheal oxygen catheters, tents, head boxes, or clear plastic hoods. Medication delivery devices include inhalers and nebulizers.
- Provide advice on appropriate activity level.
- Implement the following chest physical therapy techniques: positioning, controlled mobilization, and breathing exercises, as indicated.

Positioning
- Modify functional residual capacity using the following posture sequence, which gradually increases volume: supine, slumped sitting, half-lying, side-lying, toward prone, sitting upright, standing.
- Regular position changes should be part of the client's management plan.

Controlled Mobilization With Exercise
- Use controlled mobilization with exercise while the client is in an upright posture.
- Control activity level to increase depth of respiration slightly, and follow by relaxed standing to regain breath.
- Modify activity with transfers or walking depending on the client's abilities.
- Progress to regular graded exercise.

Breathing Exercises
- Techniques can include deep breathing, end-inspiratory hold, sniff technique, single percussion, and abdominal breathing.

PRECAUTIONS/CONTRAINDICATIONS
- Oxygen is a drug that has both side effects and risks. It should be carefully administered, precisely prescribed, and routinely monitored. Substernal pain, dyspnea, and cough may signal oxygen toxicity. In neonates, high concentrations of oxygen may cause eye damage.
- Some degree of atelectasis can develop in clients who cannot take deep breaths due to low lung volumes but are required to perform forced expiratory maneuvers.

Contraindications to CPAP and IPPB
- These devices are not intended to be used with subcutaneous emphysema, facial trauma, bronchopleural fistula, bullae, undrained pneumothorax, and recent esophageal or bronchial surgery.
- For IPPB, other cautions include pneumothorax, large emphysematous bullae in the lung, hemoptysis, active tuberculosis, or a bronchial tumor in the proximal airway.
- Clients with cystic fibrosis or emphysema can be susceptible to air trapping or pneumothorax, gastric distention, or infection.
- Improperly used nebulizers can trigger bronchospasm.

Contraindications to Head-Down Position in Postural Drainage
- abdominal distention
- acute spinal cord lesion
- arrhythmias
- breathlessness
- cardiovascular instability
- cerebral edema
- headache
- hemoptysis (recent)
- hiatal hernia
- hypertension
- obesity
- pregnancy

- pneumothorax, undrained
- pulmonary edema
- subcutaneous emphysema
- seizures

Contraindications to Postural Drainage in Any Position
- head injuries
- post esophagectomy
- aortic aneurysm
- during the filling cycle of peritoneal dialysis
- facial edema from burns, post eye surgery
  Discuss with medical staff if contraindicated technique should be risked for potential benefit.

Contraindications to Percussion and Vibration
- arrhythmias or angina (unstable)
- hemoptysis (recent)
- skin not intact due to trauma
- osteoporosis
- rib fracture or an increased risk of fracture

Contraindications to Coughing Therapy
- aneurysm
- increased intracranial pressure
- eye surgery (recent)
- subcutaneous emphysema
- pneumonectomy (recent)
  Spasm of multiple coughs can lead to fatigue, bronchospasm, and airway closure.

Contraindications and Precautions to Nasopharyngeal Suctioning
- Avoid in a client with a cerebrospinal fluid leak, clotting disorders, stridor, or pulmonary edema.
- Use caution with clients with recent esophagectomy or pneumonectomy.
- Suctioning may aggravate bronchospasm.
- Hypoxia and cardiac arrhythmias can occur during nasopharyngeal suctioning.
- Atelectasis or obstruction of the airway can be caused by suction that is too strong or too prolonged.

DESIRED OUTCOME/PROGNOSIS
- The client will have an increase in lung volume.
- The client will experience a relief of symptoms.
- The client will increase capacity for ADLs.
- The client will experience a decrease in episodes of attacks, leading to a sense of control over symptoms.
  Bronchiectasis may be reduced by childhood vaccination for whooping cough and measles.

REFERENCES

ASSESSMENT

American Physical Therapy Association. A guide to physical therapist practice, Volume I: a description of patient management. *Physical Therapy.* 1995;75:720–738. **[Ventilation, respiration, and circulation examination]**

Goodman C, Snyder TE. *Differential Diagnosis in Physical Therapy*. Philadelphia, Pa; WB Saunders, 1990:332, 337, 357, 362–363.

Functional Level

Chronic Respiratory Disease Questionnaire

Guyatt G, Berman LB, Townsend M, Pugsley SO. A measure of quality of life for clinical trials in chronic lung disease. *Thorax*. 1987;42:773–778.

Classes of Respiratory Impairment

Rothstein JM, Roy SH, Wolf SL. *The Rehabilitation Specialist's Handbook*. Philadelphia, Pa: FA Davis Co; 1991:585–626.

Visual Analogue Scale for Dyspnea

Aitken RCB. Measurement of feelings using visual analogue scales. *Proceedings of the Royal Society of Medicine*. 1969;62:989–993.

Pulmonary

Auscultation

Aweida D, Kelsey CJ. Accuracy and reliability of physical therapists in auscultating tape-recorded lung sound. *Physiotherapy Canada*. 1990;42:279–282.

Brooks D, Wilson L, Kelsey C, et al. Accuracy and reliability of specialized physical therapists in auscultating tape recorded lung sounds. *Physiotherapy Canada*. 1993;45:21–24.

Pasterkamp H, Montgomery M, Wiebicke W, et al. Nomenclature used by health care professionals to describe breath sounds in asthma. *Chest*. 1993;92:346–352.

Percussion

Bourke S, Nunes D, Stafford F, Hurley G, Graham I. Percussion of the chest re-visited: a comparison of the diagnostic value of auscultatory and conventional chest percussion. *Irish Journal of Medical Science*. 1989;158:82–84.

Special Tests to Which the PT May or May Not Have Access

Mackenzie CF, Shin B, McAslan TC. Chest physiotherapy: the effect on arterial oxygenation. *Anesthesia and Analgesia*. 1978;57:28–30. [Arterial blood gases, chest x-rays]

Respiratory Function Tests (RFTs)

American Thoracic Society. Lung function testing: selection of reference values and interpretive strategies. *American Review of Respiratory Disease*. 1991;144:1202–1218. [Vital capacity]

Downie PA. *Cash's Textbook of Chest, Heart and Vascular Disorders for Physiotherapists*. 4th ed. Philadelphia, Pa: JB Lippincott Co; 1987:83–101. [Ventilatory function: helium dilution method, whole-body plethysmography, and radiological. Tests of forced expiration: peak expiratory flow rate (PEFR), forced expiratory volume in 1 second (FEV1), and flow-volume loops]

Hough A. *Physiotherapy in Respiratory Care: A Problem-Solving Approach*. London, England: Chapman & Hall; 1991:37–41. [Peak expiratory flow rate (PEFR), total lung capacity (TLC), vital capacity (VC), forced vital capacity (FVC), forced expiratory volume in 1 second (FEV 1 *Little*), FEV1/FVC, tidal volume, functional residual capacity (FRC), inspiratory reserve volume (IRV), expiratory reserve volume (ERV), residual volume (RV), spirometry, inspiratory muscle function, airways resistance, lung volumes, and exercise testing]

O'Rourke PP, Schena JA, Thompson JE. The effects of pulmonary physiotherapy on delivered tidal volume. *Critical Care Medicine*. 1984;88:286. Abstract.

Rothstein JM, Roy SH, Wolf SL. *The Rehabilitation Specialist's Handbook*. Philadelphia, Pa: FA Davis Co; 1991:585–626. [Pulmonary function terminology, common pulmonary function tests such as spirometry, diffusing capacity, body plethysmography, nitrogen washout test, ventilation/perfusion scan, spirogram and lung volumes, low-volume loops, and normal arterial blood gas values]

Singh S. The use of field walking tests for assessment of functional capacity in patients with chronic airways obstruction. *Physiotherapy*. 1992;78:102–104.

Vital Signs

Blood Pressure
Frohlich ED. Recommendations for human blood pressure determination by sphygmomanometers: report of a special task force appointed by the steering committee, American Heart Association. *Hypertension*. 1988;11:210A–222A.
Stolt M. Reliability of auscultory method of arterial blood pressure. *Hypertension*. 1990;3:697–703.

Heart Rate
Rothstein JM. *Measurement in Physical Therapy*. New York, NY: Churchill Livingstone; 1985.

Respiratory Rate
Simeows EAF, Roark R, Berman S, Esler L, Murphy J. Respiratory rate: measurement of variability over time and accuracy at different counting periods. *Archives of Disease in Childhood*. 1991;66:1199–1203.

Treatment
Booker HA. Exercise training and breathing control in patients with chronic airflow limitation. *Physiotherapy*. 1984;70:258–260.
Brimioulle S, Moraine J, Kahn R. Passive physical therapy and respiratory therapy effects on intracranial pressure, abstracted. *Critical Care Medicine*. 1988;16:449.
Ciesla N, Rodrieguez A, Anderson P, Norton B. The incidence of extrapleural hematomas in patients with rib fractures receiving chest physical therapy. *Physical Therapy*. 1987;67:766. Abstract.
Cohen M, Hoskin TM. *Cardiopulmonary Symptoms in Physical Therapy*. New York, NY: Churchill Livingstone; 1988.
Conway JH. The effects of humidification for patients with chronic airways disease. *Physiotherapy*. 1992;78:97–101.
Crosbie WJ, Myles S. An investigation into the effect of postural modification on some aspects of normal pulmonary function. *Physiotherapy*. 1985;71:311–314.
Dean E. Effect of body position on pulmonary function. *Physical Therapy*. 1985;65:613–618.
DeGarmo C, Cerny F, Conboy K, Ellis EF. In vivo effects of theophylline on diaphragm, bicep, and quadricep strength and fatigability. *Journal of Allergy and Clinical Immunology*. 1988;82:1041–1046.
Downie PA. *Cash's Textbook of Chest, Heart and Vascular Disorders for Physiotherapists*. 4th ed. Philadelphia, Pa: JB Lippincott Co; 1987.
Downs J. Endotracheal suction: a method of tracheal washout. *Physiotherapy*. 1989;75:454.
Frownfelter D. *Chest Physical Therapy and Pulmonary Rehabilitation: An Interdisciplinary Approach*. Chicago, Ill; Year Book; 1987:239–259.
Gallon A. The use of percussion. *Physiotherapy*. 1992;78:85–89.
Harding J, Kemper M, Weissman C. Alfentanil attenuates the cardiopulmonary response of critically ill patients to an acute increase in oxygen demand induced by chest physiotherapy. *Anesthesia and Analgesia*. 1993;77:1122–1129.
Hough A. *Physiotherapy in Respiratory Care*. London, England: Chapman & Hall; 1991.
Imle PC, Mars MP, Eppinghaus CE, Anderson P, Ciesla ND. Effect of chest physiotherapy (CPT) positioning on intracracial (ICP) and cerebral perfusion pressure (CPP). *Critical Care Medicine*. 1988;16:382. Abstract.
Irwin S, Tecklin JS. *Cardiopulmonary Physical Therapy*. 2nd ed. St Louis, Mo: CV Mosby Co; 1990.
Kigin C. *Advances in Chest Physical Therapy*. Park Ridge, Ill: American College of Chest Physicians; 1984.
Kigin C. Evolution of pulmonary physical therapy in the United States. *Physiotherapy Practice*. 1986;2:22–30.
Kirilloff LH, Owens HR, Rogers RM, Mazzocco MC. Does chest physical therapy work? *Chest*. 1985;88:436–444.

Klein P, Kemper M, Weissman C, Rosenbaum SH, Askanazi J, Hyman JI. Attenuation of the hemodynamic responses to chest physical therapy. *Chest.* 1988;93:38–42.

Mackenzie CF, Imle PC, Ciesla N. *Chest Physiotherapy in the Intensive Care Unit.* 2nd ed. Baltimore, Md: Williams & Wilkins; 1989.

Mackenzie CF, Shin B. Chest physiotherapy vs bronchoscopy. *Critical Care Medicine.* 1986;14:78–79.

Mohsenifar Z, Rosenberg N, Goldberg HS, Koerner SK. Mechanical vibration and conventional chest physiotherapy in outpatients with stable chronic obstructive lung disease. *Chest.* 1985;87:483–485.

Rasanen J, Bools JC, Downs JB. Endobronchial drainage of undiagnosed lung abscess during chest physical therapy. *Physical Therapy.* 1988;68:371–373.

Webber BA. *The Brompton Hospital Guide to Chest Physiotherapy.* 5th ed. London, England: Blackwell Scientific Publications; 1988.

Webber B, Parker R, Hofmeyer J, Hodson M. Evaluation of self-percussion during postural drainage using the forced expiration technique. *Physiotherapy Practice.* 1985;1:42–45.

Witt PL, MacKinnon J. Trager psychophysical integration: a method to improve chest mobility of patients with chronic lung disease. *Physical Therapy.* 1986;66:214–217.

Young CS. Recommended guidelines for suction. *Physiotherapy.* 1984;70:106–108.

Young CS. A review of the adverse effects of airway suction. *Physiotherapy.* 1984;70:104–106.

Zadai CC. Exercise testing and training for the pulmonary impaired patient. In: Basmajian JV, Wolf S, eds. *Therapeutic Exercise.* 5th ed. Baltimore, Md: Williams & Wilkins; 1990.

Zadai CC. *Pulmonary Management in Physical Therapy.* New York, NY: Churchill Livingstone; 1992.

Chronic Bronchitis

DESCRIPTION

Chronic bronchitis is chronic inflammation of the tracheobronchial tree. This disorder is characterized by mucus hypersecretion leading to a chronic productive cough and structural changes of the bronchi. To be considered a chronic condition, the symptoms must have been present for at least 3 months for 2 consecutive years.

Chronic bronchitis is considered an obstructive disorder. Airway obstruction is characterized by an increased resistance to airflow occurring during forced expiration. Other disorders considered obstructive include asthma, bronchiectasis, cystic fibrosis, and emphysema. The disease combination of chronic bronchitis and emphysema is called various names, including *chronic obstructive pulmonary disease (COPD)* and *chronic airways obstruction.*

CAUSE

Obstructive diseases are caused by either reversible factors, such as inflammation, or irreversible factors, such as damaged alveoli. A localized lesion, such as a foreign body, may also cause airway obstruction. Chronic bronchitis can be caused by repeated exposure to pollutants that irritate the airway's sensitive lining. It is most commonly associated with cigarette smoking.

ASSESSMENT

Areas

- History, including any drug or oxygen therapy and fluid balance
- Vital signs, including temperature, blood pressure, and heart rate

- General appearance
- Cardiovascular, including results of exercise testing
- Equipment, including use of oxygen, humidification, drips, and any chest tubes
- Musculoskeletal, including posture, head and neck musculature, and chest shape
- Skin and soft tissue, including edema and condition of hands, especially nails
- Pulmonary, including breathing rate, pattern, and speech; position of trachea, chest motion, fremitus (vibration from the voice or secretion transmitted to chest wall), chest pain, diaphragmatic movement; breath sounds, extrapulmonary adventitious sounds, voice sounds; lung density and diaphragmatic excursion
- Functional level, including activities of daily living (ADLs)
- Special tests to which the PT may or may not have access

Instruments/Procedures (See References for Sources)

Functional Level
- Chronic Respiratory Disease Questionnaire
- classes of respiratory impairment
- visual analogue scale for dyspnea

Pulmonary
- palpation of abdomen, position of trachea, fremitus, scalene muscles, chest pain, diaphragmatic movement
- auscultation of breath sounds, extrapulmonary adventitious sounds, voice sounds
- percussion of lung density and diaphragmatic excursion

Special Tests to Which the PT May or May Not Have Access
- arterial blood gases
- bacterial and cytological tests of sputum
- chest x-ray
- exercise tests
- Respiratory Function Tests (RFTs)
    1. airways resistance
    2. body plethysmography
    3. diffusing capacity
    4. exercise testing
    5. expiratory reserve volume (ERV)
    6. flow-volume loops
    7. forced expiratory volume in 1 second
    8. forced vital capacity (FVC)
    9. functional residual capacity (FRC)
    10. helium dilution method
    11. inspiratory reserve volume (IRV)
    12. nitrogen washout test
    13. peak expiratory flow rate (PEFR)
    14. residual volume (RV)
    15. spirogram
    16. spirometry
    17. tidal volume

18. total lung capacity (TLC)
19. vital capacity (VC)
20. ventilation/perfusion scan

PROBLEMS

- The client usually has a productive cough, which is usually a morning cough (which may be thought of as "normal" to a smoker).
- The client can have breathlessness and fatigue.
- The breath sounds are usually decreased with crackles and wheezes.
- The disorder can lead to sleep disturbance.
- There is usually poor tolerance to exercise and labored breathing, with a decreased functional capacity and expiratory flow rates.
- The client usually has frequent respiratory infections.
- There can be cor pulmonale.

TREATMENT/MANAGEMENT

Chest PT in General

- Provide education on disease control and pain management.
- Provide clearance of secretions via hydration, humidification, nebulization, mobilization, breathing exercises, postural drainage, manual techniques, mechanical aids, cough and forced expiratory techniques, and nasopharyngeal suction.
- Consider mechanical devices to aid ventilation, such as continuous positive airways pressure (CPAP) and intermittent positive-pressure breathing (IPPB). In general, additional oxygen therapy is needed only for hypoxemia. It can be delivered through low-flow or high-flow masks, large-capacity masks, reservoir bags, nasal cannulas, transtracheal oxygen catheters, tents, or clear plastic hoods. Medication delivery devices include inhalers and nebulizers.
- Provide advice on appropriate activity level.
- Implement the following chest physical therapy techniques: positioning, controlled mobilization, and breathing exercises, as indicated.

Positioning

- Modify functional residual capacity using the following posture sequence, which gradually increases volume: supine, slumped sitting, half-lying, side-lying, toward prone, sitting upright, and standing.
- Regular position changes should be part of the client's management plan.

Controlled Mobilization With Exercise

- Use controlled mobilization with exercise while in upright posture.
- Control activity level to increase depth of respiration slightly, and follow by relaxed standing to regain breath.
- Modify activity with transfers or walking depending on the client's abilities.
- Progress to regular graded exercise.

Breathing Exercises

- Techniques may include deep breathing, end-inspiratory hold, sniff technique, single percussion, and abdominal breathing.

PRECAUTIONS/CONTRAINDICATIONS
- Oxygen is a drug that has both side effects and risks. It should be carefully administered, precisely prescribed, and routinely monitored. Substernal pain, dyspnea, and cough may signal oxygen toxicity. In neonates, high concentrations of oxygen may cause eye damage.
- Some degree of atelectasis can develop in clients who cannot take deep breaths due to low lung volumes but are required to perform forced expiratory maneuvers.

Contraindications to CPAP and IPPB
- These devices are not intended to be used with subcutaneous emphysema, facial trauma, bronchopleural fistula, bullae, undrained pneumothorax, and recent esophageal or bronchial surgery.
- For IPPB, other cautions include pneumothorax, large emphysematous bullae in lung, hemoptysis, active tuberculosis, and a bronchial tumor in the proximal airway.
- Clients with cystic fibrosis or emphysema can be susceptible to air trapping or pneumothorax, gastric distention, or infection.
- Improperly used nebulizers can trigger bronchospasm.

Contraindications to Head-Down Position in Postural Drainage
- abdominal distention
- acute spinal cord lesion
- arrhythmias
- breathlessness
- cardiovascular instability
- cerebral edema
- headache
- hemoptysis (recent)
- hiatal hernia
- hypertension
- obesity
- pregnancy
- pneumothorax, undrained
- pulmonary edema
- subcutaneous emphysema
- seizures

Contraindications to Postural Drainage in Any Position
- head injuries
- post esophagectomy
- aortic aneurysm
- during the filling cycle of peritoneal dialysis
- facial edema from burns, post eye surgery
  Discuss with medical staff if contraindications should be risked for the potential benefits.

Contraindications to Percussion and Vibration
- arrhythmias or angina (unstable)
- hemoptysis (recent)

- skin not intact due to trauma
- osteoporosis
- rib fracture or an increased risk of fracture

Contraindications to Coughing Therapy
- aneurysm
- increased intracranial pressure
- eye surgery (recent)
- subcutaneous emphysema
- pneumonectomy (recent)
  Spasm of multiple coughs can lead to fatigue, bronchospasm, and airway closure.

Contraindications and Precautions to Nasopharyngeal Suctioning
- Avoid in a client with a cerebrospinal fluid leak, clotting disorders, stridor, or pulmonary edema.
- Use caution with clients with recent esophagectomy or pneumonectomy.
- Suctioning may aggravate bronchospasm.
- Hypoxia can occur during nasopharyngeal suction as well as cardiac arrhythmias.
- Atelectasis or obstruction of the airway can be caused by suction that is too strong or too prolonged.

DESIRED OUTCOME/PROGNOSIS
- The client will have an increase in lung volume.
- The client will experience a relief of symptoms.
- The client will increase capacity for ADLs.
- The client will experience a decrease in episodes of attacks, leading to a sense of control over symptoms.
  The advent of peripheral edema with chronic bronchitis is an initial sign of cor pulmonale, which carries a grim prognosis.

REFERENCES

ASSESSMENT
American Physical Therapy Association. A guide to physical therapist practice, Volume I: a description of patient management. *Physical Therapy.* 1995;75:720–738. [**Ventilation, respiration, and circulation examination**]

Goodman C, Snyder TE. *Differential Diagnosis in Physical Therapy*. Philadelphia, Pa; WB Saunders; 1990:332, 337, 357, 362–363.

Functional Level

Chronic Respiratory Disease Questionnaire
Guyatt G, Berman LB, Townsend M, Pugsley SO. A measure of quality of life for clinical trials in chronic lung disease. *Thorax.* 1987;42:773–778.

Classes of Respiratory Impairment
Rothstein JM, Roy SH, Wolf SL. *The Rehabilitation Specialist's Handbook*. Philadelphia, Pa: FA Davis Co; 1991:585–626.

Visual Analogue Scale for Dyspnea

Aitken RCB. Measurement of feelings using visual analogue scales. *Proceedings of the Royal Society of Medicine*. 1969;62:989–993.

Pulmonary

Auscultation

Aweida D, Kelsey CJ. Accuracy and reliability of physical therapists in auscultating tape-recorded lung sound. *Physiotherapy Canada*. 1990;42:279–282.

Brooks D, Wilson L, Kelsey C, et al. Accuracy and reliability of specialized physical therapists in auscultating tape recorded lung sounds. *Physiotherapy Canada*. 1993;45:21–24.

Pasterkamp H, Montgomery M, Wiebicke W, et al. Nomenclature used by health care professionals to describe breath sounds in asthma. *Chest*. 1993;92:346–352.

Percussion

Bourke S, Nunes D, Stafford F, Hurley G, Graham I. Percussion of the chest re-visited: a comparison of the diagnostic value of auscultatory and conventional chest percussion. *Irish Journal of Medical Science*. 1989;158:82–84.

Special Tests to Which the PT May or May Not Have Access

Mackenzie CF, Shin B, McAslan TC. Chest physiotherapy: the effect on arterial oxygenation. *Anesthesia and Analgesia*. 1978;57:28–30. **[Arterial blood gases, chest x-ray]**

Respiratory Function Tests (RFTs)

American Thoracic Society. Lung function testing: selection of reference values and interpretive strategies. *American Review of Respiratory Disease*. 1991;144:1202–1218. **[Vital capacity]**

Downie PA. *Cash's Textbook of Chest, Heart and Vascular Disorders for Physiotherapists*. 4th ed. Philadelphia, Pa: JB Lippincott Co; 1987:83–101. **[Ventilatory function: helium dilution method, whole-body plethysmography, and radiological. Tests of forced expiration: peak expiratory flow rate (PEFR), forced expiratory volume in 1 second (FEV1), and flow-volume loops]**

Hough A. *Physiotherapy in Respiratory Care: A Problem-Solving Approach*. London, England: Chapman & Hall; 1991:37–41. **[Peak expiratory flow rate (PEFR), total lung capacity (TLC), vital capacity (VC), forced vital capacity (FVC), forced expiratory volume in 1 second (FEV 1 *Little*), FEV1/FVC, tidal volume, functional residual capacity (FRC), inspiratory reserve volume (IRV), expiratory reserve volume (ERV), residual volume (RV), spirometry, inspiratory muscle function, airways resistance, lung volumes, and exercise testing]**

O'Rourke PP, Schena JA, Thompson JE. The effects of pulmonary physiotherapy on delivered tidal volume. *Critical Care Medicine*. 1984;88:286. Abstract.

Rothstein JM, Roy SH, Wolf SL. *The Rehabilitation Specialist's Handbook*. Philadelphia, Pa: FA Davis Co; 1991:585-626. **[Pulmonary function terminology, common pulmonary function tests such as spirometry, diffusing capacity, body plethysmography, nitrogen washout test, ventilation/perfusion scan, spirogram and lung volumes, low-volume loops, and normal arterial blood gas values]**

Singh S. The use of field walking tests for assessment of functional capacity in patients with chronic airways obstruction. *Physiotherapy*. 1992;78:2:102–104.

Vital Signs

Blood pressure

Frohlich ED. Recommendations for human blood pressure determination by sphygmomanometers: report of a special task force appointed by the steering committee, American Heart Association. *Hypertension*. 1988;11:210A–222A.

Stolt M. Reliability of auscultory method of arterial blood pressure. *Hypertension.* 1990;3:697–703.

Heart Rate

Rothstein JM. *Measurement in Physical Therapy.* New York, NY: Churchill Livingstone; 1985.

Respiratory Rate

Simeows EAF, Roark R, Berman S, Ester L, Murphy J. Respiratory rate: measurement of variability over time and accuracy at different counting periods. *Archives of Disease in Childhood.* 1991;66:1199–1203.

TREATMENT

Booker HA. Exercise training and breathing control in patients with chronic airflow limitation. *Physiotherapy.* 1984;70:258–260.

Bracci L. Role of physical therapy in management of pulmonary alveolar proteinosis: a case report. *Physical Therapy.* 1988;68:686–689.

Brimioulle S, Moraine J, Kahn R. Passive physical therapy and respiratory therapy effects on intracranial pressure, abstracted. *Critical Care Medicine.* 1988;16:449.

Buscaglia AJ, St Marie MS. Oxygen saturation during chest physiotherapy for acute exacerbation of severe chronic obstructive pulmonary disease. *Respiratory Care.* 1983;28:1009–1013.

Busch AJ, McClements JD. Effects of a supervised home exercise program on patients with severe chronic obstructive pulmonary disease. *Physical Therapy.* 1988;68:469–474.

Campbell T, Ferguson N, McKinlay RGC. The use of a simple self-administered method of positive expiratory pressure (PEP) in chest physiotherapy after abdominal surgery. *Physiotherapy.* 1986;72:498–500.

Chung F, Dean E. Pathophysiology and cardiorespiratory consequences of interstitial lung disease—review and clinical implications: a special communication. *Physical Therapy.* 1989;69:956–966.

Ciesla N, Rodrieguez A, Anderson P, Norton B. The incidence of extrapleural hematomas in patients with rib fractures receiving chest physical therapy. *Physical Therapy.* 1987;67:766. Abstract.

Cohen M, Hoskin TM. *Cardiopulmonary Symptoms in Physical Therapy.* New York, NY: Churchill Livingstone; 1988.

Conway JH. The effects of humidification for patients with chronic airways disease. *Physiotherapy.* 1992;78:2:97–101.

Crosbie WJ, Myles S. An investigation into the effect of postural modification on some aspects of normal pulmonary function. *Physiotherapy.* 1985;71:311–314.

Dean E. Effect of body position on pulmonary function. *Physical Therapy.* 1985;65:613–618.

DeGarmo C, Cerny F, Conboy K, Ellis EF. In vivo effects of theophylline on diaphragm, bicep, and quadricep strength and fatigability. *Journal of Allergy and Clinical Immunology.* 1988;82:1041–1046.

Downie PA. *Cash's Textbook of Chest, Heart and Vascular Disorders for Physiotherapists.* 4th ed. Philadelphia, Pa: JB Lippincott Co; 1987.

Downs J. Endotracheal suction: a method of tracheal washout. *Physiotherapy.* 1989;75:454.

Frownfelter D. *Chest Physical Therapy and Pulmonary Rehabilitation: An Interdisciplinary Approach.* Chicago, Ill: Year Book; 1987:239–259.

Gallon A. The use of percussion. *Physiotherapy.* 1992;78:85–89.

Harding J, Kemper M, Weissman C. Alfentanil attenuates the cardiopulmonary response of critically ill patients to an acute increase in oxygen demand induced by chest physiotherapy. *Anesthesia and Analgesia.* 1993;77:1122–1129.

Hough A. *Physiotherapy in Respiratory Care.* London, England: Chapman & Hall; 1991.

Imle PC, Mars MP, Eppinghaus CE, Anderson P, Ciesla ND. Effect of chest physiotherapy (CPT) positioning on intracranial (ICP) and cerebral perfusion pressure (CPP). *Critical Care Medicine.* 1988;16:382. Abstract.

Irwin S, Tecklin JS. *Cardiopulmonary Physical Therapy.* 2nd ed. St Louis, Mo: CV Mosby Co; 1990.

Johnson NJ, Grindler D. Home rehabilitation for chronic obstructive pulmonary disease: a physical and occupational therapy approach. *Journal of Home Health Care Practice.* 1990;2:2:19–43.

Kigin C. *Advances in Chest Physical Therapy.* Park Ridge, Ill: American College of Chest Physicians; 1984.

Kigin C. Evolution of pulmonary physical therapy in the United States. *Physiotherapy Practice*. 1986;2:22–30.

Kirilloff LH, Owens HR, Rogers RM, Mazzocco MC. Does chest physical therapy work? 1985;88:436–444.

Klein P, Kemper M, Weissman C, Rosenbaum SH, Askanazi J, Hyman JI. Attenuation of the hemodynamic responses to chest physical therapy. *Chest*. 1988;93:38–42.

Mackenzie CF, Imle PC, Ciesla N. *Chest Physiotherapy in the Intensive Care Unit*. 2nd ed. Baltimore, Md: Williams & Wilkins; 1989.

Mackenzie CF, Shin B. Chest physiotherapy vs bronchoscopy. *Critical Care Medicine*. 1986;14:78–79.

Mohsenifar Z, Rosenberg N, Goldberg HS, Koerner SK. Mechanical vibration and conventional chest physiotherapy in outpatients with stable chronic obstructive lung disease. *Chest*. 1985;87:483–485.

O'Rourke PP, Schena JA, Thompson JE. The effects of pulmonary physiotherapy on delivered tidal volume. *Critical Care Medicine*. 1984;88:286. Abstract.

Pavia D. The role of chest physiotherapy in mucus hypersecretion. *Lung*. 1990;168(suppl):614–621.

Rasanen J, Bools JC, Downs JB. Endobronchial drainage of undiagnosed lung abscess during chest physical therapy. *Physical Therapy*. 1988;68:371–373.

Reid WD, Loveridge BM. Physiotherapy management of patients with chronic obstructive airways disease. *Physiotherapy Canada*. 1983;35:183–195.

Sutton PP, Lopez-Vidriero MT, Pavia D, et al. Assessment of percussion vibratory-shaking and breathing exercise in chest physiotherapy. *European Journal of Respiratory Diseases*. 1985;66:147–152.

Swerts PMJ, Mostert R, Wouters EFM. Comparison of corridor and treadmill walking in patients with severe chronic obstructive pulmonary disease. *Physical Therapy*. 1990;70:439–442.

Tydeman DE, Chandler AR, Graveling BM, Culot A, Harrison BDW. An investigation into the effects of exercise tolerance training on patients with chronic airways obstruction. *Physiotherapy*. 1984;70:261–264.

Webber BA. *The Brompton Hospital Guide to Chest Physiotherapy*. 5th ed. London, England: Blackwell Scientific Publications; 1988.

Webber B, Parker R, Hofmeyer J, Hodson M. Evaluation of self-percussion during postural drainage using the forced expiration technique. *Physiotherapy Practice*. 1985;1:42–45.

Witt PL, MacKinnon J. Trager psychophysical integration: a method to improve chest mobility of patients with chronic lung disease. *Physical Therapy*. 1986;66:214–217.

Wollmer P, Ursing K, Midgren B, Eriksson L. Inefficiency of chest percussion in the physical therapy of chronic bronchitis. *European Journal of Respiratory Diseases*. 1985;66:233–239.

Young CS. Recommended guidelines for suction. *Physiotherapy*. 1984;70:106–108.

Young CS. A review of the adverse effects of airway suction. *Physiotherapy*. 1984;70:104–106.

Zadai CC. Exercise testing and training for the pulmonary impaired patient. In: Basmajian JV, Wolf S, eds. *Therapeutic Exercise*. 5th ed. Baltimore, Md: Williams & Wilkins; 1990.

Zadai CC. *Pulmonary Management in Physical Therapy*. New York, NY: Churchill Livingstone; 1992.

Emphysema

DESCRIPTION

Emphysema is a disease of the alveoli with accompanying permanent damage to the airways, particularly to the air spaces distal to the terminal bronchioles. Emphysema is considered an obstructive disorder. Airway obstruction is characterized by an increased resistance to airflow occurring during forced expiration. Other disorders considered obstructive include asthma, bronchiectasis, cystic fibrosis, and chronic bronchitis. The disease combination of chronic bronchitis and emphysema is called various names, including *chronic obstructive pulmonary disease (COPD)* and *chronic airways obstruction.*

CAUSE

Obstructive diseases are caused by either reversible factors, such as inflammation, or irreversible factors, such as damaged alveoli. A localized lesion, such as a foreign body, may also cause airway obstruction. Emphysema is caused by smoking or occasionally by a congenital destruction of alveoli.

ASSESSMENT

Areas
- History, including any drug or oxygen therapy and fluid balance
- Vital signs, including temperature, blood pressure, and heart rate
- General appearance
- Cardiovascular, including results of exercise testing
- Equipment, including use of oxygen, humidification, drips, and any chest tubes
- Musculoskeletal, including posture, head and neck musculature, and chest shape
- Skin and soft tissue, including edema and condition of hands, especially nails
- Pulmonary, including breathing rate, pattern, and speech; position of trachea, chest motion, fremitus (vibration from the voice or secretion transmitted to chest wall), chest pain, diaphragmatic movement; breath sounds, extrapulmonary adventitious sounds, voice sounds, lung density and diaphragmatic excursion
- Functional level, including activities of daily living (ADLs)
- Special tests to which the PT may or may not have access

Instruments/Procedures (See References for Sources)

Functional Level
- Chronic Respiratory Disease Questionnaire
- classes of respiratory impairment
- visual analogue scale for dyspnea

Pulmonary
- palpation of abdomen, position of trachea, fremitus, scalene muscles, chest pain, diaphragmatic movement
- auscultation of breath sounds, extrapulmonary adventitious sounds, voice sounds
- percussion of lung density and diaphragmatic excursion

Special Tests to Which the PT May or May Not Have Access
- arterial blood gases
- bacterial and cytological tests of sputum
- chest x-ray
- exercise tests
- Respiratory Function Tests (RFTs)
    1. airways resistance
    2. body plethysmography
    3. diffusing capacity

4. exercise testing
5. expiratory reserve volume (ERV)
6. flow-volume loops
7. forced expiratory volume in 1 second
8. forced vital capacity (FVC)
9. functional residual capacity (FRC)
10. helium dilution method
11. inspiratory reserve volume (IRV)
12. nitrogen washout test
13. peak expiratory flow rate (PEFR)
14. residual volume (RV)
15. spirogram
16. spirometry
17. tidal volume
18. total lung capacity (TLC)
19. vital capacity (VC)
20. ventilation/perfusion scan

PROBLEMS

- The client is usually breathless, with labored breathing.
- There can be weight loss.
- The client usually has a barrel-like chest shape.
- There can be altered breath sounds, usually decreased and/or wheezing.
- There is usually strong use of accessory muscles.
- There can be clubbing of nails and cyanosis.
- There can be cor pulmonale.
- There can be an accompanying cough.
- There can be hypoxemia and hypercapnea.

TREATMENT/MANAGEMENT

Chest PT in General

- Provide education on disease control and pain management.
- Provide clearance of secretions via hydration, humidification, nebulization, mobilization, breathing exercises, postural drainage, manual techniques, mechanical aids, cough and forced expiratory techniques, and nasopharyngeal suction.
- Consider mechanical devices to aid ventilation, such as continuous positive airways pressure (CPAP) and intermittent positive-pressure breathing (IPPB). In general, additional oxygen therapy is needed only for hypoxemia. It can be delivered through low-flow or high-flow masks, large-capacity masks, reservoir bags, nasal cannulas, transtracheal oxygen catheters, tents, head boxes, or clear plastic hoods. Medication delivery devices include inhalers and nebulizers.
- Provide advice on appropriate activity level.
- Implement the following chest physical therapy techniques: positioning, controlled mobilization, and breathing exercises as indicated.

Positioning

- Modify functional residual capacity using the following posture sequence, which gradually increases volume: supine, slumped sitting, half-lying, side-lying, toward prone, sitting up-

right, and finally standing.
- Regular position changes should be part of the client's management plan.

Controlled Mobilization With Exercise
- Use controlled mobilization with exercise while in upright posture.
- Control activity level to increase depth of respiration slightly, and follow by relaxed standing to regain breath.
- Modify activity with transfers or walking depending on client's abilities.
- Progress to regular graded exercise.

Breathing Exercises
- Techniques may include deep breathing, end-inspiratory hold, sniff technique, single percussion, and abdominal breathing.

PRECAUTIONS/CONTRAINDICATIONS
- Oxygen is a drug that has both side effects and risks. It should be carefully administered, precisely prescribed, and routinely monitored. Substernal pain, dyspnea, and cough may signal oxygen toxicity. In neonates, high concentrations of oxygen may cause eye damage.
- Some degree of atelectasis can develop in clients who cannot take deep breaths due to low lung volumes but are required to perform forced expiratory maneuvers.

Contraindications to CPAP and IPPB
- These devices are not intended to be used with subcutaneous emphysema, facial trauma, bronchopleural fistula, bullae, undrained pneumothorax, and recent esophageal or bronchial surgery.
- For IPPB, other cautions include pneumothorax, large emphysematous bullae in lung, hemoptysis, active tuberculosis, and a bronchial tumor in the proximal airway.
- Clients with cystic fibrosis or emphysema can be susceptible to air trapping or pneumothorax, and gastric distention or infection can occur.
- Improperly used nebulizers can trigger bronchospasm.

Contraindications to Head-Down Position in Postural Drainage
- abdominal distention
- acute spinal cord lesion
- arrhythmias
- breathlessness
- cardiovascular instability
- cerebral edema
- headache
- hemoptysis (recent)
- hiatal hernia
- hypertension
- obesity
- pregnancy
- pneumothorax, undrained
- pulmonary edema
- subcutaneous emphysema

- seizures

Contraindications to Postural Drainage in Any Position
- head injuries
- post esophagectomy
- aortic aneurysm
- during the filling cycle of peritoneal dialysis
- facial edema from burns, post eye surgery
  Discuss with medical staff if contraindications should be risked for potential benefit.

Contraindications to Percussion and Vibration
- arrhythmias or angina (unstable)
- hemoptysis (recent)
- skin not intact due to trauma
- osteoporosis
- rib fracture or an increased risk of fracture

Precautions for Coughing Therapy
- aneurysm
- increased intracranial pressure
- eye surgery (recent)
- subcutaneous emphysema
- pneumonectomy (recent)
  Spasm of multiple coughs can lead to fatigue, bronchospasm, and airway closure.

Contraindications and Precautions to Nasopharyngeal Suctioning
- Avoid in a client with a cerebrospinal fluid leak, clotting disorders, stridor, or pulmonary edema.
- Use caution with recent esophagectomy or pneumonectomy.
- Suctioning may aggravate bronchospasm.
- Hypoxia can occur during nasopharyngeal suction as well as cardiac arrhythmias.
- Atelectasis or obstruction of the airway can be caused by suction that is too strong or too prolonged.

DESIRED OUTCOME/PROGNOSIS
- The client will have an increase in lung volume.
- The client will experience a relief of symptoms.
- The client will increase capacity for ADLs.
- The client will have a decrease in episodes of attacks, leading to a sense of control over symptoms.

REFERENCES

ASSESSMENT
American Physical Therapy Association. A guide to physical therapist practice, Volume I: a description of patient management. *Physical Therapy.* 1995;75:720-738. [**Ventilation, respiration, and circulation examination**]

Goodman C, Snyder TE. *Differential Diagnosis in Physical Therapy.* Philadelphia, Pa; 1990:332, 337, 357, 362–363.

Functional Level

Chronic Respiratory Disease Questionnaire
Guyatt G, Berman LB, Townsend M, Pugsley SO. A measure of quality of life for clinical trials in chronic lung disease. *Thorax.* 1987;42:773–778.

Classes of Respiratory Impairment
Rothstein JM, Roy SH, Wolf SL. *The Rehabilitation Specialist's Handbook.* Philadelphia, Pa: FA Davis Co; 1991:585–626.

Visual Analogue Scale for Dyspnea
Aitken RCB. Measurement of feelings using visual analogue scales. *Proceedings of the Royal Society of Medicine.* 1969;62:989–993.

Pulmonary

Auscultation
Aweida D, Kelsey CJ. Accuracy and reliability of physical therapists in auscultating tape-recorded lung sound. *Physiotherapy Canada.* 1990;42:279–282.

Brooks D, Wilson L, Kelsey C, et al. Accuracy and reliability of specialized physical therapists in auscultating tape recorded lung sounds. *Physiotherapy Canada.* 1993;45:21–24.

Pasterkamp H, et al. Nomenclature used by health care professionals to describe breath sounds in asthma. *Chest.* 1993;92:346–352.

Percussion
Bourke S, Nunes D, Stafford F, Hurley G, Graham I. Percussion of the chest re-visited: a comparison of the diagnostic value of auscultatory and conventional chest percussion. *Irish Journal of Medical Science.* 1989;158:82–84.

Special Tests to Which the PT May or May Not Have Access
Mackenzie CF, Shin B, McAslan TC. Chest physiotherapy: the effect on arterial oxygenation. *Anesthesia and Analgesia.* 1978;57:28–30. [**Arterial blood gases, chest x-ray**]

Respiratory Function Tests (RFTs)
American Thoracic Society. Lung function testing: selection of reference values and interpretive strategies. *American Review of Respiratory Disease.* 1991;144:1202–1218. [**Vital capacity**]

Downie PA. *Cash's Textbook of Chest, Heart and Vascular Disorders for Physiotherapists.* 4th ed. Philadelphia, Pa: JB Lippincott Co; 1987:83-101. [**Ventilatory function: helium dilution method, whole-body plethysmography, and radiological. Tests of forced expiration: peak expiratory flow rate (PEFR), forced expiratory volume in 1 second (FEV1), and flow-volume loops**]

Hough A. *Physiotherapy in Respiratory Care: A Problem-Solving Approach.* London, England: Chapman & Hall; 1991:37–41. [**Peak expiratory flow rate (PEFR), total lung capacity (TLC), vital capacity (VC), forced vital capacity (FVC), forced expiratory volume in 1 second (FEV 1 *Little*), FEV1/FVC, tidal volume, functional residual capacity (FRC), inspiratory reserve volume (IRV), expiratory reserve volume (ERV), residual volume (RV), spirometry, inspiratory muscle function, airways resistance, lung volumes, and exercise testing**]

O'Rourke PP, Schena JA, Thompson JE. The effects of pulmonary physiotherapy on delivered tidal volume. *Critical Care Medicine.* 1984;88:286. Abstract.

Rothstein JM, Roy SH, Wolf SL. *The Rehabilitation Specialist's Handbook.* Philadelphia, Pa: FA Davis Co; 1991:585–626. [**Pulmonary function terminology, common pulmonary function tests such as spirom-**

etry, diffusing capacity, body plethysmography, nitrogen washout test, ventilation/perfusion scan, spirogram and lung volumes, low-volume loops, and normal arterial blood gas values]

Singh S. The use of field walking tests for assessment of functional capacity in patients with chronic airways obstruction. *Physiotherapy.* 1992;78:102–104.

Vital Signs

Blood Pressure

Frohlich ED. Recommendations for human blood pressure determination by sphygmomanometers: report of a special task force appointed by the steering committee, American Heart Association. *Hypertension.* 1988;11:210A–222A.

Stolt M. Reliability of auscultory method of arterial blood pressure. *Hypertension.* 1990;3:697–703.

Heart Rate

Rothstein JM. *Measurement in Physical Therapy.* New York, NY: Churchill Livingstone; 1985.

Respiratory Rate

Simeows EAF, Roark R, Berman S, Esler L, Murphy J. Respiratory rate: measurement of variability over time and accuracy at different counting periods. *Archives of Disease in Childhood.* 1991;66:1199–1203.

TREATMENT

Booker HA. Exercise training and breathing control in patients with chronic airflow limitation. *Physiotherapy.* 1984;70:258–260.

Bracci L. Role of physical therapy in management of pulmonary alveolar proteinosis: a case report. *Physical Therapy.* 1988;68:686–689.

Brimioulle S, Moraine J, Kahn R. Passive physical therapy and respiratory therapy effects on intracranial pressure, abstracted. *Critical Care Medicine.* 1988;16:449.

Buscaglia AJ, St Marie MS. Oxygen saturation during chest physiotherapy for acute exacerbation of severe chronic obstructive pulmonary disease. *Respiratory Care.* 1983;28:1009–1013.

Busch AJ, McClements JD. Effects of a supervised home exercise program on patients with severe chronic obstructive pulmonary disease. *Physical Therapy.* 1988;68:469–474.

Campbell T, Ferguson N, McKinlay RGC. The use of a simple self-administered method of positive expiratory pressure (PEP) in chest physiotherapy after abdominal surgery. *Physiotherapy.* 1986;72:498-500.

Chung F, Dean E. Pathophysiology and cardiorespiratory consequences of interstitial lung disease—review and clinical implications: a special communication. *Physical Therapy.* 1989;69:956–966.

Ciesla N, Rodrieguez A, Anderson P, Norton B. The incidence of extrapleural hematomas in patients with rib fractures receiving chest physical therapy. *Physical Therapy.* 1987;67:766. Abstract.

Cohen M, Hoskin TM. *Cardiopulmonary Symptoms in Physical Therapy.* New York, NY: Churchill Livingstone; 1988.

Conway JH. The effects of humidification for patients with chronic airways disease. *Physiotherapy.* 1992;78:97–101.

Crosbie WJ, Myles S. An investigation into the effect of postural modification on some aspects of normal pulmonary function. *Physiotherapy.* 1985;71:311–314.

Dean E. Effect of body position on pulmonary function. *Physical Therapy.* 1985;65:613–618.

DeGarmo C, Cerny F, Conboy K, Ellis EF. In vivo effects of theophylline on diaphragm, bicep, and quadricep strength and fatigability. *Journal of Allergy and Clinical Immunology.* 1988;82:1041–1046.

Downie PA. *Cash's Textbook of Chest, Heart and Vascular Disorders for Physiotherapists.* 4th ed. Philadelphia, Pa: JB Lippincott Co; 1987.

Downs J. Endotracheal suction: a method of tracheal washout. *Physiotherapy.* 1989;75:454.

Frownfelter D. *Chest Physical Therapy and Pulmonary Rehabilitation: An Interdisciplinary Approach.* Chicago, Ill: Year Book; 1987:239–259.

Gallon A. The use of percussion. *Physiotherapy.* 1992;78:85–89.

Harding J, Kemper M, Weissman C. Alfentanil attenuates the cardiopulmonary response of critically ill patients to an acute increase in oxygen demand induced by chest physiotherapy. *Anesthesia and Analgesia.* 1993;77:1122–1129.

Holle RH, Williams DV, Vandree JC, et al. Increased muscle efficiency and sustained benefits in an outpatient community hospital-based pulmonary rehabilitation program. *Chest.* 1988;94:1161–1168.

Hough A. *Physiotherapy in Respiratory Care.* London, England: Chapman & Hall; 1991.

Imle PC, Mars MP, Eppinghaus CE, Anderson P, Ciesla ND. Effect of chest physiotherapy (CPT) positioning on intracranial (ICP) and cerebral perfusion pressure (CPP). *Critical Care Medicine.* 1988;16:382. Abstract.

Irwin S, Tecklin JS. *Cardiopulmonary Physical Therapy.* 2nd ed. St Louis, Mo: CV Mosby Co; 1990.

Johnson NJ, Grindler D. Home rehabilitation for chronic obstructive pulmonary disease: a physical and occupational therapy approach. *Journal of Home Health Care Practice.* 1990;2:2:19–43.

Kigin C. *Advances in Chest Physical Therapy.* Park Ridge, Ill: American College of Chest Physicians; 1984.

Kigin C. Evolution of pulmonary physical therapy in the United States. *Physiotherapy Practice.* 1986;2:22–30.

Kirilloff LH, Owens HR, Rogers RM, Mazzocco MC. Does chest physical therapy work? *Chest.* 1985;88:436–444.

Klein P, Kemper M, Weissman C, Rosenbaum SH, Askanazi J, Hyman JI. Attenuation of the hemodynamic responses to chest physical therapy. *Chest.* 1988;93:38–42.

Mackenzie CF, Imle PC, Ciesla N. *Chest Physiotherapy in the Intensive Care Unit,* 2nd ed. Baltimore, Md: Williams & Wilkins; 1989.

Mackenzie CF, Shin B. Chest physiotherapy vs bronchoscopy. *Critical Care Medicine.* 1986;14:78–79.

Mohsenifar Z, Rosenberg N, Goldberg HS, Koerner SK. Mechanical vibration and conventional chest physiotherapy in outpatients with stable chronic obstructive lung disease. *Chest.* 1985;87:483–485.

Rasanen J, Bools JC, Downs JB. Endobronchial drainage of undiagnosed lung abscess during chest physical therapy. *Physical Therapy.* 1988;68:371–373.

Sutton PP, Lopez-Vidriero MT, Pavia D, et al. Assessment of percussion vibratory-shaking and breathing exercise in chest physiotherapy. *European Journal of Respiratory Diseases.* 1985;66:147–152.

Swerts PMJ, Mostert R, Wouters EFM. Comparison of corridor and treadmill walking in patients with severe chronic obstructive pulmonary disease. *Physical Therapy.* 1990;70:439–442.

Tydeman DE, Chandler AR, Graveling BM, Culot A, Harrison BDW. An investigation into the effects of exercise tolerance training on patients with chronic airways obstruction. *Physiotherapy.* 1984;70:261–264.

Webber BA. Living to the limit: exercise for the chronic breathless patient. *Physiotherapy.* 1981;67:128.

Webber BA. *The Brompton Hospital Guide to Chest Physiotherapy.* 5th ed. London, England: Blackwell Scientific Publications; 1988.

Webber B, Parker R, Hofmeyer J, Hodson M. Evaluation of self-percussion during postural drainage using the forced expiration technique. *Physiotherapy Practice.* 1985;1:42–45.

Witt PL, MacKinnon J. Trager psychophysical integration: a method to improve chest mobility of patients with chronic lung disease. *Physical Therapy.* 1986;66:214–217.

Wollmer P, Ursing K, Midgren B, Eriksson L. Inefficiency of chest percussion in the physical therapy of chronic bronchitis. *European Journal of Respiratory Diseases.* 1985;66:233–239.

Zadai CC. Exercise testing and training for the pulmonary impaired patient. In: Basmajian JV, Wolf S, eds. *Therapeutic Exercise.* 5th ed. Baltimore, Md: Williams & Wilkins; 1990.

Zadai CC. *Pulmonary Management in Physical Therapy.* New York, NY: Churchill Livingstone; 1992.

Pneumonia

DESCRIPTION

Pneumonia is an infection of the lung that involves the alveolar spaces and interstitial tissue. The infection may involve only a segment of a lobe or the entire lobe. Alveolar involvement in conjunction with the bronchi is called *bronchopneumonia* and in conjunction with interstitial tissue is known as *interstitial pneumonia.*

CAUSE

Pneumonia is usually caused by bacteria. Types of bacterial pneumonia include gram-positive bacteria, gram-negative bacteria, mycoplasmal, and Legionnaires' disease. In infants and children, the main pulmonary pathogens are usually viral. A client may be predisposed to pneumonia if his or her history includes any of the following factors: alcoholism, chronic obstructive airways disease, compromised consciousness, debility, dysphagia, exposure to transmissible agents, extreme age, or immunosuppressive disorder and therapy.

ASSESSMENT

Areas

- History, including any drug or oxygen therapy and fluid balance
- Vital signs, including temperature, blood pressure, and heart rate
- General appearance
- Cardiovascular, including results of exercise testing
- Equipment, including use of oxygen, humidification, drips, and any chest tubes
- Musculoskeletal, including posture, head and neck musculature, and chest shape
- Skin and soft tissue, including edema and condition of hands, especially nails
- Pulmonary, including breathing rate, pattern, and speech; position of trachea, chest motion, fremitus (vibration from the voice or secretion transmitted to chest wall), chest pain, and diaphragmatic movement; breath sounds, extrapulmonary adventitious sounds, and voice sounds; lung density and diaphragmatic excursion
- Functional level, including activities of daily living (ADLs)
- Special tests to which the PT may or may not have access

Instruments/Procedures (See References for Sources)

Functional Level
- Chronic Respiratory Disease Questionnaire
- classes of respiratory impairment
- visual analogue scale for dyspnea

Pulmonary
- palpation of abdomen, position of trachea, chest motion, fremitus, scalene muscles, chest pain, and diaphragmatic movement
- auscultation of breath sounds, extrapulmonary adventitious sounds, and voice sounds
- percussion of lung density and diaphragmatic excursion

Special Tests to Which the PT May or May Not Have Access
- arterial blood gases
- bacterial and cytological tests of sputum

- chest x-ray
- exercise tests
- Respiratory Function Tests (RFTs)
  1. airways resistance
  2. body plethysmography
  3. diffusing capacity
  4. exercise testing
  5. expiratory reserve volume (ERV)
  6. flow-volume loops
  7. forced expiratory volume in 1 second
  8. forced vital capacity (FVC)
  9. functional residual capacity (FRC)
  10. helium dilution method
  11. inspiratory reserve volume (IRV)
  12. nitrogen washout test
  13. peak expiratory flow rate (PEFR)
  14. residual volume (RV)
  15. spirogram
  16. spirometry
  17. tidal volume
  18. total lung capacity (TLC)
  19. vital capacity (VC)
  20. ventilation/perfusion scan

PROBLEMS

Bacterial

- The client usually has a cough, fever, and shaking chills.
- The client may have chest pain and dyspnea.
- The client may have tachypnea.
- The client usually has excess sputum production that is purulent and rusty colored or blood streaked.
- The client usually has hypoxemia and hypocapnea initially leading to hypercapnea.

Viral

- The client usually has a fever and chills.
- The client usually has a dry cough.
- The breath sounds are usually decreased.
- The client usually has hypoxemia and hypocapnea.

TREATMENT/MANAGEMENT

In general:
- Teach positioning techniques and forward-leaning postures. Teach client how to splint during cough if it is painful.
- Use relaxation exercises and work adjustment strategies.
- Instruct in breathing exercises: abdominal (diaphragmatic) breathing, pursed-lips breathing, segmental breathing, low-frequency breathing, and sustained maximal breathing.
- Provide secretion clearance via traditional or modified postural drainage.

- Enhance cough by using forced expiration, manual ventilation, mechanical stimulation with suctioning, neuromuscular facilitation with ice along the paraspinal region on the thoracic spine, positioning, or pressure.
- Consider use of transcutaneous electrical nerve stimulation (TENS) for pain relief.
- Consider supplemental oxygen or mechanical ventilation as indicated.

Effect of Specific Techniques
- Abdominal (diaphragmatic) breathing exercises eliminate accessory muscle activity, decrease respiratory rate, increase tidal ventilation, increase distribution of ventilation, and decrease postoperative treatment.
- Pursed-lips breathing exercises eliminate use of accessory muscles, decrease respiratory rate, increase arterial oxygen tension, decrease carbon dioxide tension, and increase tolerance to exercise.
- Segmental breathing exercises prevent excessive pleural fluid and secretions, diminish panic, decrease paradoxical breathing, and enhance chest mobility.
- Low-frequency and sustained maximal inspiration breathing slow down the respiratory rate.
- Reduced oxygen consumption increases the dyspnea threshold for a specific activity, improves tolerance to functional activity, and increases quality of life.
- Postural drainage, percussion, and vibration increase the volume of sputum expectorated, increase the clearance of secretions, decrease airway resistance, increase lung compliance, decrease work used for breathing, increase oxygenation and ventilation, and decrease hospitalization and the number of postoperative pulmonary complications.
- Cough techniques evoke a reflex cough, decrease the risk of cough complications, and diminish retained secretions.
- Exercise conditioning increases endurance and duration of activity.
- TENS decreases pain medication and increases forced vital capacity.

PRECAUTIONS/CONTRAINDICATIONS
- Stop exercise if the following phenomena occur: premature ventricular contraction (coupled, several, or in increased frequency), atrial dysrhythmias, heart block (second- or third-degree), changes in ST-segment (greater than 2 mm), decline in heart rate or blood pressure or heart rate greater than target, increase in diastolic pressure greater than 20 mm Hg, dyspnea, nausea, fatigue, dizziness, headache, blurred vision, palor, or diaphoresis.
- TENS may possibly lead to electrocardiogram (ECG) or pacemaker interference.

DESIRED OUTCOME/PROGNOSIS
- The client will improve ventilation.
- The client will increase oxygenation and decrease oxygen consumption.
- The client will increase secretion clearance.
- The client will increase exercise tolerance.
- The client will experience a decrease in pain.

REFERENCES

ASSESSMENT
American Physical Therapy Association. A guide to physical therapist practice, Volume I: a description of patient management. *Physical Therapy.* 1995;75:720–738. [**Ventilation, respiration, and circulation examination**]

Goodman C, Snyder TE. *Differential Diagnosis in Physical Therapy.* Philadelphia, Pa: WB Saunders; 1990:332, 337, 357, 362–363.

Functional Level

Chronic Respiratory Disease Questionnaire

Guyatt G, Berman LB, Townsend M, Pugsley SO. A measure of quality of life for clinical trials in chronic lung disease. *Thorax.* 1987;42:773–778.

Classes of Respiratory Impairment

Rothstein JM, Roy SH, Wolf SL. *The Rehabilitation Specialist's Handbook.* Philadelphia, Pa: FA Davis Co; 1991:585–626.

Visual Analogue Scale for Dyspnea

Aitken RCB. Measurement of feelings using visual analogue scales. *Proceedings of the Royal Society of Medicine.* 1969;62:989–993.

Pulmonary

Auscultation

Aweida D, Kelsey CJ. Accuracy and reliability of physical therapists in auscultating tape-recorded lung sound. *Physiotherapy Canada.* 1990;42:279–282.

Brooks D, Wilson L, Kelsey C, et al. Accuracy and reliability of specialized physical therapists in auscultating tape recorded lung sounds. *Physiotherapy Canada.* 1993;45:21–24.

Pasterkamp H, Montgomery M, Wiebicke W, et al. Nomenclature used by health care professionals to describe breath sounds in asthma. *Chest.* 1993;92:346–352.

Percussion

Bourke S, Nunes D, Stafford F, Hurley G, Graham I. Percussion of the chest re-visited: a comparison of the diagnostic value of auscultatory and conventional chest percussion. *Irish Journal of Medical Science.* 1989;158:82–84.

Special Tests to Which the PT May or May Not Have Access

Mackenzie CF, Shin B, McAslan TC. Chest physiotherapy: the effect on arterial oxygenation. *Anesthesia and Analgesia.* 1978;57:28–30.

Respiratory Function Tests (RFTs)

American Thoracic Society. Lung function testing: selection of reference values and interpretive strategies. *American Review of Respiratory Disease.* 1991;144:1202–1218. [**Vital capacity**]

Downie PA. *Cash's Textbook of Chest, Heart and Vascular Disorders for Physiotherapists.* 4th ed. Philadelphia, Pa: JB Lippincott Co; 1987:83–101. [**Ventilatory function: helium dilution method, whole-body plethysmography, and radiological. Tests of forced expiration: peak expiratory flow rate (PEFR), forced expiratory volume in 1 second (FEV1), and flow-volume loops**]

Hough A. *Physiotherapy in Respiratory Care: A Problem-Solving Approach.* London, England: Chapman & Hall; 1991:37–41. [**Peak expiratory flow rate (PEFR), total lung capacity (TLC), vital capacity (VC), forced vital capacity (FVC), forced expiratory volume in 1 second (FEV 1 *Little*), FEV1/FVC, tidal volume, functional residual capacity (FRC), inspiratory reserve volume (IRV), expiratory reserve volume (ERV), residual volume (RV), spirometry, inspiratory muscle function, airways resistance, lung volumes, and exercise testing**]

O'Rourke PP, Schena JA, Thompson JE. The effects of pulmonary physiotherapy on delivered tidal volume. *Critical Care Medicine.* 1984;88:286. Abstract.

Rothstein JM, Roy SH, Wolf SL .*The Rehabilitation Specialist's Handbook.* Philadelphia, Pa: FA Davis Co; 1991:585–626. [**Pulmonary function terminology, common pulmonary function tests such as spirom-**

etry, diffusing capacity, body plethysmography, nitrogen washout test, ventilation/perfusion scan, spirogram and lung volumes, low-volume loops, and normal arterial blood gas values]
Singh S. The use of field walking tests for assessment of functional capacity in patients with chronic airways obstruction. *Physiotherapy*. 1992;78:102–104.

Vital Signs

Blood Pressure
Frohlich ED. Recommendations for human blood pressure determination by sphygmomanometers: report of a special task force appointed by the steering committee, American Heart Association. *Hypertension*. 1988;11:210A–222A.
Stolt M. Reliability of auscultory method of arterial blood pressure. *Hypertension*. 1990;3:697–703.

Heart Rate
Rothstein JM. *Measurement in Physical Therapy*. New York, NY: Churchill Livingstone; 1985.

Respiratory Rate
Simeows EAF, Roark R, Berman S, Esler L, Murphy J. Respiratory rate: measurement of variability over time and accuracy at different counting periods. *Archives of Disease in Childhood*. 1991;66:1199–1203.

TREATMENT
Brimioulle S, Moraine J, Kahn R. Passive physical therapy and respiratory therapy effects on intracranial pressure, abstracted. *Critical Care Medicine*. 1988;16:449.
Britton S, Bejstedt M, Vedin L, et al. Chest physiotherapy in primary pneumonia. *British Medical Journal*. 1985;290:1703–1704.
Chung F, Dean E. Pathophysiology and cardiorespiratory consequences of interstitial lung disease—review and clinical implications: a special communication. *Physical Therapy*. 1989;69:956–966.
Ciesla N, Rodrieguez A, Anderson P, Norton B. The incidence of extrapleural hematomas in patients with rib fractures receiving chest physical therapy. *Physical Therapy*. 1987;67:766. Abstract.
Cohen M, Hoskin TM. *Cardiopulmonary Symptoms in Physical Therapy*. New York, NY: Churchill Livingstone; 1988.
Crosbie WJ, Myles S. An investigation into the effect of postural modification on some aspects of normal pulmonary function. *Physiotherapy*. 1985;71:311–314.
Dean E. Effect of body position on pulmonary function. *Physical Therapy*. 1985;65:613–618.
DeGarmo C, Cerny F, Conboy K, Ellis EF. In vivo effects of theophylline on diaphragm, bicep, and quadricep strength and fatigability. *Journal of Allergy and Clinical Immunology*. 1988;82:1041–1046.
Downie PA. *Cash's Textbook of Chest, Heart and Vascular Disorders for Physiotherapists*. 4th ed. Philadelphia, Pa: JB Lippincott Co; 1987.
Frownfelter D. *Chest Physical Therapy and Pulmonary Rehabilitation: An Interdisciplinary Approach*. Chicago, Ill: Year Book; 1987:239–259.
Gallon A. The use of percussion. *Physiotherapy*. 1992;78:2:85–89.
Hough A. *Physiotherapy in Respiratory Care*. London, England: Chapman & Hall; 1991.
Imle PC, Mars MP, Eppinghaus CE, Anderson P, Ciesla ND. Effect of chest physiotherapy (CPT) positioning on intracracial (ICP) and cerebral perfusion pressure (CPP). *Critical Care Medicine*. 1988;16:382. Abstract.
Irwin S, Tecklin JS. *Cardiopulmonary Physical Therapy*. 2nd ed. St Louis, Mo: CV Mosby Co; 1990.
Kigin C. *Advances in Chest Physical Therapy*. Park Ridge, Ill: American College of Chest Physicians; 1984.
Kirilloff LH, Owens HR, Rogers RM, Mazzocco MC. Does chest physical therapy work? *Chest*. 1985;88:436–444.
Klein P, Kemper M, Weissman C, Rosenbaum SH, Askanazi J, Hyman JI. Attenuation of the hemodynamic responses to chest physical therapy. *Chest*. 1988;93:38–42.

Sutton PP, Lopez-Vidriero MT, Pavia D, et al. Assessment of percussion vibratory-shaking and breathing exercise in chest physiotherapy. *European Journal of Respiratory Diseases.* 1985;66:147–152.

Sutton P, Parker R, Weber B, et al. Assessment of the forced expiration technique, postural drainage and directed coughing in chest physiotherapy. *European Journal of Respiratory Disease.* 1983;64:62.

Webber BA. *The Brompton Hospital Guide to Chest Physiotherapy.* 5th ed. London, England: Blackwell Scientific Publications; 1988.

Webber B, Parker R, Hofmeyer J, Hodson M. Evaluation of self-percussion during postural drainage using the forced expiration technique. *Physiotherapy Practice.* 1985;1:42–45.

Zadai CC. Exercise testing and training for the pulmonary impaired patient. In: Basmajian JV, Wolf S, eds. *Therapeutic Exercise.* 5th ed. Baltimore, Md: Williams & Wilkins; 1990.

Zadai CC. *Pulmonary Management in Physical Therapy.* New York, NY: Churchill Livingstone; 1992.

Chapter 14

Skin Disorders

- Burns
- Pressure sores

Burns

DESCRIPTION

Burns cause localized injury to tissues through wound edema, protein denaturation, and diminished intravascular fluid volume. Burns lead to erythema, increased capillary permeability, and cell death. They also lead to systemic, life-threatening problems such as hypovolemic shock, infection, and inhalation injury. After a burn injury, the client has usually suffered many losses, but the most critical to the client is often the loss of former appearance.

Burns are described most precisely by the depth of skin tissue destroyed, although they are also classified by the degree system (see box).

Classification of Burns

Superficial (first-degree): Epidermis layer is involved.

Partial-thickness (second-degree):
 • *Superficial:* Outer level of the dermis is involved.
 • *Deep:* Much of the dermis is involved, and there may be alteration in hair follicles and sweat glands.

Full-thickness (third-degree): All of the dermis has been burned.

Subdermal (fourth-degree): All of the tissue from the epidermis to and through the subcutaneous tissue is destroyed. This may include muscle and bone.

CAUSE

Burns are caused by a chemical, electrical, or thermal mechanism of injury. Children aged 1 to 5 are most often burned by scalds from liquids. Home fires account for less than 5% of hospitalizations for burns.

ASSESSMENT

Areas
• History
• Psychological state
• Pain
• Posture
• Extent of burns: degree, percentage of body surface burned
• Mobility, including active and passive range of motion (ROM), including any contractures
• Strength
• Pulmonary, including any inhalation injury
• Neurological, including sensation
• Functional level, including activities of daily living (ADLs), transfers
• Gait, if indicated

Instruments/Procedures (See References for Sources)

Extent of Burns
• Lund–Browder charts for estimating areas
• rule of nines

Functional Level
- Barthel Index
- PULSES Profile

Strength
- manual muscle testing (only appropriate to areas not burned)
- voluntary motion

PROBLEMS
- The client has usually suffered many losses, but the most critical to the client is often the loss of former appearance.
- The client will have pain.
- The client can show signs of shock.
- There can be infection.
- The client can have pulmonary injury.
- The client usually has metabolic complications.
- The client can suffer kidney damage.
- The client can have circulatory problems due to the physiological changes post burn.

TREATMENT/MANAGEMENT

Emergent Phase (First 72 Hours After Injury)
- Physical therapy is primarily concerned with positioning to maintain proper length as the burn heals and to assist with control of edema through elevation.
- Begin active ROM exercises as soon as the client is able to tolerate; these can be combined with hydrotherapy sessions. It is usually beneficial to have clients medicated for pain in preparation for the session.
- Clients with extensive burns will need breathing exercises.

Acute Phase
- Assess for the need for splints or positioning devices.
- Monitor skin for areas of increased pressure. Use of special beds/mattresses can assist in prevention of pressure points.
- Elevate any burned extremities.
- Provide wound care with whirlpool (containing a chemical agent) and mechanical debridement if indicated, usually for 20 minutes.
- Debridement is followed by wound dressing with topical agents, if indicated.
- Continue active and functional exercise, but switch to passive exercise if the client is unable to perform active exercise.
- The skin should blanch if a stretch is applied to the area.
- Use adaptive equipment as indicated. Consult with the occupational therapist as needed.
- Exercise is usually contraindicated after skin grafting for 3 to 7 days, or 7 to 10 days after a cultured epithelial autograft. Assess for postoperative splinting.
- Ambulate as soon as possible. Consult with surgeon before ambulating post skin grafting in lower extremities. See Precautions for contraindications. Proper dressing and elastic support are needed if the client has burns on the lower extremities. Use protective and assistive devices as indicated.
- Consider use of a tilt table if the client has postural hypotension.

Common Deformities and Motions To Counteract Deformities

Joint/Area	Direction of Deformity	Motion to Counteract Deformity
Anterior neck	Flexion	Hyperextension
Shoulder/axilla area	Adduction with internal rotation	Abduction, flexion, and external rotation
Elbow	Flexion and pronation	Extension and supination
Hand	Intrinsic minus position	Wrist extension; MCP flexion, proximal IP and distal IP extension; thumb palmar abduction
Hip/groin area	Flexion and adduction	All motions, especially extension and abduction
Knee	Flexion	Extension
Ankle	Plantar flexion	All motions, especially dorsiflexion

Source: Reprinted with permission from M Staley, RL Richard, and JE Falkel, Burns, in *Physical Rehabilitation*, 3rd ed., SB O'Sullivan and TJ Schmitz, p. 525, © 1994, FA Davis Co.

Long-Term Rehabilitation Phase

- Select exercise and stretching appropriate to the client's needs, ranging from passive to resistive. Consider use of continuous passive machines, isokinetic exercise, aquatics, proprioceptive neuromuscular facilitation patterns, open- or closed-chain exercise, and functional activities. Prescribe a conditioning program and advice on use of equipment such as a stationary bicycle, a treadmill, and free-standing weights.
- Assess for use of serial splinting, casting, or dynamic splinting to avoid contractures.
- Educate the client about scar management through use of pressure therapy via appliances or garments. An ideal pressure of 25 mm Hg is recommended. Garments are usually worn 23 hours a day for over a year. Scar management equipment should be fitted by experienced personnel and can include light dressings, elastic pressure devices, gloves, stockings, and clothing with a high-pressure component such as bicycle shorts and custom garments.
- Scar massage, especially deep friction massage, may be used to mobilize scar tissue.
- Referral to a support group, such as the Phoenix Society, is recommended. See addresses in Appendix D.
- Referral to a cosmetologist who specializes in corrective makeup can be helpful for some clients, especially women with facial burns.
- Establish a discharge plan, including a home exercise program of exercise, skin care, and use of pressure garments and splints. Use of written materials and/or videotapes is helpful.
- Physical therapy may be continued on an outpatient basis:
  1. Continue exercise: ROM, strengthening, and conditioning.
  2. Monitor the use of pressure garments and splints.
  3. Provide modalities such as paraffin for scar tissue softening and ROM.
  4. Educate the client about edema prevention and skin care.
  5. Provide gait training as indicated.
  6. Treat associated injuries.
  7. Assist in preparation to return to work, such as work tolerance screening, job analysis, and work hardening.

PRECAUTIONS/CONTRAINDICATIONS
- Clients with diabetes prior to the burn are at higher risk for metabolic complications.
- Mechanical debridement should not cause bleeding.
- Avoid side effects of improper positioning:
  1. Prolonged use of a lower extremity position with hips abducted and externally rotated, knees in flexion, and ankles inverted with plantar flexion can result in peroneal nerve stretch with weakness of dorsiflexors.
  2. Avoid prolonged use of shoulder abduction of more than 90 degrees to prevent brachial plexus stretch.
  3. Avoid pressure on the ulnar nerve at the cubital space in the elbow.
  4. Avoid prolonged stretch to exposed tendon until the wound is sufficiently healed.
- Splints should not leave any pressure points.
- Monitor vital signs during initial endurance activities.
- Minimize hand contact with burned area due to pain.
- For clients with recent skin grafting, exercise is usually contraindicated after grafting for 3 to 7 days.
- Do not use direct heat. Caution client to use proper skin care protection when in the sun.
- Contraindications to ambulation post burn include
  1. cellulitis or thrombophlebitis
  2. fractures
  3. lower extremity tendon damage
  4. burned weight-bearing surface on soles of feet
  5. medically unstable condition, such as very low hemoglobin or severe burn wounds

DESIRED OUTCOME/PROGNOSIS

Acute Phase
- The client will avoid infection.
- The client will have a decrease in scarring and contracture.
- Therapy will facilitate healing and protect tissue.
- The client will maintain strength and endurance.
- Therapy will prevent pulmonary complications.
- The client will remain active.

Long-Term Phase of Rehabilitation
- The client will be independent in self-care and transfers and ambulation.
- The client will have normal strength.
- The client will be independent in a home exercise program.
- Pressure therapy will provide control of hypertrophic scarring.
- The client will be competent in skin care.
- The client will resume functioning in life.

Scars continue to mature for 1 to 2 years after initial wound healing. At maturation, the scar should no longer appear inflamed but should have a faded appearance. It is advisable for the client to use pressure garments until the scar matures.

Long-term recovery depends heavily on a client's compliance with the home program. Adjustment to alterations in appearance due to the burn usually takes much time and support.

In all phases of treatment, two key components for success are team approach and education.

REFERENCES

ASSESSMENT

American Physical Therapy Association. A guide to physical therapist practice, volume I: a description of patient management. *Physical Therapy.* 1995;75:720–738. **[Integumentary integrity examination]**

Extent of Burns

Byl N, Zellerbach LR, Pfalzer LA. Systemic issues and skin conditions: wound healing, oxygen percutaneous drug delivery, burns, and desensitized skin. In: Myers RS, ed. *Saunders Manual of Physical Therapy Practice.* Philadelphia, Pa: WB Saunders Co; 1995:610. **[Rule of nines]**

Rothstein JM, Roy SH, Wolf SL. *The Rehabilitation Specialist's Handbook.* Philadelphia, Pa: FA Davis Co; 1991:751–766. **[Degree of burn, rule of nines, Lund–Browder charts for estimating areas, biological events in response of burn injuries, topical medications used in burn treatment, and grafts]**

Staley M, Richard RL, Falkel JE. Burns. In: O'Sullivan SB, Schmitz TJ, eds. *Physical Rehabilitation.* 3rd ed. Philadelphia, Pa: FA Davis Co; 1994:509–532. **[Percentage of body surface area burned: modified Lund–Browder chart]**

Functional Level

Barthel Index

Mahoney BI, Barthel DW. Functional evaluation: the Barthel Index. *Maryland State Medical Journal.* 1965;14:61–65.

Wade DT, Collin C. The Barthel ADL Index: a standard measure of physical disability? *International Disability Studies.* 1988;10:64–67.

PULSES Profile

Granger CV, Albrecht GL, Hamilton BB. Outcome of comprehensive medical rehabilitation: measurements by PULSES profile and the Barthel Index. *Archive of Physical Medicine and Rehabilitation.* 1979:60:145–154.

Moskowitz RW, McCann CB. Classification of disability in the chronically ill and aging. *Journal of Chronic Disease.* 1957;5:342–346.

Mobility

Contractures

Cammack S, Eisenberg MG, eds. *Key Words in Physical Rehabilitation: A Guide to Contemporary Usage.* New York, NY: Springer Publishing Co; 1995:35–36.

Payton OC, DiFabio RP, Paris SV, Protas EJ, Van Sant AF, eds. *Manual of Physical Therapy.* New York, NY: Churchill Livingstone; 1989.

Thomson A, Skinner A, Piercy J. *Tidy's Physiotherapy.* Oxford, England: Butterworth-Heinemann; 1991.

TREATMENT

Baxter GD, Bell AJ, Allen JM, Ravey J. Low level laser therapy: current clinical practice in Northern Ireland. *Physiotherapy.* 1991;77:171–178.

Boardman S. Treatment in respiratory problems. In: Leveridge A, ed. *Therapy for the Burn Patient.* London, England: Chapman & Hall; 1991:29–33.

Burns SP, Conin TA. The use of paraffin wax in the treatment of burns. *Physiotherapy Canada.* 1987;39:258–260.

Burnsworth B, Krob MJ, Langer-Schnepp M. Immediate ambulation of patients with lower-extremity grafts. *Journal of Burn Care and Rehabilitation.* 1992;13:89–92.

Byl N, Cameron M, Kloth LC, Zellerbach LR. Treatment and prevention: goals and objectives. In: Myers RS, ed. *Saunders Manual of Physical Therapy Practice.* Philadelphia, Pa: WB Saunders Co; 1995:647–659.

Byl N, Zellerbach LR, Pfalzer LA. Systemic issues and skin conditions: wound healing, oxygen percutaneous drug delivery, burns, and desensitized skin. In: Myers RS, ed. *Saunders Manual of Physical Therapy Practice.* Philadelphia, Pa: WB Saunders Co; 1995:609–616.

Covey MK. Application of CPM devices with burn patients. *Journal of Burn Care and Rehabilitation.* 1988;9:496–497.

DiGregorio VR, ed. *Rehabilitation of the Burn Patient.* New York, NY: Churchill Livingstone; 1984.

Duncan CE. A gait training suggestion for lengthening gastrocnemius-soleus muscles: suggestion from the field. *Physical Therapy.* 1989;69:773–776.

Duncan CE. Use of a ramp surface for lower extemity exercise with burn-injured patients. *Journal of Burn Care and Rehabilitation.* 1989;10:346–349.

Ekes A. Burn patient cooperation in physical and occupational therapy. *Journal of Burn Care and Rehabilitation.* 1985;6:246–249.

Gairns CE, Martin DL. The use of semi-permeable membrane bags as hand burn dressings. *Physiotherapy.* 1990;76:351–352.

Gallagher J, Lakatos M, Goldfarb IW, Slater H. Discharge videotaping: a means of augmenting occupational and physical therapy. *Journal of Burn Care and Rehabilitation.* 1990;11:470–471.

Giuliani CA, Perry GA. Factors to consider in the rehabilitation aspect of burn care. *Physical Therapy.* 1985;65:619–623.

Hardy MA. The biology of scar formation. *Physical Therapy.* 1989;69:1014–1024.

Howell JW. Management of the acutely burned hand for the nonspecialized clinician. *Physical Therapy.* 1989;69:1077–1090.

Hoyrup G, Kjorvel L. Comparison of whirlpool and wax treatments for hand therapy. *Physiotherapy Canada.* 1986;38:79–82.

Johnson CL. Physical therapists as scar modifiers. *Physical Therapy.* 1984;64:1381–1387.

Johnson CL. Burn therapy: state of the art. *Journal of Burn Care and Rehabilitation.* 1985;6:64–65.

Johnson CL. The role of physical therapy. In: Boswick JA, ed. *The Art and Science of Burn Care.* Rockville, Md: Aspen Publishers, Inc; 1987:299–306.

Johnson CL, Schubert D. University of Chicago Burn Center: physical therapists care for wounds. *Journal of Burn Care and Rehabilitation.* 1987;8:56–60.

Johnson CL, Trotter MJ. Survey of burn education in entry-level physical therapy programs. *Physical Therapy.* 1988;68:530–533.

Kealey GP, Jensen KT. Aggressive approach to physical therapy management of the burned hand: a clinical report. *Physical Therapy.* 1988;68:683–685.

Keilty SEJ. Inhalation burn injured patients and physiotherapy management. *Physiotherapy.* 1993;79:87-90.

Marquez RR. Acute care of the adult burn patient. *Physical Therapy Practice.* 1994;3:37–61.

McDonald K, Johnson B, Prasad JK. Collaborative physical therapy for a 4-month-old infant with 80% full-thickness burns. *Journal of Burn Care and Rehabilitation.* 1988;9:193–195.

McNee J. The use of silicone gel in the control of hypertrophic scarring. *Physiotherapy.* 1990;76:194–197.

Meyer DO, Barnett PH, Gross JD. A school reentry program for burned children: physical therapy contribution to an existing school reentry program, part 2. *Journal of Burn Care and Rehabilitation.* 1987;8:322–324.

Morgan B, Boardman S. Burns. In: Downie PA, ed. *Cash's Textbook of General Medical and Surgical Conditions for Physiotherapists.* London, England: Faber & Faber Ltd; 1984:237–251.

Parrott M, Ryan R, Parks DH, Wainwright DJ. Structured exercise circuit program for burn patients. *Journal of Burn Care and Rehabilitation.* 1988;9:666–668.

Raeside F. Physiotherapy management of burned children: a pilot study. *Physiotherapy.* 1992;78:891–895.

Richard RL. Use of Dynasplint to correct elbow flexion burn contracture: a case report. *Journal of Burn Care.* 1986;7:151.

Richard RL. OASIS positioning: a respite for therapists. *Journal of Burn Care and Rehabilitation*. 1990;11:552–553.

Richard RL, Jones LM, Miller SF, Kinley RK Jr. Treatment of exposed bilateral Achilles tendons with use of the Dynasplint. *Physical Therapy*. 1988;68:989–991.

Richard RL, Miller SF, Staley MJ. The physiologic response of a patient with critical burns to continuous passive motion. *Journal of Burn Care and Rehabilitation*. 1990;11:554–556.

Richard RL, Staley MJ. *Burn Care and Rehabilitation: Principles and Practice*. Philadelphia, Pa: FA Davis Co; 1994.

Smith K, Owens K. Physical and occupational therapy burn unit protocol: benefits and uses. *Journal of Burn Care and Rehabilitation*. 1985;6:506–508.

Staley M, Richard R. The elderly patient with burns: treatment considerations. *Journal of Burn Care and Rehabilitation*. 1993;14:559–565.

Staley M, Richard RL, Falkel JE. Burns. In: O'Sullivan SB, Schmitz TJ, eds. *Physical Rehabilitation*. 3rd ed. Philadelphia, Pa: FA Davis Co; 1994:509–532.

Ward RS. Pressure therapy for the control of hypertrophic scar formation after burn injury: a history and review. *Journal of Burn Care and Rehabilitation*. 1991;12:257–262.

Ward RS. Reasons for the selection of burn-scar support suppliers by burn centers in the United States: a survey. *Journal of Burn Care and Rehabilitation*. 1993;14:360–367.

Ward RS, Hayes-Lundy C, Reddy R, et al. Influence of pressure supports on joint range of motion. *Burns*. 1992;18:60–62.

Ward RS, Hayes-Lundy C, Reddy R, et al. Evaluation of topical therapeutic ultrasound to improve response to physical therapy and lessen scar contracture after burn injury. *Journal of Burn Care and Rehabilitation*. 1994;15:74–79.

Ward RS, Hayes-Lundy C, Schnebly WA, et al. Rehabilitation of burn patients with concomitant limb amputation: case reports. *Burns*. 1990;16:390–392.

Ward RS, Schnebly WA, Kravitz M, et al. Have you tried the sandwich splint? A method of preventing hand deformities in children. *Journal of Burn Care and Rehabilitation*. 1989;10:83–85.

Ward RS, Schnebly WA, Warden GD, et al. The efficacy of an autonomous burn physical therapy department in a hospital setting. *Journal of Burn Care and Rehabilitation*. 1988;9:195–197.

Wright PC. Fundamentals of acute burn care and physical therapy management. *Physical Therapy*. 1984;64:1217–1231.

Pressure Sores

Also known as *decubitus ulcers* or *bedsores*.

DESCRIPTION

A pressure sore is an area of ulcerated tissue with exudate and ischemic necrosis. Sores usually occur in tissue that covers a bony prominence that has been exposed to prolonged pressure from lying in bed or pressure from a cast. Clients who are paralyzed or debilitated or who have desensitized skin are especially vulnerable to injury. Pressure sores can increase the length of hospitalization, interfere with rehabilitation, and lead to amputation. In extremes cases, a pressure sore can be life threatening.

Grades of Pressure Sores

Grade I: Limited to superficial epidermis and dermal layers
Grade II: Involves the epidermal and dermal layers and extends into the adipose tissue
Grade III: Extends through the superficial structures and adipose tissue down to and including muscle
Grade IV: Destroys all soft tissue structures down to bone, with communication with bone or joint structures or both

Courtesy of the National Spinal Cord Injury Association, Thorofare, New Jersey.

CAUSE

Pressure sores may be triggered by intrinsic or extrinsic factors. Intrinsic factors include diminished sense of pain and pressure, loss of tissue, disuse atrophy, malnutrition, infection, fever, spasticity, and loss of vasomotor control. Of extrinsic factors, pressure is the primary risk factor due to interruption of local circulation, lack of changing position, friction, wrinkles in clothing or bedding, or moisture leading to maceration of the skin.

ASSESSMENT

Areas
- History
- Skin, including cleanliness, color, dryness, edema, elasticity, moisture, and temperature changes
- Abnormal skin response, including blanching, pressure marks or areas, presence of pressure sores
- Grade/status of sore
- Functional level

Instruments/Procedures (See References for Sources)
- Norton Scale
- The Braden Scale
- Pressure Sore Status Tool

PROBLEMS
- The client has an area of skin ulceration with exudate and necrosis.

TREATMENT/MANAGEMENT
- Prevention is critical. Instruct client and caregivers in abnormal skin responses to identify early changes.
- Perform daily skin inspection regularly, such as when bathing, dressing, and undressing, after using toilet, and after transfers.
- Check main pressure points, including areas where cast, brace, or clothing may rub. Use dorsum of hand or mirror to assist in areas hard to see.
- Use positioning, turning, and pressure-relieving devices and wound care if a sore develops.

Skin Care Management Tips

Dos and Don'ts
- Do lift in the chair every 10 minutes.
- Do lift the paralyzed limbs when transferring.
- Do use a mirror for detection of marks, abrasions, blisters, and redness on buttocks, back of legs, and malleoli.
- Do watch for marks on the penis from the condom.
- Do protect the arms and legs from excessive cold.
- Do watch the temperature of bathwater; avoid too hot water.
- Don't expose the body to strong sunlight; quadriplegic patients should wear a hat.
- Don't knock arms or legs against a hard object.
- Don't rest arms or legs against a warm object or sit too close to a fire.

Source: Reprinted with permission from I Bromley, *Tetraplegia and Paraplegia: A Guide for Physiotherapy*, 3rd ed., © 1985, Churchill-Livingstone.

Treatment of Pressure Sores
- Use topical therapy debridement and dressing technique for pressure sores, grade III or grade IV, a minimum of twice daily.
- Consider use of whirlpool, hyperbaric oxygen, electrical stimulation, and laser therapy.

PRECAUTIONS/CONTRAINDICATIONS
See Appendix C for precautions when using physical agents and modalities.

EXPECTED OUTCOME/PROGNOSIS
- The client will experience healing of pressure sore.
  A pressure sore may take up to a year to heal.

REFERENCES

ASSESSMENT

American Physical Therapy Association. A guide to physical therapist practice, volume I: a description of patient management. *Physical Therapy.* 1995;75:720–738. **[Integumentary Integrity Examination]**

Bohannon RW, Pfaller BA. Documentation of wound surface area from tracings of wound perimeters: clinical report on three techniques. *Physical Therapy.* 1983;63:1622–1624.

Byl N, Zellerbach LR, Pfalzer LA. Systemic issues and skin conditions: wound healing, oxygen percutaneous drug delivery, burns, and desensitized skin. In: Myers RS, ed. *Saunders Manual of Physical Therapy Practice*. Philadelphia, Pa: WB Saunders Co; 1995:619. **[Pressure sore grades, skin dysfunction monitoring]**

Feedar JA. Wound evaluation and treatment planning. *Topics in Geriatric Rehabilitation.* 1994;9:4:35–42.

Braden Scale

Bergstrom N, Braden B. A prospective study of pressure sore risk among institutionalized elderly. *Journal of the American Geriatric Society.* 1992;40:747–758.

Norton Scale

Lincoln R, Roberts J, Maddox R, et al. Use of the Norton pressure sore risk assessment scoring system with elderly patients in acute care. *Journal of Enterostomal Therapy.* 1986;13:128–132.

Pressure Sore Status Tool

Bates-Jensen B. The Pressure Sore Status Tool: an outcome measure for pressure sores. *Topics in Geriatric Rehabilitation*. 1994;9:4:17–34.

TREATMENT

Balogun JA, Abidoye AB, Akala EO. Zinc iontophoresis in the management of bacterial colonized wounds: a case report. *Physiotherapy Canada*. 1990;42:147–151.

Baxter GD, Bell AJ, Allen JM, Ravey J. Low level laser therapy: current clinical practice in Northern Ireland. *Physiotherapy*. 1991;77:171–178.

Beckerman H, de Bies RA, Bouter LM, De Cuyper HJ, Oostendorp RAB. The efficacy of laser therapy for musculoskeletal and skin disorders: a criteria-based meta-analysis of randomized clinical trials. *Physical Therapy*. 1992;72:483–491.

Birke JA, Novick A, Graham SL, et al. Methods of treating plantar ulcers. *Physical Therapy*. 1991;71:116–122.

Charman RA. Bioelectricity and electrotherapy: towards a new paradigm? Bioelectric potentials and tissue currents, part 3. *Physiotherapy*. 1990;76:643–654.

Davis LB, McCulloch JM, Neal MB. The effectiveness of Unna boot and semipermeable film vs Unna boot alone in the healing of venous ulcers: a pilot report. *Ostomy Wound Management*. 1992;38:19–21.

Dyson M. Mechanisms involved in therapeutic ultrasound. *Physiotherapy*. 1987;73:116–120.

Feedar JA. Pressure sores. *Topics in Geriatric Rehabilitation*. 1994;9:4:1–16, 35–82.

Feedar JA, Kloth LC, Gentzkow GD. Chronic dermal ulcer healing enhanced with monophasic pulsed electrical stimulation. *Physical Therapy*. 1991;71:639–649.

Fernandez S. Physiotherapy: prevention and treatment of pressure sores. *Physiotherapy*. 1987;73:457–459.

Fitzgerald GK, Newsome D. Treatment of a large infected thoracic spine wound using high voltage pulsed monophasic current. *Physical Therapy*. 1993;73:355–360.

Griffin JW, Tooms RE, Mendius RA, et al. Efficacy of high voltage pulsed current for healing of pressure ulcers in patients with spinal cord injury. *Physical Therapy*. 1991;71:433–444.

Gogia PP. *Clinical Wound Management*. Thorofare, NJ: Slack, Inc; 1995.

Gogia PP, Hurt BS, Zirn TT. Wound management with whirlpool and infrared cold laser treatment. *Physical Therapy*. 1988;68:1239–1242.

Gogia PP, Marquez RR, Minerbo GM. Effects of high voltage galvanic stimulation on wound healing. *Ostomy Wound Management*. 1992;38:29, 31–35.

Hardy MA. The biology of scar formation. *Physical Therapy*. 1989;69:1014–1024.

Higgs JD. Pressure sores: is there a place for nutritional support? *Physiotherapy*. 1987;73:457–459.

Kitchen SS, Partridge CJ. A review of low level laser therapy. *Physiotherapy*. 1991;77:161–168.

Kitchen SS, Partridge CJ. A review of ultraviolet radiation therapy. *Physiotherapy*. 1991;77:423–432.

Kloth LC, Feedar JA. Acceleration of wound healing with high voltage, monophasic, pulsed current. *Physical Therapy*. 1988;68:503–508.

Maxwell L. Therapeutic ultrasound: its effects on the cellular and molecular mechanisms of inflammation and repair. *Physiotherapy*. 1992;78:421–426.

McCulloch JM, Kloth L, Feedar JA. *Wound Healing: Alternatives in Management*. 2nd ed. Philadelphia, Pa: FA Davis Co; 1995.

McDiarmid T, Burns PN, Lewith GT, Machin D. Ultrasound and the treatment of pressure sores. *Physiotherapy*. 1985;71:66–70.

Roche C, West J. A controlled trial investigating the effect of ultrasound on venous ulcers referred from general practitioners. *Physiotherapy*. 1984;70:475–477.

Sussman C. Physical therapy modalities and the wound recovery cycle. *Ostomy Wound Management*. 1992;38:43–47, 50–51.

Chapter 15

Women's Health Disorders

- Dysmenorrhea
- High-risk pregnancy
- Incontinence
- Interstitial cystitis
- Labor and birth
- Osteoporosis
- Pelvic floor tension myalgia
- Pelvic inflammatory disease
- Postpartum period
- Pregnancy
- Vulvar vestibulitis

Dysmenorrhea

Also known as *primary dysmenorrhea* or *functional dysmenorrhea.*

DESCRIPTION

Dysmenorrhea is painful menstruation. *Primary dysmenorrhea* is defined as pain that accompanies the menstrual cycle. The pain is usually felt in the lower abdomen and lower back during the early stages of a cycle. Pain usually decreases with an increase in blood flow. *Secondary dysmenorrhea* is painful menstruation caused by pathology.

CAUSE

Primary dysmenorrhea is thought to be caused by ischemia from uterine contractions and the release of the hormone prostaglandin. It may also be caused by hypertonicity in the uterine isthmus, leading to increased pressure and pain. Anxiety, lack of exercise, extrusion of tissue through the cervix, especially with a narrow cervical opening, or a malpositioned uterus can exacerbate the pain.

Secondary dysmenorrhea is caused by an abnormality or pathology such as endometriosis, adenomyosis, fibroids, pelvic cysts or tumors, and pelvic inflammatory disease.

ASSESSMENT

Areas
- History, including general health
- Pain
- Posture, including the effect of position on pain
- Strength, including pelvic floor muscle strength, if indicated
- Special tests to which the PT may or may not have access

Instruments/Procedures (See References for Sources)

Pain
- body diagram
- Numeric Pain Rating Scale
- visual analogue scales

Special Tests to Which the PT May or May Not Have Access
- breast exam
- examination of perineum, vagina, and cervix
- cervical cytology
- bimanual pelvic exam
- urinalysis

PROBLEMS
- The client usually has cramping in the abdominal region.
- The client can have low back pain.
- The client usually reports premenstrual tension.
- The client can also experience nausea, vomiting, or fainting.

TREATMENT/MANAGEMENT
- Consider use of modalities for pain such as transcutaneous electrical nerve stimulation (TENS) or interferential current.
- Try TENS with a conventional mode first, and then adjust parameters as indicated. Electrode placement effectiveness varies. One regimen suggests placement posteriorly at the level of uterine innervation, T10–L1, or anterolaterally, in suprapubic region of abdomen, between umbilicus and anterosuperior iliac spine. An additional option for electrode placement is at accupressure point spleen 6 and spleen 10. Over large areas of pain, additional electrodes have been used.
- With interferential current, the use of two electrodes of 100 cm^2 placed anteriorly and two electrodes of 200 cm^2 placed posteriorly is suggested. Intensity varies with client tolerance, with treatment duration of 15 to 20 minutes daily or on alternate days. Rhythmical frequency at 90 to 100 Hz has been suggested.
- Consider use of shortwave diathermy or superficial heat.
- Teach relaxation techniques or distraction techniques.
- Encourage vigorous exercise.
- Recommend specific exercises. The pelvic tilt can offer some relief, especially for a woman who has a retroverted uterus.
- Positioning and stretching should also be addressed; a supine position with knees flexed against the chest with a 10-second hold can offer relief. Leaning forward toward a wall can assist a stretch of the abdominal area that some women find beneficial.
- Soft tissue mobilization techniques, such as myofascial release, can also be used for dysmenorrhea and endometriosis.

PRECAUTIONS/CONTRAINDICATIONS
- Pain due to secondary dysmenorrhea may increase with activity.

DESIRED OUTCOME/PROGNOSIS
- The client will experience a reduction in pain and tension.
- There will be increased circulation to the abdominal region.
- The pain can diminish with age and after pregnancy.

Dysmenorrhea is one of the of the main reasons given for a hysterectomy. The physical therapist can offer a woman the option of conservative treatment, thus possibly avoiding surgery.

REFERENCES

ASSESSMENT
Ling FW, King PM, Myers CA. Screening for female urogenital system disease. In: Boissonnault WG, ed. *Examination in Physical Therapy Practice*. New York, NY: Churchill Livingstone; 1991:149. **[Female Urogenital System Checklist]**

Pain

Body Diagrams
Headley BJ. Chronic pain management. In: O'Sullivan SB, Schmitz TJ. *Physical Rehabilitation*. 3rd ed. Philadelphia, Pa: FA Davis Co; 1994:577–602.

Numeric Pain Rating Scale
Jensen MP, Faroly P, Braver S. The measurement of clinical pain intensity: a comparison of six methods. *Pain*. 1986;27:117–126.
McGuire DB. The measurement of clinical pain. *Nursing Research*. 1984;33:152–156.

Visual Analogue Scale
Carlsson AM. Assessment of chronic pain, part I: Aspects of the reliability and validity of the visual analogue scale. *Pain*. 1983;16:87–101.
Longobardi AG, Clelland JA, Knowles CJ, Jackson JR. Effects of auricular transcutaneous electrical nerve stimulation on distal extremity pain. *Physical Therapy*. 1989;69:10–17.

TREATMENT
Adams C, Frahm J. Genitourinary System. In: Myers RS, ed. *Saunders Manual of Physical Therapy Practice*. Philadelphia, Pa: WB Saunders Co; 1995:459–504.
Lee JM. *Aids to Physiotherapy*. New York, NY: Churchill Livingstone; 1988:97.
Lewers D, Clelland JA, Jackson JR, et al. Transcutaneous electrical nerve stimulation in the relief of primary dysmenorrhea. *Physical Therapy*. 1989;69:3–9.
Manheim CJ, Lavett DK. *The Myofascial Release Manual*. Thorofare, NJ: Slack Inc; 1989:76.
Mannheimer JS, Whalen EC. The efficacy of transcutaneous electrical nerve stimulation in dysmenorrhea. *Clinical Journal of Pain*. 1985;1:75–83.
O'Connor LJ, Gourley R. *Obstetric and Gynecologic Care in Physical Therapy*. Thorofare, NJ: Slack Inc; 1990:91–97.
Pauls J. Hysterectomy. In: Pauls J, *Therapeutic Approaches to Women's Health: A Program of Exercise and Education*. Gaithersburg, Md: Aspen Publishers, Inc; 1995:7-2:1–7.

High-Risk Pregnancy

DESCRIPTION

In a high-risk pregnancy, there is an increased chance of morbidity or mortality for either the mother or the baby. Reportedly, as many as 25% of pregnant women can be included in the category of high-risk pregnancy.

CAUSE

Inherent risk factors include maternal age of 16 or below or maternal age of above 35, prepregnancy weight below 100 pounds, inadequate weight gain, maternal obesity, and height below 5 feet.

Risk factors related to obstetrical history or medical conditions are numerous and carry differing levels of risk. Some of the more frequently encountered problems are disseminated intravascular coagulation, gestational diabetes, hydraminos, hypertensive disorders, intrauterine growth retardation, incompetent cervix, multifetal gestation, oligohydramnios, placenta abruptio or placenta previa, preterm labor, and premature rupture of membranes.

Preexisting medical problems such as cardiac or respiratory abnormalities or diabetes can make an otherwise normal pregnancy complicated.

ASSESSMENT

Areas
- History, including detailed obstetrical and medical history
- Vital signs at rest and with activity
- Skin and soft tissue, including edema, if indicated, using volumetrics and girth
- Strength, including voluntary movement; do not perform resistive testing
- Cardiovascular, including endurance
- Mobility, including range of motion (ROM)
- Gait, if ambulatory
- Functional level, including activities of daily living (ADLs), bed mobility, and transfers

Instruments/Procedures (See References for Sources)
- Algorithm for physical therapy decisions for high-risk pregnancy

PROBLEMS
- The client is usually on restricted activity level, often on bed rest.
- Bed rest can lead to depression about being confined.
- Deconditioning occurs secondary to bed rest.
- The client can have blood pressure irregularities.
- The client can have premature contractions in excessive number.
- The client usually has musculoskeletal problems.
- The client usually has decreased independence in ADLs.
- The client can have increased intra-abdominal pressure during ADLs.

TREATMENT/MANAGEMENT

General Guidelines

Guidelines for Planning a Treatment Program for a Woman on Bed Rest

- Consider the principal diagnosis of the patient.
- Consider the secondary diagnoses and preexisting conditions (varicose veins, obesity, prior history of low back problems, and myofascial dysfunction).
- Consider the contraindications involved in the particular case. Determinations can involve detailed reading of the chart and conversation with the physician.
- Consider the patient's complaints.

Source: Reprinted with permission from L Pipp, The Exercise Dilemma: Considerations and Guides for Treatment of the High Rish Obstetric Patients, *Journal of Obstetrical and Gynecologic Physical Therapy*, Vol. 13, No. 4, pp. 10–12, © 1989, American Physical Therapy Association.

When individualizing the treatment plan, you should include the following:
- Avoid any increased intra-abdominal pressure through straining or Valsalva maneuver.
- Teach the client relaxation techniques.
- Instruct the client in proper positioning and body mechanics for comfort and to enhance circulation.

- Consider the use of aquatic therapy for the benefit that hydrostatic pressure brings to a pregnant woman.
- Provide a list of resources and literature for the client. See Appendix D.

Upper Extremities
- Establish an exercise program for the upper extremities.
- Upper extremity exercises can include biceps, triceps, deltoids, and rotator cuff musculature.
- Consider use of devices such as Theraband® or Theratubing®. Use light weights as tolerated if no complications arise.
- Monitor for signs to stop exercise, such as dizziness, overfatigue, dyspnea, or increase in contractions.

Lower Extremities
- Assess the client's response to exercise carefully.
- Instruct the client in circulatory exercises that include leg exercises (to be done every hour, when awake) to avoid deep-vein thrombosis.
- Consider the use of the following exercises:
  1. ankle circles for circulation
  2. active assistive, passive, or active exercise as tolerated, without weights or manual resistance
- Consider the use of an aquatic program.

PRECAUTIONS/CONTRAINDICATIONS
- Avoid resistance when testing strength.
- Avoid the Valsalva maneuver and inadvertent breath holding during exercises, especially isometric exercise.
- Avoid stress on the abdominal or pelvic floor muscles.
- Monitor medical status to check for any changes such as an increase in blood pressure, any bleeding or leaking of fluid, and any increase in contractions, especially during or within 30 minutes of the exercise session.
- Avoid the plantar-flexed position at the ankle to avoid a calf cramp.

DESIRED OUTCOME/PROGNOSIS
- The woman will maintain or increase strength while on a restricted activity level.
- The woman will avoid an increase in intra-abdominal pressure or increased strain during ADLs.
- The woman will minimize the physiological effects of bed rest.
- The woman will maintain optimal uterine blood flow.
- There will be increased venous return to prevent thrombosis.
- There will be diminished stress and an increased sense of control.
- The woman will reduce musculoskeletal problems associated with pregnancy.
- The woman will prepare for optimal postpartum recovery.

REFERENCES

ASSESSMENT

Algorithm for Physical Therapy Decisions for High-Risk Pregnancy
Appel C. Obstetrical considerations. In: Myers RS, ed. *Saunders Manual of Physical Therapy Practice.* Philadelphia, Pa: WB Saunders Co; 1995:522.

TREATMENT

Appel C. Obstetrical considerations. In: Myers RS, ed. *Saunders Manual of Physical Therapy Practice.* Philadelphia, Pa: WB Saunders Co; 1995:505–541.

Frahm J, Welch RA. Physical therapy management of the high-risk antepartum patient: medical management, part 1. *Clinical Management in Physical Therapy.* 1989;9:4:14–18.

Frahm J, Welch RA. Physical therapy management of the high-risk antepartum patient: part 2. *Clinical Management in Physical Therapy.* 1989;9:5:47–49.

Frahm J, Welch RA. Physical therapy management of the high-risk antepartum patient: physical and occupational therapy treatment objectives and program, part 3. *Clinical Management in Physical Therapy.* 1989;9:6:28–33.

Pipp LM. The exercise dilemma: considerations and guidelines for treatment of the high-risk obstetric patient. *Journal of Obstetric and Gynecologic Physical Therapy.* 1989;13:4:10–13.

Pauls J. *Therapeutic Approaches to Women's Health: A Program of Exercise and Education.* Gaithersburg, Md: Aspen Publishers, Inc.; 1995.

Rasmussen B. Reimbursement for obstetric and gynecologic physical therapy. *Journal of Obstetric and Gynecologic Physical Therapy.* 1994;18:2:10–12.

Perinatal Loss Among Physiotherapists

Larson AI. Congenital malformations and exposure to high-frequency electromagnetic radiation among Danish physiotherapists. *Scandinavian Journal of Work, Environment and Health.* 1991;17:318–323.

Larson AI, Olsen J, Svane O. Gender-specific reproductive outcome and exposure to high-frequency electromagnetic radiation among physiotherapists. *Scandinavian Journal of Work, Environment and Health.* 1991;17:324–329.

Ouellet-Hellstrom R, Stewart WF. Miscarriages among female physical therapists who report using radio and microwave-frequency electromagnetic radiation. *American Journal of Epidemiology.* 1993;138:775–786.

Taskinen H, Kyyronen P, Hemminki K. Effects of ultrasound, shortwaves, and physical exertion on pregnancy outcome in physiotherapists. *Journal of Epidemiology and Community Health.* 1990;44:196–201.

Incontinence

DESCRIPTION

Urinary incontinence is the involuntary loss of urine. Incontinence can occur at any age, but it is common during pregnancy, affecting around 40% to 85% of pregnant women. There are several forms of incontinence, including the following:

- *Stress incontinence:* The loss of urine during increases in intra-abdominal pressures produced by stresses such as coughing, sneezing, and lifting or straining. Stress incontinence is the most common cause of incontinence in women.
- *Urge incontinence:* Named for an urgent need to urinate combined with the involuntary loss of urine.
- *Overflow incontinence:* Continuous or intermittent loss of urine in small amounts due to bladder overdistention.
- *Mixed incontinence:* Combination of both urge and stress incontinence.
- *Transient incontinence:* Temporary incontinence.

CAUSE

Incontinence in women is affected in part by diminished levels of estrogen during menopause. Childbirth and pelvic trauma can lead to weakness of pelvic floor muscles due to damage of the pudendal nerve, resulting in loss of urine. Chronic constipation can also lead to pelvic floor muscle damage.

Increased weight gain can increase intra-abdominal pressure, and chronic cough, usually due to smoking, can lead to urine leakage. Side effects of some medications, surgical procedures, infection in the urinary tract (UTI), diseases of the neurological system, and thyroid disorder can also trigger incontinence.

Causes of the specific types of incontinence are as follows:

- *Stress incontinence* can be caused by weakness of the urinary sphincter with relaxation of the pelvic floor muscles and downward displacement of the urethra during increases in intra-abdominal pressure. Stress incontinence may also be caused by perineal nerve damage secondary to childbirth (stretching of the perineal nerve or tearing of the perineum), excessive straining during defecation, trauma from childbirth or sexual abuse, or other trauma. In men, it can follow prostatectomy or trauma and intrinsic or neurogenic sphincter defect. In women, it can also be caused by cystocele (pelvic relaxation that allows the bladder to protrude into the vagina) .
- *Urge incontinence* is usually idiopathic, but it may be caused by UTI, uninhibited neurogenic bladder dysfunction, multiple sclerosis, obstructive neuropathy, bladder calculi, tuberculosis, interstitial cystitis, or neoplasms.
- In *overflow incontinence*, bladder overdistention is due to a defect in the detruser muscle caused by sensory neuropathy, a stricture in the urethra, or lesion. In men, overflow incontinence is caused by disease of the prostate gland. In women, it is caused by incontinence surgery or pelvic prolapse (severe).
- *Mixed incontinence* has the same causes as those listed for components of stress and urge incontinence.
- *Transient incontinence* may be caused by delirium, infection, atrophy associated with menopause, medication side effects, depression, endocrine imbalance, impacted stool, or functional incontinence associated with restricted mobility.

ASSESSMENT

Areas
- History, including occupation, surgery, menopausal state, medications, and medical conditions that may affect incontinence, such as allergy, diabetes, heart disease, neurological disease, and respiratory disorders
- Social/psychological, including emotional reaction to incontinence
- Bowel habits, including any constipation
- Functional level, including activity level
- Urogenital: perineal area, pelvic floor muscle strength, urinary frequency, urgency, stress, and nocturia
- Special tests to which the PT may or may not have access

Comparison of Four Methods To Record Pelvic Muscle Strength			
Number	Grade (Modified Oxford Grading Scale)	Traditional Rating	Description
0	Nil	Nothing	No contraction
1	Flicker	Rapid fatigue	Just a bit

2	Weak	Not full range, not against gravity	Slight bulge in posterior wall as pelvic floor moves forward
3	Moderate	Full range in gravity-eliminated position	Feel some lift
4	Good	Full range against gravity	Feels like "baby sucking on your finger"
5	Strong	Full range against resistance	Strong squeezing in with a strong lift

Source: Reprinted from J Pauls, *Therapeutic Approaches to Women's Health: A Program of Exercise and Education*, p. 5-1:16, © 1995, Aspen Publishers, Inc.

Instruments/Procedures (See References for Sources)

Special Tests to Which the PT May or May Not Have Access
- urodynamic studies
- cystourethrography
- videourodynamics
- electromyography

Urogenital
- stop test or urine stream interruption test
- 1-hour office pad test
- internal evaluation of pelvic floor muscle strength
- daily intake and output diary
- urinary stress test

PROBLEMS

Incontinence
- The client has involuntary loss of urine with exertion or sudden increase in intra-abdominal pressure.
- There is usually an increased frequency and/or urgency to urinate.
- The client can also have chronic constipation.
- The incontinence can be accompanied by backache or lower abdominal pain.
- Incontinence can lead to extreme changes in a client's activities of daily living.

Prolapse, Cystocele, Rectocele
- The client may report a feeling of heaviness in the vulvar area.
- The client may complain of backache.
- The client usually has increased frequency in urination and/or incontinence, especially stress incontinence. The client may also report pain or burning with urination.

TREATMENT/MANAGEMENT

Physical therapy for incontinence usually involves behavioral therapy. For rehabilitation purposes, the term *behavioral therapy* is used for an array of techniques, including pelvic muscle exercise, biofeedback, weight training with vaginal cones, electrical stimulation, and bladder retraining, habit (or timed) voiding, and prompted voiding.

Pelvic Muscle Exercise

Pelvic floor muscle exercise means increasing awareness and use of these muscles.
- For increasing awareness, have the client feel the muscle working and make sure she is not substituting or bearing down.
- For increasing actual strength, after the woman knows how to do a contraction, have her hold for a few seconds and relax for twice as long as the hold. See how many times she can do this. This is her baseline number. Continue to increase from the baseline number to stress the muscle. But be careful not to overfatigue, or the woman may end up more discouraged. Chart her progress. One regimen suggests a goal of 20 contractions at least 6 times a day. Another suggested schedule is a 10-10-10 schedule: 10 repetitions 10 times a day with a 10-second hold. Consider the use of very brief contractions, or flicks, to stimulate the phasic component of the pelvic floor muscles.
- For some women, being in a gravity-upright position may be too stressful at first. You can incorporate a progressive sequence for learning, going from a supine position to side-lying and then standing.

Biofeedback

Consider biofeedback using a perineometer or electronic biofeedback equipment. Auditory and/or visual feedback of information from surface or internal electrodes facilitates pelvic floor control. Follow instructions from the manufacturer or the references to this chapter for detailed instruction. A perineometer is a pneumatic device that uses pressure to measure effort. Visual feedback can be provided by simply giving the client a mirror to watch the external effects of a pelvic floor muscle contraction.

Weight Training With Vaginal Cones

Vaginal cones usually come in a set of five cone-shaped weights, numbered from 1 (20 g) to 5 (70 g). Follow instructions from the manufacturer or the references to this chapter for detailed instruction. Select the appropriate cone. Insert the lightest cone with the pointed end and string downward. The cone should be able to stand vertically above the level of the pelvic floor. Once it is in place, the client walks around. If it can be held and retained for 1 minute, the client progresses on to the next cone, which is heavier, and so on until she is unable to retain for at least 1 minute. The heaviest cone that can be retained for 1 minute is used for exercise. The client should insert the cone twice a day and walk around for 15 minutes. If it slips, it should be pushed back up. If it can be retained, the next cone can be used, or the client can try the same cone with more challenging activities, such as jumping.

Electrical Stimulation

For electrical stimulation, choose from faradic current or interferential current as indicated. Follow instructions from the manufacturer or the references to this chapter for a detailed protocol. One regimen suggests that the parameters be varied with the stimulation as follows:
- *Intensity:* per patient tolerance.
- *Frequency:* measured in Hz (hertz), pps (pulses per second), or cycles; 5 to 10 Hz is suggested for urgency and detrusor instability.
- 35 Hz is used to increase muscle awareness and elicit a cortical response.

- 50–60 Hz may fatigue the muscle.
- *Rest:* a weak muscle needs more rest than a trained muscle; the rest period should at least be equal to length of stimulation or greater (slow-twitch fiber, or slow oxidative, needs stimulation of 10 to 20 sec, fast-twitch fibers, or fast glycolytic, needs 30 to 60 sec).
- *Pulse width:* 200 to 400 microseconds ideal.

Bladder Training

Educate the client about incontinence and set up a schedule of voiding that allows for increasing longer intervals between voiding. Habit training or timed voiding is especially "helpful" or "useful" for the client needing dependent care.

Summary of Appropriate Activities Based on Muscle Grade

Weak muscles, grades 1 or 2:
- Use gravity-eliminated position.
- Facilitate muscle with quick stretch.
- Use proprioceptive neuromuscular facilitation with patterns and overflow activity from gluteal and adductor muscles.
- Use sensory stimulation with electrical stimulation.
- Repetitions should be fewer but more frequent to avoid overfatigue and promote myelin sheath development.

Stronger muscles, grades 3, 4, or 5:
- Progress with full range of motion, increasing the hold time or number of repetitions.
- Add resistance with cones.
- Vary positions with weight bearing.
- Try with full bladder and quick contractions. Quick ones are especially important to splint with contraction prior to a stress such as a cough.

PRECAUTIONS/CONTRAINDICATIONS
- Bladder retraining is not indicated for clients with stress or overflow incontinence.
- Electrical stimulation (ES) is contraindicated during menstruation or pregnancy. ES is not to be used if the client has malignancy, metal implants, or a pacemaker.
- The following information should be given to the client who uses weighted cones:
  1. Excess lubrication, as at ovulation or other times, may affect cone retention.
  2. Vaginal cones are not used during the client's menstrual cycle.
  3. A wide introitus may make retention impossible. Permanent damage of innervation to pelvic floor may leave the woman a poor candidate for cones.
  4. A woman may be challenged by as little as 10 seconds, and the times listed may be unrealistic or fatigue inducing. Concentrate on increasing duration as opposed to resistance. A woman should *not* view reaching the No. 5 cone as the final goal. Adjust schedule to tailor the program to the client's individual needs.
  5. For infection control purposes, cones should be for one client's use only.

DESIRED OUTCOME/PROGNOSIS
- The client will experience a reduction or stop in urine leaking.

- Therapy will normalize reflex activity for proper bladder functioning.
- The client will increase the strength of her pelvic floor and abdominal region.
- Therapy will stimulate proprioceptive feedback to the client, increase awareness of pelvic floor muscle function, and increase ability to differentiate and control pelvic floor contractions as opposed to contractions in regions such as adductor and abdominal musculature.
- Improved support of pelvic organs may preclude the need for surgery or enhance surgical outcomes.
- The overall outcome for client will be the restoration and increase in voluntary control of pelvic floor.

Successful Pelvic Floor Rehabilitation

Components of a Successful Pelvic Floor Exercise Program
- The client has an understanding of the anatomical aspects affecting the exercise program.
- The therapist obtains an accurate baseline of the initial degree of incontinence.
- The client is highly motivated.
- The client receives education and encouragement from the therapist.
- The client receives feedback on her efforts.
- The exercise program is customized and regularly supervised.
- Supervision includes ongoing re-evaluation for assessment and treatment purposes.

Source: Reprinted with permission from C Adams and J Frahm, Genitourinary System, in *Saunders Manual of Physical Therapy Practice*, RS Myers, pp. 459–504, © 1995, WB Saunders Company.

REFERENCES

ASSESSMENT
Ling FW, King PM, Myers CA. Screening for female urogenital system disease. In: Boissonnault WG, ed. *Examination in Physical Therapy Practice*. New York, NY: Churchill Livingstone; 1991:149. [**Female Urogenital System Checklist**]
Adams C, Frahm J. Genitourinary system. In: Myers RS, ed. *Saunders Manual of Physical Therapy Practice*. Philadelphia, Pa: WB Saunders Co; 1995:483. [**Treatment algorithm**]

Special Tests to Which the PT May or May Not Have Access
Adams C, Frahm J. Genitourinary system. In: Myers RS, ed. *Saunders Manual of Physical Therapy Practice*. Philadelphia, Pa: WB Saunders Co; 1995:459–504. [**Urodynamic studies, cystourethrography, videourodynamics, electromyography**]

Urogenital
Adams C, Frahm J. Genitourinary system. In: Myers RS, ed. *Saunders Manual of Physical Therapy Practice*. Philadelphia, Pa: WB Saunders Co; 1995:477–483. [**Stop test or urine stream interruption test, 1-hour office pad test, internal evaluation of pelvic floor muscle strength, daily intake and output diary, urinary stress test**]
Pauls J. *Therapeutic Approaches to Women's Health: A Program of Exercise and Education*. Gaithersburg, Md: Aspen Publishers, Inc; 1995:5-1:16. [**Pelvic floor muscle strength**]

TREATMENT

Adams C, Frahm J. Genitourinary system. In: Myers RS, ed. *Saunders Manual of Physical Therapy Practice.* Philadelphia, Pa: WB Saunders Co; 1995:459–504.

Ashworth PD, Hagan MT. Some social consequences of non-compliance with pelvic floor exercises. *Physiotherapy.* 1993;79:465–471.

Brubaker L, Kotarinos R. Kegel or cut? Variations on this theme. *Journal of Reproductive Medicine.* 1993;38:672–678.

Cardozo L, Kelleher C. Sex hormones and the female lower urinary tract. *Physiotherapy.* 1994;80:135–138.

Chiarelli PE. *Women's Waterworks: Curing Incontinence.* Rushcutters Bay, NSW, Australia: Gore & Osment; 1992:32.

Dunbar A. Pelvic floor dysfunction: the complexity of clinical practice. *Journal of Obstetric and Gynecologic Physical Therapy.* 1990;14:3:4.

Frahm J. Strengthening the pelvic floor. *Clinical Management in Physical Therapy.* 1985;5:3:30, 32–33.

Kahn J. *Electrotherapeutics.* New York, NY: Churchill Livingstone; 1991:156–157.

Kahn J. Electrodes and procedures for treatment of stress incontinence. *Journal of Obstetric and Gynecologic Physical Therapy.* 1993;17:1:7.

Keating JC, Schulte EA, Miller E, et al. Conservative care of urinary incontinence in the elderly. *Journal of Manipulative Physiological Therapy.* 1988;11:300–308.

Knight SJ, Laycock J. The role of biofeedback in pelvic floor re-education. *Physiotherapy.* 1994;80:145–148.

Kotarinos RK. Electromyographic and dynamometric characteristics of female pelvic floor musculature. *Physical Therapy.* 1988;68:350.

Harrison SM. Stress incontinence and the physical therapist. *Physiotherapy.* 1983;69:144–147.

Laycock J. Graded exercises for the pelvic floor muscles in the treatment of urinary incontinence. *Physiotherapy.* 1987;73:371–377.

Laycock J. Pelvic floor re-education. *Nursing: The Journal of Clinical Practice, Education and Management.* 1991;39:4:15–17.

Laycock J. Pelvic muscle exercises: physiotherapy for the pelvic floor. *Urologic Nursing.* 1994;14:136–140.

Laycock J, Green GR. Interferential therapy in the treatment of incontinence. *Physiotherapy.* 1988;74:161–168.

Laycock J, Jerwood D. Development of the Bradford Perineometer. *Physiotherapy.* 1994;80:3:139–143.

Mantle J. Focus on continence. *Physiotherapy.* 1994;80:126–131.

Mantle J, Versi E. Physiotherapy for stress urinary incontinence: a national survey. *British Medical Journal.* 1991;302:753–755.

Malone-Lee J. Recent developments in urinary incontinence in late life. *Physiotherapy.* 1994;80:133–134.

McCandless S, Mason G. Physical therapy as an effective change agent in the treatment of patients with urinary incontinence. *Journal of the Mississippi Medical Association.* 1995; 271–274.

McIntosh LJ, Frahm JE, Mallett VT, Richardson DA. Pelvic floor rehabilitation in the treatment of incontinence. *Journal of Reproductive Medicine.* 1993;38:662–666.

McIntosh LJ, Mallett VT, Frahm JD, et al. Gynecologic disorders in women with Ehlers-Danlos syndrome. *Journal of the Society for Gynecologic Investigation.* 1995;2:559–564.

Noble E. The female pelvic floor: review and commentary. *Journal of Obstetric and Gynecologic Physical Therapy.* 1993;17:3:12–15.

Olah KS, Bridges N, Denning J, Farrar DJ. The conservative management of patients with symptoms of stress incontinence: a randomized, prospective study comparing weighted vaginal cones and interferential therapy. *American Journal of Obstetrics and Gynecology.* 1990;162:87–92.

Pauls, J. Female urinary incontinence. *Therapeutic Approaches to Women's Health: A Program of Exercise and Education.* Gaithersburg, Md: Aspen Publishers, Inc; 1995:5-1:16.

Santiesteban AJ. Electromyographic and dynamometric characteristics of female pelvic floor musculature. *Physical Therapy.* 1988;68:344–351.

Sayer TR. Stress incontinence of urine: a connective tissue problem? *Physiotherapy.* 1994;80:143–144.

Tries J, Eisman E. The use of biofeedback in the treatment of urinary incontinence. *Physical Therapy Practice*. 1993;2:2:49–56.

Wall LL, Davidson TG. The role of muscular re-education by physical therapy in the treatment of genuine stress urinary incontinence. *Obstetrical and Gynecological Survey*. 1992;47:322–331.

Interstitial Cystitis

Also known as *Hunner's ulcer*.

DESCRIPTION

Interstitial cystitis (IC) is characterized by inflammation and irritation of the bladder but is not thought to be an infectious disorder.

CAUSE

IC can be a disorder of the autoimmune system, an allergic reaction, or a type of collagen disease. It may be manifested secondary to an infectious agent that is as yet unidentified.

ASSESSMENT

Areas

- History, including any medical conditions or symptoms such as bleeding or discharge, occupation, surgery, menopausal state, and medications
- Social/psychological
- Urinary symptoms; frequency, urgency, stress, and nocturia
- Bowel habits, including any constipation
- Pain, including any dyspareunia (painful intercourse)
- Functional level, including activities of daily living (ADLs)
- Perineal examination: observation and strength, if indicated

Instruments (See References for Sources)

No specific evaluation was identified for IC. Consider use of elements from evaluations for incontinence.

Urinary Symptoms
- daily intake and output diary

PROBLEMS

- The client usually has severe pelvic pain.
- There is usually painful urination with increased frequency.
- There can be increased pain after consumption of acidic or carbonated drinks, alcohol, or drinks with caffeine.

TREATMENT/MANAGEMENT

- Instruct the client in bladder training. Educate the client about incontinence, and establish a schedule of voiding that allows for increasing longer intervals between voiding.

- Teach habit training or timed voiding, especially for the client needing dependent care.
- Consider use of transcutaneous electrical nerve stimulation (TENS). One regimen suggests electrode placement using two sets of electrodes, one at the suprapubic area and another on paraspinal musculature at the T-10 level, with intensity as tolerated and frequency at BID for 2 hours.
- Consider use of interferential current; see manufacturer's suggestion for protocol and electrode placement.

PRECAUTIONS/CONTRAINDICATIONS
None mentioned.

DESIRED OUTCOME/PROGNOSIS
The client will experience a decrease in symptoms.

REFERENCES

ASSESSMENT
Ling, FW, King PM, Myers CA. Screening for female urogenital system disease. In: Boissonnault WG, ed. *Examination in Physical Therapy Practice.* New York, NY: Churchill Livingstone; 1991:149. **[Female Urogenital System Checklist]**

Urinary Symptoms
Adams C, Frahm J. Genitourinary system. In: Myers RS, ed. *Saunders Manual of Physical Therapy Practice.* Philadelphia, Pa: WB Saunders Co; 1995:477–483 **[Daily intake and output diary]**

TREATMENT
Adams C, Frahm J. Genitourinary system. In: Myers RS, ed. *Saunders Manual of Physical Therapy Practice.* Philadelphia, Pa: WB Saunders Co; 1995:459–504.
Kotarinos RK. Interstitial cystitis. *Journal of Obstetric and Gynecologic Physical Therapy.* 1994;18:4:5–7.

Labor and Birth

DESCRIPTION
Labor involves contractions of the uterus that usually progress by getting longer, stronger, and more frequent. These contractions lead to dilation and effacement of the cervix. For descriptive purposes, labor is divided into four stages:
- The first stage covers the onset of labor until the cervix is completely dilated (about 10 cm).
- The second stage, or the pushing stage, begins at full cervical dilation and ends with the birth of the baby.
- The third stage begins after the baby is born and is complete when the placenta is delivered.
- The fourth stage is an observation time lasting from the placental delivery until 4 hours postpartum.

Labor lasts between 12 to 14 hours in a first pregnancy and 6 to 8 hours in subsequent pregnancies.

CAUSE

The stimulus that triggers the beginning of labor has not been established. One theory suggests that the hormone oxytocin, which is released from the pituitary gland, begins the process.

ASSESSMENT

Areas
- History
- Respiration: rate and rhythm of breathing pattern
- Areas of tension/pain
- Uterine contractions
- Progress of labor: dilation and effacement from primary caregiver
- Pain
- Posture: positions of comfort /effect of posture on circulation and pain

Instruments/Procedures
- Palpation of areas of tension/pain
- External palpation of uterine contractions

PROBLEMS
- The client usually has gradually increasing pain with contractions.
- Approximately 25% of women feel contractions primarily in the back; this is known as back labor.
- The client may have difficulty relaxing.
- The client may have anxiety and fear about labor.

TREATMENT/MANAGEMENT
- Educate the client about pregnancy, labor, birth, and the postpartum period prior to labor with childbirth education instruction. The physical therapist can also be a childbirth educator or can refer the client to a childbirth educator. Organizations that certify educators have varied philosophies. Three of the largest organizations include Lamaze/ASPO (American Society for Psychoprophylaxis in Obstetrics, Inc.), ICEA (International Childbirth Education Association), and the Bradley method (American Academy of Husband-Coached Childbirth).
- A physical therapist may also assume the role of professional labor support and lactation consultant.

Labor Support
- Provide encouragement and emotional support.
- Provide information about the labor and birth process and the comfort measures available.
- Provide advocacy of the client's choices regarding the birth experience.
- Instruct in stress management techniques to calm the parasympathetic nervous system, including
  1. massage, especially slow, rhythmical strokes
  2. slow-paced abdominal breathing

3. soothing surroundings
4. warmth from water, moist heat packs, or compresses
5. avoiding worry
6. meditation on calming thoughts
7. muscular release through relaxation techniques
- Relaxation techniques include the Mitchell method of reciprocal relaxation, Benson's relaxation response, progressive relaxation, modified progressive relaxation, selective dissociative relaxation, and differential relaxation.
- Consider use of ice for labor pain.
- Consider use of transcutaneous electrical nerve stimulation (TENS) for labor pain, especially for pain in low back. Electrode placement may vary. One suggested option is to place one set of electrodes paraspinally at level T-10 to L-1 (level of uterine innervation) and another set paraspinally at S-2 to S-4. (An additional option includes anterior placement of the electrodes in a V shape in the suprapubic area.) Parameters may vary. One option includes a pulse rate at 80 to 120 Hz, pulse width at 150 μs, and intensity as desired by client.

Positioning During Labor
During labor, positions for pushing can be modified.
- A side-lying or partially reclined position is recommended for many disabled women, especially if they cannot use a position in which the legs are widely spread. Side-lying is also useful for a patient with the diagnosis of herniated nucleus pulposus or spinal stenosis.
- Avoid standing for women with spondylolisthesis. Avoid the lithotomy position with sacroiliac dysfunction if standing is uncomfortable. Avoid hip abduction with pubic symphysis dysfunction.
- Women with a spinal cord injury may need extra padding to avoid pressure sores when assuming positions for prolonged periods.

Selected Labor Considerations for Pregnant Women with Disabilities	
Disability	**Considerations During Labor**
Arthritis	Side-lying may be the least stressful position for second-stage labor. Epidural may not be an option
Amputation with use of prosthesis	Avoid prolonged positions, which may lead to skin breakdown under prosthesis
Asthma	Extra cortisone and adrenalin released naturally during labor provide increased protection against an asthma attack
Cerebral palsy	Cesarean is often recommended, but there is no research to support this assumption; more research needed
Diabetes	Blood sugar levels will be closely monitored
Epilepsy	Avoid any medications that might trigger convulsion. The breathing techniques might trigger an attack in some women; avoid overbreathing
Heart disease	Close monitoring during labor is warranted. Interventions may be used during second-stage labor to diminish the stress of expulsive efforts

Multiple sclerosis	Epidural may not be an option due to concerns of possibly exacerbating disorder; no research to confirm this assumption
Scoliosis	Epidural may not be an option. Pelvic size is usually unaffected by scoliosis
Spina bifida	Abdominal muscle strength is usually sufficient for second-stage labor. Careful positioning is indicated
Spinal cord injury	Instruction in manual palpation of contractions is indicated to determine when labor is beginning. Contractions of uterus are usually sufficient to expel baby during second stage. Positioning is important also. Degree of intervention needed during second stage depends on level of lesion. Spasm in pelvic floor muscle during delivery may be present

Source: Reprinted from J Pauls, *Therapeutic Approaches to Women's Health: A Program of Exercise and Education,* p. 3-1:10, © 1995, Aspen Publishers, Inc.

Back Labor

Around 25% of women experience some or all of their labor contractions in the lower back area. Back labor is often caused by a baby in an occiput-posterior position.

Comfort measures for back labor include

- changing positions—all-fours, sitting, side-lying (avoid supine)
- firm counterpressure on the back (muscular area) with the heel of partner's hand, tennis ball, or rolling pin
- passive pelvic tilt by partner with woman in side-lying position
- active pelvic tilt—any position
- massage
- heat or cold compresses—whichever works most effectively
- TENS

PRECAUTIONS/CONTRAINDICATIONS

- Occasionally, TENS may interfere with equipment such as fetal monitor if in use.

Cautions Concerning TENS Usage

TENS is contraindicated under the following conditions:

- Any electrode placement that applies current to the carotid sinus (neck) region.
- Presence of a demand-type cardiac pacemaker.
- Any electrode placement that causes current to flow transcerebrally (through the head).
- Presence of undiagnosed pain syndromes until etiology is established.
- The safety of TENS devices for use during pregnancy or delivery has not been established.
- TENS is not effective for pain of central origin (this includes headache).
- TENS devices should be used only under the continued supervision of a physician.
- TENS devices have no curative value.
- TENS is a symptomatic treatment and as such suppresses the sensation of pain that would otherwise serve as a protective mechanism.

- The user must keep the device out of the reach of children.
- Electronic monitoring equipment (such as ECG monitors and ECG alarms) may not operate properly when TENS stimulation is in use.
- If the device is capable of delivering a charge per pulse of 25 microcoulombs or greater, there should be a prominently placed statement warning that stimulus delivered by this device may be sufficient to cause electrocution. Electrical current of this magnitude must not flow through the thorax because it may cause a cardiac arrythmia.

Source: Reprinted with permission from E Pomerantz, TENS and Pregnancy: Rules for Safe Practice, *Journal of Obstetric and Gynecologic Physical Therapy*, Vol. 12, No. 3, p. 5, © 1988, American Physical Therapy Association.

DESIRED OUTCOME/PROGNOSIS
- The client will be informed about the process of labor and options for birth.
- The client will have coping measures for labor.
- The client will have a positive birth experience.

REFERENCES

TREATMENT
Appel C. Continuing education: positioning for labor and delivery for women with spinal dysfunction by J. Boissonnault. *Journal of Obstetric and Gynecologic Physical Therapy*. 1992;16:3:6.
Fenwick L, Simkin P. Maternal positioning to prevent or alleviate dystocia in labor. *Clinical Obstetrics and Gynecology*. 1987;30:1:83–89.
O'Connor LJ, Gourley R. *Obstetric and Gynecologic Care in Physical Therapy*. Thorofare, NJ: Slack, Inc. 1990.
Wilder E, ed. *Obstetric and Gynecologic Physical Therapy*. New York, NY: Churchill Livingstone; 1988.

Childbirth Education
Blankfield A. Survey of breathing exercises and natural childbirth methods. *Physiotherapy*. 1969;55:311–318.
Cole S. Changes in childbirth education. *New Zealand Journal of Physiotherapy*. 1991;19:2:19–21.
Lubic RW, Norton K, Klein M, Beernink HE, Ellis J, Simkin P. More on "the trouble with 'choice' in childbirth." *Birth: Issues in Perinatal Care and Education*. 1983;10:179–185.
Pauls J. *Therapeutic Approaches to Women's Health: A Program of Exercise and Education*. Gaithersburg, Md: Aspen Publishers, Inc; 1995.
Simkin P. Quantity, quality, and money: still more on veteran childbirth educators. Effective childbirth education: are small classes the only way? *Birth: Issues in Perinatal Care and Education*. 1984;11:176–177.
Simkin P. Is anyone listening? The lack of clinical impact of randomized controlled trials of electronic fetal monitoring. *Birth: Issues in Perinatal Care and Education*. 1986;13:219–220.
Simkin P. Stress, pain, and catecholamines in labor: a review, part 1. *Birth: Issues in Perinatal Care and Education*. 1986;13:227–233.
Simkin P. Stress, pain, and catecholamines in labor: stress associated with childbirth events. A pilot survey of new mothers, part 2. *Birth: Issues in Perinatal Care and Education*. 1986;13:234–240.
Simkin P. Electronic fetal monitoring: back to the drawing board? *Birth: Issues in Perinatal Care and Education*. 1987;14:124.
Simkin P. Midwifery comes to Canada. *Birth: Issues in Perinatal Care and Education*. 1988;15:102–103.
Simkin P. Childbearing in social context. *Women and Health*. 1989;15:3:5–21.
Simkin P. Just another day in a woman's life? Women's long-term perceptions of their first birth experience, part 1. *Birth: Issues in Perinatal Care and Education*. 1991;18:203–210.

Simkin P. Just another day in a woman's life? Nature and consistency of women's long-term memories of their first birth experiences, part 2. *Birth: Issues in Perinatal Care and Education.* 1991;19:64–81.

Simkin P. The labor support person: latest addition to the maternity care team. *International Journal of Childbirth Education.* 1992;7:1:19–27.

Simkin P. Overcoming the legacy of childhood sexual abuse: the role of caregivers and childbirth educators. *Birth: Issues in Perinatal Care and Education.* 1992;4:224–225.

Simkin P. When should a child attend a sibling's birth? A guideline for parents. *Midwifery Today and Childbirth Education.* 1993;28:37.

Simkin P. Epidural epidemic. *Birth Gazette.* 1994;10:4:28–34.

Simkin P. Potential risks of epidural anesthesia. *Midwifery Today and Childbirth Education.* 1994;31:27.

Simkin P. What you should know about active management of labor. *Childbirth Instructor Magazine.* 1995;5:1:8–10.

Simkin P, Heeran K. Index and abstracts to the current literature. *Birth: Issues in Perinatal Care and Education.* 1985;12:190–192.

TENS

Dunn PA, Rogers D, Halford K. Transcutaneous electrical nerve stimulation at acupuncture points in the induction of uterine contractions. *Obstetrics and Gynecology.* 1989;73:286–290.

Grim LC, Moray SH. Transcutaneous electrical nerve stimulation for relief of parturition pain: a clinical report. *Physical Therapy.* 1989;65:337–340.

Hill L. TENS for back pain in late pregnancy. *Physiotherapy.* 1990;76:566.

Hollinger JL. Transcutaneous electrical nerve stimulation after cesarean birth. *Physical Therapy.* 1986;66:36–38.

Keenan DL, McCrann DJ, Simonsen L. Transcutaneous electrical nerve stimulation for pain control during labor and delivery: a case report. *Physical Therapy.* 1985;65:1363–1364.

Lee EW, Chung IW, Lee JY, Lam PW, Chin RK. The role of transcutaneous electrical nerve stimulation in management of labour in obstetric patients. *Asia-Oceania Journal of Obstetrics and Gynaecology.* 1990;16:247–254.

Pipp LM. Compendium of selected TENS literature. *Journal of Obstetric and Gynecologic Physical Therapy.* 1993;17:12.

Polden M. Transcutaneous nerve stimulation in labor and post-cesarean section. *Physiotherapy.* 1985;71:3.

Pomerantz E. TENS and pregnancy: rules for safe practice. *Journal of Obstetric and Gynecologic Physical Therapy.* 1988;12:3:5.

Osteoporosis

DESCRIPTION

Osteoporosis is a progressive reduction in bone tissue mass per unit volume. This decrease in bone mass leads to skeletal weakness characterized by bone fractures. The most common adult metabolic bone disease, osteoporosis leads to between 1 and 1.5 million fractures in the United States annually. Colles fracture and vertebral crush fractures, as well as fractures in the hip and pelvic region, are often a result of osteoporosis.

CAUSE

Research suggests that diminished weight bearing leads to less stress on bones, which triggers calcium resorption, resulting in bone loss. Increased risk factors for primary osteoporosis include female gender, never having been pregnant, early menopause, white or oriental race, thinness, aging, family history, and inactivity.

There are three types of primary osteoporosis:
- idiopathic osteoporosis
- Type I or postmenopausal osteoporosis, which occurs around age 51 to 75 in women due to endocrinologic changes but can also occur in men.
- Type II or involutional osteoporosis, which occurs in clients over age 70, although it actually begins in the third decade. Women are two times as likely as men to be affected. This type is possibly related to a decrease in vitamin D synthesis.

ASSESSMENT

Areas
- History, including previous fractures, symptoms of dysmenorrhea or menopause, use of hormones, and any medications that may affect skeletal health
- Posture
- Pain
- Balance
- Gait
- Mobility, including active range of motion (ROM)
- Strength, especially trunk strength
- Neurological, including coordination and balance, in static and dynamic state
- Cardiovascular, including endurance level
- Functional level, including activities of daily living (ADLs) and leisure activities
- Equipment, including home environment
- Special tests to which the PT may or may not have access

Instruments/Procedures (See References for Sources)

Balance
- one-legged stance test (OLST)
- sharpened Rhomberg test (SR)
- step-width measurements
- quantitative muscle tester (QMT)
- get up and go test (GUGT)
- sensory organization test (SOT) for standing balance

Functional Level
- PULSES Profile

Mobility
- timed up-and-go test

Posture
- postural stress test
- posturography
- Reedco Posture Score Sheet

Special Tests to Which the PT May or May Not Have Access
- bone mineral density measurement

- trunk muscle strength testing
- isometric and isokinetic torque evaluation
- work measurements
- electromyography (EMG)

PROBLEMS
- The client usually has extreme pain.
- The pain is usually chronic.
- The pain is often in thoracic region, especially if the client shows signs of kyphosis and is a postmenopausal woman.

TREATMENT/MANAGEMENT

In General
- Provide education, including fall prevention information.

Education Topics for Osteoporosis

- unavoidable versus avoidable risk factors
- dos and don'ts of exercise and activities
- proper body mechanics, perhaps including a "back school," and work simplification
- proper posture
- consultation with nutritionist regarding diet, calcium supplements, etc
- individualized instruction in an exercise program to address identified dysfunction and needs
- supportive or orthotic devices where needed
- review of home environment and activities to minimize the risk of falls and fracture (eg, installing handrails, eliminating slippery throw rugs, not climbing on ladders)
- work consolidation
- possibly modification of diet or lifestyle to help to minimize those risk factors that are avoidable

---

- Increase functional activity level.
- Encourage weight-bearing exercise or exercise that stresses bone. Ideally, an exercise program can be started premenopausally, but even after an osteoporosis fracture, exercise such as walking, jogging, or stair climbing can be safe.
- Increase activity level and postural alignment with various activities, including calisthenics, weight lifting, swimming, cycling, walking, running, golfing, tennis, gardening, and dancing—almost all have been more or less successful in either preventing age-related bone loss in the postmenopausal woman or actually increasing bone density, especially in the extremely sedentary woman. Stress as many parts of the skeleton (safely) as possible.
- Progress by adding light weights, Theraband™, etc., for resistance. Balance, coordination, and function can be facilitated by combining many of the exercises, along the order of dynamic stabilization routines.

- Every day, try to walk briskly, keeping an erect posture and swinging arms freely.
- Excessive flexion and rotation activities should be avoided.

Tips for Avoiding Injuries

- Remove all loose or slippery area rugs.
- Keep electrical cords well out of the way.
- Keep walkways and porches clear.
- Be especially careful around pets. Man's best friend may inadvertently cause a fall, both in the home or when out for a walk.
- Monitor your medications, both prescription and over the counter. Drug interactions can account for dizziness, loss of balance, sedation, etc.
- Avoid situations where you are vulnerable to falling. Let someone else climb up on the ladder.
- Be extra careful during the winter when sidewalks, porches, and driveways may be icy.
- Be sure to have a clear path from your bed to the bathroom in case the need arises in the middle of the night.
- Use ample lighting; use plenty of nightlights.

Source: Reprinted from PB Gleeson, Osteoporosis, in J Pauls, *Therapeutic Approaches to Women's Health: A Program of Exercise and Education,* pp. 5:6-1:1-6-1:27, © 1995, Aspen Publishers, Inc.

Pain Reduction Measures
- For fracture pain, provide heat to areas of muscle spasm.
- Instruct the client in extension exercise following vertebral fracture.
- Post hip fracture, provide gait training, usually with partial weight bearing with internal fixation for 6 weeks. Consult with the surgeon on weight-bearing status.
- Any appropriate modalities may be used during the pain management aspect of treatment. Heat and/or cold and massage as well as transcutaneous electrical nerve stimulation (TENS) may provide temporary pain relief. Positioning for relaxation and proper alignment should always be emphasized. Splints, corsets, or other orthotic devices may be indicated.

PRECAUTIONS/CONTRAINDICATIONS
- Women with a significant amount of bone loss should consult their physicians before the physical therapist designs an individualized exercise program for each client.
- Avoid flexion exercises if the client has suffered vertebral fracture.
- After internal fixation, the client should avoid hip flexion (keeping the angle no less than 90 degrees), adduction past midline, and internal rotation.
- An added caution before prescribing an exercise program for the elderly population: cervical vertebrae may collapse with osteoporosis, resulting in a disruption of the vertebral artery flow. Vertebral artery syndrome may be present, with symptoms including dizziness, blurred vision, or blackouts with extension, lateral flexion, or rotation of their cervical spine. The physical therapist should determine if there is any compromise of the vertebral artery prior to prescribing neck exercises and should educate clients concerning this possibility.

Exercise and Leisure Time Dos and Don'ts

1. Do make an appointment with a physical therapist to discuss work consolidation, safe body mechanics, and ways of making your environment more "user-friendly."

2. Do follow a regular exercise program that includes a variety of different activities. Although weight-bearing activities such as walking have been shown to be the most effective in terms of preventing bone loss, all forms of activity, including swimming, are beneficial.

3. Do be sure that your exercise program includes plenty of gentle, controlled movements that emphasize extension, especially of the shoulders, trunk, and hips.

4. Don't perform unnecessary flexion activities, especially those that also involve rotation movements. Exercises such as sit-ups, toe touches from a standing position, and other forms of purposeful flexion should be avoided. Discuss with your physical therapist the safest methods of making beds, weeding gardens, etc, to minimize the flexion forces on the spine.

5. Don't engage in ballistic types of exercise routines, such as high-impact aerobics and jumping rope.

Source: Reprinted from PB Gleeson, Osteoprosis, in J Pauls, *Therapeutic Approaches to Women's Health: A Program of Exercise and Education*, pp. 5.6-1:1-6-1:27, © 1995, Aspen Publishers, Inc.

DESIRED OUTCOME/PROGNOSIS

- The client will increase soft tissue flexibility.
- The client will increase muscular strength.
- The client will increase muscular endurance.
- The client will improve balance (both static and dynamic).
- The client will improve coordination.
- The client will correct any asymmetry.
- The client will increase joint ROM.
- The client will improve function.

Exercise is only one component in the efforts to prevent the complications associated with osteoporosis. Estrogen replacement therapy, as well as nutritional considerations, must be addressed for optimum skeletal health. Exercise alone is not the complete answer to replacing bone mass in the aging skeleton.

REFERENCES

ASSESSMENT

Goodman C, Snyder TE. *Differential Diagnosis in Physical Therapy*. Philadelphia, Pa; 1990:332, 337, 357, 362–363.

Murray C, O'Brien K. Osteoporosis workup: evaluation bone loss and risk of fracture. *Geriatrics*. 1995:50:9:41–53.

Balance

Anacker SL, DiFabio RP. Influence of sensory inputs on standing balance in community-dwelling elders with a recent history of falling. *Physical Therapy*. 1992;72:575–581. [**Standing balance: sensory organization test (SOT) for standing balance, get up and go test (GUGT)**]

Briggs RC, Gossman MR, Birch R, et al. Balance performance among noninstitutionalized elderly women. *Physical Therapy.* 1989;69:748–756. **[Sharpened Rhomber test, one-legged stance test]**

Fansler CL, Poff CL, Shepard KF. Effects of mental practice on balance in elderly women. *Physical Therapy.* 1985;65:1332–1336.

Heitmann DK, Gossman MR, Shaddeau SA, Jackson JR. Balance performance and step width in noninstitutionalized elderly female fallers and nonfallers. *Physical Therapy.* 1989;69:923-931. **[Sharpened Romberg, one-legged stance test, step-width measurements]**

Iverson BD, Gossman MR, Shaddeau SA, Turner ME Jr. Balance performance, force production, and activity levels in noninstitutionalized men 60 to 90 years of age. *Physical Therapy.* 1990;70:348-355. **[Sharpened Rhomberg test (SR), one-legged stance test (OLST), quantitative muscle tester (QMT)]**

Functional Level

PULSES Profile
Granger CV, Albrecht GL, Hamilton BB. Outcome of comprehensive medical rehabilitation: measurements by PULSES Profile and the Barthel Index. *Archive of Physical Medicine and Rehabilitation.* 1979;60:145–154.

Moskowitz RW, McCann CB. Classification of disability in the chronically ill and aging. *Journal of Chronic Disease.* 1957;5:342–346.

Mobility
Duncan PW, Chandler J, Studenski S, et al. How do physiological components of balance affect mobility in elderly men? *Archives of Physical Medicine and Rehabilitation.* 1993;74:1343–1349. **[Mobility functions]**

Podsiadlo D, Richardson S. The timed "up and go": a test of basic functional mobility for frail elderly persons. *Journal of the American Geriatric Society.* 1991;39:142–148.

Posture
Chandler JM, Duncan PW, Studenski SA. Balance performance on the postural stress test: comparison of young adults, healthy elderly, and fallers. *Physical Therapy.* 1990;70:410–415. **[Postural stress test]**

Moore S, Woollacott MH. The use of biofeedback devices to improve postural stability. *Physical Therapy Practice.* 1993;2:2:1–10. **[Posturography]**

Lewis CB. The relationship between posture and psychological variables in students aged 18–25. In: Lewis CB, McNearney T. *The Functional Tool Box: Clinical Measures of Functional Outcomes.* Washington, DC. Learn Publications; 1994. **[Reedco Posture Score Sheet]**

Special Tests to Which the PT May or May Not Have Access

Bone Mineral Density and Strength
Halle JS, Smidt GL, O'Dwyer KD, Lin S. Relationship between trunk muscle torque and bone mineral content of the lumbar spine and hip in healthy postmenopausal women. *Physical Therapy.* 1990;70:690–699. **[Bone mineral density, trunk muscle strength, isometric and isokinetic torque evaluation and work measurements]**

Smidt GL, Lin SY, O'Dwyer KD, Blanpied PR. The effect of high-intensity trunk exercise on bone mineral density of postmenopausal women. *Spine.* 1992;17:280–285. **[Bone mineral density with dual photon absorptionometry and trunk muscle strength with muscle examination and exercise dosimeter 3000]**

Zimmermann CL, Smidt GL, Brooks JS, Kinsey WJ, Eekhoff TL. *Physical Therapy.* 1990;70:302-309. **[Torque and bone mineral density]**

EMG
Brunt D, Williams J, Rice RR. Analysis of EMG activity and temporal components of gait during recovery from perturbation. *Archives of Physical Medicine and Rehabilitation.* 1990;71:473–477.

TREATMENT

Aisenbrey JA. Exercise in the prevention and management of osteoporosis. *Physical Therapy.* 1987;67:1100–1104.

Bornor JA, Dilworth BB, Sullivan KM. Exercise and osteoporosis: a critique of the literature. *Physiotherapy Canada.* 1988;40:146–155.

Cirullo JA. Osteoporosis. *Clinical Management in Physical Therapy.* 1989;9:1:14–19.

Gleeson PB. Osteoporosis. In: Pauls J, *Therapeutic Approaches to Women's Health: A Program of Exercise and Education.* Gaithersburg, Md: Aspen Publishers, Inc; 1995:6-1:1-6-1:27.

Gleeson PB, Protas EJ, LeBlanc AD, Schneider VS, Evans HJ. Effects of weight lifting on bone mineral density in premenopausal women. *Journal of Bone and Mineral Research.* 1990;5:153–158.

Hertling D, Kessler RM, eds. *Management of Common Musculoskeletal Disorders.* 2nd ed. Philadelphia, Pa: JB Lippincott Co; 1990:32, 456, 559, 562.

MacKinnon JL. Osteoporosis: a review. *Physical Therapy.* 1988;68:1533–1540.

Moore S, Woollacott MH. The use of biofeedback devices to improve postural stability. *Physical Therapy Practice.* 1993;2:2:1–10.

Pawlson LG, Lewis C. Dysmobility. In: Karpman RR, Baum J, eds. *Aging and Clinical Practice: Musculoskeletal Disorders. A Regional Approach.* New York, NY: Igaku-Shoin; 1988.

Rutherford CM. The role of exercise in prevention of osteoporosis. *Physiotherapy.* 1990;76:522–526.

Shipp KM. Osteoporosis: to manage fragility. *PT—Magazine of Physical Therapy.* 1993;1:70–75.

Sinaki M. Postmenopausal spinal osteoporosis: physical therapy and rehabilitation principles. *Mayo Clinic Proceedings.* 1982;57:699–703.

Turner P. Osteoporotic back pain: its prevention and treatment. *Physiotherapy.* 1991;77:642–646.

Vandervoort AA. Effects of aging on human neuromuscular function: implications for exercise. *Canadian Journal of Sport Sciences.* 1992;17:178–184.

Woollacott MH, Shumway-Cook A. Changes in posture control across the life span: a systems approach. *Physical Therapy.* 1990;70:799–807.

Falls

Anacker SL, DiFabio RP. Influence of sensory inputs on standing balance in community-dwelling elders with a recent history of falling. *Physical Therapy.* 1992;72:575–581.

Brownlee MG, Banks MA, Crosbie WJ, Meldrum F, Nimmo MA. Consideration of spatial orientation mechanisms as related to elderly fallers. *Gerontology.* 1989;35:323–331.

Dean E, Ross J. Relationships among cane fitting, function, and falls. *Physical Therapy.* 1993;73:494–500.

Judge JO, Lindsey C, Underwood M, Winsemius D. Balance improvements in older women: effects of exercise training. *Physical Therapy.* 1993;73:254–262.

Meldrum D, Funn AM. An investigation of balance function in elderly subjects who have and have not fallen. *Physiotherapy.* 1993;79:339–342.

Obonyo T, Drummond M, Isaacs B. Domiciliary physiotherapy for old people who have fallen. *International Rehabilitation Medicine.* 1983;5:157–160.

Simpson JM. Elderly people at risk of falling: the role of muscle weakness. *Physiotherapy.* 1993;79:831–835.

Speechley M, Tinetti M. Assessment of risk and prevention of falls among elderly persons: role of the physiotherapist. *Physiotherapy Canada.* 1990;42:75–79.

Therapy Management Innovations, Inc. *Falls Assessment for the Physical Therapist.* USA, Therapy Management Innovations; 1992.

Vandervoort AA, Chesworth BM, Cunningham DA, Rechnitzer PA, Paterson DH, Koval JJ. An outcome measure to quantify passive stiffness of the ankle. *Canadian Journal of Public Health.* 1992;83(suppl 2):S19–S23.

Winter DA, Patla AE, Frank JS, Walt SE. Biomechanical walking pattern changes in the fit and healthy elderly. *Physical Therapy.* 1990;70:340–347.

Pelvic Floor Tension Myalgia

Also known as *coccygodynia, levator ani spasm, pyriformis syndrome,* and *spastica pelvic diaphragm.*

DESCRIPTION
Pelvic floor tension myalgia is pain in the pelvic floor muscles and surrounding area.

CAUSE
Pelvic floor tension myalgia can be caused by muscular imbalances of the abdominal and back musculature or habitual muscular contraction due to pain. Spasm in the levator ani muscle can be caused by trauma, surgery, pathology, or excessive anxiety.

ASSESSMENT

Areas
- History, including occupation, surgery, menopausal state, medical conditions, medications
- Psychological/social
- Urinary symptoms
- Bowel habits, including any constipation
- Pain
- Perineal examination, including strength of pelvic floor musculature
- Special tests to which the PT may or may not have access

Instruments/Procedures (See References for Sources)
- Female Urogenital System Checklist

Special Tests to Which the PT May or May Not Have Access
- perineometer
- urodynamic assessment

PROBLEMS
- There is pain in the rectum, pelvis, or back.
- There can be leg pain.
- There can be pain with bowel movement.
- There can be constipation.
- There is usually dyspareunia.

TREATMENT/MANAGEMENT
- Consider rectal diathermy or high-voltage pulsed current stimulation as per the manufacturer's instructions.
- Consider Thiele's massage.
- Instruct in relaxation exercises.
- Encourage daily warm soaks or baths.

PRECAUTIONS/CONTRAINDICATIONS
See Appendix C for precautions when using physical agents and modalities.

EXPECTED OUTCOME/PROGNOSIS
• The client will experience relaxation of the pelvic floor muscles.

REFERENCES

ASSESSMENT
Herman H. Urogenital dysfunction. In: Wilder E, ed. *Obstetric and Gynecologic Physical Therapy*. New York, NY: Churchill Livingstone; 1988:98–99. **[Assessment of excessive tension]**

Adams C, Frahm J. Genitourinary system. In: Myers RS, ed. *Saunders Manual of Physical Therapy Practice*. Philadelphia, Pa: WB Saunders Co; 1995:494. **[Perineal examination]**

Ling, FW, King PM, Myers CA. Screening for female urogenital system disease. In: Boissonnault WG, ed. *Examination in Physical Therapy Practice*. New York, NY: Churchill Livingstone; 1991:149. **[Female urogenital system checklist]**

TREATMENT
Adams C, Frahm J. Genitourinary system. In: Myers RS, ed. *Saunders Manual of Physical Therapy Practice*. Philadelphia, Pa: WB Saunders Co; 1995:459–504.

Dunbar A. Rehabilitation for the abdominal wall weakened by chronic pelvic pain: breathing, laughter, and other exercises. *Journal of Obstetric and Gynecologic Physical Therapy*. 1991;15:1:4.

Hammill JM. Relief cushion for coccygeal pain. *Clinical Management in Physical Therapy*. 1988;8:5:27.

Herman H. Urogenital dysfunction. In: Wilder E, ed. *Obstetric and Gynecologic Physical Therapy*. New York, NY: Churchill Livingstone; 1988:98–99.

Wallace K. Female pelvic floor functions, dysfunctions, and behavioural approaches to treatment. *Clinics in Sports Medicine*. 1994;13:459–481.

Pelvic Inflammatory Disease

Also known as *salpingitis.*

DESCRIPTION
Pelvic inflammatory disease (PID) is an infection of the fallopian tubes, and possibly the cervix, uterus, and ovaries as well.

CAUSE
Infection usually begins intravaginally, spreading upward due to microorganisms transmitted during intercourse. Women using an intrauterine device (IUD) are particularly vulnerable because the IUD device allows transmission of pathogens. Childbirth, ruptured ectopic pregnancy, or surgical procedures such as an abortion may also, less commonly, allow transmission of an infecting organism.

ASSESSMENT

Areas
• History, including any medical conditions or symptoms such as bleeding or discharge, occupation, surgery, menopausal state, and medications

- Psychosocial
- Urinary symptoms: frequency, urgency, stress, and nocturia
- Bowel habits, including any constipation
- Pain, including any dyspareunia (painful intercourse)
- Activities of daily living (ADLs)
- Perineal examination, including pelvic floor strength

Instruments/Procedures (See References for Sources)

No specific evaluation for PID was identified. Consider use of elements from evaluation for incontinence.

Urinary Symptoms
- daily intake and output diary

PROBLEMS
- The woman will usually have extreme pain in lower abdominal region.
- The woman can have swelling and tenderness accompanying the pain.
- The woman can have backache.
- The woman can have dysmenorrhea and may have increased menstrual flow.
- The woman can feel generally lethargic.
- The woman can have dyspareunia.

TREATMENT/MANAGEMENT
- In the acute phase of infection, the client should be receiving medical attention.
- In the chronic phase, perform gentle mobilization exercises, instruct the client in relaxation exercises, and try shortwave or microwave diathermy at daily frequency or on alternate days for a duration of 20 minutes.

PRECAUTIONS/CONTRAINDICATIONS
- See precautions for diathermy in Appendix C.

DESIRED OUTCOME/PROGNOSIS
- The client will have a decrease in pain.
- There will be a reduction in infection.

REFERENCES

ASSESSMENT
Goodman C, Snyder TE. *Differential Diagnosis in Physical Therapy*. Philadelphia, Pa; WB Saunders; 1990:332, 337, 357, 362–363.
Ling FW, King PM, Myers CA. Screening for female urogenital system disease. In: Boissonnault WG, ed. *Examination in Physical Therapy Practice*. New York, NY: Churchill Livingstone; 1991:149. **[Female urogenital system checklist]**

Urinary Symptoms
Adams C, Frahm J. Genitourinary system. In: Myers RS, ed. *Saunders Manual of Physical Therapy Practice*. Philadelphia, Pa: WB Saunders Co; 1995: 477–483. **[diaries]**

TREATMENT

Adams C, Frahm J. Genitourinary system. In: Myers RS, ed. *Saunders Manual of Physical Therapy Practice.* Philadelphia, Pa: WB Saunders Co; 1995:459–504.

Lee JM. *Aids to Physiotherapy.* New York, NY: Churchill Livingstone; 1988:97.

Polden M, Mantle J. *Physiotherapy in Obstetrics and Gynecology.* London, England: Butterworth-Heinemann; 1990:293–294.

Postpartum Period

Also known as the puerperium.

DESCRIPTION

The postpartum period describes the time following birth. The uterus undergoes a process of involution, or returning to near prepregnant size, usually 5 to 6 weeks after birth. Most describe the period as lasting 6 to 12 weeks. But each woman's adjustment period is different.

CAUSE

During the time following birth, the mother's body undergoes a physiological adjustment to the changes from pregnancy and delivery.

ASSESSMENT

Areas
- History, including type of delivery, complications, medical history
- Activity level
- Mobility, including transfers, bed, and gait
- Pain
- Strength, if indicated
- Range of motion (ROM)
- Posture
- Musculoskeletal, including joints, presence of diastasis recti after third postpartum day
- Functional level

Instruments/Procedures (See References for Sources)

Strength
- manual muscle testing (MMT)

PROBLEMS
- The woman usually feels physically exhausted.
- There are usually contractions, called *afterpains*, after birth and during nursing, which can be painful. They are usually stronger with second or subsequent deliveries.
- There can be breast discomfort.
- The abdominal muscles are usually very lax.
- There can be bladder distention.
- The client can be constipated. Hemorrhoids can be present.

- The client usually has perineal pain if she sustained a laceration or if an episiotomy was performed.
- The woman may have had perineal trauma, such as hematoma, edema, ecchymosis, or erythema.
- The woman usually has "postpartum blues" characterized by crying spells, anxiety, worry, loneliness, and mood swings.
- The woman can have postpartum depression, usually beginning as soon as 24 hours after delivery, but possibly beginning several weeks later. Symptoms of depression include feeling hopeless, being overly concerned or under concerned about baby, losing appetite, having a fear of touching the baby, being unable to sleep, and having little concern about appearance.
- Postpartum psychosis is a more extreme reaction to birth and is rare.

TREATMENT/MANAGEMENT

In General
- Referral to a support group is almost always welcome for new mothers, especially those with postpartum depression.
- Instruct in postural correction as needed. During the postpartum period, there is a tendency for a forward head and rounded shoulder posture due to holding and feeding the baby.
- Instruct in proper body mechanics. Proper instruction in activities of daily living (ADLs) for child care includes topics such as lifting, feeding, changing, and use of equipment.

Exercise
After checking for diastasis of the abdominal muscles, the therapist can teach exercises, stressing the importance of the restoration of the abdominal and the pelvic floor muscles. The synergistic nature of the pelvic floor with the abdominal muscles can also be taught. Provide the woman with guidance about exercise in general and specific exercises for after birth. These exercises can include the following:
- First 2 to 3 days after an uncomplicated delivery
  1. gentle abdominal exercise coordinated with breathing
  2. ROM exercises for the feet and ankles
  3. pelvic tilt
  4. pelvic floor toning
  5. heel slides and gluteal toning
- After first 2 to 3 days
  1. abdominal exercise as indicated by state of abdominal wall: begin with head lifts if diastasis is larger than 2 cm; if less than 2 cm, curl-ups are indicated; progress as indicated to bridging and curl-ups with diagonal or reverse components added
  2. upper back release and upper extremity exercises
  3. leg toning

Episiotomy Healing
- Ice packs can be used during the first 48 hours; then switch to mild heat, sitz baths, Kegel exercises, and a pericare bottle. Follow up with a pelvic floor rehabilitation program.

Breast-Feeding

Tips to New Mothers About How to Get Started With Breast-Feeding
- Stroke nipple near the infant's mouth to encourage reflexive rooting response and to facilitate sucking.

- Let the infant breast-feed on demand and not on a fixed schedule. It is normal for newborns to nurse 10 to 12 times in a 24-hour period.
- Refer to books, nurses, lactation consultants, hospital classes, or a support group such as La Leche League International as indicated.
- Discuss inverted nipples during pregnancy so intervention can begin before the baby arrives.

Common Problems Encountered in Breast-Feeding
- Engorgement—fullness as milk production begins
  1. Breast-feed as soon as possible after birth.
  2. Feed frequently.
  3. Use both breasts at each feeding.
  4. Apply warmth before feeding (use warm cloth or take shower).
  5. Apply cold after feeding.
- Sore nipples
  1. Use the less sore nipple first.
  2. Let air get to breasts.
  3. Coat nipples and aureola with breast milk.
  4. Make the feedings shorter and more frequent.
  5. Position the infant's chest to the mother's chest, with the infant and breast well supported under and on top.
  6. Vary nursing positions.
- Mastitis—reddened, lump in breast, painful, may begin with flulike symptoms
  1. Rest with the infant, and feed the infant every 2 to 2 1/2 hours.
  2. Use medication for fever as prescribed by physician.
  3. Generally, it is advisable to continue to breast-feed.
- Musculoskeletal conditions affecting breast-feeding mothers
  1. Discuss proper body mechanics postpartum.
  2. Recommend supports such as nursing pillows and stools for arm and foot support.

After a Cesarean Delivery
- Instruct the woman in abdominal breathing and huffing techniques with incisional support via a pillow.
- Consider transcutaneous electrical nerve stimulation (TENS) for post-cesarean delivery pain control. Electrode placement may vary depending on the type of incision. For horizontal incisions possible locations include above and below the incision, parallel at each end of the incision, or in an inverted V shape at each end of the incision.
- Beginning exercises for after cesarean delivery, as indicated by recovery, are breathing exercises, ankle ROM, isometric leg exercises. Gradually add, as recovery allows, pelvic tilt, bridging, modified curl-ups, and leg sliding exercises.

PRECAUTIONS/CONTRAINDICATIONS
- The new mother can resume aerobic activity at the 60% level after clearance from her physician and when her body feels ready.
- Referral is indicated if the pathological condition of postpartum psychosis appears. It is manifested by symptoms of persistent depression, lack of interest in the baby, thoughts of harming the baby or self, hallucinations, and/or other psychotic behavior.
- The mother should notify the primary caregiver if

1. The entire breast is hot and hard, and there is also fever, chills, nausea, or aching; the woman may have mastitis.
2. The leg has an area that is hot, swollen, and red; the woman may have thrombophlebitis.
3. There is a frequent urge to urinate, but little or no urine is passed, and there is pain in the lower abdomen or back; the woman may have cystitis.
4. Lochia, vaginal discharge, changes back to a bright red color; there may be some placental retention.
5. Vaginal discharge is foul smelling, accompanied by pain and itching; there may be infection.
6. There is a fever higher than 100.4 degrees F for more than 1 day, with persistent, intense pain from the vaginal area.

DESIRED OUTCOME/PROGNOSIS

- Pain will be diminished.
- The woman will increase strength and endurance.
- The woman will be independent in mobility and ADLs.
- The woman will be educated about body mechanics for child care with the infant.
- The woman will be continent in bladder and bowel.
- Musculoskeletal dysfunction will be corrected.

REFERENCES

ASSESSMENT

Manual Muscle Testing

Daniels L, Worthingham C. *Muscle Testing: Techniques of Manual Examination*. 6th ed. Philadelphia, Pa: WB Saunders Co; 1995.

Kendall FP, McCreary EK, Provance PG. *Muscles: Testing and Function*. 4th ed. Baltimore, Md: Williams & Wilkins; 1993.

TREATMENT

Appel C. Obstetrical considerations. In: Myers RS, ed. *Saunders Manual of Physical Therapy Practice*. Philadelphia, Pa: WB Saunders Co; 1995:522.

Boissonnault JS, Blaschak MJ. Incidence of diastasis recti abdominis during the childbearing year. *Physical Therapy*. 1988;68:1082–1086.

Boissonnault JS, Kotarinos RK. Diastasis recti. In: Wilder E, ed. *Obstetric and Gynecologic Physical Therapy*. New York, NY. Churchill Livingstone; 1988:63–82.

Gent D, Gottleib KL. Cesarean rehabilitation. *Clinical Management in Physical Therapy*. 1985;5:3:14–19.

Kotarinos RK. Diastasis recti and review of the abdominal wall. *Journal of Obstetric and Gynecologic Physical Therapy*. 1990;14:8:8–10.

Nicholson W. Mastitis and ultrasound. *Australian Journal of Physical Therapy*. 1994;40:49.

Pauls J, ed. *Therapeutic Approaches to Women's Health: A Program of Exercise and Education*. Gaithersburg, Md: Aspen Publishers, Inc; 1995;3:1:42.

Pipp LM. Compendium of selected TENS literature. *Journal of Obstetric and Gynecologic Physical Therapy*. 1993;17:12.

Pirie A, Herman H. *How to Raise Children Without Breaking Your Back*. West Somerville, Mass: IBIS Publications; 1995.

Riddoch S, Grimmer K. Developing a clinical indicator for obstructive mastitis. *Australian Journal of Physical Therapy*. 1993;39:321–322.

Simkin P. Intermittent brachial plexus neuropathy secondary to breast engorgement. *Birth: Issues in Perinatal Care and Education.* 1988;15:102–103.

Pregnancy—Musculoskeletal Conditions

DESCRIPTION

Pregnancy changes can lead to or aggravate musculoskeletal conditions. About half of all pregnant women experience back pain. Some common musculoskeletal conditions during pregnancy are

- back pain, including postural pain, sacroiliac dysfunction, disk derangement, and sciatica
- diastasis abdominis recti
- pubic symphysis pain
- coccydynia
- calf cramps
- costal margin pain
- transient osteoporosis of pregnancy
- thoracic outlet pain
- carpal tunnel syndrome

CAUSE

Low back pain has many causes, but two of the most common are faulty posture combined with poor body mechanics. During pregnancy, factors contributing to musculoskeletal dysfunction include increased weight gain, hormonal relaxation of tissues, stretching of abdominal muscle, increase in lumbar lordosis and thoracic kyphosis, genu recurvatum, and forward head posture.

ASSESSMENT

Areas
- History
- Edema
- Posture
- Range of motion (ROM)
- Gait
- Joint integrity and structural deviations/neurological involvement
- Strength
- Pain
- Functional level
- Special tests to which the PT may or may not have access

Instruments/Procedures (See References for Sources)

Edema
- volumetrics
- girth measurements

Joint Integrity and Structural Deviations/Neurological Involvement
- carpal tunnel syndrome tests
  1. Phalen's test
  2. Tinel's sign
- diastasis recti abdominis test
- lumbar lordosis measurement
- orthopedic tests for sacroiliac joint
  1. limb-length test
  2. Gillet test: palpation of anterior and posterior superior iliac spines (patient standing, then sitting), palpation of iliac crests (patient standing, then sitting)
  3. side-lying iliac compression test
  4. sitting flexion text
  5. standing flexion test
  6. standing Gillet test
  7. supine iliac gapping test
- standing march test for irritated symphysis
- thoracic outlet syndrome tests
  1. Adson's test
  2. hyperabduction test
  3. Wright's test

Special Tests to Which the PT May or May Not Have Access
- nerve conduction studies (see "Carpal Tunnel Syndrome Tests" in references)

Test for Diastasis Recti Abdominis

The therapist has the woman in the supine position with no pillow under her head. The woman lifts her chin and shoulders forward to bring the rectus muscle belly forward. The therapist palpates the gap between the rectus abdominis muscle at the level of the umbilicus and also 4.5 cm (about two fingers) above and 4.5 cm below this level. A gap equal to the width of two or more fingers (4.5 cm) is considered positive. Below the umbilical line, a separation of one finger might be significant.

Source: Reprinted from J Pauls, *Therapeutic Approaches to Women's Health: A Program of Exercise and Education*, p. 2-1:4, © 1995, Aspen Publishers, Inc.

PROBLEMS

Low Back Pain

Muscle Strain
- The woman may have localized swelling.
- The woman often has pain with movement.
- The woman often has decreased and painful ROM.
- Passive movement is often within normal limits.
- The woman may show painful recovery from movement.

- The woman may have unilateral pain.
- The woman may have pain radiate distally.

Muscle Spasm
- The woman usually has decreased ROM, pain, and tenderness over a muscle.
- There is usually increased tone in the muscles.
- The woman may find that continued spasm becomes a source of additional pain due to a self-perpetuating cycle.

Postural Syndrome
- The woman often finds that pain eases with activity.
- Usually standing or sitting posture is beyond normal limits.
- The woman can find pain only during sustained supine positions.

Sacroiliac Joint Dysfunction
   In sacroiliac joint dysfunction in general:
- The woman often complains of pain with sitting.
- The woman often has pain on leaning forward.
- The woman may have pain with an increase in intra-abdominal pressure.
- The woman can have a sudden onset of unilateral sacroiliac pain.
- The woman can have a sharp pain or catching sensation during rolling from side to side.
- The woman may feel pain in the posterior thigh.
- The woman may have anterior hip pain.
- The woman may report paresthesia in the absence of neurological signs.
- The woman may find ipsilateral sacroiliac dysfunction present with L 3–4 or L 4–5 lesions.
- A pattern of right sacroiliac dysfunction has been described as causing associated discomfort at left T-12, right T-8, left T-2, and right C2-3.
   In the case of anterior rotation of the ilium on the sacrum, the long-sitting versus supine leg-length test makes the leg appear longer when the client is in a supine position and shorter when she is in a sitting position.
   In the case of posterior rotation of the ilium on the sacrum, the long-sitting versus supine leg-length test makes the leg appear shorter when the client is in a supine position and longer when she is in a sitting position.

Pubic Symphysis Pain
- The woman can have pain over the area of the symphysis pubis and sacroiliac joints, groin, and adductor muscles.
- There can be palpable separation of the joint, especially during weight shifting.
- The woman may have pain with forward bending.
- The woman may not be able to move in bed.
- The woman may not be able to walk.
- The woman may not be able to move her legs.

Pregnancy-Associated Osteoporosis
- The woman usually has a back pain that is unexplained by another diagnosis.
- The woman may have hip fracture.

Disk Derangement
   In the case of acute posterolateral disk prolapse:
- The woman may have a sudden onset of unilateral lumbosacral pain.

- Often the pain is severe or knifelike, but it may be dull and aching.
- The woman may have aching into the leg, usually unilateral.
- Often the pain is worse with sitting or sudden straining, and it may be hard to stand up.
- The woman can have lumbar deformity with loss of lordosis.
- The woman often has lumbar scoliosis (convexity on involved side).
- Often there is marked, painful restriction of spinal movement, with a decrease of extension mobility.
- Often the pain increases with repeated flexion and/or sustained flexion.
- Often the mechanism of onset involves flexion.
  In the case of disk herniation:
- The woman may have neurological involvement (reflexes, myotome and/or dermatome).
- The woman may have pain and/or paresthesia distal to knee.
- The mechanism of onset usually involves lumbar flexion.
- The woman may have pain aggravated by sitting.
  In the case of lower lumbar disc herniation (extrusion) with nerve root impingement:
- The woman may have unilateral leg pain, but bilateral is possible.
- The woman often feels leg pain in the posterolateral thigh and the anterior lateral or posterior aspect of the lower leg.
- The woman may have back pain alone; the combination of back and leg pain is less common.
- Often lumbar extension will peripheralize pain. Extremity pain is usually worse than back pain.
- The woman often has mild segmental neurologic deficit, indicated by the presence of a specific dermatome sensory loss or specific motor weakness.
- Rarely, rupture leads to decreased pain but increased neurological signs.

Sciatica
- The woman often has pain following the course of the sciatic nerve, with radiating pain into the buttocks.

Diastasis Abdominis Recti
- This condition often goes undetected by the pregnant woman.

Piriformis Syndrome
- The woman often has persistent, severe, radiating low back pain that extends from the sacrum to the hip joint over the gluteal region and posterior portion of the upper leg (sciatic distribution).
- The hip on the involved side may demonstrate an increase in external rotation secondary to a shortened piriformis muscle.
- Often, on palpation, the buttock on the involved side is very tender. The leg on the involved side may appear shorter from contracture.

Coccydynia
- The woman is often unable to sit directly on the coccyx because of localized tenderness.

Calf Cramps
- The woman often has pain in the calf triggered by pointing the toes.

Costal Margin Pain
- The woman can often have pain on the anterior aspect of the lower ribs secondary to the changes in abdominal muscle alignment and the flaring of the ribs.

Thoracic Outlet Syndrome
- The woman often has parethesia in the upper extremity.
- The woman may complain of fatigue with arm use.
- Often, upper extremity stretching leads to pain.

Carpal Tunnel Syndrome
- The woman often has weakness in the hands.
- The woman may have thenar atrophy.
- The woman often has paresthesia, especially at night.
- The woman may have diminished median nerve conduction velocity.
- The woman may have swelling over the volar aspect of the wrist.
- Pitting edema may also be present.

TREATMENT/MANAGEMENT

Low Back Pain

Muscle Strain
　In acute cases:
- Try ice (except over the kidney area), any modalities not contraindicated during pregnancy, and relaxation techniques, as tolerated.
- The client should also be advised to rest.
　In subacute cases:
- Begin with gentle movement, and progress to full movement.
- Superficial heat and massage can be added, along with gentle stretching techniques, graded isometric exercise, and resistive dynamic exercise.
- Use the side-lying position if needed. Usually the left side-lying position is the most comfortable, and a client can perform these exercises from this position: gluteal set, pelvic tilt, and adductor set.
- Correct posture abnormalities with kinesthetic training, and correct flexibility and strength imbalances. Posture exercises include axial extension, stretching the pectoralis major muscle, strengthening the midthoracic area muscles, and toning abdominal shortening contractions of the external obliques along with the rectus abdominis.
- Stabilization exercises to promote isolation and cocontraction of muscle groups should be considered.

Muscle Spasm
　In acute cases:
- Ice or cold packs and passive support can be helpful. Avoid ice over the kidney region.
- The following techniques are also indicated: elongation of muscle to tolerance via positioning, reverse muscle action techniques, and passive to active ROM in a pain-free range.
　In subacute and chronic cases:
- Moist heat and/or ice, cold packs, and massage are indicated.
- Progress the exercise program as tolerated.

- Consider using postural retraining with kinesthetic awareness and relaxation exercises. Education should be emphasized, along with a search for the underlying cause of the pain.

Postural Syndrome

Posturally related back pain is especially suited to the self-treatment principles learned in a back school. Possible topics for back school include the following:
- *Basic information:* anatomy, biomechanics, pain, drugs, sex, stress, physical fitness, health, resources
- *Rehabilitation/prevention:* posture, awareness, movement, body/mind relationship, self-help techniques, physical interventions
- *Ergonomic principles:* human considerations, environmental conditions, work dynamics, relevance of person to equipment
- *Basic rules of working and lifting*
Supplement education with appropriate strengthening and stretching exercises.

Treatment sessions in the water can be helpful. Immersion is an effective treatment for edema, significantly decreasing swelling in the lower extremities.

Sacroiliac Joint Dysfunction

In general:
- Instruct the client in how to stretch shortened muscles and strengthen weakened muscles. Treatment aims to decrease pain and improve joint mobility and mechanics.
- The area is supported with an orthosis if it is acute and inflamed or in need of increased stability. A support with a special pad for the sacroiliac region is especially helpful. The client should be cautioned, however, that an orthosis does not substitute for strengthening exercises and can actually weaken muscles if overused. A heel lift may be indicated if leg-length difference is demonstrated. The client should avoid any painful activities or vigorous exercise, such as jogging, until the pelvis is level and she is symptom-free.
- For acute pain, the client rests with legs adducted and flexed. She may get some relief by applying pressure around the hips with an orthosis.
- Ice packs and supported weight bearing with crutches or a walker may be needed.
- The typical treatment of ultrasound or electrical stimulation over the sacral sulci is contraindicated during pregnancy (see Precautions).
- Provide education about the vulnerability of this joint. Teach posture awareness and body mechanics. Avoid high heels and prolonged standing.
- Use gentle mobilization or muscle energy techniques. Strengthen pelvic floor muscles and abdominal musculature.
- Teach proper relaxation positions (avoid the supine position after the first trimester if the client experiences symptoms of supine hypotension).
- Avoid unilateral weight bearing.
In cases of anterior rotation of the ilium on the sacrum:
- Consider eccentric contraction of hamstrings on the involved side, isometric or resisted hip extension, and knee extension to the gluteal and hamstring muscles on the involved side.
- Extreme abduction of lower extremities should be avoided.
- If tight, the hip piriformis muscle and iliotibial band should be stretched; weakened lower extremity muscles and abdominal musculature need to be strengthened.
- Progress can be facilitated with orthotic support, but the client can be weaned from the device if her pelvis can stay level on its own. If not, orthotic support will be needed during the remainder of her pregnancy and perhaps into the postpartum period.

In cases of posterior rotation of the ilium on the sacrum:
- Consider isometric contraction of the hip flexors, with the client in a position with 90-degree hip flexion and 90-degree knee flexion, squeezing the forearm between the knees during isometric hip adduction within a sitting position, and stretching and strengthening as before.

In cases of locking of the joint:
- The client lies on her back briefly, bends the knee of the involved side, and wraps her toes under the outer side of the straight leg. The therapist can gently place the client's bent knee across her body, while gently pressing the shoulder of the involved side in the opposite direction. This can be combined with a gentle rocking motion.
- A self-help position is similar. If the right side is involved, the client gently pulls her right flexed knee up and out with the right hand. With her left hand, she cups the right foot. She can also simply lie supine with the leg on the affected side crossed over the other leg with some rotation to get a traction effect to the sacroiliac joint through the weight of the leg. After staying in this position for 15 minutes or so, she cautiously resumes normal activity. The supine position should be avoided after the first trimester if the client is experiencing symptoms of supine hypotension. She follows with support and avoids overuse of any manipulation. The client rests in a side-lying position with pillows for support.
- Single weight-bearing exercises should be avoided.

Pubic Symphysis Pain
- Try moist heat or cold packs for pain relief.
- Positions in which the legs are widely separated should be avoided.
- Crutches or a walker may be needed for weight-bearing activities.
- The symphysis pubis joint can be immobilized with a binder around the hips at pubic level as tight as the client can tolerate after the joint is aligned first.
- A depressed pubis can be raised by gentle pressure to the anterior ilium and ischial tuberosity.
- Having the client squeeze the forearm between the knees during isometric hip adduction in a sitting position is also helpful.
- Another self-correction technique involves the use of the abdominals to pull on the pubis.
- Resisted hip extension also utilizes the energy and movement from the muscle action to achieve the desired effect.

Pregnancy-Associated Osteoporosis
- If hip fracture is ruled out, treatment consists of rest, pain-reducing measures, and a gentle exercise routine that progresses to partial and then full weight bearing if well tolerated.

Disk Derangement
In cases of acute posterolateral disk prolapse:
- Reduce derangement with appropriate movement; the client may find pain reduced with repeated extension.
- Maintain reduction with posture correction and restore function. Avoid poor posture with education.
- Self-treatment with repeated movements can be tried first and may progress to mobilization if indicated (see Precautions).
- Gentle traction can be tried with caution (see Precautions).
- Use appropriate modalities for pain.
- Transcutaneous electrical nerve stimulation (TENS) should be considered as a last resort (see Precautions).

- Treatments such as massage and localized moist heat packs can decrease disk pain by increasing the blood supply and facilitating relaxation.
- Massage can be done either in the water or on land, in a sitting or side-lying position. Massage can be performed prone during pregnancy if a special maternity support or table adaption is present and the client is comfortable.

In cases of disk herniation:

- For protrusion with neurological signs, use modalities and advise the client to rest. Avoid aggravation with postures that cause increased intradiscal pressure (especially sitting and flexion).
- Gentle traction can be considered (see Precautions).
- Maintain correct posture and provide education.
- External support with a pregnancy back orthosis is indicated.
- Consider a trial of extension exercises, and extension in prone lying, if this is still a tolerable position, with gentle anterior–posterior glides.
- Contact the referring physician if neurological signs progress.

In cases of lower lumbar disc herniation (extrusion) with nerve root impingement:

- TENS for pain can be considered as a last resort (see Precautions). Contact referring physician if neurological signs worsen.

Sciatica
- Reduction in activity may help in the acute stage.

Diastasis Abdominis Recti
- Treatment consists of splinting the two sides of the rectus abdominis toward midline while doing any stressful activity or during abdominal exercises. Splinting can be accomplished using the hands or with a wrap.
- An attempt should be made to approximate the rib with the pubic symphysis without bulging the abdominal wall.
- Teach the client shortening active contractions of the transversus and the internus and externus obliquus abdominal muscle in combination with breath exhalation.
- The client might consider using a maternity binder, reducing intra-abdominal stress with proper body mechanics, and avoiding a Valsalva maneuver.

Piriformis Syndrome
- Moist heat is applied, with the client in the side-lying position (affected side up) and support at the waist, abdomen, and knees.
- Tightness is treated with pressure to insertion while adducting and internally rotating hip of the affected side.
- Gentle stretching is added. With the client in a sitting position, stretching is performed with hip flexion, adduction, and internal rotation. Equal weight bearing while standing should be stressed.
- Contract/relax, proprioceptive neuromuscular facilitation techniques, friction massage, and myofascial release techniques also can be used.
- Rule out any sacroiliac dysfunction.

Coccydynia
- Treatment includes gentle mobilization when necessary.

- Myofascial techniques, examination and treatment of trigger points, and strain-counterstrain techniques can be considered.
- The use of specially designed ischial support cushions or two cushions with a gap in the middle to avoid pressure on coccyx while sitting and the application of ice or heat are helpful.
- Encourage proper sitting posture.

Calf Cramps
- "Runner's" stretch with dorsiflexion of the ankle can provide relief. Lock the foot up into supination before stretching.
- Stretching can also be performed by the therapist using a contract/relax technique on the gastrocnemius muscle tendon.
- Increase strength in the dorsiflexor muscles to counteract the strength of the cramp.
- Consider massage if no contraindications.

Costal Margin Pain
- Raising the arms and flexing the trunk to the side away from the pain usually gives relief.
- Also, a posterior stretch can be accomplished by wrapping the arms around a chair while straddling it backwards.
- Teach proper posture, with emphasis on avoiding slumped sitting.
- Prescribe exercise for upper back strengthening.
- Consider muscle energy techniques for rib region.

Thoracic Outlet Syndrome
- General treatment consists of gentle mobilization of the clavicle at either joint and posture exercises to elevate the shoulder girdle.
- More specific treatments for the three types of thoracic outlet syndrome are described below.

Scalenus Anticus and Cervical Rib Syndrome
- Treatment consists of local heat, massage, ultrasound (away from the area near the baby in utero), traction, stretching of scalenus muscles, and active strengthening of upper trapezius and levator scapular muscles.

Costoclavicular Syndrome
- Treatment consists of exercise, posture training, and mobilization of the clavicle.

Hyperabduction Syndrome
- Treatment consists of stretching pectoral muscle and postural training.

Carpal Tunnel Syndrome (CTS)
- Treatment for CTS varies and usually aims at symptomatic relief. Treatment consists of resting splints unilaterally or bilaterally, as needed.
- Splints are useful in decreasing wrist pressure.
- Splints can also be alternated during the day if both hands are involved. A splint on the wrist in a neutral position can be used as frequently as needed, perhaps even through the remainder of the pregnancy.
- Other therapists use a splint that "cocks" up the wrist into an extended position or keeps the wrist in a neutral position. The patient is told to avoid vigorous flexion and extension.

- Night splints, which may fit into a patient's lifestyle better, can also counteract the pain caused by increased heat, with subsequent increased metabolism, that occurs at night.
- Ice packs can be applied for pain relief.
- Postural exercises, such as thoracic outlet exercise, may help to alleviate brachial plexus pressure.
- Ergonomic considerations, such as maintaining 90 degrees' flexion of the elbow when working at a desk, can prevent repetitive motion strain.
- Ultrasound is sometimes helpful. Avoid sonating the abdomen, pelvis, and lumbar-sacral area (see Precautions).
- For posturally related pain, exercises, posture re-education, and conservative physical therapy may alleviate symptoms.
- Isometric and stretching exercises to consider include wrist circles, thumb and finger stretches, finger-thumb squeeze, wrist curls with the palm up and with the palm down, arm curls, and shoulder shrugs.

PRECAUTIONS/CONTRAINDICATIONS

See also Appendix C for contraindications with physical agents.

The following precautions should be observed during the examination and treatment of a pregnant woman:

- The therapist should avoid testing that leaves the client excessively uncomfortable or that she is unable to tolerate.
- Having the woman's buttocks higher than the level of her chest could possibly, in rare instances, cause an air embolism infarct; this position has been associated with introduction of air into the vaginal canal in a forced manner.
- The woman should change positions slowly to allow time for postural and circulatory changes.
- The therapist should use caution with any maneuvers that could lead to shearing forces on a joint, secondary to laxity, or transient osteoporosis. Some therapists consider manipulation contraindicated during pregnancy, but, if indicated, and if special precautions are taken, the benefits may outweigh any risk. Most pregnant clients can be treated with an appropriate mobilizing technique without any undue complication (see Maitland and Corrigan, *Practical Orthopaedic Medicine,* in references). Adequate posturing of clients needs to be considered. Mobilization grades 1 and 2 are the most commonly used techniques in the lumbar spine during pregnancy. Muscle energy techniques are also used to affect joint alignment. Vigorous thrusting techniques are contraindicated.
- Avoiding the supine position for periods longer than 3 minutes is important to prevent supine hypotension syndrome.
- The physical therapist must be careful, however, not to let pregnancy mask causes unrelated to the baby, such as a herniated disk, fibromyalgia, or ankylosing spondylosis.
- Correction of a lateral shift may cause increased back pain (a centralization effect) but should not cause increased leg pain. Discontinue the extension exercise if this happens. Extension of the spine is contraindicated if it does not decrease or centralize the pain, if bladder weakness or paresthesia in the saddle region is present, or if the patient is unable to assume a position due to pain or stage of pregnancy. Avoid flexion if it increases pain or peripheralizes the symptoms. Flexion positions and exercises may harm patients with herniated nucleus pulposus with protrusion. If any increase in mobility increases pain or an inflammatory response, try another approach.

- Clients with pain and stiffness usually progress in improvement. If a client is not following patterns of improvement, this may be a warning to consider an organic disease or psychogenic disorder.
- Special caution should be taken when using physical agents and modalities with a pregnant woman:
  1. Modalities such as deep heat (ultrasound or diathermy) or electrical stimulation are contraindicated over areas near the baby, especially the sacral sulci.
  2. Some therapists consider mechanical traction to be contraindicated during pregnancy. Traction has, however, been used successfully in the first two trimesters, provided it is with small poundage. Check with the equipment manufacturer for guidelines.
  3. TENS for pain relief in pregnancy has not been approved by the FDA and should be considered only as a last resort and only in the last two trimesters. Because TENS and other forms of electromagnetic and ultrasonic therapy have not been proved safe for use during pregnancy, they must be used with caution until the short-term and long-term effects on the fetus have been documented sufficiently (see Pomerantz, "TENS and Pregnancy," in TENS references). Some authors consider its use contraindicated in pregnancy (see Pipp, "TENS Update," in TENS references). But TENS has been used during pregnancy in areas other than over the uterus. In special circumstances, under the consultation of the physician, the benefit may outweigh any potential risk. It may also carry less risk than pharmaceutical and surgical alternatives. The conventional mode has been used.
  4. Modalities can be overused, particularly with musculoskeletal strain or sprain and inflammation. Pain relief through modalities should not cause you to ignore loss of motion and strength.
  5. Whirlpools with very hot water and saunas should be used with caution, and water temperature should be monitored carefully. If body temperature rises more than 1 degree, it is time to get out. Raised internal temperature can interfere with fetal cell division.
- Discuss with primary caregiver any of the following symptoms:
  1. swelling in feet and ankles not better after 30 minutes of elevation
  2. swelling in both hands
  3. eyes and/or face are puffy
  4. leg has painful, hot, red, or swollen area
  5. bloody vaginal discharge
  6. thin, watery discharge
  7. abdominal pain accompanied by nausea or vomiting, or dizziness or pain lasting longer than 2 minutes
  8. frequent contraction prematurely more than six times in an hour
  9. major decrease in fetal movement
  10. visual disturbances
  11. significant decrease in urine production
- Contraindications associated with aquatic exercise and pregnancy are toxemia, cerclage secondary to a dilated cervix, antepartum bleeding, and fetal hypotrophy. General contraindications include heart insufficiency, uncontrolled hypertension, respiratory insufficiency, tuberculosis, infections, incontinence, epilepsy, and diabetes.

DESIRED OUTCOME/PROGNOSIS

The goals of treatment will vary depending upon clinical findings but in general:

- The client will experience a decrease in pain and a relief of symptoms.

- The client will have an increase in movement and restore function or stabilize excessive movement.
- Therapy will prevent the progression and recurrence of the disorder.
Early intervention is important to decrease the severity of pain and disability.

REFERENCES

ASSESSMENT

O'Connor LJ, Gourley R. *Obstetric and Gynecologic Care in Physical Therapy*. Thorofare, NJ: Slack, Inc; 1990:220–221. **[Musculoskeletal evaluation for pregnant women]**

Bookout MM, Boissonnault WG. Physical therapy management of musculoskeletal disorders during pregnancy. In: Wilder E, ed. *Obstetric and Gynecologic Physical Therapy*. New York, NY: Churchill Livingstone; 1988:17–61.

Joint Integrity and Structural Deviations

Carpal Tunnel Syndrome Tests

Rothstein JM, Roy SH, Wolf SL. *The Rehabilitation Specialist's Handbook*. Philadelphia, Pa: FA Davis Co; 1991:245, 274, 277. **[Phalen's test and Tinel's sign]**

Tomberlin JP, Saunders HD. *Evaluation, Treatment and Prevention of Musculoskeletal Disorders. Vol 2: Extremities*. Chaska, Minn: The Saunders Group; 1994:233.

Hertling D, Kessler RM. *Management of Common Musculoskeletal Disorders*. Philadelphia, Pa: JB Lippincott Co; 1990:254–256. **[Median nerve pressure tests and nerve conduction studies]**

Diastasis Recti Abdominis Test

Pauls J. *Therapeutic Approaches to Women's Health: A Program of Exercise and Education*. Gaithersburg, Md: Aspen Publishers, Inc; 1995:2-1:4.

Lumbar Lordosis Measurement Device

Otman AS, Beksac MS, Bagoze O. The importance of lumbar lordosis measurement device application during pregnancy, and post-partum isometric exercise. *European Journal of Obstetrics, Gynecology, and Reproductive Biology*. 1989;31:155–162.

Orthopedic Tests for Sacroiliac Joint

Rothstein JM, Roy SH, Wolf SL. *The Rehabilitation Specialist's Handbook*. Philadelphia, Pa: FA Davis Co; 1991:127–131.

Thoracic Outlet Syndrome Tests

Tomberlin JP, Saunders HD. *Evaluation, Treatment and Prevention of Musculoskeletal Disorders. Vol 2: Extremities*. Chaska, Minn: The Saunders Group; 1994:108. **[Adson's test, Wright's test, hyperabduction test]**

TREATMENT

Ebner M. *Physiotherapy in Obstetrics*. London, England: E & S Livingstone Ltd; 1967.

Gleeson PB, Pauls JA. Obstetrical physical therapy: review of the literature. *Physical Therapy*. 1988;68:1699–1702.

Hulme J. Obstetric and gynecological analysis of movement dysfunction and physical disability. In: Scully R, Barnes M, eds. *Physical Therapy*. Philadelphia, Pa: JB Lippincott Co; 1989:598–604.

Kahn J. Electrical modalities in obstetrics and gynecology. In: Wilder E, ed. *Obstetric and Gynecologic Physical Therapy*. New York, NY: Churchill Livingstone; 1988:113–129.

Maitland GD, Corrigan B. *Practical Orthopaedic Medicine*. Cambridge, England: Butterworth & Co; 1983:297.

O'Connor LJ, Gourley R. *Obstetric and Gynecologic Care in Physical Therapy.* Thorofare, NJ: Slack, Inc; 1990.

O'Connor L, Pipp LM. Obstetric and gynecological causes. In: Scully R, Barnes M, eds. *Physical Therapy.* Philadelphia, Pa: JB Lippincott Co; 1989:299–306.

Pauls, J, ed. *Therapeutic Approaches to Women's Health: A Program of Exercise and Education.* Gaithersburg, Md: Aspen Publishers, Inc; 1995;2-1:1.

Scott CM, Paspalas J. Physical therapy for the obstetric patient: development of a program. *Clinical Management in Physical Therapy.* 1983:3:3:12–13.

Simkin P, Whalley J, Keppler A. Gracefully pregnant. *American Baby.* 1992;54:76–80.

Wilder E, ed. *Obstetric and Gynecologic Physical Therapy.* New York, NY: Churchill Livingstone; 1988.

Exercise

American Physical Therapy Association, Section on Obstetrics and Gynecology. *Perinatal Exercise Guidelines.* Alexandria, Va: American Physical Therapy Association; 1986.

Appel C. Prenatal/postpartum exercise. *Journal of Obstetric and Gynecologic Physical Therapy.* 1991;15:4:7.

Ashworth PD, Hagan MT. Some social consequences of non-compliance with pelvic floor exercises. *Physiotherapy.* 1993;79:465–471.

Bernstein S. Components and approaches of current perinatal exercise classes: part 1, a literature review. *Journal of Obstetric and Gynecologic Physical Therapy.* 1994;18:4:10–14.

Bing, E. *Moving Through Pregnancy.* New York, NY: Bantam Books; 1975.

Boissonnault JS, Blaschak MJ. Incidence of diastasis recti abdominis during the childbearing year. *Physical Therapy.* 1988;68:1082–1086.

Boissonnault JS, Kotarinos RK. Diastasis recti. In: Wilder E, ed. *Obstetric and Gynecologic Physical Therapy.* New York, NY: Churchill Livingstone; 1988: 63–82.

Danforth DN. Pregnancy and labor. *American Journal of Physical Medicine.* 1967;46:653–658.

Heardman H. *Physiotherapy in Obstetrics and Gynaecology.* 2nd ed. London, England: E & S Livingstone Ltd; 1959.

Kisner C, Colby LA. *Therapeutic Exercise: Foundations and Techniques.* 2nd ed. Philadelphia, Pa: FA Davis Co; 1990:567.

Konkler CJ. Principles of exercise for the obstetric patient. In: Kisner C, Colby LA, eds. *Therapeutic Exercise: Foundations and Techniques.* 2nd ed. Philadelphia, Pa: FA Davis Co; 1990:567.

Kotarinos RK. Diastasis recti and review of the abdominal wall. *Journal of Obstetric and Gynecologic Physical Therapy.* 1990;14:8–10.

Little J. Postural adjustments during pregnancy and implications for the childbearing woman. Bulletin of the Section of Obstetrics and Gynecology. 1984;8:3:16, 17.

Noble E. *Essential Exercises for the Childbearing Year.* 4th ed. Boston, Mass: Houghton Mifflin; 1995.

O'Connor LJ. Exercising more ways, enjoying it less. *Journal of Obstetric and Gynecologic Physical Therapy.* 1989;13:8–9.

Pipp LM. The exercise dilemma: considerations and guidelines for treatment of the high risk obstetric patient. *Journal of Obstetric and Gynecologic Physical Therapy.* 1989;13:10–12.

Polden M. Health after childbirth: are we neglecting women's problems? *Professional Care of Mother and Child.* 1993;3:121–122.

Shrock P, Simkin P, Shearer M. Teaching prenatal exercise: part II—exercise to think twice about. *Birth and Family Journal.* 1981;8:3:1675–1676.

Simons J. *Pregnant and in Perfect Shape: Exercise During Pregnancy and After.* Melbourne, Australia: Nelson Publishers; 1987:4–5.

Wilder E, ed. *Obstetric and Gynecologic Physical Therapy.* New York, NY: Churchill Livingstone; 1988:1:20:191.

Fetal Alcohol Syndrome

Harris SR, Osborn JA, Weinberg J, Loock C, Junaid K. Effects of prenatal alcohol exposure on neuromotor and cognitive development during early childhood: a series of case reports. *Physical Therapy.* 1993;73:608–617.

Osborn JA, Harris SR, Weinberg J. Fetal alcohol syndrome: review of the literature with implications for physical therapists. *Physical Therapy*. 1993;73:599–607.

High-Risk Pregnancy
Frahm J, Welch RA. Physical therapy management of the high-risk antepartum patient: medical management, part 1. *Clinical Management in Physical Therapy*. 1989;9:4:14–18.

Frahm J, Welch RA. Physical therapy management of the high-risk antepartum patient: part 2. *Clinical Management in Physical Therapy*. 1989;9:5:47–49.

Frahm J, Welch RA. Physical therapy management of the high-risk antepartum patient: physical and occupational therapy treatment objectives and program, part 3. *Clinical Management in Physical Therapy*. 1989;9:6:28–33.

Pipp LM. The exercise dilemma: considerations and guidelines for treatment of the high-risk obstetric patient. *Journal of Obstetric and Gynecologic Physical Therapy*. 1989;13:4:10–13.

Rasmussen B. Reimbursement for obstetric and gynecologic physical therapy. *Journal of Obstetric and Gynecologic Physical Therapy*. 1994;18:2:10–12.

Low Back Pain in Pregnancy
Dinniny P. Women's health issues: coming of age. *PT—Magazine of Physical Therapy*. 1995;3:9:46–55.

Dunbar A. Low back pain during pregnancy: an overview. *Journal of Obstetric and Gynecologic Physical Therapy*. 1989;13:2:4–5.

Dunbar A. Stable and steady: the lumbar spine. *Journal of Obstetric and Gynecologic Physical Therapy*. 1993;17:2:5–7.

Hill L. TNS for back pain in late pregnancy. *Physiotherapy*. 1990;76:566.

Hummel-Berry K. Obstetric low back pain: a comprehensive review. Part one: incidence and diagnosis. *Journal of Obstetric and Gynecologic Physical Therapy*. 1990;14:1:10–13.

Hummel-Berry K. Obstetric low back pain: a comprehensive review. Part two: evaluation and treatment. *Journal of Obstetric and Gynecologic Physical Therapy*. 1990;14:2:9–11.

Lile A, Hagar T. Survey of current physical therapy treatment for the pregnant client with lumbopelvic dysfunction. *Journal of Obstetric and Gynecologic Physical Therapy*. 1991;15:4:10–12.

Mantle J. Back pain in the childbearing year. In: Boyling JD, Palastanga N, eds. *Grieve's Modern Manual Therapy*. 2nd ed. New York, NY: Churchill Livingstone; 1994:799–808.

Perinatal Loss
Larson AI. Congenital malformations and exposure to high-frequency electromagnetic radiation among Danish physiotherapists. *Scandinavian Journal of Work, Environment and Health*. 1991;17:318–323.

Larson AI, Olsen J, Svane O. Gender-specific reproductive outcome and exposure to high-frequency electromagnetic radiation among physiotherapists. *Scandinavian Journal of Work, Environment and Health*. 1991;17:324–329.

Ouellet-Hellstrom R, Stewart WF. Miscarriages among female physical therapists who report using radio and microwave-frequency electromagnetic radiation. *American Journal of Epidemiology*. 1993;138:775–786.

Taskinen H, Kyyronen P, Hemminki K. Effects of ultrasound, shortwaves, and physical exertion on pregnancy outcome in physiotherapists. *Journal of Epidemiology and Community Health*. 1990;44:196–201.

TENS
Dunn PA, Rogers D, Halford K. Transcutaneous electrical nerve stimulation at acupuncture points in the induction of uterine contractions. *Obstetrics and Gynecology*. 1989;73:286–290.

Grim LC, Moray SH. Transcutaneous electrical nerve stimulation for relief of parturition pain: a clinical report. *Physical Therapy*. 1989;65:337–340.

Hill L. TNS for back pain in late pregnancy. *Physiotherapy*. 1990;76:566.

Keenan DL, McCrann DJ, Simonsen L. Transcutaneous electrical nerve stimulation for pain control during labor and delivery: a case report. *Physical Therapy*. 1985;65:1363–1364.

Lee EW, Chung IW, Lee JY, Lam PW, Chin RK. The role of transcutaneous electrical nerve stimulation in management of labour in obstetric patients. *Asia-Oceania Journal of Obstetrics and Gynaecology.* 1990;16:247–254.

Mannheimer JS. TENS: uses and effectiveness. In: Hoskins MT, ed. *International Perspectives in Physical Therapy: Pain.* New York, NY: Churchill Livingstone; 1985:77.

Pipp LM. TENS update: compendium of selected TENS literature. *Journal of Obstetric and Gynecologic Physical Therapy.* 1993;17:1:12.

Polden M. Transcutaneous nerve stimulation in labor and post-cesarean section. *Physiotherapy.* 1985;71:3.

Pomerantz E. TENS and pregnancy: rules for safe practice. *Journal of Obstetric and Gynecologic Physical Therapy.* 1988;12:3:5–7.

Vulvar Vestibulitis

DESCRIPTION
Vulvar vestibulitis is inflammation and pain in the area of the vaginal vestibule and vulva.

CAUSE
No specific cause was identified.

ASSESSMENT
No specific evaluation was identified. Consider use of elements from the evaluation for incontinence.

Areas
- History, including any medical conditions or symptoms such as bleeding or discharge, occupation, surgery, menopausal state, and medications
- Psychological/social
- Urinary symptoms: frequency, urgency, stress, and nocturia
- Bowel habits, including any constipation
- Pain, including any dyspareunia (painful intercourse)
- Activities of daily living (ADLs)
- Musculoskeletal evaluation, including any contributing postural problems and adductor muscle spasm, hip, or pelvic floor muscle imbalance
- Perineal examination: strength or spasm, if indicated

Instruments/Procedures (See References for Sources)
- Female Urogenital System Checklist

PROBLEMS
- The woman usually has severe pain localized at the vestibule of the vagina and vulvar area.
- The pain may be described as burning.
- The woman is hypersensitive in the labia minora area, especially if clothing is tight.

- There is usually dyspareunia.
- The condition can be accompanied by urgency in urination, cystitis, or interstitial cystitis.

TREATMENT/MANAGEMENT
- Consider use of acupressure, joint mobilization, soft tissue work, trigger point therapy, or myofascial release.
- Modalities can include electrotherapy, ultrasound or diathermy, superficial heat, ice, or transcutaneous electrical nerve stimulation (TENS).
- Encourage a fitness program with a stretching component.
- Instruct in relaxation techniques.

PRECAUTIONS/CONTRAINDICATIONS
See Appendix C for precautions with modalities.

DESIRED OUTCOME/PROGNOSIS
- The client will experience a relief of symptoms.

REFERENCES

ASSESSMENT
Ling, FW, King PM, Myers CA. Screening for female urogenital system disease. In: Boissonnault WG, ed. *Examination in Physical Therapy Practice*. New York, NY: Churchill Livingstone; 1991:149. **[Female Urogenital System Checklist]**

TREATMENT
Adams C, Frahm J. Genitourinary system. In: Myers RS, ed. *Saunders Manual of Physical Therapy Practice*. Philadelphia, Pa: WB Saunders Co; 1995:459–504.

Assessments—Pediatrics

Below, asterisks mark the sources containing the actual instruments.

AAHPER Youth Fitness Test

> *Hunsicker P, Reiff G. *AAHPER Youth Fitness Test*. Rev ed. Reston, Va: American Alliance for Health, Physical Education and Recreation; 1976.

Adams Forward Bending Test

> Bleck E. Adolescent idiopathic scoliosis. *Developmental Medicine and Child Neurology*. 1991;33:167–173.

Alberta Infant Motor Scale (AIMS)

> *Piper MC, Darrah J. *Motor Assessment of the Developing Infant*. Philadelphia, Pa: WB Saunders Co; 1994.
>
> Campbell SK. The child's development of functional movement. In: Campbell SR, ed. *Physical Therapy for Children*. Philadelphia, Pa: WB Saunders Co; 1994:3–37.

Alpern-Boll Developmental Profile

> *Alpern G, Boll T. *Developmental Profile*. Indianapolis, Ind: Psychological Developmental Publications; 1972.

Apgar Score

> Apgar V. (1953) Proposal for a method of evaluation of newborn infant. *Anesthesia and Analgesia* 1953;32:260–267

Assessment of Motor and Process Skills

> Campbell SK. The child's development of functional movement. In: Campbell SK, ed. *Physical Therapy for Children*. Philadelphia, Pa: WB Saunders Co; 1994:3–37.
>
> Fisher AG. Development of a functional assessment that adjusts ability measures for task simplicity and rater leniency. In: Wilson M, ed. *Objective Measurement: Theory into Practice*. Vol 2. Norwood, NJ: Ablex; 1994:145–175.

Assessment of Preterm Infants' Behavior (APIB)

> *Als H, Lester BM, Tronick EZ, Brazelton TB. Manual for the assessment of preterm infants' behavior (APIB). In: Fitzgerald HE, Yosman MW, eds. *Theory and Research in Behavior Pediatrics*. Vol 1. New York, NY: Plenum Press; 1982:65–132.

Ashworth Scale

> *Bohannon RW, Smith MB. Interrater reliability of the modified Ashworth scale of muscle spasticity. *Physical Therapy*. 1987;57:206–207.

Barthel Index

> *Mahoney FL, Barthel DW. Functional evaluation: The Barthel Index. *Maryland Medical Journal*. 1965;14:61–65.

Basic Gross Motor Assessment (BGMA)
    *Hughes JE. *Basic Motor Assessment*. Golden, Colo: Jeanne E. Hughes; 1979.

Bates Infant Characteristic Questionnaire
    *Bates JE, Feeland CAB, Lousbury ML. Measurement of infant difficultness. *Child Development.*
    1979;50:794–803.

Battelle Developmental Inventory
    Palisano RJ. Neuromotor and developmental assessment—Battelle Developmental Inventory. In: Wilhelm
    IJ, ed. *Physical Therapy Assessment in Early Infancy*. New York, NY: Churchill Livingstone; 1993.

Battelle Developmental Inventory Screening Test
    Feldman AB, Haley SM, Coryell J. Concurrent and construct validity of the Pediatric Evaluation of
    Disability Inventory. *Physical Therapy*. 1990;70:602–610.
    *Newborg J, Strock J, Wnek L. *Battelle Developmental Inventory*. Allen, Tex: DLM Teaching Re-
    sources; 1984.

Bayley Infant Neurodevelopmental Screen (BINS)
    *Aylward CP. *Bayley Infant Neurodevelopmental Screen*. San Antonio, Tex: Psychological Corpora-
    tion; 1992.
    Campbell SK. The child's development of functional movement. In: Campbell SK, ed. *Physical Therapy
    for Children*. Philadelphia, Pa: WB Saunders Co; 1994:3–37.

Bayley Scales of Infant Development (BSID) or Bayley II
    *Bayley N. *Bayley Scales of Infant Development*. New York, NY: Psychological Corporation; 1969.
    *Bayley N. *Bayley II*. San Antonio, Tex: Psychological Corporation; 1994.
    Brenneman SK. *Bayley Scales of Infant Development*. In: Tecklin JS, ed. *Pediatric Physical Therapy*.
    Philadelphia, Pa: JB Lippincott Co; 1994:42–44.
    Brenneman SK. Bayley II. In: Tecklin JS, ed. *Pediatric Physical Therapy*. Philadelphia, Pa: JB Lippincott
    Co; 1994:44–45.
    Campbell SK. The child's development of functional movement. In: Campbell SK, ed. *Physical Therapy
    for Children*. Philadelphia, Pa: WB Saunders Co; 1994:3–37.
    Harris SR. Early diagnosis of spastic diplegia, spastic hemiplegia, and quadriplegia. *American Journal
    of Diseases of Children*. 1989;143:1356–1360.
    Miedaner J, Finuf L. Effects of adaptive positioning on psychological test scores for preschool children
    with cerebral palsy. *Pediatric Physical Therapy*. 1993;5:177–182.

Behavioral Assessment Scale of Oral Function in Feeding
    *Stratton M. Behavioral Assessment Scale of Oral Functions in Feeding. *American Journal of Occupa-
    tional Therapy*. 1981;35:719–721.

Borg Exertion Scale
    *Borg GV. Psychophysical bases of perceived exertion. *Medical Science of Sports Exercise*. 1982;14:377–
    387.

Brazelton Neonatal Behavioral Assessment Scale—see *Neonatal Behavioral Assessment Scale*

Bruininks–Oseretsky Test of Motor Proficiency (BOTMP)
    Boyce WF, Gowland C, Rosenbaum PI, et al. Measuring quality of movement in cerebral palsy: a
    review of instruments. *Physical Therapy*. 1991;71:813–819.
    Brenneman SK. Bruininks–Oseretsky Test of Motor Proficiency. In: Tecklin JS, ed. *Pediatric Physical
    Therapy*. Philadelphia, Pa: JB Lippincott Co; 1994:38–41.
    *Bruininks RH. *Bruininks–Oseretsky Test of Motor Proficiency*. Circle Pines, Minn: American Guid-
    ance Service; 1978.

Stengel TJ. Assessment of motor development in children. In: Campbell SK, ed. *Pediatric Neurologic Physical Therapy*. New York, NY: Churchill Livingstone; 1991:33–65.

Canadian Occupational Performance Measure

*Law M, Baptiste S, McColl MA, Opzoomer A, Polatajko H, Pollock N. The Canadian Occupational Performance Measure: an outcome measure for occupational therapy. *Canadian Journal of Occupational Therapy*. 1990;57:82–87.

Chandler Movement Assessment of Infants—see *Movement Assessment of Infants*

Childhood Health Assessment Questionnaire

*Singh G, Athreya B, Fries JF, Goldsmith DP. Measurement of functional status in JRA. *Arthritis and Rheumatism*. In press.

Children's Orientation and Amnesia Test (COAT)

Ewing–Cobb L, Lewin HS, Fletcher JM, Miner ME, Eisenberg HM. Post-traumatic amnesia in children: assessment and outcome. Presented at the meeting of the International Neuropsychological Society; 1989; Vancouver, BC.

Clinical Assessment of Gestational Age in the Newborn Infant

*Dubowitz LMS, Dubowitz V, Goldberg D. Clinical assessment of gestational age in the newborn infant. *Journal of Pediatrics*. 1970;77:1–10.

Denver II

Brenneman SK. Denver II. In: Tecklin JS, ed. *Pediatric Physical Therapy*. Philadelphia, Pa: JB Lippincott Co; 1994:32–35.

Campbell SK. The child's development of functional movement. In: Campbell SK, ed. *Physical Therapy for Children*. Philadelphia, Pa: WB Saunders Co; 1994:3–37.

Frankenburg WK, Dodds J, Archer P. Denver II: a major revision and restandardization of the Denver Developmental Screening Test. *Pediatrics*. 1992;89:1.

*Frankenburg WK, Dodds J, Archer P, et al. *Denver II Technical Manual*. Denver, Colo: Denver Developmental Materials; 1990.

Dynamometer

Dvir Z, Bar Haim S, Arbel N. Intertester agreement in static resistance measurement using a simile uniaxial dynamometer. *Physical and Occupational Therapy in Pediatrics*. 1990;10:3:59–67.

Early Intervention Developmental Profile

*Brenneman SK. Early Intervention Developmental Profile. In: Tecklin JS, ed. *Pediatric Physical Therapy*. Philadelphia, Pa: JB Lippincott Co; 1994:48–49.

Rogers SJ, D'Eugenio DB. Assessment and application. In: Schafer DS, Moersch MS, eds. *Developmental Programming for Infants and Young Children*. Vol 1. Ann Arbor, Mich; University of Michigan Press; 1977.

Early Neuropsychological Optimality Rating Scales (ENORS)—see *Bayley Infant Neurodevelopmental Screen*

Erhardt Developmental Prehension Assessment

*Erhardt T. *Erhardt Developmental Prehension Assessment*. Phoenix, Ariz: Therapy Skill Builders; 1984.

Reddihough D, Bach T, Burgess G, Oke L, Hudson I. Comparison of subjective and objective measures of movement performance of children with cerebral palsy. *Developmental Medicine and Child Neurology*. 1991;33:578–584.

Functional Disability Scales
   Spector RC. Functional Disability Scales. In: Spilker B, ed. *Quality of Life Assessment in Clinical Trials*. New York, NY: Raven Press; 1990:115–129.

Functional Independence Measure for Children (WeeFIM)
   *Granger CV, Hamilton BB, Kayton R. *Guide for the Use of the Functional Independence Measure (WeeFIM) of the Uniform Data Set for Medical Rehabilitation*. Buffalo, NY: State University of New York, Research Foundation; 1989.

Gesell and Amatruda Development and Neurological Examination
   Knobloch H, Stevens F, Malone AF. *Manual of Developmental Diagnosis: The Administration and Interpretation of the Revised Gesell and Amatruda Developmental and Neurological Examination*. Houston, Tex: Gesell Developmental Materials, Inc; 1987.

Gesell Developmental Schedules—Revised
   Brenneman SK. Gesell Developmental Schedules. In: Tecklin JS, ed. *Pediatric Physical Therapy*. Philadelphia, Pa: JB Lippincott Co; 1994:41–42.
   Campbell SK. The child's development of functional movement. In: Campbell SK, ed. *Physical Therapy for Children*. Philadelphia, Pa: WB Saunders Co; 1994:3–37.
   *Knobloch H, Pasamanick B, eds. *Gesell and Amatruda's Developmental Diagnosis: The Evaluation and Management of Normal and Abnormal Neuropsychological Development in Infancy and Early Childhood*. Hagerstown, Md: Harper & Row; 1974.
   *Knobloch H, Stevens F, Malone AF. *Manual of Development Diagnosis*. Rev ed. New York, NY: Harper & Row; 1980.

Gross Motor Function Measure (GMFM)
   Kramer JF, MacPhail HEA. Relationships among measures of walking efficiency, gross motor ability, and isokinetic strength in adolescents with cerebral palsy. *Pediatric Physical Therapy*. 1994;6:1:3–8.
   Rosenbaum P, Cadman D, Russell D, Gowland D, Hardy S, Jarvis S. Issues in measuring change in motor function in children with cerebral palsy: a special communication. *Physical Therapy*. 1990;70:125–131.
   Russell D, Rosenbaum P, Gowland C, Hardy S, Gadman D. Validation of a gross motor measure for children with cerebral palsy. *Physiotherapy Canada*. 1990;42(suppl 3):2.
   Russell DJ, Rosenbaum PO, Cadman DT, Gowland C, Hardy S, Jarvis S. The Gross Motor Function Measure: a means to evaluate the effects of physical therapy. *Developmental Medicine and Child Neurology*. 1989;31:341–352.
   *Russell D, Rosenbaum P, Gowland C, et al. *Gross Motor Function Measure (GMFM): A Measure of Gross Motor Function in Cerebral Palsy*. Hamilton, Ontario, Canada: McMaster University.

Gross Motor Performance Measure (GMPM)
   Berg KL, Williams JI, Wood-Dauphine SL, Maki BE. Measuring balance in the elderly: validation of an instrument. *Canadian Journal of Public Health*. 1992;83:7–11.
   Boyce W, Gowland C, Russell D, et al. Consensus methodology in the development and content validation of a gross motor performance measure. *Physiotherapy Canada*. 1993;45:94–100.
   Boyce W, Gowland C, Rosenbaum P, et al. Gross Motor Performance Measure for children with cerebral palsy: study design and preliminary findings. *Canadian Journal of Public Health*. 1992;83:2:S34–S40.
   Boyce WF, Gowland C, Hardy S, et al. Development of a quality-of-movement measure for children with cerebral palsy. *Physical Therapy*. 1991;71:820–832.
   Boyce W, Gowland D, Hardy S, et al. Reliability of the gross motor performance measure of cerebral palsy. *Physiotherapy Canada*. 1990;42(suppl):1.

*Russell DJ, Rosenbaum PL, Cadman DT, Gowland C, Hardy S, Jarvis S. The Gross Motor Performance Measure: a means to evaluate the effects of physical therapy. *Developmental Medicine and Child Neurology.* 1989;31:103–120.

Juvenile Arthritis Functional Assessment Scale (JFAS)

*Lovell DJ, Howe S, Shear E, Hartner S, McGirr G, Scheulte M, Levinson J. Development of a disability measurement tool for juvenile rheumatoid arthritis: the Juvenile Arthritis Functional Assessment Scale. *Arthritis and Rheumatism.* 1989;32:1390–1395.

Klein–Bell ADL Scale

*Klein RM, Bell B. Self-care skills: behavioral measurement with Klein–Bell ADL Scale. *Archives of Physical Medicine and Rehabilitation.* 1982;63:335–338.

Manual Muscle Testing

*Daniels L, Worthingham C. *Muscle Testing: Techniques of Manual Examination.* Philadelphia, Pa: WB Saunders Co; 1995.

Milani–Comparetti Motor Development Screening Test

Boyce WF, Gowland G, Rosenbaum PI, et al. Measuring quality of movement in cerebral palsy: a review of instruments. *Physical Therapy.* 1991;71:813–819.

Brenneman SK. Milani–Comparetti Motor Development Screening Test. In: Tecklin JS, ed. *Pediatric Physical Therapy.* Philadelphia, Pa: JB Lippincott Co; 1994:30–32.

*Milani–Comparetti A, Gidoni EA. Pattern analysis of motor development and its disorders. *Development Medicine and Child Neurology.* 1967;9:625–630.

*Milani–Comparetti A, Gidoni EA. Routine developmental examination in normal and retarded children. *Developmental Medicine and Child Neurology.* 1967;9:631–638.

*Trembath J, Kliewer D, Bruce W. *The Milani–Comparetti Motor Development Screening Test.* Omaha, Neb: University of Nebraska Medical Center; 1977.

*Stuberg WA, et al. *The Milani–Comparetti Motor Development Screening Test.* 3rd ed, rev. Omaha, Neb: University of Nebraska Medical Center; 1992.

Stuberg WA, White PJ, Miedaner JA, Dehne PR. Item reliability of the Milani–Comparetti Motor Development Screening Test. *Physical Therapy.* 1989;69:328–335.

Miller Assessment of Preschoolers

Boyce WF, Gowland G, Rosenbaum PI, et al. Measuring quality of movement in cerebral palsy: a review of instruments. *Physical Therapy.* 1991;71:813–819.

*Miller LJ. *Miller Assessment for Preschoolers.* Littleton, Colo: Foundations for Knowledge in Development; 1982.

*Miller LJ. *Miller Assessment for Preschoolers.* San Antonio, Tex: Psychological Corporation; 1991.

Stengel TJ. Assessing motor development in children. In: Campbell SK, ed. *Pediatric Neurological Physical Therapy.* New York, NY: Churchill Livingstone; 1991:33–65.

Miller First Step

*Miller LJ. *Miller First Step: Screening Test for Evaluating Preschoolers.* New York, NY: Psychological Corporation; 1992.

Morgan Neonatal Neurobehavioral Examination

*Morgan A. Neuro-developmental approach to the high-risk neonate. In: Tecklin JS, ed. *Pediatric Physical Therapy.* Philadelphia, Pa: JB Lippincott Co; 1994:71–73.

Movement Assessment of Infants

Ashton B, Piper MC, Warren S, Stewin L, Byrne P. Influence of medical history on assessment of at-risk infants. *Developmental Medicine and Child Neurology.* 1991;33:412–418.

Boyce WF, Gowland C, Rosenbaum PL, et al. Measuring quality of movement in cerebral palsy: a review of instruments. *Physical Therapy.* 1991;71:813–819.

Brenneman SK. Movement Assessment of Infants. In: Tecklin JS, ed. *Pediatric Physical Therapy.* Philadelphia, Pa: JB Lippincott Co; 1994:35–36.

*Chandler LS, Andrews MS, Swanson MW. *Movement Assessment of Infants: A Manual.* Rolling Bay, Wash: Infant Movement Research, Children Development and Mental Retardation Center; 1980.

Harris SR. Early diagnosis of spastic diplegia, spastic hemiplegia, and quadriplegia. *American Journal of Diseases of Children.* 1989;143:1356–1360.

Schneider JW, Lee W, Chasnoff IJ. *Physical Therapy.* 1988;68:321–327.

Swanson MW, Bennett FC, Shy KK, Whitfield MF. Identification of neurodevelopmental abnormality at four and eight months by the Movement Assessment of Infants. *Developmental Medicine and Child Neurology.* 1992;34:321–327.

Neonatal Oral Motor Assessment Scale (NOMAS)

Neonatal Behavioral Assessment Scale

Brenneman SK. Neonatal Behavioral Assessment Scale. In: Tecklin, JS, ed. *Pediatric Physical Therapy.* Philadelphia, Pa: JB Lippincott Co; 1994:45–48.

Brazelton TB. *Neonatal Behavioral Assessment Scale.* Philadelphia, Pa: JB Lippincott Co; 1984:88. Clinics in Developmental Medicine.

Wilhelm IJ. Neurobehavioral assessment of the high-risk neonate: the Brazelton Neonatal Behavioral Assessment Scale. In: *Physical Therapy Assessment in Early Infancy.* New York, NY: Churchill Livingstone; 1993:48–52.

Neurological Assessment During the First Year of Life

*Amiel-Tison C, Grenier A. *Neurological Assessment During the First Year of Life.* New York, NY: Oxford University Press; 1986.

Neurological Assessment of the Preterm and Full-Term Newborn Infant

*Dubowitz L, Dubowitz V. *The Neurological Assessment of the Preterm and Full-Term Newborn Infant.* Philadelphia, Pa: JB Lippincott Co; 1981:79. Clinics in Developmental Medicine.

Dubowitz L. The neurological assessment of the full-term and preterm newborn infant. In: Harel S, Anastasiow N, eds. *The At-Risk Infant.* Baltimore, Md: Paul H Brooks; 1985:186–196.

Stengel TJ. Assessing motor development in children. In: *Pediatric Neurological Physical Therapy.* 2nd ed. New York, NY: Churchill Livingstone; 1991:33–65.

Neurological Development in the Full-Term and Premature Neonate

*Saint-Anne Dargassies S. *Neurological Development in the Full Term and Premature Neonate.* Amsterdam, the Netherlands: Excerpta Medica; 1977.

Saint-Anne Dargassies S. In: Harel S, Anastasiow N, eds. *The At-Risk Infant.* Baltimore, Md: Paul H Brooks; 1985:185–196.

Neurological Evaluation of the Maturity of Newborn Infants

*Amiel-Tison C. Neurological evaluation of the maturity of newborn infants. *Archives of Diseases in Children.* 1968;43:89–93.

Neurological Examination of the Full-Term Newborn Infant

*Prechtl HFR, Beintema D. *The Neurological Examination of the Full Term Newborn Infant.* Philadelphia, Pa: JB Lippincott Co; 1964:12. Clinics in Developmental Medicine.

Prechtl HFR. *The Neurological Examination of the Full Term Newborn Infant.* Philadelphia, Pa: JB Lippincott Co; 1977:63. Clinics in Developmental Medicine.

Stengel TJ. Assessment of motor development in children. In: Campbell SK, ed. *Pediatric Neurological Physical Therapy.* 2nd ed. New York, NY: Churchill Livingstone; 1991:33–65.

New York State Physical Fitness Test

*Clarke HH, Clarke DH. *Application of Measurement in Physical Education.* Englewood Cliffs, NJ: Prentice Hall; 1987:93–99.

Objective-Based Motor Skill Assessment Instrument

Boyce WF, Gowland C, Rosenbaum PI, et al. Measuring quality of movement in cerebral palsy: a review of instruments. *Physical Therapy.* 1991;71:813–819.

*Ulrich DA. *The Objectives-Based Motor Skill Assessment Instrument.* Carbondale, Ill: Southern Illinois University Press; 1982.

Peabody Developmental Motor Scales (PDMS)

Boyce WF, Gowland G, Rosenbaum PK, et al. Measuring quality of movement in cerebral palsy: a review of instruments. *Physical Therapy.* 1991;71:813–819.

Brenneman SK. Peabody Developmental Motor Scales. In: Tecklin JS, ed. *Pediatric Physical Therapy.* Philadelphia, Pa: JB Lippincott Co; 1994:36–38.

*Folio MR, Fewell RR. *Peabody Developmental Motor Scales.* Allen, Tex: DLM Teaching Resources; 1983.

Hinderer KA, Richardson PK, Atwater SW. Clinical implications of the Peabody Developmental Motor Scales: a constructive review. *Physical and Occupational Therapy in Pediatrics.* 1989;9:81–106.

Stephens TE, Haley SM. Comparison of two methods for determining change in motorically handicapped children. *Physical and Occupational Therapy in Pediatrics.* 1991;11:1–17.

Stengel TJ. Assessing motor development in children. In: Campbell SK, ed. *Pediatric Neurological Physical Therapy.* 2nd ed. New York, NY: Churchill Livingstone; 1991:33–65.

Pediatric Evaluation of Disability Inventory (PEDI)

Brenneman SK. Pediatric Evaluation of Disability Inventory. In: Tecklin JS, ed. *Pediatric Physical Therapy.* Philadelphia, Pa: JB Lippincott Co; 1994:49–53.

Campbell SK. The child's development of functional movement. In: Campbell SK, ed. *Physical Therapy for Children.* Philadelphia, Pa: WB Saunders Co; 1994:3–37.

Feldman AB, Haley SM, Coryell J. Concurrent and construct validity of the Pediatric Evaluation of Disability Inventory. *Physical Therapy.* 1990;70:602–610.

*Haley SM, Coster WJ, Ludlow LH, Haltiwanger JT, Andrellos PJ. *Pediatric Evaluation of Disability Inventory (PEDI): Developmental, Standardization and Administration Manual.* Boston, Mass: New England Medical Center Publications; 1992.

Haley SM, Coster WJ, Faas RM. A content validity study of the Pediatric Evaluation of Disability Inventory. *Pediatric Physical Therapy.* 1991;3:177–184.

Stengel TJ. Assessing motor development in children. In: Campbell SK, ed. *Pediatric Neurological Physical Therapy.* 2nd ed. New York, NY: Churchill Livingstone; 1991:33–65.

Posture and Fine Motor Assessment of Infants (PFMAI)

*Case-Smith J. Reliability and validity of the posture and fine motor assessment of infants. *Occupational Therapy Journal of Research.* 1989;9:259–272.

Posture Scale for Children

*Levine SB. Development of a posture scale for children: preliminary analysis of concurrent validity of the posture scale for children. *Pediatric Physical Therapy.* 1991;3:212. Abstract.

Problem Oriented Prenatal Risk Assessment System (POPRAS)

*Hobel CJ. Identification of the patient at risk. In: Bolognese RJ, Schwartz RH, Schneider J, eds. *Perinatal Medicine: Management of the High-Risk Fetus and Neonate.* Baltimore, Md: Williams & Wilkins; 1982:3–28.

Sitting Assessment Scale (SAS)

Myhr U, von Wendt L, Sandberg KW. Assessment of sitting in children with cerebral palsy from videofilm: a reliability study. *Physical and Occupational Therapy in Pediatrics.* 1993;12:4:21–35.

Test of Gross Motor Development (TGMD)

Ezzelle L, Moutoux L. Critical review of the Test of Gross Motor Development. *Physical and Occupational Therapy in Pediatrics.* 1993;12:4:73–87.

*Ulrich DA. *A Test of Gross Motor Development.* Austin, Tex: Pro-Ed; 1985.

Test of Infant Motor Performance (TIMP)

Campbell SK, Osten ET, Kolobe THA, Fisher AG. Development of the Test of Infant Motor Performance. In: Granger CV, Gresham GE, eds. *New Developments in Functional Assessment.* Philadelphia, Pa: WB Saunders Co; 1993:541–550.

Test of Motor and Neurological Functions

Boyce WF, Gowland C, Rosenbaum PI, et al. Measuring quality of movement in cerebral palsy: a review of instruments. *Physical Therapy.* 1991;71:813–819.

*DeGangi GA, Berk RA, Valvano J. Test of motor and neurological functions in high-risk infants: preliminary finding. *Developmental and Behavioral Pediatrics.* 1983;4:182–189.

Test of Motor Impairment (TOMI)

Boyce WF, Gowland C, Rosenbaum PI, et al. Measuring quality of movement in cerebral palsy: a review of instruments. *Physical Therapy.* 1991;71:813–819.

*Stott DH, Moyes FA, Henderson SE. *Test of Motor Impairment.* Guelph, Ontario, Canada. Brook Educational Publishing; 1966.

Test of Motor Impairment—Henderson Revision

Boyce WF, Gowland C, Rosenbaum PI, et al. Measuring quality of movement in cerebral palsy: a review of instruments. *Physical Therapy.* 1991;71:813–819.

*Stott DH, Moyes FA, Henderson SE. *Test of Motor Impairment, Henderson Revision.* Guelph, Ontario, Canada: Brook Educational Publishing; 1984.

Toddler and Infant Motor Evaluation (TIME)

*Miller LJ. *The Toddler and Infant Motor Evaluation.* Tucson, Ariz: Communication Skill Builders; 1994.

Tufts Assessment of Motor Performance (TAMP)

Gans BM, et al. Description and interobserver reliability of the Tufts Assessment of Motor Performance. *American Journal of Physical Medicine and Rehabilitation.* 1988;67:202–207.

Vineland Adaptive Behavior Scales

*Sparrow SS, Balla DA, Ciccette DV. *Vineland Adaptive Behavior Scales.* Circle Pines, Minn: American Guidance Service; 1984.

Vulpe Assessment Battery

Stengel TJ. Assessing motor development in children. In: Campbell SK, ed. *Pediatric Neurological Physical Therapy.* 2nd ed. New York, NY: Churchill Livingstone; 1991:33–65.

*Vulpe SG. *Vulpe Assessment Battery: Developmental Assessment, Performance Analysis, Individualized Programming for the Atypical Child.* Toronto, Ontario, Canada: National Institute on Mental Retardation; 1977.

WATSMART (Waterloo Spatial Motion Analysis and Recording Techniques)

Kluzik JA, Fetters L, Coryell J. Quantification of control: a preliminary study of effects of neurodevelopmental treatment on reaching in children with spastic cerebral palsy. *Physical Therapy.* 1990;70:65–76.

WeeFIM—see *Functional Independence Measure for Children*

Wolanski Gross Motor Evaluation

Boyce WF, Gowland C, Rosenbaum PI, et al. Measuring quality of movement in cerebral palsy: a review of instruments. *Physical Therapy.* 1991;71:813–819.

*Wolanski N, Zdanska-Brincken M. A graphic method for the evaluation of motor development in infants. *Development Medicine and Child Neurology.* 1969;11:238–242.

Appendix B

Aging References

Dewane JA. Dealing with dizziness and disequilibrium in older patients: a clinical approach. *Topics in Geriatric Rehabilitation*. 1995;11:1:30–38.

Goldstein TS. *Geriatric Orthopaedics: Rehabilitative Management of Common Problems*. Gaithersburg, Md: Aspen Publishers, Inc; 1991.

Guccione AA. *Geriatric Physical Therapy*. St Louis, Mo: CV Mosby Co; 1993.

Kimble E. A case study in adaptive aquatics for the geriatric population. *Clinical Management in Physical Therapy*. 1986:6:4:8.

Leseberg KA, Schunk C. TENS and geriatrics. *Clinical Management in Physical Therapy*. 1990;10:6:23.

Lewis C. What's so different about rehabilitating the older patient. *Clinical Management in Physical Therapy*. 1984;4:3:10.

Lewis C. Dysmobility and the elderly patient. *Clinical Management in Physical Therapy*. 1988;1:1:20.

Lewis CB, Bottomley JM. *Geriatric Physical Therapy: A Clinical Approach*. Norwalk, Conn: Appleton & Lange; 1994.

Lewis CB, Campanelli LC. *Health Promotion and Exercise for Older Adults: An Instructor's Guide*. Rockville, Md: Aspen Publishers, Inc; 1990.

Lord S, Mitchell D, Williams P. Effect of water exercise on balance and related factors in older people. *Australian Journal of Physical Therapy*. 1993;39:217–222.

May BJ. The Elderhostel experience: designing fitness programs for the elderly community. *Clinical Management in Physical Therapy*. 1988;3;18.

Newman LA. *Maintaining Function in Older Adults*. Boston, Mass: Butterworth-Heinemann; 1995.

Paillard M, Wilchynski JA. Exercise and health: a local seminar for the elderly. *Clinical Management in Physical Therapy*. 1985;5:4:40.

Piotrowski A, Cole J. Clinical measures of balance and functional assessment in elderly. *Australian Journal of Physiotherapy*. 1994;40:183–188.

Poluha PK. Appropriate footwear for the elderly resident. *Clinical Management in Physical Therapy*. 1981;1:4:16.

Roach KE. Community health setting. *Orthopaedic Physical Therapy Clinics of North America*. 1993;2:215–319.

Sallade JR, Adam L. Geriatrics exercise booklet. *Clinical Management in Physical Therapy*. 1986;6:1:32.

Satterfield MJ, Yasumara K, Goodman G. Impact of an engineered physical therapy program for the elderly. *International Journal of Rehabilitation Research*. 1984;7:151–162.

Smyth L. *Practical Physiotherapy With Older People*. New York, NY: Chapman & Hall; 1990.

Sobie T, Lewis C. Quantification of functional capacity in the elderly. *Clinical Management in Physical Therapy*. 1989;5:24.

Walker JM, Sue D, Miles-Elkousy N, et al. Active mobility of the extremities in older subjects. *Physical Therapy*. 1984;64:919–923.

Contraindications for Physical Agents and Modalities

CONTRAST BATHS CONTRAINDICATED
- bleeding
- cardiovascular conditions
- diminished sensation
- hypersensitivity to temperature
- peripheral vascular disease
- pregnancy—avoid temperature hot enough to raise woman's core temperature. See also section on "Pregnancy."

CRYOTHERAPY CONTRAINDICATED
- allergy to cold
- angina pectoris or cardiac disorders
- compromised circulation
- extremes of age are a relative contraindication
- history of frostbite to area
- open wounds after 48 to 72 hours
- Raynaud's disease
- regenerating peripheral nerves

CONTINUOUS PASSIVE MOTION CONTRAINDICATED
- see manufacturer's recommendations

DIRECT CURRENT CONTRAINDICATED

Ion Transfer
- anesthetic skin in area
- bleeding
- cardiac pacemaker
- embedded metal in area
- recent scars in area

ELECTROTHERAPY CONTRAINDICATED

Unipolar or Bipolar Motor Point Stimulation
- anesthestic skin area
- bleeding in area
- cardiac pacemakers
- extreme edema
- malignancies in area
- open wounds
- superficial metal implants
- when no active movement is allowed

ELECTROMYOGRAPHIC BIOFEEDBACK CONTRAINDICATED
- precaution with any skin irritation under electrode placement
- precaution with deep relaxation in clients with diabetes due to possible effect on metabolic level

HYDROTHERAPY (IMMERSION) CONTRAINDICATED
- acute rheumatoid arthritis at extreme temperatures above 95 degrees F
- bleeding
- cardiac disorders (severe)
- diarrhea
- diminished sensation
- malignancies if high temperature is used
- pregnancy—avoid temperature hot enough to raise woman's core temperature; see also section "Pregnancy"
- respiratory disorders (severe)
- selected skin conditions
- severe peripheral vascular disease, diabetes, or arterial sclerosis

IONTOPHORESIS CONTRAINDICATED
- allergy to applied substance
- any condition in which electrical stimulation is contraindicated
- bleeding
- diminished sensation
- metallic implants or wire in area to be treated
- over areas with open skin, or bruise
- pacemakers
- recent scars

POINT LOCATOR/STIMULATOR CONTRAINDICATED
- same as TENS and laser

SUPERFICIAL HEAT CONTRAINDICATED

General Contraindications
- bleeding
- compromised circulation
- deep-vein thrombophlebitis
- dysesthesia or reduced sensation
- edema
- extremes of age range
- inability to report sensations reliably
- skin or lymphatic cancer

Hot Packs
- local infection
- selected skin conditions

Paraffin
- open wounds

Fluidotherapy
- unprotected open wounds

Radiant Heat
- acute inflammation
- bleeding
- cardiac insufficiency
- extremes of age
- fever
- malignancies
- peripheral vascular disease
- tissues affected by x-ray therapy
  Use caution with
- existing edema
- diminished sensation
- unreliable ability to report

DIATHERMY CONTRAINDICATED
- acute inflammation or infection
- bleeding
- cardiac disease
- cardiac pacemakers
- compromised circulation
- general debilitation
- metal in the treatment field
- metastasis in area
- over eyes
- over epiphyses in growing children
- over genital area
- pregnancy

DIADYNAMIC CURRENT THERAPY CONTRAINDICATED
- after cryotherapy or other pain-relieving modality in the area
- on recent fracture
- on fragile skin
- over chest wall
- with threat of bleeding in area
- with malignancy in area
- with vascular disease

INTERFERENTIAL CONTRAINDICATION
- as per unipolar stimulation

INTERMITTENT PNEUMATIC COMPRESSION CONTRAINDICATED
- acute deep-vein thrombosis
- acute fracture
- acute pulmonary edema
- acute skin infection
- compromised circulation
- congestive heart failure

- edema due to cardiac or kidney dysfunction
- edema secondary to traumatic injury
- increased pain due to obstructed lymphatic channels
- metastasis in area

LASER CONTRAINDICATED
- cancerous tissue
- fontanelles on infant
- over eyes
- pregnancy

PARAFFIN CONTRAINDICATED
- as per hot packs

PHONOPHORESIS CONTRAINDICATED
- as per ultrasound and any contraindications due to drug, as per physician or *Physician's Desk Reference*

SPINAL TRACTION CONTRAINDICATED
- acute sprain or strain
- acute inflammation
- exacerbation of symptoms
- hypermobility
- if pressure of harness is too uncomfortable
- osteoporosis
- postsleeve fibrosis in lumbar area for cervical traction
- rheumatoid arthritis
- spinal cancer
- spinal cord pressure with aggravation of symptoms
- spinal infection
- TMJ dysfunction, unless traction adapted to consider condition
- vascular conditions
- when movement is prohibited

ULTRASOUND CONTRAINDICATED
- same precautions listed for superficial heat
- acute inflammatory joint pathologies
- bleeding
- cardiac pacemakers or over carotid sinus, cervical ganglia, heart, or stellate ganglia
- during treatment with deep x-ray, radium, or radioactive isotopes
- epiphyses of growing child
- infection
- malignancy
- pregnancy
- thrombophlebitis
- over eyes
- over spinal cord after laminectomy

- use with caution over areas of unhealed fracture site, post repair of ligament or tendon, over area of implants, or with osteoporosis

ULTRAVIOLET IRRADIATION CONTRAINDICATED
- active pulmonary tuberculosis
- acute diabetes
- acute skin conditions, such as eczema or dermatitis
- fever
- hyperthyroid
- pellagra
- photosensitivity
- porphyrias
- for 3 months after x-ray therapy
- sarcoidosis or xeroderma pigmentosum
- severe cardiac disorder
- systemic lupus erythematosus
  Use with caution:
- cardiac, kidney, or liver disease
- cancer or chemotherapy
- photochemical hypersensitivity
- extremes of age range—very young or very old
- fair-skinned
- immediately before treatment with superficial heat
- selected medications—consult with physician

TENS CONTRAINDICATED
- central nervous system disorders such as CVA to head area
- extreme sensitivity to adhesive tape
- may interfere with demand-type pacemaker
- open skin
- over carotid sinus
- over chest area with cardiac disease
- over eyes
- over head and neck with epilepsy
- over laryngeal or pharyngeal muscles
- over mucosal surfaces
- pregnancy—safety has not been determined; see also section "Pregnancy"
- when operating hazardous machinery

REFERENCES

Please refer also to the manufacturer's recommendations and current journals. The contraindications are based on the texts listed below.

Electrical Stimulation: An American Physical Therapy Association Anthology. Alexandria, Va: American Physical Therapy Association; 1993.

Gersh MR. *Electrotherapy in Rehabilitation.* Philadelphia, Pa: FA Davis Co; 1992.

Hayes K. *Manual for Physical Agents.* 4th ed. Norwalk, Conn: Appleton & Lange; 1993.

Hecox B, Mehreteab TA, Weisberg J, eds. *Physical Agents*. Norwalk, Conn: Appleton & Lange; 1994.
Michlovitz SL. *Thermal Agents in Rehabilitation*. 2nd ed. Philadelphia, Pa: FA Davis; 1990.
Peat M, ed. *Current Physical Therapy*. Philadelphia, Pa: BC Decker Inc; 1988.
Prentice WE. *Therapeutic Modalities in Sports Medicine*. 3rd ed. St. Louis, Mo: CV Mosby Co; 1994.

Appendix D

Addresses

AGING

American Geriatrics Society
770 Lexington Ave, Suite 300
New York, NY 10021
(212) 315-8700

National Council on Aging, Inc
409 3rd St SW, 2nd Floor
Washington, DC 20024
(202) 479-1200

AIDS

National Aids Hotline
American Society Health Association
PO Box 13827
Research Triangle Park, NC 27709
(800) 342-2437
(800) 344-7432 (Spanish)

National AIDS Information Clearinghouse
PO Box 6003
Rockville, MD 20850
(800) 458-5231 (Voice)
(800) 243-7012 (TDD)

ALZHEIMER'S DISEASE

Alzheimer's Disease Association
70 E Lake St
Chicago, IL 60601
(312) 853-3060

AMPUTATION

American Amputee Foundation
PO Box 250218
Little Rock, AR 72225
(501) 666-2523
(501) 666-8367 (Fax)

National Amputation Foundation
73 Church St
Malverne, NY 11565
(516) 887-3600
(516) 887-3667 (Fax)

Orthotic and Prosthetic Association
717 Pendleton St
Alexandria, VA 22314
(703) 836-7116

AMYOTROPHIC LATERAL SCLEROSIS

Amyotrophic Lateral Sclerosis (ALS)
   Association
21021 Ventura Blvd, Suite 321
Woodland Hills, CA 91364
(818) 340-7500

APHASIA

National Aphasia Association
Young People's Network
PO Box 1887

Murray Hill Station
New York, NY 10156-0611
(800) 922-4622

ARTHRITIS

American Juvenile Arthritis Organization
1314 Spring St NW
Atlanta, GA 30309
(800) 283-7800
(404) 872-7100
(404) 872-0457 (Fax)

National Arthritis and Musculoskeletal and
  Skin Diseases Information Clearinghouse
9000 Rockville Pike
Box AMS
Bethesda, MD 20892
(301) 495-4484

ASTHMA AND ALLERGY

Asthma and Allergy Foundation of America
1125 15th St NW, Suite 502
Washington, DC 20005
(202) 466-7643
(800) 727-8462
(202) 466-8940 (Fax)

ATAXIA

National Ataxia Foundation
750 Twelve Oaks Center
15500 Wayzata Blvd
Wayzata, MN 55391
(612) 473-7666
(612) 473-9289 (Fax)

ATHLETICS

American College of Sports Medicine
PO Box 1440
Indianapolis, IN 46206
(317) 637-9200

BALANCE DISORDERS AND DIZZINESS

The EAR Foundation
2000 Church St, Box 111

Nashville, TN 37236
(800) 545-4327 (Voice/TDD)
(615) 329-7807

BEREAVEMENT SUPPORT

AMEND (Aiding Mothers and Fathers
  Experiencing Neonatal Death)
4324 Berrywick Terrace
St Louis, MO 63128
(314) 487-7582

BLINDNESS

American Council of the Blind
1155 15th St NW, Suite 720
Washington, DC 20005
(202) 467-5081
(800) 424-8666

BRAIN DAMAGE

Andrew Blake Foundation
PO Box 866
Winona, MN 55987
(507) 452-5734

BRAIN TUMORS

American Brain Tumor Association
2720 River Rd, Suite 146
Des Plaines, IL 60018
(800) 886-2282 (Consumer Line)
(708) 827-9910
(708) 827-9918 (Fax)

BREAST CANCER

National Alliance of Breast Cancer
  Organizations
9 E 37th Street, 10th Floor
New York, NY 10016-2822
(212) 719-0154

Y-ME National Breast Cancer Organization
212 W Van Buren
Chicago, IL 60607
(800) 221-2141

BURNS

American Burn Association
Baltimore Regional Burn Center
4940 Eastern Ave
Baltimore, MD 21224
(800) 548-2876

Let's Face It
PO Box 711
Concord, MA 01742-0711
(508) 371-3186

The Phoenix Society for Burn Survivors,
    Inc.
11 Rust Hill Road
Levittown, PA 19056-2311
(215) 946-BURN

CANCER

American Cancer Society
PO Box 190429
Atlanta, GA 31119-0429
(404) 816-7800
(404) 816-9443 (Fax)

CEREBRAL PALSY

United Cerebral Palsy Association
1522 K St NW, #1112
Washington, DC 20005
(800) 872-5827
(202) 842-1266 (Voice/TDD)
(202) 842-3519 (Fax)

CLEFT PALATE

Cleft Palate Foundation
1218 Grandview Ave
Pittsburgh, PA 15211
(800) 242-5338
(412) 481-1376
(412) 481-0847 (Fax)

CRANIOFACIAL DISORDERS

AboutFace
99 Crowns Ln, 3rd Floor
Toronto, ON

Canada M5R 3P4
(800) 225-3223
(416) 944-3223
(416) 944-2488 (Fax)

Let's Face It
PO Box 711
Concord, MA 01742
(508) 371-3186

CYSTIC FIBROSIS

Cystic Fibrosis Foundation
6931 Arlington Rd
Bethesda, MD 20814
(800) 344-4823
(301) 951-4422
(301) 951-6378 (Fax)

DIABETES MELLITUS

American Diabetes Association
National Service Center
1660 Duke St
Alexandria, VA 22314
(800) 232-2472
(703) 549-1500
(703) 683-2890 (Fax)

National Diabetes Information
    Clearinghouse
1801 Rockville Pike, Suite 500
Rockville, MD 20852
(301) 468-2162

DOWN SYNDROME

National Down Syndrome Congress
1605 Chantilly Dr, Suite 250
Atlanta, GA 30324
(800) 232-6372
(404) 633-1555
(404) 633-2817 (Fax)

FETAL ALCOHOL SYNDROME

National Organization on Fetal Alcohol
    Syndrome
1815 H St NW, Suite 710
Washington, DC 20006

(800) 666-6327
(202) 466-6456 (Fax)

FIBROMYALGIA

American Fibromyalgia Syndrome
   Association
PO Box 9699
Bakersfield, CA 93389

HEAD INJURIES

National Head Injury Foundation
1776 Massachusetts Ave NW, Suite 100
Washington, DC 20036-1904
(800) 444-6443 (Helpline)
(202) 296-6443
(202) 296-8850 (Fax)

HEART DISORDERS

American Heart Association
7272 Greenville Ave
Dallas, TX 75231-4596
(800) 242-8721
(214) 373-6300
(214) 706-1341 (Fax)

Congenital Heart Anomalies—Support,
   Education, and Resources
2112 N Wilkins Rd
Swanton, OH 43558
(419) 825-5575

INCONTINENCE

Continence Restored, Inc.
407 Strawberry Hill
Stamford, CT 06902
(914) 285-1470
(203) 348-0601

National Association of Continence
   (Formerly Help for Incontinent People
   (HIP))
PO Box 8310
Spartanburg, SC 29305-8310
(800) BLADDER
(864) 579-7900

The Simon Foundation
PO Box 815
Wilmette, IL 60091
(800) 23SIMON
(708) 864-3913

International Continence Society (ICS)
c/o David Rowan
Dept of Clinical Physics and
   Bioengineering
West of Scotland Health Boards
11 W Graham St
Glasgow G4 9LF
United Kingdom

INTERNET

American Physical Therapy Association
http://apta.edoc.com

Physiotherapy WWW Server
http://cutl.cit.unisa.edu.au/pt/index.html

LEUKEMIA

Leukemia Society of America
600 Third Ave, 4th Floor
New York, NY 10016
(212) 573-8484
(212) 856-9686 (Fax)

LIMB DISORDERS

Cherub Association of Families and Friends
   of Children With Limb Disorders
936 Delaware Ave
Buffalo, NY 14209
(716) 762-9997

LUNG DISEASES

American Lung Association
1740 Broadway
New York, NY 10019
(800) 586-4872
(212) 315-8700
(212) 265-5642 (Fax)

MULTIPLE SCLEROSIS

National Multiple Sclerosis Society
733 3rd Ave, 6th Floor

New York, NY 10017
(800) 532-7667
(212) 986-3240

MUSCULAR DYSTROPHY

Facio-Scapulo-Humeral Society
3 Westwood Rd
Lexington, MA 02173
(617) 860-0501

Muscular Dystrophy Association
3300 E Sunrise Dr
Tuscon, AZ 85718-3208
(602) 529-2000
(602) 529-5300 (Fax)

MYASTHENIA GRAVIS

Myasthenia Gravis Foundation
53 W Jackson Blvd, Suite 1352
Chicago, IL 60604
(800) 541-5454

NEONATAL ILLNESS/PREMATURITY

Parent Care
9041 Colgate St
Indianapolis, IN 46268-1210
(317) 872-9913 (Voice/Fax)

OSTEOPOROSIS

National Osteoporosis Foundation
2100 M Street NW, Suite 602
Washington, DC 20037

PAIN

American Academy of Pain Medicine
5700 Old Orchard Rd, 1st Floor
Skokie, IL 60077
(708) 966-9510

American Chronic Pain Association
PO Box 850
Rocklin, CA 95677
(916) 632-0922

PARKINSON'S DISEASE

Parkinson's Disease Foundation
William Black Medical Research Building
Columbia Presbyterian Medical Center
640 W 168th St
New York, NY 10032
(800) 457-6676

United Parkinson Foundation
360 W Superior Street
Chicago, IL 60610

PEDIATRICS

American Academy of Pediatrics (AAP)
141 Northwest Point Blvd
PO Box 927
Elk Grove Village, IL 60009-0927

Children's Hospice International
700 Princess St
Alexandria, VA 22314
(800) 242-4453
(703) 684-0330
(703) 684-0226 (Fax)

March of Dimes
Birth Defects Foundation, National Office
1275 Mamaroneck Ave
White Plains, NY 10605

Parents of Chronically Ill Children
1527 Maryland St
Springfield, IL 62702
(217) 522-6810

POLIO

Polio Information Center
510 Main St, Suite A446
Roosevelt Island, NY 10044
(212) 223-0353

REFLEX SYMPATHETIC DYSTROPHY SYNDROME

Reflex Sympathetic Dystrophy Association
116 Haddon Ave, Suite D
Haddonfield, NJ 08033
(609) 795-8845
(609) 795-8845 (Fax)

REHABILITATION

National Rehabilitation Association
633 S Washington St
Alexandria, VA 22314
(703) 836-0850
(703) 836-0852 (TDD)

National Rehabilitation Information Center
(NARIC)
8455 Coleville Rd, Suite 935
Silver Spring, MD 20910-3319
(301) 588-9284
(800) 346-2742 (Voice/TDD)

Resources for Rehabilitation
33 Bedford St, Suite 19A
Lexington, MA 02173
(617) 862-6455

Technical Aids and Assistance for the
Disabled
1950 W Roosevelt Rd
Chicago, IL 60608
(312) 421-3373
(800) 346-2959

The Association for Persons With Severe
Handicaps (TASH)
7010 Roosevelt Way NE
Seattle, WA 98115
(206) 523-8446 (Voice)
(206) 524-6198 (TDD)

World Institute on Disability
510 16th St, Suite 100
Oakland, CA 94612
(510) 763-4100

SCOLIOSIS

National Scoliosis Foundation
72 Mount Auburn St
Watertown, MA 02172
(617) 926-0397
(617) 926-0398 (Fax)

SPINA BIFIDA

Spina Bifida Association of America
4590 MacArthur Blvd NW, #250

Washington, DC 20007-4226
(800) 621-3141
(202) 944-3285
(202) 944-3295 (Fax)

SPINAL CORD INJURY

American Paralysis Association
500 Morris Ave
Springfield, NJ 07081
(800) 225-0292
(201) 379-2690
(201) 912-9433 (Fax)

National Spinal Cord Injury Association
600 West Cummings Park, #2000
Woburn, MA 01801
(800) 962-9629

SPINAL MUSCULAR ATROPHY

Families of SMA
PO Box 1465
Highland Park, IL 60035-7465
(800) 886-1762
(708) 432-5551
(708) 432-5551 (Fax)

STROKE

ACTION
1100 Vermont Ave NW
Washington, DC 20525
(202) 606-4855

Administration on Aging
330 Independence Ave SW
Washington, DC 20201
(800) 677-1116

AHA Stroke Connection (formerly the
Courage Stroke Network)
American Heart Association
7272 Greenville Ave
Dallas, TX 75231-4596

American Self-Help Clearinghouse
St Clares-Riverside Medical Center
Denville, NJ 07834

National Aphasia Association
PO Box 1887
Murray Hill Station
New York, NY 10156-0611

National Easter Seal Society
230 West Monroe St, Suite 1800
Chicago, IL 60606
(312) 726-6200

National Stroke Association
96 Inverness Dr East, Suite I
Englewood, CO 80112-5112
(303) 649-9299

Rosalynn Carter Institute
Georgia Southwestern College
600 Simmons St
Americus, GA 31709

Stroke Clubs International
805 12th St
Galveston, TX 77550
(409) 762-1022

The Well Spouse Foundation
PO Box 801
New York, NY 10023
(800) 838-0879

SUDDEN INFANT DEATH SYNDROME (SIDS)

Association of SIDS Professionals
Massachusetts Center for SIDS
Boston City Hospital, Ambulatory Care
   Center 5B29
818 Harrison Ave
Boston, MA 02118
(617) 534-7437

National Sudden Infant Death Syndrome
   Alliance
10500 Little Patuxent Pkwy, #420
Columbia, MD 21044-3505
(800) 221-7437
(410) 964-8000

WOMEN'S HEALTH

American Physical Therapy Association
   Section on Women's Health
Attn: Darcy Hammar, ext 3237
PO Box 327
Alexandria, VA 22313
(800) 999-2782

Doulas of North America
Barbara Hotelling
2112 Bretton
Rochester, MI 48309

Florida Healthy Mothers, Healthy Babies
15 Southeast 1st Ave #A
Gainesville, FL 32601

Depression After Delivery-National
PO Box 1282
Morrisville, PA 19067
(800) 944-4773

High-Risk Moms, Inc
PO Box 4013
Naperville, IL 60567-4013
(708) 515-5453

Hysterectomy Educational Resources and
   Services (HERS) Foundation
422 Bryn Mawr Ave
Bala Cynwyd, PA 19004
(215) 667-7757

International Cesarean Awareness Network
   (ICAN)
PO Box 152
Syracuse, NY 13210
(315) 424-1942

La Leche League International
PO Box 1209
Franklin Park, IL 60131-8209
(708) 455-7730

National Organization of Mothers of Twins
   Clubs, Inc
PO Box 23188

Albuquerque, NM 87192-1188
(505) 275-0955

National Women's Health Network
514 10th St NW, Suite 400
Washington, DC 20004
(202) 347-1140

The American College of Obstetricians and
Gynecologists (ACOG)
409 12th St SW
Washington, DC 20024-2188

The Melpomone Institute for Women's
Health Research
1010 University Ave
St Paul, MN 55104

Index